PURCHASING HANDBOOK

OTHER McGRAW-HILL HANDBOOKS OF INTEREST

PURCHASING HANDBOOK

Standard Reference Book on Purchasing Policies, Practices, Procedures, Contracts and Forms

GEORGE W. ALJIAN
Editor-in-Chief

VICE-PRESIDENT OF PURCHASING, PACKAGING, AND TRAFFIC (RETIRED), CALIFORNIA AND HAWAIIAN SUGAR REFINING CORPORATION, LTD., SAN FRANCISCO, CALIFORNIA
FORMERLY LECTURER IN INDUSTRIAL PROCUREMENT, SCHOOL OF BUSINESS ADMINISTRATION, UNIVERSITY OF CALIFORNIA, BERKELEY, CALIFORNIA, AND PRESIDENT, NATIONAL ASSOCIATION OF PURCHASING AGENTS

SECOND EDITION

McGRAW-HILL BOOK COMPANY
New York San Francisco Toronto London Sydney

W. H. Chaffee, *Vice-president, Purchases and Traffic, American Radiator & Standard Sanitary Corporation, New York, N.Y.*

E. G. Chambers, *Executive Secretary, Purchasing Agents' Association of Northern California, Inc., San Francisco, Calif.*

C. C. Chauvin, *Manager—Purchasing Research, Corporate Purchasing Staff, Chrysler Corporation, Detroit, Mich.*

Robert W. Clark, *Project Engineering Manager, Celanese Corporation of America, Charlotte, N.C.*

W. A. Coates, *Director of Purchases, Westinghouse Electric Corporation, Metuchen, N.J.*

M. D. Coe, *Director of Purchases, The Stanley Works, New Britain, Conn.*

F. A. Coenen, *Director of Purchases, Rex Chainbelt, Inc., Milwaukee, Wis.*

*George H. Cole, *Manager of Purchases, Alabama Power Company, Birmingham, Ala.*

H. A. Cole, *Purchasing Agent, Bendix Eclipse of Canada, Limited, Windsor, Ontario, Canada*

*C. E. Colvin, *Director of Purchasing and Traffic, Ethyl Corporation, Baton Rouge, La.*

*Frank S. Conable, *Purchasing Consultant, Corning Glass Works, Corning, N.Y.*

A. R. Connolly, *Purchasing Agent—Equipment, Celanese Corporation of America, Charlotte, N.C.*

D. R. Coultrip, *Manager of Administrative Services, Dow Corning Corporation, Midland, Mich.*

*Mark B. Covell, *Superintendent of Supply Service, Union Electric Company, St. Louis, Mo.*

Dr. Kenneth Cox, *Professor, School of Business Administration, North Texas State University, Denton, Tex.*

Mrs. Joseph Cranmore, *Food Consultant, Portchester, N.Y.*

William W. Crawford, *Vice-president—Purchasing, United States Steel Corporation, Pittsburgh, Pa.*

George A. Cumming, *Deputy State Purchasing Agent, State of California, San Francisco, Calif.*

Albert J. D'Arcy, *Director of Purchases, Union Carbide Corporation, New York, N.Y.*

Lester E. Davis, *Director of Purchases, Pitman-Moore Division, The Dow Chemical Company, Indianapolis, Ind.*

Clifford H. Dawley, *Purchasing Agent, Ampco Metal, Inc., Milwaukee, Wis.*

*A. J. DeCarlo, *Staff Assistant, Central Purchasing, Burroughs Corp., Detroit, Mich.*

*Garnet T. Dickson, *General Purchasing Agent, The Goodyear Tire and Rubber Co. of Canada Ltd., New Toronto, Ontario, Canada*

Ralph Dixon, *Purchasing Agent, Datex Corporation, a Subsidiary of Gianinni Controls Corp., Monrovia, Calif.*

*Michael M. Donohue, *Director of Purchases, County of Allegheny, Pittsburgh, Pa.*

D. G. Donovan, *Director of Purchases, Pepperell Manufacturing Company, a Division of West Point—Pepperell, Inc., Boston, Mass.*

*Mary C. Donovan, *Maywood, N.J.*

C. W. Doyle, Jr., *Cost Reduction/Value Control Coordinator, General Dynamics, Fort Worth, Tex.*

Delbert J. Duncan, *Professor of Marketing, School of Business Administration, University of California, Berkeley, Calif.*

William G. East, *Manager of Field Purchasing Offices, Monsanto Company, St. Louis, Mo.*

Harold E. Edell, *Staff Assistant to Manager of Purchases, Union Carbide Corporation, New York, N.Y.*

Marshall G. Edwards, *Assistant Secretary—Professional Activities, National Association of Purchasing Agents, New York, N.Y.*

R. Ehrhardt, *California and Hawaiian Sugar Refining Corporation, Ltd., San Francisco, Calif.*

Wilbur B. England, *Professor of Business Administration, Harvard University, Boston, Mass.*

J. F. Estill, Jr., *Vice-president, Houston Lighting & Power Company, Houston, Tex.*

*J. S. Fair, Jr., *General Purchasing Agent, Pennsylvania Railroad, Philadelphia, Pa.*

Arnold D. Finley, *Manager of Purchasing Administration, Sylvania Electronic Systems —East, Sylvania Electric Products, Inc., Needham Heights, Mass.*

*Frank C. Fish, *Staff Purchasing Agent, Central Engineering, St. Regis Paper Company Jacksonville, Fla.*

Edwin Fleischmann, *Consulting Engineer, San Francisco, Calif.*

*A. Dean Foote, *Assistant Director of Purchases, Allis-Chalmers Manufacturing Company, West Allis, Wis.*

Samuel A. Forter, Jr., *Corporate Materials Control, General Dynamics Corporation, New York, N.Y.*

Ira G. Fox, *formerly Purchasing Agent, Transformer Division, Westinghouse Electric Corporation, Sharon, Pa.*

A. L. Froehlich, *Manager of Purchases, Illinois Tool Works, Inc., Chicago, Ill.*

*Owen W. Gaudern, *Manager of Purchases, The Fluor Corporation, Ltd., Los Angeles, Calif.*

Kenneth B. Gay, *Executive Director—Material, North American Aviation, Inc., El Segundo, Calif.*

Verne O. Gehringer, *Purchasing Agent, County of San Diego, San Diego, Calif.*

J. C. Good, *Manager Field Purchasing Offices, Monsanto Company, St. Louis, Mo.*

Irene Gordon, *Purchasing Agent, Wallace & Tiernan, Inc., Belleville, N.J.*

Duncan S. Gregg, *Director of Purchasing, Kaiser Aluminum & Chemical Corp., Oakland, Calif.*

*G. N. Hackett, *Staff Director, Purchases & Traffic, Thompson Products, Inc., Cleveland, Ohio*

H. A. Hamilton, Jr., *Purchasing Agent, Afro-American Purchasing Center, Inc., New York, N.Y.*

*E. Oliver Hanson, *formerly Purchasing Agent, The Crescent Company, Pawtucket, R.I.*

Dr. Clyde T. Hardwick, *Professor of Business Administration, University of Detroit, Detroit, Mich.*

George A. Harrap, *Purchasing Agent, Disston Division, H. K. Porter Company (Canada) Ltd., Acton, Ontario, Canada*

Allan S. Harrison, *formerly Director of Purchasing, Ford Motor Company of Canada Limited, Oakville, Ontario, Canada*

*G. L. Haszard, *General Purchasing Agent, British Columbia Electric Co., Ltd., Vancouver, B.C., Canada*

Charles W. Hayes, *Director of Purchases, Emory University, Atlanta, Ga.*

*William E. Hayes, *Vice-president, Peterson Industries, Burbank, Calif.*

*Wilber G. Hayward, *Director of Purchases, Forbes Lithograph Mfg. Co., Boston, Mass.*

*W. J. Heckman, *Vice-president for Purchasing & Transportation, Olin-Mathieson Chemical Corporation, New York, N.Y.*

Robert M. Hill, *Vice-president, Morgan Guaranty Trust Company of New York, New York, N.Y.*

Dr. John H. Hoagland, *Department of General Business, Michigan State University, East Lansing, Mich.*

Alice C. Hodnett, *Purchasing Officer, U.S. Atomic Energy Commission, New York, N.Y.*

L. D. Howell, *Assistant General Attorney, Celanese Corporation of America, Charlotte, N.C.*

James Hume, Jr., *Supervising Buyer, Brown & Williamson Tobacco Corporation, Louisville, Ky.*

*Paul J. Imperato, *Purchasing Agent, Associated Transport, Inc., New York, N.Y.*

C. D. Jones, *Director of Purchasing, Diamond Alkali Company, Cleveland, Ohio*

Edward R. Jones, *Director of Purchasing, New York State Thruway Authority, Albany, N.Y.*

*Emil H. Jones, *Director of Purchases, E. R. Wagner Manufacturing Co., Milwaukee, Wis.*

*Harold F. Jones, *Manager, Basic Materials Division, Purchasing Department, E. I. du Pont de Nemours & Company, Wilmington, Del.*

William Karchere, *Purchasing Research Analyst, Union Carbide Corporation, New York, N.Y.*

A. M. Kennedy, Jr., *Vice-president, Divisions General Manager, Specialty Products Group, Westinghouse Research & Development Center, Pittsburgh, Pa.*

*Stephen J. Kennedy, *Local Purchasing Agent, Springfield Gas Light Company, Springfield, Mass.*

J. M. Kinabrew, Jr., *Vice-president, Standard Supply and Hardware Company, Inc., New Orleans, La.*

E. M. Krech, *Director of Purchases, J. M. Huber Corporation, Hillside, N.J.*

John G. Krieg, *City Purchasing Agent, City of Cincinnati, Cincinnati, Ohio*

*M. L. Lampe, *General Purchasing Agent, Armstrong Cork Company, Lancaster, Pa.*

H. R. Lanser, *Purchasing Agent, Monsanto Company, St. Louis, Mo.*

*H. K. LaRowe, *Director of Purchases, American Cyanamid Company, New York, N.Y.*

Donald G. Lauck, *Assistant Director—Purchasing, Universal Atlas Cement, Division of United States Steel Corporation, New York, N.Y.*

H. J. Laufer, *Director of Purchases, The Courier-Journal—The Louisville Times, Louisville, Ky.*

*Thor C. Laugesen, *Manager of Purchases, Cochran Foil Corporation, Louisville, Ky.*

*Christian C. Lee, *Purchasing Agent, Norton Memorial Infirmary, Louisville, Ky.*

*Elsie B. Leggett, *formerly Purchasing Agent for New York and Districts, Bigelow-Sanford Carpet Co., Inc., New York, N.Y.*

*T. M. Logan, *Manager, Purchasing General Office, Caterpillar Tractor Co., Peoria, Ill.*

*M. D. MacBurney, *Director of Purchases, Witco Chemical Company, New York, N.Y.*

*R. E. McGrath, Jr., *Buyer, The Courier-Journal—The Louisville Times, Louisville, Ky.*

*James Clark McGuire, *Director, Purchasing and Administrative Services Department, The Port of New York Authority, New York, N.Y.*

*Clifton E. Mack, *Associate Commissioner, Federal Supply Service, General Services Administration, Washington, D.C.*

C. Warner McVicar, *Director of Purchasing and Traffic, Rockwell Manufacturing Company, Pittsburgh, Pa.*

*C. L. Magnuson, *Supervisor of Purchases, State of Connecticut, Hartford, Conn.*

*Wm. H. Mansfield, *General Purchasing Agent, Plumbing and Heating Division, American Radiator and Standard Sanitary Corporation, New York, N.Y.*

Josephine E. Mari, *Purchasing Agents' Association of Northern California, Inc., San Francisco, Calif.*

*P. J. Martersteck, *Director of Purchases, Joseph E. Seagram & Sons, Inc., New York, N.Y.*

*Willard L. May, *Manager, Methods & Control Division, Peoria Plant Purchasing Department, Caterpillar Tractor Co., Peoria, Ill.*

William C. Meyer, *Assistant Vice-president—Purchasing & Traffic, Crucible Steel Company of America, Pittsburgh, Pa.*

H. R. Michel, *Director of Purchases, Celanese Corporation of America, Charlotte, N.C.*

Lawrence D. Miles, *Consultant, formerly Manager, Value Service, General Electric Company, Schenectady, N.Y.*

*Ralph C. Moffitt, *Vice-president—Purchases, United States Steel Corporation, Pittsburgh, Pa.*

*Donald A. Monro, *Director of Purchases, Standard Oil Company (Indiana), Chicago, Ill.*

*W. Boyd Moon, *Purchasing Manager, Gladding, McBean & Co., Los Angeles, Calif.*

R. S. Mullen, *Purchasing Agent, Harvard University, Boston, Mass.*

D. J. Murphy, *Senior Analyst, American Oil Company, Chicago, Ill.*

*C. R. Murray, *Assistant General Purchasing Agent—System, Southern Pacific Co., San Francisco, Calif.*

Roland E. Neal, *Purchasing Agent, Dow Corning Corporation, Midland, Mich.*

J. P. Nelligan, *Manager, Transportation Services, American Radiator & Standard Sanitary Corporation, New Brunswick, N.J.*

*Ben R. Newbery (Retired), *formerly Director of Purchases and Materials, Lone Star Gas Company, Dallas, Tex.*

Harold J. Newman, *Director, Staff Services—Purchasing, Allegheny Ludlum Steel Corporation, Pittsburgh, Pa.*

*Joseph W. Nicholson, *City Purchasing Agent, Milwaukee, Wis.*

*E. G. Novotny, *Purchasing Agent, Combustion Engineering, Inc., Chattanooga, Tenn.*

G. Lloyd Nunnally, *Director, Department of Purchases and Supply, Commonwealth of Virginia, Richmond, Va.*

*Paul O'Brien, *Director of Purchases, Frank Adam Electric Company, St. Louis, Mo.*

C. F. Ogden, *Administrative Vice-president, The Detroit Edison Company, Detroit, Mich.*

Aldan F. O'Hearn, *Director of Purchases, Board of Education, Chicago, Ill.*

*E. L. O'Meara, Jr., *Purchasing Agent, Harbison-Walker Refractories Company, Pittsburgh, Pa.*

W. F. O'Toole, *Purchasing Agent, University of Tennessee, Knoxville, Tenn.*

Joseph A. Padovani, *Purchasing Agent, U. S. Steel Corporation, San Francisco, Calif.*

*A. Paget, *Administrative Assistant, Purchasing, Union Oil Company of California, Los Angeles, Calif.*

A. G. Pearson, *Executive Assistant, North American Aviation, Inc., Downey, Calif.*

W. J. Pierce, *Supervisor, Purchase Research Division, Purchasing Department, The Detroit Edison Company, Detroit, Mich.*

*W. C. Pink, *Purchasing Agent, Emco Limited, London, Ontario, Canada*

Harold C. Plant, *Manager, Computer Manufacturing Applications, RCA Electronic Data Processing, Camden, N.J.*

*L. G. Pochat, *Buyer, The Procter & Gamble Company, Cincinnati, Ohio*

*Carle F. Pohle, *Purchasing Agent, Uarco, Inc., Cleveland, Ohio*

Victor H. Pooler, Jr., *Manager of Purchasing, Carrier Air Conditioning Company, Syracuse, N.Y.*

Gaylord E. Powell, *Director of Procurement, Xerox Corporation, Rochester, N.Y.*

*Winthrop E. Prescott, *Director of Purchasing, The Kendall Company, Boston, Mass.*

G. E. Priester, *Manager—Purchasing Planning, American Oil Company, Chicago, Ill.*

Hoyt B. Pritchett, *Purchasing Director, Brown & Williamson Tobacco Corp., Louisville, Ky.*

Victor W. Quam, *Chief Deputy Purchasing Agent, County of Los Angeles, Los Angeles, Calif.*

J. T. Rapson, *Manager, Traffic Services, Ford Motor Company of Canada Limited, Oakville, Ontario, Canada*

Glenn H. Reinier, *Director of Purchases, Abbott Laboratories, North Chicago, Ill.*

George A. Renard, *Columnist, Purchasing Week, New York, N.Y.*

G. W. Riches, *Purchasing Agent, The Philip Carey Manufacturing Company, Cincinnati, Ohio*

J. J. Ritterskamp, Jr., *Vice-president for Administration, University of Chicago, Chicago, Ill.*

James F. Robjent, *Purchasing Agent, Northeast Division, Scott Paper Company, Winslow, Maine*

C. J. Rost, *Manager of Purchasing Planning, American Oil Company, Chicago, Ill.*

*J. W. Ruff, *Director of Purchases, American Blower Division, American Radiator & Standard Sanitary Corporation, Detroit, Mich.*

Jack S. Rutherford, *Buyer—Industrial, Aluminum Company of America, Pittsburgh, Pa.*

L. J. Saffores, *Assistant Manager—Purchasing & Packaging, California and Hawaiian Sugar Refining Corporation, Ltd., San Francisco, Calif.*

Alfred D. Sands, *Purchasing Agent, Corporate Purchasing Staff, Burroughs Corporation, Detroit, Mich.*

*J. Richard Sayers, *Manager, Plant Purchasing Offices, Monsanto Company, St. Louis, Mo.*

Lyle E. Schaffer, *Coordinator, Purchasing, Standard Oil Company (Indiana), Chicago, Ill.*

J. A. Schilpp, *Director, Traffic & Purchases, H. K. Porter Company, Inc., Refractories Division, Pittsburgh, Pa.*

*L. C. Schmetzer, *Staff General Traffic Manager, Thompson Products, Inc., Cleveland, Ohio*

*E. Eugene Schultz, *District Purchasing Agent, Union Oil Company of California, San Francisco, Calif.*

T. I. Elliott Shircore, *B.A., Director (Purchasing), Chiswick Products Ltd., London W. 4, England*

W. A. Small, *Managing Director, Canadian Association of Purchasing Agents, Toronto, Ontario, Canada*

Chas. A. Smith, *Engineering Consultant—Schedules, Celanese Corporation of America, Charlotte, N.C.*

Chas. F. Smith, *Director of Purchases, American Oil Company, Chicago, Ill.*

Douglas V. Smith, *Consultant—Purchasing Education, General Electric Company, New York, N.Y.*

Joseph G. Smith, *Vice-president—Purchases and Raw Materials, Pittsburgh Steel Company, Pittsburgh, Pa.*

*Raymond P. Snow (Retired), *formerly Director of Purchasing, The Cleveland Electric Illuminating Co., Cleveland, Ohio*

L. H. Somers, *Director of Purchasing and Supplies Inventory, Honolulu Construction & Draying Co., Ltd., Honolulu, Hawaii*

J. J. Staed, *Manager of Purchasing, A. B. Chance Company, Centralia, Mo.*

Russell T. Stark, Sr., *Manager of Procurement and Services, Manufacturing & Engineering Division, Burroughs Corporation, Detroit, Mich.*

David Steinberg, *Manager, Purchases and Materials, Lenkurt Electric Co., Inc., a Subsidiary of General Telephone & Electronics Corp., San Carlos, Calif.*

R. W. Stewart, *Purchasing Agent—Raw Materials and Metals, Aluminum Company of America, Pittsburgh, Pa.*

N. C. Stiles, *Manager, Process Materials, Monsanto Company, St. Louis, Mo.*

*Eugene Stroud, *Vice-president—Purchases, Modern Welding Company, Inc., Owensboro, Ky.*

*Samuel Supon, *General Purchasing Agent, Hilton Hotels, Eastern Division, Hotel Statler, New York, N.Y.*

*Robert C. Swanton, *Purchasing—Materials Management Consultant, New Haven, Conn.*

*Frederic G. Syburg, *Vice-president, Chain Belt Company, Milwaukee, Wis.*

Frank A. Taylor, Jr., *Manager Gulf Coast Regional Purchasing, The Dow Chemical Company, Houston, Tex.*

Chester F. Teeple, *Director of Purchasing & Traffic, Warner-Lambert Pharmaceutical Company, Morris Plains, N.J.*

T. R. Thompson, *Procurement Staff, Allison Div., General Motors Corporation, Indianapolis, Ind.*

Rufus B. Tobey, *District Purchasing Agent, Crown Zellerbach Corporation, Portland, Ore.*

*Leonard Tolson, *formerly Purchasing Agent, Maclean-Hunter Publishing Company, Ltd., Toronto, Ontario, Canada*

L. E. Treadway, *Purchasing Agent, The Federal Glass Co., Division of Federal Paper Board Co., Inc., Columbus, Ohio*

H. Murray Tyler, *Supply Manager, The Australian Purchasing Officers Association, Sydney, Australia*

Scott W. Tyree, *Assistant Purchasing Agent, Container Corporation of America, Chicago, Ill.*

John F. Ward, *Director of Purchases, Contracts and Supplies, City of Chicago, Chicago, Ill.*

*Carey R. Warren, *Manager, Purchasing Department, Canadian-Brazilian Services Ltd., Toronto, Ontario, Canada*

W. G. Watt, *Manager—Purchasing and Packaging, California and Hawaiian Sugar Refining Corporation, Ltd., San Francisco, Calif.*

*E. H. Weaver (Retired), *formerly Vice-president, Procurement and Contracts, Union Oil Company of California, Los Angeles, Calif.*

Raymond I. Wells, *Purchasing Agent, I. H. Schlezinger & Sons, Columbus, Ohio*

*H. Lawrence Westerdale, *Purchasing Agent, Brooks & Perkins, Inc., Detroit, Mich.*

Frank E. Whyte, *Director of Purchasing, SKF Industries, Inc., Philadelphia, Pa.*

B. A. Wilson, *Director of Engineering, Fibreboard Paper Products Corporation, San Francisco, Calif.*

*David L. Wilt (Retired), *formerly Purchasing Agent, University of California, Los Angeles, Calif.*

A. B. Wisrodt, *Purchasing Agent, Port of Galveston, Galveston, Tex.*

Frank W. Wodrich, *Director of Material, Science Services Division, Texas Instruments Incorporated, Dallas, Tex.*

Ian M. Young, *Purchasing Agent, Toronto General Hospital, Toronto, Ontario, Canada*

*William F. Zarbaugh, *Vice-president, Engineering—Purchasing & Traffic, Jones & Laughlin Steel Corporation, Strip Steel Division, Youngstown, Ohio*

FOREWORD TO THE FIRST EDITION

The *Purchasing Handbook* is a milestone in the development of purchasing as a major management responsibility for profitable operations.

It meets a long and very real need for essential, practical information and fills a gap in the literature available for management guidance. Equally important, it provides ready reference material for those working in purchasing, engineering, production, and design, as well as for students in industrial management and business administration.

The National Association of Purchasing Agents recognized this need and listed a purchasing handbook as a necessary educational objective for its members twenty years ago. It further upgraded the importance of that need, and the requirements to meet it, with the years, as purchasing continuously increased in management recognition and profit importance. This progress in purchasing and the need for a handbook were fully and very agreeably reaffirmed with the development of this project.

George W. Aljian is the logical person to serve as Editor-in-Chief. With a practical knowledge of purchasing, plus a standing in purchasing circles and organizing ability second to none, he has gathered a staff of editors, contributors, and reviewers representing a virtual "who's who" in purchasing. The usefulness and practicality of the book reflect the combined knowledge and experience of this editorial group.

Although the NAPA does not sponsor any commercial publication, it does believe in and actively supports competitive commercial enterprises. That policy has proven to be sound in the organization for the development of the *Purchasing Handbook*. With the publication of this handbook, purchasing executives can personally applaud and approve this satisfactory completion of one of the Association's major professional objectives.

We can also be assured that with such editorial competence and publication leadership future editions will reflect the progress in purchasing management.

George A. Renard

November, 1958

PREFACE

The purpose of the *Purchasing Handbook* has not been changed in this second and extensively revised edition. Its objectives were permanently blueprinted by the leaders of purchasing when this handbook was only a dream. The primary objective of the handbook is to serve as a guidebook or manual. It is intended to provide practical, dependable reference information to assist in answering the day-to-day "how to do it best" concerns of the men and women engaged in purchasing activities for small, medium, and large organizations in industry and government, as well as in other nonprofit organizations.

What has been done in this edition is to make additions and changes that fill the need for currently accurate information encompassing the latest developments in this vital segment of business management. The information presented here keeps pace with the sweeping tide of progress in the business world, in which purchasing has functioned as both an implement and an active contributor.

The task of revision was undertaken and has been well done by excellently qualified purchasing executives. Among them are not only a number from the staff responsible for the development of the first (1958) edition, but also many others new to this particular project, whose assistance has added greatly to the information contained in this new edition. The new material and substitutions that appear in this volume reflect the experience and survey research of all these men and women.

The aim of the editors of the *Purchasing Handbook* is to present for use or adaptation currently accepted purchasing policies, practices, and procedures. The sections are replete with forms, records, and tables to provide examples and illustrations of the techniques being used by purchasing departments to obtain better values.

Over one-third of the text of this edition presents new material, and the balance has been updated in every respect. There is a new and separate section on the application of data processing in purchasing. Other sections now include new techniques on negotiations; evaluating suppliers, as well as purchasing performance; improving inventory control; and blanket purchase orders, as well as "blank check" purchase orders. Also introduced are the effects of PERT, CPM, the learning curve, and certification programs and facilities on purchasing. The range of reference material for each phase of purchasing has been increased.

The *Purchasing Handbook* should continue to be particularly useful to management executives who are responsible for procurement or for the organization of a purchasing department. It should prove to be of great help to students in business courses, as it will clarify and illustrate principles and practices mentioned in the many good purchasing textbooks. Finally, its contents could well serve as guidelines to give sales executives and salesmen a better understanding of the problems of their counterparts in purchasing.

Emergence of purchasing as a profit-contributing function, with management status and recognition, has triggered highly significant developments, with the emphasis on costs—reduction in the cost of purchases or purchasing, and the related activities of supply management. Much consideration is directed to establishing controls, audits, measurements, and evaluations to gauge the results of purchasing performance. In turn, purchasing performance is interwoven with analysis of values and the selection and performance of suppliers.

The textbook fundamentals of purchasing have not changed. They are:

1. Buying the proper product or service to meet the requirements
2. Having material available at the proper time
3. Securing the proper amount
4. Paying the proper price

Within those fundamentals, however, there is almost continuous change. Value has become the key to purchasing, and cost is replacing price in determining the proper product or service required. Value in a purchase is that combination of quality, delivery, service, and price which is available and will adequately serve the need at the lowest cost.

This evolution in the activities, responsibilities, and objectives of the purchasing function has been paralleled by an escalation in the qualifications and training required of purchasing personnel. The purchasing organization is obliged to possess the technical, administrative, and commercial ability and the ethical stability demanded by modern and changing conditions.

The examples of profit opportunities for the purchasing function that are presented are pushing the expectations for performance higher and are compelling adoption of the new methods and techniques that are available.

To all editors and associate editors, each skilled in his own particular field of procurement, who guided the numerous revisions of manuscript drafts, and to everyone else who has given so readily of his time and effort, the Editor-in-Chief wishes to express thanks, individually and collectively. Fortunately, most of their names are recorded in the list of contributors. I hope to be forgiven for the inadvertent omission of names inasmuch as the list of those to whom I am indebted finally grew to unmanageable proportions.

Thanks, too, are due to the numerous authors, publishers, purchasing associations and publications, corporations, governmental agencies, and many others who so generously granted permission to quote and reproduce from their material.

The Editor-in-Chief wishes to express his debt to George A. Renard for behind-the-scenes assistance; also for preparing the Foreword soon after his retirement from the National Association of Purchasing Agents after 29 years of service as its Executive Secretary-Treasurer.

Finally, grateful acknowledgment is made to my wife, Mary Lou, for her tireless assistance and most valuable accomplishments in manuscript editing and typing, correspondence, and proofreading. Without her guidance and devotion, neither this second edition nor its predecessor would have been possible.

George W. Aljian
EDITOR-IN-CHIEF

To all men and women who by competent purchasing performance on their day-to-day assignments are contributing to the advancement of purchasing as a career in management

CONTENTS

SECTION I

THE PURCHASING FUNCTION

Editor

Russell T. Stark, Sr., Manager of Procurement and Services, Manufacturing & Engineering Division, Burroughs Corporation, Detroit, Michigan

Associate Editors

Stanley E. Bryan, M.S., D.B.A., Professor, Graduate School of Business Administration, Michigan State University, East Lansing, Michigan

Lester E. Davis, Director of Purchases, Pitman-Moore Division, The Dow Chemical Company, Indianapolis, Indiana

Stripped of all excess verbiage, *business* can be defined as the striving for profit by adding value. Value can be added by bringing ore to the surface and greater value added successively as it is transported to the smelter, refined to pure metal, alloyed for wider usefulness, fashioned into myriad shapes, assembled into complex articles and machines, and distributed throughout an industrial civilization.

Each successive related and interlocking process of adding value starts with the acquisition of the materials, supplies, tools, and services required for that stage of adding value.

Profit is that portion of the sales dollar remaining as the gain or reward for having added value after paying all the costs incurred in the process. A survey of 2,316 manufacturing corporations by the National Industrial Conference Board[1] disclosed that the weighted average profit of these businesses in 1962 amounted to 5.5 cents of each sales dollar. Another survey[2] found that the largest single portion of the sales dollar, 55 cents, was expended for materials, supplies, tools, and services.

One penny saved in the procurement of that 55 cents' worth of materials goes directly into profits. And this additional penny equals the profit earned on 18 per cent greater sales—at the above average profit of 5.5 per cent.

THE SIGNIFICANCE AND SCOPE OF THE PURCHASING FUNCTION

The function of the purchasing department is to help produce more profits for the company.

In the small proprietorship business, procurement of materials, supplies, tools, and services is performed by the proprietor. He commits his own dollars with the care and prudence necessary to ensure a satisfactory profit. As the business expands, the proprietor must turn over his purse to a trusted agent to act for him in the procurement of needed materials, tools, services, and supplies.

The *purchasing agent* is the owner's delegated and authorized agent specializing in the procurement of materials, supplies, tools, and services. In a larger business such as the modern industrial corporation, the efforts of several people are required to perform the purchasing agent's duties, and the efforts of these people are appropriately organized in a purchasing department.

The *purchasing department* is corporate management's group of professional and expert specialists for the procurement of materials, supplies, tools, and services required by all other groups in the enterprise in the over-all process of adding value.

[1] NICB "Road Maps of Industry," No. 1426, April 26, 1963.
[2] NICB "Road Maps of Industry," No. 918, July 31, 1953.

The Responsibilities of Purchasing

The purchasing agent is the custodian of his firm's purse; his first and foremost obligation is *integrity* in spending its funds. He is also responsible for the active searching out and dissemination of ideas and suggestions concerning cost saving or product improvement available from the many sources of supply with whom he deals.

Proper performance of the purchasing function is vital to the smooth operation of many other departments of the business. It is a basic responsibility of the purchasing department to obtain, at the *right price,* the *right material* at the *right time* so that the flow of production is not interrupted or impeded.

The purchasing department acts as the agent of all others in the firm in dealing with all other business supplying or aspiring to supply materials and services. *Professional competence* in representing them intelligently, honorably, and forthrightly is a mandatory responsibility.

The materials on which and with which to add value is the largest element of cost in the business process. As management's authorized agent, *prudence* in obtaining best ultimate value for the money expended is perhaps the purchasing man's heaviest burden of responsibility.

The primary or basic responsibilities of purchasing might be described in terms of the intangible qualities of personal character required for satisfactory performance of those responsibilities—*integrity, dependability, competence,* and *prudence.*

Limitations in Responsibilities

Procurement of materials and services follows a chain of decisions and events broader in scope than the clearly defined responsibility of any single functional group in the business enterprise. In the small single-proprietorship business, the owner may decide whether or not to purchase an item, the specifications of the particular item, how many to buy and when it would be needed, how he wants it delivered, and how he plans to store it pending actual use, as well as the terms he can afford in payment of his commitment.

Negotiation of the purchase is the clearly defined responsibility of the proprietor's agent for the purchase. Management (the proprietor) retains the prerogative of deciding initially whether or not to purchase, and then delegates to the appropriate using supervision primary responsibility for deciding when and how much to buy and the particular qualities to specify.

Receiving and storage supervision, who must handle the material physically, inherits the proprietor's authority to decide how to receive and store it pending actual use. Finance supervision specifies the procedure for budgeting and appropriation of funds to pay invoices.

Purchasing's responsibilities through this chain of decisions and events include not only the negotiation of the actual purchase but also that of making certain that, within reason, everything possible has been done to ensure best value to the company for the money expended.

This role is not a negative one of sitting idly by until asked for advice and opinion. It is incumbent on the purchasing agent to keep his management, his requisitioners, and his associate supervision constantly informed and advised of the right quantities to buy, the most economic quality to specify, the most practical scheduling and to insist that such procedure be followed in the absence of overriding contrary considerations.

OBJECTIVES OF THE PURCHASING FUNCTION

Creation of a purchasing department represents a recognition of purchasing as an organized activity. Organized activities are characterized by their discernible objectives. Purchasing activities, in order to make an effective contribution to the institution of which they are a part, must be oriented toward the over-all objectives of the organization. Yet the purchasing function has objectives of more specific character. These include:

1. Cost reduction or profit making
2. Control of financial commitments
3. Control of negotiations
4. Provision of information and assistance in the specialized purchasing field, to management and other groups

These classes of objectives are interdependent. In the long run all these types of objectives must be recognized and pursued if purchasing is to achieve a maximum of real economy and effectiveness.

Cost Reduction or Profit Making

Purchasing is an economic function. Some nonprofit organizations, such as hospitals, schools, and government agencies, might not stress an over-all objective of profit. Purchasing, however, in any organization is a business function. Its objectives include the well-being and survival of the organization of which it is a part. The objectives of purchasing are similar in nonprofit institutions and in business. Purchasing activities must contribute to the survival and effectiveness of the organization, and where profit is a prime objective of the organization, purchasing activities must be operated with that objective as the ultimate justification for existence.

In recent years much attention has been given to the direct contribution which purchasing activities can make to the profits of the organization. In part this is measurable in dollar figures. In some companies the saving of one dollar in purchased materials and supplies is equivalent to the profit obtainable by a ten dollar increase in sales. This ratio varies in various companies, but the ratio should be known by the executive responsible in a particular company for purchasing activities.

The profit objective is implicit in the concept of obtaining proper materials at the proper price in the proper quantity from the proper vendor at the proper time. The proper materials are those proper for the job at hand irrespective of grade or market designation of quality. In one case the very finest grade obtainable in the market might be proper quality, while for another purpose the proper quality would be the grade deemed by the market as its poorest grade. The purchasing department represents a judging operation to consider *all* the factors involved in a purchase, ranging from cost of material and machine capabilities to factors of vendor and administrative relations. By considering the profit objective in securing the proper balance of factors the purchasing function brings together the experience and judgment of all parties concerned.

To perform the economic function of contributing to profit and to serve his organization effectively, a buyer must exercise professional competence. Professional competence is utilized in acting as an agent for others who need materials, supplies, and purchased services. To become professionally competent, the buyer must strive to increase his knowledge in many fields. As a professional buyer such an individual must wear many "hats," and wear them effectively. A measure of professional competence is how well a buyer can secure the willing cooperation of users and others in the company with special knowledge of the factors that determine the value of a given purchase.

Adherence to the profit objective as a goal and motivation requires prudence in judging the best value for the money spent. A logical balance exists between price and value in use. A production operation about to halt for lack of materials or supplies emphasizes the close relationship existing between cost and value. Much greater savings might be obtained by purchasing at a higher price to avoid a halt of production than in striving for lowest direct cost. To ensure supply may require seemingly uneconomical short-term purchasing activities. Examples include such policies and practices as the following:

1. The maintenance of stock known to be costly to store
2. The division of purchases between two or more vendors

3. The maintenance of buying relations with firms whose prices appear to be higher than competitors
4. Reciprocal relationships with certain customers
5. Payment of premiums for quick delivery

Service

The service objective of purchasing is a recognized need. To allow the larger organization to operate effectively in the long run, the purchasing function might have to operate at less than maximum efficiency in the short run. The purchasing department must occasionally stand ready to contribute service even though this represents uneconomical buying. Purchasing has the important objective of supporting the operating program of the organization. In the longer run cooperation among operating departments and purchasing activities can result in maximizing the purchasing department's contribution to service and profit. On the other hand, service is only one of the purchasing functions. Purchasing must always seek optimum value for goods and services to be purchased. Where service must take precedence, prices paid in excess of optimum value should be documented.

Certain specific responsibilities grow out of the service objectives of the purchasing function. Some of these functions might be fully delegated to the purchasing department. Others are shared. And there are additional functions or responsibilities in which the purchasing department has considerable interest. Included in these classifications are the following:

1. Responsibilities often fully delegated to the purchasing function
   - *a.* Obtaining prices
   - *b.* Selecting vendors
   - *c.* Awarding purchase orders
   - *d.* Following up on delivery promises
   - *e.* Adjusting and settling complaints
   - *f.* Selecting and training of purchasing personnel
   - *g.* Vendor relations
2. Responsibilities often shared with functions other than the purchasing function[3]
   - *a.* Obtaining technical information and advice
   - *b.* Receiving sales presentations and arranging for sales opportunities with interested personnel
   - *c.* Establishing specifications
   - *d.* Scheduling orders and deliveries
   - *e.* Specifying delivery method and routing

[3] Refer to Section 2 for analysis of some of these shared functions.

   f. Inspecting
   g. Expediting
   h. Accounting
   i. Purchasing and market research
   j. Inventory and warehousing policy and/or control
   k. Forward buying and hedging policies and procedures
   l. Construction contracting
   m. Service contracts and agreements
   n. Sales of scrap, salvage, and surplus
   o. Purchasing for employees
   p. Contracting for machines and equipment
   q. Development of specifications
   r. General considerations of quantities or timing on planning deliveries
   s. Transportation and traffic
   t. Determination of whether to make or buy
   u. Customs
   v. Other functions
3. Responsibilities often divorced from purchasing, but of particular interest to purchasing
   a. Receiving and warehousing
   b. Payment of invoices
   c. Other functions

This listing is exemplary, not exhaustive. Company policy varies in the division of these responsibilities. Purchasing responsibilities in any company should be well defined to encourage effectiveness in operations. One criterion of success in purchasing is how well the purchasing personnel can motivate the actions of persons beyond their direct areas of responsibility. Good purchasing personnel will accomplish results each day far beyond their immediate sphere of responsibilities. Because of their position, purchasing people are well fitted to know both the function of their business and the thoughts, ideas, processes, and products of the many businesses with which they deal to stimulate the imagination of others in their company to make use of these things. A type of objective which must be recognized in purchasing is the goal of securing recognition and respect from others for the contributions which ability and knowledge can make to the total operations.

Control of Financial Commitments

With purchased materials and service amounting on the average to more than 50 per cent of the sales volume, outstanding commitments at any one time represent a very substantial financial obligation in any company. It is imperative that the members of management know at all times exactly what commitments have been made and that they have centralized control over the making of commitments. The purchasing department provides that control by:

1. Insisting that no commitments be made except by authorized members of the purchasing department or by approved delegated authority.
2. Setting up strict procedure for the issuance of purchase orders and keeping a record of them.
3. Providing management with control point in establishing inventory policies and ensuring that these policies are being observed.
4. Providing a control point for purchases of other than inventory items such as construction contracts and other items.

Without centralized control the financial stability of a company might easily be endangered; therefore the purchasing department must of necessity maintain very strict rules with respect to the making of commitments.

Control of Negotiations and Vendor Relations

It is an inherent function of the purchasing department to maintain careful control of negotiations and vendor relations for a number of reasons:

1. A purchasing department negotiator's effectiveness is greatly weakened if he is not recognized as the man to deal with from the very beginning. He should control all contacts with vendors.
2. In negotiating with suppliers over price or other conditions, unwise disclosures can be very harmful to the company's interest. Other departments are asked to confine their discussions with suppliers to specifications and performance and leave price negotiations to the purchasing department.
3. Suppliers are more likely to deal on a confidential basis with a tightly controlled organization.
4. In many industries, there are a relatively few highly competitive firms. Technological progress may be rapid. The advantage of getting there first with the best may mean the difference between success and failure. The purchasing department is charged with supervision and control of negotiations with suppliers in order to minimize the possibility of unwise disclosures of information.
5. Effective vendor relations are necessary to achieve assurance of supply and to protect the company's good reputation.

Staff Functions

In all organizations, one of the important functions of the purchasing staff is to provide information and assistance to management and other departments, in the specialized purchasing field. In the larger, multiplant companies, this may be one of the major functions of the central purchasing staff. In such instances much, if not most, of the actual purchasing may be done by the plant purchasing departments, with the central staff concerned with the development and administration of policies, with the training and instruction of scattered buying personnel, and with provision of advisory service to the general and plant managements.

ORGANIZATION OF THE PURCHASING FUNCTION

Purchasing is a part of management and should be organized to operate accordingly. The purchasing department should be organized to embrace all aspects of the purchasing function and may include purchasing, inventory control, stores, and general materials control. Management expects the purchasing department to accept responsibility to secure the right material, at the right price, at the right time, and to maintain a good relationship with suppliers. To accomplish this, the department must be organized on sound management principles. As described in Section 2, lines of authority should be clear and well defined. Policies should be formulated only after determination of what is required in the relationship of the purchasing department with other departments.

In the absence of a clearly established directive from management, the purchasing department should assume the responsibility for preparation of a guide, frequently called a policy manual, setting forth its functions to be submitted to management for approval. Examples will be found in Section 3 of this handbook.

The purchasing department must constantly keep in mind that one of its most important functions is to act as a line of communication between the suppliers' representatives and the representatives of the purchasers' departments that specify and/or use materials and services. The line of communication must be maintained either through transmittal of information through the purchasing department or by arranging meetings between the concerned parties. Information and ideas must be exchanged to ensure constantly the acquisition of the most suitable material, at the best price available, in the quantities necessary to maintain production rates and consistent with established inventory policies.

The purchasing department should be organized so that it has a knowledge of the company's plans, both as to the present and future needs.

It must maintain proper relationship with manufacturing, sales, legal, and engineering divisions. Policies and procedures should be developed, after consultation with other divisions, which clearly state the department's procedures and responsibilities.

RELATIONSHIP OF PURCHASING WITH OTHER FUNCTIONS

The coordinated efforts of many people performing many duties are necessary to attain the final objective of any business establishment. Certain closely allied groups of duties or areas of work, called "functions," are virtually common to all business, differing widely from one enterprise to another only in size and scope and importance in accordance with the individual or peculiar requirements of the separate business entities.

The purchasing "function," comprising all the duties necessary to procure materials, supplies, and services for the business, performs its assigned tasks in concert with the efforts of the production "function" to manufacture or process the product, the sales "function" to market, and all the other "functions" doing their part in the over-all organized effort. How smoothly these functions mesh together to produce an efficient and harmonious group effort depends in large measure on the degree of comprehension; also on the understanding, on the part of all personnel involved, of the reasons underlying the relationships recognized in and provided for in the organization manual.

Organization charts and manuals are as varied as the businesses they describe and serve; but all are founded on universally recognized common-sense precepts of ideal basic relationships between departments, or groups, or functions. Questions arising as to proper relationships, though seemingly perplexing and contradictory, usually become greatly simplified merely on thoughtful examination in the light of the basic reasons underlying the relationship between the purchasing department and other functional groups as follows.

Production. This is the function of the group actually engaged in producing the product, be it manufacturing, processing, refining operations, or performing salable services. As such, at least in most industrial business, *production* is the principal function to be served by the purchasing organization. The cardinal relationship, therefore, between purchasing and production is that of purchasing to procure the materials needed for production and of production to rely on purchasing for such service. It is the mutual responsibility of purchasing and production to fulfill their function, as it relates one to the other, in such a way as to ensure the most economical results.

Purchasing's responsibility is to procure the materials, supplies, and services required by production and to arrange these deliveries as required for optimum rate and continuity of production operations. This does not relieve purchasing of its responsibility to recommend new products, more practical quality, and more economical quantities to the production department.

Production management enjoys a fundamental right to expect not only unfailing delivery of its material and service needs, but a reliable measure of intelligence as well from its purchasing agency to anticipate future supply conditions and to advise well in advance or with utmost promptness concerning events which are likely to influence future production schedules and operations. It is the right of purchasing people to expect from production advice of anticipated changes of policy or plans of production, so that the purchasing function can be carried out.

While production usually specifies the quantities, quality, and required delivery dates, in one relationship both purchasing and production share an equal and dual obligation to management; both are accountable for costs. The production superintendent's cost performance depends in large part on the purchasing agent's ability to obtain maximum value per dollar expended. Conversely, the purchasing agent's ability to buy to best advantage depends in large measure on the production supervision's willingness to devise or accept most economic specifications. There may be important differences of opinion on what constitutes greatest value, with the production and purchasing departments unable to reach agreement. In such instances, the dispute may be referred to higher authority for a decision.

Among the most common causes of interdepartmental friction between production and purchasing are supply failures, in which production is at the mercy of its purchasing agent, and insufficient notice from production for purchasing to secure delivery or to obtain optimum value.

Harmonious relationships depend on mutual confidence and cooperation between the two groups engendered by the full understanding of each as to the prerogatives and objectives of the other.

In public purchasing, i.e., government, education, hospital, and other nonprofit institutions, the same principles are applicable except that purchases are almost exclusively for use rather than for manufacture or resale. Thus the operating department in industry becomes the using department in public purchasing, all as described in Section 19, "Public Purchasing."

Sales. The relationship between purchasing and sales may be close and vital or no more than casual, according to the peculiarities of the specific business. The sales function is to market the end product of the group effort; the success of that marketing effort depends on function of the product, price, quality, and reliability of delivery, for which sales is dependent on the efficiency of its purchasing department, among others.

The price at which sales can offer goods or services always depends in part on the prices paid by purchasing for component materials, and in many businesses this may be the determining factor in quoting the sales price. A firm obligation to sell at a price may require a simultaneous firm commitment to purchase basic components at a corresponding price or a hedging order on a future market for the corresponding raw materials.

The ability of sales to present additions to or improvements in its product line is often dependent on purchasing's ability to obtain information on new developments from supply sources and to recognize their value. When sales or research departments are promptly advised of these developments, they can better secure a position of leadership.

A delivery date promised by sales, in many businesses, depends on and can be no more reliable than the delivery schedules negotiated by purchasing for the component or raw materials. A custom equipment salesman cannot fulfill a promised delivery unless his purchasing department can procure the component subcontract castings on the corresponding schedule.

The quality of product which sales delivers, and on which the reputation of the business rides with every transaction, depends in varying measure on the quality of materials and components bought for the product by purchasing. Sales suffers the consequence of customer complaint, for example, when its product machine stops running because the insulation in a purchased motor breaks down.

Purchasing's relationship with sales may be as the expert agent buying for sales what it needs to perform its functions, or as a full partner in working out the problems of a desirable product: price, protection of profit margin, delivery schedules, and quality guarantees on the products marketed by sales.

Purchasing may also be in a strategic position to render effective assistance to sales through reciprocal business relations. With other considerations essentially equal and with due precaution against the ever-present hazard of reciprocity abuses, any business prefers to patronize a valued customer.

It behooves the purchasing agent to make a thorough study of his firm's sales function to determine all the ways in which he can contribute and to define and promote his relationship with sales to best serve that end.

Scheduling and Planning. These functions are always performed in the business, though frequently not separately identified as an organizational entity. Perhaps it is production supervision that "schedules" incoming supplies, or executive management that "plans" longer-range activities and objectives. Wherever those functions are performed, the basic purchasing relationship is the same: to serve those functions (*a*) by complying with the schedules of supply or giving reasons for requesting changes; (*b*) by being alert to market developments and rendering prompt advice of changes which are likely to influence schedules and plans; (*c*) by developing forecast information on material supplies and markets, and by scheduling deliveries if assigned this responsibility.

There is a corollary relationship between these scheduling and planning functions and purchasing; an obligation to keep the purchasing agent fully informed of future plans so that he can perform effectively.

Stores.[4] The stores function, defined broadly, includes the requisitioning of needed material, the physical handling of incoming supplies, and the materials control related to them. Stores operations include receiving and checking material purchases, systematic storage and protection of stocks, and dispensing materials to the direct operations personnel. The stores function is closely allied to the inventory data processing function and the inventory control process and is frequently combined with purchasing, but may also be found under the jurisdiction of production, production control, maintenance, or financial management. Accordingly, the stores relationship with purchasing, as actually practiced, varies widely.

The management pressure on purchasing to achieve optimum value per dollar expended is diametrically opposed in view to management's pressure on stores supervision to minimize inventories, it being axiomatic that best prices obtain on greatest volume, whereas minimum inventories follow least volume.

Actual achievement of an optimum balance of these two pressures, the real objective of an enlightened management, requires a high degree of competence on the part of both stores and purchasing supervision.

Other influences complicating relationships between purchasing and stores include the necessity, in an efficient stores operation, to mechanize handling and systematize control. These methods of increasing internal efficiency in stores often impinge upon the flexibility and effectiveness of purchasing in its pursuit of increased value in the external environment. High-speed data processing for stores, automated handling systems, and the increasing use of computer control of inventories result in requirements that are often inconsistent with optimum purchase quantities, vendor lead-time requirements, packaging procedures, and delivery practices.

[4] Covered in detail in Section 13, "Quantity Determination Through Inventory Management."

The relationship between purchasing and stores must be such that neither tends to be dominated by the objectives of the other. Stores must not be unduly handicapped in its management of storage space, manpower, materials movement, and inventories; and purchasing must not be hampered by the need to place uneconomic hand-to-mouth orders and by the necessity of dissipating its skill in purchasing and vendor relations by having to concentrate on follow-up to meet arbitrary delivery schedules. Good management must ensure that these two diverse functions operate effectively together.

Basically, it is the responsibility of the stores function, with or without the aid of an effective data processing system for inventory control, to requisition needed materials, specifying the needed amount and the time requirements in the delivery schedule. This responsibility should be carried out, however, with regard to purchasing's function of maintaining effective vendor relations and achieving value in purchases.

Fundamentally, it is the responsibility of purchasing to procure the needed materials as specified and see that they are delivered on time, while achieving value and maintaining good vendor relations at the same time. To aid proper data processing, the purchasing department has the responsibility of keeping the stores department advised in advance as to optimum purchase quantities and feasible delivery schedules.

Stores supervision, as the physical handler of materials and supplies and the originator of requisitions for replenishment, is in a position to be tempted to assume greater authority in its relationship with purchasing than its responsibility warrants. The purchasing agent who permits such encroachment to curtail the effectiveness of his procurement is remiss in the discharge of his responsibility to his management.

Maintenance. This is basically a service function to keep facilities in good operable condition. In so doing, it consumes repair and maintenance materials and supplies. While maintenance is considered a service function, it is most important. It is imperative that production be continuous, without a slowdown or shutdown because of delayed procurement of repair parts. Its relationships with purchasing, therefore, parallel those between the production and purchasing functions.

Construction.[5] Virtually all industrial business requires construction, performed by maintenance forces, by a separate construction group, or by independent contractor. Purchasing's relationship with the construction function may range from minimum contact or responsibility, usually in the case of construction contracted to outside general contractors; to active participation in all phases of contract negotiation, especially when the work is subcontracted; to serving the construction group by procure-

[5] Detailed in Section 16, "Considerations in Nonrepetitive Major Purchases."

ment of requisitioned materials; responsibility for delivery of all bills of material items to the job site; and subsequent disposal of surpluses remaining at completion.

Engineering. The engineering function usually includes a variety of responsibilities: the design of physical facilities; the designation of equipment standards; the evaluation of proposed alterations and additions to facilities; the technical definition of specifications for materials and supplies; the testing of items requiring proof of quality or claims.

The relationship between purchasing and engineering, more nearly than in the case of any other function, is one of mutual service. Purchasing serves engineering by the procurement of supplies and equipment requisitioned under engineering authority, by the obtaining of quotations and technical assistance from suppliers as assistance in the preparation and evaluation of alternatives, and by market surveys and searches for new and better materials and equipment.

Engineering, in turn, renders invaluable assistance to purchasing in the advice of its expert specialists on questions of optimum specifications of a given item for its particular application, desirable purchase standardizations, and in reconciling conflicting nonexpert ideas on specification matters.

Research. The search for improved methods and products is the function of research. Purchasing, therefore, being familiar with methods and products used in and being developed in other industries, has the responsibility for keeping research advised of them. Purchasing also has access to the ideas and plans of other industries and should give research all the helpful information their position provides. The relationship of research with purchasing closely parallels the engineering-purchasing relationship, with purchasing obligated to procure the wide variety of unusual and unpredictable specialties required for research projects and research obligated to contribute expert technical opinion and formal testing assistance.

It is axiomatic that the full and most reliable resources of the business should be available for bringing to bear on any problems; an alert purchasing executive can increase his department's effectiveness by cultivating rather than neglecting the assistance that is his for the asking from his engineering and research organization.

Accounting. This is a triple function in most businesses: keeping account of and handling monetary transactions of both income and expenditures; arranging and budgeting the necessary working capital; and auditing procedural details of performance to ensure conformity with management policies and directives. Purchasing has vital relationships in all three accounting areas.

The ideal relationship is that of equal partners. Purchasing makes expenditures; accounting on due proof of supplier performance makes the payment. Purchasing requires a deep pocketbook to keep the materials and supplies rolling into the business; accounting must see to it that adequate funds are available. Purchasing personnel are entrusted with the custodianship of a large proportion of the firm's income. In some organizations accounting's auditing staff maintains a continual check for the benefit of purchasing management to ensure that sound business practices prevail, focusing a spotlight on transgressions of oversight, thoughtlessness, and ignorance, before they grow serious and uncovering the first indication of dishonesty.

It is not accounting's prerogative to pass judgment on value received by purchasing in its negotiations, but it is accounting's responsibility to determine by appropriate audit whether specified authorizations and procedures are adhered to. It is not accounting's responsibility to adjust errors in procurement transactions, but it is their responsibility to determine that material receipts and invoiced prices are in strict accord with the terms of the purchase order before payment is released, calling deviations to the purchasing agent's attention for appropriate corrective measures.

Cost Control. The function of pinpointing costs to the specific responsible supervision and of focusing management attention on variances from predetermined standards may be performed within the accounting organization or by a specialized (and often technical) staff group. The relationship of purchasing to this function is the same in either event.

Purchasing supplies price data for the establishment of budgetary or standards forecasts and identifies each purchase with the appropriate cost-code charges as specified on the purchase authorization. Variances which are caused by price fluctuations are the purchasing agent's responsibility.

Cost control is management's mechanism, be it formal or informal, complex or simple, for rewarding good cost performance or taking action to correct an unsatisfactory condition. The effective purchasing executive is constantly alert for opportunity to contribute toward improved cost indices.

Traffic.[6] The traffic function closely resembles the purchasing function; indeed traffic is but the purchase of transportation service and purchasing is often traffic's principal client. Traffic's objective is to specify the most economic mode of delivery for the particular item and to meet the required delivery timing. Since transportation cost is an integral part of the delivered cost of any item purchased, the relationship between purchasing and traffic is that of traffic rendering the same kind of expert,

[6] Also see Section 18, "Traffic and Transportation Considerations."

specialized service to purchasing that is expected of purchasing by material requisitioners.

The purchasing agent is obligated to call upon traffic to determine and specify the best method of transportation, the delivery routing, and the applicable rates. The purchasing agent is further advised to inform traffic of any routing or method of shipment a supplier has developed or discovered which will reduce costs or give better service.

Legal. The function of legal counsel is to provide all segments of the business with expert legal interpretation of laws, contractual obligations, commitment agreements, and protective policies. The purchasing agent operates perpetually in an environment of legal restriction. The legal relationship is that of service to the purchasing agent when and to the extent requested.

Personnel. The function of hiring, training, and developing personnel is a service available to the entire business, including the purchasing department. The purchasing agent is no less obligated than other supervision to utilize this available specialized assistance in problems of salary administration, preliminary training, job rotation, and aptitude testing. He will undoubtedly, however, find it necessary to develop and train his buying personnel in the performance of the buying function.

Public Relations. The primary function of public relations is to foster those policies throughout the business which will deserve favorable public notice and acceptance. The public relations department cannot create good public relations except as it influences all those having contact with the public to do unto others as they would have others do unto them.

The purchasing function by reason of its wide and intimate contact throughout its supply circles is a major influence on the firm's public relations, for better or worse. Its relationship, therefore, with the public relations function is that of a valuable ally.

If the purchasing department treats its visiting sales representatives with the consideration and courtesy its own salesmen desire, and if it awards its orders to those who deserve the orders—in the American competitive system, those who freely offer the most value—then the purchasing executive will have contributed his full quota to his firm's public relations aspirations. Not to be excluded from this same objective are the public relations responsibilities of the purchasing staff in outside activities, such as civic and professional.

INFLUENCE OF VENDOR RELATIONS ON COMPANY REPUTATION

Reputation is the sum total of public opinion formed from all the favorable and unfavorable instances of personal and corporate experience. Vendor personnel respond to emotional stimuli in the characteristic human pattern. They trust or distrust, admire or deplore, like or dislike as personal experience influences them.

A company can hardly gain or hold a reputation for integrity if those selling to it feel that its purchasing is inclined to cheat, or a reputation for reliability if they cannot depend on the purchasing department to live up to its promises.

Cooperation is the give and take of meeting each other halfway. If the vendor finds in the purchasing agent a warm and friendly spirit of understanding and cooperativeness, he can hardly look upon the company as a cold and uncooperative enterprise, and vice versa. No amount of advertising will persuade a vendor that the company is a good place to do business if he finds the purchasing agent cold and uncooperative.

Fortunately for the deserving and unfortunately for the rest, salesmen talk shop, and personalities, as they chance to meet each other on their rounds. They swap experiences and opinions; and this word-of-mouth advertising, if honestly stated, pegs the purchasing agent and his company according to their due deserts.

It is disappointing to the vendor salesman when he fails to make a sale. The purchasing agent is handicapped in his "relations" in that for every purchase he makes, pleasing to one vendor, he disappoints perhaps ten others. Courtesy is the balm that takes the sting from such disappointment. The salesman who has been accorded genuine courtesy and knows that the purchasing agent has placed his order fairly and squarely maintains his respect despite his natural no-sale disappointment. If he feels, however, that he has been given a brush-off or is the victim of an unfair favoritism, the purchasing agent and his company suffer the consequent damage to their reputation wherever salesmen meet.

Reciprocity is a stern test of the purchasing agent's judgment and integrity because there is no clear-cut delineation between right and wrong. At one extreme is the evident mutual advantage and desirability of patronizing one's own customer but at the other is the abuse of pressure toward an uneconomic and unfair purchase simply because the vendor is a customer.

The purchasing agent who hopes to maintain an unsullied reputation for fair and ethical dealing must apply to every reciprocity transaction the test of whether or not it is at least just as advantageous as any other freely offered proposal.

THE PHYSICAL REQUIREMENTS FOR PURCHASING

The size of the purchasing staff and its physical requirements depend not only on the size and complexity of the organization it serves but also on the scope envisioned as to the thoroughness of the purchasing job to be performed. One man can relay a vast quantity of orders by telephone downtown to a well-stocked supply house; but he can perform a thorough shopping job on only a fraction of that volume. One man can place orders for an infinite variety of merchandise but he can do an intelligent buying job only on the items in the fields in which he specializes. How large a staff and, consequently, its physical needs, depends on how expertly the business wants its purchasing function performed.

An adequate staff of expert purchasing manpower to shop, negotiate, and follow through on all purchase requirements is the fundamental to be provided. Adequate stenographic service must be furnished the buying staff for typing quotation requests, purchase orders, and transcribing correspondence. An adequate filing service is essential.

The purchasing agent's most vital tool is rapid communication; hence telephone, telegraph, and teletype service, in addition to his specialized purchasing forms and stationery, is mandatory. He needs also for convenient reference a library of the pertinent catalogs, price lists, and supplier directories, as well as trade papers and magazines.

The purchasing department in most companies receives the major proportion of visitors; it can hardly function without these vendor sales visits. A convenient, pleasant, and adequate reception facility is a necessity, and it is highly desirable that each buyer be furnished a place, preferably his own private office, or a convenient access to a reception room where he can conduct sales interviews in private.

The budgetary needs of the purchasing function depend on the manpower assigned, the corresponding office and reception space, and the general business office and communications facilities and expenses required.

The procurement of materials, supplies, and service is a necessary function in any business; personnel must be delegated to perform that function. The overhead expense of the function can be rigidly limited almost to any degree dictated by the controlling management. An enlightened management desiring the cost savings inherent in an effective and thorough purchasing performance will authorize a budget sufficient to provide adequate staff and facilities, most probably in proportion to the ability demonstrated by the purchasing executive for profitable utilization.

FUNCTIONAL OPERATIONS IN PURCHASING

The purchasing system includes all the functions involved in the procurement of material from the time a need or possible need is first known until the material is received and approved for use. Steps involved in the process are:

1. Obtaining preliminary information on specifications, availability, performance, and price
2. Routing of requisitions to proper buyer
3. Editing of requisition and assignment of supplier, routing, and other pertinent instructions by buyer
4. Obtaining competitive bids
5. Typing of purchase order and distribution of copies
6. Expediting if necessary
7. Receiving of material
8. Price checking
9. Approval of invoice for payment
10. Providing records and information for data processing system

No two systems can be identical, and need not be to be effective. However, one thing common to all systems is the necessity of eliminating red tape. Avoid unnecessary record keeping. In some cases, it is found that the purchasing department is maintaining records to develop statistics which can be secured from the accounting or other divisions.

Preliminary Survey. The sooner the purchasing department is informed of requirements or possible requirements, the more effective and helpful they can be and the less chance of misunderstandings with vendors. This applies, particularly, to special or nonstandard materials. Thus all except routine preliminary inquiries should be made through the purchasing department who will arrange interviews with other interested personnel as required.

Points to be considered in developing a system are:

Requisition. The requisition should follow the purchase order in form as much as possible. After it has cleared all required approvals, it should require a minimum of editing by the executing buyer. Many firms use a traveling requisition[7] for repetitive buying.

Purchase Order. The purchase order, where accepted by the supplier without exception, becomes a contract and must be considered as such. It should contain all the information necessary for the supplier to perform delivery and invoice in accordance with the buyer's wishes. Copies should be made for all concerned within the purchasing department. Additional copies should be provided for accounting, budgeting, and other divisions as may be required. However, the number of copies provided should be limited to the minimum required to do the job.

An acceptance copy may be mailed with the original to the supplier for execution and return. Many companies reserve the acceptance copy

[7] Refer to Section 25, "Forms and Records."

for use only on orders for machinery, equipment, and other than routine purchases.

Much red tape can be avoided by using a purchase order copy for a receiving report. Except in rare instances, all purchase orders should be priced.

In an integrated electronic data-processing purchase order system, a computer program uses machine-stored data to choose automatically among programmed alternatives and print out a purchase order. The buyer's role is to furnish basic data for the program, to work closely with the programmer, and to review the resulting printed purchase orders before they are released. He modifies them where necessary and approves them.

Claims. A clear-cut means of handling claims must be designed into the system. Claims generally fall into two classes, either against the supplier or the carrier.

Claims against carriers should be made by purchaser when material is shipped f.o.b. shipping point. Claims should be prepared and filed by the traffic department, working closely with the receiving and purchasing department to develop the required information. The carrier should be notified as soon as damage is discovered.

Ordinarily the supplier should handle claims only when material is shipped f.o.b. destination. Sometimes a supplier is in better position to effect a fair settlement promptly because of greater patronage to the carrier involved and will handle a claim, if asked to do so, even though shipment was made on an f.o.b. mill basis.

Claims against suppliers should be handled immediately. Delays in notification will cause less serious consideration of claims.

STANDARDS OF PERFORMANCE IN THE PURCHASING FUNCTION[8]

Purchasing Standards

Performance Standards. Definite performance standards should be developed and assigned to each job in the department. In the development of these standards, consideration must be given to the amount of mental effort and physical effort required on each job that is appraised. It is readily apparent that the same standards cannot be used to appraise a buyer's work load as are used to figure an invoice clerk's or typist's load.

Personnel Standards. Simply stated, the purchasing department personnel should be the best obtainable within the permitted budget. Avoid people with limitations which make it difficult to promote them. They

[8] Also see Section 24, "Evaluating Purchasing Performance."

eventually become dissatisfied. Also, others then look upon these people as roadblocks around whom they cannot progress. Be sure that anyone employed has a real interest in purchasing and has an active imagination and the ingenuity to utilize it to the fullest extent.

Tangible Measures

No flat percentage figure can be assigned arbitrarily to the cost of purchasing. The actual cost of purchasing without other considerations cannot be used as a denominator of operating efficiency or performance. For example, the purchasing department of a blast furnace operation producing merchant pig iron would show a low ratio of purchasing cost to purchasing volume because of the large amount of bulk raw materials purchased, such as iron ore, limestone, and coke. The actual cost of writing a purchase order for 100,000 tons of iron ore is no more than the cost of an order for one keg of nails or one small electric motor. Cost-of-purchasing indices and ratios must be established within the purchasing department and these used as a basis from which to improve performances. They must be regarded as a challenge.

The establishment of a cost-reduction program, regularly audited, is another means of tangible measure.

Intangible Measures

Intangible measures as indicated are those standards to which it is impossible to apply a measurable criterion. However, intangible values do exist and can be appraised negatively, positively, or by degree. Some of these intangible considerations are:

1. Are vendor relations on a high level? Is the department known as being fair in its dealings or is it known to engage in sharp practice? Does the department personnel realize that it, at all times, is "the company" to everyone with whom it comes in contact? Does it at all times, regardless of the circumstances, reflect credit on the company? Is the department personnel among the first to hear of new products and processes from suppliers, indicating good relationships?

2. Does the department personnel cooperate with and receive the cooperation of the other departments with which it must work closely? Is the personnel of other departments receptive to the suggestions and ideas of the department personnel, indicating a harmonious and mutually profitable relationship?

3. Are the departmental policies clearly stated and understood by everyone concerned?

4. Does the department have high morale with the proper attitude toward its supervision?

5. Does the department take steps to reach all objectives and carry out all policies of its general management?

FUNCTIONS OF A COMPLETE PURCHASING OPERATION

The sequence of events leading up to and following through a complete procurement cycle in a business involves many functions other than purchasing but the purchasing function is called upon to take part at each step. The degree of formality and the details of procedure may vary from firm to firm and in degree from item to item in each firm, but each transaction is subject to the following typical sequence.

Original Consideration of the Purchase. Before an item can be bought, someone must decide whether or not to buy it; and, if so, specifically what should be bought. According to the degree of importance, the value involved or the complexity of the problem, purchasing has the responsibility of developing prices, alternatives, and other relevant information.

Origination of the Purchasing Request. When the decision is reached by the appropriate individual, that decision is transmitted in the form of a duly authorized requisition. It may take any one of three typical forms: (*a*) a repetitive reorder card, (*b*) a routine requisition form, or (*c*) a specific memorandum requesting an unusual procurement not provided for in existing routine procedures.

Whatever the form, the request to purchase or requisition is purchasing's signal to proceed and provides three essentials: (*a*) purchasing's authority to make the commitment; (*b*) the identity, quantity, and specification of what is to be purchased; and (*c*) the date when the item is required.

The requisition form usually provides certain additional information for the convenience of subsequent receiving and handling as well as accounting and cost control records, such as specific destination identification and the appropriate cost codes to be charged.

Determination of Possible Sources. It is purchasing's function at this point to take over the direct procurement responsibility. Based on knowledge and experience as to potential vendors, the purchasing agent determines whom to invite to quote. According to circumstance and his judgment, he may elect to telephone, telegraph, or mail his quotation requests or to invite vendor representatives in for personal discussion. When time allows, it is advisable to send a formal quotation request form even when a single supplier is asked to quote.

Selection of the Source. Negotiation of the commitment is an important feature of the purchasing agent's responsibility. His object is to determine who in his objective and honest judgment freely offers the most ultimate value for the money in the combined factors of price, service, and quality.

Traffic and Routing. It is a purchasing function to select the most economic method of delivery and routing, based on the traffic department's expert advice, consistent with the reliability of delivery within the permissible delivery timing. The selection should be specified.

If there is indicated a need or desirability for special arrangements or shipment tracing with the transportation agency, this function usually is performed by the traffic department as requested by the purchasing agent.

Issuance of Purchase Order. When agreement with the chosen vendor is reached, all pertinent provisions of the agreement are formally confirmed by the preparation and issuance of the purchase order. The purchase order is a legally binding obligation and the authority to incur such obligation is a function entrusted to the intelligence, prudent judgment, and integrity of the purchasing agent. It is essential that the obligation be stated on the purchase order clearly and completely.

Usually the purchase order is imprinted with the standard conditions on which the firm is willing to do business and the particular purchase agreement is thereby stated as subject to the vendor's acceptance of those standard conditions. Specific provisions negotiated for the particular order include quantity and identification, specifications, price, f.o.b., and discount terms, delivery instructions covering mode of transportation, carrier, routing, destination and required delivery (or shipping) date, and such pertinent special instructions as provisions for inspection, certification, packaging, preshipment samples, and notification of shipments.

While the primary purpose of the purchase order is to state the detailed agreement reached with the vendor and authorize his delivery of the purchased material, copies of the document serve the additional purpose of notifying and advising all other affected departments of the details of the transaction. Thus, the requisitioner is notified that his material has been ordered, the terms of the purchase, and when he may expect delivery. Receiving personnel are notified what incoming material to expect, when and how it is scheduled to be delivered, what inspection to make and whom to notify on arrival. The accounting department's copy notifies of the expenditure committed and furnishes the price and terms to be verified and paid on the subsequent invoice. Other copies may be used for additional notifications according to the organization and needs of the particular firm.

Purchase Follow-up and Expediting. Follow-up is the process or function of checking up on the vendor to ensure his fulfillment of his promised delivery obligation. While the term "expediting" is frequently used loosely or interchangeably with "follow-up," it is more accurate to define expediting as the effort to improve a promised or scheduled delivery. Follow-up is a function almost always performed by the purchasing department. While commonly a purchasing function, expediting frequently requires technical talents and assistance so that it is not uncommon for this function to be performed by others such as engineering or inspection personnel as requested and authorized by the purchasing agent.

Follow-up is the purchasing agent's most onerous chore; a necessity in the satisfactory discharge of his responsibility to see to it that his requisitioner's needs are delivered on time. The first step in effective follow-up is a clearly understood, firm agreement on delivery before the order is awarded. The burden of follow-up can be lightened by insistence on delivery reliability and systematic weeding out of vendors who fail to fulfill glib and irresponsible delivery promises. *The burden of follow-up can be further lightened by insistence that vendors regularly supply up-to-date information on the status of orders already placed.* It is a major point of importance for the purchasing agent to develop effective and inclusive follow-up and expediting procedures and to establish clearly understood policies rewarding reliable delivery performance and penalizing the unreliable.

Receiving and Inspection. The function of receiving and physically handling delivered materials, together with verifying that the deliveries correspond exactly to that specified in the purchase order, is usually performed not by the purchasing department but by a specialized group, independent of purchasing from internal audit standpoint, working in conjunction with allied functions of stores, warehousing, or materials handling.

Inspection ranges from simple count and verification of the packing list or delivery ticket to prescribed laboratory testing for the verification of specified quality and on to elaborate technical inspections and demonstrations of performance. The inspection function, because of its wide and varying scope, may be performed by any one of several functional groups from receiving personnel on up according to the governing circumstances. Instructions for inspections may be (and usually are in the significant instances) specified by the requisitioner, thereafter becoming the purchasing agent's responsibility to make the appropriate arrangements. It is the purchasing agent's responsibility to see that the matter of inspection is not overlooked or neglected during the purchasing process.

Invoice Check and Payment. It is a generally recognized accounting function to verify or check the accuracy of invoices and thereupon to transmit payment to the vendor. Invoices require three checks: first, verification by comparison with receiving documents that the billed material has been received complete and in proper condition; second, verification by comparison with the purchase order that the prices and terms conform to the purchasing agent's commitment; third, machine extension of the invoice to verify arithmetical accuracy.

The accounting department in some firms provides the routine service of (*a*) verifying the mathematical accuracy of invoices, (*b*) rendering payments with due promptness, (*c*) earning cash discounts in accordance with the purchasing agent's purchase agreement, and (*d*) in some concerns, ascertaining all instances of variance between invoices rendered and the purchase agreement, referring such instances back to the purchasing agent for appropriate correction and/or renegotiation. *Such variances which are obviously clerical error are generally adjusted by direct handling between the respective accounting departments to avoid unnecessary burden on the respective purchasing and sales departments.* It is the responsibility and prerogative of the purchasing function to obtain satisfactory settlement of delivery and invoice deviations from the original purchase agreement.

A thorough purchasing operation requires, for complete open-order control, notification of material receipts, invoice payments, and comparison of invoice and purchase order terms. The purchasing department's process of checking receipts and invoices against original purchase commitments to signal the completion of open order, thereupon closing it out to inactive status, is a significant duplication of accounting's verification process. Such duplication can be eliminated by integration of purchasing and accounts payable clerical functions and personnel, which is practiced in some firms. The inherent hazard from possible dishonesty when the same individuals are committing, checking, and paying invoices necessitates exceptional measures for adequate audit control wherever this organizational practice is chosen.

Material and Inventory Control.[9] The function of controlling the variety and quantity of materials on hand may be performed either by a specialized group, by personnel charged with the responsibility for physical handling and/or warehousing, or by the purchasing department; or all three related functions may be integrated in an over-all materials management function. The organizational choice depends on the nature of the business in question.

The material and inventory control function, regardless of where assigned, is that of ensuring enough but not too much supply on hand of all the materials and supplies of the proper quality essential to the business. Reorders must be initiated on a lead-time schedule determined by purchasing as adequate for economical negotiation and delivery, varying

[9] Detailed in Section 13, "Quantity Determination Through Inventory Management."

in accordance with supply conditions. Reorder quantities must be determined within the capacity for satisfactory and economic storage and with due regard for optimum purchase economies. Inventory levels must be maintained between the minimum limit of adequate stocks to ensure continuity of operations and a maximum determined by space limitations, working capital limitations, optimum purchase quantities, and expense penalties of physical handling of excessive delivery frequency.

Optimum inventory investment for a given business can be determined only by establishing optimum inventory of each item under prevailing market conditions and totaling the differing individual items.

The function of inventory control profoundly influences the efficiency of the procurement function and, in turn, is dependent upon purchasing's appraisal of prevailing markets for its own efficiency.

Value Analysis and Purchasing Research. Getting his money's worth has always been the businessman's principal procurement objective; unless he can buy at the right price, he cannot sell at the right price. Hence his purchasing agent is chosen largely and perhaps mainly on the basis of exceptional ability to weigh and judge values. The function of "value analysis," therefore, is the body itself of every purchasing entity, as described in Section 11.

The growing complexity of modern business and industry has mothered the invention of specialized and organized methods for analyzing values. Such terms as "value analysis," "purchasing research," and "purchase analysis" have evolved to denote specific organizational group effort toward improved purchasing.

Purchasing research specialists, working either within the purchasing department itself or separately as an allied group, aim to discover "the one best way" for the firm to procure its necessary materials and supplies. Such effort is concentrated on items purchased repetitively, with priority assigned according to dollar significance.

The procedure parallels that of any other research effort: identifying and establishing the scope of the project, assembling the known facts, suggesting potential alternatives, examining all possibilities, and deciding on the optimum final solution.

The purchase analysis starts with determining what is bought, its cost, why it is bought, what alternate items might be used, how the various alternates are sold, what are the optimum procurement methods, and finally what is "the one best way" for the firm to obtain that particular supply. Data, opinion, suggestion, and other talent must be solicited from all sources both within the organization itself and from suppliers.

As in any research, the qualities which determine the productive worth of the effort are thoroughness and ingenuity, thoroughness in developing all the relevant facts, and ingenuity in generating ideas of better alternatives.

The purchasing agent is a key figure in the purchasing research function. In a small firm he may be the function. In any size firm and however it may be organized, the purchasing agent is the one for whose benefit the research is performed and who must in final analysis implement the research results by making his purchases accordingly.

Purchasing Administration. The administrative function is that of organizing and supervising the efforts of the group toward the accomplishment of the assigned purchasing responsibilities. It encompasses the establishment of guiding purchasing policies, the definition of procedures to be employed, the delegation of duties to be performed, the employment and training of personnel, and the supervision of assigned tasks.

Administration includes keeping all members of the group informed as to corporate developments and objectives, maintaining cordial working relations within the group, obtaining cooperation from other functional groups, and coordinating individual efforts with the activities of others both within and outside the department.

The complete purchasing operation is a chain reaction starting long before an actual requisition is delivered on the purchasing agent's desk and continuing far beyond his award of the order; it is the administrative function to guide the purchasing crew toward the end of linking its contributions in the proper sequence in the over-all chain of events.

Salvage and Surplus Disposal. This function, as explained in Section 21, is most usually assigned to the purchasing department for reasons of expediency. While salvage and surplus disposal is essentially a sales rather than purchase function, its relation to the sales department is further removed than from the purchasing department. There are three main destinations for such material for disposal: reuse by some other segment of the company; return to original supplier for restocking; and sale to used-material dealers or to other users. The purchasing department by the nature of its function is in the strategic position to direct surplus to reuse or to deal with the original supplier for return for credit. Its normal business relations, too, keep the purchasing department in direct contact with used-material dealers and facilitate salvage and surplus disposal through those channels.

Periodic Audit of the Purchasing Department. The audit function is performed by specialized audit personnel usually located organizationally within the accounting department. The objective of periodic audit is to verify that authorized procedures have been followed throughout the procurement operation, or else to focus appropriate management attention on deviations so that corrective measures may be instituted. The function is performed as a service to purchasing (and higher) supervision; the purchasing agent is obligated both to cooperate by furnishing the auditors with all requested facts and information and to utilize the resultant audit report by according conscientious consideration to the recommendations.

REPORTS TO TOP MANAGEMENT

Different top managements give different emphasis to the kinds of reports they want. But any top management must have reports from the various departments in order to have information to use in planning, organizing, and controlling operations. Such reports should be prepared with an eye to the needs of top management for significant key-point summary data, and reports should exclude voluminous operating detail that does not particularly concern top management. From purchasing, for example, top management normally wants periodic reports on the significant trends in prices, materials availability, and the events that will significantly affect material costs. Annual performance reports giving a summary of the purchasing department's activities and accomplishments help management to appraise purchasing performance.

Periodic reports, presented at specified time intervals, should be in such a form and continuity that they allow management to compare present and past period results and to make projections into the future. Some reports are appropriate covering monthly, quarterly, or annual periods, while others are desirable daily. Electronic data processing now makes it possible for top management to have daily reports of key figures that once required days or weeks to compile. In periodic and current reports a meaningful figure might be all that is necessary to communicate essential information. The trend is to present effective timely data that is currently useful for top management control and decision-making and to minimize the number of specific reports that require considerable management reading-time.

Lengthy reports are being replaced by the use of index numbers, percentage figures, ratios, and significant dollar figures that can be compared with programmed standards to indicate present actual status. A meaningful figure such as the current inventory turnover figure might carry all the information specifically necessary for top management action initiation. Top management, upon review of the figure, might ask for some kind of special report interpreting the significance of the change in the figure during the period, or it might prefer to make the interpretation itself. Unless top management specifies otherwise, reports should be expository rather than descriptive. Brief interpretations might be appropriate in written reports, even if not asked for, if the prime purpose is to clarify the meaning of the report and not to try to excuse failures or promote personal position.

Kinds of Reports Going to Top Management

Periodic Reports. Some of the periodic reports that are sent to top management monthly, quarterly, or yearly include the following:

1. The dollar value of purchases—further divided into various inventory categories (raw materials, finished components, supplies, etc.)
2. The operating costs of the purchasing department—further divided into accounting categories (direct purchasing personnel, clerical personnel, office expense, etc.)
3. Analysis of work performance of the purchasing department
   a. Number of orders issued and dollar value of purchase commitments
   b. Number of invoices processed and dollar value of payments to vendors
   c. Annual progress and performance report describing department activities and accomplishments
4. Inventory performance and status
   a. Inventory turnover figures—total and by category
   b. Comparison of actual to programmed inventory
   c. Surplus and inactive inventory
5. Cash discount performance
   a. Total possible cash discounts
   b. Total cash discounts earned
6. Vendor performance and buyer responsibility
   a. Percentage of late deliveries
   b. Percentage of defects in delivered materials
7. Cost reduction and value achievement
   a. Period index of prices actually paid compared with period index of industrial price level
   b. Results of cost reduction program
8. Miscellaneous
   a. Cost of reciprocity purchases
   b. "Make or Buy" decisions during period
   c. Results of international purchases program

Current and Special Reports. Top management often wants current and special reports that include the following:

1. Current inventory status
   a. Critical materials shortages

   b. Surplus and aging inventory
   c. Actual inventory size and programmed inventory size
2. Current and imminent cost and price changes
   a. Current or imminent changes in commodity prices or purchasing costs
   b. Current or imminent changes in freight rates and materials handling costs
3. Current market and materials developments
   a. Significant market developments, threats of strikes or other stoppages, and other events that might affect assurance of supply
   b. Information concerning new materials and processes of significance to the firm

Purchasing Department Reports in the Particular Enterprise

Inventory Control. The purchasing department should qualify itself to assume all or part of inventory control reporting because of its strategic position. If the department exercises complete control, it should make the report directly to top management. If the department shares control with other departments, it must share the report and a decision has to be reached as to what department compiles the final report. In any event, it is of vital importance that top management be given current and accurate information on inventory status and supply conditions affecting inventory.

Commitments versus Working Capital. Working capital must be available to meet purchase commitments. The purchasing department, by keeping a continuous record of commitments and a schedule of deliveries, can assist the treasurer and controller in preparing reports relative to working capital needs. The purchasing department is the source of information on commitments and must provide a means for transferring the accumulated data to the reporting department.

Price Trends. Purchasing is responsible for keeping top management informed on price trends. In this particular report the purchasing department should feel free to editorialize and "go out on a limb" with its predictions. The purchasing department must take full responsibility for the prediction of price trends.

Performance, Cost Reduction, and Value Realization. In large organizations, formal methods of communications must take the place of the informal methods possible in smaller organizations. The performance report in large organizations is used by top management to appraise a department's performance and plan for the future. The departmental performance report gives the purchasing manager an opportunity to explain his department's objectives, its accomplishments, and its plans for the future.

Often the performance report can be augmented by a report on documented and audited cost savings accomplished through a formal cost reduction and value realization program.

SUMMARY

The object of this section is to highlight the over-all function of purchasing. Each of the following sections elaborates in detail practically every sentence. Collectively, it demonstrates that successful purchasing has no short cut. There is no magic formula to buy the right commodity at the right price. A continuing project of study, analysis, and straight thinking by competent personnel and organization is required to attain that objective.

It is recognized that purchasing has come a long way since the days when it was merely a mechanical job of obtaining a few competitive bids and affixing a signature to a purchase order to the lowest bidder. In those days, purchasing did very little in challenging specifications, suggesting substitute material, participating in the acquisition of equipment, or sitting in on top management discussions. Today, management looks to purchasing to supply accurate and factual information faster through modern methods (such as data processing when available to them) of contributing to the expansion of its engineering base through better source selection, and to provide its full share in cost improvement of its products.

It is also recognized that the purchasing function, as outlined in this handbook, will not remain static. Decisions now being made by top management in all business functions must necessarily have their effect on purchasing. That will determine in the years to come the span of the purchasing man's responsibilities and how the job is to be executed.

BIBLIOGRAPHY

For reference books on the purchasing function, see Section 26, "Library and Catalog File." This lists current books and magazines on subjects directly related to all phases of purchasing, and on general business matters.

SECTION 2

PURCHASING DEPARTMENT ORGANIZATION

Editor

Harold A. Berry, President, Afro-American Purchasing Center, Inc., New York, N.Y. (Section written while Vice-president and Director of Management Services, Chicago, Rock Island and Pacific Railroad Company, Chicago, Illinois)

Associate Editors

C. Dwight Brooks, Manager, Purchasing Administration, Burroughs Corporation, Detroit, Michigan

Victor H. Pooler, Jr., Manager of Purchasing, Carrier Air Conditioning Company, Syracuse, New York

With the purchasing department controlling the outflow of over 50 per cent of the average company's sales dollar, management has come to recognize the part purchasing can play in the over-all success of the business. It also recognizes that the greater the complexity of the materials purchased or of the products manufactured, or the higher the percentage of company expenditures for procurement of materials, supplies, and services, the more important the purchasing department should be considered in establishing the company organization. It will, therefore, select the type of organization that will grow with the company while helping the company grow and prosper.

Management further recognizes that a dollar saved by sound purchasing represents the profits earned by an average company on an additional $10 of sales. While most companies expend great effort to increase their sales to gain an increased profit, unfortunately not all companies have realized that an efficient purchasing department with equal effort and with management cooperation can achieve so much with no additional investment.

RESPONSIBILITY AND AUTHORITY

The chief executive officer of the progressive company, regardless of the size of his company, will delegate full responsibility and authority for the procurement function to a responsible and capable purchasing department officer. This is true whether the latter functions as a "one-man" department or directs the purchasing activities of a large corporation.

The term "responsibility" in this sense is accountability for the performance of duties, and "authority" is the formal right to require action of others. To fulfill his responsibility, the purchasing officer must be given authority which is equal to the responsibility in every respect. The delegation of responsibility without an accompanying and commensurate authority is, in effect, no delegation at all. For effective operation of the purchasing department, responsibility and authority are inseparable. In written policies, a clear definition of one is in effect a clear definition of the other. Thus, the limits of authority and responsibility can be combined into one composite statement. This is usually put in writing so that the purchasing officer will know what is expected of him, and the limits of his authority. Such a statement avoids overlapping of authority with other departments and consequently avoids confusion. An example follows of such a written statement by the top management of a medium-sized manufacturer where the purchasing agent reports to a director of purchasing, who in turn is responsible to a vice-president. The examples include all information from the company organization management guide covering the purchasing function.

Director of Purchasing—Job Description

Function

Develop for the approval of the Vice-President and put into effect approved objectives, policies, and programs to govern purchasing activities.

Responsibilities and Authority

Establish policies concerning the procurement of materials and supplies and the rental of equipment for the company's use in such a manner that the maximum value will be obtained per company dollar expended.

Negotiate in company with other departments directly involved for the services of whatever outside consultants and engineers may be required to implement programs of modernization, expansion, etc., of the company's physical properties, and establish policies for administering their activities as they affect contractual considerations.

Assure the constant exploration for new sources, products, materials, processes, and ideas, and assure that information will be available to other departments in changing specifications or adopting such substitutions as will perform the required function of all purchases at the least cost to the company over the period of their life.

Assure that purchase sources deliver purchases in the quantity and at the price, quality, and time required, and follow up on major purchase orders to assure delivery on schedule.

Provide for advantageous sales of obsolete, damaged, scrap, or excess equipment, materials, and supplies.

Administer the securing of priorities and allotments from appropriate governmental agencies during periods of governmental control of material.

Administer the order writing and clerical activities involved in purchasing, such as the distribution of bids or inquiries, the receipt of quotations, negotiations, and the receipt and checking of invoices for payment.

Keep currently informed of laws, rules, and regulations affecting the purchasing and delivery of required materials.

Keep abreast of current developments in the purchasing profession.

Furnish timely information to the Vice-President and appropriate department heads concerning market conditions and trends and the probable effect on the supply and price of materials used in the manufacture of our products.

Relationships

THE VICE-PRESIDENT

Be accountable to the Vice-President for the fulfillment of his function, responsibilities and authority, and relationships, and for their proper interpretations.

DIRECTOR OF TRAFFIC

Seek the advice and counsel of the Director of Traffic with respect to transportation and outside warehousing aspects of purchases.

PLANT SUPERINTENDENTS—STOREKEEPERS

Counsel with and advise the Plant Superintendents and Storekeepers on sound inventory policies for containers, materials, and supplies.

DIRECTOR OF MARKET PLANNING

Seek the advice and counsel of the Director of Market Planning with respect to future production plans and purchasing and inventory requirements which may arise therefrom.

OTHER MEMBERS OF MANAGEMENT

Seek advance information from members of management on anticipated purchasing requirements.

LABORATORY

Work closely with all sections of the Laboratory in the development of improved major supplies and materials.

ATTORNEY

Seek the advice of the Company Attorney on the form of major purchase contracts.

VENDORS

Assure maintenance of sound relations with vendors and work with them through subordinates to improve items purchased, while seeking constantly to develop new and better sources of supplies.

Purchasing Agent—Job Description

FUNCTION

Develop, for approval of the Director of Purchasing, and put into effect approved policies and programs which will assure procurement of materials, supplies, and services at all times at all company plants and offices.

RESPONSIBILITIES AND AUTHORITY

OPERATIONS

Be responsible for the purchase of all materials and supplies required at the plants and offices.

Be responsible for materials and supplies investigation activities within the scope of the Purchasing Department responsibilities involving possible economies, new products, changes in quality, and changes in design. Report to the Director of Purchasing on all such activities and, as may be directed by him, transmit reports and recommendations to the Plant Superintendents.

Examine daily Purchasing Department copies of all orders placed by buyers on preceding day.

Develop, for the approval of Director of Purchasing, new sources of supply or changes in status of old sources where major or critical purchases are concerned.

Serve on special committees involving matters pertaining to procurement and allied interests.

Keep informed on all laws and regulations affecting purchase and delivery of items procured by the Department.

Keep abreast of current developments within the purchasing profession.

Handle any special assignments which may be delegated by the Director of Purchasing.

Keep abreast of all developments and plans at the plants which will affect the purchasing function.

Assure that all information available to the Purchasing Department on new materials, products, processes, supply situation, etc., is passed along to plant and/or office officials.

Assume the full responsibilities of the Director of Purchasing in his absence.

PERSONNEL

Supervise the activities of the Purchasing Department through the Head Buyer for Production, the Head Buyer for Non-production, the Advertising and Special Services Buyer, and the Office Supplies Buyer.

RELATIONSHIPS

THE DIRECTOR OF PURCHASING

Be accountable to the Director of Purchasing for the fulfillment of his function, responsibilities and authority, and relationships, and for their proper interpretation.

Counsel with the Director of Purchasing on sound inventory policies on all items procured.

THE DIRECTOR OF MARKET PLANNING

Seek the advice and counsel of the Director of Market Planning with respect to future production plans and purchasing and inventory requirements which may arise therefrom.

THE GENERAL SALES MANAGER

Work with the General Sales Manager on matters involving customer complaints involving packages, and special requirements involving changes in plans covering Government container specifications and/or requirements.

PLANT SUPERINTENDENTS—STOREKEEPERS

Make recommendations to the Plant Superintendents and Storekeepers regarding sound inventory policies.

THE TRAFFIC DEPARTMENT

Cooperate with the Traffic Department in handling damage complaints which may result from excessive rough handling of containers or possible improper container specifications or quality in so far as these may affect the purchasing function.

VENDORS

Assure maintenance of sound relations with all vendors, present and prospective.

All Department Heads—Job Description

All department heads have certain responsibilities and authority regardless of their specialty. These are covered under duties and responsibilities listed below.

Duties and Responsibilities

Within the limits of Company policies, approved programs and control procedures, assume responsibility for and have commensurate authority to accomplish the fulfillment of duties as set forth in the organization manual. Appropriate portions of responsibilities may be delegated to subordinate personnel, together with proportionate authority for their fulfillment—but over-all responsibility and accountability for results may not be delegated nor relinquished.

A. PLANNING AND REVIEW:

1. Plan near and long-term programs covering operations, to implement major Company objectives and policies, seeking advice and counsel of immediate superiors as necessary.
2. Keep immediate superiors currently informed of major plans and programs and of the progress and the problems of operations for which responsible.
3. Develop for approval of immediate superiors such budgets as are necessary or as are requested to maintain departmental functions at lowest possible cost consistent with quality, and operate within the limits of the budget approved.

B. ORGANIZATION:

1. Maintain a sound plan of organization, and propose for approval of immediate superiors modifications in and deviations from the basic plan of organization as may be required by changing circumstances to best facilitate the management control and coordination of departmental activities.
2. Subject to approval of immediate superiors, select immediate subordinates—and approve, in turn, selection of their immediate subordinates.
3. Assure that competent employees are available at all times and in training for effective conduct of operations directed, and that subordinates concerned are kept sufficiently informed on current activities so that they are qualified to take over effectively in a superior's absence.

C. PERSONNEL:

1. Establish high standards of performance for departmental personnel, and require performance in accordance with standards established.
2. Regularly appraise the performance of immediate subordinates, measuring such performance against established goals and making necessary recommendations thereon.
3. Maintain satisfactory personnel relations to assure just and equitable treatment of all personnel in accordance with the policies and contracts of the Company and to promote cooperation through the department and stimulate all employees to their best efforts.

D. OPERATIONS:

1. Through proper direction, control, coordination and delegation, put into effect and assure the prosecution of approved departmental policies, plans, programs and assignments and the attainment of approved objectives.
2. Approve detailed operating programs and procedures recommended by immediate subordinates, which fall within the framework of established division or department objectives and policies.
3. Review progress against approved programs, and counsel with departmental personnel on means of improving the operation of the division or department.
4. Coordinate the work of directly responsible department or section heads or

group leaders, and interpret and delegate to them their responsibility for effecting approved objectives, policies and programs.

5. Assist in promoting the acceptance and installation of modern management techniques with the objective of promoting efficiency, economy and team work.
6. Consult with other department heads to coordinate department programs and collaborate with other departments in such activities, projects and programs as are of mutual interest and concern.
7. Serve, as required, on regular or special committees and execute assignments connected therewith.
8. Conduct such relationships not elsewhere specifically defined which are necessary to the accomplishment of Company functions.

Channels of Communication

While the organization structure and chart define lines of responsibility, authority, and accountability, they do not indicate or limit channels of contact or flow of information between or among members of the organization. It is obvious that the best and most productive efforts of the staff cannot be obtained unless they are kept currently informed of all developments with which they are concerned. Therefore, it is the responsibility of each member of the organization to take such steps as may be necessary to inform those associated with any project or problem of all developments. Organization policy permits and expects the exercise of common sense and good judgment, at all organization levels, in determining the best channels of contact for expeditious handling of company work.

Contacts and flow of information between members of the organization should be carried out in the simplest and most direct way practicable. Normally this can be accomplished simply by adequate distribution of certain copies of memorandums, reports, and letters. In making such contacts, however, it is the duty of each member of the organization to keep his superior promptly informed regarding any matters:

1. For which his superior may be held properly accountable by others
2. Which are likely to cause disagreement or controversy, particularly between different departments of the organization
3. Which require the advice of his superior or coordination by his superior with other components of the organization
4. Which involve recommendations for change in, or variance from, established policies

Any Head of Purchasing

Alternate methods of delegating responsibility and authority toward the accomplishment of the purchasing objective are numerous, regardless of the size of the organization. The larger the size, the greater the need for the department head to concentrate on planning, forecasting, organizing, administering, coordinating, and controlling.

The typical examples already cited have been presented in order to illustrate major points of the place of purchasing in the management function. The duties of the director of purchasing and the purchasing agent can be consolidated, and this is true in thousands of small purchasing departments in the United States and Canada. Regardless of size, formulation of objectives and assignment of duties is highly essential if the company is to survive and prosper.

In this and other examples of responsibilities and authority, great emphasis is placed on relationships with the divisions and departments in the organization.

Teamwork and complete cooperative effort is essential to the proper discharging of purchasing responsibilities. Purchasing is not an end in itself. It is in existence to supply the company's material and service requirements. To function properly, it must assist and be assisted by the other departments. Purchasing is in a position to make definite contributions to all departments and, by using this opportunity to set the right example, it can normally earn complete cooperation in its dealings with the other departments.

Section 1 examined the need for the proper relationship of purchasing with other departments, groups, or functions and listed theoretical considerations for the major ones involved. This requires the constant and daily attention of every purchasing executive.

To Whom Purchasing Reports

Since the purchasing agent in any sizable company has executive or policy-making status, the trend today, as is shown in Table 2–1, is toward having the head of the purchasing department report to the president or to a vice-president. In the case of decentralized operations, district or plant purchasing reports to the local chief executive such as the general manager or plant manager. With executive status the purchasing agent is in a position to make over-all contributions for the good of the company.

The purchasing officer is becoming recognized as an authority not only on material market conditions and price trends, but on general economic and particularly competitive conditions. His timely word of caution or suggestion for revising material and production schedules may well affect the profit picture.

Having direct contact with top management the purchasing department head has access to advance information which enables him to alert his department to future changes, thereby saving lead time to incorporate such changes. His alert judgment and the opportunity to apply it makes the company as a whole more flexible in the face of changing economic or marketing conditions.

Table 2–1. To Whom Purchasing Reports[1]

	Under $5 million, %	$5 to $50 million, %	Over $50 million, %	Total, %
President	56.1	30.8	19.0	34.7
Vice-president*	15.8	20.5	41.3	25.4
Executive vice-president	5.3	10.2	27.6	13.9
Plant manager†	5.3	8.9	...	5.2
General manager†	8.8	13.0	1.7	8.3
Treasurer (or secretary and treasurer)	1.7	5.1	...	2.6
Miscellaneous‡	7.0	11.5	10.4	9.9

* Includes vice-president for material management, manufacturing and engineering, finance, planning and development, operations, administrative and general services.

† Usually a decentralized plant reporting to a general manager or plant manager.

‡ Manager of manufacturing, controller, administration manager, business manager, material manager, chairman of the board.

The development of this trend is recognition that the purchasing department must be free to act on its own initiative without working through some other department or division that may not be cognizant of the market conditions or appreciative of the problem or opportunities for the purchasing department.

For example, some years ago approximately 25 per cent of the industrial purchasing agents reported to some production executive. However, as can be seen in Table 2–1, the error of this approach has generally been recognized and the situation somewhat rectified.

PROPER ORGANIZATION ESSENTIAL TO EFFICIENT OPERATIONS

Effective company organization eliminates friction, duplication of effort, and noncoverage by defining responsibilities and authority. Job specifications make possible the better utilization of personnel.

The purchasing organization should be fitted to the job to be done. Utmost care should be taken to see that the assignment of responsibilities is not tailored to an inelastic type of organization.

[1] Table 2-1 and many other tables in this section were based on a survey of 350 nationally recognized leaders of the purchasing profession, conducted by the editor during 1963. Figures shown are for annual purchases.

The scope of responsibilities will vary not only from industry to industry but also from company to company within an industry. Therefore, the best form of organization for the department will not necessarily be identical to or even similar to that of other companies.

Procedures and Job Analysis

The development of understandable and workable procedures and job analysis is the first step in organizing and standardizing the efforts and activities of purchasing.

Organization tends to promote greater efficiency and effectiveness with a minimum of waste motion. It also provides for the development of experts or specialists in various phases of the procurement work.

Published procedures or manuals such as illustrated in Section 3 spell out the procedures and systems within the department. They also define the relationship of the department with other departments or divisions of the company. They cover all routine situations and the operations of the department, and they provide for meeting the unusual conditions or problems that so frequently face purchasing.

In setting up or reviewing the organization of the small purchasing department, it is helpful to study the organizations and procedures of larger departments. While it may be natural to ignore large company organizations as being too dissimilar, the knowledge and responsibility that are required to develop a successful purchasing department are found in equal proportion in the large or the small company.

Generally the large organizations have succeeded because they have given more than usual attention to proper organization within their companies. As a result such companies usually have purchasing departments that gain the greater return for the money expended.

Except for the volume of purchases, many small and medium-sized purchasing departments handle an equal number of diversified commodities as the larger departments. Some small departments must also procure thousands of separate items per year. Their solution is to specialize in a limited number of major purchases and to investigate improved buying procedures for the smaller commitments through experience on the job, through contacts with fellow buyers, and finally from services of professional purchasing associations.

One of the problems that confront some purchasing departments, both large and small, is based on custom or precedent. In companies where one raw material, such as soybeans, tobacco, corn, coffee, cocoa, rubber, silk, or sugar, is the basis of the company's production, that major material may be purchased by a commodity expert of executive rank who is not a part of the purchasing department. To rectify the situation, either the executive and his duties are transferred into the purchasing department or his successor is selected and trained from the ranks of purchasing personnel.

Organization Qualifications

Procedures are but tools of the profession. More important is sound knowledge of purchasing qualifications, systems, and practices. These are basic requirements, whether for a single or multiplant department, and are outlined in the remaining pages of this section. Among the points to be covered are:

1. The degree of centralization, based on:
   a. The single plant or plants geographically grouped close together
   b. The multiplant company, geographically widespread or with diversified products
2. Rules and regulations of department
3. Staffing the department
4. Operating procedures
5. Relation with other functions

POLICIES AND PRACTICES

As previously mentioned, the responsibility and authority of the purchasing executive should be spelled out and thoroughly understood by top management and heads of all departments, as a matter of good company planning and effectiveness.

However, this responsibility must be extended into basic policies and practices understood by everyone in the organization who has direct or indirect dealings with the purchasing department. They must know, for example, the specific policies concerning vendor relations, negotiation of price and other conditions, issuance of the purchase order, and discussions of all related points such as delivery, quality, and price after the order is in force. Among the media for communicating this information to the company employees are (1) published rules or regulations, (2) company informational booklets, and (3) departmental manuals.

One industrial company in the nonferrous industry has defined its policies and procedures through the following published rules and regulations.

General Policy

The authority and responsibility for purchasing rests with a Purchasing Department. This places the responsibility on those who have the interest and the skill to do the work properly and whose primary concern is in the performance of this special task. It permits the setting up of uniform policies with respect to seller relationships. It facilitates the prescribing of procedure, records and routine, and also expedites inspection and approval of materials. It promotes economy by consolidating requirements and by setting up material standards for inventories.

Provisions

1. All requests for prices or for repair service, and all purchases, must be made by the Purchasing Department.
2. Salesmen should be received in other departments only at the request of the Purchasing Department.
3. If necessary to interview salesmen regarding special details of their products, other departments should request such visits through the Purchasing Department.
4. In interviews with salesmen, no one who is not a member of the Purchasing Department should commit himself on preference for any product, the Company's source of supply for any product, or give any information regarding performance or price which might in any way embarrass the Purchasing Department or the Company.
5. All correspondence with suppliers should be through the Purchasing Department, except in special cases where the technical details involved make it advisable to delegate authority to others. In such cases, the Purchasing Department should receive copies of all correspondence.
6. With the exception of freight adjustments which are handled by the Accounting Department, the Purchasing Department should conduct all adjustment negotiations.
7. The Purchasing Department has full authority to question the quality and kind of material asked for, in order that the best interests of the Company may be served.
8. It is within the province of the General Purchasing Agent to delegate to representatives of the different departments authority to select material, but the actual purchasing can be done only on the Company's approved purchase order through the Purchasing Department.
9. In cases of extreme emergency, and only in such cases, an exception to the above rule may be made with the understanding that the head of the department placing the emergency order personally assumes the responsibility of immediately following up the verbal order, given by himself or his representative, with the proper department requisition.

With the official rules and regulations in writing, all departments will understand the authority and the responsibilities of the purchasing department. This will also make known why vendor relations must be conducted or at least initiated through the purchasing department. If vendors look to others than purchasing personnel for business, the purchasing department becomes ineffective and company policies are weakened. Purchasing needs the complete cooperation of all management to maintain its responsibilities. If employees of other departments insist on interviewing sales people without the approval of purchasing, this situation should be resolved with the department head or, failing that, through the chief officer of the company or plant.

Conversely, if purchasing is to be maintained as the only door between the company and the fulfillment of its needs, the door must open two ways. Purchasing must be ever ready to bring in new ideas to the organization. It should see that vendors' representatives who offer worthwhile contributions for the company's welfare obtain prompt audiences with the proper people in the organization.

DEPARTMENT ORGANIZATION FOR A SINGLE-PLANT COMPANY

The basic single-plant organization is the foundation of practically all purchasing departments, regardless of the type and size of corporation, the number of plants, the types of products manufactured, or the geographical spread of the plants.

Simplicity Desired in Purchasing Department

A purchasing department should not be established merely for the sake of having an organization, but should try to achieve the stated objectives as simply and efficiently as possible. An example of this type of department is shown in Fig. 2–1.

The main purpose of the purchasing department is to fill the company's requirements for materials, supplies, and services when they are required and at a price that is competitive. All the other services and goals of the purchasing department are established to assist in this basic directive.

Red tape should be cut to the minimum required for orderly buying procedures. When it is recognized that every possible phase of business activity is reviewed by or passes through the purchasing department, there can be a strong tendency to develop policies and procedures bound in so much red tape that they become unwieldy and unworkable.

To permit reasonable growth without disturbing the basic structure and the functions performed by the department, the organization should not be rigid. The department that includes the fundamentals of good organization can expand naturally, for the elements of good purchasing departments are practically identical regardless of size. The responsibilities and duties of the various members of the department will remain basically the same as they and their department grow. The growth of the department remains directly under the control of the purchasing executive who has responsibility for its activities. With expansion can come the specialization that will make it more effective.

The plan should permit expansion and contraction without disrupting the basic organization. It should withstand boom or depression and should anticipate new products and the phasing out of old ones. Good purchasing organization is not a strait jacket.

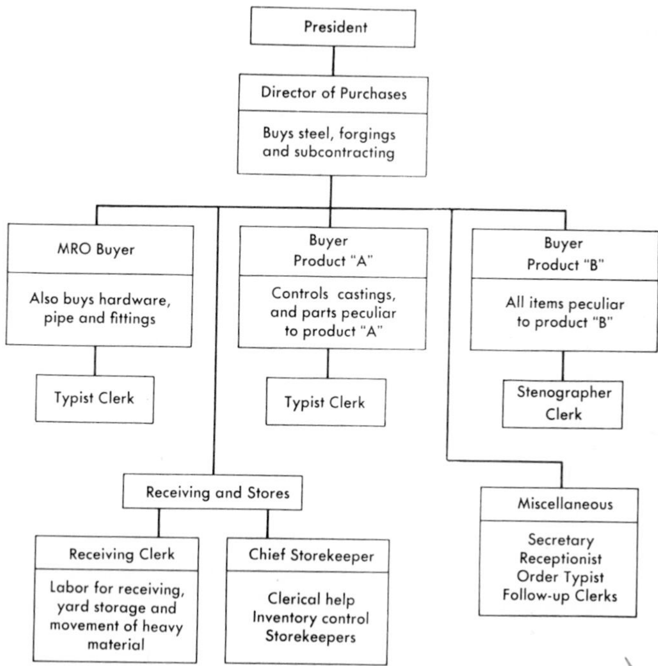

FIG. 2–1. Purchasing department for a company with sales volume of 10 to 15 million dollars annually manufacturing two basic products, each of high value.

Even with forward planning, there may come a time when the department should be reorganized to meet changing conditions. It is then advisable to break with tradition rather than to continue under an outmoded organizational structure. One should plan for the future but should not hesitate to break with the past. A comparison of the organization and the results it is achieving with the goals of the department should be made periodically.

Purchasing Department Must Be Functional

An organization to be flexible, quick to react to change, and competitive must be completely functional with the accent on the job to be done.

In many organizations, specific responsibilities are assigned based on the peculiarities or the personality of some individual or individuals. Naturally, allowances must be made for some outstanding individuals, but only those positions should be established that are essential to the over-all success and efficiency of the department and of the company.

On the other hand, the scope of purchasing is so varied that frequently even the larger companies have functions within the purchasing department that are logically there in those specific cases, while in the average company these responsibilities are normally found elsewhere.

Simplicity should be the goal in setting up the organization, writing procedures for its operation, developing the required printed forms, and making contact with others within and outside the company.

Regardless of the size of the department, its manpower, or the value of its purchases, the same end results are expected. The goal is the same although the manner of achievement will vary, depending upon the size of the department and the type of product or products purchased and manufactured.

Members of small purchasing departments often complain that most of the literature and aids offered them are either developed by or are applicable only to large purchasing departments. However, the procedures and policies developed at great expense by large corporations are usually available to and adaptable at least in part to the smallest company.

The larger purchasing departments may be practically self-sustaining for many services such as engineering, inspection, and records, while in the case of the smaller departments those services must be secured from other departments or individuals.

Naturally, the smaller the company, the more versatile its personnel must be to combine successfully functions that are the responsibilities of individuals or in some cases even of sections or departments in the larger corporations.

Also, in the small companies, it may be necessary to seek information from or borrow personnel on a temporary basis from other departments, such as the inspection, engineering, or manufacturing departments, in order to complete the functions of the purchasing department.

In the one-man purchasing department, we come up with a greater concentration of varied activities, as the ultimate is the concentration of all the responsibilities and duties of purchasing in this individual.

Job Determines Size of Department

Generally speaking, volume will determine the size of the organization and types of supplemental personnel as well as the number of buyers required. (See Table 2–2.)

The complexity of the materials purchased and of the end products produced will also affect the choice of service personnel, such as purchasing engineers and quality-control men. And the greater the complexity, the greater the need for more specialized or expert buyers and the smaller the output of orders per buyer.

Table 2–2. The Number of Buyers in Addition to the Department Head

Buyers	Under $5 million, %	$5 to $50 million, %	Over $50 million, %	Total, %
None	36.4	2.7	...	12.0
1–3	58.2	58.1	3.7	42.1
4–10	5.4	33.8	27.8	23.5
Over 10	...	5.4	68.5	22.4

Purchasing should be sufficiently flexible even in its planned organization to meet changing conditions or new demands. For example, the availability or nonavailability of the right type of personnel may force compromises in establishing the anticipated ideal organization. It may even be desirable to revise the intended organization structure to best utilize the unusual abilities of an available outstanding individual although he may not exactly fit the job description.

The type of materials to be purchased, the length of material coverage, and similar factors affect the ratio of buyers to service and clerical personnel (e.g., in times of material scarcity, expediting is of relatively greater importance).

Managers of smaller departments may wish to concentrate on a higher ratio of skilled buyers, who do their own expediting, specification analysis, etc., with less clerical personnel. An organization of this type can rapidly expand its capacity for work through the addition of inexperienced clerical personnel. This approach would be in direct contrast to the time-honored "one-man department" with one high salaried individual to make all decisions and a clerical group to support him.

Such a policy of being relatively long on buying and technical talent anticipates greater growth potential, better servicing of manufacturing facilities, more contributions in value analysis, added production aids through improved materials, supplies, methods, and equipment, and further continuing cost reductions for materials procured.

In order to be competitive, smaller companies have an even greater need to do an effective procurement job than have the larger companies whose cash reserves may allow them to withstand a major error without fatal consequences.

For these reasons, it is practically impossible to compare intelligently variations in the amount expended for purchasing department operations. The size of the department staff and their salaries vary with the complexity of products purchased, total responsibility for policy and duty, geographical areas, and a host of other reasons.

Title of the Purchasing Executive

The titles of the department head and of his subordinates are of secondary importance to the authority exercised by the executive and of that delegated to his subordinates. As is shown in Table 2–3, there

Table 2–3. Title of the Head of the Purchasing Department

	Under $5 million, %	$5 to $50 million, %	Over $50 million, %	Total, %
Purchasing agent	62.2	61.0	34.0	53.3
Director of purchasing*	15.1	15.6	28.0	19.1
Manager of purchasing†	13.2	15.6	22.0	16.8
Vice-president‡	5.7	3.1	14.0	7.2
General purchasing agent	3.8	4.7	2.0	3.6

* Includes stores, traffic, and transportation responsibility in some titles.
† Includes personnel and administration responsibility in some titles.
‡ Includes production and real estate responsibility in some titles.

is a tendency to standardize on titles. Normally the department head is a vice-president when he is an officer of the company. Either director of purchasing or manager of purchasing is the title used in larger purchasing departments where the supervisor reports to the president or to a vice-president who is possibly a vice-president of purchasing and some other function or vice-president of materials. A few companies have changed the designation from director to manager of purchasing to eliminate any possibility of misunderstanding that the director of purchasing was a director of the company. Small and medium-sized purchasing departments are usually under the leadership of a purchasing agent.

In larger companies the department head will generally concern himself only with policy and administration. In medium-sized companies he may buy a few commodities or products because he is expert in those fields, to keep the "feel of buying" or because the time required for his other duties does not preclude buying. He is primarily an administrator, more concerned with personnel selection, training and supervision of personnel, forward planning, and coordinating with other departments.

He is secondarily a buyer. He should have a general knowledge of all the items purchased and of their ultimate use, but he should not be expected to have detailed technical knowledge of all fields.

The smaller the company, the more buying will be done by the department manager down to the so-called "one-man department," where he will obviously perform all purchasing tasks. In a small company he may even have duties beyond the normal scope of the purchasing function.

Title of the First Assistant

In larger companies the executive may have one or more direct assistants, variously titled in accord with their different duties. They will supervise the people performing certain phases of the procurement func-

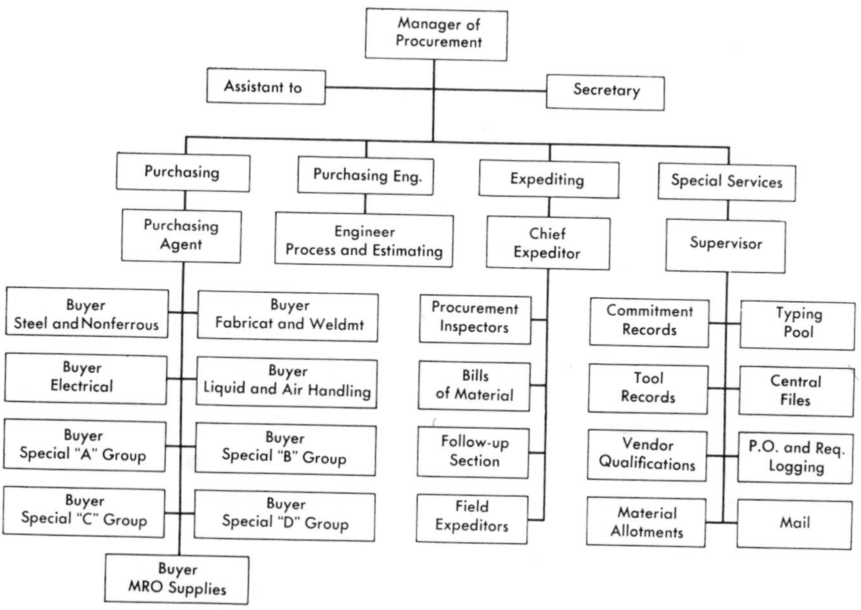

FIG. 2–2. Completely centralized purchasing department for a company with five plants manufacturing identical products with only MRO supplies purchased locally.

tion such as buying, inventory control or requisitioning, specification or value analysis, expediting, quality control, and an array of clerical functions that include filing, maintaining of records, typing, priorities, and material allotments.

A representative highly centralized purchasing department employing more than one assistant is shown in Fig. 2–2.

As is shown in Table 2–4, the first or only assistant is usually so designated by his title such as assistant purchasing agent, purchasing agent, or assistant director of purchasing. In this case, the purchasing agent obviously reports to a manager, director, or a vice-president.

Table 2–4. Title of First Assistant in the Purchasing Department

	Under $5 million, %	$5 to $50 million, %	Over $50 million, %	Total, %
Assistant purchasing agent	31.1	39.1	14.6	29.9
Purchasing agent	13.8	17.2	41.4	23.9
Buyer	48.3	29.7	7.6	26.8
Assistant director of purchasing	3.4	3.1	9.7	5.2
Assistant manager of purchasing	...	3.1	9.7	4.5
Miscellaneous*	3.4	7.8	17.0	9.7

* Reported in all groups are inventory control managers. Reported in the group over $50 million, administration manager, assistant manager purchasing and traffic, manager purchasing administration, and division head.

Need for Experienced Buyers

Those members of the department who, through proper training and experience, can study markets, forecast trends, chart economic conditions, analyze values, and review new materials, new techniques, and new equipment should specialize in buying, and be freed from time-consuming clerical duties. Each buyer should be backed with adequate clerical help to assist him and allow him to devote most of his time to the more technical phases of his assignment.

This arrangement allows the review of specifications by those who know materials, the possible substitution of standard items in place of special materials, the placing of orders with proper timing and in the best quantity brackets, and similar advantages.

It takes a trained purchasing man to buy from the vendor who will make the greatest ultimate contribution. The type of tooling to be purchased, the f.o.b. point, cash discounts, the intangibles that give quality, and suggested component substitutions are all points to recognize in the determination of the supplier.

The vendor's personnel, skills, equipment, facilities, forward planning, research personnel and facilities, and general performance are points of ultimate strength or weakness to be carefully studied in selecting one supplier over another.

Experienced buyers recognize that if the low bid is the criterion for the selection of the supplier, the apparent low bidder may later build up additional expediting costs, clerical expense for material deviations, and additional labor costs to avoid rework and production stoppages. There may also be a sacrifice in quality.

The buyers' primary function is to buy the categories assigned to them by reviewing specifications; locating potential suppliers; securing and analyzing quotations; selecting the suppliers; negotiating price, delivery, and any unusual conditions; signing the purchase order; and discussing quality, acceptance, and replacements. Buyers are responsible for the completeness and accuracy of purchase orders that carry their signatures.

Guidance for a Buyer

A Middle Western utility in its Purchasing Manual has set forth purchasing objectives, principles, and buying practices that provide excellent guidance for a buyer.

PURCHASING OBJECTIVES

To buy the right items in the right volume at the right time from the right sources at the right price; and to have them delivered at the right time.

PURCHASING PRINCIPLES

Be loyal to the Company in all business dealings.
Be just to all with whom you deal.
Be courteous to everyone.
Promote the interests and policies of the Company.
Be receptive to counsel from other departments.
Buy without prejudice.
Promote honesty and truth in buying and selling.
Respect our obligations.
Avoid sharp practices.
Obtain the maximum ultimate value for every dollar spent.
Increase our knowledge of materials and manufacturing processes.
Accord prompt and courteous reception to salesmen.

BUYING PRACTICES

We believe that to buy successfully our buyers must be completely familiar with all procurement factors. This includes:

Complete information as to the product they are buying, its design, use, and the length of time required for manufacture.

Knowledge of general business conditions and specific commodity trends.

A good idea of the cost of production.

Stocks on hand, and

Who are the other large users of the important basic commodities, such as copper and steel.

Also, buyers should be familiar with and use cost analysis to determine whether or not the prices they are paying are fair.

Specialization by Buyers

In larger companies the buying function is normally divided, on the basis of categories of material or products, into sections and assigned to buyers. In some companies, groups of buyers may be under the supervision of senior buyers or purchasing agents who in turn report to the department head or to his assistant.

Buyers are usually given assignments based on their abilities and interests or degree of specialization, recognizing that they can best perform in assignments that they like. The purchasing department shown in Fig. 2–3 is representative.

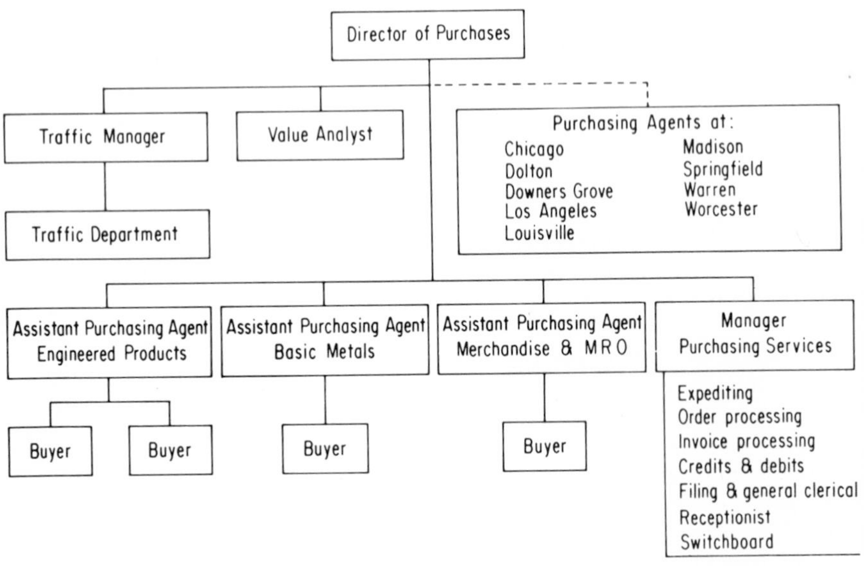

FIG. 2–3. **Purchasing Department, Rex Chainbelt, Inc. Organized into three distinct buying groups with a service group responsible for auxiliary functions.** (*By permission of Rex Chainbelt, Inc., Milwaukee, Wis.*)

In well-organized companies no one outside the purchasing department may make a purchase commitment for materials or services which, according to policy, fall within the scope of the purchasing department. And to keep the purchasing organization functioning properly, no one in purchasing makes a commitment for a buyer within his categories unless he is expressly acting for him and with his knowledge.

If a buyer purchases all of a company's needs in given categories, his experience in procuring for certain end products should reflect itself in purchasing for new but similar requirements. For example, one major appliance company introduced a new line of products for manufacture and assembly. The purchased parts were distributed to the company buyers who, based on their experience, were able to procure the bill of material at a total cost of approximately 20 per cent under the estimate, while the only additional personnel required was one expediter to assist the buyer of hardware and fastening devices.

The procedure should also make the buyer the expert on purchasing the proper "end-use function" rather than merely objectively buying an item to print, to specification, or from a catalog or stock list. The example above in which large savings were achieved was made possible by the buyers being allowed to make substitutions based on their and their vendors' experience.

The procedure wherein one buyer is solely responsible for a category of material makes for better vendor relations by restricting contacts within and without the company, by cutting down the number of vendors' calls, and by establishing a specialist for the vendor to deal with.

Frequently, buyers operate as section supervisors with other subordinate buyers, follow-up clerks, and all necessary clerical help reporting to them. This procedure gives strength to the department as the follow-up clerk, buyer's secretary, and order typist concentrate, as does the buyer, on only a phase of the purchasing department job and in consequence they become more expert in that phase. The education of the group is more rapid through concentration. They may substitute for the buyer in his absence and may relieve him of the more time-consuming duties, allowing him more time to do a better buying job with all of its attendant intangibles.

The procedure also provides excellent training for a follow-up clerk who has buyer capabilities, allowing him to expand his activities as rapidly as he qualifies.

The buyer's responsibility normally includes expediting materials into the plant and through receiving inspection. Regular visits through his company's plants and periodic visits to his suppliers keep the buyer up to date in his buying and problem solution.

The "pickup buyer" is finding his way into more organization charts, particularly for those companies having large plants requiring a great variety of MRO items, with many emergency requirements.

This individual works under the direction of the MRO buyer or the purchasing agent, is supplied with a company car or pickup truck, and purchases emergency requirements or low-dollar items with petty cash, releases against blanket orders, or with preissued checks drawn against a special account.

He not only takes a burden off the MRO buyer, but also off receiving, order typing, accounts payable, and inspection, and he saves countless calls and checking between the requisitioner, purchasing department, and the supplier by directly picking up and delivering emergency and miscellaneous small-order requirements.

Such an individual must have the follow-through to see that all requirements are handled promptly and that the necessary paper work is promptly and adequately processed.

Follow-up or Expediting

As is shown in Table 2–5, the follow-up or expediting function is almost universally assigned to the purchasing department.

Table 2–5. Department Responsible for Follow-up or Expediting

	Under $5 million, %	$5 to $50 million, %	Over $50 million, %	Total, %
Purchasing	96.8	95.5	90.6	95.5
Miscellaneous*	3.2	4.5	9.4	4.5

* Reported in the group under $5 million are production, operating departments, accounting, and purchasing and sales.

Reported in the middle group are production, operating departments, requisitioner, stores, and purchasing and stores.

Reported in the third group are requisitioning department, purchasing and operations, and local plant responsibility.

It may rarely be assigned to production, operations, stores, and even to the requisitioning department. The expediting function may be set up in the purchasing department as a unit reporting separately as a subdepartment or the follow-up clerks may work through and report to the separate buyers, functioning as assistant buyers as well as follow-up clerks.

National economic conditions or company characteristics may make one approach temporarily or permanently better.

There is a danger in relieving the buyer of his responsibility for delivery. He is the man of authority in the eyes of the vendor and his requests are met with great respect and cooperation.

If it is found desirable to set up a separate follow-up section, particularly during periods of emergency, it is still necessary for the buyer, the follow-up clerk, and the field expediter to work closely as a unit. Friction or rivalry within this group will break down vendor relations.

It must be recognized that the buyer, by selecting the vendor, still retains the responsibility to assist where possible.

The follow-up duties normally begin with the receipt of the requisition in the purchasing department. Then, with the mailing of the purchase order, sufficient time is allowed for the return of the signed acknowledgment. Failing its receipt, the expediter must see that the acknowledgment is received without alteration so that a contract exists.

It may even be necessary to determine that the supplier has his orders placed with his subcontractors for adequate delivery and that production is properly scheduled. The reputation of the supplier and the condition of the inventory will have much to do with the degree of expediting effort required.

Once the follow-up clerk has assurance that the material has been shipped, he should work with the traffic department and upon its receipt check with inspection reports to determine that the material is acceptable before his responsibility is finished.

The follow-up section normally issues material status or shortage reports periodically to reflect the anticipated delivery dates of unreceived material. It may also issue, acting for the buyers, current lead-time requirements reports to requisitioning departments as a preventive measure to ease the future expediting task.

Other Functions Frequently Assigned to Purchasing

Many functions, related to but not a part of purchasing, fall under the supervision of the purchasing manager by inclusion in his title (e.g., manager of purchasing and stores, director of purchasing and packaging, or manager of materials) and sometimes by assignment on the company organization chart or in a statement of company policy. Such exceptions are based on the peculiar nature of the business, grouping of related activities, or because of the unusual talents of the manager or his staff. Other companies may assign these extra functions or duties by implication or probably through their understanding that such functions, being closer to purchasing than other departments, are as much a part of the purchasing duties as is the actual buying function. Some assignments vary widely in their scope, including in rare cases probably every function performed in business.

There are, however, certain activities that are included with greater frequency in the over-all purchasing function. These often include: (1) traffic, (2) inventory control, (3) stores, (4) statistician, (5) accounts payable or invoice checking, (6) government controls, priorities, and allocations, (7) purchasing quality control, (8) purchasing engineer, (9) value analysis, (10) purchasing research, and (11) sale of scrap and surplus.

Traffic

While Traffic is the subject of Section 18, the survey summarized in Table 2–6 for complete traffic responsibility (both purchased goods and finished products) shows that it is closely allied to purchasing, either as a function of purchasing or a closely cooperating allied department.

Table 2–6. Department Responsible for Traffic for Both Incoming Supplies and Outgoing Products

	Under $5 million, %	$5 to $50 million, %	Over $50 million, %	Total, %
Purchasing	61.2	35.0	24.2	45.3
Traffic	28.1	52.6	63.6	43.1
Purchasing and traffic	3.3	4.2	...	3.3
Materials	...	3.3	6.0	2.2
Production or manufacturing	1.7	2.5	...	1.8
Shipping	3.3	...	...	1.5
Miscellaneous*	2.4	2.4	6.2	2.8

* Reported in the group under $5 million are order, receiving, and service departments; in the middle group are plant manager, accounting, and sales departments; and in the third group are requisitioning department and commercial manager.

Inventory Control

Inventory Control is the subject of Section 13. It is most frequently within the province of purchasing as is shown in Table 2–7.

Table 2–7. Responsibility for Inventory Control (Based on a Survey Made by *Purchasing* magazine)*

	Raw materials, %	Fabricated parts and components, %	Maintenance and operating supplies, %
Purchasing department	69.2	54.1	64.5
Stores department	16.1	16.1	28.3
Production department	17.3	35.5	26.8
Materials control department	11.4	11.4	2.9
Executive and other	17.8	11.2	3.9

* As 20 per cent of replies mentioned dual responsibility, total percentage adds to more than 100 per cent.

Storeskeeping, the physical control, storage, and disbursement function, frequently is broken into two responsibilities—productive and nonproductive stores—which of their nature and frequency of use may call for separate organizations.

The stores department, in addition to storing the material physically so that it may readily be located and available in adequate amounts, exercises all precautions to avoid shrinkage from any cause, attempts to use as little valuable factory space as possible, and strives for standardization and the reduction in the number of items stocked. The stores department should work closely with the buyers, be appraised of changes in order lead time, and cooperate with purchasing to receive maximum quantity discounts. The stores department should also work closely with purchasing research or value analysis, pointing out areas of apparent saving, usage trends, or changes in material rate of use.

In nonproductve storeskeeping, the inventory control records are usually set up on a minimum-maximum basis and are retained and posted in the stores department.

Nonproductive stores may be under the supervision of the MRO supplies buyer, who in this capacity operates similar to a merchandising manager or to the purchasing agent of a mill supply house, literally buying for resale to his own organization, using shop requisitions in place of funds.

Productive stores when combined with purchasing will usually be tied to the buying function through inventory control, the record keeping and requisitioning function.

Depending on the nature, physical size, dollar value and volume, productive material may be stored in warehouses and cribs and requisitioned to the assembly lines or it may be stored on the lines, adjacent to them or on conveyors flowing toward the assembly lines, used as required and accounted for by periodic physical checks. In mass production standby stocks alone are segregated to cover emergencies that arise in the free flowing supplies of components. Good storeskeeping, in essence, is as little storeskeeping as possible. Purchasing is the active partner in making such a goal allowable. The manner of stock control is of concern to the buying group who will be forced to replace shrinkages of materials in emergency cases if inventories are held down. If inventories of unguarded materials are held at levels sufficient to avoid such shortages, the over-all inventory will probably require too great a share of the company's investments. Purchasing is therefore the rope in the inventory tug of war.

Statistician

The statistician, whether on a full-time or part-time basis, maintains necessary records and issues all statistical reports. He forecasts trends for commodity prices and seasonal conditions governing supply and reports on a variety of items that may be peculiar to his industry, such as percentages of dollar volume of purchases from multiple suppliers or statements of purchases where reciprocity is involved.

Based on past experience he should be in a position to point out to buyers and requisitioners seasonal problems such as the ever-present cement shortage that comes in the autumn, the fact that Southern pine may be delayed by spring floods, that Canadian and Pacific Northwestern lumber may be delayed by winter blizzards, etc.

Suppliers who participate in a percentage of a purchased product frequently worry about whether they are receiving their anticipated share of the volume. The buyer should have monthly reports of receipts together with complete quality reports to aid him in his discussions with these suppliers.

Returns of various surveys show that statisticians are employed by very few purchasing departments. These surveys point out that several purchasing departments call on company statisticians for assistance or that statistical assignments are handled by some other member of the purchasing department.

Checking Invoices

The purchasing department shares the responsibility for checking invoices in many companies; however, the trend is to relieve the buyer of this accounting function. Some of these assignments include the complete accounts payable function through the preparation and mailing of the checks. Others limit the responsibility merely to invoice checking, which covers matching all invoices with purchase orders before they are passed for payment, bringing all discrepancies to the cognizant buyer's attention, and securing either corrected invoices or revised purchase orders, so that there is complete agreement before giving approval for payment. Others assign the full accounts payable responsibility to the accounting department, arguing that matching of figures, cost calculation, extension of figures, applications of discounts, and similar duties are more in the realm of accounting than purchasing. In such instances, only invoices with discrepancies are referred to purchasing for the buyer's corrective action. Regardless of the manner in which these responsibilities are allocated, they should be discharged promptly in the interest of vendor relations.

Traveling Inspectors

The employment by purchasing departments of traveling inspectors who visit vendors' plants is an excellent step in the direction of guaranteeing timely receipts of high-quality materials if the volume of purchases can substantiate the expense.

The traveling inspector should survey plants, equipment, quality of workmanship, and the like, of possible vendors to determine whether they should be seriously considered by the buyer as potential suppliers.

When a new vendor is selected, the inspector should review the planned operations and the quality checks that will be applied. He will also approve vendor's tooling prior to authorizing fabrication and will approve the first good product of such tooling before allowing additional production and the next productive step, whether it will be additional operations, assembly, or shipment.

The purchasing inspector will periodically pay routine visits to the vendors to recheck the sequence of operations and the quality of the purchased product. And if incoming shipments of material fall dangerously below acceptable standards or the material in any way appears to point a trend that will fall below acceptable quality, the buyer should arrange to have an inspector go immediately to the source of the trouble.

Inspectors employed by the purchasing department must work very closely with the company's chief inspector so that acceptance standards are identical, so that the purchasing department inspector gets promptly to the root of troubles as they develop, and so that there is complete harmony.

Purchasing department inspectors should receive their original training and periodic briefing in the company's inspection department.

It may even be desirable for the traveling inspectors to receive technical instruction from the company's chief inspector, although the actual routine and approval of expenses are the responsibility of the purchasing executive.

These inspectors, being representatives of purchasing, must be trained to the purchasing outlook, that is, they must be firm, fair, and diplomatic, keeping the vendors as well as the buyers honestly appraised of true conditions. Their authority should extend to having the right to halt production in vendors' plants until the product will meet acceptance standards.

If a separate inspection group is not maintained in purchasing, it may be mutually beneficial to borrow personnel from the company's inspection department to make periodic quality checks at sources.

Such traveling inspectors may also double as field expediters when necessary as many of the problems of nondelivery are traceable to quality. As representatives of purchasing, they should be briefed to handle almost any problems in geographical areas covered by their itineraries.

Purchasing Engineers

Purchasing engineers are employed by some of the larger companies. They have a variety of responsibilities, most of which are included in the following:

Specification analysis—reviewing and translating current specifications and working with buyers, value analysts, and vendors on specification substitution for product availability, cost reductions, or quality improvements.

Processing and estimating new purchased parts or changes in parts to supply the buyers with bench marks to check vendors' quotations for new parts or to check vendors' estimates of cost increases due to authorized changes.

Reviewing, with the buyer, equipment and facility lists submitted by potential vendors to be certain that they can qualify as suppliers prior to the issuance of requests for quotations.

Liaison between purchasing and engineering on technical problems when requested by buyers or the purchasing agent.

Value Analyst

Value analysis (Section 11, "Value Analysis Techniques"), the study of functions, has the job of determining that every element of cost—whatever it may be—contributes in proportion to its cost. The survey summarized in Table 2–8 shows that it may also be designated as cost analysis or as purchasing research.

Table 2–8. Companies Employing Cost or Value Analysis

	Under $5 million, %	$5 to $50 million, %	Over $50 million, %	Total, %
Cost analysis	3.1	5.0	36.4	7.8
Value analysis	...	...	3.0	0.3
Procurement research	...	...	3.0	0.3

In addition to the companies employing individuals or groups to discharge these functions, several companies report that their buyers or some member of their purchasing department have received value analysis or purchasing research training and that formal programs are being conducted by them.

Normally the term value analysis is considered to apply to productive materials particularly in large volume; however, a complete value analysis program demands the analysis of material, labor, supplies, design, and service costs.

There is some question as to whether the purchasing department should have a separate value analysis section, whether the function should be left to the buyers to work out detailed plans with progressive vendors, or whether the value analyst should work closely with the buyers as the coordinator of the program. As the coordinator he would be a consultant to the buyers or to their vendors and the moving force to keep the program in operation. The answer will vary based on the type and volume of products manufactured.

It has generally been agreed that the buyer is the key man in the value analysis program. He knows what items lend themselves to improvement, in what area the high dollar is spent, what vendors can assist in the program, where the new ideas originate, and the timing necessary to inject changes developed in the program. On the other hand, due to the pressure of keeping production flowing, the buyer can too easily set aside a cost improvement program unless there is some organized effort to keep him on target. The third choice, wherein value analysis is a staff service for the buying personnel, is therefore normally most successful in achieving results where the bulk of a company's purchases are in high-volume repetitive buying.

Value analysis of material is but one phase of purchasing research that analyzes and reevaluates policies, procedures, operations, job assignments, and programs relating to purchasing and allied functions.

Manager of Purchasing Research—Job Description

Representative of extremely successful research programs are the duties of manager of purchasing research, as developed by one large purchasing organization:

PLANNING AND PROGRAM DEVELOPMENT

1. Designs and institutes programs for the evaluation of the performance of procurement duties.
2. Analyzes operations of the Purchasing Divisions and prepares studies of improved techniques, systems, and controls.
3. Contacts purchasing executives of other companies to ascertain methods employed in executing procurement responsibilities, and determines applicability of such methods to this corporation.
4. Develops methods of performing operations incidental to actual procurement, for the purpose of increased efficiency and reduction in administrative expenses.
5. Designs and administers Savings Objective Program of the Purchasing Division.
6. Reviews, interprets, and controls development of statistical reports and information required by the Purchasing Division.
7. Is responsible for the coordination of information on the acquisition and delivery of major purchase requirements with consumption rate and standard inventory levels to maintain proper balance of procurement with availability of requirements.
8. Represents the Purchasing Division in development of programs concerned with disposal of surplus and waste purchased materials, including salvage activities.

9. Provides staff services to Chief Purchasing Officers of other General Operating Divisions and Associated Subsidiaries on request of the Director of Purchases.

COMMERCIAL RESEARCH

10. Evaluates source of supply of purchased goods and services in terms of vendor performance, facilities and capacity to produce, financial standing, and commercial significance by reviewing publications, industry reports and vendor statements, by coordinating information concerning suppliers from other Corporation departments with such information from the Purchasing Division, and by direct contact with suppliers and visitations to their plants. Also assists in the development of new sources of supply for purchased commodities.
11. Ascertains and investigates new products and materials introduced on the market and determines the possibility of satisfying procurement needs more efficiently with such products or materials.
12. Analyzes and interprets trends of business in general and supply-demand relationship of specific purchased commodities.
13. Analyzes prices of purchased commodities in terms of market conditions and cost of production.
14. Prepares long-range economic studies concerning major purchased commodities to assist in resolution of procurement policy. Such studies involve contacts with suppliers, industry associations, and governmental agencies.

VALUE ANALYSIS

15. Designs, establishes, and develops on behalf of the Purchasing Division programs and projects concerned with evaluating the quality of purchased commodities, including considerations of standardization, specifications, substitution, inspection, and testing of such commodities. Coordinates commercial considerations of Purchasing Division with considerations of other Corporation departments regarding the use of purchased commodities to obtain maximum economic advantage through the purchasing function.
16. Is responsible for development and execution of projects in the Purchasing Division concerned with obtaining greater value in purchased goods and services through analysis of product design, packaging, transportation, manufacturing methods, and materials handling. Contacts sales and operating executives of suppliers and industry and trade associations, and works with executives of other Corporation departments in performance of these functions.
17. Coordinates exchange of Purchasing Research information among Purchasing Divisions of General Operating Divisions and Associated Subsidiaries.

Clerical Operations

Though often taken for granted, clerical operations are just as important as any other functions of the purchasing department. The ratio of clerical help to buyers normally increases with the size of the company and the volume purchased. Such clerical functions usually include typing, filing, reporting, record keeping, logging, operations of business and communications machines, and receptionist.

A well-organized, smoothly operating department expresses itself by promptly processing paper work, having accurate, necessary records readily available, and seeing that buyers and others do not meet roadblocks in the performance of their duties through delays or because information is misplaced.

Centralized filing in some degree is normal in the purchasing department, as described in Section 25.

The central filing section usually includes the requisitions, numerical purchase order files, vendor purchase order files, and any current informational data generally referred to.

Each operating member of the department such as the buyer should have readily available to him records and correspondence needed to handle the business at hand or for his future projects. On the other hand each office should not be an empire to itself, burdened with retaining old files of records and correspondence and with the issuance of periodic reports.

Records and correspondence that should be retained by the company but have no current value to the original users should be removed to central files, as described in Section 25.

Central files should also retain all records and correspondence generally referred to by more than one individual or section.

Catalog files may generally be the responsibility of central filing, although some purchasing departments may choose that each buyer maintain his own library. Again, who uses the catalogs and the frequency of references should be the basis for the determination.

Miscellaneous Services

Central order typing, wherein all orders are channeled through a typists' pool, is frequently used in larger departments. This has the advantages of spreading the work load from various buyers over available typists and theoretically evens out the work flow. It has the disadvantage of different typists working on a buyer's orders, with the need for the operators to acquire a great variety of technical knowledge, thereby increasing the margin of error, particularly when jobs of this nature are usually training positions with employees not too desirous of remaining long on this assignment. The preparation of "request to quote" forms is on some occasions similarly routed through general typing but normally is the responsibility of the buyer's secretary or whoever handles his general correspondence.

Stenographic pools are established in some purchasing departments.

However, due to the involved nature of purchasing correspondence and the fact that in the former research, gathering of documents, and background are frequently required, pool assignments usually do not prove as successful as assignments to individual buyers. With the latter choice the stenographer will have better opportunity to learn the habits, routines, and commodities of her superior and by performing more of his clerical work can extend his value to his company.

Miscellaneous services such as issuance of reports, and the maintenance of logs of requisitions, purchase orders, etc., and of records such as record of vendor tooling (its location, value, condition, and insurance status) if not assigned to other sections may fall into an over-all clerical or special services section, supervised by the purchasing office manager, supervisor of purchasing office services, or by whatever title fits in with the over-all company policy. Receptionists, telephone, telegraph and teletype operators, their reliefs, and the mailing section are normally included in this general service group for supervisory purposes.

DEPARTMENTAL ORGANIZATION FOR A MULTIPLANT COMPANY

In the multiplant company there may be a need for decentralized purchasing, of which there are many variations. Except for the requirements of better controls, the internal structure, rules, and regulations are practically identical to those of a single-plant purchasing department.

To eliminate any misunderstanding relative to the use of the word "centralized," in the following pages, it is assumed that all companies reaching this stage of organization have centralized all purchasing activities within the company. "Centralization or decentralization" therefore refers to physical centralization or decentralization of the purchasing function on a geographical basis.

In those plants where "decentralized purchasing" is the policy, all plant purchasing is handled by one local purchasing department.

In many multiplant organizations, purchasing is highly centralized with the home office purchasing department buying all productive and high dollar items, allowing the local purchasing departments to make only emergency purchases. Other companies allow the local offices to procure all MRO supplies and some allow all follow-up functions to be performed locally.

There is also a tendency developing among large companies with far-flung and even diversified operations to develop regional purchasing offices. These centralized offices will do all buying in their assigned regions that is not handled at the home office and will thereby eliminate the plant purchasing departments.

Others even allow local procurement of all parts or materials peculiar to that operation. An example of this type of organizational planning is shown in Fig. 2–4.

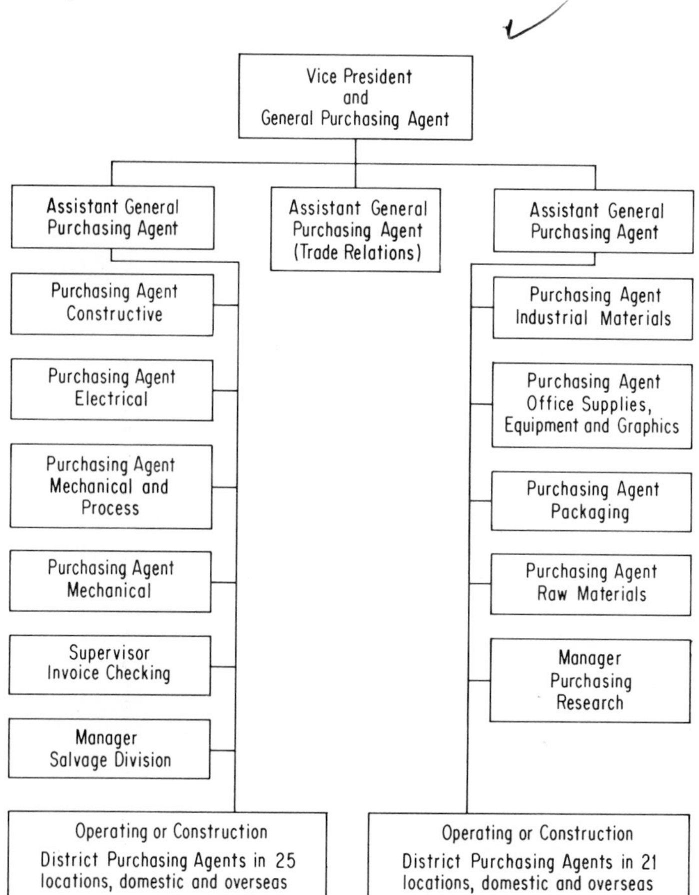

FIG. 2–4. **Purchasing Department, The Aluminum Company of America.** (*Reproduced by permission of The Aluminum Company of America, Pittsburgh, Pa.*)

There is a shading from the tightly centralized purchasing department at the home office with little local freedom of action to the other extreme of complete local autonomy.

No company or its purchasing department should function merely for the benefit of organized procedures, but the procedures should be established or revised to assist the company to prosper and grow.

The choice of a centralized or decentralized purchasing organization should be based on ultimate rather than temporary benefits and take into consideration all facts and unusual conditions. The decision should be governed by three major conditions:

1. The similarity of products produced in the various plants
2. The geographical distribution of the plants
3. The over-all size of the company and the volume of purchases in total and by major commodity or product categories

For Plants Producing Similar Products at Relatively Close Distances

Centralized purchasing permits a greater specialization in the buying function. Each buyer can concentrate on fewer items and there are fewer duplications of effort in similar categories of materials. Particularly when

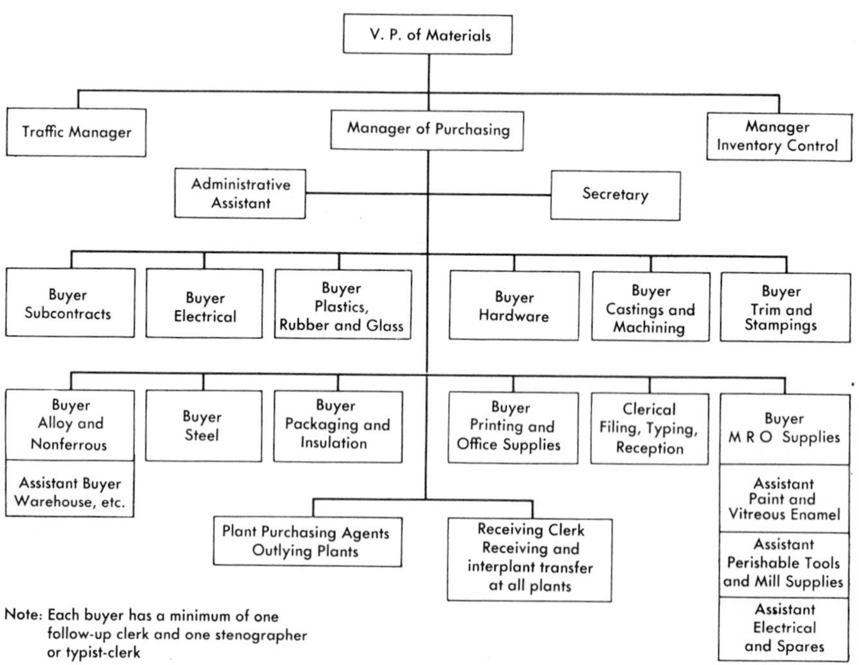

FIG. 2–5. Purchasing department of a major appliance manufacturer with annual purchases of 50 million dollars.

new products are to be introduced and for purposes of value analysis or cost control, this specialization is of inestimable value. An example of this type of organization is shown in Fig. 2–5.

Each year this company has added a new product to its line. With an organization of the type shown, new items that were similar to those already purchased were delegated to the buyers who had the experience to recognize and immediately apply value analysis to the component parts before the engineering was completed. They were able to call upon known and proven suppliers for engineering, styling, and even marketing assistance. As a result, new products reached the market faster, more competitively priced, and production had fewer interruptions.

Centralized purchasing can do a more effective and thorough job in purchasing research, market analysis, cost reduction, and inventory control.

Centralized purchasing retains strict authority and control at the home office without sacrificing (where plants are closely concentrated) the advantages of local purchasing.

One multiplant company that manufactures electrical products, in lieu of centralized purchasing, channels all copper buying through a plant purchasing agent who is acknowledged as an expert in that field. Textile requisitions go through a different plant purchasing agent, and so on. This is acknowledged by that company as a substitute for a central organization and came about through a series of mergers in which a few top-quality purchasing agents of equal ability were absorbed within a short time. Each man thus employs his administrative ability in his local plant while having over-all responsibility for some material or materials for the entire company. Such a system has obvious pitfalls and is mentioned because it is a successful exception. Its continued success calls for close cooperation and understanding.

Centralized purchasing, without any real sacrifice in authority or control or loss of effectiveness, can permit MRO, emergency, or peculiar parts purchases by the local plant purchasing department.

This type of local buying has the twin advantages of allowing the local plant some necessary flexibility and it also helps improve its community relations. With such a system the home office would still buy a large proportion of productive materials and components and place all high-value orders.

Centralized purchasing should encourage the local purchasing agents "to shop" their areas for productive parts that may be the specialties of some local producers in their areas, regardless of where the parts are used in the company. Quotations developed from local sources should be summarized in competition with those secured by the central buyer and the resulting orders would be placed by the central buyer or whoever has the preassigned responsibility for making the purchase.

It may be advisable to decentralize the follow-up function for "on-the-spot" expediting. The advisability of this step would depend on the nature of the products produced, the geographical proximity of the various plants to each other and to the sources of supply, and the seriousness of the delivery problem.

For Plants with Dissimilar Products or Which Are Widespread Geographically

Plants producing unlike products and widely separated geographically often resort to decentralized procurement with each plant practically autonomous. In such cases the home office normally dictates policy and in some instances even detailed procedures. In this type of an organization the home office usually employs commodity or product specialists to advise the local purchasing departments. The home office frequently groups purchases of items or materials in general use, in order to gain maximum discounts. An example of such a national organization is shown in Fig. 2–6.

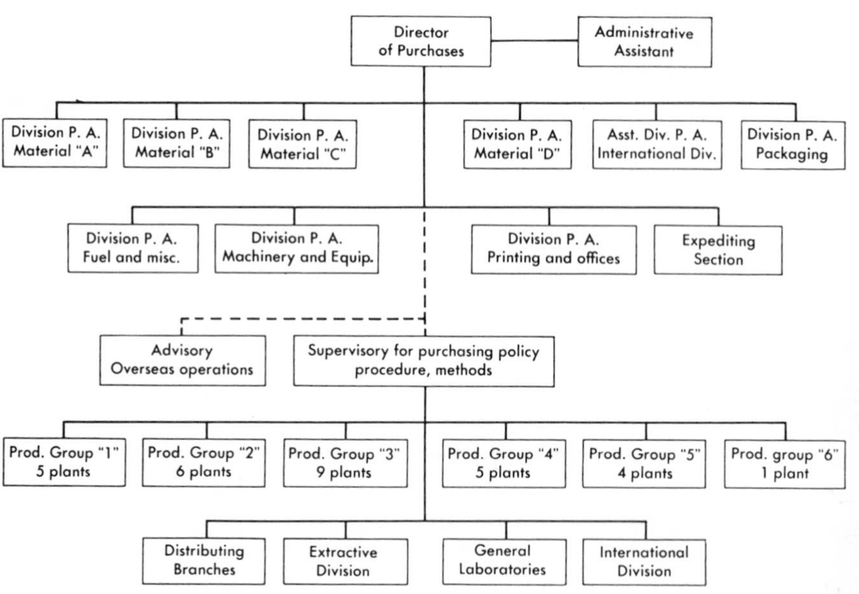

FIG. 2–6. Purchasing department of a large multiplant company where basic materials are centrally purchased for decentralized operations.

Other companies may choose to treat all problems as local problems and in no way dictate even policies and procedures.

Decentralized purchasing gives the local plant organization close control over its material and components. The plant purchasing agent, being closer to his suppliers, can better operate with smaller inventories and can better meet emergency requirements.

Where plants are widespread geographically, decentralized purchasing avoids possible problems due to transportation, loss of time, and poor communications between the local organization and the supplier.

Where plants produce dissimilar products from unlike components, specialization in the buying function is not practical above the individual plant level. Therefore, a decentralized purchasing organization does not seriously hamper buying efficiency.

For a Widespread Organization with Decentralized Purchasing and Central Control

In the large corporations with producing units spread throughout the country, decentralized purchasing has often become the policy regardless of the products produced. However, there is now a tendency for closer corporate control of these outlying units. For example, even if it is not feasible to maintain central control over the entire operations of the company, there are more instances of plants being grouped into a few geographical areas with control exercised on a semiautonomous basis.

Decentralized purchasing with central control permits local purchase of supplies and services peculiar to each plant, while common items can be centrally purchased or at least contracted for on a blanket-order basis subject to local release.

In this type of organization the central office normally has the responsibility of purchasing construction, equipment, and supplies for a new plant during its construction period. If lead time makes such a step necessary, it may also procure all materials to commence production. The central office frequently lets national contracts for materials and MRO supplies used in quantity by more than one plant, allowing local plant purchasing agents to release against these contracts. It is also responsible for trade relations and the determination of percentages of business to be placed with various suppliers when such action is beneficial. It assists local plants, at their request, in locating materials and in expediting deliveries against open orders. It also advises the plant purchasing agents of changes in government regulations, secures legal interpretations, and secures legal approval for agreements incorporating unusual terms or conditions.

It generally has responsibility for interplant transfer of machinery, equipment, materials, and supplies, for the disposal of surplus, for the standardization of tools, equipment, and supplies, and for the over-all inventory position of the company.

It advises management and the plant purchasing department on general business conditions, commodity price trends, and unusual conditions that may influence future operations of the company.

The plant purchasing department normally conducts all purchasing activities except those expressly retained by the central purchasing department. It keeps the central purchasing department advised of local conditions, unusual aspects of vendor performance, and any developments that may affect the plant or company's welfare or future planning. It normally procures supplies and disposes of locally generated scrap within limits defined by central procurement or company policy. Even when plant purchasing agents report to the local plant managers, they conduct all purchasing activities in accordance with policies established by the central procurement department.

Central control guards against multiple tooling and multiple inventories with possible concurrent shortages of the same parts.

This procedure also allows the realization of maximum discounts through the grouping of requirements for largest quantity purchases.

Central Authority in Decentralized Organizations

How far the authority of the home office purchasing executive should extend into other plants in multiplant organizations should be carefully determined by:

1. The degree of centralization or decentralization established in the company's policy
2. The specific responsibilities of central and of plant purchasing being spelled out in practical detail to avoid overlapping functions and possible confusion within the company organization and among the vendors
3. Plant purchasing agents reporting to their general managers except for over-all purchasing policy versus (4)
4. Plant purchasing agents reporting to the home office purchasing executive except for strictly local problems, such as working hours

When the authority, duties, and responsibilities of the home office and of each of the local plant purchasing organizations are clearly spelled out, they must be understood by all who are affected by such policies.

For example, the Celanese Corporation of America includes the following in its "Manual of Policies and Procedures":

> The Director of Purchases administers the procurement function through a Purchasing Organization composed of a Central Purchasing group, located at headquarters, and several plant purchasing departments or representatives, one at each plant or office. He manages the activities of the Central Purchasing group and exercises functional supervision over the plant purchasing departments. Each plant purchasing agent is responsible:
>
> *a.* to his plant manager, for the proper management of his department in accordance with plant policies and directives, and for the efficient performance of the plant procurement function, and

b. to the Director of Purchases, for carrying out Corporate procurement policies and standard practices and procedures, and for maintaining procurement performances at a high level of quality.

Particularly in corporations where decentralization is the rule, local management is usually strong and independent and may resist apparent home office pressure unless the authority, duties, and responsibilities of each are clearly defined, understood, and agreed upon.

An understanding and acceptance of such purchasing policies is necessary for the company to guard against a claim of a plant purchasing department that it is too restricted to function effectively, or against the complaint from headquarters that individual plants have too much freedom of decision and action.

The lines of communication between the home office and the local plant purchasing organizations must be kept open—both ways—at all times.

This permits the free exchange of buying information between the home office and the local purchasing organizations.

The local purchasing agent should be conversant with all local conditions and problems relating to his activity. He should keep the central purchasing executive appraised of unusual local developments affecting purchasing.

The home office should make available to the local purchasing agents whatever information has been developed or is available to help the plant purchasing agents to improve their functions.

There may be a strong desire at one or both ends to cut the ties, but it is imperative that home office and plants cooperate in assisting each other.

Open lines of communication are essential to prevent absolute chaos. For example, the home office of a company, in one instance, purchased pattern equipment for a common part. Plant A found they could get a better price from a new vendor and moved the pattern equipment to the new vendor. Shortly after, plant B, not desiring to deal with this new vendor, moved the patterns to still another supplier. Then the home office required an emergency quantity of the parts for service orders and after a few days was advised by the original supplier that the patterns were no longer in their possession. More time was lost before the home office discovered where plant A had sent the patterns and a new rush order was sent to the supplier only to have this order returned with the notation that tooling was no longer in their possession. By the time the patterns were located, castings produced and shipped, much time and temper had been lost. As this was but one of several similar situations arising during a short period of time, the company is now a staunch advocate of highly centralized control of all purchasing activities.

Intracompany cooperation can assist the promotion of worthy personnel from plant to plant or in staffing new plants. It will also spread the experience among the various divisions and reduce the tendency to overstaff at the local plant level.

The home office is normally the clearinghouse or court of appeals, regardless of its degree of authority, on such basic matters as the use of reciprocity or trade relations, the compilation with the assistance of plant purchasing agents of a list of acceptable bidders or vendors, the maintenance of a record of the location of common tooling, the issuance of national contracts, the establishment of staff functions such as market analysis, vendor analysis, comparative quality studies, credit-rating information, and seeking the solution of legal questions.

General Considerations of Centralized versus Decentralized Purchasing

The degree of decentralization of the purchasing department should normally parallel the decentralization of management responsibilities so that there is a prompt, free, and on-the-spot interchange of information or ideas in the solution of normal and emergency problems. However, the advantages of combining the total volume of purchases and the use of buying specialists should not be overlooked.

No organization should be centralized to the degree that local productive operations can be paralyzed or where cooperation is lost due to distance between procurement and production.

There is little point in having a highly centralized department if the various plants use dissimilar materials or if the materials are readily available in each locality with a minimum of tooling or setup expense.

In the recent past the trend has been toward decentralization, that is, to getting the job done by those who are sufficiently close to it, who have a primary interest in getting it done, and to avoiding loss of local perspective by routing the requirements through the home office where they could add to an accumulation of detail and would necessitate the cooperation of many people who do not have the local problem as a primary interest.

Decentralization of an activity builds men by spreading responsibilities and giving more opportunity to grow with a quicker recognition for achievements possible.

Conversely, an able man with limitations, who could be lost in a large organization would show his true value when on his own (for example, an able buyer may be so limited in exercising supervisory or executive ability that an opportunity will show that he should remain a successful buyer rather than an unsuccessful purchasing agent).

This trend to decentralization is recently reversing. Today, the move to closer centralization, with better control, is apparent. The advantages of establishing profit centers of control do not measure up to the advantages obtainable with central control, allowing the use of buying specialists and securing the savings of larger volume purchases.

Table 2–9. When Plants Are Geographically Separated and Purchasing Is Decentralized, Is Control of Purchasing Centralized?

	Under $5 million, %	$5 to $50 million	Over $50 million, %	Total, %
Central control	79.7	75.4	80.6	77.7
Local control	20.3	24.6	19.4	22.3

It is recognized that decentralization means the duplication of many charges that could quickly liquidate savings effected by a change to decentralization. Some of these are:

1. Fixed charges carry on.
2. There is a tendency to overstaff outlying units.
3. With duplications, a lack of specialization normally follows.

Summarizing, no one form of organization can be arbitrarily applied to all companies. It is first necessary to study the particular operation, giving thought to the job to be done and then developing the most logical organization to do it as efficiently as possible. The examples used in the preceding pages have been eminently successful in other companies and may serve as a guide in making this study.

BIBLIOGRAPHY

For reference books on purchasing department organization, see Section 26, "Library and Catalog File." This lists current books and magazines on subjects directly related to all phases of purchasing and on general business matters.

SECTION 3

POLICY AND PROCEDURE MANUALS

Editor

C. Warner McVicar, Director of Purchasing and Traffic, Rockwell Manufacturing Company, Pittsburgh, Pennsylvania

Associate Editors

J. F. Estill, Jr., Vice-president, Houston Lighting & Power Company, Houston, Texas

A. B. Wisrodt, Purchasing Agent, Port of Galveston, Galveston, Texas

With the increased complexity of the purchasing function in both profit and nonprofit enterprises, written statements of departmental functions and activities have become essential. This is particularly true in purchasing because of its increasing diversification into all areas of the organization. Such statements of purchasing policy have been issued in four basic forms according to the purpose intended.

TYPES OF PURCHASING MANUALS

Policy and Procedure Manuals

This type is fundamental and is necessary in order to establish written policies and procedures for distribution to other staff members and all purchasing personnel within a company. It may consist of a loose-leaf binder containing 20 sections or more; its 8½- by 11-in. pages will total anywhere from 80 to 300. An outstanding manual of this type is reproduced in this section following the heading "Example of Policy and Procedure Manual."

Policy Manuals

This type, which explains the company's purchasing policies, usually consists of an 8½- by 11-in. booklet containing from 20 to 36 pages. It is distributed to other departments within the company as well as to purchasing personnel, and it is often made available to vendors to acquaint them with the company's policies. Allegheny Ludlum Steel Corporation has issued a fine example of this type of booklet entitled "Statement of Purchasing Policies and Principles."

Procedure Manuals

As procedures change frequently, while policies, if sound, rarely change, some companies issue separate procedure manuals for internal distribution, which include samples of the various forms used and explain their usage in detail. Manuals vary in size and content according to the company involved and the complexity and number of the forms used. Companies engaged in government contracts, for example, find it advisable to prepare procedure manuals which include government forms that are necessary in the company's area of responsibility.

Welcome Booklets

These are intended for distribution by receptionists to salesmen, to aid them in contacting the individual in the purchasing department whom they should see. Welcome booklets are designed to create good will for the company but also contain other information such as products manufactured, other plant locations, and personnel. They are pocket-size and may contain from a four-page minimum of information to a more complete story requiring 24 pages.

NEED AND VALUE OF MANUALS

The American Management Association in its Research Study No. 66, *Evaluating Purchasing Performance,*[1] includes these statements concerning the establishment of the area of purchasing responsibility:

[1] Copyright © 1964 by the American Management Association, Inc., 135 West 50th Street, New York, N.Y. 10020.

The scope of the purchasing department's responsibility should logically be defined before evaluation is attempted. It is impractical to try to decide *how well* a job is being done until the nature of the job needed and expected has been determined. The first step is to secure managerial agreement on *what* the job is, and on what priorities should be given to its various elements.

A summary of the results of this research study by the editors, F. Albert Hayes and George A. Renard, continues:

The survey found that 62 per cent (125) of the companies reporting have a manual of purchasing policy, and that 71 per cent (143) have a manual of purchasing procedures. Job descriptions, policy statements, or memoranda of understanding as to authority are other media for outlining the responsibilities of the department. These various documents are natural starting points in planning for evaluation, since it would be unfair to hold a department accountable for the effectiveness of activities over which it has little control. Where no such agreements exist beforehand, it is reasonable to define purchasing responsibilities as a first step toward future evaluation.

There is a greater need for manuals in decentralized purchasing, where plant purchasing agents are separated from the headquarters responsible for centralizing purchasing control. For the decentralized company, as well as for the single-plant operation, written statements have numerous advantages, such as:

1. Spelling out the responsibilities and authority of purchasing. Management backing is needed to make purchasing policies authoritative.
2. Apprising other departments of purchasing's prerogatives, in order to avoid misunderstandings and friction.
3. Helping to promote consistent and fair relations with vendors, both old and new.
4. Facilitating uniform action by all purchasing personnel in dealings both within and without the company.
5. Standardizing routine purchasing procedures, thus relieving administrators of the task of close supervision.
6. Facilitating training of new members in the department and of veteran members assigned to new positions.
7. Stimulating new ideas and suggestions for improving and streamlining purchasing operations.

Tailoring Manuals to Individual Needs

There is no standard concept of the contents of a purchasing manual, and thus variations will be noted from one company to another. As a whole, manuals incorporate such matters as organization, responsibility, authority, functions, company policy, department policy, procedures, references, specifications, and specific instructions regarding company purchase orders and acceptances. The individual manual, however, is tailored to the needs and requirements of its own organization.

Even the style of manual must be tailored to the individual needs. Memorandums may suffice in some companies. Irrespective of style, manuals are usually indexed and placed in standard loose-leaf binders so that amendments can be made easily when necessary. Purchasing is not static. It is alive. As changes in policies or procedures become advisable, they should be made without delay. A purchasing manual is as necessary to a modern purchasing department as a sales manual is to the sales department, as an accounting manual is to the accounting department, or as any manual is to a department where a definition is required of what is to be done and how it is to be accomplished.

An example of a comprehensive type of manual is included in this section. It represents the function and activity of purchasing. In its entirety, it sketches the whole story of purchasing. The theories, practical considerations, and extensions of the individual areas are covered more specifically in other sections of this handbook.

The example in this section explains how to prepare purchasing policy and procedure manuals for small, medium, or large purchasing departments in industry and government and in nonprofit organizations as well. Obviously, it is in greater detail than might be necessary for a small organization, but sections required for the department's own purposes can be extracted. Examples of forms mentioned in this model manual will be found throughout this handbook.

F. Albert Hayes, Consulting Editor of *Purchasing Week,* internationally known among purchasing executives, wrote for that magazine a three-part article entitled "Purchasing Manuals Have Many Values."[2] Excerpts from this article follow:

A small "welcome" booklet with simple statement of policies is perhaps the easiest and quickest to produce. Man-hours may be numbered in 2–3 weeks. The intent here is to let the supplier know whom to see, what you buy, and your over-all purchasing policy.

What does a good purchasing manual contain? Exactly what you need, not what someone else has developed for his needs. Like a hand-fitted glove, a good purchasing policy manual is tailored to the company.

But there is probably something else you should have determined before you request initial approval for carrying out the project. Will a purchasing manual strengthen the contribution purchasing can make to company success?

[2] Reprinted by special permission from *Purchasing Week,* McGraw-Hill Publications, New York, Mar. 9, 16, and 23, 1959.

PROGRAM FOR PREPARING A PURCHASING MANUAL

Mr. Hayes includes in his article a "Program for Preparing a Purchasing Manual," as shown in Fig. 3–1.

Program for Preparing a Purchasing Manual

1. Do your own thinking. Decide what you want, why you want it.
2. Get permission of top operating executive to cross department lines in exploring and formulating policies. (Policies to be submitted again for final approval.)
3. Collect and compile material:
   a. Start a tentative index of subjects.
   b. Jot down unwritten policies carried in minds of old-timers or observed by company custom.
   c. Record information already appearing in company bulletins, letters, or pamphlets that concern purchasing.
   d. Collect other information defining purchasing subjects from organization charts, job descriptions, procedure manuals, correspondence, reports, etc.
   e. Collect manuals issued by other companies. Request information on their development.
4. Evaluate this material. Are existing policies compatible with stated objectives of the company or those of other departments?
5. Select and edit retained material so evolved policy has companywide applicability and value for frequent and permanent reference.
6. Make a draft of policy manual.
7. Circulate draft to other department heads and associates in purchasing department. Ask for suggestions, confer personally with each man. Try to reconcile all possible points of controversy.
8. Rewrite and resubmit on basis that document now reflects participation by all concerned.
9. If manual is also intended for vendors, submit it to a few of them for comment and review at this point.
10. Submit document to chief executive officer. Include summary of all expressed comments secured for or against policies.
11. If top executive approves, get his foreword and signature to make it an official company statement of purchasing objectives and policies.

FIG. 3–1. Preparation of a purchasing manual. (*Reprinted by special permission.*)

The steps for preparing a manual, as outlined in Fig. 3–1, may appear to be time-consuming and elaborate. However, experience has shown that they are necessary and minimal. A manual prepared for circulation in a purchasing department only, for example, is not effective beyond that department. The program recommended in Fig. 3–1 lets other members of management know what purchasing is trying to do and how it is to be accomplished. Consequently, other departments will feel they have had a part in the development of purchasing policy and will cooperate with it. After suggestions agreed upon have been incorporated in the proposed manual, copies should be distributed by the head of the purchasing department to the chief executive officer of the company, to each department head, and to the assistants and buyers in the purchasing department.

A reasonable length of time should be allowed for purchasing personnel to familiarize themselves with the contents of the manual. Then the head of the purchasing department should meet with them and discuss the manual's contents chapter by chapter. He will thus learn whether or not the contents of the manual are understood and be able to correct any existing misunderstandings. He should also make certain that his employees understand, appreciate, and use the purchasing manual policies and procedures in their dealings with others within the company, as well as in their outside contacts. The manual will then be an effective tool for improved interdepartmental relations, better relations with vendors, and more successful and outstanding purchasing performance.

The best manuals are those that are easy to read. They should be printed in large type on a good grade of 8½- by 11-in. paper, with indices separating the various sections. It is well to letter the front cover of the loose-leaf binder to show the company name, trademark, and the words "Purchasing Manual."

Be sure that the finished manual is one of which your company will be proud, and one that may be made available to other companies for their use in developing a similar manual.

EXAMPLE OF POLICY AND PROCEDURE MANUAL

Policies and procedures, including data and forms, on all sections in this sample manual are defined, explained, and illustrated in other sections of this handbook. Refer to the Index for their page locations.

Details follow regarding the basic contents of a purchasing manual for use in any company. Most of the material is from the "Purchasing Manual" of the Rockwell Manufacturing Company and is reproduced with their permission.

In preparing a similar manual for use in your company, the first step is to use the sections which follow, if they are applicable. Sections may be shortened or lengthened as necessary, in order to provide ideal purchasing conditions. Procedures not outlined in this handbook will have to be prepared independently to fit particular company requirements.

Many purchasing manuals contain 20 or more sections. A typical index contains a listing describing the content of each section, as shown in Fig. 3–2.

(COMPANY NAME)

(Date)

PURCHASING MANUAL INDEX

FIG. 3–2. Purchasing manual index.

The Foreword, Section 1

This section should contain a signed copy of a letter from the president of the company, or chief executive officer, addressed to the company's executive staff, general managers, and purchasing agents. This gives official approval to the policies and procedures that follow. One such letter is shown in Fig. 3–3.

Organization, Section 2

This section contains an organization chart of the titles and names of personnel in the purchasing department and often indicates to whom the head of the purchasing department reports.

The director of purchasing (or purchasing agent, depending on company organization) has various functions and responsibilities. These are defined as follows:

1. Develop company-wide purchasing objectives, policies, programs, and procedures for the negotiation and acquisition of materials, equipment, supplies, and services.

THE ROCKWELL BUILDING • PITTSBURGH, PENNSYLVANIA 15208 • TELEPHONE: (412) 241-8400

Rockwell Executive Staff
General Managers, Divisions and Subsidiaries
Purchasing Agents, Divisions and Subsidiaries

The General Purchasing Department of the Rockwell Manufacturing Company has prepared this "Purchasing Manual" for its Divisions and Subsidiaries. It is the basis for the Company's purchasing policies and procedures. The term "Division" as used throughout this manual for the sake of brevity, means all Divisions as well as all Subsidiaries of the Company.

When changes become necessary, new pages covering such changes will be sent to all recipients of the Manual. Those who have copies are requested to keep them up to date by inserting the new sheets and removing those which they replace.

The purchase function involves the procurement of materials, supplies, equipment and services at the lowest possible cost consistent with the quality needed for the production of merchandise which will meet the required standards of the Rockwell Manufacturing Company. Although procedures change, fundamentals do not. Our goal is the promotion of the Company's best interests through intelligent action and fair dealing which will result in obtaining the maximum projected value for each dollar of expenditures.

This manual has been prepared for all purchasing personnel as a guide to performing the procurement function in accordance with Company policies. It is intended to serve as a continuing reminder of the duties and responsibilities involved in procuring required items, while at the same time maintaining the Company's reputation for fairness and integrity.

A. C. Daugherty
A. C. Daugherty
President

FIG. 3–3. The foreword.

2. Coordinate purchasing procedures throughout the company.
3. Act as company spokesman on all matters pertaining to purchasing.
4. Institute the reports necessary to permit analysis of purchasing department performance.
5. Develop and administer a program for the development of personnel suitable for promotion within the company.
6. Disseminate to other departments information designed to promote efficient operation of their function.
7. Negotiate and approve term contracts and leases with suppliers to the best interest of the company.
8. Consolidate purchases of like or common items to obtain the maximum economical benefits.

9. Purchase all equipment, supplies, and services for company use in such a manner that the maximum value will be obtained for the money expended. Purchases shall be made from qualified manufacturers whose reputations, financial positions, and price structures are sufficiently adequate for consideration as logical sources of supply.
10. Arrange for the disposal or negotiate the sale of surplus materials and equipment, including obsolete stock, scrap, and turnings.
11. Cooperate with other departments of the company to maintain inventories at a satisfactory operating and dollar-value level.
12. Study markets to analyze prices paid for materials and equipment, generally define how to obtain savings through improved specifications and supervision of supply sources, and recommend changes in quantities to be ordered when conditions warrant.
13. Utilize known contacts and sources to expedite deliveries of needed material and equipment.
14. Work with other departments of the company to promote better customer and supplier relations.
15. Work with the standards committee in establishing standardization of materials and supplies used throughout the company.
16. Provide liaison with government agencies for handling requests for information concerning the company's ability to handle contracts which may be proposed in the event of mobilization.
17. Prepare and submit for approval annual purchasing department operating budgets. Control budget expenditures by before-the-fact authorizations and after-the-fact approval of such expenditures.

For Use in Companies Having More than One Plant

18. Conduct periodic audits of division and subsidiary purchasing departments to ensure compliance with approved policies and procedures as outlined in the purchasing manual.
19. Purchase or assist in the purchase of materials, equipment, supplies, and services for divisions or subsidiaries when requested to do so.

For Use When Purchasing and Traffic Departments Are Combined

20. Establish and administer policies and procedures related to the use of carrier or transportation facilities, including agency to be employed, rate compliance, expediting action, liability protection, and filing of claims, etc.
21. Protect company's interest in all matters involving freight rates, freight classifications, transportation costs, and transportation services. Represent the company before carrier rate committees and individual carriers in the negotiation of transportation rates.

22. Maintain adequate rate tariff files and follow proceedings of regulatory bodies and carrier rate committees on matters affecting rates on the company's traffic as well as on the traffic of competitors.
23. Arrange travel accommodations for employees and secure transportation tickets when requested to do so.

Purchasing Policy, Section 3

This is one of the most important sections of the manual because it places the authority and responsibility for purchasing in the purchasing department.

Good purchasing policy is defined as follows:

PURCHASING POLICY: Purchasing is one of the most common of business activities. It means the acquisition of some kind of property and the giving of an accepted price or consideration in return.

Every transaction between a buyer and a seller involving the transfer of property is a contract. Some contracts are of the simplest form, while others are made the subject of lengthy written agreements defining in technical terms the nature of the material, method of payment, and other contractual conditions.

From the inception to the consummation of a transaction between a buyer and a seller, many important problems are involved; and the proper handling of these and the administering of the business features connected with them are vital factors in the successful operation of the company.

For these reasons, the authority and responsibility of purchasing rests with the purchasing department. This places the responsibility on those who have the interest and the skill to do the work properly and whose primary concern is in the performance of this special task. It permits the establishing of uniform policies with respect to seller relationships.

Dependable records of sources of supply are necessary to successful purchasing. These records must be kept up to date and be instantly available. Purchasing personnel must systematically select useful information from the mass of material received every day. They are constantly looking for new manufacturers, new lines and grades of material, and better prices. They endeavor to purchase in accordance with market conditions, placing orders for future delivery when advisable. The successful buyer must constantly study markets and keep informed concerning materials purchased. Carefully compiled and easily available records of purchases must be maintained extending over a period of years.

Purchasing requires careful study and training. It is a function for specialists. Only the purchasing department is to conduct and conclude the negotiations affecting purchases, such as prices, terms, and deliveries.

The purchasing department is to establish and administer purchasing policies, institute reports necessary to permit analysis of purchasing performance, negotiate and approve term contracts, consolidate purchases of like or common items, analyze prices paid for materials and equipment, and generally define how to obtain savings and to coordinate purchasing procedures.

Additional policies are summarized briefly:

1. All requests for prices or for repair service and all purchases must be made by the purchasing department. In some instances, authority to request prices may be delegated to others.
2. Salesmen may be received in other departments only at the request or permission of the purchasing department.
3. If necessary to interview salesmen regarding details of their products, other departments should request such visits through the purchasing department.
4. In interviews with salesmen, no one who is not a member of the purchasing department may commit himself on preference for any product, on the company's source of supply for any product, or give any information regarding performance or price which might in any way embarrass the purchasing department or the company.
5. All correspondence with suppliers is to be through the purchasing department, except in special cases where the technical details involved make it advisable to delegate authority to others. In such cases, the purchasing department must receive copies of all correspondence.
6. With the exception of freight adjustments which are handled by the traffic department, the purchasing department will conduct all adjustment negotiations.
7. The purchasing department has full authority to question the quality, quantity, and kind of material asked for, in order that the best interests of the company may be served.
8. In cases of extreme emergency, and only in such cases, an exception to the above rule may be made with the understanding that the head of the department placing the emergency order personally assumes the responsibility of immediately following up the verbal order, given by himself or his representative, with the proper department requisition.
9. (If your company has a policy regarding the purchasing of foreign materials, equipment, or supplies, whether direct or through domestic representatives, it should be included here.)

In general, product purchasing responsibility is determined by the nature of the material or fabricated part in question, the attempt being made to see that all identical, similar, or closely related items are handled in the same buying office. This allows for substitutions to be made of one material or part for another when desirable from a price or delivery standpoint.

Where it is possible to do so without conflicting with the above principle, the attempt will be made to concentrate all items purchased from a given supplier in one buying office in order to have each supplier deal with only one buyer. However, there will be cases where this will not be possible when a supplier handles several dissimilar or entirely unrelated types of products.

Responsibilities of Purchasing Personnel

1. Scrutinize requisitions, letters, memos, and quotations for correctness and clarity.
2. Keep interested departments informed on proper lead times required and on all unusual supply situations.
3. Follow-up and expedite delivery as deemed desirable or necessary after issuance of purchase orders.
4. Cooperate to adjust deliveries up or down when necessary.

Replacement Parts

Manufacturers of machinery, equipment, and tools include many standard items in their lists of repair or replacement parts. Only special or patented parts should normally be ordered from them. Repair parts for their equipment such as switches, electric cable, plugs, cap screws, bolts, nuts, washers, etc., may be requisitioned as special parts. These are expensive when purchased from the equipment manufacturers. Use or purchase standard parts from stock or from standard supply sources, rather than from the equipment manufacturers.

Plant Visits

Plant visits to learn other types of manufacturing processes are an excellent means of increasing knowledge. Visiting suppliers should be a regular part of every purchasing agent's and buyer's policy and practice. Plant visitations are justified on the basis that the purchasing officer is responsible to his company for the selection of the proper sources of supply. This decision is one of the most important factors in purchasing because finding the right source determines the reliability, quality, delivery, and cost of the materials purchased.

A buyer cannot hope to know as much about any product that he buys as does the producer of that product. But one good look at the actual production processes of a part or product, showing the operations involved and the methods used, enables the buyer to see that product in a new light and with greater understanding whenever it appears on a requisition.

Purchasing Agents' Association

Membership and active participation in the meetings and activities of a local purchasing agents' association is a desirable way to expand knowledge of purchasing. Meeting with other purchasing personnel and exchanging viewpoints and experiences with them may bring valuable ideas or changes to company practices. The opportunity to become an officer or committee member of a purchasing agents' association should be grasped and the assignment carried out in an enthusiastic and intelligent manner.

Projects

Every member of the purchasing department who is responsible for issuing purchase orders should at all times be working on at least one purchasing project. An individual item or class of material should be selected and a specific program laid out with the thought of eventually reducing the price or improving the quality. This is done by locating more efficient and more economical suppliers; changing the specification to follow commercial practices and yet continue to meet requirements; purchasing in larger quantities; or in any other way reducing costs to the lowest possible level. By concentrating efforts on a few items at a time, a thorough job can be done which will reflect an efficient buying program.

The monthly activity report (Fig. 3–4 on p. 3–54) furnished to the director of purchasing or purchasing agent provides a means of informing him of projects and of their results. It is an opportunity to do a creative job over and above that required just to meet current demands.

Systems and Procedures

Systems and procedures should be examined frequently to see if changes can be made to incorporate improved methods. Consider the adoption of new systems and procedures described in purchasing and other professional or trade magazines and innovations discussed at purchasing agents' association meetings. Learn how other companies handle purchasing problems comparable to yours and consider whether their solutions can be adopted to streamline your operations. Look for novel features —promote efficiency for greater economy.

Employee Purchases

A procedure has been established through our personnel department for the purchase by employees of company-manufactured products. The laws of many states prohibit the use of company purchase orders for the procurement of materials for sale to employees other than for products manufactured by that company. It is our policy that purchases of articles to be paid for by our employees will not be made by our purchasing departments at any location. This policy shall not apply to the sale or distribution of meals, candy, beverages, cigarettes, cigars, or tobacco; company-sponsored recreation-activity clothing or supplies; or tools and materials such as safety shoes, goggles, gloves, etc., used or worn by employees to promote their safety and health or improve their working conditions. However, whenever surplus or obsolete machinery, tools, furniture, supplies, or equipment become available for disposition by our purchasing departments, in accordance with the section on surplus and obsolete materials in this manual, such items may be sold to employees only at prices at least equal to those obtainable through normal outlets.

When we can assist employees by referring them to suppliers who welcome such referrals, it is common courtesy to do so and secures good will for the company. But it should be understood that the supplier and the employee must complete their own transaction by mutual agreement without the use of company purchase orders and without requiring purchasing department employees to spend time locating suppliers or securing quotations.

Conflict of Interest

Any purchasing department employee who has any financial or other interest in a supplier company either directly, or indirectly through members of his immediate family, shall so report such financial or other interest, in writing, to his supervisor. The supervisor will decide whether the interest in question is of sufficient magnitude as to warrant the disqualification of the purchasing department employee concerned from negotiating proposed purchases with, or issuing purchase orders to, that supplier.

Legal Aspects of Purchasing, Section 4

This section points out that a purchase order is a legal document; that a buyer legally obligates his company and that he also may be personally liable for his acts. The section follows:

LEGAL ASPECTS OF PURCHASING: Purchasing agents and buyers should have a general knowledge of the legal aspects of purchasing. The company legal counsel is available and purchasing agents and buyers should call upon him for assistance in answering any legal problems.

Every purchasing agent or buyer must have sufficient understanding of law to know the relationship between the company and its buyers and the legal consequences of the acts which he performs in the company's name. Without this knowledge, he may unconsciously commit acts which may cost the company more than he can save in months of careful buying.

This does not mean that the buyer must be a legal expert, nor that he should rely upon his own judgment when questionable points arise. In fact, the opposite is true.

Legal decisions, as published from time to time in reports, magazines, and books, may be misleading. In order to avoid getting into legal entanglements, it is important for the buyer to learn the fundamentals so that he will recognize the need for legal guidance and call for it when necessary.

The company authorizes the head of the purchasing department and he authorizes his assistant and buyers to make such contracts in the purchasing field as are usual and necessary in the performance of their duties. When anyone acts within his authority, express or apparent, his actions are binding upon the company.

The head of the purchasing department is a general agent and has authority to make such contracts as are usual and necessary in the performance of his duty. He is liable to the company if he damages the latter through active fault, bad faith, or dishonesty, or through negligence.

The acts of purchasing agents, assistants, and buyers, as agents, are binding upon the company within the limits of the authority given them. When acting within the scope of their authority, their acts are binding upon the company; when allowed to exceed their authority so that the sellers dealing with them are justified in believing they possess the authority exercised, their acts are equally as binding. If a purchasing agent or buyer who is granted general authority is replaced, the sellers accustomed to dealing with him are justified in believing that his successor will have the same degree of authority.

In order to avoid personal liability, it must be made clear to the seller that the buyer is acting as an agent. In fact, to avoid conclusively any question of personal liability on the part of the agent, the buyer must disclose not only the fact that he is acting as an agent, but actually disclose the name of the company for whom he is acting. In executing the agreement, the addition of the word "agent" after the signature does not of itself relieve the agent of personal liability. Such addition of the word "agent" or similar term, unless it otherwise sufficiently appears from the instrument that the agent executed the agreement for his principal, is usually construed by the courts to be mere description. The buyer's name, therefore, must always be below the company name.

There is a personal liability:

1. If the buyer makes a false statement concerning his authority with intent to deceive, or if his misrepresentation has the natural and probable consequence of being misleading.
2. If he performs, without authority, a damaging act, even though believing he has such authority.
3. If he performs an illegal act, even with authority of his employer.

In each of these cases, the seller may have no recourse to the company, since no valid contract may exist between the seller and the company; and since such a contract may not exist, the only recourse which the seller may have is to sue the buyer personally. However, if there were limitations on the latter unknown to the seller, it may still follow that the company can be held. Under these circumstances, the agent has put himself in a difficult position and is, of course, answerable to the company. He may also be answerable to the seller with whom he has dealt, on the ground of deceit, on the charge that he is the real contracting party, or for breach of warranty that he was authorized to make precisely the contract he undertook to make for the company.

Subject to many exceptions arising out of varying circumstances, a salesman's authority ordinarily is to solicit orders and send them to his employer for ratification and acceptance. In order, therefore, that a supplier may be held legally liable, it is necessary for the purchaser to know definitely that the salesman is authorized to conclude a contract without referring it to the company he represents for acceptance. If the purchaser does not have this definite knowledge, he should secure the signature of an authorized official of the supplier on his purchase order acceptance.

It is well established that a buyer who inspects goods before entering into a contract of sale is put on his guard and is deemed to have shown an intention to rely upon his own judgment with respect to quality, quantity, and other characteristics of the merchandise.

When a purchaser accepts merchandise after such inspection, either as to quality or quantity, he is usually barred from raising an issue respecting defects apparent from such inspection.

Also, a seller often cannot be held responsible for the failure of equipment to perform the work which the buyer expected of it, if the latter ordered it on specification or by trademark or brand, without indicating to the seller the purposes for which the equipment or goods were intended.

In fact, in order to hold the seller responsible on an implied warranty for the performance of the goods for the purpose for which they are intended by the buyer, the buyer must not only make this known to the seller, but must also clearly indicate that he relies with respect thereto on the seller's skill and judgment. The Uniform Sales Act[3] reads:

> Where the buyer, expressly or by implication, makes known to the seller the particular purpose for which the goods are required and it appears that the buyer relies on the seller's skill or judgment, there is an implied warranty that the goods shall be fit for such purpose.

Once a contract is made, both parties are legally obligated to perform in accordance with the terms. Occasionally, however, one party or the other may seek to cancel the contract, or by his acts fail to perform his obligations under its terms.

In so far as the seller is concerned, a breach occurs if he refuses to manufacture the goods, or if he delays delivery beyond the period stipulated in the agreement. In such event, the seller is liable to the buyer for such breach, and the buyer may:

1. Treat the contract as breached and by notification seek to cause the seller to pay damages sustained as a result of the breach.
2. Waive the breach and keep the contract alive for the benefit of both parties, being at all times himself ready and able to perform.
3. Accept a delayed shipment and seek to recover the difference between the contract price and the value of the goods at time of delivery.

The seller may, however, without liability, delay delivering the purchased goods when the purchaser orders a change in the original agreement, or if after delay of shipment, purchaser subsequently agrees to accept delivery.

Relations with Other Departments, Section 5

This section stresses the need for the purchasing department to cooperate with other departments of the company. The section may be summarized as follows:

RELATIONS WITH OTHER DEPARTMENTS: The purchasing department exists in order to supply the needs of the company. The attitude of the other departments will be a reflection of the purchasing department's service to them, and to a large extent, the standard by which its efficiency will be measured.

The purchasing department is in constant contact with other departments, and cooperation and mutual confidence are essential. The buyer

[3] Full text will be found in Section 28.

must have an understanding of the particular requirements of the several users of materials and services. This knowledge takes time to acquire but it is time well spent. Through keen observation, discussions with users in the plant, talks with salesmen, and by keeping informed of latest methods by reading applicable technical publications, the buyer establishes himself as one who is sincerely trying to advance the interests of his company.

Other departments should keep the purchasing department advised of current and anticipated activities, such as production schedules, volume of business, new business, new products, new design, etc., in such detail as will assist in advance competitive negotiations. The information should be given far enough in advance to allow for study and adequate manufacturing lead time. The purchasing department in every instance must be careful not to divulge confidential information.

If there are points of contact where there is any question of the work overlapping that of another department, the duties of each should be clearly defined and arranged to the best interests of the company.

The production department, in particular, has so much direct contact with the purchasing department that there must be a large degree of cooperation between them.

Often the production department, on the basis of its records, will requisition a quantity of material which carries a higher purchase price than would apply to a moderately larger quantity. It is the duty of the purchasing department to advise the production department of this so that it can determine the advisability of increasing the quantity and make proper record of the economical quantity to order. On the other hand, if the production department requisitions a quantity of material which is high in price and a reduction is anticipated, the purchasing department should recommend reducing the quantity to just enough to meet requirements until the reduction in price becomes effective. At times, the purchasing department may make valuable suggestions on substitute materials and changes in quality or specifications which will reduce costs.

The stores department also must maintain close contact with the production department. It must be able to supply needed materials promptly from stock, and it must eliminate items which become obsolete and are no longer required.

The engineering department is responsible for the design of units and parts as well as for the successful operation of machinery and equipment. It is also responsible for the efficient layout and operation of equipment. Its men have definite ideas and requirements expressed in terms of strength, rigidity, toughness, hardness, ductility, or other physical properties; they also have good working knowledge of the various materials available which embrace the desired properties; but in determining which of the materials can be obtained most advantageously, the purchasing department's training and experience are required.

It is at this point that relations between the two departments are given the acid test. The engineering department should not be too exacting in its specifications; it should recognize the fact that considerations of price, economy, and convenience in production should be weighed along with those of design and that the purchasing department should have reasonable latitude in making the purchase. The engineer does his best job when he allows for plenty of competition, as competition brings out the best in latest developments as well as the best price. On the other hand, the purchasing department should not push the matter of price or supplier to the point where it interferes with real engineering requirements.

The functions of the two departments are complementary and supplementary, and close cooperation is essential if the best results are to be obtained. This is especially true in the present period when it is so important to incorporate in design every possible advantage that can be derived from intelligent purchasing. Good design can suffer tremendously if it is not backed up by intelligent selection and purchase of materials and parts.

The engineering department cannot be expected to know all about prices, size, and quantity extras, time required for delivery, extras for special tolerances, etc. It is often practicable for purchasing to suggest a slight change in specification to permit use of standard sizes, shapes, lengths, or grades of material so that costs may be reduced without sacrifice of any necessary characteristic. The purchasing department should advise engineering of any change in specification or substitute material which in its opinion would lower the cost without sacrifice of results.

The engineering department should request information on engineering materials, supplies, and equipment through the purchasing department and no major engineering service should be accepted from any company without first determining whether the company would be acceptable to the purchasing department as the supplier.

Conversely, many new technical developments are brought to the attention of purchasing department personnel. These in turn must be referred to the cognizant engineering department for possible inclusion in our products.

Cooperation with the sales department is essential. Unless the company's products can be sold at a profit, it cannot stay in business. On the one hand, the company's customers are entitled to an even chance at the business awarded by the purchasing department. On the other hand, the company's customers should be told that their quotations to the purchasing department will be analyzed and the purchase order placed, on the basis of quality, service, and price.

Relations with Salesmen, Section 6

This section is so important that it is one of the largest in a purchasing manual.

RELATIONS WITH SALESMEN: The purchasing department has more contact with other companies and suppliers than any other department with the possible exception of the sales department. It has the power to enhance or detract from the company's good name in its relations with salesmen. It has long been considered good sales policy to develop good will on the part of the customer toward the seller. This good will has been developed through the use of a trademark, extensive advertising, and long and hard missionary work on the part of the sales department. It has real commercial value and is recognized as an asset by courts of law. It is just as essential to develop good will between the company and its suppliers as it is to have good will between the company and its customers.

In general, one's opinion of a company is formed by contacts with its employees. The purchasing department has a real opportunity and a major responsibility in forwarding the reputation of the company and the good will it commands.

Fairness. We can and should promote the reputation of (insert your company name) for fair dealing:

1. By giving all salesmen a full, fair, prompt, and courteous hearing on any subject that is justified by the nature of their products
2. By keeping competition open and fair
3. By declining to take advantage of a seller's errors
4. By discouraging revision of bids after submission and insisting on receiving the best price first and holding the bidder to it
5. By keeping buying specifications fair and clear and avoiding impractical or unnecessary specifications
6. By showing consideration for the seller's difficulties and cooperating with him when possible
7. By avoiding the rejection and return of petty items or items for petty reasons
8. By using material which is not strictly up to specifications if it is usable without sacrifice
9. By not putting the seller to unnecessary expense on returned goods

10. By having buying policies and principles consistent with our selling policies
11. By not soliciting bids from a potential supplier unless we are willing to use that supplier should he offer an acceptable material at a satisfactory price and delivery; qualifications of a supplier will be determined before requesting his quotation

Integrity. We can and should promote the reputation of (company name) for integrity:

1. By observing strict truthfulness in all transactions with salesmen and in correspondence
2. By respecting the confidence of the salesman or his company as to quotations or other confidential information
3. By keeping ourselves free from obligation to any vendor

Service. We can and should promote the reputation of (company name) for service:

1. By answering letters promptly
2. By expediting, when possible, tests of samples submitted and by rendering prompt reports to the company which submitted the sample
3. By furnishing complete information to the seller and by sending samples, blueprints, or other information when needed
4. By an efficient follow-up system

Progressiveness. We can and should promote the reputation of (company name) for progressiveness:

1. By keeping an open mind on new methods and materials offered
2. By encouraging the making of tests or trials on materials that may be of value to our company
3. By visiting, when advisable, major sources of supply and keeping informed as to their stability and methods

In addition, the members of the purchasing department have a further duty and responsibility. Each one should be product-minded and a sincere booster for the products manufactured by his company. Potentially, our influence on the company's sales is much greater than we may think. We may have the opportunity to create interest and lighten the task of the sales department.

Friendship. This has been and always will be an important factor in business. On a proper plane, it is to be encouraged between buyer and seller, for it can be of great advantage to both parties. To confer with business friends when a new item is suddenly required is the quickest and surest way to find the best market and the best price. When it is difficult for a buyer to secure an article quickly, a seller, for the sake of friendship, will undertake to supply it and will put himself to much inconvenience to do so.

Friendship can even be cultivated by the manner in which a salesman is told he has lost, or cannot have, an order. These may seem small things, but courtesy, square dealing, honesty, and straightforwardness beget friendship. They are appreciated by sellers and the buyer benefits largely from them. The salesman who receives brusque treatment is not likely to make an extra effort to render special services, to offer new ideas readily, or to speak as favorably of either the buyer or the company as he would if he felt he had been given fair and courteous treatment.

There is nothing questionable or unethical in lunching with a salesman either to give him a better opportunity to present his case or to cultivate friendship, provided the buyer accepts such attentions as he would from any other friend and keeps himself free of obligations. The buyer should pay for luncheons as well as the prospective seller.

Entertainment or Gifts from Suppliers. Acceptance of gifts other than advertising novelties is at all times prohibited. Employees must not become obligated to any supplier and shall not conclude any company transaction from which they may personally benefit.

Reciprocity. Good will is an essential factor in business. One means of developing good will, other things being equal, is to give business to those who return the favor. There is no more favorable way of ensuring satisfactory quality, service, and price than by extending favors to friendly companies, particularly if those favors yield a profit to the company. If, in the process, anything is sacrificed in the way of price, quality, or service, it is not efficient purchasing. Customers are seldom willing to pay more for the same quality or the same price for a poorer quality just as a matter of friendship. In general, they buy from the company because they obtain a superior product, better service, or a better price. The company which pleads or demands that business be given on a reciprocal basis is rarely satisfied with an even break. It is unsound policy for a company to base its hopes for success on any other basis than the value of its product and service to potential buyers. If, on consideration of all the factors which enter into good buying, it is found that a good customer is on an equality with the rest, or better, let him have the business; but if he is not, the purchasing department cannot assume the responsibility of making a purchase which involves a departure from the fundamental principles of good buying.

All members of the purchasing department must be careful not to antagonize actual or potential customers or create ill will toward the company's products. Never under any circumstances should a member of the purchasing department tell a salesman that the company will not buy his product because the salesman's company does not buy from them. A friendly attitude may influence him to do all in his power to have his company buy our products. If antagonized, he will do everything possible to harm our company's business.

Much of the success of the company's operations depends on the purchasing department acquiring materials in sufficient quantities, when needed, at an economical price, regardless of the source from which they are obtained. Therefore, these important requirements should not be superseded by good will. In negotiations with salesmen, buyers should be firm but reasonable and insistent that vendors meet requirements and specifications. This must and can be done without impairing good will. All questions of policy must be referred to the head of the purchasing department.

Great responsibility is placed upon purchasing agents and buyers to use their authority in such a manner in their contacts with salesmen that there will be a continuity in mutual understanding and responsibility so that the company's manufacturing activities are properly supported. In negotiating with salesmen, there are certain points of personal character and ethical conduct that are requisites of a good purchasing agent or buyer. Courtesy, honesty, fairness, and firmness each have their place in this activity.

Commercial Bribery. This is an evil for which there is no justification. Fortunately most buyers cannot be influenced in this manner. However, bribery in any form is a most serious evil because it is frequently hard to detect and very insidious in its nature. Open bribery is seldom attempted; usually it consists of an attempt to secure favoritism by gifts or entertainment. Attempts to influence decisions unfairly may be directed against company officials, plant managers, purchasing personnel, plant foremen, and even the workmen, when they can in any way influence the selection of materials to be purchased. That this condition, though uncommon, does exist is proved by unfortunate occurrences that come to light occasionally. All the codes list as unfair trade practice, commercial bribery in any form. Legally, there are a number of court decisions bearing on the matter of bribery, and many states have laws making commercial bribery a criminal offense. It is important that purchasing people do not place themselves in a position which permits suspicion of their ethics.

Letter Writing. Remember that when a letter is written on company letterhead, as far as the recipient is concerned he has received a letter from the company. The impression created by such a letter often remains long after its contents are forgotten.

There are several fundamentals to be observed when writing a business letter: be brief, courteous, and natural; avoid slang and catch phrases; and use good, clear, grammatical English. Never mislay courtesy when striving for brevity. Remember that printed or written words are subject to just the interpretation that the reader of the words gives them. Be sure only one meaning can be taken and that it is expressed clearly. Never say "we expect" or "you will" when "will you please" will accomplish the same result more pleasantly.

The quality of naturalness is often missing in business correspondence. Too many letters sound a false note, contain antiquated words and stilted phrases, that the writer would not use were he speaking instead of writing.

Telegrams. Always answer wire messages promptly, no later than the day after they are received. This courtesy to the sender of the original telegram is advisable even though the answer is incomplete, in which case it is well to include a reason as to the cause of the delay, together with an estimate as to when the complete answer can be given.

Courtesy. It is company policy to maintain an "open door" to all companies desiring to sell to it. When this door is entered by a seller, he must receive courteous, cordial, wholehearted, and friendly consideration. The buyer must never take the attitude that any product offered is unimportant even though it is not presently purchased. The buyer must realize that the products the salesman offers are to him the most important products in the world. If this attitude of buying is always employed in the handling of people, circles of friendship and influence are extended with a resultant benefit to the company.

It is a fundamental policy to conserve the salesman's time and reduce the waiting period to a minimum. If it is necessary for the salesman to wait for more than ten minutes, the buyer should personally advise him of the fact and explain the reason. Remember his time is also valuable.

The salesman should be given an opportunity to tell his story under conditions of privacy, with a minimum of interruptions such as telephone calls or other time-consuming delays.

Good telephone and letter writing manners are essential and it is important to train ourselves and those under our jurisdiction so that courtesy, tact, proper presentation, and a friendly attitude become matters of habit. Success in our work requires that we leave the individual we have contacted with a willingness and a desire to serve us.

In the handling of controversial situations, we are entitled to a belief in our own convictions, but at the same time we must never be intolerant of our correspondent's views.

We must exercise care and discretion when informing suppliers of the reasons relative to specific objections to their equipment or material. The facts, such as the results of tests, performance, etc., should be presented clearly and in detail but never in such a manner as to cause irritation or cause the seller mistakenly to feel an unwarranted prejudice exists.

A competent salesman can be of unlimited assistance to the buyer and he appreciates receiving a full and complete story to refer to his employers, but it is only human nature to resent unwarranted criticism or opinions not based on fact.

In the buying profession, the buyer should create a positive, constructive, aggressive approach. This manner will enable him to present his problem, locate new or better sources, or improve the present source by substitution or elimination of waste, and secure the most out of his interviews. The present-day salesman has usually been given complete, intensive training in the manufacture and application of the product he is selling. A buyer will find it good policy to hear each salesman's story and to convince himself whether or not the salesman has something which will fit current or future requirements. If the product has merit but is not currently being purchased, the buyer should arrange to pass the information along to his company's user of the product, or else arrange for the saleman to demonstrate to the using department the superiorities of the recommended item.

Interviewing Hours. It is company policy not to limit the hours of the working day during which salesmen will be interviewed. One of the basic reasons for this policy is that limited interviewing hours would result in less efficient utilization of time by our vendors' salesmen so that our costs for purchased materials might increase. Another reason is that if our customers limited the hours during which our salesmen could call on them, it would necessitate greatly increased costs for additional salesmen to represent our company.

Buying Proper Quality, Section 7

This section describes procedures necessary to ensure that the right quality will be purchased to fulfill, but not exceed, the requirements for which the goods are intended. The section follows:

BUYING PROPER QUALITY: Quality and service are just as important as price, and it is the duty of the purchasing department to secure the best quality for the purpose intended. Quality buying is the buying of supplies, materials, goods, or services of a grade that will fulfill but not exceed the requirements for which the goods are intended.

In some instances, the primary consideration is durability. The question of immediate cost or ease of installation or repair is secondary. In other cases, the life of the item is not the most important factor but rather its efficiency in operation.

Proper specifications help to obtain proper quality. Purchasing personnel must work with production and engineering personnel in securing adequate specifications for all material.

Purchase Specifications. Buying proper quality depends upon (1) having proper specifications and (2) checking material bought against specifications.

A specification is no more than an accurate description of the material to be purchased. There are many forms of specifications, such as:

1. Brand or trade name
2. Blueprint or dimension sheet
3. Chemical analysis or physical properties
4. Description of material and method of manufacture
5. Description of performance, purpose, or use
6. Identification with standard specification known to the trade generally and to the vendor
7. Sample

Specification by Brand or Trade Name. This places the buyer in entire dependence upon the seller's reputation for quality. It should be used in cases where branded products have been found to be superior to others for the purpose intended and when their composition is secret, unknown, or patented. It should also be used for standard products when the extent of their use does not justify the expenses of investigation and detailed specifications. The purchasing department should have approval on at least two and preferably more than two brands. There are comparatively few brands that do not have competitive and equal grades.

Specification by Blueprint or Dimension Sheet. Such specifications are advisable for the purchase of forgings, castings, machines, machine parts, construction of new facilities, etc. Blueprints provide a safe method of checking against specifications when material is received and inspected.

Specification by Chemical Analysis or Physical Properties. Either one or both are ideal for many materials since such specifications can be checked accurately by laboratory tests or other methods.

Specification by Description of Material and Method of Manufacture. This type of specification should be used rarely. Ordinarily, the seller, if he knows the use for which the goods are intended, is in better position to determine the proper materials and method of manufacture than the buyer. It should be used only for very particular and special requirements, as the responsibility is entirely the buyer's if goods have been manufactured in accordance with his instructions.

Specification by Performance, Purpose, or Use. This is an excellent form of specification, for if the vendor is dependable and accepts such a specification, the responsibility is entirely his. This type of specification is the easiest to prepare and is recommended especially in the purchase of machinery and tools. The vendor, if progressive, will offer the latest developments, which might not be mentioned if the specifications were incomplete. The buyer is not concerned with the materials or the method of manufacture as long as the product accomplishes the desired results by the most efficient method. The vendor is left free to make the best product at the lowest cost to suit the service. He can take advantage of all modern technical knowledge and methods of manufacture. When materials are covered by this type of specification, it is advisable to obtain plenty of competition, since only one bidder, being responsible for results, may suggest a better but more expensive article than is justified or required.

Specification by Identification with Standard Specification Known to the Trade Generally and to the Vendor. This is a satisfactory form of specification, provided it meets all requirements and can be accepted without undue and unnecessary expense. Examples of this are the ASME, ASA, ASTM Specifications, and Lumber Grading Rules.

Specification by Sample. Avoid samples unless no other type of specification is possible. Samples are subject to physical change or substitution and their use as standards often causes disputes.

A good specification should be:

1. As simple as is consistent with exactness, but so specific that a loophole will not allow a bidder to evade any of the provisions and thereby take advantage of his competitors or the buyer.
2. Identified, when possible, with some brand or specification already on the market. Special goods are expensive.
3. Capable of being checked. It should describe the method of checking which will govern acceptance or rejection. A specification which cannot be checked is of little value and where checking methods vary in accuracy, only confusion can result.
4. Reasonable in its tolerances. Unnecessary precision is expensive.
5. As fair to the seller as possible.
6. Capable of being met by several bidders for the sake of competition.
7. Clear. Misunderstandings are expensive.
8. Flexible. Inflexible specifications defeat progress. Invite vendors to suggest cost-saving alternates or substitutes.

Inspection as a Check on Specifications. All specifications must be reasonably checked. Inspection is not a function of the purchasing department, but the purchasing department should be informed of results so that it can place orders with the sellers who supply the most satisfactory goods and services.

The purchasing department should make certain that the first castings from a new pattern or mold, the first stampings from a new die, or the first shipment of materials made to blueprints or specifications are checked and approved by engineering, production, or other authority before production quantities are released.

The buyer should show on purchase orders for patterns, tools, dies, molds, jigs, and fixtures that "Payment will not be approved until production samples have been inspected and approved by purchaser." The purchase order should also state who owns, maintains, and insures these special production facilities.

Savings through Specification Examination. One additional method used to promote money savings is to continually examine specifications from which production, maintenance, and operating materials are purchased. A study of such specifications may result in modifications wherein the function performed will not be altered but its cost will be reduced. It is important to determine the origin of specifications currently in use. A thorough investigation by competent purchasing personnel might indicate that specifications should be modernized to include newer, improved materials.

Buying Proper Quantity, Section 8

Buying proper quantity usually includes a formula for purchasing minimum and maximum quantities and a typical section on this subject follows:

BUYING PROPER QUANTITY: The quantities to be bought are determined from known factors of demand, supply, and cost. The demand factor appears from the estimates of the sales, production, or maintenance departments, or from the records of the stores department showing withdrawals from stock. The supply factor is drawn from the reserve stock of any item carried in inventory and from the time required to secure delivery. The cost factor is derived from the inventory carrying charges and the price advantages possible on quantity purchases. In order to establish the quantity to be bought, these factors must be combined in such a manner that the material will cost the least in terms of ultimate cost.

Since the most economical quantity to order at any one time seldom meets the requirements of demand, some storage of materials is desirable from an ultimate cost standpoint. Storage is also necessary to ensure that materials will be available when and where they are needed.

It is not usually a function of the purchasing department to determine the demand. This must be decided by the manufacturing, planning, scheduling, or stores departments. The purchasing department, however, should continuously keep informed about operating conditions and any anticipated changes which will affect demand. The other two factors which determine quantity—availability and cost—are for the purchasing department to determine. It is, therefore, logical that the interested departments need to cooperate to assemble all the factors and determine the proper quantities to order.

Formula for Minimum Ordering Quantity. Stated simply, a good working formula is: immediate net demand, minus stock on hand, plus the estimated demand during the delivery period, plus a reasonable margin of safety.

This formula makes no allowance for a possible minimum charge per order, possible savings by ordering a larger quantity, or for fluctuations in market prices. Minimum ordering quantity should be used as an actual ordering quantity when it is as economical to buy this amount as any larger quantity, or when a drop in prices is probable, or when storage of a larger order would be impractical.

Optimum Ordering Quantity. This quantity should be established at a point where the carrying costs and risks on inventory balance the gains obtained by ordering in larger quantities.

A number of formulas for determining the proper quantities have been published in purchasing, inventory control, and production control textbooks (as well as in other sections[4] of this handbook). Some of the factors considered are:

1. The cost of procurement from the time the purchase is requisitioned until the goods have been received, checked, inspected, and placed in stores. This includes the expense of receiving and inspecting, the expense of the purchasing department chargeable to the order, and that of the accounting department in handling the invoice and payment.
2. The quantity to be purchased for a given period.
3. The interest charges for carrying the inventory.
4. The storage charges on the goods.
5. The reserve stock necessary for emergencies.
6. The unit purchase price.

[4] See Sections 13 and 29.

In many cases, the use of formulas results in a higher inventory of low dollar value items and a lower inventory of high dollar value items. This has the obvious advantage of eliminating frequent and costly orders for small value items.

Formulas cannot completely substitute for the buyer's good judgment. Judgment on such factors as obsolescence, deterioration, expansions, and anticipated market price changes should override the formula answer when applicable.

The optimum order quantity should appear on each traveling requisition. When the price of the item changes, the order quantity should be recalculated. An important part of this system is the determination of order point. If the normal lead-time usage is added to the safety factor of reserve stock, this will give a reasonable order point.

The purchasing department can do a great deal toward reducing the number of invoices by attention to proper ordering quantity, grouping requisitions, and combining those to the same supplier on one order for standard stock items. However, a separate purchase order should be issued for each item of production material. This makes it easier to check purchase orders with receiving reports, to issue change orders revising the original quantity ordered, and to secure follow-up information by mail, wire, or telephone.

Buying at a Proper Price, Section 9

This section describes the need for purchasing men to base their knowledge of prices on value rather than on quotations. Quotations may be secured from many companies, but not one of them may be to the best advantage of the purchaser if he has not yet located the best source of supply. This section contains the following information:

BUYING AT A PROPER PRICE: Delivery, quality, and service as well as price must be considered in determining the value of goods purchased. Good buying demands something more than a comparison and scrutiny of prices, for price is sometimes of secondary consideration. The buyer is expected to get the greatest ultimate value possible for the company. Before the buyer agrees to spend the company's money for any item, it is his duty to study the prices quoted, the quality of material offered, the use for which it is intended, and the service likely to be obtained. To do this intelligently, the buyer must have an intimate knowledge of the uses of the material, a wide knowledge of the many variations in the material he is buying, and a good knowledge of prices.

Price Knowledge. The buyer must familiarize himself with current prices and with the prices of recent purchases. The policy of securing quotations for purposes of price comparison is universal, is sound in theory, and is uniformly successful in securing prices for most proposed purchases. But when these quotations are obtained, the buyer's price knowledge has not been broadened because he has not learned why prices are high or why they are low. The mere securing of prices does not increase his knowledge of the relation between price and demand, the relation between trade cycles and prices, how advancing prices may be anticipated, and how declines in prices may be foreseen. Even though items are covered by catalogs and price lists, the buyer, assuming the cost warrants such action, should determine the factors that go to make up the price, especially those that are important in its remaining at that point or in causing its movement up or down.

Countless numbers and varieties of materials are bought by the purchasing department, and it is not supposed that their prices can be remembered. Proper records of previous purchases must be kept and used for price checking.

Manipulated Prices. An analysis of the factors which determine prices, a knowledge of market conditions, and records of past purchases will indicate to buyers when prices are manipulated or artificial.

In the case of a patented process or article, the manufacturer may be entitled to a fair and legitimate profit not only on his manufacturing costs but also on his work in developing and perfecting the process or article. But when, by manipulation or collusion, a price unwarranted by known and existing conditions is quoted, the buyer has every justification in attempting to get the materials elsewhere at their correct value.

Relation of Cost to Prices. Costs determine the minimum price at which goods can be sold profitably. Vendors cannot operate unless profits are earned and satisfactory cooperation between buyer and seller cannot be expected until the supplier is able to make a profit on the business obtained from the buyer. However, the seller is not entitled to a profit on inefficient or obsolete equipment or on outmoded methods of high cost operation.

It is obvious that no supplier remains long in business selling at cost or below. A manufacturer cannot expect a profit unless he can keep his costs down to a point where he is reasonably efficient. In order to keep (company name) in a position where it can operate efficiently, it is necessary to keep costs down by efficient buying. It is the buyer's duty to be sure that he does not pay too much.

Purchasing materials from only one source is sometimes dangerous, especially if their continuous production is vital to the company. In case of fire, strikes, natural hazards, or other events at a vendor's plant, the purchaser may also be forced to shut down or curtail operations. Developing competition where necessary is another one of a buyer's duties.

Items in a competitive field not only offer additional security but, in most cases, cost less to buy.

The purchase price alone, however, is not and should not be the governing factor in placing an order unless all other factors are equal. Price differentials are often due to differences in quality. It is necessary for the buyer to determine whether the poorer quality should be purchased at a lower cost or a better quality at a higher cost in order to receive the utmost projected value.

Differences in promised delivery dates need to be analyzed. Quite often the lowest bid specifies a late delivery date and it may be advisable to place the order at a higher price in order to secure delivery at an earlier time.

Occasionally the terms of payment offer a sufficiently large cash discount to justify placing the order at a higher unit price that will result in the lowest net price when the invoice is paid and the cash discount deducted.

A number of vendors may quote identical prices and terms. When this occurs, the order should be placed on the basis of quality and service. Usually one vendor will be preferable to the others when quotations are analyzed on the basis of quality and service.

Transportation Costs. Continuing increases in transportation costs have become an important factor in evaluating vendor quotations. Higher transportation costs plus time lost in transit could negate a lower price from a distant vendor in favor of a higher price from a nearer vendor. In fact, the cost of freight to destination must be included in any tabulation of prices if a fair comparison is to be made. Transportation rates must constantly be reviewed to determine the most economical method of transportation and the name of the preferred carrier (or carriers, if the materials must move by more than a one-line haul). This information should be specified on purchase orders to ensure that materials are received at the lowest possible cost.

Contracts, Section 10

This section describes the procedures to be followed when a company's standard purchase order is considered inadequate to cover unusual terms and conditions, or when a vendor offers better terms under a contract than he will accept on individual purchase orders. A section on contracts may contain all or part of the following:

CONTRACTS: It is desired that contracts, other than the standard purchase order, be entered into when the purchase order is considered inadequate to cover unusual terms and conditions.

All purchasing contracts are necessarily both buyer and seller contracts.

When contracts offered by sellers on their own forms are considered, it is natural that the seller's interest has been fully protected. In accepting such a contract, the buyer must make sure that he is equally well protected.

However, purchasing agents and buyers can do much to have contracts drawn in the proper manner and reduce delay and legal expense. Buyers should try to have fine print on contracts enlarged and made more legible.

The following factors should be kept in mind:

1. Every clause of the contract should be definite to the point of making any misunderstanding unlikely.
2. All necessary provisions must be placed in the contract and it must include the entire agreement between the parties.
3. Printed matter anywhere referred to in the body of a purchasing contract, no matter how small the type, is binding.
4. Any additions or revisions that might be required in the original text of a contract must be signed by both parties. Verbal modifications bind neither buyer nor seller and must not be permitted.

Long-term Contracts. Production materials are usually placed under relatively long-term contracts for insurance of supply, price advantage, or for other considerations. Some long-term contracts are based on cost plus a predetermined rate of profit; others are based on an existing wage formula or a published raw material price or a combination of both. They cover large quantities of requirements, usually at fixed prices with periodical deliveries at the purchaser's convenience to reduce inventory investment. They are of advantage to the seller by reducing sales expense and by keeping his production in continuous operation. They also eliminate the need for the buyer to place numerous small contracts or purchase orders.

Except in special cases, one-year purchase contracts are most desirable. This policy gives the purchasing agent or buyer an opportunity to thoroughly review the situation at each new contract period. It is not advisable to provide for continuance by a clause automatically renewing them for some future period.

Programming or Planned Purchasing. These have a definite place in buying procedures. Properly used, they have the following advantages:

1. Reduce paper work by eliminating the use of purchase requisitions.
2. Make it necessary to plan purchases on a long-range over-all basis for greatest price advantage.
3. Provide a means of effective control of commodities purchased in large quantities.

4. Stimulate the close examination of one-supplier situations with the objective of eventually obtaining additional sources of supply.

In general, there are three types of supply situations which lend themselves to programming or planned purchasing. One is where the ability to choose from more than one source of supply is restricted. Such cases include those in which a design may be set for a particular product requiring the purchase of a number of components. These components may be negotiated at the start to find the lowest cost vendors. Once those decisions are made, all the business for at least a reasonable period must be placed with the same suppliers in order to amortize nonrepetitive tooling costs. Similarly, there may be requirements for which the engineering or production approval covers only one supplier. In such cases, continued submission of purchase requisitions bearing the same story increases the volume of paper work which must be handled, without altering control of the purchasing situation.

In the same way, "programs" should be established for limited periods of time where prices quoted by suppliers are substantially the same, all furnish the same or equivalent products, and all are able to provide satisfactory deliveries. The important aspect in such situations is the proper distribution of business between suppliers over a period of time rather than the placement of any individual purchase order. This objective can be best reached through use of a planned program.

The third possible type of program covers similar materials and parts purchased from the same group of suppliers but on different specifications and stock numbers or to different style numbers. Each individual material or part may be a true one-supplier item and is usually not interchangeable with any other material or part. It cannot be programmed, however, without taking into account the purchases of other materials or parts in the same general classification which are purchased from the same group of suppliers. Examples of this type of program would be steel castings and malleable iron castings.

There are a large number of individual purchases which are most efficiently handled as single transactions and are not adapted to purchasing programs. These purchases include those unrelated to other requisitions, bulk purchases in a fluctuating price market with variance between suppliers, and items on which the purchaser is in the process of developing a change of source. In these cases, the purchase requisition form can be made to tell the whole story.

Blanket Contracts. These are a useful and popular tool in buying materials used repetitively. When an order is written against a contract, it is necessary to write the price on the purchase order and to refer to the contract, giving the contract number. This will facilitate invoice checking. Where the company has several contracts covering the same material, the one giving the best price and service is to be given the orders.

Releases. Except under special arrangements, releases on contracts must be made on regular purchase orders. Such orders must contain an added clause, "Price and all terms are in accordance with and governed by Contract No. ________."

These contracts and agreements may provide for the purchase of partial requirements. This procedure is designed to permit the most advantageous placement of purchase orders.

Price. Prices may be fixed at a determined figure by contract. In some cases, it is desirable to make a provision that the price be based on the market price at the date of shipment. In such a contract, it is necessary to state accurately the means of determining the market price. This is done by reference to some standard price-reporting medium, such as a reputable trade paper. When it is possible, sliding scale price agreements should be safeguarded by inserting a maximum price which the seller shall not exceed, regardless of market changes. A most favorable type of price agreement is one in which the seller fixes the current price as a maximum price and agrees to give the buyer the advantage of all declines in market prices.

In the case of contracts where the seller retains the right to increase prices, the buyer must try to include a provision requiring the vendor to give notice to the company at least 30 days or more prior to the effective date of the new price schedule.

The company must have the right to determine within the 30-day period whether or not to continue the contract at the new price. A typical protective provision is the following:

> Such revised price shall become effective not earlier than thirty days after the seller shall give notice in writing thereof to the purchaser. If after the giving of such notice the purchaser is not willing to pay such revised price, the purchaser, within thirty days thereafter, may terminate this agreement by giving to the seller ten days prior written notice of such termination.

Another good protective clause is:

> The purchaser shall have the right to cancel this contract at any time in the event that such price revisions are not satisfactory to the purchaser.

Occasionally a supplier insists on an escalator clause providing for a price increase due to certain contingencies. It is company policy to make certain that the clause to be used also provides for a price decrease in the event that market conditions or costs of manufacture decline.

Penalties. Special attention must be given to the right to cancel the contract and to the penalty to the purchaser or vendor for nonperformance. Exceptions to this penalty, such as fires, floods, labor disturbances, wars, casualties, shortage of cars or raw materials, or other causes beyond control must be agreed to by both parties. Final agreement must be written into the contract.

Conditions and Instructions. An agreement shall not be made with suppliers to exempt or supplement the conditions and instructions of the printed purchase order or contract without the approval of the head of the purchasing department.

Time Clauses. Delivery may be agreed to be made within a certain period, on a certain date, or in accordance with the purchaser's instructions. The most favorable type of contract with respect to time is one that calls for delivery "within the period from ______ to ______ as desired by the purchaser." In any event, performance desired by the purchaser and promised by the vendor must be established during negotiations and qualified in writing in the contract.

Time is of the essence in buying contracts. A clear statement of the right to cancel and refuse deliveries if not made on time should be included in all contracts. Every contract should contain a definite statement of termination, either by lapse of time or the action of the parties to it.

Special Conditions. These are sometimes necessary in purchasing contracts for the protection of the purchaser's or vendor's interests. Such conditions must be stated plainly and not left to mutual understanding.

In some cases it is advisable to include a liquidated damage clause to protect the purchaser and to ensure completion of the contract by the required time.

It should be remembered that a purchasing contract is at one and the same time both a sales contract and a buying contract. The vendor may submit a contract form which has been written by the legal department for protection from all contingencies and with little or no protection to the purchaser from these same contingencies. One clause found in many such contracts is:

> The vendor shall not be liable for non-performance of this contract in whole or in part if non-performance is the result of fires, labor troubles, wars, casualties, shortages of cars or raw materials, or any other cause beyond his control.

This clause would excuse nonperformance by the seller without protecting the buyer under similar conditions. The following is preferable:

> The consequences, direct or indirect, of labor troubles, fires, accident, war, shortages of cars, failure of supply of raw materials, suspension or curtailment

of manufacturing operations, and any and all like or different causes which are beyond the control of the parties hereto shall excuse performance hereunder, in whole or in part, to the extent by which performance has been prevented by such consequences. Upon removal of the cause of any such interruption, the performance shall be resumed at the specified rates.

The value of such a clause is that the purchaser is also protected from liability to receive materials during the existence of any of the several calamities named.

Guaranties. A guaranty adds nothing to a contract unless it is a definite guaranty of a specific item not covered by the general contract. A guaranty of service for a fixed period after delivery or against defects discovered within a fixed period is valuable protection in many cases. So far as possible, the guaranty should be specific as to what constitutes failure, inherent or otherwise, as applying to the particular item coming under the guaranty.

In case of failure, the purchasing department is to be given a complete statement of facts regarding the failure. Such facts must be reported within the guaranty period. The buyer who placed the order should handle the complaint with the seller.

Surplus and Obsolete Material, Section 11

This section describes the procedure to be followed when the disposal of such materials is the responsibility of the purchasing department. If a special salvage section handles the problem, this section would not be included in the purchasing manual. A typical section on this subject follows:

SURPLUS AND OBSOLETE MATERIALS: The company's inventories should be kept at a point commensurate with the rate of production. It is a function of the purchasing department to handle the disposal of surplus and/or obsolete materials and equipment in order to keep inventories as low as possible and to standardize material used so as to minimize the number of articles carried in stock.

The disposal of surplus and/or obsolete materials, machinery, and equipment may be handled in one of the following ways:

1. Substitution for more active material
2. Transfer to other company-operated plants
3. Return to manufacturer or supplier
4. Outright sale or exchange for other material
5. Scrap, and charge off the resulting loss

When operating conditions change, the existing stock items to be made obsolete should, if practicable, be used before acquiring stock of the new standard. However, when material or equipment becomes surplus or obsolete, a surplus report is to be prepared for the head of the purchasing department by the department which has the material. This report must include this information:

1. Quantity and unit
2. Description—part number, size, material, how packed, and serial number, etc.
3. Condition
4. Date of purchase
5. Cost when purchased
6. Present book value
7. Location

When machinery or equipment is being scrapped, transferred, or sold, all spare parts held in stock for that equipment are to be listed for disposal with the equipment.

When materials of this nature are to be sold, bids should be solicited by the purchasing department from financially reliable potential purchasers. Complete records should be maintained regarding the disposition of the material.

Quotation Requests, Section 12

This section describes when requests for quotation forms are to be used and with what limitations. A typical section is as follows:

QUOTATION REQUESTS: When a purchase requisition has received a purchaser's approval as to quantity, form, and propriety, he must then decide where to place the order. His first duty is to select from available vendors one or more whom he believes will offer value in terms of price, quality, and service. He then solicits quotations from them.

The inquiry method of securing bids from two or more sellers should be employed, irrespective of the buyer's knowledge of prices. The firms asked to quote must be competent to handle the business. Any company whose bid may not be considered when the bids are analyzed should not be asked to quote.

Firms requested to quote must be selected so as to get the broadest possible price information. It is desirable on some materials to secure quotations from different geographical locations as well as from local sources, as some variation of prices can be expected, depending upon trade conditions in different localities. It is advisable on some goods which are usually purchased from a dealer to check his prices occasionally by sending an inquiry to a manufacturer. On the other hand, if the goods are purchased in small quantities, the dealer may allow a greater cash discount, a lower price, or better service than the manufacturer. The question of whether to deal with manufacturers or jobbers for products which can be secured from both without price advantage either way is one that cannot be answered except by a careful study of all factors involved. If the manufacturer charges extra for broken packages and delays delivery, while the dealer makes no extra charge for broken packages and makes prompt deliveries, thus permitting the company to operate on a lower inventory, then if price and quality are equal, the orders should be placed with the dealer.

The (company name) has a standard Request for Quotation form which is to be used for all requests for quotation unless special details require a letter. Two copies are sent to each vendor to be filled in. One copy is retained by the vendor while the other is to be returned.

As a rule, inquiries should be sent to not less than three possible sources of supply before making purchase commitments in excess of $250. If it is considered impractical to do so, an explanatory notation should be made on the purchase requisition.

Written confirmation is desirable on all verbal quotations amounting to $250 or more.

Whenever the vendor selected is not the lowest bidder, an explanatory notation should be made on the purchase requisition to indicate the reason for the choice.

When bids on identical specifications show wide variations, the buyer should immediately find out whether any double meaning could be read into the specifications. It is also advisable to interview both the highest and lowest bidders and go over their proposals, since this will generally bring to light any misconceptions which may exist. Variations in quoted prices often occur in the purchase of tools and machinery because it is the practice of some makers to quote for the bare machine, while others will include additional parts and attachments. For this reason, all quotations for equipment and appliances should be carefully scrutinized.

In order to get the best projected value, quotations must be:

1. Analyzed on the basis of quality, service, and price. Quality and service being equal, the award should be made to the lowest bidder, except under unusual circumstances.
2. Considered as final with regard to figure submitted. Allowing revision of bids or quotations after submission may bring a better price on one transaction. But when it becomes known that it is the buyer's general practice, he can seldom obtain by a first request truly competitive quotations with best obtainable prices.
3. Considered confidential by the buyer. The policy of hinting to com-

petitors the nature of quotations destroys confidence and bona fide competition. In the long run, it is expensive.

Quotations, after receipt and action, become part of the purchasing department's records, and all losing as well as winning bids are to be retained in the company for the length of time required by Federal or state statutes.

Many of the standard items that recur often in nonproduction purchasing are pipe, valves, fittings, firebrick, fuses, conduit pipe and fittings, electrical supplies, bolts, nuts, and screws. These items are usually sold on the basis of catalog list prices less a trade discount which varies according to the nature of the buyer's business or to the dollar value of the proposed purchases.

As prices on these items normally do not fluctuate as much as others, it is advisable to send out quotation requests prior to each calendar quarter, requesting quotations on general groups of items that may be required during the ensuing period. The quotation request would not name specific quantities, however, as requirements are indefinite and would not be known until requisitions for material are received during the period covered.

After tabulating and analyzing the bids, a blanket purchase order may be issued to the best source. It should specify the period covered; description of prices or discounts at which deliveries are to be made; and state that formal purchase orders or releases will be furnished for any material that is to be delivered on that particular order. This procedure saves time for both buyer and seller as quotation requests are sent out only four times each year instead of telephoning or securing quotations each time a requisition is received. It also enables the vendors to quote lower prices because of the larger volume resulting by receiving a blanket order for three months' requirements.

The Purchase Order, Section 13

This section explains the importance of the purchase order and includes the following information:

THE PURCHASE ORDER: The (company name) purchase order is the seller's authority to ship and invoice for the goods specified on the order and is the purchaser's commitment for the value of the goods ordered. It is a legal document. When the order is written as an acceptance of an offer, a contractual relation is established immediately upon its issuance; otherwise, the order itself is an offer to such a contractual relation, which is completed by an acceptance form or upon acceptance by the seller.

The purchase order is the most important of the purchasing forms.

While it is unnecessary to employ intricate legal phraseology in the text of the order, its importance as a legal document should not be slighted. It should cover definitely and precisely the essential elements of the purchase to be made in a manner which will render future misunderstandings impossible and minimize the necessity of additional correspondence.

It is important to note that only the terms and conditions appearing on the purchase order and on the reverse side are considered part of the contract. Acceptance of the order is conditional on acceptance of all terms and conditions.

As a background for placing orders, buyers must be familiar with the conditions printed on the back of the vendor and acceptance copies of the purchase order. These have been approved by the legal department for the protection of the company. By knowing them, buyers have a better understanding of procedures and will not verbally require suppliers to perform acts contrary to purchase order conditions.

Name and Address of Seller. The seller's name on the purchase order must be the same as the name of the company that will invoice the order. If the order is placed with a sales agent who is acting for the seller, the order is to be addressed to the seller showing the agent's name on the next line as the representative of the seller. For example:

The Blank Corporation
John J. Agent, Representative

Delivery Required. Delivery required should be shown as two dates—"not earlier than" and "not later than." By establishing a time range for delivery, the arrival of material is assured when it is needed, but not prior to that time. The establishing of a maximum date shifts the responsibility of transportation delays to the seller. These dates should be definite dates, not "Rush," "A.S.A.P.," or "Urgent." By failing to establish definite dates, the recourse to cancellation for nondelivery becomes questionable.

Prices. When prices are based on a quotation or an agreement as to prices, reference should be made to such quotations or agreements. If the order is to be placed against a contract, it is necessary to show the price and to refer to the contract by giving the contract number. Since the company sometimes has blanket contracts or agreements with more than one seller who can supply the same material, the buyer should check these contracts to be sure of obtaining the best price.

Terms. Payment terms, including cash discounts, are usually at the option of the seller. They should be obtained whenever possible. Cash discounts usually apply only to the value of the material and not to transportation charges or Federal, state or local taxes. For accounting reasons, the company prefers to pay the seller only once each month. The preferred terms are 2 per cent for cash on the 10th of the month for shipments made during the preceding month (i.e., 2 per cent 10th prox.).

F.o.b. Point. This should be clearly defined on the purchase order to avoid misunderstandings. The delivered price is the cost to the company and an indefinite statement of f.o.b. point may cost more than the saving made by careful work on all other details of the order. It is important to remember that the title to goods and all risks of ownership vest in the purchaser at the f.o.b. point. Actually, the f.o.b. point is preferably at the buyer's plant, since this leaves the title to the goods in the seller and at his risk during their transportation. When purchases are made f.o.b. destination, the freight should be prepaid. This will eliminate the accounting required to pay the transportation charges and deduct them from the invoice. Every purchase order must clearly show the f.o.b. terms which apply. The commonly used ones are:

1. F.o.b. destination
2. F.o.b. shipping point, freight prepaid and allowed
3. F.o.b. shipping point, freight allowed
4. F.o.b. shipping point, freight prepaid and charged
5. F.o.b. shipping point, freight equalized with named point
6. F.o.b. shipping point

The words "ship prepaid" or "installed" are not part of any f.o.b. point and should not be so used. The words "ship prepaid" should be shown with the "routing" instructions and the word "installed" should be shown as part of the "price."

Test or Trial of Materials, Goods, or Equipment. It is sometimes desirable to make a test or trial of certain materials, goods, or equipment before completing a purchase. In general, our company policy is that anything worth trying or testing is worth the cost of the test.

If the seller is paid and the material proves unsatisfactory or undesirable, the company is not under any obligation. However, if the seller supplies a free sample which is unsatisfactory and then makes changes which cost money, time, and effort in an attempt to meet requirements, he may feel that he has been poorly treated if another source is selected and he is not given a further opportunity to try his material.

Under no circumstances should either materials or equipment be accepted for trial, test, or demonstration before a purchase order outlining all terms and conditions of the trial is issued. As an exception to the general policy, however, free samples may be accepted for trial when the value of the sample is less than the cost of the paper work involved in completing a purchase.

It is usual for suppliers to invoice the company when the material is shipped, even when they have agreed that acceptance is dependent upon approval after trial. To avoid payment before approval is given, the words "Trial Order" are to be written on the purchase order on the line where terms of payment are usually written. This will indicate that payment is not to be made without special approval. The proposed cost and the following statement should also be typed in the "price" column:

> *Trial Order–Invoice not to be paid until approved by individual who signs this order.*

In addition to this, this clause must be typed on the purchase order:

> *It is understood and agreed that the goods described in this order are for test or trial purposes. The buyer may, at his option, either return them with no obligation and at no cost other than transportation charges from and to your factory or retain them. It is further agreed that the buyer shall be the sole judge of the results of this test or trial. If the buyer decides to purchase the goods on this order, he agrees to pay the seller the sum of $.................*

Note that the two clauses above are to be typed on all copies of the Purchase Order to ensure complete understanding by the vendor as well as by those in the company who receive copies. Do not use rubber stamps.

Personal Signature Required on Purchase Orders. As purchase orders are legal documents obligating the company, it is advisable that authorized purchasing personnel personally sign each purchase order. Rubber-stamp signatures are not permissible. (This paragraph in a purchasing manual must be rewritten if company policy does not require personal signature. Also see Section 4 of this handbook, "Facsimile Signatures" and Section 5, "Purchase Order Signatures.")

Purchase Order Acceptances, Section 14

This section of the manual stresses the importance of the purchase order acceptance when it is properly signed, dated, and returned. It also specifies actions that are to be taken if the document is not returned promptly.

PURCHASE ORDER ACCEPTANCES: All acceptances of purchase orders sent in by suppliers to the purchasing department are to be forwarded to the responsible buyer. If the acceptance is properly signed and dated, it should be filed. When the acceptance copy contains one or more exceptions, such as those following, the buyer is to take whatever action may be necessary:

1. Change in quantity
2. Change in price

3. Alteration in any way of the reading of the purchase order
4. Exception to the terms or conditions of the purchase order
5. Promised delivery date later than the requested delivery date
6. Discrepancy between the specific delivery date negotiated by the buyer at the time of placement and the actual promised date
7. Unsigned acceptance

Acceptances need not be sent out with every order. They are not required if the material, by a verbal order, has been shipped or received, as these conditions are acceptances of purchase orders. For these reasons, the company's original copy of the purchase order does not refer to the acceptance copy.

It is important that all suppliers return signed copies of purchase order acceptances whenever they are sent out with the purchase order. Unless the acceptance is signed and returned by the supplier, a legal contract does not exist. The buyer shall follow each order within 15 days after placement of the order in an effort to obtain a properly executed acceptance.

When acceptable changes are made in the acceptance that affect quantity, specification, price, terms, or conditions, they should be confirmed by a purchase order supplement or change notice. If the changes are unsatisfactory, the order should be canceled.

Purchase orders should be priced when issued. However, in some cases it is necessary to send the original purchase order, unpriced, to the seller. The supplier should be requested to return the acceptance with his price shown thereon. If the supplier's price is satisfactory, the buyer should initial the acceptance, note his records accordingly, and have the other copies of the purchase order changed to agree.

When the supplier returns the purchase order acceptance unsigned, the buyer must send it back to the supplier with a request that it be signed and returned. Without this signature, the purchase order terms and conditions have not been formally accepted or agreed upon. In fact, without the vendor's acceptance the purchase order itself is incomplete and not a binding contract.

Follow-up and Tracing of Orders, Section 15

This section describes the procedure to be followed after a purchase order is issued to make reasonably sure that the material will be received at the time required. A typical section follows:

FOLLOW-UP AND TRACING OF ORDERS: The function of a purchasing department is to supply materials to fulfill the company's requirements. This is not accomplished by issuing an order and securing a promise from the vendor. The process is not complete until satisfactory delivery has been made. To ensure that the delivery will be made when required, some form of follow-up is necessary, and the purchasing department must be organized to take care of this as needed.

There are various methods of handling follow-up procedure. In many purchasing departments, follow-up on an order is the responsibility of the buyer who placed the order. To assist the buyer, it can be efficiently handled by a clerk who keeps the records for this purpose and takes the ordinary routine follow-up steps on his own responsibility, referring particular orders to the appropriate buyer as special action may become necessary. In cases where follow-up is a major activity, requiring a large amount of time and personal attention that would seriously interfere with the buyer's primary responsibilities of negotiating purchase agreements, it calls for a specialized staff, including expediters in the field. Under these conditions, it is best to have a follow-up and expediting division in the purchasing department, with cooperation and assistance from the buyers as the need arises.

The basis for successful follow-up lies first of all in the proper stipulations of purchase. The purchase order must state when delivery is required. By previous negotiation, the buyer secures quotations for materials, specifying that delivery will be required at a definite date, or at a definite period of time after the vendor receives the purchase order. Delivery promises made on quotations determine to some extent which vendors will share the business. Without this preliminary consideration on the part of the buyer, expediting may degenerate into mere pressure which is the least effective of all follow-up methods.

The next procedure is to secure the vendor's signed agreement on the acceptance copy of the purchase order, to deliver the material on the date or dates requested. *The promise,* not the request, *is the proper basis of the follow-up.* It is often desirable to try to get a seller to better his delivery promise. But when such promises are honestly made and represent the best service that the seller can reasonably expect to give on an order, it is the function of follow-up to hold him strictly to that promise. Thus the acceptance copy serves a double purpose. It completes the contract agreement by acceptance of the order, and it determines the delivery schedule. Every effort should be made to have the acceptances returned promptly with automatic postal card follow-up in every case where acknowledgment or actual shipment is not promptly forthcoming. By consistent education of vendors on this point, buyers have reached a point where practically all acceptances are returned without special follow-up.

Setting the date for follow-up is a matter calling for the exercise of judgment and depends on the nature of the purchase order. On some standard stock items follow-up is not necessary as the material will arrive on the promised delivery date. But on major projects and made-to-order items that involve not only a place on the vendor's manufacturing schedule but a considerable production cycle as well, such action would be too late to accomplish any practical good in overcoming possible delay and ensuring delivery as promised. In such cases, the follow-up would be scheduled for some days or even weeks in advance of the delivery promise, and the follow-up action would be adjusted accordingly.

Routine follow-up, according to such a schedule, can usually be effected by simple routine methods to be handled by competent clerical assistants. A printed double postal reply card requesting specific delivery information, with a reference to the order number and vendor's delivery promise, is the usual first step. The return postal card is preferable to a letter in facilitating the vendor's reply. By inserting the purchase order number, a complete communication can be prepared in a matter of seconds. The inquiry is strengthened by a printed notice at the bottom of the postal card:

> We are trying to conserve your time as well as ours by using this form. It is sent in duplicate to enable you to use one copy for your reply and to keep the other for your files.

Beyond the suggested postal card, as the need for additional follow-up becomes more acute, the tone and method of follow-up becomes stronger and more personalized. The usual sequence is: personal letter, telegram, telephone, and personal interview by expediter or buyer at the vendor's plant.

To avoid the waste of time and money spent in follow-up by wire and telephone, it is our responsibility to instruct our vendors and their salesmen that it is their duty, after a purchase order is received from us and until the material is shipped, to keep us informed as to whether it will be shipped in accordance with our delivery requirements as shown on the purchase order. How much information and when we should receive it depends on the importance to us of the material ordered.

The buyer should take appropriate action to correct any purchase order change proposed by the vendor in delivery date, quantity, price, or any other aspect. If the vendor still cannot meet our original terms, the buyer must take whatever measures seem advisable—place the order with another vendor, develop a new source, or refer to the requisitioning department to see if it will accept the vendor's revised shipping promise.

When repetitive troubles occur with one vendor, efforts should be made to place some or all of the requirements elsewhere, even if it becomes necessary to purchase additional dies or patterns to be used at other sources for substantial production runs. A one-vendor production item frequently causes trouble due to the many factors that arise to delay deliveries. Occasionally one of two or more vendors of the same production material is unable to deliver as scheduled. When this happens, it may be a relatively simple matter to increase orders with the other source or sources until such time as the vendor who has failed to deliver is able to resume shipments. If the vendor who has delayed deliveries cannot resume production, the buyer shops around for another vendor who will offer better deliveries. Dies or patterns may then be transferred without serious interruption in production schedules.

The various sources of supply should be studied carefully in order to find the most dependable ones and eliminate from consideration those whose history clearly shows a record of broken delivery promises. Where it is not possible or advisable to drop these vendors from the supplier lists, a campaign of education, carried, if necessary, to the higher officials of the delinquent companies, will generally bring results.

Often a particular item will be ordered frequently enough from the same vendor with the result that a number of purchase orders will accumulate for identical material. In these instances, it is the purchasing department's responsibility to see that vendors apply shipments against the oldest purchase orders first. This procedure keeps the number of outstanding purchase orders at a minimum as well as simplifying paper work in the receiving and accounting departments.

Open purchase orders on which small quantities remain unshipped should be considered complete and removed from the active file if the balances do not represent economical production runs. However, the vendor must be notified by a purchase order cancellation notice that the order has been considered complete, and agree to it by accepting, signing, and returning the acceptance copy.

If the requisitioning departments work closely with the purchasing department, many needless rush orders for material will be forestalled and there will not be any need for other than routine follow-up.

Constant requests to suppliers for rush service destroy their effectiveness. Extra expenses for telegrams, long-distance telephone calls, and special services add to both buyer's and seller's costs, resulting in smaller profit for both.

The objective of follow-up is to secure delivery in accordance with the delivery promise, or better. Failing of this, it is necessary to get a revised delivery promise which is capable of fulfillment and which will be even more aggressively followed. The follow-up action should be recorded in every case.

Invoices, Section 16

This section refers to the need for pricing purchase orders correctly so that invoices may be processed for payment without delay. Invoice checking and approval should not be a function of the purchasing department. Ideally, the purchasing department should prepare purchase orders in complete detail as to quantity, description, price, f.o.b. point, routing, discount terms, and any other details that affect payment to the vendors, and a copy of the purchase order should be sent to the accounting department. When the purchasing department has made certain that the material has been received at the time required, its function has been completed. It is the accounting department's responsibility to verify from the receiving report that the material has been received by authorized personnel. It should also be the accounting department's responsibility to determine that the invoice and transportation charges are in accordance with the terms specified on the purchase order and to complete the transaction by paying the vendor, taking advantage of such cash discount terms as may have been specified on the purchase order. Therefore, this section of the purchasing manual on invoices should be somewhat as follows:

Invoices are the seller's charges against the company on the basis of which the seller is paid for materials or services furnished. The invoice is based upon the purchase order and should refer to it and follow it in all details of description, terms, and prices.

To the extent that purchase orders are correctly priced when placed, a great deal of burdensome clerical work is later avoided. Each buyer should make every effort to do as near a 100 per cent job of pricing all his orders correctly as is consistent with good purchasing practice. The buyer must consider all factors such as dollar value of purchase order, urgency of delivery, date of most recent quotation or previous purchase order, and extent of competition.

It is necessary that accounting personnel see that invoices are processed for payment without delay or hindrance. It is company policy that the payment of invoices will not be delayed beyond the dates they are due.

All invoices from local vendors that do not agree with the purchase order, along with the accounting copy of the order, are to be referred by accounting to the person who originated the order. The order originator will then make any changes or additions that are necessary on the accounting and purchasing department copies of the order, initial and date them, and refile the purchasing department copies. The corrected accounting papers are to be returned to that department within 48 hours, exclusive of weekends and holidays. The originator of the order should not sign or approve the invoices for payment, as this is the accounting department's function, based on the completeness of the order. Questions regarding invoices from out-of-town vendors referred to purchasing by accounting are to be handled by letter, wire, or telephone and returned to accounting as promptly as possible with definite information about the adjustments that have been agreed upon. In all cases, get the vendor to agree as soon as possible to the invoice changes or corrections that are necessary.

Records, Section 17

This section describes the necessity for the maintenance of basic records in the purchasing department. The following information forms a good basis for this section:

Record of Material Specifications. All approved specifications for purchased material are to be filed and indexed for availability and ready reference.

Vendor Record. Each buyer is to keep a loose-leaf binder or card file containing in alphabetical order the vendors' names, local and home office addresses, telephone numbers, names of sales managers, salesmen's names, f.o.b. points, cash discount terms, and routing instructions. This information is of great value when calling, wiring, or writing vendors for urgent quotations, placing orders, or following up on orders.

Purchase Record. A purchase record of commodities purchased must be maintained. Typically, it consists of a card for each item, material, or part in regular use. It shows, in the heading or indexing margin, the item name, number, ordering description or reference to the applicable purchase specification, and a list of vendors from whom it has been or may be purchased. When a purchase requisition is received, refer to this card and have requests for quotation forms typed and mailed to the firms listed thereon, filing the card again for future use. When the inquiries are returned by the vendors quoting prices, terms, shipping date, and possibly suggested substitutions or alternates, they are then entered and tabulated on the purchase requisition. This tabulation gives complete, condensed data. When analyzed, the bids make it possible to select the company which is entitled to receive the purchase order, based on lowest cost, quickest delivery, or other known factors. The purchase requisition bearing these data will also provide a complete reference in case of need to refer to the transaction at a later date.

Posted from a copy of the purchase order are: the order number, date of order, vendor's name, quantity ordered, price, terms, f.o.b. point, and division or department for which the material is ordered. The record should be so arranged as to allow quick and accurate comparison between different purchases of the same commodity. There should be a separate card by size or number for each commodity. This record is in many respects the heart of a purchasing system. It gives the buyer an opportunity to place each order with the full facts available as to: choice of vendors, previous volume of purchases, prices, discounts, terms, and names of the requisitioning departments.

Adequate price records include:

1. Statement of methods of pricing used by various suppliers when they differ, and yet the material supplied meets a single specification.
2. Statement of any other factors which are more important than price to selection of supplier, such as quality, delivery, and service.
3. Statement of actual check made to make sure that premiums are not involved in purchasing from a distributor rather than the manufacturer.
4. Statement that continued usage of lower-priced substitutes was questioned and not recommended when their original use was necessitated by an emergency.
5. Statement that quotations were required, even from single sources of supply, to prove that every effort to know prices was made. Also quotations from other suppliers even though the order had to be placed immediately for other reasons.

Contract Record. It is essential to have available at all times the complete record of purchase contract commitments. Where only a few contracts are in force, a separate record is not required as a file on contracts will be more convenient. Where a large number of contracts are filed, the buyer will find it convenient to record his contracts on a card which can be used as a desk index. Contract files should be kept locked and care should be taken to keep all conditions of the contracts confidential.

Miscellaneous Records. Various other records are essential to some purchasing offices. These will vary with the nature of the business and other factors. Records of pattern location, possession of tools needed for manufacture of purchased goods, trial or testing of sample materials, sale or disposition of surplus or obsolete equipment, returnable container record, special arrangements of various sorts, and the like are often necessary.

Care should be taken that systems, whether in use or proposed, are not too elaborate. The value of a record should be considered in the same manner as a purchase. If it costs more than it is worth, some other system should be adopted.

Reports, Section 18

This section provides for a monthly activity report to be made by the head of the purchasing department to his supervisor. It may provide for monthly reports of a purchasing agent's staff to be made to him.

This section also provides an opportunity for purchasing agents and buyers to make savings reports. Savings reports prove the value of purchasing, but they are only one of the means of measuring the efficiency of purchasing personnel. This section, as is true of all others, should be enlarged or reduced to fit conditions existing in each company. Detailed explanations of typical monthly activity and savings reports follow:

Monthly Activity Reports

This instruction establishes the procedure to be followed by each buyer in submitting to the director of purchasing (or purchasing agent) a monthly report of general activities and market conditions affecting the department.

Reporting Requirements. Each buyer will:

1. Follow the pattern shown in Fig. 3–4.
2. Submit the report each month to the director of purchasing (or purchasing agent) by the tenth of the month following the month reported upon.

Reporting Elements. In reporting general market and economic conditions, personal experiences and knowledge of price fluctuations are to be used as the informational sources, rather than printed publications. Also report local conditions affecting purchasing.

Work Load. A numerical list of all purchase orders as issued is to be maintained showing the consecutive order numbers and the total dollar value of each order. In those instances where the price is not definitely known, the buyer is to write an estimate of the cost on the requisition and then circle that figure. This will indicate to the order typist that the estimate is to be used to compile the value of purchase orders issued for this report and is not to be typed on the purchase order.

Report to Management. The monthly activity reports will be summarized by the head of the purchasing department for a composite report to management.

Savings Reports

Good purchasing performance continually contributes to company

ROCKWELL MANUFACTURING COMPANY AND DIVISIONS
PURCHASING MANUAL

Section 18-Page 2

(Use the Internal Correspondence form)

Subject: PURCHASING DEPARTMENT ACTIVITY REPORT.

Month of ________ ________________Division. Date ________

1. GENERAL CONDITIONS
   (General conditions and their effect on your plant.)

2. MARKETS AND DELIVERIES
   1. Raw Materials.
   2. Other Production Materials.
   3. MRO Supplies.
   4. Most Critical Items.

3. PRICES
   1. Total savings reported for this month and cumulative for calendar year.
   2. Price reductions reported by vendors.
   3. Price increases reported by vendors.

4. PLANT VISITS
   (Vendor - Location - Product - Date of Visit - Buyer)

5. PURCHASING AGENTS ASSOCIATIONS (Meetings attended, committee activities, etc.)

6. WORK LOAD
   1. A. Number of purchase orders issued.
      B. Number of purchase order change notices and/or releases issued.
      C. Number of "X" series purchase requisitions used in lieu of purchase orders.
      D. Total of Items 1A, 1B and 1C.
   2. Total value of purchases this month.
   3. Value of invoices or receipts this month.
   4. Total commitments end of month.

7. ORGANIZATION AND PERSONNEL
   1. Employed end of this month - Female Male Total
   2. Changes, Completed or Planned -

8. PROJECTS (As described in this Manual, Section 3, Purchasing Policy).

9. OTHER COMMENTS AND SUGGESTIONS
   (Such as new sources, substitutions, standardizations, or improved operations that might be helpful to our other plants.)

____
Division Purchasing Agent

FIG. 3–4. Activity report.

profits as a result of money savings that ensue from activities such as the following:

1. Lower prices obtained by developing new sources of supply.
2. Price reductions other than normal market fluctuations made through negotiations with suppliers.
3. Price reductions resulting from the development of nonrestrictive specifications, resulting in increased competition.

4. Savings ensuing from the use of standard items or sizes as compared with special purchases previously made. These include the elimination of price extras; inventory savings when fewer items are stocked; and purchases of standard materials instead of those originally requisitioned at higher costs.
5. Savings resulting from the utilization of new or substitute materials, as compared with previous materials specified.
6. Savings from negotiating better trade discount, cash discount, or quantity discount classifications and terms.
7. Savings made through the utilization or salvage of surplus and obsolete supplies and equipment as compared with the cost of new purchases for comparable requirements.
8. Savings made by the purchase of fabricated or semifinished components previously manufactured by the company, or vice versa.
9. Savings made through better purchasing procedures and lower costs of departmental operation.

It is an important function of purchasing to compile a savings report whenever any of these suggested revisions may be measured. However, these reports may be prepared only when money savings are made as a result of some activity or request which originated in the purchasing department. This report is to be sent to the director of purchasing (or purchasing agent) at the time that the saving is made (see Fig. 3–5).

The saving made on a particular purchase order shown on a savings report is only a measure of the buyer's saving on the first order. As the material will be reordered a number of times each year, the buyer should receive credit for his saving on an annual basis. Thus it is also necessary to estimate the total annual saving on each item. The last two lines on the report provide for this information which may be based on estimated quantities, as the actual annual quantities to be ordered may not be known.

The head of the purchasing department will compile a consolidated savings report that will show the total reported results of the purchasing department cost-reduction activities.

Patents, Section 19

This section gives information about patents that all purchasing department personnel need to know.

PATENTS: Patents are issued, after due proceedings, on application to the Commissioner of Patents, Washington, D.C. Patents grant their owners, for a limited period, the exclusive right to make, use, or sell a new and useful article, machine, manufacture, or composition of matter.

ROCKWELL MANUFACTURING COMPANY AND DIVISIONS

PURCHASING MANUAL

(Use the Internal Correspondence form)

Subject: PURCHASING DEPARTMENT REPORT OF SAVING

________________ Division. Date __________

Purchasing Agent or Buyer

Description of Material

Reason for Revision (state reason, for example—substitute material, standardization, change of vendor, quantity increased, negotiation, purchasing recommendations, quality improvement, or other.)

Former Price $ Former Vendor's Name ________________

Price this Order $ Present Vendor's Name ________________

Savings per Unit $

Quantity this Order

Savings this Order $

* * * * * *

Estimated Quantity Purchased Annually

Estimated Annual Savings this Item $

____

Plant Purchasing Agent

Send original to Director of Purchasing and Traffic, Pittsburgh.
Send one copy to General Manager.
Retain one copy for Purchasing Department file.

FIG. 3–5. Report of saving.

Patents may cover particular articles, machinery, apparatus, compositions of matter, and also methods or processes by which a particular result or product is obtained.

Liability for Patent Infringement. In the event of infringement of a patent, not only the maker or seller, but also the user may be liable. In negotiating purchases involving a patented article or process, the policy is to protect the company against financial loss, by reason of infringement, by including in the purchase order or agreement a patent indemnity clause. The clause used by the company is required printing on the back of all purchase orders.

Adversely Held Patents. If the buyer knows of an adverse patent situation in which either the supplier or the company might be charged with a patent infringement, the buyer must obtain the approval of the director of purchasing (or purchasing agent) before placing the order, even though the supplier may agree to the patent indemnity clause. Remember that the indemnity is no stronger than the finances of the supplier.

Licenses under Valid Patents. The (company name) will respect the rights of holders of valid patents. Nevertheless, it may not be necessary to use the invention covered by a patent as there may be other processes, materials, or devices of a noninfringing nature that will accomplish the same result or perform a similar function.

Confidential or Secret Disclosures. If anyone in the purchasing department is approached by a supplier or patentee who offers to disclose information about a particular article, machine, apparatus, method, or process upon the condition that such information is to be kept in confidence, or if the buyer is asked to give assurance that no use will be made of the information, the buyer should refuse to permit the supplier to disclose such information. Likewise, if a supplier or patentee offers to show or demonstrate to the buyer an article, machine, apparatus, method, or process with the understanding that the buyer will not disclose any information about it, the buyer must not permit any such demonstration or showing. Such persons must be referred to the company's patent attorney.

Special Instructions, Section 20

This section provides a place for whatever special policies or procedures have not been previously referred to in the manual, such as:

1. Tax policies affecting purchasing
2. Accounting policies affecting purchasing
3. Data processing procedures for or affecting the purchasing department
4. Purchasing requisitions and/or traveling requisitions
5. Movement of household goods when a company employee is transferred from one location to another
6. Special instructions regarding issuance of purchase orders for materials to be used on government orders

SELECTED BIBLIOGRAPHY

Evaluating Purchasing Performance, AMA Research Study No. 66, American Management Association, Inc., 135 West 50th Street, New York, N.Y. 10020, 1964

"Manual of Purchasing Policies and Principles," *Purchasing Week,* booklet reprint from Feb. 22, 1960, issue, McGraw-Hill Publications, New York, N.Y. 10036, 1960

Pooler, Victor H.: *The Purchasing Man and His Job,* American Management

Association, Inc., 135 West 50th St., New York, N.Y. 10020, pages 211–217, 1964

"Purchasing Department Manual—J. M. Huber Corporation," *The Philadelphia Purchasor,* Purchasing Agents Association of Philadelphia, Inc., Philadelphia, Pa. 19102, February, 1964

"The Purchasing Manual," *Purchasing,* Conover-Mast Publications, Inc., New York, N.Y. 10017, Oct. 9, 1961

"Purchasing Manuals Have Many Values," *Purchasing Week,* McGraw-Hill Publications, New York, N.Y. 10036, March 9, 16 and 23, 1959

Rockwell Purchasing Manual, Rockwell Manufacturing Company, Pittsburgh, Pa. 15208

Statement of Purchasing Policies and Principles, Allegheny Ludlum Steel Corporation, Pittsburgh, Pa. 15222

For other references, see list of purchasing books in Section 26, "Library and Catalog File."

SECTION 4

LEGAL INFLUENCES IN PURCHASING

Editor

Gordon Burt Affleck, Managing Director—Church Procurement, The Church of Jesus Christ of Latter-Day Saints, Salt Lake City, Utah

Associate Editors

J. J. Ritterskamp, Jr., Vice-president for Administration, University of Chicago, Chicago, Illinois

Joseph G. Smith, Vice-president—Purchases and Raw Materials, Pittsburgh Steel Company, Pittsburgh, Pennsylvania

EDITOR-IN-CHIEF'S NOTE: Sections 4 and 5, "Legal Influences in Purchasing" and "Purchase Order Essentials," are both about problems in the same field. They may seem repetitious. This is especially true of Section 4 and the first part of Section 5. *However,* these two sections, in different parts, have been written, rewritten, edited, and arranged by many practical purchasing men. The approach in the two sections is from different angles. After careful consideration and study it has been deemed wise to include both sections "as is." Any seeming repetition should merely emphasize the extent of interest and experience purchasing men have in these areas. If any doubt exists, even the experienced purchasing official seeks the advice of an attorney. Litigation should be avoided, especially where compromise or arbitration is possible.

This section of the handbook is not intended as an exhaustive study of the legal principles having to do with the purchasing function. Only the general principles are discussed and interpreted in the hope that with some basic understanding of his rights and liabilities, the buyer may at least avoid serious controversy and litigation. Another point of view will be given in Section 5.

It is the sincere hope of those who have worked on this section and on Section 5 that the necessarily short outline as given will induce the reader (buyer) to seek further information as to the nature and application of legal principles involved in the day-to-day duties of a purchasing agent.

He should avail himself of legal counsel whenever and to the extent necessary. He will recognize that a sound sense of ethics is by far the most potent tool of his profession. Without it the law is powerless to aid him in the proper and effective discharge of his responsibilities.

PURCHASING AND THE LAW OF AGENCY

Agency is the relationship that exists when one is authorized to act for or represent another in a transaction with a third party. The person undertaking the performance of the act is known as the agent. The person represented is referred to as the principal. Thus, the purchasing agent is an agent performing the procurement function for a principal (his company). The typical act of agency is a purchase made by the purchasing agent with the intention that his company will receive the commodity and will pay the agreed price. The negotiation and the purchase are consummated by the agent with the supplier, but the whole transaction is performed for the benefit of the company. We thus have a typical agency relationship.

Creation of Agency

The relationship of principal and agent is created by agreement between the two parties.

In the case of a purchasing agent, the agency is usually created by his employment to perform the procurement function. Thus, his employment makes the laws of agency applicable to him and to his work.

Modification or Termination of Agency

An agency agreement or contract may be modified at any time by mutual consent of the parties. It may also be terminated at will (in the absence of contractual provision to the contrary) by either party, or by operation of law in the case of inability of either party to continue the arrangement, i.e., death, insanity, or bankruptcy.

Authority of Agent

It is desirable to have the employment and contractual relationship spelled out as a protection and safeguard to both the purchasing agent and his company. Unfortunately, most purchasing agents are employed without a written contract and no expression of the agreement is available. Tables of organization and job descriptions, such as those described in Sections 2 and 3, are sources where one may find the duties of the purchasing agent reduced to writing. In the absence of such evidence, the contract may be deduced from the oral agreement and employment between the purchasing agent and his employer.

Express Authority

Whenever the authority of the agent is to be exactly prescribed, restricted, or limited, it is best to reduce the agreement of authority to writing. To avoid the usual implied conditions or limits of "reasonable" authority, the written instrument should clearly state that the writing contains the whole agreement and "is not to be interpreted to imply more or less" than stated. When the agreement is so definite, oral or written, it is referred to as an "express agreement" giving "express authority."

If the power to delegate authority to an assistant or subordinate is not stated in the written instrument which gives "express authority," then the authority does not exist. This is true of such matters as signing purchase orders, hiring or discharging employees, and any other related or similar acts which should be stated in writing if the purchasing agent is to have such authority. If such authority is given, then the acts of the assistants and subordinates will obligate the principal or company in the same manner as the acts of the purchasing agent.

Implied Authority

Implied authority is authority the agent is reasonably presumed to have in order for him to accomplish the objectives for which the actual authority was granted. This implied authority is assumed to have been agreed upon by the principal and agent, although it is not reduced to writing. A purchasing agent is expected to perform his work and further his company's interests with all the ability, resourcefulness, and ingenuity at his command. Much of his authority lies in this classification of "implied authority." It is difficult to provide for every eventuality that may be faced by the purchasing agent in the performance of his normal duties. The usual intent of the company is to give the purchasing agent adequate opportunity to accomplish his function by every legitimate means at his command. Consequently, his implied authority can be interpreted to be very broad as long as it does not conflict with any authority expressly denied him.

Apparent Authority

There is a third type of authority, known as apparent authority. In the characteristic principal and agency relationship a third party is involved, namely, the person with whom the agent deals or contracts for his principal. Apparent authority is that authority which this third person may be led to believe the agent possesses because of words or conduct of the principal. The principal may not have intended the agent to have this authority, but the principal's conduct has given the impression to the third party. Under these circumstances, if the principal accepts the results of the performance by the agent, even if the performance is beyond the agent's authority, the principal will be bound. If the principal accepts or fails to notify the third party of the agent's lack of authority, this acceptance or silence, which lulls the third party into a sense of security, may be considered as implying authority in the agent or be considered as apparent authority. In either case the principal generally would be bound. Consequently, under this theory of apparent authority, a principal may be held for acts performed by an agent, even though the principal granted neither permission nor authority for their performance and even if this permission could not be reasonably implied from the agent's granted authority. The law imposes this responsibility upon the principal because of the need of protecting an innocent third party dealing with the agent in good faith.

Unauthorized procurement may be made by an agent going beyond his authority or by other individuals not designated as agents. For example, a company may permit the purchasing agent to purchase materials beyond his authority as to type and amount involved, that is, beyond his stated authority. Or the company may allow others in the company to make purchases without any stated agency authority. If the company accepts the material and pays for it, third parties then would have a right to consider that the purchases were made with authority. Subsequent purchases under similar circumstances would bind the principal unless he clearly discloses that the parties do not have the authority.

Authority of Sales Agents

While reviewing the types of authority possessed by an agent, it is well to consider the people with whom a purchasing agent deals in his procurement routine. The customary supplier contact is a salesman. This salesman is a representative of his company, but as an agent the degree of authority he possesses may be somewhat limited. Courts long have regarded a salesman as an emissary to solicit business for his employer, not a duly authorized agent of the company possessing authority to consummate transactions. This means that representations and offers the salesman may make are not binding and valid until such time as they are confirmed by the office of the supplier.

Some salesmen and sales officers do possess the authority to represent their company fully in all transactions, but the purchasing agent dealing with such salesmen should make certain they do possess such authority, since as a general rule they do not. This can be determined by inquiry directed to the vendor's office (also see Section 5).

Duties of an Agent

There are many and varied duties that an agent owes to his principal. An attempt will be made here to outline briefly those that primarily pertain to purchasing agents.

1. A purchasing agent is expected to follow instructions—to proceed in his work in the manner that is prescribed by his company and to follow the established general procedures. Failure could be interpreted to be breach of contract and grounds for dismissal.

He should not exceed the purchasing authority granted him by his company. It is incumbent upon the company to define clearly the nature and extent of the authority given the head of the purchasing department. This is particularly true if the company for special reasons should desire to limit the scope of his work in any manner. It is equally essential that the purchasing executive determine the full scope of authority granted him to avoid unintentionally exceeding it.

In the absence of any written or specific expression of authority granted to a purchasing agent, the following statement would be a fair appraisal of his commission:

> To purchase in the usual manner for his company; to solicit offers to sell, enter into negotiations to obtain the best price and terms for his company as well as the best value; to complete the contract to purchase in the usual and customary form; and at all times to act in the best interest of his company in any and all circumstances.

2. An agent has the obligation of loyalty to his principal. In the case of the purchasing agent or buyer, this would mean that he is not secretly to represent conflicting interests in his negotiations but devote himself exclusively to the welfare of his company. Should the purchasing agent have an interest in any company that is a potential or actual supplier to his principal, this would appear to prevent him from contracting with that company unless he made full disclosure to his employer and secured approval beforehand.[1]

Loyalty also implies confidence. Any confidential information given the purchasing agent by his company must be kept in complete confidence and not divulged. This duty applies even after the purchasing agent leaves the employ of his company.

3. An agent has the duty to seek out information diligently and to report to his company all pertinent facts that he discovers while acting as an agent. Information of value that is discovered by the agent should be disclosed promptly to his principal.

Disclosure of Agency Relationships

A purchasing agent should disclose the fact that he is acting as an agent for his company, when making a purchase (also see Section 5). To accomplish this, the purchase order in addition to the customary information should show the name of the company, the name of the purchasing agent, and a clear indication that he is acting as purchasing agent of his company. Thus:

Smith Manufacturing Co.
By John Jones
Purchasing Agent

[1] Also discussed in Section 6, "Ethical Practices in Purchasing."

An assistant purchasing agent or a buyer, if authorized to sign purchase orders, should do so in the same manner as the purchasing agent.

Facsimile Signatures

Any signature, to be valid, must (1) be an authorized signature and (2) be intended as a legally binding signature. The mode of affixation is immaterial if it meets these two prerequisites. Typewritten, rubber-stamped, and preprinted signatures or even initials are valid and can be used. The danger of unauthorized use is increased, however, in such instances where a preprinted or rubber-stamped signature is utilized.

Legal Liabilities of the Purchasing Officer

An individual acting in any capacity is expected to act in a legal manner. Society demands an individual be responsible for damage or injury resulting from his unlawful actions. In the consideration of the legal liabilities of the purchasing officer many of the so-called areas of liability are common to any person acting in any capacity. Only a few specific areas of responsibility arise because of the agent and principal relationship.

Responsibility for Errors

A purchasing agent represents to his company that he has the necessary skill and training to perform the purchasing function satisfactorily. He also represents that he will perform his work with the degree of care that an ordinary prudent man could be expected to exercise. This should not be interpreted that the purchasing agent insures his company against all losses occasioned by the commission of errors and mistakes of judgment. He has the duty to exercise ordinary care as any reasonably prudent purchasing agent would exercise under similar circumstances. Acting in that manner generally relieves him from responsibility.

Errors made by other personnel of the purchasing department fall in the same category. The purchasing agent is responsible for the successful operation of his department. This usually implies the exercise of ordinary care in selecting employees and in training them adequately. Due observance of careful selection, proper training, and adequate supervision satisfies the requirement of ordinary care.

Contractual Liabilities

Two potential sources of liability of the purchasing agent for the contracts he may make are with his company and with its suppliers. Neither source of liability is of much consequence if the purchasing agent follows the true intent of his agency with his company. The law implies that the purchasing agent act within the scope of the authority granted him by his company. If he does act in that manner, and acts with reasonable care, under all circumstances, no contractual liability can arise between him and his company. And if he acts within the scope of his authority and makes adequate disclosure of his agency to suppliers and third parties, no liability arises between him and them in relation to his acts as an agent.

It is only when the purchasing agent acts outside the scope of his authority—either express or implied—that he becomes subject to potential liability. If his company is forced to honor a contract negotiated by the purchasing agent that was not within the scope of his authority (in the case where the supplier believed the purchasing agent had the apparent authority to make the contract), his company may hold the purchasing agent for any loss which it may sustain. The company may, of course, elect to ratify and accept the actions of the purchasing agent, in which case the purchasing agent will be relieved of liability for his unauthorized acts.

The purchasing agent may be unexpectedly bound on a contract he has negotiated for his company if he fails to disclose the fact of his agency to the supplier. He may recover from his company in such instances, provided he acted in good faith for the company and within the scope of his authority.

The purchasing agent may be held personally under a contract with a supplier if he does not have the express or implied authority to make such a contract *and* the supplier does not believe that the purchasing agent has authority from his company and so informs the purchasing agent. The purchasing agent is then in the position of contracting for himself and must accept the liabilities involved. The fact that he feigned agency for his company does not lessen his liability.

Liability for Negligence

Everyone is expected to assume the responsibility of his negligent acts. Purchasing agents are no exception. Should a purchasing agent injure someone because of negligent action, he is expected to make full restitution for the damage caused. This applies to damage caused while operating a vehicle in a negligent manner, trespassing, damaging another's property, and any of the other acts for which the law imposes responsibility on the average citizen.

Such negligence, occurring in the performance of his official duties as purchasing agent, can also be imputed to his company. If he is acting within the scope of his employment, his company can be made to bear the cost of any damage occasioned by his negligent action. This means that the person injured has the opportunity to collect his damages from the company, or the purchasing agent, or both. An injured party is inclined toward suing both the purchasing agent and the company for such damage occasioned since the opportunity of collecting is greater. The company has the privilege of seeking restitution from the purchasing agent for any damages it is forced to pay because of the agent's negligence.

Criminal Liability

The commission of a criminal offense subjects the wrongdoer to the penalties provided by law. A purchasing agent must assume full responsibility if he commits a crime while performing his duties. The fact he is acting as the agent of his company is no excuse. The law imposes the penalty for commission of the illegal act and it is imposed upon the person committing the act.

The purchasing agent may unintentionally violate a so-called regulatory law in the performance of his official duties. The court's usual attitude in such cases is to hold his company responsible for the act.

Other similar legal questions have arisen in regard to regulatory acts and laws. Some of these concern such matters as monopoly, price discrimination, labor, and wages and hours. See Section 28, Appendix, "Supreme Court Decisions Affecting Purchasing" for two enlightening decisions.

Commercial bribery has been the subject of considerable thought and discussion, and it is interesting to note that in at least one state—New York—there is a law concerning it. Section 439 of the Penal Laws of New York states in part:

> A person who gives, offers or promises to an agent, employee or servant of another, any gift or gratuity whatever, without the knowledge or consent of the principal, employer or master of such agent, employee or servant, with intent to influence such agent's, employee's or servant's action in relation to his principal's, employer's or master's business, . . . or agent, employee or servant, who, being authorized to procure materials, supplies or other merchandise either by purchase or contract . . . for his principal, employer or master, receives directly or indirectly, for himself or for another, a commission, discount, gift, gratuity or bonus from the person who makes such sale or contract . . . is guilty of a misdemeanor.

This statute holds both the donor and recipient of the gift guilty of violating the intent of the law. This phase is also discussed in Section 6, "Ethical Practices in Purchasing."

CONTRACTS

Nature of a Contract

An agreement, verbal or written, should have the following five essentials: (1) competent parties, (2) proper subject matter, (3) consideration, (4) mutuality of agreement, and (5) mutuality of obligation. Briefly the rules covering these five essentials are as follows:

1. The parties to an agreement should be legally competent. Infants, mentally deficient persons, criminals under some circumstances, and others have been declared as lacking the capacity to enter into a binding agreement or contract. However, as a general rule a contract will not be set aside on grounds of incompetence if the party had the legal capacity to enter into the contract from the beginning and if there is no fraud or concealment. For example, if A, a purchasing agent for B Company, agrees to purchase 50,000 bricks from the X Company at a given price with delivery in one hundred twenty days, and before the delivery date A has a mental breakdown and is declared incompetent, the agreement will stand between B Company and X Company. If in the above case A were acting for himself, his subsequent incompetency alone would not be reason to set aside the agreement.

If a party to an agreement is in fact an infant (generally not twenty-one years of age), the agreement may be set aside on the grounds of lack of contractual capacity—"infancy." But the infant must disaffirm the agreement if he wishes to be relieved. The election to affirm or disaffirm after reaching maturity lies with the infant (see Section 5).

2. In the case of "proper subject matter," it should be noted that agreements contrary to public policy, in conflict with existing laws, or against morality are void. Examples of improper subject matter include smuggling, narcotics, obscene literature, gambling (in some states and under some circumstances), etc.

3. Consideration, as a general rule, may be defined as any benefit to a promisor, or any detriment to a promisee, the promise of which is the inducement to the transaction. The test of good consideration was laid down a number of years ago in the case *Presbyterian Board of Foreign Missions v. Smith,* 209 Pa. 361, 59 A 689. A promise at the instance of the promisor to do or forbear doing something which he is not legally bound to do constitutes good consideration whether it be some act or forbearance, or the payment of money, or other matter of value.

4. The term "mutuality of agreement" is used to express the need for the same understanding about the agreement which is to be consummated. Sometimes, with or without fraud or misrepresentation, one party

thinks he is agreeing to do, or to purchase, or forbear from doing something and the other party to the proposed agreement has some other act or thing or forbearance in mind. Under such circumstances, even if written and signed, the absence of "mutual agreement" or understanding will usually void the contract. Both parties should assent to substantially the same thing in the same sense and to the same terms without reservation.

5. Mutuality of obligation implies that there is an obligation on each party to do or permit something to be done in consideration of the act of the other. Where one party is required to perform or abstain and rights exist at the option of only one party, usually no agreement results. The chief exceptions to this rule are gratuitous promises to relatives, bequests to schools, churches, and similar institutions. Sometimes the terms "consideration" and "mutuality" seem to imply an equality of performance or consideration, but this is not the case. The meaning of these rules is that there must be some value exchanged from each side of the agreement. Where a contract has been partially or wholly performed in good faith by one of the parties, he is entitled to recover on a reasonable basis for value rendered.

The validity of a contract is usually tested by the law of the state where the contract is made. Unless the agreement is in conflict with the laws of other states, it will usually be recognized and enforced.

The Purchase Order as a Contract[2]

Verbal orders should be avoided. Written agreements reduce chances for misunderstanding. Courts are reluctant to permit evidence of oral agreements at variance with written terms of a contract. Writing should be clear and definite as to amount, quality, price, time of delivery, and payment. Where language is broad, ambiguous, or uncertain, or where it is subject to more than one interpretation, courts attach such ordinary meaning and intent as would be construed by reasonable persons under the same or similar circumstances; at most, such meanings as attached to them by the trade or profession involved.

One section of a contract may not be used to nullify or change terms and conditions of another part. The known intent, not the phraseology, determines whether a contract is a lease, sale, or consignment. Courts will not go outside a written agreement to allow a showing of custom or usage if the intent of the parties is clearly stated.

Contractual mistakes fall into two categories: law and fact. Mistake of law and ignorance of law are so similar, within the scope and application

[2] Also see Section 5, "Purchase Order Essentials."

of this work, as to be treated as one. Ordinarily a mistake of law will not affect the validity of a contract or relieve the parties of their respective obligations under it.

A mistake of fact, in order to relieve the complaining party, should be as to (1) identity of subject matter, or (2) as to the existence of the subject matter or the ability to produce, or (3) where the mistake is due to the failure of one party to reveal a material fact which was not reasonably ascertainable by the other party. If the complaining party enters into an agreement with knowledge of his ignorance of a material fact, he cannot cancel. The law imposes an unmistakable duty on every party to a contract to know the contents of the document he signs. A plea that one understood the meaning but not the legal consequences of his agreement is no defense. A mistake of fact not only must be material to the contract but also must relate to past or existing conditions. A mistake as to facts not yet in existence amounts only to conjecture. A certain amount of risk is inherent in most normal business transactions.

If the subject matter has been substantially altered, damaged, or destroyed, this may render an agreement impossible of performance. This would not entirely void the agreement unless such contingencies were anticipated in the agreement itself. Usually specific performance would not be required; perhaps it would be impossible under the circumstances. However, the other party to the agreement may recover damages if the contingencies were not anticipated and made a part of the agreement. Mere difficulty, expense, inconvenience, or loss, even though unforeseeable, will not discharge a party to an agreement.

The fact that an order is signed and given to a salesman or mailed directly to the seller does not necessarily constitute a contract. Normally such action is merely an offer. To be a contract, there must be acceptance. Acceptance is spelled out in many ways. The formal method is for the purchaser to send a written acceptance form with the purchase order. When this is returned in the manner prescribed in the purchase order (offer), there is a contract. Some purchase orders ask the vendor to send his own written acceptance form. Much of the business of this country is done every day by telephone and followed by confirming purchase orders. And much of the business of the country is done by vendors and sellers who rely upon the pattern established in the trade. If buyers and sellers go on month after month sending purchase orders and filling or accepting them without any formal acceptance, a pattern is established and acceptance usually would be implied in these circumstances. In most cases, however, acceptance is accomplished by shipment or some other affirmative act on the part of seller in relation to the purchase order and within the established buying pattern. If the order is an unqualified acceptance of an offer made by seller, then the purchase order would be the necessary step in acceptance and the contract agreement thereby completed.

As noted in the section treating agency, any signature, to be valid, must (1) be an authorized signature and (2) be intended as a legally binding signature. Terms and conditions of purchase or a reference to them should be clear and readable and should appear above the signature in order to avoid doubt as to authenticity.

IDENTIFICATION OF SALES

Bailment Distinguished from Sale

Buyers frequently are required to furnish suppliers with tools or material from which to fabricate parts, or to warehouse merchandise. This transfer of property is in the nature of a trust upon a contract and not a transfer of title. In a transaction of bailment the person who makes the delivery is called the *bailor,* the one who receives the goods is the *bailee.* Problems most frequently arising in connection with bailments have to do with the degree of care which the law imposes on the bailee in exercising his trust. The commonly accepted standard of diligence and care required of a bailee is that degree of vigilance which he would normally be expected to exercise if the property were his own and commensurate with the value of the article affected. Adequate insurance and a careful selection of contractors should be the rule.

Consignment, Sale or Return, Approval, Etc.

A consignment should not be confused with a sale. A consignment refers to goods entrusted to another for care or sale. The relationship is that of agency and title remains in the consignor. A consignment is likewise a bailment, for reasons previously explained. Suits involving consignments usually include seizure of property by creditors in the hands of third persons. The legal test of whether a transaction is a sale or consignment hinges on the purpose. If the goods are transferred from one party to another to be sold for the first party, it is a consignment. If the goods are to be disposed of as the property of the second party, whether paid for or not, it is a sale. Reservation of title in seller until full payment is made does not necessarily alter the essentials of a sale; to constitute a consignment, whereby creditors may be denied the right to attachment and possession, more than mere retention of title in the seller is needed.

The following will show some typical situations concerning title:

A purchase under a "sale or return" agreement transfers title to the buyer, but gives the buyer the option to return the goods within a specified time, or if no time is fixed, then within a reasonable time.

Under an ordinary purchase the buyer has the privilege of inspecting the goods. Should they fail to conform to the representations of the seller, either express or implied, he may return the goods and rescind the sale. Under a "sale or return" purchase, however, the buyer has an option to return the goods *irrespective of their quality*. With the exercise of this option the *transaction is closed and the purchase contract becomes terminated.*

On the other hand, if the buyer fails to exercise this option or right of return within a specified or reasonable time, should no time be set, the purchase becomes absolute and the buyer liable for the price in an action for goods sold and delivered.

Distinction between "Approval" and "Sale or Return"

Under a sale on approval, however, the buyer does not become the owner of the goods until he has expressed his approval either directly or by his conduct. In a "sale or return" transaction the buyer becomes the owner upon the delivery of the goods with the privilege of divesting himself of ownership if he so determines.

This distinction between the title to goods acquired under a "sale or return" contract and under a consignment contract *becomes vital upon the loss or destruction of the property.*[3]

Conditional Sales

A conditional sales contract is one in which the purchaser or buyer is given possession of the merchandise but the vendor or seller retains title. This is frequently true in the sale of automobiles. The condition whereby titles finally pass is not always the same. Conditional sales contracts constitute a large growing portion of all commercial transactions in this country. The most common form of the conditional sales contract is the modern "installment contract." In such cases the seller retains the title until the last payment is made.

This reservation of title in the seller alone does not give the seller's creditors any right to repossess the merchandise. The creditors can only stand in the seller's shoes and if the buyer keeps up his payments and is not otherwise in default, he cannot be disturbed in his possession.

The next question arises when the buyer attempts to sell the merchandise without title. Does an innocent third party have any protection? Can the seller repossess the merchandise in the hands of the third party if there is a default in the conditional sales contract? To overcome the difficulty raised by these and similar questions, the majority of the states

[3] Albert Woodruff Gray, *Purchase Law Manual,* listed in Selected Bibliography at end of this section.

have adopted laws providing that such conditional sales contracts should be recorded, usually in the county recorder's office. If so recorded, as specified in the statute, all third parties are assumed to have notice that the seller retains title. In other words, these laws do away with the "innocent third party."

Suppose that a third party purchases goods from the original buyer. Also assume that such third party actually or constructively knows that a conditional sales contract exists between original seller and original buyer. If the original buyer defaults in his conditional sales contract, the seller may repossess the goods from the third party even if the conditional sales contract was not recorded. In this case the third party had notice and was not innocent. Here again, if in doubt, consult an attorney.

DISCHARGE FROM CONTRACTUAL OBLIGATIONS

There are a number of ways by which a contract may be discharged or terminated. A buyer should be aware of his rights and liabilities in this connection. In most cases a party is legally discharged from contractual obligations and may recover damages for loss suffered if fraud can be proved. Failure to perform by one of the parties releases the other of his obligations, although he may sue for damages or for specific performance—one or the other, but not both.

For instance, X Company may have a purchase order agreement with Y Company for the manufacture of Z number of machines—the machines to be made in accordance with the specifications of X Company. Y Company was given the order upon acceptance of its bid and at a guaranteed price and delivery date. Y defaults, does not deliver, and does not actually commence to manufacture the machines. X Company is not obligated to pay or otherwise perform its part. In fact, if X Company has suffered or will suffer any loss by reason of Y's default, X Company may recover damages from Y Company. If Y Company did in fact make the machines but decided to hold them for a better price from another party, then X Company could bring an action for specific performance and recover by court order directing that the machines be delivered in accordance with the terms of the contract.

A contract may be terminated by mutual agreement. And unless otherwise prohibited by terms of the agreement, a party may assign his rights, but he may not assign to another his liabilities to pay the contract price.

A contract may be terminated by operation of law in a number of circumstances—by death of one of the parties, bankruptcy, destruction of subject matter, impossibility of performance, or where some act or condition of one party makes performance by the other impossible or inequitable.

The fact that contracts may be terminated by operation of law would not necessarily release the other side of liability. For example, assume that in case of death, the deceased party was a manufacturer and that under a purchase order agreement he had produced some part of the items agreed upon, and these could be used by the purchaser, and that some delivery had been made. In this case the estate of the deceased could recover for the items produced and delivered, or both, unless the agreement required full delivery as a material condition of the contract. Of course, specific performance for the balance could not be required if the skill of the deceased was necessary or the company did not go on in the business. Contrary to popular belief, so-called acts of God (earthquake, fire, flood, etc.) generally will not terminate a contract or discharge the parties, unless provided for in the agreement.

COMMON CARRIERS[4]

If the place of delivery is stated in the bill of lading as the place of business of the buyer, then delivery of material must be made by the carrier within a reasonable time after arrival at the carrier's premises. Unreasonable delay by the carrier constitutes a breach of the delivery contract recoverable in damages. If the goods were sold f.o.b. cars at the manufacturer's plant and the title passed to the buyer as soon as they were placed in the hands of the common carrier, then the buyer would be obliged to accept the goods and look to the carrier for recovery of any damages which the goods may have suffered. If title was to remain in the seller until goods were delivered and accepted by the buyer, then the buyer might take delivery of the goods for the seller and without accepting the goods as and for his own. In this case the buyer would hold the goods for the seller and would not be responsible to the seller for payment or for goods if they were not as ordered or were received in damaged condition. Under these circumstances the seller could recover from the carrier for any loss or damage suffered by reason of careless handling of the goods or because of buyer's refusal to accept the goods because of unreasonable delay in delivery.

If the terms of the purchase agreement call for full shipment and clearly state that partial shipment will not be acceptable, then as stated before, the buyer might accept the partial delivery of the goods from the carrier but he would only do so as an agent of the seller. The buyer would

[4] Also see Section 18, "Traffic and Transportation Considerations."

then notify seller that he was holding the goods at the expense of and for the seller and would ask for instructions covering the return of the goods. Under these circumstances the buyer could even recover damages for his losses because of partial or faulty delivery.

A consignee is not required to accept shipments at unreasonable hours. By weight of Federal decision a carrier may not abandon incorrectly addressed merchandise but must ascertain the correct address and deliver with reasonable promptness thereafter. When a carrier's established route does not reach the destination specified in the bill of lading, he is only required to deliver as near the destination as possible and to notify the consignee promptly. Should a consignee refuse a shipment, justified or not, a carrier may not abandon goods. He must remove them to a convenient and appropriate place and store at shipper's expense. The buyer is not entitled to inspect a c.o.d. shipment before payment. He is not deemed to have accepted it, however, until he has had a reasonable opportunity for examination to determine whether it is in accordance with contract (see Section 5).

The f.o.b. point (free on board) not only transfers ownership of material but automatically determines responsibility for transportation charges, insurance, and applicable taxes. The careless definition of a point at which title passes can have far-reaching and serious results. "Freight allowed" means that the vendor will pay the freight bill. It does not mean that title passes at the vendor's dock. The f.o.b. point is the controlling point for the passing of title; therefore if vendor quotes you "freight allowed" f.o.b. Grand Rapids, the title passes to you when goods are delivered to the common carrier at Grand Rapids even if vendor pays the freight.

WARRANTIES

Seller's Warranties

The law pertaining to seller's warranties has developed from the common law of England (the law merchant), by court decisions based on the common law, customs, and usages of the trade, state statutes, and the codification of all these legal rules and opinions into the Uniform Sales Act, commonly called the Sales Act.[5] A more liberal and far-reaching step in the law of warranties was the recent adoption by Pennsylvania of the Uniform Commercial Code.[6] However, for this discussion we shall look to the rules followed by most states of the union under the Uniform Sales Act and also refer to this new Uniform Commercial Code.

Many years ago the doctrine of *caveat emptor* (let the buyer beware)

[5] See copy of act in Section 28, "Appendix."
[6] See comments on code in Section 28, "Appendix."

was the rule in nearly all commercial transactions involving personal property. Under this ancient doctrine the seller was under no obligation to disclose any faults in the merchandise he was trying to sell; the buyer supposedly, with reasonable diligence, could determine any faults for himself. However, as industry expanded, commerce increased, and transportation and communication methods improved, the courts began to take a more liberal view of the rights of buyers. The courts felt that the doctrine of *caveat emptor* should not apply where the buyer did not deal on equal terms with the seller. It was the belief of many that if buyers could not rely on the statements of sellers, prospective buyers would be reluctant to do business and commerce would suffer as a result. As a result of this liberal attitude the implied warranty doctrine came into being as a matter of public policy.

Implied warranties are created by operation of law. They do not arise out of contractual agreement between the parties. For example, they may be invoked when it appears that the buyer is actually relying on some apparent skill, knowledge, or judgment of the seller. The Sales Act divides implied warranties into four main groups: (1) implied warranty of title, (2) implied warranty in sale by description, (3) implied warranties of quality, and (4) implied warranties in sale by sample.

Implied Warranty of Title (Section 13 Sales Act)

In a contract to sell or a sale, unless a contrary intention appears, there is an implied warranty on the part of the seller that (1) in case of a sale he has the right to sell the goods, and that in the case of a contract to sell he will have the right to sell the goods at the time when the property is to pass; that (2) the buyer shall have and enjoy quiet possession of the goods as against any lawful claims existing at the time of the sale; that (3) the goods shall be free at the time of the sale of any charge or encumbrance in favor of any third person, not declared or known to the buyer before or at the time when the contract or sale is made.

Under present statute, as under common law, the buyer does not assume the risk that the seller's title might be defective. However, if buyer knows that seller does not have good title, then no implied warranty of title arises. A seller does not have title to lost or stolen goods, chattel mortgages, or goods he is selling by virtue of authority given him by law, as a sheriff or auctioneer.

Implied Warranty in Sale by Description (Section 14 Sales Act)

The Sales Act states that where there is a contract to sell or a sale of goods by description there is an implied warranty that the goods shall correspond with that description. Further, if the contract or sale is by sample as well as by description, the bulk of the goods shall correspond with that description as well as with the sample. Whether this situation is treated as an express or as an implied warranty, in either case the buyer is afforded adequate legal remedy.

Implied Warranties of Quality (Section 15 Sales Act)

Where the buyer, expressly or by reasonable implication, makes known to the seller the particular purpose for which the goods are required, and the seller knows that the buyer relies on the seller's skill or judgment, there is an implied warranty that the seller has the skill and that the goods produced shall be reasonably fit for such purpose. However, if the buyer has examined the goods, there is no implied warranty as regards defects which such examination ought to have revealed. There is also no implied warranty as to fitness for any particular purpose where there is a sale of a specific article under its patent or other trade name. An implied warranty as to the quality or fitness for any particular purpose may be relied on by the usage of the trade.

Implied Warranties in Sale by Sample (Section 16 Sales Act)

In the case of a sale by sample there is an implied warranty that (1) the bulk shall correspond with the sample in quality, that (2) the buyer shall have a reasonable opportunity of comparing the bulk with the sample (except so far as otherwise provided in section 47 (3) which deals with c.o.d. transactions), and that (3) if the seller is a dealer in goods of that kind, the goods shall be free from any defect rendering them unmerchantable which would not be apparent on reasonable examination of the sample. When the buyer has examined the goods or the sample or model as fully as he desired or if the buyer refuses to examine the goods, there is no implied warranty as regards defects which an examination ought, under the circumstances, to have revealed to him.

A distinction must be made between sale by sample and description, which gives rise to a warranty, and sale by sample on inspection, which does not give rise to a warranty. If under the circumstances, the parties are apparently dealing with the sample, the description will be totally immaterial, and the sale would be described as a sale by sample on inspection. If, however, the buyer was apparently relying upon the superior skill or knowledge of the seller, the bulk delivered not only must correspond with the sample, but the sample must likewise correspond with the description given to it.

In those cases where there is an express warranty, the law of implied warranties applies unless an implied warranty is clearly inconsistent with the express warranty.

Express Warranties (Section 12 Sales Act)

In addition to implied warranties there may be express warranties in sales or contracts to sell. Unlike an implied warranty, which is imposed by law, an express warranty is imposed by the parties to the contract. No particular words or forms of expression are necessary to create an express warranty; e.g., the word warranty or guaranty need not be used to constitute an express warranty [*MacAndrews & Forbes Company v. Mechanical Manufacturing Company* (11 N.E., 2d 382)].

Wherever a seller induces a buyer to enter into a contract, under the terms of which the seller expressly guaranties to the buyer some particular quality or characteristic of the subject matter of the sale, undertaking to assume responsibility to the buyer should the terms of the guaranty be breached, there is an express warranty (46 *Am. Jur.* 482, Sales Section 299).

Both the Sales Act and the Uniform Commercial Code provide that a warranty is created when the natural tendency of an affirmation on the part of a seller is to induce the buyer's purchase and the buyer does in fact purchase in reliance on that representation. Thus, it is not necessarily the form of the seller's statement that controls, but rather the intention of the seller to be bound by his promise and the buyer's reliance on it.

An affirmation merely of the value of the goods or a statement purporting to be merely the seller's opinion or commendation of the goods, sometimes referred to as "dealers' puffing or sales talk," does not of itself create a warranty. From a practical standpoint it is often difficult to determine when a statement is mere "puffing" and when it is a warranty. In general, whenever the parties are dealing, not on the basis of equality and the buyer relies on the seller's apparent superior skill or judgment, any statements by the seller having to do with the use to which the subject matter of the sale might be put, or its fitness for a particular purpose upon which a reasonable man in the buyer's position could justifiably rely, would be construed as an express warranty.

Both the Sales Act and the Uniform Commercial Code provide that there is a warranty that the bulk of the goods must correspond with the sample whenever there is a sale of unascertained or future goods. It should be noted that future or unascertained goods are goods which are either not in existence at the time the contract is entered into or goods which the seller does not own or possess at the time the contract is entered into. Specific goods are goods which are in existence at the time the contract is made. The only difference between the two laws is that under the Sales Act this is regarded as an implied warranty, while under the Uniform Commercial Code it is an express warranty.

In addition to the express warranties discussed above, a seller may make any other warranties he pleases, which will be binding upon him if the buyer relies thereon to his detriment. However, it is important to distinguish a warranty from an insurance agreement. A warranty provides for compensation to the purchaser solely for defects in the article itself. When a warranty or guaranty calls for an indemnity against hazards outside of the article to which it relates, it becomes an insurance policy subject to statutory provisions regulating the conduct of business insurance.

Exclusion and Waiver of Warranty (Section 71 Sales Act)

Where an agreement creates an express warranty, words disclaiming the warranty do not eliminate the warranty. The theory supporting this rule is that where the same agreement both creates and seeks to negate an express warranty an inconsistency is created which the law will usually resolve against the seller and in favor of the buyer. The rule concerning implied warranties, however, is different. The Sales Act provides that where any right or duty or liability would arise under a contract to sell or a sale by implication of law, it may be negatived or varied by express agreement or by the course of dealing between the parties, or by custom, if the custom be such as to bind both parties to the contract or sale. Thus, it is the law in most states that a seller can limit his liability by express agreement. It is legal for the parties to stipulate that there shall be no warranty or liability other than that expressed in the contract, and a warranty of fitness will not be implied in conflict therewith. But, to eliminate an implied warranty of fitness, there must be a definite stipulation to that effect. Such words must not be ambiguous or they will be construed against the seller. For example, where sellers' acknowledgments state that the sellers warrant nothing, there is no implied or express warranty unless the body of the sales contract calls for a warranty.

Where the sale is designated "as is" or with words that clearly indicate that no warranties were intended, then no warranties arise, except that the seller has good title. However, the goods must be of the type that were ordered, e.g., where a milling machine is sold "as is" and a punch press is delivered, no sale takes place. It is also the rule that an implied warranty can be excluded or modified in course of dealing or performance or usage of trade.

Waiver of Breach of Warranty (Section 49 Sales Act)

The Sales Act provides that "In the absence of an express or implied agreement of the parties, acceptance of the goods by the buyer shall not discharge the seller from liability in damages or other legal remedy for breach of any promise or warranty in the contract to sell or the sale. But if after the acceptance of the goods the buyer fails to give notice to the seller of the breach of any promise or warranty within a reasonable time after the buyer knows or ought to know of such breach, the seller shall not be liable therefor." This section of the Sales Act is a radical change from the common law. If the buyer accepted the goods after examining them, or after he had an opportunity to examine them, under the common law he had no opportunity to return the goods or avoid the sale. But note, even under the Sales Act the buyer must give prompt notice in order to hold the seller liable for a breach of warranty.

Remedies for Breach of Warranty (Section 69 Sales Act)

It is advisable that competent legal counsel be consulted whenever it is felt that a breach of warranty has taken place, as the laws of the several states differ with regard to remedies for breach of warranty. The Sales Act provides for the following remedies: (1) Where there is a breach of warranty by the seller, the buyer may, at his election: (*a*) accept or keep the goods and set up against the seller the breach of warranty by way of recoupment in diminution or extinction of the price; (*b*) accept or keep the goods and maintain an action against the seller for damages for the breach of warranty; (*c*) refuse to accept the goods, if the property therein has not passed, and maintain an action against the seller for damages for the breach of warranty; (*d*) rescind the contract to sell or the sale and refuse to receive the goods, or if the goods have already been received, return them or offer to return them to the seller and recover the price or any part thereof which has been paid. (2) When the buyer has claimed and been granted a remedy in any one of these ways, no other remedy can thereafter be granted. (3) Where the goods have been delivered to the buyer, he cannot rescind the sale if he knew of the breach of warranty when he accepted the goods, or if he fails to notify the seller within a reasonable time of the election to rescind, or if he fails to return or to offer to return the goods to the seller in substantially as good condition as they were in at the time the property was transferred to the buyer. But if deterioration or injury of the goods is due to the breach of warranty, such deterioration or injury shall not prevent the buyer from returning or offering to return the goods to the seller and rescinding the sale. (4) Where the buyer is entitled to rescind the sale and elects to do so, he shall cease to be liable for the price upon returning or offering to return the goods. If the price or any part thereof has already been paid, the seller shall be liable to repay so much thereof as has been paid, concurrently with the return of the goods, or immediately after an offer to return the goods in exchange for repayment of the price. (5) Where the buyer is entitled to rescind the sale and elects to do so, if the seller refuses to accept an offer of the buyer to return the goods, the buyer shall thereafter be deemed to hold the goods as bailee for the seller, but subject to a lien to secure the repayment of any portion of the price which has been paid, and with the remedies for the enforcement of such lien allowed to an unpaid seller by section 53 of the Sales Act. (6) The measure of damages for breach of warranty is the loss directly and naturally resulting, in the ordinary course of events, from the breach of warranty. (7) In the case of breach of warranty of quality, such loss, in the absence of special circumstances showing proximate damage of a greater amount, is the difference between the value of the goods at the time of delivery to the buyer and the value they would have had if they had answered to the warranty.

PATENT LAWS[7]

Definition

A patent is a grant by the Federal government through the Patent Office to an inventor, his agents, heirs, or assigns of certain exclusive rights to his invention for a period of seventeen years, throughout the United States, its territories and possessions. Legally speaking, a patent grant does not confer the right to make use of or sell an invention, but the right to exclude others from doing so.

Matters relating to patentability and patent protection in foreign countries should be referred to an attorney specializing in this field. Laws in foreign countries differ with respect to patents, taxes, imports, licenses, and reciprocal agreements. Space required to deal with foreign patents would exceed the scope and purpose of this work.

Subject Matter

The law provides that patentable matter may be any new and useful process, machine, manufacture, composition of matter, or any new and useful improvement thereof. An idea or suggestion without the actual machine, process, or composition cannot be patented. The term "new" means that the invention in question must not have been known or used by others in this country, its territories and possessions, prior to discovery or invention thereof, and must not have been in public use or on sale for more than one year prior to patent application. To qualify as "useful," the subject matter must have some useful purpose and must, in fact, be operable. Frivolous, mischievous, or immoral material cannot

[7] Also see Section 5, "Purchase Order Essentials."

qualify under statutory requirements. The Atomic Energy Act of 1946 prohibits the granting of patents where the invention will be used exclusively in producing fissionable material or atomic energy for military purposes.

Art or process, as distinguished from a mere idea or plan, is any method or act capable of producing a tangible product or change in the essential character of some material object. Permanent change is not essential in order to qualify within the meaning of the statute.

Machine is any device, even if usable only in combination with some other mechanism, capable of producing by its own operation, certain predetermined physical effects. A machine need not be automatic to qualify under statute. The "principle" or distinguishing characteristic of a machine is not patentable, although such information must be set forth in the specifications embodied in the patent application.

Manufacture is any article or object made by man, not produced on a machine, and which cannot be classed either as a natural product or natural element. Buildings, monuments, bridges, and electronic instruments so qualify.

Composition of matter covers all compounds, compositions, or mixtures resulting from the union of two or more specific ingredients. The method as well as the composition may be patentable whether produced mechanically or chemically. An improvement of a previously patented compound is patentable if it produces a new and useful result.

Plant, other than tuber-propagated, may be patented by the inventor, provided it is asexually (artificially) reproduced and qualifies as a new type or variety not previously known or patented.

Design, another class of patentable matter, is any physical substance or shape which gives a peculiar or distinctive appearance to the article under application. If ornamental rather than useful, the subject may be copyrighted. No design is patentable which cannot be reproduced.

Applicant

The original inventor, if alive and sane, or if deceased, his executor or administrator, may file application for a patent. Two or more persons may file jointly if actually coinventors. Persons hired to make drawings or models, to prepare legal documents, or to provide capital do not thereby become joint inventors. They may, however, be joint patentees.

Procedure

Patent applications must be signed by the inventor and filed by him or his attorney with the Commissioner of Patents, Washington, D.C.

"Rules of Practice," "Patent Laws," and "Patents" may be obtained from the Superintendent of Documents, Washington, D.C. 20402.

Application and Fee. The application must include a petition or request for a patent; complete specifications and claims; drawings when applicable; oath signed by applicant under seal. The minimum filing fee is $65. Because of recent changes, applicants should consult a patent attorney or write for details to the Department of Commerce, Washington, D.C. 20230. A patent application will be held abandoned if response is not made to the Patent Office within six months of notice (or shorter period if specified) on matters relating to claim rejections or requests to amend. In cases where an application has been "abandoned" it can, upon proper presentation be revived, but it cannot relate back to filing date of the original application for the purpose of establishing completion date of the invention. It must be treated as a new application.

Specifications and descriptions are not required to be furnished in minute detail, provided the information as a whole would be clear to one trained in the art or science to which the invention relates. Where applicable, both generic (general) and specific claims should be made in an application. It may develop that the invention is broadly new in which case both claims would be valid. Conversely, if some prior specific application of the invention subsequently came to light and had been included under the general but not under the specific claim, the specific claim would still be sufficient to support the application.

An applicant has six months after allowance of an application in which to pay the final fee, otherwise the patent is withheld. The Commissioner is authorized, at his discretion, to issue a patent if final fee is paid within one year after the six months' period has expired.

Interferences. An application for a patent constitutes an interference or counterclaim for the same or similar invention when there is: (1) another pending application; (2) a patent previously issued, but less than one year prior to date of application in question; (3) a reissued patent, the original of which was granted less than a year prior to date of the application in question. Claims for determination as to the original or first inventor or "pleading in interference" require highly specialized and competent counsel in this field of law.

Infringements. A patent right or grant is personal to the owner thereof, and has no definite situs apart from the individual holding it, but is coexistent in every state. Suit for infringement (unauthorized use or application) may be brought in any judicial district where a defendant resides, does business, or where acts of infringement occurred.

Reissue of Patent. If an original patent is found to be defective through oversight or error, the mistake may be rectified by surrender of the patent within reasonable time of discovery, provided application for reissue is for the same invention as originally issued. A reissued patent expires on the same date applicable to the original.

Licenses. A patentee may grant to others an exclusive or nonexclusive right to the use of his invention. Such license or permission need not be in writing to be binding on all parties to the agreement. Licensing provisions, however, may not be made in restraint of trade or on matters against public interest.

Sales and Assignments. Sale of a patent must be made by an instrument in writing and recorded in the Patent Office within three months of contract date in order legally to provide constructive notice to all parties at interest. A patent is personal property and as such may be owned individually or jointly. In the absence of agreement to the contrary, joint owners, regardless of size of interest, may make, use, and sell without legal accountability to the other for royalties derived therefrom. One may assign all or any portion of his title or interest in an invention. If assignment or transfer is acknowledged before a notary in writing, such acknowledgment constitutes prima-facie evidence of the assignment.

Inventions by Employees. Many companies require written agreements at time of employment providing that patentable inventions shall be the property of the employer. Even in the absence of express agreement, an employer may acquire a nonexclusive royalty-free license to make and use if his time, material, and facilities contributed in making the invention.

Identification of Patented Material. Damages for patent infringement cannot be recovered where the patentee has failed to identify the articles in question with the word "patent" together with day and year granted. Where the character of the article does not permit such identification to be so affixed, this information may be printed on a package, tag, or label. This rule does not apply to a patent for a process.

Fraudulent Marking. Anyone who, having no patent therefor, marks an article with the word "patent," or any word implying that a patent exists thereon and for the purpose of deceiving the public, is subject to a penalty of $100 with costs; half to go to the party suing, half to the United States, to be recovered in the jurisdiction where the act occurred.

Time to Sue. An inventor cannot sue for infringement until after a patent has been issued, nor can he recover for an act of infringement occurring more than six years prior to the date suit is brought.

Corporations. Ordinarily, officers, directors, and stockholders of a corporation are not personally liable for patent infringements by the company unless they virtually control all stock and direct its activities. Any officer, agent, or employee acting beyond the scope of his authority may become personally liable for damages or profits resulting directly from such infringement.

COPYRIGHTS

Historical

Under the Constitution of the United States, Congress has the power to enact laws "to promote the progress of science and useful arts, by securing for limited times to authors and inventors the exclusive right to their respective writings and discoveries." The Copyright Act of 1909, as amended, is the present law, superseding all former statutes relating to copyrights in the United States and its territories and possessions.

Copyrightable Material

For purposes of administration and convenience, statute divides copyrightable material into thirteen classifications; this does not, however, limit subject matter of copyright strictly and literally to this list. The principal difference between a copyright and patent is that a patent confers an exclusive right, whereas a copyright permits fair use by all persons of the work copyrighted. The following have been recognized as valid subjects of copyright protection:

1. Books, including composite and cyclopedic works, directories, gazetteers, letters, and other compilations. A book need not be bound or printed to qualify, and may consist of a single sheet so long as it has been reduced to material form.
2. Newspapers and periodicals.
3. Lectures, sermons, addresses, and manuscripts (prepared for oral delivery); they may be copyrighted as unpublished works; when published they should be copyrighted as books. The term manuscript does not include pictures.
4. Dramatic or dramatico-musical compositions. A mere dance, song, act, voice, or motion will not qualify. The work or presentation must tell a story. Mechanical instrumentalities incidental to a scene or act are not copyrightable.
5. Musical compositions—with or without words. A new arrangement or adaptation of an old piece is copyrightable. Phonograph records, or recordings, are not included.
6. Maps. Information charts and graphs are not within the meaning of the statute. Maps, when accompanied by written matter, qualify as a book.
7. Works of art, models, and designs for works of art. This includes drawings, paintings, and sculpture.
8. Reproductions of works of art include drawings, etchings, paintings,

photographs, and statuary reproductions of originals. Reproductions are copyrightable provided they indicate the exercise of intellect and skill, or present some new concept of the former.

9. Drawings and plaster works of a technical or scientific nature. These include blueprints, graphs, technical charts, industrial "mock-ups," and anatomical figures.

10. Photographs include both artistic and mechanical conceptions. A photograph may be a photograph of another picture if sufficiently different and new so as not to constitute piracy. The artistic quality or physical condition of a photograph has no bearing with respect to copyrightability.

11. Prints and pictorial illustrations include almost any technical or commercial illustration, labels, displays, and scroll work for stock certificates and playing cards.

12. Motion pictures, photoplays. This category includes both sound and silent pictures. A script or scenario may be copyrighted separately.

13. Motion pictures, other than photoplays, include travelogs, newsreels, and educational and industrial films.

Commercial prints, illustrations, and labels are registered in the Library of Congress with the Registrar of Copyrights. Such material must first be published by the owner (proprietor) or his agent with notice of claim on all copies offered for sale in the United States and its territories and possessions.

Material Not Copyrightable

Material that is not copyrightable includes trademarks, titles consisting of common words which lack originality, business forms, governmental publications, the original version of any work in the public domain, except compilations of same, and fraudulent, libelous, immoral, or seditious material. News items transmitted by wire are not subject to copyright. Translations of books and articles from a foreign language are original works under provisions of statute and qualify. Official letters, papers, and documents may be copyrighted by the owner, provided publication is not against public policy; the government, however, reserves the right to publish if in the public interest.

Statutory Requirements

Persons. The author, his executors, administrators, or assigns may apply for a copyright. A person to whom the copyright is assigned becomes the owner or "proprietor." In order to obtain a copyright, one must be a citizen of the United States, or if a foreigner, he must be domiciled within the United States, the District of Columbia, or one of the territories or possessions. A citizen of a "proclaimed" country (under reciprocal agreement) may also secure a copyright.

Procedure. A copyright is secured by publications with notice of copyright. Publication may be made anywhere in the United States or its possessions, or in any foreign country or "proclaimed" country whose citizens are entitled to benefits under the statute. Publication consists of printing, or otherwise producing, selling, or by public distribution by proprietor of the copyright, or by one so authorized. Publication with notice of copyright is a condition precedent to formal application, the absence of which has been held to constitute abandonment of claim.

Application and Fee. Promptly (within reasonable time) following publication, the proprietor must file two copies of his work, together with application, with the Registrar of Copyrights, Library of Congress, Washington, D.C. 20025. Applications should be accompanied by the prescribed fee. For schedules of fees for applications, photographs, unpublished works, labels, or prints relating to merchandise for advertising and/or sale, write the Registrar of Copyrights.

Notice. The statute requires that notice of copyright consist of the word "copyright" or the abbreviation "copr.," accompanied by name of the proprietor. In the case of literary, musical, and dramatic works, notice must be accompanied by the year. In the case of illustrations, maps, pictures, and works of an artistic or scientific nature, notice may consist of the letter © enclosed within a circle, and followed by the initials, monogram, or personal mark of the proprietor. This mark must be placed on some accessible part of the article so identified. Notice of copyright, in the case of a book or other printed publication, must appear on the title page or the page immediately following; if a periodical, then on the title page or first page of text of each separate number or under the title heading; if a musical work, either on title page or first page of music. For a contribution to magazine or journal, notice may be placed under the title, or if a one-page work, at the end thereof.

Term. Copyrights are not perpetual; the term is for 28 years with privilege of renewal for an additional 28 years. The Copyright Act of 1909 and also prior acts provide that the right of renewal must accrue in order that an author or inventor may not bar himself, or widow and children, from claiming renewal by making contracts in advance.

Ad Interim Copyright. In the case of a book published abroad in English an interim copyright good for five years may be obtained from the copyright office.

Mistake. Where an omission or mistake has occurred with respect to the prescribed notice, a proprietor will not be barred in an action for damages after the error has been rectified except in case of innocent infringement.

TRADEMARKS

Historical

Trademarks are not created by statute, having existed from early common law. Laws providing for registration and protection merely fortify the right by conferring a statutory title. A trademark is not property in the usual sense, being an intangible privilege by reason of its exclusiveness. It is property only in the very limited sense that it is a personal right to the enjoyment, reputation, and profit that result from the legal exclusion of others from its use and benefits.

Definition

A trademark, as defined in section 45 of the Act of 1946, is "any word, symbol, device, or combination thereof adopted and used by a manufacturer or merchant to identify his goods and distinguish them from those manufactured or sold by others." In order to qualify under section 45, a trademark must be in use in commerce and thereby become subject to lawful regulation by Congress. A mark shall be deemed used in commerce: (*a*) on goods when it is placed in any manner on the goods or their containers, or the displays associated therewith, or on the tags or labels affixed thereto, and the goods are sold or transported in commerce; (*b*) on services when used or displayed in the sale or advertising of services, and the services are rendered in commerce. Trade and commercial names adopted by corporations, associations, professions, institutions, and individuals do not come within the meaning of the statute unless actually used as trademarks.

Monopoly. The owner of a trademark acquires no right to prevent others from making or selling the same article. Exclusive rights to goods under trademark may be obtained only under patent or copyright. Ownership of a trademark does not confer the right to fix terms under which a vendee may sell a trademarked article.

Marks Not Subject to Registration. A mark cannot be registered if it (*a*) comprises fraudulent, immoral, scandalous, or seditious matter; (*b*) comprises or simulates the flag, coat-of-arms, or other insignia of the United States, or of any state, municipality, or of any foreign nation; (*c*) comprises the name, portrait, or signature of any living person without his consent, or the name, portrait, or signature of a deceased President of the United States during the life of his widow, if any, except by written consent of the widow; (*d*) comprises or resembles a mark registered in the Patent Office, or a mark or trademark previously used in the United States by another and not abandoned, and which if used, may cause confusion or mistake.

Principal and Supplemental Registers

The Trade-Mark Act of 1946 provides for the establishment of two registers to be known as the Principal and Supplemental Registers. Coined or arbitrary marks known as "technical marks" may, if otherwise qualified, be registered on the Principal Register. Marks not so qualified, but which can, in fact, distinguish an applicant's goods, and which have been in lawful use and commerce for at least one year, may be placed on the Supplemental Register.

Applications and Correspondence

All correspondence relating to patent matters, unless otherwise directed, should be addressed to The Commissioner of Patents, Washington, D.C. 20025. A separate letter should, in every instance, accompany each subject of inquiry or application. The application must be filed in the name of the owner, and by him or his attorney. Copies of Trade-mark Registrations and Rules of Practice in Trade-mark Cases may be purchased from the Patent Office. Application forms are not supplied by the Patent Office; the latter should be prepared only with the assistance of a qualified attorney since particular forms may be used only in cases to which they are applicable.

The elements of an application are:

1. Written application on approved form
2. A drawing of the mark to be registered
3. Five specimens (actual trademark to be used)
4. Filing fee: consult an attorney or The Commissioner of Patents for details

Term of Registrations

Under the Act of 1946 registrations remain in force for twenty years from date of issue, and may be renewed for periods of twenty years unless previously cancelled or surrendered.

Renewal

In order to qualify for renewal a mark must be in use in commerce which lawfully may be regulated by Congress at the time application for renewal is made. Application must be made in the name of person holding title to the registration. An application for renewal may be filed at any time within six months prior to expiration of certificate of registration. Application may be made within three months following such expiration upon payment of an additional fee.

Foreign Trademarks

To effect registration in most foreign countries, it is required that registration be effective in the United States. Duration of certificates and use of trademarks vary with the laws of each country. The trademark laws of the United States, like those relating to patents and copyrights, have no extraterritorial effect with respect to foreign countries except in cases of treaty or special agreement.

SELECTED BIBLIOGRAPHY

Anderson's Uniform Commercial Code (2 volumes), The Lawyers Cooperative Publishing Co., Rochester, N.Y.

Christ, Jay F.: *Fundamental Business Law,* American Technical Society, Chicago, Ill., 1948

Coppola, Andrew J., and Harry Katz: *Law of Business Contracts,* John Wiley & Sons, Inc., New York, 1962

Credit Manual of Commercial Laws, National Association of Credit Management, New York, 1963

Edwards, Gorwin D.: *Price Discrimination Law: A Review of Experience,* Brookings Institute, Washington, D.C., 1959

Gray, Albert Woodruff: *Purchase Law Manual,* Conover-Mast Publications, New York, 1954

Guide to U.S. Government Contracts and Sub-contracts, Joint Committee on Continuing Legal Education, American Law Institute, Philadelphia, Pa.

Hawkland, William D.: *Sales and Bulk Sales,* Joint Committee on Continuing Legal Education, American Law Institute, Philadelphia, Pa., 1958

Hewitt, Charles: *American Business Law Journal,* Valentine Hall, Indiana University, Bloomington, Ind.

Phalon, Reed T.: *Business Law under the Uniform Commercial Code,* Prentice-Hall, Inc., Englewood Cliffs, N.J., 1959

Uniform Commercial Code—1962: Official Text with Comments, West Publishing Company, St. Paul, Minn.

SECTION 5

PURCHASE ORDER ESSENTIALS

Editor

L. E. Treadway, Purchasing Agent, The Federal Glass Co., Division of Federal Paper Board Co., Inc., Columbus, Ohio

Associate Editors

Kenneth B. Gay, Executive Director—Material, North American Aviation, Inc., El Segundo, California

Duncan S. Gregg, Director of Purchasing, Kaiser Aluminum & Chemical Corp., Oakland, California

As mentioned in the EDITOR-IN-CHIEF'S NOTE on the title page of Section 4, "Legal Influences in Purchasing," that section and this section, "Purchase Order Essentials," are both about problems in the same field. They may seem repetitious. This is especially true of Section 4 and the first part of Section 5. *However,* these two sections, in different parts, have been written, rewritten, edited, and arranged by many practical purchasing men. The approach in the two sections is from different angles. After careful consideration and study it has been deemed wise to include both sections "as is." Any seeming repetition should merely emphasize the extent of interest and experience purchasing men have in these areas. If any doubt exists, even the experienced purchasing official seeks the advice of an attorney. Litigation should be avoided, especially where compromise or arbitration is possible.

FUNCTIONS OF THE PURCHASE ORDER

The purchase order form serves a variety of purposes in most business organizations. Its most essential function is to inform a supplier that the buyer desires to purchase the items specified on the order. Through the use of multiple copies, however, the order form may, in addition, serve many other purposes, such as (1) an acknowledgment form to be executed and returned by the supplier, (2) a source of information for the accounting department, (3) a receiving report, (4) a source of information for inspection and quality control personnel, (5) confirmation of purchase for the requisitioning department, and (6) a working copy for the purchasing department in expediting delivery of the goods or performance of the service.

In addition to the internal functions of the purchase order for accounting, etc., it should always be kept in mind that the purchase order is a contractual instrument and has important legal functions affecting the rights and obligations of the purchaser. The terms and conditions contained in the printed order form should include those which are essential to protection of the buyer's interests.

The forms and procedures commonly used in connection with purchase orders are discussed and illustrated in this section.[1] Also included is a discussion of requisition forms and procedures. In addition, the basic legal aspects of purchase orders are discussed with a review of the terms and conditions commonly used in purchase order forms.

LEGAL CONSIDERATIONS

As noted above (and discussed in the preceding Section 4), a purchase order is a legal instrument which expresses the buyer's part of a contract of sale. Every purchase is a contract in contemplation of law. For this reason, a knowledge of the fundamentals of contract law is highly desirable for the professional buyer. This does not mean that the purchasing agent needs an extensive legal education. But he should have a grasp of certain essentials of commercial law to help him avoid legal pitfalls

[1] Also illustrated in Section 25, "Forms and Records."

and enable him to recognize situations of doubt in which the advice of professional counsel should be sought.

Applicable Statutes

To a large extent, the legal rights and obligations of buyers are now determined by statutory law which specifically covers the purchase and sale of goods. These statutes have been enacted by state legislatures and are patterned after certain uniform laws developed and recommended by the Conference of Commissioners on Uniform State Laws. Certain Federal legislation, such as the Fair Trade Act, Clayton Anti-Trust Act, and Robinson-Patman Act, also have direct bearing on the activities of the purchasing agent.

At present, 40 states have "uniform" laws in effect. Of this total, 22 still have the older Uniform Sales Act while 29 have enacted the newer Uniform Commercial Code.[2]

The Uniform Sales Act was generally adopted by state legislatures in the period 1900 to 1910, while the Uniform Commercial Code was first promulgated in 1951. The first state to adopt the new code was Pennsylvania, where it became effective in 1954. In the following ten years 17 additional states enacted the code.

Both of the statutes under consideration spell out in considerable detail the legal rules respecting purchase and sale of goods. The Uniform Commercial Code is broader in its coverage of all phases of the subject, including certain questions related to the offer, acceptance, and formation of a sales contract and to other matters, not included in the Uniform Sales Act.

These statutes are of such importance in industrial purchasing that individual purchasing agents are well advised to determine which law applies in their particular state or jurisdiction and then to endeavor to become reasonably familiar with the salient provisions.

There are, of course, several states in which there is no statutory law covering the sale of goods, as such. In these states there are legislative enactments, however, which affect certain specific questions related to the purchase of goods. These statutes, together with the law developed by court decisions in these states, result in a set of rules which is closely related to those prevailing in states having the Uniform Sales Act. Purchasing agents located in states not having either "uniform" statute, however, should resolve all doubts on any important question by consulting professional counsel.

[2] See Section 28, "Appendix," for a copy of the Uniform Sales Act. Also three explanatory, detailed references to the Uniform Commercial Code.

Which Law Governs?

Where the laws of two or more jurisdictions involved in a business transaction are in conflict, it becomes important to determine which law governs. For example, a buyer in Illinois may issue a purchase order to a seller in New York for goods to be delivered in Ohio. Generally, the formation of the contract and the interpretation of its provisions will be governed by the law of the jurisdiction in which the last act that brings the contract into existence was executed. Usually, the last act is that of acceptance of the offer. In this example, therefore, interpretation of the contract would be governed by the law of New York. However, the legal rules relating to delivery of goods and their acceptance are determined by the laws of the jurisdiction in which the delivery is to be made or accepted, unless the parties have agreed to the contrary. In this example, therefore, delivery and acceptance of goods would be governed by the laws of Ohio.

For various reasons, purchasing agents may find it desirable to specify that the laws of a particular state shall govern a purchase transaction. Sometimes, a provision to this effect is printed on the purchase order form. Even if this is done, however, it is advisable for the buyer to make certain that nothing in the seller's acknowledgment is in conflict with respect to which law shall govern the sale. If such conflicts are discovered, the problem should be resolved with the supplier so that both parties understand which laws are to apply.

Formation of Contract

The time-honored requirements of a legally enforceable contract are:

1. Offer and acceptance
2. Parties competent to contract
3. Legality of subject matter
4. A sufficient consideration

The courts were, historically, very strict in insisting that a contract was formed only when there was an exact meeting of the minds, i.e., when offer and acceptance were completely identical. Suppose B ordered "1,000 tractor tires" and specified "ship at once" and the seller wired in reply "shipping 700 tires tomorrow, balance Thursday." The older decisions would hold that there was no contract because the offer said nothing about part shipments and it would be presumed that the entire lot must be shipped at once.

The Uniform Commercial Code takes a more realistic attitude in conformity with actual business practices and, under it, a contract would arise in the above example. On this point, section 2–206 of the Code provides:

OFFER AND ACCEPTANCE IN FORMATION OF CONTRACT

(1) Unless otherwise unambiguously indicated by the language or circumstances
   (*a*) an offer to make a contract shall be construed as inviting acceptance in any manner and by any medium reasonable in the circumstances;
   (*b*) an order or other offer to buy goods for prompt or current shipment shall be construed as inviting acceptance either by a prompt promise to ship or by the prompt or current shipment of conforming or non-conforming goods but such a shipment of non-conforming goods does not constitute an acceptance if the seller reasonably notifies the buyer that the shipment is offered only as an accommodation to the buyer.

(2) Where the beginning of a requested performance is a reasonable mode of acceptance an offeror who is not notified of acceptance within a reasonable time may treat the offer as having lapsed before acceptance.

Buyers should take careful note that this section permits the seller to accept simply by making shipment, if the order calls for prompt shipment. However, if the purchase order calls for delayed shipment or specifies that the seller must accept or acknowledge the order, then no contract is created until the seller signifies acceptance.

Normally, contractual obligations attach as soon as a legally effective acceptance is made. The purchase order may be either an offer or an acceptance, depending on the circumstances of each purchase. The order can be issued as an acceptance of a proposal or quotation given by the seller and a contract comes into being at that time. This is very rarely done. In the more common situation, the purchase order constitutes an offer to buy, and the contract is created when the seller accepts by signing the acknowledgment copy of the purchase order (or by delivering, if the order so states). Advertisements and price lists, published by a potential supplier, are not "offers" from the standpoint of contract law. They are interpreted only as inviting buyers to make offers at the prices shown. Ordinarily, a purchase order issued on an oral quotation made by a salesman does not create a contract until the order is accepted by an authorized agent of the supplier.

Firm Offers

The problem of firm offers to buy or sell can be of great importance. An example of this problem arose in a situation in which a purchasing agent received a quotation for certain electrical component units priced at $29 each in lots of 2,000. The proposal stated that prices were firm for 30 days after date. The agent transmitted this information to the sales department of his company which, in turn, used the quotation to price the assembled unit at $130. Because of a competitive situation, this price represented a margin of only $5, i.e., the total projected cost was $125.

A few days later the company in question received an order for 2,000 complete assemblies at $130 and, on the same day, the purchasing agent received a letter revising the price on electrical components. The letter to the buyer revised the quotation to $42 each, placing the responsibility for this change on an increase in price of certain imported materials.

In this example, where the buyer had not yet placed an order, a question immediately arose as to whether the seller could be held to his original offer of $29 each.

In jurisdictions not following the U.C.C. the buyer's company would be faced with loss, because, prior to acceptance, the seller would have a right to revoke his offer.

The Uniform Commercial Code, however, contains a provision on firm offers in section 2–205 reading as follows:

> FIRM OFFERS: An offer by a merchant to buy or sell goods in a signed writing which by its terms gives assurance that it will be held open is not revocable, for lack of consideration, during the time stated or if no time is stated for a reasonable time, but in no event may such period of irrevocability exceed three months.

If, in this example, the offer were governed by the U.C.C., the buyer could have held the seller to the quoted price of $29 each. It should be noted that this section applies only where "a signed writing . . . gives assurance that it will be held open." Ordinarily, there is no such provision in purchase order forms so that, generally, purchasing agents will be able to withdraw orders without obligation until the seller accepts. It is a rule which will probably work more in favor of the buyer in holding sellers to firm offers which are expressly open for stated periods.

Order-Acknowledgment Conflicts

The printed order and acknowledgment forms used by business organizations commonly contain numerous terms and conditions. Sometimes these are shown on the reverse of the form and may be in small print. They are intended, of course, as protection of the legal interests of the respective parties. A survey of such terms and conditions appears later in this section.

There is often disagreement and conflict between the terms of the purchase order and the seller's acknowledgment form. This is sometimes facetiously described as "the battle of forms." In spite of these conflicts, however, both buyer and seller sometimes pay little attention to the printed terms and conditions and proceed with the transaction on the assumption that a contract to buy and sell has been made.

The legal results of conflict between acknowledgment and order are different in various jurisdictions of the United States. Basically, the states can be classified into two groups in this regard, i.e., (1) states having the Uniform Commercial Code and (2) states without the Code.

The latter group may be said to follow the common law rules, based on court decisions. The Uniform Sales Act does not materially change the common law rules with respect to order-acknowledgment conflicts. In common law jurisdictions, therefore, there are two problems arising from disagreement between the order and acknowledgment forms which the purchasing agent should carefully watch. First, the existence of disagreement in forms may mean that there is no enforceable contract so that the buyer has no assurance of delivery of the material he intended to purchase. Secondly, if he accepts shipment without checking the disagreements he may find himself bound by undesirable terms and conditions specified by the supplier.

In states which have enacted the Uniform Commercial Code the rules are substantially different, but in some respects the hazards for the purchasing agent are just as great. Provisions of the Code concerning conflict between purchase orders and acknowledgments are quite explicit and seem in harmony with the actual understanding and practice of businessmen. On this question, section 2–207 provides:

ADDITIONAL TERMS IN ACCEPTANCE OR CONFIRMATION

(*A*) A definite and seasonable expression of acceptance or a written confirmation which is sent within a reasonable time operates as an acceptance even though it states terms additional or different from those offered or agreed upon, unless acceptance is expressly made conditional on assent to the additional or different terms.

(*B*) The additional terms are to be construed as proposals for addition to the contract. Between merchants such terms become part of the contract unless:
  (1) the offer expressly limits acceptance to the terms of the offer;
  (2) they materially alter it; or
  (3) notification of objection to them has already been given or is given within a reasonable time after notice of them is received.

It is clear from the language of this section that the purchasing agent must take action to protect his interests where there are unacceptable terms in the seller's acknowledgment. Perhaps the easiest and most obvious method of protection is to incorporate provisions in the purchase order that no variation from the terms of the order is acceptable unless approved in writing by the buyer. In any case, however, the buyer is well advised to examine the terms of the seller's acknowledgment and give prompt objection to any unacceptable features.

Unpriced Orders

It is sometimes necessary to issue purchase orders without a definite price being shown for the items ordered. This may occur when time does not permit lengthy cost calculations on the part of the supplier before beginning fabrication or because some emergency requires immediate purchase without advance quotation. Buyers generally strive to keep "advise price" orders at a minimum.

There has been much uncertainty about the price which the seller can legally charge on an open price order. There have been fears that such an order is the equivalent of a blank check. While no court has ever taken the view that the seller could charge any price, no matter how high, under these circumstances, there has been uncertainty in the law on this question.

The Uniform Commercial Code resolves the problem of open price orders in section 2–305:

OPEN PRICE TERM

(1) The parties if they so intend can conclude a contract for sale even though the price is not settled. In such a case the price is a reasonable price at the time for delivery if
   (*a*) nothing is said as to price; or
   (*b*) the price is left to be agreed by the parties and they fail to agree; or
   (*c*) the price is to be fixed in terms of some agreed market or other standard as set or recorded by a third person or agency and it is not so set or recorded.

(2) A price to be fixed by the seller or by the buyer means a price for him to fix in good faith.

(3) When a price left to be fixed otherwise than by agreement of the parties fails to be fixed through fault of one party the other may at his option treat the contract as cancelled or himself fix a reasonable price.

(4) Where, however, the parties intend not to be bound unless the price be fixed or agreed and it is not fixed or agreed there is no contract. In such a case the buyer must return any goods already received or if unable so to do must pay their reasonable value at the time of delivery and the seller must return any portion of the price paid on account.

Oral Commitments

Not all purchase commitments are made in writing. At times it is necessary to place orders orally, particularly by telephone. This is standard practice in many companies, especially in doing business with established sources of supply known to be satisfactory.

To protect against unfounded claims based on commitments alleged to be made orally, the law long ago provided certain safeguards. The British Parliament, over two centuries ago, adopted the Statute of Frauds establishing limits on the kinds of oral contracts which could be sued upon in the courts. The title of this law is still used to describe the statutory limits on enforceability of oral contracts, even under the new Uniform Commercial Code.

The rules are very similar under both the new Code and the older Uniform Sales Act. However, there is a new provision in the U.C.C. concerning written confirmation of oral agreements which is interesting and important. It is included in section 2–201 which, in part, reads as follows:

FORMAL REQUIREMENTS: STATUTE OF FRAUDS

(1) Except as otherwise provided in this section a contract for the sale of goods for the price of $500 or more is not enforceable by way of action or defense unless there is some writing sufficient to indicate that a contract for sale has been made between the parties and signed by the party against whom enforcement is sought or by his authorized agent or broker. A writing is not insufficient because it omits or incorrectly states a term agreed upon but the contract is not enforceable under this paragraph beyond the quantity of goods shown in such writing.

(2) Between merchants, if within a reasonable time a writing in confirmation of the contract and sufficient against the sender is received and the party receiving it has reason to know its contents, it satisfies the requirements of sub-section (1) against such party unless written notice of objection to its contents is given within ten days after it is received.

From paragraph (2) of the foregoing, it is readily apparent that buyers should promptly examine any confirmation of an oral agreement sent by the seller and object within ten days if there is any statement not in accordance with the buyer's understanding.

PURCHASE REQUISITIONS[3]

In most concerns the purchase requisition is the basis for the developing and issuing of a purchase order. The requisition furnishes the buyer with his authority for purchasing the items listed on the requisition. The requisitions originate with the various departments of the concern and while usually dictated by an individual in the department, are approved by the department head who is authorized to approve expenditures up to a certain amount. The purchasing department is furnished with all procedures or regulations pertaining to the amount for which the de-

[3] Also referred to in Section 25.

partment head might approve without having a special appropriation issued.

Numbering of Requisitions

Most requisitions are numbered consecutively and often have a letter or letters preceding the number which identify the originating department. For instance, a requisition coming from general stores might be GS-156, one coming from machine shop might be MS-190, one coming from the treasury department might be TR-110, etc. Of course, these symbols are all worked out and are familiar to purchasing and cost departments.

Description

The requisitions should contain a complete description of the item or items required. If blueprints are referred to, the numbers should be given together with the latest revision dates and copies should be available that can be sent out for bids. The number of the items required should be shown, the delivery date required, the point to which the delivery should be made, if for some particular job this should be shown, and the account number to which the items are to be charged. Where material is required for stock, requisitions should show the amount on hand and the estimated time the material being ordered will last. This helps the buyer to determine whether or not he should recommend that amounts be increased or decreased. If by increasing the amount a better price can be obtained, he would recommend the increase. If the amount specified would increase the inventory needlessly, he naturally would recommend that a lesser amount be purchased. The latter becomes especially important if purchasing is responsible for stores inventory.

Requisitions for stock are usually made in duplicate, the original copy going to the purchasing department and the duplicate being held in the department requiring the material. Requisitions for items for special jobs are often in triplicate with the copy going to the cost department so that job's department charge can be checked. In many concerns the cost department does not check charge numbers on requisitions for special jobs, preferring to check the charge number on the copy of invoice sent to the cost department.

Some companies require that the original and a copy of requisition be sent to the purchasing department. The original goes to the buyer purchasing the material listed and the copy to the file clerk. The file clerk shows on his copy the buyer handling the original. This gives purchasing a system for locating all invoices by number and making certain that requisitions are not held for long periods or lost.

A typical requisition is reproduced in Fig. 5–1. Another example is shown in Section 25, "Forms and Records."

FORM 32-R

REQUISITION TO PURCHASING DEPARTMENT
FEDERAL GLASS DIVISION

No. ______

DEPARTMENT ______ DATE ______

TO BE USED FOR ______

DATE NEEDED ______ SPECIAL FOLLOW-UP DATE ______

(DO NOT WRITE IN THIS SPACE)

ACCOUNT No. ______ SALES TAX EXEMPT

QUANTITY	DESCRIPTION	PRICE

Competitive Bidding

Unless otherwise indicated, it will be assumed that competitive quotations can be considered. If you believe competitive bidding should not be used in this instance, please check the appropriate square.

☐ Urgent – insufficient time for bidding.
☐ Emergency – Order placed by requisitioner before notice to Purchasing.
☐ Only one known source of supply.
☐ Other Reason. (Explain) ______
(Please use reverse or attach separate sheet if necessary)

SUPPLIERS AND QUOTATIONS

ORDER PLACED WITH ______

CONFIRMING ______

ORDER PLACED BY ______

DATE ______ ORDER No. ______

FOLLOW UP: T - TELEPHONE W - WIRE L - LETTER

ITEM NO.	DATE	METHOD	SHIPPING PROMISE

PRICE INFORMATION
REFER TO SUPPLIER'S PRICE LIST ☐
REFER TO PURCH. DEPT. PRICE BOOK ☐
REFER TO PREVIOUS INVOICE ☐
OBTAIN NEW QUOTATIONS ☐
ENTER ON: ORDER RECORD ☐ PRICE RECORD ☐

FOREMAN OR DEPARTMENT HEAD ______

SEND ORDER COPIES TO ______

DELIVERY OR STORAGE POINT ______ APPROVED BY ______

FIG. 5–1. Typical requisition form.

PURCHASE ORDER FORMS

There are almost as many different purchase order forms in use as there are purchasing departments. A review of those issued by hundreds of companies, large and small, reveals numerous shapes, sizes, and colors, as well as subject matter and its arrangement. Uniformity in purchase orders is not necessary, although greater standardization among buyers undoubtedly would be of assistance to the sellers.

The chief requirement is that the purchase orders contain a clear description of the material or services required, the terms of purchase and sale, and time, manner, and place of delivery. The arrangement should be such as to facilitate writing the order and its interpretation and transcription by the seller. The information usually found in a purchase order includes the following items.

Identification

The buyer's company name should stand out on the order. Identification symbols applying to the order occupy a prominent position on the order form and frequently are put in a box in the upper right-hand corner with instructions that they are to be shown on all documents and packages. For that reason they should be as brief and simple as possible. The most commonly used identification symbols are the following:

Purchase Order Number. Most purchasing agents prefer purchase order forms numbered consecutively by the printer to facilitate accounting for each form. Supplements may carry an entirely new number or unnumbered forms may be used on which the original order number and the supplement numbers are typed. Letter prefixes may be used before the purchase order number to distinguish orders for different plants or departments, or letter suffixes after the number may designate the buyer.

Some purchasing agents prefer not to use prenumbered purchase order forms but to fill in the purchase order number as each order is typed. This makes it more difficult to account for each issued order, but makes it possible to use the number for classification purposes. For example, a separate number series may be used for each buyer, for each class of purchase, each department, or any other classification.

Requisition Number. The purpose of this number is to show purchasing department authorization and to enable the requisitioning unit to match purchase orders against requisitions. It may be advisable that the requisition number not show on the original and acknowledgment copies of the purchase order, since the requisition number is usually an internal identification symbol. An exception to this might be where a purchasing department has a file with copies of requisitions in numerical order. Then when individual in buyer's company or vendor refers to requisition number instead of purchase order number the copy of requisition will show just what buyer is handling the transaction.

"For"

Information given under this designation is to enable the receiving department to direct material to proper locations such as the stock room, job site, department, etc. Numbers are quite often used. It is not desirable to give names of individuals as this encourages direct contacts by supplier representatives, either in connection with the order in question or subsequently.

Most companies have all less carload and packaged materials delivered to a central receiving department. Carload shipments and truckload shipments usually are delivered where the materials are to be used or stocked. Many concerns show on the purchase order the department or individual requesting the material. The name of the department or the individual can be kept off the original which goes to the vendor. For most receiving departments the initials of the person requesting the material is sufficient to indicate where delivery should be made.

Supplier's Name and Address

One of the most important essentials of the purchase order is the supplier's name and address. To save time in mailing and to avoid the possibility of mistakes in addressing envelopes or by putting purchase orders in the wrong envelope, most purchase order forms are designed for mailing in window envelopes. Space for typing the name and address of the supplier is clearly defined in the upper part of the purchase order.

Shipping Instructions

Adequate space should be available in a prominent location on every purchase order to give complete shipping instructions as to destination and routing.

If a separate series of purchase orders is used for each geographical location, it may be desirable to have the destination, name, and address printed on the purchase order form to avoid unnecessary typing and to prevent mistakes.

Terms of Purchase[4]

Cash discounts and f.o.b. points are important factors in total price, but these conditions usually are shown on the purchase order separate from the basic unit prices for ease of reference and to make sure they are not overlooked.

Cash Discounts. Each vendor usually has an established policy on cash discount allowances which may be fairly uniform for various products throughout an industry. Alert buyers do not allow this to discourage them from negotiating cash discount terms with each vendor since the total of cash discounts in any one period may do much toward paying purchasing department expenses. The most frequent terms are 2 per cent 10 days net 30 days, but variations are numerous. Vendors whose standard terms may be _____ per cent 10 days may permit customers who buy frequently to pay on the 10th proximo, or twice a month, to avoid

[4] Described in more detail in Sections 9, 18, and 27.

numerous remittances. Such terms as "prompt" or "net cash" are indefinite and should be avoided.

F.o.b. Points. The f.o.b. point usually determines when ownership passes from seller to buyer as well as who pays transportation charges. Thus, it is very important to take careful note of f.o.b. point in making a purchase, as well as to show it clearly on the purchase order. It is often important that the f.o.b. point be so definite as to show that it is f.o.b. vendor's plant with the name of the city where the plant is located. The f.o.b. terms on foreign purchases are rather complicated (see Section 17). In writing orders for materials to be imported, it would be well to check with a reliable importer to make certain that the proper terms are being used. The more frequent f.o.b. terms and the effect on ownership are the following:

1. "Delivered." This means that the seller will pay transportation charges and that title does not pass to the buyer until he receives the goods.
2. "Collect." This indicates that the purchase was made f.o.b. shipping point and that the buyer will pay transportation charges. Ownership is vested in the buyer as soon as the goods are delivered to a common carrier.
3. "Prepaid." Unless otherwise qualified, this indicates that the purchase was made on a delivered basis and that the seller will pay transportation charges. Ownership remains with the seller until goods are delivered to the destination specified.
4. "Freight Allowed." This may also be stated more explicitly as "f.o.b. shipping point, freight allowed to destination." Either form indicates that title passes as soon as the goods are delivered to a common carrier but that the seller will reimburse the buyer for the transportation charges.
5. "F.o.b. Shipping Point, Freight Prepaid." More explicitly this is "f.o.b. shipping point, freight prepaid to destination." The effect of this condition is the same as "freight allowed" except that the seller prepays transportation charges. Prepayment of freight in such instances saves clerical work for both buyer and seller and is gaining increasing acceptance.

Laws governing passage of title and ownership are of extreme importance to buyers and are summarized more fully in Section 4.

Date of Shipment or Delivery

Unless otherwise specified, it would be presumed that shipment against a purchase order is to be made as soon as possible and any unreasonable delay would make the contract void or voidable.

Definite dates for shipments and/or deliveries should be indicated on every purchase order. The "soon as possible," "promptly," "rush," etc., mean little to vendors because nearly all the orders they receive carry similar instructions. Usually it is more satisfactory and will save time if the buyer and seller can agree on a delivery date prior to writing the purchase order. This date shown on the order gives helpful information to the buyer's company's manufacturing and planning departments.

It is well for purchasing to keep various departments informed regarding the time required to obtain certain materials so that requisitions will be issued in time for buyers to obtain the needed deliveries.

The buyer should insist on realistic delivery dates from the party requisitioning material and should be careful not to greatly misrepresent to vendors the dates when materials are needed. If the party requisitioning material shows that material is needed much sooner than it actually is, increased delivery costs such as high express charges instead of truck or freight charges result.

Direction to Ship

Many purchase orders do not contain any form or specific statement requesting the seller to ship, the title "purchase order" being considered sufficient. In the interest of completeness, however, it seems desirable to insert a statement under the address and above the description of the material ordered such as: "Please ship the material described below, subject to all the terms and conditions shown on the face and reverse side of this order" (if there are conditions on the reverse side of the order). Also see Sections 4, 19, and 26.

Body of Order

Most purchase order forms are fairly uniform in dividing the body of the form into two vertical sections with Quantity shown on the left side and Description in the center. Many include the third column for Price on the right. This data is then typed in as the order is issued. When dealing with suppliers of long standing who are quite familiar with requirements, there is a temptation for buyers to become careless in describing the material ordered or in specifying quantities and prices. It is important to remember that the purchase order is a legal document and should be accurate and definitive. Besides the danger of error on the part of new personnel in one organization or the other, descriptions shown on purchase orders frequently are carried over into other records, and poor ones may cause much delay or confusion.

Quantities. Quantities should be specific in terms of pricing units. For example, material purchased at so much per pound should be described as "1 C/L (one carload) approximately 50,000 pounds" not merely as "one carload." Also, a tank carload should specify "1 T/C (10,000 gal) No. 2 fuel oil" and not merely say "one tank carload." Similarly, the number of units in a case, the number of gallons or pounds in a drum, or the number of units in a bag should be stated, as well as the unit of shipment. Some carload items have different freight rates for different tonnages. As an example, where nitrate of soda has a freight rate of 32 cents per hundredweight for a minimum carload of 40,000 to 60,000 pounds, a carload of 60,000 to 80,000 pounds has a freight rate of 29 cents per hundredweight, and a carload of 80,000 pounds and over has a freight rate of 27 cents per hundredweight. With rail rates increasing rather steadily, buyers and traffic managers are obtaining more concessions on freight rates for the large tonnages.

The quantity column should be kept free of other information.

Description. The description should be as brief as possible, and yet long enough to describe the purchase clearly and definitely. For quick reference, it is desirable to start with a short general title or description and follow with details such as "one–centrifugal pump," and then give size, capacity, materials of construction, etc. Any specific instructions, such as part numbers, drawings for approval, test reports, reference to company standards, etc., should be included in the description.

In discussing the requisition leading to the purchase order, emphasis was also put on the importance of complete and accurate description. It is the buyer's responsibility to check this, even going so far as to check his company's engineering department when reference is made to a blueprint to make certain that the correct print with latest revision is being used.

If the purchase order represents acceptance of an offer by the seller, reference to such offer should be made, but this should not take the place of giving the more important specifications in the order itself. If this description is lengthy, frequently the general description of the article or material is given first and then on a separate line below is the statement: "Specifications, prices, and delivery as per your quotation (proposal date)."

With repetitive purchases it is customary to agree on specifications and other terms in advance by means of a formal contract or otherwise, and to agree that such specifications and terms will apply to all purchases until mutually agreed otherwise. This eliminates the need for repetition of details, but the need for proper identification of the item purchased still remains.

Price.[5] Unless there is a very good reason for not doing so, the items

[5] Also covered in Sections 9 and 10.

listed on a purchase order should be priced. This is mandatory in a company where the accounts payable division checks and pays invoices without having them approved in purchasing. It is also necessary where a total of daily commitments is kept. The number of purchase orders with "advise price" should be kept to a minimum. This type of order could be costly (see Section 4). Price in most instances is by unit and is extended for the total dollar value of the purchase order. At times it may be advisable for price to be indicated for the total quantity purchased without showing unit prices of the items. If the purchase order covers shipping instructions for material purchased in accordance with terms of an existing general contract, the price may be stated merely as "A/C contract" or "account of contract." In such instances, it is usually desirable to insert the contract price on the buyer's copies to facilitate the approval of invoices, etc. Leaving the contract price off the purchase order copy for the receiving department helps to protect the contract price.

In buying repetitive items it is desirable to ask the seller to quote in terms of list unit prices less specified discounts, if any, rather than to quote net unit prices or a total price for a given quantity. This makes it easier to compare prices quoted by other suppliers and also makes it easier for the buyer's organization to set up unit prices and to allocate charges. If part shipments are made, it is usually desirable to have invoices issued for each shipment, and this is easier if unit prices are designated on the purchase order.

Invoicing Instructions. Many concerns require more than one copy of the invoice and may or may not wish to have invoices mailed to the place of destination or to the home office. To avoid confusion, the purchase order should include in a prominent place a statement that an invoice should be rendered promptly for each shipment with a designated number of copies and to a specified address.

Shipping Paper Instructions. Shipping papers assume a vital role in the purchase transaction, and are of particular importance when purchases are for several locations. Specific instructions should be given as to the number of copies, mailing address, etc., including a statement that papers covering final shipment of an order show that it completes the order.

Cancellation Provisions. It frequently happens that a buyer may contract for engineering services, construction of a building[6] or a machine, or may place an order for special materials to be made, only to find that conditions have changed so that it becomes necessary for him to cancel the order after the supplier has already done considerable work on the order. First of all, it should be definite what the settlement will be if the

[6] See Sections 3 and 16.

seller cannot produce the material or equipment in the specified time. Second, a definite understanding should be reached when order is issued showing the buyer's obligation if conditions so change that the buyer must cancel before order is completed.

Prior to writing an order, buyer and seller should work out definite cancellation provisions. One of the most common is, should it become necessary for the buyer to cancel an order before completion for any reason other than the seller's inability to fulfill the order, the buyer will pay the seller the actual cost of the work plus a certain overhead and profit which will be clearly defined in the order.

An example of what can happen where cancellation conditions are not spelled out follows.

A buyer for a manufacturing concern obtained competitive bids on five million parts to go out as accessories with his company's product. The order for five million was placed at a firm unit price. After receiving about two million of these parts, the buyer found it necessary to cancel the order. The cancellation provision on the order was not definite. The seller claimed that he had bought tools and equipment which could be amortized by furnishing the five million parts but could not be on the two million furnished. The seller also claimed that he had purchased special material for the job and had rented outside space to store the material in order to complete the order on time. The seller's claims at first were so extravagant that they would have made the cost for two million parts practically the same as the cost for the five million. Much time was spent in trying to reach an agreement with the seller. Finally, the transaction was completed by the buyer purchasing all the special stock, the machinery which was definitely ordered by the seller for the job, and allowing the seller a considerably higher price per unit for the two million pieces furnished, as the price which had originally been billed was based on furnishing five million. It is clear that much time and argument could have been prevented had the order contained a complete cancellation understanding.

In some instances where it becomes necessary for a buyer to place an order for special products to be produced, some concerns have found it necessary to send out a form covering possible cancellation. This practice was started when concerns had defense orders, parts of which had to be filled by subcontractors. Conditions were necessary which would satisfy those agents negotiating a settlement of defense contract cancelled by the government. Some concerns, in special cases, have continued to use forms similar to the one illustrated by Fig. 5–2.

For many purchases, buyer may not need to include as much as is given here. A brief statement on the face of the order, or cancellation provisions, if any, on the back of the purchase order, may suffice.

Corning Glass Works Purchase Order____________

This purchase order is subject to cancellation in whole or in part at the option of Corning at any time before it has been completely filled by the Seller on the following terms and conditions:

1. Corning shall notify Seller in writing or by Telegram of Corning's intention to cancel and the extent thereof.

2. Immediately upon notice of cancellation, Seller shall cease all work under this purchase order and shall take all possible steps to cancel all orders which Seller may have placed for the purchase of materials and supplies to be used by Seller in the manufacture of goods covered by this purchase order. Failure of Seller to use due diligence in cancelling such orders shall deprive Seller of the benefits of Paragraph 5 as they apply to such orders.

3. Corning agrees to pay Seller for all finished goods covered by this purchase order which have previously been delivered to Corning or are in Seller's possession and not therefore paid for on receipt of notice of cancellation, at the rate set forth in this purchase order.

4. Corning agrees to pay Seller for all finished goods covered by this purchase order which are in process of manufacture on receipt of notice of cancellation, the price for such goods in process to be the cost thereof to Seller at cancellation as determined by accepted accounting practices and including Seller's factory overhead, plus profit percentage established at time of placing the order.

5. Corning agrees to pay Seller at actual cost to Seller plus handling charges for all raw materials in Seller's possession or covered by uncancellable orders placed by Seller to the extent (a) that such raw materials have been ordered specially by Seller in reliance on this purchase order, and (b) that such raw materials are useful solely in the manufacture of the goods covered by this purchase order.

6. All goods, work in process, and raw materials paid for by Corning under the foregoing Paragraphs 3-5 inclusive shall thereupon become Corning's property, and Seller shall deliver same to Corning in accordance with Corning's instructions.

7. Seller shall have no claim against Corning under this purchase order in the event of cancellation thereof except as expressly provided in the foregoing Paragraphs 2-5 inclusive.

FIG. 5–2. Cancellation notice form.

Purchase Order Signatures. Purchase orders customarily are signed by the buyer's purchasing agent or by someone authorized by him (also see Section 4). The name of the company is printed on the purchase form followed by a line for signature. Typical forms are:

XYZ Company	XYZ Company	XYZ Company
____________	____________	____________
Purchasing Agent	Dir. of Purchases	Purchasing Agent
		By ____________
XYZ Company	XYZ Company	XYZ Company
____________	____________	By ____________
Dir. of Purchases	(Signed with Title)	Purchasing Department
By ____________		

In a small organization the purchasing agent may sign all purchase orders, and his name and signature will be used. In larger organizations, assistant purchasing agents, or buyers, or assistant buyers may sign the orders, but some companies feel that it is desirable to have the name of the purchasing agent or director of purchases printed on the order. When the buyer signing the order is not readily available, the supplier will want to contact the purchasing agent, and can do so quickly if the purchasing agent's name appears on the order.

Indications are that more and more it is becoming the practice of purchasing departments to have the purchase order signed by the individual handling the purchasing transaction. It makes for more efficiency in the purchasing department where the order is issued, and also in the order and sales department of the vendor.

GENERAL CONDITIONS OF PURCHASE

Some of the general information which applies to all orders is usually found on the face of the order. Included are statements showing that the purchase order number must appear on all invoices, shipping papers, packages, invoice instructions, and the number of copies of invoices required. Specific instructions or information which may change with each individual order are usually typed in the body of the order. An example of this is where the buyer orders an item or items to be made from special molds, tools, or dies. The purchase order should show the cost of the molds, tools, or dies. It should also be clearly stated whether or not the special equipment becomes the property of the purchaser and will be delivered to the buyer whenever delivery is requested. A definite agreement should be worked out with the vendor and clearly stated in the order. If it is agreed that the equipment is to be used exclusively for producing items for the buyer's company, this should be included in the order. Many general conditions are often shown on the back of the order and on the front of the order is a statement to the effect that all conditions on the back of the order do apply.

Many years back, purchase orders covered few general conditions. This was also true of most of the acknowledgments sent out by vendors. During the past twelve to fifteen years both the purchaser on purchase orders and vendor on acknowledgments have thought it necessary to add more and more general conditions.

Many of the purchase orders are accompanied by an acknowledgment form which the vendor is requested to sign and return, as mentioned in Section 4. If a buyer insists, most vendors will return this acknowledgment form. It so happens, however, that many vendors insist on sending their own acknowledgment form. They naturally prefer to use this to the exclusion of the purchase order acknowledgment form but, if pressed, will usually use the purchase order acknowledgment form and also send their own form. This is a rather awkward situation because many of the vendor's forms carry conditions which are not acceptable to the buyer. There are many companies whose sales order departments use one manifold copy of their form which is sent to their production and shipping departments as an acknowledgment to the customer.

From the foregoing, it is readily seen that much confusion can result and much working together between the buyer and the vendor is necessary to bring about the filling of the order without delay or misunderstanding. It is the responsibility of the buyer to see that orders which he issues are acknowledged promptly by the vendor and to see that the items and conditions on the acknowledgment meet with the requirements on the buyer's purchase orders.

A review of conditions on many acknowledgments and on many purchase orders indicates that there is possibility for considerable simplification. Buyers can work toward simplifying conditions on their own order forms and can also encourage suppliers to simplify their acknowledgment forms.

An example of what one concern found by experience to be necessary in the way of an acknowledgment form is shown in Figs. 5–3 and 5–4, front and back.

It is possible that many of these conditions would be contrary to those included in the buyer's purchase order. In contrast to the acknowledgment which has been reproduced, a fairly simple one is reproduced in Fig. 5–5 with all the conditions showing on the face.

Purchase Order Conditions

A buyer may find it advisable to have several general conditions shown on his purchase order. These could be chosen from the typical clauses commonly found on purchase orders.

Terms and Conditions. This order is subject to the following terms and conditions and by accepting the order, or any part thereof, the seller agrees to and accepts said terms and conditions:

1. If seller refuses to accept this order exactly as written, he will return it at once with explanation.
2. Purchaser will not be responsible for any goods delivered without purchase order.
3. Seller will send separate invoice for each purchase order number.
4. Seller will deliver no invoice to purchaser's employee. They must be mailed to buyer's company.

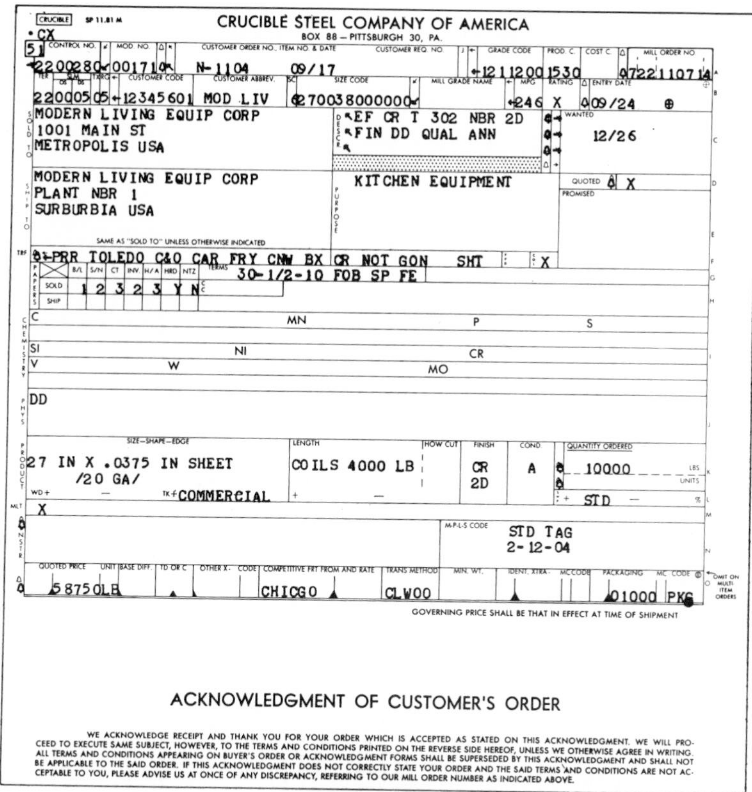

CRUCIBLE SP 11.81 M

CRUCIBLE STEEL COMPANY OF AMERICA
BOX 88 — PITTSBURGH 30, PA.

• CX
51

CONTROL NO. 220028 — MOD. NO. 00171 — CUSTOMER ORDER NO., ITEM NO. & DATE N-1104 09/17 — CUSTOMER REQ. NO. — GRADE CODE 1211200 — PROD. C. 1530 — COST C. — MILL ORDER NO. 0722110714

TER 2 — SLM OS/DS 200 05 — TXRG 05 — CUSTOMER CODE 12345601 — CUSTOMER ABBREV. MOD LIV — SC — SIZE CODE 270038000000 — MILL GRADE NAME — MPG 246 — RATING X — ENTRY DATE 09/24

SOLD TO: MODEN LIVING EQUIP CORP / 1001 MAIN ST / METROPOLIS USA

DESCR: EF CR T 302 NBR 2D / FIN DD QUAL ANN

WANTED 12/26

SHIP TO: MODERN LIVING EQUIP CORP / PLANT NBR 1 / SURBURBIA USA

SAME AS "SOLD TO" UNLESS OTHERWISE INDICATED

PURPOSE: KITCHEN EQUIPMENT

QUOTED X

PROMISED

TRF: PRR TOLEDO C&O CAR FRY CNW BX — CR NOT GON — SHT — X

PAPERS: B/L S/N CT INV. H/A HRD NTZ — SOLD 1 2 3 2 3 Y N — SHIP

TERMS 30-1/2-10 FOB SP FE

CHEMISTRY: C — MN — P — S — SI — NI — CR — V — W — MO

PHYS: DD

PRODUCT: SIZE—SHAPE—EDGE 27 IN X .0375 IN SHEET /20 GA/ — WD + — TK + COMMERCIAL — LENGTH COILS 4000 LB — HOW CUT — FINISH CR 2D — COND. A — QUANTITY ORDERED 10000 LBS — UNITS — + STD — %

MLT X

INSTR — M-P-L-S CODE STD TAG 2-12-04

QUOTED PRICE 58750 — UNIT LB — BASE DIFF. — TD OR C — OTHER X- — CODE — COMPETITIVE FRT FROM AND RATE CHICGO — TRANS METHOD CLW00 — MIN. WT. — IDENT. XTRA- — MC CODE — PACKAGING 01000 PKG — MC CODE — OMIT ON MULTI ITEM ORDERS

GOVERNING PRICE SHALL BE THAT IN EFFECT AT TIME OF SHIPMENT

ACKNOWLEDGMENT OF CUSTOMER'S ORDER

WE ACKNOWLEDGE RECEIPT AND THANK YOU FOR YOUR ORDER WHICH IS ACCEPTED AS STATED ON THIS ACKNOWLEDGMENT. WE WILL PROCEED TO EXECUTE SAME SUBJECT, HOWEVER, TO THE TERMS AND CONDITIONS PRINTED ON THE REVERSE SIDE HEREOF, UNLESS WE OTHERWISE AGREE IN WRITING. ALL TERMS AND CONDITIONS APPEARING ON BUYER'S ORDER OR ACKNOWLEDGMENT FORMS SHALL BE SUPERSEDED BY THIS ACKNOWLEDGMENT AND SHALL NOT BE APPLICABLE TO THE SAID ORDER. IF THIS ACKNOWLEDGMENT DOES NOT CORRECTLY STATE YOUR ORDER AND THE SAID TERMS AND CONDITIONS ARE NOT ACCEPTABLE TO YOU, PLEASE ADVISE US AT ONCE OF ANY DISCREPANCY, REFERRING TO OUR MILL ORDER NUMBER AS INDICATED ABOVE.

FIG. 5–3. Acknowledgment of customer's order form (front). (*By permission of Crucible Steel Company of America, Pittsburgh, Pa.*)

5. No boxing, packing, or cartage charges will be allowed by purchaser unless specifically authorized on the face of this order.
6. Goods must be shipped as per instructions; otherwise any extra handling charge will be billed back to seller.
7. It shall be understood that the cash discount period to purchaser will date from the receipt of the invoice and not from the date of the invoice.
8. If price is omitted on order, except where order is given in acceptance of quoted prices, it is agreed that seller's price will be the lowest prevailing market price and in no event is this order to be filled at higher prices than last previously quoted or charged without purchaser's written consent.
9. In the event of seller's failure to deliver as and when specified, purchaser reserves the right to cancel this order, or any part thereof, without prejudice to its other rights, and seller agrees that purchaser may return part or all of any shipment so made and may charge seller with any loss or expense sustained as a result of such failure to deliver.

TERMS AND CONDITIONS OF SALE

1. Seller shall not be liable for delay or failure to perform due to causes beyond the control of the Seller, such as, but specifically not limited to, the unavailability of goods, law or governmental regulation, judgment of a competent court, difficulties with labor, accidents, delays in transportation, acts of God, or war.

2. Claim for errors, deficiencies or imperfections will not be considered unless made with reasonable promptness after receipt of material and unless the Buyer promptly discontinues the use of said material. Material proving defective in the hands of the Buyer, when used for the purposes for which such material is intended, will be replaced or credit will be allowed for the price thereof at the Seller's option. Seller shall not be liable for any claims for labor, expenses or damages (whether direct or consequential) resulting from or occasioned by use of defective material and material must not be returned except by written permission of Seller.

3. The material may be inspected by the Buyer prior to shipment.

4. Seller warrants only that its ownership of the material will be complete and not subject to liens incurred by Seller.

5. Seller will indemnify and save harmless the Buyer from any judgment for damages and costs which may be awarded by a court of competent jurisdiction against the Buyer on account of the infringement of any United States patent by the material, per se, supplied by the Seller under this order, provided prompt written notice be given the Seller of any notice of infringement or the beginning of any such suit, or both. Upon receipt of such written notice from the Buyer, the Seller may, notwithstanding the foregoing indemnity, at its election and at its own expense: defend the suit; or procure for the Buyer the right to continue using said material; or replace the same with non-infringing material suitable to the Buyer; or modify the material so that it becomes non-infringing; or remove the material and refund the purchase price and transportation costs thereof. In case the Seller elects to defend the suit, the Buyer shall render to the Seller every reasonable assistance which the Seller may require in such defense. The foregoing states the entire liability of the Seller with respect to patent infringement by said material.

6. The order represented by this acknowledgment can be cancelled, terminated or modified only with the Seller's consent and then only upon terms and conditions to be agreed upon which shall include protection of the Seller against all loss.

7. The price for the material covered hereby shall be adjusted to the Seller's price in effect at the time of shipment. All changes in freight rates or transportation charges used in determining delivered prices occurring after the date of this acknowledgment will be for the Buyer's account. If the Buyer should change the point at which the material is to be delivered f.o.b., the Buyer shall pay all increased freight or transportation charges including freight on the tare. Seller shall not be responsible for spotting, switching, drayage or other transportation charges incurred at destination.

8. Terms of payment: the terms of payment, unless otherwise stated on the face of this acknowledgment, are thirty days net from date of invoice, or ½ of 1% cash discount for payment on or before the 25th of the month for invoices dating from the 1st to the 15th day inclusive of the same month, and for payment on or before the 10th of the month for invoices dating from the 16th to the last day of the previous month. This cash discount is only allowable when payment is made within the discount periods aforesaid and the date of invoice governs.

9. For the purpose of invoicing and billing, each shipment shall be treated as a separate and independent contract. All shipments and deliveries made hereunder shall be at all times subject to the approval of the Seller's credit department, and if at any time in the judgment of Seller's credit manager there is any doubt as to the Buyer's responsibility, the Seller may decline to continue production or to make any further shipments hereunder except upon receipt of satisfactory security or cash; if this security or cash be not received, Seller may terminate this order.

10. Waiver by the Seller of any breach of contract shall not be construed as a waiver of any other existing or future breach, or as an estoppel.

11. All taxes of every sort which the Seller may be required to pay or collect under any existing or future Federal or State law upon or with respect to the sale, delivery, storage, processing, use, consumption or transportation of any of the material covered hereby shall be for the account of the Buyer, and the Buyer will pay the amount thereof to the Seller upon request.

12. Unless otherwise shown on the face hereof, material shall be within the limits and of the sizes manufactured by the Seller, and shall be subject to Seller's standard variations and manufacturing practices. Material purchased on the basis of weight is subject to customary quantity variations recognized by trade practice.

13. We hereby certify that this material will be produced in compliance with all applicable requirements of Sections 6, 7, and 12 of the Fair Labor Standards Act of 1938, as amended, and of regulations and orders of the Administrator of the Wage and Hour Division issued under Section 14 thereof.

14. If terms or conditions contained in the Buyer's purchase order are inconsistent with the terms and conditions of this acknowledgment, the Seller's terms and conditions shall govern.

FIG. 5–4. Acknowledgment of customer's order form (back) with conditions. *(By permission of Crucible Steel Company of America, Pittsburgh, Pa.)*

ORDER ACKNOWLEDGEMENT

THE H. A. SMITH MACHINERY COMPANY

PRODUCTION – TOOL ROOM – SPECIAL MACHINERY

3402 Court Street
East Syracuse, N. Y.
Phone: HO3-8606

July 2, 19

OUR ORDER NO. C-10259-S

CUSTOMER'S ORDER NO. B26538-K 6/28/

TO The Monarch Machine Tool Co.
Sidney, Ohio

SHIP TO Corning Glass Works
Corning, New York

We wish to thank you for your order covering the following equipment which we accept subject to the terms and conditions below:

DELIVERY Needed Last Wk. of Aug.

VIA

1 - MONARCH Series "90" Model 2501 x 132" Center Distance Dyna-Shift Lathe for 440 volt, 3 phase, 60 cycle	$ 33,734.00
1 - Type "C" Swiveling Air-Gage Tracer	12,395.00
1 - Regular Tailstock	1,396.00
1 - Oil Pan	1,150.00
1 - Special Cross Feed Gearing	750.00
1 - Motor driven coolant pump and piping	687.00
1 - Carriage dial indicator type stop	215.00
1 - 18" 4-Jaw Chuck	490.00
1 - 42" Face Plate	371.00
1 - Set of (4) 10" single key face plate jaws	464.00
	$51,652.00

TERMS: Net 30 Days F. O. B. Sidney, Ohio

CONDITIONS

All reasonable means will be used to make shipment at time specified, but we assume no liability for loss or damage arising from delays due to fires, strikes, or any causes beyond our control. All prices quoted cover machines and equipment only as specified. If any subsequent changes are made in methods or design, the right is reserved to revise prices.

This order is accepted with the mutual understanding that it is not subject to cancellation.

THE H. A. SMITH MACHINERY COMPANY

PER John Smith

FIG. 5–5. Order acknowledgment form—simplified type. (*By permission of The H. A. Smith Machinery Co., East Syracuse, N.Y.*)

10. In the event any article sold and delivered hereunder shall be covered by any patent, copyright, or application therefor, seller will indemnify and save harmless purchaser from any and all loss, cost, or expenses on account of any and all claims, suits, or judgments on account of the use or sale of such article in violation of rights under such patent, copyright, or application.
11. In the event any article sold and delivered hereunder shall be defective in any respect whatsoever, seller will indemnify and save harmless purchaser from all loss or the payment of all sums of money by reason of all accidents, injuries, or damages to persons or property that may happen or occur in

connection with the use or sale of such article and are contributed to by said defective condition.

12. If seller performs services or constructs, erects, inspects or delivers hereunder, seller will indemnify and save harmless buyer from all loss or the payment of all sums of money by reason of all accidents, injuries, or damages to persons or property that may happen or occur in connection therewith.
13. Purchaser reserves the right to place in seller's plant, at purchaser's expense, an inspector or inspectors who shall be permitted to inspect before shipment, or during the process of manufacture, any material on this order.
14. Seller agrees not to release any advertising copy mentioning purchaser or quoting the opinion of any of purchaser's employees unless such copy is approved by purchaser before release.
15. Seller represents and warrants that no Federal or state statute or regulation, or municipal ordinance, has been or will be violated in the manufacturing, sale, and delivery of any article or service sold and delivered hereunder and if such violation has or does occur, seller will indemnify and save harmless purchaser from all loss, penalties, or the payment of all sums of money on account of such violation.
16. Any contractor supplying both services and materials shall pay all sales or use taxes on materials so furnished and shall indemnify and save harmless purchaser from any damage, costs, expenses, or penalties on account of such taxes.
17. Purchaser may at any time insist upon strict compliance with these terms and conditions, notwithstanding any previous custom, practice, or course of dealing to the contrary.
18. The terms and conditions of sale as stated in this order govern in event of conflict with any terms of seller's proposal, and are not subject to change by reason of any written or verbal statements, by seller or by any terms stated in seller's acknowledgment unless same be accepted in writing.

From these terms and conditions, a buyer should be able to select the ones required for his particular order.

Patentable Items[7]

When a buyer is placing an order for equipment developed by his company, the buyer should consult the legal department of his company to determine if the equipment is patentable. If so, the buyer's legal department should assist in developing the wording to go into the purchase order to protect the buyer's company.

Insurance[8]

On purchase orders where the supplier does work on the buyer's property or constructs equipment to perform certain jobs for the buyer's

[7] Covered in detail in Section 4.

[8] Also covered in Sections 9, 16, and 17.

company, specific insurance protection should become part of the specifications and terms of the order. This again is important on the face of the order even if it is shown in general conditions on the back of the order.

A general insurance protection clause may not be sufficient in many cases. The buyer should check with his company's insurance chief and

SHEET 1 OF 2

WELLSVILLE PUMP COMPANY
Purchasing Department
Wellsville, New York

ORIGINAL

Stuart Stoker Corp.
Elmira, New York

Req. 1809 2/1/

Order No. CO-56-001-K
Must be shown on all packages and invoices

Stuart Stoker Corporation, Elmira, N.Y. (hereinafter called the contractor) and Wellsville Pump Company, Wellsville, N.Y. (hereinafter called the purchaser) agree as follows:

Contractor shall furnish and install one (1) Stuart Steam Generating Unit Type XX for indoor service for coal firing with Stuart traveling grate spreader stoker as described in contractor's proposal number 4026 of 1/20/ .

Contractor shall furnish purchaser with approved prints of the installation from Factory Insurance Association, Factory Mutual Engineering Division, and any required approvals of the State of New York.

Delivery and erection of equipment covered by this order are to be completed so that full operation may be had on or before August 15, 19 .

Price per contractor's letters of 1/20/ and 1/26/ $130,000,000

Terms: 70% - On shipment of all materials
20% - 30 days from date of shipment
Balance - On acceptance by purchaser of complete installation

Invoices are to be rendered in quadruplicate to Wellsville Pump Company, Purchasing Dept., Wellsville, New York.

Shipments of all materials are to be made to: Wellsville Pump Co.
Main Plant - Bldg. 9
Wellsville, New York

Each box, crate or separate piece shall show purchaser's order No. CO-56-001-K.

Transportation charges from point of shipment to destination shall be paid by contractor.

Unloading, hauling and handling between the points of delivery by the transporter and the site of erection shall be done by contractor. If hauling is done by contractor, purchaser shall provide railroad siding for use of contractor within 200 feet of boiler site.

NOTICE TO CONTRACTOR

No changes in this order will be recognized unless made and confirmed in writing by Wellsville Pump Company's Purchasing Dept. All information and communications regarding this order, including those with respect to delivery or completion, are to be handled only through Wellsville Pump Company's Purchasing Department.

Insurance Clause

Contractor is to maintain all necessary insurance to protect himself against claims for bodily injuries or death of any person or persons whether or not employed by contractor which may arise from any operation in connection with work covered by this order. Required insurance in all cases will be

FIG. 5–6*a*. Contract purchase order form (sheet 1).

SHEET 2 OF 2

WELLSVILLE PUMP COMPANY
Purchasing Department
Wellsville, New York

ORIGINAL

Order No. CO -56-001- K
Must be shown on all packages and invoices

Stuart Stoker Corporation
(Continued)

Req. 1809 2/1/

Workmen's Compensation and Employer's Liability for the state involved and Public Liability Insurance with limits of $100,000 per person and $300,000 per accident.

If contractor is to sublet any portion of this order, it will be necessary that he carry contractor's protective liability insurance in limits similar to those enumerated above.

If the work to be performed by the contractor under this order will subject property of Wellsville Pump Company and/or of the public to damage, it will be necessary to provide adequate property damage insurance. $100,000 limits should be provided in this instance.

The contractor is to furnish Wellsville Pump Company with certificates of insurance per above prior to proceeding with the work covered by this contract.

Contractor shall also assume full liability for all Federal and State contributions for Unemployment Insurance, Disability Benefits Insurance, Federal Insurance Contributions Act payments and proper deductions of the Federal Withholding Tax of his employees.

MAIL INVOICE IN QUADRUPLICATE TO ADDRESS SHOWN AT TOP OF THIS ORDER.

Order number must appear on all invoices, shipping papers and packages.

Please sign duplicate (blue) copy and return to us as your acceptance.

No statement of our account is necessary unless invoices are past due.

Accepted ______________ 19 __ WELLSVILLE PUMP COMPANY

______________________ J. J. Knight
Purchasing Agent

By ______________________
Title

FIG. 5–6*b*. Contract purchase order form continued (sheet 2).

be sure to include the insurance limits that will properly protect the buyer's company and not make the insurance cost for the contractor (supplier) prohibitive. The limits will naturally vary with the different types of jobs and will be governed considerably by what buyer's own company insurance covers.

Examples of insurance protection clauses are evident in the contract orders reproduced in this section.

Conditions Covering Work on Buyer's Premises

Reference has been made to some conditions that should be included in purchase orders where work is to be done on the buyer's premises.

Many concerns have found it advisable to use what might be called a "contract purchase order" to handle agreements for constructing buildings, special machinery, etc. These usually include all the main points covered by the seller's or the builder's proposal and many of the conditions necessary to satisfy the financing and accounting rules of the buyer's company.

A typical contract order is reproduced in Fig. 5–6*a* and *b*, but more information on such nonrepetitive purchases will be found in Section 16.

PURCHASE ORDER COPIES AND SAMPLES

The purchase order is usually made up so that several copies can be produced at one typing. Smaller companies usually use purchase order pads in which they insert carbons to make up to six copies. When the number of purchase orders required per day is high, a continuous form with one-time carbon is often used. This will give up to six or eight good copies. If more than eight copies are required, or if reproduction of

FORM 31

VENDOR'S COPY

PURCHASE ORDER

TELEPHONE
444-1101

AREA CODE
614

THE FEDERAL GLASS COMPANY
DIVISION OF FEDERAL PAPER BOARD COMPANY, INC.
COLUMBUS 7, OHIO

IMPORTANT
OUR PURCHASE ORDER NUMBER MUST APPEAR ON ALL PACKAGES, INVOICES, PACKING SLIPS, AND CORRESPONDENCE.

No.

SCHEDULE this order for PROMPT shipment unless otherwise indicated.

SHIP cheapest way unless otherwise indicated.

PLEASE ENTER OUR ORDER FOR THE FOLLOWING SUBJECT TO TERMS AND CONDITIONS STATED HEREIN:

SHIP VIA	DELIVERY REQUIRED IN OUR PLANT	CONTRACT OR QUOTE NO.	DATE OF ORDER

QUANTITY	DESCRIPTION	PRICE

DELIVERIES accepted only between 8 A.M. and 2:30 P.M. Monday thru Friday, except by special arrangement. Please instruct carrier accordingly.

CONDITIONS OF PURCHASE

1. ACKNOWLEDGMENT: If this order is accepted, the acknowledgment copy, indicating your acceptance of the order and all conditions herein stated, must be signed and returned immediately.
2. INVOICES AND PACKING SLIPS: Invoice in triplicate and mail with Bill of Lading or Express Receipt immediately after each shipment. Packing slip must accompany each shipment.
3. QUALITY AND INSPECTION: We reserve the right to inspect all shipments after delivery to us and to reject any material which may be defective or not in accordance with specifications as to quality or performance.
4. PATENTS AND COPYRIGHTS: Seller warrants that there is no violation of patent rights or copyrights in manufacturing, producing or selling the material or equipment covered by this order or in the use of such material or equipment by the buyer in the usual or intended manner, and seller agrees to hold the purchaser harmless from any and all liability, loss, or expense occasioned by any such violation.
5. NON-PERFORMANCE: Time is of the essence of this order. Buyer reserves the right to cancel this order or any portion hereof if delivery or performance is not made within specified time.
6. PRICE: Except with our prior agreement, this order must not be shipped or invoiced at prices higher than those shown hereon.
7. FAIR LABOR STANDARDS ACT: Seller shall insert a certificate on all invoices submitted in connection with this order stating that the goods covered by the invoice were produced in compliance with the requirements of the Fair Labor Standards Act of 1938, as amended, including Section 6, 7, and 12, and regulations and orders issued under Section 14 thereof.
8. INSURANCE: If seller performs labor or services under this order within the plant or on the premises of buyer, Workmen's Compensation and Liability Insurance Certificates must be submitted to and approved by buyer before such labor or services begin.
9. ADDRESS ALL QUESTIONS AND CORRESPONDENCE CONCERNING THIS ORDER TO THE BUYER WHOSE NAME APPEARS IN THE LOWER RIGHT CORNER OF THIS ORDER.

THE FEDERAL GLASS COMPANY
DIVISION OF FEDERAL PAPER BOARD COMPANY, INC.

GENERAL PURCHASING AGENT

PURCHASING AGENT OR BUYER

FIG. 5–7. Purchase order form: Illustration 1.

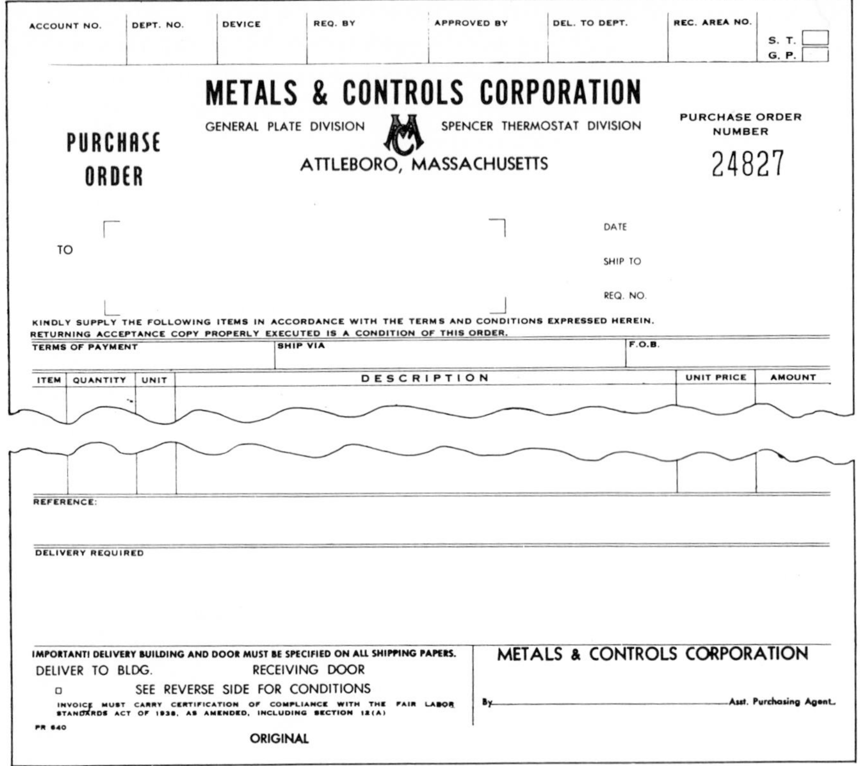

ACCOUNT NO.	DEPT. NO.	DEVICE	REQ. BY	APPROVED BY	DEL. TO DEPT.	REC. AREA NO.	S. T. / G. P.

PURCHASE ORDER

METALS & CONTROLS CORPORATION

GENERAL PLATE DIVISION SPENCER THERMOSTAT DIVISION

ATTLEBORO, MASSACHUSETTS

PURCHASE ORDER NUMBER

24827

TO

DATE

SHIP TO

REQ. NO.

KINDLY SUPPLY THE FOLLOWING ITEMS IN ACCORDANCE WITH THE TERMS AND CONDITIONS EXPRESSED HEREIN. RETURNING ACCEPTANCE COPY PROPERLY EXECUTED IS A CONDITION OF THIS ORDER.

TERMS OF PAYMENT	SHIP VIA	F.O.B.

ITEM	QUANTITY	UNIT	DESCRIPTION	UNIT PRICE	AMOUNT

REFERENCE:

DELIVERY REQUIRED

IMPORTANT! DELIVERY BUILDING AND DOOR MUST BE SPECIFIED ON ALL SHIPPING PAPERS.

DELIVER TO BLDG. RECEIVING DOOR

☐ SEE REVERSE SIDE FOR CONDITIONS

INVOICE MUST CARRY CERTIFICATION OF COMPLIANCE WITH THE FAIR LABOR STANDARDS ACT OF 1938, AS AMENDED, INCLUDING SECTION 12(A)

PR 640

ORIGINAL

METALS & CONTROLS CORPORATION

By ________ Asst. Purchasing Agent.

FIG. 5–8. Purchase order form: Illustration 2. (*By permission of Metals & Controls Corporation, Attleboro, Mass.*)

the order becomes necessary for the receiving department or others, a master copy is produced in writing the original order so that as many copies as are needed can be reproduced on some system such as Ditto or Ozalid. It has also been developed that as many as eight or nine copies of a snap-out order form with carbon inserted can be obtained and typed satisfactorily with an electric typewriter. As a rule the original copy is white and the other copies of various different colors. Of course, the same color always goes to receiving department, the same to cost department, etc. In the reproduction, information can be omitted by blanking out certain portions. Terms and conditions which are printed on the purchase order would not ordinarily be required on copies other than the original and acknowledgment which go to the vendor. Omission of this printing on the other copies is likely to make the order sets cost less.

Reproductions of three routine purchase orders are shown in Figs. 5–7 to 5–9. Since this particular form plays such an important role in the purchasing department, it is discussed and illustrated in many other sections of this handbook. If nothing else, its repetition and emphasis in the following sections demonstrate its commanding position of all forms used by purchasing: Section 19, "Public Purchasing"; Section 20, "Purchasing in Canada"; and Section 25, "Forms and Records."

Supplier's or Seller's Copy

The original copy of purchase order usually goes to the seller or supplier. If it is desirable to omit some information on the seller's copy which is needed on the buyer's copy or other copies, a blank piece of paper is inserted to prevent typing on the original copy. While some purchase orders have an acknowledgment form on the bottom and are so perforated that this bottom portion can be torn off and returned to buyer, this type of acknowledgment has pretty much passed out of use.

Acknowledgment

A review of purchase order forms shows that many concerns do use an acknowledgment copy of a purchase order which is to be signed by the seller and returned to the buyer. This copy is usually identical with the original except that it shows that it is an acknowledgment copy and is a different color from the original.

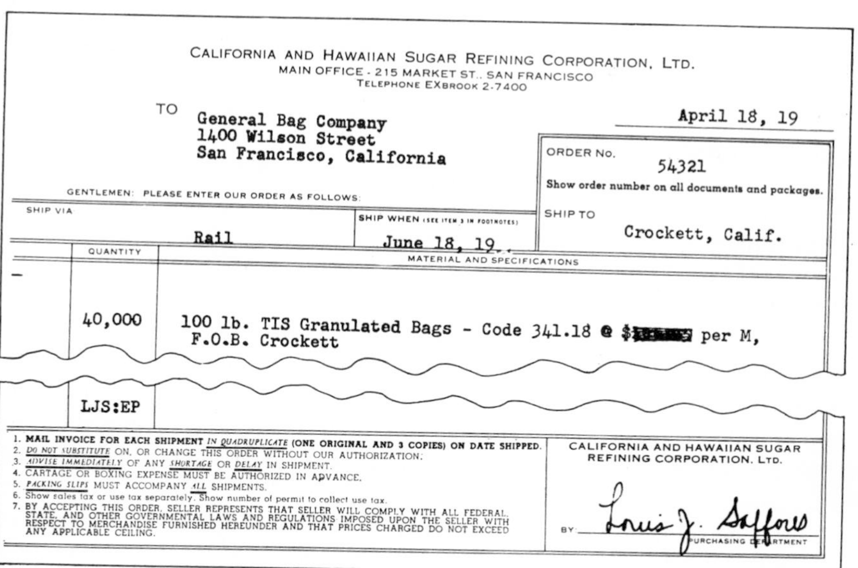

CALIFORNIA AND HAWAIIAN SUGAR REFINING CORPORATION, LTD.
MAIN OFFICE - 215 MARKET ST., SAN FRANCISCO
TELEPHONE EXBROOK 2-7400

TO General Bag Company
1400 Wilson Street
San Francisco, California

April 18, 19

ORDER No. 54321
Show order number on all documents and packages.

GENTLEMEN: PLEASE ENTER OUR ORDER AS FOLLOWS:

SHIP VIA	SHIP WHEN (SEE ITEM 3 IN FOOTNOTES)	SHIP TO
Rail	June 18, 19	Crockett, Calif.

QUANTITY	MATERIAL AND SPECIFICATIONS
40,000	100 lb. TIS Granulated Bags - Code 341.18 @ $[illegible] per M, F.O.B. Crockett
LJS:EP	

1. MAIL INVOICE FOR EACH SHIPMENT *IN QUADRUPLICATE* (ONE ORIGINAL AND 3 COPIES) ON DATE SHIPPED.
2. *DO NOT SUBSTITUTE* ON, OR CHANGE THIS ORDER WITHOUT OUR AUTHORIZATION.
3. *ADVISE IMMEDIATELY* OF ANY *SHORTAGE* OR *DELAY* IN SHIPMENT.
4. CARTAGE OR BOXING EXPENSE MUST BE AUTHORIZED IN ADVANCE.
5. *PACKING SLIPS* MUST ACCOMPANY *ALL* SHIPMENTS.
6. Show sales tax or use tax separately. Show number of permit to collect use tax.
7. BY ACCEPTING THIS ORDER, SELLER REPRESENTS THAT SELLER WILL COMPLY WITH ALL FEDERAL, STATE, AND OTHER GOVERNMENTAL LAWS AND REGULATIONS IMPOSED UPON THE SELLER WITH RESPECT TO MERCHANDISE FURNISHED HEREUNDER AND THAT PRICES CHARGED DO NOT EXCEED ANY APPLICABLE CEILING.

CALIFORNIA AND HAWAIIAN SUGAR REFINING CORPORATION, LTD.

BY Louis J. Saffores
PURCHASING DEPARTMENT

FIG. 5–9. Purchase order form: Illustration 3.

Purchasing Record

One copy is usually retained by the issuing purchasing department as evidence of the purchase and for the purpose of comparing invoice prices and terms if such checking is done in the purchasing department. Provision is often made on the bottom or reverse side of this copy to show dates and amounts of invoices and other information of interest to the purchasing department.

Expediting Copy

In most purchasing organizations it is desirable to make a separate expediting copy of the order filed by date of follow-up. The purchasing copy is used to carry all interim correspondence and information, and the expediting copy is brought up to date by reference to the purchasing copy at the time of follow-up. It may be advisable to block out prices on the expediting copy. Where purchasing departments give the expediting copy fairly rough usage, they have provided for this by having this particular copy on slightly heavier weight paper. Many purchasing departments have special lines printed on the back of the expediting copy for the purpose of delivery records and follow-up history.

Receiving Copy

The receiving department must have information on material scheduled for arrival so that they can be prepared to receive it and count and inspect it on arrival. In some instances, quantities are not indicated on receiving department copies to ensure a careful and accurate count. The most usual practice is to show quantities and to set up other safeguards against careless receiving department performance. Prices usually are blocked out on receiving department copies. Various systems are used, including the use of multiple copies of purchase orders to record part shipments and to avoid the writing of receiving reports.

Accounting Copy

The accounting department usually receives an exact copy of the purchase order for the purpose of compiling commitment reports for the treasurer and for aid in auditing invoices. In many organizations invoices are sent directly to the accounts payable department rather than the purchasing department, and the accounts payable department is responsible for checking the extensions on the invoices.

Some accounting departments check the invoices against the purchase order for specifications, prices, etc., check them against copies of receiving slips which are received in accounts payable department, and approve the invoice for payment. Other accounting departments have the accounts payable department "spot check" invoices against purchase orders and receiving slips but have the routine checking of all invoices against purchase orders and receiving slips done by the invoice section and buyers in the purchasing department. The buyer should be best qualified to determine whether the invoice meets all requirements of the purchase order.

Copy for Requisitioning Department

The individual or department for whom the materials or services are ordered usually receives a copy of the purchase order. This shows that the order has been placed and gives the party requisitioning the material a chance to check the specifications on the order and the delivery date. In some instances, such as a large engineering department, numerous copies of the purchase order may be needed. If so, it is desirable to show the price only on those few copies where such information is necessary and to block out prices on other copies.

Numerical Reference Copy

It is desirable to file one copy of each purchase order in numerical sequence for purposes of identification when the purchase order number is known but not the name of the supplier, and to provide a quick reference not always possible while other copies are in active use. Usually the numerically filed copies are kept for only a limited period of time such as six months.

Some purchasing departments prefer the numerical listing of all purchase orders showing supplier, brief description of material, etc., instead of carrying the copies of purchase orders in a numerical order file.

Revision of Purchase Order

Frequently it becomes necessary to revise a purchase order after it has been issued. (An example is illustrated in Section 25.) Changes in the quantity, price, or description of some items are needed. While some buyers handle this by letters, sending copies to all those holding copy of original order, the preferred method is to write a supplemental purchase order.

In a majority of instances the supplemental or revised order bears the same order number as the original with an affix to indicate that it is not the original. For instance, if on purchase order E-157 of June 4, 1965, one item called for "10 bars cast iron—1¾″ Dia. x 6′ Long—Spec. #13" and it was desired to increase this to 14 bars, a supplemental order would be written. The number of this order could be E-157-1A. It should carry the date it is written and also show that it revises E-157 of June 4, 1965. If a second revision to E-157 were necessary, this could be E-157-2A. Entire or partial cancellations of orders are often made by issuing supplemental or revised orders.

Whenever revision or cancellation of an order is made, it is important that the number and date of revision be shown on the original purchasing record copy of the order. It is also well to show on purchasing copy the reason for the revision and the authority, especially if the change is costly.

PASSING OF TITLE

Under "Terms of Purchase" and "F.o.b. Points," it was stated that the f.o.b. point usually determines when title to the material passes to the buyer. The statements made covered everyday purchasing practices. No mention was made about shortages due to transportation, the obtaining of refunds for shortages, and the transfer of ownership in some of the more unusual contract transactions. See Section 4 for further particulars.

Shortages in Transit

When a buyer receives shipment of materials that do not contain the amount of materials shown on a seller's invoice, his receiving department should promptly notify the transportation company making delivery. That enables the carrier's representative to verify shortage and determine if there was evidence of theft in transit.

If material was sold "f.o.b. seller's plant," or "f.o.b. seller's plant freight allowed to destination," the buyer usually enters the claim for shortage against the transportation company. If material was sold "delivered to buyer's plant," the seller usually makes replacement shipment to cover the shortage and enters claim with the shipper for the shortage.

Claims for material lost in transit are usually handled in the same way as shortage claims. It is true, however, that in some instances either the buyer or the seller handles all claims regardless of the f.o.b. conditions and passing of title. The buyer and seller agree as to which is in better position to handle the claim and act accordingly. This subject is also discussed in Section 4.

Transfer of Ownership

In order to take advantage of foreseen price increases buyers sometimes purchase material and become owners of it before it is delivered to any carrier. The terms of the purchase may call for immediate payment or at some future date. The buyer usually becomes owner of the material as soon as it is invoiced and should see that it is covered by his company's insurance against loss or damage.

Sight Draft

Occasionally it is necessary for a buyer to receive material by paying for it on a sight draft bill of lading. The seller, instead of sending the bill of lading to the buyer, forwards it together with all costs of the shipment to a bank in the buyer's town or city. The bank on receipt of the buyer's payment for the material delivers the bill of lading to the buyer, who may then receive the material.

Some of the reasons a seller insists on this form of selling are (1) his company is short of funds and does not want to wait nearly 30 days for payment; (2) he is in doubt about credit rating of buyer's company; or (3) he may have to put all his sales through his company's bank because of the seller's indebtedness to that bank.

C.o.d. Sales

A c.o.d. sale provides for payment immediately on delivery to the buyer. Some of the reasons for this type of sale are (1) the seller's company may be one which makes all sales c.o.d.; (2) the seller is in doubt about the buyer's credit rating; or (3) the seller may have a ruling that all sales under a certain amount, such as $5, must be c.o.d.

Sale on Approval

A contract to buy goods on approval after "trying them out" is not a sale until the buyer signifies his approval of the goods to the seller. Keeping the goods beyond the time fixed by the "conditional purchase" constitutes a sale and obligates the buyer to pay in accordance with the agreement.

ARBITRATION

Most purchasers and vendors dislike disagreements about performance under purchase or sales agreements and do all that is possible to prevent court action.

Differences of opinion regarding the quality of the seller's material or the cost to the buyer due to the seller's late delivery are two common causes of disagreements. If buyer and seller cannot reach an agreement, it would be well to refer the matter to an arbitrator or group of arbitrators[9] with agreement in advance to abide by the decision rather than to resort to the courts.

[9] Rules and procedures for arbitration are described in Section 28, "Appendix."

PURCHASE ORDER VERSUS SUPPLIER'S INVOICE

An invoice is an itemized statement of merchandise shipped or services rendered to a purchaser or consignee with the quantity, value or prices, and charges shown. It is the seller's charges against the purchaser on the basis of which the seller expects to be paid for materials or services furnished.

Invoice Must Agree with Purchase Order

To the extent that purchase orders contain all the details of each transaction, a great deal of burdensome clerical work is later avoided, particularly when checking invoices. That explains why every purchase order must be complete as to the quantity ordered, description, price, shipping point, whether shipping charges are to be prepaid or collect, and whether terms are net cash or whether a discount is allowed for prompt payment. Each purchase order must be as complete as is consistent with good purchasing practice, taking into consideration all factors, such as the value of the purchase order, urgency of delivery, and date of most recent quotation or previous purchase.

Invoice Checking

Some form of receiving record or receiving report is needed which, when signed and dated by the receiving or stores department, certifies to the purchasing department that the materials have been received and to the purchasing or accounting department that the company is obligated to pay for the material.

In a small company, the receiving department copy of the purchase order or the vendor's packing slip is signed and dated and becomes the only record of the receipt of material.

In medium or large companies, the receiving department has as many copies of the purchase order, or separate multipart receiving forms, as are needed to record the purchase order number, date, vendor's name, quantity, and kind of material received. Copies of each receival are then sent to the purchasing department, and at times to the accounting and inspection departments, with another copy to accompany the material through the plant, and whatever other copies may be required.

In all companies, however, a record of receivals is made. When deliveries requested by the purchase order have been completed, the purchasing department (if not responsible for invoice checking) transfers its purchase order copy from the open to the closed file, and then releases the receiving report to the accounting department so that it can be matched with their copy of the purchase order and with the invoice, when it is received. If the receiving report indicates that only a portion of the quantity ordered has been received, the record of the partial shipment and the date received is to be made on the purchasing department copy of the purchase order. The copy of the order is kept in the open file so that the purchasing department can follow up and expedite shipment of the balance of the order. In this case, it is the accounting department's responsibility to make a complete and careful check of all vendors' invoices by comparing quantities charged with quantities ordered and shipped, prices charged, invoice extensions and totals, terms of payment, f.o.b. point, and the freight charges if they are not paid by the vendor. However, any differences between the purchase order and the invoice are referred to the purchasing department for settlement.

Companies have saved many dollars in invoice audit by finding charges not in accordance with the terms of the purchase order. Another source of savings is through the detection of arithmetical or typing errors in billing extensions from unit prices to invoice totals.

Invoice checking, accomplished by comparing the invoice with the corresponding purchase order and receiving report, is in many cases a function of purchasing departments. Available data indicate that over 65 per cent of purchasing departments are responsible for this function. This plan particularly works well for the small and medium-sized purchasing departments.

The checking of transportation charges to ensure that the correct classifications and rates have been applied, and that the most economical routing and method of transportation have been used, are usually traffic department responsibilities. As transportation charges on incoming materials represent a large item of purchasing cost, the traffic function is often a part of the responsibility of the head of the purchasing department.

Settlement of Invoices

When invoices from vendors are received, one or more copies may have been requested. It is important that only the original invoice copy be used for approving payment to the vendor. This original invoice is identified with a rubber stamp or printed attachment providing spaces for entering and initialing each of the necessary verifications before the bill is paid. This rubber stamp usually includes spaces for:

1. Date material received
2. Quantity and quality O.K.
3. Price O.K.
4. Extensions checked

5. F.o.b.
6. Terms
7. Account

These clerical functions are accomplished by comparing the invoice with the corresponding purchase order and receiving report. By providing spaces for initialing by those who check these invoices, the invoice becomes a certified document supporting the expenditure of the company's money.

PURCHASE ORDER DRAFT SYSTEM

A relatively new method of reducing the cost of handling small orders is the use of the purchase order draft system. Potential users should evaluate their accounting department as well as their purchasing department systems and procedures before deciding whether the system will reduce their costs. Basically the system is a simple method of combining a purchase order with a blank check to pay for the material described in the purchase order. The blank check can be either a bank draft or a regular check. The simplicity is deceptive because the underlying controls of a properly designed system are equal to those in the more conventional methods. The benefits to the buyer are:

1. Reduction in total paper work resulting from purchasing department action
2. Standard, simple method for issuing releases against blanket orders
3. Increase in cash discounts
4. Substantial reduction in back orders
5. Potential use in the automation of small dollar purchases

From the seller's standpoint the benefits are:

1. Immediate cash payment for materials sold
2. Reduction or elimination of internal paper work related to the sale
3. Opportunity to eliminate or reduce the discounting of his own bills to obtain operating capital

Usually the purchasing agent is delegated authority by the accounting or finance department to sign the checks. In a large purchasing department, buyers may also be delegated such authority. The system lends itself to computer preparation of the orders, and the check is mechanically signed when used in this manner.

The controls of this system include a post-audit of all invoices; prenumbering of both the purchase order and the check; a printed statement on the reverse side of the check that the check can be deposited only to he account of the payee; a printed limitation on the face of the check o a maximum amount such as $1,000; limitation of the period during which the check is valid, such as 90 days from the date on the face of he check. The system is usually used for purchases from vendors who ave a past history of reliability and satisfactory performance and who will ship the order complete. It is almost foolproof when used as a release gainst blanket orders.

Variations of the system include the use of separate checks which may e pasted to standard purchase orders at the discretion of the purchasing gent, thereby converting such orders into purchase order drafts. See ection 19, "Public Purchasing," for a further variation of this system.

An even more novel application is the use of a combination requisiion-purchase order form which is preaddressed by Addressograph plates nd given to selected vendors of noninventory items such as automotive epair parts, saw-blade sharpening, electric motor repairs, and ready-mix oncrete. In this application the vendor, who has been selected by the purhasing department, upon receiving a telephone order from an authorized mployee of the buyer, lists the items on the form and retains one copy or his record. The vendor delivers the material using the prepared form n place of a delivery ticket. The buyer's receiving department takes ossession of the material, retains one copy of the form, and forwards the emaining copies to the purchasing department. The purchasing department then prepares a separate blank-check form, pastes it to the purchase rder, and returns the purchase order to the vendor. The vendor extends and totals the order, inserts the correct amount on the check, and ays himself.

There are other methods of using a check payment system. One of hese involves computing the exact amount of the charge and then writng the check to that amount. As in the purchase order draft system, the heck is a part of the purchase order form. This method requires a high egree of accuracy on the part of both the buyer and the seller; otherwise, there will be more, rather than less, paper handling, in order to alance the account through refunds, additional payments, or exchange f goods.

Another method is payment issued immediately upon receipt of maerials. In this system a check is also part of the purchase order form, but he check portion of the form is not mailed to the supplier when the urchase order is mailed. The buyer negotiates the purchase, including he exact charges. When the material is received, it is checked for corectness, and the check is immediately completed and forwarded to the upplier. This check is issued by authorized personnel either in purhasing or in some other department, but not necessarily by the accounts payable group. This variation provides fast payment to the supplier and reduces some of the paper work normally involved in paying an invoice.

Under any of the check payment order systems, a separate bank account is usually maintained to assure strict accounting. The basic advantage of check payment systems is the reduction of workload in processing invoices for the small-order and the nonrecurring types of purchase. If the limitation to the face amount of the check is set at $1,000, most

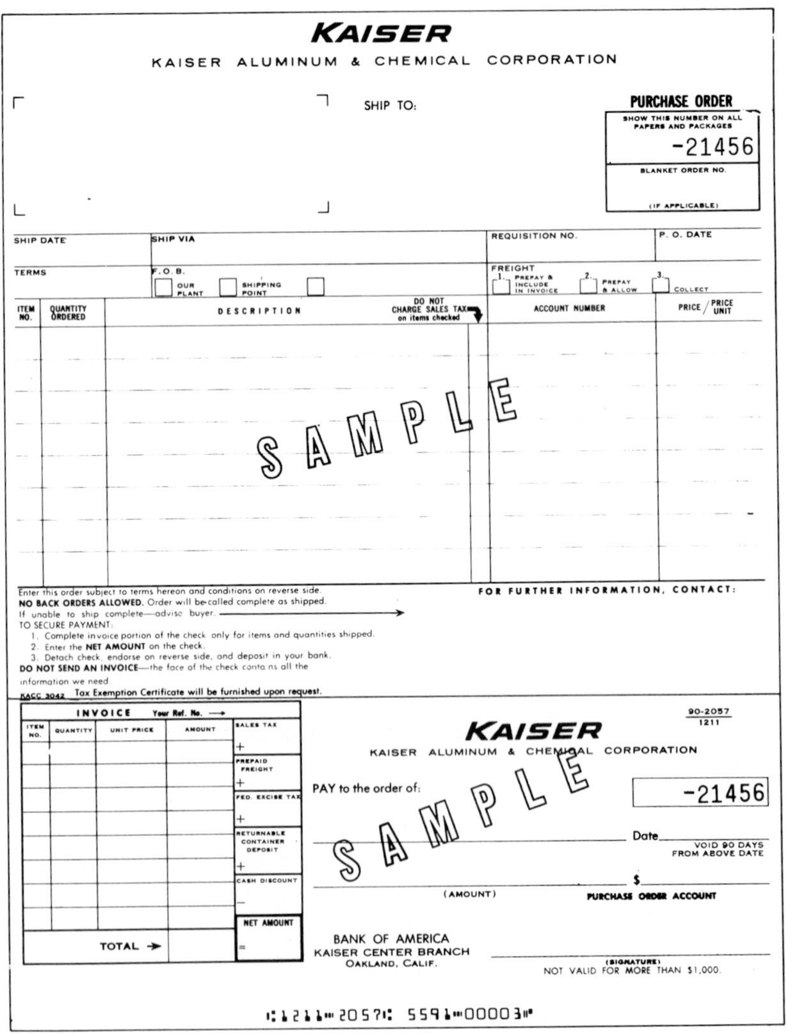

KAISER

KAISER ALUMINUM & CHEMICAL CORPORATION

SHIP TO:

PURCHASE ORDER
SHOW THIS NUMBER ON ALL PAPERS AND PACKAGES
-21456
BLANKET ORDER NO.
(IF APPLICABLE)

SHIP DATE	SHIP VIA	REQUISITION NO.	P. O. DATE
TERMS	F. O. B. ☐ OUR PLANT ☐ SHIPPING POINT ☐	FREIGHT 1. ☐ PREPAY & INCLUDE IN INVOICE 2. ☐ PREPAY & ALLOW	3. ☐ COLLECT

ITEM NO.	QUANTITY ORDERED	DESCRIPTION	DO NOT CHARGE SALES TAX on items checked	ACCOUNT NUMBER	PRICE / PRICE UNIT

SAMPLE

Enter this order subject to terms hereon and conditions on reverse side.
NO BACK ORDERS ALLOWED. Order will be called complete as shipped.
If unable to ship complete—advise buyer.
TO SECURE PAYMENT:
1. Complete invoice portion of the check only for items and quantities shipped.
2. Enter the **NET AMOUNT** on the check.
3. Detach check, endorse on reverse side, and deposit in your bank.

DO NOT SEND AN INVOICE—the face of the check contains all the information we need.
KACC 3042 **Tax Exemption Certificate will be furnished upon request.**

FOR FURTHER INFORMATION, CONTACT:

INVOICE Your Ref. No. →

ITEM NO.	QUANTITY	UNIT PRICE	AMOUNT	
				SALES TAX +
				PREPAID FREIGHT +
				FED. EXCISE TAX +
				RETURNABLE CONTAINER DEPOSIT +
				CASH DISCOUNT −
				NET AMOUNT
	TOTAL →			=

90-2057
1211

KAISER

KAISER ALUMINUM & CHEMICAL CORPORATION

PAY to the order of: -21456

SAMPLE

Date
VOID 90 DAYS FROM ABOVE DATE

(AMOUNT) $
PURCHASE ORDER ACCOUNT

BANK OF AMERICA
KAISER CENTER BRANCH
OAKLAND, CALIF.

(SIGNATURE)
NOT VALID FOR MORE THAN $1,000.

⑆1211⑈2057⑆ 5591⑈00003⑈

FIG. 5–10. The combination purchase order with attached blank-check form. Prenumbered-snap-out. Terms and conditions on back of this form are shown in Fig. 25–4. (*Reproduced by permission.*)

companies could apply such a system to between 80 and 90 per cent of all purchase orders issued and would find that this volume of paper work covers approximately 15 per cent of the purchasing-dollar commitments.

A form combining the purchase order and blank check is illustrated by Fig. 5–10. Its printed limitation is $1,000; however, this figure was $200 when the system was started by the company. The separate check form used by the County of Los Angeles is shown in Fig. 19–16.

BLANKET PURCHASE ORDERS

"Blanket purchase order" is a rather broad term frequently used to cover a number of different types of agreements: price agreements, standard orders, open orders, open-end orders, staggered delivery orders, requisition orders, scheduled orders, orders of intent, and open-end contracts. The basic differences between these various agreements are minor. In general, a blanket order may be described as an incomplete contract with a given vendor to purchase certain items from that vendor. The blanket order will normally spell out all terms, conditions, delivering instructions, and other constant information, including prices, for a specified period of time. The blanket order may or may not be backed up by a formal contract.

A blanket order is *incomplete* in that it is not usually an authorization to ship anything. Only when the specified vendor receives a bona fide shipping requisition or other type of release, written or verbal, does the act of purchasing become effective.

Blanket orders may cover nearly every type of material from chemicals and inks to bread and window-washing services. Reasons for using blanket orders and the typical manner in which they assist in the purchasing function are:

1. Reduce paper work on those items bought repetitively.
2. Provide a means for obtaining the advantages of quantity purchasing power. The total quantity representing an organization's purchasing power on a given item might come from combining the requirements of various plants or from merely determining the total requirements for a given year at a single facility.
3. Decentralize the actual act of ordering materials on a day-by-day basis while maintaining centralized control over the selection of vendors and the establishment of prices, terms, and other conditions.
4. Reduce the amount of routine information exchanged through the purchasing department after an order has been placed. Since all terms, prices, and conditions are present, the feeling here is that the physical

checking of invoices and the receiving of information become an accounting responsibility.

5. Release professional purchasing people from the tasks of handling repetitive, routine transactions. By covering such transactions in the mechanics of the blanket order, purchasing agents and buyers can then concentrate their efforts on nonroutine acquisitions, with only periodic reviews of the various blanket orders.
6. Other:
   a. Provide price protection for a specified period of time.
   b. Minimize in-plant inventories. Vendors receiving blanket orders are expected to maintain an inventory on the items covered.
   c. Provide organized procedure for reviewing purchases of groups of commodities on a regular basis.

Under any blanket-order system the procedure for establishing and instituting the form should be such that purchasing will maintain its basic responsibility for providing materials as needed and controlling the dollars spent for them. This control need not be lost when purchasing delegates authority to another department to issue releases directly to the supplier. One copy of the release form should be sent to purchasing, enabling the department to maintain a clear record of the purchases throughout the life of the order. Normally, blanket orders should not be used for items involving large sums of money if the needs and schedules can be rather accurately determined. Maximum benefits are achieved when they are used to eliminate a large number of rush and routine small dollar-value transactions.

BIBLIOGRAPHY

Same as for Section 4, "Legal Influences in Purchasing."

Other books on purchase orders are listed in Section 26, "Library and Catalog File."

Additional samples of purchase order forms are illustrated in Section 25, "Forms and Records."

SECTION 6

ETHICAL PRACTICES IN PURCHASING

Editor

William W. Crawford, Vice-president—Purchasing, United States Steel Corporation, Pittsburgh, Pennsylvania

Associate Editors

M. D. Coe, Director of Purchases, The Stanley Works, New Britain, Connecticut

F. A. Coenen, Director of Purchases, Rex Chainbelt, Inc., Milwaukee, Wisconsin

Gaylord E. Powell, Director of Procurement, Xerox Corporation, Rochester, New York

Ethics have a prominent place in the conduct of industrial and public purchasing. Problems of ethics are ever present in commercial transactions and must be handled in a sound and generally acceptable manner if the company and individual involved are to prosper and command respect in the trade.

CONCEPT OF ETHICS

Consciously or unconsciously, man began to develop a code of ethics very early in his development into a civilized individual. He began to respect the rights of others, not to steal, not to lie, to have his word accepted as reliable, and to cooperate with others in joint endeavors such as hunting and fishing. As trade developed, certain customs and practices grew up and were accepted by the business community. These were later recorded as laws to cover many situations. Through all this history, man has had to understand the difference between what is right and what is wrong. This in turn has meant that a concept of what is ethical and what is unethical would evolve. The daily decisions by countless persons as to what is the right or wrong course of action in all of life's varied situations have been the cornerstone of man's tremendous progress and accomplishment.

Ethical standards vary from person to person, business to business, country to country, and from one people to another. However, in the United States and in most areas of the world where the Christian religion predominates, fundamental Christian principles as outlined in the Bible establish the basic ethical standards practiced in business. It, of course must be understood that the study and application of ethics is not an exact science. Actually, it is a very inexact science, because no one has ever recorded a comprehensive set of ethical standards that any significant number of people have agreed to abide by in every detail. Each individual is inclined to have his own ideas as to just what is ethical and what is not.

However, as the writer views this subject, the best starting point for guidance on ethical practices is the Golden Rule: "Do unto others as you would have them do unto you." This advice has stood the test of time and should be reflected upon when in doubt about an ethical question. One cannot escape the fact that ethical standards are necessary to organized human endeavors. This is true from both a moral and a practical business standpoint. A businessman must know or be able to assume approximately what other businessmen's ethical standards are. This requires that one's action on ethical questions be steady and consistent. Recognition of this need is found in the business policies charted by many successful companies in phrases such as "develop and maintain public good will, respect the valid rights of others, promote mutual understanding between management and employees, make equitable set tlement of all claims." Vacillation undermines the confidence of one's associates and destroys the stature of the individual involved.

Code of Ethics

Purchasing people must be above the suspicion of unethical behavior at all times and under all circumstances. To do this requires strict adherence to a sound code of ethics. Such a code has been developed by the National Association of Purchasing Agents.[1] This code is as follows:

1. To consider, first, the interest of his company in all transactions and to carry out and believe in its established policies.
2. To be receptive to competent counsel from his colleagues and to be guided by such counsel without impairing the dignity and responsibility of his office.
3. To buy without prejudice, seeking to obtain the maximum ultimate value for each dollar of expenditure.
4. To strive consistently for knowledge of the materials and processes of manufacture, and to establish practical methods for the conduct of his office.
5. To subscribe to and work for honesty and truth in buying and selling, and to denounce all forms and manifestations of commercial bribery.
6. To accord a prompt and courteous reception, so far as conditions will permit, to all who call on a legitimate business mission.
7. To respect his obligations and to require that obligations to him and his company be respected, consistent with good business ethics.
8. To avoid sharp practice.
9. To counsel and assist fellow purchasing agents in the performance of their duties, whenever occasion permits.
10. To cooperate with all organizations and individuals engaged in activities designed to enhance the development and standing of purchasing.

PERSONAL ETHICAL CONSIDERATIONS

Honesty and integrity are vital. Those with whom a buyer is associated must be satisfied from personal experience or general reputation that the individual is reliable. The background and environment of an individual from birth through his business career have a bearing on his

[1] Full statement of this code, also advocated by the Canadian Association of Purchasing Agents, is located in Section 28, "Appendix," under NAPA Standards of Conduct. Also see codes of other associations in Section 28.

ability to measure up to the fundamentals of honesty and integrity. This is a significant matter to consider both at time of potential employment and promotion.

A buyer should have dignity in a pleasant and informal way. He should reflect the policies of his concern, assuming always that he is employed by an honorable concern. This rules out highhandedness regardless of the circumstances. It also means "prima donnas" do not fit.

Fairness and impartiality are vital to sound ethical practices. Everyone calling on a purchasing department should know that the treatment he receives will be neither better nor worse, but just the same as that given to all other callers.

People employed in purchasing must avoid compromising situations. A buyer cannot use one supplier's summer cottage for a week-end stay in the mountains without other suppliers concluding that this particular supplier will get an advantage when the buyer must make decisions affecting them all.

A buyer must rely on a sense of what is right rather than whether something is legal or illegal. Actions not only must *be* right, but must *look* right to other people. A buyer should be conscious at all times of the necessity of keeping himself above suspicion.

An excellent way to keep oneself above suspicion is to evidence character and good judgment, thereby setting a good example. A supervisor in purchasing work must be meticulous in seeing that he "practices what he preaches." The questionable relationship or action sooner or later reduces the stature of the individual and his company, and is reflected in the attitude of the personnel he supervises.

Numerous ethical questions arise in connection with business entertainment. However, one must be careful not to confuse manners, which concern social conduct, with ethics, which concern moral principles. Many phases of business entertainment involve nothing more than established social conduct for getting a job done. Examples would be meeting a business associate for lunch or dinner in order to become better acquainted, to discuss a lengthy business matter, or to bring up a particularly difficult subject under informal circumstances. On the other hand, entertainment solely for the sake of entertainment and particularly on a repetitive basis goes beyond acceptable social conduct for people engaged in purchasing work and will be treated later in this section under "Questionable Influences." Business entertainment of the normal type should be reciprocated at the expense of the employer; in other words, as an expense account item. If management cannot be convinced that this is proper, it is vital that the buyer avoid accepting the attitude of some people that a buyer should be entertained and not do any entertaining.

Fortunately, this attitude on the part of management is rapidly giving way to a more enlightened position. However, if reciprocating legitimate business entertainment at company expense is not approved, an adequate job at reasonable cost can often be done in one's home. An example would be a buffet dinner and bridge for business associates to whom a buyer owes return entertainment.

OBLIGATIONS TO COMPANY

An employer is entitled to undivided loyalty from all employees, and particularly from those charged with purchasing the goods and services necessary to operate the business. There is no excuse for volunteering information concerning the employer's business to outsiders unless the employer stands to gain thereby. For example, revealing total requirements of a commodity purchased in speculative markets can result in an unnecessary price advance to the detriment of the employer. Such information is the property of the employer, and there is no ethical consideration involved in declining to reveal it. On the other hand, if a change in source of supply is planned or a substitute material is to be used or the user decides to produce the material himself, it is only fair that the current supplier be given as much advance notice as possible so that he will have a reasonable amount of time in which to try to establish another outlet or make other arrangements.

An employer is entitled to ethical conduct by responsible employees at all times regardless of whether in the office or away from the office. For example, information that would not be revealed to a supplier in the office must not be divulged under the more informal circumstances of a cocktail party or other social event. Buyers are people and cannot be expected to divorce themselves wholly from their business associates after business hours. However, on the other hand, the amenities of social contact should not include conduct incompatible with the employer's interests.

It is unethical to disagree with company policies in public. The place to discuss and thrash out such matters is with one's supervisors or in one's own management councils, but not elsewhere. Although it is not necessarily an ethical matter, it is sound advice to stand your ground in your own organization if you have the facts and believe your position is right.

A purchasing employee must not have outside interests that conflict with his obligations to his employer. An example of such a conflicting interest would be a buyer having part ownership in a supplier. Obviously, one cannot serve two masters simultaneously. The ownership of a supplier's stock is only questionable where the per cent of ownership is significant (say 5 per cent or over) and the volume of business involved (say 10 per cent or over) is substantial in relation to the supplier's total volume. For example, there would be nothing wrong with a buyer owning 100 shares of stock of a large automobile manufacturer even though he might buy trucks from this company. On the other hand, it would be ethically wrong for him or his family to own 100 shares of a coal company having 1,000 shares of stock outstanding if his purchases of coal from that company had any significant bearing on the profitableness of the business and consequent ability to pay dividends.

OBLIGATIONS TO SUPPLIERS

Exchange of money for material or services is the fundamental purpose of the salesman's developing relations with the buyer. The determination of whether such exchange will occur is an exclusive right of the buyer.

Selling is merely the art of influencing a buyer to do what the salesman wants—to make a decision in his favor. The principal influences upon a buyer should be those considerations which reflect to the benefit of the company for which he works, but the range of such considerations will be dependent upon the authority and quality of the particular buyer involved. Modern purchasing has extended these considerations beyond the factors of price and delivery. Today's buyer is vitally interested in changes in specifications or substitute commodities which will reduce costs or improve performance. He is imbued with the philosophy of saving while spending.

The day of classifying buyers as "order placers" is disappearing. Large-scale introduction of new and better commodities and processes resulting from technological developments in recent decades has expanded the capacity of the buyer to contribute to the profitability of his company. This change in the role of purchasing has had direct impact on the buyer-seller relationship, which is no longer governed exclusively by the fact that the buyer has something the salesman wants. The buyer now recognizes that the supplier's technical knowledge can be utilized to reduce costs related to purchased goods and services and he knows that management will judge buying performance on the basis of his ability to capitalize on such knowledge.

Today's buyer-seller relationship is based upon mutual dependence and cooperation. Shortages of supplies and equipment in recent years have also contributed to the buyer's dependence upon harmonious relations with suppliers. He has been compelled to attempt to influence suppliers to furnish materials required for operations of his company under conditions of extreme shortages.

The relationship of buyer to seller evokes many ethical considerations. Although it is impossible to prescribe the most ethical courses of action to govern all the situations arising from this relationship, it is important that the buyer examine and understand the ethical significance of certain repetitive circumstances which make up this relationship. Recognition of ethical obligations is primary; determination of how to meet these obligations is secondary.

The first obligation to a supplier is to give his representatives a prompt and courteous reception. Of course buyers may have to schedule their interviews and budget their time, but a salesman's time is also of value. Refusal to let a salesman tell his story or keeping visitors waiting unduly long, if often indulged in, becomes more than bad manners. Such action disregards the rights and feelings of others and would be classed as unethical.

Information furnished suppliers or potential suppliers should be reliable. It is unethical to mislead a supplier. An example would be indicating to a supplier that if he takes an initial order for a large quantity on a cost basis he can expect repeat orders at a satisfactory profit margin when actually the buyer merely plans to drop that particular supplier after the first order is filled. There are those who consider such practices smart and shrewd. However, they are not only unethical, but in the long run result in so much unfavorable reaction that the buyer's ability to obtain aggressive competition on his requirements is seriously impaired. Moreover, if a buyer cannot supply information requested by a supplier, he should say so frankly, but diplomatically. Furnishing erroneous information in order to avoid handling difficult questions is a sign of weakness and inexperience on the part of the buyer.

Every reasonable consideration should be given to the supplier's commodities and he should be told honestly whether the company can use them or not. He is entitled to a frank "no" if that is the answer rather than an answer which leaves him hopeful for business at a later date when the buyer never really intends to buy because the commodity in question is too costly for application to his business or for some other reason is of no use to him.

Unreasonable demands for service should be avoided. For example, a buyer should not urge a supplier to cut his delivery promise unless he actually needs the item prior to the quoted delivery date. If it is continually demonstrated to the salesman that such requests are well considered before they are made, he will learn to take them seriously and will become a valuable ally in times of emergency.

Sending a supplier an inquiry generally implies that, if his offering of quality and price is the best and his delivery is acceptable, he would get the order. If it is known in advance that the purchaser would not buy from a certain supplier, then to send him an inquiry borders on giving misleading information and is unethical.

It is unethical to betray confidences entered into with suppliers. If a buyer is not willing to live up to such confidences, they should be declined when proposed. For example, a supplier may be in a position to offer an extra discount on a particular lot of his production with the understanding that subsequent sales will be at the regular price. In order to avoid embarrassment with those customers unable to place orders at the time, he may propose that the special offer be kept confidential. If this relationship cannot be maintained, it should not be entered into in the first place.

The buyer has an ethical obligation to protect unique and novel ideas furnished by suppliers. This is not only ethical, but very practical as suppliers capable of submitting such ideas will soon stop doing so unless security of the information is maintained. For example, suppose a conveying system is to be purchased and an inquiry based on the owner's specifications is sent to four bidders. Three of the bidders quote as requested. The fourth bidder quotes as requested, but also offers an alternate which significantly reduces the installation cost and results in a faster as well as simpler and more dependable system. Obviously, the fourth bidder has offered something unique and novel for which he is entitled to consideration. If the prospective buyer takes these ideas and asks others to quote on them, he is violating the relationship established with the fourth bidder who will not only feel that he is being treated unethically, but who will probably not make such suggestions in the future.

On the other hand, in the case of repetitive items, it is not necessary for a buyer to perpetuate a monopolistic position which the supplier may have achieved through development of a design or formula or product best adapted to the buyer's need. The supplier may have spent substantial sums in preliminary development and engineering services and is legitimately entitled to recoup them. A fair arrangement should be worked out giving the supplier all the business on such items for a year or so, depending on the quantities involved, so that he is well rewarded for his ingenuity as well as reimbursed for his experimental and developmental costs in addition to normal production profits. The business can then be opened to general competition with a resultant lowering of price since the development costs will not be reflected in new prices. The original supplier will have benefited from his preferred position, will already have developed production know-how, and will be a step ahead of the field. He may also have succeeded in totally depreciating his patterns, dies, and tooling during the protected period. Release of the supplier's process on this basis would be justified, unless there are specific agreements that this will not be done.

Fair-minded buyers do not maintain that "the customer is always right." It is especially important in negotiating settlement of claims that buyers do not arbitrarily use the weight of their company's purchases to enforce unfair settlements on their suppliers. On the other hand, one must be alert to the unethical supplier who will submit a particularly favorable proposition in order to "get his foot in the door," and start negotiating for "extras."

In general, anything that is worth securing for trial is worth buying, unless the cost of the paper work exceeds the cost of the article to be tested. Therefore, a buyer should avoid imposing upon suppliers for free sample lots or free demonstration units. Free samples can also give rise to other problems such as appropriation for personal use. An example would be hack-saw blades finding their way into a home workshop.

Personal and friendly relationships with salesmen are desirable. However, a buyer must remain impartial in all business phases of such relationships. This requires a broad perspective and the ability to act from a detached viewpoint. It is a measure of the "big man" against the "little man." There must be no "inside information" to anyone. All suppliers should receive identical information. Giving one supplier "an edge" is unethical. An example would be agreeing with one bidder that it is not mandatory to hold to the $\frac{1}{32}$ in. tolerance limits on certain castings and that anything within $\frac{1}{16}$ in. tolerance will be accepted. Obviously, such information would give that bidder an advantage over his competitors.

Being impartial means treating everyone alike. If one supplier asks for an extension of time, then it is proper that all bidders be notified that they can have the same extension. If one supplier or contractor asks for and receives a clarification or interpretation of a specification forming part of an inquiry, then the same clarification or interpretation should be given to all bidders.

A buyer must take all reasonable steps to safeguard confidential information within his own responsibility as well as elsewhere in his company. This includes suppliers' prices. Specific and comprehensive procedures should be established designating the persons who should receive restricted information and their responsibility for keeping it confidential. An example would be test results on competitors' products. Such tests may be conducted solely to establish certain data pertinent to one application. However, if the information were inadvertently divulged to the trade, it could be misinterpreted to the serious damage of a manufacturer whose product might be excellent for most applications.

A buyer should provide his suppliers with the opportunity to correct their honest mistakes without being penalized. For example, a supplier quotes a $1\frac{1}{2}$-ton dump truck at $346.30 when he obviously means $3,463. It would certainly be unethical to try to hold the bidder to the erroneous price.

However, the buyer should not be expected to pay more than he would otherwise have paid just because he is willing to let a supplier correct an error. If correction of a mistake placed this particular supplier's quotation considerably above the price quoted by other acceptable suppliers, then the order should go to the seller offering the best value; or if the order has already been placed and changing vendors is not feasible, then correction could be allowed up to the next lowest bidder. This would keep the buyer from losing money and would give some measure of relief to the one who made the error.

There are various ethical considerations involved in handling the negotiations prior to award of business. Negotiations concern themselves with such matters as quality, price, escalation, terms and conditions, delivery, f.o.b. point, insurance, packaging, and freight allowance. There are various methods employed in placing business. Among them are sealed bids, competitive bids without further negotiation, and competitive bids with a round of negotiation just prior to award. Regardless of the system followed, it is considered unethical to reveal competitive prices and then in effect "shop" for the lowest price. This practice is sometimes referred to as putting the business "up for grabs." A bidder has every right to expect that his price will not only be kept confidential, but that any negotiation of his initial price will be pointed toward finding more economical ways of accomplishing the work or producing the product rather than squeezing his profit margin, unless the buyer can demonstrate that the contemplated profit margin is unreasonable. It is unethical for a buyer to furnish information to a bidder regarding price, terms, or other factors that would influence or assure that bidder of securing the business. Freedom of competition among qualified sources promotes healthy business relationships. Giving certain bidders "second chances" after all proposals have been evaluated should not be condoned as an ethical practice. In this connection it should be mentioned that the reputation of fairness is a very valuable business asset.

Negotiations should be approached as a mutual problem, in the correct solution of which both buyer and seller have an equal interest. Beyond having such an attitude, each buyer should conduct his company's business with the same careful attention and interest he would give to buying for his own family. In so doing, he will appreciate that there is no such thing as "something for nothing."

In addition to ethical practices by buyers, it is well to remember that "it takes two to make a bargain." In other words, deal with ethical suppliers. Sellers have definite obligations to buyers. A buyer should be able to trust his suppliers. Suppliers who promote unethical relationships and situations are dangerous and should be avoided, for in the long run it will mean higher prices for poorer quality than available from ethical suppliers. The old idea of *caveat emptor* (let the buyer beware) is proving unsound. Sellers must tell the truth if they are to be successful over an extended period of time.

QUESTIONABLE INFLUENCES

Anything of a personal nature flowing from a supplier to a buyer, which it is hoped would result in favored treatment of that supplier in preference to another, is improper. The degree of impropriety varies tremendously. Common sense and judgment must often be called upon to judge specific situations. There simply are no specific rules or standards that can be applied generally. Probably as good a yardstick as any to use in evaluating questionable situations is "What would my reaction be if I were an outsider and were exposed to all the facts of the case?" Of course, different individuals will arrive at different conclusions in such matters, but there seems to be no way to avoid this situation, since no two individuals have exactly the same ethical standards. However, as a general statement, the higher or more "strait-laced" one's ethical standards, the more general will be one's acceptance by his business associates.

Lunches or dinners with suppliers can be entirely acceptable and desirable experiences if they serve as vehicles to facilitate normal business objectives. However, if they become a steady thing with one or two suppliers and thereby fall into the category of "free drinks and food," they become questionable influences and should be avoided. In this connection, it should be mentioned that a salesman who notices alcohol on a buyer's breath during an afternoon call may wonder if the buyer had lunch with a competitor who possibly obtained confidential information over the lunch table. Obviously, the cause for wonderment should be avoided.

Cocktail parties and buffet lunches or dinners at business conventions can be either constructive mediums through which to expand contacts and friendships or places where a buyer stays too long to the embarrassment of both himself and his company. Each individual must handle this problem for himself. However, if he will keep prominently in mind that he is participating to widen his associations and knowledge, rather than to get a "free lunch," he will reap the benefits and avoid the pitfalls.

Buyers making even the most desirable educational visits to suppliers' plants may become questionable recipients of favors, particularly when *all-expense trips* to distant points are involved for *both* the *buyer* and his *wife.* Falling in this same classification are sizable cash awards to winners of supplier-sponsored contests exclusively for purchasing men and women, unless, of course, the prize becomes the property of the company for which the buyer works.

Gifts of any type at any time from a supplier to a buyer are very questionable. Stated in a very general way, there are probably no such gifts that are not questionable. However, advertising novelties such as pencils, pens, lighters, calendars, and wallets are generally acceptable without raising an ethical question. Of course, even here one must use judgment. For example, a solid gold pen and pencil set would be very questionable.

Examples of No-gift Christmas Letters. Because of the difficulty of establishing standards on what is acceptable and what is not when gifts other than advertising novelties are involved, many purchasing managers are formally asking suppliers not to make gifts to buying personnel. Here are four examples which have been used successfully to get the point across firmly and politely:

EXAMPLE 1 of a "no-gift" card mailed each October to suppliers of the Sacramento Municipal Utility District:[2]

> While custom and precedent and sheer friendliness in the past have prompted some suppliers to send gifts and other tokens of value to employees of the District at this season of the year, we request that this practice be discontinued.
>
> It is felt that your cooperation in this matter will best serve our mutual interests and the true spirit of Christmas.

EXAMPLE 2 of a "no-gift" letter signed by the president of the firm:[3]

> To All of Our Suppliers:
>
> Again—Holiday Greetings from All of us at Fred Meyer, Inc.
>
> Again—we request your observance and assistance in respecting our policy of no holiday gifts or undue lavish entertainment.
>
> High quality, proper service and profitable cost price (to you and us) is the solid basis for a lasting business relationship and a lasting friendship.

[2] By permission from Sacramento Municipal Utility District, Sacramento, California.

[3] By permission from Fred Meyer, Inc., Portland, Oregon.

So again, to emphasize, no gifts please to any employee of Fred Meyer, Inc.

We all wish you and your firm a pleasant and profitable New Year with Good Will toward men.

EXAMPLE 3 of a "no-gift" letter:[4]

In the past, the fine spirit of Christmas has prompted some of our business friends and others to express good will and appreciation by sending various forms of gifts to members of our organization.

Without being presumptuous, and in the utmost spirit of friendliness and good will, we would like to suggest that you omit the names of our employees from any Christmas lists you may contemplate.

A card or letter will serve as well to express holiday greetings and help us maintain impartial, but cordial relations.

EXAMPLE 4 of another approach:

This is a frank and friendly word about the annual problem of business Christmas gifts.

We thought it might be helpful if we dropped our supplier friends a little reminder concerning our policy, with a word or two of explanation.

We have chosen to buy your product or service over the year solely because of its excellence, and we confidently hope to do so in the future. Product excellence is the best gift we can receive at any time. Hence, at this time of year, we know you will refrain from presenting seasonal gifts of a more personal nature to those of us you meet and work with.

Actually, it's a policy based on our own feeling—which we know you share—that the best thing companies like ours can do for their customers is to deliver a high quality product at a fair price and then service it with the utmost efficiency and courtesy.

As Christmas rolls around again, we would like to express our appreciation for the very satisfactory business relationship we have enjoyed with you during the year, and we extend our very best wishes for a happy and prosperous New Year.

Trend in Christmas Gifts. The giving of Christmas gifts to customers seems to be firmly embedded in American business life. To some, the practice raises serious ethical problems. To others, any profound discussion of the Christmas gift problem is "much ado about nothing." The purchasing agent, who plays such an important role in the distribution of business, is naturally a target when it comes to Christmas giving. Therefore *Purchasing* magazine asked purchasing executives in all parts of the country for their views on the subject. Their combined answers follow.

[4] By permission from Research Institute of America, Inc., New York City.

Question	*Increase*	*Decrease*	*No Change*
Have you noticed an increase or decrease in the number of suppliers giving or attempting to give Christmas gifts to purchasing personnel during the past few years?	14%	41%	45%
Has there been an increase in the value of the gifts that are given or offered?	13%	23%	64%

In addition, 12 per cent stated that gift *giving* as practiced in industry posed a serious ethical problem, 50 per cent reported it was merely a general nuisance for all concerned, and 38 per cent indicated it was not a problem at all.

Gifts Other than Christmas. The question of gifts to buying personnel arises most prominently at Christmas; however, there are suppliers who will take almost anything as an excuse to proffer a gift to a buyer. Easter, Thanksgiving, and birthdays are examples. There can be no question but that such gifts have only one motivating force: buying a favored position as a supplier. Improper gifts should be returned. Silent acceptance will probably be interpreted as approval of the practice. Although the subject of gifts to buying personnel is a complex one, it is not a difficult one if approached in a firm, yet diplomatic, manner. It is largely a matter of applying clear ethical principles. The individual who protests that the subject is too tough to handle is only rationalizing his basic weakness to succumb to temptation. This points up the fundamental personnel problem of selecting individuals of high integrity for purchasing work, and then compensating them on a basis fully commensurate with their responsibilities.

At times, suppliers will offer buyers the use of certain facilities such as automobiles, airplanes, boats, lodges, or private clubs. Although the use of these facilities often raises many eyebrows and cannot be justified on a business basis, it should not be automatically assumed that the practice is wrong. Suppliers often provide such facilities as a convenience to get the buyer to visit a particular plant or mine which is or can become a source of his needs. The buyer gains through wider knowledge as a result of such visits, and the facilities are merely part of the supplier's selling tools. There are occasions on which plant or mine visits would be impossible because of time or other factors if such facilities as those mentioned above were not made available. On the other hand, if the use of such facilities is designed only or primarily for "having a good time" or avoiding personal expense that would otherwise accrue, it is ethically wrong and should be avoided. It should be mentioned that the buyer has the normal social obligation of reciprocating favors that are extended in business matters. His employer should see that if he is obligated to accept such favors in the line of his employment, then he must in some manner be able to repay them. Such an atmosphere avoids a feeling of obligation that might otherwise exist regardless of the propriety of the activity.

Joint vacations and "night-clubbing"-type parties between a buyer and a seller are almost universally questionable. Regardless of what the actual facts may be, competitors and others will assume the buyer is off for a "free ride," and draw their conclusions accordingly.

The right attitude and a mature sense of balance are vital in handling the questionable influences that arise in purchasing work. To be compatible with one's employment, the activity must significantly serve the employer's interest or be of such a nominal nature that the propriety of the activity is unquestionable.

PERSONAL PURCHASES FOR EMPLOYEES

In some companies, the facilities of the purchasing department are employed to make personal purchases for employees as a part of the general employee relations program. Rapidly growing companies or organizations that require highly trained technical personnel or have a labor shortage frequently encourage the practice. It is also in widespread usage in the educational and institutional fields since salary scales are usually lower than in industry and profit sharing or bonus plans are not available. In fact, there are probably few purchasing agents who do not, at some time or other, assist a company official in making a personal purchase. Yet, the majority of companies frown upon adopting it as a general policy for the benefit of all employees for ethical, economic, or practical reasons.

In the strictest sense, this is not an ethical problem. However, it is so frequently referred to as being an "unethical purchasing practice," and it has become so universal a problem, that its inclusion is a must in the treatment of purchasing ethics.

Yet, as with most activities, the *manner* in which the thing is done frequently does make the deed unethical. Certainly, it would be ethically wrong for a commercial concern to use its purchasing volume to force a distributor or other supplier to make price concessions inconsistent with his general commercial position. For example, it would be improper for a large industrial buyer of valves and plumbing supplies to ask a plumbing distributor to sell an employee a hot-water heater wholesale if such action would result in embarrassing the distributor with his customers operating retail stores.

It is generally agreed that even the most ethical practices can be abused until they become reprehensible. Buyers should be familiar with trade practices and marketing policies and are, therefore, the people best qualified to judge the ethics of a transaction. They should rely on their own judgment and conscience and consider all elements of the transaction in this perspective.

The first test is to determine whether any subterfuge is involved. Subterfuge is in itself unethical. The presumption is that orders placed with a supplier by the purchasing agent are for the exclusive use and benefit of the company. If such items are being purchased surreptitiously by the company for the personal use of an employee and such facts are unknown to the supplier, this would be unethical.

The second test is whether or not the supplier's consent has been obtained under duress. For example, if the buyer obtained compliance with the request by pointedly alluding to the business placed by his company with that supplier in the past, this would be a grossly improper use of the company's purchasing power. It would seem, in fact, that any reluctance on the part of the supplier should indicate to the buyer that he should tactfully steer the conversation to other channels and save the supplier further embarrassment.

Some states have statutes prohibiting personal purchases for employees. They are generally known as "trade diversion laws." Such acts make it unlawful to sell articles to employees not of the employer's own production or not handled in the regular course of his trade. Exemptions are listed which include meals, candy bars, cigarettes, tobacco, or such items as may be required for the employee's safety or health. For example, safety shoes, safety gloves, and safety glasses or goggles of various types as well as uniforms and specially prescribed work clothes might be purchased in quantity by the purchasing department and charged at cost to the employee. The company's best way of ensuring standard quality is to obtain such equipment in this manner. Wisconsin, Pennsylvania, Illinois, Ohio, Michigan, and Minnesota are examples of states having such legislation. Enforcement of such laws has been lax. Yet, if it is a violation of business ethics for a company to engage in business practices which it knows are in violation of the law, however loose the enforcement of that law may be, such activity is surely subject to censure.

The most common condemnation of the practice arises because company purchases are in competition with other established outlets for merchandising the product for private use, to the disadvantage of distributors and dealers. This, to be sure, tends to break down normal channels of distribution. In our national business structure, the general availability of goods depends on strong and well-organized channels of distribution and purchasing agents and their respective managements should be concerned with maintaining a stable and orderly distribution system.

Particularly, where the plant is located in a small or medium-sized city, the effect of these activities can become quite serious to the retail outlets handling the commodities in question. Often much local antagonism toward the company is aroused which can lead to adverse regulations by local governing agencies, such as refusal to grant changes in zoning regulations necessary to the plant's expansion.

Finally, there are many practical objections. It is but a short step from an occasional request from a company official to a constant stream of demands from any and every person in the company wishing to make personal purchases at wholesale. The purchasing department may well find itself neglecting the company purchasing program, which is its primary function and responsibility. Moreover, such purchases are expensive purchases since they must be considered individually and become special items, often outside the regular line of company procurement. As a consequence, more time and effort is required than on standard requirements. Indeed, cost per order is one of the established criteria of efficiency and this ratio will be unfavorably increased by large numbers of personal purchases. Additional accounting records would be required in the processing of invoices, distribution of costs, maintenance of ledgers and the collection of accounts, whether by cash payment or payroll deduction.

The company's credit is involved. Employees' commitments must be promptly and properly met, whether the transaction is made with the company or some cooperating supplier. Also, the employee may leave the company before the transaction or payment is completed.

If the service is to be self-sustaining, a service or handling charge must be made. Few employees would understand the necessity for this and would consider it a "profit" to the company and resent it, thereby destroying the very benefit to employee relations which the company had hoped to achieve.

In a certain percentage of the cases, a mechanical failure will occur and the items will not be covered by the normal dealer service and guarantees. The employee will feel that he has recourse to his purchasing department for assistance. Again, he is likely to blame the company when he finds that he cannot obtain satisfactory adjustments, repairs, or returns through this medium.

The completeness of these services varies from the occasional call by an executive associate of the purchasing agent to entire buying organizations set up for the purpose. Many companies have company stores where such articles can be purchased, often at cost plus 10 per cent. One large Chicago company employs more than 40 buyers who are in constant contact with sources of supply of every kind of product. Some authorities have made surveys which show that this trend is on the increase. One survey[5] of 599 purchasing agents reports results as follows:

Question	*Yes*	*No*	*Occasionally*
Does your company assist its personnel in making personal purchases to obtain advantages not available through regular channels?	34%	14%	52%

Question	*All*		*Certain Groups*
To what personnel is this service available?	65%		35%
	Yes	*No*	
Do you use company purchase orders in making purchases for employees?	68%	32%	
	Good	*Poor*	*No Effect*
What is the "public relations" effect among employees?	71%	8%	21%

An earlier survey[6] indicated that 15 per cent of the companies responding had some such plan. Discounts ranged from 20 to 40 per cent, and the plans have been in operation anywhere from three to thirty years.

That these plans are considered employee benefits by most of the companies that use them is indicated by the following quotation from the employee handbook of a large industrial company:

> Company requisitions. The company will make purchases for any employee on those items on which the company can save the employee some money or which the employees cannot purchase for themselves. These purchases will only be made from firms with whom the company has an active account. Such purchases will be deducted from the employee's paycheck. The personnel department can give you full particulars.[7]

The majority of purchasing agents are still opposed to the policy of personal purchases, for reasons of ethics, economic soundness, or practicality, or of all three; but it still remains a business fact. It is a question that must be decided in every organization, and not just by the purchasing agent. It is a question of general concern to the management of the

[5] By permission from *Purchasing* magazine, New York.
[6] By permission from Printers' Ink Publishing Co., Inc., New York.
[7] By permission from Printers' Ink Publishing Co., Inc., New York.

company and should be decided as a matter of general policy. It would not be proper to state categorically that the practice is right or wrong, wise or unwise. Rather, the various factors that must be considered have been presented with the hope that they will help the reader in arriving at the right decision for his company.

LEADERSHIP FROM PURCHASING

Nowhere is purchasing personnel more greatly challenged then when confronted with the opportunity to provide leadership within their company in the area of ethical conduct. Ethical conduct with suppliers not only involves purchasing personnel but also involves design engineers, quality control personnel, and the various departments using purchased materials, equipment, and supplies. Therefore, a climate of ethical conduct must be created throughout the company wherever contact with suppliers is involved. Nothing can be more embarrassing to the image of a company or its purchasing department than to see a double standard of conduct being applied by separate departments within the company.

It has often been said that presidents of companies are more inclined to accept guidance in ethical conduct than are most purchasing people prepared to take initiative to provide this leadership themselves in this area. This presents a true challenge to the purchasing manager to, first, ensure top notch ethical conduct in his own department, and second, provide leadership in establishing this same ethical climate in regard to suppliers throughout his company.

This impact of a purchasing manager aggressively insisting upon high ethical conduct on the part of all company personnel will do more to elevate the status of professional purchasing than any other single contribution that they may make.

Purchasing can communicate this ethical conduct leadership in several ways. The best manner to communicate it is through their own strict adherence to the established concept of ethical conduct. This, however, raises the question of what exactly are the practices that should or should not be entered into by both purchasing and other department personnel. It cannot be assumed that all people automatically know what is the proper or improper thing to do under a given situation.

A lengthy ethical conduct policy containing many specific do's and don'ts cannot be expected to cover every situation to be encountered and often substitutes adherence to rules rather than conformance to good ethical judgment. A relatively short, more broadly written ethical conduct policy, that is capable of being communicated to all company personnel can, however, serve as a sound basis for securing an understanding

Business activities of the Procurement Division of Xerox Corporation shall be conducted on the highest level of ethical conduct. Our relations with our suppliers and carriers will be motivated by the promotion of mutual respect and goodwill.

The following is intended to serve as the framework for our daily decisions in this area of ethical conduct for all personnel of the Procurement Division.

1. *N.A.P.A. Principles and Standards*

   We subscribe to the principles and standards of purchasing practice advocated by the National Association of Purchasing Agents and the Purchasing Agents Association of Rochester.

2. *Laws and Legal Regulations*

   We adhere to both the letter and the spirit of all federal, state and local laws and regulations in all of our business contracts and transactions.

3. *Purchase without Prejudice*

   We will strive to place our business without prejudice, seeking to obtain the maximum ultimate value for each dollar of expenditure, consistent with our quality, cost, service, capacity and time requirements.

4. *Visitor Reception*

   We will strive to accord a prompt and courteous reception and maintain reasonable visiting hours, so far as conditions will permit, for all who call on us.

5. *Lunch with Suppliers and Carriers*

   Lunch with suppliers and carriers is not to be encouraged. When justified by necessary business relations, the buyer shall act as host for the luncheon with subsequent luncheons on a reciprocal basis. If three or more Xerox personnel are present at lunch, the buyer shall act as host for the luncheon.

6. *Evening & Weekend Entertainment and Dinner*

   Evening & weekend dinner and entertainment with suppliers and carriers is to be avoided. When justified by necessary business relations, the buyer shall secure the prior approval of his supervisor.

7. *Gifts*

   Gifts of any kind from suppliers and carriers are to be discouraged. When acceptance is unavoidable, without embarrassment to the buyer and/or the supplier or carrier, a nominal gift, not exceeding $10.00 in value, may be accepted. Gifts of more than nominal value shall be diplomatically returned to the giver. Advertising novelties are exempted from this policy. Gifts seemingly intended to represent an attempt to improperly influence the buyer shall be reported to the Vice President—Procurement & Distribution Division for mutual disposition.

8. *Supplier and Carrier Paid Expenses and Services*

   Supplier and carrier paid loans, travel and accommodation expenses, services and remuneration of any kind are to be avoided at all times.

9. *Security of Confidential Business Information*

   Prices, quotations, contract terms, sources of supply, patentable and secret processes, production schedules and competitive product information, belonging to either a supplier, carrier or Xerox Corporation, shall be kept in the strictest of confidence.

(Signed) ____________________

Vice President, Procurement & Distribution Division

FIG. 6–1. Policy of ethical conduct.

and acceptance of ethical conduct objectives. Purchasing can provide the necessary leadership in communicating and securing the understanding and acceptance of these ethical conduct objectives.

Full statements of the NAPA Code and other purchasing association codes of ethics are located in Section 28, "Appendix." Two examples of departmental policy of ethical conduct, which add some specific areas of interest to the NAPA Code, are included in this handbook. The one for The Detroit Edison Company is reproduced in Section 28. That for the Procurement Division of the Xerox Corporation at Rochester, N.Y., is identified as Fig. 6–1.

ELEVATING THE PURCHASING PROFESSION

A considerate and thoughtful buyer dedicated to sound ethical standards can do much to raise the stature of his employer, himself, and the purchasing profession. It has been said that a buyer should be "honest, decent, courteous, cheerful, thoughtful, helpful, fair, capable, cooperative, morally responsible, gentlemanly, patient, tactful, friendly, open-minded, good natured, humble, emotionally stable, respectable, dependable, 'extrovertive,' energetic, and able to handle his own financial affairs capably." This is an almost impossible order, but by perseverance and hard work these objectives can be approached to the high credit of all those doing purchasing work. It must be remembered, one can't "buy" an ethical reputation; it must be earned.

BIBLIOGRAPHY

For reference books on ethical aspects of purchasing, see Section 26, "Library and Catalog File." This lists current books which include various concepts of ethics, reciprocity, gratuities, and other areas related to this over-all subject.

SECTION 7

HOW TO SELECT SOURCES OF SUPPLY

Editor

Arnold D. Finley, Manager of Purchasing Administration, Sylvania Electronic Systems—East, Sylvania Electric Products, Inc., Needham Heights, Massachusetts

Associate Editors

J. C. Good, Manager, Field Purchasing Offices, Monsanto Company, St. Louis, Missouri

G. W. Riches, Purchasing Agent, The Philip Carey Manufacturing Company, Cincinnati, Ohio

James F. Robjent, Purchasing Agent, Northeast Division, Scott Paper Company, Winslow, Maine

NATURE OF THE TASK

The selection of the sources of supply is, and must be, at the same time, both the right and the responsibility of the purchasing agent. Even with failure to exercise this right, he has not escaped his essential responsibility.

In the exercise of judgment, the purchasing agent realizes his highest potential as a creative contributor to executive management. It is in the area of source selection that his capability is most heavily taxed and most gratefully recognized.

Moreover, source selection is a continuing challenge. A decision cannot be once made and then rested upon. It becomes the leverage and the tool whereby the purchasing agent first achieves and then retains the level of performance which distinguishes the professional, the expert, in this materials supply function.

The factors that bear upon these judgments will be many in number and complex in nature. The purpose of this section is to indicate the primary ones. However, many others, such as price evaluation,[1] are themselves complete subjects which are justifiably handled as such elsewhere in this handbook.

CHARACTERISTICS OF ITEMS TO BE PURCHASED

There are certain basic facts that must be known about an item to be purchased before the first steps can be taken toward source selection. They are elements which in themselves either qualify or disqualify certain types of companies as possible suppliers, and hence narrow the field of selection.

Industry Classification. By what industry is the required product produced? As soon as this is known, the number of possible suppliers is reduced to the group of companies composing that industry. Reference to trade registers or directories, many of which are indexed by industry, will then provide a list of the names and locations of possible sources.

The commonly used commercial name of a product usually indicates the type of industry producing it. In some instances, however, the name indicates only the form of the product, and in order to identify the producing industry it is necessary also to know the material of which it is made.

The type of industry producing a product frequently determines the number of potential sources available from which to select. Some industries are composed of many producing companies, varying widely in size and capacity; others consist of only a few potential sources from which to choose.

Commercial Availability of the Product. Is the product regularly produced in standardized form? If so, is it available from manufacturers' and/or distributors' stocks; or is it manufactured only on specific customer order?

There are many products which are manufactured in standardized form, but of which only certain sizes are produced in quantity for stock, these being known as stock sizes. Other sizes which are in smaller demand,

[1] See Section 10, "Price Evaluation."

although made to standard specifications or dimensions, are made only after receipt of a customer's order, and are known as made-to-order sizes. Catalogs of such products usually indicate the distinction between the stock sizes and those which are made to order. Stock sizes, in addition to their greater availability, are usually lower in price.

Is the product nonstandard, requiring special manufacture? Some products by their very nature are nonstandard. Most forgings, castings, molded plastics, molded and extruded rubber products, to name a few, are made to customer's design, usually from dies, patterns, or molds paid for by the customer. They are produced only on order and in the quantities specified by the customer. Nonstandard products of this nature are not to be confused with special variations of standardized products, which are usually considered undesirable and costly but sometimes unavoidable. Both types, however, require special production.

Quantity to Be Purchased. Is the required quantity small, moderate, or large? As these are relative terms, they must be considered in relation to the physical size of the product, its unit value, and the production facilities that the potential sources have available for making it. A quantity of one thousand, for example, is large in one instance, small in another.

Whether the quantity is small, moderate, or large will decisively influence the choice of the type of source to be considered—whether it shall be a distributor or manufacturer; if a manufacturer, whether it shall be a large-volume, medium-volume, or short-run producer. Many manufacturers are not equipped to produce large quantities at competitive prices, but are better able to manufacture in small lots than their larger competitors.

Many standardized products are manufactured in much larger quantities than are usually purchased at one time by the user. They are made available to the purchaser by being carried in distributors' stocks where they may be bought for immediate delivery in whatever quantity required. Some such products are available only from distributors. Others may be purchased from either a distributor or manufacturer.

Time Element of the Purchase Requirement. When is the product needed? Time will have an important bearing on the kind of supplier to be selected.

When the time available for procurement is less than the minimum required for manufacture, the potential sources must be either distributors or manufacturers who ordinarily carry the product in stock.

When the time available for procurement is equal to or greater than the minimum required for manufacture, the logical potential sources will be manufacturers (assuming that manufacturing quantities are required), provided that manufacturers' backlogs of unfilled orders permit actual deliveries in the minimum processing time. Manufacturers' quoted deliveries, often referred to as lead time, fluctuate widely and at any given time are a reflection of the processing time plus order book status and/or material supply.

Purpose of the Purchase. Will the product be repeatedly required:

1. For use as material or a component part in the manufacture of the purchaser's product?
2. For use or consumption in the purchaser's operation?

Will the product be purchased only once or occasionally:

1. For use as productive or capital equipment?
2. For use as material or a component in the manufacture of a special or nonrepetitive product of the purchaser?
3. For subcontracting of operations normally performed in the purchaser's plant? Subcontracting here may be defined as: fabrication, machining, assembly, or other processing normally performed by the purchaser, which due to insufficient production facilities, material, or manpower, cannot be performed in time to satisfy the purchaser's production schedule.

Knowing the purpose for which the purchase is to be made assists the buyer to select the type of supplier needed. Some manufacturers may be equipped to produce economically both in large repetitive volume and in short runs, but this is not usually the case. The volume producer has high-production equipment and tools which give him low costs on long runs, but do not permit economical production of short runs; the job shop or moderate-volume producer has greater flexibility to make quick changes and has lower equipment overhead to offset higher labor cost per unit.

Physical Size of the Required Item. Is the size of the product, in terms of weight and/or dimensions, such as to restrict the number of potential sources capable of producing it? For example, relatively few companies have the equipment to produce:

1. Steel stampings ¼ in. or more in thickness and/or over 30 in. in diameter, width, or length
2. Products or parts requiring machining on exceptionally large machine tools
3. Iron or steel castings weighing 10 tons or more

It is sometimes necessary to purchase a product with dimensional tolerances closer than the commercial standard. Sources must then be found that are capable of maintaining the greater accuracy.

PRELIMINARY SELECTION OF SOURCES

Sources from which almost every required product may possibly be purchased are so numerous that a preliminary selection is necessary to narrow the field to those most likely to fulfill the requirements successfully. The purpose of such preliminary selection is to establish a list of bidders from whom quotations may be requested.

Sources of Information. The sources of information available to the buyer for making preliminary selections can be generally classified as those in printed form available in the purchasing office.

Listings in the paragraphs which follow should not be construed as suggesting any order of approach to a problem. The nature of the item plus special circumstances always present will endow one or more of these approaches with improved effectiveness over the balance of the paths. This is where the experience of a buying agent and his ability to grow through it will be visible to those evaluating him.

Sources of assistance in printed form include:[2]

1. *Classified Telephone Directories.* Useful in identifying services and locally available items where small value and speed of acquisition are major factors.
2. *Buyers' Guides.* Available in large variety; usually embracing a particular industry such as chemistry, construction material, or electronics. Such yearly issues as *Radio Master's, EEM,* and *Sweet's Catalogs* are examples. These are excellent guides to sources, but are frequently incomplete in description unless the item desired is common or basic.
3. *Registers.* Semiofficial listing vehicles such as:
   a. *Thomas's Register of American Manufacturers*
   b. *MacRae's Blue Book*
   c. *Conover-Mast Purchasing Directory*
   d. An ever-expanding group of regional volumes promoted through Chambers of Commerce or regional development agencies

   The value of all these registers is in identifying sources for specific contact. Seldom does one prove a source from their pages. Retaining all the books listed above might be repetitive, but full coverage of the area of interest with several of them is certainly a must for any efficient purchasing operation.
4. *Projection Display of Film Data.* This new medium of data review is showing great vitality in the market of industry, and deserves serious consideration whenever new engineering or development is a part of purchasing's "customer within the walls" market. These systems utilize

[2] See Sections 26 and 28 for detailed listings.

a permanent projector and display screen in conjunction with either microfilm or aperture card libraries. The libraries are kept up-to-date by a service organization on a yearly subscription basis.[3] These libraries have the capacity for storing huge quantities of manufacturers' literature in modest space, and most important, the automatic replacement, obtained as a service, makes timeliness of information a reality without clerical effort. With the complete data on the products of over 100,000 suppliers already in this form, this system has much to recommend it.

5. *Catalogs and Advertising Literature.* This material is excellent for specific references. If it is well cross-referenced by commodity and kept current on almost a daily basis, this is among the best methods of preliminary source selection. The limitation exists in that this material consumes much space and becomes almost useless very quickly unless it is well organized and constantly updated.

The second group of sources is that based upon personal contacts and experience. It includes:

1. *Interviews with Salesmen and Manufacturers' Representatives.* This is the most productive source possible, since the area of commodity need will tend to encourage calls by representatives related to these areas. This source should make all necessary data available, helping crystallize the need and contributing the basis for a comparative weighing of value and the final decision. The shortcomings of this source arise from the variable degree of knowledge of individual representatives, and the ever-necessary discrimination by the buyer, when eagerness to sell is heavily reflected in the information.
2. *Internal Specialist Sources.* There is usually far more of this available than the false pride of most purchasing organizations will admit. Granted that the selection of proper sources is a purchasing responsibility, the assembly of facts upon which to base source selection is too important for the buyer to fail to draw upon the trained and technical knowledge in his own house. Research or engineering departments, planning and production, quality and inspection—these are or should be concentrations of specialized knowledge whose judgment should be solicited.
3. *Vendor Index File.* An accurate up-to-date vendor index file is a major purchasing aid which enables placement of telephone calls with a minimum of delay, ensures mailing to proper addresses, and promotes courteous and friendly relations with suppliers. To obtain the data required for a permanent file, a letter of transmittal with a form at-

[3] Examples: VSMF by Information Handling Services, Inc., 800 Acoma St., Denver, Colo. 80204; and the Thomas System, Micro-catalogs, New York, N.Y. 10001.

tached explains to suppliers the reason the information is required. Upon its return, the information is transferred to file cards, which also double as an approved vendor list. Figure 7–1 illustrates such a card in simple form.

VENDOR INDEX

Name Badger Malleable & Mfg. Co.

Address: Street 223 N. Chicago Avenue

City South Milwaukee **Zip** ____ **State** Wis.

Terms Net 30 **F.O.B.** Seller's Plant

Type of Operation Malleable Iron Fdy.

District Office None

FIG. 7–1. A 3- by 5-in. card printed in duplicate with one-time carbon inserted. Cross index is provided by filing original alphabetically by supplier name, duplicate by commodity classification. File includes complete listing of established sources and of potential sources who have displayed interest and capability by solicitation or advertising.

It is tempting and useful to make the slight improvement necessary in these form-cards to make them records of past purchases. This is illustrated in Figs. 7–2 to 7–4. However, there is an overlap of interest

PURCHASE ORDER OR QUOTATION RECORD

Ven No.	Vendor Name and Address	Cash Discount Terms	F.O.B. Point
1	Acme Glove Company, Oconto, Wisconsin	1-10-30	S.P. F/A to WA
2	City Glove Company, Milwaukee, Wisconsin	2-10-30	S.P.
3	Wisconsin Glove Company, Milwaukee, Wisconsin	2-20-40	F/A to Dest.

Purchase Order or Inquiry No.	Date	Ven No.	Quantity	Unit	Unit Price	Trade Discount		Remarks
646143	1/17/65	2	960 pr.	doz. pr.	9.25	net		Our Inq. 59389 their quote 1/14/65
58089	4/29/65	2	1000 pr.	doz. pr.	8.65			
58089	4/30/65	1	1008 pr.	doz. pr.	9.00			

Freight Classification Card 1 of 1

Commodity Name: Gloves - Leather Faced Drawing No.: Q 0015870 Size or Type: ACM #66

FIG. 7–2. A 5- by 8-in. visible index card, filed numerically by part or drawing number, or alphabetically by part name. Record shows previous sources or potential sources, their locations, terms, and f.o.b. points, with chronological listing of quotations and purchase orders placed.

COMPANY NAME		FRANKLIN SUPPLY COMPANY
ADDRESS STREET CITY & STATE TELEPHONE		945 WESTMINSTER STREET PROVIDENCE, RHODE ISLAND PLANTATIONS 1-3000
SALES REPRESENTATIVE NAME STREET CITY & STATE TELEPHONE		DANIEL KAYE 843 HOPE STREET PROVIDENCE, RHODE ISLAND GASPEE 1-5721
PERSON TO CONTACT: ORDER PLACEMENT	MR.	HERBERT L. ROSEN
ORDER DELIVERY	MR.	ERNEST DANDREA
INVOICE MATTERS	MR.	DONALD GOULD
ENGINEERING	MR.	DANIEL KAYE
QUALITY	MR.	HERBERT L. ROSEN
CLAIMS	MR.	DONALD GOULD
REJECT CLAIMS MADE		10 DAYS AFTER RECEIPT OF MATERIAL

VENDOR RECORD
FORM 8197-BOSTITCH, INC.

FIG. 7–3. Vendor data cards, 5- by 8-in., filed alphabetically in standard metal file case. Cards make immediately available the correct address and telephone number of vendor and sales representative. The front side of the card also lists vendor contacts for handling of various problems. (*By permission of Bostitch, Inc., Westerly, R.I.*)

TERMS NET

TRANSPORTATION	
RAILROAD ROUTING	N.Y., N.H., & H. R.R.
MOTOR FREIGHT ROUTING	ARROW TRANSPORTATION
AIR EXPRESS ROUTING	
FREIGHT * CHARGES	☐ DELIVERED ☐ FOB DESTINATION ☐ FOB SHIPPING POINT ☐ FREIGHT ALLOWED ON LBS OR MORE

*DEPENDENT ON ITEM

COMMODITIES HANDLED

DAYTON V BELTS & SHEAVES
ALEMITE LUBRICANTS & FITTINGS
SCHRADER AIR DEVICES
DEVILBISS SPRAY EQUIPMENT
BLACK & DECKER ELECTRIC TOOLS
INGERSOLL-RAND AIR COMPRESSORS
ARO AIR TOOLS

FIG. 7–4. Reverse side of card in Fig. 7–3 gives discount terms and transportation data. A list of commodities supplied by vendor is also included in data shown. The vendor data file also serves as a list of approved vendors, as only accepted suppliers have cards preserved in the file. (*By permission of Bostitch, Inc., Westerly, R.I.*)

developing here. It may be most desirable to develop a "parts history" file, as discussed later in this section, and to index it by commodity type. The system planner will want to design the vendor and commodity files to be complementary to each other and not repetitive with a duplicate entry of data.

4. *Professional Organizations.* The local chapters of purchasing organizations, such as the National Association of Purchasing Agents, the Canadian Association of Purchasing Agents, and the National Institute of Governmental Purchasing, are invaluable training grounds for purchasers of all levels of experience. Personal involvement in the activities of such organizations, however, is the key to enjoyment of most of the benefits. A full listing of organizations will be found in Sections 26 and 28.
5. *Trade Shows and Exhibits.* Practically all fields of industry have their periodic trade shows and exhibits. The value of these varies greatly and is greater for the less experienced visitor than for the veteran purchasing agent. For the purchaser's own area of interest, such shows must be seriously tried by self-exposure, with knowledge-gathering as the objective. When regarded as an entertaining "reward" for past routine labor, show and convention trekking casts an unfavorable image on the purchasing profession and on the individual buyer.

SELECTION FOR QUOTATIONS

Factors to Be Considered in Preliminary Selection. *Number of Bidders Desired.* The number of potential sources selected to bid must be sufficient to ensure competition. That is the main objective of the bidders' list. The list must be broad enough to ensure that it will bring to bear all the types of competition desired, including:

1. *Price competition.* It must seek out the lowest-cost producers or distribution outlets.
2. *Technological competition.* It must seek out the differences that exist between potential suppliers in the field of ideas, in engineering solutions, design, materials, and production techniques.
3. *Service competition.* It must seek out those who are best able to deliver at the times and in the quantities required.

Three is considered the practical minimum number of bidders when the product to be purchased is standardized or the specifications definitely established. A greater number is desirable, even necessary, when alternates are to be considered, and particularly when specification recommendations are being sought. There is no limit to the number from whom quotations may be requested, but it is regarded as poor practice to include in the bidders' list the names of companies who cannot be given serious consideration in the final selection.

Size and Facilities. It should be considered whether, from the preliminary information obtainable, the indicated size of a company is suitable for supplying the requirement, and whether its indicated facilities give reasonable assurance of successful performance. The biggest possible suppliers are not necessarily the best qualified; small companies may often prove to be the best sources for nonrepetitive requirements, for moderate-volume repetitive items, and for specialized or precision work. Large or small, however, the potential supplier's equipment must be adequate.

Geographical Location. Certainly, one or more local sources should be the start of the search. Net cost of an item of the needed quality at the point of use is the good buyer's criterion. All other things being equal, the nearest source will be the best value. But all things seldom are equal, and only by testing the market fairly and broadly can one know whether basic price at a distance may offset transportation costs, or quality of the local offering decrease the real value. Whenever excessive communication, whether by personal visit or other media, during the seller's performance is anticipated, it should be remembered that its cost will be higher for remote sources.

Sales Representation. Consider the sales representation of potential suppliers. Are there representatives readily accessible at the point of purchase and/or the point of use? Are they conscientious workers for their customer's benefit?

Reciprocity Considerations. Reciprocity is often an influential factor in both the solicitation of quotations and the actual buying decision. This matter will be considered in more detail later in this section under the subtitle "Factors Influencing Final Selection of Source—Original Purchase." Here let it suffice to say that whether or not a purchasing agent willingly embraces the implications of reciprocity, he cannot put the question behind him. Nor can he settle, once and for all, upon a policy openly "accepting" or "rejecting" and expect to have his problem solved. He will be remeeting this question throughout his career and will learn that the only irrefutable fact is that his course must be "open." For the original solicitation of bids, the buyer owes both favored and neutral sources equal opportunity to bid and must supply all sources with equal factual data, to enable fair and comparable bids to be generated.

SOLICITING AND EVALUATING QUOTATIONS

A seller frequently quotes prices for his products to present customers or prospective customers on his own initiative; that is, without being formally requested to do so. Furthermore, current prices of many commodities are published. Thus, buyers have available the means of keeping abreast of the "market" for a range of items. However, the buyer is naïve indeed who assumes that published or "standard" prices are necessarily the best ones available. But even if they prove to be so, before a specific purchase can be made from a particular seller, there must be complete agreement between buyer and seller on price and other terms and conditions of purchase. This agreement is most effectively arrived at by means of an inquiry sent by the buyer to his selection of prospective sellers, whose responses are in the form of bids.

The Inquiry or Invitation to Bid. Careful preparation of this document is essential for all future understanding between buyer and seller. It should be definite on the following points:

1. Quantity required. When the total quantity is to be delivered over a period of time, quantity per delivery and the frequencies of deliveries should be stated.
2. Description and/or specification of item(s) to be purchased. This must be exact and should include, where necessary, drawings and formal specifications. These specifications and drawings should not describe the peculiar item of a single manufacturer, and then be sent broadside to all competitors for bid. This practice makes a mockery of open competition. The best procurement specifications are those which describe the function of the item and its maximum physical dimensions and leave the detail optional to include as broad a field of competition as possible. Sometimes specifications are allowed to define one manufacturer's item but then are broadened by the phrase "or equal." This is an "off-the-hook" gesture, so to speak, since *theoretically* the competition is open. In many cases this is the only solution, but it is much abused and should be discouraged.

   Proprietory rights of the buyer's company may be involved in some of the drawings sent out. If so, a legend on the drawing itself should state this. Similarly, a buyer may receive answers to bid invitations which include such drawings. Such cases involve both ethics and law, subjects which are covered elsewhere in this handbook.
3. Required point of delivery.
4. Required time or times of delivery.
5. Transportation method, if of importance to the buyer.
6. The date by which quotations must be received. This should be firmly stated and even more firmly adhered to by the buyer. It may not be extended for any one bidder, even upon the most heartrending entreaties, unless it is similarly extended for all bidders.

7. All special conditions which will affect price or the bidder's ability to perform. These include:
   a. Material or information to be supplied in whole or in part by the buyer after the award of the business.
   b. Description of tools or patterns available to the performing vendor.
   c. Notification of interface with other sub-vendors where such exists (such as receiving patterns from a foundry, machining, and passing on to a plater).
   d. Any special requirements, such as delivery or installation on a weekend or holiday, etc.
8. It should require bidders to identify:
   a. The basis of the price in relation to the quantity range to which it applies.
   b. The basis of price in relation to the number and span in time of deliveries.
   c. The period of time, after date of the bid, for which the bid prices are "firm." This is usually not less than 90 days and may be extended on specific request and agreement.
   d. Any exceptions or events which can invalidate the prices quoted (such as strikes, union renegotiations, etc.).
9. It should include a reprint of the buyer's uniform terms and conditions, popularly called the "boiler plate," if such is used by the buyer's firm. It is frequently most convenient to satisfy this requirement by printing these on the reverse side of the inquiry form itself.

A fairly satisfactory inquiry form is illustrated in Fig. 7–5.[4] This provides for an original copy to be retained by the buyer with three carbons produced at the same time to be directed to each of three potential sources. As much fixed information as possible is, therefore, conveyed with a single typing; any single vendor is barred from identifying his competition, while at the same time he is gently advised that he has competitors by the very nature of the form itself.

Evaluation of Quotations. Quotations are sometimes so simple that they appear to be easily compared just by being read, or by writing down the essentials as they are received over the telephone. This is often the case with standardized products where the differences (or uniformity) in specifications and quality between the acceptable bidders are known and understood by the buyer beforehand. Price and delivery and a quick decision loom as the paramount issues in the buyer's mind, and with sufficient experience, he is justified in treating them so. But it is hazardous

[4] See Section 25, "Forms and Records," for another illustration of "Invitation to Bid" form.

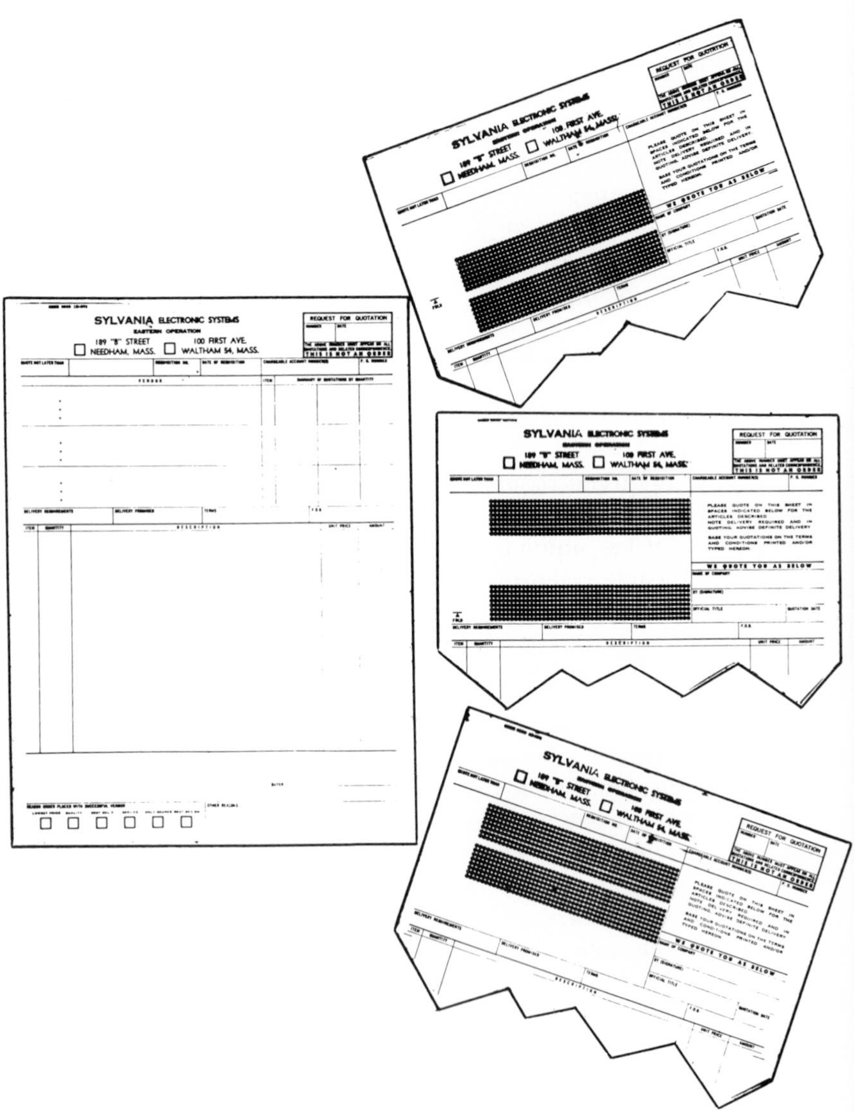

SYLVANIA ELECTRONIC SYSTEMS

EASTERN OPERATION

☐ 189 "B" STREET NEEDHAM, MASS. ☐ 100 FIRST AVE. WALTHAM 54, MASS.

REQUEST FOR QUOTATION

THIS IS NOT AN ORDER

VENDOR

DELIVERY REQUIREMENTS | DELIVERY PROMISED | TERMS | F.O.B.

ITEM | QUANTITY | DESCRIPTION | UNIT PRICE | AMOUNT

PLEASE QUOTE ON THIS SHEET IN SPACES INDICATED BELOW FOR THE ARTICLES DESCRIBED

NOTE DELIVERY REQUIRED AND IN QUOTING ADVISE DEFINITE DELIVERY

BASE YOUR QUOTATIONS ON THE TERMS AND CONDITIONS PRINTED AND/OR TYPED HEREON.

WE QUOTE YOU AS BELOW

FIG. 7–5. Quotation solicitation form. (*Courtesy of Sylvania Electronic Systems Division, Sylvania Electric Products, Inc., Needham Heights, Mass.*)

to assume regularly that other quotation elements are of no importance or that there are no obscure differences of consequence in the quotations. A check list or tabulation will minimize the chances of embarrassing oversight. Tabulation, in fact, is the only safe method of comparing complicated quotations involving distinct differences in the products offered.

It is hardly possible to devise a tabulation form that will have wide application. Variations in the specific points to be compared are too great. Every tabulation should, however, provide for easy comparison of the following:

1. Cost factors (also see Section 10)
   a. Price
   b. Transportation cost; to be calculated by buyer if not included in quotation
   c. Installation cost, if any
   d. Tooling or other preparation costs
   e. Sales or excise taxes to be added; amount
   f. Terms of payment; cash discount
   g. Price basis, if multiple deliveries are involved
   h. Price subject to acceptance within ______ days
   i. Price protection: firm; protected against decline; or subject to escalation
2. Delivery (also see Section 18)
3. Design or specification factors
   a. Specification compliance
   b. Specification deviation
   c. Specification advantages
   d. Important dimensions
   e. Weights
4. Legal factors (also see Sections 4 and 5)
   a. Warranty
   b. Cancellation provisions
   c. Patent protection
   d. Public liability and workmen's compensation protection
   e. Federal law and regulation compliance

In evaluating complex or highly competitive procurements, it is sometimes useful to assign relative "weights" to the factors being compared and then to grade each potential vendor as to his competitive position for that factor. Thus quality might be considered as worth 20 per cent; price, 20 per cent; technical excellence, 30 per cent; delivery availability, 20 per cent; and business confidence factor, 10 per cent, rounding out the 100 per cent. Each vendor could be graded from 1 to 10 on each of these points. As illustrated in Fig. 7–6, a prospective seller might earn all 10 points for quality, for example. Under his name and opposite "quality," therefore, would be entered the figure "20." (If he had earned only seven points, the buyer would enter "14," since quality was given twice 10 points, or 20 per cent, in the weighting.)

Quotation Evaluation Summary						
Factor	Weight	Ace Industries	F. J. Joslyn	Premier Mfg.		Range
Quality	20%	14	20 *	16		7 - 10
Price	20%	$3.70 20 *	$4.05 18	$3.95 19		9 - 10
Tech. Value	30%	18	27 *	24		6 - 9
Deliv. Probabil.	20%	14	10	20 *		5 - 10
Financial Comp.	10%	6	10 *	9		6 - 10
		72	85	(88)		

FIG. 7–6. Quotation evaluation summary—suggested format for statistically rating quotations.

Proceeding in this way, the buyer will have a matrix where the horizontal lines give the spread by each point of comparison and the vertical columns show the points earned by each potential vendor. Adding the vertical columns will disclose the seller with the highest point count and the maximum potential value per dollar of cost.

Quotation Records. Records of past and current quotations and of the action taken are a distinct asset to a purchasing operation and will become a necessity as a small activity grows into a larger one. Economy of effort suggests concurrent use of two methods of maintaining such quotation records:

1. Item card. This is a simple identification of a standard catalog product, repetitively purchased. This includes most supplies and operating items and much of the so-called "hardware" used in production iself. Figure 7–2 illustrates a simple card record which can be adapted for such use and filed by commodity.

2. Item folder. This is a fairly sophisticated record, one version of which is illustrated in Fig. 7–7. Both outside and inner surfaces are printed to create data space, while the folder construction enables it to hold correspondence, quotations, applicable drawings, etc. Very large dollar value procurements, those of special custom design, the procurement of items continuously required for the output product, large investments in capital equipment, etc., are the areas that justify quotation records as complete as this medium provides.

PART IDENTIFICATION FOLDER

PART NO.:
REVISION:

QUOTATION HISTORY

Date	Vendor	Address	Quantity	Quoted Price	Tooling	Remarks

Reference Part Nos.

Normal Lead Time	Entered By	Date

NAME AND DESCRIPTION OF PART

CLASSIFICATION CODE:

Vendor and Address	Terms	Code	Vendor and Address	Terms	Code	Vendor and Address	Terms	Code
1			4			7		
2			5			8		
3			6			9		

Use Above Code Column As Follows: V—Approved Vendor, O—Not Tested, M—Mftr., A—Mftrs. Agent, —Distributor, —Foundry, M/C—Machine Shop, SM—Sheet Metal Shop, S—Service, Such As Plating, Painting, Etc.

Date of Order	P. O. Number	Vendor	Quantity Ordered	Dash No.	Buyer	Unit Net Price	F.O.B. Pt. (City & State)	Date Completed	Remarks

SESE 1783 (6-63)

FIG. 7–7. Parts history folder. This is in the form of a manila file folder, the ruling of the front and back inner surface of which is illustrated. The outside back surface (not shown) has been ruled for a pattern and tooling control.

The buyer should think about the indexing of this file. Most small organizations will correctly consider that filing by alphabetical sequence of the commodity group and sub-group will be adequate. As the company grows substantially, this system will certainly become unwieldy. A parts numbering system is the only means of regaining rapid retrievability. This has a side advantage as well. A good parts numbering system is a necessary base for all degrees of electronic data processing, covered in Section 14. The United States government's Federal stock numbering system will give buyers some ideas.

FACTORS INFLUENCING FINAL SELECTION OF SOURCE—ORIGINAL PURCHASE

This subsection considers the factors which exert influence on the supplier selection for a transaction involving:

1. A nonrepetitive purchase such as:
   a. Plant capital equipment
   b. An item required for incorporation in a special product
   c. An item required for resale in conjunction with a regular product
   d. An item of special nature required for an experimental effort
2. The *first* purchase of any item required. Even if the purchase is subsequently repetitive, the first time is an "original."

In all the above, the following will apply with varying emphasis because of the size, nature, cost, etc., of the item.

Financial Considerations

Price. If price is defined as the ultimate cost to the user, then it is the base of reference against which all other factors are measured. Price as quoted by a supplier is not, however, such a cost. It is part of the total cost and often the only flexible part. The buyer must use price to determine cost at point of his use. The latter, however, becomes his tool of decision.

Nor is a price final just because it may be the lowest quoted in multibid competition. Price is only justified by value. It is a basic buyer responsibility, and a perfectly ethical one, to relate price to value and to seek an equitable relationship between the two, however much higher priced the competition may have been. In Section 10, much more is said on the subject of negotiation. The practice and policy noted there are applicable under conditions of original purchase as well.

Transportation Cost. This cost, if not included in the price of the delivered unit to the buyer's point of use, must be calculated from the quoted shipping weight, the point of origin, and the proper carrier's transportation rate. Full consideration of proper tariff classification, travel media, and competition between carriers must be applied at this point in the evaluation. For further details, see Section 18, "Traffic and Transportation Considerations."

Installation Cost. This is the cost of putting the purchase into use. It may be found to differ materially between quoting sources, as assembly is considered.

Preparation Cost. The cost of accessories, tools, dies, fixtures, etc., is a variable in quoting policy of various suppliers. Who furnishes what of that which is needed?

Sales Taxes. These are seldom included in the bidder's price. They apply to transactions initiated and/or consummated within certain states or cities. Some of these taxes are, in effect, "use" taxes, applying to all deliveries made within a state, regardless of the point of shipment (see Section 9) .

Terms of Payment. While cash discounts tend to follow a pattern within a given industry, this is not invariably true. In the accounting sense, a cash discount is not a portion of the price of an item. If the buying company adheres to a uniform policy of "discounting," however, the magnitude of a cash discount and the days allowed will have the same effect as a price differential and should be treated as such. Cash discount tables can be found in Section 29, "Reference Tables." Considerable variance between vendors may be found. Partial payments, for example, may be required as work progresses.

Price Protection. Will the supplier's price remain firm after an order is placed and until shipment is made? If so, how soon must the quotation be accepted? Will supplier's prices be revised downward in event of market decline before shipment? Will supplier's price be subject to escalation or increase after an order has been accepted and if so, for what cause and within what limits? Answers to these questions have a heavy bearing on the purchasing decision, particularly when final delivery will not be made for several months or more. They are a lesser influence on short delivery purchases.

Product Quality. Quality of a product as viewed by the purchasing agent is that degree of quality which will result in the product's most economically useful life for the purpose intended. It is the measure of the desired characteristics of the product, rather than its perfection; hence it must be judged in the light of its suitability for the purchaser's needs. Since quality determination, then, is a matter of judgment, and the use of good buying judgment is the purchasing agent's most necessary qualification, here is the factor in source selection deserving his utmost attention. It calls for careful examination of the following points.

Specifications and/or design. The bid tabulation or similar check list is a most useful tool for this purpose. Study of bidders' catalogs and literature and thorough discussion of specification and design features with sales representatives are also necessary steps for the full understanding of comparative quality.

Demonstrations or samples. Visual inspection and comparison, whenever feasible, are unexcelled as means of product evaluation.

Experience of other users. Users of a product are usually willing to tell a prospective purchaser what their experiences have been with that product, although they may not always be willing to do so in writing. Direct contact in person or by telephone is the best means of obtaining a user's confidential opinion of any product. Testimonials written or printed for general distribution are of doubtful reliability.

Reputation. The degree of respect which a product commands on the market is an indication of its quality and reliability for the purpose intended. It is a factor of particular importance when the product is to be incorporated as a component in the purchaser's product.

EXAMPLE:

> A manufacturer of garden tractors buys the gasoline engines to power them. The reputation and customer acceptance of the make of engine selected directly affect the reputation and marketability of the tractor.

Product reputation cannot reliably be determined by vendor discussions alone; broad investigation is frequently necessary.

Prospective Supplier Service. The service factor in industrial transactions is not simple. It commences with the sales representative's first call of solicitation; his demonstration of competence; his prompt, complete, and imaginative response to an inquiry. It continues with efficient entry and acknowledgment of orders; prompt, accurate handling of order status requests, revisions in specification or delivery instructions; self-initiated follow-through on delivery performance; proper packing, routing, and tracing of shipments; prompt and accurate billing. It includes technical advice or instructions on installation and use of the seller's product; quick response to complaints and undelayed, fair adjustments thereof; prompt supply of repair parts; and exhibited seller interest in product performance throughout the product's useful life.

It is hardly possible to determine in advance the effectiveness of a prospective supplier's service. There are, however, several indicators which can be investigated and compared by the buyer, and which will give him a good basis for judging probable service performance. They include:

Availability and capability of sales and technical personnel. Investigation should include not only supplier's representation in the buyer's immediate area, but the home office or factory staff as well.

Availability of replacement parts. This is an important consideration when purchasing:

1. Capital equipment or tools for use in the purchaser's operations
2. Components to be incorporated into purchaser's product

EXAMPLE:

A lift-truck manufacturer who purchases gasoline engines for assembly into his trucks will wish to be certain that engine parts are available promptly to users of those trucks from well-located service stocks throughout the country.

Capacity to supply anticipated volume. Before making the initial purchase of a repetitive production item which is expected to develop into substantial quantity, the buyer's investigation should provide assurance that the supplier selected will have sufficient capacity to meet the volume requirements. This is an especially important consideration if expensive tooling is involved so that a single source must be relied upon.

Commitments to others whose requirements may at times absorb a large portion of supplier's capacity, such as obligations to (*a*) parent, subsidiary, or affiliated companies or (*b*) unusually large customers. Such obligations are likely to have an effect on a supplier's ability to serve additional repetitive requirements regularly and without interruption.

Transit time from shipping point. When uninterrupted or definitely scheduled receipts of the item are essential to maintain purchaser's production, the shorter the transit time, the less chance of costly delays.

Labor Relations. The relationship that exists between management and labor in a supplier's plant is of great concern to a buyer who relies on that plant for consistent, regular supply of a product. A good labor relations history is no guarantee against disrupting strikes or slowdowns in the future, but it is a sufficiently good sign to merit important consideration by the prudent buyer.

Financial Responsibility. The financial standing of a supplier, or prospective supplier, is a factor warranting thoughtful consideration by the buyer; it is the key to evaluation of:

Ability to stand behind a product in case of failure. It would be foolhardy to purchase a large piece of plant equipment at a cost of thousands of dollars from a source whose resources would be seriously strained if it were required to make good on a major defect. A well-financed supplier is able to back up its product and is the most likely to provide good repair and technical service over an extended period.

Dependability of supply. There are many elements necessary in the make-up of a dependable source, but financial soundness is one of the most essential. High credit rating is an indicator of good management in production as well as in financial control. (See Section 28, "Appendix," under Credit Reports.) Lack of adequate financing or good credit may prove a serious handicap to reliable, smooth, continuous operation.

The financial position of a company is evidence of the extent of its past success, and is the best possible guide to the character of its future performance.

Reciprocal Relations. The comments above which referred to solicitation of quotations apply equally in the selection of actual suppliers. "Reciprocity can be neither wholly served nor wholly ignored. One can, perhaps, steal a phrase from the language of international diplomacy—"most favored nation treatment." In other words, no supplier shall be given a better opportunity than the "related" one. No other supplier shall be given more assistance than he. Every avenue to his success shall be strictly open. But when the points are tabulated and the various factors weighed, good procurement demands that the better bidder win!

It would be less than realistic not to note that pressures will be very strong to vary this policy and that some industrial climates will ignore it. In a manual of good procurement practice, however, the reader should expect to find exactly that, and good procurement is open, equal, and fair procurement.

Reciprocity philosophy that violates the above policy is self-defeating. In our complex society, every seller is potentially a customer and vice versa. The larger and more diversified the company affiliation, the more this is true. To practice flagrant reciprocal favoritism is to espouse a policy which tends to limit the growth of one's own enterprise and to deny it business from its larger growth market.

FACTORS INFLUENCING SELECTION OF SOURCE—REPETITIVE PURCHASES

Past Performance of Seller. This criterion is a most significant one where past experience with a seller exists. Broad "memory" impressions are only valid, however, by accident, if at all. They tend to crystallize around one happy or unhappy experience and not to be a measure of total performance.

Modern progress in procurement methods has seen increasing emphasis placed upon meaningful evaluation of seller performance. In simple fairness to one's suppliers and oneself, this must be reduced to a quantitative basis. An adequate and effective system for measuring the merit of suppliers can thus become the unassailable proof of a purchasing opertion's honesty and efficiency. It is the final answer to every charge of bias and favoritism.

As ever, when truth is to be constructed, it must be the result of adding together a series of facts each of which must be valid. One must really and fairly measure performance in those aspects which, collectively, make a good procurement.

With suppliers with whom one is doing continuing business there are only three criteria of good performance to measure. They are:

1. Quality. The level achieved in terms of adequacy of average product to the defined level of need, and the per cent of rejected material reaching you, the customer.
2. Price. The consistency of a fair cost for the quality level required.
3. Service. The fulfillment of promises; the effort expended to recoup schedule and problem situations; the evidence of sanctity of promises.

The National Association of Purchasing Agents has established a Development Projects Committee which prepared a report[6] with the following suggestions. All three of the methods of seller evaluation noted by the Committee give full recognition to the fact that it is net cost for fulfillment of the function that is being purchased which is significant and that dollar payment for the item itself seldom determines this. The three methods noted are:

1. The Categorical Plan
2. The Weighted-point Plan
3. The Cost-ratio Plan

These represent three levels of sophistication in arriving at a total evaluation of seller effectiveness and depend for their effectiveness on three different levels of data gathering capability, such as might be available from a moderate-sized enterprise, a medium-large one, or a large and fully automated business.

The Categorical Plan. This assumes keen and able evaluation by all members of the buying staff. Each buyer keeps a listing of his major suppliers at hand. As events occur, he notes them against the list. A monthly meeting is held at which each seller is reviewed with the intent of weighing the plus notations against the minus ones, and each seller is assigned to a "preferred," "neutral," or "unsatisfactory" category.

This plan is easy and effective. It does not permit corrective action with a vendor, since provable data do not exist. However, it far surpasses depending on the personal whim of the buyer or on his vague impressions.

[6] "Evaluation of Supplier Performance," National Association of Purchasing Agents, New York, 1963.

The Weighted-point Plan. This plan is identical in approach to the method of bid evaluation of similar name, described earlier in this section. Quality, price, and service are given "weights," and sellers are rated for quality and service in terms of percentage of good performance to the total performance and, in the case of price, in terms of delivered total cost to the buyer.

The resulting ratings are then changed to a composite one which becomes a portion of 100 per cent. There will emerge a seller with an absolute nearer approach to 100 per cent than the others. The basis will be supported by factual data which can be used for corrective action with the faltering suppliers, if such is mutually desired.

With the approval of the National Association of Purchasing Agents, Figs. 7–8 through 7–11 are reproduced below to illustrate use of this approach. In this example, decision has been made to weight the factors as follows:

Quality . . . . .40 points
Price . . . . .35 points
Service . . . . .25 points

Figure 7–8 shows the relative simplicity of arriving at the quality portion of the rating.

(Insert drawing & part no.)	Lots received	Lots accepted	Lots rejected	Percentage accepted × Factor		Quality control rating
Supplier A	60	54	6	90.0	40	36.0
Supplier B	60	56	4	93.3	40	37.3
Supplier C	20	16	4	80.0	40	32.0

Note: To rate lots closer a system of fractional lots can be used. Thus, if an unacceptable lot is only half or one-tenth bad, it could be said 0.5 or 0.1 lots were unacceptable, etc. This would distinguish between suppliers with a total lot unacceptable and only a small part of a lot unacceptable.

FIG. 7–8. Quality rating under the Weighted-point Plan.

In Fig. 7–9, the price factor is illustrated as being more complex, since one must first determine real cost delivered to the buyer, which is done in Fig. 7–9, Part A. Then, the buyer must convert this into a merit value, which is illustrated in Part B of Fig. 7–9. Here the lowest cost is rated as 100 per cent, and the others are related thereto by dividing them into this lowest cost.

Part A

	Unit price	– Discount		+ Transportation charge	= Net price
Supplier A	$1.00	10%	($ .90)	$ .03	$ .93
Supplier B	1.25	15%	($1.06)	.06	1.12
Supplier C	1.50	20%	($1.20)	.03	1.23

Part B

	Lowest price ÷	Net price =	Percentage ×	Factor =	Price rating
Supplier A	$ .93	$ .93	100%	35	35.0
Supplier B	.93	1.12	83%	35	29.1
Supplier C	.93	1.23	76%	35	26.6

FIG. 7–9. Price rating under the Weighted-point Plan.

In Fig. 7–10, the service factor (fulfilled promises, etc.) has been tabulated similarly to the quality one.

	Promises kept ×	Service factor =	Service rating
Supplier A	90%	25	22.5
Supplier B	95%	25	23.8
Supplier C	100%	25	25.0

FIG. 7–10. Service rating under the Weighted-point Plan.

By compositing these (Fig. 7–11), we have a true qualitative proof of the greater economic value resulting from dealing with "Supplier A."

Rating	Supplier A	Supplier B	Supplier C
Quality (40 points)	36.0	37.3	32.0
Price (35 points)	35.0	29.1	26.6
Service (25 points)	22.5	23.8	25.0
Total rating	93.5	90.2	83.6

FIG. 7–11. Composite rating under the Weighted-point Plan.

The Cost-ratio Plan. This plan assumes a flow of extensive cost and time data to purchasing, presumably from an over-all data processing system. The net price is, again, set down for each seller. All subsequent actions in obtaining seller's performance are then reduced to dollars and cents. Letters, telephone calls, visits, etc., are "charged to his account," so to speak. The cost of the item through this vendor can be a quite literal accumulation of fact. Frequently, items like "number of days of lateness" are standardized as penalty points per day which are assigned a real dollar value. Items like transportation, whether planned or of premium variety to cover lateness, can be charged at actual value.

VENDOR EVALUATION RATING SYSTEM

VENDOR EVALUATION—DELIVERY FACTOR
PER CENT ALLOWABLE OF FACTOR RATING OF 35 MAX. POINTS

0 DAYS LATE EXCELLENT	ONE DAY LATE GOOD	TWO DAYS LATE FAIR	THREE DAYS LATE QUESTIONABLE	FOUR DAYS LATE UNSATISFACTORY
100 35	85 29.75	70 24.50	55 19.25	40 14.0

DAYS LATE FIGURED AFTER FIVE DAYS FROM VENDOR'S AGREED SHIPPING DATE
FIG. (underlined) = PERCENT OF POINT VALUE.
FIG. = ACTUAL POINT VALUE.
* % OF ACCEPTABLE LOTS BY Q C

VENDOR EVALUATION—QUALITY CONTROL FACTOR
PER CENT ALLOWABLE OF FACTOR RATING OF 50 MAX. POINTS*

	EXCELLENT	GOOD	FAIR	QUESTIONABLE	UNSATISFACTORY
MAXIMUM	100 50	99 49.5	94 47.0	89 44.5	84 42.0
AVERAGE		97 48.5	92 46.0	87 43.5	82 41.0
MINIMUM		95 47.5	90 45.0	85 42.5	80 40.0

QUALITY = 50
DELIVERY = 35
PRICE = 15
100

QUESTIONABLE - CAUSE FOR IMMEDIATE REVIEW

UNACCEPTABLE - CAUSE FOR REMOVAL FROM BIDDER'S LIST

VENDOR EVALUATION—COMPOSITE RATING

	EXCELLENT	GOOD	FAIR	QUESTIONABLE	UNACCEPTABLE
QUALITY	100 50	97 48.50	92 46.0	87 43.50	82 41.0
DELIVERY	100 35	85 29.75	90 24.50	55 19.25	40 14.0
PRICE	100 15	100 15	100 15	100 15.00	100 15.0
	100	93.25	85.50	77.75	70.0
SPREAD		99-92.25	92.24-84.50	84.49-76.75	76.74-69.0

PRICE - ALL VENDORS WILL RECEIVE 15 POINTS IN COMPOSITE RATINGS UNLESS THE RATING IS BEING APPLIED TO A CURRENT BID COMPARISON.

FIG. 7–12. Display of vendor evaluation system as used at Sylvania Electronic Systems—East, Needham Heights, Mass. (*Reproduced through courtesy and permission.*)

It is intended that the flow of information to this record be on a continuous basis. Therefore, the real cost of an identical item from several sellers varies with the skill and dependability of the seller. It is common to notify suppliers of their ratings periodically. Thus, purchasing impartially upgrades the performance of all sellers who seriously want to do business, by selecting suppliers for maximum net value to the buyer.

If the buyer's organization is geared to produce data on all rejection percentages and delivery delinquencies and to segregate certain overhead cost factors to vendor accounts, the cost-ratio plan of vendor control is most desirable because of its fairness and accuracy.

The majority of readers will probably have to be satisfied with the quite effective weighted-point plan, modified to suit specific conditions.

Before leaving this subject of evaluation, there is an important factor of judgment to be noted. All three of the above systems, and others that might be devised, involve an arbitrary assignment of importance to one or more of the quality, service, and price factors. One must remember that this was arbitrary. In the previous illustration, 40, 35, and 25 per cent were chosen respectively. Figures 7–12 and 7–13 illustrate a company using the weighted-point plan and assigning weights of 50, 15, and 35 per cent. By giving every vendor 15 points on price, it has removed price from impact on the rating and left this factor for the buyer to evaluate.

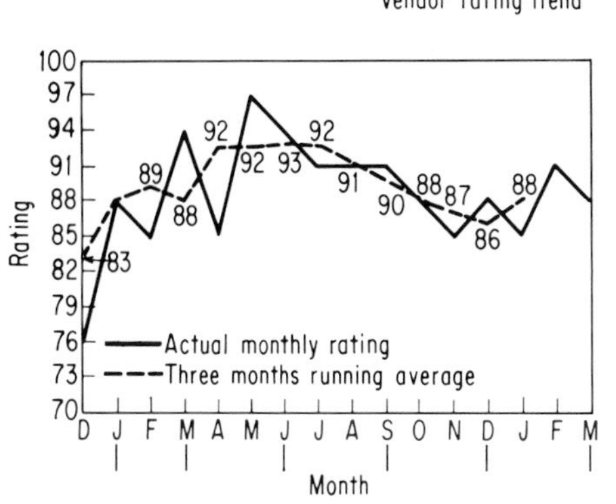

FIG. 7–13. Procurement vendor evaluation. A study of a single supplier, using system described in Fig. 7–12. (*Reproduced by permission Sylvania Electronic Systems.*)

The actual weights assigned to factors should be a measure of (*a*) the importance of that factor to the buyer and (*b*) the difficulty in obtaining that factor. For example, if the tolerances of a mechanical part are so broad as to be easily realizable from any half competent seller, quality might have a very nominal value. If, however, the tolerances are so unusual that a high order of sophistication is required of a vendor to realize, quality would tend to rise in esteem and points.

FACTORS INFLUENCING SELECTION OF SOURCE—ALL MAJOR PURCHASES

Particular factors of measurement for both original and repetitive procurements have been considered in the preceding pages. There are, of course, a group of universal factors which control the success of a seller relationship of any duration, but which increase in importance as one's involvement with the supplier becomes larger financially or more critical to the welfare of the buyer's organization.

Financial Adequacy. Normally, financial adequacy and stability is foremost among these. However, with relation to any given level of purchase commitment, the buyer need only concern himself with adequacy to sustain that level. For example, if the purchases may not exceed $100,000 per year, why should a billion-dollar supplier be considered better than a million-dollar one? Thus, capital adequacy is a "yes" or "no" judgment; if "yes," it can be watched to assure continuance but otherwise dropped as a comparative measure.

Cooperative Capability. Evidence of the ability of an organization to work cooperatively with a buyer's needs will reveal itself from previous experience or, lacking that, will be indicated in talks with sales representatives and sales managers. Both willingness and ability to act maturely will be betrayed to the discerning buyer.

Samples. Sometimes a resort to careful examination of samples will reveal a host of decisive factors and provide reassurance. However, reservations with respect to dependence upon samples are distinctly in order.

1. Remember that samples may be selected carefully to impress the buyer and may not necessarily be representative of a production run.
2. Acceptance of samples should be carefully controlled with the following criteria as guides:
   a. They should be authorized to be received only by and through the buyer and as a result of his issuing a memorandum purchase order.
   b. Usually, they should be paid for, and the buyer should so insist. Items of the most nominal value are sometimes properly furnished at no charge because of the excessive cost of paper work. However, the tendency of the seller's representative will be to overstate this "nominalness"; the buyer is advised to establish a policy of paying.
   c. Evaluation of the sample and report to the supplier is an ethical responsibility of the buyer. If he has paid for the samples, this is a minimum trade courtesy; if he has accepted them at no charge, he is under direct moral responsibility to do so.

No hint of obligation, moral or otherwise, should be permitted to color judgment prior to the selection of a supplier.

Plant Visits to Potential Vendors. When any major procurement is involved, plant visits can be the most valuable tool of decision making. The buyer himself should make such visits and draw upon whatever special assistance he may want in technical support as team members. As technology complexes our needs in this modern environment, the plant visit has assumed a justified prominence.

For this to be true, however, such a visit must be a planned, productive meeting of two organizations, not a pleasure junket. The difference between the two is represented by (*a*) an agenda prepared in advance, including visits to specific management people of the plant and the obtainment of answers to specific areas of inquiry, and by (*b*) a formal report of the visit which goes into the vendor file of that supplier for future use. The effectiveness of the plant visit becomes a question of who maintains control of it. If the buyer does not do so, it will be the duty of the prospective supplier, as a courteous host, if for no more selfish reason. The buyer who has a formal written agenda of "things to find out," who obtains those answers in succession, and who can summarize his findings in a formal report will control the visit to his company's advantage.

What constitutes a proper agenda for such a "buyer-controlled" visit? This varies with the nature of the need prompting the visit. However, there are two broad areas of such need:

1. The monitoring, negotiating, or expediting visit. Merely to define the circumstances prompting the visit is to suggest the proper agenda.
   a. If quality level is deteriorating, why? Where is the fabrication process failing? How, and by whom, can recovery be achieved?
   b. If delivery is sagging, what isn't happening on time and who is responsible for the delay? What must happen to reinstate performance, and what can be done to recover the lost time?
2. The exploratory, or "evaluating," first visit. The purpose of this visit is to determine whether a potential source has the capability to discharge a contract well, or which source, among several, can do so best.

This second type of visit demands some useful observations which are almost always measures of capability.

1. Adequacy and maintenance of the plant and equipment. This is answered by the following observations:
   a. Is the plant antique, modernized, or relatively new?
   b. Is care and maintenance a planned program or a sporadic accident?
   c. What limitations of work are determined by the size capacity of the tools and machines?
   d. Does the presence of ingenious methods and set-ups reveal deep and imaginative experience in the field?
2. Housekeeping, cleanliness, and maintenance of order. These factors reflect the habits of management itself. Chaos on floors and benches and in stockrooms is hardly likely to not also exist in the offices and administration. It will exist, too, in their business relations with customers.
3. Trade or technical knowledge at all levels. This is a factor of importance to the buyer in every area of responsibility. If the buyer buys only fingers and muscle, he accepts responsibility to direct and control these himself. He should want to delegate this control to the seller. He must, therefore, discover whether the capacity to control labor and machines exists where it is needed.

4. A program of controlled quality of output. In larger buying organizations, a member of the quality assurance department will frequently be called upon by the buyer as a member of the visiting team. Often, however, the preliminary decision, at least, resides with the buyer. Control of quality is not measured by the degree of gold-plating and precision that *can* be achieved. It is measured by the knowledge of quality that is regularly created and can be recognized at every important check-point. Whether quality exists can be answered by such observations as:
   a. Do gauges and instruments exist to adequately test the item?
   b. Are the inspection points at the proper stages of fabrication?
   c. Are gauges and instruments calibrated and corrected on a regular cyclical plan?
   d. Are records kept of the results of instrument checks and production inspections? Are these records available, retrievable, and traceable to the exact items tested?
   e. Is incoming material inspected and evaluated prior to adding the in-plant labor cost to it? (Failure here will be the basis of missed delivery dates for the buyer.)
   f. Is quality assurance, as an organization, situated in the management organization so that its integrity cannot be influenced by either the design group, who "fathered" the design, or by the manufacturing group, who "mothered" the fabrication?
   g. Does the quality assurance department use the statistics gathered to apply statistical control and corrective techniques where needed?
5. Morale of the total organization. This is important down to the lowest tier. In this judgment, however, a "happy family" atmosphere is not necessarily one of high morale. The critical element is mutual respect. This should be disclosed in all personnel relationships, even in the most chance interchanges to which the buyer may be a witness.
6. Management competence. Without this, almost all else is lost. However, if the preceding five aspects have been favorable, management competence will nearly certainly exist. Thus, the buyer has much help in judging this factor, apart from profit and loss statements.

A closing word is in order regarding the impact of financial statements on a buyer's selective judgment. These documents are frequently supplied as proofs of competence. Usually they are some measure of such, but the buyer should recognize them for what they are—financial snapshots taken at a point in time. They indicate a future capability, but they do not make it inevitable; nor do they preclude improved future performance.

The buyer should remember that the impact of his potential business will either bolster a sagging workload at the seller's plant, fit into a normal production cycle to maintain a planned workload, or create a new level of workload. What the buyer observes in a plant visit should be interpreted in the context of whichever of the above three situations will be true. Hence, the evidence of the past characteristics of the seller must be weighted against the impact of the proposed business. The question is how the seller is likely to perform under the presumed workload.

ALTERNATE SOURCES OF SUPPLY

Advantages. As long as our economy is one wherein costs are assumed to be kept reasonable through the force of competition, more than one source for all materials needed will be the healthy environment for good procurement. This is a universal fact. However, price integrity is not the only area improved by multiple sourcing. At least three other advantages are involved.

1. Without warning, "disasters" can eliminate the effectiveness of any seller, guilty or not. Fires, earthquakes, windstorms, strikes, legal suits in injunctions—these are in part unpreventable and their losses are usually irretrievable. Frequently, "blame" simply is not involved, and even when it is, the buyer is not helped by fixing it on someone.
2. Improvement of product, generation of new ideas, imagination applied to the buyer's needs—these are stimulated by honest, open, and continuing competition.
3. Open encouragement to multiple sources helps a buyer create a more favorable trade or public image for his company. The broader the buying base of the company, the more the rest of society regards it as an honorable and fair-minded enterprise.

Limitations of Application. With the principle established that multiple sources constitute good procurement, it must still be noted that circumstances limit application in practice. Note that the word "limit" is used. Some circumstances involving the following factors will prohibit multiple sourcing, some will determine the number of sources that should be used at one time, and some will point the way to an "open ball game."

1. If, perhaps, the buyer does not actually need identical items from all suppliers, he most likely can take advantage of easy and uncostly interchangeability. The specifications to which he buys should be as open as the technology of the item will permit; but barriers to such interchangeability can exist, and, if genuine, must govern the procurement.
2. Consistent with the remarks made above on the evaluation of various sources, a "best" source will have emerged. Other sources are, therefore, somewhat inferior, and multiple sourcing implies that the buyer accepts a penalty in this respect. This penalty must be offset by the benefits of "second sourcing."

3. Total cost of the item to the buyer is usually a function of quantity. The curve of price is not a uniform slope. It is usually steep in the area of the lower quantities, flattening out as quantity becomes large. Multiple sourcing, therefore, presumes that the buyer is purchasing in enough quantity to enable him to reach the flattened part of the price curve with each of two or more sellers.
4. All of the factors such as price, delivery, and service apply to all sources of an item when weighing the advantage to the buyer. Parallel sources must improve themselves and be improved by the buyer's action so that they will move in the direction of being truly identical to the primary source. The environment is thus created for the best kind of competition when repeat purchases of the item occur.

Leverage of Multiple Sources. In the distribution of business among multiple sources, the buyer has the opportunity to use his buying leverage to steadily improve every factor of the procurement for his company. It is quite ethical and healthy to frankly use this percentage of division as reward and punishment. The right to compete for a buyer's business is an inherent one; the right to enjoy continuance of business is an earned one. The buyer who does not reward a seller for especial virtue is destroying the incentive of that seller to continue his extra effort.

SELLER RELATIONS—THE PRACTICE OF TOTAL GOOD BUSINESS

The procuring agent approaches his full stature of businessman in his conduct of buyer-seller relationships. He is living continuously before the bar of judgment and is measured, by both his company and the suppliers, by the same scale of merit. Respect is engendered in both by the same criteria. The selling fraternity will necessarily take advantage of poor and "rubber stamp" buying to boost its sales—it cannot afford not to. But it will enjoy selling to, competing for the business of, and earning the favor of astute, intelligent, and capable buying agents. The purchasing agent is a salesman. He has money to sell. Money is exactly as much of a commodity as any item purchased, and the supplier is buying money with his goods or services. The value for which a buying agent sells his company's money is determined both by the wisdom with which he selects the customers for his money and by the control he maintains over the business relationships that result.

BIBLIOGRAPHY

For other reference literature than that noted in the text of this section, see Section 26, "Library and Catalog File."

SECTION 8

QUALITY: THE MAJOR ASSIGNMENT

Editor

Raymond W. Brick, Executive Secretary-Treasurer, Purchasing Agents Association of Los Angeles, Los Angeles, California

Associate Editors

Clifford H. Dawley, Purchasing Agent, Ampco Metal, Inc., Milwaukee, Wisconsin

E. M. Barrow, Purchasing Manager, Knight Electronics Corp., Division of Allied Radio Corp., Maywood, Illinois

What is quality? Why is it necessary? How is it obtained? The quality of a product is not just one feature of that product, but rather the degree to which the product meets the requirements of the immediate purchaser, the intermediate fabricator or assembler, the distributor, and the ultimate consumer of the end product.

BASIC FACTS ON QUALITY

Quality requirements may include, but are not limited to:

Dimension
Weight
Chemical analysis
Physical properties
Performance and life characteristics
Finish
Appearance
Design
Value for the price

Quality is necessary for user satisfaction whether the user be the immediate purchaser, an intermediate processor or handler, or the ultimate consumer.

Quality is obtained:

By adequately specifying the requirements
By selecting vendors who have the capabilities and know-how
By mutual understanding of purchaser's needs
By the exercise of adequate quality control in producer's and purchaser's operations

Quality specifications cannot be written in detail into every purchase order or purchase agreement; but, a quality specification must be a necessary part of every purchase agreement. This may be accomplished by reference to:

Established buyer specifications
Established vendor specifications
Blueprints

Catalog references
Engineering association specifications
Industry association standards
Government specifications

Selection of vendors may be made:[1]

By a specific investigation involving one supplier and a single transaction (See Section 28, "Appendix," under Procedure for Initiating and Concluding Trials or Tests of Materials or Equipment, a suggested procedure to establish new or alternate sources.)
By a choice from an established list
By a routine selection based on experience
By use of a well-established well-known company

Mutual understanding of purchaser's quality needs is an essential element of good vendor-user relationships and is accomplished:

Through adequate specifications
Through education of vendor by visitations of qualified purchasing personnel
Through review of vendor's performance to ensure compliance
Through prompt contact on quality problems through established channels

Quality control in its broadest concept includes:

The organization and procedure through which a producer controls the quality of the product manufactured
The specifying of purchase requirements
The inspection and acceptance of incoming parts
The assurance of compliance on the part of the supplier to specified quality levels by education, including field representative reviews
The contacting of vendors on quality problems
The handling of rejected items
The financial and accounting aspects of rejections

Quality control is the responsibility in some degree of all of the following functions or departments whether separately organized or in combination:

Sales
Engineering
Manufacturing engineering
Production
Quality control
Purchasing
Technical
Receiving
Incoming inspection

[1] Also see Section 7, "How to Select Sources of Supply."

QUALITY DEFINITIONS

The definition of the word "quality" and the meaning of "quality control" have gained much significance in modern manufacturing needs. These help in the close control of necessary requirements of material analysis, dimensions, make-up, and performance specifications. Of Webster's several definitions, the following will best describe quality from the buyer's standpoint:

"The power to accomplish—capability of doing a certain thing."

From this it will be seen that as far as the buyer is concerned, the mere fact that an article is "good," or "best," or "highest priced" does not necessarily mean that it has the required "quality" (from the standpoint of the purchase order specification) unless it does the required thing in the needed manner.

It may be assumed from this that job specifications or performance requirements must be written into every purchase order or purchase agreement. To attempt to do so on every order is impossible from a practical standpoint and is too time-consuming and costly for the benefits it may bring.

What it does mean is that the *quality specification* is a necessary part of every purchase transaction. The purchase order must state what the item is required to be and/or do. The quality specification may be expressed in terms of size, weight, dimension, color, kind, performance, or in any other terms necessary so that the vendor supplies what the buyer needs. To assist in the use of the information which follows, please keep the following definitions in mind. They will help to avoid confusion with terms which are sometimes used to describe different activities which are not covered here:

Quality. The power to accomplish—
Capability of doing a certain thing.
The establishment of a specification capable of doing a certain thing.

Quality Control. Often the buyer's quality-control people may function in a dual capacity and assist the purchasing department and the receiving department inspection on control of received material quality. For the purpose of this publication "quality control" is meant to apply only in the area of purchased items obtained from suppliers. It is not to be confused with the quality control of items produced within the buyer's own plant or business. See also page 8–10, "Responsibility in the Quality Department."

Necessity and Benefits of Quality Control

There are many reasons for the control of quality on purchased items, all of which will add up to profit dollars for the buyer's company. One important reason is that it avoids confusion between buyer and seller in determining what is required, etc., which will result in improved supplier relationships.

The legal aspects of a quality-control program are important. Without a clear statement of needs on the purchase agreement and without full understanding of the needs by the vendor, there can be legal responsibility on the buyer's part if the vendor shipped under an honest misunderstanding. The buyer may then find himself responsible for all or for a part of the defective goods if the quality requirement on the purchase order was incomplete or not clear.

Production requirements are met in time and in the needed quality by material or parts which meet the quality specification. High costs always result from:

Rejection of shipments
Resultant production delays
Extra handling of rejections and replacements
Extra inspection of rejections and replacements
Lowered quality of finished items made from or with poor quality components
Increased production time in buyer's plant

Lowered costs will result from the right thing (acceptable quality) at the right time for the buyer's needs. As in the case of all purchases, a lower price may also result when the vendor is able to produce well and in continuous production material and parts which meet the buyer's quality specifications on delivery.

HISTORY OF QUALITY CONTROL

In many items and in many industries, the matter of quality is so simple or so well established over a long period of time that its expression is simple and sure. Precision manufacture, however, has introduced the necessity of spelling out quality specifications in detail and sometimes also requires substantial vendor education to ensure acceptable quality of the purchased items.

New automation techniques and other advances in technology are being adapted to all types of business activity (both manufacturing and commercial) and have consequently required new materials, new parts, new processes, and new tolerances. These new items, along with increasingly critical requirements on new uses for old established materials and parts, have introduced the necessity of detailed specifications to be furnished a supplier with the purchase order. Good judgment will determine the extent to which it is necessary to detail the purchase specification, and it is desirable that the buyer make it as brief and as easy to understand as possible. It will be obvious that it is not necessary to specify gauge and quality of wire on a paper-clip requirement if the only need is a standard pattern and size.

It will be equally plain that where special needs or performance are desired, such information shall be furnished in as simple a fashion as possible to bidders on the request for bids, and to the vendor on the purchase order. A clear understanding of the specification goes far toward the development of quality-control needs and methods. Historically, many industries have established products where delivery of acceptable quality items is a matter of record. On such items and often with such established vendors, the control methods discussed in this section will not be necessary or needed, until there has been a quality rejection.

Many industries and many companies will be in the position of operating with materials and parts where there are no stringent quality requirements. In such activities the quality specification and the quality control will be simple. The continued development of precision manufacture in the metalworking industries, the expansion of possibilities in the atomic field and other areas of supply appear to forecast the need for increased attention on the part of the buyer for quality control involving detailed inspection of purchased materials and parts.

In the more complex activities and products, the buyer will carefully appraise his quality requirements, clearly pass them on to the bidders and to vendors, and take any necessary steps to ensure the receipt of purchased items which meet the quality requirements and to secure vendors who can satisfactorily meet those requirements.

Although "quality" is a basic concept in modern buying and selling, it is reaching a highly sophisticated place in some of the "space age" requirements—aircraft, missiles, and electronics. In many applications (especially those in which products are being produced for outer space travel), the performance specification is very rigid and gives a whole new view of quality to both buyer and seller.

Included in this concept is a new quality requirement which is being termed "traceability," meaning that a part is completely traceable in all of its handlings and processings—sometimes even to the basic raw material as produced (metals as they come from the mine, etc.).

Although "traceability" is not a feasible characteristic for ordinary commercial products, the alert purchaser should be aware of this highly technical quality requirement, as the impact of such programs may well have an effect on many of our commercial and industrial activities.

RESPONSIBILITY FOR QUALITY CONTROL

The need for quality control, broadly speaking, is the responsibility of everyone in the buying and selling company. Its cost benefits are so great that every good employee of both buyer and seller will do everything possible to ensure good material and parts on the first delivery.

From a practical standpoint, however, it is well to pinpoint some of the areas of responsibility. These will vary from industry to industry and may be different within companies in the same industry, depending on conditions and products, and sometimes on organizational setup. It may be necessary to examine several plans and company setups and alter them to suit the particular problem or industry.

The following ideas work in some instances. One of them, a combination of several, or parts of them may give the most workable setup for effective quality control.

Responsibility in the Purchasing Department

Quality is a prime responsibility in the purchasing department regardless of where the quality specifications actually originate. The buyer's job is not finished with the placing of a purchase order; the purchased item must be delivered on time and be of the correct quality.

Where quality specifications are not severe and where the purchase requisition may be originated in the purchasing department, the quality specification is often established or coordinated with the issuance of the requisition.

Where the quality specification may be complicated and particularly where performance is expressed as a function of the purchased item, the quality specification may be the responsibility of other departments within the buyer's company.

There are several departments and activities where the prime responsibility of quality specification on purchased materials may be placed. Some of these are discussed under appropriate headings.

Whether or not the purchasing department has the responsibility of originating or coordinating the quality specification, it is accountable for seeing that the quality specification is part of purchase agreements.

The purchasing department *must:*

1. Know what is wanted and pass the information on to the bidders and to the vendors.

2. See that the vendor performs according to the purchase quality specification.
3. Take necessary steps to protect the buyer's company against financial loss from material or parts which do not meet the purchase specification.

To accomplish the above, it will be necessary for the buyer on occasion to enlist the assistance of others (both inside and outside the buyer's company) to develop and make workable the purchase quality specification.

The purchasing department buyer does not start negotiations or ask for bids on an item of purchase (the nature of which requires a quality specification) without having available to him sufficient information to permit the prospective supplier to submit an intelligent and realistic bid. Under such circumstances the buyer sees to it that a proper specification is developed so that the buyer's company, and the prospective vendor, may be protected from financial loss which can result from poor-quality material, or defective parts, or from claims arising out of lack of understanding of what is required. In some instances the vendor may be given an opportunity to review and participate in establishing the quality specification.

When in spite of all preliminary precautions, material is rejected by the buyer's receiving inspection as not meeting the purchase quality specification, the purchasing department is responsible for the negotiations leading to the disposition of any extra costs which may have been incurred.

The vendor notification of rejected items and the subsequent negotiations regarding the disposition, credit, etc., involved should be the responsibility of the purchasing department. It is desirable that these negotiations be handled with the vendor by the same buyer who handled the original purchase. The person who does the buying is in a better position to handle rejections of materials than others in the buyer's company for several reasons, among which are the following:

1. The buyer knows what was wanted and handled the papers which spelled out the quality specification.
2. The vendor will find it easier and more satisfactory to deal with the buyer than the other individuals within the buying company. For this reason, it is frequently to the buying company's advantage since a vendor is easier to negotiate with on a rejection if he feels that he is dealing with someone who is familiar with the entire picture.

The purchasing department is the focal point for the buying company's quality-control program and will enlist all the help necessary from within the company to make it function effectively on purchased items.

In this connection, it is important to note that in a survey conducted by the National Industrial Conference Board in 1948, 280 purchasing agents reported on responsibility for the quality-control function, i.e., inspecting and testing incoming materials. Only 14 per cent indicated primary responsibility for the function, while 80 per cent responded that they held joint or secondary responsibility.

Responsibility in the Engineering Department

The establishment of the purchase quality specification is the responsibility of the engineering department in many companies and in many industries. Where proprietary design or when the item required involves complicated manufacture, the engineering department may be charged with the duty of developing and transmitting such quality specifications to the purchasing department or to the people who issue the purchase requisitions. Some engineering departments also actively supervise the incoming inspection activities. In some cases the quality specification is originated by engineering and other departments handle the incoming inspection.

Responsibility in Production Engineering Departments

In some industries, production engineering is responsible for the quality specification of purchased items. This duty may be prime, that is, the production engineering department may originate the specification or they may coordinate it with the material requirement (such as on the bill of material, etc.) so that the quality specification appears on the requisition to purchase.

Responsibility in the Production Department

In some instances it is advisable to have the production department establish or cooperate in the development of the purchase quality specification. This is especially true in the case of capital equipment intended for production use and for facilities used by, or under the control of, the production or operating department.

It is also customary for the purchase quality specification on supply items (such as expendable tools, wheels, bits, etc.) to be originated by or controlled by the production or operating department.

Where not primarily responsible for the origin of the purchase quality specification for raw materials or component parts, it is important that the needs of the production department be carefully established and reflected in the development of the quality specification. Cooperation with the production or operating departments at this point, as well as after receipt and during use of purchased items, pays big dividends in lowering production costs and increasing profits.

Responsibility in the Quality Department

Sometimes it is useful to have one group responsible for quality problems and for exercising quality control over the buyer's produced items. Where such a function exists in the buyer's company, it may be advisable, and it is frequently the custom, to charge the quality group with responsibility for quality of items purchased as well as for quality of items to be produced or processed in the buyer's plant. Where this is the case, the quality department may have the prime responsibility for issuing the purchase quality specification. In other cases it is desirable to leave this prime duty in other departments (as engineering, etc., as before mentioned) with the quality department acting in an advisory capacity in the preparing of this specification. Where a quality group exists within the buyer's company, it is desirable that such group have responsibility for incoming inspection. It is also useful and very helpful to enlist the aid of the quality group in the education of vendors, preferably at the time of establishing a new source.

Responsibility in the Receiving Department

This is the point at which deviations from the purchase quality specification may become evident. Adequate inspection facilities (people, space, and tools) are a prime requisite of receiving and of receiving inspection functions. Where possible the inspection activity should be carried on in, or closely adjacent to, the receiving area. Where necessary to perform one or more of the inspection checks at a point removed from the receiving area, in-transit check should be controlled by the receiving department until the incoming shipment has been accepted or rejected. When rejections are made, the receiving department will see that proper notification is forwarded to the purchasing department with sufficient details as to the reason for the rejection so that the vendor may be notified. The receiving department will continue to have physical jurisdiction over rejected material until disposition is received from the purchasing department or will release it to some function that has been agreed upon which will retain the shipment until such disposition. (Among the latter will be the segregated area which is designated for rejected materials awaiting disposition and the so-called Material Review Board, MRB, which has become popular in metalworking industries such as the aircraft industry.) Regardless of how the organization may be set up (that is, wherever the quality specifications may originate), it appears that the following items are a necessary part of the receiving department's contribution to a smooth-working quality-control program:

1. Incoming shipments must be checked immediately on receipt for possible shipping damage and to see that the weight, count, etc., agree with the shipper's forwarding documents and appear to be substantially within the quantity or amount specified on the buyer's purchase order.
2. Receiving inspection must be performed as soon as possible to determine whether the quality specification on the purchase order has been met and the received item is within the specified quality limits. (See "Determination of Quality" later in this section.)
3. Where unacceptable parts (or material) have been received, the shipment must be segregated and notification forwarded to the purchasing department of the reasons for rejection.

Responsibility in Other Departments

There will be other departments in many companies which have an interest in and some responsibility for the quality specification for purchase and for the quality-control program on purchased items. These will vary with the industry, the company, and sometimes with the product but a few of the activities which have some interest are listed here:

Matériel or materials division	Production scheduling
Material control	Research
Production control	Technical

Often activities such as these will have the responsibility of originating purchase requisitions against which the purchasing department issues an order. Some of these may have the prime responsibility of the purchase quality specification and may operate from a central specification file. Where they do not have the prime responsibility for the purchase quality specification, it is necessary that they be accountable for coordinating the quality specification so that it appears on the requisition at the time of issuance or that reference be made in such a way that the quality requirement becomes an integral part of the requisition to purchase. The buyer's sales department also has an interest in proper quality control, although perhaps on a more general basis. For example, it may be desirable (or even necessary) that sales departments obtain from customers their needs in the form of definite and acceptable quality standards. These quality requirements will be passed on to other departments within the buyer's company so that they in turn will be reflected in the buyer's quality purchase specification.

EFFECTIVE QUALITY-CONTROL PROGRAM REQUIREMENTS

1. Specifications of quality which may develop from:
   a. The needs of buyer's own products of production
   b. Customers
   c. Those within buyer's company who design, plan, schedule, control, purchase, etc.
2. Responsibility for the establishment of the quality specification such as engineering, production engineering, etc., as already enumerated
3. Responsibility for passing the quality specification to the vendors
4. Responsibility for adequate incoming inspection to be assured of receiving the required quality
5. Responsibility for checking and reporting to the purchasing departments any items rejected for quality deviation
6. Responsibility for negotiation for the return and replacement, for credit, etc., of rejected materials

HOW QUALITY IS EXPRESSED

Quality may be expressed in various ways, but it is important to do it in a manner which will clearly show what the item is intended to be, to do, and what the buyer expects to receive. It is important not to overspecify and it is not necessarily true that the highest-priced material is the best quality for the intended use. Methods of expressing the purchase quality specification follow:

By Blueprint or Dimension Sheet

This is a common way of establishing the quality specification in metalworking, building, and in other industries where dimensional limits are required. When using these, the information must be clear, the dimensions completely specified, the tolerances (if any) expressed, and the language or terminology not ambiguous. Blueprints or dimension sheets may originate from sources such as the following:

1. Customers' drawings or specifications
2. Central specifications file (some purchasing departments have their own or a duplicate of their engineering department's specifications file)
3. The engineers or others in the company who prepare the requisition for the purchasing department

The blueprint or dimension-sheet method has the advantage of inviting competition and establishing the buyer's right to inspection and rejection on agreed standards. Its disadvantages include the cost and time of preparing specifications.

By Industry Standard

Particular requirements of certain industries and industry groups have developed a type of need which has come to be expressed as an industry standard. Such standards are frequently outlined in sufficient detail and with enough exactness to make it satisfactory to refer to them as part of the purchase quality specification. An industry standard may also be an American Standard.

In addition to industry or company standards, various common-use standards are frequently used as an American Standard issued by the American Standards Association. These include:

ASME—American Society of Mechanical Engineers
ASTM—American Society for Testing and Materials
NEMA—National Electric Manufacturers Association
SAE—Society of Automotive Engineers
AN—Army and Navy Specifications
USP—United States Pharmacopoeia
Federal and State Specifications

(See Fig. 8–1 as a typical AMS steel specification, and Fig. 8–2 as a typical instrument specification published by the Society of Automotive Engineers.)

Standards such as the above, and many others which are not listed, are the outgrowth of much experience in use and represent an accurate and understandable quality specification. Where they fit the buyer's needs or when the needs can be adjusted to take advantage of an existing industry standard item, important savings of time and money can often be made because such items are quickly available at lower cost, and with better quality acceptance, than are many tailor-made products or materials.

By Brand or Trade Names

Continued manufacture and merchandising of a product or material to consistent quality standards over a long period of time will often establish the "brand" or trade name as an effective and dependable standard of quality. Where such a brand or trade name has been found satisfactory, the buyer is often safe in specifying it as his purchase quality specification. Often it may be satisfactory to specify a brand name or trade name "or equal."

AERONAUTICAL MATERIAL SPECIFICATIONS | **AMS 5755**

SOCIETY OF AUTOMOTIVE ENGINEERS, Inc. 485 Lexington Ave., New York 17, N.Y.

Issued
Revised

ALLOY, CORROSION AND HEAT RESISTANT
Nickel Base - 5Cr - 24.5Mo - 5.5Fe

1. ACKNOWLEDGMENT: A vendor shall mention this specification number in all quotations and when acknowledging purchase orders.

2. FORM: Bars, forgings, and forging stock.

3. APPLICATION: Primarily for parts and assemblies, such as turbine shrouds and seals, requiring oxidation resistance up to 1600 F, good strength up to 1200 F, and low coefficient of expansion.

4. COMPOSITION:

		Check Analysis	
		Under Min	or Over Max
Carbon	0.12 max	--	0.01
Manganese	1.00 max	--	0.03
Silicon	1.00 max	--	0.05
Phosphorus	0.050 max	--	0.005
Sulfur	0.050 max	--	0.005
Chromium	4.00 - 6.00	0.10	0.10
Molybdenum	23.00 - 26.00	0.10	0.10
Iron	4.00 - 7.00	--	--
Vanadium	0.60 max	--	0.01
Nickel + Cobalt	remainder		
Cobalt, if determined	2.50 max	--	--

5. CONDITION:

5.1 Bars: Hot rolled, solution heat treated, and descaled. Rounds 0.75 in. and over in diameter shall be centerless ground.

5.2 Forgings: Solution heat treated and descaled.

5.3 Forging Stock: As ordered by the forging manufacturer.

6. TECHNICAL REQUIREMENTS:

6.1 Heat Treatment: Material shall be solution heat treated by heating to 2150 F ± 25, holding at heat for not less than the time indicated below, and quenching in water or rapid air cooling.

FIG. 8–1. Typical AMS steel specification. (*Reproduced by permission of Society of Automotive Engineers, Inc., New York.*)

There are many brand or trade names of industrial and commercia products which have been well established through long usage and whic can be used as acceptable quality standards. The buyer may establish list of his own which will provide an effective and convenient way o

SOCIETY OF AUTOMOTIVE ENGINEERS, Inc. 485 LEXINGTON AVENUE NEW YORK 17, N.Y.	AERONAUTICAL STANDARD	AS412A
CARBON MONOXIDE DETECTOR INSTRUMENTS		Issued Revised

1. PURPOSE: To specify minimum requirements for carbon monoxide detector instruments for use in aircraft, the operation of which may subject the instrument to the environmental conditions specified in Paragraph 3.3. This standard is not intended to cover fire detectors.

2. SCOPE: This Aeronautical Standard covers the basic type of carbon monoxide detector instrument used to determine toxic concentrations of carbon monoxide by the measurement of heat changes through catalytic oxidation.

3. GENERAL REQUIREMENTS:

3.1 Material and Workmanship:

3.1.1 Materials: Materials shall be of a quality which experience and/or tests have demonstrated to be suitable and dependable for use in aircraft instruments.

3.1.2 Workmanship: Workmanship shall be consistent with high grade aircraft instrument manufacturing practice.

3.2 Identification: The following information shall be legibly and permanently marked on the instrument or attached thereto:

(a) Name of instrument (Carbon Monoxide Detector)
(b) SAE Aeronautical Standard AS412A
(c) Manufacturer's part number
(d) Manufacturer's serial number or date of manufacture
(e) Manufacturer's name and/or trademark
(f) Rating

3.3 Environmental Conditions: The following conditions have been established as design requirements only. Tests shall be conducted as specified in Sections 5, 6, and 7.

3.3.1 Temperature: When installed in accordance with the instrument manufacturer's instructions, the instrument shall function over the range of ambient temperature indicated in Column A below, and shall not be adversely affected by exposure to the temperatures shown in Column B below.

Instrument Location	A	B
Heated Areas (Temp. controlled)	-30 to 50 C	-65 to 70 C
Unheated Areas (Temp. uncontrolled)	-55 to 70 C	-65 to 70 C

3.3.2 Humidity: The instrument shall function and shall not be adversely affected when exposed to any relative humidity in the range from 0 to 95 percent at a temperature of approximately 32 C.

3.3.3 Altitude: The instrument shall function and not be adversely affected when subjected to a pressure and temperature range equivalent to -1000 feet to 40,000 feet standard altitude except that the instrument temperature shall not be lower than -30 C.

FIG. 8–2. Typical AS instrument specification. (*Reproduced by permission of Society of Automotive Engineers, Inc., New York.*)

transmitting the purchase quality specification to bidders and to suppliers. Using brand names has the advantage of simplicity but may limit buying to a single source for a particular product and thus destroys the competitive element in sound procurement.

By Chemical or Physical Specification

In the case of chemicals, metals, etc., it is sometimes necessary or desirable to specify composition of purchased materials.

Companies in the chemical business and firms that compound purchased items for resale frequently have their own chemical specifications on the material which they purchase. Where such specifications exist, they should be attached to the purchase order to establish the quality specification desired. Another way to handle this is to furnish the bidders and vendors with a master copy of the specification which is coded or identified in such a way that a purchase order reference will clearly establish the quality specification desired. (An example of this might be a paint company which specified on its purchase order "our XYZ specification aluminum bronze," to a supplier who had a copy of the XYZ specification.) Where metal alloys are purchased and industry standards do not cover the necessary requirements, the chemistry of the alloy should be specified to make sure that the vendor will furnish the correct quality.

By Performance

On occasion the function of performance of a purchased item is a part, or the principal portion, of the quality specification. Where performance is specified, it is important that the required behavior be as simply expressed as possible with the performance limits or variables (where such exist) clearly specified. It is not unusual for the purchaser to disregard completely the appearance or the composition of a purchased material and simply specify work which is expected of the purchased material. As an example, the purchase order may specify a metal as follows:

> Must be suitable for forming 90-deg. bends by drop hammer without rupturing and must withstand operating temperatures of 1100°F without appreciable surface oxidation evident after 72 hours of such temperature.

In this case it will be seen that appearance apparently does not have any bearing on the quality specification and that the purchaser does not care about the chemical make-up of the metal as long as it meets the performance requirements.

By Sample

Where the quality specification cannot be established clearly or satisfactorily by any of the previously mentioned means, it is well to furnish a sample of the item desired to the vendor for duplication. In using the sample for quality specification the following points are important:

1. The sample must be of sufficient size or quantity to permit easy matching.
2. The limits within which acceptance can be effected should be specified. (As an example, color samples are often furnished in textiles, paints, etc. Wherever possible, the color variation permissible should be expressed in relation to a common factor of whiteness such as magnesia and to a color-rating scale such as that furnished by Keuffel & Esser and others. Paint color should be rated both "wet" and "dry.")

Combination of Specifications

Where the needs (the quality specifications) cannot be clearly expressed by any one of the means covered, a combination of two or more may be used to advantage. The quality specifications should be as short and as concise as possible but should not sacrifice exactness or clearness for brevity. In whatever manner quality is specified, the buyer should know what he wants and needs, and the vendor must also know what the buyer expects to get. Any compromise with this means the possibility of shipments which will not meet the quality specifications and which will result in expensive rejection.

Summary for Expressing Quality

Just how quality is expressed on the purchase order depends on a great variety of conditions, particularly the type of industry and the effectiveness of the purchasing department. To obtain a cross-sectional summary on how quality is specified, *Purchasing* magazine published in its March, 1955, issue the results of a series of questions asked of purchasing agents all over the country.

In answer to the question of how quality was designated, 31 per cent responded that purchases were established by specification, 30 per cent by brand name, 27 per cent by ordinary commercial designation, and 12 per cent by other methods. It was important to note, however, that 92 per cent of the purchasing men further indicated that the purchasing department had the prerogative of purchasing a brand other than specified, if it was of equal quality. Furthermore, 91 per cent reported that even with a given brand, samples and prices of competing brands were periodically obtained for consideration.

THE APPROVED BIDDERS' LIST[2]

Where an item or material is substantially a tailor-made one for a particular purpose, an approved bidders' list may be established by the

[2] Also see Section 7, "How to Select Sources of Supply."

buyer which will consist of those vendors who can satisfactorily supply to the buyer's quality specification. The problems involved in establishing an approved bidders' (or vendors') list are too numerous to allow a complete coverage in a quality specification or quality-control discussion. However, it is not possible to establish such a list without carefully appraising vendors from the quality standpoint.

As an important and effective tool of the quality-control program and its contribution to lower costs, it is necessary that alternate sources be established on all purchased items. At least two sources should be maintained at all times and where possible it may be desirable to have more than two vendors on the approved list of suppliers. In having an alternate source, the buyer will be able to maintain production within his own plant pending resolution of any problem which is a development of a quality rejection of purchased materials or parts. There will be other ways of specifying quality to vendors. The vendor must know what the buyer wants and what the buyer expects him to do.

DETERMINATION OF QUALITY

Determining compliance with the required quality is perhaps the most involved and probably one of the most important parts of a good quality-control program. To function effectively, quality determination should be made immediately on receipt of the shipment. For this reason the receiving inspection function should be located in the receiving area or as close to it as possible. This will avoid expensive handling and re-handling and save time in releasing correct material or parts to the production department or to production stores. The physical layout, the personnel, and the equipment of receiving inspection is not often the responsibility of the purchasing department, but the purchasing department will have a substantial interest in the workings of this group and will closely cooperate with it in the quality-determination efforts and standards as well as in the prompt handling and disposition of rejected shipments. The starting point for receiving inspection is a copy of the purchase order with the quality specification clearly spelled out or supported by referenced standards or attached documents. Figure 8–3 shows a specimen purchase order attachment.

The purchasing department will see that receiving inspection is supplied with copies of purchase orders and will assist in providing copies of specifications on any standard quality call-outs which may appear on such purchase orders. (This might include copies of specifications such as applicable SAE or ASME specifications where these appear as material or specification call-outs on the orders.) See Fig. 8–4 for the first page of a specimen SAE steel specification.

Military Standard MIL-STD-105A (Sept. 11, 1950) may be found useful in setting up a control program. It can be had from the Government Printing Office at a nominal cost.

The receiving (receiving inspection) department is responsible for the verification of materials with the purchase order to determine whether they meet the quality specification on the order. Such determinations

---

RELIABILITY TEST REQUIREMENTS

GENERAL

This purchase order attachment requires that parts manufactured for ______ as specified on this order be tested to the requirements on Form 3260. These tests are performed periodically on sample units taken in accordance with the instructions contained herein. Performance of these tests prior to shipment of the lot shipments sampled is not required but should be completed as promptly as possible after the end of the manufacturing period. Although double sampling and testing is permissible, ______ will pay only for first sample tests and for the units destroyed in these tests. Payment for these tests is subject to acceptance by ______ of the certified test results reported on Form 3260. These test results should be sent to ______ Receiving Department.

1. *GROUP C TESTS*

1.1 Testing to measure the reliability of a component, or to test the conformity of the design, construction, and materials shall be conducted by the seller at periodic intervals. The Group C tests shall be performed in the order listed on Form 3260.

1.2 Units of the same general construction shall be grouped for the purpose of Group C inspection Classification of units for such grouping is supplied by the buyer. Sample size to be tested will be governed by the sampling table referenced on Form 3260. An exception to grouping shall be made when the part is first produced or production is resumed after a lapse of more than four months. In this case samples from the parts produced will be subjected to Group C tests in accordance with test requirements of Form 3260.

1.2.1 Those characteristics which assure conformance to the procurement specification and which measure the conformity to design, processes and material shall be designated as Group C.

1.2.2 Life tests shall be designated as Group D.

1.2.3 The list of Group C and Group D characteristics shall be supplied to the seller on ______ Company Form 3260 (Reliability Test Certification).

1.3 All units withheld for Group C inspection shall have successfully passed Group A and Group B inspection.

1.4 A portion of each week's production shall be randomly selected during a three-month or other specified manufacturing period and held as samples for Group C tests. The number withheld shall be proportional to the rate of production and be sufficiently large to provide for both the first and second sample. The samples selected shall be as evenly distributed and as representative as possible. At the end of the manufacturing period as specified in Section 1.4 or 1.5, the seller shall perform, or have performed by a testing laboratory approved by the buyer, all required tests listed on Form 3260. At the completion of the testing, the results shall be immediately forwarded to ______ Company Receiving Department.

1.5 The sampling interval set forth in Section 1.4 shall be increased to four months when three successive lots have successfully passed Group C tests.

1.6 If an outside testing laboratory is used, so indicate in the proper column and supply the name and address of the laboratory on the form.

1.7 All units manufactured for the buyer shall be identified with a unique mark or code to identify manufacturing period. This mark or code shall be supplied to the buyer on Form 3260.

1.8 If any sample unit fails any of the Group C tests, the seller shall immediately notify the buyer and furnish a written record of the cause of failure and proposed corrective action. The buyer will reply as promptly as possible as to whether the proposed corrective action is acceptable or whether additional information or alternative steps will be required.

1.9 No further shipments of the type represented by the sample shall be made until authorized by the buyer.

1.10 Units which have been subjected to Group C inspection shall not be shipped to the buyer, unless specifically requested.

1.11 If, in the manufacture of a unit, seller proposes a change in (*a*) materials used, (*b*) manufacturing process, (*c*) construction, (*d*) place of manufacture, the buyer is to be notified in detail. However, changes shall not be binding upon buyer unless evidenced by a purchase order Change Notice issued and signed by buyer.

2.0 GROUP D INSPECTION:

2.1 Where the item is of a type that requires life testing, details of the test will be supplied by the buyer on ______ Company Form 3260 (Reliability Test Certification). Group D testing need not be performed prior to shipment.

2.2 Sample size shall be in accordance with the sampling table referenced on Form 3260. The sampling interval shall be the same as provided for Group C inspection unless otherwise specified.

2.3 Samples for Group D testing shall be selected in the same manner as set forth in Section 1.4. Samples shall have passed Group A and Group B tests, but shall not have been submitted to Group C tests.

2.4 Group D test results shall be forwarded in accordance with Section 1.4.

2.5 Failure to pass Group D inspection shall be handled as established in Section 1.8 and 1.9.

2.6 Samples which have been subjected to Group D tests and second set of samples not requiring testing shall be shipped to the buyer only on issue of a Change Notice to the purchase order. Overshipments against production orders will not be accepted.

2.8 Questions concerning these requirements or need for additional copies of instructions, forms or sample tables should be referred to the responsible ______ Buyer.

THIS ATTACHMENT, WITH ITS TERMS AND CONDITIONS,
IS AN INTEGRAL PART OF THIS PURCHASE ORDER.

NAME OF COMPANY PURCHASE ORDER ATTACHMENT

FIG. 8–3. Specimen purchase order attachment on reliability test requirements.

might include (but may not be limited to) quantity, weight, size, count, appearance, odor, dimension, color, performance, composition, etc.

Such verification is not always completely possible within the geographical area of receipt and will be supplemented by additional or supplementary checks performed by engineers, chemists, production men, etc., at points which may be far removed from the receiving area itself.

Where such verification must be performed at another point and in another department, it is important that the responsibility for the material being tested remain with the receiving inspection department until final approval, or until deviation has been established which results in rejection.

High-Strength, Low-Alloy Steel, SAE 950

SAE Recommended Practice

High-strength, low-alloy steel represents a specific type of steel in which enhanced mechanical properties and, in most cases, good resistance to atmospheric corrosion are obtained by the addition of moderate amounts of one or more alloying elements other than carbon.

Steels of this type are normally furnished in the hot-rolled or annealed condition to minimum mechanical properties. They are not intended for quenching and tempering. The user should not subject them to such treatment without assuming responsibility for the ensuing mechanical properties. Where these steels are used for fabrication by welding, no pre-heat or post-heat is required. In certain complex structures, stress relieving may be desirable. These steels may be obtained in any of the standard shapes or forms normally available in carbon steel.

TABLE 1—*Minimum Properties of Steel as Furnished by the Mill*

PROPERTY	THICKNESS OR DIAMETER, IN.				
	Up to 0.0709 inclusive	0.0710 to 0.2299 inclusive	0.2300 to ½ inclusive	Over ½ to 1 inclusive	Over 1 to 2 inclusive
Minimum yield point[a], psi	50,000	50,000	50,000	47,000	45,000
Minimum tensile strength[a], psi	70,000	70,000	70,000	67,000	65,000
Elongation[b] in 2 in., %	20	22[c,d]	22	22[e]	22[e]
Elongation[d] in 8 in.	—	—	1,500,000/tensile strength		
Bend test[f], 180 deg	D = 1T	D = 1T	D = 1T	D = 2T	D = 3T

[a] For severe cold-forming operations requiring greater ductility, relaxation of the yield-point and tensile-strength requirements is commonly negotiated between producer and consumer.

[b] ASTM standard rectangular specimen, 2-in. gage length. (ASTM E 8).

[c] Minimum thickness for plates over 48 in. wide is 0.180 in.

[d] For plates, material 0.180 in. and heavier is customarily tested in 8-in. gage length using ASTM standard rectangular specimen subject to modification of ASTM A 242.

[e] For 0.505-in. diameter, use ASTM standard round specimen 2-in. gage length. (ASTM E 8.)

[f] Use ASTM A 242 bend test.

Application—These steels because of their enhanced strength, corrosion- and erosion-resistance, and their high strength-to-weight ratio and service life, are adapted particularly for use in mobile equipment and other structures where substantial weight savings are generally desirable. Typical applications are automotive bumper face bars, truck bodies, frames and structural members, scrapers, dump wagons, cranes, shovels, booms, chutes, conveyors, railroad and industrial cars.

Qualification Tests—At the option of the purchaser of a new or modified grade or radically different range of thickness, samples from one to three mill heats may be initially supplied for qualification tests for resistance welding, metallic arc welding, and for notched-bar impact properties of the particular grade or thickness range to be furnished. (The qualification is for information as to these and other desired properties and their variance from mill heat to mill heat.)

Chemical Composition Limitations—The maximum limits of the several elements are to be as given in Table 2 unless otherwise negotiated between producer and consumer.

TABLE 2—*Chemical Composition Limits*

ELEMENT	CHEMICAL LIMIT	REMARKS
Carbon Manganese	0.12 max. 1.00 max.	For resistance welding.
Carbon Manganese	0.20 max. 1.25 max.	For other-than-resistance welding and non-welded applications.
Sulfur	0.050 max.	—
Phosphorus	0.150 max.	Phosphorus is beneficial as a strengthener and improves corrosion resistance, but it should be considered in conjunction with other elements in resistance welding applications where in satisfactory low-temperature properties are required. To avoid excessive brittleness, severely cold-formed high-phosphorus material should be stress relieved.
Silicon	0.90 max.	Silicon is a strengthening element, but must be considered in connection with other elements and their effect on resistance welding.
Copper	—	Where copper exceeds 0.70% unless adjustments are made in composition, the phenomenon of precipitation hardening in heating should be given due consideration.
Other alloying elements	—	The choice of, and limits for alloying elements other than those mentioned necessary to attain required mechanical properties, are commonly negotiated between producer and consumer. The type of alloy combination should not be changed without the knowledge and consent of the purchaser and in accordance with the requirements implied by the above qualification tests.

Tolerances—The standard manufacturing tolerances for dimensions shall apply to the respective commodities procured under this specification. (Tolerances for carbon steel are given in the AISI Steel Products Manual.)

FIG. 8–1. Specimen SAE steel specification. (*Reproduced by permission of Society of Automotive Engineers, Inc., New York.*)

Sampling

Where material or parts are received in large volume, it is expensive and time-consuming to inspect 100 per cent of the material or parts so received. Several shorter methods of determining quality have been developed which are found satisfactory in some industries and for some products or materials. As an illustration, the custom of physically counting small parts will often give way to an agreed weight-quantity determination between the vendor and buyer. (For example, miniature bearings may be sold and accepted on the agreed basis of 1 lb avoirdupois being equal to 10,000 bearings. This eliminates the Herculean task of physically counting, which may not be worth the time and expense involved.)

Among the methods of quality determination the *statistical sampling method* has recently become quite popular. This method operates on the basis of taking samples of a predetermined size or quantity, inspecting them, and accepting or rejecting the entire shipment on the basis of the quality evaluation of the sample. Mathematically it has been proved that statistical sampling will operate satisfactorily within predictable limits and savings of inspection time and money can be realized without adversely affecting the accuracy of quality determination in the receiving department (receiving inspection). Statistical sampling operates on the basis of published mathematical tables. It is not necessary to understand the mathematical background of these frequency tables to be able to use them successfully. Tables such as "Computation of Sampling Inspection Tables" by H. F. Dodge and H. G. Romig (John Wiley & Sons, Inc., New York) have successfully replaced the haphazard selection of arbitrarily selecting any given percentage with a method of predictable success. The interest in this method and the rather widespread use of the statistical sampling method warrant a brief statement of its use as follows:

After the routine inspection in the receiving department to establish identity, size, weight, shipping damage, etc., is completed, the following must be determined so that inspection may be made by statistical sampling method:

1. Lot size (number or quantity in shipment)
2. The acceptance quality level (AQL) (lowest lot quality which can be accepted)
3. The sample size (the number of pieces from the lot which will be inspected and which will determine the acceptance or rejection of the whole lot)
4. Acceptance number (maximum defective pieces in the sample which will still allow the acceptance of the entire lot based on the sample inspection)

Variations of the sampling procedure will be found useful. For instance, on small amounts the "single sampling" method is used satisfactorily. The single sampling method may be illustrated by the following:

> One hundred parts are received which have an AQL (acceptance quality level) of 0.06 per cent. From the table we find that 27 pieces should

be inspected and at an AQL of 0.06 per cent not more than 1 piece can be found defective; otherwise the whole lot of 100 would be rejected.

This single sampling method is employed to maintain a high quality level on small quantities.

Where quantities are larger, the "double sampling" method is employed. This method reduces inspection time over the single sampling method while maintaining an acceptable quality determination. In the double sampling the original sample withdrawn from the lot (entire shipment) is smaller than that taken in the single sampling method. A second sample is taken which tends to check the first sample taken in the double sampling method. Where the first sample is not productive of the results desired, a second sample is taken to check the results of the first sample. Since this second sample is taken only when results from the first sample are not conclusive, it will be seen that the total number of samples withdrawn under the double method will tend to be less on the average than those taken under the single method. An example of how double sampling might operate follows:

1. Lot size	4,000 pieces	
2. AQL	1 per cent maximum	
3. Sample size	first sample—150	second sample—300
4. Acceptance number	first sample—3	second sample—7

From the above it will be seen that if the rejections are 3 or less on the inspection of the first sample (150), the entire lot will be accepted. If more than 3 but less than 7 are rejected in the first sampling, a second sample of 300 is taken. (If more than 7 are rejected in the first sampling, the entire lot is then rejected.)

In checking the second sampling, the number of rejects from the first sampling are added to those found in the second sampling. If they do not total more than 7, the entire lot is accepted; if they exceed 7, the entire lot is rejected. See Fig. 8–5 which shows a typical inspection form which can be used with either single or double sampling methods.

Another type of inspection technique is termed "sequential sampling." This is a continuing type of inspection until the decision is reached to accept or to reject the entire lot. This method also employs the use of a mathematically developed chart which assists the inspector in determining the point at which he will accept or reject the entire lot. The chart which is shown as Fig. 8–6 is one which is used in sequential sampling procedures. The parallel lines represent the limits within which the purchased items must fall to ensure their meeting the quality specification. In use, the inspector plots acceptances individually by a cross or check mark, continuing horizontally in a line until he reaches a reject. At this

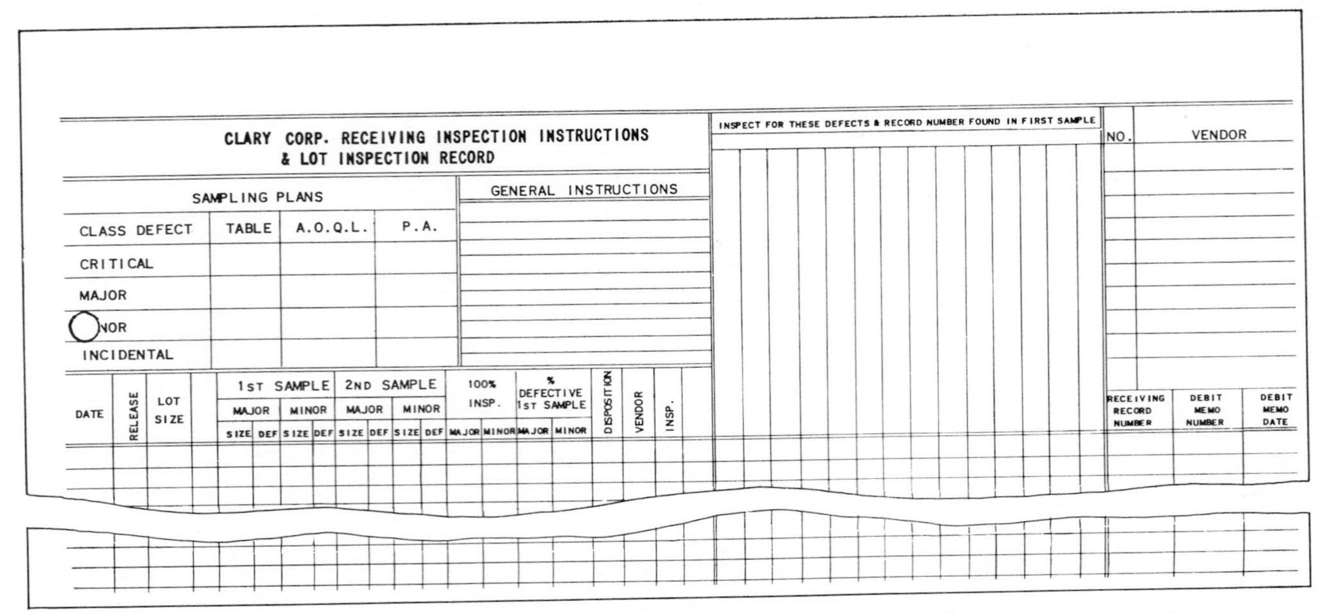

CLARY CORP. RECEIVING INSPECTION INSTRUCTIONS
& LOT INSPECTION RECORD

SAMPLING PLANS			
CLASS DEFECT	TABLE	A.O.Q.L.	P.A.
CRITICAL			
MAJOR			
MINOR			
INCIDENTAL			

GENERAL INSTRUCTIONS

INSPECT FOR THESE DEFECTS & RECORD NUMBER FOUND IN FIRST SAMPLE

NO.	VENDOR

DATE	RELEASE	LOT SIZE		1ST SAMPLE				2ND SAMPLE				100% INSP.		% DEFECTIVE 1ST SAMPLE		DISPOSITION	VENDOR	INSP.
				MAJOR		MINOR		MAJOR		MINOR								
				SIZE	DEF	SIZE	DEF	SIZE	DEF	SIZE	DEF	MAJOR	MINOR	MAJOR	MINOR			

RECEIVING RECORD NUMBER	DEBIT MEMO NUMBER	DEBIT MEMO DATE

FIG. 8–5. Inspection form. This can be used for single or double sampling methods. It also serves as a vendor quality performance record. (*Reproduced by permission of Clary Corporation, San Gabriel, California.*)

point he moves up one division and starts a new horizontal line of acceptance crosses. This procedure is continued until the acceptance symbols either cross the top parallel line, which results in the rejection of the entire lot, or they cross the bottom parallel, which results in the entire lot being accepted.

The above inspection procedures seem to be particularly adaptable to the precision metalworking industry, although the sampling method is used with great success in the petroleum and chemical industries, to mention two. (The petroleum industry takes samples from bulk con-

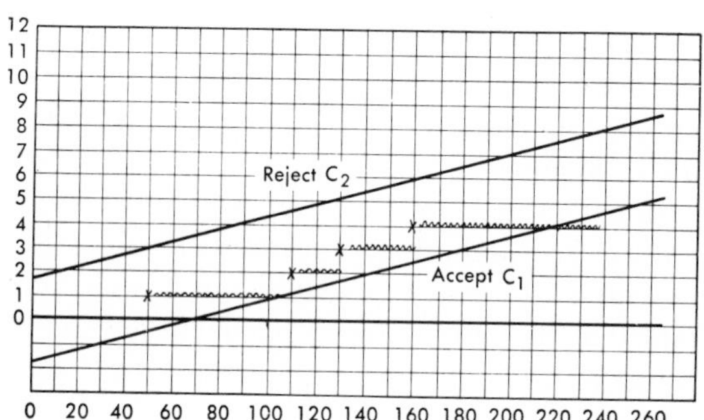

FIG. 8–6. Sequential sampling chart. (*C. W. Kennedy, Quality Control Methods, copyright by Prentice-Hall, Inc., Englewood Cliffs, N.J. Reprinted by permission of the publisher.*)

tainers such as storage tanks and tank cars by dropping a container to various levels, opening it there, and obtaining a sample at that level. Averaging test results from several levels often gives a sufficiently accurate check of the entire lot.)

The success or failure of the various techniques suggested here, and others which may be in use, will depend on samples of the proper size and distribution so that sufficiently accurate results are obtained. Where heavy mortality occurs suddenly with an old established vendor on an item which he has been producing successfully, it will be desirable to "back up" on inspection techniques by increasing the size or frequency of sampling. This remedial action may take the form of 100 per cent inspection of all shipments until the cause for the discrepancy has been determined and the remedy made effective. Among other methods of receiving inspection techniques will be those required by special products or requirements, particularly where performance checks must be run prior to acceptance.

REJECTIONS

Rejections should be handled promptly and with good judgment. There are many sound reasons for such action, a few of which follow. The protection of the buyer's production needs and the cost factor which is so quickly affected by poor parts and material are probably the prime reasons for handling rejections quickly and carefully. The matter of public relations with suppliers, the obtaining of maximum cooperation in speed of remedy of the trouble causing the rejection—as well as reducing the costs of rejections—are also important aspects of this activity.

The mechanics of rejection should be such that notification and complete details are given to the purchasing department as soon as possible after the rejection. The paper-work phase of this procedure is quite important in some companies and it is not uncommon to use a copy of the receiving department's rejection notice for the vendor's notification after proper approval by the purchasing department. See Fig. 8–7 for a sample rejection form, which also serves as vendor notification of rejection.

It is important that the purchasing department get the rejection notice promptly with full information for cause of rejection. The vendor should have full information at once so that he can take the necessary steps to replace the defective shipment with proper parts or material which will meet the purchase quality specification.

The responsibility for actual rejection lies with the receiving department inspection. The responsibility for handling with the vendor should be with the purchasing department and preferably should be in the hands of the buyer who handled the purchase negotiation.

As previously stated, there are several advantages in having the buyer who originally purchased the item handle the rejection notification and subsequent negotiation with the vendor. He has the advantage of knowing the details of the purchase quality specification as agreed upon at the time of placement of the order. The vendor will be more likely to respect the buyer's opinion and wishes than those of a third party who is not completely familiar with the transaction.

The buyer who made the original purchase, and who will probably place additional business with the vendor, is often in the best psychological position to handle rejection negotiations with the vendor.

Promptness in determining the quality of a shipment is the first requirement. The second is immediate notification of the purchasing department along with full details as to the reason for rejection if the quality specification has not been met. After this is accomplished, the

Form 6301-1

UNION PACIFIC RAILROAD COMPANY Order No. ____

REPORT OF OVER, SHORT, REJECTED OR DAMAGED MATERIAL

Report No. ____

Firm Name ____ ____ (Location) Date ____ 19__

Street ____

City ____ State ____ Order No. ____ Date ____ 19__

MATERIAL ORDERED		MATERIAL RECEIVED Shipping Notice No. ____ Date ____ 19__	
QUANTITY	DESCRIPTION	QUANTITY	DESCRIPTION

REMARKS:

Rejected Account ____
Nature of Defect or Damage ____

MATERIAL PREVIOUSLY RECEIVED ____

What does waybill cover? ____ (No. & kind of containers)
Were all items shown on waybill received? ____

Over ____
Short ____

Receiving Sheet No. ____ Date ____ Car No. ____ W.B. ____ Date ____

Seals (Side) ____ (End) ____ Condition of Container when received ____ F. B. ____ Date ____

Weight Gross ____ Tare ____ Net ____ Whose Scale? ____

ACTION TO BE TAKEN AS INDICATED IN SPACES MARKED (X) BELOW:

1. ( ) Make immediate shipment {of material reported short / to replace rejected material} {transportation charges prepaid / transportation charges collect}
2. ( ) Furnish disposition together with return goods tags for material to be returned to you {transportation charges collect / transportation charges prepaid}
3. ( ) Render credit memorandum for incorrect or rejected material promptly upon receipt of return shipment
4. ( ) Excess or incorrect material will be retained
5. ( ) Adjust charges for material retained
6. ( ) Form {5805 / 5846} No. ____ Date ____ has been rendered reporting loss or damage in transit

Above rechecked and found to be correct ____ Storekeeper ____ Stockman

NOTE: All correspondence, return goods tags and other pertinent data pertaining to this report should be mailed to the undersigned promptly showing action taken. Please show reference to the order number as well as number and date of this Form 6301-1 on Invoice, Credit Memorandum, and all Correspondence.

Yours very truly,

FIG. 8–7. Combination rejection form. Also serves as vendor notification of rejection. *(Reproduced by permission of Union Pacific Railroad Co., Los Angeles, California.)*

buyer will have several choices of action in the disposition of the rejected shipment.

The action selected by the buyer will vary depending upon the circumstances but will include the following:

After the buyer is satisfied that the information given him is complete and accurate enough to justify the rejection of the shipment, he will:

1. Explore (with the help of others within his company) the possibility of salvaging the shipment by:
   a. Diversion to another less critical use within the buyer's plant.
   b. Take corrective action on the rejected shipment in the shape of rework procedures which may make it comply with the purchase quality specification. (This rework may be performed by the buyer, the seller, or another, based on an agreement which should be reached with the vendor in advance of the work and the rework expense.)
2. Reject the shipment and ask the vendor for disposition and credit.

The investigation of salvage is always a sound one. It not only will save time in getting the correct item into the buyer's production but also keeps the seller's cost at a minimum. Rework or diversion to another less critical use will often save much, if not all, the cost of items which may otherwise have only scrap value. When a vendor's costs are kept at a minimum by such a common-sense approach to the rejection problem, relations with the supplier will most certainly improve.

The cost of rejected shipments will not prove to be entirely the worry of the vendor, even if he credits in full or replaces at no charge the particular item which is rejected. The vendor's own over-all cost, upon which his price to the buyer on future orders must be based, will be affected by expensive rejections. It will be to the buyer's interest to work closely with the supplier on rejections and on the remedy which will be desirable following such rejections (see "Vendor Quality Rating" and "Vendor Quality Education" in the following pages of this section).

The rejection form should include such information as dimensional and chemical discrepancies, preferably listed along with the purchase quality specification so that a quick and easy check may be made by both the buyer and the vendor. Where special check fixtures or tools are used in the receiving inspection, it should be so specified on the original purchase order or on the rejection notice (or both). Some of the forms which have been found useful in handling rejections are shown in Figs. 8–7 and 8–8. Where possible a single rejection form should be adapted to cover several items. A sample of such a form is shown in Fig. 8–7.

During the period of time in which the rejection is under discussion and prior to the time when disposition of the rejected shipment is determined, it is desirable to segregate the rejected shipment. Unless this is done, there is possibility of loss or damage occurring during the time in which the return or replacement is being negotiated. There is also the possibility that the material or parts may be placed into the buyer's production or production stores by mistake if not segregated and clearly

Form 3021

ORDER NUMBER

UNION PACIFIC RAILROAD COMPANY
RESEARCH AND STANDARDS ENGINEER
CERTIFICATE OF INSPECTION

REPORT NUMBER

SHT._____OF_____SHTS.

OF__________STEEL RAILS__________LBS. PER YARD__________SECTION

MANUFACTURED BY__________AT__________WORKS

FOR__________DATE__________

THE FOLLOWING STEEL RAILS HAVE BEEN INSPECTED AND ARE ACCEPTED.

SPECIFICATIONS__________DATES
NO. OF RAILS ROLLED__________NO. OF HEATS ROLLED__________NO. OF HEATS REJECTED__________OF ROLLING__________

NO. OF RAILS ACCEPTED	TOTAL	NO. OF RAILS REJECTED ACCOUNT OF		ACTUALLY REJECTED	ACCEPTED AS X RAYLS
1. AS NO. 1. FROM THIS ROLLING		12. TOP RAIL TEST PIECE (OR PIECES)	BREAKING		
2. " " 2. " " "		13. " " " " "	FAILING IN DUCTILITY		
3. " " 1. FROM STOCK. SEE REPORT NO.		14. " " " " "	SHOWING INTERIOR DEFECT		
4. " " 2. " " " " "		15. SECOND " " "	BREAKING		
5. TOTAL ACCEPTED AND SHIPPED		16. " " " " "	FAILING IN DUCTILITY		
6. NO. 1. RAILS STOCKED FROM THIS ROLLING		17. " " " " "	SHOWING INTERIOR DEFECT		
7. " 2. " " " " "		18. THIRD" " " "	BREAKING		
8.		19. " " " " "	FAILING IN DUCTILITY		
9. RAILS RESTRAIGHTENED		20. " " " " "	SHOWING INTERIOR DEFECT		
10. RAILS CUT FOR FLAWS — FOR OTHER REASONS		21. SURFACE DEFECTS	OTHER REASONS		
10A. RAILS BROKEN BACK ACCOUNT NICK & BREAK PIECE DEFECT, WITH NO DEFECT AT END OF RAIL OR IN BOLT HOLES		22. TOTAL REJECTED			
10B. RAILS UNDER 10A SHOWING NO DEFECT AT BREAK BACK					
11. RAILS MADE NO. 2 FOR FLAWS — FOR OTHER REASONS					

NUMBER OF RAILS OF EACH LENGTH

	39′	38′	37′	36′	35′	34′	33′	32′	31′	30′	29′	28′	27′	26′	25′		TOTAL
NO. 1																	
NO. 2																	

	CALCULATED WEIGHT			SHIPPER'S SCALE WEIGHT				HOT TRIAL WEIGHTS	
	TOTAL POUNDS	TONS	LBS.	TOTAL POUNDS	TONS	LBS.	%	MAXIMUM	
NO. 1								MINIMUM	
NO. 2								AVERAGE	
TOTAL									

	TOTAL ORDER TONS	TOTAL ACC. INCL. THIS CERTIFICATE			BALANCE DUE	
		TONS	LBS.	%	TONS	LBS.
NO. 1 RAIL						
NO. 2 RAIL						
TOTAL						

NOTE: TOTAL PERMISSABLE WEIGHT NO. 2 PER SPEC. — TONS LBS.

SEE "NOTICE OF RAILS SHIPPED" NOS.

FIG. 8–8. Another type of rejection form used for a specific commodity—in this case steel rails. (*Reproduced by permission of Union Pacific Railroad Co., Los Angeles, California.*)

marked with rejection tags, etc. Where there are frequent rejections, or where it takes a long time to resolve disposition of rejected shipments, it will be found useful to provide a separate area for rejected shipments. This area should be removed from the receiving and receiving inspection departments until disposition can be determined.

The policy of segregation of rejected shipments has several advantage in addition to the protection against unauthorized usage by the buyer' production department. One advantage is that it provides an "as is an where is" location where the vendor can physically inspect the rejecte material. If there is a discussion on quality and on quality determination the buyer should arrange for the meeting and conduct the proceeding in order to ensure proper control of the negotiations. During such discus sions, it is often possible to determine the possibility of rework either b the buyer or the seller.

Minor differences can often be adjusted by work which the buyer ca conveniently perform at his plant. Where this can be done, the expens of boxing, transportation, handling, etc., for return to the seller can ofte be saved. Where such salvage is not possible, the vendor may be able t make the necessary adjustments on the rejected items, or will replace th shipment with items meeting the purchase quality specification. Whe determining the method of diversion, rework, or return, the buyer wil keep in mind the relative cost of the method and the possibility of pro viding from it an acceptable item under the purchase quality specification

Under whatever method selected, or combination of methods that fi the case, the buyer should determine as soon as possible the vendor's re sponsibility and the amount of the costs involved which the vendor i expected to assume. In establishing the financial basis on which rejecte shipments are returned, it will be useful to determine the following:

1. The point of shipment of the rejected item and with what identifica tion so that it can be quickly handled in the vendor's plant.
2. Whether shipment is to be made collect or prepaid, the method o shipment, and/or the carrier. (When a vendor is paying this bill, h may want to select his choice of these items.)
3. Whether the incidental costs of transportation, packaging, handling etc., are for the vendor's account on both the original and the replace ment shipment (if there is a replacement).

Among the steps necessary in connection with adjustments will be th following (the selection of any one or any combination will depend o the circumstances of the rejection and on other factors which will influ ence each particular case):

1. Withhold payment of invoices for items received until after acceptanc by receiving inspection.
2. Where a bill has been paid and rejection made after payment, debi the vendor's account with the value of the rejected shipment or with hold payment of a like amount in other billings of the vendor.

3. Arrange for replacement shipment (if there is a replacement) or an even exchange for the returned shipment, or bill the rejected shipment to the vendor and instruct him to invoice for the replacement shipment.
4. Instruct the vendor as to whether he is to make replacement shipment on the original purchase order or whether a new purchase order will be issued to cover the replacement.
5. Agree with the vendor on the procedure to be followed in the settling of any other financial details which may include items such as the following:
   a. Transportation charges
   b. Packaging charges and handling
   c. Cost of extra inspection time
   d. Cost of lost production time
   e. Loss of associated parts or materials
   f. Any other loss or damage which may have occurred

In most cases, the rejection of shipments and the settlement for them is simple and clear-cut; however, the matter of contingent liabilities may be quite involved. Where there are contingent costs involved, the original purchase order with a clearly stated purchase quality specification will be found invaluable.

With a complete and clear understanding at the time of purchase and with a written record of the purchase quality specification, it is usually only a question of mechanics and careful handling on the part of the buyer in order to effect a speedy and fair settlement with any good supplier. In large companies where there is usually a large volume of paper work in the purchasing, receiving, and accounting functions, it is common practice to debit the vendor for rejected material and to have him remit, or the buyer will deduct on the basis of the vendor's credit memorandum. A replacement shipment can then be billed in the regular manner by the vendor and any difference in count, etc., which may occur will be a matter of written record.

VENDOR QUALITY RATING[3]

A valuable purchasing tool is a vendor rating based on the quality of material or parts which he delivers to the buyer. Often this can be included with the vendor's performance rating in so far as delivery schedules are concerned. Receiving inspection records (where the results can be tabulated and watched over a period of time) will soon show the

[3] Also see Section 7, "How to Select Sources of Supply."

purchasing department whether the vendor is a good one, and whether the buyer is buying at the lowest "cost" considering the quality of the vendor's shipments and his performance over a period of time. Many types of analyses and reports can be developed from a vendor's performance study and most of them will be tailored to the needs of a particular company or to a particular product or material.

An arbitrary determination of unsatisfactory performances based strictly on a flat percentage of failures may be unfair to vendor and buyer alike. As an example, where the "major" and "minor" type of discrepancy is the basis for acceptance and rejection, the proper weight and evaluation should be given to the vendor who is heavy in one or the other. It is unfair to penalize a vendor who has a high percentage of deviations in the "minor" range, but it may be necessary to take decisive action against a vendor who has a relatively low percentage of rejects but which are all in the "major" category.

Samples of such vendor performance rating charts are shown in the numerous figures in this section. Although differing by company and by item, it will be seen that they include the following:

1. Vendor's name
2. Material or part identification
3. Period of time covered
4. Quantity delivered
5. Quantity acceped, rejected, or both

In some cases the above will be expanded to show the number of items in the total requiring inspection. In other cases it will be desirable to show the major and minor (see "Determination of Quality") performance of the vendor. Other variations will suggest themselves, but it is important that the conclusions drawn from such evaluation be arrived at with care and with complete and up-to-date information. It may be possible to obtain a vendor performance check very simply, such as by accumulation of copies of rejection notices against particular vendors and making calculations from the totals which they show. Samples of methods which have been useful in vendor quality performance evaluation are shown in Figs. 8–9 and 8–10. Before developing a form for purchasing department use, the receiving and receiving inspection forms should be examined to see whether the information is not already being accumulated on a form which can be adapted to purchasing department use.

Since quality determination is so much a community responsibility and activity, it is recommended that the purchasing function work closely with all related functions which have interest in or information to contribute to the vendor quality performance rating chart.

INSPECTION & TEST CERTIFICATION

PART NUMBER	PART NAME	REPLACES ISSUE	ISSUE DATE
984541-3	Transformer, Power, Step-Up	ORDER TYPE	DATE
SELLER	ADDRESS		18 November 19
		PURCHASE ORDER NO.	RECEIVING REPORT NO.
		HAC DRAWING NUMBER 984541-3	SPECIFICATION MIL-T-27 984541 & MIL-STD-202

ISSUE DATE: 18 November 19

INSP. CLASS	DEFECT CODE	INSPECTION & TEST CHARACTERISTICS	NO. OF DEFECTS	STAMP OR INITIALS
		GROUP "A" INSPECTION TESTS		
1	931	Marking		
1	707	Dimensions, Mounting		
2	495	Terminals		
2	714	Dimensions, Over-All		
		GROUP "B" INSPECTION TESTS		
2	197	Over-Voltage (Condition 1)		
1	186	Rated Load		
1	316	Polarity		
2	183	Electrostatic Shield		

PREPARED: [signature] APPROVED: [signature]

USE SAMPLE TABLE NO. 1

QUALITY SUMMARY

INSP. CLASS	n	c	NUMBER DEFECTIVES
1			
2			
3			
4			

LOT SIZE	ACCEPTED	IDENT. MARK OR CODE

DISPOSITION

SCREENED	REPAIRED	REPLACED

EXPLAIN YES ITEMS BELOW	YES	NO
CHANGE IN MATERIAL		
CHANGE IN CONSTRUCTION		
CHANGE IN MFG. PROCESS		
CHANGE IN PLACE OF MFG.		
COMMENTS:		

THE UNITS ACCOMPANYING THIS FORM HAVE BEEN INSPECTED TO THE LISTED REQUIREMENTS AND THE RECORDED RESULTS ARE COMPLETE AND ACCURATE

SIGNATURE

TITLE

FIG. 8–9. Inspection and test certification form. May also be used to determine vendor quality performance.

Rejection Code	Pieces	Pct	VENDOR'S QUALITY RATING											
	Orders	Pct												
Vendor	Code No.													

FIG. 8–10. Vendor quality rating form. (*Reproduced by permission of Northrop Aircraft, Inc., Hawthorne, California.*)

VENDOR QUALITY EDUCATION

A sound quality-control program begins with the following:

The vendor must know what the buyer wants.
The vendor must know how to meet the buyer's quality.
Specification as covered in the purchase negotiation and by the purchase order.

Earlier discussions cover the matter of telling the vendor what is wanted. How to meet such requirements is equally important. Primarily, it can be considered the vendor's responsibility and interest to know how to produce properly the item on which he bids and for which he accepts orders.

It is the buyer's responsibility to select vendors who by their experience, facilities, and knowledge (as well as their past performance) are fitted to fill a purchase order in accordance with the buyer's purchase quality specification. The buyer will select alternate sources of supply, each vendor being considered capable of supplying in a satisfactory manner the items required by the buyer. On such a basis the vendor education phase of a buyer's responsibility starts with the selection of the bidders, each one of whom should be potentially a satisfactory supplier from the standpoint of the purchase quality specification.

In purchasing standard items which require only superficial inspection much reliance can be placed by the buyer on sources who have supplied satisfactory products over a long period with no appreciable difficulty in so far as quality is concerned. Where the item is new, where the application is new, or where the specifications take on new significance because of the new use, a new selection of vendors is frequently indicated.

FIELD LIAISON REPORT ON
PROSPECTIVE SUBCONTRACTOR

NAME OF COMPANY ____________

ADDRESS ____________ TELEPHONE NUMBER ____________

ACTIVITIES ENGAGED IN ____________

NAMES AND TITLES OF EXECUTIVES

____

I GENERAL INFORMATION

1. STATE NUMBER OF PRODUCTION EMPLOYEES ____________
2. STATE NUMBER OF EMPLOYEES BOTH PRODUCTIVE AND NON-PRODUCTIVE ____________
3. HAS COMPANY PREVIOUSLY DONE SUBCONTRACT WORK FOR RYAN? ____________
4. IS COMPANY INTERESTED IN DOING SUBCONTRACT WORK FOR RYAN? ____________
5. IF SO, WHAT CLASS OF WORK? ____________
6. TOTAL FLOOR SPACE AVAILABLE ____________
7. TYPE OF BUILDING OR BUILDINGS ____________
8. CONDITION OF BUILDINGS AND OFFICES ____________
9. GENERAL HOUSEKEEPING CONDITIONS ____________
10. ARE LIGHTING FACILITIES ADEQUATE? ____________
11. DOES THIS COMPANY UNDERSTAND THAT IF FOR ANY REASON RYAN WORK IS FARMED OUT, THE RYAN LIAISON INSPECTOR MUST BE NOTIFIED IMMEDIATELY?

____

II INSPECTION FACILITIES

1. DOES THIS COMPANY HAVE A SATISFACTORY INSPECTION ORGANIZATION? ____________
2. NAME OF CHIEF INSPECTOR ____________
3. CHIEF INSPECTOR'S PAST EXPERIENCE ____________

____

4. TO WHOM IS THE CHIEF INSPECTOR RESPONSIBLE? ____________
5. DOES THE CHIEF INSPECTOR HAVE FINAL AUTHORITY TO ACCEPT OR REJECT WORK? ____________
6. ARE INSPECTORS RESPONSIBLE TO ANYONE OTHER THAN INSPECTION SUPERVISORS OR THE CHIEF INSPECTOR?

____

7. IN THE EVENT THAT THIS COMPANY DECIDES TO ACCEPT SUB-CONTRACT WORK FROM THE RYAN AERONAUTICAL COMPANY WILL IT AGREE TO MAINTAIN AN INSPECTION ORGANIZATION ACCEPTABLE TO THE RYAN QUALITY CONTROL DEPARTMENT?

____

8. THIS FACILITY HAS BEEN ASSIGNED CLASS RATING* ____________

GENERAL COMMENTS

*CLASS
A LIMITED ONLY AS TO TYPE OF WORK
B QUALIFIED WITH LIMITATIONS LISTED IN GENERAL REMARKS
C NOT APPROVED BY INSPECTION DEPARTMENT

DATE ____________ PREPARED BY: ____________

FIG. 8–11. Check sheet used to rate a prospective vendor. (*Reproduced by permission of Ryan Aeronautical Company, San Diego, California.*)

The selection of new vendors should be approached with care. Th buyer should enlist the help of engineers, production people, quality de partment personnel, and any others who can help in the factual analysi of prospective suppliers. Often the basic requirements of a good vendo will be summarized on a check or rating sheet similar to that shown o Figs. 8–11 and 8–12. Such a preliminary analysis of a prospective sup plier will help the buyer in establishing a good dependable source in s far as the vendor's potential production of quality items is concerned

In order that we may evaluate your facilities, please answer the following questions:

1. Full name of Company: ____________________

2. Address of Office: ____________________ Phone: __________
   TWX NO:

3. Address of Plant: ____________________ Phone: __________

4. a. Individual: __________ Partnership: __________ Corporation: __________

   b. If not a Corporation, is Company name or Partnership legally registered? __________

   c. Subsidiary of ____________________

5. List Principal Officials: Citizen Yes or No

   ____________________ Name ____________________ Title

   ____________________ Name ____________________ Title

   ____________________ Name ____________________ Title

6. List names of companies for whom work is being done:

   ____________________ Name ____________________ Address

   ____________________ Name ____________________ Address

   ____________________ Name ____________________ Address

7. a. Total number of shop employees: __________ c. Area covered __________

   Area uncovered __________

   b. Number of shifts being worked: __________ Hours per shift __________

FIG. 8–12. Another type of vendor rating form. (*Reproduced by permission of Northro Aircraft, Inc., Hawthorne, California.*)

The preparation of such charts or rating sheets will follow the needs which are indicated by the buyer's business and by the products which are to be purchased. Care should be exercised that all the critical items, the potential trouble spots, be recognized and covered thoroughly in the survey.

The vendor survey is the opening part of the buyer's vendor quality education. In the survey the buyer's requirements, his method of operation, and frequently his manufacturing and inspection methods are covered in enough detail so that the vendor knows what will be expected when he gets a purchase order.

Further education may be necessary after a vendor has been placed on the approved list, and this will be governed by the items which are to be furnished and the quality specification to be applied. When further education is needed, it should be apparent to the buyer at the time the requisition is received and the buyer should then prepare to assist, where necessary, the vendor's efforts to meet the quality specification of the purchase order. Such education may take several forms (as discussed in "Methods Used in Vendor Quality Education") and the type of education, as well as the extent of the effort expended by the buyer's company, is something which will be varied with the buyer's judgment of the benefit to be gained. It is not wise to attempt to lead vendors by the hand in quality education matters. It is better to carefully select sources who have the knowledge and the facilities to produce the quality specified by the buyer. The buyer should interest his own company in vendor quality education and in quality supervision of a vendor's production only to the minimum extent necessary to provide a quality product at the lowest possible cost. A vendor who requires constant supervision, even though his quality performance is good, may be leaning too heavily upon the buyer for technical support and for that reason be a costly supplier. The buyer should keep his education and technical advice efforts to suppliers at a minimum in order to protect the buyer's own cost.

METHODS USED IN VENDOR QUALITY EDUCATION

Some of the education required by the vendor is basic and must be supplied by the buyer no matter how simple the quality specification. To take care of this basic information need, the following items are frequently found helpful:

Explain the quality specification.

Show the vendor the buyer's plant, operation, or use of the purchased item.

Discuss the quality specification and/or the use of the item with other members of the buyer's company such as engineers, production men, inspectors, etc.

Demonstrate to vendor any special tools or procedures used to determine quality of incoming items.

Buyer will visit vendor's plant and may also be accompanied by technical people in his organization who can help in vendor evaluation and vendor operations in so far as they affect quality of parts to be furnished to buyer.

The purchasing department, with the support of technical help from within the buyer's company, should establish the extent and the method of the vendor's education. Where such education, and particularly vendor supervision, is required in any substantial amount, other sources of supply should be established.

Where necessary or desirable, particularly in the beginning of production of a new part or material (or one which is tailored to the buyer's specification), the purchasing department should request the help of engineers, production quality personnel, etc., in whatever efforts are necessary. In some cases this may result in the vendor having the buyer's technical men stationed in the vendor's plant during initial production of the item.

SUMMARY

A good, effective quality-control program has the following objectives:

Quality consistent with the requirements of the purchased items.

Lowest possible cost consistent with delivery of the required quality to the buyer's production point with minimum handling and supervision.

The responsibility of a good quality-control program is a wide one, and probably rests in some degree on everyone in both the vendor's and the buyer's organizations. Pinpointed responsibilities are necessary to make a good quality-control program work. These will vary from industry to industry, from company to company, and even in the same company, depending on products involved.

The responsibility of the purchasing department in a good quality-control program is usually in the category of transmission of specifications to, and negotiation with, the vendors. In some companies the purchasing department may have other responsibilities, including the creation of adequate quality specifications. If departments other than purchasing have the responsibility of originating the purchase quality specification, they have the responsibility of transmitting that specification to the purchasing department along with the purchase requisition.

Quality and the purchase quality specification may be expressed in several ways. It is important that a clear and unmistakable expression of the buyer's needs is part of every purchase order. Among the ways in which quality can be expressed are the following:

1. By blueprint or dimension sheet
2. By industry standard
3. By brand or trade name, by catalog number
4. By chemical or physical specification
5. By performance
6. By sample
7. By an approved bidders' list
8. By combination of the above

The determination of quality and the comparison of received items from various vendors is usually a function of the receiving department and/or the receiving inspection activity which should be closely located and allied with the receiving area. This inspection group should be required to furnish a rejection notice and rejection details to the purchasing department.

When an incoming shipment is rejected as not meeting the purchase quality specification, the purchasing department should be so notified with sufficient information so that the vendor can be contacted. Negotiations with the vendor on the points of replacement costs should be the responsibility of the purchasing department and should preferably be handled by the buyer who negotiated the purchase. The buyer, with the aid of others in his organization, will carefully explore all possibilities of diversion or salvage by rework, etc., where this results in lower cost than outright rejection and return. The buyer will protect his company by negotiating cost settlements with the vendor and will establish the method of handling such settlements with a minimum of confusion and paper work.

Vendor performance ratings on quality will be found useful in reducing the buyer's cost by eliminating vendors with a high rejection record.

The buyer will take whatever precautions are necessary to ensure that the vendor has the necessary education and know-how to produce items to the buyer's quality specification. Such education will be simple or involved as the circumstances may dictate and will include others in the buyer's organization who can assist the vendor in meeting the purchasing quality specification.

The broad aspects and the substantial benefits of a successful quality-control program are many and the buyer will carefully and intelligently approach all angles of this problem, beginning with the time the purchase requisition is received, so that the purchase order when issued has a complete and easy to understand purchase quality specification.

SELECTED BIBLIOGRAPHY

Duncan, Acheson J.: *Quality Control and Industrial Statistics,* Richard D. Irwin, Inc., 1818 Ridge Road, Homewood, Ill., 1952

Feigenbaum, A. V.: *Total Quality Control–Engineering and Management,* McGraw-Hill Book Company, 330 West 42d Street, New York, 1961

Juran, J. M.: *Quality Control Handbook,* McGraw-Hill Book Company, 330 West 42d Street, New York, 1962

Manual on Quality Control of Materials, STP 15–C, American Society for Testing and Materials, 1916 Race Street, Philadelphia, Pa.

Publications of the American Society of Quality Control, 161 W. Wisconsin Avenue, Milwaukee, Wis.

Publications of the American Society for Testing and Materials, 1916 Race Street, Philadelphia, Pa.

Schrock, Edward M.: *Quality Control and Statistical Methods,* Reinhold Publishing Corporation, 430 Park Avenue, New York, 1957

Titchen, Robert S., *et al.: Quality Control and Applied Statistics,* Loose-leaf Abstract Service, Interscience Publishers, Inc., 250 Fifth Avenue, New York

Also Section 26, "Library and Catalog File," listing other reference books and periodicals on quality consideration.

SECTION 9

PRICING CONSIDERATIONS

Editor

William G. East, Manager of Field Purchasing Offices, Monsanto Company, St. Louis, Missouri

Associate Editors

J. M. Kinabrew, Jr., Vice-president, Standard Supply and Hardware Company, Inc., New Orleans, Louisiana

J. J. Staed, Manager of Purchasing, A. B. Chance Company, Centralia, Missouri

A price in terms of cents per pound or dollars per square yard is not sufficient, in itself, to describe what a buyer's company may actually pay for a product. The many factors which modify the invoice price and influence the ultimate delivered cost of the product are discussed in this section.

The question of price as it relates to cost of manufacture or as compelled by conditions of supply and demand will be covered in Section 10. A discussion of price from the standpoint of the value of the article to the buyer's company is the subject of Section 11.

Pricing considerations fall into four general categories:

1. The terms of the price, payment, and price adjustment clauses, which have a direct effect upon the price itself, and which must be covered on the purchase order
2. Price schedules as they vary with the quantity purchased, size of shipment, quality specified, containers used, level of distribution, and buying industry (discounts)
3. Price schedules as they are fixed and affected by law
4. Additional costs which are incident to the purchase and add to the ultimate delivered cost of the material

Finally, ways and means open to the buyer to develop his own sources of pricing information are discussed. In an economy as dynamic as that of the United States, no attempt is made to set forth specific practices of any trades or industries. That remains for the buyer himself to ascertain.

PRICE TERMS

In arriving at a basis on which business is to be transacted, many elements must be considered collectively. While it cannot be considered alone, the price to be paid is certainly an essential element.

It is necessary in arriving at a binding contract to establish a definite consideration such as a specific price or a basis on which the price may be calculated. In the following paragraphs the most commonly used price terms are set forth.

Firm Price. This price term is used in many day-to-day purchasing transactions. It means that the price quoted at the time the contract is signed or the order is accepted will remain the same until delivery has been effected and the transaction completed. The purchase may cover a specific quantity of material for either immediate delivery or delivery over an extended length of time. It may also apply to an unspecified quantity for delivery within a specific length of time. Firm prices, based on published price schedules, are covered later under "Price Schedule."

Price in Effect at Time of Shipment. Since the close of World War II and the Korean conflict, spiraling wage and material costs have made it difficult for manufacturers to gauge their costs over any extended period of time. As a result the use of the above price term has become common in many industries. This price term means that the price you pay at time of shipment is the one then in effect regardless of what the quoted price may have been. Generally, the price is tied to published market data or based on the specific suppliers' published prices.

In recent years the practice of quoting prices in effect at time of shipment has been meeting buyer resistance and is being replaced by prices with 30- to 90-day protection extended.

Cost Plus.[1] Cost-plus agreements are frequently used in construction contracts, service contracts, and certain specialized manufacturing industries. Such contracts contemplate reimbursement to the contractor or supplier for the actual cost of the work involved plus a specified compensation or rate of compensation.

The term "cost" usually includes the following:

1. Cost of all materials and labor and services directly applicable to the job
2. Any taxes applicable to the job payroll and any premiums on insurance or bonds specified in the contract
3. Cost of hand tools and rental of any special equipment necessary for the job
4. Other overhead costs as defined and agreed to

The compensation is generally agreed to in advance to be a fixed amount or a percentage of the actual cost as defined above. It is important for the buyer to keep in mind the essential difference between "a cost-plus percentage contract" and "a cost-plus-fixed-fee contract."

The compensation usually includes the carefully defined contractor's overhead, general supervision, administrative and general expenses, and

[1] Also see Section 16, "Considerations in Nonrepetitive Major Purchases."

profit. A fixed dollar amount provides an incentive to the contractor to do the work efficiently and promptly in order to minimize his overhead expenses and thereby provide him with a maximum profit.

Contrariwise, when the contractor's compensation is arrived at as a percentage of cost, such an incentive does not exist. In fact, circumstances could arise on the job which would actually gain the contractor more profit through the percentage fee as a result of inefficient prosecution of the work.

Both methods for determining a contractor's compensation on cost-plus contracts are widely used. The facts of each job and the division of risks between buyer and seller are the determining elements.

In all cases involving cost-plus contracts, the contracting parties should have a clearly defined understanding of the cost elements and compensation involved. To the extent practicable these are spelled out in the formal contract.

Best buying practice suggests keeping cost-plus contracts to a minimum. However, cost-plus, either as a per cent or a fee, can be considered a good practice in a new or unknown area of technology or process. Only the use of fixed price bidding, or such contracting practices as described later can ensure adequate incentive for efficient performance on the part of the seller.

Recapture Clause. Recapture clauses are included in some equipment rental contracts. These clauses permit the lessee to purchase the equipment for an agreed-upon amount at any time during the rental period. Any rentals or a percentage of such rentals paid are applied against the purchase price.

Guaranteed Maximum Price. Contracts may be negotiated on the basis of actual costs plus overhead and profit but with an agreement that the final price will not exceed a guaranteed maximum.

Renegotiation. Certain governmental contracts are subject to renegotiation provisions which provide for reopening of the contract where the final profit margin falls outside limits considered to be reasonable.

PRICE ADJUSTMENTS

Escalator Clauses. The objective of an escalator clause is to allocate certain elements of cost risk equitably between buyer and seller. They are generally used in situations where a firm price is not desirable when considered in light of other conditions of the contract, term, basic price level, extent and kind of risks, etc. Any price which is not firm must have some provision for arriving at the final price.

The application and use of escalator clauses in contracts frequently raise controversial questions. The buyer for his own protection needs to exercise considerable care in the selection of elements on which the price is based. As an example: if it is agreed that provisions should be made to reflect labor costs, the use of straight time rate or of an average industry rate would serve to insulate the buyer from costs occasioned by excessive overtime on the part of the seller. In such an instance, if several classifications of labor are used on the job, use of industry rates further maintains the incentive for the seller to produce efficiently. Likewise, in providing for price adjustments to compensate for material cost, it is generally desirable to use a basis which is subject to normal competitive forces. The successful application of any formula depends importantly on careful analysis of all the elements in light of the buyer's and seller's objective.

Following is a list of commonly used types of price adjustment clauses whose sequence has no bearing on their importance. There may be many variations and combinations of these clauses depending on specific conditions.

Price in Effect at Time of Shipment (*see Price Terms*). This method of permitting price adjustment:

1. Does not necessarily relate or tie the billing price to actual cost changes
2. Permits the billing price to reflect actual market conditions at time of delivery (this, however, obligates the buyer, if accepted by him, to accept the basis on which the price is established by the seller)

A variation would be a limit on any increase or decrease in per cent and/or a limit on the time within which shipment would have to be made. A few examples of these clauses are:

> The price herein quoted is subject to adjustment to seller's published price in effect at time of shipment.
>
> Prices stated herein shall be subject to adjustment to the company's prices in effect at time of shipment and any increase hereunder not to exceed 10 per cent.
>
> The prices quoted are subject to change without notice; however, orders shipped within 90 days from date of order will be invoiced at the price at which the order was accepted. Orders specifying delivery over 90 days from date of order and less than 180 days from date of order will be invoiced at the price in effect at time of shipment, but no more than 10 per cent higher than the price at which the order was accepted.

Price Subject to Adjustment to Reflect Changes in Costs and/or Market Prices of Components. Changes in materials and/or labor costs as determined by published indices (U.S. Department of Labor, *Iron Age,* American Iron and Steel Institute, etc.), as well as changes in transportation costs, taxes, and fixed costs may be used as the basis for adjustment. An example of this would be:

Because of the seller's inability to secure firm prices for material and auxiliary equipment and its inability to forecast what labor rates will prevail at the time of manufacture of the equipment to be furnished hereunder, the contract price is to be adjusted as follows:

For each 1 per cent increase or decrease in the price of finished steel as published in the magazine *Iron Age*, from (date) to the date midway between the beginning and completion of fabrication of the equipment manufactured by the seller and furnished under this contract, the contract price shall be adjusted $________. If the per cent of increase or decrease in the price of finished steel is fractional, the adjustment is to be made proportionately.

For each 1 per cent increase or decrease in the average earnings per hour in the iron and steel industry as compiled by the American Iron and Steel Institute, from (date) to the date midway between the beginning and completion of fabrication of the equipment manufactured by the seller and furnished under this contract, the contract price shall be adjusted $________. If the per cent of increase or decrease in the said average hourly rate is fractional, the adjustment is to be made proportionately.

The amounts included in this proposal for equipment and for services not manufactured or performed by the seller are based upon prices current at (date). In the event the suppliers of such equipment and/or services increased or decreased prices to the seller, the contract price shall be adjusted by the actual increase or decrease which the seller must pay to such suppliers.

Payments of all such price adjustments shall be due upon receipt of the invoice or credit, as the case may be. The total amount of price adjustment resulting from paragraphs above will not exceed 20 per cent of the total contract price.

Changes in cost of material and/or labor as determined by a specific formula can be used (for example, labor represented by 40 per cent of the price, material 45 per cent, fixed portion of the price 15 per cent not subject to change). An example of this would be:

The contract price quoted for equipment is based on labor and material costs in effect (date), and such price shall be increased or decreased in accordance with the following formula to adjust for increases or decreases in the seller's labor and material costs occurring thereafter.

Material. For the purpose of this adjustment, the proportion of the contract price representing cost of materials is accepted as 40 per cent. The amount accepted as representing material costs shall be increased or decreased by a percentage thereof equal to the percentage by which the average monthly index of metals and metal products as contained in the Wholesale (Primary Market) Price Index published by the Bureau of Labor Statistics of the United States Department of Labor (computed on the same basis and by the same methods as are used on the date hereof for the period commencing with the month within which actual fabrication of the equipment is commenced in the factories of the seller, and ending with the month within which final shipment is made from the factories of the seller) shall exceed or be less than the index number published as aforesaid for the month of (date).

Adjustment in the contract price shall be made in accordance with the foregoing formula immediately following the release by the Bureau of Labor Statistics of the monthly indices for the specified period of months.

Labor. For the purpose of this adjustment, the proportion of the contract price representing cost of labor is accepted as 45 per cent. The amount accepted as representing labor costs shall be increased or decreased by a percentage thereof equal to the percentage by which the average gross hourly earnings boiler-shop products as contained under Fabricated Metal Products in the Employment and Earnings report published by the Bureau of Labor Statistics of the United States Department of Labor (computed on the same basis and by the same methods as are used on the date hereof for the period commencing with the month within which actual fabrication of the equipment is commenced in the factories of the seller, and ending with the month within which final shipment is made from the factories of the seller) shall exceed or be less than the average hourly earnings published as aforesaid for the month of (date). Adjustment in the contract price shall be made in accordance with the foregoing formula immediately following the release by the Bureau of Labor Statistics of the monthly indices for the specified period of months.

Limitation. Total price adjustments determined in accordance with the above shall not exceed 20 per cent of the contract price.

A firm price may be established for a specified time, for instance, twelve months, and then be subject to adjustment as determined by a specific formula or other method.

The price of a product may be subject to adjustment during the life of the contract to reflect changes in published market price of the product or its components. For example, crude coal tar and tar acid oils are generally priced to reflect a percentage of the market price of naphthalene, tar acids, phenol, and creosote.

Another example of this is found in the purchase of alloy solder consisting of 40 per cent tin and 60 per cent lead. The price paid would be the *American Metal Market* carload price of tin and lead delivered, in effect on date of shipment plus $6 per hundredweight, representing the seller's conversion costs. A price breakdown using this escalator would be as follows:

	Price Structure per Hundredweight AMM (5–17–65)		Conversion Cost	Net Cost
Tin, 40%	$97 = $38.80	$48.40 +	$6	= $54.40
Lead, 60%	16 = 9.60			

Cumulative Discounts. Cumulative or earned discounts differ slightly from straight quantity discounts in that they are generally applied to contract purchases which continue over a period of time. For example, in the purchase of some steel goods the base price is paid on invoices rendered for each order, and the contract provides that at the end of a calendar year the total quantity of material purchased against the contract will be matched with a previously agreed-upon schedule of discounts. The buyer is then reimbursed by the seller at the discount level appropriate to the quantity purchased during the year.

Price Decline Protection Clauses. It is common practice in the purchase of process materials and other goods bought on a regular recurring basis to sign contracts, with one or more sellers, which establish a basis on which the business will be done. These contracts often name a price which is not firm for the duration of the contract but rather can be reduced to reflect downward market price movements. The following are typical "price decline protection clauses" found in the chemical and coal-tar industries.

> *Chemical.* Should the buyer at any time any shipment is due under this contract, be offered a lower delivered price on material of equal quality in like quantity for the same use by a reputable manufacturer of such material, he will furnish the seller satisfactory proof of same; in which event the seller will either supply such shipment at a lower price or permit the buyer to purchase such quantity elsewhere, and the quantity so purchased elsewhere will be deducted from the total quantity of this contract.

> *Coal-tar Industry.* If material of similar grade of domestic origin is offered by a responsible manufacturer for delivery to the same destination, in similar quantities and on like terms as herein provided at a lower delivered cost to buyer than the delivered cost hereunder, seller, upon receipt of written evidence of same, shall either meet such lower delivered cost or permit buyer to purchase from such manufacturer at said cost the quantity so offered, which quantity, if so purchased shall be deducted from the quantity covered by this contract.

PAYMENT TERMS

The terms of payment, as specified on the purchase order, fall into two general categories from the buyer's standpoint:

1. Those terms which influence the ultimate delivered cost
2. Those terms which merely designate method of payment

For example, a cash discount of 2 per cent 10 days makes possible a saving of 2 per cent of the invoice price and is, therefore, a cost factor.

An irrevocable letter of credit, set up for a foreign purchase, establishes the buyer's ability to pay but does not, in itself, affect cost.

Payment terms which do affect the delivered price may be further subdivided into those which require cash on or before delivery and those which extend credit in some form (open account). Both types of payment may involve discount terms.

Establishing payment terms is the prerogative of the seller, but as a condition of the contract they are generally considered a subject for negotiation by the buyer.

Cash Discount.[2] Payment terms which include cash-discount provisions are common throughout industry and were developed initially as an inducement for prompt payment. There is now considerable question as to whether the discount reflects the interest cost on the seller's working capital tied up in overdue accounts receivable, or whether the discount covers the extra cost of collection from slow payers and interest charges for one or two months beyond the invoice due date. From the standpoint of the buyer, the discounted price is really the price of the goods, and the discount represents a penalty for late payment, despite the fact that it may be referred to as a financial earning and shown as income credit on the profit and loss statement.

Assuming his company is financially able to pay its bills promptly, the purchasing officer is responsible for taking all cash discounts granted. This is an obvious factor to be considered in price analysis and in arriving at lowest net cost. This also requires a knowledge of trade practices (as not all discounts for cash are openly offered), inclusion of pertinent discount terms on the order, and securing and processing invoices promptly so that discounts can be legitimately taken.

Payment terms, in general use, which include cash discount provisions that influence ultimate delivered costs are:

Net 30 days. Payment of entire invoice amount within 30 days from invoice date.

Net 10 prox. Payment of entire invoice amount by the 10th of the month following the month of date of invoice.

2% 10/net 30. If payment is made within 10 days from date of invoice, the amount of invoice may be discounted 2%. The invoice becomes overdue 30 days after the invoice date. Discount percentages and due dates vary; however, they rarely exceed 3% and 90 days.

2% 10th and 25th. If payment is made on bills dated between the 1st and 15th by the 25th of the month and bills dated between the 15th and

[2] For computations of cash discounts, see Tables 29–12 and 29–13.

30th by the 10th of the following month, the amount of the invoice may be discounted 2%.

2% 10 days e.o.m. If payment is made by the 10th of the month following the month the invoice was issued, the amount may be discounted 2%.

Cash at Time of Purchase. Payment terms which require payment with the order, payment in advance of shipment, or payment on delivery are designed to protect the seller from bad credit risks or to avoid complex billing and collection procedures. They are also an advantage to the purchasing department when they avoid costly invoice handling and disbursement operations. However, purchasing can be placed in an almost untenable position in the forcing of settlements on claims.

The advantages and controls for cash at time of purchase terms will be discussed later under "Incidental Purchasing Costs."

Prepayment Discounts. Prepayment or anticipation discounts and deferred terms are payment methods which extend credit, recognizing the seasonal nature and/or frequent short cash position inherent in the nature of some businesses.

Prepayment discount terms extend credit for two to three months, allowing time for the buyer to convert and sell the goods before the actual invoice due date, but also offering him the opportunity to earn a discount by making early payment. This type of discount is similar to the normal discount payment provisions with two exceptions; the time allowed for payment is considerably longer, and the discount rate reflects a more realistic interest rate of 6 to 9 per cent per year. Several examples of prepayment discount terms are:

Net 10/60 extra. Invoices under these terms are due 70 days after invoice date, and the buyer is given the opportunity to prepay, discounting at the rate of 6% per annum. Payment before 10 days yields a 1% discount. Payment in 40 days entitles the buyer to ½%.

Net 90 days, ½% per month anticipation. The invoice is due in 90 days and may be discounted ½% for each 30 days prepayment, permitting a maximum discount of 1½%.

Deferred terms are designed by sellers to fit the seasonal pattern of the buyer's business. For example, agricultural supplies which are sold to the farmer in May and June must be produced in the fall and winter. To induce the dealers to take in stock many months before their sales materialize and thereby take advantage of the dealers' warehouse space, agricultural supply manufacturers ship throughout the winter on terms of, for example, 1 or 2 per cent May 1 net June 15.

Consignment Terms. Consignment terms, frequently used in merchandising activity, simply defer payment until the goods are resold by the buyer. They are an inducement to provide space for inventory and to promote resale. In contrast to deferred terms and other types of credit terms, title to the materials on consignment is retained by the seller and payment is demanded only after resale or use by the buyer. There are seldom any cash discount provisions associated with consignment buying.

Progressive Payment Terms. Payment terms which call for progressive payments are common in the purchase of major equipment and in on-site construction contracts. This type of payment is discussed in detail in Section 16, "Considerations in Nonrepetitive Major Purchases." It is appropriate here to state that progressive payments by the buyer for goods and services which have not been delivered or are not complete and usable to him require that he surrender working capital that might otherwise be used by him for production and profit-making purposes. The capital necessary to finance the construction of a major piece of equipment requiring many months to build is a part of the cost of that construction. If the buyer has agreed to buy the piece of equipment by irrevocable contract, then the cost of obtaining the working capital should quite rightfully fall upon the seller, not the buyer, and no progressive payments should be involved. Two examples of progressive payment terms for major equipment are:

EXAMPLE 1

The contract price shall be payable in New York exchange free from collection charges to the seller and to be paid as follows: For the equipment delivered, including erection supervision and tools, 10 per cent net cash six months after notice of award; 30 per cent net cash in six bimonthly payments, the first payment due eight months after notice of award and the last payment due eighteen months after notice of award. If shipment is started prior to eighteen months after notice of award, the balance of the 30 per cent then remaining unpaid shall be due upon start of shipment; 30 per cent net cash on shipment, prorated as shipments go forward; 25 per cent net cash one month from date of shipment; 5 per cent net cash on completion of erection. (If an acceptance test is required, the final 5 per cent shall be due upon satisfactory completion of the test. If through no fault of the seller, the completion of the test is delayed, then the final 5 per cent shall be due 30 days from the date of notice from the seller that the equipment furnished by the seller is ready for test.) In the event that erection is abandoned or wholly or partially postponed as hereinafter provided, then the final 5 per cent of such contract price, less a proportionate adjustment of the amount included in the contract price for erection supervision and tools, shall be due upon such abandonment or postponement.

Nevertheless, when the equipment is ready for shipment and shipment is delayed or postponed beyond the contract shipping date through any causes beyond the control of the seller, the first 70 per cent of the contract price, less previous payments, shall be due on the contract shipping date; 25 per cent of such contract price shall be due 30 days from date of actual shipment and the balance of the contract price shall be due on completion of erection. In the event that, after shipment following such delay or postponement, erection is abandoned or wholly or partially postponed as hereinafter provided, then the final 5 per cent of such contract price, less a proportionate adjustment of the amount included in the contract price for erection supervision and tools, shall be due upon such abandonment or postponement. In the event that shipment is delayed or postponed for six months beyond the contract shipping date, the final 30 per cent of the contract price shall be due at the expiration of such period of six months, less a proportionate adjustment of the amount included in the contract price for erection supervision and tools. Upon the due date of the final percentage of the contract price, as set forth above, any further obligations of the seller under this contract, of whatever nature, shall terminate.

EXAMPLE 2

The contract shall be $________, payable in New York exchange free from collection charges to the seller and to be paid as follows, and, if this contract comprises more than one unit, applied with respect to individual units: 70 per cent net cash on shipment, or on presentation of sight draft with bills of lading attached, at the option of the seller, prorated as shipments go forward; 25 per cent net cash 30 days from date of shipment, prorated in accordance with shipments made; 5 per cent net cash upon completion of erection or upon satisfactory completion of acceptance tests, if acceptance test is required, but not later than 30 days after notice from the seller that the equipment is ready for test. If, through no fault of the seller, the completion of such test, or of any necessary or desirable mechanical or operational adjustments, is delayed or deferred beyond the date when the equipment is placed in commercial operation, then this payment shall be due not later than 90 days after the equipment is placed in commercial operation.

Notwithstanding any of the above provisions, when the equipment is ready for shipment and shipment is deferred beyond the contract shipping date through no fault of the seller, 70 per cent of the difference between the contract price and the seller's estimated cost of superintendence shall be due on the contract shipping date; the remaining 30 per cent of said difference shall be due 30 days from date of actual shipment and the balance of the contract price shall be due on completion of erection. In the event of shipment being so deferred for six months beyond the contract shipping date, the remaining 30 per cent of the said difference between the contract price and the seller's estimated cost of superintendence shall be due and payable at the expiration of such period of six months, and any further obligations of the seller under this contract, of whatever nature, shall thereupon terminate. The purchaser shall also pay to the seller all storage, painting, and handling charges resulting from such delays in shipment.

In the case of on-site construction, the situation is somewhat different. Here the contractor delivers a combination of goods and services which he surrenders to the buyer's possession. Generally, the buyer is easily able to assess the value of that part of the contract which has been executed, and payment terms of 80 to 90 per cent of monthly expenditures on the part of the contractor can be justified. One of the practical considerations in the type of contract negotiation which supports the desirability of such progressive payments is the characteristic method of financing construction in progress used by contractors, coupled with legal restrictions surrounding the sale and installation of materials which become improvements to real estate. An example of a progressive payment clause used for on-site construction under a cost-plus-fixed-fee contract follows:

> The terms of payment applicable to this agreement shall be 90 per cent payment of all work performed by the contractor as performed and billed monthly, and $________ (one-half of the fixed fee) on a pro rata basis monthly. The balance (i.e., 10 per cent of all subcontract work plus the remaining one-half of the fixed fee) is to be retained by the buyer until satisfactory completion of the work. Paid bills or waivers of lien will accompany each month's billing to cover all the monthly bills paid for in the previous month's billing.
>
> The buyer shall pay such monthly bills as found to be in order within ten days after they are received from the contractor. At the completion of the job and when it has been accepted by the buyer the balance due under this contract shall be paid within thirty days. With the final statement the contractor shall submit evidence satisfactory to the buyer that all labor and material bills and other indebtedness connected with the work have been paid.

PRICE SCHEDULE

Many materials and services are bought and sold at prices standardized by the seller in a formal price schedule. This is in contrast to purchases of nonstandard materials or commodities in which the price agreed upon is peculiar to one transaction only.

Price schedules present a pattern of prices which vary with quantity purchased, size of shipment, quality specified, container, level of distribution, and at times with the season and the buying industry.

Price Variation with Order Size. It is possible for the seller to achieve economies in production, packaging, billing, and sales expenses with large orders. A large order enables the vendor to plan his operation and attain rapid cash turnover. Typical price variation with order size, reflecting savings in selling, billing, and shipping expenses, occurs in the purchase of chlorinated solvents where there are successively lower prices offered for 1-, 5-, 10-, and 25-drum orders.

Another example of price variation with order size occurs in the purchase of mild steel welding electrodes. The standard package contains 50 lb. There are price breaks for less than standard package, 1 to 4 packages, 10 to 19 packages, 20 to 399 packages, 400 to 799 packages, and 800 and over. Normally, the price per pound purchased in quantities of 800 packages and over is less than half the price of the material purchased in less than standard package amounts.

Additional examples of this type of price variation exist in the purchase of printing paper with price breaks for less than standard packages, full packages, 1 carton, 4 cartons, 16 cartons, 5,000 lb, 10,000 lb, 20,000 lb, carload of 36,000 lb, with a spread in price of 55 cents per pound on broken package to 20 cents per pound in carload lots. Also on common sizes of envelopes, price schedules from 5,000 to 500,000 vary about 100 per cent.

Lower prices for large orders are often offered as an inducement for a larger share of business rather than as a reflection of lower cost.

Price Variation with Savings in Loading and Transportation Costs. Real cost savings are experienced by the seller in the handling of full carload (c.l.), truckload (t.l.), or bargeload orders in contrast to less-than-carload (l.c.l.) or truckload (l.t.l.) movements. When handling larger shipments, the seller can use his warehouse labor more efficiently and the applicable freight cost per unit charged by the carrier is less. Many price schedules reflect this variation in cost by offering different prices for c.l. or t.l. and for l.c.l. or l.t.l. shipments.

For certain products shipped in carload lots different rates are available, depending on the size of the minimum carload. For example, steel pipe may be shipped in 40,000- or 80,000-lb minimum carloads, or in 200-, 400-, or 600-ton bargeloads. Lower freight rates applicable to larger shipments are reflected in lower delivered costs.

In recent years the practice of allowing the carload or truckload price on orders covering several materials which, when combined, will total a full load movement, has increased. These orders are termed mixed car, truck, or lot orders. Excessive freight charges may be incurred in mixed shipments if the total weight does not meet or exceed the weight requirements for the product with highest minimum weight provision.

Even if the quantity ordered is less than a bargeload, carload, or truckload, it may be shipped as a minimum barge-, car-, or truckload and the minimum freight charges prorated over the quantity actually shipped. Often the prorated freight per unit will be less than the freight per unit if shipped at the order's actual weight.

Price Variation with Quality or Grade. The price schedules for many materials show a variation in price for different levels of quality (see Section 8). Ether is sold, in order of increasing price, as ether concentrated, ether USP, ether purified, ether (analytical reagent), and ether anhydrous (analytical). The variation in price in this case is primarily based on increased cost of manufacture to obtain higher purity.

A material such as nitrogenous tankage, used in the fertilizer industry, is sold at a price which varies in direct relation to the concentration of the desired ingredient, organic nitrogen. As the concentrations of this factor increase, the cost per ton of the material also increases.

Price Variation with Container Size and Type. In answer to customer demands, the packaging industry has developed a wide range of package types and sizes. Many years ago, sulfuric acid was shipped in glass carboys of 13 gal capacity only. The material is now sold in a range of containers including 300,000-gal barges.

If a liquid product is sold in a 1-gal tin can the container cost is about 25 cents per gallon and the container is considered nonreusable. If the material is sold in a 1-gal steel drum, the container cost is closer to 90 cents per gallon, added protection is afforded the products, but the container is still technically a single-trip unit. If the same product can be shipped in the standard 55-gal steel drum which costs between $6 and $7, the container cost per gallon of product is reduced to only 12 cents and, in addition, the drum has some salvage or reuse value. If the material were to be shipped in an 8,000-gal tank car costing about $12,000, but usable for many years, the container cost would be reduced to less than 1 cent per gallon. From the above, it is apparent that the buyer must consider carefully his needs and the appropriate container cost, weighing such factors as deterioration, obsolescence, and waste of product when specifying the container on his order. Figure 9–1 is a comparison of packaging costs for a variety of typical containers.

Price Variation with Level of Distributive Function. As set forth above, product prices vary with quantity and other conditions of purchase, the range generally reflecting costs which are incurred in manufacturing or handling the individual order quantities involved. There are many other elements which affect the price the buyer pays, and he must know the relationship of his demand and his position as a buyer to the over-all distribution of the product if he is to correctly evaluate them.

Broadly speaking, pricing systems under which all similar items or related products are distributed to the ultimate user tend to reflect costs which are incurred in the distributive processes (which may involve several channels of trade between the prime producer and the ultimate consumer).

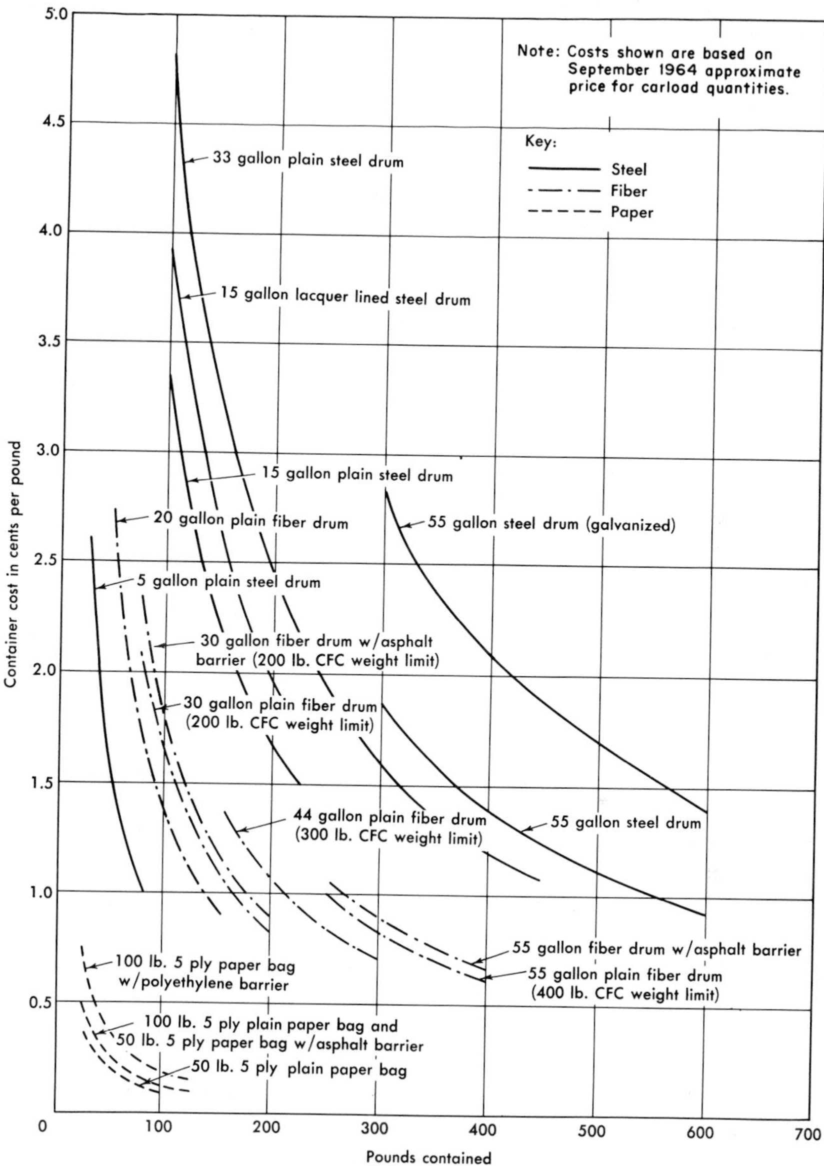

FIG. 9–1. Nonreturnable container costs per pound of contained product.

Published Price Schedules. The prime producers of many products follow the practice of publishing price schedules. It is here that pricing systems come into play. Schedules may be on a net basis to all buyers or to a restricted class of buyers. Generally, consumer goods are priced so that the schedule or list price represents the retail price to be paid by the ultimate consumer. With industrial-type items, list prices are frequently used to establish the prices of individual types or sizes and remain in effect for many years. In this case only the discount or multiplier is changed to reflect current conditions. Likewise, the schedules may be subject to a number of discount practices for various classes of buyers. These are known as trade discounts. Handy discount tables will be found in Section 29.

Wholesale. The term wholesale, as used generally, refers to large lots. Within this meaning there are several subdivisions in so far as variation of price on a product may occur. The titles of the subdivisions within the meaning of the word "wholesale" vary widely from one segment of industry to another. Familiarity with the buyer's own segment of industry is essential for proper evaluation of the discount applicable in each circumstance.

Distributor. The term distributor refers to an agency for the marketing of goods. A distributor warehouses and distributes a manufacturer's products in an area on an exclusive or nonexclusive basis. He sells to other "middlemen" (wholesalers, dealers, retailers, etc.) and/or to industrial consumers. The price to the distributor and/or the list price, subject to a distributor's discount, generally reflects only the margin of cost to the prime manufacturer for moving the goods in large lots to the distributor's area. In general, distributors (jobbers and wholesalers) sell to industrial consumers at a price comparable to that at which they sell to dealers, and often at a lower price, if volume warrants.

Jobber (or Wholesaler). The term jobber refers to one who buys and resells to dealers or others. He is a middleman usually dealing in larger quantities and carrying stocks for service to the area. In marketing of some goods, the distinction between jobber and distributor may disappear. In the marketing of other goods, the distributor is closer to the manufacturer than the jobber.

Broker. The term broker refers to a middleman who for a fee brings buyer and seller together. The broker, depending on whether he is operating for the buyer or for the seller, receives his fee for his services from one or the other. Transactions are between buyer and seller in so far as payment of bills, credit arrangements, etc., are concerned. In the distribution of goods commonly handled by brokers, fees are generally well established. It should be noted that in dealing with an unusual sale such as sale of used capital equipment, a broker will frequently offer to turn up prospects for a negotiated finder's fee at which point the negotiation between buyer and seller continues directly.

Dealer. The term dealer refers to one who buys and sells for his own account. In some instances, a dealer may act as a broker, at other times, as a retailer.

Retail. The term retail, as used generally, refers to sale at the ultimate consumer's level. In dealing with manufactured goods, many manufacturers recognize in their price and/or their discount lists the position of the ultimate user and his demand in relation to the over-all distribution of the manufacturer's product. Consequently, a final sale at retail implies the sale of several or a few items in a small quantity.

Manufacturer's Price. In addition to the levels of distribution referred to above which bring about varying prices and varying discounts off list for a product, the price established by the prime manufacturer may recognize that his product is used in large volume by other manufacturers in the assembling of their products. A good example would be the manufacturer of motors who sells to a washing-machine manufacturer. Consequently, manufacturers' price lists frequently reflect "sales to other manufacturers" or "sales for resale" as distinguished from "sales for further distribution to market" or "sales to ultimate consumers."

Open-market Pricing. Many products, primarily basic commodities, and/or materials in the early stage of process, are quoted on daily basis on open markets. Common examples of these are nonferrous metals, ferrous metals, and petroleum products.

Effect of Certain Laws on Price Schedules. It is not the purpose of this section to treat legal matters as such, particularly when they are controversial. However, over the past several decades, the Congress of the United States has enacted a number of laws which have had broad effect, directly or indirectly, on commercial buying and selling practices. These include the Sherman Act, Federal Trade Act, Clayton Antitrust Act, and the Robinson-Patman Act. These statutes are representative of an area designed to protect what is essentially a competitive economy from monopolistic practices and to eliminate "unfair competition." Section 4, "Legal Influences in Purchasing," furnishes further details of these laws.

Robinson-Patman Act. The act which is of particular interest to buyers is the Robinson-Patman Act. This was intended as an "anti-chain-store" law having been enacted during a period when there was considerable feeling against chain-store operations. The particular problem for a buyer arises from the fact that certain prohibitions apply to the buyer as well as to the seller.

The pertinent part of the Robinson-Patman Act which deserves mention in this connection has to do with that part which amended section 2 of the Clayton Act. These two acts are referred to in this connection as one.

Section 2(a) outlaws direct and indirect discriminations in price. Mere differences are not unlawful, but become so only when the effect of such differences may be to substantially lessen competition, may tend to create a monopoly, or may injure, destroy, or prevent competition. Price differences which make only due allowance for differences in cost of manufacturing, sale, or delivery resulting from differing methods or quantities in which goods are sold or delivered are not prohibited.

Section 2(b) also provides that a seller may escape the prohibitions of the section if he can prove "that his lower price or the furnishing of services or facilities to any purchaser or purchasers was made in good faith to meet an equally low price of a competitor, or the services or facilities furnished by a competitor."

Section 2(c) prohibits "a commission, brokerage, or other compensation or any allowance or discount in lieu thereof" to or for the benefit of the other party to a transaction. Such payments can be made by a seller only to one who represents him and only for services actually rendered. It is unlawful for a buyer or intermediary to accept such prohibited payment.

Section 2(f) provides "that it shall be unlawful for any person engaged in commerce, in the course of such commerce, knowingly to *induce* or *receive* a discrimination in price which is prohibited by this section."

In summing up, it is important to recognize that the buyer is liable for "knowingly" inducing or receiving price discrimination which is prohibited under section 2(a) or for receiving, with or *without* knowledge, brokerage payments or allowances prohibited under section 2(c). The act, however, is not specific nor is it clear-cut in its reference to the buyer's liabilities. There is a lack of court decisions that clearly interpret this section, and therefore no specific rules can be formulated to aid the buyer.

Fair Trade Laws. Another area of the law which has a bearing on commercial purchase-sales contracts involves the so-called "fair trade" laws. These laws are designed to permit a manufacturer to establish legally and enforce uniform prices at which his products are resold. The application of this so-called fair trade practice largely involves products which are distributed by multiple marketing methods on a national scale where the manufacturer has spent considerable sums in advertising and promotion to develop demand at the consumer level for his particular product.

California passed the first act permitting such resale price maintenance. The California act provided for enforcement of price maintenance contracts between the contractors. Shortly thereafter (1933) California added a "nonsigner" clause to its Fair Trade Act which provided that everyone in the state was bound by a minimum price which was established by the contract whether or not such a person is a party of the contract.

In 1937 over forty states had laws patterned after California. In that year Congress amended the Sherman Act by passing the Miller-Tydings Act. This act permitted "vertical" price maintenance contracts.

In 1951 the United States Supreme Court in Schwegmann *v.* Calvert Corporation (71 S. Ct. 745) declared that the Miller-Tydings Act did not legalize the "nonsigner" clause in Fair Trade Acts. Congress subsequently (1952) passed the McGuire Act which makes it legal to bind nonsigners if such is legal under applicable state laws. Consequently, if a manufacturer and one or more retailers want to agree, combine, or conspire to fix a minimum price they can do so if state law permits. Of the forty-eight states, forty-five passed Fair Trade Enabling Acts. However, as of early 1958, the highest courts of nine states and lower courts in three other states had ruled these laws unconstitutional. It accordingly seems apparent that the future of such legal regulation of pricing practices is in considerable doubt. Probably because of this doubt, some of the larger manufacturers had discontinued fair trading their products by early 1958.

As indicated at the outset, it is not within the scope of this section to treat legal matters as such but only to call attention to those areas of the law which may have a direct bearing on a buyer's activity in connection with his own pricing considerations. It is readily apparent that a prudent buyer will ascertain from his own legal counsel the extent of any liabilities that may arise as the result of his actions in his own field of activity.

Parity Price Supports. A final area of the law which may become a price consideration in the purchase of certain commodities concerns the government's agricultural support program. The Department of Agriculture administers this program of price support operations through loans to farmers, purchase agreements, purchases, and payments, of which the loans constitute by far the most important support method. Price minimums are established for many agricultural commodities by what is known as the parity price system which Congress first gave legislative recognition to in the Agricultural Adjustment Act of 1933. These prices are now computed under the Agricultural Adjustment Act of 1938 as amended by the Agricultural Acts of 1948, 1949, 1954, and 1956.

Parity prices are the dollars and cents prices calculated to give farm commodities the same purchasing power they had in the 1910–1914 base period when prices received for farm products were considered in balance with the rest of the economy (prices paid by farmers). The market prices of some supported commodities in weak markets at times drop below the current parity support level for a number of reasons, among which is failure of some farmers to participate in the program and because of sales by nonfarmers ineligible to receive support loans.

Buyers of the commodities listed in Table 9–1 may find specific discussion of Federal price support programs in the United States Department of Agriculture "Price Support Handbook," June, 1960.

Table 9–1. A List of Selected Basic and Nonbasic Commodities

Basic Commodities	*Nonbasic Commodities*	
Corn	Milkfat, in cream	Flaxseed
Cotton, American upland	All milk, wholesale	Oats
extra long staple	Honey, extracted	Rye
Wheat	Wool	Sorghums–grain
Rice	Mohair	Soybeans
Tobacco	Barley	Crude pine gum
Peanuts	Beans, dry edible	Tung nuts
	Cottonseed	

TRANSPORTATION COSTS

The following discussion sets forth the obligations of the seller and buyer with respect to transportation costs, liabilities, and procedures involved in delivering goods sold at one location to the buyer's point of receipt. Each obligation affects the ultimate cost of the goods.

Usual trade practices in quoting and ordering goods where transportation is involved may be broken down into the following groups:

Shipments Involving Only Inland Transportation Facilities (Other than Water)

1. *F.o.b. point of release of goods to carrier (rail, truck, air, or mail).* Seller places goods on carrier's conveyance and sends buyer the collect transportation receipt or bill of lading. Buyer takes title to the goods and pays for all charges to his destination from the loading point, i.e., transportation, insurance, loss and damage in transit, unloading, and handling.
2. *F.o.b. point of release of goods to carrier (rail, truck, air, or mail) with full transportation allowed to buyer's named point (usually a rail destination, transportation zone, or area where price is based).* Seller places goods on carrier's conveyance and sends buyer the collect transportation receipt or bill of lading. Seller deducts transportation charges from his invoice. Buyer takes title to the goods at the loading point and pays all charges from that point to destination the same as in (1) above.
3. *F.o.b. point of release of goods to carrier (rail or truck) freight equalized with another shipping point (usually the location of a competing plant).* Seller places goods on carrier's conveyance and sends buyer the collect transportation receipt or bill of lading. Seller deducts actual

transportation charges from his invoice and adds transportation from point of equalization to his invoice. Buyer takes title to the goods at the loading point and pays all charges from that point to destination the same as in (1) above, although net cost is the same as if shipment had been made from the equalization point.

4. *F.o.b. delivered to buyer's named point (usually a rail destination, warehouse, transportation zone, or area where price is based) via rail, truck, air, or mail.* Seller pays all charges and is responsible until goods are actually turned over to buyer, at which point title to the goods passes to the buyer.

Shipments Involving Ocean Vessels or Other Water Conveyances

1. *F.a.s. vessel named port of shipment.* Seller pays for all charges involved in placing goods alongside vessel at the port and provides buyer with dock or ship's receipt. Buyer takes title to the goods aboard the vessel and pays all charges for loading onto vessel and for ocean transportation; also any other charges to destination.
2. *F.o.b. vessel named port of shipment.* Seller pays for all charges until goods have been placed aboard vessel at the port. Buyer takes title to the goods aboard the vessel and pays for ocean transportation and any other charges to destination.
3. *Free overboard; ex ship; overside; c.i.f.: named port.* Seller pays for all charges until goods have been unloaded from the vessel. Buyer takes title to the goods at the dock, port of destination, and pays only transportation from that point to destination.

See Section 17, "Purchasing Internationally," Section 18, "Traffic and Transportation Considerations," and Section 27, "Glossary of Terms." For detailed information on trade definitions refer to "Revised American Foreign Trade Definitions," reprinted in Section 17.

TAXES ON TANGIBLES, SERVICES, AND IMPORTS

Among the multiplicity of taxes levied by the national, state, and local governments there are certain ones which, for special reasons, become price considerations to the purchasing agent.

Those which do so are in general taxes where (1) the sales transaction as such provides the measure of the tax. Further, it is important to know precisely (2) on whom the tax is legally levied and (3) the legal provisions for collection.

Because of the complexity of tax laws and their interpretations, discussion of this phase of purchasing must be limited to an outline of certain fundamental principles. It is essential that the buyer have a working knowledge of the tax laws which are applicable to his area of operations. However, he must then rely on guidance by his own legal counsel.

One of the first things to consider is on whom the tax is legally levied. Certain governmental units do permit some taxes to be absorbed by the seller and consideration must be given as to whether the tax is being absorbed (as a cost component) or passed on to the buyer as an addition to the price.

A second consideration concerns the legal procedure for collecting the tax. This becomes a procedural matter for the buyer which may be settled because of legal requirements or which may be handled by mutual agreement with the seller where the law so permits.

The procedure of collecting state use taxes is one example. For instance, all states employing use taxes require the ultimate consumer to pay the tax. This is the only way the state can collect where goods are shipped from another state by suppliers not doing business in the using state. In all states the law provides that the seller is to collect the tax if he is licensed by the state to do so but it falls upon the buyer as user to recognize that he may need to establish a procedure to accumulate such tax charges and report to the taxing unit directly.

Another instance of this procedure involves the collection of gasoline taxes. Many state gasoline taxes are legally levied on the consumer but provide for the collection of these taxes by the service station which makes the sale. Taxes collected on gasoline used for non-highway purposes may be subject to a refund upon filing of the proper claim forms with the appropriate taxing agency.

Gasoline purchased for non-highway use is wholly or partially exempt from state gasoline taxes in the following states at the rates shown:

Table 9–2. State Gasoline Tax Exemptions per Gallon for Non-highway Use as of September 1, 1964

State	Exemption	State	Exemption
Arizona	5¢	Missouri	5¢
California	6¢	New Jersey	6¢
Connecticut	6¢	New Mexico	6¢
Georgia	5½¢	New York	6¢
Illinois	5¢	Ohio	7¢
Indiana	6¢	Texas	5¢
Kansas	5¢	(partial 5¢ less 1½% from amount refunded)	
Massachusetts	5½¢		
Michigan	6¢	Washington	7½¢
Mississippi	7¢	West Virginia	7¢
(partial 6¢)		Wisconsin	6¢

Likewise, in many states, while a sales tax is levied on the seller from whom it is legally collectible, the law may permit the seller to absorb the tax as part of his price or pass it on and collect it as such from the buyer. In the former instance, absorption of the tax or adding it to the quoted price on the invoice may become a trade practice.

Taxes on Tangibles. Taxes on the manufacture, sale, and use of tangible personal property which become pricing considerations generally fall into one of three categories. These are sales taxes, use taxes, and excise taxes.

Sales Taxes. Sales taxes in general are imposed either upon the seller for the privilege of selling tangible personal property or upon the sale itself and are usually levied at the retail level. The law may be mandatory or permissive as to the seller passing the tax on to the buyer.

Use Taxes. Use taxes are levied against the storage, use, or consumption within the taxing unit (usually a state) and are primarily designed as a compensating tax in connection with sales taxes for the purpose of reaching property used in the area but purchased elsewhere. The user is in all instances required to pay the tax whether it be to the seller or directly to the taxing agency.

Excise Taxes. Excise taxes are taxes levied on the manufacture of specific items. They are levied both at the manufacturing and the retail level by the Federal government as well as by many states and local taxing units.

Sales and use taxes in effect in each state are shown in Table 9–3.

Many counties and cities levy sales, use, or gross receipts taxes, and some states collect such local taxes. For information concerning such local problems, the buyer may refer to one of the current tax service publications.

Taxes on Services. In addition to the above taxes there are certain other taxes which become pricing considerations.

Transportation Taxes. These are the taxes levied on the transportation of materials and persons. Where applicable, they are generally paid by the carriers which issue the freight bill or sell the tickets and are shown as a separate item to be added to the tariff.

Taxes on Labor. Buyers who purchase services involving labor on a cost-plus basis need to consider the social security taxes which are levied on wage payments as such. These taxes are the Federal Old Age and Survivor's Insurance tax, and the Federal Unemployment tax under which all states have established their own unemployment insurance acts.

As pointed out at the outset, because of the complexity of tax laws and their interpretations, it is essential that the buyer have a working knowledge of the laws which are applicable to his area of operations. Among the best-known services which are available on the subject of taxes are those published by Commerce Clearing House, Inc., and Prentice-Hall, Inc.

Table 9–3. State Sales and Use Taxes as of February, 1964

State	Type of Tax	Rate
Alabama	Sales and use	4%
Alaska	Gross receipts tax	½% over $20,000
		¼% over $100,000
Arizona	Gross income	Varies
	Use	3%
Arkansas	Sales and use	3%
California	Sales and use	3%
Colorado	Sales and use	2%
Connecticut	Sales and use	3½%
Delaware	Manufacturers' license	$5 plus 0.025% of gross receipts
	Merchants' license	$5 plus 1/7 of 1% of cost over $5,000
District of Columbia	Sales and use	3%
Florida	Sales, use, and rental	3%
Georgia	Sales, use, and rental	3%
Hawaii	Gross income	Varies
	Consumption, use	3½%
	Compensating, use	½%
Idaho	No state tax	
Illinois	Retailers' occupational and use	3½%
Indiana	Sales and use	2%
Iowa	Sales and use	2%
Kansas	Sales and use	2½%
Kentucky	Sales and use	3%
Louisiana	Sales, use, and rental	2%
	Occupational license	Varies
Maine	Sales and use	4%
Maryland	Sales and use	3%
Massachusetts	Meals excise tax	
Michigan	Sales and use	4%
Minnesota	No state tax	
Mississippi	Sales and use	3%
	Wholesale use	⅛ of 1%
Missouri	Sales	3%
Montana	Admissions tax	
Nebraska	No state tax	
Nevada	Sales and use	2%
New Hampshire	No state tax	
New Jersey	No state tax	
New Mexico	Occupational gross income	Varies
	Sales and use	3%
	Merchants' license	From $5 to $150
New York	No state tax	
North Carolina	Sales and use	3%
North Dakota	Sales and use	2¼%
Ohio	Sales and use	3%
Oklahoma	Sales and use	2%
Oregon	No state tax	

Table 9–3. State Sales and Use Taxes as of February, 1964 (*Continued*)

State	Type of Tax	Rate
Pennsylvania	Sales and use	5%
Rhode Island	Unincorporated business gross receipts	Varies
	Sales and use	3%
South Carolina	Sales and use	3%
South Dakota	Sales and use	2%
Tennessee	Sales, use, and rental	3%
Texas	Sales and use	2%
Utah	Sales and use	3%
Vermont	No state tax	
Virginia	Merchants' license	$20 plus 20 cents per $100 over $2,000
Washington	Sales and use	4%
	Occupational gross income	Varies—0.25% for retailers
West Virginia	Sales and use	2%
	Occupational gross income	Varies 0.5% less 5% for retailers
Wisconsin	Sales and use	3%
Wyoming	Sales and use	2%

Import Duties. An import duty or tariff is a tax which is levied on certain goods entering a country. The United States began levying import duties in 1789, primarily to produce revenue for government operation. This has changed somewhat and the present Tariff Act of 1930 lists four reasons for our import duties:

1. To provide revenue
2. To regulate commerce with foreign countries
3. To encourage the industries of the United States
4. To protect American labor, and for other purposes

The last two, encouraging United States industries and protecting American labor, are now the most important.

Not all goods entering this country are dutiable. Coffee, natural rubber, sulfur, cocoa beans, fertilizers, rough and uncut diamonds, wood pulp, newsprint paper, and many other materials enter duty free. The goods which are dutiable are assessed for duty in three different ways.

1. *Specific duty* is a fixed charge per unit of material. Example: 10 cents per pound; 3 cents per gallon; $2 per ton, etc.
2. *Ad valorem duty* is a percentage of the foreign value of the product.
3. *Compound duty* includes both a specific and an ad valorem duty.

Example: $3\frac{1}{2}$ cents a pound and 15 per cent ad valorem. Here again the ad valorem is usually based on the foreign value; the exception is in paragraphs 27 and 28 (organic chemicals) of the Tariff Act of 1930 where the ad valorem duty is based on the American selling price, which is approximately the lowest price in the domestic price schedule.

The rates of duty applied to articles imported into the United States are covered by the publication "United States Import Duties (1952)" and amendments issued by the United States Tariff Commission, Washington, D.C.

For articles not specifically listed by the Tariff Commission, an answer as to what the duty might be may be obtained from the Bureau of Customs, Treasury Department, Washington, D.C. Customs will not give a definite decision on the duty applying unless and until an article has been imported. Further information on "Import Duties" will be found in Section 17, "Purchasing Internationally."

INSURANCE REQUIREMENTS—BONDS

It has been generally assumed throughout this section that the goods or services under consideration are available and/or will be delivered according to the terms of the contract. However, consideration of prices is meaningless unless performance is to be carried out in accordance with needs.

It is important, in some instances, to consider protection against exposure to risks or liabilities which may arise out of the performance by the contractor or supplier. The cost of such protection becomes a pricing consideration.

Contract Bonds. Occasions may arise, generally in contracting for services but occasionally covering the delivery of goods, where it is desirable to ensure performance by requiring a contract bond. Such bonding is a common requirement in procurement by governmental bodies but is generally discretionary in private business. Thus the cost of such a contract bond, if such bond is deemed advisable, becomes a pricing consideration in appraising the proposals of individual bidders.

Workmen's Compensation—Public Liability Insurance. It is usually of concern to an owner of property, when contracting for services, to be adequately protected against liabilities which may arise from the performance of such services. It is common practice to require contractors to provide evidence of insurance coverage of sufficient limits, effective for the duration of the contract, to afford adequate protection for the owner. Usually these include such coverage as workmen's compensation and occupational disease (under the laws of the state in which work is to be performed), bodily injury liability, and property damage liability. Many other insurance coverages are available. In selecting suppliers or contractors, the cost (or the additional cost) of providing sufficient insurance coverage must be taken into account as a price consideration.

A somewhat special case arises in connection with cost-plus contracts. As the premiums for the types of coverage mentioned above are based on hours worked, the cost of the insurance is usually included as an item of cost. As the rates charged are usually based on a contractor's casualty experience, the varying experience of different contractors may introduce a pricing consideration.

Another very important factor on cost-plus contracts is the fact that unsatisfied claims arising out of the work may be held to be items of cost and charged to the owner by the contractor. As the risks involved frequently have little relationship to value of the work, this is a highly important consideration.

All-risk Insurance (Transportation). This is a special case involving shipment of extremely large or valuable items. The carrier is normally responsible for the safe delivery of goods but under various tariffs the carriers' liabilities are limited to certain values and to certain causes of loss or damage. Insurance coverage is available to cover cases which may exceed the carrier's liability, the cost of which constitutes a pricing consideration.

INCIDENTAL PURCHASING COSTS

There are many costs incidental to a particular purchase which may not appear in the terms of a purchase order, but which need to be considered in arriving at purchase decisions. Those most commonly encountered can be placed in two categories, small-order costs and material-handling costs. Both affect ultimate delivered costs of any particular material.

Small-order Costs. The high relative cost of processing small orders is a problem for both buyer and seller. It generally costs no less to process the paper work for a small purchase than for a large one, and it costs the supplier as much to invoice a 50-cent order as it does a $5,000 order. Another problem to both buyer and seller is the cost of handling small items. An order may be large in the aggregate but consist of many small items. Considering each item as a unit of work (a "line of billing" is the term used by many suppliers), such an order may be costly to handle. To requisition, inquire for price and delivery order, receive, process invoice, store, and disburse one item costs just about as much as another, although the first may have ten times the value of the second. On the seller's side, entering, disbursing, checking, pricing, extending, and invoicing likewise cost about the same per item, regardless of size. Although there are some situations in which purchasing small quantities is unavoidable, there are many ways in which the purchasing agent can work to reduce the number of small-value orders which he is writing.

The storeroom and consuming departments should be urged to consolidate small orders and the purchasing agent himself should be alert to possibilities for further consolidation of requisitions into a large order.

National surveys have shown that there is a wide variation in the cost of a purchase order with its attendant invoice handling costs. These variations are due to differences in the volume of work, efficiency of operation, location, and system employed, and it is necessary that the purchasing agent determine the appropriate purchase order cost for use as a guide when considering his small-order problem.

Many purchasing departments have set up petty cash purchasing systems for use in connection with small money value purchases. A limited number of carefully chosen people in the storeroom and office service departments are permitted to pay cash on delivery of materials received against "cash purchase orders." This system is controlled by:

1. Limiting the size of an invoice which can be paid for by cash
2. Permitting payments to be made only for material covered by signed purchase orders
3. Limiting the total cash available for disbursement to a few hundred dollars
4. Requiring a check of the delivery tickets by an authorized member of the purchasing department before these tickets can be turned over to the cashier to support a make-up withdrawal of more cash

By using a system such as outlined above, it is possible to avoid the invoice matching and invoice processing procedures in the accounting department which culminate in the writing of a check for the vendor. There is a simplification of purchasing procedure also, as the order may be written on a simple two-part form and there is no permanent filing or purchase record entry required. Some companies have gone a step further, and as a part of their purchase order are enclosing blank, signed checks for completion of the amount by the supplier. See "Purchase Order Draft System" in Section 5.

The high relative cost of expediting a small order is aggravated by the fact that small orders are often emergency or rush orders which require expensive expediting and telephoning.

Minimum order charges are an effort by suppliers to defray partially the cost of handling small orders. It is general practice among suppliers to suggest to the customer that he order additional material and bring his total purchase up to or over the minimum.

One method of reducing purchasing costs which has been used by many large companies is the issuance of blanket orders against which purchases are applied and billed monthly with control established by the buyer on each individual order. Different types of blanket orders are explained in Section 5.

Material-handling Costs. It is sometimes necessary for the buyer to provide the special containers, special alloy drums, tank cars, and tank trucks to handle the movement of material to his plant. Providing the equipment necessary to package and transport materials involves not only an initial capital charge but also regular operating expenses. Vendors often sell in reusable equipment. Examples of these are: reels for wire and cable, cases for soft drinks, carboys for acids, and nickel and stainless steel drums for corrosive materials. It is a common practice for the vendor to charge a deposit which is redeemable upon return of the container. Container deposits require that the buyer's company tie up capital which could otherwise be used and there is therefore an interest charge on this money.

Another expense in this connection is the cost of the return of the seller's containers to his plant when empty. The question as to whether the freight charges for the return of the reusable containers are for the seller's or buyer's account becomes a pricing consideration.

The buyer needs to be alert to minimize material-handling charges on the material he is receiving.

Under some circumstances, bags can be handled easier than drums; 70- to 80-lb bags can be handled by one man whereas 120-lb bags require two, and the palletizing of bags makes it possible to unload a car with one-twentieth of the labor normally required. In order to achieve minimum over-all cost to his company, the purchasing agent's knowledge of materials and the package in which they are offered needs to be coordinated with that of the storeroom and using personnel with respect to material-handling costs.

Demurrage charges are levied on cars which are not returned to the carrier within the free time allotted. Demurrage charges can be avoided by:

1. Careful scheduling of inbound shipments
2. Obtaining lease agreements when a holdup of the car is recognized as unavoidable
3. Attention to the prompt unloading of all inbound shipments

There are many miscellaneous charges connected with the importation of materials from overseas. The cost of lighterage, custom broker fees, insurance, dockage, and other charges associated with international purchasing will be discussed in Section 17.

PRICE INFORMATION

Development of reliable current price information is important in all purchasing activity. Knowledge of prices is essential to many engaged in other functions of company activities. Determination of prices and the maintenance of adequate company price records is therefore an important function of the purchasing department. Price information generally falls into six categories:

1. Prices published by vendors in their catalogs and price sheets
2. Prices submitted by vendors upon direct request for bids
3. Prices developed during negotiation
4. Prices developed by the operation of open commodity markets such as the grain market operated by the Chicago Board of Trade
5. Prices of commodities not traded on exchanges but which, due largely to the breadth and activity of the market, are reasonably uniform and are published on a daily basis. This category for the most part is represented by raw and semifinished materials, such as metals, lumber, basic chemicals, etc.
6. Price indices designed to be generally representative of widely traded materials but which due to variations within the market do not represent specific item prices or the price of a given material in a specific market. These indices form a very valuable source of widely published pricing information. They are developed and published by government agencies, industry groups and associations, and private organizations engaged in the sale of economic services and counseling services.

Maintaining a current catalog and price-sheet file is difficult if it is to be complete. Catalogs and price sheets are printed in a multitude of sizes, shapes, and arrangements and do not lend themselves to shelving and filing in an orderly and economical way. Most companies develop and maintain pricing information designed to meet their own needs. Consequently, many such price files are selective, relying on past purchase records and local vendor representatives for price information when desired.

A widely used method for securing prices for major nonrepetitive purchases is to secure competitive bids from several logical suppliers. For a simplification of the bid procedure many purchasing departments use a standard bid or inquiry form, such as shown in Fig. 9–2. Other examples of this form are shown in Section 7, "How to Select Sources of Supply," and in Section 25, "Forms and Records."

AJAX SUPPLY COMPANY

Purchasing Department

1700 South 2nd Street St. Louis, Mo.

INQUIRY

NO.

DATE

REQUEST FOR QUOTATION

TO:

THIS IS NOT AN ORDER

Gentlemen:
You are invited to submit quotation on material listed below:

VIA F.O.B. Terms:

QUANTITY	MATERIAL	PRICE

If unable to make delivery required advise best delivery you will guarantee to make.
All quotations to include boxing, crating and cartage charges.
We reserve the right to reject any or all bids.

Yours very truly,

PURCHASING DEPT.

FIG. 9–2. Inquiry form.

Obtaining formal bids requires time that can usually be justified only for purchases of some magnitude. Often for purchases of small and intermediate value, the use of the telephone to obtain quotations from several suppliers is a satisfactory substitute for the formal bid. If a record is desired, it may simply be notes on the requisition form.

When the issuance of a formal "request for quotation" is indicated, it is necessary to exercise the same care in its preparation as in the writing of a purchase order. The request should specify the material in detail and spell out the quantity, delivery requirements, and terms under which the bid will be considered. In addition, it may be desirable, though not necessary, to state if the bids should be itemized, if partial bids will be accepted, and the date and time at which the bidding will close.

BID EVALUATION SHEET

Engineering Department

Prepared by: ____________

Description:

Estimated Cost: ____________

Required Delivery Date: ____________

Eng. Auth. No. ______

Project No. ______

Item No. ______

Spec. No. ______

Date ______

Company				
Compliance With Specs.				
Base Price				
Extras or Deductions				
Freight				
Sales Tax				
Discount or Other				
Total Purchase Price				
Est. Diff. Installation Cost				
Comparative Installed Cost				
Est. Annual Savings Repairs " " " Oper. Labor " " " Utilities " " " Total				
Incremental Cost Over Low Bid				
Delivery				
Terms of Payment				
Escalation				

Remarks

Approvals: Process ____ Date ____ E. & I. ____ Date ____
Design ____ Date ____ Const. ____ Date ____
Recommended Supplier: ____________
Basis for Recommendation: ____________

FIG. 9–3. Bid evaluation sheet.

Bids may be obtained verbally, by letter, or as is common practice in government purchasing, by advertising in newspapers and posting on the bulletin board of a public building.

Tabulation of bids on a form designed for this purpose is the first step in bid analysis. An example of this form is shown in Fig. 9–3, and also in Section 7, "How to Select Sources of Supply."

The bidding, to be fair and useful, must be on identical goods or services and any variations should be shown on the summary sheet. If the variation is significant, it is best to reject all bids, rewrite the specifications, incorporating the best features from each vendor's suggestions, and send out new bid requests to all of the original bidders. When the transaction is complete, the summary provides an important part of the department's price records and pricing information.

While the industrial buyer is under no obligation to purchase from the lowest bidder and uses the request for bid technique as a convenient method for securing price information, the buyer for a governmental agency must under normal circumstances award the business at the lowest price. Government purchasing will be discussed in detail in Section 19, "Public Purchasing."

A third method for securing prices is by negotiation. This approach is particularly suited to the purchase of nonstandard materials or materials which can be made to order at a saving to the buyer and/or the seller. Techniques of negotiation are described in Section 10.

A variation of negotiated prices is "contract buying" or "stockless purchasing." Bids are requested for all of, or a substantial part of, a plant's or company's requirements on a particular category of goods or supplies, for a given period of time. In addition to the advantages mentioned in the preceding paragraphs, contract buying allows a company to reduce substantially its investment in storeroom facilities and stocks and to reduce its payroll as well. Furthermore, it establishes definitely the maximum price for a given future period. These agreements usually contain downward escalator clauses.

The profit the seller shall make is also a subject for negotiation and this in turn requires a consideration of the risks involved in the seller's manufacture and the buyer's use. Through skillful negotiation the buyer is able to combine a strong competitive feature of bidding with the additional advantage of a detailed discussion of the factors which make the price. This discussion often leads to opportunities for price reductions which are developed mutually by buyer and seller. A detailed discussion of price analysis and price negotiation is covered in Section 10, "Price Evaluation." Mention is made here only because negotiated prices become an important division of pricing records to a company.

Many materials which are produced in large volume, by a large number of manufacturers, and/or sold to a large number of buyers are bought and sold on commodity exchanges, or so widely as to produce an effectively free open market. Prices of many such commodities are widely reported in the press and in a number of daily and weekly publications.

Listed below are a number of publications which offer valuable sources of current pricing information. These are shown first in alphabetical order and in the second list are regrouped under the broad commodity divisions which they regularly cover.

These are presented as representative of the more widely used sources of such information. Most daily newspapers publish commodity market prices for their own locality, as well as cover national markets. The United States government, through the Department of Commerce, publishes certain pricing information which forms a valuable source of such information for the use of the buyer. The Department of Labor also publishes data concerning labor costs and price indices which are useful to the buyer in price analysis. Many of these periodicals are listed in other sections of this handbook, particularly Sections 15, 26 and 28.

In addition to these sources, which may be considered sources of public information, there are innumerable sources available to the buyer on a private basis. Many trade associations collect and disseminate market information solely for the use of their membership. In this category also are the large number of economic services which furnish their clients with information on prices and price trends. Probably the most readily available source to the buyer is that furnished by suppliers on a regularly published basis.

SELECTED REFERENCES ON PRICING CONSIDERATIONS

Alphabetical Listing

American Lumberman & Building Products Merchandiser, H. A. Vance, 139 North Clark Street, Chicago, Ill. 60602

American Metal Market, American Metal Market Co., Inc., 525 W. 42d St., New York, N.Y. 10036

American Paint Journal, American Paint Journal Co., 2911 Washington Avenue, St. Louis, Mo. 63103

America's Textile Reporter, Frank P. Bennett & Co., 286 Congress Street, Boston, Mass. 02110

Black Diamond, The, The Black Diamond Co., 431 South Dearborn Street, Chicago, Ill. 60605

Commercial Bulletin, Curtis Guild & Co., 156 High Street, Boston, Mass. 02110

Cotton Trade Journal, Francis G. Hickman, Hickman Building, Memphis, Tenn. 38103

Daily News Record, Fairchild Publications, Inc., 7 East 12th Street, New York, N.Y. 10003

Drovers Journal, 836 Exchange Avenue, Chicago, Ill. 60609

E & M J Metal and Mineral Markets, McGraw-Hill Publications, 330 West 42nd Street, New York, N.Y. 10036

Engineering and Mining Journal, McGraw-Hill Publications, 330 West 42nd Street, New York, N.Y. 10036

Engineering News-Record, McGraw-Hill Publications, 330 West 42nd Street, New York, N.Y. 10036

Feedstuffs, Miller Publishing Co., 2501 Wayzata Blvd., Minneapolis, Minn. 55440

COAL AND COKE

American Metal Market
Black Diamond, The
Commercial Bulletin
Iron Age
Saward's Journal

CHEMICALS AND PAINT MATERIALS

American Paint Journal
Journal of Commerce and Commercial
Oil, Paint & Drug Reporter
Rubber Age

COTTON, TEXTILES, AND WOOL

America's Textile Reporter
Cotton Trade Journal
Daily News Record
Journal of Commerce and Commercial
Mill Stock Reporter
Modern Textiles
Wall Street Journal
Women's Wear Daily

FATS AND OILS

Journal of Commerce and Commercial
National Provisioner, The
Wall Street Journal

GRAINS AND FEEDSTUFFS

Feedstuffs
Journal of Commerce and Commercial
Northwestern Miller, The
Wall Street Journal

HIDES AND LEATHER

Journal of Commerce and Commercial
Leather & Shoes
National Provisioner, The
Pratt's Report
Shoe & Leather Reporter
Wall Street Journal

LIVESTOCK

Drover's Journal
National Provisioner, The
Wall Street Journal

LUMBER AND WOOD

American Lumberman & Building Products Merchandiser
Commercial Bulletin
Hardwood Market Report
Timberman, The

METALS AND MINERALS

American Metal Market
E & M J Metal and Mineral Markets
Engineering and Mining Journal
Iron Age
Journal of Commerce and Commercial
Metal Reporter
Steel
Wall Street Journal

PAPER AND PULPWOOD

Journal of Commerce and Commercial
Mill Stock Reporter
Paper Industry
Paper Mill News
Paper Trade Journal

PETROLEUM AND PETROLEUM PRODUCTS

American Metal Market
Commercial Bulletin
Journal of Commerce and Commercial
National Petroleum News
Plat's Oilgram Daily
Wall Street Journal

PRODUCE AND DAIRY PRODUCTS

American Egg & Poultry Review
Journal of Commerce and Commercial
Packer
Produce Packer
Wall Street Journal

RUBBER AND RUBBER PRODUCTS

Journal of Commerce and Commercial
Rubber Age
Rubber World
Wall Street Journal

METALS AND MINERALS

American Metal Market
E & M J Metal and Mineral Markets
Engineering and Mining Journal
Iron Age
Journal of Commerce
Steel
Wall Street Journal

PAPER AND PULPWOOD

Journal of Commerce
Paper Industry
Paper Mill News
Paper Trade Journal
Waste Trade Journal and Mill Stock Reporter

PETROLEUM AND PETROLEUM PRODUCTS

American Metal Market
Commercial Bulletin
Journal of Commerce
National Petroleum News
Platt's Oilgram Price Service
Wall Street Journal

PRODUCE AND DAIRY PRODUCTS

Journal of Commerce
Packer
Poultry & Egg Weekly
Wall Street Journal

RUBBER AND RUBBER PRODUCTS

Journal of Commerce
Rubber Age
Rubber World
Wall Street Journal

Refer to Section 15, "Buying Considerations: Representative Commodities," for additional sources of price and other information on apparel, automotive and parts, chemicals and plastics, ferrous and nonferrous metals, food and kindred products, fuels, lumber and timber, mill supplies, office equipment and supplies, pulp and paper, textiles and utilities.

Section 28, "Appendix," lists organizations and professional associations that supply prices and price trend information. In addition, Section 26 furnishes names and addresses of magazines issued by many of these organizations and associations.

SECTION 10

PRICE EVALUATION

Editor

Harold J. Newman, Director, Staff Services–Purchasing, Allegheny Ludlum Steel Corporation, Pittsburgh, Pennsylvania

Associate Editors

Samuel A. Forter, Jr., Corporate Materials Control, General Dynamics Corporation, New York, New York

H. R. Lanser, Purchasing Agent, Monsanto Company, St. Louis, Missouri

INFLUENCES ON PRICE EVALUATION

Price may be defined as the sum or amount of money at which a thing is valued, or the value which a seller sets on his goods in the market. Consequently, to obtain an article you pay in money, barter, or services.

Price is one of the greatest variables in purchasing. Dollars and cents alone are just one of the aspects. This medium is often camouflaged with many misleading adjectives, such as the best price, lowest price, most economical price, etc. It may appear bewildering to one seeking the right or fair price. Theoretically, price is the suggested figure at which a seller can deliver his goods at a profit and which the buyer pays, expecting to receive full value for use or manufacture. The profit must be sufficient to encourage a continuous supply of the proper quality to him who needs it, where and when he needs it, at a cost to him commensurate with that of his competitors.

Price knowledge is based upon experience and familiarity with general price conditions. This does not necessarily imply quoted prices on inquiries or printed lists are fair or the lowest available. To gain price vision, the buyer should understand the conditions affecting the particular industry with respect to the commodities or items priced. To determine the right price, it is essential for a buyer to be conversant with business trends, trade cycles, supply and demand, how price advances and declines may be anticipated, quantity discounts, and many other factors discussed in Section 9 as making up the price.

As a guide toward achieving a sense of good judgment about price, a buyer should read current trade journals and books, such as listed in Sections 9 and 26, maintain a continuous record of prices paid previously, make plant visits, be familiar with trade customs, alliances that may exist, and special conditions of manufacture and sale.

Besides listing names of publications and books on pricing considerations, Section 9 also describes the basic factors of price, per se, such as:

1. Price terms
2. Price adjustments
3. Payment terms
4. Price schedules
5. Transportation costs
6. Taxes
7. Insurance
8. Incidental purchasing costs, and
9. Developing price information

The purpose of Section 9 is to define all factors affecting price. This section, 10, however, recapitulates those price considerations not only in Section 9, but also many others for effective evaluation by the buyer. Thus some repetition is demanded in this section to minimize reference to Section 9.

Price versus Cost

Any study of price evaluation or pricing influences must of necessity place the element of price in its true perspective in relation to cost. Price should be regarded as only one of the elements in the formula for cost. It must never be overlooked that such factors as transportation, receiving, handling, recording, and storage are in themselves expenses to the purchaser which must be added to the price to determine the ultimate cost. Still other factors, among them quality as related to the function to be performed, service, obsolescence, and spoilage, must also be considered in determining the ultimate cost, though they may be more difficult to evaluate and convert to dollars and cents.

It should be noted, too, that buying at a lower price is not necessarily a criterion of good procurement and, in fact, may be a very easily attainable objective. The buyer who sets as his objective the attainment of a lower ultimate cost, has, however, established a solid basis for an intelligent job of purchasing. For example, the purchase of a grinding wheel at a higher price than others offer in the market may well be justified if tests indicate that under the user's conditions it will remove more metal over a longer period of time than competing wheels.

None of this is intended to minimize the importance of price in the buying decision, but rather to call attention also to the many other considerations vital to the determination of the ultimate cost of the goods purchased.

Another interesting facet is the influence of the supplier's cost in the establishment of his selling price. While every producer must eventually recover his costs plus a margin of profit if he is to remain in business, it is primarily the marketplace which will determine the selling price of his product.

The Right Price

Generally speaking, there are three basic methods of pricing: (1) published *price lists* (with quantity and other discount setups); (2) *bids* on individual specifications; (3) *negotiated prices* on specific jobs or lots of material.

Published Market Price Lists

Many manufacturers publish price lists which represent the prices to be charged all customers. This standard list does not mean all customers will pay the same price, but it does mean all customers who qualify for a certain category as described in the list will be charged the same price.

This so called "one-price" policy has considerable backing among major national manufacturers. It is probably the easiest to administer by relieving the pressure of price selling on the part of the sales force. Selling can then be done on the basis of service and quality, and differences between the price schedules of competitors will be rationalized on those factors.

Under this method of pricing, retailers, wholesalers, and manufacturers may each have an appropriate price list and quantity price brackets may also be shown. In addition, a quantity discount may be available to each class of purchaser, based on annual volume or dollar value of material purchased. The purchasing agent should know the several categories into which the price schedule is organized and should ensure that he is obtaining the prices applicable to the status of his company for each class of purchase. This, of course, suggests the practice of combining purchase records of all plants in the same company to become eligible for a higher discount at all plants.

An aggressive buyer will go beyond this point and attempt to assess the economic justification for differences in prices between the classes of customers. Original Equipment Manufacturers (called OEM) are usually entitled to special discounts on standard products incorporated into a finished product. The purchasing agent for an OEM is negligent if he is not obtaining this benefit for his company. The purchasing agent for a large user of similar items, but not for incorporation into final product, may well attempt to have his own category accorded equivalent price treatment and he should exert effort to this end.

Typical illustrations of published price lists are shown by the following three samples of extracts from a hardware jobber's catalog.

EXAMPLE 1

	1–6	*6–12*	*12–72*	*Gross*
Axe, hand, "Apache"	Ea. $1.69	1.63	1.55	1.45
Axe, hand, "Warrior"	Ea. $0.89	0.86	0.80	0.72

EXAMPLE 2

	1–10	*10–25*	*26 and up*
Switch, Start-Stop Cat. #73 & 79	Ea. $6.00	6.00	4.80
	Net	−15%	Net

EXAMPLE 3

	Less Pkg.	*Pkg. (25)*	*10 Pkg.*
Screw, set, hollow head			
¼ − 32 × ½	Ea. $0.03	Pkg. 0.42	Pkg. 0.36

The following tabulation shows an example of a "quantity discount" schedule. This figure is adapted from an electric-motor manufacturer's price list.

EXAMPLE OF DISCOUNT SCHEDULES

¼-hp single-phase induction motor
110/220 volts, 1—ϕ, 60-cycle, alternating current

Number	*List*	*Small industrial*	*Large industrial*	*Jobber*	*OEM*
1–24	$34.50	−15%	−32%	−40%	−41%
25–99	$34.50	−20%	−32%	−45%	−50%
100–500	$34.50	−23%	−35%	−50%	−55%
500 plus	Price on application				

Above prices are based on single-order quantity, f.o.b. shipping point with freight prepaid and allowed to first destination within continental United States.

Many sellers may not have list price with discount setups and any possibility of achieving such rests with the buyer. Therefore, it is the responsibility of the buyer to negotiate to this, where his purchases indicate an economic and legal basis for special treatment.[1]

Prices of many items in the raw material or semifinished categories are published daily for well-established market grades. While not price lists, as such, they are effective as published price information and are so used in business. These prices usually are a reflection of the demand and the

[1] See Sections 4 and 9, references to Robinson-Patman Act and other laws.

availability, or the apparent availability, of the commodity. They tend to fluctuate quite markedly on the basis of factors which control output or availability of the commodity such as weather, labor for processing, strikes, floods, etc. If the future supply appears to be shorter, users of the product will buy heavily and the price may advance quickly. The condition of surpluses in these markets may also occur quickly with the consuming industry finding itself committed for large stocks of commodities at inflated prices. The purchase and sale of futures and hedging[2] are devices used to minimize fluctuations which may occur in the production and price of some of these commodities.

Bids on Individual Specifications

This approach to pricing really involves two different problems:

1. Bids on individual detailed specification
2. Competitive bidding on standard items

Some materials and parts are made according to the buyer's *detailed specifications* and bought on the basis of bids by producers. This is one of the most highly competitive forms of pricing, since many of the economic forces can be brought to bear and the price level may be determined by the extent to which the supplier needs the business. In this method of pricing, careful and complete specification, good bidding procedures, and careful bid analysis are essential.

Suppliers from time to time will vary prices even when they have published price lists. Among the many reasons are: to maintain volume, clear inventories, aspire to additional volume so that they can themselves buy in more economical quantities, and to meet competition. Purchasing will frequently request bids on the basis of performance specifications or other less detailed specifications to obtain benefits from these temporary conditions in the market, in effect inviting the bidders to quote standard items at the best price available.

Negotiated Prices

The two previously discussed basic methods of determining the right or fair price depend largely on the existence of a competitive market and/or the ability to set forth the exact, detailed specifications of the equipment or materials to be purchased. Very often, however, these and other criteria are lacking or totally absent and the buyer must resort to negotiations with the supplier to secure the best advantage for his company.

[2] See Section 12, "Forecasting and Forward Buying."

Sometimes when certain kinds of equipment or materials are to be purchased, or a specific job is to be done, direct competition may not be present because the offerings of the various bidders are not identical. Different pieces of equipment have individual features, although they may be intended to do the same job. Technical assistance may be required to evaluate the bids.

When a construction or installment project is to be accomplished, the ability of all interested contractors to perform may be questionable to the point where only one is considered qualified. Familiarity with plant facilities, specially trained employees, or a record of previous accomplishment may favor one contractor to the exclusion of all others. In such circumstances, negotiations may be used to establish the scope of the project and the right or fair price.

It should be noted here that while this section concerns itself with pricing matters, it is not intended to imply that the area of negotiations is thus limited. To the contrary, negotiations with suppliers will often involve other matters such as transportation, tooling, scrap disposition, tolerance, or any of the host of considerations that are part of a procurement decision.

The art of negotiation provides the purchasing executive with perhaps his finest opportunity to improve his company's profits and to obtain the recognition not usually accorded the mere checker of price lists or bids. His knowledge of value analysis and learning curve techniques, discussed later in this section, will strengthen his negotiating skill. As with any art, the practitioner must develop and refine his skills through repeated exposure, but basic to this is an understanding of the art itself. The United States Air Force comments on negotiations in the following manner:

> Procurement by negotiation is the art of arriving at a common understanding through bargaining on the essentials of a contract, such as delivery, specifications, price, and terms. Because of the interrelation of these factors with many others, it is a difficult art and requires the exercise of judgment, tact, and common sense. The effective negotiator must be a real shopper, alive to the possibilities of bargaining with the seller. Only through an awareness of relative bargaining strength can a negotiator know where to be firm or where he may make permissive concessions in price or terms.

Negotiations involve the psychology of persuasion. Nothing contributes more toward successful negotiations than advance planning of objectives and strategy. The purchasing agent should enter the session with a positive attitude toward achieving his objectives, as well as having decided upon the maximum extent of his potential concessions. All pertinent facts should be collected and studied before the meeting so that the buyer will be ready to answer promptly and speak with determination on any points the opposition may bring up to weaken his position. An agenda should be developed and be made known to all participants.

Selection of those who are to participate is a vital consideration of planning. Quite often the purchasing agent will be the sole negotiator for his company. At other times where technical or other considerations predominate, he may ask qualified persons from engineering or other departments to join him. While he will derive certain advantage from the presence of these experts, there is also the danger that one of them, if not experienced in negotiating strategy, may expose a weak point in the buyer's position or prematurely commit the buyer with a thoughtless remark.

An appreciation and understanding of the emotional factors are important to the successful conducting of negotiating sessions. A personal contact between buyer and seller is involved, with both presumably dealing in good faith and each having his company's and his own best interest uppermost in his thoughts. The buyer should learn all that he can about those with whom he is to negotiate and appraise the position they are likely to take on the issues involved. Displays of temper or generation of anger by the purchasing agent will generally avail him little and may even be a handicap to logical, clear-headed thinking.

Even the physical environment of the negotiating session is an important consideration. Pleasant surroundings make it easier to successfully complete negotiations. Inadequate ventilation, lighting, or space may present unnecessary obstacles to an otherwise pleasant and fruitful discussion. Recess periods may be desirable, both for a change of pace and for a review of progress.

The negotiation process provides a legitimate and ethical means for the buyer and seller, through give and take, to eliminate unjustified or unnecessary increments of cost. It should not be construed as a means for stripping the vendor of a fair profit or an opportunity for extracting unreasonable concessions. In reality, the most successful negotiations are those which produce results satisfying to both sides and which provide the framework for a long-term, mutually beneficial relationship.

It should be remembered that the conditions on which an agreement has been based may well change over a period of time. Therefore, the prudent purchasing agent will not file away and forget a contract or agreement he has just negotiated but will regard his responsibility as one of continuing administration. He will remain alert not only to his company's and the vendor's observance of all provisions, but also to the possibility of reopening negotiations if and when it is to his company's advantage to do so.

One author offers several "do's" and "don'ts" which may be helpful in negotiation sessions.[3]

Don't:

1. Tip your hand too early. Withhold something for later concession in return for a point.
2. Get so bogged down in details that the overall objectives are lost. A suggestion: After close scrutiny to details, give way relatively generously to a compromise which is still satisfactory.
3. Try to prove the vendor is wrong. You may win the point, but you won't reduce the price and leave him room to back off gracefully from a stated position.

Do:

1. Negotiate at home when possible. Isolate members of the selling team by seating buying members between them to break up their attack.
2. Negotiate with those who can make concessions. It is useless to attempt negotiations with a salesman on items such as mill steel, where prices are set at the home office—although it will help if his sales reports back up your position. Many salesmen, however, have a range of prices to submit, and they may be able to drop a figure 5 per cent without contacting management.
3. Remain silent at times. Often greater concessions result from a seller's fear of losing business. Vendors may talk themselves into a better settlement than expected.
4. Know what you can expect to gain by negotiating and keep your target in mind. Analyze the amount of "give" the vendor can reasonably be expected to have.
5. Plan ahead. Prepare the agenda to your advantage and brief team members beforehand to be sure none of them tip your hand or give in on a point before you do.
6. Negotiate for the long pull—not the short-sighted advantage which may backfire at the first turn of economic conditions.
7. Be confident of facts presented. Don't use information that you may have to acknowledge as wrong.
8. Use new techniques such as the learning curve and price/cost analysis.
9. Divert attention if the negotiation hits your weak points. Shift the strategy of attack to minor points which you may later concede.
10. Call a recess if talk hits a snag, or arrange for a lunch break. Set the meeting for a time that will allow the vendor to relax at lunch with company people (at the buyer's expense, of course).
11. Enlist the aid of specialists in manufacturing, methods, finance and engineering to help evaluate tooling and other special costs. Purchasing research will help supply basic data for negotiating in depth.
12. Always be fair.

[3] Victor H. Pooler, Jr., *The Purchasing Man and His Job,* American Management Association, New York, 1964, pp. 120–121.

Supply and Demand

In a capitalistic society, supply-and-demand relationships contribute significantly to the direction and shape of the business activity curve. This does not, however, deny the influence of government regulations, politics, and other factors on the free operation of supply and demand, and on business trends in general. It is not pertinent here to examine in detail the operation and effect of supply-demand curves; nevertheless, the subject will be discussed as one of the factors influencing the buyers' and sellers' markets.

The progressive manufacturing company must be aware of basic supply-and-demand ratios as they concern the sale of its own products. The alert purchasing agent not only should be concerned with the materials he must purchase to meet the varying levels of output, but also must be concerned with these same relationships in the several other markets in which he is obtaining his supplies, parts, etc. His concern is with specific commodity markets, competitive markets, and also with the over-all business levels. He must know these relationships as they affect his purchased commodities and as they affect commodities which may be alternate sources. A short supply of one or more alternates might cause absorption of some of the supply of his commodity to meet other demands, and the over-all business picture may cause fluctuations in demand or supply in each separate industry or commodity.

Trade journals publish news items, editorial comment, and statistical information giving knowledge about the current supply-demand relationship. One of the most reputable and reliable sources for this information is the weekly *Bulletin* of the National Association of Purchasing Agents. An example of this report is reproduced in Fig. 10–1.

Continuous reference to this report (or other reports) will keep the purchasing agent informed in regard to current relationships and in addition will alert him to changes in prices, deliveries, and other purchasing problems which may result therefrom. Use of such reports demands that they be read thoughtfully and the information gleaned from them be related to the reader's own business circumstances. Reading these reports will help the purchasing agent who is versed in his field, who knows his own company's problems and circumstances, and who has the general knowledge and experience to appreciate the significance of the opinions and facts presented.

Buyers' and Sellers' Markets

For price evaluation, a buyers' market is considered that state in which the buyer has a distinct bargaining advantage. In a sellers' market the

The Lumber Market

Report Prepared by the Lumber Committee of the National Association of Purchasing Agents.

ITEMS	*Supplies*	*Prices*	*Purchase Recommendations*
Hardwood Lumber			
Northern	Ample	Steady	60 to 90 Days
Southern	Ample	Steady	60 to 90 Days
Softwood Lumber			
Construction	Ample	Steady	Current Needs
Southern	Ample	Steady	Current Needs
West Coast	Ample	Steady	Current Needs
Softwood Lumber—Factory (Shop, etc.)			
Southern	Ample	Steady	Current Needs
West Coast	Ample	Steady	Current Needs
Plywood			
Hardwood	Ample	Steady	Current Needs
Softwood	Ample	Steady	Current Needs
Imported	Ample	Steady	60 to 90 Days
Hardwood Flooring			
Oak	Ample	Steady	Current Needs
Maple	Ample	Steady	Current Needs

CENTRAL STATES—Reported by Chairman Carl J. Culmann.

A shake-up in the structure of the American Lumber Standards Committee is under way. This was confirmed recently in testimony by J. Herbert Holloman Assistant Secretary of Commerce before a sub-Committee of the House of Representatives. Testimony on the make-up of the American Lumber Standards Committee included views expressed by A. J. Agather, Chairman of the A.L.S.C. and A. S. Boisfontaine, Manager of S.P.I.B., that the Committee is broadly representative of the industry. At the same time, statements by Aaron Jones, W.C.L.I.B. Chairman, and several other West Coast representatives, asserted the Committee membership should be broadened. That this will be done is a foregone conclusion. Another item of interest to lumbermen is the export of logs from the Pacific Northwest which has totaled about 400 million feet for the first six months of 1964. This volume compares with 252 million feet for the same period in 1963, or an increase of 58%. These have been bound mainly for Japan, Korea and Canada, and what is particularly galling to northern Washington manufacturers is that lumber from these same logs is later resold in the Atlantic Coast Cargo market. In this area the combination of sales to Japan and British Columbia has made log buying unprofitable, with the result a number of mills do not appear to be building winter log decks at a normal pace.

NORTH PACIFIC STATES—Report of Regional Chairman, R. H. Brayne, *Weyerhaeuser Company, Wood Products Division,* Longview, Wash.

Mixed cars of dry dimension are having the heaviest percentage of orders. Transit sales are light. Standard and better dimensions are rather active with sales leaning heavily to specified. Low grades show no signs of immediate improvement.

Green Framing Lumber: A few scattered downward prices instituted by producers mostly to random narrow widths. Straight cars of 2x10-14′ scarce. Straight cars of long dimension find the prices down $1-2. Sales of 2x4 are good in relation to other sizes.

Dry Framing Lumber: Dry dimension fir is still fairly good in mixed car business. Straight cars in both standard and better and utility grades are found to be a little soft.

Standard and better hemlock random length is available in the lower $60s for 2x4s; 2x6s are approximately $65, and 2x8 prices remain fairly firm.

Plywood: Most mills have a fairly good order file, but a shortage of wide door cars is disturbing some shipping schedules. Prices still on $62 list. Sheathing sales run good with prices remaining firm.

NORTHEASTERN STATES—Report of Regional Chairman, William B. Lambert, *The Frank S. Harden Company,* McConnellsville, N. Y.

The fourth quarter of 1964 should find very little change in the prices of either logs or lumber. Inventories appear to be at a level that will take care of increased requirements over the next six months.

Report of Associate Regional Chairman, Mitchell P. Krach, *H. F. Lynch, Lumber Company,* West Springfield, Mass.

East Coast sales are almost as active as "politicking." Prices are holding firm as heavy demand continues. Outlook is very optimistic for the third quarter, reflecting a good backlog of orders by both the industrials and the building trades.

Hardwoods, plywoods, eastern and western pines, eastern and western white spruce prices are all holding their own Supplies are ample to take care of all requirements. Blanket orders and contracts continue to be the "buy words."

SOUTHEASTERN STATES—Report of Regional Chairman, Jerry F. Nelems, *Raines Lumber Company,* Birmingham, Alabama.

The lumber situation is good. There has been no drastic change within the past month.

Construction on residence is still up in this part of the country and this helps the lumber dealer.

Supplies of most lumber are adequate.

LAKE STATES—Report of Regional Chairman, Lawrence S. Clark, *Twin City Hardwood Lumber Company,* St. Paul, Minn.

Conditions in this area seem to be good, with a steady amount of business flowing through distributors and retailers. Weather has improved with sufficient rain, so conditions for fall trade look very good.

The corn crop in this area is spotted with some of it ruined by drought; but other areas, sometimes almost across the road, have exceptionally good anticipated yields. The total crop of all items will not be as large as a year ago; but, as a general rule, farmers seem to be satisfied.

CENTRAL STATES—Report of Regional Chairman, Clifford Kleier, *Boland-Maloney Lumber Company,* Louisville 6, Ky.

Hot, dry September is again with us bringing with it visions of cool autumn days; a period which should bring increased activity to this industry. There are no abnormal happenings of any kind. Prices are steady, deliveries are normal and supplies ample for this season of the year.

FIG. 10–1. Example of commodity report by NAPA. (*Reproduced by permission.*)

seller has a distinct bargaining advantage. Either condition may exist in a particular industry in contrast to the over-all business picture. In fact, the relationship may even be with regard to a single item in a product line in an industry.

Buyers' Market

A *buyers' market* is first shown by a willingness on the part of sellers to grant concessions such as: quality changes, more favorable delivery, or better packaging at no increase in price. It may be evidenced by price concessions, or more generous payment terms. An alert buyer will detect a softening in his vendors' attitude long before the press confirms the existence of a buyers' market.

Primarily a buyers' market exists when supply is greater than demand. In practice a buyers' market comes into existence when one or more suppliers think that supply will exceed demand. Not all buyers' and sellers' markets are directly caused by this supply-demand relationship, but in the great majority of cases this influence is at least contributory.

At least one source has estimated that a difference of only 2 or 3 per cent in supply or demand will change the market to a buyers' or sellers' market.

Economists, sales executives, and purchasing agents all tend to agree that a mild buyers' market is a healthy economic condition. Under this condition sellers are required to devote energies to produce at lowest cost possible, to utilize personnel and equipment at an optimum rate, to stimulate research for product improvement, including both new component materials as well as new uses, and to improve product quality.

A buyers' market may exist under conditions of short supply if there is potential threat of increased supply from idle production facilities or substitute materials. Under this situation the buyer assumes bargaining strength from the threat of potential new suppliers in the field.

Purchasing policies must recognize that a buyers' market is not to be used as a lever to whip suppliers for past grievances, real or imagine[1] It is an opportunity for the buyer to improve purchasing performance and contribute to the company's profit picture by intelligent negotiation based on knowledge of his own requirements and the willingness of his vendors to cooperate for mutual benefit. The buyer, having at this time the dominant bargaining position, will have principal influence in determining the fair price.

Opportunities may be offered to obtain new materials, to develop additional sources of supply, or to improve scheduling of shipments. In a buyers' market marginal producers tend to drop out of the picture, some suppliers may cease to produce certain items, and some suppliers may offer drastic price concessions to capture a greater share of the business Any of these could have a reverse effect and the buyer must be alert to detect any indication that his own suppliers may be contemplating leaving the market, or that reduced prices may be a last-straw effort to stay in business. Usually a buyers' market finds more suppliers offering products than before, as sellers seek additional customers for their output o offer new (to them) product lines to keep the factory busy. These latte offerings may be legitimate, in that the supplier will continue to offe them to his new customers when his normal volume is again up to hi level. They may be transient, in that he may drop the new product o refuse to serve new customers when business returns to a normal leve

Over a substantial period the American economy has expanded and a predictions are that such expansion will continue through the futur This dynamic condition means that the purchasing agent can look fo more varied sources for more varied materials in the long pull, bu periodic temporary imbalances can be expected. He must remain alert and flexible; alert to detect shifts in his bargaining strength and flexible in his thinking and practices to utilize his strength to best advantage for the competitive well-being of his company.

Sellers' Market

A *sellers' market* tends to encourage economic waste, and such waste is more or less proportional to the intensity of the market. At its worst, particularly as demonstrated during the World War II years of shortages, "getting the goods" is more important than how the goods are obtained or at what cost. Purchasing people are then required to negotiate from a poor starting position. Costs of procurement are high and costs of expediting can be substantial.

Material costs are high because of many "legitimate" but wasteful practices. Overtime is expended, employee production levels usually are low, quality control usually slips, and transportation costs are increased because of rush shipments or partial shipments. Control over these can become impossible for either seller or buyer. The buyer will doubtless try to minimize these extra cost factors and some real good can result from his efforts. But in the end his principal function is to get the materials required to keep his own production lines moving. Added costs usually can be passed on in his selling price.

Probably the toughest purchasing job in the whole field belongs to the buyer in a depressed industry when the general business level is one of shortages. Every ounce of skillful effort must be exerted for every purchase. Everything he buys is difficult to obtain and his bargaining power is low, but every possible price savings must be obtained, every disadvantage must be challenged in order to hold his own company's costs low enough to attract the maximum level of sales. Value analysis must be practiced, every requisition must be checked for quality specification and quantity point, routings and other transportation and handling costs must be examined, each possible source must be evaluated, and taxes and insurance costs must be assessed. He must do a real purchasing job if his company is to weather these adverse conditions.

Evaluation of Suppliers

Price evaluation is predicated on vendors' costs. For standard competitive articles this aspect of evaluation is not susceptible to searching study but for special products and construction services detailed cost studies may be required. In competitive bidding such studies will be based mainly on general industry figures, not necessarily those of any particular supplier. Material estimates will be based on generally published quotations such as commodity exchange reports. Labor estimates will be based on established or prevailing rates at estimated man-hours. If the buyer's estimate differs from the competitive bids, discussions with the bidders may be held and these will be concerned with generalized figures not usually in great detail. Sufficient information should develop to assure the purchasing agent that he has at least closely approximated the fair price.

Failing to achieve such assurance, he can then either accept the most favorable bid, reject all bids and submit to a new bidder list, or select a limited number of suppliers and negotiate with them on a "negotiated price" basis.

Selection of these bidders[4] should be done on the basis of generally accepted criteria. As related to price evaluation, it is emphasized that negotiations will be based on the particular bidder's costs. If a marginal high-costs producer is selected, the computed price may be "fair" to him but may in fact be based on costs that are out of line. Improper selection of sources will penalize the buyer. The buyer must ensure that his source is at least of average efficiency, based on production equipment, worker output, labor rates, incoming material costs, overhead, and all the other factors contributing to cost and price. Though reference material to assist the buyer in vendor evaluation is available, his own knowledge and judgment must ultimately prevail.

The purchasing agent who refuses to do business with a particular source of supply should be in a position to justify his decision. This may involve price, quality, performance, integrity, or numerous other considerations. It may simply reflect the impracticalities and poor economics of dividing one's business among an overabundance of suppliers who may wish to participate. Nevertheless, it is likely that the rejected or excluded sources will inquire as to the reason for rejection or exclusion, and pressure may be brought to bear on ownership, management, or government alleging prejudice or discrimination. A logical and intelligent evaluation of suppliers will assist the purchasing agent in maintaining his prerogatives in source selection.

Escalation[5]

Price adjustment clauses have become prevalent because of uncertainty as to sellers' future costs. Although they are used in connection with many routine purchases, they are principally required for purchase of capital equipment, raw materials, component parts, and other items where a long-term delivery is expected. Historically, the first use of "escalation"

[4] See Section 7 on factors influencing selection of bidders.

[5] Refer to Section 9 for examples of various types of escalator clauses.

was in connection with raw or semifinished materials where prices fluctuated in accordance with commodity exchange quotations. Immediately following World War II inflationary forces assisted in popularizing "escalator clauses" because it was virtually impossible to reach price agreement without them.

Such clauses should be neither rejected nor encouraged by the buyer without first giving full consideration to the specific situation. Generally it is most desirable to agree on a firm price to facilitate cost planning, forecast of expenditure, and market stability. If the seller cannot reasonably predict his own costs, then a firm price quotation may involve either unreasonable risk or a large factor for contingency. The buyer may well consider either factor to be unjustified since one may leave him with no supply and the other with an unreasonable price.

In arriving at a fair price, provision for price adjustment frequently is the only solution. In Section 9 are shown several possible "price adjustment clauses." The purchasing agent should be familiar with these clauses, he should recognize the possible results from the use of each, and he should know what result he wishes the clause to attain.

Basis for Selection of Clauses

Primarily, the use of an escalator clause is designed to ensure that the vendor will continue to produce and sell at a profit and that the buyer will continue to buy at as low a price as possible. Stated otherwise, the escalator clause is used to attain the fair or right price over a period of time.

The simple "price in effect at time of shipment" clause may be satisfactory if the particular commodity is a standard production-run item sold in competition with similar products of other manufacturers and at published or established prices. Thus pencils, tumbler switches, standard welding rods, and similar types of commodities can safely be purchased with this type of clause covering the unpredictable future.

Other items, such as small compressors, electric motors, and office machines, may be purchased on this same basis except that since the monetary value is higher, some limit (per cent of base price) should be set so that the amount of escalation will not have an undue effect on the buyer's product or cost of operation. Here again the justification for use of the clause is that competitive factors tend to restrict the vendor's freedom to change prices at will.

Certain other items including steel, finished copper products, and refractories are usually sold on a "price in effect" basis. The individual buyer cannot force a change in this sales policy. The individual seller cannot, however, easily effect changes in prices. Except for the largest users, who may have long-term contracts, the buyers can safely consider that the competitive forces of other manufacturers as well as alternate materials will provide adequate protection.

The more complicated price adjustment clauses are required for component parts, capital equipment, and construction work. Generally the use of indices is preferable to a clause that provides for the seller passing on his "actual increases in cost." Use of the indices permits verification without auditing the seller's books and accounts. It provides necessary price relief and does not admit of questioning the seller's diligence or efficiency of production. Indices are beyond effective control of either buyer or seller and represent averages for the particular economic activity measured.

To the extent that the agreed-upon index or indices relate to the seller's cost factors they should be adequate to closely approximate his cost changes. If the vendor is a foundry, it would be illogical to utilize as a determinant an index measuring changes in labor costs in the electrica industry. Appropriate indices are available that reflect costs of foundrie and one of these should be selected.

Bureau of Labor Statistics indices[6] are widely used, primarily because of the integrity of the Bureau and of the statistical information and computations entering into the indices. Those in widest use are published monthly and are easily obtainable. The quantity of indices provide coverage for nearly any conceivable industry or job. Figures are computed from information obtained on a nationwide basis and thus represen "average" conditions. Some of the indices are also given for designated areas.

For certain uses the buyer and vendor may well agree on a mor localized index such as the construction cost information, including aver age prices presented in *Engineering News-Record* or selected prices pub lished in *Steel* or *Iron Age*. The basis for this judgment is to maintain th impartiality offered by these sources but to base adjustments on average representing the geographical area in which the vendor is operating. Th philosophy in this instance is that changes in other geographical areas d not directly result in changes in the immediate area.

Most difficult to administer is the adjustment clause that bases change on "actual increases in seller's costs." This clause can only be justifie where:

1. The seller's base costs are clearly known
2. Material, labor, and assigned overheads can be completely accounte for
3. The buyer has implicit faith in the diligence and efficiency of the sell

[6] Information on published indices can be obtained by writing to Director, Burea of Labor Statistics, Department of Labor, Washington, D.C. 20210.

If these three primary requisites are met, then "actual cost" escalation is he perfect assurance of a fair price.

Figure 10–2 graphically shows a comparison of price increases with rends in certain of the manufacturer's costs as determined from Bureau of Labor Statistics indices.

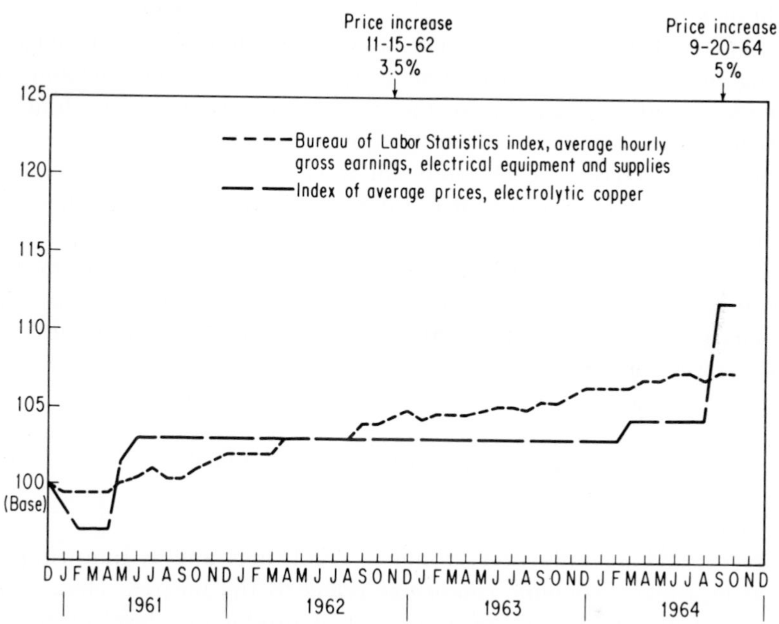

FIG. 10–2. Comparison of price increases with Bureau of Labor Statistics indices.

Government Price Evaluation

All units of government, including most of the special districts and public corporations, are restricted by law in their freedom of action[7] as contrasted to industries in purchasing. Price evaluation is not foreign to government agencies and in fact certain branches of the government, notably the Department of Defense, have aggressive price evaluation programs in effect.

Price evaluation by public bodies necessitates extreme accuracy and attention to all factors for the frequent result of price evaluation is that the lowest bid price is not the most advantageous or fair price. The lowest bidder generally thinks himself entitled to the order and in fact may have "cut corners" so as to offer this low bid. Pressures exerted and investigations conducted are by-products of price evaluation under such circumstances. Fortunately, enough good work has been done by these

[7] See Section 19, "Public Purchasing."

public agencies that the practice of placing orders after price evaluatio is becoming accepted as logical and legally correct.

Most contracts for large military expenditures and for the Atomi Energy Commission expenditures are negotiated, and price analysis i an essential preliminary to execution of the contract.

Government purchases are made for *service* requirements and not fo profit-making objectives. Usually timing of purchase is based on the neces sity of performing a service and not with direct reference to advantageou timing of the business cycle. The factors of supply and demand an economic conditions emphasize the necessity of verifying specification determining functional need, and adjusting quantity. While most gov ernmental purchases are of small dollar value, some regular purchase represent the major portion of the industry's production and they hav considerable resultant impact on supply-and-demand relationships.

Certain government purchasing programs are directly tied in wit planned influence on the economic level. These are exemplified by pric support purchases in agricultural products, certain aspects of the "mil tary reserves" program of stockpiling strategic materials, and public work projects.

FACTORS IN PRICE EVALUATION

Economic Conditions

Every purchase influences economic conditions and is in turn infl enced by them. Economic conditions refers to the business climate an is a result of supply and demand, level of production, level of emplo ment, general price level, the price curve, and all other economic i fluences. Every purchasing agent should equip himself with informatio on economic conditions of (*a*) general business activity, (*b*) activity withi the industry of which his company is a part, and (*c*) activity of the princ pal industries supplying his company's needs.

Generally available information of this nature appears in the dai newspapers, in daily or weekly trade journals,[8] in the commercial pre (*Wall Street Journal* and *Journal of Commerce*), and in periodica (*Time* and *Harvard Business Review*). Supplementary information available through subscription to special reports such as *Kiplinge Forbes' Magazine,* or even to clipping services. Each buyer must select h own best source but he must have some source for information beyo his own immediate experiences.

Examples of these reports are shown in Figs. 10–3 and 10–4.

[8] Such as *Bulletin* of the National Association of Purchasing Agents, *Daily Paci Builder,* and *Engineering News-Record.*

Examples in Figs. 10–3 and 10–4 are presented mainly to illustrate the type of statistical and interpretive material available. There is information available on almost any product and in almost any degree of detail. Lists can be found in Sections 9, 15, 26, and 28.

The Bulletin of the National Association of Purchasing Agents

Wholesale Price Index

Average primary market prices, during the week ended August 25, 1964, advanced 0.5% from the previous week. At 101.0% of the 1957-1959 base, the index was 0.6% above the average Wholesale Price index for July, 1964.

Farm products advanced 2.1%; processed foods advanced 1.5%, and the index of all commodities other than farm and foods advanced 0.1%.

The Bureau's daily index of spot market prices for 22 selective commodities, most of which are raw materials, for the week ended August 27, 1964, was 98.8%, compared with 92.2%, for August 29, 1963.

—*U. S. Department of Labor. Bureau of Labor Statistics.*

Volume of Business

Physical volume of business, in the week ended August 22, 1964, advanced to 90.2 from 90.0 in the preceding week, according to Barron's index adjusted for long-term industry and population growth. The year-earlier figure was 84.0 —*Barron's.*

Trade Review

The total dollar volume of retail sales in the week ended August 26, ranged from 3% to 7% higher than a year ago, according to spot estimates.

Avid demand for cotton gray goods continued early last week, but subsided in the last few days. Shortages are very common particularly in wide sheetings. Cotton yarn specifications are running heavy in Philadelphia and backlogs are piling up, but forward buying is slow for this time of year. Orders for cotton yarn have ebbed in New York. However, Providence reports a continuation of its brisk yarn pace and orders are pouring into Charlotte for ten to twelve weeks ahead. While there was a slight step up in carpet wool demand in Philadelphia and mohair top in Boston, both markets remained sluggish on the whole.

Steel output mounted to 2,392,000 net tons in the latest week, an 0.5% fractional edge over the previous week's production. The increase was the industry's third in a row, although its smallest of the three. Production outpaced last year's level by 35.8%, just 2.2% short of the widest year-to-year margin so far in 1964. Auto plants boosted demand for steel as they began placing heavier orders for delivery in September and October than had been expected.

New-car production continued to spurt in the latest week as auto makers attempted to stock all dealer showrooms with 1965 models in case of a strike. While reaching a three-week high of 66,730 assemblies, production was only about one third its usual level in 1964, due to the change-overs. Nevertheless, output ran 58.5% ahead of the prior week's 42,109 (revised) units and 57.3% ahead of last year's. For the present, labor talks appear stalemated with the UAW not satisfied with the size of the "Big Three's" proposals generally, and with the omission of improved working conditions specifically.

After its climb to a record high last week, paperboard production eased 0.5% to 402,568 net tons. In a like manner, unfilled orders slackened to a four-week low of 607,884 net tons, a slip of 2.2%. New orders diminished by a comparable 2.3% to 386,832 net tons. While production raced 7.0% ahead of last year's figure, unfilled and new orders saw only mild gains of 1.3% and 1.5%, respectively, from 1964 levels. —*Dun & Bradstreet, Inc.*

Weekly Commodity Price Indices—1926 = 100

Prepared for the National Association of Purchasing Agents, by McGill Commodity Service, Inc.

	Prewar Aug. 18, 1939	Aug. 29, 1958	Aug. 28, 1959	Aug. 26 1960	Aug. 25, 1961	Aug. 31, 1962	Aug. 30, 1963	Jan. 3, 1964	Aug. 21, 1964	Aug. 28, 1964
ALL COMMODITIES	63.7	177.8	175.4	172.0	175.8	179.1	176.1	174.8	174.1	**177.5**+
Industrial	70.9	196.9	203.7	197.9	199.1	199.3	198.7	199.3	199.4	199.4
Agricultural	53.2	136.1	133.5	131.6	135.4	136.8	142.3	151.5	135.9	**136.4**+
Livestock	56.2	184.8	157.7	156.6	170.0	182.8	162.9	143.2	159.0	**174.0**+
Building Materials	85.5	285.3	308.4	278.0	283.7	289.9	288.3	276.6	274.5	274.5
Chemicals	87.5	145.7	147.5	148.3	148.7	148.2	148.2	148.4	151.7	151.7
Fuels	65.4	191.4	189.5	191.2	186.7	188.3	189.1	189.0	189.0	189.0
Hides and Leather	76.7	147.9	228.1	159.4	184.3	164.4	132.3	133.5	150.9	*150.1*–
Nonferrous Metals	70.9	157.4	175.5	184.7	179.6	175.0	182.8	191.3	203.9	**204.5**+
Ferrous Metals	100.1	263.4	264.1	262.1	262.6	261.0	260.2	266.3	267.3	*267.2*–
Paint Materials	68.5	160.2	160.0	168.7	164.9	162.1	153.4	156.6	155.3	**156.1**+
Paper and Pulp	75.5	215.8	216.7	217.8	211.7	213.1	209.4	214.4	215.0	215.0
Fine Textiles	58.6	160.3	162.8	159.0	165.0	167.5	169.3	174.5	168.6	*168.5*–
Coarse Textiles	49.5	128.4	140.9	151.6	151.6	149.7	150.3	152.5	152.5	**154.0**+
Vegetable Oils	59.1	131.8	134.6	123.5	142.8	126.3	125.3	123.5	124.9	*123.6*–
Sensitive Agricultural	56.6	147.1	147.0	143.4	146.6	146.3	151.1	157.9	136.5	**136.7**+
Sensitive Industrial	58.2	189.6	205.0	195.6	191.6	192.2	192.4	189.6	190.7	**190.8**+

Note: Price declines are emphasized by *italics* and price increases by **bold type**.

Higher this week: Belting Leather, Rosin, Shellac, Quicksilver, Tin, Print Cloth, Sheetings, Silk, Burlap, Soybean Oil, Cattle, Hogs, Sheep, Lambs, Wheat, Corn, Oats, Rye, Eggs, Butter, Lard.

Lower this week: Calfskins, Steel Scrap, Cotton, Coconut Oil, Corn Oil, Cottonseed Oil, Potatoes, Coffee, Turpentine.

IG. 10–3. Example of report on economic conditions from September 2, 1964, issue of he *Bulletin* of the NAPA. (*Reproduced by permission.*)

Use of this information requires that the user know what it says. How vas it prepared? What methods are used to collect and measure the facors entering into the chart, graph, curve, or comment? What is being neasured? Are the same standards used throughout? What is its past reiability? Do these measures reflect the user's real interest?

In addition to these over-all indicators the buyer's company probably as its own statistical information on its own sales volume, profitability,

The Fuel Oil Market

COMPOSITE REGIONAL SUMMARY

Report based on information of Purchasing Agents who comprise the Fuel Oil Committee of the NAPA.

Descriptive words indicate trends as compared with previous report.

Regions	*Inventories*		*Consumption*		*Wholesale prices*			*Buying policy*		*Status of transportation*
	Residual	Distillate	Residual	Distillate	Residual	Distillate	Gasoline	Residual	Distillate	
New England	Steady	Increasing	Increasing	Increasing	Firm	Firm	Weak	Mostly contract	Mostly contract	Ample
Seaboard	Normal	Increasing	Steady	Steady	Steady	Steady	Weak	Mostly contract	Mostly contract	Ample
Detroit area	Normal	Normal	Steady	Steady	Steady	Steady	Weak	Contract	Contract	Normal
Ohio Valley	Increasing	Steady	Steady	Down	Firm	Weak	Weak	Current	Current	Normal
Upper Lakes	Steady	Steady	Steady	Steady	Weak	Weak	Weak	Mostly contract	Mostly contract	Good
Midcontinent	Steady	Steady	Steady	Steady	Steady	Steady	Steady	Mostly contract	Mostly contract	Good
Pacific West	Steady	Steady	Normal	Normal	Steady	Steady	Steady	Contract	Contract	Ample

FIG. 10–4. Example of report on economic conditions of fuel oil from September 23, 1964, issue of the *Bulletin* of the NAPA. (*Reproduced by permission.*)

production levels, etc. These will assist in determining the buyer's position in the over-all economic picture.

Utilizing this information the purchasing agent can be guided in his performance and placement of orders. When this information is properly interpreted, he can hold back placement when prices are high but indicators show softening in the market ahead. If he detects a strengthening, he may buy more heavily, anticipating future higher prices. Seasonal trends should be considered and the buyer should commit as much as possible during the low-price–high-availability period.

A purchasing department faced with the assignment of replacing a power or heating plant must consider the increasingly large foreign markets for United States coal and also the unrest in the Middle East, which affect the price of fuel oil and gasoline. Consideration might be given to the purchase of combination oil and gas burners in conjunction with coal-fired equipment. This combination would permit use of either type fuel as world conditions affect these markets.

The strengthened economic position of the Common Market countries created new and expanding markets for coffee which did not exist prior to and during World War II. This condition forced the price of coffee upward in the United States.

Rapidly increasing population within the various age groups has created new markets. People in general live longer, and are healthier. This has driven the cost of medical care upward. Such costs are tied to an increasing number of labor union contracts, which in turn influence purchase prices.

Quality

Quality is the nature or state of a material. The buyer's specification of proper quality and the seller's interpretation of the proper degree of quality, in terms of selling price, is probably the most difficult single aspect (and therefore the most important) of the many-phase function of price evaluation.

Well-planned specifications, carefully worked out in terms of generally accepted industry standards, are prerequisite to price determinations. Many companies are unduly penalized in buying because of highly restrictive specifications or because of quality factors emphasized far beyond the point of necessity. The purchasing agent must be aware of the cost factors built into the specification used. He should seek management assistance in buying suitable qualities of materials and not materials which are of far higher quality than necessary. Specials[9] of any sort in-

[9] See Section 11, "Value Analysis Techniques."

crease the price considerably and cause other procurement difficulties since they have to be worked into production schedules and are not stocked either by manufacturers or by their jobbers. Ambiguous or left-out parts of a specification will make it impossible to negotiate from a firm basis.

Once quality standards are established, a buyer should develop and maintain contact only with firms which have the facilities and which demonstrate ability to consistently deliver the merchandise of the quality which meets those quality standards.

The following is a realistic approach to setting quality standards:[10]

The problem: To secure an abrasion-resistant steel plate of established quality and reasonable price.

The purchasing agent responsible for multiplant steel purchases in a steam-electric generating operation noted that all plant superintendents were requisitioning separate type (analyses) plates for repair and maintenance of coal-handling and ash-disposal systems. The steels ranged from low-carbon steel at 5 cents per pound to certain alloys at 43 cents per pound.

The purchasing agent established that a steel plate which was highly resistant to abrasion and easily formed cold was needed in all cases, and that the several analyses being purchased could be combined in one type for all plants.

Sales representatives of several steel companies were consulted. Metallurgists from several companies were accompanied to the plants by the purchasing agent. After a thorough study a suitable product was found. Alloy "X," an alloy developed by one of the steel companies and licensed to other manufacturers was the choice made. This material had been proved in use to possess high tensile strength, high abrasion resistance, and cold-forming properties. At first it was used as wear plates and to patch holes worn in the chutes from coal bunkers to pulverizers. Later, its use was extended to include coal pipes, ash lines, and other systems subjected to the extreme abrasive action of coal and ash in motion.

The study leading to the selection of Alloy "X" also developed the need for corrosion-resistant steel where wet high-sulfur coal came in constant contact with steel. A metallurgist suggested the use of stainless-steel-clad plates which would give the full protection against corrosion at a much lower cost. A trial order of stainless-clad plates was purchased. Troubles developed in the fabrication of this new material, due to the inexperience of the company welders with it. The purchasing agent arranged for a demonstration of proper welding techniques by qualified technicians and the troubles ended.

Results: While it is too soon to determine the full economic benefit which will result from this experience, it is already established that an annual savings of $100,000 has been effected by the purchase of the Alloy "X" over the various higher-priced alloy steels previously used. There is good reason to believe that Alloy "X" will outlast the previous steels used and create additional savings

[10] See Section 8, "Quality: The Major Assignment."

through longer life, less labor for fabrication, repair and installation, and more continuity of plant service.

The stainless-clad, while higher priced than the previously used alloy plate, gives promise of substantial savings due to its much greater life in service.

The purchasing agent is now investigating the possibility of using Alloy "X" in pipe, forgings and castings, and replacements for short-lived items in the ash and coal systems not made of plate.

These all-important quality standards must be maintained from the outset by the use of clearly outlined specifications. Specifications, as far as is possible, must not be so restrictive as to limit the number of potential suppliers to so few that the element of competition is destroyed. Specifications must be broad enough to give equal opportunity to qualified bidders, and yet stringent enough to ensure the maintenance of quality standards and the exclusion of offerings which may be undesirable from a quality standpoint. A good specification will tell a qualified bidder the characteristics which he must include in his product or service to produce the results desired by the buyer. Below is such an example for board used in cartons filled by a manufacturer.

EXAMPLE

	Specification for Clay-coated Newsback Board
Grade	Clay-coated Newsback Board
Caliper	.016 plus or minus .001
Basis Weight	69 to 73 lb per 1,000 sq ft, blue-white shade, as per color standards
Brightness	70 to 73 G.E.
Folder	The carton when assembled shall show no cracking on the scores
Sealing Properties	The board must be sized for Brightwood machine
Water-drop Test	In the water-drop test the board shall show an initial penetration on both top and back surfaces in 2 sec. max. The time for complete disappearance of the water drop shall be 2,400 sec. max. on the top surface and 6 sec. on the back surface.
Odor	The board must not impart odor to products contained.

Tests are conducted for conformance to specified quality from each production run, both by the buyer and the seller in their respective laboratories.

There is a broadly stated and somewhat generally believed axiom to the effect that "You get what you pay for." The corollary point of emphasis here is that there is nothing to be gained, and there is much to be lost, by paying for quality which cannot be fully used. A case in point is the following:

EXAMPLE

A large mill used rotary scrubbing brushes costing $72 each and which tests showed had a usable life of 168 hr. Another vendor offered a brush at $80 each with a life of 210 hr. The respective hourly costs were about $0.42 and $0.38 per hour. Seemingly the second brush would be the better buy at approximately $0.04 per hour difference. The *quality* of the second brush was beyond requirements, however, as the brushes were replaced every 152 hours for operational reasons. On the basis of *usable* quality the brushes compare:

Brush A ($72 each)	$0.47 per hour
Brush B ($80 each)	0.52 per hour
Savings (A over B)	$0.05 per hour

Very often the application of quality specifications brings out the need for modification and amendment, both from a cost and a practical standpoint. The following demonstrates this:

The specification for ground beef delivered and sold under contract to a group of charitable institutions stipulated that "ground beef shall be processed and fabricated from U.S. Good graded boneless chucks under the constant supervision of an official grader of the U.S. Department of Agriculture, etc., etc., ... The price shall be . . ." (in this case the bid price was 39 cents per pound).

Protests from the institutions about the high price for ground beef revealed that the supplier was unable to use fresh, lean, and perfectly acceptable trimmings of the same and often higher (U.S. Choice or U.S. Prime) grades of beef. If a supplier had no chucks from which to make ground beef, he was forced to purchase them in order to meet the terms of the contract. At the same time he could have furnished good ground beef from trimmings, except the specification prohibited this practice.

The amended specification provided that "ground beef shall be processed from U.S. Good graded chucks, or from lean beef trimmings taken from carcasses processed in the vendor's plant the same day, under the constant supervision of an official grader of the U.S. Department of Agriculture . . . etc., etc., ... The price shall be . . ." (and the price per pound was reduced to 33 cents per pound).

An additional case in point here is that ground beef produced from only chuck at 39 cents per pound was no more acceptable than ground beef produced from trimmings or chuck, at the supplier's discretion, for which the price was only 33 cents per pound.

A buyer who is familiar with the quality standards of his company should constantly encourage his suppliers to offer substitute materials, new materials, and recommendations that offer potential savings to the buyer and maintain his quality standards.

There will always be some items which must be purchased from one source and for which only one quality or grade is available. In such cases, price cannot be the determining factor, although the buyer should do his utmost to negotiate the lowest possible price under such conditions. Machinery repair parts fall into this category, and in some cases the decision or determination of the best price becomes one of "make or buy" discussed near the end of this section. Where repair parts purchased from a proprietary source are prohibitively high, and the cost of making the same parts in the buyer's plant is equally high, there is a good opportunity for the buyer to recommend purchase of machinery which does not offer such an expensive handicap in terms of parts replacement.

In the case of a patented process or article, the manufacturer is entitled to a fair and legitimate profit. But, if by manipulation or opportunism, an unwarranted price is quoted, the buyer should try to find a substitute or should negotiate with the vendor toward a fair price. All legitimate steps should be taken to get a fair price.

Service

This is an element within the price which must be considered in price evaluation. It generally consists of deliveries made on time, packaged or crated according to specifications, routed properly and economically, providing of technical service when needed, the prompt response to emergency requests, and furnishing of regular reports from the supplier's quality-control laboratory. Some elements of service may constitute an additional expense which can be avoided, if proper technical and professional personnel are available within the buyer's own company.

Conversely, whether or not such personnel are available, it may well be that the supplier is in a position to provide certain services at lower cost to the buyer than if they were to be performed within the buyer's own organization.

Service can be a cloak for complacency. An excellent case in point is the following:

EXAMPLE

> X-ray equipment is highly technical and is used in a specialized field; yet the actual working parts of most common pieces of this equipment are quite simple. The practice among users of X-ray equipment has long been to pay full price for all film and development supplies to the X-ray jobber, who, in turn, renders 24-hr "free service" to any and all types of X-ray equipment within a given area. Within the past two years, an alert buyer of X-ray equipment and supplies consummated an

agreement with a jobber, under which a 10 per cent discount was taken on all invoices for film and supplies. The jobber, on the other hand, was paid a charge of $5 per hour for service calls. At the end of the first year, on $60,000 worth of film and supplies, the savings on initial purchases of film were:

On purchases of	$60,000
10 per cent discount on purchases	6,000
Service at $5 per hour	1,200
Net savings	$4,800

The determination of required service is important because great numbers of businesses have added technical personnel, equipment, and other means of furnishing their own services during critical periods. This type of service is often cut back by sellers, and many times eliminated entirely. Survival of the purchaser's company may depend upon its being able to provide the service from within. Technological development in new materials has spread at such a rapid rate that all industries must be in constant contact with all markets in order to remain abreast of the advantages which new developments may offer.

Sellers' services in this field will outweigh the price paid for materials. A good example occurs in the use of glue:

> For many years all large users of glue depended solely upon their suppliers' laboratory and/or field service men to keep them out of difficulty and to ease such troubles as occurred. However, today, large users maintain their own laboratories equipped to run tests for proper content and condition, and their own engineering staff who often are better versed on the properties and uses of the glue than the manufacturer's representatives.
>
> If the glue buyer is paying a high price in order to be certain that he has access to the seller's laboratories or field services, he is wasting money. He must, however, be conversant with all new glue products as they appear on the market, and he should have the value of the new products evaluated by his own technical staff.
>
> There are many small users of glue who have not found it economically practical to establish laboratory controls and engineering staffs. In such cases, the buyer would be foolishly frugal if he failed to make use of his source of supply in this regard to avoid production "down time" and high material waste, even though he were forced to pay a higher initial price for the glue.

Of necessity, certain industries must emphasize service at the sacrifice of price savings. A manufacturer operating a production line must have consistent schedules, deliveries of the specified quality, with immediate attention to the purchaser's emergency requirements. Any delivery or service failure which would hold up a production line would cost much more than an initial reasonable difference in price. For this reason, buyers in many industries are reluctant to take a chance with suppliers who have not proven ability to provide service, even though such suppliers may have offered a price advantage.

Under such circumstances, a buyer's continued efforts should be given to improvement in the price of the supplier whose service ability has been proved, while he continues to study and develop the service ability of the new or potential supplier who offers lower price.

Beware of the seller whose staff consists merely of production personnel and salesmen. Even though the buyer maintains his own laboratory, conducts his own inspections, and renders all the necessary services at his own expense (thereby paying a lower price), he still must rely on the vendor to conduct research toward product improvement. In other words, the buyer cannot rely on a source that is not constantly endeavoring to offer a better product in the marketplace. This is not to say that such a vendor should be scorned and turned away. At any given time, this vendor can well be the most advantageous source for his product, and the intelligent buyer will use him. Good ethics and good business sense demand that he be warned that progressive competitors may gradually diminish his advantage.

Price Paid by Competitors

Direct comparison with competitors' purchase prices is unnecessary to efficient purchasing. Each purchasing agent should exert his efforts toward buying at the lowest attainable fair price. This price will be in line with those paid by his competitors if the purchasing agent has done his job diligently. It may be higher or lower than his competitors' prices because of differences in specified quality, services required, order quantities, transportation costs, etc. All the factors that influence the determination of the *fair price* should be examined, evaluated, and modified or retained to meet the optimum needs of the individual company. To the extent that the purchasing agent errs in any of these considerations he is liable to penalty—obtaining other than his actual needs at other than his fair cost—as compared to his competitors.

Indirect comparison with competitors' purchase prices is ethical, and in fact is a business necessity. Sufficient information, to permit this comparison, is generally common knowledge. Such information will be proffered by salesmen, published in trade journals, or mentioned at professional meetings. Rarely will this information include price figures, but price figures are not necessary, nor would they be pertinent. This general information will trigger the trained buyer to reexamine his purchasing evaluations should it intimate any alterations of previously established patterns of procurement by the competitors.

The manner in which comparison of one's purchase prices with those of competitors' is conducted takes on legal significance, and the buyer is cautioned to consider this as well as the ethical aspects of his comparisons.

Vendors' Costs

A vendor's costs determine the minimum price at which his goods can be sold profitably.[11] Satisfactory cooperation between buyer and seller cannot be expected, unless the supplier is able to make a profit on the business obtained from the buyer. Since profit is the remainder after all costs are subtracted, it is necessary, in determining the fair price, to develop costs accurately. True cost information is not usually available to the buyer, and except as indicated below should not be known to the buyer.

Excessively low or high quotations on bids should alert the buyer to possible clerical errors. This may mean improper cost estimating by the bidder. This is the simplest form of vendor cost evaluation. Should the vendor, if low, confirm his bid price, the buyer will be required to form his own cost analysis to determine if there may be a possible risk in accepting the bid. Generally the bidder will volunteer his basis, such as "We want to close out this line" or "We have ample material left over from a previous job" or "Business is off and we need something to keep the shop busy for a week."

In the event the bidder merely confirms his price without elaboration, the buyer will be required, keeping in mind the various price elements shown in Section 9, to determine to his own satisfaction the probability that the vendor can and will deliver as quoted. His knowledge of the product and generalized cost information will be his guides.

Detailed evaluation of vendors' costs are required in cases concerned with special products and large construction work. Such evaluations will generally require cooperative efforts of technical personnel such as engineering, accounting, and design departments.

It may be of advantage to the buyer's firm in some instances to make every effort to provide cost-reduction assistance to his suppliers. This program can include help in plant layout and materials flow, selection of equipment, training of personnel, assistance in procurement of raw materials, transportation advice, and in extreme examples financial assistance or support. Even the smallest manufacturer can be in the position of having some of these expert services available on his staff which could be made available to his suppliers to the mutual advantage of both.

[11] Refer to Section 9.

Every component in the supplier's product must be analyzed as to its proper share of the cost of the product. Value analysis programs are extremely useful in making these determinations. In many cases the redesigning of a component will materially reduce the total cost of the part and will greatly affect the cost of the finished product. This is particularly true in large quantities of mass-produced items and the parts that go into such items.[12]

Undue effort should not be expended on items of small value. Small savings in large unit quantities are very effective in establishing the profit position of a manufacturing company. On the other hand, even relatively large savings on items which are used in small quantity have little net effect. This is not to say that small dollar value purchases should be completely ignored. From time to time *every item purchased* should receive a thorough review including price analysis. It cannot be assumed that once a fair price is established on minor items, conditions will hold steady.

In buying construction services, cost analysis usually consists of the preparation of an "owner's estimate," frequently called the "engineer's estimate." Purchasing will generally assist in the preparation of this estimate although the engineering department or outside engineering consultants are better equipped to assume this responsibility. This estimate is prepared on the basis of man-hours of labor at established rates and quantities of material at estimated prices. If the purchaser's own engineers are not familiar with current costs, it may be advantageous to engage outside consultants in this specialized field.

The Learning Curve

Analyses in certain manufacturing industries have shown continuing relationships between the reduction in direct labor hours and the increase in cumulative units produced. These studies, primarily in the airframe and aerospace industries, have led to the development of mathematical statements defining the inverse relationships between labor hours per unit and the number of units produced. These statements are called learning or progress curves, although design, methods, tooling, and managerial reinforcements typically play roles in the relationship supplementing worker learning.

The concept is based on the premise that a "learning" factor is injected into the repetitive production of a new item and that a worker gains in speed and efficiency as he acquires experience in the operation. In addition, better scheduling, higher quality, and more effective over-all management may reasonably be expected to improve the cost picture as production continues. The learning curve is an attempt through scientific

[12] Refer to the following paragraphs and to Section 11, "Value Analysis Techniques."

means to determine what measure of reduced cost may be expected at successive levels of production.

If it is determined that labor costs decline by 10 per cent on a particular item each time production is doubled, the learning rate is 90 per cent. The rate is always expressed as a percentage calculated on the basis of declining labor utilization associated with a doubling of the number of units produced. The learning curve can be reproduced graphically either on regular graph paper or on log-log paper as shown in Fig. 10–5.

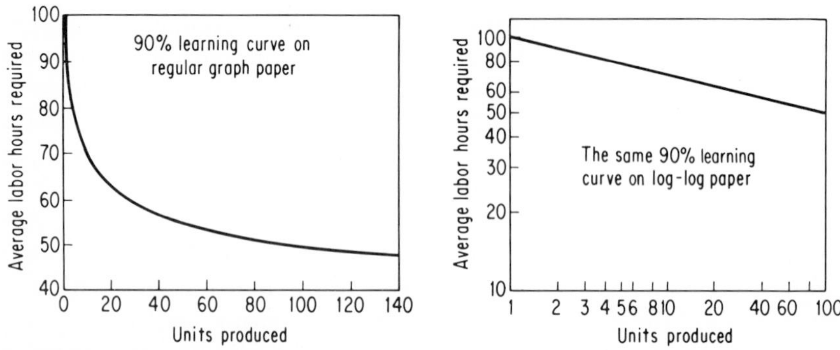

FIG. 10–5. Examples of learning-curve graphs. (*Reprinted by special permission from the April 2, 1962, issue of Purchasing Week. Copyright © 1962 by McGraw-Hill, Inc.*)

Application of the learning curve theory to price analysis can provide the buyer with a useful negotiating technique by permitting him to point out the need for improved cost performance by suppliers. Care must be exercised in selection of the proper learning rate, however, as this will vary according to industry and product. A cost analysis tailored to a specific situation in which the supplier understands and cooperates in determination of vital factors will yield the most satisfactory results. It should also be understood that results will be most rewarding where the products subjected to learning curve analysis are new and nonstandard and involve considerable labor.

Quantity

Quantity purchases generally represent a saving over smaller purchases, and rightfully so. But there are many facts to be considered, before seeking price reduction through quantity alone.[13] One of the chief factors to be considered is the cost of possession, or carrying charges. The cost of possession includes among other things obsolescence, interest on capital, possible deterioration, handling and distribution, taxes, insurance, and storage.

[13] Refer to previous pages and to Section 9 where discussion of this occurs.

Obsolescence is one of the gravest dangers to which inventories are subjected and should receive foremost consideration where quantity purchases are contemplated. For example, if the shelf life of an item is 90 days, it would be unwise to buy in excess of a 90-day supply for the sake of price reduction. Also, if the particular item is susceptible to obsolescence due to design changes or other factors, it would be unwise to stock beyond normal lead time plus safety factor.

Quantity purchases, as all other purchases, should be made on the relationship of the dollar value of the item to the ratio of its turnover, and not on the possible price reduction of a given quantity.

In most purchases, in addition to the purchase price, there is the cost of owning. This cost of "getting" versus cost of "keeping"[14] is of utmost importance. For instance, if a buyer can save 3 per cent by purchasing in larger quantities, and yet the carrying charges amount to 6 per cent, then he obviously loses money rather than saves on the large-order price. The cost of possession is of such importance that it is usually advisable to consult with the finance department.

One of the easiest ways to secure lower prices is to consolidate quantities. This is one basic reason why central purchasing departments in multiplant companies were established. By consolidating quantities and by having proper stores-inventory facilities and controls, the materials required by the company can be on hand at the time needed without an excessive investment in inventory scattered through numerous departments of a plant. This invites standardization of products, parts, and raw materials to the highest degree feasible.

EXAMPLE

PROBLEM

The plant operating personnel for a group of large steam-electric generating stations were requisitioning lubricants by manufacturer and brand name. Each plant had particular preferences which were based upon prejudice, acquaintanceship, and other nonobjective factors. Brands acceptable at one plant were not acceptable at other plants. Construction and maintenance personnel had divided opinions and preferences. There was a wide range of prices paid among the several brands.

SOLUTION

The purchasing division, using considerable ingenuity, tact, and practical psychology in its approach, held discussions with the heads of the various using divisions. Attention was called to the varying preferences of the individuals concerned and a statement was presented showing the wide range of prices being paid. Some of the price differential was due to pricing policy of the

[14] See Section 13, "Quantity Determination through Inventory Management."

various manufacturers and some was due to the small quantities of certain purchases.

A list of all items of equipment—turbines, generators, tractors, pumps, etc.—was prepared together with the manufacturers' recommendations for lubricants. The physical and chemical properties of each manufacturer's recommendation were determined. Based on these analyses, a list of standard lubricant specifications was prepared which covered each type of equipment owned by the company.

Each lubricant manufacturer was then sent a questionnaire, asking for the physical and chemical properties of each of their lubricants. This information was then related to the standard specifications developed by the company. Agreement was reached by the using organizations and purchasing as to acceptable brands for each use.

Contracts are now made annually for all the plants. As a result, lubricants are bought by specification instead of manufacturer's brand. Competition is secured among the several manufacturers. Lowest prices are secured, as purchase is made for large annual requirements instead of much smaller quantities.

In those cases where the equipment manufacturer stated in his warranty that a brand-name lubricant should be used, its use is being continued during the period of warranty.

In the case of large turbines and generators, the initial filling of oil is purchased by specification. However, current additions are made of the same brand of oil in order to avoid any problem which might result from noncompatibility of different oils.

The result is that savings are tremendous. One type of lubricant used at the rate of 200,000 gal annually is now purchased at an average of 25 cents per gallon below previous prices. The total annual savings for all lubricants purchased under the new plan is estimated at a quarter of a million dollars.

The grouping of orders to larger quantities and into classifications commonly sold by vendors requires that the purchasing agent have a voice in planning of production and also have at least partial control and responsibility of stores and inventory.

The purchasing agent must also be aware of new developments within his own company involving design and engineering changes so as to prevent overstocking items which soon will no longer be used. He must become an effective member of the management team and must devote the time necessary within his own company in order that purchasing considerations, as well as manufacturing considerations, can be determined when products are in the planning stage.

In no case can all small or emergency orders be eliminated. The purchasing agent, however, should constantly strive to see that their impact is minimized and that the large important orders in terms of dollar value or production significance are not lost in the shuffle of servicing many numerous small and rush requisitions. Attention can then be given to doing a better job in commodities used in large quantities which involve large sums of money. As numerous repetitive small orders of certain classifications come up, procedures should be worked out to consolidate small requirements into larger and fewer orders.

Freight Costs[15]

Freight is an integral part of the cost of any commodity purchased. The basic factors in freight are weight, distance of shipment, classification, and number and type of carriers.

Weight may be reduced and classification changed to lower (cost) classification by using the best packing method. Packing and loading have probably been the biggest factors in reducing costs of freight in recent years. Any number of new rates and classification changes have come about by improved packing methods, because of reduction of carrier handling costs and risk of damage. Often the reductions in handling cost by proper packing and loading are greater than those realized in freight costs only. The labor and material cost in packing, and the handling cost by shipper and customer, have been reduced in such proportions as to greatly overshadow the freight savings, even though the original impetus for research was to bring about the freight savings.

> An example of cost reductions brought about by revision and packing methods can be seen in the refrigerator industry which some years ago packed its product in wirebound crates over heavy excelsior pads. The first step in improvement of packing was the use of corrugated board reinforced with wood.
>
> Now the industry is packing in corrugated cartons over preassembled corrugated forms at a cost of one-third the former package cost and with more than two-thirds reduction in weight.

Freight rates are not entirely static and changes can be obtained. Many items are shipped at miscellaneous or unclassified rates or at rates based on low-volume freight movements. Working through buyer's and seller's traffic departments the purchasing agent can make application to the railroads and tariff bureaus (or barge lines or other media) for a hearing to request a lower rate, for approval by the Interstate Commerce Commission. If a sufficient case can be made based on tonnages as compared to tonnages and rates on related commodities, there is an excellent chance of favorable action. Examination of the tariff books or rate books in any traffic department will effectively demonstrate the fruitfulness of such efforts.

In addition to the reductions that might be brought about through reduction in weight and handling and packing, there can be brought about

[15] See Section 18, "Traffic and Transportation Considerations."

low freight costs by various techniques with no change in this product or the classification. Some of these are stopover and pool car shipping with other users of the same product from the same shipper. By working with distributors of products the buyer can purchase in carload, trailerload, or boatload quantity and this often results in freight-cost reductions. Buyers, whose businesses are so located that a large percentage has a transfer or break point in one other city, can usually make arrangements to have an accumulation and pooling of these shipments into either truckload or trailerload lots with far greater freight savings than the collection and loading costs.

Freight cost on raw materials usually is a major cost in the finished product. These costs may be analyzed from the standpoint of available carriers—rail, truck, contract truck, river barge, ocean-rail-seatrain, muletrain, yours or the vendor's own conveyance and others.

Consideration of the most economical size of shipment must be made since rates are based on quantity. It may be possible to pool products or shipments or develop closer sources to obtain best weight.

Much success can be achieved in gaining price reductions through proper attention to freight costs. Attention should be given to the method of transportation, the distances involved, and the speed with which shipments must be made. Plants located on navigable streams or lakes will save much by ship and barge transportation. Railroad freight rates in full carloads, of course, are much cheaper than less-than-carload rates of mixed commodities. Full trailer loads carried by motor freight lines are cheaper again than l.t.l. lots. Parcel post and railway express rates are expensive, as are air freight, air express, or air parcel post. Proper planning and larger quantity orders can eliminate to a great extent higher-priced methods of transportation.

The purchase of any product should be based on the cost of delivery of this product to the operator or machine using this product and the purchasing agent should not stop at the selling price quoted but should analyze completely other subsequent costs.

Packaging and Materials Handling

The previous topic on transportation considerations has introduced the subject of price evaluation possibilities through better packaging and handling so as to reduce manpower requirements.

Packaging improvements may consist of such a small thing as specifying smaller containers to permit one-man handling or to prevent losses due to opened partially emptied containers which permit loss, deterioration, or contamination. They may consist of larger elements such as palletizing so that a number of individual containers may be handled in short order by one man and one piece of equipment rather than many men hand-moving for many hours.

Shipment of bulk materials in tanks can eliminate small containers.

EXAMPLE

> Acids were delivered in 13-gal carboys which required handling manually and increased the risk of damage to plant and personnel from breakage.[16] Those using sufficient volume now have installed large storage tanks connected by pipelines to their process equipment. Acid is delivered by tank car or tank truck involving less manpower, less danger, and reducing the cost of transport equipment and freight charges.

Other changes consist of substituting packaging materials such as fiberboard boxes for shook. These result in lower-cost containers and more satisfactory packaging.

EXAMPLE

> Nails were exclusively packaged in 100-lb wooden kegs costing approximately 65 cents each. Properly designed fiberboard containers costing approximately 40 cents each are now used. In addition to this economy, filling can now be done more efficiently, costs of storage and handling of the empty knocked-down containers are less, storage of filled containers permits more boxes per unit of space (can stock higher), boxes palletize better, spillage is reduced, rusting of partly empty boxes is reduced since the top is no longer broken when opening, and an attractive package can be made by printing, including better readability of the "size" stamp.

Taxes[17]

Taxes come in varying rates on various products and services. Generally the taxes which are likely to affect the purchase of products are severance taxes, personal property tax (inventory), excise taxes, sales and use taxes, and payroll taxes.

Severance taxes are generally applicable only on raw material. The cost of the severance tax and the cost of the accounting and clerical personnel to handle the paper work required in the payment of these taxes must be definitely considered in the purchase. In cases where severance taxes are being paid, it is advisable to investigate primary processing in the state from which purchase is made rather than in the buyer's own plant.

Inventory is the greatest safety factor; yet it is the greatest risk factor that a purchasing agent faces. In forming his opinion of what inventories

[16] See also "Insurance," on pages that follow.

[17] See Section 9, "Pricing Considerations."

are advisable, he must bear in mind that taxes are paid on inventory and that even without a drop in market price, a constantly high inventory is a tax burden to his company and thereby a profit consumer. He can reduce this tax burden through working with sources of supply, who are often willing to manufacture in volume but ship on a schedule very close to the buyer's production needs. While this does not in any way affect the buyer's liability or reduce his risk in market changes, it does bring about a tax savings for his company.

Timing of purchase and/or delivery can frequently be adjusted to take advantage of "assessment day" in those cities and states where taxes are levied based on ownership on a specific day or days. Thus if personal property taxes are levied on inventory on hand on March 1, the buyer should schedule deliveries so as to have on hand, on March 1, the minimum safe working inventory and to build up inventories after that date.

Payroll taxes related to purchases are directly related to the labor used in handling, receiving, recording, etc. Reductions in these services brought about by improved materials handling will reflect in direct reduction of payroll tax.

Purchasing departments should be aware of the direct taxes and hidden taxes involved in the cost of merchandise which they secure. They should work through business organizations, chambers of commerce, and trade associations, so that as few special taxes or excise taxes as possible are levied on products which they buy. This, of course, is of interest to the entire business community. All businessmen should be interested in equitable and reasonable bases for taxation, rather than the selection of special products which throw undue burdens on certain industries to the advantage of other industries.

Insurance

Insurance is purchased against an adverse occurrence. Insurance is a method of spreading a risk among many people or companies and is based on mathematical probabilities. The more probable it is that an adverse situation will occur, the higher the cost ("premium") to each insured. To reduce this cost, the "probability of catastrophe" must be lessened and the insurance carrier must be shown that such lessening of hazard has been made.

It is beyond the scope of this handbook to examine this subject in detail. There are highly technical and highly informative books on the subject to which the reader should refer to the extent compatible with his responsibilities for insurance purchases. Where the purchasing officer of a company is also the insurance officer, he should have adequate knowledge of that specialized field. If the amount of insurance premiums paid is too small to justify extensive knowledge of the subject, this officer should acquaint himself with reputable brokers and rely on them for counsel and advice.

Insurance is a field where some knowledge by the purchasing agent can be advantageous in effecting price reductions, even where a company has a special insurance department. With only limited knowledge the buyer can assist, and seek the assistance of, these specialists. Ideally, if there is no risk, there is no need to carry insurance. If there is 100 per cent risk, then 100 per cent insurance coverage would be indicated. Therefore, the buyer should make an appraisal of the risk with other departments concerned (such as treasury, operating, traffic, engineering). Once the risk has been established, the buyer can go to work evaluating it and attempting to lessen it.

EXAMPLE

Cargo Insurance for a canned food packed in plain fiberboard containers was .32 cents per $100. Evaluation showed that this high cost was due to high risk of (1) handling damage and (2) water damage. Use of wooden cases would give a rate of .21 cents per $100. Use of asphalt laminated fiber boxes would give a rate of .19 cents per $100.

SOLUTION

Continue packaging in plain fiberboard. Additional cost of wooden box (about 30 cents per box) or laminated fiber box (about 16 cents per box) would be many times the savings on insurance.

* * * * * *

EXAMPLE

Machinery packaged on skid and wrapped with tarpaulin. Insurance rate $1.60 per $100. Each skidload valued at approximately $350. Similar material packaged on unitized principle with fiberboard box reinforced with wooden struts and simple wood skid-type bottom carried a rate of $1.12. Additional cost for unitized package is about 80 cents. Savings on premium is 3½ times 48 cents, or $1.68. Deduct 80 cents for additional cost for net savings of 88 cents per package.

Dramatic savings can be made in insurance costs by lessening the chances for fire, theft, explosion, deterioration, or almost any type of hazard. This can be done by changing the formulation of goods, changing the shape, modifying the packaging, and perhaps by providing new and improved storage and handling techniques. The "price" can be reduced by reducing this almost hidden component of price by modifications at the suppliers' level, in transporting, and at the buyer's plant.

The product must be accurately described so that the premium charged is the proper one and not that which applies to some similar but higher-rated risk.

Both the volume and the type of product purchased affect insurance costs. Each purchase should be analyzed to see if quantity of purchase can be adjusted. Substitution should be sought for materials which represent a storage hazard, as that might be causing increased insurance rates on all the inventories and installations of the business. Dangerous materials can increase fire, workmen's compensation, casualty, and practically any other kind of insurance.

Another type of insurance which affects buyers is product liability on which there is a risk of customer recourse. This coverage relates to the final product and is of direct concern to the purchasing man only if he is the company's insurance officer.

Workmen's compensation is normally beyond control of the purchasing agent except as his efforts may change the number of personnel employed.

Public liability coverages will be his direct concern more from the defensive standpoint; he should ensure that vendors performing services at his plant site have sufficient liability coverages to meet any anticipated risk to his company's facility or to third parties.

In many cases, insurance costs can be minimized by proper classifications, proper percentages of coverages, elimination of fire hazards, and proper protective clothing. Here again the purchasing agent should be familiar with his plant and its problems, if he is to do a good purchasing job on insurance coverage.

Duties[18]

A purchasing agent should endeavor to purchase duty-free materials, if available. He should retain imported goods "in bond" to avoid payment on materials exported which include such dutiable goods. He should be familiar with the duty rates and political possibilities for the future.

Those buyers who are dependent on using a considerable volume of products from foreign sources should become thoroughly familiar with all tariffs and other costs contingent upon importation. Only by being thoroughly familiar with these regulations will they be able to select a proper source of supply as to the country in which it is located and the classification of the products. The importer who avoids the products of a particular country because of high duties should, nevertheless, remain in contact with business within that country, just as every buyer should be working with sources in his own town on products which he is buying

[18] See Section 17, "Purchasing Internationally."

rom distant points within his own country. A government policy of eciprocal trade agreements, such as the policy of the United States, tends o bring about continual changes in importation costs. A buyer should, herefore, keep informed on possible sources in countries other than those rom which he is currently buying, so that he may take advantage of any agreements which remove tariffs on the product in which he is interested, rom a country from which he is not currently buying.

Where buying from foreign sources is small or sporadic, the purchasng agent will do well to obtain the services of importation organizations pecializing in this field. He will generally realize greater savings than heir fee and at the very least will remove the risk of encountering unexpected costs after he is too committed to do anything about it.

Value Analysis[19]

Value analysis is the other side of the price analysis coin. This section s not complete without emphasizing this point, even though Section 11 deals more fully with this subject matter. Regardless of any dollar amount hat may be set as being the "right" price for a product, that price cannot be right unless the buyer is utilizing the maximum value.

In the paragraphs above it has been repeated many times that the right price is in part determined by that price aspect relating to quality. Value analysis relates quality to function. Carried to a logical conclusion then, here cannot be a right price unless the material or service is *the* proper one for the specific requirement. Value analysis thus is a critical part of rue price analysis and must be the cornerstone for proper determination of the right price.

The buyer must go beyond the requisition for the solid foundation on which to build his price analysis. He must seek the true quality requirenent by use of the principles and techniques of value analysis. He must irst determine *what* the material is to do. What is its purpose? What does t do? Next, *why* is it used? Why is it of a particular shape, size, grade? *How* is it used? Is it reshaped? Is it fitted to other parts by weldments or bolts? Is it used temporarily and then scrapped? *When* is it used? Is it used even though it serves no useful purpose? Is it used sometimes but not all the time? *Where* does its real value lie—in its physical shape, chemical formulation, wearability, surface appearance? *Who* uses it?

The answers to these questions will provide the key to effective analysis. From here it can be determined if the function is really required. If not, of course, there then is no value. If the function is required, then the naterial can be examined in the light of improvements to quality to provide greater wearability or strength or other characteristics, or perhaps

[19] See Section 11, "Value Analysis Techniques."

be modified to do away with unnecessary strength or wearability or other feature. Perhaps a change in shape, size, surface condition, or modification of process or tolerances can achieve the same or better functional results at lower cost. Perhaps the study will indicate that another material will do an equal or better job at lower cost.

Surprisingly, many products in use today are like the human appendix. They once performed a service no longer needed, but they are still assembled into each unit produced. And like the appendix, the whole unit may be disabled when this useless part flares up.

Many companies, large and small, have organized teams to give an inquisitive look at almost everything that is bought in quantity. Much time is spent with vendor production and engineering as well as with the using departments in their own plant. Remarkable savings are being achieved by standardizing, by simplifying design, by using new products, and by analytically looking at what goes into the cost of a unit.

The purchasing agent who feels that he does not have time to get into these problems will find, however, that his time could be spent in no better way than in using imaginative inquisitiveness in thinking about the products, the raw materials, and the parts that he buys constantly and routinely. He may find in many cases that a rigid specification is in use long after the need has vanished. He may find that new methods of manufacture greatly lower the cost of parts and are perhaps making them more functional and with better design.

The purchasing department is in a strategic position not only to know what is going on in its own company but also to know what is available from its numerous sources of supply. The purchasing agent must so organize his work that he has time to give proper attention to the most important part of his job, the achieving of substantial cost reductions for his company. It has generally been found that a small team, divorced from routine day-to-day purchasing activities, and yet with a great deal of experience within the company and with vendors, will achieve the best results in the sphere of value analysis. Purchasing should guide this team.

The purchasing executive himself must be sold on this program if he is to pave the way for this group to work effectively with all departments of the company. The whole company must be receptive to the possibility of savings achieved through a value analysis program.

One distinct advantage of the value analysis program is the dramatic appeal to the cost consciousness of all other personnel that can be attained by properly demonstrating the results of specific problems. These results are obtained by the teamwork of all departments and all levels within the departments. By publicizing some selected examples of comparisons between the old and the new all personnel can see the possibilities. When hese are examples from their own plants, sought for and achieved by their co-workers, the stimulus to all workers reaches toward a peak level of interest and participation.

Mere "price analysis" by the buyer rarely will be able to achieve a potential equal to that which may be reached by united effort.

MAKE OR BUY

"Make or buy" decisions must be based on a considerable number of factors, many of which are not susceptible to straight cost analysis. Such decisions, except when concerning relatively minor matters, cannot be the responsibility of any one department. In owner-operated enterprises, the owner may presume to make his own decision, but unless he has the counsel of others, including purchasing, he is only guessing.

To "buy" is generally the easy way out. The cost can usually be determined in advance and included in the selling price. Unfortunately, if everything is "bought" and assembled, the product may not be salable because of the lack of quality control in manufacture, or the final selling price may be too high.

To "make" everything would also be an easy decision, and for certain products this is done for all items except standardized operating supplies, standard production and processing equipment, and materials not entering directly into product or production. In cases where this is practical, the final product is new, highly complicated, and of relatively high monetary value.

Almost every company makes some items and buys other items. This handbook is not concerned with the reasons for any particular decision made in the past, but rather it is concerned with the factors to be considered in arriving at decisions in reexamining past practices, or in determining "make or buy" for new items. Make or buy is certainly a valid question to be included in value analysis programs. Make or buy is a valid consideration in any cost-reduction or product-improvement program. Make or buy is important in any facilities expansion (or contraction) project.

To Make

To "make" requires production equipment, personnel, material, space, supervision, and in varying degrees, overhead, maintenance, taxes, insurance, management attention, and other indirect or hidden costs.

To "make" returns immediate control of quality. It may also provide work for idle equipment or personnel, utilize scrap material, shorten delivery time, permit use of a part which outside suppliers are not able to produce, permit experimentation, promote flexibility when dimensions are variable, ensure continuity of supply, train personnel for more complicated operations, cost less than purchased items, and keep design information secret.

To Buy

To "buy" permits lower investment in facilities, smaller labor force lower plant cost for building and upkeep, less overhead for taxes, insurance, supervision, etc.

To "buy" permits specialization, manufacture by the most efficient equipment, lower inventories, scheduling of material deliveries as required, change of design without loss of investment in equipment or inventory, obtaining lowest real cost by competitive bidding, and obtaining best price and product by suppliers' more varied experience.

Arriving at the Decision

In arriving at the decision, purchasing will generally be best equipped to counsel in regard to the "buy" side of the decision-making process. Since purchasing is the contact with outside suppliers, purchasing should have knowledge of suppliers' capabilities and reliability. Purchasing effort should be directed toward obtaining all necessary information in this regard and should concern itself not with the details of costs of "make" but only that the appropriate departments have given adequate attention to them.

Depending upon the production level at which the company is operating in comparison with the general level of economic activity, each of the various advantages of "make or buy" will assume varying importance, as will each of the disadvantages. If the company is producing at a maximum level, then "buy" will be more attractive in order to permit the company to utilize personnel and equipment to produce the maximum for sale. At lower levels of operation it may be desirable to "make" as much as possible, to spread fixed costs over as wide a range as possible, to produce the best product through direct quality control, and to maintain the work force with minimum layoffs. In either level the decision may be made even though the other alternate might have resulted in a lower actual cost for the particular item.

When producing at *normal levels of operation* it becomes more difficult to reach "make or buy" decisions. True costs "to make" a particular item are difficult to determine. Cost accounting necessarily makes arbitrary assignments of various overhead factors, which in a particular instance may miss the actual cost by wide margins on either the high or low side.

Use of existing production equipment may not actually be free, since it wears the unit, uses power, requires heating of the space, dilutes supervision, and may require special costs. Purchase of new equipment may not be justified, since it dissipates working capital, involves depreciation which may continue after product changes make the part obsolete, requires floor space, and may involve new personnel.

Buying of the item is indicated if satisfactory sources are available and can meet quality, delivery, and service requirements at a satisfactory price. If the reliability of suppliers is not good, inspection costs may be increased even though the supplier stands the costs of rejects. His labor difficulties become the buyer's too, and transportation to buyer's plants opens opportunity for transit damage or delays.

Positive Approach to Make or Buy

The foregoing has tended toward the negative side of the decision-making process. In practical application the negative approach tends to encourage continuity of past practices. Aggressive companies have determined "make or buy" on the basis of positive thinking after examination of the disadvantages of each as applied to specific problems.

One world-known manufacturer is reputed to follow a policy of making one-half of the required quantity of each component and buying the other half. The basis of the policy is said to be to ensure continuity of supply in the event of labor difficulties in either plant. This has a further benefit in that both plants act as cost checks on each other.

One major automobile maker carried integration to a high degree, owning and operating rubber plantations, foundries, and a myriad of other facilities which supplied automobile parts to his assembly plants. Other automobile companies were considerably less integrated; some did not even make their own engines. The various companies appear to have moved toward a middle ground from the two extremes to a point where they make the more significant (cost as well as technical) parts and buy the less significant items (accessories, trim, etc.).

Shortage of skilled personnel has tended to encourage "buying" in recent years. Many technical experts have formed small companies and offer new or improved products which are advantageous to incorporate into other goods and which the buyer cannot make himself for want of personnel to design or manufacture.

Conversely automation tends to encourage "making" insofar as automobiles and other large products are concerned. The high cost of some of these automated machines prohibits any but the largest companies purchasing them. Small manufacturers have neither sufficient money to purchase nor output to justify these units.

Other types of automated equipment do encourage "buying" by the average purchasing agent. These machines produce at lower costs than conventional equipment, but must be kept busy to be justified. Prices quoted by specialists in these fields are so much more attractive than the buyer's costs that in many instances companies are closing certain departments and utilizing space, personnel, and facilities to increase production of final product.

	Small (work force under 5,000)	Large (work force over 5,000)	Total company mentions
Reasons for buying:			
Volume not big enough to justify capital and inventory investment	9	3	12
Plant space	6	5	11
Benefit of outside supplier's specialized ability	11	10	21
Demand varies; we buy overflows	7	1	8
Lack of skilled personnel			
Quicker delivery—quantity	2	...	2
Higher quality			
Less expensive	9	6	15
Reasons for making:			
Integration of plant operations	9	6	15
Transportation delivery and expense—quantity	6	...	6
Unreliability of suppliers	1	...	1
Unusual complex parts requiring direct supervision	6	5	11
Helps carry overhead	11	2	13
Secrecy (do not want designs widely known)	3	2	5
Higher quality	5	4	9
Less expensive	6	6	12

FIG. 10–6. Major factors influencing manufacturers' decisions to make and to buy (2[illegible] companies). (*Source: Survey by Worcester Pressed Steel Company, in article by Carter C. Higgins, "Make or Buy Re-examined," Harvard Business Review. Reproduced by permission.*)

Labor, in periods of low operating levels, tends to encourage "making" by various stratagems including walkouts. For this reason and others, some companies may decide to "make" rather than face the dual unpleasantness of labor disruptions and the always difficult prospect of laying off or terminating members of the industrial family.

In periods of high production, particularly of temporary peaks, some companies tend to "buy" even at a price disadvantage to transfer to a seller the unpleasant job of an ultimate reduction in forces, and thereby attempt to minimize their prospective labor difficulties.

The exhibit in Fig. 10–6 indicates the importance of various factors considered in arriving at a "make or buy" decision. Although the survey made by Worcester Pressed Steel Company was related to a specific material, it is highly informative of customer thinking. Note that all customers considered their own personnel and quality of product to be equal to outside suppliers' even though they "bought." Presumably those who required exceptional quality did not buy, since nine who made their own stampings gave "higher quality" as their reason.

Nearly as many *large* as *small* companies buy to achieve the benefits of outside suppliers' knowledge and specialized abilities.

Clearly demonstrating one of the confusing aspects of the make or buy problem is the fact that almost as many "make" (12) as "buy" (15) on the basis that it is "less expensive." This seems to correlate, respectively, with "integration" and "capital investment." The actual correlation between the two is not revealed by the survey, but other information leads to the belief that companies concerned with integration of operations frequently assign little or no overhead to functions related to but not directly a part of normal production. Companies that are not integration-minded tend to assign full or heavy overhead to these fringe operations.

PRICE RECORDS

Countless numbers of articles are bought by the purchasing department, and it is not supposed that their prices can be remembered. Proper records of previous purchases must be kept and used for price checking and to assist in analyzing price.

The purchasing executive must be constantly aware of prices and price trends, certainly on major items which he purchases. A good inventory system may incorporate price information. In many cases, this can be used without duplicating records within the purchasing department itself. The purchasing department must, however, keep track of prices, quantities, and sources of supply of major items in order to evaluate properly its own performance in terms of general economic trends and to evaluate sources of supply with whom it deals.

Price information must be timely and must be accurate. Trends of prices gathered from all sorts of sources, including weekly commodity price indices, Bureau of Labor Statistics, charts and forecasts from financial papers and magazines, and even from the intelligent reading of a magazine and the proper evaluation of current events, all must be kept up to date. Many markets fluctuate rapidly. The trend may be more important than the spot prices of any particular day.

Many purchasing agents have found it worthwhile to develop charts or other visual aids to cover price trends on items that are of major importance to their company. Here the trend becomes very apparent and graphical. Such visual aids are of interest and assistance to top management as well as to purchasing department personnel.

Price records are a basic tool in analyzing price. They are essential for the buyer to make a fair and adequate comparison of price among vendors. How extensive price records will be is a matter requiring considerable judgment. "You can't see the forest for the trees" if too much effort is made to keep detailed records on items of small value. A carefully indexed record of prices and quantities purchased should be kept for all important, repetitive items. These records may be in price books, card files, or visible tray indices. They may be filed alphabetically by commodity or numerically by code. One card system is explained at the end of this section.

With the growth of integrated data processing, more and more companies of all sizes are utilizing tabulating and computer equipment. One particular company, among many others, has adopted the use of punch card control of all stores and materials. Thus, every item is assigned a code number, and all receipts, issuances, and changes are handled mechanically by tabulating equipment. In this company's purchasing department, a set of these material cards is maintained, filed numerically by code number. Basic information, including the code number, item description, and standard cost, is automatically printed by the tabulating machine.

Actual purchase prices, quantities bought, and vendor information is clerically recorded on these cards. The numerical filing actually speeds up location of the cards for most uses of this file, since all purchase requisitions must bear the code number. Numerical location is considerably faster than alphabetical location, as cards can be arranged numerically by the tabulating machine.

The disadvantage of this system comes when one is searching for an item without knowing its code number. Of course, code numbers are systematically assigned and cross reference is relatively easy. An important advantage of this system is its utilization of cards which are mechanically printed, thus eliminating a considerable clerical job of preparing a card for each item.

In summary, the extent to which price records are kept is a matter of judgment—the ability to draw the line at that point where the value of the record justifies the cost of keeping it. High dollar volume materials certainly justify careful complete price records. The actual system of record keeping must be adapted to the nature of the business, the organization of the department, and the commodities purchased.

Description of the Purchasing Price Record System of The Courier-Journal—The Louisville Times of Louisville, Kentucky

The purchasing price records of this organization are kept on two cards, one of which is known as the "vendor card" and the other as the "price record card." These cards are 5 by 8 in. and are made of a ledger paper rather than card stock, so that a number of cards can be accommodated in each pocket of the filing cabinet.

A visible filing cabinet is used. This cabinet has pockets to accommodate the cards. With this type of filing equipment, one of the cards is placed in the pocket at the back of the preceding card so that the two cards face each other.

The vendor card fits into the back of the preceding pocket. This card has in the upper left-hand corner a space for the general description of the particular item. Below it is a space for "specifications," which is a description of the item, so that the entries on the price card can be held to a minimum. Below the "specifications" section are eleven spaces for recording the names of vendors, their addresses, and telephone numbers. Each vendor is given a number, so that when a purchase is recorded on the price card below only the vendor's number is shown.

The price card fits in a pocket facing the vendor card above. This card is printed on both sides so that a greater number of purchases can be recorded on the one card. This card has columns for the date of purchase, the order number, the vendor's number, which is taken from the vendor's card, and for a description of the particular item, provided the general description on the vendor card does not cover it. There are also columns for the quantity purchased, the list or unit price, and the discount applying. There are three columns to give the transportation cost of parcel post, express, or freight.

Operation of Price Record System. When a purchasing transaction has been completed and the quantities, price, and extensions checked and the invoice approved, the purchasing department file copy of the purchase order is passed on to the individual who is responsible for posting the price records. The person checking the invoice has placed on it all the essential information needed for the price record. The person handling the posting then enters on the cards the necessary information. When this has been done, the order is filed numerically in a permanent completed order file.

SELECTED BIBLIOGRAPHY

Books

Air Force Guide for Pricing, Government Printing Office, Washington, D.C., 1962

De Rose, Louis J.: *Negotiated Purchasing,* Materials Management Institute, Boston, Mass., 1963

Evaluation of Supplier Performance, National Association of Purchasing Agents, New York, 1963

Jordan, Raymond: *How to Use the Learning Curve,* Materials Management Institute, Boston, Mass., 1964

McDonald, Paul: *Government Price Contracts and Subcontracts,* Procurement Associates, Glendora, Calif., 1964

Refer also to books listed in Section 26, "Library and Catalog File."

Articles

Bloom, Harold: "The Techniques of Negotiation," *Connecticut Purchasor,* Purchasing Agents Association of Connecticut, Inc., Ansonia, Conn., November, 1962

Edelman, Franz: "Art and Science of Competitive Bidding," *Harvard Business Review,* Boston, Mass., July–August, 1965

Hirschman, Winifred B.: "Profit from the Learning Curve," *Harvard Business Review,* Boston, Mass., January–February, 1964

"How to Negotiate," *Purchasing,* New York, Feb. 12 and 26, March 12, 1962

"How to Use Learning Curves as a Tool in Price Analysis," *Purchasing Week,* New York, April 2, 1962

Krech, Edward M.: "Negotiation," *Connecticut Purchasor,* Purchasing Agents Association of Connecticut, Inc., Ansonia, Conn., September, 1964

Pierce, Wilbur J.: "Negotiations and Negotiating," *Bulletin* of the National Association of Purchasing Agents, New York, Dec. 18, 1963

Smith, Spencer B.: "The Learning Curve: Basic Purchasing Tool and Two Ways to Use It," *Purchasing,* New York, Mar. 11 and 25, 1965

"The Use of Price Indexes in Escalator Contracts," technical note from the *Monthly Labor Review,* Bureau of Labor Statistics, U.S. Department of Labor, Government Printing Office, Washington, D.C., August, 1963

SECTION 11

VALUE ANALYSIS TECHNIQUES

Editor

Lawrence D. Miles, Consultant, formerly Manager, Value Service, General Electric Company, Schenectady, New York

Associate Editor

C. W. Doyle, Jr., Cost Reduction/Value Control Coordinator, General Dynamics, Fort Worth, Texas

THE PURCHASING AGENT'S JOB AND OPPORTUNITIES

The minimum that is expected of a purchasing agent is that he provide *specified* material at the right place and time and at a price that *satisfies* is employer. This definition involves *no* extra contribution on the part f the purchasing agent and the rewards and recognition for doing a minimum job are few. To make a maximum contribution and to gai the rewards for such a contribution, the purchasing agent has only t redefine his job as follows:

"In its fullest sense, the responsibility of the purchasing agent is to pro vide *exactly the right material* for the job at the right place and time an at a price which he *knows* is best." Some ways and aids to help the pur chasing agent move to this "maximum" definition and its opportunitie are the concern of this section.

The engineer's job is to get sure performance and effective design fo as good value as he can. The manufacturer's job is to make schedule shipments of quality-controlled materials reliably from the most eco nomical processes and equipment, developing human resources to thei fullest. The purchasing agent's job is to have the material when neede and to guarantee that when he spends one of the management's dollar he gets a dollar's worth of value.

An Over-all Understanding of Value Analysis

Some concepts, approaches, and techniques of value analysis are appli cable to each phase of an enterprise—some to management, some t marketing, some to engineering, some to manufacturing, some to pur chasing, etc.

Furthermore, the same techniques are now sometimes called value en gineering techniques. The following definitions will clarify this.

Definitions

Value analysis is an arrangement of *techniques* which makes clear th functions the user wants from a product or service; establishes by com parison the appropriate cost for each function; then causes the require knowledge, creativity, and initiative to be used to provide each functio for that cost.

Value engineering is the process of applying value analysis technique in the engineering sphere of responsibility.

Purchasing value analysis is the process of applying value analysis tech niques in the sphere of materials procurement.

A value analyst is one who has learned the techniques of value analysis has developed skill in using them, and is currently engaged in the occupa tion of applying them. Value analysts may also be called *value specialists*

A value engineer is one who, by training, is professionally entitled t use the engineering title, who has learned the techniques of value analy sis, has developed skill in using them, and is currently engaged in the occupation of applying them.

A value consultant is the same as either value analyst or value engineer.

A purchase value analyst is one who has learned the techniques of value analysis, has developed skill in using them, and is currently applying them in the sphere of materials procurement.

System Nature of Value Analysis

Value analysis is a system—a system requiring the organized application of specific techniques, designed and arranged in a rational dependence, to accomplish the end objective of enhancing total value.

This should not be construed to mean that the value analysis techniques are entirely new. To the contrary, purchasing agents applying some techniques of value analysis will recognize many techniques that have been successfully used in other effective management disciplines for many years. A closer examination, however, will reveal that these well-known techniques may be used "as is" or may be modified, refined, and more important, organized in a logical sequence to produce a specific result. Some new techniques may be added to this over-all system. The logic of this statement can perhaps be supported by a simple analogy regarding the use of wood, steel wire, and ivory.

Scholars tell us that the use of wood has been understood since the time of prehistoric man. Primitive man found that the branch of a tree could be used to provide the function of a club. The club provided him a means of protection against his natural enemies and also a means of obtaining the food necessary to sustain his life. Moreover, man discovered that wood used for fires could warm his cave. It could also be used to cook his food to make it more palatable.

Man has, for many years, used steel wire in many forms and fashions. For example, wire can be used as a snare to trap animals. Used as a fence, it can confine animals to a desired area and/or prevent intruders from entering certain areas.

Admirers of primitive art have long been fascinated by the tools, household implements, and objects of art that have been fashioned from ivory with the very crudest of tools. Examples of this art may be found in northern regions where Eskimos have utilized the ivory tusk of the walrus for hundreds of years. Similar items made of ivory obtained from elephant tusks may also be found in primitive villages in Africa.

Although each of these items was known and used for many years in its own individual applications, it wasn't until early in the 18th century that Bartolomeo Cristofori combined these three basic ingredients into a single system which resulted in a stringed, percussion instrument commonly known as the piano. What a startling difference in the result!

As illustrated by this simple analogy, the techniques comprising the system of value analysis have been carefully blended into an organized system to present a completely different *end result.* Although any note on the piano will produce sound when struck, the keys must be touched in proper sequence if the *end objective* is music. So the necessary techniques of value analysis must all be used and must be applied in proper sequence if the desired *end result* is to be achieved.

The system of value analysis is a method by which value is brought into proper perspective. This can be illustrated by the definition of method according to René Descartes, French philosopher and mathematician of the 17th century. "Method," said Descartes, "consists entirely in the order and arrangement of those things upon which the powers of the mind are to be concentrated in order to discover some truth."

The basic purpose of the value analysis system is to provide the necessary techniques in order of rational dependence. These techniques will enable the practitioner to:

1. Accumulate facts
2. Identify areas of knowledge required
3. Provide efficient knowledge search
4. Apply creative skills
5. Apply precise evaluation techniques

The combination of these techniques will in turn provide the means of placing functions and their value in their proper relationship.

The Basic Approach of Value Analysis

In the process of getting lower-cost alternatives into consideration, three basic steps are used:

1. Identify the function
2. Evaluate the function by comparison
3. Develop value alternatives

Step One—Identify the Function. Any useful product or service has a prime function. In addition, there may be secondary functions involved. A light source may be required to resist shock; a pump for domestic use may have to operate at a low noise level; a clock or watch may need to provide attractiveness.

In this functional approach, it will also often prove helpful to separate the parts and costs of a product or service into functional areas. If we take a device like an electrical switch, for instance, we can break it down into electrical function, mechanical function, enclosing function, and assembly.

The cost figures will indicate what areas hold the best promise for profitable value analysis.

Step Two—Evaluate Function by Comparison. Since value is a relative rather than absolute measure, the approach of comparison must be used in evaluating functions. The basic question, "Is the function accomplished reliably at the best cost?," can be answered only by comparison.

The larger and the more complicated the object for analysis is, the greater will be the number of comparisons necessary to make the analysis sufficiently comprehensive to establish the best value for each included function. Evaluation, then, is a result of the comparison involved.

Step Three—Develop Value Alternatives. Realistic situations must be faced, objections overcome, and alternatives effectively developed.

The Job Plan—Steps Which Carry Through the Basic Approach

The Understanding Phase

What is to be accomplished?

What is it that the customer really needs or wants?

What are the desirable characteristics in respect to size, weight, appearance, durability, etc.?

The Information Phase

Secure all pertinent information: costs, quantities, vendors, drawings, specifications, planning cards, manufacturing methods data, actual samples of parts, and assemblies where practicable.

Examine the basic engineering and manufacturing functions involved. Ask questions, listen, and develop a thorough understanding.

The Speculative Phase

When understanding and information have been acquired, the foundation is laid for application of various techniques to generate every possible solution to the over-all problems involved, to the parts of problems, and to the individual problems. To derive the fullest benefit from our creative power, we must now:

Encourage and arrange for free use of the imagination
Consult others who may contribute
Utilize the various parts of any and all techniques that will help in effectively accomplishing this phase

The Analytical Phase

Estimate the dollar value of each exposed idea.

Investigate thoroughly those ideas with a large dollar value to objectively determine their good and bad points, and then seek to eliminate, overcome, or minimize objections.

Select the ideas and approaches which are indicated to have the most promise.

The Program-planning Phase

Break the job down into a progression of functional areas, e.g., a fastening job, an electrical-contact job, a support job, a dust-protection job, etc.

Apply the applicable value analysis techniques.

Select the best vendors for consultation.

Supply all needed information to the specialists and to the vendors.

The Program-execution Phase

Pursue constantly, regularly, thoroughly, and intensely each of the avenues set up in the program-planning phase until all of the suggestions have been appraised and evaluated.

Stay with each promising suggestion and help to overcome difficulties until definite, tangible, and usable results are secured.

Status Summary and Conclusion

What will be most appropriate as a status summary depends upon the particular situation. If the purchasing agent or buyer has worked through the value analysis job plan for the product on which he will make decisions and take action, he can move immediately into the decision making and action taking. If on the other hand, as often happens, the decisions of others are also involved, the method of documentation is of great importance. A suggestion sheet which should be concise, meaningful, and readable should then be issued. It must be drawn up in the "manager's language," and should usually not be more than one page. Engineering information and supporting data must not be a part of it but should be accumulated separately.

Over-all Techniques of Value Analysis and Their Application to Purchasing

1. Avoid generalities; get down to specifics.
2. Get all available costs; understand their meaning and limitations; cause meaningful costs to be developed or provided.
3. Give credence only to information from the most reliable source.

4. Blast, create, then refine.
5. Use real creativity.
6. Identify and overcome roadblocks.
7. Use industry specialists to extend specialized knowledge.
8. Get a dollar sign on the key tolerances.
9. Utilize vendors' available functional products.
10. Utilize and pay for vendors' skills and knowledge.
11. Utilize specialty processes.
12. Utilize applicable standards.
13. Use the criterion "If it were my money, would I spend it this way?"

While the purchasing agent will occasionally contribute through the use of all of the techniques, his contact outside of the enterprise puts him in the position to be a major contributor through the use of the above techniques 7, 9, and 10.

Use Industry Specialists to Extend Specialized Knowledge. Through the contacts of purchasing, good industrial specialists can be found to help solve the specific product or service problems more efficiently. Better answers are needed.

To get better answers establish clearly in mind exactly what is to be accomplished, i.e., precisely what functions are desired; communicate this need to suitable specialists; and assist in getting their services. This places better alternatives before the decision makers.

Utilize Vendors' Available Functional Products. All products are developed to perform one or more main functions. The bicycle, the turbine generator, and the airplane, for example, all provide principal functions for which they are purchased. Every main function, however, is accomplished by a group of subfunctions, each of which often has a functional relationship to other components.

The main function of the airplane, for instance, is accomplished through a number of contributing subfunctional components—the wings, the motors, the body, the tail, etc. In turn, the functions of these various components are accomplished by their functional components. The wing function may be accomplished, for example, by sheet aluminum, structural aluminum or magnesium, rivets, fastenings, hinges, and supports.

Often need has fostered development, and specific functional products have resulted, such as special hinges, special rivets, special tapered structural shapes, and special gasoline-containing bags. The use of these products often provides a total function reliably and more economically than specially designed components.

Available functional products commonly have low costs. Buyers, knowing well what is needed, will search out and find these functional offerings and present the alternative to the company's decision makers.

Utilize and Pay for Vendors' Skills and Knowledge. Many users will design and, buying raw materials, build their own special parts. The alternative is to indicate to suppliers who have the proper general type of equipment and accumulation of skills precisely the functions that are required. Suppliers will gladly provide suggestions and quotations. Often the costs of this procedure are from one fourth to one half the costs of the "do it yourself" method.

The technique of utilizing and paying for vendor's skill and knowledge yields exceptionally high returns when effectively used, for the following reasons:

1. Large amounts of special knowledge exist in every field, and much of this knowledge is not possessed by people in other fields.
2. Only a relatively small amount of the total special knowledge bearing on any technology exists in any one place at any one time.
3. New developments, known only to the engineers concerned with them, are in progress in most good suppliers' plants.
4. Suppliers want their new developments to meet actual needs in the market.

The purchasing agent can find these skills and this knowledge and negotiate suitable arrangements for their use.

The Fundamental Concept of Value

The value of a service, material, or product is not determined by its cost. To determine value, the lowest cost for the needed function must be found.

Defining Function

Function describes the element of usefulness in a product or service. Function can usually be reduced to a two-word definition. For instance, a part may "exclude dust," "support handle," "prevent rust," or "protect customer."

What Function Will the Purchase Serve?

When buying material for a product, the buyer should know what job it will do. If the purchase will help the product do a functional job, it is utilitarian or serviceable. If the purchase adds something which the customer likes, such as more pleasing appearance or interesting "extras," but does *not* make the product *work* better, it is an attraction to help *sell* the product. These functions are worth money. Expense for anything which does not do either is needlessly wasted money. The job of analyzing values is the job of evaluating useful and attractive functions.

An Example of Evaluation

Evaluation *always* includes:

1. Function—what does it do?
2. Cost to perform the function.
3. Development of alternates. How else can the job be done?
4. Comparison of and with alternates. For example:
   a. Hold two small steel plates together with threaded portion. [Defined function: "hold plates"; see (2).]
   b. Keep small steel plates an exact distance apart.

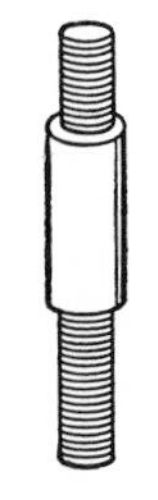

FIG. 11–1.

A vendor of a screw-machine part has been supplying it as described by Fig. 11– for 8 cents. How else might the job be done? Who else might do it? What would it cost made by the alternate methods?

One vendor submits the following information and drawing in Fig. 11–2:

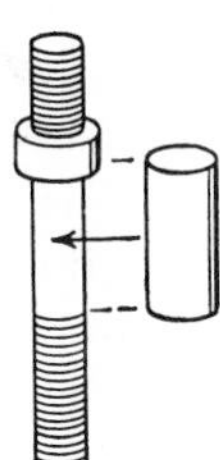

FIG. 11–2.

Start with proper size wire.
Cold head a shoulder and roll thread it.
Provide spacer.

Cost—$1\frac{1}{3}$ cents.
The same function for $\frac{1}{6}$ of the cost.

Another vendor submits:

Make as above except upset two shoulders on it, as illustrated by Fig. 11–3. Cost—$\frac{8}{10}$ cent.
The value of the part needed is $\frac{8}{10}$ cent—and *not* 8 cents.

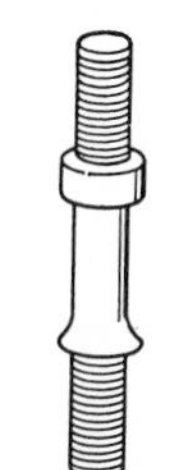

FIG. 11–3.

The *value* of this part has probably been fairly accurately determined by these comparisons!

What Is Value?

Value is determined by the *lowest* cost at which an *essential function* can be *reliably provided*. "Lowest cost" is determined *not* only by studying the present design or manufacture but also by considering the *best* combination of ideas, methods, materials, equipment, etc., which could do the job equally well. "Essential function" is the function which the item must accomplish without the inclusion of other costs which add neither serviceability nor attractiveness. "Reliably provided" means that equivalent quality must be provided.

Some Wrong Ideas about Value

Value is often confused with price or cost, and it is neither. Another common erroneous belief is that lowering the cost of an item lowers its quality. This is not true. Also, the value of a protective device is often thought to be the replacement cost of the equipment it protects, whereas the real *value* of the protective device is the lowest cost of providing equivalent protection.

A Check List for Evaluation of Any Item

Understand fully what it is.
Understand fully what it does.
Know what it costs.
Make sure that each feature that adds cost, adds essential function.
Determine what else will provide the essential function.
Determine the costs of alternates.
Select the lowest cost alternate which, with equal reliability, performs the essential function.
The dollar-and-cents cost of the item which will reliably perform the essential functions at the lowest cost is the *value*.

ALTERNATES

This section is offered as a quick source for determining the practicality of using certain materials and processes. It does not contain information on all materials, but is offered as a rapid means of approximate selection. It is hoped that this information will help in selection of alternate materials, processes, and services.

Machine Speeds*

Machine	*Operations per minute*	*Average shop cost per 1,000*
Punch press—high-speed auto. 4 tons	250–400	$ 0.25
Cold header, ⅛-in. stock	100–500	0.35
Punch press—high-speed auto. 15 tons	150–550	0.40–.28
Punch press—high speed auto. 25 tons	125–200	0.50
Cold header, ¼-in. stock	90–450	0.60
4-slide machine, light	75–175	0.60
Punch press, 60 tons	75–150	0.65
Cold header, heavy 1-in. stock	80–400	0.75
4-slide machine, heavy	50–125	0.75
Punch press—hand feed (blanking), 75 tons	50–125	0.75
Punch press—hand feed (blanking), 300 tons	40–80	1.25
Thread roller	40–80	1.25
Screw-head slotter	30–60	1.50
Automatic wire cutter and stripper	30–60	1.50
Dial tapper	30–50	1.80
Punch press—forming—slide feed	30–40	2.25
Punch press—forming—hand feed	15–30	3.00
Tapping machine—foot-operated	15–25	3.75
Tubular riveting machine	8–15	5.50
Resistance welding machine	5–10	10.00
Centerless grinding machine	2–8	12.00
Molding machine—thermoplastic	1–4	25.00
Brazing machine	1–2	40.00
Molding machine—thermosetting	½–1	100.00

* These are average figures and are based upon one operator and one machine.

Operation Speeds

Operation	*Operations per minute*	*Average shop cost per 1,000*
Take micrometer reading	5–8	$12.00
Use GO and NOGO snap gauge	10–15	6.00
Stamp part with hammer	15–20	5.00
Stamp part with rubber stamp	20–30	3.00
Drill small hole—drill press	4–8	15.00
Pierce small hole—punch	20–30	3.00
Wrap part in tissue and seal in carton	2–5	25.00
Position part in "egg-crate" carton	10–15	6.00
Pick up and position part in fixture	15–30	4.00
Pick up and drop part in fixture	30–50	2.00

Operation Speeds (*Continued*)

Operation	*Operations per minute*	*Average shop cost per 1,000*
Pick up, start, and hand drive small screw	3–6	$20.00
Pick up, start, and air drive small screw	10–12	7.00
Power drive small screw—hopper feed	10–20	4.00
Rivet with high-speed hammer (2) parts	4–8	15.00
Resistance weld (2) parts	5–10	10.00
Tubular rivet (2) parts	8–15	5.00
Cut off small tubing—screw machine	5–10	10.00
Cut off small tubing—abrasive wheel	30–60	1.50
Count parts visibly	60–120	0.75
Sort handful of parts (2) stacks	60–100	1.00
Deburr small screw-machine parts	7–12	10.00
Polish head of chrome-plated screw	5–12	15.00
Draw arc and hand weld 1 in. pass	3–6	20.00
Ream hole—drill press	2–10	20.00

Steel: Miscellaneous Forms

Relative Costs: Hot-rolled .20 Carbon = 1.00

Name	*Relative price*			
	Bar	*Sheet*	*Strip*	*Plate*
Hot-rolled—.20 carbon	1.00	0.91	0.91	
Hot-rolled—medium steel	1.01			
Cold-drawn	1.24			
Cold-rolled—.20 carbon	1.26	1.12	1.36	
Cold-drawn—chem. base	1.27			
Cold-drawn—sulfurized carbon	1.39			
Cold-drawn—screw stock	1.36			
Cold-drawn—.4 to .8 carbon	1.45			
Galvanized sheet steel (10 gauge)		1.23		
Enameling sheet steel		1.24		
Aluminum deoxidizing strip—cold-rolled			1.22	
Ingot iron strip—cold-rolled			1.23	
Plate—structural quality—under 1½ in. thick				1.05
Plate—welding quality—over 1½ in. thick				0.97
Plate—copper bearing				0.98
Plate—boiler—flange quality				1.01
Plate—.35 to .45 carbon—under 1½ in. thick silicon-killed				1.09
Plate—silicon-carbon				0.98
Plate—chrome-silicon—flange quality—under 1½ in. thick				1.15
Plate—carbon-silicon—flange quality—under 1½ in. thick				1.15

Stainless Steel

Relative Costs with Steel = 1.00
Base Price Including Chemical Extras Only, 1965

Name	*Relative price* Bar and rod	Sheet	Strip—cold roll	Strip—hot roll
13% chrome—no nickel—magnetic	6.43		7.54	5.89
Free machining	6.53			
High chrome—decorative—magnetic	6.53	7.72	7.74	6.05
Chrome iron—heat resisting—magnetic	6.74			
Turbine quality—magnetic	7.16			
18–8—nonmagnetic	8.06	9.36	9.36	7.26
18–8—low-carbon—nonmagnetic	8.47			
18–8—free machining—nonmagnetic	8.64			
27% chrome—heat resisting—magnetic	8.84	13.31	13.31	11.21
18–10 titanium stabilized—nonmagnetic	9.53	11.42	11.41	9.32
18–10 columbian stabilized—nonmagnetic	11.27	14.00	14.00	11.21
25–12 heat resisting—nonmagnetic	11.52	14.12	14.10	11.27
25–20 heat resisting—nonmagnetic	15.48	16.58	16.58	14.41
18–8 Ni-Cr-Mo—heat resisting	15.69			

Brass and Bronze Rod

Relative Costs with Steel = 1.00
Base Price as of 1965 Does Not Include Extras

Name	*Relative price*
Yellow brass (free cutting)	8.93
Yellow brass (leaded—high)	8.93
Yellow brass (semifree cutting)	8.93
Forging rod (drawn)	8.93
Muntz metal	10.42
Naval brass	10.50
Yellow brass (high)	10.98
Low brass	11.88
Red brass	12.21
Commercial bronze	12.65
Phosphor bronze (2% tin)	13.98
Rotor bar bronze (2% tin)	13.98
Everdur	13.83
Phosphor bronze (free cutting—4% tin)	16.04
Cupronickel—15%	17.00
Nickel silver—18%	16.02
Phosphor bronze—Grade B (leaded)	17.09
Phosphor bronze—Grade A	17.14
Phosphor bronze—Grade C (8% tin)	17.78
Phosphor bronze—Grade D (10% tin)	18.42
Beryllium copper (Berylco 25S)	34.32

Brass and Bronze Sheet

Relative Costs with Steel = 1.00
Base Price as of 1965 Does Not Include Extras

Name		*Relative price*
Muntz metal	½ in. thick and over	10.26
Naval brass	½ in. thick and over	10.65
Yellow brass	(65–35)	11.07
Yellow brass	(High)	11.07
Yellow brass	(2.5% lead)	11.07
Yellow brass	(Clock)	11.07
Extra quality brass	(70–30)	11.07
Low brass		11.92
Red brass		12.22
Commercial bronze		12.68
Muntz metal	Less than ½ in. thick	11.31
Cartridge bronze	(Low) 95–5 gilding metal	13.00
Manganese bronze	½ in. thick and over	11.24
Naval brass	Less than ½ in. thick	11.71
Admiralty	Less than ½ in. thick	12.70
Everdur		14.01
Manganese	Less than ½ in. thick	12.50
Nickel silver		14.65
Oreide bronze		13.08
Phosphor bronze	Grade E (1% tin)	15.99
Ambraloy (Aluminum bronze)		15.54
Phosphor bronze	Grade A (4% tin)	17.03
Phosphor bronze	Grade A (4% tin)	17.03
Phosphor bronze	Grade C (8% tin)	17.68
Phosphor bronze	Grade D (10% tin)	18.33
Trodoloy	(Berylco 10)	34.32
Beryllium copper	(Berylco 25S)	38.75

Brass and Bronze—Wire

Relative Costs with Steel = 1.00
Base Price as of 1965 Does Not Include Extras

Name	*Relative price*
Yellow brass	11.11
Yellow brass (high)	11.11
Commercial bronze	12.79
Everdur (3% silicon)	14.01
Everdur (silicon-manganese)	14.01
Phosphor bronze—Grade A (5% tin)	17.14
Phosphor bronze—Grade C (8% tin)	17.78
Beryllium bronze (Berylco 25S)	38.10

Brass and Copper—Seamless Tubing

Relative Costs with Steel = 1.00
Base Price as of 1965 Does Not Include Extras

Name	*Relative price*
Deoxidized copper	13.32
Yellow brass (high)	11.60
Yellow brass (high flange quality)	11.60
Deoxidized copper	13.32
Deoxidized copper	13.32
Red brass (cold-drawn)	12.82
Commercial bronze	13.20
Everdur	17.68
Nickel silver	17.91

Copper

Relative Costs with Steel = 1.00
Base Price as of 1965 Does Not Include Extras

Name	*Relative price*	
	Bar and rod	*Sheet and strip*
Hot-rolled rods tough pitch	12.43	
Hot-rolled rods tough pitch (hot forging)	12.43	
Hot-rolled rods tough pitch (cold forging)	12.43	
Drawn rods tough pitch	12.71	
Drawn rods tough pitch (bus bars)	12.71	
Hot-rolled rods tough pitch (switch blades)	12.71	
Commutator copper (scalped)	13.81	
Plain extruded copper sections	13.57	
Commutator copper (high silver bearing)	13.91	
Strip tough pitch—rolls		12.88
Sheet and plate—hot-rolled—tough pitch		13.29
Sheet and plate—cold-worked—tough pitch		13.29
Strip—silver bearing		13.55
Spring and brush copper		13.49

Metal-forming Processes

Metal-forming processes are listed. In general, size, quantity, shape, and adaptation of a part to the process vary considerably.

1. Casting
   - Sand casting
   - Die casting
   - Permanent-mold casting
   - Centrifugal casting
   - Plaster-mold casting
   - Investment casting
2. Forging
   - Cold heading
   - Drop forging
   - Cold and impact extrusion
   - Hot upsetting
   - Cold drawing
   - Hot extrusion

Die rolling
Thread and form rolling

3. Forming
   - Stamping
   - Deep drawing
   - Roll forming
   - Wire forming
   - Metal spinning
   - Brake forming
   - Section contour forming
   - Rotary swaging and hammernig
4. Deposition
   - Metal spraying
   - Electroforming
5. Treating
   - Shot peening
   - Cold treating
   - Heat treating
6. Nonmetallic Molding
   - Plastic molding
   - Powder metallurgy
   - Rubber molding
   - Ceramics molding

Materials and Processes Normally Used to Provide Various Functions

	Brackets and supports	*Decoration*	*Electric conductors*	*Enclosures*	*Fasteners*	*Gaskets*	*Gears*	*Handles*	*Heat conductors*	*Hinges*	*Housings*	*Linkages*	*Protective surfaces*	*Springs*
Aluminum	x	x	x	x	x			x	x		x	x	x	
Brass	x	x		x	x	x	x	x		x	x	x	x	x
Cadmium		x											x	
Copper		x	x			x			x					
Cork						x								
Fiber	x			x	x	x	x					x		
Glass	x	x		x				x				x		
Paints		x	x			x							x	
Paper		x	x	x		x							x	
Plastic—thermosets	x	x		x	x	x		x			x	x		
Plastic—thermoplastics	x	x		x	x	x		x			x	x	x	
Plastic glass reinforced	x	x		x	x		x	x			x	x		
Plastics—other	x	x		x	x	x	x	x			x	x	x	
Rubbers	x			x	x	x		x				x	x	x
Silver		x	x						x				x	
Steel	x	x	x	x	x		x	x	x	x	x	x	x	x
Textiles		x				x							x	
Tin		x											x	
Zinc	x	x		x	x	x		x	x	x	x	x	x	
Nickel	x	x	x	x	x				x			x	x	x
Castings	x	x	x	x	x		x	x	x	x	x	x		
Extruded materials	x		x	x	x		x	x	x	x	x	x		
Fabrications	x			x	x		x	x	x	x	x	x		
Forgings	x		x	x	x		x	x	x	x	x	x		
Stampings	x	x	x	x	x	x	x	x	x	x	x	x	x	x
Tubing	x		x	x	x				x		x	x		
Roll forming	x	x	x	x	x				x	x	x	x		

Comparison of Cost in Metal-removal Methods

These are general guides. Size, quantity, shape, and adaptation of part to process will vary relationships considerably. Typical operation from steel is used in all cases excepting die casting. Cost will, in general, be the inverse of pieces per hour.

Process	*Pc/hr*
Contouring (6 in. diam. by 1/4 in. thick):	
Die trimming and blanking	100
Flame cutting	20
Contour sawing	10
Milling	5
Planing–shaping–slotting	3
Surfacing (4- by 6-in. long):	
Broaching	60
Abrasive belt grinding	15
Milling	6
Grinding	3
Planing–shaping–slotting	3
Lapping	2
Cylindrical (2 in. diam. by 4 in. long):	
Automatic lathe turning	20
Turret lathe turning	10
Hollow milling	8
Engine lathe turning	4
Grinding	4
Superfinishing	2

Process	*Pc/hr*
Hole forming (1 in. diam. by 1/8 in.):	
Punching	400
Reaming	60
Drilling	40
Boring	30
Broaching	30
Honing	20
Grinding	12
Lapping	3
Gear manufacturing (4 in. diam. by 1 in. face):	
Casting	60
Broaching	30
Shaving	20
Lapping	10
Hobbing	5
Shaping	4
Generating	2
Grinding	2

Common Metals: Relative Costs by Weight and Volume

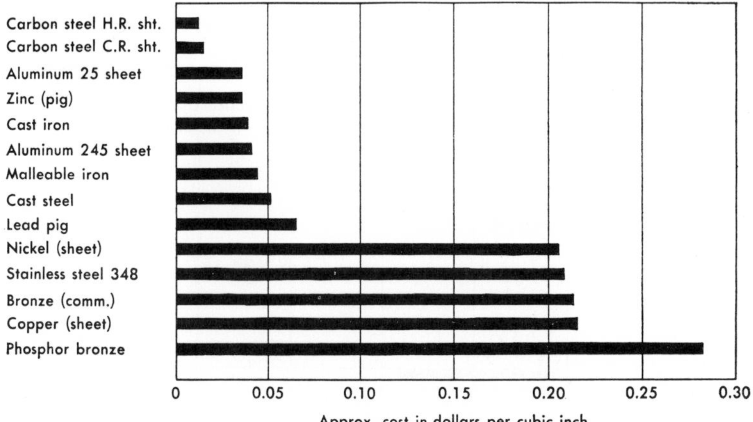

FIG. 11–4. Common metals—relative cost by volume.

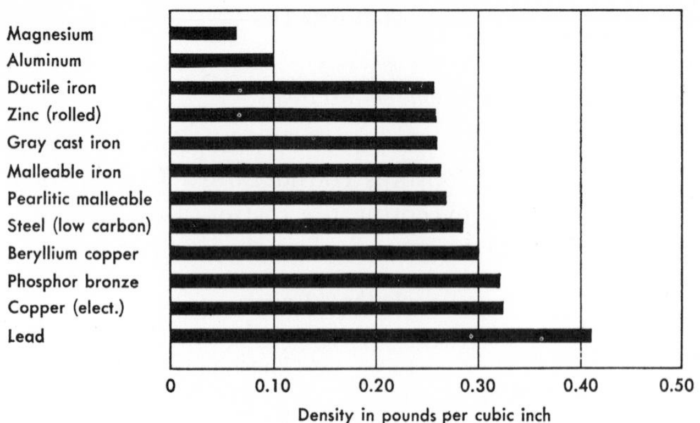

FIG. 11–5. Common metals—weight/volume relationship.

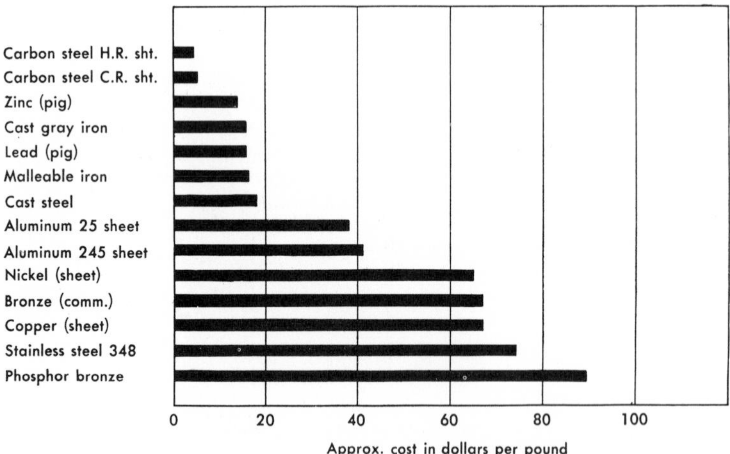

FIG. 11–6. Common metals—relative cost by weight.

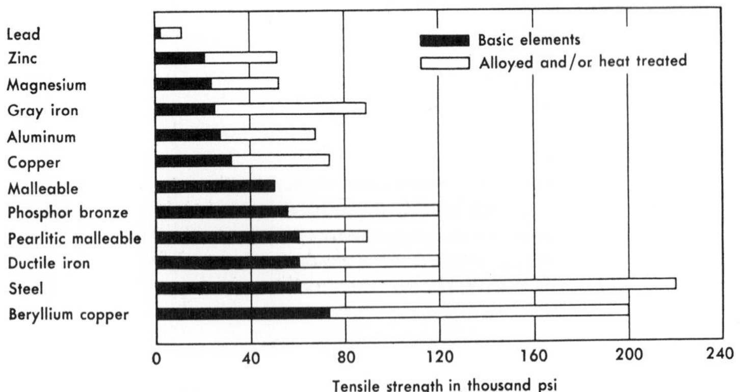

FIG. 11–7. Representative tensile strengths—common metals.

Possible Elements of Value in Metal Products

Value Considerations

A. Chemical composition
   1. Availability of the elements
B. Physical properties
   1. Strength
      a. Tensile, compressive, shear
      b. Hot and cold strength
      c. Fatigue
      d. Creep
      e. Stress–rupture
      f. Hardness
      g. Elasticity
      h. Impact resistance
C. Thermal properties
   1. Coefficient of thermal expansion
   2. Thermal conductivity
D. Electrical properties
   1. Conductivity
   2. Magnetic
E. Production considerations
   1. Melting range
   2. Forging temperature
   3. Ductility–castability
   4. Machinability
   5. Weldability
   6. Finish characteristics
   7. Heat-treatment characteristics
F. Application factors
   1. Corrosion resistance
      a. Mechanical
      b. Chemical
   2. Resistance to abrasion
   3. Friction qualities
   4. Refractory qualities
   5. Appearance
      a. Plating, etc.

MATERIALS AND PRODUCTS

Adhesives

Type	*Cost in cents per fluid ounce*	*Application and information*
White glues	15–20	Good general-purpose glues suitable for most applications
Resorcin resin	30–35	These are intended for items which will be subjected to humid conditions and for these applications the higher cost is justified; may also be subjected to high temperatures; must be mixed just before using
Liquid animal and fish glues	20–23	These are apt to have an unpleasant odor and should be avoided except for special applications
Urea resin glue	13–15	Both of these are suited to items which will be subjected to moderately high temperatures and humidity; they must be mixed just before using
Casein glue	8–10	
Synthetic resin adhesives	.....	Epoxy, polyester, alkyd phenolic adhesives cured by chemical reaction and suitable for all kinds of joints
Rubber cements	.....	Solvent solutions of various synthetic or natural rubbers. Suitable for joining all kinds of materials as well as rubbers

Natural adhesives (poor fungus or mold resistance) include the following:

Glue

1. Animal and fish glues have good strength; poor water resistance.
2. Casein, soya, and corn protein glues have better water resistance than animal or fish glue.
3. Most glues are good for bonding paper, leather, wood, and fabrics.

Paste and Mucilage

These have a starch, dextrin, or gum base; dry rapidly; have little water resistance. These are good for bonding paper, leather, wood, and fabrics.

Natural Resins

1. Resin: These are used for hot melt applications in addition to solution.
2. Shellac.
3. Asphalt: Forms, floor-tile cements, and paper impregnants.

Synthetic adhesives (good fungus and mold resistance) include the following:

Elastomers

These are solutions and emulsions of natural and synthetic rubber and rubberlike materials; have a wide range of properties and uses; bond rubber, wood, steel, synthetic materials, cloth, felt, etc.

Thermoplastic Resins

1. Cellulose derivatives of acetate and nitrate; household cements; are inflammable; poor heat resistance; good bonding to most materials.
2. Polyvinyl acetates of butyrate and alcohol; clear films; heat-sealing safety glasses is an application; good resistance to oils and greases.

Thermosetting Adhesives

These are the strongest organic adhesives; usually require heat to "cure" or "set"; have good resistance to heat, chemicals, and oils, and excellent resistance to fungus or mold.

1. Phenol formaldehyde, urea formaldehyde, resorcinol formaldehyde, formaldehyde; standard synthetic adhesives; bond wood (plywood), metals, and plastics.
2. Polyurethanes; excellent adhesion to wood, plastics, metals, and rubber.
3. Polyesters; good water and solvent resistance; most popular use is in glass-plastic laminates (cars, boats, building panels, etc.).
4. Epoxies; recently developed materials, excellent resistance to most solvents and corrosive liquids; excellent strength with glass, ceramics, metals; currently popular; used in Europe to bond aircraft panels and to bond steel laminations, aluminum components, hypodermic needles, etc.
5. Silicones; broad temperature range; best heat resistance of all organic adhesives; used to bond silicone rubber, metals, plastics, ceramics; bond strength not as high as epoxy or phenolic.

Bearings and Bearing Materials

Essentially, properties of bearing materials may be summarized in four groups:

1. Oil-film bearings for a wide variety of machinery.

Bearing material	*Typical uses*
Tin-base babbitt	Steam turbines, electric generators
Lead-base babbitt	Electric motors, gas engines, diesels
Copper-lead	Diesels, gas engines
Bronze	Electric motors, aircraft engines
Cast iron	Refrigerator compressors
Silver (overlay)	Aircraft engines
Aluminum	Electric motors

2. Porous metals, plastic, and other nonmetallic materials, for boundary lubricated bearings which operate under light-load conditions, as i household appliances and office machinery. Lubricant film does no completely separate moving parts. Sometimes, under light loads, n lubricant is used.

Bearing material	*Typical uses*
Sintered porous bronze	Small appliances, fans, mixers
Carbon-graphite	Toasters, bearings (water lubricated)
Nylon	Office furniture, toys, textile and food machinery
Teflon	Food machinery, textiles, aircraft accessories, refrigerator-fan bearings
Graphited bronze	Actuator mechanism (low velocity)
Rubber	Ships' stern tube bearings

3. High-temperature bearings, as for missiles, high-speed aircraft, an nuclear propulsion systems.

Bearing material	*Approximate service temperatures (°F)*
Conventional carbon-graphite	To 700
Carbon-graphite treated	To 1,000
Low-alloy steel (52100)	To 400
Tool steels	To 700
Nickel-base alloys	1,000+
Cobalt-base alloys	1,000+
Cermets and ceramics	1,000+

Lubricants include liquid metals, silicone-base oils, and gases (air helium, etc.).

4. The rolling contact bearing (ball and roller type), where high hardnes and high fatigue strength materials are used, as in vacuum cleaners gyro gimbals, aircraft generators, instrument bearings, electric motors and locomotives.

Most commonly used rolling-element bearing materials	*Rolling-element bearing materials for special use*
AISI52100*	MHT
AISI4320	M1 tool steel
AISI6120	M50 tool steel
AISI8620	T1 tool steel
AISI3115	Stellite 3
AISI420	Stellite 19
AISI440	Stellite 25

* AISI—American Iron and Steel Institute

Castings

How to Analyze Values in Castings. There are three main types o castings: sand castings, die castings, and permanent-mold castings.

Sand castings are made by pouring molten metal into a sand mold

Considerable machining is usually required on sand castings; therefore they are primarily used for small lots or for large and complex shapes. Materials used in sand castings include iron, bronze, aluminum, and magnesium.

Die castings are made by injecting molten metal into machined dies or molds. These dies are used continuously. The initial tooling charge is high but the unit cost is low, as little machining is required on a die casting. A die casting is practical when the quantity is high—in the neighborhood of 15,000 per year or more. Until recently, die castings were small parts; now large pieces are die-cast (for example, the automobile grill).

The initial tool cost for a die casting is very high; changes are also very expensive. The tool cost for a four-barrel carburetor die casting will run around $15,000. In many industries, sand castings are used for new designs; when the design is stabilized and production is known, die castings are considered.

Intermediate between sand castings and die castings are permanent-mold castings, which are also necessary where porosity could be a factor. They require more machining than die castings but less than sand castings. The same materials used in sand castings are used in permanent-mold castings. The tool cost is higher than for sand castings but much less than for die castings, as noted in Fig. 11–8.

In addition, specialty methods such as precision mercury, lost wax, shell molding, etc., often perform particular functions most economically.

Chemicals

Chemicals are combinations of elemental materials. This field includes plastics, paints, synthetic rubber, and fuels. Chemicals are divided into two major categories:

Inorganic. These are usually in bulk quantities, large tonnage, and have a relatively low price per pound.

Organic. These are greater in dollar sales than inorganic; include synthetics; may be tailored by processing to needs or specific applications. Major factors affecting costs are purity and type of material required.

1. Production quantities. A chemical that could be cheap in tonnage quantities may be very expensive when it is made by the pound to satisfy a limited demand.
2. Character and extent of processing required. This includes something of labor and equipment, but has also to do with yields, heat, or other energy requirements, etc.
3. Process equipment required; size, type, construction.
4. Marketing services required.

	Metal mold				Centrifugal	Shell m
	External pressure casting					
	Die casting	Pressure casting (cold chamber)	Permanent mold	Semipermanent mold		
Description	Pressure injection steel die. Casting mechanism continuously immersed in molten metal	Pressure injection steel die; metal ladled into chamber each shot	Metal molds and cores; gravity pour	Metal mold; sand or graphite core; gravity feed	Sand, plaster, graphite, or metal mold; cast at 600 to 3,000 rpm	Accurate pattern; resin mo gravity p
Tools, patterns, and/or molds; Order of cost preference	6	6	5	5	1—Graphite mold 2—Metal mold	4
Typical die and/or pattern cost for small part; order of 15 cu in.	$4,000–$6,000	$4,000–$6,000	$1,500–$5,000 Lowest cost metal mold	$1,500–$5,000		$750–$
Metals	Lead, tin, aluminum, zinc, low melting-point alloys	Copper, aluminum zinc, magnesium alloys	Copper, aluminum, magnesium	Nonferrous alloys and cast iron	Most all depending upon pattern	All except carbon st
Die and/or pattern; pattern life—a function of metal temperature and pressure	Medium to high	Medium except brasses and bronzes	High except brasses and bronzes	Good with low melting-point alloys		Very high life; one- mold
Blowholes and/or Porosity	5 Sound at skin; porous at thick sections	4 Sound at skin; porous in thick sections	3 Low; dense fine-grain structure	Fair to good	1—metal mold (excellent)	2
Order of tolerances, typical	3 ±.003 to ±.010 Usually smaller because of smaller part	2 ±.003 ±.008	4 ±.005 ±.020	Same as permanent for metal mold; same as sand for core	6 Variable—depends on metal, temperature, speed and mold material	5 ±.005 to 1/32 or c long part
Possible savings machining-preference	4	3	5	4	7	2
Sizes, approximate maximum	10#	100#	200–300#	200–300#	1000#	300
Strength same alloy	2	1	3	3–5	4 Metal mold; higher elongation and hardness	Compares ably to s
Labor in process —large quantities	Least	More than die casting but less "down" time for maintenance. Very low	Low	More than permanent mold, less than sand		Higher tha
Cycles per 8-hr day (size a major factor in cooling time)	200–1,000	100–1,000	50–400	Between sand and permanent	1–50	300 shells day—on Two men to 300 per c
Where to use	Stable design; high production; reduce machining; hard skin; softer core; machining through skin not recommended for critical section	Stable design; high production; reduce machining; save expensive material; hard skin; softer core; thinner sections than die casting; machining through skin not recommended for critical section	Stable design; medium quantity; reduce machining; save expensive material; critical sections may be machined	Same as permanent mold except to achieve undercuts and involved internal coring	Long and large hollow shapes; gear blanks; pressure vessels; babbitt liners; small squirrel-cage rotors; rings	Low to me quantity; if mechan reduce m ing; save sive mate

NOTE: This chart is intended for use only as a guide in selecting a process. It is recognized that most parts could not be produ all of the above processes and that tolerances, costs, etc., could be greater or less than shown.

Other processes which should be considered are punch press, forging, extrusion (including steel and impact extrusions) co casting, slush casting, and fabrication.

casting	Investment castings		*Powdered metal		Molded plastics	
					Thermoplastic	Thermosetting
metal ı; sand gravity	Metal pattern—plaster investment mold; part usually has parting line	Metal die—wax, plaster, mercury, or low melting-point alloy pattern; plaster investment; no parting line	Steel die; heat and pressure	Carbide die; heat and pressure	Steel mold; pressure injection	Steel mold; compression or transfer type
1	3				7	7
500			$200	$600		
All	Most all metals up to 3000°F melting point		Copper, tin, iron, brass, aluminum			
attern— etal pat- very high; ot mold	High pattern life	Highest die life; one-shot pattern	Medium	High	High	High
6	2		Porosity partially controllable, as sintered; impregnate at extra cost		Seldom	None; compression; seldom-transfer
7 small arge motor)	1 Must have taper ±.005 to ±.010	No taper ±.002 to ±.010 ±.0015 with mercury	±.001" up to 1½" Diam. ±.002" over 2½" Diam. ±.010" up to 1½ Lg. ±.020" over 3" Lg. Closer by coining		Varies with material	¼" ±.002–±.005 1" ±.003–±.006 6" ±.008–±.014
6	1					
imited	Limited by facilities—approximately 60# to date		Projected area 6–8 sq in.—average maximum 18¼" diam. By one vendor		Projected area 1,400 sq in.	Projected area 400 sq in.
5	6 Somewhat lower than sand in metals subject to grain growth		Good Improved by impregnation			
High	Higher than sand	Highest	Least		Very Low	Low
–140	Complete cycle—one day or longer		1,000–5,000		400	175
ble design; oduction; rge parts; arts with achining; s lends itself icavity	Changeable design; high-temperature alloy; unmachinable alloy; Generally not competitive above 25,000–50,000 pieces where part is acceptable as die casting; process lends itself to multicavity molds Shape limited by extraction of pattern; good finish, high accuracy, moderately high production	 Complex shapes, intricate cores; either Laboratory development or high production process; close tolerances; difficult to do by any other casting or machining process	Small gears, screw-machine parts to save material and machining; min. qty. approx. 500; bearings, carbides, tungsten, permanent magnet materials * Process not comparable to others		High production items; appearance appeal; medium tolerances; intricate shapes; low weight; insulating properties	Medium high production; good tolerances; insulating properties; low weight; intricate shapes; higher temperatures than thermoplastic but not as good as metals Tolerances for phenolics, compression molded only—tolerances for transfer molding are closer. Use transfer molding for closer tolerances, delicate mold sections, fragile inserts

FIG. 11–8. Casting and molding processes chart.

Minor factors influencing cost of chemicals are:

1. General unit cost of labor
2. Special packaging
3. Research and development
4. Shipping and all elements which are included in this term

A check list by price range of several common chemicals follows:

High. Pharmaceuticals, reagents, tracers
Medium. Plastics, fibers, solvents, resins for formulation and fabricatio
Low. Heavy chemicals for general industrial and process uses, e.g., acid and alkalis

Considerations for a purchasing agent's buying of chemicals are i four major categories: (1) price, (2) quality, (3) delivery, and (4) con tinuity.

The price of a substance should be in line with the market. *Chemica and Engineering News* (a weekly magazine, published by America Chemical Society, 20th and North Hampton Streets, Easton, Pa.) publishe four times a year the prices of all important chemicals. Attempts shoul be made to negotiate quantity discounts. Sometimes a jobber will carr six months' supply of an item, enabling buying at a quantity price.

The quantity of a chemical to order depends upon the applicatior For example, if acetylene is used in large quantities for welding, it i not economical to buy it in cylinders. Acetylene generators will provid gas of satisfactory purity. Another example is nitrogen. Generators shoul be used where the purity of nitrogen is not critical, as in purging c furnaces. Nitrogen generators used in this way are one-half the cost o the same gas in cylinders. In inert-arc welding, helium can be replaced b less expensive argon or carbon dioxide for many welding applications.

Delivery is extremely important. A plant might shut down if shortage of some essential chemicals were to develop. A reasonable lead tim should be allowed, but then delivery should be expected on time. Habi ually late vendors should be dropped.

Continuity means that a firm has been in the same line for a numbe of years and seems to have built up a satisfied list of clients. Check wit other people who are doing business with a prospective supplier.

Copper

Special characteristics of copper and copper-base alloys and the com bination of characteristics available are unique and of particular interes to the electrical industry. Some of these characteristics are:

onductivity	Ease of finishing and plating
orrosion resistance	Solderability
uctility	Color
ttractive combination of physical properties	Fatigue resistance
	Nonmagnetic characteristics

These can best be discussed by grouping the copper and copper alloys ito several broad classes, as follows:

. Copper
. Brasses
. Bronzes
. Nickel alloys
. Modified brasses
. Special alloys

The coppers include not only electrolytic tough pitch copper but also xygen-free high-conductivity deoxidized copper, free-machining copper, rsenical copper, and several others. As a broad class, these are distin-uished by extremely high conductivity, high ductility, good solderability, nd nonmagnetic properties. They will always be in demand for electrical pplications of a wide variety.

The brasses, varying from Muntz metal with 60 per cent copper to Gilding metal with 95 per cent copper, offer a wide variety of physical haracteristics and they have an equally wide application. The yellow rasses of 64 to 70 per cent copper are undoubtedly the most widely used f any of the copper-base alloys. They offer a range of physical properties rom softness approaching that of copper to spring characteristics of ellow brass rolled 8 Nos. hard. They are all, practically speaking, non-nagnetic and are fabricated and finished easily.

The bronzes fall into several classifications. To name three, the phos-hor bronzes, which are essentially tin bronzes with very small amounts f phosphorus, the silicon bronzes, and the aluminum bronzes. The first f these, the so-called phosphor bronzes, have very attractive spring char-cteristics at a reasonable price and their main application is for springs. *The silicon bronzes,* while having good spring characteristics, offer a vider range of characteristics and are used extensively for fasteners such s bolts as well as for engineering applications. *The aluminum bronzes* re particularly good for wear resistance, and are quite widely used for gears, bearings, etc.

The nickel alloys can be classed in two groups: first, the cupronickels nd, second, the nickel silvers. The cupronickels offer excellent corrosion resistance and are widely used for condenser tubes and heat-exchange applications. Their ductility is such that they should be even more widel used than they are in engineering applications. In the future their appl cation will broaden and they will be used much more widely than the are at present. *The nickel silvers* are one of the oldest of the copper-bas alloys and their applications are generally well known.

The modified brasses and the special alloys cover such a wide rang that it is difficult to detail any specific application, but they do fill a ver real need in the industrial picture. In general, they are tailor-made for specific application.

Muntz metal is the lowest-cost brass but is of such limited applicatio that companies normally base their cost or price comparisons on yello brass as being the lowest-cost, generally applicable material. In genera the price per pound increases with increase in copper content. If th metal is modified by the addition of a third element, this increases th price in direct proportion to the percentage of the third element addec Quantity on an order very seriously affects the price, and the price based on a certain quantity, which generally is five to ten thousan pounds. For quantities less than this, the price increases quite sharply for quantities greater than the base quantity, the price decreases rathe slowly.

On size, again there is a base grouping of size which represents th most economical range of sizes to make in our present mills. For size either above or below this, the price increases. Likewise, for shapes othe than standard, there is an increase in price. Standard tolerances hav been established for all the important shapes and classifications and, fo tolerances less than the standard, there is an extra charge. Also, for specia handling such as special straightness, nonstandard lengths, etc., there ar special charges which have been established to compensate the mills fo the additional work involved in maintaining the special characteristics.

Containers[1]

Cartons are paperboard boxes used for protective, decorative, an shipping purposes. They are not usually reused. Shipping cartons ar bought in varying degrees of reliability, depending upon the weight o the contents and the usage they will receive. A 30-lb test carton is stanc ard. For shipping fragile items, an inner 30-lb light carton is nested, wit some protective cushioning material, inside a 100-lb test outer carton.

Metallic containers are usually reusable and include cylinders, barrels and drums. Cylinders are built to withstand high pressures and roug

[1] See also "Packaging," page 11–14.

sage. Substances shipped in cylinders are oxygen, acetylene, hydrogen, itrogen, chloride, carbonic gas, helium, etc.

Tin cans. This title covers a variety of tin containers most familiar in onsumer applications such as the packing of vegetables, coffee, etc. Cans re used in industry whenever protection of the product will be necessary or an extended period of time. For example, the armed forces use tin ans for the packaging of spare parts, and industry is even using them to ackage items like small motors.

Barrels are built of heavy-gauge steel, aluminum, or magnesium, and re intended to withstand extreme abuse. They are usually of 30- to 50-al capacity and have bulged sides. They are primarily used for shipment f liquids such as beer, soap, liquid wax, etc.

Drums are a type of container with straight sides, usually of steel. When intended for the shipment of liquids, they have threaded holes to ermit the insertion of a tap. When they are used for the shipment of olids, the tap is usually removable. These drums cost approximately $3 ach and should be returned for credit, if possible.

Glass containers are used for shipment of drugs, alcohols, and other hemicals in small quantities. They are fragile, but inexpensive, and are lean, durable, and sanitary.

Plastic bags and other containers are now often used even for liquids nd should be investigated.

lectrical Components

The field of electrical components is extremely competitive. An effort hould be made to accumulate purchases to obtain a discount on a quantity order.

Where the consumption of articles can be predicted (light bulbs, fuses, onnectors, etc.), a year's supply should be ordered. Batteries are an xception. Only one or two months' supply should be ordered, as there s approximately 10 per cent loss of life every month.

When quantities are large, substantial discounts can be realized in ome cases by buying direct from the manufacturer. To facilitate quantity purchasing, it is best to determine the general areas in which the lectrical components will be applied. When purchasing electric motors, nowing the application will often permit the purchase of less expensive motors than those which have been specified.

A general list of a few single-phase motors and their applications is iven below:

Motors—universal

Used for drills, food mixers, sewing machines, a-c or d-c speed varied by a rheostat and by amount of load

Motors—repulsion-induction
  High starting torque
  Starting current must be kept low
Motors—capacitor
  Motor must start under load
  Refrigerator, freezer, pumps
Motors—split-phase
  Low cost
  Easily started—low starting torque

Fabrications

A general definition of fabrication is: The building up of complicate shapes from simple stock materials.

Fabrications are assemblies joined together by such means as rivets brazing, crimping, or gas, arc, or spot (electric) welding. Usually sheet metal parts make up the assembly, but sometimes extruded shapes, tub ing, or machined parts are used. No general rule for cost reduction ca be made beyond the general advisability of obtaining competitive quotes

Usually gas welding or brazing is restricted to small quantities; ar welding and spot welding are used for larger quantities.

Fabricated parts are often proposed as replacements for large castings Sometimes this is practical. Sometimes the reverse brings better valu However, large parts are difficult to control dimensionwise. If the appli cation is a critical one, there may be a high percentage of rejects. Som cost-reduction possibilities are the use of weld bolts and weld nuts, t eliminate machining studs, riveting, and tapping holes.

Fasteners

The general category of fasteners includes nuts and bolts, headed an threaded, snap-ons, clamps, insert threads, nails, clips, machine screws locking screws, and tapping screws.

The major factors affecting the purchase price of the above are strength size, quantity, stock item or special, and machine time—if the purchase i "special."

Labor rates in the industry are roughly comparable among companie and are not an important variant in cost.

Material is generally dictated by the application. If 1010 steel will d the job, no customer would order brass, stainless, or other more expen sive material. The percentage of material to cost will vary greatly, sinc other costs do not vary in proportion to material as a rule.

Burden or "overhead expense" is the third important factor and thi ill vary substantially among manufacturers, depending upon such fac- ors as:

. The degree of automation in a plant
. The willingness of a plant to vary its production schedules to accommodate customers
. The engineering talent available to solve the more difficult problems of a customer
. The speed with which orders are processed
. The willingness of the company to manufacture small as well as large quantities for the benefit of their customers

There are few items in the product line for which a lower-priced sub- titute cannot be found. Also the opposite affords savings. The thread- utting screw is more expensive than a machine screw; however, it elimi- ates the cost of tapping, which more than offsets the higher material nd processing costs essential to its manufacture.

Some special locking devices cost more than a loose screw or lock vasher, but assembly-line hand labor is far more costly than the small remium added to the price for the preassembly process.

Plastic rivets, grommets, and supports may cost more than their metal ubstitutes, but enameled surfaces are not crazed in their application nd substantial assembly-line savings result from the use of a one-piece astener.

Suitable alternates for many fastening problems are clips, which come n many forms—stampings, springs, wire formed, and plastic—and can ave in assembly costs as well as material.

Convenient adhesives are now available for many permanent fastening obs. Sometimes they are lower in cost, and some times they have better perating properties.

orgings and Cold-headed Parts

Forgings are parts made by the hammering or squeezing of metal while ot. The hammer head and die have forms cut out so that the required hape is obtained. In the case of difficult shapes, several forging operations nay be necessary. The forging operation results in a very strong part, uitable for highly stressed applications, as an automobile crankshaft. Considerable machining is necessary on most forgings. Forgings are ex- ensive and are usually made one at a time; when several parts can be nade at once, the cost is materially reduced.

Cold heading is similar to forging except that the stock is not heated. The stock is wire up to 1 in. diameter. It is fed to heading dies by cylindrical rolls; the stock is held while the head is upset. Typical part made by cold heading include bolts, rivets, valve spring retainers, com mutator segments, drum plugs, screws, studs, etc. Cold heading is usuall used only for high production parts, over 20,000 items per year.

Because of the high speed at which parts are headed (50 to 230 pe minute) and because there is little or no waste of material, the cost o headed parts is from 50 to 85 per cent less than screw-machine parts.

When designing a part to be made by header, it should be remembere that the tolerances common to screw machines are not applicable t headers, nor are sharp corners, double shoulders, or undercuts.

Fuels[2]

Fuels are generally defined as materials which react with oxygen t produce heat. The major factor of cost is shipping, which is affecte by the kinds of heating material chosen and the transportation to poin of use.

The major types of fuels are gas, bituminous coal, fuel oil, and anthra cite coal. Cost reductions are difficult where facilities are already installe for burning a costly fuel; however, costs should be kept in mind for nev installations or replacements. The accompanying table shows the relativ annual cost of heating in major cities across the country in 1955 based o keeping the dwelling at 70°F. In buying fuel oil, bulk quantities usuall carry a substantial discount. Have a fuel oil tank of 10,000-gal capacity since it permits loads of 5,000 gal, a tank truckload.

Relative Annual Cost of Dwelling Heating

City	Coal	Oil	Gas
Atlanta	$ 84	$136	$ 73
Boston	276	259	381
Chicago	348	282	209
Detroit	220	314	220
Kansas City	176	210	115
Los Angeles	...	53	32
Milwaukee	337	342	295
Montreal	226	378	...
New Haven	276	252	389
New York City	209	238	365
Pittsburgh	103	245	131
Portland, Maine	321	322	497
St. Louis	158	203	145
San Francisco	...	124	60
Washington, D.C.	195	206	230

[2] Also see Section 15, "Buying Considerations: Representative Commodities."

lass

Technically, glass is a liquid with a very high viscosity; it has no clearly efined melting point. Selenium, silicon, and some arsenic and borax ompounds are the major glasses. Clays and ceramics are sometimes ıcluded in the glass family. The major cost factor in producing glass is ıe processing required.

Glass is a compound of sand, soda, lime, niter, feldspar, etc. Its outanding properties are transmission of light, high chemical and temperaıre resistance, good mechanical strength, and cheapness.

The major categories of flat glass are window glass, glass plate, and ire glass.

Other major uses of glass are for containers, pressed and blown glassare, and for decorative and architectural purposes.

Glass cloth is being used for electrical purposes; when impregnated ith plastic, it is used for high-temperature and high-dielectric purposes.

Glass is used extensively in fiber form to provide strength in plastics, eauty and fireproofness in fabrics, and special properties in many prodcts.

ısulation

Insulation materials are those which will not conduct electricity, heat, nd sound. Insulation may be divided into three categories: electrical ısulation, building insulation, and sound or acoustic insulation.

Electrical insulation may be paper, rubber, plastic, asbestos, silicone, r ceramic. For many purposes, the least expensive insulation should e furnished. Only where unusually high temperatures or adverse operting conditions exist should the more costly silicones or ceramics be sed. Plastic laminates with glass fibers or mica are replacing ceramics in ome high-temperature applications.

Building insulation is of four types: mineral wool, glass wool, reflective ıeeting, and mica pellets. Mineral wool is the least expensive, but is not esirable for many applications because it tends to absorb moisture. Glass ool is replacing mineral wool in wall and ceiling applications. Reflective ısulation is aluminum foil, used where reflection of heat is desired. Mica ellets are suited for filling irregular areas or hard-to-reach areas. A table f the relative prices is given below:

Insulation Prices

Material	*Dollars per 20-ft. roll 16 in. wide*
Mineral wool	1.50
Glass wool	2.50
Reflective sheeting	2.75
Mica pellets	1.75 (4 in. coverage)

Sound insulation has received considerable attention in the past fe years. Ceiling acoustic tile costs no more than standard ceiling materia and adds to the comfort of the occupants. Mineral wool or glass wool ca be used in interior partitions to cut down on transmission of sound.

Lubricants

Lubricants are generally used to reduce friction between moving par and may also be used as cutting compounds, coolants, rust preventiv cleansing compounds, and sealing materials. The major classificatior are:

Solid graphite
Liquid hydrocarbons
Semiliquid greases

Lubricants include cutting oils, machine oils, and greases. The amour of a lubricant to buy at one time depends upon the usage, but if sul stantial quantities are used, one or two months is normal. Oils should b purchased in bulk; the packaging of a quart can of oil may add 10 t 15 per cent to the cost.

In some cases, a variety of cutting oils can be replaced by a singl general-purpose oil. This can be determined by a factory representativ conferring with tool engineers, machine-room foremen, etc. In bul quantities, a single cutting fluid can be purchased and substantial saving may be realized.

If the quantity of lubricating oil used is substantial, it may be wortl while to have three general-purpose oil specifications made up. The oi could be the following:

Light oil—10 to 15 viscosity motors, lock, hinges, pins, etc.
Medium oil—20 to 30 viscosity internal-combustion engines, lathe an drill-press spindles
Heavy oil—50 to 75 viscosity turbine compressors, transmissions, etc.

The oil companies have numerous oils which fall within the broa viscosity limits given.

Maintenance, Repair, and Operating Supplies (MRO)

While automation has decreased the time required to turn out man products, it has increased maintenance expense. We must have bigge and better buildings to house the new equipment. To keep both equip ment and building in good operating condition requires considerabl expenditures.

It is the responsibility of the buyer to understand the maintenanc problems of his plant. By recommending materials and services to fit the needs of the plant, he helps to reduce overhead.

If the plant has a central stockroom, with a competent man in control, quantity purchases are practical. If the stock is stored in a number of unattended stockrooms, quantities should be kept as low as possible to discourage pilferage. Items such as light bulbs, toilet paper, cleaning cloths, tools, etc., are apt to disappear in large quantities.

Automatic oiling systems on large equipment eliminate or reduce the time required to oil machines. The quantity of lubricant used is apt to be less and human error is eliminated.

If considerable work must be sent out to be welded or metal sprayed, the desirability of purchasing equipment should be considered.

Replacement of all light bulbs in a plant on a periodic schedule should be considered. This practice, which is recommended by one of the largest firms in lighting, is said to be practical for plants of over 150,000 sq ft.

COMMENTS: Factory supplies include, for example, drills, taps, reamers, screwdrivers, brushes, etc.; brooms, mops, pails, aprons, gloves, lubricants, cleaning compounds, paper, etc.; and fuels.

Value is controlled largely by three factors:

1. Selecting the right grade
2. Negotiating and buying from the right suppliers
3. Controlling dispensing and use

Large *value* losses occur from high inventories. Many supplies deteriorate. They dry out, mildew, oxidize, or rust. A supply inventory must be an active inventory.

It is the buyer's responsibility to know the products he is buying; what functions they will perform; facilities required to achieve this performance, including workmen and/or machines; sources that will furnish these supplies of the quality required and at the most economical prices.

Machine Parts

Machine parts are any parts made on machine tools. The parts are made from rod, tubing, bars, or other solid stock.

Machine parts are used for small lots or for precision applications. Their cost is usually high and considerable tooling may be necessary, depending on the complexity of the part. When the part is relatively small and production is high, a machine tool called a screw machine is often used.

Screw machines are multiple-spindle lathes which require little attention from the operator. Parts from the screw machine are usually finished, with no secondary operations required. A typical small screw-machine part is the metal tip of mechanical pencils, costing about 2½ cents. A typical large screw-machine part is the automobile piston, costing about $3.50.

Screw machines are rarely used to make screws except for small runs or for close-tolerance screws (see "Forgings").

Machine Tools

A metal-cutting machine tool is a power-driven machine, not portable by hand, used for the purpose of removing metal in the form of chips by one of five basic methods: drilling, turning, milling, planing or shaping, or grinding. There are over 250 types of these machine tools, varying from 1 ft to over 30 ft in height.

A metal-forming machine tool differs from a metal-cutting machine tool in that it forms metal by means of pressure. If the metal thus formed is hot, the process is known as forging. Forging machines hammer or press the hot metal into the cavities of dies. Other machine tools, such as shears, brakes, and presses, form cold sheet metal or plate. Shears cut large sheets of metal into smaller pieces. Brakes bend sheet metal or plate steel to form flanges or other shapes by squeezing the metal into a stationary, long, narrow, concave die with downward pressure of a complementary convex die. Presses consist of fixed beds over which are platens having an up-and-down movement. By stamping or squeezing the metal between appropriate complementary dies on the fixed bed and the platen, presses can shear and bend sheet metal and, in addition, can perform such operations as embossing and drawing. Embossing stiffens a flat area by indenting it; drawing causes the cold metal to flow in a hollow shape usually with vertical sides.

Special-purpose machine tools are often designed to "mass produce" identical parts. Many of these machines cannot be adapted to other work; others can be adapted but only after being rebuilt. The efficiency and the economies of special-purpose machines in the production of numerous identical parts greatly offset the disadvantage of their inflexibility. Aluminum pistons, for example, are automatically polished on their sides, tops, and beveled edges in 15 sec by a machine specially designed for that purpose; performing the same operation on nonautomatic machines requires 10 min, or 40 times as long. Before investing in a machine tool for a special purpose, make a study of the future business in the part. For example, if a machine tool must be amortized over a ten-year period, and the parts will only be produced for five years, it is a poor investment.

Large benefits—in the form of better repeatability, less time to change from job to job, less operator error, often with lower costs—are secured by the use of numerical- or tape-controlled machines. The operator usually places the raw material and a roll of tape in the machine and closes the switch. The tape gives all machining instructions to the tools of the machine.

Ordinarily, the larger machine tools are more costly, but a 6-in. precision lathe may cost twice as much as an 8-in. production lathe. The precision lathe would be used by toolmakers, the production lathe for shop or maintenance work.

The life expectancy of a machine tool is considerable—twenty to thirty years is not unusual. Newer machines with greater productivity and flexibility may cause replacement before the machine is worn out.

Often a machine tool can be rebuilt (preferably by the original manufacturer) at a substantial saving over a new machine.

The purchasing agent should keep catalogs of all the machine-tool companies, and familiarize himself with their capabilities and advantages in regard to cutting speeds, special features, and accessories. Close cooperation with the manufacturing engineer will enable the best possible purchases to be made.

Metals

The two major categories of metals are ferrous and nonferrous. Ferrous metals are iron, steel, and steel alloys. All other metals are included under nonferrous. See Section 29 for the chemical symbols of the metals. Earlier in this section the average costs of the metals are given. Steel and aluminum are generally the most stably priced metals, whereas others are prone to major fluctuations.

The purchase of an adequate supply of steel has not been a great problem of late. However, it has been difficult on several occasions. One of the best ways of ensuring an adequate supply of steel is to maintain good relations with one or more jobbers. Become regarded as a steady customer for an ensured supply in times of scarcity.

Large quantities are usually bought direct from the mill. There should be several sources of supply in case one mill should fail to deliver. The same pattern applies to nonferrous metals, except that here quantities are not apt to be as large and more orders will go to jobbers and specialty suppliers. Companies faced with periodic shutdowns because of metal shortages might well determine if carrying large inventories of some metals would not be advantageous.

Metals should be purchased in the shape as close as possible to that desired in the finished product. This applies primarily to rod and tubing, as well as extrusion and structural shapes.

Office Equipment and Supplies[3]

When purchases for the office are constantly checked with the needs of the office, the greatest values are realized. Procedures in an office are constantly changing: some forms become obsolete; use of others increases; new types are necessary. To do the best job for the office, the buyer must know both its procedures and equipment and must be able to recommend new equipment to do the job more efficiently.

Four categories of office equipment and supplies are:

Furniture	Printing services
Office machines	Stationery items

Furniture includes desks, chairs, filing cabinets, tables, etc. Wood was standard until recently; now the trend is to more costly but more durable steel furniture. Extremes of styling should be avoided; the square-legged style is always available and conservatively styled equipment will look better longer. Purchase all office furniture in the same color. Office furniture is constantly being shifted and the appearance of an office is much improved if all the equipment is the same color and shade.

Printing. A buyer may be responsible for the purchasing of printing services such as typesetting, engraving, and art work. This type of service is extremely specialized and it is difficult to apply general rules to all jobs. Bring together the using department and the printer on all new or unusual jobs.

The quality of the printing should be in proportion to the requirements of the job. Often mimeograph, multilith, or offset can be substituted for the more costly letterpress.

The buyer should educate the advertising or art departments to put its art out on a schedule so that the printer has sufficient lead time. When the printer must get the job out in short order, the costs go up.

Considerable savings can be realized by combination runs of printed forms. This is applicable to forms of a similar size and quantity. The advantages of the new types of forms such as snap-out and fanfold should be reviewed every so often with the using department.

Office Machines. Office machines include typewriters, desk calculators, adding machines, multilith equipment, time clocks, ozalid machines, etc. Typewriters are often purchased with economy in mind; however, the more expensive heavy-duty models give less maintenance trouble. Electric typewriters and electric calculators should be considered when the equipment is in constant use.

[3] Also see Section 15, "Buying Considerations: Representative Commodities."

A year's guarantee should accompany each office machine. This is available on most equipment with the exception of manual typewriters, which are usually guaranteed for 90 days. Place orders with concerns which have local service facilities. Balance service contracts against the cost of maintaining equipment. Perhaps lease a group of typewriters on a yearly rental basis so that all service charges are handled by the rental agency.

Stationery Items. The cost and delivery of quality items purchased locally should be balanced against the cost of the same items purchased direct from the manufacturer or a large mail-order stationer.

An effort should be made to restrict purchasing of supplies to a small number of suppliers, as small orders receive more attention from a supplier from whom you do considerable buying.

Several low-quantity items such as binders, notebooks, etc., can sometimes be replaced by a single type for quantity discounts. Purchases of special items from petty cash should be encouraged.

Packaging

Packaging (see also "Containers," page 11–30) today is the world's largest business volumewise. It is estimated that between 10 and 15 billion dollars are being spent annually for packaging materials. Besides consumer goods items which are packaged to help sell the merchandise, most other items are packaged at least once during the manufacturing cycle. It is very important that every effort be made to reduce this huge expense, for packaging lends nothing to the quality of the product once it reaches the customer. In fact, it sometimes presents a problem to dispose of the packaging material. As we further the science of package design and testing, larger products will be packaged in corrugated instead of wire-bound boxes and crates or in dimensioned wooden containers or crates. In 1950, refrigerators, ranges, washing machines, air conditioners, television sets, and many other products were packaged in wooden containers. Today, they are packaged in all-corrugated containers of various designs to suit the product. Some designs have certain features that are not incorporated in other designs. This may make one particular design more suitable. The quality of linerboard and better methods of fabricating the linerboard to the medium have assisted in obtaining better containers at lower cost. This naturally increases the strength of the material, and with material evaluation performed for you by the vendor, there are many ways to place a value on the various pieces that make a corrugated box. Evaluate and use containers that have the right amount of strength, meet the railroad requirements, use less material, and provide designs easy to assemble—resulting in lower material, labor, and transportation costs.

Plastics

Plastics in packaging take many forms. Foam plastic for cushioning and product protection is probably the largest use of plastics in packaging. Another important use of plastics is as thermoplastics in the form of skin and blister packaging for card displays. The combination of plastics and fiberboard to form moisture- and freeze-resistant containers is a new and important development. Plastic-coated materials are probably second only to plastic bags for use in the movement of products. Wherever moisture is a hazard to the product, plastic packages should be considered. Whenever fragile items must be moved, foam-plastic cushions should be evaluated. The light weight of foam plastics and the transparency of many thermoplastics will continue to increase their use throughout the packaging field.

The term plastics usually refers to a class of synthetic organic materials, solid in finished form but, at some stage in their processing, fluid enough to be shaped by heat and pressure. Of these, there are two basic types.

Thermoplastics

These become soft when heated and harden when cooled, no matter how often the process is repeated; they may be molded, extruded, and formed, and quickly ejected at high output rates (similar to glass processing). They include acrylics, cellulosics, nylon, polyethylene, styrene, polyfluorocarbons (teflon), vinyls, ABS, acetals, polypropylene, phenoxies, polyallomers, and chlorinated polyether.

Thermosets

These are chemically changed and set into permanent shape when heat and/or pressure is applied and will not soften with reheating; to allow this chemical change to take place, a part remains in its mold for a curing period. Thermosets include phenolics, melamine, urea, polyesters, epoxies, silicones, and alkyds.

As engineering materials, plastics are unique in three rather important respects: (1) they are inherently resistant to corrosion; (2) they have good *combinations* of properties, rather than extremes of any single property; and (3) plastics often permit the bypassing of steps in fabrication and the combining of functions of design by integrating components and simplifying parts.

No plastic is as strong as steel (though some have strength-to-weight ratios which are as high). They are as light in solid form as most woods, and thin-wall design and coring can be utilized to achieve even lower weights. Plastics are as elastic as soft rubbers (though a wide degree of rigidity-flexibility is available) and as scratch-free as glass (yet within a few percentiles of duplication). But plastics are the only available materials which are *simultaneously* strong, light, flexible, and transparent. They also require a minimum of finishing after processing. Color, glossy or textured finishes, threads, undercuts, bosses, metal inserts, and holes may all be produced right in the mold.

Furthermore, because of their inherent versatility, plastic parts may combine several functions, serving as both mechanism and housing, frame and insulator, and case and lens. A single plastic unit may even function as bearing, gear, shaft, boss, and sleeve altogether. As a result, the relative cost of a plastic part tends to be lower than the price per pound or per cubic inch would indicate. The following comparison of an electrically driven appliance part of die-cast aluminum with an identical part made of plastic is a typical example of the cost saving which can be obtained with plastic.

Two parts	*Two parts*	*One part*
Original aluminum frame and general-purpose plastic cover	High-performance plastic frame and general-purpose plastic cover	All high-performance plastic, integral frame and cover
$0.55 frame 0.45 cover	$0.51 frame 0.45 cover	integral frame and cover
$1.00	$0.96	$0.95
0.6 lb frame 0.5 lb cover	0.24 lb frame 0.45 lb cover	integral frame and cover
1.1 lb	0.69 lb	0.55 lb

Other advantages of plastic are that it is a nonconductive, nonbrittle, material, with automatic color finish, better corrosion resistance, and better impact resistance. Its performance is more dependable, its assembly is simplified, and it meets and holds closer tolerances than most die-casts.

When comparing cost figures for plastics with those for metals, processing and finishing costs (not to mention shipping costs, which are significant, since plastics are much lighter than metals) can usually be more significant than material costs. This can be seen by considering finishing costs alone (cost of converting one cubic inch of material into a one cubic-inch part), as in the following table.

Costs	Die-cast zince	Die-cast aluminum	Premium-priced plastic
Minimum finishing:			
Labor	4¢	4¢	4.0¢
Material	3	3	4.5
Total	7¢	7¢	8.5¢
Average finishing:			
Labor	6¢	5¢	3.5¢
Material	3	3	5.0
Total	9¢	8¢	8.5¢
Maximum finishing:			
Labor	10¢	11.5¢	6¢
Material	3	3.0	5
Total	13¢	14.5¢	11¢
Painting and plating:			
Labor	11¢	10¢	5¢
Material	11	3	6
Total	22¢	13¢	11¢

Plastics versus Metals

Properties which may be *favorable* to plastics when compared with metals:

1. Lighter weight
2. Better corrosion resistance
3. Better resistance to shock and vibration
4. Transparent or translucent
5. Quieter—tend to absorb vibration and sound
6. Higher abrasion and wear resistance
7. Self-lubricating
8. Often easier to fabricate
9. Have integral color and finish
10. Cost trend is downward
11. Cost less per finished part

Properties which may be *unfavorable* to plastics when compared with metals:

1. Lower strength
2. Much higher thermal expansion
3. More susceptible to creep, cold flow, and deformation under load

4. Lower resistance to thermal degradation and heat distortion
5. More subject to embrittlement at low temperatures
6. Softer
7. Less ductile
8. Absorption of moisture or solvents may change dimensions
9. Flammable
10. Ultraviolet degradation for some varieties
11. Most cost more per cubic inch or per pound

Properties of plastics which may be *either favorable or unfavorable* when compared with metals:

1. Flexibility. Even rigid varieties are more resilient than metals
2. Nonconductors of electricity
3. Thermal insulators
4. Formed by heat and pressure

Exceptions to the above general characteristics:[4]

1. Some reinforced plastics (glass-reinforced epoxies, polyesters and phenolics) are nearly as rigid and strong (particularly in relation to weight) as most steels. They may be even more dimensionally stable.
2. Some oriented films and sheets (oriented polyesters) may have greater strength-to-weight ratios than cold-rolled steels.
3. Some plastics are now cheaper than competing metals (nylons vs brass, acetal vs zinc, acrylic vs stainless steel).
4. Some plastics are tougher at low than at normal temperatures (acrylic has no known brittle point).
5. Many plastic-metal combinations extend the range of useful applications of both (metal-vinyl laminates, leaded vinyls, metallized polyesters, and copper-filled TFE).
6. Plastic and metal components may be combined to produce a desired balance of properties (plastic parts with molded-in, threaded metal inserts; gears with cast-iron hubs and nylon teeth; gear trains with alternate steel and phenolic gears; and rotating bearings with metal shaft and housing and nylon or TFE bearing liner).
7. Metallic fillers in plastics can make them electrically or thermally conductive or give them magnetic properties.

Which Plastic?

Although there are many plastics, the choice for any application should lie within a relatively narrow band or family, as prescribed by the per-

[4] Reprinted by permission from *Machine Design,* "The Plastics Reference Issue," Sept. 17, 1964. Copyright by The Penton Publishing Company, Cleveland. Condensed from article "Selecting Plastics," by Richard J. Jacob, President, Cadillac Plastic and Chemical Co., Detroit, Michigan.

formance required. Within this band, though, there will probably be several plastics suitable. Selecting the best is a matter of weighing the performance of each and comparing this data with what is expected of the particular part.

Thus, the first step toward selection of a plastic is a primary knowledge of the performance parameters of the application—what the part will do, under what conditions, and to what it may possibly be exposed (damaging effects, etc.). These performance parameters are usually available in engineering terms, often measured or dictated by standard ASTM (American Society for Testing and Materials) test conditions and specifications.

The second step is to select the family or type of plastic. When this has been done, the plastic suppliers should be able to recommend the right formulation within that family or type to do the best job. It is advantageous to test the plastic chosen in a prototype model of the design before releasing materials specifications. This is because average ASTM properties obtained under laboratory conditions are only approximate guides to performance, which may vary with design and environment.

Plastic Materials Application Guides for Comparative Purposes[5]

Bearings, Bushings, Slides, Guides, Valve Liners, Wear Surfaces

PROPERTIES REQUIRED

Low coefficient of friction, even when nonlubricated. High resistance to abrasion. Fair or better form stability, heat resistance, and corrosion resistance.

CONSIDER PLASTICS WHEN

1. Corrosives or abrasives are present. 2. Lubrication might contaminate product being processed. 3. Assembly must operate above or below useful temperature of conventional lubricants. 4. Maintenance-free operation is desirable. 5. Complex lubrication systems would otherwise be required. 6. Weight is a major consideration. 7. Electrical insulation must be provided. 8. Noise must be controlled. 9. Galling and scoring must be minimized. 10. High-load low-speed operation would squeeze out conventional lubricants. 11. Stickslip characteristics would be objectionable.

		Cost (¢ per cu in.)
Fluorocarbons TFE	Lowest coefficient of friction of any material. Nothing sticks to it with any strength. No stickslip. Highest heat and chemical re-	25 to 40

[5] Reprinted by permission from *Machine Design,* "The Plastics Reference Issue," Sept. 17, 1964. Copyright by The Penton Publishing Company, Cleveland. Condensed from article "Selecting Plastics," by Richard J. Jacob, President, Cadillac Plastic and Chemical Co., Detroit, Michigan.

	sistance (virtually inert). Excellent abrasion resistance. Does not mar polished surfaces. Mechanical properties, only fair to good, remain virtually unaffected from −430°F to 550°F. Zero moisture absorption. Must be compression molded or machined from stock shapes.	
FEP	Readily injection molded and extruded, does not adhere to tacky materials; chemically inert.	43
TFE fabric	Has higher mechanical properties than pure TFE and best PV rating (dry) in group. Recommended for high load capacities at low speeds (50,000 psi at 0 fpm) not over 200 fpm and rarely over 50 fpm. Does not take set (deform) under heavy static loads. Clearance requirements between shaft and bearing are extremely low.	106
Filled TFE	Fillers of fibrous glass will improve mechanical and electrical properties. Fillers of graphite compounds will increase mechanical strength and reduce starting friction and initial wear. (Should not be used for electrical applications.) Molybdenum disulphide-fibrous glass fillers will increase hardness, stiffness, and wear resistance—and even lower starting friction—without appreciable effect on desirable electrical and chemical properties of TFE.	26 to 58
Nylons	Best wear and abrasion resistance in group. Strong, tough. Very resilient. Does not mar polished surfaces. Absorbs vibration and noise. Excellent chemical resistance, except against acids. Only tough plastic available in large sections.	3.7
Acetals	Has virtually no stickslip. Outstanding fatigue resistance (best in group): stiffest of the unfilled mechanical plastics. Excellent dimensional stability at normal temperature (better than nylon). Can withstand repeated important stress better than any other plastic. Tough and resilient. Good resistance to creep. Low moisture absorption.	3.3

Acetal, TFE fiber-filled	Combines the strength and stiffness of acetal with the exceptional low-friction properties of TFE fluorocarbons. Low-friction properties almost as good as fluorocarbons'. Stiffness even better than acetal's. PV values (dry) are up to five times greater than pure acetal's, up to 15 times greater than pure TFE's. Creep resistant. Excellent wear life. Is most efficient at high loads and low speeds.	26.5
Polyethylenes, high-density	High resistance to abrasion. Moisture resistance second only to fluorocarbons in this group. Excellent chemical resistance. However, high thermal expansion and low heat-distortion point limit use to applications involving low speeds and loads.	0.9

PROPERTY SUMMARY. *Nylon* recommended for general-purpose bearings and wear surfaces. *Fluorocarbons* (especially TFE) for sliding or low-speed-rotating dry bearings, for highly corrosive service, or service in extreme temperatures (—430 to +500 F). *Acetals* for submerged or humid service, and when resistance to creep is important. *Acetals* and *fluorocarbons* for valve liners or slides to eliminate jerky starts and stickslip. *Filled fluorocarbons* for heavier loadings and high creep resistance. *TFE-filled acetal* for heavy duty sleeve or sliding bearings. *TFE fabric* for ball-and-socket and thrust bearings; sliding bearings under heavy load, low speed. *High-density polyethylene* for lowest cost at very low speeds and loads. *Fluorocarbons* for nonstick surfaces.

Gears, Cams, Racks, Couplings, Rollers, Heavily Stressed Mechanical Components

PROPERTIES REQUIRED

High tensile plus high impact strength. Good fatigue resistance and stability at elevated temperatures. Machinable or moldable to close tolerance.

CONSIDER PLASTICS WHEN

1. Weight reduction is important. 2. Ambient conditions are gritty, abrasive, or corrosive. 3. Part is to be subjected to flexing. 4. Noise or vibration must be controlled. 5. Combined functions are desired.

		Cost (¢ per cu. in.)
Nylons	Best wear and abrasion resistance in group. Strong, tough. Very resilient. Low coefficient of friction, even when not lubricated. Does not mar polished surfaces. Absorbs vi-	3.7

	bration and noise. Excellent chemical resistance, except against acids. Only tough plastic available in large sections.	
Acetals	Outstanding fatigue resistance (best of any thermoplastic) : stiffest unfilled mechanical plastics, can withstand repeated prolonged stress better than any other plastic. Lowest moisture absorption in group. Offers excellent dimensional stability at normal temperature (better than nylon, though not as good as polycarbonate). Good low-friction properties, even when not lubricated. Good resistance to creep. Poor chemical resistance to acids and alkalis.	2.2
Acetal, TFE fiber-filled	Combines the strength and stiffness of acetal with the exceptional low-friction properties of TFE fluorocarbons. Low friction properties almost as good as fluorocarbons'. Stiffness even better than acetal's. PV values (dry) are up to five times greater than pure acetal's, up to 15 times greater than pure TFE's. Creep resistant. Excellent wear life.	26.5
Polycarbonates	Outstanding impact strength—best in group, by far. Exceptional creep resistance and heat and dimensional stability. Excellent high- and low-temperature strength. However, because of low fatigue resistance, performs indifferently under cyclic stress conditions (e.g., spur gear). Low moisture absorption. Resistance to oils and solvents only fair. Only transparent plastic in this group.	4.5
Phenolics, fabric-filled	In sheet form, lowest cost of rigid plastic shapes. (However, rods cost three times more than sheets, so recommended mostly for inexpensive thin-stamped gears or parts.) Outstanding dimensional stability, heat resistance. Hardest in this group. Fair resistance to acids and alkalis.	1.5 to 3

PROPERTY SUMMARY. Nylons are recommended for general-purpose gears, and other mechanical components. Acetals for maximum fatigue life, for highly accurate parts or exposure to extremely humid conditions. Phenolic-fabric laminates for low-cost, thin-stamped gears or parts. Polycarbonates for intermittent, very high impacts (not recommended for applications involving repeated cyclical stress). TFE-filled acetals for heavy-duty applications.

Chemical and Thermal Equipment Parts, Missiles, Plating Components

PROPERTIES REQUIRED

Resistance to extremes of temperatures and to an exceptionally wide range of chemical attack. Minimum moisture absorption. Fair or better strength.

CONSIDER PLASTICS WHEN

1. Cost is a primary consideration. 2. Ultimate in corrosion resistance is required. 3. Abrasives may be present in combination with corrosives. 4. Minimum maintenance is desired. 5. Thermal insulation is a requirement.

		Cost (¢ per cu. in.)
Fluorocarbons: TFE and FEP	Highest chemical and heat resistance of any plastic. Extremely high impact strength. Mechanical properties, only fair to good, remain virtually unaffected from −430°F to 400°F or 550°F. Lowest coefficient of friction of any material, and best nonstick properties. Virtually no breakaway friction. Zero moisture absorption. Extremely good dielectric properties. FEP is more expensive and has a slightly lower continuous-use thermal rating (400°F vs 550°F), but is easier to fabricate. (TFE must be compression molded or machined from stock shapes.)	25 to 40
CTFE	Only transparent plastic in this group. Zero moisture absorption. Excellent weathering properties. Greater tensile and compressive strength than TFE and FEP. Better resistance to radiation under atmospheric conditions. However, does not perform as well at extremely high or low temperatures, chemical resistance and lubricity are not as outstanding and dielectric strength is lower.	45
Chlorinated polyether	Exceptional heat and chemical resistance (except to fuming nitric and sulphuric acids). Extremely good dimensional stability at high temperatures and in corrosive situations. Good strength and abrasion resistance. Very low moisture absorption.	12.6

PVC	Extremely tough, hard, and chemically resistant. Good abrasion resistance. Highest tensile strength among thermoplastic pipes. 50% heavier than polyethylene.	1.16 to 2.07
Polypropylene	Similar in properties and appearance to high-density polyethylene, but even stronger and lighter (lightest of all plastics), and has a continuous-use thermal rating of 230°F–320°F (compared to 170°F–260°F for high-density polyethylene). High flexing strength. Excellent resistance to creep and stress cracking.	0.9 to 1.1
High-density polyethylene	Excellent chemical and wear resistance. Good mechanical strength. Lighter than water.	0.9
Epoxy-glass	Thermosetting resin-and-glass fabric laminate that can be easily laid up into large structures or parts. Outstanding tensile and impact strength (by far the highest of this group). Outstanding chemical and heat resistance (highest heat distortion point under load). Adheres tightly to most substances. Easily patched.	3.4 to 6.5

PROPERTY SUMMARY. TFE fluorocarbons for general-purpose chemical and extreme temperature applications. Polypropylene and high-density polyethylene for plating and less severe chemical exposures. Chlorinated polyether, PVC and CTFE for extreme resistance in combination with mechanical strength and stiffness. CTFE for transparency. Epoxy-glass for greatest mechanical strength and large structures.

Housings, Shrouds, Containers, Ducts

PROPERTIES REQUIRED

Good to excellent impact strength and stiffness. Good formability and moldability. Moderate cost. Good environmental resistance. Fair or better tensile strength and dimensional stability.

CONSIDER PLASTICS WHEN

1. Resonance must be prevented and sound transmission minimized. 2. Elastic deformation is required to prevent dents and cracks in case of random impacts. 3. Producing complex shapes difficult by metalworking techniques. 4. Post-fabrication finishing is undesirable. 5. Integral thermal or electrical insulation must be provided. 6. Corrosion and moisture resistance are required.

		Cost (¢ per cu. in.)
ABS	Best all-around combination of properties in this group. Retains its strength right up to its maximum recommended range. Hard, smooth surface with excellent gloss. Not quite as formable as high-impact styrene.	1.5 to 1.8
High-impact styrenes	Easy to form. Has lowest forming temperature.	0.8 to 1.2
Polypropylenes	Similar in properties and appearance to high-density polyethylene, but even stronger and lighter (lightest of all plastics), and more heat resistant. (Sterilizable.) Has unique ability to be used as a hinge material by properly thinning the material at the point at which flexing is to occur. The strength of such a hinge seems to improve with age.	0.9 to 1.1
High-density polyethylenes	Excellent formability. Excellent chemical and wear resistance. Lighter than water. Very low water absorption.	0.9
Cellulose acetate butyrates	Only transparent thermoplastic in this group. Very rough in thin section. Glossy. Able to withstand shock and maintain toughness over a wide temperature range. Easily formed to very deep draws.	2.7
Modified acrylics	Has excellent formability, better than ABS, but lower impact strength and a lower continuous-use heat resistance. Best outdoor-weathering plastic in high-impact group.	1.6 to 2.0
Polyester-glass	Layup of resin and glass is simplest method of molding large, complex parts or structures. Resulting laminates are about 3–8 times stronger than thermoplastics in this group, have 2½ times greater impact strength, and 7–10 times better stiffness. Remarkable dimensional stability and heat resistance. Excellent adhesion to nonmetallics. Easily repaired.	2.2 to 3.2
Epoxy-glass	Epoxy is about twice as expensive as polyester and not quite so easy to layup, but its laminates offer even greater stiffness,	3.4 to 6.5

tensile strength, dimensional stability, and heat resistance. Thermal expansion is even less than steel's. Outstanding chemical and weather resistance. Excellent adhesion to most surfaces—both nonmetallic and metallic.

ROPERTY SUMMARY. High-impact styrene and ABS recommended for general-urpose applications at lowest cost. Polyester-glass and epoxy-glass for maximum rength-to-weight ratios, stiffness, and heat resistance. Cellulose acetate butyrate or transparent housings. Modified acrylic for resistance to sunlight and to staining. Polypropylene, high-density polyethylene, and epoxy-glass for applications in orrosive environments. Polypropylene when its high flexing strength can be tilized in design.

IGHT-TRANSMISSION COMPONENTS, SURFACES, TRANSPARENT PACKAGING, SIGNS, IODELS

ROPERTIES REQUIRED

ood light transmission in transparent or translucent colors. Good to excellent ormability and moldability. Shatter resistance. Fair to good tensile strength.

ONSIDER PLASTICS WHEN

. Shatter resistance is required. 2. Vibration resistance is important. 3. Flexibility required. 4. Colored transparency is desired. 5. Maximum strength-to-weight atios are required. 6. Translucency must be obtained with the material rather an by surface treatment. 7. Ease of forming in complex shapes is required. 8. Iand fabrication of prototypes is required.

		Cost (¢ *per cu. in.*)
crylics	Has best optical properties of all plastics—outstanding transparency and light reflectance (sparkle) and diffusion. Outstanding weather resistance. Can transmit light around corners and be edge lighted. Good structural strength. Nontoxic. Excellent formability.	2.2
olystyrenes	Pipes light. Excellent low-temperature properties. However, is brittle and has poor formability.	0.6
cetates	Excellent clarity, toughness, and high impact strength. Maintains properties over a wide temperature range (—40°F to 200°F). Stable at room temperature, with good resistance to discoloration or deterioration. (Long-term exposure to outside	1.8 to 2.4

	weathering not recommended.) Poor to fair chemical resistance.	
Cellulose acetate butyrates	Better impact strength, weathering properties, and chemical resistance than acetate. Lower moisture absorption and better surface. Very tough. Has poor formability, but can be drawn more deeply than acetate. Poor resistance to acids and alkalis, but good against solvents and excellent against oils.	2.7 to 3.3
Vinyls, rigid	Excellent clarity, dimensional stability (even in humid environments), toughness, flexibility, and formability. Good abrasion and chemical resistance. Printable.	1.2 to 2.1
Polycarbonates	Outstanding impact strength—best in group, by far. Exceptional creep resistance and heat and dimensional stability. Excellent high-and-low-temperature strength. Low moisture absorption. Good chemical resistance (but only fair against oils). Fades when subjected to ultraviolet. Excellent formability.	4.5
Medium-impact styrenes	Addition of rubbers to pure styrene makes material flexible, tougher, easier to form, improves its resistance to chemicals and, with added stabilizers, to ultraviolet. Since this greatly reduces light transmission, is available translucent but not transparent.	0.7 to 1.1

PROPERTY SUMMARY. Acrylics recommended for general-purpose applicatio especially for optical, decorative, and outdoor use. In sheet stock, cast acryl has greater strength and transparency; extruded acrylic has lower cost (especiall in thin thicknesses) and better formability. Polycarbonates for maximum strengt as in explosion shields. Butyrates for excellent impact resistance, and deep forn ability. Vinyls for maximum formability and printability. Acetates and viny for flexible glazing and guards. Medium-impact styrene and rigid vinyls fc lowest cost translucent lighting applications. Polystyrene for lowest cost molde transparent parts.

ELECTROSTRUCTURAL PARTS, HOUSINGS, SWITCHGEAR, TERMINAL BOARDS, PLUG SOCKETS, INSULATORS, COIL FORMS

PROPERTIES REQUIRED

Excellent electrical resistance in low to medium frequencies. High strength an impact properties, good fatigue resistance, and heat resistance. Good dime sional stability at elevated temperatures.

ONSIDER PLASTICS WHEN

. Shock loadings are high. 2. Weight reduction is important. 3. Dimensional ccuracy must be close. 4. Complex integral conductor-insulator parts are needed :.g., printed circuitry and slip-ring assemblies).

		Cost (¢ per cu. in.)
.llylics	Exceptional dimensional stability. Outstanding heat resistance. Excellent electrical properties remain stable even under conditions of high heat and humidity. Excellent chemical resistance. Low water absorption.	4.5 to 22.0
.lkyds	Superior dimensional stability, high strength, good thermal properties. High dry-insulation resistance. Retains good dielectric characteristics at relatively high temperatures. Uniform, low shrinkage during cure.	3.0 to 4.5
.minos	Hard, scratch-resistant surface. Good resistance to solvent, oils, and greases. Fast moldability. Unlimited color possibilities. Fibrous-glass fillers will increase impact strength, heat resistance, and electric properties. Asbestos fillers will give maximum arc and heat resistance and dielectric strength.	1.0 to 3.0
poxies	Outstanding dimensional stability over a wide temperature range, impact and flexural strength (highest in this group), and heat and chemical resistance. Excellent continuous-use heat resistance. Low shrinkage rate in encapsulation.	2.4 to 5.0
henolics	Outstanding dimensional stability. Excellent flexural strength and heat resistance. Available in low-cost sheet form, recommended for punched, stamped parts, and in both casting or molding compounds.	1.5 to 3.0
olycarbonates	Outstanding impact strength and dielectric strength—both, best in group. Exceptional creep resistance and heat and dimensional stability. Low moisture absorption. Transparent.	4.5

Polyesters	Excellent chemical resistance. Outstanding strength, impact resistance, and dimensional stability. Available in rigid or flexible forms. Readily colorable. Laminates cure without pressure.	0.9 to 3.2
Silicones	Highest continuous-use heat resistance in this group: retains strength and electrical properties during continuous use at elevated temperatures as high as 500°F and above. Stays flexible at temperatures below −100°F. Excellent electrical properties. General inertness—resistance to weathering, ozone, and most chemicals. Not corrosive to other materials. Has ability to prevent other materials from sticking.	13.0 to 25.0

PROPERTY SUMMARY. Polycarbonates for transparent parts requiring high impa strength. Cast epoxies for encapsulating electric or electronic assemblies f maximum environmental resistance. Molded epoxies for uses which requi dimensional stability over wide temperature ranges. Melamines for extra har ness. Silicones for highest heat resistance. Aminos for lowest cost. Phenolic lam nates for punched, stamped parts.

Powdered Metal Parts

Powdered metal parts are molded from metal powder, usually iron bronze, and a binding agent of a volatile resin.

Powdered metals are molded in a press to the desired shape. They a then sintered (baked in an oven) to strengthen them and are then reac for use. Ordinarily no finishing operations are necessary.

Quantities of 10,000 pieces per year are considered the minimum f powdered metal parts. This technique is used to advantage in replacin certain small castings and forgings, gears, subassemblies, and screw-m chine parts.

The most widespread use of powdered metals is in bronze bearing The porous structure of the bronze allows it to act as a reservoir for oi The small bronze bearing used in an 8-in. electric fan costs about 3 cent Larger parts are priced accordingly.

Raw Stock

Most raw materials are supplied as strip, sheet, or rod, but extrude shapes (angles, tees, or channels) are also requested. Some shapes ar called for more often than others; substitute these for the more unusu shapes wherever possible. It costs more for a mill to set up to run a sp ial lot. It also costs more for special alloys. Substitute standard alloys wherever practical.

Expensive chemical analysis may be necessary if stocks should become nixed in transit or in receiving. In the case of steels, the melt number s stamped on the ends of the bar or rods.

ubber

Rubber is a generic term covering a large variety of synthetic rubbers s well as the older natural rubber. Synthetics are becoming more and nore important and include butadiene-styrene (GR-S), nitrile, neoprene, utyl, polysulfide, silicone, and urethane rubber. Each of these rubbers, s well as natural rubber, has its advantages in mechanical properties, n resistance to heat, cold, weathering, or chemicals, and in processing haracteristics.

Butadiene-styrene GR-S is used in tires and tubes, belts, hose, seals, and ound absorption.

Nitrile rubber is resistant to oils and some chemicals—used in seals, uel tanks, hose, and cables.

Neoprene is resistant to oils, chemicals, and weathering—used in hose, eals, belting, shoe soles, coated fabrics, and adhesives.

Butyl is very impermeable to gases—used in inner tubes, hose, seals, nd electrical insulation.

Polysulfide rubber (*Thiokol*) is resistant to oils and chemicals but poor n heat aging—used in hose, seals, and caulking.

Silicone is very resistant to heat, cold, and weathering and processes asily—used in electrical insulation, seals, rollers, caulking, adhesives, and nolds for casting plastics.

Urethane is resistant to oils, chemicals, abrasion, and cold—used in a ariety of applications including urethane foam cushions.

etal Spinning

Metal spinning is an ancient art (the ancient Egyptians were experts) nd is now used by industry for the production of small numbers or unsual sizes of metal parts at low tooling cost.

prings

The cost of producing springs depends in large measure on quantity, olerances, material, and finish. Tolerances should never be specified oser than necessary since they control the speed of production, the type f inspection, and affect the amount of discard. Choice of material should e flexible, since more expensive material often results in lower ultimate osts through longer life attained. Special finishes also add to the cost.

The more the springmaker knows about where the spring is to fit and what it is to do, the better the result obtained, both from a cost and per formance standpoint.

Stampings

Stampings are sheet-metal parts made from flat stock, usually steel. Th stock can be of any thickness, although it usually does not exceed ⅛ in The parts are stamped out on presses, several operations on a part often being performed at one stroke of the press. The process of stamping ou parts is essentially a high-production process; however, with a small pres and simple tools, small runs (500 to 1,000) are sometimes feasible.

Stampings require setting up dies on a press for each run; however once the tools are paid for, a great many parts can be made for a low unit price. Only a small amount of finishing is required on a stamped part.

	Short run		Conventional
	Temporary	Semipermanent	
Tools	22.00	95.00	325.00
Setup charge	2.50	4.00	6.50
Piece price in lots of 1,000	0.031	0.019	0.004
Cost of 1,000	55.50	118.00	325.50
Cost of 5,000	179.50	194.00	351.50
Cost of 10,000	334.50	289.00	398.00
Cost of 15,000	489.50	384.00	391.00
Cost of 20,000	644.50	479.00	411.00

FIG. 11–9. Cost comparisons of short- and long-run stampings (Dayton Manufacturin Company, Minneapolis, Minnesota).

Examples of large stampings are the body panels of an automobile. An example of a small stamping is the metal screw base of a light bulb. These bases are made on a special multiple plunger press called an eyelet ma chine. The hood of a car represents a $50 stamping; the screw base of light bulb costs less than 1 cent.

Surface Protection Products

Surface protection products fall into three categories: (1) paint, lac quer, and varnish, (2) plating, and (3) chemical finishes.

1. A *paint* is a compound of three ingredients: a pigment, a bindin

gent, and a solvent. The four major types of paints are the oil base, the ubber base, the alkyd base, and ne enamels. Oil-base paints are rimarily used for outside wood nd metal structures. Rubber-base nd alkyd-base paints are extensively used for inside woodwork, artitions, walls, etc.; flat oil paints re also used here. Lacquers are ompounded of a gum or resin and quick-drying solvent. They are sed for finishing metals, either clear r pigmented. Most machine tools re protected with lacquer. Varnishes re tough, hard-wearing finishes used rimarily for floors. Shellac is a arnish with alcohol as a solvent. 'arnishes are also used to protect office furniture, electrical coils, boats, tc.

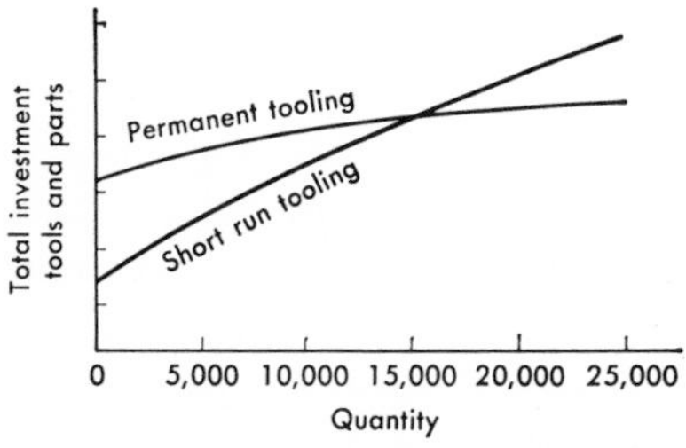

FIG. 11–10. Graph showing economic advantage in purchasing parts made by stamping rather than by other processes. At some point in the operation, there will be an economic advantage in purchasing parts made by stamping rather than by other processes. Typical cost curves such as this will assist in determining the point at which there is an advantage in switching to permanent tooling (Dayton Manufacturing Company, Minneapolis, Minnesota).

It is important to specify outside paint for outside work and inside aint for inside work. Prices of some popular paints are given:

Outside oil-base paint	\$6.00–\$7.00 per gal
Inside paints:	
Flat rubber base	5.25– 6.00 per gal
Flat alkyd base	4.00– 5.50 per gal
Flat oil base	3.50– 4.50 per gal
Gloss enamel	7.50– 8.00 per gal

2. *Plating* is divided into hot metal dipping and electroplating. Hot etal dipping is the application of coatings of tin and zinc by immersion f the article in the molten metal. Hot tin coatings are applied to steel n the tin can), cast iron, copper, and brass (for articles in contact with ood). Zinc is used to protect steel used in building (hot dipped nails).

The most used types of electroplating are brass, cadmium, and chrome. *Brass* is used primarily on steel hardware for decorative purposes.

Cadmium plating is applied largely to steel because it protects steel lectrochemically and does not form corrosion products as easily as does nc. It takes solder readily and is widely used in the electronics industry or this reason.

Chromium plating is most often used as a decorative finish. It shoul be applied over preliminary applications of copper and nickel. Som heavy chrome plating is applied to tools to prevent wear or to build u tools that are worn.

3. *Chemical finishes* are used both for corrosion protection and to serv as bases for paint or other organic finishes. Steel and zinc are phosphite and zinc and cadmium are treated in chromate solutions for salt-spra resistance. Magnesium is treated with chromate solutions to lessen corro sion and to facilitate painting. Aluminum is treated with an oxidizin electrochemical process which forms an oxide coating. This is very har and can be tinted a variety of colors; the process is called anodizing.

Textiles

Textiles is a term for the raw and finished materials made from cotto wool, silk, linen, rayon, and other fibers. The following table lists th commercially important textile materials:

Commercial Fibers

Animal fibers	Wool, silk, mohair
Vegetable fibers	Cotton, flax, jute, ramie, hemp
Mineral fibers	Asbestos, tinsel, metallic threads, glass
Salvaged material	Reprocessed wool
Synthetic material	Rayon, nylon, orlon, Dacron, Acrilan, Dynel

Wool is primarily used for clothing. Its use is diminishing in contra to woollike synthetics which have replaced it in some applications. Th most durable wool fabrics are hard finished worsted, sharkskin, or gal ardines. Soft finished wools are desired for warm outer garments an blankets.

Cotton is the most used textile; its uses are too well known to requir description. The quality of a cotton fabric is determined by the threa count; the higher the count, the better the fabric. Cotton cloth of mor than 200 by 200 threads per inch is percale; below this count is muslin.

Asbestos and glass are the most important mineral fibers. Asbestos i used for both electrically and thermally fireproof garments and insula tion. Glass is very important in the reinforcement of plastics for a variet of structural applications, from boats to rockets.

Salvaged materials are becoming increasingly important; approximatel 20 per cent of the wool used today is reprocessed. It is used in rugs, blar kets, felt hats, etc. Cotton rags are used for making high-quality pape

Synthetic fabrics can simulate the qualities of almost all other fabric They are being used more and more because of their low cost and eas of processing. They are durable and easily cleaned. Synthetic fibers ar ringing new and far better properties to textiles, such as resistance to vear, rot, shrinking, humidity, and fungi. In addition, synthetics are nore uniform and often process better.

In purchasing synthetics, the use to which they will be put should be ept in mind. Nylon is affected by heat and caustic fumes; cotton is affected by acids which do not damage wool fabrics.

WHAT BUSINESSES CAN BENEFIT FROM VALUE ANALYSIS?

or All Sizes and Types of Businesses

Problems will vary somewhat according to the size of the business. The ollowing suggestions, based on experience in dealing with a variety of ases, will serve as a guide in solving the problems that may arise.

1. Start with simple items and progress to the biggest ones. One recalls hat major league ball players all started on the sand lots.
2. Everyone in the "job environment" should be given an understanding of value analysis activity. Value work is integrated into existing funcions and into each man's ideas of his own job so that he will become a elper rather than a competitor.
3. It is necessary to make sure that engineering, manufacturing, and ther management personnel understand the reason for the interest in *unction*. Think function, talk function, and demonstrate function to supliers and others.
4. Specific examples are used for teaching. Avoid generalities which ome from adding examples together. Avoid examples that prove emarrassing to certain individuals. (It is far better to use examples of a imilar nature but ones with which the personnel have not been identied. However, in the smaller businesses especially, this may not always e possible.)
5. One does not press to hard for immediate results. Instead, one mainains professional perseverance, while giving people time to think differntly and to change attitudes where necessary. Some people take longer han others to accept change. Work first with those who most readily ccept and understand the different and the new. Then, as the new way radually becomes the normal way, others will accept it.
6. The smart buyer avoids being a "credit grabber." Instead he takes ositive steps to show that the opposite is the case.

or Small Businesses

The greatest problems that might arise in the case of small businesses em from two causes: First, lack of competent, active leadership, the kind that is necessary to keep other pressures from gradually forcing good value work into the background of men's minds. Second, making value analysis a part-time job. It then is often reduced to a token effort by the pressure of everyday duties. Good analyzing of values, while extremely profitable and beneficial to the company, does not force its own deadline and is consequently pushed aside for the jobs that require immediate attention. In order to overcome these problems, the small business may profitably be guided by these procedures:

1. Choose a member of top management to promote and support the work of analyzing values. He should establish a value analysis program, organize it with sufficient authority to ensure results, and provide for periodic review and measurement of progress.
2. Secure an understanding that designated individuals will spend a certain percentage of their time in analyzing value.
3. Establish a self-training program so that those assigned responsibility will develop knowledge, understanding, and ability.
4. List the men in all functions of the organization from the foreman or equivalent on up. Determine what each man should know about evaluation techniques and value analysis work and then form groups according to similar needs. Make effective plans to see that each group receives the required teaching and information.
5. Put emphasis on value analysis work by means of special comments, awards, promotions, etc., so that, like any other essential activity, its importance becomes increasingly recognized by all.

For Medium-sized Businesses

1. Follow item 1 for "Small Businesses."
2. Select a qualified man and assign value analysis work to him as a full-time job. He should combine talent, training, experience, and ability in purchasing with the same characteristics in either engineering or manufacturing. Ideally, he should have these qualifications:
   - Experience in engineering or methods and planning, supported by a general understanding of the properties of materials and their uses.
   - A good creative imagination.
   - Enough initiative and organizational skill to push a job through to completion with little or no supervision.
   - An appreciation of the importance of value.
   - The ability to get along well with others.
   - From three to thirty years of work experience.
3. Follow item 4 for "Small Businesses."

4. Make the most effective proportionment of time and effort among these four areas:
   - Integration (with other activities of the company).
   - Evaluation (of whatever costs money—particular products, processes, or services).
   - Consultation (assistance when requested by others on specific items).
   - Education (to constantly increase the value content of original designs, original tooling, etc.).
5. Provide an activity report every two months.

For Large Businesses

1. Follow item 1 for "Small Businesses."
2. Provide three men for value analysis work full time. (Others may be added as needs arise and as results are proved.) One man should have excellent talents, training, abilities, and experience in purchasing, the second should have the same in engineering, and the third in manufacturing. They should have the qualifications listed in item 2 for "Medium-sized Businesses."
3. Have the men work near each other. Appoint one as the leader responsible for the activity. From an accounting standpoint the three men may be on the payrolls of three functions (purchasing, engineering, and manufacturing) until they have proved themselves and established their work as a separate function.
4. Follow item 4 for "Small Businesses."
5. Follow items 4 and 5 for "Medium-sized Businesses."

General

Some purchasing agents extend the value analysis technique to office routine in order to make more man-hours available for concentrated value analysis toward the procurement of materials, supplies, etc. Time savers pointing in that direction include:

1. More blanket orders, especially for MRO orders
2. A cash purchasing system for rush MRO needs
3. Traveling requisitions
4. Purchase order draft payment system
5. Processing of invoices transferred to accounting
6. Expediting simplified by mandatory reports from suppliers on order balances
7. Delegating, after analysis, the maximum amount of routine work from buyers to clerical personnel
8. Greatest of all, eliminating unnecessary reports and similar paper work

Value analysis considerations between the buyer and the seller add or increase many benefits.

1. It is the "service" factor in the buyer's trilogy of quality, price, and service.
2. It is a fundamental requirement in establishing reliability of supply and acceptability of sources.
3. It is a new technique and formula for selecting and rating vendors.
4. It gives tremendous impetus to the important public relations aspects of purchasing.

It is summarized in the maxims that a good vendor list is the buyer's greatest asset, and that the right buying decision is all wrapped up in selection of the vendor.

This section on value analysis is offered not as the *last word* on the subject, but as a starting point. The job of value analysis must go beyond this section and, when it does, the lists of handbooks, standards, trade shows, etc., presented in the following references, will serve as the beginning of a better knowledge of this subject and the job.

REFERENCES: VALUE ANALYSIS TECHNIQUES[6]

Handbooks for Useful Supporting Knowledge

American Society of Tool and Manufacturing Engineers: *Manufacturing Planning and Estimating Handbook,* McGraw-Hill Book Company, New York

"Army-Navy Material Specifications," Superintendent of Documents, Government Printing Office, Washington, D.C.

Maynard, H. B.: *Industrial Engineering Handbook,* McGraw-Hill Book Company, New York

The Metals Handbook, American Society for Metals, 7301 Euclid Avenue, Cleveland, Ohio

Miner, Douglas F., and John B. Scastone: *Handbook of Engineering Materials,* John Wiley & Sons, Inc., New York

Society of Plastics Industry: *Plastics Engineering Handbook,* Reinhold Publishing Corporation, New York

Books, Films, and Teaching Aids

BOOKS AND MAGAZINES

Cutting Costs by Analyzing Values, National Association of Purchasing Agents, New York, 1952

Department of Defense Value Engineering Handbook, Government Printing Office, Washington, D.C., 1963

[6] See Section 26, which lists other books.

alcon, W. D.: *Value Analysis, Value Engineering: The Implications for Managers,* American Management Association, New York, 1965

Iandelkorn, R. S.: *Value Engineering 1959,* Reinhold Publishing Corporation, New York

——: *Value Engineering, Volume II,* Reinhold Publishing Corporation, New York

Iiles, L. D.: *Techniques of Value Analysis and Engineering,* McGraw-Hill Book Company, New York, 1961

ierce, Wilbur J.: *Value Analysis, Guide to Purchasing,* National Association of Purchasing Agents, New York, 1965

urchasing, Conover-Mast Publications, New York. In May or June of nearly each year since 1950, *Purchasing* has devoted an entire issue to value analysis and engineering.

alue Analysis—An Aid for the Buyer, National Association of Purchasing Agents, New York, 1960

alue Engineering Weekly, Industry Reports, Inc., Washington, D.C.

LMS

The Evaluation of Function, Cost and Worth," Merit Film Productions, Mission Hills, Calif.

The Search for Savings," Industrial Education Films, Princeton, N.J.

/alue Analysis in Action," National Association of Purchasing Agents, New York

:ACHING AIDS

ellen, J. S.: "A Two-Hour Introduction to Value Analysis" (Instructor's Manual and Trainee's Workbook), *Value Engineering Weekly,* Industry Reports, Inc., Washington, D.C.

'alue Analysis: An Advanced Purchasing Technique" (Slide Script Presentation), National Association of Purchasing Agents, New York

andards

nerican Standards Association, 70 East 45th Street, New York, N.Y.

des and Regulations

bbott, A. L.: *National Electrical Code Handbook,* 9th ed., McGraw-Hill Book Company, New York, 1957

uilding Codes," National Board of Fire Underwriters, New York

ade Shows, Conventions, and Meetings

Practically all important industrial groups hold trade shows or conven-
ns. At the trade shows, the members of an industry display their wares d attempt to draw interested buyers to the show in order to build up eir interest and, if possible, make sales. At the trade show, exhibitors splay their latest products and have their engineering and sales per-

sonnel available to discuss the product as it may apply to the purchaser's industry. In many cases the purchasing agent can actually operate or participate in a demonstration of the product. It offers the purchasing agent an opportunity to visit the exhibits of the important manufacturers in an industry group and to obtain literature, specifications, and price information.

The convention is usually a meeting of trade associations or professional groups designed primarily as a forum for the exchange of ideas. Many conventions arrange to have display space for the display of equipment and products of interest to members. Such conventions are ideal places for a supplier to show his line to a concentrated group of interested prospects and offers the purchasing agent an opportunity to find out about new products and suppliers. A list of sources of information in regard to trade shows, conventions, and meetings follows.

Sales Meeting (magazine) has a listing of sales meetings, conventions, and trade shows. Published quarterly by Meetings, Inc., 386 Fourth Avenue, New York, N.Y. 10016

Another source of information in regard to shows and exhibits is prepared by Exhibits Advisory Council, Inc., 39 Cortland Street, New York, N.Y. 10007

Still another source is Deutsch and Shea, Inc., 230 West 41st Street, New York, N.Y. 10036

SECTION 12

FORECASTING AND FORWARD BUYING

Editor

E. F. Andrews, Vice-president–Purchases, Allegheny Ludlum Steel Corporation, Pittsburgh, Pennsylvania

Associate Editors

D. G. Donovan, Director of Purchases, Pepperell Manufacturing Company, A Division of West Point–Pepperell, Inc., Boston, Massachusetts

A. L. Froehlich, Manager of Purchases, Illinois Tool Works Inc., Chicago, Illinois

It is difficult to pinpoint exactly the time at which a purchase might be classified as forward buying as contrasted with buying for immediate needs and for immediate delivery. The term could well have different meanings to different people. Generally speaking, however, it refers to the time or timing element in connection with a purchase, a time or times in the future when the several parts or all of a purchase will be shipped or delivered, title will transfer to the buyer, and terms will become effective. Forward buying, then, is the purchase of commodities and/or services for future delivery and/or performance under agreed conditions including the element of price.

REASONS FOR FORWARD BUYING

Brief comment may be desirable as to the reasons for treatment of this subject, as well as reasons for considering forward buying—in other words—why practice forward buying. There are a variety of reasons. There may be a desire to ensure future continuity of supply, projected or anticipated production, and sales. Obviously another reason would be to protect price structure paid over a longer than usual period of time. This is not without the element of risk which will be treated later. It might be considered as a safeguard of a standard or a quality. Because of seasonal requirements or seasonal production (largely agricultural and forest products) it is often necessary to resort to forward buying. In some instances, forward buying might be requested, entirely reasonably, by a supplier as assistance to him in planning production, facilities, and expansion, possibly resulting in improvement of service, quality, or price to the buyer.

There is a much broader reason for considering this subject quit thoroughly in this handbook. The entire scope of the activity of a purchasing agent or a director of purchases can be divided into *present* an *future*. For the *present*, he organizes and administers a department, supplies current requirements for materials and services, and seeks top value in what he buys through adequate specifications, competition, reasonabl volumes, and substitute materials. As much as a half of his job deals wit the *future*, and it is in this area that he really becomes a part of management.

Management plans for the future, and in this sense forward buying i an essential part of the purchasing executive's management responsibi ity. He has the responsibility of knowing at all times the long-ter conditions and trends in price and the supply levels of the items whic his company uses. He must recognize and forecast economic trend natural conditions, and the effect of political situations on his supp lines, so that sound forward buying decisions can be made.

Under these circumstances, it can be seen that forward buying becomes not a *method* but really the heart of the procurement function and an important part of total company planning for profit. It can well be the area where purchasing is really doing a purchasing job and can make its greatest contribution to the profits, growth, or condition of a company. Forward buying can, of course, be practiced in connection with any commodity, material, component, assembly, or other item, although in this instance, reference is made generally to commodities and raw materials –items that bulk large in importance and basic to any finished product.

TYPES OF FORWARD BUYING

In a general sense, all buying is forward, since receipt of goods is at some date after order placement. However, "hand-to-mouth" or "quick turnover" of material is not what is being discussed in this section. Forward buying falls generally into two categories. The first is that of purchases being made to meet a definite, known production schedule. In the second category are those purchases being made in anticipation of future, presently unscheduled, production. It is not our intention to discuss speculation on the commodity market under this heading. The usual connotation of the term speculation is that of an end rather than a means, the end being to make a profit by selling the commodity itself. Such decisions are not usually the sole responsibility of the purchasing executive but involve, rather, a management prerogative to choose between alternative investment opportunities. While dealing in futures is practiced in certain types of industry, it is not normally an industrial purchasing executive's concern and will not be discussed here. The Commodity Exchange, the seven industrial materials traded on the Exchange, and the practice of hedging to minimize the risk are discussed later.

Under the first classification above, that of forward buying to supply only a definite production schedule, the advantages might be to fix a firm price of raw materials or to ensure an adequate supply. Generally speaking, delivery of this type of purchase would be reasonably close. Quantity would be based on actual orders on hand for production. The main reason for separating this from those purchases made in anticipation of orders is the somewhat lower risk involved. At least there exists an assurance that the material can and will be used. Comparatively little planning is necessary on this. However, in arranging schedules of delivery, inventory carrying charges must be taken into consideration.

The subject of price is another matter. Under most circumstances, the only sure way of definitely being assured of a firm price is to take delivery or at least to own title to the material. In a few industries it is common practice to adjust prices downward if other related prices in that market decrease, but still maintain the contract price as a maximum if prices increase. These are probably the exception. In most cases, contracts or future orders are priced at a firm price, as negotiated or current as of the date of the contract, or at prices in effect at time of delivery. Obviously the cost of carrying inventory must be weighed against market factors under some of these circumstances, and also the need and importance for firm prices or price protection according to the manner in which the finished product is sold.

Largely the discussion that follows will relate more in detail to the second type, as it is in this category where the greatest potential risk exists, and since there is generally a need for the consideration of many more factors and possibilities than in the first type.

It should be emphasized that all forward buying involves more risks of one kind or another than buying nominal quantities at fixed price for immediate or prompt delivery. While the contents of this section may not be entirely complete, the purpose is to call attention to as many pitfalls and measures of protection as possible. In the final analysis, forward buying is almost entirely a matter of taking calculated risks, balancing and weighing the various factors and possibilities.

COST OF CARRYING INVENTORY[1]

Forward buying may involve an increase in inventory. This cost must then be taken into consideration as part of the cost of performing forward buying. Since this can be a substantial part of cost over and above any costs due to loss or gain through price movements, it must not be overlooked. Such costs will vary among industries and materials, and thus they must be figured in the light of any particular situation. A recent survey of costs of carrying inventory of purchased or unworked materials ranged from an annual 10 per cent of the value of that inventory to 35 per cent, with the average about 20 per cent, slightly under 2 per cent per month. It is obvious that any possible price advantage gained through forward buying can be considerably reduced by this inventory carrying cost factor. If a loss incurs, this cost must be added to the loss.

According to the above survey, the elements of cost most generally considered are:

1. Interest
2. Taxes
3. Insurance
4. Rent—space

[1] See Section 13, "Quantity Determination through Inventory Management."

5. Stores operation
6. Depreciation–deterioration
7. Obsolescence
8. Purchasing

The assembly of this information is generally accomplished by the accounting department. It is usually expressed in terms of a percentage of the value of the material being stored. In isolated instances, it may be well to state this cost in terms of a physical unit of the material, which will lead to a more exact figure. The intent of the above figures are based on a cross section of all materials. Obviously, storage costs of lightweight materials, such as cloth, will be quite different from steel bars, which will vary from steel shapes or castings (see range of costs in Table 29–16). At the same time, unit value, another factor in calculating carrying costs, will deviate for various materials. Figures for cost of carrying inventory will therefore differ by industry, company, commodity, and time, to mention but a few variables.

It should be noted that inventory carrying costs are usually not figured on the total amount of a purchase, but on the average inventory or an average increment of inventory. For instance, if the cost of carrying inventory is figured on the value of a given purchase, the value of this purchase is never 100 per cent inventory after the time that the first withdrawal is made. When only 10 per cent of the purchase remains on hand, the inventory charges are considerably less than when the lot was first received.

While the terms used above appear to be self-explanatory, some explanation might be of interest.

Interest. While working capital is invested in inventory, it is not available for other purposes. Since this conceivably could lead to an increased need of borrowing or the loss of interest on invested funds, some similar charge must be applied against the additional inventory.

Taxes. In areas where inventories are taxed, as inventories or as personal property, an additional quantity of inventory may invite added tax charges.

Insurance. If insurance is necessary on the material bought ahead, this is a necessary charge against the advantages or savings of forward buying.

Rent—Space. Added inventory means added storage space requirements. This might take the form of actual rent paid for space for the increased inventory or perhaps charges at a more nominal rate when it takes space away from other materials or functions that lead to inefficiencies. In some cases, charges for such incidentals as refrigeration, heating, and other necessary special conditions, etc., might need to be included.

Stores Operation. Aside from the paper work necessary to record the material placed in inventory, there can be actual additional labor costs due to the need for physical inventorying of the material. The stores responsibility is increased in one manner or another; there must be extra costs in this area.

Depreciation—Deterioration. Generally speaking, depreciation charges will be negligible, but deterioration possibilities, through shrinkage and spoilage, are very real. This will, of course, depend considerably on the type of material.

Obsolescence. More than likely, any possibility of obsolescence will have been discounted at the time the decision to purchase is made. It is inconceivable that any substantial forward purchase would be made in the face of any obsolescence possibility, but this should not be overlooked in calculating the costs of carrying extra inventories.

Purchasing. This is a real cost in any inventory, although it is very possible that in buying ahead, purchasing costs may be a credit rather than a debit against carrying costs. This is particularly true if more than the usual quantity or coverage was purchased, since expenses and time of negotiation and of processing orders will be substantially the same for 100,000 pounds or 500,000 pounds.

ECONOMIC TRENDS, MARKETS, PRICES

The most important single factor in forward buying is economic forecasting in the particular commodity in question. Economics is not an exact science and so economic forecasting cannot be exact. However, it is probable that the accuracy of the forecasting will be in direct proportion to the effort and time spent in securing background on a commodity or material and in the completeness in considering all factors.

In this area, as in many types of purchasing, the maintenance of *good vendor relations* is basic. Maintaining such relations keeps a buyer in a position to secure valuable information relating to the current and future price movement and availability of materials, not only as related to an individual company but to that industry as a whole. The interest of the buyer and seller in market conditions, price trends, and supply cannot be separated. This is one of several sources of information to assist in economic forecasting.

The more obvious sources of information are through *economic surveys and forecasts* made by private agencies, trade papers, and government bureaus. These cover a specific range of materials, as well as broad economic predictions and forecasts.

Sources of Economic Data

Some of the various sources of economic information available are listed below. Their suitability to your specific problems will vary. Generally speaking, they have been found to be suitable and helpful in economic analyses.

1. The NAPA "Business Survey Report"[2] published monthly in the NAPA *Bulletin*.
2. Economic data and commodity indices published periodically in the NAPA *Bulletin*.[2]
3. *Economic Indicators* published monthly for the Joint Economic Committee by the Council of Economic Advisers, U.S. Government Printing Office.
4. *Survey of Current Business,* U.S. Department of Commerce, Office of Business Economics, published monthly.
5. *Business Cycle Developments,* U.S. Department of Commerce, Bureau of the Census, published monthly.
6. Commodity data by purchasing executives and outside experts as reported in the NAPA *Bulletin* on coal, containers, fuel oil, lumber, nonferrous metals, paper, steel, textiles, and others.[2]

Needless to say, there are many other private and industrial sources of economic data available on request.

Factors Influencing Decisions

The background secured can be just as voluminous as desired, and again it is emphasized that the thoroughness with which information is gathered and analyzed will have a direct relationship to the wisdom of the decisions.

Some of the factors that may be examined in order to arrive at a decision on the desirability of forward buying are enumerated below.

Price. The price, of course, is one of the most important factors of concern. An examination of past price trends may give certain clues as to the behavior of prices in the future. The important thing is to examine the underlying reasons for past price activities. Examination and analysis of movements and the reasons for them will not necessarily provide the answer to probable future trends, but it may be helpful in determining the magnitude and general direction of price swings and whether future changes will be erratic, leisurely, violent, inflationary, or deflationary.

Supply and Demand. Price cannot be separated from the supply-and-

[2] Survey printed monthly in NAPA *Bulletin,* available to members only. The official title of this periodical is *The Bulletin of the National Association of Purchasing Agents,* published weekly except during the summer months.

demand picture of a given material, as supply and demand will have a definite effect on price. It is important to have basic information about the over-all industry productive capacity and consumption. If natural resources of a material are plentiful, then examination of other factors affecting the flow to the marketplace is essential. If basic quantity of supply is limited, then studies regarding substitutes and the development of additional sources must be made.

Technological Change. It is important to examine the history of a commodity to see the frequency of technological change that has occurred. An item that is changing quite rapidly should not be committed too far in the future, as such a commitment will undoubtedly lead to excessive obsolescence.

Number and Location of Suppliers. The number and location of suppliers of a given commodity will have a bearing on your future buying decisions. A commodity with many reliable suppliers located close at hand need not be committed as far in the future as a commodity with few suppliers located at greater distances from your production facility. The size and financial stability of these suppliers should also be taken into your consideration.

Labor Conditions. If the commodity under consideration is being produced by an industry fraught with frequent labor instability, then close attention to labor contracts and awareness of the possibility of interrupted work schedules are necessary in order to make sound forward buying decisions.

Transportation. Transportation considerations will bear upon the amount of inventory being carried and the length of forward commitment. The best example of this is the relationship of iron ore, brought in by lake boats, to the steel industry. Due to weather conditions and freezing in the lake area, delivery cannot be assured during the winter months. The forward buying problems of such a situation are obvious.

Government Action. Possible government actions must be considered, particularly if the commodity is an item in the government stockpile or an item affected by import-export regulations.

Cost of Possession. The cost of ownership (discussed elsewhere in this book) will have a bearing upon the length into the future of your inventories. Affecting this will be the cost of storage itself (for example, refrigerated storage) or the perishability of the commodity under consideration.

International Politics. If the commodity under consideration is a vulnerable material with its source in a foreign country, one must be kept informed of the international political situation regarding the country controlling this commodity. Recent examples are the problems of copper buyers when the flare-up in the Congo occurred and the loss to nickel buyers of their nickel supply in Cuba.

These and other considerations must all have a bearing on forward buying policy.

How to Forecast

A classical theory, now considered by some to be old-fashioned, is that business trends move in cycles. An examination of the history of almost any indicator will reveal a certain rhythm; and, in retrospect, one cannot deny the existence of a certain number of cyclical influences. However, one must remember that in the past our economy was smaller and much less complicated than modern commercial activity, with its sophisticated interrelationship of supply, demand, price, and political influences.

Fundamental to economic forecasting are analysis of trends and measurement of change. Available indicators fall into two basic categories. One is the actual measurement of given statistical data and the subsequent analysis is of the trends indicated and the degree of change. The second is the so-called "opinion survey" as used by the National Association of Purchasing Agents in its "Business Survey Report." The forecaster must pick the indicators most suited to the type of forecasting he is planning. It must be recognized that certain indicators will lead, while others will lag behind economic turning points. It is suggested that more than one indicator be used, since even the most reliable and accurate of economic indicators will misbehave at times.

After the indicator has been selected, the next step is to examine and thoroughly understand the makeup of the data used in the indicator—where it comes from, what influences it, and how reliable the sources for gathering the information are. Examination as to whether it is seasonally adjusted or what other adjustments may be applicable is suggested. This should then be followed by a series of tests for the accuracy of the indicator. Historical examination of the behavior of the indicator at times of change is most important. Accuracy measurements on indicators are sometimes available.[3]

Once the effectiveness of an indicator is established, the next step is to examine its timeliness. Unless the indicator will give more information and point the direction in time for decisions, it is useless.

When the group of indicators to be used has been selected, tested, and proven, an examination must be made of its sensitivity to various outside influences such as political situations, labor, weather, etc. When this is completed, we are finally ready to address ourselves to the forecast. By

[3] A report on the effectiveness of the NAPA "Business Survey Report" is available through the National Association of Purchasing Agents.

analyzing the trends or plotting the opinions, making allowances for the current outside influences and examining past behavior, reasonably accurate forecasts can be developed. Generally, it is not wise to accept the popular view without question, since the behavior of individual industries may, at times, be completely opposite to the general direction.

It must be remembered that the indicators discussed above furnish information; they do not make decisions. This is where the knowledge and judgment of the individual are brought to bear. It must also be remembered that all accurate, widely read, influential economic forecasting is self-defeating if corrective measures are taken in time by enough people. Nevertheless, past experience has proved that the time and effort spent in intelligently and accurately forecasting future business conditions is a rewarding personal experience and is usually profitable to you and your company.

COMPANY INDICES

Having selected the services, indices, and economic indicators to watch, a buyer should be able to determine the economic trend that will affect price. At best this is an over-all picture and may or may not be applicable to a particular business. As an example, an index on nonferrous metals contains all the metals in that group. These metals do not usually move together pricewise. Tin may be up due to foreign economic conditions. At the same time, lead and zinc may be down due to supply-and-demand conditions in the United States.

Then, too, the weight of the individual metals in the group index might be, and probably is, entirely different from the weights by use of the buyer, even though he buys some of all of the metals in the nonferrous group. A number of purchasing agents, in order to check their over-all price movements, have successfully developed an index weighted to the company use similar to Fig. 12–1, Price Index Weighted to Individual Company Use.

1. First list the dollar value of important materials purchased for a period (Example: the year 1948).
2. Determine a minimum point value for the materials to be included in the index (Example: $50,000).
3. Weight the materials to be used by the point value determined (see column 2), i.e., having purchased $3,000,000 of copper in 1948, 3,000,000 ÷ 50,000 = 60 weight points in the index for copper.
4. Next determine the percentage of each commodity weighted to the total weight points in column 2, i.e., copper has 60 points of a total of 256. Equals 23 per cent of the index of 100 (see column 3).

(1) Commodity	(2) Weight points based on $50,000	(3) Index per cent of weight points	(4) Prices Jan. 1, 1949	(5) Prices July 1, 1949	(6) Change from January base	(7) Per cent change from January base	(8) Index point change
1. Copper	60	23	23.5	16	7.50	32	7.36
2. Zinc	16	6.2	18.5	10	8.50	46	2.75
3. Lead	29	11.5	21.5	12	9.50	44	5.06
4. Coal	12.5	5	12.05	10.75	1.31	10.6	0.53
	256	100%					27.49
						July 1 Index:	72.51

FIG. 12–1. Price index weighted to individual company use.

5. List the market prices of the index materials as of the first of the month in which the index is started; in this case January 1, 1949, was used (see column 4).
6. The first of each month thereafter list the current market prices of the index materials (see column 5). List as in column 6 the amount of change, plus or minus, from the starting index prices.
7. Determine the percentages or price changes (see column 7), i.e., copper having dropped from 23½ cents in January to 16 cents in July, a decrease of 7½ cents, the per cent of reduction in copper is 32 per cent.
8. Then determine the index point change in each material in the index by multiplying the index points (column 3) by the percentage price change (column 7) and arrive at the index point change (column 8). Thus copper, being 23 per cent of the weighted index of 100, has a percentage decrease over the period of 32 per cent; $.32 \times 23 = 7.36$, which is the number of points by which the starting index of 100 is reduced by price reductions in that commodity.

Listing all the changes in column 8, plus and minus, and subtracting the pluses from the minuses, will give the net change in the index (see column 8). Here all the price changes in the 24 commodities selected for the index, from January 1 to July 1, work out to a net point reduction as of July 1 of 27.49, establishing the index as of that date at 72.51.

PLANNING WITHIN THE COMPANY

It is obvious that any decision to buy materials for longer than normal periods into the future must be accompanied by a certain amount of planning and preparation within the company. Reference to the need for price and availability forecasting has already been made. It is important that a policy be established on approvals for forward buying of any substantial quantity of materials. While the purchasing department investigates and develops the program, and while such activity is considered a real and important part of the purchasing function, it is generally recognized that other areas of management must have a voice in final decisions. Large purchases could ultimately affect all other departments of the business, if not carefully planned and executed. The financial officer's counseling on availability of funds and the production and sales departments' forecasts of probable need must be weighed in order to maximize total return on total investment. Time for planning within the company for such investments is essential.

TYPES OF CONTRACTS

In a discussion of planning for this phase of purchasing, the subject of contracts and types of contracts must be considered. It would not be reasonable or plausible to expect that enumeration here of suggestions to cope with all situations or circumstances would be possible, but a partial check list is presented below. Obviously some of the required provisions will relate to factors already discussed, i.e., the reasons forward buying is being done, the type of market, current market conditions, competitive conditions, etc. For this reason, the comments below follow no order of importance. In many instances, there will be little choice on the part of the buyer, since a standard form of contract will be in use by a whole industry. However, it is always possible to try to negotiate a contract that is desirable to the buyer in every respect.

Price.[4] Since price can be a major reason for forward purchasing, it is obvious that a considerable amount of thought is necessary to secure proper price conditions on the contract. The most desirable terms from the buyer's viewpoint would be a *fixed price, with price protection,* i.e., downward adjustment in case of general market decline. This will depend to a great degree on the type of market and the supplier's position in that market. Under a price clause of this type the buyer can hardly lose, except by scheduling deliveries in a manner that leads to higher than optimum inventory. The next best choice would be a *fixed price for the life of the contract.* It is here that background of the price movement of the commodity and other price information is most necessary in forming a judgment to determine the probable price trend. The least desirable would be an *escalator price clause,* allowing for increases in price according to the then existing market.

COMMODITY EXCHANGES—HEDGING

The operations of the commodity exchanges and hedging are subjects too big, having many ramifications and divergencies, to brief in a purchasing handbook. Presenting case histories of deals will not be very useful, as two deals are seldom exactly alike in purpose, timing, quantity, and market conditions. The use of these markets is a job for a specialist. Like the stock market, it is no place for an amateur. No standard formula exists for all dealing. The formula must be tailored by *competent specialists* to the particular needs of the buyer for a particular deal. A

[4] Also see Section 9, "Pricing Considerations."

popular misconception of the uninitiated is that trading in commodity futures on the exchanges and operating hedges will eliminate all price risk. There is no such guarantee; in fact, a poorly managed deal can result in a loss.

Of the thirty-odd commodities traded on the exchanges, only seven are industrial materials: copper, cotton, lead, zinc, tin, hides, and rubber. The others are mostly agricultural products, and while many of them are of interest to industries, as processors, they are of no interest to the average industrial buyer. The bulk of the agricultural product trades are known as "trade" or "merchant" deals, and they far outweigh any industrial interest in the market.

However, the judicious, well-planned use of the commodity exchange services can minimize some price risks. A buyer contemplating the use of these markets will do well to consult a member of the Exchange, an expert in trading in the commodity of interest, tell him the problem and desired result, and make a decision based on expert advice.

Of the commodities traded, cotton may well be classed as the major item. Despite the inroads of synthetic fibers, cotton still outranks all other fibers used in the huge world-wide textile industries. Its production is the economic backlog of many areas of the United States and many more countries. Its fabrication into finished products is said to have built and maintained more American communities than any other single commodity.

The largest and possibly the oldest exchange (founded in 1870) is the New York Cotton Exchange. They have published a booklet, "Cotton and Cotton Futures," covering the operation of the Exchange and the methods used to secure price insurance.

In the fabricating of cotton into finished products, we can find all the conditions facing material procurement found in the types of forward buying discussed in the early part of this section. From the time cotton is baled until it is processed into a finished product may run into six months or more. The fabricator may have to take a position even before the cotton is harvested.

An example of how he may ensure against price fluctuation by hedging is illustrated in Fig. 12–2, Example of Production Hedge by Mill Pending Cloth Sale, taken from the New York Cotton Exchange booklet mentioned above. To better understand the example (Fig. 12–2), the following should be kept in mind.

Hedging means that a business making a transaction (buying or selling) will, at the same time, make an opposite transaction (selling or buying cotton futures). As prices may fluctuate thereafter, a profit in the actual transaction will be offset by a corresponding loss in the futures, or

Date	Price per pound	Total price
Sept. 15—Manufacturer buys 500 bales of Middling 1 inch cotton needed for early use at 200 points on December, New York, for prompt shipment. He immediately "fixes" the price; i.e., pays the current price of December futures of 23.60¢ plus 200 points or....................	25.60¢	$64,000.00
The 250,000 pounds of cotton so purchased will make about 850,000 yards of the cloth he is manufacturing, weighing about 212,500 pounds. The 37,500 pounds difference between cotton weight and cloth weight represents tare and manufacturing waste, but part of the waste loss is recoverable by sale of the waste. The manufacturer calculates that his costs including cost of cotton after waste allowance, manufacturing, sales, and other expenses, will be 51¢ per pound for the 212,500 cloth pounds, or $108,375.00. While he thinks the cloth should be worth 52¢ a pound, giving him 1¢ a pound or $2,125.00 profit, the cloth market is dormant and he can make no satisfactory sale. Therefore, simultaneously on—		
Sept. 15—He sells 500 bales of December, New York, futures at.........	23.60¢	59,000.00
Nov. 10—Cotton and cloth prices have fallen. Demand for cloth is better. The manufacturer having the 212,500 pounds of cloth ready for sale is offered 50¢ a pound. He sells it at...........................	50.00¢	106,250.00
Nov. 10—Simultaneously he buys in the 500 bale hedge in New York December futures at.......................................	21.60¢	54,000.00

* * *

Results of the manufacturer's hedged operation follow:

Cotton and Cloth		Cotton Futures	
Total cost (51¢ per cloth pound) of production and sale of 212,500 pounds of cloth, including cost of 250,000 pounds of Middling inch cotton bought, with waste loss adjusted for amount realized on waste resale................	$108,375.00	500 bales sold at...............	$59,000.00
Received for cloth............	106,250.00	500 bales bought at.............	54,000.00
		Gain on futures..............	$ 5,000.00
		*Less commissions.............	87.50
Loss..................	$ 2,125.00	Profit....................	$ 4,912.50

Manufacturer's net profit (futures gain less loss on manufacturing operation) ....$ 2,787.50

Manufacturer operated his plant successfully in a difficult market, kept employees at work, and profited, where had he not hedged he would have lost $2,125.00 net.

* Member rate.

By permission from "Cotton and Cotton Futures," The New York Cotton Exchange, 60 Beaver St., New York City.

FIG. 12–2. Example of production hedge by mill pending cloth sale. (*From "Cotton and Cotton Futures," New York Cotton Exchange.*)

a loss in the actual transaction will be offset by a profit in the futures. The risk of price change is thus reduced to a minimum.

There are several grades of cotton. The base price on all exchange transactions is "middling grade," as shown in the example. Higher or lower grades may be delivered at the buyer's option by paying premiums or receiving discounts. The figures used are arbitrary, not an actual transaction, and are only intended to demonstrate the hedging principle.

The example assumes a declining cotton market with losses offset by profits in futures. If it were a rising market, the hedger would profit on spot cotton, and its products, and lose on futures. The buyer using a hedge operation eliminates the chance of a large profit to ensure the business against the risk of a large loss.

SELECTED BIBLIOGRAPHY

Abramson, Adolph G., and Russell H. Mack: *Business Forecasting in Practice: Principles and Cases,* John Wiley & Sons, Inc., New York, 1956

Bratt, Elmer Clark: *Business Cycles and Forecasting,* 5th ed., Richard D. Irwin, Inc., Homewood, Ill., 1961

Chambers, Edward J.: *Economic Fluctuations and Forecasting,* Prentice-Hall, Inc., Englewood Cliffs, N.J., 1961

Lee, Maurice W.: *Macroeconomics: Fluctuation, Growth and Stability,* 3d ed., Richard D. Irwin, Inc., Homewood, Ill., 1963

McKinley, David H., Murray G. Lee, and Helene Duffy: *Forecasting Business Conditions,* The American Bankers Association, New York, 1965

Newgarden, Albert: *Evaluation and Using Business Indicators,* AMA Management Report No. 25, American Management Association, Inc., New York, 1959

Shiskin, Julius, *Signals of Recession and Recovery,* Occasional Paper 77, National Bureau of Economic Research, New York, 1961

Spencer, Milton A., *et al.: Business and Economic Forecasting: An Econometric Approach,* Richard D. Irwin, Inc., Homewood, Ill., 1961

SECTION 13

QUANTITY DETERMINATION THROUGH INVENTORY MANAGEMENT

Editor

Ira G. Fox, formerly Purchasing Agent, Transformer Division, Westinghouse Electric Corporation, Sharon, Pennsylvania

Associate Editors

David Steinberg, Manager, Purchases and Materials, Lenkurt Electric Co., Inc., a subsidiary of General Telephone & Electronics Corp., San Carlos, California

A. M. Kennedy, Jr., Vice-president, Divisions General Manager, Specialty Products Group,[1] Westinghouse Research & Development Center, Pittsburgh, Pennsylvania

W. A. Coates, Director of Purchases, Westinghouse Electric Corporation, Metuchen, New Jersey

[1] Formerly Vice-president, Purchases & Traffic, Westinghouse Electric Corporation, ittsburgh, Pennsylvania.

The importance of the inventory portion of the total financial investment of a business enterprise can never be overstated. The influence which the size of inventories has upon operating costs and profits is something which is too often neglected, or is completely overlooked in planning the operation of a business.

However, a successful business enterprise, large or small, industrial or retail, can continually deprive itself of substantial profit dollars, and even commit economic suicide, as a result of poor or improper inventory control. It is important to realize that inventory, which in many enterprises represents from 30 to 50 per cent of the total invested in the business, is actually dollars—the "lifeblood" of the business. These are dollars upon which the business pays insurance charges, interest, storage costs, and at the same time assumes risks of devaluation, deterioration, damage, or obsolescence.

Large inventories tie up large amounts of cash which might necessitate borrowing money at interest. A heavy inventory also increases the potential for devaluation because of unfavorable price or cost changes and loss due to design obsolescence.

On the other hand, with too little inventory, added costs of operation appear in the form of reduced manufacturing efficiency and increased overhead costs such as work stoppages, extra machine setups, short runs, and increased personnel turnover—to say nothing of the lost sales and customer good will because of inability to deliver the product.

It becomes important, therefore, that a going business determine and maintain an adequate inventory for a given volume of business which yields the greatest dollar return on the total business assets. This is *inventory control* in its fundamental meaning. Figure 13–1 shows a summary tabulation of the cost-creating factors which are affected by a condition of excessive inventory, or a condition of insufficient inventory. It is these costs which are reduced or eliminated through sound planning and control of inventory.

Area of cost	Condition *A* excessive inventory	Condition *B* insufficient inventory
I. Material costs	1. Greater risk of *loss* due to: *a.* Devaluation through changes in price or manufacturing cost *b.* Obsolete stock c. Shelf deterioration or damage	1. *Higher* prices and manufacturing costs due to small quantity "rush" orders
II. Factory costs	1. *Increase* in factory costs due to: *a.* Lack of storage space resulting in crowded floor conditions, and inefficient working conditions	1. *Increase* in factory costs due to: *a.* Work stoppages *b.* Lay-offs and rehiring—added expense of training new people c. Extra machine setups *d.* "Emergency" type of operation
III. Overhead expense	1. *Increased* overhead expense due to: *a.* Additional insurance cost *b.* Interest on cash borrowed if necessary c. Possible requirements for added storage space in the form of outside rentals 2. Loss of available cash for income-producing investments	1. *Increased* overhead expense due to: *a.* Added clerical costs in purchasing, receiving, inspection, accounting as a result of many small orders *b.* Increased handling of materials

FIG. 13–1. Inventory effects on cost of operations.

SCOPE OF INVENTORY CONTROL

But what is the scope of inventory control? It is a mistaken impression that inventory control invariably means added overhead investment in the form of people, clerical office machines, and the paper work and delays of an elaborate system. The extent and means of control must always be commensurate with the company's needs. For example, it is an erroneous conclusion that inventory is not being "controlled" in the five-man shop where the "boss" does all the planning, purchasing, and accounting. If this individual has given due consideration to the economic and other factors applicable to his business and its inventory, he is "controlling" his inventory even though all the planning and records are retained in his head. On the other hand, this enterprise may have grown during the course of years into a variety of products, or volume of production, to the point where it is necessary to publish written instructions and procedures to ensure that policies and practices are carried out which are consistent and economic. It is impossible in this situation for one man to handle properly the extent of the inventory-control problem.

In considering the scope of inventory control for minimum cost of operation, we must at this point define the classes of inventory generally found in an industrial inventory asset.

Stores inventory. Recognized generally as the stock of raw materials (such as steel, copper, etc.), and fabricated parts awaiting processing or assembly.

Work in process. Work in process includes parts in progressive stages of completion, such as raw material just issued from stores, material in various stages of processing, and parts or assemblies awaiting final acceptances as finished stock.

Finished stock. Units of the manufactured product awaiting sale or consignment.

Supplies. The expendable items which are required to manufacture the product, but do not become a part of that product, such as tools, cleaning materials, cutting oils, etc. These are commonly termed MRO, i.e., maintenance, repair, and operating supplies.

The above categories are not to be considered fixed or all-inclusive, since it is understandable that the broad classifications and the constituents of inventory will vary with the particular industry.

Because of the closer relationship of the purchasing agent to the *stores inventory,* its control, and potential cost reduction, the balance of this chapter will be devoted to techniques for control of inventory principally in this category.

Before proceeding to some of the specific techniques for control of inventory, it is necessary to have a clear understanding of the purpose of inventory and some of the factors which influence our inventory decisions.

PURPOSE OF INVENTORY

Inventory is created for two general purposes, namely, protection and economy:

1. To provide sufficient material to meet demands for the particular raw material, fabricated part, or finished product with a minimum of delay (i.e., protection)
2. To effect lower product costs by realizing the economies resulting from longer manufacturing runs, and from purchasing larger quantities per order (i.e., economy)

Although there may be a variety of individual reasons for creating inventory under a given set of circumstances, if closely examined, they will all fall into one of the two categories mentioned above.

FACTORS INFLUENCING INVENTORY

In the act of creating inventory, there are two fundamental questions which must be answered in every instance, namely:

1. How much to buy (or manufacture) at one time.
2. When to buy (or manufacture) this quantity.

Answers to these two questions must come from a proper consideration and evaluation of a number of different factors having a bearing on inventory and its control. Four of these factors are fundamental, and, without consideration for costs, could form the basis for any decision on how much to buy and when to buy. These are as follows:

1. *Requirements,* or demand, on a unit/time basis. This is based upon information from a production or sales forecast schedule.
2. *Quantity in stock and on order.* This is usually obtained from a ledger record showing a stock balance plus any open purchase or manufacturing orders for previously known requirements.
3. *Procurement time,* or lead time, is the total length of time to obtain a fresh supply of the item.
4. *Obsolescence.* Consideration must always be given to the possibility of design changes or other factors which would make the material obsolete.

If purchasing or manufacturing is to be done strictly to requirements, consideration of the above factors will be sufficient to determine "how much" and "when" to order. However, if attention is to be given to reducing inventory costs, then the following considerations must be added to the above list; namely:

1. *Ordering cost.* This includes the cost of processing the purchase order, receiving and inspection costs, freight charges, and accounts payable costs to pay the vendors' invoices.
2. *Inventory carrying cost.* This factor includes interest rate on average dollars in stock, insurance, cost of depreciation and obsolescence, and cost of storage facilities (rent, light, heat) based upon floor space of storage area, taxes, and handling costs.

While the application of these cost factors to specific control techniques will be discussed in more detail later in this section, it should be noted at this point that the proper evaluation of the ordering and carrying costs is the key to one of the largest areas for reducing cost by inventory control.

It should be readily understandable that the ordering cost, or carrying costs, will vary from industry to industry, and even between two plants in the same industry. However, the determination of these cost factors is a "must" if real "cost control" of inventory is to exist. Since these costs are the direct result of the frequency of ordering and size of inventory, proper evaluation and comparison of the ordering and carrying cost under various ordering frequencies will reveal a most economical frequency or size of order, as will be discussed later in this section.

Ordering Cost (Variable)

Computation of this cost should be based on a period of not less than one year.

Accuracy in establishing the cost elements needed to arrive at the ordering cost is essential to sound inventory policies. Determining the "fixed" and "variable" portions of this cost should be the result of careful consideration.

The following data are required:

1. Total number of purchase orders issued.
2. Labor costs (and payroll costs) for the entire purchasing department, material control, receiving, and stores. Some of these costs are fixed, whereas some will vary with the number of orders issued. For example, the purchasing agent and the senior buyers would be "fixed costs"; other purchasing department personnel would be "variable." Stockroom personnel are charged either to the cost of carrying inventory or to the cost of ordering. (Usually these costs are 75 per cent for carrying inventory and 25 per cent for ordering.)

3. Cost of supplies (expense items). These include printed forms, paper, ribbons, pencils, etc. About half of these costs would be considered variable.
4. Floorspace and maintenance. Cost of office space occupied by purchasing and material control. About 75 per cent is variable.
5. Incoming inspection. Cost of inspection personnel, of which about 25 per cent is variable.
6. Accounts payable. Labor and payroll costs. About 90 per cent variable.
7. Inbound freight. About 25 per cent of this cost item is considered variable.
8. Telephone and telegraph. About 50 per cent of these costs incurred by buying personnel are variable costs.

Once all the above cost elements have been assembled and divided between fixed and variable costs, tabulation like the following can be made.

EXAMPLE

Expenditure	Actual cost	% of actual cost	Variable cost
Labor	$400,000	60	$240,000
Supplies	18,000	50	9,000
Space–occupancy	40,000	75	30,000
Incoming inspection	100,000	25	25,000
Accounts payable	20,000	90	18,000
Inbound freight	100,000	25	25,000
Telephone and telegraph	16,000	50	8,000
Total	$694,000		$355,000

Total number of purchase orders for the year: 20,000

Actual cost per purchase order: $\frac{\$694{,}000}{20{,}000} = \$34.70$

Variable cost per purchase order: $\frac{355{,}000}{20{,}000} = \$17.75$

Average number of items per purchase order: 2.5

Variable cost per item: $\frac{\$17.75}{2.5} = \$7.10$

Inventory Carrying Cost (Variable)

Accuracy and careful consideration are again of primary importance. The following data are needed to establish the cost of owning inventory:

1. Average monthly inventory for the period (year) under review.
2. Interest. This is the current bank rate, charged for the use of money (4 to 8 per cent would seem about right). Variable 100 per cent.

3. Taxes. This may vary from state to state, but will probably be 2 to 3 per cent of average inventory. Variable 100 per cent.
4. Insurance. This, too, will vary, with a figure of 10 cents per $1,000 probably close to most rates. This, too, is a 100 per cent variable cost.
5. Obsolescence. Actual amounts of purchased material, written off as obsolete, are used here. Normally this would be between 2 and 8 per cent, and it is 100 per cent variable.
6. Shrinkage. Where this is a factor, allowance should be made for it; 1 per cent seems about the permissible maximum, and about 20 per cent of the cost would be variable.
7. Labor costs. These costs were used above in determining the cost of ordering, except for a portion of stockroom personnel. Stores people will "vary" in accordance with factory requirements (manufacturing orders), and the cost is not considered variable with inventory levels.
8. Floorspace and maintenance. The floorspace and other costs for the stores areas are usually variable 90 per cent, with 10 per cent fixed costs. This must be determined separately for each plant operation.
9. Scrap. Actual amount of scrapped (purchased) materials is a variable cost. This would normally be less than 0.5 per cent of the average inventory.

After assembling and apportioning the above cost elements, a tabulation, similar to the following, can be made.

EXAMPLE

Expenditure	Actual cost	% of actual cost	Variable costs, %
Interest on investment	$144,000	100	6
Taxes	72,000	100	3
Insurance	240	100	0.01
Obsolescence	144,000	100	6
Shrinkage	2,400	20	0.02
Labor	70,000		
Space—occupancy	80,000	90	5
Scrap	7,500	100	0.31
Total	$520,140		20.34

Average monthly inventory: $2,400,000
Variable cost (per cent) of carrying inventory = 20.34%*
Variable cost of carrying inventory: $2,400,000 × 20.34% = $488,160

* See Table 29–16 for a composite of estimates involved in carrying charges for inventory.

ORGANIZING FOR INVENTORY CONTROL

In its broadest sense, effective inventory control requires more than just the creation of a control organization and delegation of responsibilities. It encompasses three general areas of study, namely:

1. Forecasting future requirements and inventory turnover
2. Characteristics of the inventory and classification of accounts
3. Organization of manpower and delegation of responsibility

Forecasting Future Requirements and Inventory Turnover

Forecasting. If an objective survey were made of companies experiencing a serious financial condition today due to excessive investment in inventory, the dominant contributing factor would be inaccurate forecasting of future sales. The accuracy of sales forecasts as translated into production and inventory requirements decidedly affects cost of inventory and cost of factory operations. Investigation will prove that excessive inventory tends to go hand in hand with a short cash position—a particularly serious condition for any company with limited working capital. It is important to be cognizant of the following relationships:

1. The inventory level is directly related to sales and production requirements.
2. Attempts to change production rates as frequently as sales of finished goods fluctuate will result in excessive factory costs.
3. Inaccurate sales and production forecasts will result in excessive or insufficient inventory, plus the associated extra costs which are shown in Fig. 13–1.

These considerations highlight the need for a close working relationship between the sales department and inventory-control organizations, and emphasize the need for a flexible inventory plan capable of quick adjustment to current conditions.

Inventory Turnover. The inventory manager may well ask, "Is the inventory policy keyed to a 'barometer' that will provide adequate and timely warning of a change in the economic picture? Does the inventory-control system provide a means for detecting future increases or decreases in materials usage in time to allow corrective measures for adjusting the inventory level to meet the changing picture?" Many companies use as a "barometer" inventory movement or turnover, which is simply the ratio of sales to stocks on hand. The method used to develop the ratio is of significance; it should incorporate sales forecasting, stocks on hand, and open commitments, as well as a comparison of past inventory movement. A general discussion of the techniques applied is advisable. To find turnover of materials in manufacturing, one may take the requisitions during the period and divide by the average materials inventory. This will give an index of the movement of materials independent of the production process. The turnover of materials may also be computed in terms of production process by using the material component of goods completed. However, it is most normal to use the disbursements from stock, or usage as it may be called, as the basis of arriving at the number of months' inventory in stock. The work-in-process turnover may be computed by dividing total production cost by the average inventory of work in process. The turnover of finished stock may be computed as purchased merchandise, that is, the average inventory of materials, work in process, and finished goods would be divided into the cost of goods sold in order to arrive at a rough measure of operating inventory turnover.

Frequency of Turnover. How many times should an inventory turn over per year? Surveys have indicated that industry tends to average approximately ten stock turnovers annually, but this figure differs widel in the type of business. For example, the retail dairy and poultry products have a turnover of 36. Meat markets operate at a turnover of 38 Fur shops manage to make a profit in turning their inventory only twic a year. Let us recognize, however, that there is a danger in being over aggressive in increasing the frequency of turnover, since this can lead tc serious consequences. Elaborating, we may say, turnover is not the cure all that some consider it to be. Nor do all inventory rules go by the boarc when the ratio of turnover to investment is boosted, and when the number of annual stock turns increases, total costs decline and profits ris —but only to a certain point. Beyond this point in many instances, th reverse occurs. The nature of the industry and the unique conditions ir individual companies are the final determining factors. It is importan to emphasize that inventory turnover in terms of total inventory ma be greatly misleading and one must break it down into classes relatin the impact of frequency of turnover to operations and net profits in orde to value the movement more concisely.

To illustrate, in one firm under review, the inventory level stood a 1.7 months on hand with a turnover of approximately seven times year. On the surface, this looked excellent, but this firm was sufferin a substantial loss due to parts shortages. It is necessary, therefore, tha the degree of inventory turnover be consistent with the tolerable num ber of shortages that would not adversely affect production. As a genera rule, a turnover of four to six times a year in the manufacturing an servicing types of industries may be considered acceptable.

Characteristics of the Inventory and Classification of Accounts. One of he first steps in organizing for more effective inventory control, and erhaps the key to ultimate success of a control plan, is the making of n analysis, tabulation, and classification of the characteristics of the comnodities being carried in inventory. The thoughtful classification of ccounts will permit sound financial control of inventory, by directing he attention of the inventory planner to those accounts which control he majority of dollars. Some of the more important points of consideraion in making such a classification or analysis of commodities are:

1. Classification by Usage. An analysis of usage (sometimes called acivity) has been found to be most useful when prepared in the form of listing of commodities in order f descending dollar activity; this s sometimes expressed as the ABC oncept. This list, when totaled in umulative fashion, will indicate at glance which accounts control the ulk of dollars in inventory. It is f interest to note that the curve hown in Fig. 13–2 is typical of a nanufacturing inventory. Approxinately 10 per cent of the items tocked account for 70 per cent of he dollar investment; at the other xtreme, 70 per cent of the items epresent only 10 per cent of inestment, with the remaining 20 er cent of the items representing 20 per cent of the investment. This elationship is shown in bar chart form in Fig. 13–3.

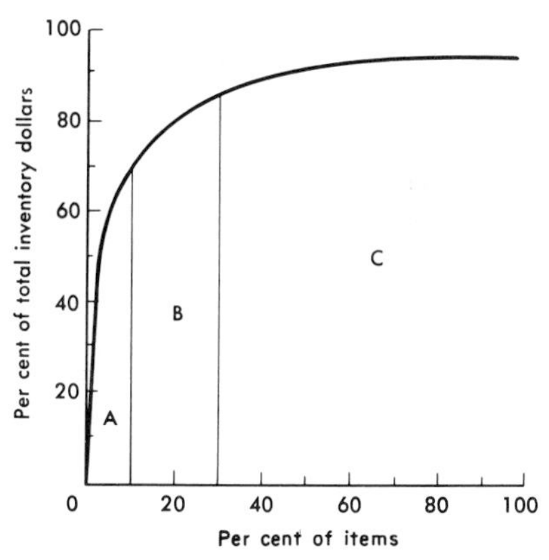

FIG. 13–2. Distribution of inventory items by inventory dollars.

Here, then, is one of the keys to better inventory control. The control olicies and techniques which apply to the few items representing 70 er cent of the total inventory value (classification A) would be designed or close supervision, through continual review of requirements, stock alances, and scheduled materials deliveries to maintain a minimum of nventory. In the automotive and consumer appliance industries, it is ommon practice to schedule these commodities in such a manner that he factory uses the material right out of the railroad car or delivery ruck. The only inventory which exists, in this case, is that which is in ansit from the supplier to the factory.

The 70 per cent of inventory items (classification C) which comrise the balance of 10 per cent of dollars may be controlled by the aximum-minimum method, by a statistically developed formula which provides a "protective" stock, or some other means which creates an economical ordering frequency. The reordering and control of these items should be reduced to an automatic basis, such as "stockless" purchasing under long-term contracts or blanket purchase orders, described in Section 5.

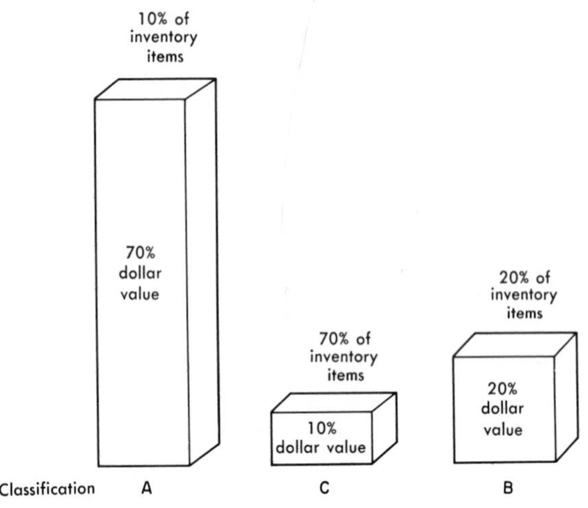

Classification A. Controlling items for inventory investment.
Maintain conservative stock level.
Constantly review and adjust scheduled open commitments.
Classification C. Avoid shortages by maintaining adequate stock levels with low risk due to minimum investment. Reorder stock on automatic basis.
Classification B. Maintain adequate stock levels with scheduled deliveries and periodic reviews of key items.

FIG. 13–3. ABC selective technique of inventory control.

This classification of accounts by activity is a tool which can be applied to the items in inventory as a whole, as suggested above, or to the inventory items in one selected commodity. In either case, the important result is that such an analysis permits a ledger controller to devote his time to "controlling" those items which significantly affect inventory dollars.

In addition to the savings which can be effected by applying special ordering and scheduling of the high dollar value inventory accounts, an analysis of the type mentioned above will also enable the best application of efforts for reduction of costs in other areas of inventory control such as transportation, storage facilities, and material handling.

2. Transportation Analysis. In connection with transportation, for example, the particular problems of those accounts affecting the bulk c

nventory and incoming freight expense should be given special study by he inventory controller and the traffic department. Techniques such as he consolidation of shipments into truckloads from a given area, establishment of special rates with one trucking company based on a sustained olume, reduction of the number of different truck lines being used by uppliers, improved in-transit packaging for reduced loss due to damage, nd others are all ways of obtaining a more efficient inventory operation vith reduced costs.

3. Storage and Handling Analyses. Likewise, in the area of storage and aterial handling, attention should be pinpointed to those items involvng the largest volume to be stored or handled. Such things as special ackaging to permit easier handling or reduction of storage space, better tilization of "air space" by stacking or use of racks, establishment of a nit package as received from the supplier containing a specified quantity accommodate the normal factory requirement for a given period, and onveyorization within storeroom and from storeroom to the area of se are just a few of the many profit-making ideas which should be iven study.

Organization of Manpower and Delegation of Responsibility. In the eld of inventory management, there is no standard of optimum organiation which can be applied to any industry or company. Because inentory control has an effect upon so many different phases of a business nterprise, the responsibility for inventory management and organizaonal structure to discharge this responsibility may take different forms. n some companies the purchasing department is charged with this reonsibility; in others, the production department handles it. In still thers, the control is divided between purchasing and production accordg to commodity. In recent years, many large companies have set up parate inventory planning and control organizations or committees, ith responsibility for establishing policies and practices. This committee ould include representation from the accounting, purchasing, producon, engineering, and sales departments.

Fundamentally, the organization for inventory control should be esblished with careful regard for four basic considerations:

The heavy influence which inventory control has upon all departments of the company.

Qualifications of inventory-control personnel, particularly the person to be charged with over-all responsibility.

Need for flexibility in the systems and control measures established.

Importance of communication. Regardless of the organizational assignments with respect to inventory control, there must be open channels of communication for the free and prompt exchange of information relative to inventory.

A few of the large manufacturing concerns have solved this "communication" problem by establishing a "manager of materials" with line responsibility over the purchasing, material planning, stores, receiving, and traffic departments. This centralization of responsibility facilitates the accomplishment of a planned and coordinated program of inventory control.

Of all the departments having an interest in inventory control, the purchasing department is probably the most directly affected by, and in turn, can most influence, the inventory control measures which are applied. The purchasing agent, or director of purchases, almost without exception, should participate strongly in the establishment of inventory policies regardless of the extent of his direct responsibility for inventory control. Three degrees of purchasing participation might, therefore, be considered:

1. Purchasing agent is directly responsible for control of stores. Delegation of stores control to the purchasing agent has a number of advantages among which are:
   a. Communication problems reduced to a minimum.
   b. Highest degree of flexibility for changes in production rate or inventory level.
   c. Opportunity for integration with suppliers with respect to combined inventory investment.
   d. Optimization of over-all acquisition and inventory cost.
   e. Direct responsibility for stores shortages and their control. This places purchasing in a key position in the manufacturing cycle, through expeditious handling and minimizing lost production time due to shortages.
2. Purchasing helps establish policies. Under this type of operation, the purchasing department would be a member of an inventory-control committee. This committee would establish policies on such matters as inventory standards, sales forecasting, load planning, etc., the formulation of which requires data and analysis which only purchasing can logically furnish. The importance of having a well-qualified purchasing representative is self-evident.
3. Purchasing has no responsibilities. Even though purchasing may no be a part of the inventory policy-making group, the responsibilit still prevails for formulating a purchasing program based on soun inventory control. Bargaining position, procurement efficiency, long term favorable relations with suppliers, maximizing profit opportun

ties cannot be attained without effective inventory planning and control on the part of the cognizant department.

Table 2–7, Section 2 shows the purchasing department responsible for ıventory control in the majority of cases. However, it should be con-.dered that in some cases purchasing may only play a minor role in ›rmulating inventory policy with little or no responsibility for setting ıe level of investment, being relegated only to the clerical task of keeping the ledgers." Real responsibility for the inventory-control func-on exists when purchasing establishes the concepts and devises the sys-em and procedure for control. Among many criteria the size of the ompany, the kind of business, the types of commodities, the nature of ıe system, and the degree of control required by management are each etermining factors in establishing the place of purchasing in inventory ıanagement.

FUNDAMENTALS OF ORDER POINT AND ORDER QUANTITY

Inventory is created for two reasons:

. To reduce over-all operating costs (economy)
. To provide protection against unpredictable demands (protection)

It is usually difficult to isolate these two characteristics when examining given stock account, but it is necessary to do so if effective methods of ıventory control are to be installed. The following sections will illustrate ıe economy function alone, then the economy and protection functions ›mbined, and finally, the protection function alone.

conomy Function

An inventory of purchased raw material and fabricated parts may be ·eated even though the company in question could operate with no in-entory at all. For example, assume that X Company makes a product hose sales can be predicted, item by item, for a period of a year or more ›r whose production schedule is firm for a year, and the finished prod-cts which are not sold are put into finished stock inventory). In this tuation, each product could be "exploded" into all the required raw ıaterial and parts, and the requirements of each piece of purchased ıaterial could be pinpointed to the exact day it would be needed. All ıaterial could be brought in daily and routed directly to the manufac-ıring area where it was needed. The only inventory would be in-process ıventory. Assuming that X Company has 5,000 different items which are urchased regularly, such a policy would mean scheduling hundreds of incoming shipments daily, with all the associated paper work, checking and following. Therefore, X Company would quickly conclude that i would be more economical to buy, receive, and store these items *in ac vance of need.* They would accomplish this by creating raw materia stock accounts. The creation of this raw material inventory would, o course, result in additional costs associated with storing the materia obsolescence, depreciation, etc. These so-called inventory carrying cost when compared with the previously mentioned costs associated with o dering and receiving, may be used to calculate the most economical polic of ordering and storing the inventory. To repeat, inventory would b created in advance of its actual need, and held for weeks or perhap months, because it would prove cheaper to carry that inventory for tha period of time, rather than incur the costs of daily or weekly orderin and/or receiving.

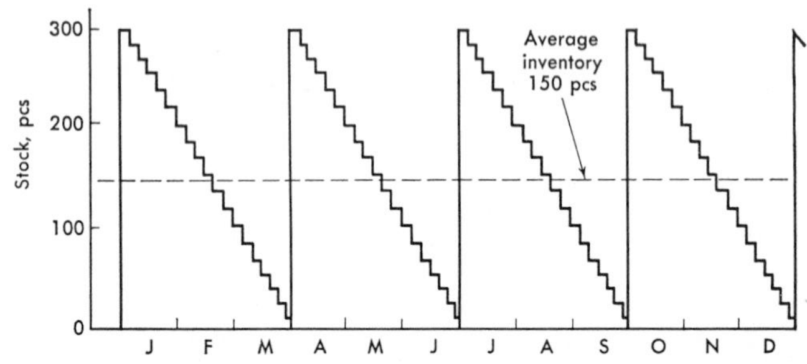

FIG. 13–4. Predictable monthly usage—100 pieces order quantity—300 pieces.

Figure 13–4 shows the rise and fall of the stock level for a given stoc item whose predictable usage is 100 pieces per month. Assume that fc this particular item the most economical method of ordering[2] is in quar tities of 300 pieces, once every three months. The stock controller woul place his orders so that each new order would arrive just as the stoc reached zero. The stock level would fluctuate between 300 and zero, r sulting in an average inventory of 150 pieces, or 1½ months' supply.

The inventory which is created by the use of a predetermined orde quantity is directly related to that order quantity, provided the sam quantity is used on all subsequent orders. Figure 13–4 shows this to b true:

Average active stock = ½ order quantity

In this example, the inventory is composed entirely of active stock, th is, every piece of stock "turns over" during the period between receiving

[2] See calculation under "Using the Economical Order Quantity," page 13–26.

Applying this principle to every item in the inventory, it provides a means for forecasting the total inventory. The total inventory would be one-half times the sum of each order quantity.[3]

This illustration is oversimplified to illustrate how the active stock portion of the inventory is created. Except for companies whose production schedules are 100 per cent predictable, most raw material inventories must contain an additional segment of inventory, called "safety stock." This subject is discussed next.

Protection Function (Safety Stock) and Economy Function

A more typical situation than the case of X Company is found in Y Company. The latter organization manufactures a product which can be forecasted only to general product lines. The individual items within those product lines may be required by its customers upon short notice.

Month	Usage	
January	970	
February	850	
March	1,010	
April	900	
May	910	
June	980	
July	1,770	(maximum monthly usage)
August	910	
September	830	
October	980	
November	910	
December	980	
	12)12,000	
	1,000	(average monthly usage)

FIG. 13–5. Stock issue record.

This short lead time does not allow time enough to purchase the material for each individual customer's order. Therefore, there is an obvious need for the creation of raw material inventory, to be available for these periodic demands. The stock level of each stock item may be set initially by guess or intention, but after a period of months, the issue pattern from the stock ledger should provide for a more factual approach. That is, past activity may be used to forecast probable future requirements. An example of such a historical record is shown in Fig. 13–5.

This example is shown to illustrate two points:

1. If the item in question is a stable item, used frequently, so that many demands are made upon it each month, there will be an issue pattern

[3] This neglects the "safety stock" portion of the inventory. See "Calculation of Safety Stock," page 13–29.

which may be used to forecast future activity. This rate of usage may be expressed as "average monthly usage," or usage per any convenient time period.

2. Even the most stable of the items will occasionally experience a period of unusually high activity. This may be called "maximum monthly usage," and may exceed the "average monthly usage" by a significant amount.

Figure 13–5 illustrates an item whose "maximum monthly usage" (1,770 pieces) is almost twice its "average monthly usage" (1,000 pieces).

Lacking any other means to forecast his future requirements, the controller of this stock item would do two things:

1. He would establish a pattern for reordering his stock so that he would receive about 12,000 pieces during the following year.
2. He would select an order point which was sufficient to cover the expected usage during the reorder period.

Using the data from Fig. 13–5, he might do the following:

1. Use an order quantity of 2,000 pieces, every two months.
2. Assuming a supplier's lead time of one month, use an order point of 1,000 pieces.

If this policy were followed, the stock level might follow a pattern as shown in Fig. 13–6*a*. As long as the monthly demands on the item did not exceed 1,000 pieces, the stock would be adequate to cover these demands. But as soon as a high activity month occurred (August), the stock would reach zero before the next order arrived. A stockout period of a week or two could result.

This policy, then, must be adjusted so that some extra stock is provided in the system to cover these occasional periods of maximum usage. This is done by raising the order point, and hence the stock level, as shown in Fig. 13–6*b*. The order point should be based on the *maximum* expected usage, rather than the *average* usage during the lead-time period. In this example, the lead time is one month. The maximum expected usage might be arbitrarily set at 2,000 pieces, and this would be used as the order point. The result of this policy is to create additional stock, to be used only during periods of above-average usage. This is called the "safety stock" portion of the inventory. Once established, this safety stock need not be reordered. This is true because each period of high activity would be offset by periods of below-average activity, which would tend to keep the safety stock at its original level. In this example then, the order quantity would remain unchanged, at 2,000 pieces, ever wo months. The stock level would not drop below the safety stock level 1,000 pieces) until the high activity during August would deplete it emporarily. The stockout period shown in Fig. 13–6*a* would be pre-ented by the introduction of safety stock (Fig. 13–6*b*).

NOTE: The rise and fall of the stock level, on the typical stock item, is ot as symmetrical as the ones illustrated, which have been deliberately versimplified. The safety stock portion of the inventory is therefore dif-icult to visualize. It may be measured, however, by simply measuring he points of minimum stock over a period of months, and calculating heir average value. The active stock portion of the inventory is then alculated by subtracting the safety stock from the average inventory ver that period.

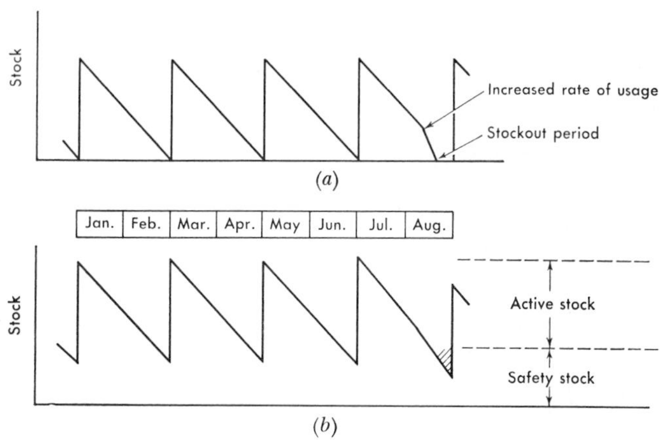

FIG. 13–6*a* and *b*. Stock flow and replenishment chart.

It should be emphasized that the order quantity is not increased to rovide protection against periods of unusually high usage. The order uantity is based upon the average usage, in this example 12,000 pieces er year. Protection is provided by maintaining a safety stock level, rough adjustment of the order point. To recap these principles, the fol-wing definitions should be reemphasized.

Active Stock—Order Quantity. The active stock portion of the inven-ry is that portion which is created for the purpose of satisfying the *pected* requirements of material. It is directly related to the order *uantity.* The order quantity is simply the expected annual requirements, ivided by that number of orders which has proved to be most economical sed upon the cost of ordering and carrying inventory (see Fig. 13–11).

Safety Stock—Order Point. The safety stock portion of the inventory that portion which is created to take care of above-average or unexpected demands on the inventory. It is directly related to the order point. The amount of stock is determined not on ordering-carrying cost considerations, but on the need for protection against stockoutages for each stock item under consideration. Some items will need more safety stock than others, depending upon the amount of deviation that has been experienced between the forecasted material usage and the actual material usage for any given time period, plus the reliability of the suppliers' deliveries, and of the order lead time (the longer the lead time, the more uncertain is the forecast of sales, and the resultant material requirements). (Those items whose future activity can be forecasted with 100 per cent accuracy will require, theoretically, no safety stock.)

Protection Function Alone

An example of a stock item which is composed almost entirely of safety stock would be a maintenance spare part whose unit cost was high and rate of usage low. Figure 13–7 shows such an item, whose activity is only

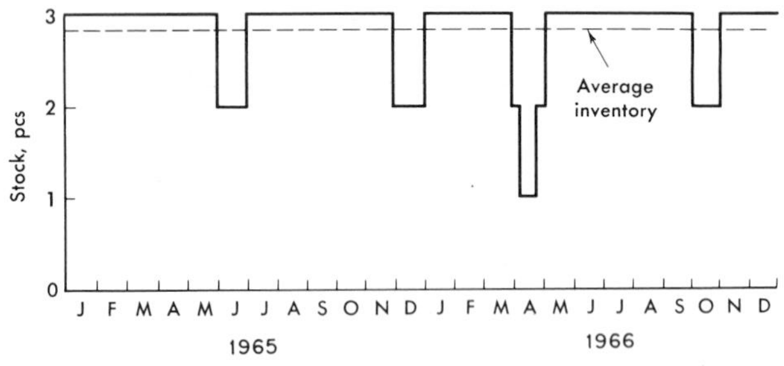

FIG. 13–7. Irregular stock flow and replenishment chart.

two or three units a year. The inventory level, on the average, is close to three units, or $300. Assuming any reasonable cost factors for ordering and carrying this inventory,[4] it would be cheaper to carry no inventory, and order each piece as needed. The three units of stock, then, are carried purely for reasons of protection, rather than economies of ordering or carrying stock. Such an item, although used infrequently, may be extremely valuable if it can prevent the breakdown of some piece of vital equipment. Since it takes a month to procure the item, there is the possibility that two units could be needed in a given month, and very rarely three units. The stock level is therefore set at three units.

The foregoing discussion of "active stock" and "safety stock" does not suggest that a given stock item should be physically separated into two parts. It does suggest that the two functions be recognized and analyzed

[4] See discussion of cost factors under "Factors Influencing Inventory," page 13–5.

separately, so that an inventory policy may be established which will result in the desired amount of protection against stockoutages at the minimum over-all cost.

ORDER QUANTITY

Maximum-minimum System

Before discussing the concept of "economical order quantity," the maximum-minimum system will be considered. This system combines order quantity and order point and operates as follows: Two arbitrary levels of stock are selected, usually expressed in weeks' or months' supply. The stock controllers are instructed to order their stock in such a manner that it stays within the two specified limits. For example, in Fig. 13–8,

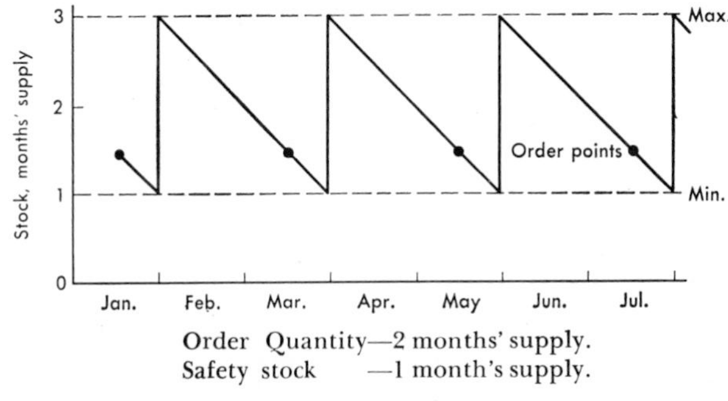

Order Quantity—2 months' supply.
Safety stock —1 month's supply.

FIG. 13–8. Maximum-minimum system.

the following conditions have been assumed: maximum stock level, three months' supply; minimum stock level, one month's supply; supplier lead time, one-half month. To maintain his stock above the one-month minimum, the stock controller must reorder before his stock drops below 1½ months. He expects the order to arrive when the stock is about one month's supply. He must not order in quantities in excess of two months' supply, because this order, plus his minimum stock, must not exceed three months. This system has some advantages as well as some serious disadvantages.

Advantages:

1. It prevents excessive build-up of stock on any given item, because of the three-month maximum.
2. It provides a level of protection against unusual demands on the stock, because of the minimum level.

3. The system is easy to explain to operating personnel.
4. Actual performance can easily be checked against the standard.

Disadvantages:

1. It is not necessarily the most economical system, when costs of processing orders and carrying inventory are considered.
2. The minimum stock may give either too much or too little protection for specific stock items.
3. The system tends to be *too automatic.* Repeatedly ordering to raise a minimum stock to the maximum level can lead to an overstocked position automatically; frequently design changes are given too little consideration in the strict compliance with maximum-minimum principles. An appropriate check against future requirements must be made to avoid reorders based only upon past experience.
4. Quantity discounts may be lost because of order-quantity restrictions.
5. It does not specifically define either the order point or the order quantity.

To illustrate point 5, under "disadvantages," it can be seen in Fig. 13–9 that there can be an almost limitless combination of order points

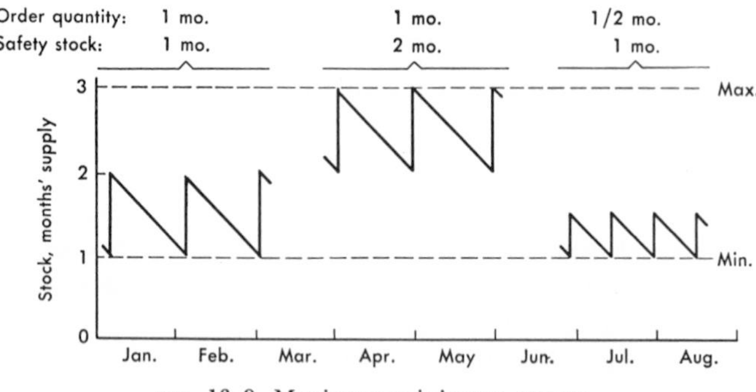

FIG. 13–9. Maximum-minimum system.

and order quantities which will maintain the stock within the prescribed limits. Figure 13–8 shows one method, where the stock fluctuates the full range between maximum and minimum. Each of the patterns in Fig. 13–9 also satisfies the requirements, but each was a different order quantity or order point. There is no assurance that the maximum-minimum restrictions will be interpreted the same way by each stock controller, so that a nonuniform system among stock controllers may result. These objections may be overcome by calculating the safety stock and order quantity on a more scientific basis.

If any systematic means, other than pure intuition on the part of the stock controller, is to be used to determine the order quantity, there must first be some method for estimating the expected future usage of each stock item. In many cases, the estimates, or forecasts, may be in error by as much as 25 to 50 per cent, but this is not necessarily a deterrent to ordering in large quantities, provided the following is true:

1. The item is not likely to become obsolete in the near future (the product line is not being redesigned).
2. The item does not have a limited shelf life.
3. Large quantities do not present an unreasonable storage problem.

Assuming, then, that there is available an estimate of the annual activity of each item, the stock controller must make a decision as to the quantity of each item he should order. (This assumes that he is not operating under a system which limits his stock on every item to two or three months' supply.) The decision which he makes as to his order quantity will, in turn, reflect itself in his inventory level. Figure 13–9 illustrates the variety of methods that may be employed to reorder his annual requirements.

In this example, the only restrictions on order quantity are a one month's supply minimum, twelve months' supply maximum. Obviously, some practical limit must be imposed at either extreme. Ordering more frequently than once a month per item will usually result in excessive costs of paperwork, material checking, etc. Ordering more than a year's supply will frequently exceed the limits of predictable future activity.

The item shown in Fig. 13–10 has an estimated annual activity of 1,200 pieces and costs $1 per piece. If the entire year's supply were purchased in one order, the active[5] stock would fluctuate from a maximum of $1,200 to a minimum of zero, with an average active stock of about $600. Alternate methods of ordering this same item may be chosen. If the order frequency is increased, the resulting active stock is reduced. If ordered monthly, in this example, the average active stock would be reduced to about $50. In general, this rule applies:

$$\text{Average active stock} = \tfrac{1}{2} \text{ order quantity}$$

In this example, assume an ordering cost of $3 per order, a carrying cost of 10 per cent per year.

The illustration, which shows five different order quantities, is given to emphasize the point that there are many ways in which the annual requirements of a given item may be ordered. In this case, the resulting

[5] That portion of inventory created by order quantity.

inventory could vary from $50 to $600. Given the costs associated with each alternative, however, it is possible to select the most economical method. Without such an analysis, the stock controller must rely on intuition or experience to make these decisions.

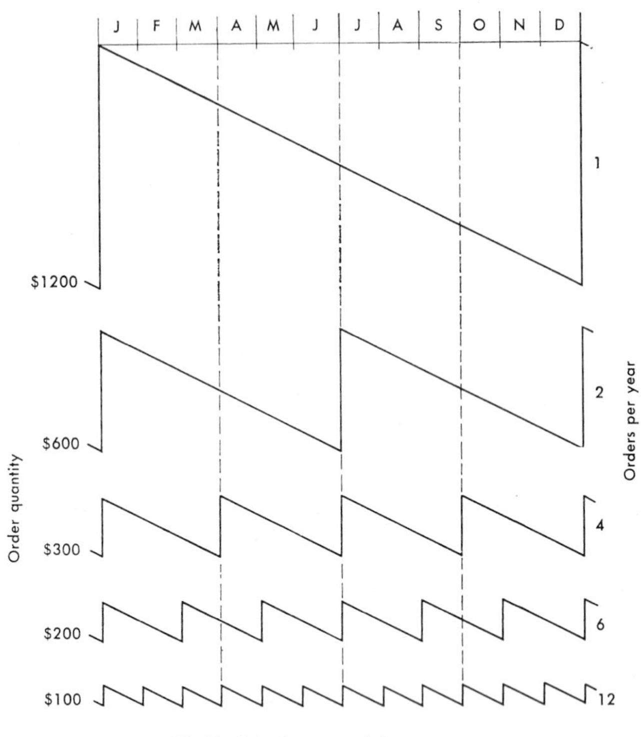

FIG. 13–10. Maximum-minimum system.

Figure 13–11 illustrates that the costs associated with carrying inventory vary inversely with the number of orders. (These costs are reduced from $60 down to $5, as the number of orders is increased from one to twelve.)

Figure 13–11 also shows that the ordering costs increase directly with the number of orders (going from $3 up to $36, in this case). Since the total cost is made up of both the ordering and carrying cost, it is this cost which must be minimized, rather than either of the other two costs. In this case, the total cost appears to reach a minimum point somewhere between two and six orders per year. If the costs are plotted as curves (Fig. 13–11), it can be demonstrated that the point of minimum total cost is at the point of intersection of the ordering and carrying cost curves.

This will always be true, regardless of the cost factors involved. Other items, having different annual activities, could be analyzed in a similar

Number of orders	Order size	Average inventory	Inventory carrying cost	Ordering cost	Total cost
1	$1,200	$600	$60	$ 3	$63
2	600	300	30	6	36
4	300	150	15	12	27
6	200	100	10	18	28
12	100	50	5	36	41

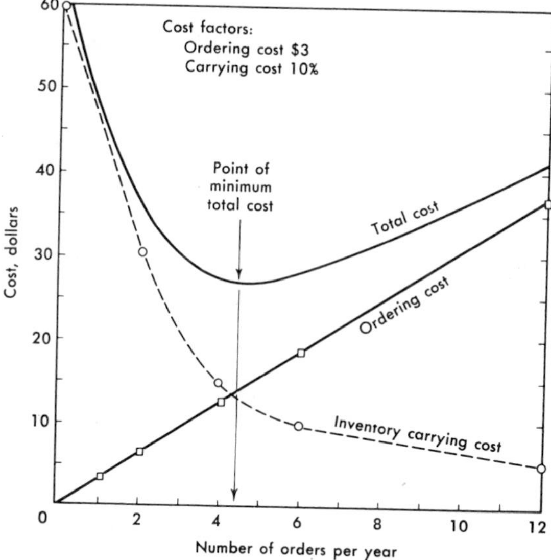

FIG. 13–11. Economical order quantity.

manner, but this is impractical for a large number of items. Therefore, the following formula may be employed:

$A =$ annual requirements ($) $\quad N =$ number of orders

$C =$ carrying cost–variable (% per year) $\quad$ Average inventory $= \frac{1}{2}\frac{A}{N}$

$K =$ ordering cost–variable (per order)

$$\text{Annual ordering cost} = \text{annual carrying cost}$$

$$KN = C\left[\frac{1}{2}\frac{A}{N}\right]$$

Solving for N, which in this case is the most economical number of orders,

$$N = \sqrt{\frac{CA}{2K}}$$

This formula is a general formula, which may be used for any combination of ordering and carrying costs. The specific cost factors which any given company may have developed can be inserted in this formula. In the example shown, these were \$3 and 10 per cent.

$$N = \sqrt{\frac{CA}{2K}} = \sqrt{\frac{0.10A}{2(3)}} = 0.13\sqrt{A}$$

This formula may be used to construct a table which relates the annual usage of any stock item to its most economical number of orders per year:

\$ Annual usage A	*No. of orders* N
60	1
240	2
540	3
960	4
2,160	6
4,860	9
8,640	12

Using the Economical Order Quantity[6]

The EOQ table may be made with many increments, or with just a few, as shown. If computations are done longhand, by the stock controller, it is best that the table be simple and easy to use. The following case shows how the table may be used on a sample item:

1. These facts should be available to the stock controller:
   a. Estimated annual usage, in pieces 4,000
   b. Approximate unit cost 50 cents
2. He performs this calculation:
   Annual usage (pieces) × unit cost = annual usage (\$)

$$4{,}000 \times 50 \text{ cents} = \$2{,}000$$

3. He refers to table for correct number of orders per year:

$$A = \$2{,}000 \qquad N = 6 \text{ (approx.)}$$

4. He calculates this order quantity:

$$\frac{\text{Annual activity}}{\text{No. of orders per year}} = \frac{4{,}000}{6} = 666 \text{ pieces, or } \$333$$

[6] See tables in Section 29 on how you can order scientifically via the Economic Order Value method.

The calculations described here are simple, and no attempt should be nade to carry calculations out to the last decimal place, as this will soon liscourage use of the table. By reasonable "rounding of his figures," a tock controller should be able to compute his order quantity within 10 o 15 per cent, without resorting to tedious calculations.

)rder Quantity Relative to Lead Time

The situation may arise where the most economical order quantity is mall (say, one month's supply), but the lead time is longer than the rder quantity coverage (say, three months). In such cases, in order to over the procurement cycle, it would be necessary to have several orders pen at any given time. In such cases, it may be more convenient to consider the use of a "blanket order," with monthly shipments of specified uantities.

ORDER POINT

The order point is a predetermined signal which will indicate to the tock controller that he should consider the possibility of reordering the tock item in question. It is expressed in units of material as it is stocked nd ordered (pounds, pieces, etc.). Whenever an issue from stock causes he coverage of an item (equivalent to stock balance + open orders) to rop below this predetermined point, the item should be investigated.

The order point must be selected at a figure high enough so that the tock will be sufficient to satisfy the maximum number of expected denands upon the stock during the period when the replacement stock is n order. In brief:

Order point = maximum expected usage during lead time

There are two problems which are inherent in the selection of the roper order point.[7]

. The lead time cannot always be accurately determined.
. The usage during the lead time cannot always be accurately forecasted.

In those exceptional cases where both the usage of material and the ead time are absolutely predictable, the order point is simply stated:

Order point = known requirements during lead time

In Fig. 13–12, the lead time is two months, and the known requirements re 100 pieces per month. The order point is therefore 200 pieces.

[7] One exception is in the case of a local supplier who can deliver on a moment's otice. The order point here might be simply zero stock.

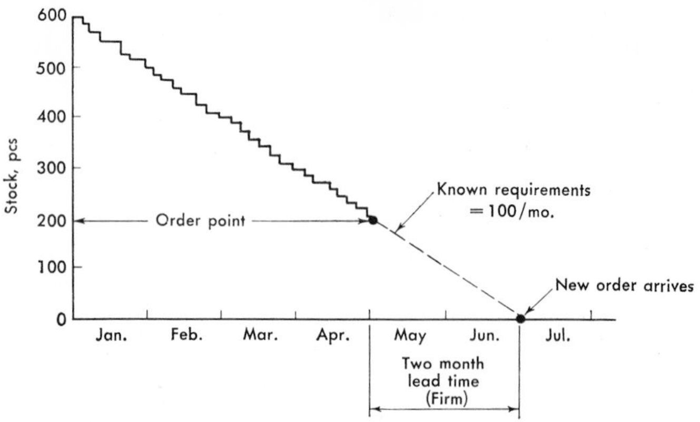

FIG. 13–12. Chart of order-point system.

In the more typical situation, however, the material usage can only be estimated, and the lead time is subject to variations. In the previou example, either a late delivery or a period of above-average activity would have caused the stock to reach zero before the new stock arrived. There fore, when material usage rates and/or lead times are based on estimate rather than firm figures, it is expedient to make an upward adjustmen of the order point. This is done through introduction of safety stock The order point now becomes:

$$\text{Order point} = \text{expected lead time usage} + \text{safety stock}$$

In the example given previously, there was no safety factor to absorb unexpected usage or delayed delivery. In Fig. 13–13, the order point ha

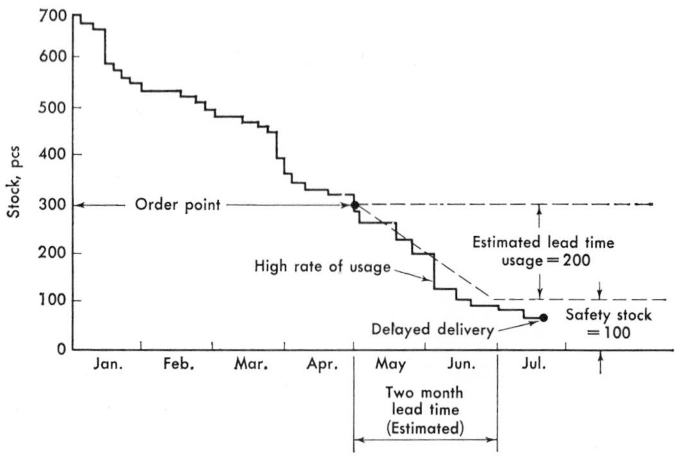

FIG. 13–13. Chart of order-point system with safety stock provision.

been raised 100 pieces, providing a buffer stock which can absorb these unexpected demands.

Calculation of Safety Stock

The amount of safety stock necessary to provide adequate protection will vary from item to item. This is true because forecasts can be made with greater accuracy for some items than for others. Lacking accurate forecasts, the stock controller may examine past stock records in order to help him estimate the maximum rate of usage which could be expected to occur during the reorder period. He might also determine the longest recorded delivery time for the item. Judgment should be used, however, so that nontypical, nonrecurring situations will be excluded. Based on such an analysis, the stock controller may decide upon an amount of safety stock sufficient to cover those occurrences which are in excess of the average usage and/or lead time.

Lengthy analyses, which may be valuable for an occasional stock item which is critical or of high dollar value, are usually impractical to apply to all items. The problem may be resolved by the use of an across-the-board safety stock. Such a generalized safety stock is often defined as "one month's supply." It means that the stock controller will order in such a manner that he will always have at least one month's supply of stock on hand, if conditions remain normal. If not, he will have the extra month's supply of stock to carry him over the period of high usage or delayed delivery.

Where safety stock is expressed in months' supply, it is convenient to use this formula:

$$[\text{Safety stock (months)} + \text{lead time (months)}] \times [\text{average monthly usage (units)}] = \text{order point (units)}$$

Following are three items, with different activities and lead times. In each case, assume a safety stock of one month's supply.

Item No.	Monthly usage, pieces	Lead time, months	Safety stock, months
1	100	1.0	1.0
2	500	2.0	1.0
3	20	2.5	1.0

The order points are computed as follows:

(Safety stock + lead time) (average month's usage) = order point
Item 1 (1.0 + 1.0) 100 = 200 pieces
Item 2 (1.0 + 2.0) 500 = 1,500 pieces
Item 3 (1.0 + 2.5) 20 = 70 pieces

Relationship of Safety Stock, Stockout Rate, and Stockout Cost

The distinction has been made between active stock and safety stock to point out that the active stock is created for purposes of economies of ordering, whereas the safety stock is added only to cover above-average usage or delayed deliveries. Some industries refer to this protection as "contingency stock." The costs associated with carrying this part of the inventory are therefore high. Any effort to reduce the safety stock, however, will automatically increase the number of stockoutages. It is theoretically possible to compare the cost of a stockout with the cost of carrying safety stock, and thereby arrive at the most economical level of safety stock, considering both costs. However, the cost of a stockout for a given item could vary greatly from one occurrence to the next, depending upon its effect upon the production line each time. The actual costs incurred in such a situation are largely a matter of opinion. This makes it impossible, in most cases, to determine a realistic stockout cost.

Although the actual costs associated with a stockout may be difficult to determine, it is not difficult to tabulate the rate of stockouts and the average duration of the stockouts. These data can be analyzed to determine if the inventory is "in control." Past history, combined with management judgment, should be enough to determine an acceptable maximum stockout rate, beyond which the manufacturer of the product will suffer. This rate might be different for various commodities. A reporting system should be set up so that actual stockouts per month may be compared with the standard. When stockouts become excessive, the safety stock must be increased until the stockouts are reduced to an acceptable level. It should be noted that an item which never goes on shortage should be reviewed critically. It may be that the stock is excessively high, and that an occasional stockout would cost less than carrying excess inventory year after year.

Refinements in Safety Stock—Order-point Calculations

Although it is true that the stockout rate will decrease as the safety stock is increased, it is not a simple matter to determine the exact amount of safety stock necessary to keep the stockouts within a given limit. Such rule-of-thumb methods as a month's supply across-the-board safety stock may be successful in keeping the over-all rate down, but individual items may go on shortage much more frequently than desired for good control. This emphasizes the need for an adjustable safety stock, tailored to the needs of each individual stock item.

Some of the factors which influence the level of safety stock are intuitively considered by most stock controllers. An examination of many stock edgers will show different levels of safety stock from item to item in line vith these factors.

The following list suggests some of the factors which should be considered in determining the correct level of safety stock.

'actors which suggest low safety tock

. High permissible stockout rate (one stockout every year, per item)
. Short delivery time (one-half month)
. Large-order quantities (twelve months' supply per order)
. Stable item
  a. Issued many times per month
  b. Predictable usage
  c. Used in a variety of products

Factors which suggest high safety stock

1. Low permissible stockout rate (one stockout every ten years, per item)
2. Long delivery time (six months)
3. Small-order quantities (one month's supply per order)
4. Erratic item
   a. Issued only once a month or less
   b. Unpredictable usage
   c. Used in only one or two products

Applying these factors to an inventory which contained a wide variety of items could result in a range of safety stocks from a one-half month upply for short-lead-time, fast-moving items to as much as a six-month upply for relatively slow movers with long lead times. The relation etween the factors and the resulting safety stock can best be determined y extensive statistical analysis. Many of the larger companies have successfully made such studies and, by application of the laws of probability, levised control tables which give the correct safety stock or order point or a wide variety of conditions.

QUANTITY DISCOUNTS

If an item of raw material or a purchased part is being purchased for special application, rather than for inventory, there arises the problem of whether or not to increase the requested quantity to take advantage of a quantity discount. An item for which future activity seems unlikely hould be purchased in the quantity requested, since there is a known equirement for that amount only. The person, frequently the design ngineer, who specified the item in question could probably give the buyer some idea of the likelihood for future use; the buyer might consider increasing the order quantity, provided that the resulting price eduction was justified, in the light of existing inventory policies.

The two factors which must be considered are the potential reduction in material cost versus the increase in inventory. Because the inherent risk of obsolescence is great, in such cases, it is advisable that the potential price reduction be significant compared to the increased inventory investment. The ratio of the former to the latter may be expressed as a percentage. Frequently an arbitrary minimum percentage is decided upon, below which the discount will not be taken. For example, it may be decided that no item of a certain commodity will be ordered in excess of actual requirements unless a 30 per cent return on investment can be realized.

EXAMPLE:

S = requested order quantity (units) = 200 pieces
S_d = minimum order quantity for discount (units) = 1,000 pieces
P = unit price at requested order quantity = \$1.00
P_d = unit price at discount quantity = \$0.80
Q = requested order quantity in \$ = $S \times P$ = 200 × \$1 = \$200
Q_d = discount order quantity in \$ = $S_d \times P_d$ = 1,000 × \$0.80 = \$800
Material price reduction = $S_d (P - P_d)$ = 1,000 (\$1 − \$0.80) = \$200
Increase in inventory value = $Q_d - Q$ = \$800 − \$200 = \$600

X' = per cent return on additional investment

$$= 100 \times S_d \frac{(P - P_d)}{Q_d - Q} = 100 \times \frac{200}{600} = 33\tfrac{1}{3} \text{ per cent}$$

Since the actual per cent return exceeds the 30 per cent minimum, the discount would be taken on 1,000 pieces.

A more scientific method is to tabulate a "before and after" price-break chart. If the savings exceed the cost of carrying the additional inventory,

Total dollar amount *after* quantity discount	Total dollar amount *before* quantity discount						
	10	50	100	150	200	500	1,000
20	0.60						
50	2.40						
100	5.40	3.00					
200	11.40	9.00	6.00	3.00			
300		15.00	12.00	9.00	6.00		
400			18.00	15.00	12.00		
500				21.00	18.00		
700					30.00	12.00	
900						24.00	
1,200						42.00	12.00
1,500						60.00	30.00

FIG. 13–14. Added inventory costs.

the discount is taken. If the savings are less than the cost of carrying the additional inventory, the lower quantity, at the higher unit price, would be more economical.

Assuming a (variable) carrying cost of 12 per cent, and basing the average inventory on one-half the (additional) order quantity, a sample price-break chart would look like Fig. 13–14. The horizontal column headings are the total dollar amounts for an item in the required quantity. The vertical headings are the total dollar amounts to be spent if the quantity unit-price discount is to be taken. As an example, take the column indicating a "before" cost of $100. If an expenditure of $200 is required to take the discount, then a carrying cost of $6 is incurred. (By going from $100 to $200 an additional order amount of $100 is committed. Average inventory would be $\frac{1}{2} \times \$100 = \$50$. Carrying costs of 12 per cent produce an inventory cost of $6.)

EXAMPLE 1:

The economic order quantity for an item is 110 pieces, at a cost of 90 cents each, for a total of $99. The unit cost reduces to 80 cents each in a quantity of 250 and up, for a total of $200. Annual usage is 150 pieces. The chart shows that an inventory cost of $6 is incurred by going to the larger quantity. The usage of 150 pieces produces savings of $150 \times \$0.10 = \$15$ per year. There is a net gain of $9 on an annual basis, and the discount should be taken.

EXAMPLE 2:

The economic order quantity for an item is 40 pieces at $5 each, for a total of $200. A reduction of the unit price to $4.70 each is available in a minimum quantity of 150 pieces, requiring an investment of $705. Annual usage of this item is 80 pieces. Reference to the chart shows added-inventory carrying costs of $30. Annual savings ($80 \times \$0.30 = \$24$) are less than the cost of carrying the additional inventory. The discount should not be taken.

INVENTORY CONTROL AND EXPEDITING

Effect of Expediting on Inventory

A study of inventory-control techniques would not be complete without a discussion of the effect of expediting on inventories. The expediting of delivery of procured materials has a major effect upon inventory levels since it influences directly the lead time or procurement-cycle time.

As indicated in previous discussions, a predetermined inventory level is usually maintained through proper consideration of the procurement-cycle time when placing orders for a new supply of material. This consideration includes a knowledge of the supplier's manufacturing cycle, transportation time, and expected usage of the material during the procurement cycle. Accordingly, under a good inventory-control plan, and with reasonably accurate knowledge of these factors, materials would be ordered in sufficient quantity and at the proper time to have at least a small reserve stock on hand when the new material is received. However, there are many circumstances which may lengthen the lead time, or cause a shortage of materials, namely, there may be an unexpected increase in usage, a breakdown or delay which lengthens the supplier's manufacturing cycle, or a simple delay in transit from the supplier's plant. It can be seen that under these circumstances, the most elaborate inventory-control system may still be troubled with an inventory shortage.

Here, then, is the point where a good expediting operation may supplement a good inventory-control plan. Effective expediting may result in obtaining the needed materials on time, in spite of the unexpected increases in requirements or delays in manufacturing which are encountered.

Organizing for Effective Expediting

Since expediting has such an important effect on inventories, an effective expediting organization should be considered a part of the over-all organizing for good inventory control. The organization for carrying out the expediting function may assume one of four basic structures:

1. Centralized
2. Decentralized within purchasing
3. Integrated with buying function
4. Field expediting

Any one of these basic expediting organization structures may provide the necessary supplement to effective inventory control. Application of the most effective type of expediting organization will largely be determined by the nature of the product and the expediting problems associated with it. The discussion below will point out some of the advantages and disadvantages normally expected from each of these expediting structures.

When the expediting function is "centralized," it may be separated organizationally and physically from any other department, although it may report to either purchasing or production. Under this setup, expediting usually operates independently of the other involved departments and places its major emphasis on obtaining delivery as requested. This setup offers the advantages of fewer personnel, less expense, and the possibility of more concentrated effort. The disadvantages of this system are the difficulty of communication and coordination with purchasing, material control, and production; possible disruption of long-range supplier agreements and relationships; and overemphasis on production at the expense of established inventory and purchasing policies.

Centralized expediting may also be an integral part of the purchasing department organization. In this instance, the disadvantages of poor communication and misinterpretation of inventory and purchasing policies are reduced, since of necessity, expediting would work more closely with purchasing and inventory control.

A "decentralized" expediting activity exists when an expediter is an integral part of each separate buying section within the purchasing department. Here, the expediting responsibility rests with the various buying sections, and results in close coordination between the buyer and expediter, with both functions under the supervision of the head of the buying section. This setup offers the obvious advantages of closer coordination between expediting and purchasing and the common understanding of long-range purchasing policies and agreements with suppliers. Also in line with its other inventory-control objectives, it allows the purchasing department to have closer control over the lead-time variable. This system offers the disadvantages of greater cost due to a greater number of people required as expediters.

The "integrated" form of expediting has the greatest control from a purchasing standpoint over the lead-time variable, regardless of where inventory responsibility resides. "Integrated expediting" exists when the individual buyer is responsible not only for obtaining a supplier and placing the order but also for ensuring delivery at a specified future date. In this manner, the purchasing department has optimum control over its long-range buying plans and supplier relationships to obtain the best possible assurance of supply. On the other hand, this setup requires a greater number of higher-priced buyers who, many companies feel, should be spending more productive time on "prebuying" or "planned purchasing" techniques instead of expediting.

A "field" expediting organization is usually utilized only under unusual circumstances in times of shortage or where several subdivisions of a large company find that their varied expediting requirements can be combined in one or several men covering a specific geographical territory. Field expediting is performed as an emergency measure or for economic purposes where a great deal of travel might otherwise be required of several men into the same area. It must be recognized here, however, that extreme material shortages, and emergency situations at suppliers' plants, make field expediting a necessary part of the over-all control of inventory. Prolonged continuance of these shortages and/or emergencies, on the other hand, should indicate to the purchasing department the necessity for improved long-range planning and commitments within the period covered by their sales, production, and inventory forecasts. Field expediting offers the big advantages of reduced expense and on-the-spot appraisal of supplier performance and capacity. On the liability side, it usually means less control over the expediter's effort and lack of coordination with buying policies.

In summary, it can be said that, regardless of the organizational form which the expediting function assumes, its success in controlling the lead-time variable and its influence on inventory are dependent upon the following factors:

1. Its understanding of, and coordination with, the established long-range purchasing objectives to attain assurance of supply
2. Reasonable familiarity with the company's inventory policies and objectives
3. An appreciation of the importance of the lead-time variable and its effect on inventory

Expediting Procedures

Stores Control. In the practical application of expediting to the control of inventories, many different office procedures are in use. The systems and the forms used therein are usually tailored to suit the particular needs of the business. However, there are a number of basic requirements to be considered in the establishment of a good expediting system.

1. There should be common identification between stores and purchasing of the item and purchase order to be expedited.
2. Forms must be simple and concise to permit rapid communication.
3. Communication between stores and purchasing should be on a direct basis.
4. Definition of "critical" item must be mutually understood, i.e., "out of stock," "10 days' supply," or "safety stock broken."

Figure 13–15, "Critical Item Report," illustrates a simple form designed to be issued by the stores department stock controller to advise purchasing of the need for expediting. Note that the form provides for designating the criticalness of the item; i.e., 1, 2, or 3.

Purchasing Control. In the area of expediting between purchasing and outside suppliers, these general conditions must be considered:

1. Forms used must be brief, simple, and designed to handle different materials and suppliers; for example, raw materials versus component parts.
2. The supplier's order department system should be clearly understood.
3. Maximum reconciliation of supplier's records and purchasing records must exist.

CRITICAL ITEM REPORT

Date Reported ____________ Class 1 / 2 / 3 Critical Item

Received by Production Planning { 1. ________ 2. ________

	REQ. OR P.O.	SUPPLIER	QTY. ON ORDER
1.			
2.			
3.			

MATERIAL

Style-Dwg. & Item ____________

Size ____________

Description ____________

P. D. S. ____________

Quantity Required ____________

Immed. Req. ________ Date Req. ________

Qty. on Hand ________ No. Wks. Supply ________

PURCHASING DEPT.

	REQ. OR P.O.	DATE PROM.	QUANTITY
1.			
2.			
3.			

ORIGINATED BY

Production (CLASS 1) ________ DEPT. ________ BY

Ledger (CLASS 2 OR 3) ________ BY

Productrol Line: ____________

☐ Main Stores: ____________

☐ Sub-Stores: ____________

____________ BY EXPEDITER

Remarks ____________

FIG. 13–15. Critical item report.

PLEASE RETURN THIS FORM PROMPTLY WITH INFORMATION REQUESTED ON ITEMS CHECKED

Subject Order No. ________ **Your No.** ________

___ 1. Acknowledgement not received. Please forward.

___ 2. Rush balance and advise shipping date.

___ 3. Did you ship as promised ____________ ? If not, give best shipping date.

___ 4, Advise if shipped, when and how.

___ 5. Material urgently needed. Give best possible shipping date.

___ 6. This is second request for information. Immediate reply is necessary to avoid telegraph or telephone expense.

Your pencil remarks are sufficient.

____

____

____

____

Yours very truly,

Smith Metal Co.

Purchasing Department

FIG. 13–16. Typical follow-up form to suppliers.

Forms which are generally used to contact outside suppliers consist of the "mail telegrams," specially designed postal cards, and form letters. A typical form letter is shown in Fig. 13–16, which indicates the type of information usually requested, and, in many instances, receives only routine attention. An eye-catching form used for quick dispatch, at minimum cost, is a "mail telegram," since suppliers in many cases ignore printed forms. Much time and money can be saved by using the form which is most appropriate for the situation, both from the standpoint of the supplier who acts upon the communication and the critical nature of the item. It is always a good idea to reach an understanding with the supplier concerning the methods of written communication you employ in order that he will direct the degree of attention you expect.

ELECTRONIC DATA PROCESSING OF INVENTORY CONTROL

Obviously many of the functions and computations described in this section can be performed most quickly and with greatest accuracy on electronic data processing equipment. The utilization of this equipment for purchasing, including its adaptability to inventory control systems, is covered more fully in the following section of this handbook, "Electronic Data Processing Applications in Purchasing."

BIBLIOGRAPHY

It was the intent of this section to outline a practical operating guide to scientific inventory control which would fill the gap between elementary practices and the advanced or theoretical techniques. The latter are covered in detail in books on inventory listed in Sec. 26, "Library and Catalog File."

SECTION 14

ELECTRONIC DATA PROCESSING APPLICATIONS IN PURCHASING

Editor

Joseph A. Padovani, Purchasing Agent, U. S. Steel Corporation, San Francisco, California

Associate Editor

Harold C. Plant, Manager, Computer Manufacturing Applications, RCA Electronic Data Processing, Camden, New Jersey

INTRODUCTION

Electronic data processing (EDP), as its name implies, is the application of high-speed electronic computers in the recording, processing, and printing out of statistical information.

The purpose of EDP in any company is to provide management with timely information of a form that can be used to make judgments and decisions. The EDP system, coincident with providing information for management decisions, should also offer opportunities for cost reduction. Finally, an EDP system develops information oriented to the requirements of a business.

A very basic principle that applies with respect to the above stated objectives of EDP systems is that to the extent requirements are uniform, the systems employed should be uniform.

Unfortunately, there are no reliable and established rules to determine when an EDP system should be installed in a company, and certainly there are no standards to point out how to design and install a system which meets particular needs, nor whether the "payout" will make an EDP system a success or a failure. Each installation must be tailored to the organization, needs, financial structure, and business objectives of the specific company.

EDP systems cost money. Not all functions or operations can or should be computerized. In most cases where EDP is being considered, the majority or all of the functions of a business should be analyzed for operations which can be included in an EDP system if the return on investment for the system (payout) is to be practical and successful. This corralling of functions for inclusion in an EDP system can be termed a *total systems approach.*

Scope of Total Systems

Although many technological advances have been made by the manufacturers of EDP equipment in all areas of design, including higher processing speeds, increased storage capacity, more compact size, greater reliability, and comparatively lower costs, the fact remains that the cost of an EDP system remains significantly high. Consequently, there are few, if any, individual business functions, such as purchasing, which can economically justify an EDP system for its own specific use.

The fundamental work flow of any one company can be classified into three basic groups for sequenced processing of data. These are shown below with major functions.

1. *Sales Process*
   - Order entry and order writing
   - Production planning and scheduling
   - Inventories
   - Shipping
   - Invoicing
   - Accounts receivable
   - Statistics
2. *Production Process*
   - Labor
   - Material
   - Facilities
   - Inventories
   - Costs
   - Statistics—reporting and management
3. *Purchasing Process*
   - Inventory management
   - Requisitioning
   - Order processing
   - Receipts
   - Accounts payable
   - Cost distribution
   - Statistics and reports
     - Expediting
     - Vendor rating and performance
     - Economic order quantities

Obviously, these sequences stimulate integrated handling. Notice, too, they are not at all affected by departmental lines of responsibility and authority. Nor is any specific type of equipment or system implied. Instead, this concept concentrates on the logical relationship between the elements in a process and the information each *requires* or *contributes to* the total system.

As to equipment, one needs to observe only two very fundamental principles.

1. Initial data must be created at their point of origin for mechanical handling.
2. From there on, in subsequent operations, whether data are in punched tape, tab cards, or whatever the medium may be, those data are processed exclusively in a mechanical or electronic manner.

Consequently, any line of equipment capable of reading or writing from coded or mechanical media is compatible with the concept of electronic data processing.

To prescribe equipment capable of producing a needed result is not difficult. To utilize it fully and profitably involves many, many problems.

Purchasing's Role in EDP

A complete EDP system should include the purchasing process, as outlined above. Even though the purchasing process crosses over other departmental lines, the alert purchasing manager must not sit passively on the sidelines while the dominant department plans and designs a system. The purchasing manager must contribute know-how, experience, and technical ability in his specialized field. This active participation can make the difference between a successful, practical program and one which increases purchasing costs and provides information which serves no useful or practical purpose.

The first objective, then, for purchasing is to stay educated and knowledgeable in the field of EDP. Secondly, the purchasing manager should get on the planning team at the very outset and contribute purchasing-oriented ideas. And finally, he should secure the kind of information output which will provide a practical, useful, and low-cost contribution to the purchasing process.

Small Company and EDP

Even the smaller companies who cannot have their own computer system need not be completely denied its benefits if they are near one of the many cities where service bureaus provide access to such equipment on a fee basis. Recent developments in data transmission are even removing the geographical deterrent. Programming and other services are also available, but the client should take an active part in the program layout or he may be headed for trouble.

The service bureau client will probably want to limit the degree of automation more than would someone with a captive operation, but areas of interest to the purchasing department, such as accounts payable and, under proper conditions, inventory control, might well be promising areas for EDP. With the proper commodity, item, buyer, and vendor codes, a computerized accounts-payable routine will develop a great number of stored data from which it is possible to very quickly generate reports of much value to purchasing people. Typical uses for such data will be discussed later.

Another possibility which may develop and be of help to even very small companies involves banks. Over 700 banks now have EDP equipment. Some are already offering an almost complete accounts-payable service. Invoices are "batched" by the customer-depositor at regular intervals (i.e., daily, etc.) and mailed or delivered to the bank where they are processed, checks to vendors written and mailed, and the depositor's account changed—all automatically. It would be very interesting to see what an imaginative purchasing agent and a progressive banker might be able to work out if they really applied themselves to this area.

Electronic accounting machines (EAM) or tabulating equipment can still perform many special tasks much less expensively than a computer. Usually, EAM equipment is used to supplement EDP equipment in data processing centers.

When the computer began to show up in the business world, after proving itself in the scientific field, there was a strong tendency to regard it as essentially a high-speed accounting machine. Banks and insurance companies made wide use of it, and among the first jobs most industrial companies put on a computer were payroll, general ledgers, and related activities.

Essentially accounting applications were fine as initial programs because they involved a considerable number of detailed calculations which had to be done in a hurry against a tight time schedule. They had the further advantage that what was wanted, as well as how to get it, was known in precise detail. There exists, however, a very real danger that too much preoccupation with such programs stifles thinking in some other important areas.

That this frequently happens is attested by the fact that in spite of their tremendous capabilities, many computer installations are failures and quite a number of the successful ones are yielding little more than marginal economic benefits. Entirely too many companies approach EDP solely on the basis of an evaluation of the cost of their present systems and procedures and then try to estimate what the cost will be to convert these procedures to a computer operation.

PLANNING FOR EDP

Passive Resistance

One of the greatest management problems in planning for an EDP system is the passive resistance of operating department heads and staff members down the line. This resistance is often the result of poor communications concerning objectives and of ignorance of the concepts. The resistance is manifested in the pointing up of problems, the finding of reasons for delay, and a display of discreet skepticism about the entire program. Often the pointing up of problems and the viewpoints are well founded and provide clues applicable in planning the system design.

It is certain that to be successful an EDP program needs friends. It is important to establish good communications and provide opportunity for viewpoints and ideas to be heard and evaluated. The method for accomplishing this can be determined by management. Committees and meetings are two means often employed. The groups should be small and the order of business planned and controlled by a chairman.

Scope of Planning

Companies whose efforts in EDP succeed from the start are a minority. This is based on actual studies. The successful companies, though a minority, do exist, and their approaches to planning and managing their EDP programs, although different in detail, do share certain common factors. These factors can be considered basic steps for a planning and control program:

1. *Identify key objectives.*

   As stated previously, the selection of equipment capable of producing a needed result is not difficult. The finding of dozens of potential applications is also fairly easy. The problem is to apply EDP where it can be utilized fully and profitably.

   Identifying the broad EDP objectives will usually orient the EDP effort beyond the narrow area of accounting. These objectives should be planned for functions coming under the three basic areas previously outlined, namely sales process, production process, and purchasing process.

   Agreement on these objectives by the department heads will avert most conflicts over EDP priorities and facilitate the development of detailed plans.

2. *List details for potential applications—long and short range.*

After agreement has been reached on key objectives and they have been defined in terms of feasibility and need, the systems staff should develop a comprehensive catalog of the potential specific EDP applications. This catalog should list the major areas of application; the objective; the type of function; requirements in terms of both (1) staff (man-months) and (2) machine time (hours per month); and net savings per year (dollars).

The preliminary estimates of savings and other benefits expected and the required investment in systems development and programming time and people are factors requiring very critical review by management. Underestimating cost and time required for development of systems is the most common deficiency of poorly conceived programs.

A very controversial element in determining "payout" is *tangible benefits* versus *intangible benefits.* Tangible benefits are verifiable or measurable reductions in cost, whereas intangible benefits can result, for example, from advantages due to greater efficiency, more timely and better decision making information.

The preparation of the detailed applications catalog will obviously require the help of the operating and staff department heads whose functions are affected by the applications involved.

A typical catalog of detailed EDP systems applications is shown in Fig. 14–1, "Data Processing Analysis Catalog."

3. *Analyze benefits and profit potential.*

Management must make the final decision concerning approval of the "go ahead" applications. This in effect is to choose among the "feasible" applications those which will produce the greatest profit or other intangible benefits.

The judgment and analysis of profitability is difficult because there is a great tendency to credit the computer with efficiencies and benefits that might be achieved with a revised manual system, or at least with mechanical-electrical equipment in lieu of a computer system. There is more discussion of this latter dangerous trap in this section under "Purchasing Programs in Preparation for Future EDP Systems."

Any established manual system or clerical procedure should be flow charted, evaluated in terms of personnel man-hours and efficiency, and then studied for complete modernization and improvement before comparing it with the EDP equivalent. Often it will be found that better or equal savings and benefits can be obtained with an updated,

Production Process
Fabrication Division

Function	Clerical force		Net reduction/year		Machine required		Procedure required		Supply costs/year	
	Present	Proposed	Positions	Savings	Hr/mo	Value/yr	Man-mo	Value/yr	Reduction	Addition
Labor:										
Scheduling	8	4	4	$ 28,000						
Time recording	7	3	4	28,000						
Payroll	15	6	9	63,000						
Payroll statistics	3	..	3	21,000						
Distribution—incurred cost	2	..	2	14,000						
Distribution—sold cost	2	..	2	14,000						
Earnings generation	6	3	3	21,000						
Labor statistics	1	..	1	7,000						
Data processing	..	4	(4)	(28,000)	30	$ 54,000	24	$192,000		$ 1,800
Material:										
Production scheduling	15	5	10	70,000						
Production recording	5	7	(2)	(14,000)						
Production control	6	5	1	7,000						
Inventories in product control	4	2	2	14,000						
Distribution—material cost	1	1								1,500
Earnings generation	4	1	3	21,000						450
Production statistics	1	..	1	7,000						1,350
Data processing	..	4	(4)	(28,000)	60	108,000	36	288,000		6,300
Total	80	45	35	$245,000	90	$162,000	60	$480,000		$11,400

Net savings per year—$71,610. **Cost Recovery-Procedure Effort—*6.9 years.***

FIG. 14–1. Data processing analysis catalog—mechanization of clerical functions.

improved manual system. Overestimating future clerical- and volume-growth projections results in biased decisions and invalid EDP savings and efficiency potential.

4. *Consider implementation and design.*

Before the actual installation is reached, much planning and preliminary systems-design work will have been completed. A comprehensive time schedule detailing every element of each phase of the system must be prepared. This schedule should include timetable objectives for recruitment and training of computer operations personnel, equipment orders, and delivery and site preparation. In addition, the schedule will identify times, objectives, and status for data gathering, flow charting, forms integration and design, and coding for computer input requirements. During the actual process of systems design, it is helpful and important to survey other firms who have completed similar installations. Visitations and studies of as many systems as possible will often enable systems designers to avoid costly delays, problems, and difficulties not readily apparent. Good concepts and usable ideas are also exchanged which may considerably improve the system under design.

An accumulative cost record of man-hours, machine time, and other related costs is an advisable means of effective control on design objectives. This monitoring of financial progress can be maintained on a monthly or quarterly "spread sheet" (cost versus savings).

Cooperation and coordination with all operating department heads outside the systems and procedure staff is of continuing importance during this stage of conversion to EDP. It is top management's responsibility to maintain the climate which enables "team effort" to reach established time and savings objectives. Figs. 14–2a and 14–2b provide

Purpose:

To analyze existing operations in this functional area in order to develop and design an inventory-management system for spares, stores, supplies, raw materials, and operating process supplies. The system to be programmed to integrate inventory management with procurement and operating processes to attain the following objectives.

Objectives:

1. **Establish and maintain stock levels and reorder quantities on the basis of economic order quantity principles, but within the realm of projected operating needs and good purchasing management policies and judgment.**
2. **Simplify, consolidate, and develop economical clerical processes consistent with sound business practice in order to implement the operation of the system.**
3. **Develop "real time" information in terms of specific items, quantities, usage, costs, and historical data as they relate to procurement and inventory management functions.**
4. **Control the Company's dollar investment in inventory and maintain acquisition costs to the lowest possible level consistent with sound operating and purchasing practices.**

FIG. 14–2a. Inventory management—data processing system objectives.

I. Define scope of system in terms of types of materials by class and plant and operating locations to be included.

II. Develop a comprehensive program for reclassification, standardization of nomenclature and specifications, and uniform commodity coding.
   A. Prepare time completion schedule.
   B. Develop procedures for carrying out all steps to achieve objectives.
   C. Establish controls to measure progress and status of program steps.

III. Correlate all data and programs required for procurement, accounting, and operating practices.
   A. Uniform units of measure.
   B. Standard order units.
   C. Standard package units.
   D. Economic order quantities and formulas.
   E. Vendor codes—multiple vendor addresses.
      1. Maintenance and control of vendor files.

IV. Apply and consolidate data processing parameters which correlate the entire purchasing process.
   A. Inventory management.
   B. Accounts payable.
   C. Receiving and quality control.
   D. Requisitioning and purchasing.
   E. Vendor rating.
   F. Perpetuation of data to other functions in operating and accounting.
   G. Obtaining statistics for application to management by exception principles.

V. Develop programs and procedures to implement the objectives.
   A. Computer-oriented data.
      1. Programs.
      2. Equipment and costs.
      3. Personnel requirements.
      4. Cost analysis.
         a. Savings.
         b. Accrued expenses.
         c. Return on investment.
      5. Input and output requirements.

VI. Accounting applications.
   A. Accounts payable.
      1. Invoice verification.
      2. Receipt and disbursement.
      3. Check writing.
      4. Audit controls.
      5. Freight bill—verification and payment.
   B. Distribution and perpetuation of data.
      1. Standard costs.
      2. Cost accounting.
      3. Work in process.
      4. Purchase order writing.

VII. Physical stocking requisites.
   A. Consolidation of warehouse facilities.
      1. Standard binning practices.
      2. Coding.
      3. Disbursement procedures.
   B. Inventory costs.
      1. Space requirements.
      2. Stocking costs.
      3. Stock-level theory.

VIII. Procedures, policy, and systems manual.
   A. Prepare manual to implement, maintain, and control the system.
   B. Obtain management approval.

FIG. 14–2b. Inventory material management system—design, development, and installation.

actual illustrations of detailed design program schedules on inventory management.

5. *Establish flexibility in thinking and design.*

During the design and implementation of the EDP system, it is of considerable importance to build in maximum flexibility to anticipate probable future advances in equipment and methods. This flexibility should be limited only by the imagination and ingenuity of those participating in the system's design. The flexibility in design applies to the basic concepts of the system which in turn determine the logic for programming the computer.

This is the area where the purchasing manager can contribute his specialized know-how and obtain the specific data or system required for his needs. It is at this point of an EDP program that a computer programmer or systems designer may impose inflexible thinking which may be based on a desire to achieve simplified or conventional programming. Often what a systems designer or programmer considers impossible or impractical from a programming or systems perspective *does have* a solution which satisfies both the needs of the purchasing responsibility and the technical restrictions of the computer. The purchasing manager should not accept as gospel the explanation that technical computer restrictions will prevent his ideas and specific needs from being designed into the system.

6. *Acknowledge inflexibilities.*

While flexibility should predominate, there are certain elements of rigidity in the electronic data processing system. Although magnetic tape provides high-speed input, in order to lift information from the tape file for any special or nonroutine need extensive scanning may be required. If this interrupts scheduled computer routines, it may present operating and cost problems.

Similarly, the planning of an elaborate routine requires comprehensive step-by-step analysis and the preparation of thousands of programmed instructions, all interrelated in precise pattern to produce one planned result—and no other. To modify the program may involve considerable time and cost.

Summary

The achievement of maximum benefits from EDP programs is nothing more than the use of sound management discipline in planning and control, incorporating:

1. A sound, practical, and economically justified plan of applications
2. Knowledgeable and careful selection of hardware

3. Clear-cut objectives
4. Realistic and valid economic analyses
5. Detailed scheduling
6. Effective cost controls
7. Regular progress reports and post-installation appraisal

Selection of Personnel for Systems Design

Some companies are motivated to engage consultants, representatives of equipment manufacturers, or other outside experts to conduct their systems study and develop the concept for EDP or IDP (integrated data processing) systems. There is ample evidence in actual case examples to indicate that this work can be done more effectively by the company's own people. The so-called outside consultants and equipment manufacturer's representatives can contribute important service in rendering technical advice and in training company employees; however, outsiders usually are not familiar enough with a company's operations, policies, practices and objectives to develop the most practical system.

An equally ineffective and costly act is to staff this activity with company personnel who are not capable of carrying out a systems design job.

The people selected to do this job should be analytical, imaginative, aggressive, highly rated individuals who have demonstrated objective and successful accomplishments in other responsibilities. Most important of all requisites is the ability to get along well with people. Salesmanship and persuasiveness are essential in reaching objectives.

It should be obvious that the area of systems development embraces many functions and provides an unmatched challenge in resolving problems of a technical, administrative, and operational nature.

The purchasing manager will be well advised to select the best man in his organization to represent the purchasing responsibilities on the EDP team. Obviously, this candidate should be thoroughly experienced in purchasing operations.

Categories of Automation in Purchasing

Although this concept is principally concerned with EDP, there are several concepts and designations which are applied in the area of purchasing automation. At present, the various categories of automation include:

EDP (electronic data processing). This involves data processing equipment in which data are stored either magnetically or electronically.

IDP (integrated data processing). This covers automatic systems in which data are stored mechanically, as in punched cards and tapes.

ADP (automatic data processing). This processing includes both EDP and IDP in any combination.

Punched-card system. This covers any system, whether ADP or nonautomatic, in which data are stored on punched cards.

A more detailed review is given in the succeeding paragraphs.

The Function and Scope of the Electronic Data Processing Equipment

The central processing unit is the heart of an EDP system. It is often called the "computer." This processing unit receives data and instructions, stores them in memory cells, and calls the data out of memory as needed in the processing routine. It performs the arithmetic operations of addition, subtraction, multiplication, and division and has the further important ability—found only in a very limited degree in mechanical systems—to make comparisons between numbers and characters and to take action called for by the result.

The central processing unit also directs the processing operations within itself and controls the flow and manipulation of both input and output information as dictated by the programmed instructions.

All the foregoing operations are performed at electronic speed. Electronic pulses, magnetic fields, and other electrical manifestations are symbolic representations of numbers and characters in the functional operation of the unit.

Since all computers will do only what they are directed to do, the data processing plan must be of human creation. The plan of instructions to the computer is called a "program."

The processing unit consists of a control unit, a storage device, and an arithmetic unit. The control unit interprets the program instructions and directs the various data processing operations. The storage unit, or "memory," receives the instructions and data from the input device, stores intermeditae solutions, and releases information, all as instructed by the program through the control unit. The arithmetic unit performs the arithmetic and comparison operations upon data and instructions sent to from the storage device, again as directed by the control unit.

Linked electrically by cable to the processing unit are devices which "read" information into it and "write" (print out) information out of it. These devices are referred to as input equipment and output equipment. Like the processing unit they are electronic in principle. The function of the input devices is to translate from an input medium, i.e., tape or card, the data of the problem and the programmed instructions necessary to obtain its solution and to put them into the processing unit. The function of the output devices, on the other hand, is to receive the information emitted from the processing unit and dispose of it as directe by the control unit.

There is a tendency for some laymen to visualize the electronic da processing system as one that handles all steps in the data processin routine. This is a misconception with practical implications which b come apparent by considering the operations performed by the inpu preparation equipment. The data processing routine generally begins the source documents which constitute the record of the transactions. is necessary to prepare input information from a source document into medium acceptable to the processing unit. The practical significance this is twofold: first, to perform these input preparation operations ma require the services of many people who would be operating a large ba tery of similar types of equipment, such as card and tape punches, th same as those used in mechanical systems; and second, the speed of pe forming these operations is still bound by human and mechanical limit tions.

Data processing per se is therefore not completely electronic in concep or operation at the present time. It is most important for a purchasin manager to understand the significance of this fact, for it impinges o the design of a system and affects the recovery of timely data required purchasing.

Integrated Data Processing

A variety of new devices have been developed since about 1951, som of which are not electronic in principle. These devices are intended increase the speed of data production and transmission. Specially d signed attachments to adding machines, desk calculators, bookkeepin machines, cash registers, typewriters, Flexowriters, and teletype machin make possible the preparation of original documents and also simult neous production of perforated tapes or cards for subsequent use in ele tronic data processing. There are many new advanced techniques an devices to transmit data over long distances using telephone and telegrap lines.

Output from these devices is used as input to the electronic systen Thus, these conventional electrical-mechanical machines may be employe not only to prepare documents, their primary function, but also produce a common-language medium (coded tape or card) which compatible with the electronic system. The effect is an integration functions which eliminates those manual operations which would be r quired to convert source data (i.e., data on an original document such a purchase order, invoice, receiving report, etc.) to the language of th electronic system.

This concept of data integration is known as "integrated data processing." This is a broad subject in itself, one upon which much could be said. Future developments in this area of input functions may overshadow all other future advances in data processing.

The importance of the above concept relates to the fact that a purchasing operation can be mechanized by applying the principles of IDP and the available devices at comparatively low cost without investment in electronic data processing equipment. The use of IDP devices and systems concepts is the basis for future moves into electronic data processing. For example, purchase order preparation can be mechanized by employing Flexowriter equipment as described in "Automation in Purchasing." Some principles relating to the foregoing concept are outlined in the following subsection.

Purchasing Programs in Preparation for Future EDP Systems

There have been many articles authored which attempt with much logic to build a case for applying EDP for automated purchasing, thus doing a more effective job of reducing both product and administrative costs. As was stated at the very outset of this section there are no clear-cut "how to do it" paths to achieve these lofty objectives. It is possible to design and develop a "buy by computer" purchasing system, but it must be tailored to the organization, needs, financial structure, and business objectives. Most important, "buy by computer" can be practical only for repetitively purchased items under a computer-controlled inventory system. It should be obvious that the materials which are not highly repetitive and which are not identified by commodity codes and standard specifications cannot be economically or feasibly "purchased" by a computer.

Another equally important factor to be considered in the "buy by computer" approach is the volume or number of items falling in the highly repetitive category. A determination of this factor in terms of computer time and programming costs must be made. Unless the reorder volume warrants this approach, the computer ordering technique may not be practical in terms of economic consideration.

The foregoing points are brought into clearer focus if the section on page 14–13, "The Function and Scope of the Electronic Data Processing Equipment," is recalled. And in this connection, one should consider the fact that input to the computer for preparing a print out in the form of a purchase order requires preparation of data in acceptable code format, including: commodity description; commodity code; quantity; price; terms; discount; applicable tax; f.o.b. point; routing instructions; shipping information; distribution of costs to proper cost center or account;

vendor's name, address, and code; shipping date. This is to name only the basic data.

The problems imposed by the above considerations indicate that along with the "buy by computer" concept, one should consider alternate means to mechanically prepare purchase orders and inquiries and to develop the statistical information for management control and guidance in decision making.

The solution for those purchasing operations which buy both highly repetitive inventory or process materials and nonrepetitive inventory or process materials may be to employ both an EDP system and a mechanized purchase order writing system. The latter mechanical writing approach would utilize a device which can be used to prepare source documents (purchase order, inquiry, work sheet, or requisition), while simultaneously and automatically capturing coded data for input to the total EDP system (e.g., Flexowriter machine).

Do not overlook the fact that the electrical-mechanical device which is referred to above can be used to mechanically prepare highly repetitive, nonrepetitive, and one-shot item purchase documents. See the sections "Automation in Purchasing," which illustrates the use of Flexowriter

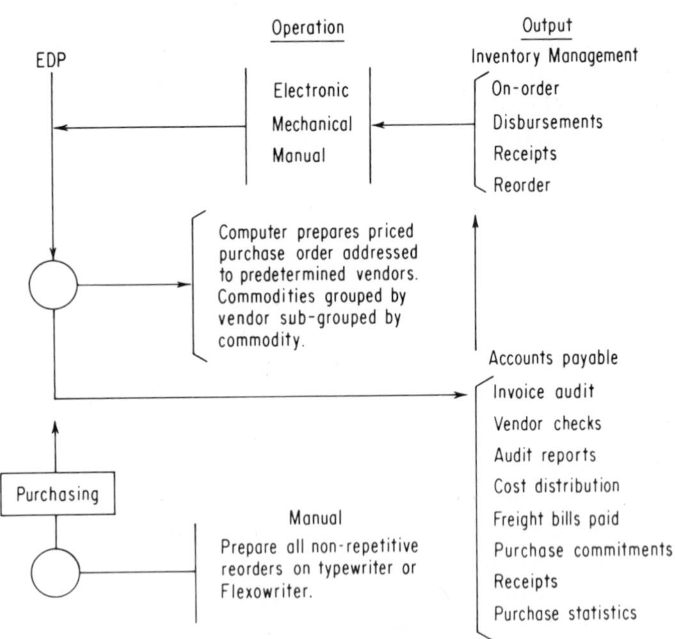

FIG. 14–3. EDP purchasing system—computer order preparation.

and traveling requisitions to achieve this type of approach to automation.

In either concept, the use of integrated data processing techniques is essential.

Typical Systems Approaches to EDP

Several general and simplified flow diagrams are shown in Figs. 14–3 and 14–4 to illustrate possible combinations of EDP and mechanized order writing techniques. These are intended to illustrate typical approaches to EDP. Fig. 14–5 illustrates a Flexowriter prepared purchase order and the data perpetuated in a computer oriented system for accounts payable and inventory control. Figures 14–6a, 14–6b and 14–6c are illustrations of a computer originated purchase request, a manual originated purchase request, and a computer written purchase order. An analysis of these documents will reveal the scope of data which can be

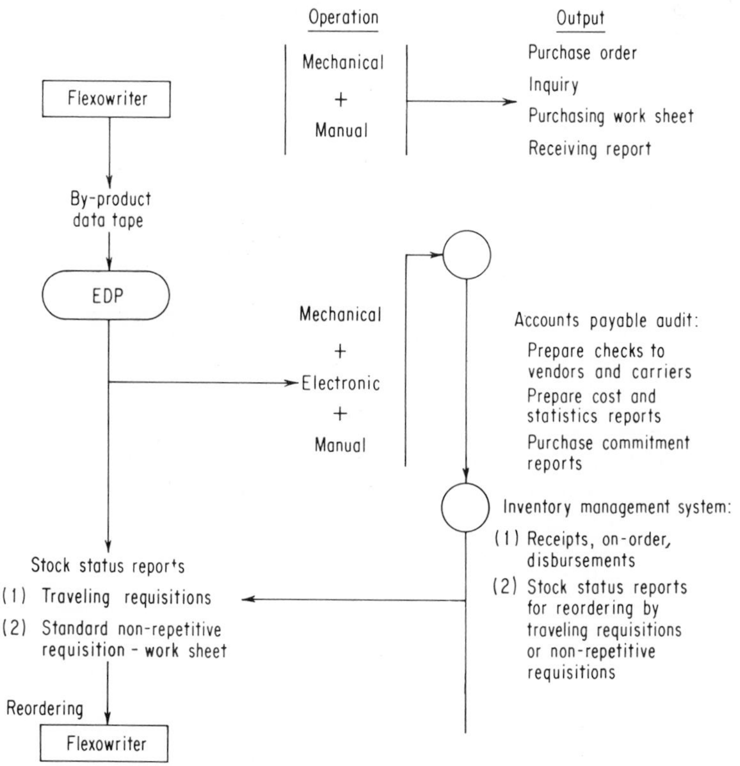

FIG. 14–4. Purchasing system using IDP—EDP.

applied to enable purchasing to make precise decisions in their buyin functions.

These latter exhibits represent one of the most sophisticated and mod ern computer oriented purchasing systems. It is operational at Lockhee Missiles & Space Company, Sunnyvale, California.

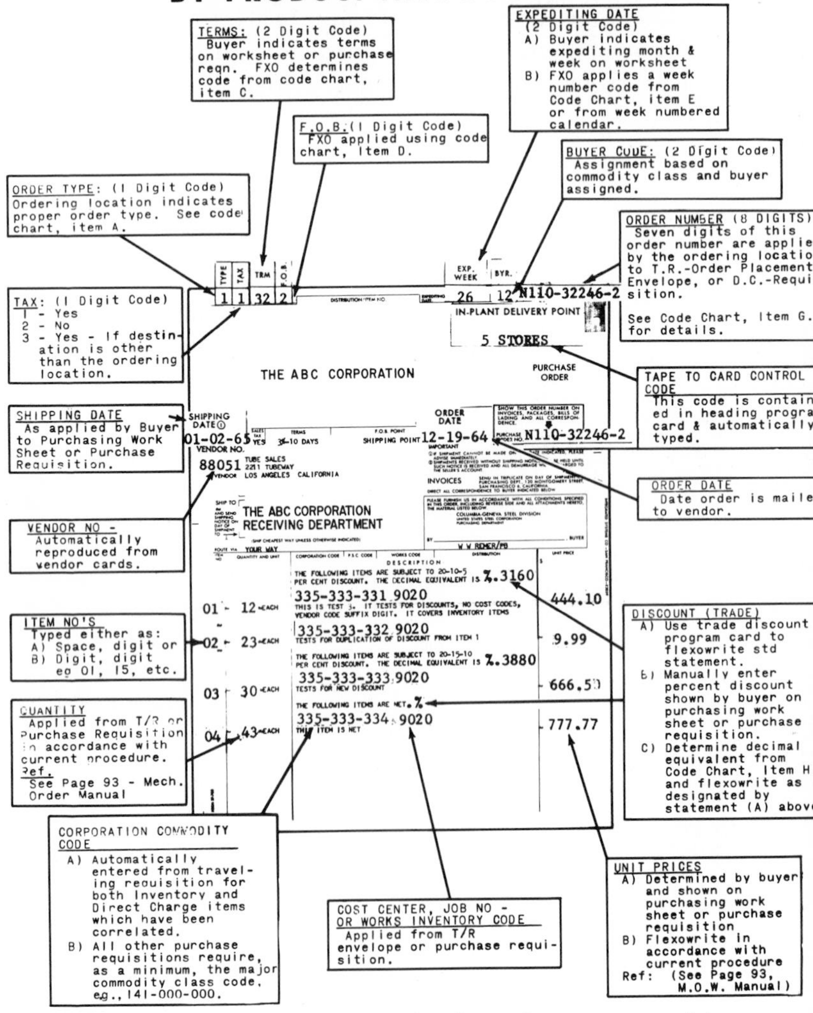

FIG. 14–5. Purchase data processing—by-product tape-source data.

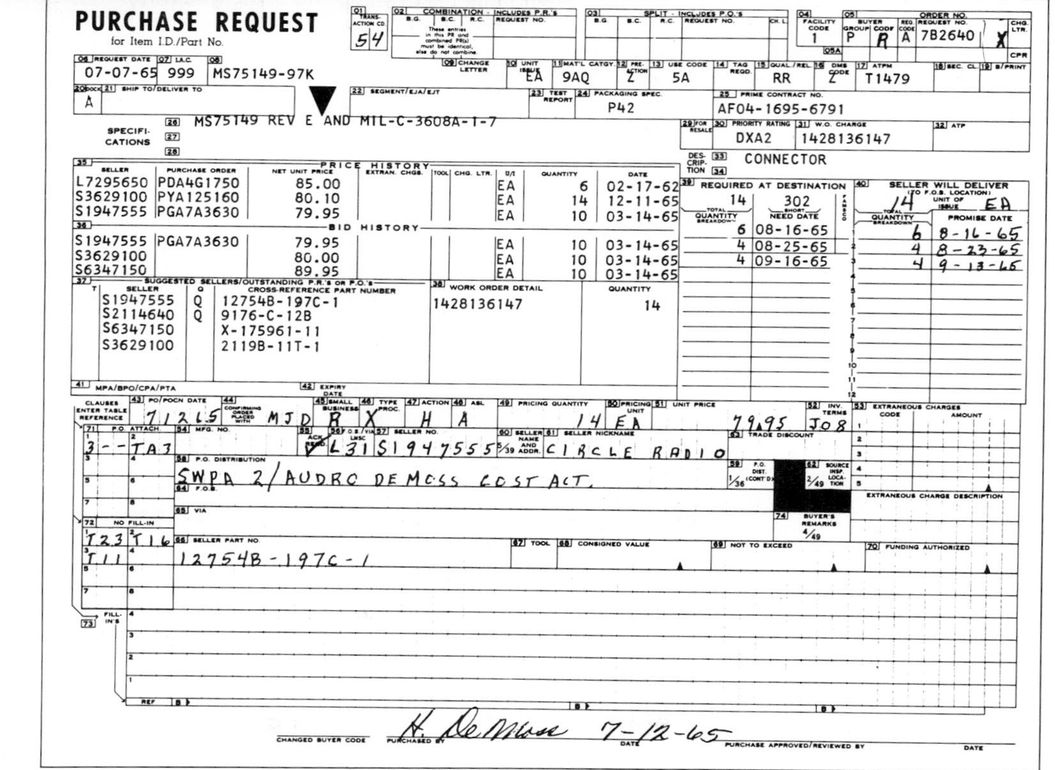

PURCHASE REQUEST
for Item I.D./Part No.

01 TRANS-ACTION CD.: 54
02 COMBINATION - INCLUDES P.R.'s: B.G. | B.C. | R.C. | REQUEST NO. (These entries in this PR and combined PR(s) must be identical, else do not combine.)
03 SPLIT - INCLUDES P.O.'s: B.G. | B.C. | R.C. | REQUEST NO. | CH. L.
04 FACILITY CODE: 1
05 BUYER GROUP: P — BUYER CODE: R — 05A REQ. CODE: A — ORDER NO. REQUEST NO.: 7B2640 — CHG. LTR.: X — CPR

06 REQUEST DATE: 07-07-65 | 07 I.A.C.: 999 | 08: MS75149-97K
09 CHANGE LETTER | 10 UNIT ISSUE: EA | 11 MAT'L CATGY: 9AQ | 12 PRE-ACTION: Z | 13 USE CODE: 5A | 14 TAG REQD. | 15 QUAL./REL.: RR | 16 DMS CODE: Z | 17 ATPM: T1479 | 18 SEC. CL. | 19 B/PRINT
20 DOCK: A | 21 SHIP TO/DELIVER TO | 22 SEGMENT/EJA/EJT | 23 TEST REPORT | 24 PACKAGING SPEC.: P42 | 25 PRIME CONTRACT NO.: AF04-1695-6791
SPECIFICATIONS: 26 MS75149 REV E AND MIL-C-3608A-1-7 | 27 | 28
29 FOR RESALE | 30 PRIORITY RATING: DXA2 | 31 W.O. CHARGE: 1428136147 | 32 ATP
DESCRIPTION: 33 CONNECTOR | 34

35 PRICE HISTORY

SELLER	PURCHASE ORDER	NET UNIT PRICE	EXTRAN. CHGS.	TOOL	CHG. LTR.	U/I	QUANTITY	DATE
L7295650	PDA4G1750	85.00				EA	6	02-17-62
S3629100	PYA125160	80.10				EA	14	12-11-65
S1947555	PGA7A3630	79.95				EA	10	03-14-65

36 BID HISTORY

SELLER	PURCHASE ORDER	NET UNIT PRICE	EXTRAN. CHGS.	TOOL	CHG. LTR.	U/I	QUANTITY	DATE
S1947555	PGA7A3630	79.95				EA	10	03-14-65
S3629100		80.00				EA	10	03-14-65
S6347150		89.95				EA	10	03-14-65

37 SUGGESTED SELLERS/OUTSTANDING P.R.'s OR P.O.'s

T	SELLER	Q	CROSS-REFERENCE PART NUMBER
	S1947555	Q	12754B-197C-1
	S2114640	Q	9176-C-12B
	S6347150		X-175961-11
	S3629100		2119B-11T-1

38 WORK ORDER DETAIL: 1428136147 — QUANTITY: 14

39 REQUIRED AT DESTINATION: 14 — 302

TOTAL QUANTITY BREAKDOWN	SHORT NEED DATE
6	08-16-65
4	08-25-65
4	09-16-65

40 SELLER WILL DELIVER (TO F.O.B. LOCATION): 14 — UNIT OF ISSUE: EA

TOTAL QUANTITY BREAKDOWN	PROMISE DATE
6	8-16-65
4	8-23-65
4	9-13-65

41 MPA/BPO/CPA/PTA | 42 EXPIRY DATE
CLAUSES ENTER TABLE REFERENCE | 43 PO/POCN DATE: 71265 | 44 CONFIRMING ORDER PLACED WITH: MJD | 45 SMALL BUSINESS: R | 46 TYPE PROC.: X | 47 ACTION: H | 48 ASL: A | 49 PRICING QUANTITY: 14 | 50 PRICING UNIT: EA | 51 UNIT PRICE: 79.95 | 52 INV. TERMS: J08 | 53 EXTRANEOUS CHARGES CODE / AMOUNT
71 P.O. ATTACH: 3--TA3 | 54 MFG. NO. | 55 ACK: ✓ | 56 F.O.B./VIA LMSC: L31 | 57 SELLER NO.: S1947555 | 60 SELLER NAME AND ADDR.: 5/39 | 61 SELLER NICKNAME: CIRCLE RADIO | 63 TRADE DISCOUNT
58 P.O. DISTRIBUTION: SWPA 2/AUDRC DEMCSS COST ACT. | 59 P.O. DIST. (CONT'D): 1/36 | 62 SOURCE INSP. LOCATION: 2/49
64 F.O.B. | EXTRANEOUS CHARGE DESCRIPTION
65 VIA | 74 BUYER'S REMARKS: 4/49
72 NO FILL-IN: T23 T16 T11 | 66 SELLER PART NO.: 12754B-197C-1 | 67 TOOL | 68 CONSIGNED VALUE | 69 NOT TO EXCEED | 70 FUNDING AUTHORIZED
73 FILL-IN'S
REF

CHANGED BUYER CODE | PURCHASED BY: H. DeMoss | DATE: 7-12-65 | PURCHASE APPROVED/REVIEWED BY | DATE

FIG. 14–6a. Computer originated purchase request. Reproduced by permission of Lockheed Missiles & Space Co., Sunnyvale, California.

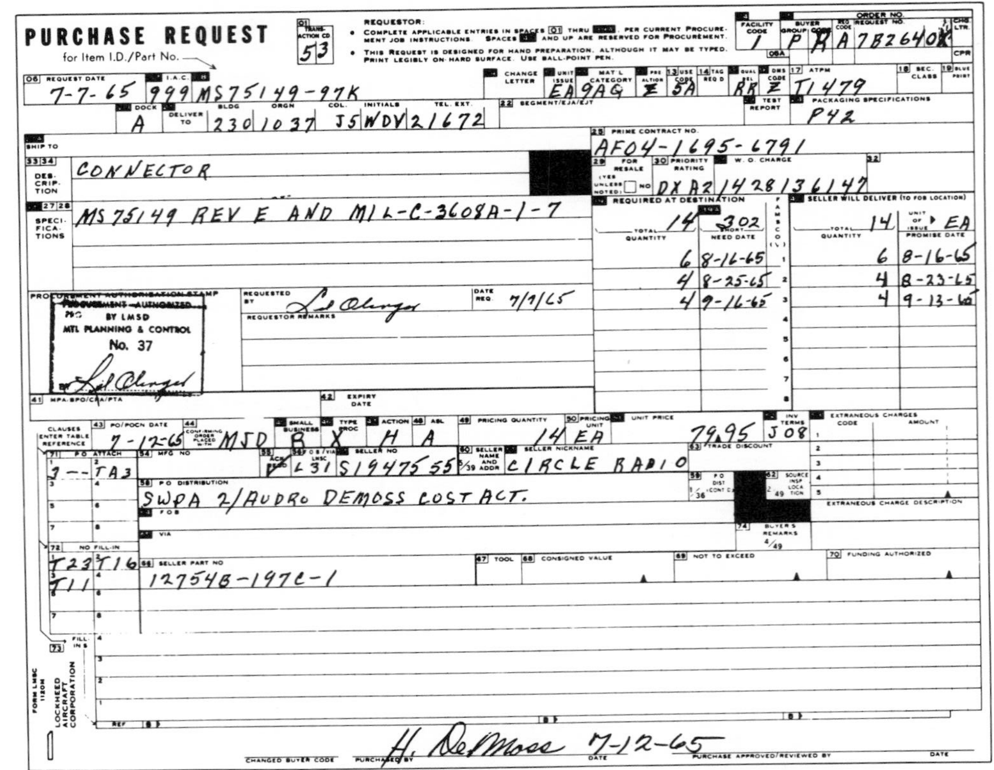

PURCHASE REQUEST
for Item I.D./Part No.

01 TRANS-ACTION CD: 53

REQUESTOR:
• COMPLETE APPLICABLE ENTRIES IN SPACES 01 THRU ___, PER CURRENT PROCUREMENT JOB INSTRUCTIONS. SPACES ___ AND UP ARE RESERVED FOR PROCUREMENT.
• THIS REQUEST IS DESIGNED FOR HAND PREPARATION, ALTHOUGH IT MAY BE TYPED. PRINT LEGIBLY ON HARD SURFACE. USE BALL-POINT PEN.

FACILITY CODE: 1 | BUYER GROUP CODE: P | REQ CODE: R | ORDER NO. REQUEST NO.: A7B2640K | CHG LTR. | CPR

06 REQUEST DATE: 7-7-65 | I.A.C.: 999 | MS75149-97K | CHANGE LETTER | UNIT ISSUE: EA | MAT'L CATEGORY: 9AG | PRE ALTION: Z | 13 USE CODE: 5A | 14 TAG REQ D | QUAL REL: RR | DMS CODE: Z | 17 ATPM: T1479 | 18 SEC. CLASS | 19 BLUE PRINT

DOCK: A | DELIVER TO | BLDG: 230 | ORGN: 1037 | COL.: J5 | INITIALS: WDV | TEL. EXT.: 21672 | 22 SEGMENT/EJA/EJT | TEST REPORT | PACKAGING SPECIFICATIONS: P42

SHIP TO | 25 PRIME CONTRACT NO.: AF04-1695-6791

33 34 DESCRIPTION: CONNECTOR | 29 FOR RESALE (YES UNLESS NOTED) NO | 30 PRIORITY RATING: DXA2 | W. O. CHARGE: 1428136147 | 32

27 28 SPECIFICATIONS: MS75149 REV E AND MIL-C-3608A-1-7

REQUIRED AT DESTINATION: TOTAL QUANTITY 14 | SHORT 302 | NEED DATE

	QUANTITY	NEED DATE		QUANTITY	PROMISE DATE
1	6	8-16-65		6	8-16-65
2	4	8-25-65		4	8-23-65
3	4	9-16-65		4	9-13-65

SELLER WILL DELIVER (TO FOB LOCATION): TOTAL QUANTITY 14 | UNIT OF ISSUE: EA

PROCUREMENT AUTHORIZATION STAMP: PROCUREMENT AUTHORIZED BY LMSD MTL PLANNING & CONTROL No. 37 BY [signature]

REQUESTED BY: [signature] | DATE REQ.: 7/7/65
REQUESTOR REMARKS

41 MPA-BPO/CRA/PTA | 42 EXPIRY DATE

CLAUSES ENTER TABLE REFERENCE | 43 PO/POCN DATE: 7-12-65 | 44 CONFIRMING ORDER PLACED WITH: MJD | SMALL BUSINESS: B | TYPE PROC: X | ACTION: H | 48 ASL: A | 49 PRICING QUANTITY: 14 | 50 PRICING UNIT: EA | UNIT PRICE: 79.95 | INV TERMS: J08 | EXTRANEOUS CHARGES CODE / AMOUNT

71 PO ATTACH: 1 --- 2 TA3 | 54 MFG NO | 55 ACK REQD | F O B/VIA LMSC: L31 | SELLER NO: S1947555 | 60 SELLER NAME AND ADDR: 39 | SELLER NICKNAME: CIRCLE RADIO | 63 TRADE DISCOUNT

58 P O DISTRIBUTION: SWPA 2/AUDRO DEMOSS COST ACT. | 59 P O DIST (CONT C) 36 | 62 SOURCE INSP LOCATION 49 | EXTRANEOUS CHARGE DESCRIPTION

FOB
VIA | 74 BUYER'S REMARKS 4/49

72 NO FILL-IN: T23 T16 T11 | 66 SELLER PART NO: 12754B-197C-1 | 67 TOOL | 68 CONSIGNED VALUE | 69 NOT TO EXCEED | 70 FUNDING AUTHORIZED

73 FILL-INS

REF

FORM LMSC 1120H LOCKHEED AIRCRAFT CORPORATION

CHANGED BUYER CODE | PURCHASED BY: H. DeMoss | DATE: 7-12-65 | PURCHASE APPROVED/REVIEWED BY | DATE

FIG. 14–6b. Manual originated purchase request. Reproduced by permission of Lockheed Missiles & Space Co., Sunnyvale, California.

PURCHASE ORDER

FACILITY: 1 | IAC: 999 | WORK ORDER OR ACCOUNT: 14-2813-6147
SMALL BUSN.: R | TYPE PROC.: X | ASL: A | SELLER NO.: S-19475-55
DOCK — SHIP TO/DELIVER TO: A 1037 230 J5 21672
MAT'L CTGY.: 9AQ | PRE-ACTION: Z | USE CODE: 5A | QR: HY | DMS CODE: Z
ATPN: T1479
UNIT OF ORDER: EA = 1.0000 UNIT OF ISSUE: EA

INVOICES: Mail original and two (2) copies to — ACCOUNTS PAYABLE, LOCKHEED MISSILES & SPACE COMPANY
NO INVOICES REQUIRED

IMPORTANT: Codes identify clauses on attachments hereto which are incorporated herein by reference: RR 3-- TA3

CIRCLE RADIO AND ELECTRONICS INC.
49716 WELDON WAY
LOS ANGELES, CALIF. 24715

DATE: 7-12-65
PURCHASE ORDER NUMBER: PRA7B2640X | CHANGE LETTER:

SELLER PRICING — QUANTITY: 14 | UNIT PRICE: 79.95 | UNIT: EA
TERMS: 1 PCT 10 DAYS
TRADE DISCOUNT: | NOT TO EXCEED:
BPO/CPA MPA/PTA: | CONSIGNED VALUE:
DIRECT ALL INQUIRIES REGARDING THIS ORDER TO: DEMOSS H.
THIS CONFIRMS ORDER PLACED WITH: MJD | DO NOT REPEAT | ACK. REQD.: NO | FOR RESALE?: YES
LMSC PART NO.: MS75149-97K | CHANGE LETTER:
SELLER PART NO.: 12754B-197C-1
GOVERNMENT CONTRACT NO.: AF04-1695-6791
PACKAGING SPEC.: P42 | DMS REG # 1 | CERTIFIED UNDER PRIORITY RATING: DX-A2

SHIP TO: ATTENTION: D.A. DIXON
LOCKHEED MISSILES & SPACE CO
BLDG. 152 SUNNYVALE, CALIF.

FOB ▶ OUR PLANT
VIA ▶ YOUR DELIVERY
SPECIFICATIONS:
MS75149 REV E AND MIL-C-3608A-1-7

DESCRIPTION: CONNECTOR

PURCHASE ORDER DISTRIBUTION:
SWPA 2/AUDRO
DEMOSS
COST ACT.

SCHEDULE: SHIP A TOTAL OF 14 EA as follows

	QUANTITY	DATE		QUANTITY	DATE		QUANTITY	DATE		QUANTITY	DATE
1	6	8-16-65	2	4	8-23-65	3	4	9-13-65	4		
5			6			7			8		
9			10			11			12		

SPECIAL INSTRUCTIONS TO SELLER:

LMSC SOURCE SURVEILLANCE MANDATORY-SUPPLIER TO NOTIFY NEAREST PRODUCT ASSURANCE FIELD OFFICE PRIOR TO MANUFACTURE.

ATTACHED TEXT IS INCORPORATED HEREIN BY REFERENCE

CERTIFY ON THE ABSOLUTE LIFE LIMIT RECORD/ALLRI/THAT ALL LIMITED CALENDAR LIFE/LCL/MATERIALS OR PARTS WERE CONTROLLED IN ACCORDANCE WITH PB29 OR THAT NONE WERE USED

FIG. 14–6c. Computer written purchase order. Reproduced by permission of Lockheed Missiles & Space Co., Sunnyvale, California.

AUTOMATION IN PURCHASING

Application of Integrated Data Processing Principles to Mechanized Order Writing

Here is a brief outline of the basic elements of a system as they relate to IDP principles.

1. *Original data are recorded at their point of origin in a mechanical form.* In a mechanized purchase order writing system this is accomplished as follows:
   a. A traveling requisition containing uniform commodity codes, commodity descriptions or specifications, standard ordering units, and other purchasing historical data is prepared for all items included within the scope of the system.
   b. All the specific data in (*a*) above, as well as predetermined, functional machine codes, are also recorded in coded form on an edge punched card. Both the traveling requisition and its corresponding coded edge punched card are retained as a unit under the control of the storeskeeper at each respective operating location.
   c. As materials are required for reorder, determined by the plant's inventory-control systems, the traveling requisitions are grouped into appropriate ordering arrangements and transmitted to the centralized purchasing department.

2. *Once in mechanical form, data are processed exclusively in a mechanical manner.* In the mechanized purchase order writing system this is accomplished as follows:

   a. Purchase orders are prepared automatically by mechanically reading traveling-requisition constant-reorder data in the form of edge punched card codes and thereby automatically typing the purchase order.
   b. Variable data only, such as price, quantity, shipping date, etc., are entered manually through the keyboard of the programmatic Flexowriter.

3. *All processing of data is integrated so that original data in mechanical form can serve all subsequent applications.* In the mechanized purchase order writing system this is accomplished as follows:

   Selected purchase data are automatically recorded in coded form in a by-product tape simultaneously with the mechanical writing of purchase orders. The tape may be converted to tab cards which assist in controlling subsequent processes such as receiving, invoice processing, inventory control, preparation of expediting reports, various usage reports, commodity by vendor, vendor by commodity, and other purchasing statistical reports. These processes can be handled by EDP systems in operation or planned for future installation as various segments of the purchasing cycle are completed.

Importance of Uniform Data

A most important requisite in planning for a mechanized system is the provision of a uniform *base* relative to commodity and purchase data.

This is the reason for a commodity-standardization program. Its purpose is to standardize for all requisitioning operations the format, ordering specifications, nomenclature, standard ordering unit, unit of measure, and commodity codes of all repetitively purchased materials and stores items.

Standardization of commodity and purchase data is essential in the procurement cycle of a mechanized system because these data are perpetuated in mechanical form for subsequent processing in other functions in the business cycle.

The standardization program of the system can be conducted as a part of the document-preparation phase of the mechanized purchase order writing system. The two programs are coordinated to proceed simultaneously for maximum efficiency and in order to complete the work in a minimum period of time.

It is possible to reduce costs and increase efficiency by integrating as many operations and documents as possible. The number of initial documents and their use must, of course, be tailor-made to satisfy conditions peculiar to the type of industry, organization, and scope of purchasing. In the system discussed here, the following documents are planned requisites:

1. Traveling requisition
2. On-order card
3. Edge punched item card
4. Edge punched item detail label
5. Item control card
6. Commodity-catalog tab card
7. Division commodity catalog
8. Edge punched vendor card

Through forms integration and machine programming techniques, items 1 to 5 are produced simultaneously.

The traveling-requisition–form set consists of the following integrated parts:

1. Traveling-requisition insert
2. On-order card
3. Identification label for edge punched card
4. Purchasing department item control card

All parts are filled in simultaneously on the programmatic Flexowriter. The edge punched item card is produced in the punch unit during the preparation of these documents.

It is of note that the traveling-requisition insert and edge punched item card are housed in a traveling-requisition envelope. The envelope, which may be discarded when its spaces have been filled, eliminates the cost of retyping a new traveling requisition and also serves to protect the traveling-requisition insert, containing basic specification data, from wear and soiling.

An on-order card is the ordering location's record of the commodity. It provides for the manual entry of ordering information, receipts, and historical data.

The purchasing department item control card is the basic centralized record for each commodity and item included in the mechanized system. It is used in controlling changes in descriptions, codes, and specifications and in adding new items. This control file is essential in commodity classification and standardization and in mechanized order-writing functions.

In establishing the traveling-requisition file, work is reduced by a Flexowriter programming method. This permits the automatic reproduction of constant information for all items within a subclass group. Repetitive data are captured on a secondary program card when the first traveling-requisition item for the group is prepared. Thereafter, the data are reproduced automatically for the items following. Only a limited number of variable data are entered manually. This is work simplification resulting in clerical economies, even during the preparation phase for the ultimate mechanized system.

The concluding phase in the preparation of the traveling requisition is the proof-listing operation. This operation serves two purposes:

1. To create a listing of items from edge punched item cards which enables the original Flexowriting to be proofed
2. To create a by-product punched tape for conversion to item tabulating cards.

The by-product tape from the proof-listing operation noted above contains all codes, descriptions, and specification for each item. Because of the flexibility of the tape-to-card converter, it is possible to punch all this information in the first (or "header") card for a group and still allow the succeeding cards to pass over without punching the repetitive descriptive information. If the information for the first item exceeds the field established for the card, the card is automatically released and the remaining data punched in a second card. Header cards are distinguished from detail cards by an automatic indicative punch. These tab cards are used to prepare mechanically a commodity catalog. The commodity catalog also indicates to each ordering location the items stocked at the other locations.

Vendor Cards

The edge punched vendor card is essential in the mechanical preparation of the request for quotation or purchase order. It is produced simultaneously with its identification label. The cards are listed on multilith masters to proof the accuracy of the Flexowriting operation. The multilith masters are then used to prepare vendor catalogs. During the proof-listing operation, only the vendor code number is punched in the by-product tape. This tape is then used to reproduce automatically vendor code-number indexes for locating the edge punched vendor cards in the tab files.

The vendor cards are filed in card-type files. Vendor-card indexing is based on the primary digits of the vendor code number (00 through 99). Single indexes are visible from both sides of the tab, and placement of Flexowriter equipment on each side of the file enables easy selection and refiling from either side and gives several Flexowriter operators the use of the same file.

Principal Features

There are a number of significant and unique features in the mechanized purchase order writing system. Several of the most important items are described below.

Purchasing Work Sheet

The purchasing work sheet is the first document that is prepared from single and/or grouped traveling-requisition edge punched item cards. This form is basic to the system, since all subsequent forms required in the purchasing transaction are automatically reproduced from the by-product tape obtained when preparing the purchasing work sheet. Thus, the quotation request or purchase order is always reproduced from the purchasing work sheet by-product tape.

The purchasing work sheet eliminates the handling by the buyer of voluminous numbers of individual traveling requisitions. Other advantages are:

1. All traveling requisitions can, immediately after preparation of the purchasing work sheet, be returned to the ordering location.
2. Clerical handling and temporary filing are simplified by reducing the number of documents handled.
3. A single source document provides a historical work record of each purchase transaction and also provides a means of transmitting buyer's instructions to the Flexowriter operators.
4. Adequate planning of programs makes the purchasing requirements extremely flexible since quantities can be modified and items split into several purchase orders or requests for quotation.
5. The historical reference of supply sources for the items being ordered (f.o.b. point, terms, etc.) is reproduced on the purchasing work sheet for the buyer's reference. This is accomplished by maintaining in the purchase-data project-control file the master vendor edge punched cards, which are filed in commodity sequence. These cards are removed from the control file as required during the preparation of the purchasing work sheet.

Indexing Quantity and Price Data

In the mechanized system, price- and quantity numeric data must be entered as a whole and/or fractional number. It is necessary that the Flexowriter operation enter the numeric data in their proper decimal position on the form. Failure to do so will cause erroneous quantity and/or price information to appear on the tab cards obtained from the purchase order by-product tape during the tape-to-card conversion process. This requirement can cause difficulties since these data are variable and are entered manually.

Design of forms and programs has provided for a mechanical margin alignment check which visually indicates when a quantity figure has been indexed incorrectly. For example: maximum quantity is 6 decimal places, or 999,000; maximum price is 8 decimal places, or $999,000.00. Quantity figures greater than 999,000 are entered in multiples of 1,000 using a symbol M to represent three ciphers, e.g., 1,999,000 would be written as 1,999M.

Changes in quantity in the purchasing statistics code and commodity code may be made during the preparation of purchase orders without special handling or delay.

Unit prices in combination with chain discounts can be indexed on the purchase order and captured in by-product tape for subsequent mechanical processing and computation of extensions and totals.

The system's inherent flexibility opens many avenues for exploration from the purchasing standpoint. The purchasing department using this system, with multiple-plant operations, is keeping pace with the most modern data processing methods in carrying out its purchasing responsibilities.

Conclusions

Installation of a mechanized purchase order writing system provides the purchasing department with immediate and potential benefits. Automation, however, cannot replace human judgment, creative thinking, knowledge, and experience.

Automation in purchasing is merely a new mechanical tool for assembling, finalizing, and perpetuating data swiftly and economically. This information can then assist the purchasing man in formulating judgment and arriving at sound purchasing decisions.

In the long-term planning for the purchase order writing system, there is only one matter of real concern, and that is the possible danger of complacency in the use of buying judgment and reasoning—will buyers become a breed of robot "order placers"? Evaluation of projected plans will conclude that this tendency need not be a problem if the purchasing staff is carefully selected and is of high caliber and if the administrative supervision of the department is competent. In the actual case example, no major disadvantages to office automation in the purchasing function have been detected. On the contrary, the top management of the company believes the purchasing staff is doing a more proficient and more intelligent job of modern scientific purchasing.

TOTAL SYSTEMS CONCEPT

The data handled by the clerical processes represent a series of activities by various organizational responsibilities joined together in making and selling the product. Each clerical process is interdependent in that automation in one function comprehends the input- and output-data requirements of the preceding or succeeding functions.

In addition to originating and perpetuating data for use in other functions such as inventory control, invoice processing, receiving, etc., mechanized purchase order writing also results in work simplification and clerical economies and correlates well with the department's value analysis and other cost-reduction activities. It increases the scope and accuracy of purchase data and improves timeliness of reports to management on purchasing operations. Analysis of material-cost trends, buying performance, and forecasts for long-range materials planning are also in the realm of possible benefits.

The system does not change basic purchasing principles, practice policies, techniques, or prerogatives. It is flexible, makes use of standar historical data and other control features, and is practical and economica

Purchasing Process

A flow diagram is shown in Figs. 14–7a to 14–7h, which illustrate i some detail the functional operation of an EDP mechanized purchas order writing system. This system incorporates the use of IDP and ED concepts, as well as manual operations in some functions of the system

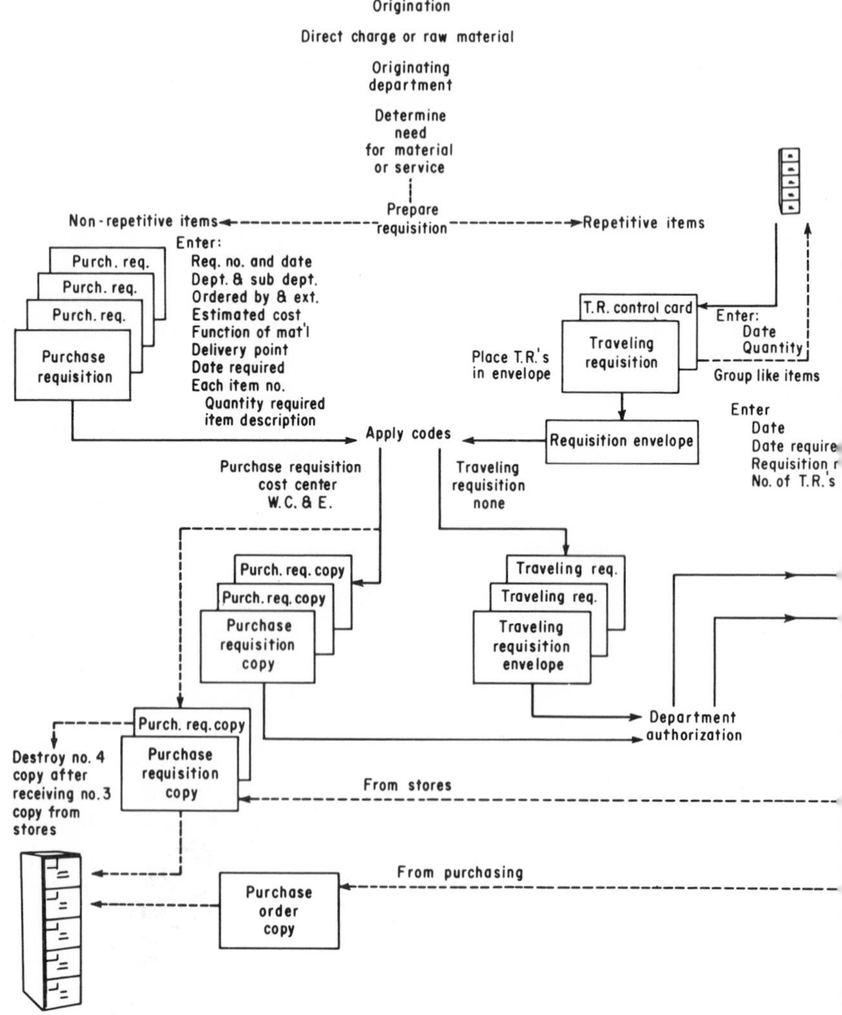

FIG. 14–7a. *Manual requisitioning* in a mechanized purchase order writing system— employing manual, Flexowriter, key-punch, tape-to-card, and computer processes.

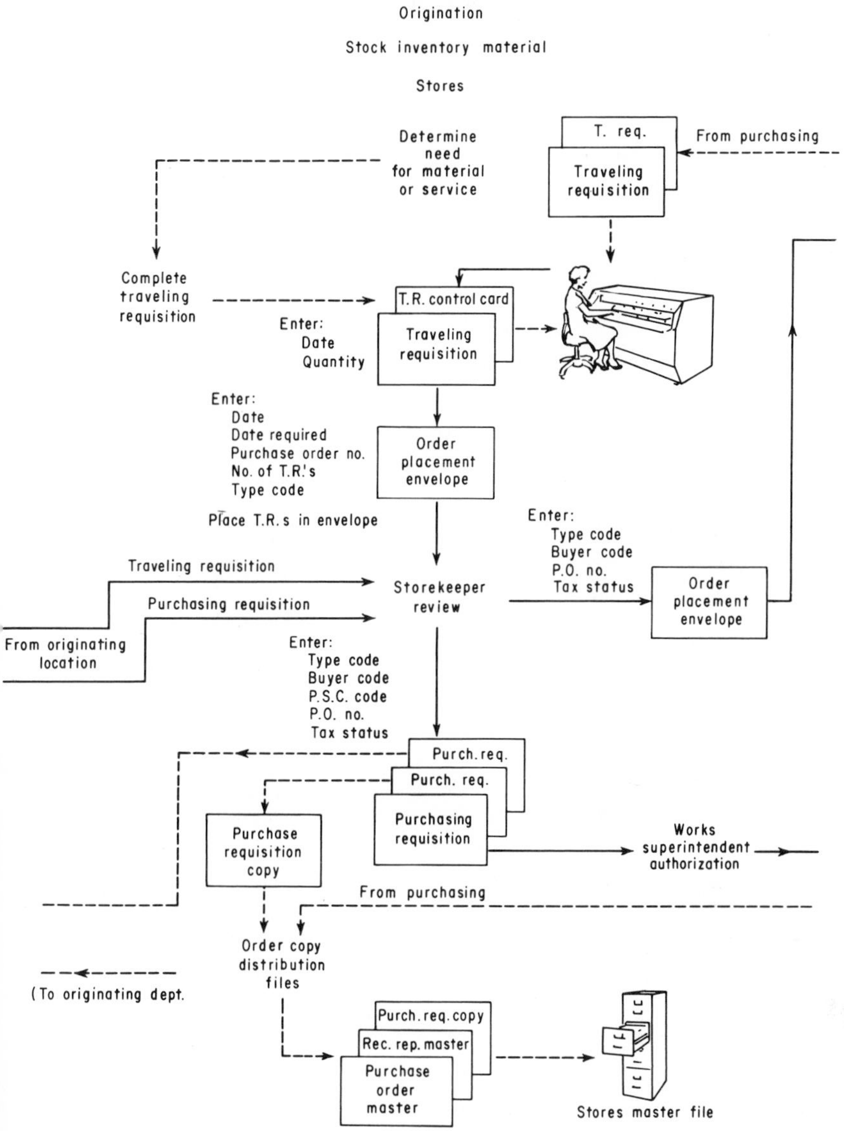

FIG. 14–7b. *Ordering by traveling requisitions* in a mechanized purchase order writing system—employing manual, Flexowriter, key-punch, tape-to-card, and computer processes.

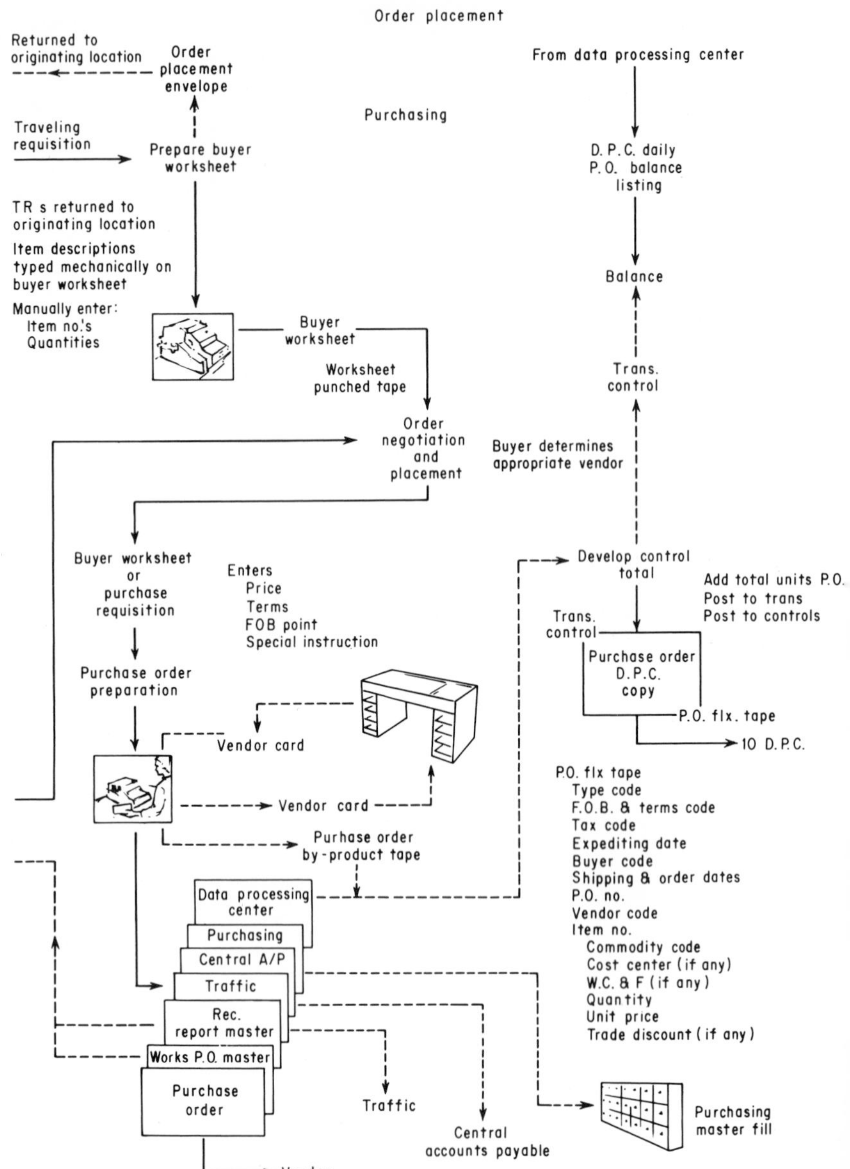

FIG. 14–7C. *Buyer processing and purchase document preparation* in a mechanized purchase order writing system—employing manual, Flexowriter, key-punch, tape-to-card, and computer processes.

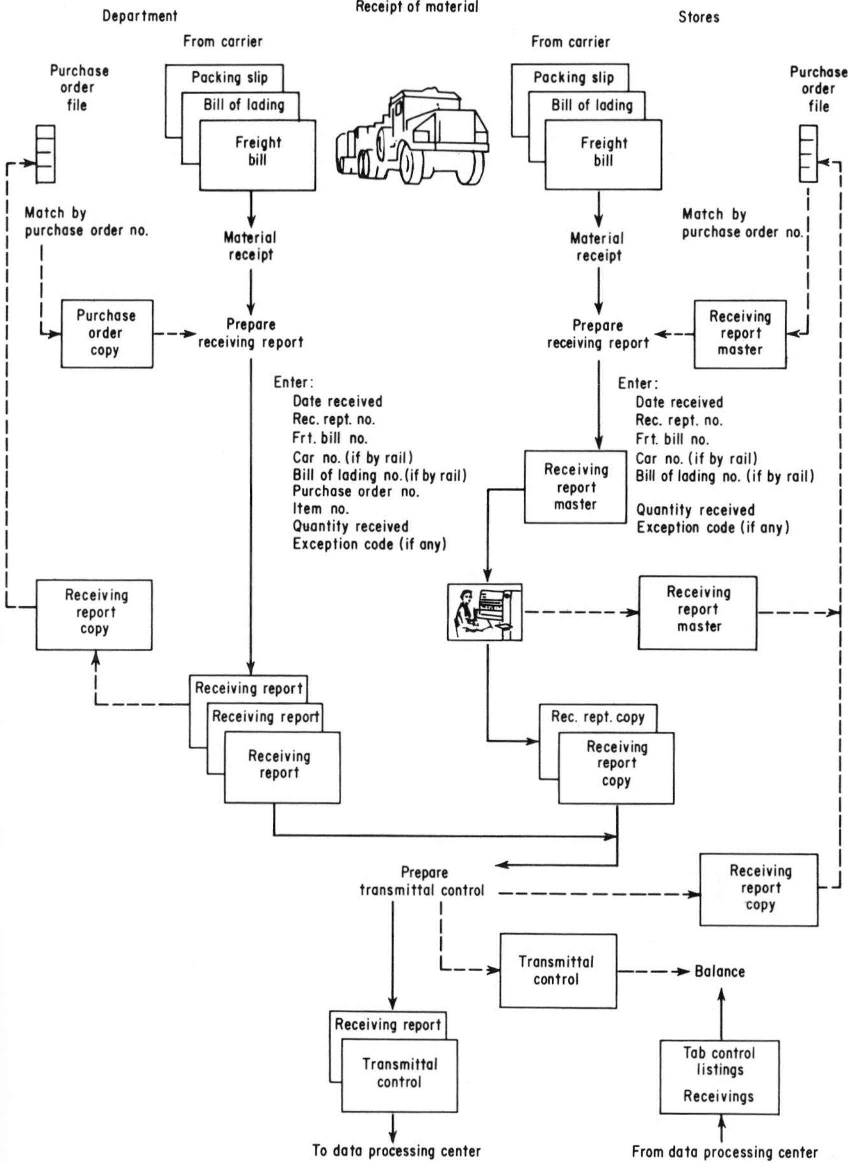

FIG. 14–7d. *Receipt of materials processing* in a mechanized purchase order writing system—employing manual, Flexowriter, key-punch, tape-to-card, and computer processes.

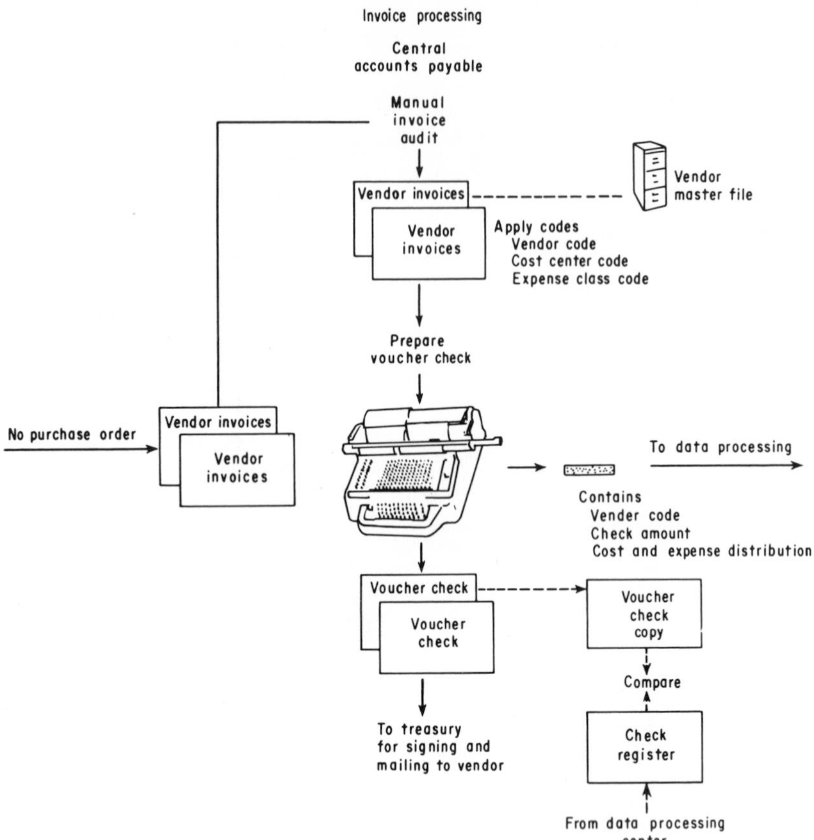

FIG. 14–7e. *Manual invoice processing* in a mechanized purchase order writing system—employing manual, Flexowriter, key-punch, tape-to-card, and computer processes.

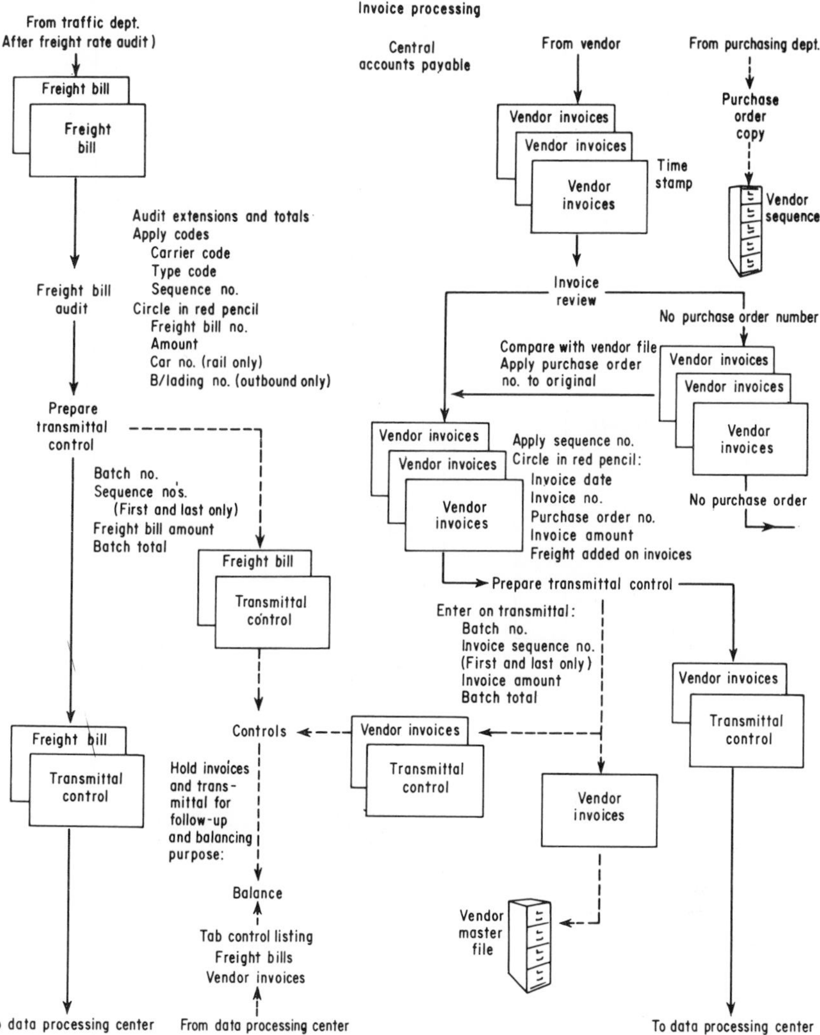

FIG. 14–7f. *Preparation of freight and invoice computer data* in a mechanized purchase order writing system—employing manual, Flexowriter, key-punch, tape-to-card, and computer processes.

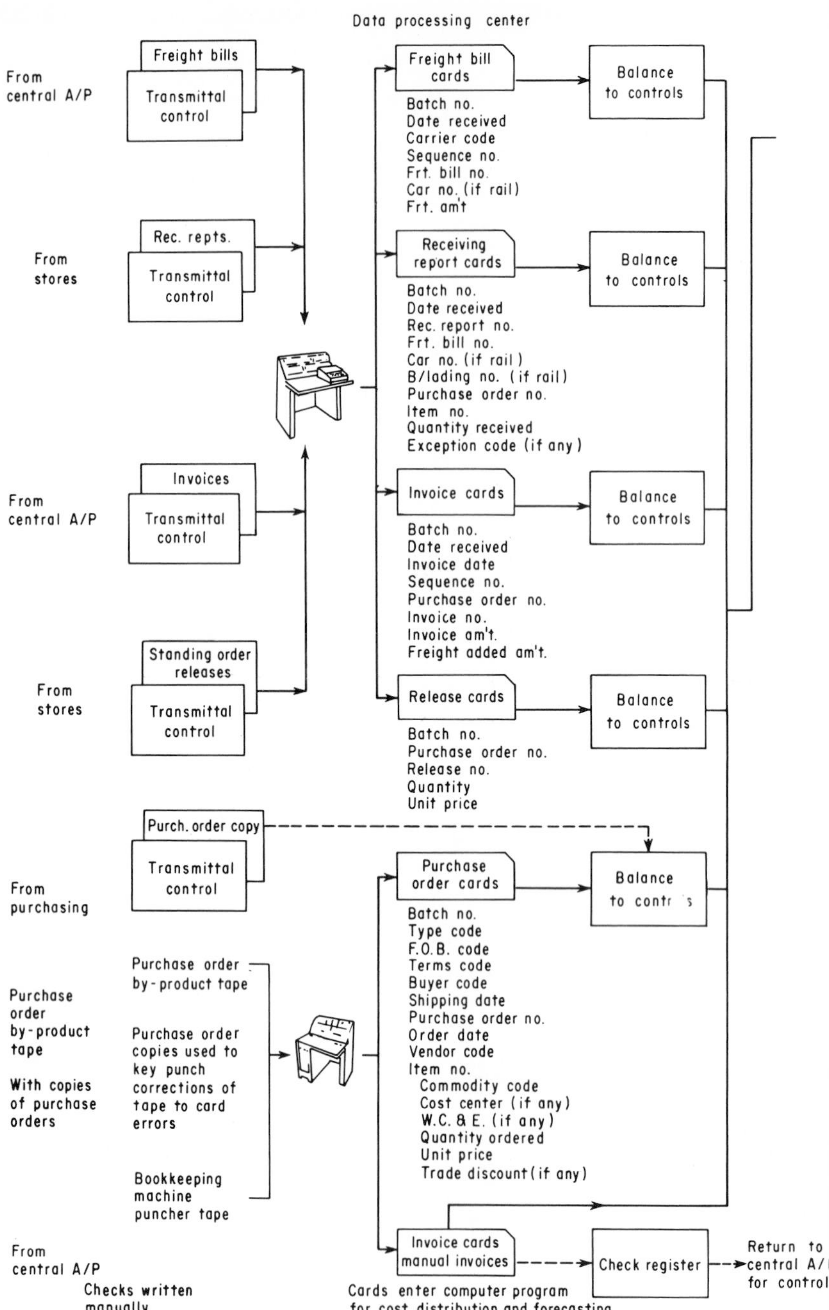

FIG. 14–7g. *Accounts payable computer input and output processing* in a mechanized purchase order writing system—employing manual, Flexowriter, key-punch, tape-to-card, and computer processes.

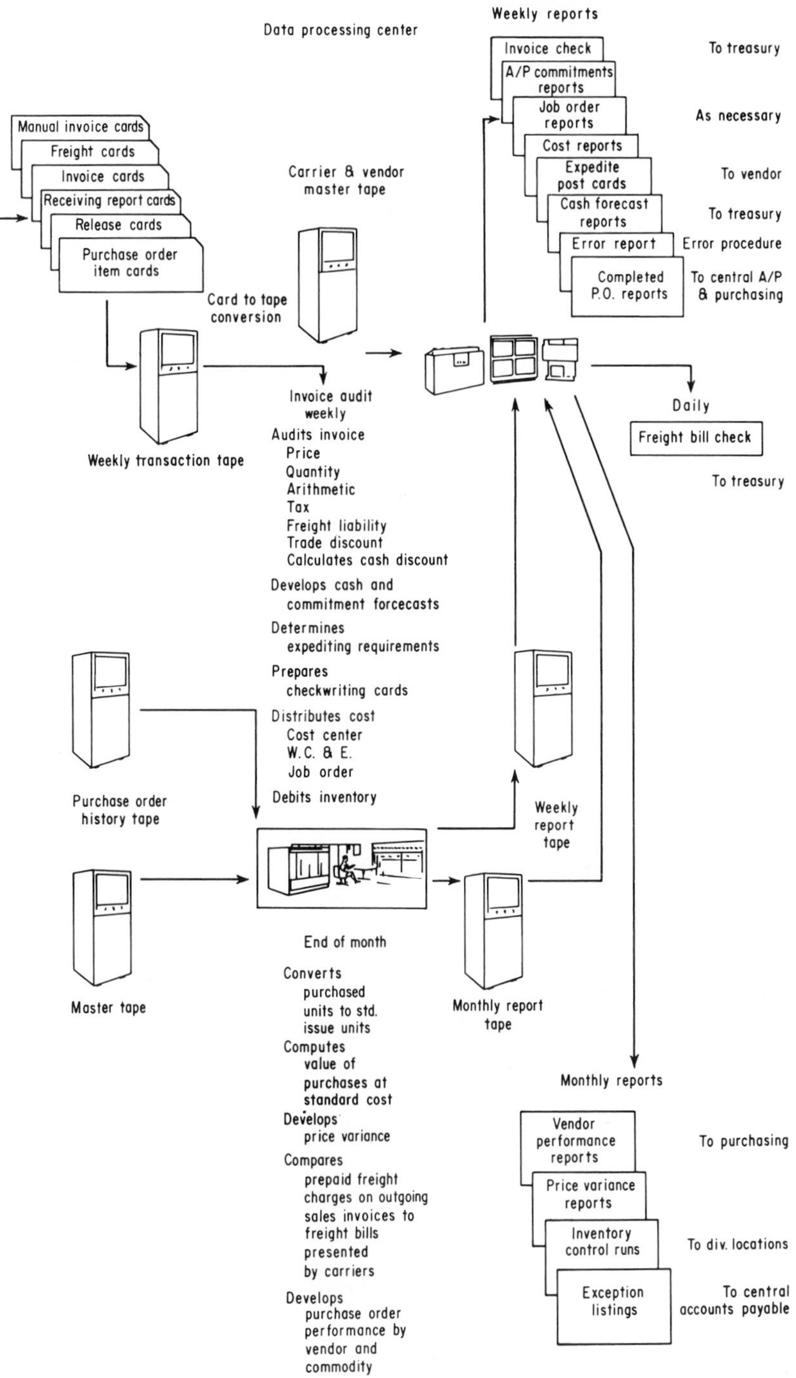

FIG. 14–7h. *Accounts payable computer processing and purchasing statistics developments* in a mechanized purchase order writing system—employing manual, Flexowriter, key-punch, tape-to-card, and computer processes.

This system is dependent on a uniform commodity code and uniform specifications as its bases. Although the mechanical order writing system uses Flexowriters and combines principles of both EDP and IDP, it is flexibly designed and would enable a transition to buying highly repetitive items by computer to be made with a minimum of cost and effort if this course of action is desired by the company.

EXPEDITING, VENDOR PERFORMANCE, EOQ

The complete EDP purchasing cycle, as noted, provides all of the basic data to initiate expediting, vendor performance, economic order quantities (EOQ), and other types of management tools. There exist so many varied approaches and possibilities for obtaining controls and information relative to the above that it would be impractical to discuss details. Again the development and design of these programs will depend on the company EDP objectives, and each tool must be tailored to fit specific needs of each company.

INVENTORY MANAGEMENT

Since the theory of inventory control and reordering is so closely allied to purchasing functions, a detailed discussion will follow on this particular subject. The balance of this section will deal exclusively with the principles, concept, and theory which relate to inventory management through EDP.

1. There is a description in some detail of how a mathematical model is constructed.
2. The importance of using operating or functional people in planning, particularly that of the input, is underlined.
3. The need for absolute accuracy of data is stressed, as is the importance of training people to properly provide it and appreciate its importance.
4. The principle of management by exception using control limits is outlined, and it is pointed out that these limits should be consistent with the cost of adhering to them.
5. The point is made that extreme precision of the model, obtained at high cost, is unwarranted when the forecast of demand is itself incapable of such precision.
6. There is an exhibit of a typical "exception report" and a discussion of its use.
7. Performance reporting is discussed.
8. The importance of coupling human judgment and power of decision

with computational and data storage and the manipulative powers of a computer system is emphasized

Influences of Electronic Data Processing on Inventory Control

Purchasing people should be vitally interested in inventory control, especially in the raw material, purchased components, and MRO (maintenance, repair, and operating supplies) areas, and a great many of them undoubtedly are. They have constant access to information on outside factors influencing inventory control, such as availability, lead times, prices (including quantity discounts), set-up charges, and the like. Purchasing is thus in a position to influence inventory policy and, in fact, shirks its responsibility when it does not. Most certainly, the procurement function is affected by the manner in which the inventory control operation is conducted, as anyone who is plagued by inadequate lead times will attest. Close communication between these two functions is necessary. Many company managements have recognized this need by placing control of this stage of inventory under the purchasing department or by having both functions report to a common boss, embracing the materials management concept.

The impact of electronic data processing, with its emphasis on systems integration, further highlights the interrelationship of these two functions.

Interpretation of Inventory Control

This part treats inventory as it is handled in Section 13 of this handbook. However, some interpretation is desirable since inventory may exist in a number of forms, only a few of which are responsive to control.

The type of inventory to be considered here is a planned inventory. This is defined as an inventory which is designed to accomplish a specific purpose. It is an inventory established to supply a definite level of service at a minimum cost consistent with that service level. Such an inventory contains items which, in general, have a relatively long life cycle.

Conversely, one also encounters unplanned inventories. In such cases, inventory is created not by intent, but as a result of unpredictable situations, such as cancellations, quality changes, and the like. This type of inventory is suitable for mechanized recording, but very little control can be exercised over it except through an analysis of what the inventory consists of in terms of number of units, specification or description, commodity code, etc. From this analysis, decisions can be made to apply items of inventory against new orders. The explanation that follows concerns planned inventories only.

The approaches discussed here must be basic. In that connection recognition should be given to the effect of individual company policies upon the method by which inventory is controlled. However, most of these special conditions do not negate accepted general procedures in inventory control, but simply impose limitations and adjustments which can be made at the time of application.

Computer Concepts

Before pursuing in detail the procedures by which an EDP system operates, it is desirable to describe generally a number of concepts that have proved helpful when building an inventory system around computer control.

Computer—Manual Balance

In the beginning, it should be made clear that a balance must be drawn betweeen mechanically oriented activities and those best performed by people. Contrary to popular concept, a computer cannot think. It can merely accomplish at great speed the activities which have been planned for it by a manually conceived program. Consequently, a computer is capable of performing speedily and very accurately the routine calculations and the elementary decisions which are part of the logic designed into the control model. This eliminates time-consuming routine as a manual responsibility. However, inventory in certain instances is not routine. When abnormal conditions arise it is vital that people take over and adjust the model to suit these exceptional conditions. At times, for example, inventory may be the means for accumulating production in advance of need in order that the load level on a plant may be stabilized. Other unexpected factors operate similarly to require personal intervention.

An additional objective of a more positive nature demands personal action—a continuing and concentrated effort on the part of supervision to use computed control data to improve the operating characteristics of computer control itself and to thus reduce cost. The proper balance is to exploit the computer's data manipulation and computing power and couple with this the power of humans to apply judgment and make required decisions.

Dynamic Operation

Many of the activities performed by EDP in inventory control are continuations of what was done manually. There is, nonetheless, a considerable difference in these two processes. The difference pertains to the speed with which computations may be performed by EDP, permitting a much more dynamic system than is possible under manual control.

Control limits, such as safety stocks and economic purchasing quantities, may be updated at a frequency compatible with changing demand patterns. Furthermore, the system of order points may be made flexible rather than fixed. This provides a close and economic relationship between existing inventory, forecast sales, and the replacement cycle. The monitoring of replacement cycles and safety-stock penetrations makes it possible to adjust safety stocks to suit their purpose with a flexibility hitherto unknown. Control reports so closely follow inventory movements that supervision and management are enabled to reduce inventory levels safely, since time and knowledge permit immediate preventive action, should unforeseen circumstances require it.

Operating Participation

The participation of operating personnel is an extremely important part of a sound operation. This point deserves emphasis since the tendency sometimes develops to expect that system design will be the complete responsibility of the data processing organization. To have an effective performance, operating personnel should be actively involved in the design of the system. They are, by experience, in a superior position to know what features should be included to make the operation both practical and economical. Given these essential ingredients, the data processing organization may then assume the responsibility for designing these requirements into the data processing operating system.

Especially important is the participation of operating people in the planning of data input. A system can be only as accurate as its input data. Factors to be aware of are the timeliness of the data, its accuracy, and the format and sequence necessary for its introduction into the system. A computer operation cannot accept the level of error frequently associated with a tab system and compensated for by alert people. It is especially important that operating manuals be prepared jointly with the people who are responsible for the inventory operation itself. Clear definition is needed of the personal responsibility for each task. Output reports should be designed around the requirements of those people who are to make use of them. This will ensure that the reports will be adequate to stimulate necessary action at various levels of authority without carrying redundant and expensive information. The data processing procedures to accomplish this purpose will, of course, be the responsibility of systems-programming and equipment-operating personnel.

Control Model Design

Certain features concerning the design of inventory control models should be pointed out. Since inventory management is quite a common problem, considerable attention has been focused on it. This has given rise to an extensive amount of literature and a wide number of approaches to inventory control. Some of these have become quite complex and in many instances have created a great deal of confusion. Some effort should be made to clarify this condition. In the first place, inventory control is not an exact science, since it is based on demand which is often difficult to forecast. This makes it evident that extreme manipulation of data for ultra precision is usually unwarranted. The emphasis should be on good operating logic rather than absolute accuracy. A review of effective inventory systems suggests some conclusions. In broad perspective, the management of inventory has three basic objectives:

1. To provide a management-stipulated level of service to customers and/or the production organization
2. To achieve a minimum level of total inventory cost, consistent with the required service level
3. To provide a set of control reports which supply management with the necessary information for taking effective action when needed and for periodically comparing the performance of the operation with policy standards

To accomplish the preceding objectives, an inventory control system must be supported by the best logic applicable to the specific inventory problem encountered. However, this logic should be implemented by the simplest mathematical tools that will accomplish the desired result within the accuracy range of the input data. It should be recognized that the people who will operate the system must understand how it works in order that their modifying actions will amplify the benefits produced by the inventory model through its routine control.

Evaluation of Performance

Traditionally, rate of turnover has been considered an important measurement of the effectiveness of inventory control. It can still be said that when looking at inventory as an aggregate this measure is of some value. However, it should be noted that if turnover is taken as an exclusive indicator of performance, it fails to achieve the most important measure of all. That measure is the total cost of an inventory item. Total cost consists of the carrying cost, the cost of replacing inventory, and the cost of shortages (failure to supply material when needed). Other factors are also very important, especially those applicable to an inventory that is built through purchases. Such factors are the effects upon prime material cost of the purchased quantities and discount possibilities, as they are influenced by the mechanics of the inventory control model.

Consequently, we see a need for a different type of evaluation. That is usually best achieved by a type of performance reporting structure which measures the effectiveness of the inventory organization in terms of the cost results of deviation from the accepted policies dictated by management. This method tends to eliminate some of the discrepancies which are apt to be created by strict adherence to turnover.

Impact of Design Changes

A potential danger exists in inventory control using EDP methods. This danger is the tendency for the system to be considered routine and completely self-operative. Actually, such a concept of operation is very desirable with respect to the minimization of clerical requirements and the making of simple routine decisions based upon the operating-model logic. However, there are other decisions which are not routine and may have a profound effect upon the efficiency of the system. Of special significance is the type of inventory where parts are obsoleted by design changes. The point is that the inventory control system, operating through the model, cannot foresee impending changes. Ordering is controlled strictly by the statistics of demand.

To offset that potential weakness, the overall organizational control plan should treat the management of inventory as an entity to be integrated with purchasing practice, design change procedures, production requirements, and the needs of the distribution system. One way in which to handle this problem is for stock-control personnel to monitor any orders for replacement material prepared automatically by the EDP system. Prior to release, the parts involved can be checked back against engineering plans for changes, and the quantities adjusted accordingly. The order itself may be delayed or cancelled. A variation of that approach is for engineering to be given the prerogative of coding items to indicate that no order should be released for such items prior to engineering approval. This feature eliminates redundant checking. This type of code can be specific to an order period or a permanent limitation upon ordering practice where items are known to be characteristically unstable.

Anticipated Results

One of the extremely important considerations when contemplating the use of EDP for inventory control is its effect upon the cost performance of the system. It would be exceedingly difficult to indicate an anticipated level of benefit that would apply consistently. However, from a number of observations certain conclusions may be conservatively drawn. When converting from a well-established tab-manual type of system to a computer-manual system, cost benefits run in the range of 15 to 25 per

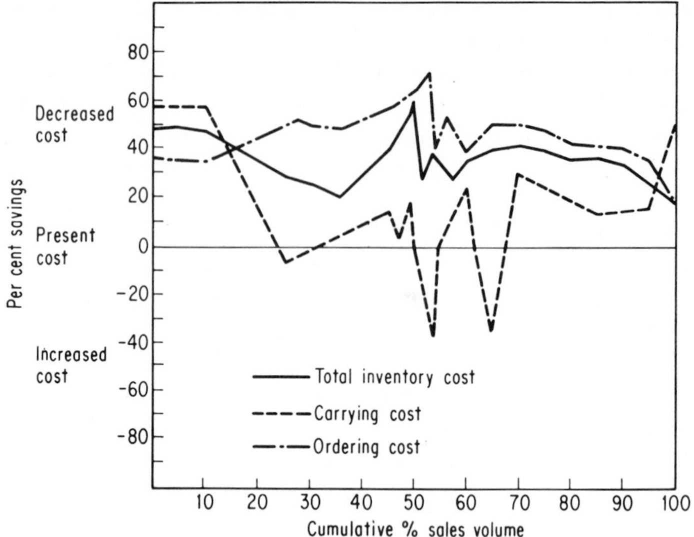

FIG. 14–8. Cost reduction through inventory control. (Items with random demand patterns.) NOTE: Items are arranged horizontally in order of their respective positions in the cumulative per cent of sales volume. By this sequence, the highest volume items appear furthest to the left.

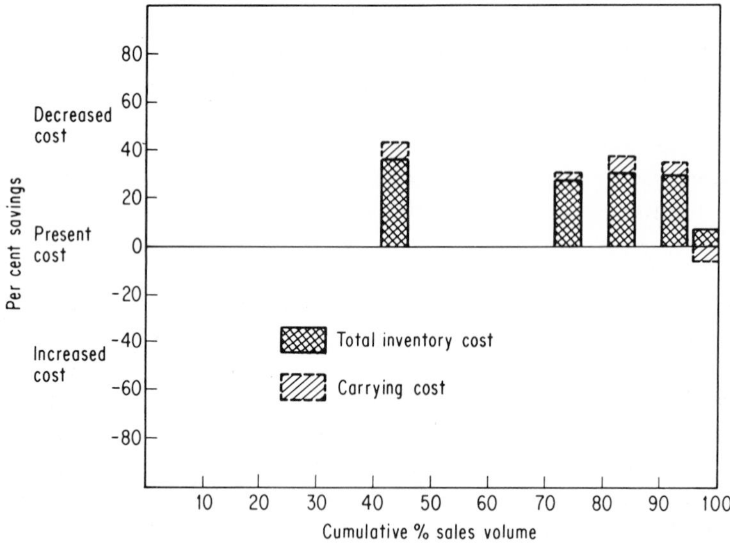

FIG. 14–9. Cost reduction through inventory control. (Items with seasonal demand patterns.) NOTE: Items are arranged horizontally in order of their respective positions in the cumulative per cent of sales volume. By this sequence, the highest volume items appear furthest to the left.

cent savings in the total cost of inventory. As indicated before, this applies to planned inventories only.

To illustrate a typical situation, Figs. 14–8 and 14–9 on "Cost Reduction through Inventory Control" show respectively the results of inventory control on items with random demand patterns and items with seasonal demands. Short-range forecasting for the random demands was accomplished by a modified moving-average projection. The seasonal items were handled by "line ratio" prediction. In Fig. 14–8 the volume range through 50 per cent shows items which are active and closely controlled. Items in the 50 to 100 per cent range are of limited activity and are controlled by a simple maximum-minimum method.

The inventory represented by Figs. 14–8 and 14–9 covers items which are obtained through purchasing and then distributed to a series of retail outlets geographically centered about a warehouse. Note that the several graph lines in Fig. 14–8 indicate total cost benefit, savings in inventory, and savings in ordering. Fig. 14–9, illustrating items with seasonal patterns, shows over-all savings and inventory savings only. It should be mentioned that both figures show savings in the cost of *maintaining inventory* only. Additional savings are possible by ordering combinations to take advantage of quantity discounts on *prime cost.*

Specific Operating Procedures

General

It should be stressed that all the following procedures to be discussed relate to the basic section on inventory control as a cost-reducing procedure. The specific approaches described here supplement or modify the still-valid procedures discussed in Section 13. Consequently, the details discussed in this section were selected as representing areas of universal interest and significant change.

Forecast Explosion Versus Statistical Controls

All inventory control starts with some form of forecast. If we consider individual factors, the forecast for economic order quantity computation is an annual forecast of requirements. Then, routinely, as the inventory is sampled for ordering, statistical forecasting covers the short-range period of the replacement cycle. Safety-stock allowances are based on the statistical variation of actual demand from a forecast taken over a representative period. Thus, it is seen that the control of parts inventories in a planned system is truly a statistical procedure.

When the production of end products, involving many parts and component assemblies, is considered, the inventory procedure may take two different paths.

Assume that end products are made to customer order. In such case there is unlikely to be an inventory of finished goods. However, it i customary to carry an inventory of finished parts and certain componen assemblies. This is especially true if parts and components are commo to many end products. In such cases, a sound procedure is to determin parts and component-assembly requirements for ordering purposes b exploding the end-product forecasts. By summarizing the results of th several explosions, the total requirements for components and detaile parts may be developed. However, this method leaves much to be desired since the tendency is to order parts and components in terms of immediate needs rather than in accordance with economic purchasing or production lot sizes. In addition, the mechanics of forecast explosion are costly

A variation of this method is to control detailed parts statistically a previously described, leaving only the component assemblies which ar close to the end-product level to be ordered by forecast explosion.

However, providing the products are reasonably stable, a much mor economical procedure is to handle both parts and component assemblie statistically. All demands against an item projected into the future serv as a short-range forecast. Furthermore, annual forecasting for EPQ (economic purchase quantity) purposes can be easily done by a modifie projection of year-to-date usage. By this procedure, all demands for common items are unified. They may be ordered in economic lot sizes and th whole procedure effectively handled by a computer inventory model.

Computation of Protective Stocks

Protective stock is an extremely important control limit in inventory management since it determines the level of service to be maintained Yet this important item is frequently left to conjecture rather than factua computation.

Actually, protective stocks, or safety stocks, as they are sometimes called may be computed with considerable reliability. At this point it is suggested that Fig. 14–10 be reviewed. Since protective stock is a buffe against changes in demand, it is desirable that it be established quantitatively as a function of these changes. Statistically, it is possible to do jus that. Figure 14–10 represents a data distribution. The magnitude o period demands is shown on the horizontal axis and the frequencies with which the given magnitudes occur is plotted on the vertical axis. Thi gives the familiar curve of a normal distribution of data although th distribution does not have to be absolutely normal, by statistical definition, to make the following procedure practically reliable.

Statistically it is possible to measure the expected variation from average by making use of what is known as a standard deviation, represented by the Greek letter sigma. Figure 14–10 shows the classic compu ation for the standard deviation. However, for data as erratic as those encountered in inventory control, a better procedure is to use the relationship that the standard deviation equals 1.25 times the mean absolute deviation. This is much less expensive to compute and will give accuracies within a close percentage of the classic formula.

The standard deviation is a uniquely desirable measure of deviation in a demand pattern because each multiple of the standard deviation covers a definite percentage of the area under the distribution curve. For example, plus or minus one standard deviation will cover 68 per cent of the area under the curve. Plus or minus two standard deviations will cover 96 per cent of the area. Consequently, if it is assumed that a demand forecast in itself will give a 50 per cent probability of service, one

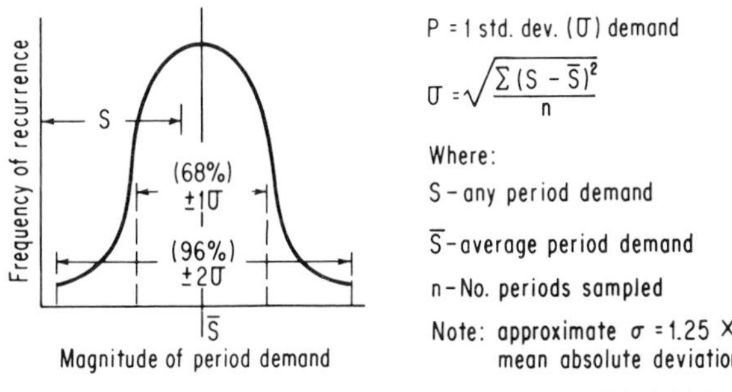

FIG. 14–10. Protective stock (P). NOTE: Approximate $\sigma = 1.25 \times$ mean absolute deviation.

standard deviation of protective stock added will give 50 per cent plus 34 per cent, or an 84 per cent protection against a stockout. Similarly, when two standard deviations of protective stock are used, the result is 50 per cent plus 48 per cent, or a 98 per cent level of service. Extending this analysis further, it is seen that management may set up any desired protection against stockouts. Within close statistical limits this is possible by specifying the appropriate multiple of the standard deviation.

A few words are in order regarding the mechanics of computing the standard deviation. It is suggested that the approximate method be used, i.e., 1.25 times the mean absolute deviation equals the standard deviation. It is suggested, also, that the actual demand for any part or component for a given interval, say one week, be compared with a modified moving-average demand as a forecast. It is suggested that a ten-week modified moving average is a good statistical demand indicator as well as a simple item to compute. It is further recommended that the deviations of actual demand from forecast be carried as a ten-week modified moving average. This will then give directly a mean absolute deviation which may be used in the relationship just indicated. The procedure would operate like the following one. The terms listed below will be used in the development of the standard deviation:

D = deviation between actual weekly demand and forecast
n = any week in a series
D_n = deviation for any given week

Then

$$\text{Any ten weeks' sum of the deviations} = \sum_{n-9}^{n} D_n$$

Also

$$\text{Average weekly deviation} = \left(\sum_{n-9}^{n} D_n\right) \div 10$$

Updating the average deviation as a modified moving average would give an expression such as the following if it is assumed that the start is at week zero and the modified moving average for week one is desired:

$$\sum_{n=-9}^{n=0} D_n - \left(\sum_{n=-9}^{n=0} D_n\right) \div 10 + D_{n=1} = \sum_{n=-8}^{n=1} D_n$$

Then

$$\text{Modified moving average for week one} = \left(\sum_{n=-8}^{n=1} D_n\right) \div 10$$

Notice that in the foregoing only one memory location is required to update from week to week. That is the value for the summations of D_n. Note also that using a ten-week modified moving average means dividing by 10 which is simply the movement of a decimal point, a simple operation for a computer. One subtraction and one addition remain to complete the updating. It was previously stated that the standard deviation is equivalent to 1.25 times the mean absolute deviation. Since the standard deviation for any item must be based on the replacement-cycle time period, the formula for protective stock would then be as follows:

$$PS = kn\,\sigma\sqrt{RC}$$

Where PS = protective stock
k = adjustment factor ranging between 0 and 1 to be used at the discretion of the stock-control supervisor
n = multiple of the standard deviation needed for the service level prescribed by policy
σ = standard deviation
RC = the replacement cycle in weeks (assuming that the standard deviation was computed on weekly demands)

Note in the equation for protective stock that the constant k offers discretionary supervisory modification, which will be explained under "Control Reports." The $\sqrt{RC}$ is used as an adjustment factor to convert one week's standard deviation to that of a specific replacement-cycle period. It makes use of the fact that the standard deviation for any period of time will vary approximately with the square root of the length of this period. A monthly computation of protective stock is a recommended frequency for this control limit.

EPQ's Reflecting Discount Rates

Unlike manufacturing economic lot sizes, the economic purchase quantities must reflect more than one unit price, depending upon the various price breaks listed. The EPQ can be determined by using an arbitrary return-on-investment figure above which the price break will be taken and below which it will be rejected. However, there is a way of determining the best price-quantity relationship more exactly when using a computer. One can compute the total annual inventory cost for the various combinations of price breaks, by using the following equation:

Total annual cost = number of orders × (purchase order cost + inventory carrying cost + order processing cost)

The following describes the method of determining the various terms in the above equation.

The purchase order cost equals the unit price times the quantity at which that price is given, plus the set-up, plus tool costs and any other costs which are associated with an order regardless of quantities. The inventory carrying cost is determined from the demand record of the item in question. This is usually carried in the computer files. Dividing any selected quantity by the demand per unit of time will give the period of time over which that order quantity is spread. Since the average inventory level is half the purchased quantity, this value is multiplied by the annual carrying-cost factor (usually 15 to 25 per cent) and the unit price. The result is the annual carrying cost on the purchased quantity. In order to arrive at the cost of carrying inventory on a single purchasing quantity, the annual carrying cost is multiplied by the period over which the quantity will be spread, divided by the total time units in a year. If usage is in terms of days, the divisor would be 365. If the usage is in weeks, the value would be 52. The order-processing cost is roughly the cost of the organizations responsible for order processing divided by the number of orders processed. Some companies may prefer to use an incremental order-processing cost. Since the effect on total cost varies as the square root of the order-processing cost, an approximate value is sufficient.

The final item to be determined is the number of orders, which is de fined as the number of time units in a year divided by the number c time units over which the ordered quantity is spread. This value ma also be determined from an annual forecast divided by the orderin quantity.

This cost combination is computed for as many price breaks as ar considered significant. All other things being equal, the EPQ giving th lowest annual inventory cost is selected. Management may wish to pu an arbitrary maximum limit on the EPQ. One that has been suggeste is that where the calculated EPQ exceeds one year's requirements an a value of $100, only one year's requirements are ordered.

Order Point Computations

Once the economic purchase quantity and the protective stock limi for inventory have been determined, it becomes important to establis a scheduling procedure for either purchases or production in order to be utilize these limits. Specifically, this is a matter of order points. Manua and EAM (electronic accounting machines) systems often rely on fixe order points. Preferably, the system should use a procedure which estab lishes floating or dynamic order points which coordinate inventory statu replacement cycle, and short-range demand patterns. Figure 14–11 illu trates how this is done. When it is desired to determine candidate par or assemblies for scheduling action, the computations shown on the illu tration are added to the inventory updating run. The frequency wit which this ordering pattern is used depends largely upon the deman pattern as well as upon the production or purchasing cycle. Normall candidates for production or purchasing can be determined about onc a week.

The procedure operates in the following manner: the inventory leve is compared to the product of the replacement cycle for the item times i current running forecast, plus the protective stock level, plus any shor ages that may have accumulated, minus any lots which have been cu rently ordered. If the comparison indicates that actual inventory excee the control inventory, then no action is needed. However, if the actua inventory is equal to or less than the control inventory, a lot must b entered. The equations for this comparison are shown in Fig. 14–1 "Forecasting Order Points."

The importance of dynamic order points is shown by the diagram i Fig. 14–11. Note that of the two order points illustrated, the one on th left is at a much higher level of inventory than the one on the right. I fact, this can amount to a significant difference in inventory investmen More important still is the fact that if the forecast shows a declini emand, it is imperative that a low order point be determined, or an nventory excess will inevitably result. This plan is designed to *avoid* nventory excesses rather than to reduce them once they have occurred. The latter is a very difficult task. If an inventory excess has developed, nly two expedients may lower it within a reasonable period of time. Both of them present difficulties. If slow moving items or dormant stock re scrapped, the condemnation of wasted investment can be made. If, n the other hand, inventory is reduced by not ordering the rapidly noving items, shortages will occur. This cannot be permitted if satisfac- ory customer service is to be maintained.

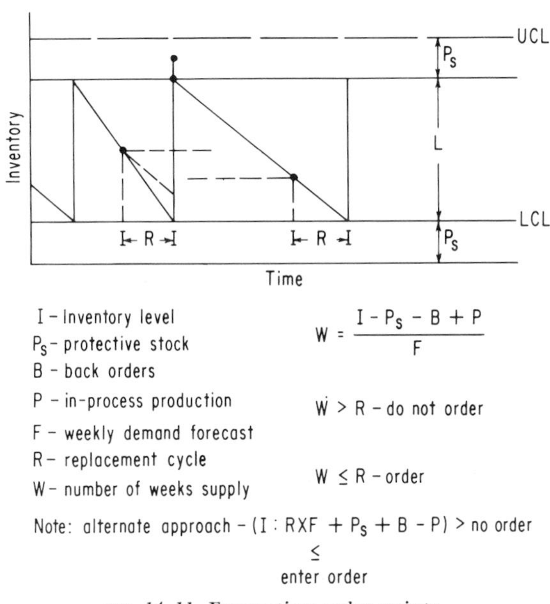

FIG. 14–11. Forecasting order points.

All the items in the formula given for determining dynamic order oints are clear and definite. However, the short-range forecast is an item or which some explanation is needed. At the outset it should be recog- ized that the short-range forecast is useful only for the replacement ycle. A number of procedures have been developed for this type of fore- asting. If the demand is random, a modified ten-week moving average is uggested. The mechanics of updating such a forecast are exactly the same s the procedure described for protective stocks and standard deviations. The only difference is that in forecasting demand, the basic element is he weekly demand for individual product items. Comparative tests of xponential smoothing (a currently popular procedure) against the modified ten-week moving-average method indicate that rarely is the addition expense and complexity of exponential smoothing justified by the eco nomic benefits. Some modification of that statement should be made, o course. It is true that if actual demand follows a long period of constan slope, exponential smoothing will forecast this slope more closely tha a modified moving average, particularly if the alpha factor is high. An other ideal application for exponential smoothing is a highly errat demand pattern coupled with an exceedingly short replacement cycle.

It should be pointed out that if a true cyclic demand pattern is encoun tered, a different forecasting procedure would be recommended—"lin ratio" forecasting. Figure 14–12 illustrates the concept of line ratio fore

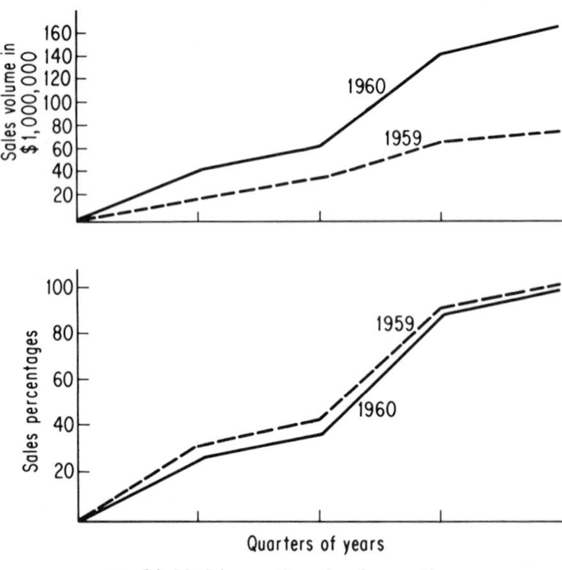

FIG. 14–12. Line ratio sales forecasting.

casting. The demand history is accumulated by months and converte into cumulative per cent sales achievements over yearly periods. Th history can be updated without taking undue memory space by treatin it as a modified three-year moving average by month. Although the sale from year to year may vary widely as Fig. 14–12 illustrates, the per cen cumulative sales achievement will remain fairly constant. Forecasts ma then be made by taking the sales achievement in dollars or units up t the point of time at which the forecast is made, and multiplying this b the ratio of the cumulative-sales percentage for the period to be fore casted over the cumulative-sales percentage at the time at which the fore cast is made. This is a simple but effective procedure.

Filters on Demand and Deviation

When using a modified moving average for forecasting demand and collecting deviations against the forecast, the results can be impaired by excessive values for some specific period. This situation can be avoided by inserting a filtering process which operates in the following manner. The current weekly demand should be compared with the moving average plus two standard deviations. If the weekly demand is equal or less, it is used. However, if the current demand is greater than the average plus two standard deviations, the latter is substituted for the current demand figure. This protects the moving average against abnormal fluctuations, yet if the condition continues, it will gradually produce an adjustment. Of even more importance, this type of filter prevents deviations from becoming so wide either above or below average that they develop protective stocks of excessive magnitude.

Seasonality

Previously, a method was described for handling the control of seasonal items. It is equally important to define seasonality. Basically, it may be defined as that degree of cyclic fluctuation that cannot be handled by a modified moving average or similar system. Specifically, the following criteria have been found quite workable. Using them, seasonality is indicated if actual demand exceeds the average by 50 per cent for three consecutive months *and* actual demand is half average demand for three consecutive months. Also, seasonality may be indicated if the actual demand exceeds the average by 75 per cent for two consecutive months *or* if the actual demand is less than one-fourth of the average for two consecutive months. Furthermore, seasonality may be indicated if actual demand is twice the average for a single month or if actual demand is zero for a given month.

Control Reports

One of the most essential features of an EDP system of inventory control is the power of the control reports which may be designed into the system. These usually consist of exception reports in which item weaknesses are identified for preventive supervisory action. These require no supervisory search through voluminous detailed data. In addition to exception reports, performance reports should be set up indicating quantitatively the degree to which the system is following managerial policy. Finally, in order that supervision may analyze and progressively improve the operation of the system, analytical reports covering the major elements of importance should be prepared at suitable frequencies.

Exception Reports

Figure 14–13 illustrates a typical inventory exception report. This gives product code and description as well as indications of those items which carry stock in excess of the upper control limit. The upper control limit is also shown. Conversely, those items which have passed either into penetration of protective stock or into actual back-order status are shown. Moreover, other important information is revealed. The item which is followed by an asterisk in Fig. 14–13 requires special expediting.

Above upper control limit	Upper control limit	Product code	Product name	Protective stock	Penetration into protective stock	Back order
40	150‡	024-11020-02	Plate			
10	50	131-13094-03	Shield			
70	200	131-12990-02	Tube			
		025-23502-01	Board	300	200†	
		086-20851-02	Cable	150	160	10
5	60	038-93830-01	Bushing			
		024-12045-46	Liner	200	50*	
		121-10949-03	Lock	125	25	
15	125	086-17376-02	Modulator			

* Requires special expediting.
† No production order entered.
‡ Over 75 per cent lot completed.

FIG. 14–13. Production control—inventory exception report.

This signifies that the time left in the replacement cycle prior to receipt of replacement stock multiplied by the short-range forecast exceeds the inventory on hand. The implication here is that unless the demand pattern changes, the item will have to be expedited in order to obtain replacement stock prior to a shortage.

A dagger following an item indicates not only that the stock level is in jeopardy but that no order has been issued for a replacement lot. An emergency order must be placed immediately.

A double dagger following an item indicates not only that it is above the upper control limit but that 75 per cent of the lot has been completed or shipped. This is important to the stock-control supervisor in deciding whether to complete the remainder of the lot or to cancel the balance since variations in lot size above 75 per cent of standard represent very small increments of additional cost, barring specific price breaks. It is recommended that this exception report be prepared daily.

The types of exception data shown above are the most significant; however, in some cases it is desirable to show dormant stocks. A dormant stock may be defined as one against which there has been no demand for a stipulated period of time. The period of aging would be an item for managerial designation.

Performance Reporting

Performance reporting is essentially a tool used by upper levels of management. Its importance becomes evident when related to management's responsibility. In general, management is expected to perform the following functions:

1. Establish policy
2. Delegate responsibility for executing policy
3. Evaluate performance against policy
4. Endorse, redirect, or initiate action

Although somewhat oversimplified, this establishes management as a form of feedback loop in which one of the most important links is the evaluation of performance *quantitatively* against policy. Without such performance data, management will be unaware of whether the function

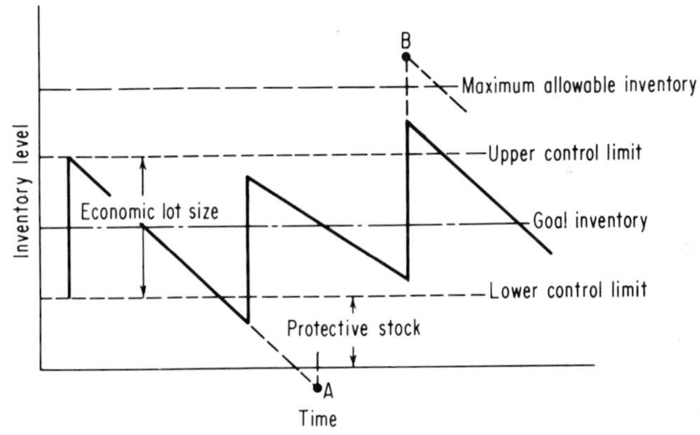

FIG. 14–14. Production and inventory cycle.

is improving or losing ground. A number of ways to evaluate performance are available to management. One of the simplest and most effective approaches is to treat performance as a summation of the costs of deviations from control limits. For example, Fig. 14–14 shows point A as a deviation of inventory on the low side. That item has penetrated through protective stock into an actual condition of shortage or back order. When updating inventory (at the time a performance report is scheduled), the units in shortage status should be evaluated by taking the product of tl number of units times their cost times the back-order cost factor. reasonable value for the back-order cost factor is about five times tl inventory carrying-cost factor. This will vary from one company to a other, according to the importance of serving the customer promptl Point B in Fig. 14–14 shows an item which has entered an excess stoc level status. This would be evaluated by taking the number of units i excess times their cost times the carrying-cost constant. The comput memory would be used as an accumulator for all cost penalties. Turnin to Fig. 14–15, still another cost should be entered. This is the cost

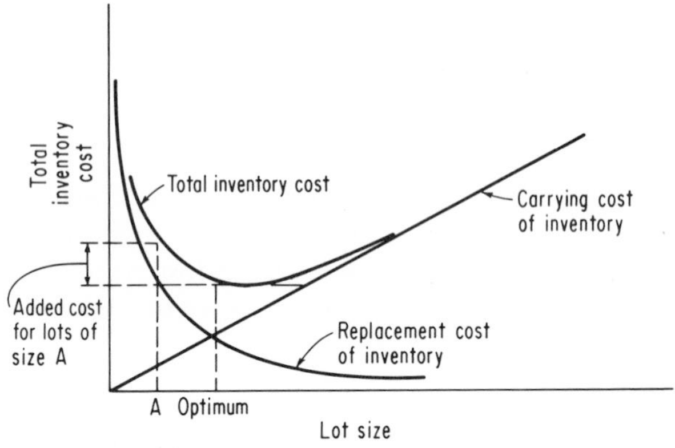

FIG. 4–15. Economic (optimum) lot-size determination.

short lots. It may be evaluated by using the table shown in Fig. 14–1 which would be carried in memory. If one starts with the per cent of normal lot, the per cent additional cost for that size lot may then b determined. From the normal annual-cost figure and the per cent co increment, the dollar cost may be computed and added to the memo accumulation.

Per cent of economic order quantity	*Per cent increase in annual cost*
125	2.5
100	0
75	4.0
50	25.0
25	112.0

FIG. 14–16. Effect of lot size on annual inventory cost.

From the foregoing it is seen that management is given performan relating to the three primary things expected of an inventory. First, in ventory must provide service, as indicated by absence of shortages. Secon t must not exceed a maximum permissible level. Third, it must be re-laced in economic lot sizes or purchasing quantities rather than in a eries of small emergency batches. Figure 14–17 shows a composite per-ormance report covering inventory. Such a report should be graphic in rder to establish trends and should cover a reasonable period for analy-is. Half a year is suggested. The chart should show the annual cost of eviation from standard limits in terms of dollars. The chart format ermits performance to be shown in comparison with a goal indicating he ultimate performance of which the system is capable. Shown also is maximum limit, which is established at the discretion of management. f inventory is above this limit, an investigation is in order.

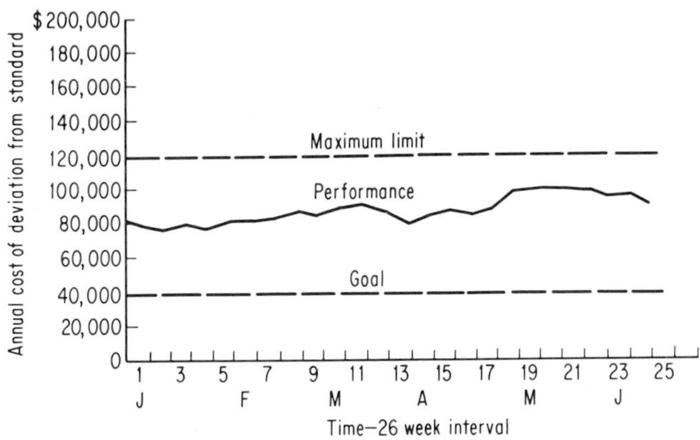

FIG. 14–17. Production control—composite performance report.

Generally speaking, management is interested in only the over-all per-ormance of the organization. However, if consistent deviations beyond he maximum limits occur, management may wish to break down the esponsibility for operating weakness. This can be done by showing the espective performances by operating functions in a chart prepared by nalyzing deviations from standard against the exception reports in the arious operating functions. The source of data would be the exception eports for the short-range period stored in computer magnetic tape or andom access files. Figure 14–18 illustrates a functional performance hart.

An important aspect of good control reports should be emphasized. Everyone from operating levels to top management uses the same set of tandards. This provides for consistency and is really more of a protection o lower levels of organization than where performance evaluation is omewhat subjective and where interpretations may vary widely.

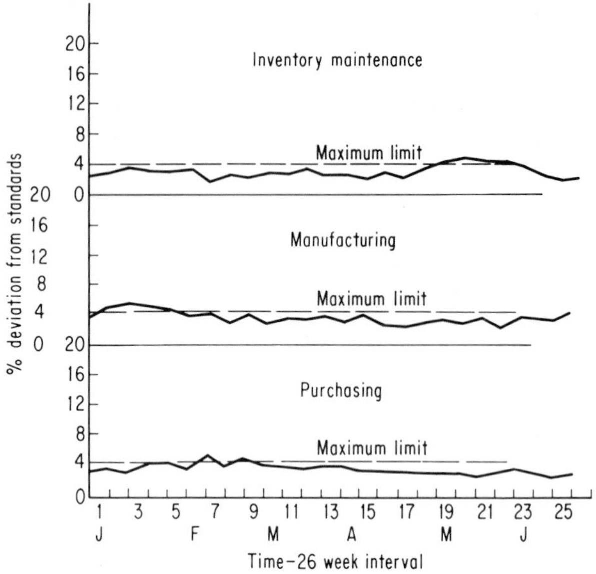

FIG. 14–18. Production control—functional performance.

Analytical Reports

In all systems of manufacturing control, the best operation is four where the judgment and power of decision associated with human bein is coupled with a computer system's powers of computation, data storag and manipulation. Certain reports are essential to give supervision th ability to take knowledgeable action. Two items are especially importa to supervision in the field of inventory management. One is the preserv tion and *improvement* of the standard replacement cycles pertaining the various items controlled. In fact, every possible means should exerted to reduce replacement cycles to just short of the point where fu ther reduction will increase cost. This has three important results. In th first place, by reducing the production cycle one automatically lowe work-in-process inventory. Secondly, a short replacement cycle permits r ordering at such a low level of inventory that the risk associated with fo cast error is minimized. Third, the length of the replacement cycle has very pronounced effect on the level of the protective stock, since the pr tective stock must be adjusted to suit the period over which the risk shortage exists.

In order for supervision to have a grasp of changes in the replaceme cycle, it is suggested that a historical review of these periods be ma on a running basis covering the various lots received. This should spa period of three to six months. Current values should be compared ith the previous year's average cycle.

Another important item with which supervision should be concerned s the degree of penetration into protective stock. Obviously, if protective tock is not used at some time it should not be carried. Consequently, it s suggested that a report be issued once a month covering the previous uarter's record of penetrations into protective stock, particularly with espect to the maximum range of penetration. If this is less than 100 per ent, supervision may wish to enter a factor less than unity in the formula or protective stock. The effect would be to reduce automatically the rotective stock when it is computed monthly (see "Computation of Proective Stocks"). By entering this adjustment as a known factor, it is posible to convert to normal model operation again by a simple change of he factor to unity if the system ever gets out of control as a result of mproper supervisory decisions.

eal-time Operation

No description of inventory control would be complete without some nention of real-time operation. In this connection, it is quite important o define what is actually meant by real-time operation as compared with n-line operation.

Generally speaking, an on-line system may be described as one in which here can be interfacing and communication with a computer from renote locations. This is usually limited to interrogations with rather retricted answering capabilities. In such a system there is very little rocessing permitted on any given individual transaction.

In contrast to on-line systems, a real-time system has all the capabilities f on-line plus completely simultaneous processing of data with the action hat created it. Both on-line and real-time systems have been centers of conomics controversy. For the purposes of this section, let it suffice to ay that where companies are large and inventory is controlled centrally, t is sometimes desirable to have very fast interrogation of inventory posiion. If the interrogation is to mean anything, the inventory itself has to e updated in a time frequency consistent with the interrogation. This neans that all transactions must be updated on a real-time basis. Consequently, before employing a system which has certain complexities, it is xtremely desirable to carefully evaluate the need for interrogations ather than exception reports, which are effective and economical in a tatistically controlled inventory.

The foregoing treatment of automated inventory control is obviously nly a small piece of what must be considered in the design of a complete nanagement information system. It not only is of special interest to purchasing people but also indicates the sort of considerations necessa in automating other areas.

Management information systems (MIS) is a term which now has wi acceptance but also seems to be widely misunderstood. It is described a completely integrated system of data gathering, transmission, and pro essing, and information storage and retrieval, as these processes conce the entire business enterprise. But more than this, it is the means which management can check performance against established policy. provides the information for evaluation and thus for decision making.

Perhaps we can more readily understand this concept if we consid MIS as made up of three things:

1. *Operation.* This consists of the model plus operating people. Aft management decides what it wants, a study is undertaken to determi how these aims will be achieved. Purchase of hardware such as dat gathering devices, telecommunication lines and equipment, compute auxiliary storage units of the random-access variety, interrogation d vices and their feedback units of printers, displays, and plotters is a operational consideration. For a MIS system, at least one on-li processor is required and one or more off-line processors may be i cluded. Where applicable, data and message switching and proce computers will be integrated to take advantage of real-time capab ities. Systems design and programming are also in the area of operatio
2. *Supervision.* This is the area where exceptions are reported so supe vision can take the necessary action.
3. *Evaluation.* This is where higher management gets into the act. E ceptions are evaluated on an over-all basis to compare performan with policy and objectives, and the information available is used i deciding the course for the future.

As this handbook goes to press, there are probably no complete man facturing information systems in operation, but a number of compani are making progress in this direction. Some of these systems were initial implemented in 1964 with major benefits anticipated to occur after tw to three years. For many companies, these benefits will be delayed we beyond that period.

A properly conceived and designed inventory management system obv ously must include purchasing knowledge and experience in applyi certain information and data. As was stated at the beginning of th section, purchasing management should be interested in and capable contributing its experience and know-how at the very outset of plannin for EDP.

SELECTED BIBLIOGRAPHY

Administration of Electronic Data Processing, Studies in Business Policy, No. 98, National Industrial Conference Board, Inc., New York, 1961

Anyon, G. Jay: *Managing an Integrated Purchasing Process,* Holt, Rinehart and Winston, Inc., New York, 1963

"Case Histories in Electronic Data Processing" (Bendix), *Purchasing,* May 20, 1963; (Kodak), *Purchasing,* June 17, 1963

Computer Dictionary, Howard W, Sams & Co., Inc., Indianapolis, Ind., 1965

Diebold, J.: "EDP—The Still Sleeping Giant," *Harvard Business Review,* September–October, 1964

Gregory, R. H., and R. L. Van Horn: *Automatic Data-Processing Systems—Principles and Procedures,* Wadsworth Publishing Co., Inc., Belmont, Calif., 1960

"How EDP Speeds Purchasing" (Thompson-Ramo-Woolridge), *Purchasing,* August 27, 1963

"How Electronic Purchasing Works," *Purchasing,* February 27, 1961

Huskey, Harry D., and G. A. Korn: *Computer Handbook,* McGraw-Hill Book Company, New York, 1962

Lytel, Allen: *ABC of Computers,* Howard W. Sams & Co., Inc., Indianapolis, Ind., 1961

Management's Role in Electronic Data Processing, Studies in Business Policy, No. 92, National Industrial Conference Board, Inc., New York, 1959

Neet, R., and S. A. Hetzler: *An Introduction to Electronic Data Processing,* The Free Press of Glencoe, New York, 1963

Plant, H.: "What Can EDP Do for Purchasing?" *Purchasing,* April 22, 1963

Schmidt, Richard, and William E. Meyers: *Electronic Business Data Processing,* Holt, Rinehart and Winston, Inc., New York, 1963

"What the Computer Can Do for the Small Company," *Purchasing,* September 9, 1963

Widing, J. William, Jr., and C. Gerald Diamond: "Buy by Computer," *Harvard Business Review,* March–April, 1964

Wright, J.: "What Will Automation Do to Purchasing?" *Purchasing,* January 14, 1963

SECTION 15

BUYING CONSIDERATIONS: REPRESENTATIVE COMMODITIES

Editor

Albert J. D'Arcy, Director of Purchases, Union Carbide Corporation, New York, New York

Associate Editors

Mrs. Joseph Cranmore, Food Consultant, Portchester, New York

Harold E. Edell, Staff Assistant to Manager of Purchases, Union Carbide Corporation, New York, New York

Edwin Fleischmann, Consulting Engineer, San Francisco, California

William Karchere, Purchasing Research Analyst, Union Carbide Corporation, New York, New York

Donald G. Lauck, Assistant Director–Purchasing, Universal Atlas Cement, Division of United States Steel Corporation, New York, New York

Chester F. Teeple, Director of Purchasing & Traffic, Warner-Lambert Pharmaceutical Company, Morris Plains, New Jersey

There are many markets or commodity classes, as shown by the contents of this section, which do not even touch the thousands of other classifications confronting purchasing departments in the United States and Canada. To attempt a coverage of every classification and the hundreds of individual items in each, or to define singular purchasing procedures, would involve an impossible task.

Principles, obviously, are the major considerations. These are outlined in other sections of this handbook.

It shall be the basic purpose of this section to direct the buyer's attention to those details in the more prominent commodity classes which might be termed "uncommon." To do this, much emphasis must necessarily be placed on pricing the items within each class. It has been claimed that once a buyer knows how to compute the price of the items he buys, he then knows how to purchase them. This is probably true about such items as have published price lists and true to some degree about items on which no price lists are published. However, the study of raw materials and commodity markets will provide an excellent guide with which to measure prices of those items.

It is probably for that reason that purchasing functionalizes departments by commodity types. Buyers can achieve better results if activities are confined to the purchase of fewer types of commodities. Specialization thus allows more study of markets, production, and methods of distribution. The amount of specialization that is justified depends upon the size of the department and the character of the business.

As outlined in Section 2 of this handbook, a division of one or more buyers in a large-sized organization will be responsible for raw material; another for castings and forgings; one for made-up parts; and others for capital and construction, MRO (maintenance, repair, and operating supplies), stationery and office supplies, advertising material, etc. In the small department, one man or woman handles all classes of all commodities. Necessarily, time prevents becoming a specialist in more than a dozen or so classifications.

That type of buyer in a medium- or small-sized department, plus, of course, those in much smaller companies that do not have a purchasing department, may require basic reference material for effective buying. That is the primary function of this section.

CONSIDERATIONS ON COMMODITY BUYING

Irrespective of commodity classifications, certain general basic considerations confront the buyer. Detailed principles and concepts are outlined in other sections of this handbook and can be located by reference to the Index. A brief review, however, may be helpful here as an introduction to the fifteen classifications alphabetically embodied in this section.

Basic Considerations

Quality. The term "quality" is usually accepted as referring to the "best or finest" product. To a buyer the word can have no exact meaning until the specification of quality is associated with its end use. When this association is established, the term "quality" will mean the most economical grade of material for the particular use intended. The majority of quality specifications are prepared by either the engineering or production department, using standard specifications such as ASTM or ASA, etc., discussed in Section 8. This should not, however, prevent the buyer's offering a substitute or a change in specifications if an advantage in ultimate cost or availability is to be gained. Under present concepts, that function called value analysis is one of the principal responsibilities and duties of the purchasing organization.

Price. The price of an article or product consists of many factors in addition to the quoted figure. Among these factors are terms of payment, transportation costs, and taxes. These might be termed "out-of-pocket" costs which are carefully analyzed to determine the low bidder or the lowest cost of the item. Purchasing, internal handling, storage, accounting, etc., are costs which might be called "fixed expenses" and are seldom considered when placing an order but should be included in any survey of the cost of procurement or the cost of carrying inventory. Sections 10, 11 and 13 detail these considerations.

Availability. Quality, price, and availability, plus service, are the primary considerations of all purchases. Each depends upon the others in varying degrees. Without intimate knowledge of the factors which established a requirement, it is difficult to say which is the most important. However, availability under all market and economic conditions is of great concern to the procurement officer. If, because of certain quality and price policies exercised during a long market, the purchaser finds restricted availability on a short market, then this feature has not been given the consideration it deserves. Availability and service are first considerations when selecting a source of supply.

Company Policy. There are three levels of purchasing policy: first, the textbook which discusses the pros and cons of procurement; second, the policy of the company which is a written or oral statement of those procedures which guide the buyer in making purchases to the best interest of the company, and is the result of the experiences of the company's purchasing executives; third, the policy of the purchasing department in the protection of their sources to ensure a continued flow of goods under all economic conditions. The department policy operates, of course, within the company policy and at the same time is a supplement to it.

There is great advantage in the written company policy as a means of keeping personnel at all levels informed as to how the procurement function is operated. The lack of such a statement on the part of top management leads to misunderstanding and disagreement as to responsibility. Usually, it delegates to the purchasing agent and no others the authority to commit the company to a purchase, thereby centralizing the function in this department. All this is described with examples in Sections 2 and 3.

At the department level, the policy is concerned with establishing good will for the company by the manner in which they negotiate with sales representatives. One very important phase of this policy explains how the department operates and why the salesman will or will not receive an order. With this information the salesman knows how to conduct future contacts. This policy also determines the advantages or disadvantages of spreading purchases among many sources or concentrating them among a few carefully chosen suppliers to create a history of requirements. The department policy is oral or written depending on its complexity, but there should be a policy.

General Considerations

Trade Customs. Trade customs or habits are those procedures and practices which have become uniform through common usage in a trade or business. As material sources have multiplied, each new producer has, in general, accepted the customs which have been identified with earlier producers. Thus steel, textiles, paper, and many other commodities are uniform in packaging, terms of payment, and f.o.b. points. Many trade customs can be common to all commodities. The careful buyer watches for deviations from the established pattern in each commodity.

For example, the trade custom of pricing within a market has become quite uniform. This fact may be attributed to pricing methods used by the manufacturers or producers and continued by the distributors. In arriving at net prices, pipe fittings are quoted at a list price subject to specified multipliers. These multipliers may be the resultant of both additions and deductions. Similarly, folding cartons are quoted at so much per thousand, tonnage steel at a price per hundred pounds, and tool steel at a price per pound. To the beginner in purchasing this may seem to be very confusing, but careful study and constant usage will develop a rather complete knowledge of these pricing habits.

Even as pricing, the f.o.b. point becomes uniform in markets and commodity classes. It can usually be said that for a given product, the f.o.b. point will be the same. Trade customs and competition seem to produce this condition. It is, however, the exception to these standard practices which the buyer must guard against.

Distribution Methods. The method by which each market distributes its goods has a bearing on the price. For every handling by an intermediate distributor or jobber, something is added to the cost because each handler must make a profit. In some markets, such as steel, a buyer may deal directly with the producer, provided he meets certain minimum tonnage requirements in each commodity. Other markets, notably most mill supplies, are sold only through distributors or jobbers. These distribution methods tend to remain firm and rather inflexible, so that it is necessary for the buyer to study and understand this situation for each market in which he operates.

Reciprocity. This is a subject which most purchasing agents prefer to avoid because they feel it tends to restrict the freedom of competition. To some degrees reciprocal buying is a factor in the placement of business in a majority of industries. Under proper control it has a definite place in purchasing procedures. Therefore, in recognition of this fact, the purchasing agent, working with top management, develops the general rules to produce such control. Sales, production, and purchasing management make a good committee to decide when reciprocal demands are sound or unsound. In all cases, a buyer gratefully acknowledges business given the company by those who seek reciprocal sales whether or not he is able to place business with them.

Speculation. The primary task of the purchasing agent is the acquisition of the necessary raw materials and supplies to support orderly production at the lowest ultimate cost. Other sections (particularly Sec. 12) of this handbook discuss the subjects of speculation, hand-to-mouth buying, and forward buying, in great detail, so that it seems beside the point to more than draw attention to the references at this time. It is sufficient to say that speculation, in the true sense, is not a function of purchasing.

Deterioration and Obsolescence. Many of the products used by industry have a relatively short storage life. If kept in stock too long, they become useless and must be scrapped. When buying this class of material, care is exercised and coverage is maintained within the expected useful "shelf life" of the product. This condition leads to the buying of small and costly quantities and so the possibilities of spaced or scheduled deliveries should be investigated.

Technological advances and developments and changes in processing or equipment can obsolete materials held in inventory for too long a period. In commodity classes which may be influenced by these factors, the buyer exercises care in determining the quantity to be purchased in relation to unit cost.

Storage Space. The space occupied by productive operations in industry may be considered profit-making areas, while that space which is devoted to the storage of supplies might be termed an item of expense. It can probably be claimed that most industrial operations are short of storage space. In view of this situation, the quantities of material of large bulk are carefully considered at the time of buying.

Cost of Carrying Inventory. Many factors are considered when approaching this phase of operations. Some of these are as follows:

1. Maximum stock to be carried
2. The use period
3. Deterioration and obsolescence
4. Cost of storage, including taxes
5. Handling charges, internal
6. Cost of transportation, delivery
7. Interest on investment
8. Insurance
9. Purchasing costs
10. Receiving and accounting costs
11. Lead time for delivery
12. Economic conditions and price trends

The accounting department of most firms maintains cost figures that can be used to determine whether or not the purchase of a larger quantity at a lower price will be economical over the using period. Where procurement personnel are in charge of inventory, careful study is made of the entire subject, as outlined in Sections 12, 13, and 29.

Areas of Purchasing

Raw Materials. The definition of "raw materials" varies widely from one company to another. In general, these are the materials which are used and consumed in making the finished product. The finished products of the seller become the raw materials of the buyer.

A constant and uniform flow of raw materials is, of course, necessary to ensure smooth and uninterrupted production. If, for any reason, this flow is disturbed, a slowdown or stoppage of production occurs, resulting in heavy losses. The assurance of a constant supply is the first duty of the procurement officer.

The ebb and flow of raw materials will be in direct proportion to the volume or rate of production. Control of this increasing and decreasing rate of supply calls for a high degree of cooperation between the purchasing department and the department which plans the production. The problem of supply becomes more complicated as the number of markets and raw materials increase.

It is in the buying of raw materials that a study of markets becomes important. These materials represent a large part of the cost of goods sold and their proper purchasing could be the difference between a profit or a loss in the operation. Trends in these markets usually develop rather slowly and all are discussed in some detail in most trade papers.

Component Parts. The purchase of component units or an assembly of units to be incorporated in an end product, presents interesting prol lems for the purchasing department.

"Make or buy" is a question that arises whenever an assembly, com ponent, or part is to be bought. In-plant costs accurately and compre hensively prepared must be compared with the price of the item as quote by a reliable supplier. The quantity involved, frequency of purchase, an the importance of delivery are some of the items to be considered i reaching a decision.

The "make or buy" problem also includes a determination of whethe the item is of standard or special design. If standard, it will probably b less expensive to buy because the item may be produced in large volum by the maker. If special, the above-mentioned considerations will appl

Contractors. The investigation of potential subcontractors usually pre cedes the bidding or quotation phase when buying components or part This is necessary to determine the suitability of the subcontractor's equi ment and facilities in relation to the service to be rendered. When sui able sources have been found, the competitive determination of pric follows the usual pattern. All details of raw materials, production, in spection, scrap disposal, shipping, and accounting are carefully discusse

Control of subcontractors for construction may be maintained eithe by having a member of the buying organization constantly present durin the working hours or by periodic inspections. The importance of the iter in relation to production or the complexity of production and deliver determines the extent of such control. The close proximity of contractua sources is desirable and is a consideration in the selection, because tran portation and inspection costs are important factors.

Operating Supplies. Operating supplies are those items commonl carried in the storeroom to support maintenance, repairs, and operation or MRO requirements in the language of purchasing. They include suc items as lubricating oils and greases, fuels, fasteners, small tools, etc.

The importance of these items cannot be minimized for the lack o them could cause an interruption in production as quickly as a lack o raw material. Skillful handling of the stores operation is a great asset t the plant management. Hundreds of items are involved and thousand of dollars are tied up in this inventory. To have sufficient stock on han for every situation and still keep the total investment within reason re quires constant attention.

It is desirable, but not always possible, to procure operating supplie from sources near the operation. Local suppliers more frequently sell o a "delivered" basis and can make more rapid deliveries. There is als the advantage of creating a history of requirements with local supplier to provide constant availability under all economic conditions.

Recording the daily flow of items in and out of the stores inventory is handled either by the storeskeeper or by some individual in the purchasing department. The assignment of this responsibility is a management function. In any event, an accurate accounting is essential. The records show, for every item, stock on hand, quantity on order, maximum and minimum stocks, order point, lead time, inventory unit, standard package quantities, and such other information as seems desirable in the operation. Postings to inventory records are kept on a current basis for both incoming and outgoing items. Periodic physical checks are made to verify the stock record cards.

While operating supplies are not incorporated in the end product of a plant, they are included in the cost of that product. They are essential to operations and maintenance and so become part of the expense of doing business. Any economies effected in their purchase or handling, and any reduction of stores inventory or transportation costs, will be reflected in the cost of the final product of the plant.

Perhaps operating supplies can become obsolete more rapidly than other items. Changes in production can make many tools obsolete or new products may prove to be more useful or safer. Close liaison between all departments involved keeps obsolescence at a minimum.

References

The subjects covered in these general considerations are mentioned in practically every section of this handbook. Thus the reader is referred to the Index for locating further, and in some cases, more complete information. Lists of outside references will be found in Section 26, "Library and Catalog File," and in Section 28, "Appendix."

APPAREL

The terms "uniforms" and "work clothes" are really synonymous, for they describe the type or style of apparel worn by an employee at work. "Uniforms" are generally considered as custom-tailored garments, while "work clothes" might be "shelf-item" garments of standard sizes offered for sale through the commissary or employee sales department. Whether purchased for male or female use, there is little difference in the factors to be considered.

Uniforms. Important factors in buying uniforms are requirements of intended use, cost of material selected, cost of cleaning according to method and required frequency, proper workmanship, and styling and color.

Uniforms or regulation dress are fundamentally work clothes, whether for male or female employees. They are designed for specific use by such employees as doormen, waitresses, stewards, waiters, chauffeurs, maids laundry workers, laboratory workers, chemists, technicians, nurses, and others. Some uniforms may include gloves, hats, caps, jackets, coats, o capes. A complete evaluation of the particular function should be made in selecting the proper material, tailoring, styling, and color.

There are many synthetic fabrics available in today's market that ar practical for certain types of uniforms. All fabrics—woolens, silks, cottons and synthetics—should be laboratory tested for tensile strength, resistanc to fading, staining, and creasing. It should also be predetermined tha the fabric can be satisfactorily laundered, or dry-cleaned.

It is desirable that buyers request a sample garment (uniform) from the manufacturer for wear test. The garment (uniform) should allow fo sufficient freedom of movement at the shoulders, armpits, and waistlin for employees who work as maids, waitresses, elevator operators, and porters, to name a few. Trimmings, such as buttons, braids, frogs, facings etc., should be chosen for easy removal before the required cleanin process, or should withstand necessary cleaning. All garments (uniforms should be reinforced at points of strain, depending upon the job classifi cation of the worker.

Appearance is also an important factor. Consideration should be given to the decor of the particular surroundings of the worker to establish harmonious atmosphere, particularly in public places. For example, i the worker is a waitress, the garment (uniform) should be of a color and style to blend with the decor of the dining room.

Work Clothes. When buying these items, one must consider the natur of the plant operations and the preference of the employees. The cost t the employee is always important, as is resistance to the hazards of th job. Fabrics can be found which will resist tear from snagging or will no permit acids to burn through and injure the employee. Such garment would not necessarily be considered as safety equipment.

Any reputable source can advise the buyer regarding the sizes to b carried, based upon the number of employees at the operation.

It would be advantageous at the time of negotiation to set up a pro cedure for the exchange of sizes and styles which do not move. When considering female work clothes, there are many advantages in establish ing a small "style committee" to approve the garment before the purchas is made. Such a committee should work with the buyer during the selec tion of items to be considered.

Both the male and female garments should be viewed from the safet angle. Plain durable items with no trimmings, or a minimum of trim mings which might be caught in moving machinery, should receive first consideration. Because this class of clothing is laundered and maintained by the employee, the items selected should be easy for him to handle.

Gloves. Regardless of the material, gloves may be considered safety equipment. The buyer should consult with the safety engineer regarding the types of gloves to be used at the plant. Gloves are a commodity whose first cost per pair may not present the true value of the item. Consideration must be given to the dexterity of the operator when using the gloves, the fabric of which they are made, and the cost per hour of useful life. Consideration must also be given to the construction of the gloves. The fewer the seams, the better. A reversible glove may be worn on either hand, thereby offering a possible double wear-life feature.

Gloves may be distributed at cost, part cost, or free, depending upon company policy. If the operation provides "free" issue, then some form of salvage and repair service should be investigated as an economy measure.

Safety Equipment. The purchase of safety equipment, including safety and protective apparel, is usually on specifications from the safety department or engineer. The specifications are exacting and should be carefully filled. To permit variations to obtain low prices may completely defeat the object of the purchase—the protection of personnel on hazardous work.

Safety shoes are considered to be in the class of safety equipment. There are several manufacturers who produce safety shoes which will meet standard requirements. They are sold directly to large operations where a store is maintained or through distributors and jobbers who sometimes offer them under their own trade names. Some manufacturers will enter into a consignment arrangement for safety shoes which requires no investment by the company. If, however, the shoes are purchased by the company, some understanding should be reached concerning the exchange of slow-moving sizes or styles. In some industrial areas retail stores carry safety shoes in stock or will order them from the factory on demand.

The important factor is, of course, the steel or plastic toe box which protects the toes from injury. To further encourage the use of safety shoes, they should be comfortable to wear. This indicates they must be carefully fitted to the employee. Style and reasonable quality are other features to consider. Floor conditions may dictate the kind of sole and heel to be used, and there are safety shoes on which no metal fasteners are used so as to provide extra protection for electrical workers. Close cooperation with the safety engineer must be maintained on all safety equipment purchases.

References

National Safety News, Annual Safety Equipment Issue, published by National Safety Council, Inc., 270 Madison Avenue, New York, N.Y. 10016

Safety Maintenance and Production, 75 Fulton Street, New York, N.Y. 10038

AUTOMOTIVE AND PARTS

Passenger Vehicles

Manufacturer. Large companies operating several plants in different localities or companies operating fleets of passenger cars may purchase directly from the manufacturer. This fleet sales department can be very helpful in effecting a substantial savings and, if desired, assist the authorized dealer of your choice in completing the transaction. Cars purchased under these arrangements would, of course, be new.

Dealer. Smaller operators usually purchase either new or used cars from dealers. When the make and model have been determined, the buying is done on competitive bidding among dealers handling that particular make of car. If a used car is to be considered, the buyer should contact both new and used car agencies. In some localities used car wholesalers and auctions are additional sources. In any event, clear title and the condition of the vehicle are of prime importance; therefore the reliability of the source should receive equal consideration with the price.

Rental. The rental of passenger cars has increased considerably in recent years. Many companies have switched from ownership to rental plans for the following reasons:

1. Investment in cars
2. Predetermined operating cost
3. Relief of maintaining repair shops and related problems of supervision, labor, inventory of parts, and shop equipment
4. Relief of problem in disposing of cars to be replaced
5. Fixed replacement date
6. Tax savings

Rental companies offer among others the following basic types of leasing plans: management plan, straight rental plan, and strip rental plan.

Management plan: the lessor furnishes the car, license, insurance, and maintenance. The agreed monthly rate includes a service or management charge. Lease period generally covers a period of one to two years.

A specific part of the monthly rate is set aside as a reserve for depreciation. The lessor will, because of experience and records he maintains, make the decision when a car should be replaced, which may be because of excessive repair costs or because the current price of used cars is attractive. When the car is disposed of, any difference between the book value and the selling price accrues to the lessee whether it be a profit or a loss.

Under the management plan, the rental rate may appear to be lower nitially, but the actual net cost is dependent on the price that used cars will bring.

Straight rental plan: This is an all-inclusive plan. The lessor provides he car, license, insurance, and maintenance. The car is replaced at the end of the lease period, and the lessee is in no way involved with profit or disposal of car.

Strip rental plan: This plan is generally accepted for one-year rental deals because the monthly rate does not provide for maintenance and may or may not include insurance. In many instances the lessee may be n a position to furnish the necessary insurance at a lower cost than the lessor. Because cars will be disposed of at the end of the one-year period, he lessee may feel that maintenance cost will be negligible and pay for he repairs as they become necessary, thereby reducing fixed monthly rate. As a general rule, in all plans the lessee furnishes gasoline, add-on oil, torage, and washing, unless the agreement provides otherwise.

When discussing rental contracts, the following items (also outlined under "Lease versus Purchase" in Section 16) should be considered and esponsibility clearly defined:

- Payment of state and local sales taxes, also cost of licensing, if cars will be stationed in various states.
- Cost of delivery of new cars to destination if more than one location is involved, also cost of returning replacement cars.
- Number of miles allowable during contract period.
- Type and model of car and accessories to be included.
- The liability of lessee when car is returned to lessor because of the condition of car, i.e., mechanically, body (inside and out), and tires.
- The types and limits of insurance should be carefully examined for proper coverage. Ascertain if carrier is a mutual or stock insurance company.
- nclude option to purchase car in the event of a national emergency and cars are difficult to obtain.
- Who will handle filing of warranty claims for mechanical or tire failures before warranty expires.
- Your legal department should examine agreement to ensure that it is not a contract of sale in the event a repurchase clause is in the agreement.

Trucks

Manufacturer. Truck-fleet operators can, as a rule, deal directly wit the manufacturers of those types of equipment which they propose purchase. The equipment is usually purchased to carefully prepared spe ifications. This detail alone would take it out of the so-called "standar line" item which would be offered by the dealer.

Dealer. 1. New: This would be the best source for the smaller operat needing light delivery or light dump trucks. Such an operation is usual satisfied with vehicles of standard specifications which are included the manufacturer's line.

2. Used: The purchase of used vehicles should be approached wit great care. The original owner usually retains the vehicles until the have outlived their usefulness and operation is uneconomical. Howeve there are instances where a company decides to make a change in the typ of unit recently purchased and will offer their present equipment f sale at a reasonable price. If used equipment is to be purchased, the fo lowing points are offered as a guide.

Contact factory branch or authorized dealer and specify type, size, an age of equipment you desire.

Verify the cost of the unit when new to assist in evaluating the pric quoted.

If possible, obtain the name of the original owner; this will provide a idea as to annual mileage and type of service in which the vehicle h operated.

Inspect the vehicle to determine present condition and extent of previo maintenance.

Rental. In recent years there has been a trend toward leasing inste of owning. This is especially true in the case of operators of ten units less. When considering the lease of equipment, prepare a specification the vehicle desired including an estimate of the annual mileage. Subm these details to the various rental companies in your community and as for information concerning both straight rental and purchase optic leasing.

1. The straight rental plan establishes a weekly rate which allows fixed number of miles of operation. Additional mileage is billed at fixed rate per mile. All services, such as registration, maintenance repai tire replacement or repair, full insurance, washing, servicing, gasolin and oil are included. However, title to the vehicle remains with the less at the expiration of the contract.

2. The purchase option lease permits the lessee to take title at the expiration of the contract. This type of contract should be carefully checked by an attorney since it may be considered a conditional sales contract by he Internal Revenue Department.

3. When considering either type of rental, the costs should be compared with the operation of an owned vehicle. In making the final decision, bear in mind that the cost of leasing makes no allowance for the salvage value of the vehicle at the end of the contract period. This might be 15 to 20 per cent of the original cost at the end of a five-year period.

Quality Considerations

Description. As a rule, operators of large fleets develop their own specfications; however, the operator of a single unit or small fleet can accomplish the same results. From the following, prepare a list of the equisites as they apply to your particular business. All truck manufacurers offer engineering service without charge to assist the buyer in developing such specifications for the equipment best suited to their operations.

1. Type, size, weight, and value of product or commodity to be hauled. Maximum weight to be loaded on unit, to determine if straight truck or ractor and trailer is required for your operation.

2. Use of truck—within city limits or rural delivery service, intercity ervice.

3. Type of body requirements, such as closed van, open-top, stake or platform body, tank body for hauling liquids, or tractor-trailer unit. Parcel-delivery-type bodies for door-to-door delivery where driver has access to body from cab. In connection with body style, consider the potential advertising value.

4. Local traffic conditions and restrictions to determine maximum length of chassis, width, and height of body. Should chassis be conventional cab forward or cab over engine type? Also investigate vehicle codes in the states where vehicles will operate to determine axle-load restrictions nd maximum gross vehicle weight for a given wheelbase.

5. Terrain of routes to be covered by vehicles, road conditions, etc. In territory with steep hills, units must be equipped with sufficient horsepower, heavy-duty brakes, and correct gear ratios in differential with single-speed or two-speed rear axles with correct and proper number of ransmission forward speeds.

6. Selection of special-equipment, refrigerator bodies for perishables. Tarpaulins for open-top bodies to protect cargo from rain and snow and power lift gates to expedite loading and unloading of heavy pieces. Winch

equipment for handling extra-heavy pieces of freight. Alarm systems t protect valuable cargo. Side doors for sidewalk deliveries.

7. Discuss with your drivers the units they now operate and obtai their ideas and suggestions on what could be done to improve operatio of vehicles, from standpoint of safety, such as type and placing of mirror extra step plate for getting in and out of cab, loading and unloading, et

8. Check with tire companies to verify correct number and size of tir required based on gross vehicle weight.

9. Companies that are equipped with complete maintenance faciliti under the direction of a supervisor will naturally review contemplate purchase for purpose of reviewing operating costs of vehicles to be r placed and obtain recommendations that will reduce maintenance cost reduce mechanical and tire road failure, and reduce number of units ou of service.

Parts—Repair and/or Replacements

The "guaranteed maintenance service contract" offered by truck manu facturers' factory branches and dealers includes the following:

Period of contract–four to five years depending upon number of mil operated.
Rate generally set up on graduated scale for each succeeding year.
Door glass, windshield, body and fenders, and accident repairs are nc included.
Delivery service to and from customer's plant is not included in rate.
Vehicle must be made available for inspection and service in accordanc with agreement.
Provision must be made if spare units are required in event of road fai ures or emergency.

When investigating the guaranteed maintenance plan and comparin the costs with your own, consider the following:

Elimination of your own facilities, personnel, and supervision.
Elimination of stocking of parts and supplies which relieves inventor and increases working capital.
Elimination of need of purchasing special shop and garage equipment.
Gives fixed per mile cost of operation.

When the comparison of maintenance costs has been made and figur reflect that the customer can do the job cheaper than is possible with service plan, the maintenance supervisor should take part in meeting with a factory representative or dealer before the deal is completed. Th maintenance supervisor should be given the opportunity of carefull hecking the servicing and parts manuals of the various makes of trucks ou contemplate purchasing. The purpose is to ascertain what will be necessary to set up a preventive maintenance program; will special tools or equipment have to be purchased to perform services and repairs? Determine the parts that have to be stocked and the disposition to be made of the parts that may become obsolete with the purchase of new models. Price comparisons should be made of the interchangeable parts, such as bearings, brake lining, etc., with parts supply firms. The cost of rebuilt assemblies, such as engines, differentials, clutches, and transmissions on an exchange basis should be discussed, as it may prove cheaper than doing he work in your own shops; also consider the down time involved.

Commercial sources for spare or repair parts can supply equivalent equipment which may offer a price advantage. Care must be exercised in checking the specifications to be sure that proper quality is obtained.

Another source of parts for old models is the salvage yard. While the parts available are quite obviously used, it may be the only place where uch items can be found.

Quality. Parts are always associated with the manufacturer's name, ear, and model on which they are to be used. Those purchased from the quipment manufacturer or his regular dealer will usually be of suitable quality. More care should be taken when other sources are used.

The standard for spare parts should be the manufacturer's catalog.

References

Automotive Industries, Chestnut and 56th Streets, Philadelphia, Pa. 19139

Automotive Service Industry Association, 168 North Michigan Avenue, Chicago, Ill., 60601

Business Car Allowances, Practices, & Controls, The Dartnell Corporation, 4660 North Ravenswood Avenue, Chicago, Ill. 60640

Chilton Automotive Buyer's Guide, Chilton Company, Chestnut and 56th Streets. Philadelphia, Pa. 19139

Commercial Car Journal, Chilton Company, Chestnut and 56th Streets, Philadelphia, Pa. 19139

Construction Methods and Equipment, McGraw-Hill Publications, 330 West 42d Street, New York, N.Y. 10036

Fleet Owner, McGraw-Hill Publications, 330 West 42d Street, New York, N.Y. 10036

"Leasing vs. Buying," National Association of Purchasing Agents, New York, 10007

Lee, Samuel J.: *Automotive Transportation in Industry,* Lloyd R. Wolfe, Publisher, 476 Park Street, Chicago, Ill., 60622

Motor Age, Chilton Company, Chestnut and 56th Streets, Philadelphia, Pa. 19139

National Automobile Dealers Association Official Used Car Guide, National Automobile Dealers Association, 2000 K Street, N.W., Washington, D.C., 20006

National Automotive Parts Association, 29 East Madison, Chicago, Ill., 60602
National Truck Leasing System, 23 East Jackson Boulevard, Chicago, Ill., 6060
SAE Journal, Society of Automotive Engineers, 485 Lexington Avenue, Ne York, N.Y. 10017
Tire & Rim Association, Inc., 2001 First National Tower, Akron, Ohio, 44308
Truck Fleet Operator, 5252 North Broadway, Chicago, Ill. 60640
Truck-Trailer Manufacturers Association, Inc., 1413 K Street, N.W. Washingto D.C.

CHEMICALS AND PLASTICS

Chemicals

On the basis of their source or derivation, chemicals are considered fall into the following basic categories:[1]

Organics—such as coal, petroleum, animal fats and oils, grains; their d rivatives and compounds
Inorganics—such as minerals and metals; their derivatives and compoun
Petrochemicals (considered organics)—such as crude oil, natural gas, a other hydrocarbon streams; their derivatives and compounds

The above three categories are further broken down into the followi classifications:

Heavy chemicals (industrial or basic)
- Acids
- Alkalies
- Fertilizers
- Minerals
- Salts
- Sulfur

Intermediate chemicals
- Materials generally requiring further processing or finishing

Fine chemicals
- Specialty compounds usually produced in small quantities

Pharmaceuticals
- Bulk chemicals used for formulating drugs and medicines

End products
- Chemicals ready for final consumption by the consumer, such as co metics, drugs, fertilizers, paints, soaps, detergents, and waxes

Plastics

Plastics are furnished as a bulk commodity in the form of plastic res beads, granules, or powders to be fabricated into semifinished and finish products by such methods as molding, casting, extruding, and rolling. T basic raw materials, plastic resins, are chemical compounds produc

[1] *The Chemical Industry Facts Book,* 1st and 2d eds., Manufacturing Chemists' A sociation, Inc., Washington, D.C.

by the chemical and petrochemical industry. Plastic materials are generally regarded as economical substitutes for the more traditional materials such as metal, wood, glass, and rubber. In fact, many properties have been developed in plastic materials which are superior to those of the more conventional materials. Plastics are separated into two main categories: thermoplastics and thermosetting plastics.

Thermoplastics—Plastics in this group become soft when heated and harden when cooled no matter how often the process is repeated.

Thermosetting plastics—These plastics are set into permanent shape when heat and pressure are applied to them during forming.

Plastic	*Examples of use*
Thermoplastics:	
Acrylics	Combs, costume jewelry, display stands
Nylon	Textile fibers and filaments, gears and mechanical parts
Cellulose acetate	Toys, vacuum-cleaner parts, tool handles
Polyethylene	Squeeze bottles, ice-cube trays, food bags
Polystyrene	Wall tile, instrument panels
Thermosetting plastics:	
Allylics	Electronic parts, laminates
Amino plastics	Tableware, appliance housings
Epoxies	Protective coatings, adhesives
Phenolics	TV cabinets, washing-machine agitators
Polyesters	Impregnation of woven or fibrous materials

The foregoing table gives examples of only the most common plastic materials. Others are listed under "Plastics" in Section 11. Buyers are cautioned to consult with the technical representatives of plastics producing companies to determine the type of plastic best suited for the specific purpose intended.

Purchase Considerations

The main considerations in purchasing chemicals, plastics, and allied products include quantity, containers, quality, availability, price, and contracts. These are discussed below.

Quantity. Most chemicals and plastics are sold directly through the manufacturers' sales organizations. Technical products are sold according to specification; therefore, direct sale from the manufacturer in carload, truckload, and bulk quantities is most typical in the chemical industry.

Small quantities (less than carload or truckload lots) are purchased from a distributor[2] or jobber[3] instead of from a manufacturer. The im-

[2] An individual or company acting as a manufacturer's representative or a distributor of a manufacturer's products, selling such products under the brand name of the producer, acts only as a broker and seldom carries material in local inventory.

[3] An individual or company who purchases carload or truckload lots of chemicals and resells them in less than carload or truckload quantities, either under the brand name of the producer or under his own brand name.

portant purchasing considerations of unit price, availability, and method of delivery and packaging are heavily related to the quantities being purchased.

As mentioned in Section 17, purchases of smaller quantities from foreign sources are usually made through a domestic agent of the foreign producer. Large quantities are usually negotiated directly with the foreign producer.[4]

Packaging and Storage. In the important role of maintaining plant inventories at the most effective and economical level possible, the buyer must be familiar with the following situations at his plant before negotiating the purchase of chemicals:

1. Transportation, unloading, storage, and material-handling facilities
2. Types of production carried on, particularly whether continuous or batch process operations
3. Past, present, and future plant usage requirements

If storage facilities are adequate and usage requirements are predictable, the buyer can take advantage of low unit prices on bulk purchase direct from the manufacturer. Prior to such decisions, calculations should be made to weigh the effect of added inventory costs against potential price reductions.

The packaging of chemicals depends on such considerations as temperature, pressure, gravity, corrosion, and toxicity. Gases are packaged in pressure cylinders, if ordered in less than carload or truckload lots. Bulk purchases of gas are transported by pipeline, barge, tank car, or tank truck, thus eliminating the expense of handling small cylinders. Bulk purchase of solid chemicals in barges, railroad cars, or large bulk containers is more economical than purchase of small lots in boxes, barrels, or drums. This also applies to bulk purchase of liquid chemicals in barge or tank-car lots as opposed to buying in drums, carboys, or cans.

Highly volatile, poisonous, or toxic chemicals require special packaging designed to minimize hazard. An example would be the requirement of lead-shielded containers to protect the handler against harmful rays of radioactive material. Some chemical containers are constructed with special corrosion-resistant linings to prevent contamination of high-purity chemicals.

Many containers are reusable and involve an extra charge which is refunded when the container is returned to the shipper. Railroad cars and barges are subject to demurrage if not unloaded and released promptly by the receiver. These types of charges have a direct effect on

[4] *International Trade Handbook,* Committee for Economic Development, Bureau of Foreign and Domestic Commerce, U.S. Department of Commerce, Washington, D.C.

increasing the final price paid for the product. The common units of measurements used to designate shipping and packaging units are:

- Cubic feet
- Gallons
- Grams
- Kilograms
- Milligrams
- Ounces
- Pounds
- Short and long tons

Quality. Most chemicals and plastics are produced and sold to rigid specifications of the industry, producer, buyer, government agency, or technical association. Some of the more common quality designations include:

- Commercially acceptable
- Industry specifications
- User specifications
- Tried and tested brand names
- CP (chemically pure)

Others worth mentioning are USP, ASTM, AWWA, NF, and ACS Reagent.[5]

Many purchasers require pre-shipment samples for testing in order to determine whether or not the bulk shipment will be satisfactory for their use. A most important factor affecting successful procurement of chemicals and plastics is sound specifications.

Sources of Supply and Availability. Dependable sources of supply usually are developed and proved only over long periods of time. There are many occasions, however, when the buyer must locate a spot supplier or a special chemical on short notice. The following are various sources of information for such purposes:

1. The yearly Buyers' Directory Issue of *Chemical Week,* which contains a comprehensive list of sources of supply for chemicals and related process materials and is recognized as one of the most complete references.
2. Trade journals received in the mail. *Paint, Oil and Chemical Review, Chemical Week,* and *Paint Journal* are this type of literature.
3. Sales representatives of chemical suppliers making calls.
4. *Thomas' Register of American Manufacturers.*
5. The "yellow page" classified business listing of telephone directories.
6. Listings in Section 26, "Library and Catalog File," and Section 28, "Appendix."

[5] Latest *United States Pharmacopeia* (USP), published by authority of the United States Pharmacopoeial Convention; American Society for Testing and Materials (ASTM), 1916 Race Street, Philadelphia, Pa.; American Water Works Association (AWWA), 2 Park Avenue, New York; *National Formulary* (NF), published by American Pharmaceutical Association, 2215 Constitution Avenue, N.W., Washington, D.C.; American Chemical Society (ACS), 2 Park Avenue, New York.

Availability depends on three basic considerations, namely: (1) th source of supply, its reliability, geographic location, method of shipmen and historical trade performance; (2) the industry's capacity to suppl the product itself in comparison to the demand; (3) the availability raw materials going into the product.

Price Guides. Most chemical and plastics prices are posted periodicall as so-called "published market" prices. Of many publications availabl listing these prices, the most important is the *Oil, Paint and Drug Re porter,* issued each Monday.

These publications do not establish the published market prices. The are simply mediums for placing general going price levels before th purchaser. Actually, published market prices are determined by on or a combination of the following: (1) manufacturers establishing price for their product which allows for a reasonable profit return; (manufacturers establishing a price to meet a special competitive situatio and (3) manufacturers meeting special requirements of individual pu chasers. The publications mentioned above have specialty editors whos responsibilities include maintaining constant contact with manufacture to determine the price levels to be published. These publications are ge erally accurate and can be used as one bench mark for making everyda procurement decisions.

The delivery or f.o.b. (point where title passes to buyer) terms of th purchase are one major factor of final price determination. Naturall the most desirable basis of price establishment is f.o.b. destination becaus delivery of the material is taken at the point of consumption, with r sponsibility for delivery, insurance claims, and losses being borne by th supplier at his expense and risk.

For a more complete explanation of delivery terms, the reader is r ferred to Thomas G. Bugan, *When Does Title Pass?*[6] Also see Sectio 4, 5, 17, and 18 of this handbook.

Contracts. In addition to the common purchase order used for sp requirements, two types of contracts are most prevalent in the chemica industry: price protection contracts and requirements contracts.

In a price protection contract, the supplier guarantees establishe pricing for a specified period of, for example, one quarter. The supplie usually protects himself against a near-future general industry price ris by means of a contract provision that the agreed-upon pricing shall co tinue beyond the specified period unless notice to the contrary is serve by either party 30 days before the start of the next quarter. There a many other types of price protection arrangements based on formulas an for different periods of time. It is frequently provided that the buye

[6] Published by W. C. Brown Company, 9151 Main Street, Dubuque, Iowa.

may order additional quantities of chemicals at the established contract price prior to the effective date of a forthcoming price increase.

In what is known as a requirements contract, the buyer's total or partial requirements of a certain chemical for a specific period are contracted for.

Summary

The industrial buyer of chemicals and plastics utilized in production of finished goods can be a major contributor to higher profits and lower costs for his firm when he is doing an effective buying job. He must be more than a good negotiator; he must strive to attain the stature of a recognized authority in the commodity and market areas within which he operates.

The industrial chemicals and plastics field is one of the largest, most diversified, and most complicated of all the commodity fields. The buyer should not only have a comprehensive knowledge of his company's production and marketing operations, but also keep abreast of technological developments of new chemicals. Knowledge of alternative sources of supply for immediate shipments, of effective price negotiation for low bulk unit prices, and of the effect of supply and demand must be part of his everyday job.

There are thousands of chemicals being manufactured and sold; therefore, no attempt has been made here to classify them in detail or to describe chemical properties. For purchasing purposes, the main problem areas in buying were set forth and a broad explanation of material classification was attempted. Complex product information must be secured from product books written by manufacturers[7] and handbooks[8] written especially for this purpose.

References

American Chemical Society, 1155 16th Street, N.W., Washington, D.C. 20036

Chemical & Engineering News, 1155 16th Street, N.W., Washington, D.C. 20036

Chemical Engineering, McGraw-Hill Publications, 330 West 42d Street, New York, N.Y. 10036

Chemical Engineering Catalog, Reinhold Publishing Corporation, 430 Park Avenue, New York, N.Y. 10022

Chemical Materials Catalog and Directory of Producers, Reinhold Publishing Corporation, 430 Park Avenue, New York, N.Y. 10022

Chemical Week Buyers' Guide Issue, McGraw-Hill Publications, 330 West 42d Street, New York, N.Y. 10036

[7] Allied Chemical Corporation, Dow Chemical Company, E. I. du Pont de Nemours & Company, Union Carbide Corporation, Monsanto Company.

[8] G. S. Brady, *Materials Handbook,* McGraw-Hill Book Company, New York.

Green Book (*Oil, Paint and Drug Reporter* Buyers' Directory), Schnell Publish-ing Company, 100 Church Street, New York, N.Y. 10007

Journal of Commerce, 80 Varick Street, New York, N.Y., 10013

Manufacturing Chemists' Association, 1825 Connecticut Avenue, N.W., Washing-ton, D.C., 20009

National Paint, Varnish & Lacquer Association, 1500 Rhode Island Avenu N.W., Washington, D.C., 20005

Oil, Paint and Drug Reporter, Schnell Publishing Company, 100 Church Stree New York, N.Y. 10007

United States Pharmacopeia, 46 Park Avenue, New York, N.Y. 10016

Wall Street Journal, 44 Broad Street, New York, N.Y., 10004

CONTRACT SERVICES

In contracting for outside services it is customary to refer to the buye as the "owner" and to the seller as the "contractor." The negotiation award, and administration of contracts for services are often complex an difficult, due to the more intangible nature of services as opposed t goods. Such contracts often involve large expenditures and high risk and liabilities on the part of both owner and contractor. Particular car in the preparation of service contracts is necessary to minimize monetary legal, and business risks and to protect the rights of both parties. Som of the problems which are not common to other purchasing situation are the following:

1. The activities of the contractor's personnel working on the owner' property expose the owner to liability in the event of personal injur or death on the premises.
2. Small- to medium-sized contractors, engaged for most work, usuall perform in regional markets and sometimes operate with minimum o marginal finances.
3. The work to be performed often cannot be fully defined at the tim the job is started. Consequently, the opportunity for obtaining firm prices is often limited. Alterations and additions to the work can b frequent; therefore, the methods used to alter the contract price mus be carefully defined.

The basic elements of a service contract include a description of th work, a time for starting and completing the work, a definition of pay-ment for the work, and other customary and legal terms and condition which must be agreed to by both parties.

It is important that the owner understand the difference between ar "independent contractor" and an "agent" in order to clearly define th relationship between the owner and the contractor in the contract. This difference is explained below:

1. An independent contractor is one who agrees to accomplish a certain result and has full control over the manner and method to be pursued. The person receiving the benefit of the services of an independent contractor is not responsible for the actions of said independent contractor.
2. An agent is someone under the control of and authorized to act for some other person or company known as the principal. A special agent cannot bind the company beyond his specific authority. The general agent conducts a series of transactions involving a continuity of service.

Some Types of Service Contracts

Sanitary Housekeeping and Janitorial Services. Areas of work should be clearly defined, as well as means of access to the areas. The frequency of washing interior glass and lighting fixtures, washing and waxing floors, cleaning toilets and washrooms, etc., should be mutually agreed upon. Care must be taken in the areas frequently used by employees that the chemicals and cleaning agents used are not persistently obnoxious or toxic. Remuneration for tools, appliances, and supplies must be clearly set forth in the contract.

Building Construction. The owner may decide to act as his own prime contractor and employ several subcontractors for the various specialty phases of construction. He may elect to employ a general contractor to execute the total work according to the owner's requirements. In either situation there may be several special subcontracts to be awarded by the owner or the general contractor. Some of these are as follows:

1. Site preparation (clearing, grading, drainage, etc.)
2. Foundations, concrete, and masonry work
3. Mechanical (including piping, plumbing, millwrighting, etc.)
4. Structural steel
5. Roofing and siding
6. Carpentry and glazing
7. Electrical
8. Heating, ventilating, and air conditioning
9. Fire-protection systems
10. Glazing, painting, and decorating

Clear and complete specifications are vital for all phases of the work, as detailed in Section 16 with sample contracts. The furnishing of and payment for tools, equipment, and supplies should be clearly established and stated in the contract. Since the contract may be performed in a location not served by utilities, it should be established whether the owner or contractor shall provide utilities during construction. For samples of service contracts, see Section 16.

Installations and Rigging. When purchasing new equipment, it is sometimes advantageous to obtain field installation services from the manufacturer. Such contracts may be performed by the manufacturer or by subcontractors engaged by the manufacturer. In addition to the installation of new equipment, it is sometimes necessary to move existing equipment to a new location. In such cases a rigging and millwrighting contractor can be engaged to perform work beyond the owner's capabilities.

Here again, such contracts must clearly define all details of foundations, utilities, equipment specifications, sizes and weights, storage of tools and supplies, site conditions, etc.

Contract Fundamentals

Contracts can be, and usually are, prepared for any type of work or service required. For example, contracts are quite common for advertising, packaging, procurement, office and plant layouts, product or machinery maintenance, painting, landscaping, gardening, office-machinery maintenance, tabulating-equipment rental, clocks, cleaning inside and outside of building, servicing plant equipment, electric sign maintenance, fire-protection equipment, and guard protection. In each case the specific work to be done or the service to be rendered must be carefully and completely described, and the completion time and the amount and method of remuneration to the contractor must be clearly established.

The following will cover some major considerations fundamental to the development, administration, and completion of contracts for services:

Prepurchase Planning. Keeping abreast of the company's future requirements and timing is essential to prepurchase planning, if purchasing's participation is to result in a meaningful contribution toward obtaining maximum value. This can be accomplished by purchasing developing a close working relationship with engineering and operating personnel. Purchasing can also keep informed of company developments by reviewing such internal documents as engineering department progress reports, capital project requests and authorizations, work order requests and approvals, and long-range planning information.

Purchase Requisition. The purchase requisition normally is purchasing's release to start contract negotiations. Therefore, the purchase requisition should cover the following points carefully:

1. Description and location of the work.
2. Detailed specifications prepared by the engineer in charge of the job. These should be separate and apart from the requisition, have a title, a date, and page numbers.
3. A complete set of drawings, suitably identified.
4. Site-visitation instructions.
5. If this information is transmitted by letter, care should be taken to eliminate conflicts among the specifications, requisition, and drawings.

Prequalification of Bidders. Preparation of a good bid list is a major factor in the successful procurement of services. Although prequalification of bidders may not be necessary when purchasing standard or catalog items, it is considered important when contemplating commitments involving large expenditures for complex services.

Invitations to Bidders. A letter of invitation is considered good practice in lieu of the usual purchase inquiry form. The invitation letter should be accompanied by all referenced specifications, drawings, and the general conditions of the proposed contract. The letter invitation to bid should contain:

1. Description and location of the work.
2. References to applicable specifications, drawings, and general conditions.
3. Information as to whom to contact for site-visitation appointment and on what date or dates visitations will be conducted. The owner should follow up and make sure these contacts are made.
4. The date on which the bids are due.
5. Request that the bidder include with his bid statements of the types of insurance he will carry if awarded the job.
6. Request for bidders to immediately notify the owner if they do not wish to bid and to return the complete invitation, including specifications and drawings, to the owner.
7. Statement from the contractor declaring that he will employ field labor in accordance with the local trade requirements and meet the schedule of progress without additional compensation from the owner.
8. The owner's proposed method of reimbursing the contractor, i.e., progress payments, lump-sum at completion of work, etc.
9. Where time permits, it can be advantageous to include a pre-prepared contract document providing appropriate spaces for the bidders to enter pricing, completion schedules, and other bid information required by the owner. This document, properly prepared by the owner, and completed and signed by the contractor, can constitute the completed contract, upon acceptance and execution by the owner.

It may also be necessary to require the contractor to carry special insurance, such as longshoreman's, rigger's, builder's risk, marine, cargo, products, or others. It is the owner's responsibility to judge the adequacy of insurance offered by the bidder.

If it becomes necessary to make any changes in the specifications, drawings, terms, conditions, schedule, etc., during the bidding period, the owner should notify all bidders and confirm such changes in writing. Any change in drawings or specifications will necessitate a formal revision, which should be dated on or before the date an award is made.

Contract Document. If the requisition and the invitation to bid have been properly prepared, negotiation and preparation of the contract document should be simplified. After the bids have been evaluated and all concerned are in agreement on the contractor selection and award, the successful bidder should be notified by telephone or telegram, if time dictates; otherwise, by preparing and mailing the contract document. Unsuccessful bidders should be notified promptly that the job was awarded elsewhere, thanked for their cooperation, and requested to return the bid drawings and specifications to the owner.

Completion of the Contract—Final Acceptance of the Work. A contract is considered to be completed when all the obligations contained therein have been fulfilled by both parties. The obligations to which the contractor has agreed may not be obvious or clear-cut at the time the work is complete because of potential difficulties with technical and legal aspects of the work which may not develop until a later date.

Since one of the contractor's obligations is to satisfy the owner, the contractor may request the owner's written acceptance of the work upon completion. A letter of acceptance may be given after inspection and approval by the owner's inspectors, but such a letter should contain the following statement: "This acceptance is promulgated without releasing the contractor from his continuing obligations under this contract." This will establish that there is no intent to release the contractor from any guarantee, patent indemnification, hold-harmless provisions, etc., assumed under the contract.

Before final payment is made to the contractor, a release of liens should always be obtained. These releases usually differ for each state; therefore they should be obtained from a local attorney. Once the release of liens has been obtained, the contract is considered closed.

ELECTRICAL EQUIPMENT

This commodity area presents the buyer with a broad market in which to exercise his skills. Space does not permit a discussion of the buying procedures for all electrical items; there are too many. The buyer will find literally hundreds of products, varying in size and electrical characteristics, to produce thousands of items, offered by both manufacturer and distributor. There are items which are suitable for volume buying and annual contracts, such as carbon brushes, lamps, and small motors, and there are other items which require well-prepared specifications for nonrepetitive custom applications, such as switchgears, power transformers, and turbine generators.

The buyer is urged to study his company's over-all requirements for possibilities of requirements contracts or price agreements based on volumes commensurate with those needs. There are sufficient jobbers and manufacturers in this field to provide ample competition.

Batteries. Battery types and sizes range from the tiny ones used in hearing aids and pencil flashlights to the large ones used in motive power applications on industrial trucks and locomotives. The high-volume small batteries are frequently committed on a contractual basis where the volume is sufficient. The small- to medium-sized wet-cell or storage-battery type may also be contracted for, if there is sufficient volume. The larger storage battery for electric industrial trucks is usually purchased as a spot requirement. Defective batteries are replaced under the manufacturer's warranty in most cases. In the purchase of large storage batteries, price agreements over a period of time are frequently arranged and the so-called "rebuild feature" may be included. This feature is actually a greater-than-scrap allowance for an old battery and is an effective means of reducing replacement cost. For large users, the rental of large batteries should be evaluated against the cost of purchase.

The description of dry-cell batteries can be handled by a statement of size and voltage and a specification which will cover minimum performance. On the other hand, storage batteries require a more detailed specification as well as information concerning their intended use.

Cable and Wire. Most commonly used types of low-voltage wire and cable can usually be located in jobber's stock. If the cable and wire is for high-voltage service, or requires special insulation or construction, bids should be obtained from manufacturers. Shipments are normally made on returnable metal or wooden spools or reels, carrying a special charge which is refunded upon return in good condition to the seller. Descriptions must include size, number, construction and material of the conductor(s), voltage and service rating, and if insulated, the type of insulation. Prices are affected mainly by the price fluctuations of the conductor metal and the prevailing competitive situation.

Electric Furnaces. Electric furnaces range in size from the home craftsman's electric kiln for baking ceramics up to 200-ton capacity electric furnaces in which alloy steels are melted. Smaller purchases present few problems since they are usually clearly identified catalog items. The larger more complex types require well-engineered specifications for developing bids. Details on application, capacity or volume, methods of charging and discharging, type of lining, maximum temperature, controls, safety features, and other needs must be stated in the formal specification which is made a part of the inquiry.

Generators. Includes devices used to generate an electric current or to change the characteristics of an electric current. These range from the tiny hand-cranked generator for military field telephones to large turbine generators for public utilities. Catalog or shelf items can be purchased in a conventional manner, by list price with appropriate discounts. Special items require detailed specifications for the generator as well as for the prime mover for driving the generator. As such equipment usually represents a major investment with a long service life, time spent on engineering and specifying is well invested. Competitive bids based on carefully prepared specifications are recommended.

Lamps. Lamp producers prefer to execute requirements contracts which offer discounts from established list prices based on annual consumption estimates with large-volume purchasers. Such contracts normally include provision for multi-point distribution close to the using locations if required. Significant factors contributing to maximum lighting value per dollar expended for lamps, which should be considered in addition to price, include lamp life, lumen output, utilization of proper lamp design for each requirement, and manufacturer reliability.

Motors. Most motors are designated by NEMA[9] design and frame size power, type of enclosure, class of insulation and electrical characteristics Small motors may be obtained from jobber's stock. Competitive bids are recommended. When volume purchases of standard items are predictable the requirements contract approach should be used. Manufacturers will negotiate contracts based on quantity and end use, such as motors for assembly on original equipment (OEM basis). Such arrangements are based on "list" prices subject to prevailing discounts applying to various quantity brackets.

In addition to the above, consideration should be given to special motors installed as drivers for purchased capital equipment. Savings are often possible when the motor is purchased direct by the buyer instead of from the equipment manufacturer in a "package." However, such savings should be evaluated against the desirability of placing complete responsibility with the equipment manufacturer by ordering the unit complete with drive.

[9] National Association of Electrical Manufacturers.

X-ray Equipment. Whether purchased for medical, inspection, or product control applications, the purchasing procedures for X-ray equipment vary only slightly. Standard machines for medical purposes are available from several sources and only the size and performance characteristics need be determined. Much information can be obtained from catalogs and consultations with the medical director. Custom installations designed for product inspection or manufacturing control may have to be specially designed for specific application. All installations must provide for ample lead or concrete shielding to protect the operators. When detailed specifications have been prepared, competitive bid procedures are employed.

Miscellaneous. Finally, there are the hundreds of supply items required to maintain operations, such as light fixtures, receptacles, plugs, fuses, sockets, switches, starters, and others. Jobbers carry well-known manufacturers' lines. Here availability takes on much importance, for these items are frequently needed on an emergency basis, and price can be secondary. On these supply items it is customary to issue semiannual inquiries for volume requirements categorized by commodity groups, i.e., conduit, house wire, connectors and fittings, fuses, switches, etc. On price agreements frequently used, it is not necessary to guarantee volume; however, an estimate is of value to both buyer and seller in establishing terms. Multiple inquiries will develop competition for requirements or price agreements.

References

Sections 26 and 28 list handbooks, trade publications, and associations specializing in electrical equipment.

FERROUS METALS

Ferrous metals, most universally used products, are produced in many forms and alloys. Ferrous metals may be purchased from two principal sources: manufacturer or mill and warehouse or distributor. The function of these sources remains rather constant regardless of the particular product to be purchased. The problems of buying vary only as one moves from one class of steel product to another and will be discussed here on that basis.

Factors Affecting Purchases

The mill is the point of manufacture of nearly all wrought-steel products. Production at the mill is in large volume so that it is necessary to schedule the work very carefully. To keep production on an economical basis, certain minimum quantities of a product become acceptable orders. All this means that the lead time must be extended when buying from the mill. The magazine *Steel* (see References) has prepared and published a "Guide for Steel Buyers." It lists steel products and maximum size available by producing mill and also indicates the location of the mill. This is a valuable reference for any steel buyer.

The various warehouse operations throughout the country provide a source for those orders which are not acceptable to the mill. It may be that the order is below the mill minimum or that earlier delivery is required than can be obtained from the mill. There are two general classes of warehouses (1) those which are a direct or subsidiary operation of the mill (captive warehouses) and (2) the independent operator, who has no financial relation with the mill other than as a customer. Neither the captive nor the independent warehouse is necessarily restricted as to the source of the products which it carries, but the captive operation would quite naturally favor the ownership source for all products which it produces.

Trade Customs

Availability. When preparing to buy steel, it is recommended that the buyer carefully analyze his requirements by product on the basis of annual needs. With this information and knowledge of the cost of carrying inventory, he can determine whether it is more economical to buy from the mill or warehouse. Using the mill as a source requires careful planning because of the extended lead time.

All mills do not produce all sizes and shapes of all their products every month. Nor do they produce in the same rotation of sizes. Some sizes and shapes, because of small demand are made bimonthly, quarterly, semiannually, or when orders on hand justify a mill run. It is advisable that the probable mill schedules be obtained by the buyer from the sources where he may place orders.

It is not intended, by the statements above, to suggest that warehouse buying requires no planning. The careful assembly of combinable items on one order will produce a lower unit cost as the total tonnage involved moves into various quantity brackets.

Acceptable Quantities—Mill versus Warehouse. For each form of steel which a mill produces there is a minimum acceptable quantity for which the mill will accept an order. These minimum acceptable quantities may change as the total demand for steel increases or decreases. A steel buyer who expects to deal with the mill as a source of supply should arrange to be constantly supplied with this information. On the other hand warehouses are established to handle any quantity of a product no matter how small. To buy minimum mill quantities repeatedly from a warehouse seems obviously uneconomical.

Distribution

Area Served. The area served by a mill may be limited by the cost of the material when delivered at the door. This is true when the shipment is f.o.b. shipping point, but not always true when the basing point method of shipment is used. Warehouses might be called "community" operations. They serve two areas (*a*) the area of so-called free delivery, f.o.b. destination, transportation costs being included in the warehouse price, and (*b*) the area beyond the free delivery zone, sometimes called the "country area." In the latter, shipments are f.o.b. shipping point. Points of delivery which are on or near the boundary between these zones would do well to analyze both methods of pricing.

Shipping Methods–Rail and Truck. Because the weight and volume of warehouse shipments are usually, but not necessarily, small and distances between drops relatively short, rail shipments are seldom used. Quick delivery of orders is a service feature of warehousing and trucking is a natural result. Depending upon the quantity involved as well as the cost of transportation, a choice must be made on mill shipments, rail, truck, boat, or barge.

Quality. For the purpose of this discussion it is assumed that all sources produce a uniform quality in all products. Therefore, it becomes simply a problem of describing the desired item in terms which will be completely clear, as to quality, to the seller. The American Iron and Steel Institute (150 East 42d Street, New York) has done much to standardize terminology within the industry. They have prepared and published a series of steel products manuals, each covering one form in which steel is made. The steel buyer should be equipped with this excellent reference file.

Prices. The pricing of steel products may at first appear to be quite complex. Upon study it resolves into a rather fixed formula of base price plus various extras. Approximately twenty possible types of "extras" that hinge on either quality or quantity requirements can be incurred when buying steel sheet and strip. In addition to the basic twenty there are hundreds of different lengths, widths, and thicknesses in common use. When reviewing the "extra" problem, pay particular attention to such items as gauge, width, length, restricted thickness, items of quantity, stretcher level standard, forming, heat-treatment, restricted chemical requirements, packing, and marking. Carefully check the extras and be sure that the end use of the product demands that the specification must be such as to make them necessary. Many times they may be unnecessary.

The base prices for mill items with extra lists are available from the manufacturer's sales office. Warehouse prices can be obtained from the distributor. *The ability of the steel buyer to compute his own prices is a great asset.* It permits him to verify quotations or prepare costs before placing an order. The pricing unit will vary from one product to another within the industry. Orders should be specified in the same units as those in the price.

F.O.B. This expression has come to indicate the point at which the buyer becomes the legal owner of the product described on the purchase order. On mill shipments the f.o.b. is nearly always "point of shipment." The exception would occur when the shipper is willing to, or must, meet competition by adjusting the transportation costs to those of a competing mill which is nearer the buyer's plant. In such a situation the f.o.b. would remain point of shipment, and this phrase is then followed by a statement that freight will be equalized with a named shipping point.

Steel—Hot-rolled. By far the largest tonnage and the greatest number of products are included in this classification. They are available from both mill and warehouse sources. The mills will perform a special service known as "conversion," when they have idle capacity in some departments. Should a buyer have a fairly large tonnage of steel, in a form which is not suitable for current production, he may negotiate with the mill to convert it into a usable form. Such conversion orders should clearly state the form in which the steel will be delivered to the mill, who pays the cost of transportation to the mill, the percentage of recovery after conversion, and f.o.b. point on the completed product.

Mills do not permit the grouping of hot-rolled products to build tonnage for pricing purposes. Like items, such as sheet or plates of the same thickness and width but different lengths or structural shapes of the same dimensions but different weights per foot, may be combined, according to price schedules, to build tonnage. On the other hand, many items from a warehouse can be combined for price advantage. Not only may various products be combined on one order, but all orders received from a single buyer on one day may be grouped to obtain tonnage and price advantage. Hot-rolled steel is sold at a price per hundred pounds.

Steel—Cold-finished. Cold-finishing mills are dependent upon the tonnage mills for their raw materials, which are various forms of hot-rolled steel. It is therefore advisable that your source of cold-finished products be carefully selected whether it be a mill or warehouse. The important feature is to determine that the mill selected will have a uniform flow of raw material to process, or that the warehouse will receive its fair share of products, both under all economic circumstances.

Mill shipments are priced according to mill pricing schedules. Warehouse pricing policy permits grouping to avoid extreme small quantity extras only. Each item is priced according to the weight involved and there are extra charges for both small items and/or small orders. Prices are quoted on a basis of so much per hundred pounds.

Pipe—Iron or Steel. In this market, standard iron or steel pipe, the distribution is through distributors or jobbers only. Carload orders of 40,000 lb or more, of mixed sizes, may be purchased from either the mill or distributor at the same price. On oil-country tubular goods the mill will deal direct. To determine your source, therefore, one must first know the product to be purchased. The distributor will handle small orders from his stocks or will broker carload orders with a mill. The latter are shipped directly to the buyer and invoiced by the distributor.

Prices to the distributor are calculated on a list price less discounts and include a factor covering transportation. The distributor sells at what is commonly called "local list" on less than carload deliveries. Such orders are usually sold on an "f.o.b. destination" basis. Prices are quoted on a per hundred foot basis.

Tubing—Steel. This product follows the same pattern of source, distribution, and pricing as pipe–iron and steel.

Steel-alloy—Hot-rolled or Cold-finished. Sources for these products are mills and warehouses. If the minimum order requirements are met, the mills will produce any standard alloy which you may require. Warehouses, however, tend to stock only the most popular alloys. Their stock lists will show all the items carried as well as the sizes and condition, annealed or heat-treated.

In pricing this product, no grouping for tonnage is permitted by either mill or warehouse. Each item or order stands alone except for protection against extreme extras for small items. Some reduction for large quantities and/or penalty for small quantities exists. Prices are quoted per hundred pounds.

Steel—Tool. *Sources.* Most grades of tool steel, either carbon or alloy, are available from both mills and warehouses. All grades are produced under rigid controls in electric furnaces. The producers of tool steel do not enforce the minimum mill order feature to the same extent that is found in the tonnage mills. The buyer, therefore, may choose to place his orders on either the mill or warehouse depending on the urgency of delivery. The mill will produce any of its regularly advertised grades. On the other hand, warehouses may carry only those grades which sell in reasonable volume in their community.

Quality. The term "quality" in tool steel can mean only the selection of the proper grade of steel for the work to be done. It must be assumed that all the leading producers have equal quality in terms of comparable or equivalent items. Grade may be specified by trade name. This method tends to restrict the buyer to a single producer and limits the stocks upon which he may draw for his needs. Many companies have prepared their own tool-steel specifications which are published to their suppliers. These specifications take into consideration the comparable grades among all producers and consequently make it possible to draw on many stocks. *The Steel Products Manual, Tool Steels,* published by the American Iron and Steel Institute (150 East 42d Street, New York) has a section devoted to "Identification and Type Classification of Tool Steels." This and other data in the manual will be of help to the buyer.

Pricing. Tool steel is priced by the pound. The price is developed from a base price for a particular grade to which are added extras for such items as annealing, quantity, size, cutting, boxing, warehousing, etc. Among producers the base prices for alloys of the same composition are identical. A list of base prices and extras can be obtained from either the producer or warehouse with which the buyer deals. It is recommended that the buyer become familiar with the detail of price construction.

Steel—Stainless. The sources are either mills or warehouses. Warehouses tend to stock only those grades of stainless products for which the demand will show a turnover. The mills will produce any grade, provided the minimum order quantity is met. Some mills specialize in the production of stainless steels and at times will stock overruns. Such a stock often provides a greater selection of grades, but there is no assurance that either the grade or form which is sought will be available. These sources, however, are worth knowing.

The producers of stainless steel distribute almost exclusively through warehouses. The warehouse or distributor buys on the regular price schedule and receives a discount, usually from the base price. Both mill and warehouse prices are calculated from the same list, and whether the shipment comes from the mill or warehouse stock the price is the same. The cost of stainless steels varies widely, depending upon the grade and surface finish. Care should be taken to relate both factors to the specifications and final use. Prices are usually quoted on a per pound basis.

Steel—Billets. This product is offered only by the producing mills and is "made to order." It is made in several forms and alloys and is the raw material for other fabricating departments or nonintegrated mills. Warehouses seldom, if ever, offer billets for sale. Prices are based on grade or alloy and quantity involved. Quotations are on the basis of net tons (2,000 lb).

Pig Iron. Tonnage mills and custom smelters are the sources for this product. It is distributed by mill sales offices and sometimes by brokers.

The dealings are usually directly with the producer. Description of the grade desired is of great importance. Prices are available from the source and are quoted on a gross ton basis (2,240 lb).

Steel Forgings. These are produced in many forms and grades and by several methods, depending somewhat on size. They are always "custom-made" to the buyer's specifications. Sources range from the large mills which cast forging billets and then form them on enormous hammers down to the shop which produces drop forgings of small dimensions. The selection of a source must depend upon the size of the forging desired. Regardless of the type of forging, rough, smooth, or die, it is customary to specify the amount of metal to be left on the piece to provide for finish machining. There is no price list for forgings. Prices are calculated upon the size of the piece, the amount of work necessary to produce the desired form, and the amount of metal involved. Quotations are usually on a pound basis, although some die forgings are on a piece basis because there is better control of weight.

Steel and Iron Castings. Mills usually produce large sand castings in various grades, but seldom compete with the local foundries on the items which are bench molded. This is not intended to suggest that local sources do not produce large castings; however, their equipment is usually limited in this field. Castings are produced to the design of the buyer and require patterns. These may be supplied by the buyer, either from his shop or a local patternmaker, or they may be ordered with the castings. In the latter case, adequate drawings are supplied. Other than the removal of sprues and risers the amount of finishing of castings must be clearly described in the order. Finishing adds to the cost; thus this detail should be carefully considered. Prices are determined by the complexity of production and degree of finishing done by the foundry. Size and the amount of metal are also a consideration. Generally, prices are on a per pound basis, but large runs from bench molding equipment may be negotiated on a unit price.

Steel Wire. Both mills and warehouses are a source for this product. The buyer of large quantities of special items will find much advantage in developing a mill source. Warehouses carry only those items which are common to many uses and therefore in constant demand. In spite of this, large quantities of wire move through warehouses. There are many grades, and distributors show some tendency to specialize in the grades carried. Prices are developed from a base plus extras and may be quoted either on a pound or per hundred pound basis, depending upon the grade.

References

American Iron and Steel Institute, 150 East 42d Street, New York, N.Y. 10017
American Metal Market, 525 West 42d Street, New York, N.Y. 10036
American Society for Metals, Metals Park, Novelty, Ohio 44072
Gray Iron Founders Society, National City, E. 6th Building, Cleveland, Ohio 44072
Iron Age, Chilton Company, Chestnut and 56th Streets, Philadelphia, Pa. 19139
Steel, The Penton Publishing Co., 1213 West Third Street, Cleveland, Ohio 44113
Steel Processing, Grant Building, Pittsburgh, Pa. 15219

FOOD AND KINDRED PRODUCTS

Meats (Beef, Lamb, Pork, Veal)

Sources. When the animal reaches marketable age or weight to produce the best grade in its class, it is transported from the raiser to the stockyards or feed lots, from which the packers usually obtain their meats for distribution. Buyers' sources are categorized below:

1. Fresh meats are purchased from abattoirs, packinghouses, wholesale distributors, or wholesale butchers. Freshness is maintained most generally by refrigeration. Various new methods are being tried but are not yet in general use.
2. Frozen meat is available through the same general sources mentioned in paragraph 1 above. Freezing is used to (*a*) preserve the product over a longer period, (*b*) permit the source to carry inventories and await favorable markets, (*c*) provide for preportioning and prepackaging, and (*d*) allow safe long-distance distribution.
3. Canned and processed meats and meat products are prepared by packers, processors, and canners and marketed through wholesale jobbers and distributors.

Trade Customs. It is possible for the buyer with limited storage facilities, or who wishes to buy on a favorable market, to purchase and store meat with his source. Such purchases are subdivided into the usual wholesale or retail cuts. When withdrawn from storage, the delivery may be as carcass, as parts, or in the cuts desired. Preboning the greatest percentage of the carcass is recommended.

Some sources specialize in a particular variety or grade of meat, and the buyer should become familiar with his sources' specialties in order to obtain the best values.

Quality. The quality of meats is determined by government specifications setting forth various grades for beef, lamb, pork, and veal. The buyer should familiarize himself with these government specifications and follow them in selecting the appropriate quality of meat for his needs.

Interstate shipments of foods are government-inspected and must meet the quality standards established by the Federal Food and Drug Act and the specifications set by the U.S. Department of Agriculture.

Descriptions of quality for various kinds of meat are too long to be included. Detailed information is available from the U.S. Department of Agriculture, Production and Marketing Administration, and *The National Live Stock and Meat Board Publication* (7th ed., 407 South Dearborn Street, Chicago, Ill.). Buyers who operate in this market should maintain on file the aforesaid information, as well as similar data available from trade associations, such as the National Restaurant Association, Supermarket Institute, and Institutional Food Manufacturers Association.

Pricing. The prices of meat and meat products are regulated by supply and demand. Commodity market fluctuations and national and local supplies are the determining factors. Prices are on a unit-weight basis, per pound or per hundredweight.

Poultry (Chicken, Turkey, Duck, Goose)

Sources. In some localities these products may be obtained fresh from the farmer. In metropolitan areas, this is usually not the case and the buyer generally purchases from packers and wholesale jobbers. Some sources which specialize in a particular product offer a better selection and quality in their specialty. Buyers' sources are:

1. Fresh poultry and game held by the distributors under refrigeration for a short time
2. Frozen products often stored and held for favorable market conditions
3. Canned items available through packing houses and wholesale jobbers
4. Freeze-dried items available through wholesale jobbers and having a shelf life of up to two years
5. Newer methods of preservation, which will soon provide greater shelf life to these items

Quality. Local, state, and Federal laws establish standards and specifications for the quality of these items. The buyer who operates in this market should have copies of all regulations available to use as a guide to quality.

Pricing. Poultry prices tend to be seasonal in nature and, of course, depend on supply and demand. Market sources are able to quote daily prices by grade.

Fish and Shellfish

Fresh Fish. The availability of varieties of fish is seasonal. Local fish dealers can give information about their best seasonal offerings and the varieties that can be obtained at the best price.

Tests for Whole and Drawn Fish. Fresh fish have the following characteristics:

1. Flesh. Firm and elastic; not separating from the bones.
2. Odor. Fresh and mild. A fish just taken from the water has practically no "fishy" odor. The fishy odor becomes more pronounced with age.
3. Eyes. Bright, clear, and full. The eyes of fresh fish are bright and transparent; as the fish becomes stale, the eyes become cloudy and often turn pink.
4. Gills. Red and free from slime. The color gradually fades with age to a light pink, then gray.
5. Skin. Shiny, with color unfaded. When first taken from the water, most fish have an iridescent appearance.

Frozen Fish. Frozen varieties are usually packed during seasons of abundance at reasonable prices and now are available the year round in practically all sections of the country. Since frozen fish are the equal of fresh fish in appearance and food value, the two forms may be used interchangeably.

Shellfish. Shellfish are sold in many varieties, of which some of the more important groups are described below:

Shrimp. (The number of shrimp per pound determine specified size—medium, large, jumbo.)

Fresh, whole (heads on); mainly around New Orleans and near harvest points.

Fresh-cooked; generally peeled (shells removed) and cleaned.

Frozen—shell on and raw.

Frozen—shelled and deveined.

Frozen—prepared for cooking; breaded, fanned.

Freeze-dried; cooked and ready for use with a short rehydration. (Same treatment used for crab meat and lobster.)

Clams and Oysters. Clams and oysters in the shell should be alive, and the shells should close tightly when tapped gently.

Shucked oysters should be plump and have a natural, creamy color with clear liquid. If in the original package or can, there should not be more than 10 per cent liquid (by weight). Oysters with an excess amount of liquid should be avoided, as this indicates that they have been improperly handled. Excessive water results in bloating of the oyster meat and partial loss of flavor and food value. Oysters are sold on a size basis. The price differential between the various sizes does not reflect their quality.

Crabs and Lobsters. When bought alive, crabs, lobsters, and spiny lobsters should show movement of the legs. The tail of live lobsters curls under the body and does not hang down when the lobster is picked up.

Spiny lobster or rock lobstertails, frozen, should have meat of clear, whitish color. There are several kinds on the market. Those from Florida, Cuba, and the Bahamas have a smooth, brownish-green shell with white spots; those from South Africa, Australia, and New Zealand have a rough shell with color varying from dark maroon to brown; those from Southern California and the west coast of Mexico are smooth and yellow-green. As is true with other frozen fish and shellfish, frozen lobstertails should be hard-frozen when bought and should have no odor.

Blue Crabs. The meat from blue crabs is packed as:

Lump meat. Whole lumps of white meat from the large body muscles that operate the swimming legs.
Flake meat. Small pieces of white meat from the body.
Flakes and lump. A combination of the two above kinds.
Claw meat. Brownish-tinted meat from the claws.

Rock Crabs. Crab meat from the New England rock crab is marketed in only one grade and is brownish in color.

Dungeness Crabs. Crab meat from the Dungeness crab of the Pacific Coast includes that from both the body and the claws. The claw or leg meat is reddish; the body meat is white.

King Crabs. Crab meat from the king crab of Alaska is taken mostly from the legs and then frozen and packed. The entire leg sections, cooked and frozen, are also marketed. King crabs are also available freeze-dried.

Soft-shelled Crabs. These are Atlantic Coast blue crabs that have shed their old hard shells. They should be alive when bought fresh. They are also obtainable frozen.

Scallops. Scallop meat consists of only the muscle that closes the shell of the sea scallop or the bay scallop. The meat of the large sea scallop is white; the meat of the smaller bay scallop is creamy white, light tan, or pinkish. Fresh scallops and frozen scallops when thawed should have a sweetish odor. When bought in packages, they should be practically free of liquid.

Fruits and Vegetables

Sources. Fruits and vegetables are available from the following sources:

1. Fresh fruits and vegetables are available directly from the grower or through jobbers, wholesale distributors, auctioneers, and growers' co-

operatives or syndicates. Sources for your area may be located in the Yellow Pages of the Telephone Directory.

2. Frozen and canned fruits and vegetables are obtained directly from the packers or processors or through wholesale jobbers and distributors.

Quality Standards. Obviously, not all fresh fruits and vegetables grow to the same degree of perfection, nor are they all of uniform pattern. Climate, soil, weather, and the district in which a product is grown affect its quality as much as does the kind of care it receives during harvesting, packing, and shipping.

It can be seen, however, that with thousands of growers engaged in producing commercial crops for shipment to distant markets, some kind of standards must exist in order that buying and selling be carried on effectively. The United States government has therefore established a grading system for fresh produce based on appearance, condition, and other factors that might affect eating quality. This, supplemented in some instances by state grading regulations, is the basis upon which trading is carried on.

Copies of the government specifications established for fresh fruits and vegetables are available from the U.S. Department of Agriculture. The grades of each of these products should be studied to determine which grade fits the individual's need.

For most commodities, U.S. No. 1 grade is top quality, followed by U.S. Combination and U.S. No. 2. The United States standards for some products, such as snap beans and sweet corn, provide for U.S. Fancy grade, which is superior to U.S. No. 1. However, for all practical purposes, U.S. No. 1 grade produce is adequate. The northwestern states have established their own standards for apples which are generally used by the trade. Extra fancy and fancy are commonly recognized grades. A wealth of free information is available from the Fruit and Vegetable Growers Association.

Pricing. The prices of fresh, frozen, or canned fruits and vegetables are largely dependent upon supply and demand. When buying, consider variety, price, quality characteristics of the item, and, most important, its ultimate use. Fruits and vegetables are usually purchased to Department of Agriculture specifications and inspected to ensure quality and weight.

Dairy Products

Distribution. The farmer who specializes in milk production usually sells his product to milk companies or cooperatives in his local area. These processors in turn process and distribute dairy products to wholesalers and distributors. Poultry raisers sell their eggs to the local wholesaler, distributor, or cooperative warehouse.

Quality. Each class and kind of dairy product is handled according to the pure food laws. Intrastate distribution may also be governed by municipal and/or state regulations, while interstate shipments come within the Federal regulations. Quality is further measured by the butterfat content in milk, cream, and ice cream, and by weight and size when dealing with eggs.

Price. The buyer should check dairy produce reports and obtain prices periodically from local suppliers. One of the best sources for information on current market conditions is the U.S. Department of Agriculture. This department will issue daily market reports upon request. Prices shown in these reports are controlled by the auction sale price of each classification. Another source of information is *Producer's Price-Current.* The buyer should refer to market bulletins on a daily basis. Prices fluctuate seasonally as well as according to supply and demand.

Staple Foods

Sources. Staples include such items as flour, sugar, cereals, spices, coffee, and tea. This wide variety of products obviously comes from many sources, originating with the grower, and on through brokers, processors, wholesalers, and distributors.

Distribution. The source or grower sells to brokers and/or processors who in turn sell to wholesale distributors and jobbers. The buyer contacts the distributor or jobber for information about the availability and price of the individual items.

Quality. The quality of all items is governed by pure food laws—either Federal, state, or municipal. On imported items, the buyer must determine what regulations apply at the time of purchase.

Price. Current price information is readily obtainable from the U.S. Department of Agriculture, Marketing Administration.

References

American Dairy Association, 20 North Wacker Drive, Chicago, Ill. 60606

American Dry Milk Institute, 221 North LaSalle Street, Chicago, Ill. 60601

American Meat Institute, 59 East Van Buren Street, Chicago, Ill. 60605

The Food Buyer's Guide, Food Publications, Inc., 442 North LaCienga Boulevard, Los Angeles, Calif. 90048

Milk Industry Foundation, 1145 19th Street, N.W., Washington, D.C. 20006

National Cheese Institute, Inc., 110 North Franklin Street, Chicago, Ill. 60606

National Provisioner, Inc., 15 West Huron Street, Chicago, Ill. 60610

National Restaurant Association, 1530 North Lakeshore Drive, Chicago, Ill. 60610

New York Produce Exchange, 2 Broadway, New York, N.Y. 10006

Olsen Publishing Company, 1445 North 5th Street, Milwaukee, Wis. 53212 (Publishers of many magazines devoted to the dairy industry.)

Produce News and Products Barometer, 6 Harrison Street, New York, N.Y. 10013

Producer's Price-Current, 92 Warren Street, New York, N.Y. 10007

Purchasing Guide for the Meat Industry, 15 West Huron Street, Chicago, Ill.

United Fresh Fruit & Vegetables Association, Wyatt Building, 777 14th Street, N.W., Washington, D.C. 20005

U.S. Department of Interior, Fish and Wild Life Department, Washington, D.C. 20240 (Excellent material on fish.)

FUELS—COAL AND PETROLEUM

Coal

The purchase of coal for an industrial operation is an important function and should not be delegated to a novice. Spot buying has almost disappeared and annual, or longer, coverage is the objective of the buyer.

Sources. Coal is mined by two general processes: Openpit or strip method which includes the boring or auger process and the deep mining or underground method.

The openpit, strip, and auger method consists of removing the overburden and excavating by means of mechanical shovels or other equipment.

When the overburden is too great to remove, operations are conducted underground. Access to the seam is gained by means of shafts, slopes, or tunnels and the removal of coal is by hand or, in the more up-to-date mines, by mechanical miners operated by air or electricity.

The best reference available covering sources, sales agencies, description of seams, and directory of mines is the *Keystone Coal Buyers Manual,* published by McGraw-Hill Publications, New York.

Distribution. In large mining operations the buyer may find that the operator has his own sales force. These salesmen will offer only the product of company-owned and -operated mines. The many medium and small operators sell their product through agents who represent many mines and therefore many grades of coal. These sources are for the buyer who has handling equipment and can purchase in carload lots. The smaller user who cannot handle carloads must turn to the retail yard, which will make convenient truckload deliveries.

Freight. The cost of transportation of coal varies, in most cases, directly with the distance of the buyer from the mine. When selecting suppliers of coal, always determine the freight cost as an important part of the delivered price. Do not overlook the use of dockside deliveries where transportation by water is available. If the volume is large, the savings may justify the purchase of handling equipment.

Quality. Coal is not a uniformly packaged product of the same quality from all sources. It varies widely from seam to seam, and often as the seam is progressively removed. An exact description of quality which would suit all types of burning equipment cannot be prepared. The buyer should determine from the equipment manufacturer the analysis of the fuel best suited for that equipment. Some buyers have used the cost per million Btu as a measure of value. It is seriously doubted that this method of buying will produce the best fuel for the operation. Rather it is the relation of all the elements in coal and their proper balance as used in the equipment. The following should be considered:

Moisture
Volatility
Carbon
Ash
Friability
Abrasiveness
Grindability
Sulfur
Btu as received
Btu dry
Fusion temperature of ash

Space does not permit a discussion of these elements in detail, but it should be clear that there is no economy in paying freight on moisture and ash in coal. To buy a product of known high ash content is to increase the handling costs on a waste product. Low sulfur is considered by the trade to be anything below 2½ per cent. For further and more technical details, the reader is referred to any modern text on steam power plants. From the foregoing it will be seen that the buyer should develop a commercially economic specification by consulting with the coal producers, the engineering department, and the equipment manufacturers.

Pricing. Coal is priced f.o.b. the mine. The buyer, since he is paying the freight charges, has the right to determine the routing and carrier who will deliver to his siding. Annual contracts will usually carry an escalation clause. Should a firm annual price be asked and quoted it will surely be hedged against possible increase in the cost of production. The firm price contract should be negotiated with great care.

Payment of invoices covering shipments of coal is usually on a monthly basis. All shipments made during a calendar month would be payable on the tenth or fifteenth of the following month. These terms are to be determined at the time of purchase.

Summary. When two or more sources are used to supply a single operation, the uniformity of the product becomes extremely important. It may not be possible to find several mines which ship an identical analysis, but it is possible to find several which will have similar burning characteristics. Once this has been done, it becomes necessary to ensure a constant supply. A knowledge of the mine reserves and labor conditions is very important. The necessity for a uniform flow of coal is often more important than either quality or price.

Petroleum (Fuel Oils)

The most commonly used grades of liquid fuel are No. 2, No. 6 low sulfur, and No. 6 regular. The latter are usually called Bunker "C" oil.

Sources. The producers are the integrated companies which start with crude oil and refine it through various steps which provide many petroleum products. Among these will be found the No. 2 fuel oil, while the No. 6 oils are the residuals. There appears to be a trend toward more and more refining which can reduce the quantity of residual oil to be used as fuel.

The distributors or independents purchase these products in bulk and store and deliver. Some of the smaller distributors do not operate storage facilities but draw directly from the producer's storage or that of other and larger distributors.

Distribution. The areas served by these sources will vary from the small dealer who serves domestic requirements in his community to the largest producer who ships his products country-wide. It has been noted that the competition is very vigorous in the sale of No. 2 fuel oil among both the producers and independent distributors. On the other hand the producers seem less interested than the independents in the No. 6 market. The buyer should survey his market with care before calling for bids to obtain maximum competition.

Depending upon the size of the operation, various methods of shipment are used; tanker, barge, tank car, tank truck, or drum. Other than producers and distributors there are few buyers who would use tanker shipments. The barge of about 2,000 to 20,000 barrels, the tank car of about 200 barrels, and the tank truck of about 110 barrels are the most common.

Each method of delivery requires its own equipment for unloading. Based upon the volume of purchases the buyer should suggest to management the most economical method of delivery.

Quality. Since certain impurities may appear in all oils mentioned above, it is advisable to buy according to specifications. The best specification can, of course, be developed as a result of analyzing the efficiencies of various fuel oils, under specific combustion conditions. The supplier should be more than willing to cooperate along these lines. As a base from which to start, the use of the U.S. Bureau of Standards, Commercial Standards Specification CS12–48 is suggested.

Pricing. Fuel oils are a product on which daily quotations may be found in the public press. The *Journal of Commerce* devotes a section of its paper to reporting the news and prices of petroleum products. On the industrial purchasing level No. 2 oil is sold by the gallon, while No. 6 oils are sold by the barrel of 42 gal each. Both No. 2 and No. 6 oils are adjusted to the temperature at time of delivery from tank trucks. The daily quotations in the press show prices loaded on tank car or truck at harbor of delivery point; transportation charges are collect. In general, the quoted prices do not yield to negotiation, but transport charges do. When buying these products, the use of competitive bidding is recommended.

Also recommended is an engineering study comparing ultimate value of fuel oils (as well as coal) with use of firm or interruptible gas described under "Utility Services" in the last part of this section.

References

American Petroleum Institute, 1271 Avenue of the Americas, New York, N.Y. 10020

Anthracite Institute, 237 Old River Road, Wilkes-Barre, Pa. 18700

Bituminous Coal Institute, 1130 17th Street, N.W., Washington, D.C. 20006

Black Diamond Co., 431 South Dearborn Street, Chicago, Ill. 60603

Keystone Coal Buyers Manual, McGraw-Hill Publications, 330 West 42d Street, New York, N.Y. 10036

National Coal Association, 1130 17th Street, N.W., Washington, D.C. 20006

National Petroleum News, McGraw-Hill Publications, 330 West 42d Street, New York, N.Y. 10036

Oil and Gas Journal, 211 South Cheyenne Street, Tulsa, Okla. 74101

The Petroleum Engineer, Davis Building, Dallas, Tex. 75202

Petroleum Refiner, 3301 Allen Parkway, Houston, Tex. 77019

LUMBER AND TIMBER

Lumber

Sources. Lumber mills may or may not own and cut their own logs from which the lumber is sawn. The size of the mill operation may vary from large permanent installations to the small portable mill which moves from one cutting to another. The species of lumber handled, size of operation, and destination of shipment will determine the minimum order which will be acceptable—truckloads to points in nearby areas or carloads to more distant points. Assorted thicknesses of the same species may be combined in one load. Obviously the mill is a source for the volume buyer.

Dealers or lumberyards acquire their stocks of various woods from the mills and distribute in smaller quantities to their customers. Since they deliver from stocks on hand, the lead time is nil.

The agricultural departments of many states publish a directory of sources of lumber and manufactured wood products existing within the state boundaries. Such a volume for your own state and those around you may be a great aid in soliciting sources.

Distribution. Mills are, in general, represented by agents or brokers. These sales representatives may handle the products of several mills producing nearly all species of lumber. Shipments are made by truck or freight as the size of the order and distance to destination indicate.

The local dealers are represented by their own salesmen who seek business in the area which they choose to serve. Some dealers specialize in serving industrial accounts, while others prefer to handle material for builders. Both should be investigated in the area in which you buy. These sources usually maintain or employ trucks or truckers to make their deliveries.

Quality. There are many degrees of quality within each species of lumber. All buyers should be familiar to some extent with the various grades; the volume buyer must be practically an expert if he is to guard the interests of his company. The description of the lumber to be purchased should indicate its quality in careful detail. There must be no area of misunderstanding between the buyer and seller.

Standard grading rules have been prepared and published by the several associations and bureaus specializing in different species. These books are available to the buyer and are truly a must for any department library. The titles and addresses from which they may be obtained are listed below:

1. Standard Grading and Dressing Rules, West Coast Lumbermen's Association, Portland, Ore.
2. Standard Grading Rules, Southern Pine Inspection Bureau, New Orleans, La.
3. Standard Grading Rules, Western Pine Association, Portland, Ore.
4. Measurement and Inspection Rules, National Hardwood Lumber Association, Chicago, Ill.

When buying lumber from distant sources, and where the exact grade is important in the end use, the buyer may secure the assurance of the bureau or association by requesting a certificate of inspection and measurement. Another means of checking grades at destination is to demand "grade marking" on the end of the boards. There may be a fee for these services, but when quality is of prime importance, the insurance pro nium is small. The details of these services will be found in the grading rulebooks mentioned above.

Problems often occur in the use or selection of lumber for industrial purposes. Such problems may be referred to the U.S. Department of Agriculture, Washington, D.C., Forest Products Laboratory, Madison, Wisconsin, or the forestry schools of nearby colleges or universities. Before assigning the problem to any agency, determine the cost of the service, if any.

Prices. Supply and demand influence the price of lumber. The occasional small-lot buyer is forced to buy on a spot basis from local dealers. The volume buyer who is constantly in the market can purchase from the mills with some price advantage. The main problem of such an operation is a constant flow of market prices over his desk. There are two publications which will supply information on prices and assist in developing a background of costs. The first is "Hardwood Market Report," *Lumber News Letter* (P.O. Box 4042, Memphis, Tenn.), and the second is *Building Materials Merchandiser* (59 East Monroe Street, Chicago, Ill.).

The f.o.b. point and transportation charges should be clearly defined by the seller at the time of quotation.

Timber

The detailed comments pertaining to the purchase of lumber also apply to the purchase of cut timber. However, purchasing of standing timber presents peculiar problems. The buyer must first find a stand of timber of the species he wishes to buy. It must then be determined in what manner the owner wishes to sell. Must the land be purchased to secure the timber or may the timber be bought without the land? If the land is involved in the purchase, will the buyer also acquire mineral rights? In some areas these can become more valuable than the timber. Survey carefully the means of transporting the logs to the mill for manufacture. Would it be more economical to use a portable mill on the site rather than to haul logs which will include all the cutting waste? Determine the demands of the owner regarding cleanup, reseeding, or other items which might be a cost against the operation.

Quality. The quality of standing timber may be determined by having a competent engineer make a survey of the tract being considered. His report should show an estimate of the number of board feet which can be cut from each of the species found growing there.

Price. The price to be paid for standing timber must be related directly to quantity and quality of lumber which it will yield. Consideration must also be given to the costs of removing the logs to the mill and such other items as may appear in the purchase agreement.

References

American Forestry Association, 919 17th Street, N.W., Washington, D.C. 20006
Forest Service, United States Department of Agriculture, Washington, D.C. 2025C
"Hardwood Market Report," *Lumber News Letter,* Post Office Box 4042, Mem-phis, Tenn. 38104
Hardwood Plywood Institute, 2310 South Walter Reed Drive, Arlington, Va.
The Lumberman, 71 Columbia Street, Seattle, Wash. 98104
National Lumber Manufacturers Association, 1619 Massachusetts Avenue, N.W. Washington, D.C. 20036
The Timberman, Miller Freeman Publications, Inc., 500 Howard Street, Sar Francisco, Calif. 94105

MILL SUPPLIES

The term "mill supplies" covers a vast number of hardware and too items used daily for construction, expansion, maintenance, production and repair work. Such products are made to manufacturers', industrial or association standards, are easily identified as to description and lis price in catalogs, and can be readily obtained from local distributors' o manufacturers' stocks. It is impractical to discuss these item by item be cause of space limitations. This section will, however, cover the six prin cipal commodity groups in which most of this type of buying activit occurs.

Flanges, Fittings, and Valves. These products are manufactured of fer rous metals such as cast iron, cast steel, forged steel, and stainless stee as well as of nonferrous metals such as cast or forged brass or bronze an aluminum. Vendor selection must be carefully considered because of th importance of local availability and service for this type of product. A the sources are usually supply warehouses or distributors, it is importan to determine that the prospective source represents the particular manu facturer's products desired.

Price. The manufacturers of flanges, fittings, and valves appear to hav rather traditional practices on pricing, as covered below:

1. Some manufacturers of flanges, fittings, and valves distribute thei products through their own outlets, but most use regular distributor and jobbers. List prices are established by the manufacturers in thei catalogs. The distributor, when buying from the manufacturer, re ceives a distributor's discount from the list price which is availabl only to established distributors. Based on his costs, the distributor the establishes the resale prices, which are more or less predicated on th quantity specified on the order or on the volume involved in a negoti ated account.

2. In most areas, distributors of pipe fittings and kindred items offer these items f.o.b. delivered to the buyer's receiving dock. Such distributors maintain their own delivery trucks for prompt service. Care must be taken to ensure that the supplier maintains adequate delivery facilities.

Metal-Working and Cutting Tools. Most mill supply houses carry complete lines of metal-working and cutting tools made by major manufacturers. The most logical local source of supply may best be determined by a competitive evaluation of prices and services available. Many reputable distributors offer prices at industrial discounts from list if purchases are in sufficient volume. As industrial discounts can vary by distributor, it is wise to check the competitive situation. Generally all tools are priced f.o.b. delivered at the buyer's plant.

Power Tools. These are broadly separated into two classifications, electric-powered tools and air-powered tools, and vary from small electric drills to contractors' air jackhammers. Some power tools are sold only by the manufacturer, but most are available through distributors. In this category the buyer can recommend a "brand name," but it is usually good practice to check with his own production and maintenance personnel for the desired choice of tools.

Some power tools distributed by mill supply houses are available at standard industrial discounts, f.o.b. buyer's plant. Tools sold directly by the manufacturer are usually at a fixed price, f.o.b. shipping point.

Paint and Painters' Supplies. The recommended basis for buying paint, varnish, lacquer, and other protective coatings is to strict specification, of which there are many, including government and Defense Department specifications. Purchasing to specification enables the buyer to secure competitive prices from several manufacturers. Many large using companies conduct extensive tests and write their own specifications. Sample test inspection is necessary to determine that the product meets the specification.

If, however, a brand name is used, it is not possible to buy competitively. Contrary to general opinion, the paint market is highly competitive and the buyer should investigate price opportunities. When unable to specify, it is satisfactory to purchase well-known brands which have been laboratory tested and given a satisfactory performance rating.

Painters' supplies, such as brushes, scrapers, and solvents, are also available from mill supply houses and paint dealers. The comments concerning paints also apply to supplies, particularly brushes. Where large quantities are involved, the buyer can obtain lower prices by dealing with major manufacturers at discounts on a requirements-contract basis.

Fasteners. Fasteners are comprised of all items used for mechanically joining materials, such as nails, rivets, bolts, nuts, and screws. Mill quantity purchases of fasteners are generally not practical for the average industrial buyer.

The development of sources must be most carefully considered. After first determining the reliability of a source, consider the following:

1. Are the products of good commercial manufacturing standard?
2. Are they (or most of them) stocked by the supplier?
3. Based on volume of annual purchases, are broken packages obtainable at full package prices?
4. Are maximum available discounts from reliable sources being obtained on quantities purchased over a period of time?

Try to avoid nonstandard "specials" if standard fasteners can be used. If specials are unavoidable, buy the largest quantity possible, so that the conventional "setup charge" will be lower per unit purchased.

Fasteners are priced f.o.b. destination except for some nonstandard items where the f.o.b. point is the manufacturer's plant.

Transmission Equipment (Mechanical). This group consists of power-transmission belts, both V and flat, stock gears, sheaves, roller chain, sprockets, speed changes, etc. Since they are normally available from mill supply houses, they are considered mill supplies. In heavy industrial areas there are supply houses which specialize in large transmission equipment, including heavy items such as large speed reducers and increasers.

Prices on transmission equipment are generally well established by the manufacturer. The reliability of the vendor, therefore, is of prime importance.

References

Factory, McGraw-Hill Publications, 330 West 42d Street, New York, N.Y. 10036

Industrial Distribution, McGraw-Hill Publications, 330 West 42d Street, New York, N.Y. 10036

Mill & Factory, 205 East 42d Street, New York, N.Y. 10017

NONFERROUS METALS

The nonferrous metal group covers a wide variety of metals; some are used in the pure condition, while others are used as alloying agents to improve the qualities of the pure metals. This section will deal only with the pure or virgin metals and will not discuss the reclaiming or refining of secondary metal from scrap. Very few metals within this group are found in the pure state but must be separated by refining methods and techniques which have been developed over the years. These methods may be reviewed, and technical information secured from metal handbooks and metal dictionaries.

Nonferrous metals, ores, and oxides originate in countries around the world. They may be refined locally or shipped to other countries for processing. As a result of these widely separated sources both the availability and price may be influenced by world politics and economics. Many of these metals are vital to the production of arms and munitions for war and defense. Because of this they may, if necessary, be completely controlled by the government, both as to production and distribution. The buyer must always be aware of this situation and keep constantly informed on the status of such items. Trade customs have developed for the distribution of these metals and tend to remain rather fixed.

Distribution of the raw material is through refineries and brokers, while semifabricated items in the form of pigs, ingots, bars, sheets, etc., are handled by warehouses, distributors, and jobbers. These outlets offer the more commonly used forms from shelf stocks. They will also accept mill orders for direct shipment to the user.

As in all buying, the description of the quality is important. These specifications should be determined by engineering and production departments and be clearly defined on the requisition. Most distribution sources prepare catalogs and/or handbooks which will assist the buyer in further describing the product quality.

There are two trading centers which have great influence on the world prices of nonferrous metals, New York and London. Many of the metals in this group are traded daily in these markets, both spot and future deliveries.

Aluminum. Primary aluminum is not traded in the metal market, but is sold by aluminum producers in its basic form.

The two basic forms of aluminum are pig and ingot. To produce pig, aluminum is cast directly from the smelting furnace. To produce ingot, aluminum is kept molten in a holding furnace until unreduced alumina (aluminum oxide) and bath materials have been removed and alloying materials (if any) have been added. Ingot may be cast from new metal that has been kept molten, or from pig that has been remelted.

The price of basic aluminum is established by aluminum producers, and is derived from cost, demand, and competition. Price structure consists of a base figure to which extras are added for such factors as high purity, quantity, and packing.

Both integrated and nonintegrated fabricators sell alloys in ingot form, and in the form of semifabricated mill products such as sheet, plate, extruded shapes, forgings, castings, wire, rod, and bar. These items are sold either direct by the producer or through distributors and jobbers.

The price of semifabricated items is derived from the cost of the basic metal plus additional costs involved in fabrication. Extras are added for quantity, packing, and similar aspects of the order.

Warehouse prices follow the same general pattern, although the warehouse price may be lower on small quantities of aluminum items.

Copper. In its primary forms, ingots, wire, bars, cathodes, slabs, cakes and billets, copper is available from smelters or mills. Other standard forms may be purchased from either mill or warehouse. All grades and forms are not available from the warehouse; however, the buyer can usually check this rather quickly.

The price of copper in its primary forms is influenced by world politics and economics and can fluctuate widely. Semifabricated forms are priced according to the quantity involved, using the base and extras formula.

Lead. The smelters or refineries offer lead in cakes of approximately one hundred pounds. Manufacturing mills produce many and varied products which reach the market directly and through warehouses and jobbers.

The price of cakes (pigs) has a degree of control by the primary producer, but it is also influenced by the world market. Prices on fabricated products will follow the primary market in a general way but tend to be more stable and are usually competitive.

Magnesium. Magnesium is available from the primary smelter in the form of pigs or ingots. Several manufacturers produce other forms such as sheet, strip, plate, rods, bars, extrusions, castings, etc. Technical advice should be sought regarding the handling of this metal in final fabrication because it ignites easily and burns with great heat and rapidity.

Pig and ingot prices are established by the producing smelter. Prices on other products are competitive among the manufacturers of those products. This metal is not traded and in general follows the economic trend.

Nickel. In its primary forms, pigs, ingots, cathodes, etc., nickel is available from a limited number of sources. Forms such as sheets, bars, tubes and alloys (Monel, nickel–silver, etc.), will be found among specialty manufacturers and warehouses.

The price of nickel in primary forms is established by the producer. In the case of manufactured items, prices may vary, depending upon the article and the number of sources from which it is available.

Tin. The most common commercial form of tin is pig (ingot) of approximately one hundred pounds. Purchases may be made from brokers and if the quantity is large, directly from the producer. The price is more or less established by the London Metal Exchange. Because of this fact and because of the large production of tin in British spheres of influence, the price is further affected by sterling exchange, visible supplies, and possible political unrest. Either spot or futures may be purchased.

Zinc. Smelters or brokers are the sources for this metal. The primary shape may be ingot or slabs, commonly known as spelter, and weighing from 42 to 100 lb. Other forms may be found among specialty manufacturers. The price is established by the primary producer on such forms as they produce. Competition will be keener among the specialty manufacturers.

Mercury (Quicksilver). The usual source of mercury is through a broker. Sometimes purchases, in large volume, can be made directly from the mine. The standard market form is a flask of approximately 76 lb. Mercury compounds are poisonous and some are explosive. A basic price may be found daily in the *American Metal Market.*

Antimony. This metal is mainly produced outside the American continent. Sources would therefore be import brokers. It is not used in the pure state commercially, but is alloyed with other metals. Standard forms are pigs of 35 to 40 lb or lumps. Prices are established by the producer.

Cadmium. This element is available as metallic cadmium from producers and as cadmium compounds from manufacturers and both forms are marketed through distributors. Prices are not controlled and may fluctuate widely, as affected by the law of supply and demand. Quotations in the press are based on cents per pound of cadmium sticks and bars in lots of 1 to 5 tons delivered.

Titanium. Until recently the available forms of titanium were sponge, oxide (white) and ilmenite (concentrates). Sources of these forms are distributed around the world. Distribution is through the producer, import brokers, and agents. Within the past few years there have been developed commercial methods of producing both alloyed and unalloyed metallic titanium. Fabricating processes are being improved constantly and at this time several forms can be purchased: sheet, strip, plate, billets, bars, tubing, and wire. The sources for these forms are smelters and processors. The metal will not usually be found in distributors' warehouses.

Because of the widespread production of ilmenite, oxide, and sponge, the prices of these items are influenced by world conditions and visible supply. On the other hand, the fabricated metallic forms have a price structure established by the smelters and processors. These prices follow the rather basic pattern of a base price (for grade specified) plus quantity extras.

Gold. A precious metal, the use of gold in industry is not too common. It is available from smelters and/or refiners. It is marketed in cast ingots approximately ½ by 2 in., sheets, wire, and leaf. Price is controlled by the Federal government. Gold is sold by the troy ounce.

Silver. Silver is available from smelters and refiners in the forms of sheets, blanks, circles, wire, anodes for plating, ingots, and solder. The United States Treasury is obligated by law to purchase all newly mined silver, but it is also permitted to sell to private industry at approximately market price. Foreign markets also provide a source for this metal depending upon conditions in their sphere of operations. Like other precious metals, silver is sold by the troy ounce. The international character of the metal as a basis for coinage precludes complete control of price. Both New York and London markets move in rather narrow range.

Platinum. Platinum is one of the precious metal group which is available from smelters and refiners. It is available in ingots, sheets, strip, wire, and leaf. This is a very expensive metal and not in general use by industry. Prices are quoted by the troy ounce and are established by the producer.

Cobalt. This metal is marketed in oxides for various uses and in lump form for alloying with other metals. Sources are domestic smelters and refiners and import brokers. Prices are established by the producers and yield to the law of supply and demand.

Chromium. Smelters, refiners, and import brokers are the sources for this product. It is available as ore, metal, and powder for use in alloying and plating. For use in the latter, contact plating supply houses. Prices are established on the various forms by the producer and are influenced by supply and demand.

Molybdenum. This is marketed by smelters, refiners, and import brokers as ore, metal and metallic powder, and commercial chemicals for alloying purposes. Prices are established by the producers.

Tungsten. Since most of this metal is imported, the source is the import broker. The usual forms are powder, sheets, rods, and salts. World market conditions influence prices.

Vanadium. Most production of vanadium is outside the United States and import brokers are the usual source. It is marketed as salts in lump form and as an oxide. Prices are affected by world market conditions.

Bismuth. Bismuth is available from smelters, refiners, and brokers. It can be found in several forms, bars, metals and/or alloys, and pharmaceutical compounds. American bismuth is obtained chiefly as a by-product of the refining of copper and lead. Prices of the various forms are established by the producers.

Alloys. Metals are alloyed to produce certain qualities of strength, hardness, abrasion resistance, or resistance to corrosion. These alloys of the basic metal are produced by the manufacturer or smelter to either standard or special analysis. Any manufacturer or smelter can supply a list of the standard alloys he produces together with their composition and physical characteristics.

References

American Metal Market Co., 525 West 42d Street, New York, N.Y. 10036

American Mining Congress, 1102 Ring Building, Washington, D.C. 20036

Aluminum Association, 420 Lexington Avenue, New York, N.Y. 10017

Copper and Brass Research Association, 420 Lexington Avenue, New York, N.Y. 10017

E & MJ Metal and Mineral Markets, McGraw-Hill Publications, 330 West 42d Street, New York, N.Y. 10036

Engineering & Mining Guidebook & Buying Directory, McGraw-Hill Publications, 330 West 42d Street, New York, N.Y. 10036

Iron Age, Chestnut and 56th Streets, Philadelphia, Pa. 19139

Lead Industries Association, 292 Madison Avenue, New York, N.Y. 10017

Metal Mining & Processing, MacLean-Hunter Publishing Corp., 500 Howard Street, San Francisco, Calif. 94105

Mining Engineering, 345 East 47th Street, New York, N.Y. 10017

Steel, The Penton Publishing Company, Penton Building, 1213 West Third Street, Cleveland, Ohio, 44113

OFFICE EQUIPMENT AND SUPPLIES

Furniture

This commodity includes such articles as desks, chairs, tables, desk lamps, files and storage cabinets, and other items with which an office is furnished. The careful selection of these items may well improve the efficiency of the office.

Types. Office furniture is made of steel, wood, and aluminum, and some smaller items of plastic. Today metal furniture is replacing wooden items, because of its durability and low maintenance cost. In addition to its many adjustable features, metal equipment is more nearly fireproof and is resistant to serious damage by the operation of janitorial cleaning equipment or when being moved for any reason.

Design-life. Office furniture is constantly changing in design. Care should be exercised when selecting all items so that additions to the equipment will be of the same or harmonizing design, to maintain a uniform or pleasing appearance in the area furnished. It would be short-sighted to equip an office with furniture of a design which might soon become obsolete.

Finish. The selection of a finish must also receive careful consideration. Furniture does not always stay in the same area. Therefore if various finishes are selected, they may, when moved from one department to another, create a problem. Finishes can be replaced, but this always adds to maintenance costs.

Distribution. As a general practice the manufacturer of metal furniture does not sell directly to the buyer, the distribution being through either independent dealers or a chain of company-owned outlets. This seems to be a logical arrangement in order to provide adequate service in many areas.

Furniture distributors usually carry representative samples of the line offered. They also have a sales organization through which advice as to design and decorating suggestions may be obtained. In addition to these services they frequently operate a retail department which will make either shop or field repairs when necessary.

Quality Standards. If large quantities of furniture are to be purchased, it is recommended that standards be established. The American Standards Association, Inc. (10 East 40th Street, New York, N.Y. 10016) publishes information under the following subjects: Chairs, posture definition; Furniture, office; Office equipment and supplies. These are excellent guides in preparing specifications.

Pricing. Prices are established by the manufacturer on the basis of production costs. Discounts from list prices are allowed to distributors and retail stores. Many outlets will accept used furniture as a "trade-in allowance" on the purchase of new items.

F.O.B. As a general practice, dealers in furniture price their line to include delivery charges. Therefore, the f.o.b. would be "shipping point —transportation allowed" or "destination." The latter is to be preferred.

Machines

Sources

Manufacturer. Many office machines are sold through a group of sales offices which are direct factory representatives. This system of distribution provides for close coverage of the sales territory, a convenient point from which deliveries can be made, and, because many of these offices maintain a repair service section, the buyer can be assured of expert service on the equipment. The repair service can be rendered in either the owner's office or in the service shop if more complicated repairs are needed. Quite naturally, these representatives handle only the product of the parent firm.

Distributor. This group will usually handle the products of many manufacturers and will have an assortment of machines. They provide a convenient source for retail outlets as well as sales representation for the lines that they carry. Shop repair services are frequently available from the distributor on all the machines of the manufacturers they represent.

Rental. The desirability of renting equipment can arise when the need for extra machines is of a temporary nature. Such a situation could be the equipping of a temporary office for political campaigns, charity fund drives, or special research groups. At the time of rental determine the possibility of having rental charges applied to the purchase price if ownership seems advisable before the rental period expires.

Another field in which rented equipment is frequently used is for accounting and computing. The use of machines for this purpose is rapidly gaining favor. Stores records, payrolls, asset records, and accounts payable are some of the possible uses. In some areas accounting firms use this type of equipment to keep the records for small companies where the expense of installation of equipment in the companies' own offices is not justified. The details of rental or possible purchase must be carefully checked, and the problems of service and/or replacement clearly defined.

New Equipment. When considering the rental of new equipment, the original cost of purchase and the market value of the used equipment should be carefully studied and compared with the total rental charges for the period involved. Thus, if the equipment can be purchased, used, and sold at the end of the period at a total cost which is less than the total rental charges, the economical action becomes quite obvious. One advantage of renting new equipment is that of being assured of constantly having machines equipped with the latest improvements. This is particularly true when renting some of the larger electronic equipment. Another advantage in renting is that the rental charges are a business expense rather than a capital investment. This point of view should be carefully checked with the management before proceeding too far with the purchase.

Used Equipment. The rental of used equipment should be for a period of short duration. The rental rates would probably be lower, but the life of the equipment would also be shorter. Usually the latest model machines would not be available in this market. But if used equipment will satisfy the requirement, by all means use it for the sake of economy.

Repairs and Service. Whether the rental agreement covers new or used equipment, be sure that the details of repairs, service, and replacement are carefully defined. The agreement should also clearly indicate the duration of the rental period and the conditions under which it may be terminated by either party.

Quality Standards

The standards for office machines have been well established by competition among manufacturers. Similar machines perform in much the same manner, producing like results. To equip an office with the products of many manufacturers may present a problem in maintenance or service. It might be sound to standardize on certain types and makes throughout the operation, or in certain segments thereof. Literature published by manufacturers will provide ready information on the design and capacity of office equipment.

Pricing

Prices for office machines have been well established by list prices published by the manufacturers. Large industrial concerns involving multiple operations may negotiate company-wide purchase contracts based upon volume purchases. In this situation the buying against such a contract is usually done by the main or central purchasing department unless the contract makes other provisions.

F.O.B. This detail of the purchase should be carefully determined at the time of negotiation. In any event the equipment should be ready for use upon arrival.

Supplies

An individual discussion of the hundreds of items which are included in this category would be impossible in this section. It would include such items as pens, pencils, paper, paper clips, stationery, typewriter supplies, standard and special forms, etc. The size of the operation being considered must govern the approach to the problem. It is from this point of view that the following suggestions are made.

Sources

Manufacturer. Large companies operating several plants and offices will find it economical to standardize their supplies. In so doing, sizable purchases may be made, stored in a central warehouse, and distributed throughout the system. These purchases would be from the manufacturer when possible, and would be of either standard or special design.

Distributor. In effect this source operates much the same as the centralized warehouse of the large company. They buy standard office supplies and sell to the retailer and small and medium-sized operations. A real service is performed by this group in providing a ready supply of the more common items needed by all businesses.

Retailer. From this source may be purchased broken package quantities and small lots of supplies such as are used by many offices. The variety of items available does not always compare with those available from the distributor. Most industrial operations will use the retailer only for emergencies or convenience.

Make or Buy. This question seems to apply to the printing of forms of special design and which are for use only within the operation. Production is by means of some sort of reproducing equipment. The problem applies to short runs which may or may not be of a repetitive nature. Careful study and analysis is required in every case to determine the proper answer to the question "make or buy." Such consideration should be given to both standard and special items.

Distribution. Both manufacturers and distributors of supplies maintain sales forces which contact prospective buyers. Usually the distributor has a catalog describing the items carried and every purchasing department should have one or more in its library.

Pricing

Prices will vary directly in relation to quantity and quality. In considering price, therefore, the quality factor must be kept constantly in mind to arrive at proper value.

F.O.B. A wide variety of f.o.b. points will be found among these items. Since transportation costs are part of the cost of goods purchased, the question of f.o.b. is important.

References

American Standards Association, Inc., 10 East 40th Street, New York, N.Y. 10016

Geyer's Dealer Topics (*Who Makes It and Where*), 212 Fifth Avenue, New York, N.Y. 10010

Life Office Management Association, 757 Third Avenue, New York, N.Y. 10017

Office Publications Inc., 60 East 42d Street, New York, N.Y. 10017

Office Appliances Buyers Index, 288 Park Avenue West, Elmhurst, Ill. 60126

PULP AND PAPER

Pulp

Sources. The United States, Canada, and Northern Europe produce approximately 95 per cent of the world's supply of wood pulp. Most of the wood pulp production is consumed by the producer, only a small portion, about 15 per cent, being sold as wood pulp.

There are two broad markets which use this material, the producers of paper in many grades from ground wood pulp and the chemical industry. The latter uses a dissolving wood pulp, a highly purified form of chemical cellulose, to make rayon, cellophane, plastics, and explosives.

The domestic production is available from the producer and sometimes through agents. Foreign wood pulp can be obtained from import brokers.

Distribution. Being a raw material, purchases usually are in reasonable tonnage and there appears to be no reason for other than direct shipment from the producer. The agent or import broker seldom warehouses for his own account on either exports or imports.

Quality

Description. The end product must determine both the quality and the proper description by which it can be obtained. This information is also necessary to determine the source, since all producers do not have all grades available.

Standards. No standards have been established within the industry. It is, therefore, the buyer's responsibility to work with his source to determine the extent of uniformity that can be expected in the product which he is purchasing.

Pricing. Prices are established by the producers and are quoted on a short-ton basis. Imported grades must sell on a competitive basis with domestic grades. Because of the expansion of domestic production facilities which provide an adequate supply, the law of supply and demand has little effect on the market. A heavy demand for the production of explosives might, however, upset this situation.

In most cases sales are made f.o.b. producer's mill with freight allowed in full or part.

Paper

Sources. The mill is the production source for all grades of paper. Large-volume buying can, in most cases, be placed directly with the producing mill. All mills do not produce all grades of paper; thus the selection of a source must be made on the basis of the grade or grades desired.

The distributor, sometimes referred to as merchant, jobber, or wholesaler, serves the retail trade by delivering from stocks carried in his warehouse. He may also represent one or more mills in his territory, calling on prospects who are not on the mill's customer list. Some mills make it a practice of selling only through distributors, while others will deal direct. There is no uniform custom in this respect.

Distribution. This is determined by the source selected, either mill or distributor. If the order is large enough, the mill will ship directly to the buyer and the distributor becomes a broker because he does not actually handle the shipment. If the delivery is from the distributor's warehouse, it is usually conveyed by truck to the seller's plant. Depending upon the source, lead time becomes a factor. Mill shipments are sometimes rather extended but represent a lower cost than warehouse shipments. Hence the urgency of the requirement may dictate the source and price.

Quality

Description. The end use must determine the quality as well as its description. This type of information can be secured through the sales representatives or by direct contact with the source. In general, the mills specialize in certain grades, but if the tonnage is large they will give special attention to the production of special finishes and/or quality.

Most paper grades are fairly well standardized as to raw material content, basis weight, gauge, color, and finishes. The paper and printing industries have converted the old ream of 480 sheets to one of 500 sheets. Basis weight, therefore, is the weight of 500 sheets of basic size. It is in the basic size that standards appear to be lacking because among the various grades the basic size differs. For book papers the basic size is 25 by 38 in., for cover papers 20 by 26 in., for ledgers and writing papers 17 by 22 in., for kraft paper 24 by 36 in., and for cardboards 22½ by 28½ in. Within each grade there may be several other sizes for the convenience of the trade. The buyer needs a full understanding of these factors as a guide to value.

Pricing. Paper ordered on a specified basic weight is priced by the pound or by the hundred pounds. When sold on this basis, it is charged on the figurative weight, unless it exceeds the allowable tolerance, generally plus or minus 5 per cent. In that case it is sold on scale weight. The producers control prices. Selling prices of various grades are developed from the base roll price. Extras are added for sheeting, trimming, packing, colors, or special characteristics.

Producers usually ship f.o.b. point of manufacture with full or part of the freight allowed. Distributors' sales are generally on a delivered basis.

Folding Cartons

Sources. Folding cartons are usually a custom-made product. This is true because of the great variety of sizes, shapes, and materials used in their production. The manufacturer is therefore the natural source. It must be noted that the methods of production are such that only large volume is desirable to the producer and will produce an attractive price. Buyers will seldom find any large selection of folding cartons available from jobber sources; however, some commonly used items, such as egg, bakery, gift, and suit boxes, are available from stocks.

Trade Customs

Art Work. Most folding cartons are used to pack consumer merchandise and may require extensive art work. There are specialists in this field who can be employed or the buyer may seek the assistance of the art department of the manufacturer. In either case, the costs involved should be predetermined. Carton decoration will require printing rolls or plates which are made to fit the manufacturer's equipment. In all probability such rolls or plates will not be adaptable to other equipment; therefore any change in source will necessitate another roll purchase.

Dies. Folding cartons are die-cut and the folding scores are made after printing. Dies for this purpose are made for the buyer's account. As in the case of printing rolls, it will probably be found that such dies cannot be transferred to another source.

Quality

Description. Many folding cartons are delivered flat and must be machine formed and glued prior to filling. This operation can present many problems. When discussing the description of the item, consider the grade of base material in relation to its qualities of folding, ready gluing, and holding together in transit and on the shelf. Surface finish becomes important in relation to ease of printing and resultant intensity of color in the design. Packing by the producer should be discussed to provide flat blanks which will process through the forming machinery. The type of closure used is also important from the point of ease and permanence.

Standards. Few if any standards have been established for folding cartons, unless one wishes to consider general design. The materials used in their construction, however, have many standards. The buyer should be familiar with the latter.

Pricing. Prices are established by the manufacturer and will be based upon quantity. They are expressed in terms of thousands. The materials used in the construction of the carton will have an influence on price. Shipments may be f.o.b. destination or shipping point, with all or part of the freight allowed.

Setup Boxes

Sources. Because of the variety of shapes, sizes, and trim, special printing, and other features the buyer can seldom find this product ready-made to his requirement. Therefore, the manufacturer becomes the only source. There are two general types of setup boxes. The first is the plain chipboard container with corner stays with or without interior packing. These containers are designed to protect the product in shipment, and not for display purposes. The other group covers the fancy setup boxes. These are trimmed with colored paper, printed, and/or embossed and while they protect the product during shipment they are also a display container.

Distribution. The producer's salesmen solicit orders, and shipments are made directly from the manufacturing plant. In some cases, paper distributors act as sales representatives for the boxmaker. This is a case of brokerage because the paper distributor does not handle the shipment in any way except for invoicing.

Quality. In this field the end use will most frequently determine the quality of the item to be purchased. It will progress from the relatively inexpensive, plain, undecorated chipboard container with corner stays to the beautifully trimmed consumer packages. In shipping containers adequate protection of the product is sought at the most economical price. On the other hand, consumer packaging requires both product protection and customer appeal, while still seeking a reasonable cost. The description used on the inquiry must be complete and in terms of the trade. Incoming inspection is the method used to ensure that the product delivered meets the quality described on both the inquiry and order. The production, packaging, and sales departments will all be involved when the question of "what to buy" arises.

Pricing. The cost of setup boxes will be established by the manufacturer on the basis of the quality described. The prices quoted depend on the cost of the materials which are used. The use of multiple inquiries is recommended when buying these items. As a general rule the price quoted is f.o.b. buyer's plant.

Corrugated Boxes

Sources

Manufacturer. Because corrugated boxes are designed to meet specific packaging requirements they are custom-built for each packing problem. This fact makes the manufacturer the logical source. When selecting a source for this product the buyer must consider several important items.

1. Will the producer have access to an adequate supply of raw materials under all economic conditions? Is he integrated or nonintegrated?
2. Is there sufficient capacity to provide prompt delivery of orders at all times?
3. Does the supplier have a means of testing the proposed package? Close control of quality in manufacturing is important.
4. Is the producing plant a reasonable distance from destination so as to provide a minimum of transit time?
5. Do they have an art department to assist the buyer when designing exterior printing?

Jobber. Some paper jobbers carry a number of plain corrugated boxes in stock to meet the demands of the small occasional buyer. The range of sizes, under such circumstances, is usually limited. Such jobbers may also represent a boxmaker and handle orders on a brokerage basis.

Trade Customs

Art Work. Many users of corrugated boxes take advantage of the advertising opportunity offered by a printed message on the container. Most producers have specialists in this field and offer their services to the buyer to assist in the design of the printing. Such service is usually rendered without charge.

Dies. Some packages by their very nature or design and some items of interior packing must be die-cut. The boxmaker will purchase these for the account of the buyer. The cost of such dies may be paid as a separate item or amortized over a number of orders. In either event the ownership of the dies should be clearly established.

Quality

Description. The common carriers have established certain rules with which boxes must conform. These rules have, to some extent, become a determination of quality. A further expression of quality may be effected by specifying the grades of paper or board with which the box shall be constructed. A little research will produce enough information to establish a good specification.

Standards. The corrugated board industry is well standardized on the various flutes which are produced, namely, A, B, and C. While all producers do not have equipment to produce all three flutes in every plant, it will be found that one large flute, A or C, and B flute are available from all sources. The carrier rules also contribute to general standardization within the industry.

References. Most producers distribute a handbook on corrugated fiber board boxes and products which is very helpful. In addition to a list of definitions of the terms used by the industry it includes illustrations of the various forms of boxes and quotes the carrier rules. The *Official Container Directory* published by Board Products Publishing Co. (228 North LaSalle Street, Chicago, Illinois) provides much information concerning sources for corrugated products as well as many other paper container items.

Pricing. Prices are established by the manufacturer and show some tendency to follow the market price of kraft paper. The basis of pricing is the number of square feet of board required to make a given box. This is then reduced to a price per thousand boxes which includes a setup charge. Quantity factors are part of the cost expressed in the price per thousand and the setup covers the preparation for printing and closing the manufacturer's joint by gluing, stitching, or taping. A buyer who has many items in his line of boxes will do well to have his prices quoted on a per thousand basis plus a separate setup charge. Prices are usually quoted f.o.b. buyer's plant.

Bags

Sources

Manufacturer. Paper or a combination of paper, thermoplastic, and textile bags are available from the manufacturer if the quantity is large enough or the specification is of a special nature. There are a great many combinations of material with which bags are made. Probably the best course to follow is first to contact the producer as a possible source. If he is not interested, the buyer can secure the names of several jobbers who handle the type of container he requires.

Jobbers. The hundreds of standard bags used by many businesses are readily available through jobbers. These sources carry large stocks and can usually make prompt deliveries.

Quality

Description. The end use or product to be packaged must determine the description of quality. The supplier will usually work closely with the buyer to make this determination. The use of sample bags and trial packages is a sound practice to follow on new products for which there is little precedence.

Standards. Many of the bags used by industry and business are well standardized both as to size and materials used. These are the items commonly found in jobbers' stocks.

Pricing. Prices are quoted on the basis of one hundred or one thousand units. The commodity markets of the necessary raw materials will influence the prices to be paid. The f.o.b. point shows a mixed pattern. The producers sell both f.o.b. shipping point and destination, depending upon individual policy. Jobbers usually ship on a delivered basis.

References

Aerosol Age, P.O. Box 31, Caldwell, N.J. 07006

American Boxmaker Directory, Peacock Business Press, Inc., 200 South Prospect, Park Ridge, Ill. 60068

American Forest Products Industries, Inc., 2 West 45th Street, New York, N.Y. 10036

Consumer Packaging, Haywood Publishing Company, 6 North Michigan Avenue, Chicago, Ill. 60602

Daily Mill Stock Reporter, 130 West 42d Street, New York, N.Y. 10036

The Dictionary of Paper, Including Pulps, Boards, Paper Properties and Related Papermaking Terms, 2d ed., The American Paper & Pulp Association, 122 East 42d Street, New York, N.Y. 10017

Fibre Box Association, 224 South Michigan Avenue, Chicago, Ill. 60604

Fibre Drum Manufacturers Association, Post Office Box 1328, Grand Central Station, New York, N.Y. 10017

The Folding Carton, The Folding Paper Box Association of America, 220 West Adams, Chicago, Ill. 60606

Industrial Bag & Cover Association, 11 West 42d Street, New York, N.Y. 10036

Industrial Packaging, 6 North Michigan Avenue, Chicago, Ill. 60602

Kraft Paper Association, 122 East 42d Street, New York, N.Y. 10017

Lockwood's Directory of the Paper and Allied Trades, 89th ed., Lockwood Trade Journal Co., Inc., 49 West 45th Street, New York, N.Y. 10036 (published annually)

Modern Packaging, 770 Lexington Avenue, New York, N.Y. 10021

Modern Packaging Encyclopedia Issue, 770 Lexington Avenue, New York, N.Y. 10021

Modern Plastic Encyclopedia, 770 Lexington Avenue, New York, N.Y. 10021

National Barrel & Drum Association, 1343 L Street, N.W., Washington, D.C. 20005

Official Container Directory, Board Products Publishing Company, 228 North LaSalle Street, Chicago, Ill. 60601

Paper and Paper Products, 466 Kinderkamack Road, Oradell, N.J. 07649

Paper Bag Institute, Inc., 41 East 42d Street, New York, N.Y. 10017

Paperboard Packaging, Board Products Publishing Company, 228 North LaSalle Street, Chicago, Ill. 60601

Paper Shipping Sack Manufacturers Association, 60 East 42d Street, New York, N.Y. 10017

Paper Trade Terms, rev. ed., William Bond Wheelwright, Silton, Callaway & Hoffman, Inc., 131 Clarendon Street, Boston, Mass. 02116

The Paper Year Book, Ojibway Press, 1 East First Street, Duluth, Minn. 55802

Pulp, Paper and Board, Industry Report, U.S. Department of Commerce, Business & Defense Services Administration, Washington, D.C. 20230

Rennicke, G. N.: *The Manufacture of Paperboard,* Board Products Publishing Company, 228 North LaSalle Street, Chicago, Ill. 60601

Steel Shipping Container Institute, 600 Fifth Avenue, New York, N.Y. 10020

Stern, Walter: *The Package Engineering Handbook,* Board Products Publishing Company, 228 North LaSalle Street, Chicago, Ill. 60601

Technical Association of the Pulp and Paper Industry, 360 Lexington Avenue New York, N.Y. 10017

Textile Bag Manufacturers Association, 518 Davis Street, Evanston, Ill.

Waterproof Paper Manufacturers Association, Inc., 122 East 42d Street, New York, N.Y.

Waxed Paper Institute, Inc., 38 South Dearborn Street, Chicago, Ill.

Werner, A. W.: *The Manufacture of Fibre Boxes,* Board Products Publishing Company, 228 North LaSalle Street, Chicago, Ill. 60601

TEXTILES

Cotton

Cotton is a white fiber obtained from the blossom of the cotton plant. A ginning operation separates the fibers from the seeds and pulp. After this process the fibers are baled and sold by brokers, in the United States, through the New York and New Orleans cotton exchanges. The worldwide nature of this commodity makes it reflect economic and political conditions as well as weather conditions. In the United States the government restricts the acreage to be planted and all these factors have their influence on the price of cotton in the exchanges. Baled cotton is sold at a price per pound established in relation to the grade.

Cotton-textile fabrics are produced and sold in many forms. The terms used to describe quality and quantity are well standardized within the industry.

Purchases can be made directly from the producing mills when the quantity is large enough. Sometimes the mills prefer to deal through commission houses or brokers, which collect a commission for their services.

Lightweight fabrics are sold by the yard and heavyweight fabrics, such as hose and belting duck, by the pound. The buyer must be careful to reduce all prices quoted to a common denominator when comparing bids. The buyer should also remember that the raw material and goods markets do not always move together. Prices are further affected by weather and world economic and political conditions, as well as insect plagues. All things considered, this is a complicated market in which to operate. Extensive research and study is therefore recommended.

Silk

Japan, China, India, Italy, and France are the principal silk-producing countries of the world. Raw silk is shipped in bales of the following approximate weights: Japanese, 133.3 lb; Chinese, 106.6 lb; and European, 220.5 lb. Purchases can be made through importers or dealers on a spot or future delivery basis. The majority of importers and dealers are located in the metropolitan area of New York City. Prices are quoted in the daily press on a per pound basis.

Silk yarns may be produced either in the country of origin or by manufacturers of yarn in the United States. Packaging takes the form of boxes, paper wrapped skeins, bobbins, and cones. Quality and ordering specifications are important and should be given careful attention by the buyer. Purchases can be made from the manufacturer of silk yarn.

Silk fabrics are rarely imported because of import duties; furthermore, the United States is one of the largest producers of such fabrics. Quantity purchases may be made directly from the manufacturer and smaller lots from brokers or textile jobbers. Shipment is usually made in rolls on a paper core or in "bookfold" form. Prices for both silk yarns and silk fabrics are established by the manufacturer on the basis of "costs." The world-wide nature of this product causes prices to be influenced by world economic and political conditions as well as supply and demand and competition from other filaments and fabrics.

Synthetic Fibers

Recent years have seen a variety of "man-made" fibers make their appearance on the market. The extent to which they may be used for industrial purposes has not yet been fully determined. They are widely used alone and in combination with natural fibers. Production in the United States is by a relatively small group of manufacturers. The producer does not further process the material, but sells to textile mills in the usual form of bales, skeins, and cones. Prices are affected by cost and may be influenced by the prices of competing fibers and by the law of supply and demand.

Materials fabricated of synthetic fibers can be made to look like those produced from natural fibers. In many cases superior wearing qualities exist in the synthetic materials. The nature of the material desired will dictate the source, because mills tend to specialize in certain types of production. Specifications should be developed with the producer on the basis of the end use. Packaging will be as standardized within the industry. Prices are established by the manufacturer on the basis of costs.

Wool

Wool is second only to cotton in importance in the field of textiles. Australia is the largest producer, although wool is produced around the world. Wool is graded by length and fineness of fiber. Each grade finds its way into the product for which it is best fitted. It is shipped in bales of varying weights, uncleaned so that the natural oils will protect it. Bulk purchases are made through dealers and brokers. The center of the wool market is Boston. The dealers and brokers are also importers and frequently have substantial stocks on hand. Prices are quoted in the daily press. World politics, economics, supply and demand, or adverse weather conditions can influence both price and quality.

Wool fabrics are available in many industrial forms from the manufacturers and jobbers and distributors. Purchase specifications must be prepared with a view toward end use. Packing will tend to be uniform within each product group. Prices are established by the manufacturer on the basis of costs. Clothing fabrics sell by the lineal yard, carpet by the square yard, and felt by the pound or by the piece when die-cut to shape. Carefully controlled competitive bids should be used to establish the best price of the quality described.

Burlap

Burlap is the American name of the cloth woven from jute fibers mostly grown in India and Pakistan. Jute is quantitatively the third-ranking fiber in world-wide commercial use, being outdone only by cotton and wool.

The weight of burlap in the United States is usually stated in terms of ounces per yard of 40-in. width and is written "40″ 10½ oz." If any other width is mentioned, for instance, 36″ 10½ oz, it is usually understood that this means 36″ 10½ oz to 40″. In other countries, it is more likely to mean 36″ 10½ oz to 36″.

The warp or porter threads of a given sample are those running parallel to the selvage. Those running across the goods from selvage to selvage are called weft, shotting, woof, or filling threads.

A sizable percentage of the burlap bags in use at one time are secondhand. Hundreds of dealers in the United States and Canada are engaged in this business which consists of collecting, buying, and reconditioning bags after they are emptied of commodities shipped in them. It is said that 75 per cent of all burlap bags are reconditioned and reused, and the average number of trips per bag is five.

Burlap and cotton fabrics, chiefly osnaburg and coarse sheeting, frequently compete with each other in the bag and baling trade. A more important competitive factor has been the increased use of paper in containers and wrapping materials at the expense of both burlap and cotton fabrics. Under some conditions it becomes economical to use containers of corrugated cardboard or wood or to ship in bulk.

Ordinarily burlap is imported into the United States either by bag manufacturers who purchase primarily for their own use or by traders who import for resale. Some of the burlap traders are agents for Calcutta mills or selling houses; others buy burlap wherever available. Variations in weights, widths, and constructions differentiate more than a hundred kinds of burlaps.

Bag manufacturers who import directly usually sell any surplus to the bale trade (comprising all uses other than for bags). Importers of burlap for resale sell either to the nonimporting bag manufacturers or to the bale trade.

Hard Fibers and Hard-fiber Products

This market covers a group of vegetable fibers. About 85 per cent o all the hard fibers grown in the world are used for the manufacture o ropes and twines. Small quantities are used in making mats, baskets rugs, etc.

Among the many hard fibers included in this market, the most commor are as follows: abacá (manila hemp), sisal (sisalana), and henequen. Non of these are grown in the United States; all must be imported. Bot abacá and sisal are in the government strategic stockpile. Because thes fibers are subject to deterioration after long storage, the manufacturer of cordage deliver their new imports to the government and accept in ex change a like quantity and quality of the ordered material from the stock pile. Henequen is not stockpiled.

The principal hard-fiber products with which we are concerned ar rope, binder twine, baler twine, and tying twine. The source for smal quantities would be the jobber or distributor of packaging supplies Large quantities could be purchased directly from the manufacturer o his representative. A proper description of the product to be purchase is very important. The end use will determine the fiber to be used, th construction, lay, and finish of the final rope. This is also true, but to a lesser degree, when buying twines.

The cost of hard fibers is influenced by world economic and politica conditions and these factors plus government stockpiling have an effec upon the cost of the finished products. Buying upon the basis of competitive bids is recommended in this market.

Rags—Cloth

The purchase of rags to be used as wipers presents some very interesting problems. The product is basically scrap fabric which has outlived its original purpose. It finds its way to reuse markets through collectors, junk shops, and graders. Finally, it is laundered and distributed.

The basic objective of the buyer should be to obtain, at the best price, rags which are 100 per cent usable by the employees of his company. To do this, it must first be determined what grade of rag is required. Usually rags are discussed by weight and so considered as wipers. Each wiping problem needs to be classified and rags purchased to meet each need.

A description of the quality of rags presents the greatest difficulty because there is no general standardization of terms within this market. The Sanitary Institute of America, which is a national association of industrial wiping cloth manufacturers, is doing much to overcome this situation. They have established descriptions for several grades as well as a specification for sterilized wiping cloths. Their members can offer the buyer a certificate covering sterilization and weight. Rags which have not been sterilized can be a menace to the health of the employees.

Price alone can never be the measure of a "good buy" when dealing with rags. Should lightweight cotton wipers be required and the shipment includes medium and heavy material, which cannot be used, then the cost for the usable wipers will have risen. Control is through the selection of a source of supply and intelligent incoming inspection.

Wipers—Cloth

This product is fabricated from new material, sold in several standard sizes, and is reusable. Many firms purchase wipers and operate their own laundries for cleaning these wipers or contract the laundering to outside specialists. Usually the same sources distribute both rags and wipers. Shipments are made from the producing mill in bales of uniform quantities. Quality is determined by the weight or density of the fabric.

The fabricated cloth wiper is frequently offered on a rental basis. In general, the service provides that a quantity of wipers be purchased. These are then used and returned to the laundry once or twice weekly, being replaced by an equal number upon each occasion. Worn-out wipers are replaced at no cost, but lost wipers are invoiced at the contract price. In approaching the question of ownership or rental of wipers, the buyer should investigate completely the itemized costs of each, including a captive laundry and a contract laundry.

References

Association of Cotton Textile Merchants of New York, 40 Worth Street, New York, N.Y. 10013

Burlap and Jute Association, 160 Broadway, New York, N.Y. 10038

Daily Mill Stock Reporter, National Business Press, 130 West 42d Street, New York, N.Y. 10036

Davison's Rayon, Silk and Synthetic Textiles, Davison Publishing Co., 2 Franklin Avenue, Ridgewood, N.J. 07450

National Association of Secondary Materials Industries, Inc., 271 Madison Avenue, New York, N.Y. 10016

Sanitary Institute of America, 173 West Madison Street, Chicago, Ill. 60602

Textile Bag Manufacturers Association, 518 Davis Street, Evanston, Ill. 60201

Textile World, McGraw-Hill Publications, 330 West 42d Street, New York, N.Y. 10036

Waste Trade Journal, 130 West 42d Street, New York, N.Y. 10036

Wool Bureau, Inc., 360 Lexington Avenue, New York, N.Y. 10016

UTILITY SERVICES

General

Sizable savings may be realized by exercising care in arranging for supplies of electricity, gas, water, telephones, and steam. Public suppliers of these services are of two types, and it is well for the buyer to be familiar with the special restrictions surrounding the operation of each.

Privately or Investor Owned Utilities. These are corporations rendering one or more types of utility service. They are found in every state. Almost everywhere, their rates, conditions of service, and many other phases of their operations and financing are subject to regulation by a state commission. Table 15–1 at the end of this section shows the status of regulation in the various states and territories. Even where the table indicates that the commission does not have jurisdiction over rates, they may be set or regulated by individual municipalities under franchises or other agreements.

The rates of regulated utilities are prescribed or approved by the regulatory body and are uniform for the same type of service and characteristics of use for all customers similarly situated. In arranging for service under such circumstances it is important to examine the possibility that more than one optional schedule may be available. Most utilities will point this out to present or prospective customers and will assist them in selecting the most economical rate, thus making it unnecessary to employ outside help for this work. Utilities usually require the customer to make his own election, after the facts are made available to him, and to abide by the consequences thereof at least during the initial contract term.

Publicly Owned or Municipal Utilities and Cooperatives. In many communities, one or more of the utilities may be owned by the municipality itself, by a utility district formed by some or all of the residents of an area for the purpose, or by a cooperative formed by users of the service.

Publicly owned electric and water systems are the most frequently encountered. Table 15–1 shows, for electric suppliers in this group, the degree of regulation to which they are subject.

In general, while publicly owned utilities are not subject to regulation by the state, municipal utilities' rates are set by city ordinance and cannot be varied. They are thus in much the same position as regulated private utilities so far as rate uniformity is concerned. They are usually unable to enter into special contracts with customers under arrangements other than those specified in the ordinances.

Unregulated cooperatives and utility districts are in a somewhat more flexible situation, since their rates need only be approved by their own directors. But, here again, uniformity is most important, and the well-operated cooperative or district will refuse to make special deals to get business. This is doubly important to them because they do not have the protective umbrella of regulation to rely on, and must maintain uniformity of their own volition, in fairness to all their customers.

As many municipal and cooperative utilities are small, it is most important to be sure that the supply of the service is adequate for present and prospective usages and that adequate financing will be available to take care of growth.

Check List of Important Items to Consider in Contracting for Utility Services

All Utility Services

1. Location of nearest available line. Most utilities will extend their lines or services some nominal distance from an existing line to reach a new customer. If the customer is at a greater distance, the extension will be made only if the customer agrees to pay for the excess length, either in a lump sum before service is connected or as a surcharge on the bills for a period of years. The advance payment, if required, may be subject to refund after a lapse of time or be dependent on the size of the customer's bill.
2. Location on the purchaser's property where the service will enter. This is usually designated by the utility so as to require the minimum run from its existing lines. Consultation in advance, where there is some valid reason for another point of entrance, may result in a more satisfactory location to the customer.
3. Definition of "premises" in the utility's rules and regulations. It is customary for utilities to state in their rules that a separate service line shall be required for each individual premises, and the latter are usually defined as a single building or a plot of land undivided by streets or highways. There are exceptions in some cases. It is well to check such definitions, since a large enterprise may have to take service at more than one point, with a consequent increase in billing over single-point delivery.
4. The extent to which the readings of separate meters will be combined for billing purposes. Ordinarily, utilities' rules provide that readings of separate meters will be combined for billing purposes only when the separate metering is done for the convenience of the utility, and the latter term is variously defined.
5. Escalation. Rate schedules of all types of utilities often contain blanket escalator clauses, which tie the stated prices to (*a*) taxes paid at a given

time, providing for upward adjustment for new or higher ones imposed subsequently; or (*b*) some national index like the Bureau of Labor Statistics Index of Consumer Prices, or Wholesale Prices; or (*c*) local statistics, if available. In order to determine the full cost of service, such adjustments must be taken into account.

6. Length of the normal billing period. There is at present a movement, begun during World War II, toward bimonthly billing to save meter-reading, billing, and collecting labor. The question becomes important when comparing rates in different areas.

Electricity

1. The type of service desired. Utilities often offer general service schedules under which lighting, power, and heating service can all be obtained. In other cases, separate rates are provided for each type of use and each must be separately metered.
2. Characteristics of service.
   a. Frequency. Sixty-cycle alternating current is the most commonly used, although some areas still have other frequencies. In downtown areas of many cities, direct current is also in use.
   b. Single- or three-phase alternating current. This may, in some cases, be determined by the starting current of motors to be used, or by the size of the total load.
   c. Voltage. It may be economical to take service at a high voltage in order to distribute it at lower cost around the purchaser's establishment, or a higher voltage may be needed for special purposes. Many utilities offer discounts for such higher-voltage service because the user supplies his own transformers.
3. Demand determination. Many schedules utilize a measured or estimated demand in kilowatts. When measured, this may be based on various time intervals: 1, 5, 15, 30, and 60 min being the more usual ones. Of these, 15 is the most popular. Special rules may make one or another interval mandatory.

   The demand used for billing purposes is likely to include not only the demand established in the current billing month but also some effect of higher demands, if any were established previously. Thus billing demand may be defined as the measured demand but not less than 50 per cent of the highest demand which has occurred in the twelve months ending with the current month. This is called a 50 per cent ratchet. If electricity is an important cost and the demand charge per kilowatt and the ratchet percentages are high, plant operation may be importantly affected.
4. Escalation. Some electric rates, particularly those for industrial service,

provide that the prices shall go up or down with the cost of fuel. Since fuel is a major variable cost in electric generation and is subject to wide variations, it may properly be thus reflected in rates. However, the escalation should take account of the proportion of the utility's supply which actually comes from fuel-fired plants, some portion of it frequently being produced in hydroelectric stations.

5. Minimum charge. This item becomes important where service is taken for highly fluctuating or seasonal use. Some schedules provide for an annual cumulative minimum charge, and, if available and applicable, might be selected for such a purpose. Minima are variously based, usually on demand or connected load.
6. Off-peak service. Many utilities offer favorable rates or demand charge concessions to large users who can take service at night and on holidays and weekends when other load is low.
7. Power factor. Industrial schedules often provide some penalty for customers who tax the utility's capacity by operating at low power factor. In other cases, the utility's rules provide that the company can require the user to maintain a given average power factor. Such provisions may be expensive either in penalties on the monthly bills or in investment to make the correction.
8. Auxiliary or standby service. Many industries require process steam, and have substantial boiler installations from which some or all of the plant's electric requirements may be generated. This will, however, only prove economical if the plant electric peak load, or some portion of it, coincides substantially with the time when maximum steam usage occurs.

   When owned generation is feasible, it may prove desirable to have some sort of standby service from the local utility, so that operations may be continued in case of emergency outages of owned generation, or to supplement local generation during all or certain portions of the year. Schedules for this type of service are usually at quite high rates, since they involve a sort of back-up insurance for what utilities generally consider to be a competing source of electricity.

   Where parallel operation of utility supply and owned generation are involved, specially negotiated contracts may be required, and these must usually be approved by the appropriate regulatory commission before they can become effective.
9. Total energy supply with gas. As described below, gas utilities have recently undertaken to supply all fuel and electric needs of certain customers with gas-turbine-driven electric generators. Process and/or heating steam and air conditioning are also often included in such a proposal.

Gas

1. Type of service
   a. Natural gas
      (1) Firm service. This is available at all times, although the amount which can be contracted for by industrial users may be limited.
      (2) Interruptible service. A price concession is available in many areas to customers who will cut off in winter, when gas is needed to supply the heating demands of firm customers. Standby supplies of coal, fuel oil, or liquefied petroleum gas are required if there is to be no interruption of the purchaser's operation. It is important when contracting for this type of service to find out what the present and future prospects of curtailment are.
      (3) Total energy. A number of gas utilities across the country are now offering, either directly or through affiliated companies, to supply all the fuel and electric needs and air-conditioning service for large industrial or commercial customers, through the use of gas-turbine-driven electric generators and compressors, so that no connection with an electric utility is required. Process and/or heating steam can also be furnished in such cases.

         Such a proposal must be carefully analyzed to make sure all costs and possible savings are evaluated. A principal attraction of this sort of arrangement is often the saving in plant investment in boilers, generating equipment, and compressors, which is replaced by annual charges for rental or amortization and cost of operation and maintenance of the equipment, as well as payments to the affiliate for gas fuel.
   b. Manufactured or mixed gas
      (1) Firm service. This is the only type of service usually available.
2. Pressure at which gas is delivered and measured. Operation of equipment in the purchaser's establishment may be seriously affected by pressure variations. The utility usually supplies a regulator.
3. Heat content of gas. Since heat units are being purchased, it is important to be sure that proper adjustment is provided in the rate schedule for variations in the heat content of the gas. Natural gas may vary from about 500 to 1200 Btu per cu ft; manufactured or mixed gas from 500 to 1000.
4. Escalation
   a. Natural gas. Because natural gas can, for many operations, be replaced by other fuels, schedules, particularly for interruptible service, are sometimes escalated with the price of a competitive fuel. In times of fuel-supply stringency, gas may rise rapidly in cost, unless there is a ceiling on escalation. (Some distribution utilities

escalate all schedules with the cost to them of purchased gas.)

b. Manufactured or mixed gas. Escalation in these schedules is usually based on the cost of gas-making fuel oil or coal, in much the same manner as in electric schedules.

. Minimum charge. Where seasonal or small fluctuating operations are involved, the minimum charge becomes important. Some schedules provide for an annual cumulative minimum charge and, if available and applicable, might be selected for such a purpose.

Vater

. Type of service

a. General industrial or commercial service for all purposes.

b. Nonpotable industrial water for special purposes, available in some areas.

c. Fire-protection service. Special rates are charged for hydrants and sprinkler connections which may affect insurance costs.

d. Partial or standby service. Where wells or other sources of water are available on the property, a special arrangement may be appropriate. These are usually not set forth in rate schedules.

. Size of metering installation. Most water utilities base the service charge or minimum charge on the size of meter to be installed. Care should be exercised to see that the service pipe is adequate, but not oversize.

. Pressure. Where industrial processes require the maintenance of pressure at a given level, investigation will reveal whether the utility is equipped to do this. If it is, important investment in pumps or water towers or both may be saved.

. Quality of water. If quality is important, an analytical study of the water should be made to determine what purifying or treating equipment must be installed.

. Adequacy of supply. In many parts of the country, water supplies have been outgrown in recent years. Firm assurance of an adequate supply is particularly important here.

elephone

. General. Of all the utilities, the telephone systems of subsidiaries of the American Telephone & Telegraph Company offer more assistance to prospective purchasers, and have the most complete and meticulously drawn rate schedules. In addition to the Bell System, there are several thousand independent telephone systems in the United States, some of them quite large. The most important item to check, if located in the territory of an independent, is the ability of the utility to handle an expansion in its plant and service, which may, in the case of a

Table 15–1. State Regulatory Commission Jurisdiction Over Rates Charged to Ultimate Consumers by Various Utilities in the United States and Territories

Commission	Electricity		Gas	Water	Telephone	Steam
	Privately owned	Publicly owned (municipals and co-operatives)				
Alabama Public Service Commission, Montgomery	Yes	No	Yes	Yes	Yes	Yes
Alaska Public Service Commission, Anchorage[a]	...	...	...	...	...	...
Arizona Corporation Commission, Phoenix	Yes	No[b]	Yes	Yes	Yes	No
Arkansas Public Service Commission, Little Rock	Yes[c]	No	Yes[c]	Yes	Yes	Yes
California Public Utilities Commission, San Francisco	Yes	No[b]	Yes	Yes	Yes	Yes
Colorado Public Utilities Commission, Denver	Yes	No[d]	Yes	Yes	Yes	Yes
Connecticut Public Utilities Commission, Hartford	Yes	No[e]	Yes	Yes	Yes	No
Delaware Public Service Commission, Dover	Yes	No[b]	Yes	Yes	Yes	No
District of Columbia Public Utilities Commission, Washington	Yes	[f]	Yes	No	Yes	No
Florida Railroad and Public Utilities Commission, Tallahassee	Yes	No	Yes[g]	[h]	Yes	No
Georgia Public Service Commission, Atlanta	Yes	No	Yes	No	Yes	No
Hawaii Public Utilities Commission, Honolulu	Yes	No[e]	Yes	Yes	Yes	No
Idaho Public Utilities Commission, Boise	Yes	No	Yes	Yes	Yes	No
Illinois Commerce Commission, Chicago	Yes	No[i]	Yes	Yes	Yes	Yes
Indiana Public Service Commission, Indianapolis	Yes	Yes	Yes	Yes	Yes	Yes
Iowa State Commerce Commission, Des Moines[j]	...	...	...	...	...	No
Kansas State Corporation Commission, Topeka[k]	Yes	No[b]	Yes	Yes	Yes	Yes

Commission	Electricity		Gas	Water	Telephone	Steam
	Privately owned	Publicly owned (municipals and co-operatives)				
Kentucky Public Service Commission, Frankfort	Yes	Yes[l]	Yes	Yes	Yes	No
Louisiana Public Service Commission, Baton Rouge	Yes	No[m]	Yes	Yes	Yes	No
Maine Public Utilities Commission, Augusta	Yes	Yes[n]	Yes	Yes	Yes	Yes
Maryland Public Service Commission, Baltimore	Yes	Yes	Yes	Yes	Yes	Yes
Massachusetts Department of Public Utilities, Boston	Yes	No[o]	Yes	Yes	Yes	No
Michigan Public Service Commission, Lansing	Yes	No[b]	Yes	Yes	Yes	Yes
Minnesota Railroad and Warehouse Commission, St. Paul	No	No	No	No	Yes	No
Mississippi Public Service Commission, Jackson	Yes	No	Yes	Yes	Yes	No
Missouri Public Service Commission, Jefferson City	Yes	No	Yes	Yes	Yes	Yes
Montana Board of Railroad Commissioners, Helena[p]	Yes	Yes[n]	Yes	Yes	Yes	Yes
Nebraska State Railway Commission, Lincoln	No[q]	No[q]	No[r]	Yes	Yes	No
Nevada Public Service Commission, Carson City	Yes	No[s]	Yes	Yes	Yes	No
New Hampshire Public Utilities Commission, Concord	Yes	No[b]	Yes	Yes	Yes	Yes
New Jersey Board of Public Utility Commissioners, Trenton	Yes	No[t]	Yes	Yes	Yes	Yes
New Mexico Public Service Commission, Santa Fe	Yes	No	Yes	Yes	...	Yes
New Mexico State Corporation Commission, Santa Fe	...	...	...	...	Yes	...
New York Public Service Commission, Albany	Yes	Yes[n]	Yes	Yes[u]	Yes	Yes
North Carolina Utilities Commission, Raleigh	Yes	No	Yes	Yes	Yes	No
North Dakota Public Service Commission, Bismarck	Yes	No	Yes	Yes	Yes	Yes
Ohio Public Utilities Commission, Columbus	Yes[v]	No	Yes[v]	Yes	Yes	Yes
Oklahoma Corporation Commission, Oklahoma City	Yes	No	Yes	Yes	Yes	No
Oregon Public Utilities Commissioner, Salem	Yes	No	Yes	Yes	Yes	Yes
Pennsylvania Public Utility Commission, Harrisburg	Yes	No[w]	Yes	Yes	Yes	Yes

Table 15–1. State Regulatory Commission Jurisdiction Over Rates Charged to Ultimate Consumers by Various Utilities in the United States and Territories (*Continued*)

Commission	Electricity		Gas	Water	Telephone	Steam
	Privately owned	Publicly owned (municipals and co-operatives)				
Rhode Island Department of Business Regulation, Providence	Yes	Yes[e]	Yes	Yes	Yes	Yes
South Carolina Public Service Commission, Columbia	Yes	No	Yes	Yes	Yes	No
South Dakota Public Utilities Commission, Pierre	No	No	No	No	Yes	No
Tennessee Public Service Commission, Nashville	Yes	No	Yes	Yes	Yes	No
Texas Railroad Commission, Austin	No	No	Yes	No	No	No
Utah Public Service Commission, Salt Lake City	Yes	No	Yes	Yes	Yes	Yes
Vermont Public Service Board, Montpelier	Yes	No[q]	Yes	Yes	Yes	No
Virginia State Corporation Commission, Richmond	Yes	No[b]	Yes	Yes	Yes	No
Washington Utility and Transportation Commission, Olympia	Yes	No	Yes	Yes	Yes	No
West Virginia Public Service Commission, Charleston	Yes	Yes	Yes	Yes	Yes	No
Wisconsin Public Service Commission, Madison	Yes	Yes[z]	Yes	Yes	Yes	Yes
Wyoming Public Service Commission, Cheyenne	Yes	Yes	Yes	Yes	Yes	Yes
Puerto Rico Public Service Commission, Rio Piedras	[y]	[z]	Yes	No	Yes	No

[a] The Alaska Public Service Commission Act effective May 9, 1959, created a commission. Legislation in 1963 gave Commission jurisdiction over certain utilities, but it is not as yet active (1964).

[b] Cooperatives "yes."

[c] Cities and commission have concurrent jurisdiction over electric and gas rates of privately owned utilities to the extent shown. However,

[d] Except for rates of publicly owned utilities outside corporate limits of municipalities and except for those cooperatively owned utilities which have been granted certificates of public convenience and necessity.

[e] No cooperatives in the state.

[f] No publicly owned utilities or cooperatives.

[g] Except natural gas pipelines selling wholesale only to direct industrial customers.

[h] Only in the counties of Palm Beach, Seminole, Volusia, Broward, Osceola, Orange, and Santa Rosa.

[i] Jurisdiction over cooperatives not asserted.

[j] Effective July 4, 1963, Commission was given jurisdiction over electric, gas, water, and telephone rates. As of August, 1964, it had not yet begun to exercise its authority.

[k] Primary power to regulate utilities operating within a single city rests with the city council, with appeal to the commission of any ordinance of such city setting rates or standards of service. Ten or more taxpayers may also appeal such city ordinances.

[l] Except for rates of municipals inside corporate limits of municipalities.

[m] Full regulatory power over municipals lies in municipal authority unless surrendered to the commission by a public election. Cooperatives "no."

[n] Cooperatives "no."

[o] Except as to rate of return and depreciation practices. No cooperatives in state.

[p] Ex-officio Public Service Commission.

[q] Except that rates outside corporate limits may be considered on application or complaint. Rates of public power districts are not subject to regulation.

[r] Except "yes" when classified as a common carrier.

[s] Except Mineral County Power System. Cooperatives "no."

[t] Except for rates of municipals outside corporate limits of municipalities. Cooperatives "yes."

[u] Except for systems with property value of less than $30,000 and municipal systems.

[v] Primary power to regulate utilities in cities rests with the City Council with appeals to the commission if City Council fails to act.

[w] Except for rates of municipals outside corporate limits.

[x] Cooperatives "no" unless they extend activities to include functions that make them utilities under the statutes.

[y] No privately owned electric utilities.

[z] Except for service rendered by Cayey electric power plant regulated by the commission, all electric service is supplied through water resources authority over which the commission has no jurisdiction.

Source: *State Commission Jurisdiction and Regulation of Electric and Gas Utilities*, Federal Power Commission Publication FPC S-147, 1960. Somewhat less comprehensive data are published annually in the Special Features Section of *Moody's Public Utility Manual*, Moody's Investors Service, New York. The information in the table has been brought up-to-date to the extent possible by comparison with the tabulation in *Moody's* for 1964.

large new customer, involve several times the amount of service cur rently rendered.

2. Type of service
   a. Metered service is commonly the only type available for busines use in large centers.
   b. Flat-rate service, formerly widely used, is gradually being displaced
3. Type of incoming facility
   a. Number of lines needed (telephone company studies will assist ir this determination).
   b. Switching arrangements. The companies have complete informa tion on the circumstances under which manual, automatic, in-dial ing, or other types of facilities are best and most economical.
   c. Off-premise extensions requiring mileage payments for lines to : distant station, compared with payment for message units or tol calls.
   d. Special arrangements such as conference facilities, autocall, publi address systems, wide-area toll service and data transmission.

Steam

1. General. Steam for building heating and process work is available fron utilities in many of the larger communities, particularly where stean electric generating plants are located near the cities. In most cases lines will not be extended to serve new customers, and in some in stances service is restricted to present customers alone.
2. Escalation. The rate for steam is usually varied with the cost of fue burned to make it.
3. Quality of steam. If process use makes a particular dryness or tempera ture of the steam important, special equipment may be needed.
4. Pressure. Since most steam supply systems are primarily for heating the delivery pressure is likely to be low. This may militate against it use for certain industrial or commercial applications.

References

For details of the rates available, contact should first be made with the utilit (gas, electric, water, telephone, steam) supplying the area where service is desire If questions arise, they may be referred to the state regulatory body (names an locations given in Table 15–1).

BIBLIOGRAPHY

Pages of this section on major considerations involved in the procuremer of the more prominent types of commodities are replete with selected reference Additional ones can be located in other sections of this handbook, particularl Section 26, "Library and Catalog File," and Section 28, "Appendix."

SECTION 16

CONSIDERATIONS IN NONREPETITIVE MAJOR PURCHASES

Editor

H. R. Michel, Director of Purchases, Celanese Corporation of America, Charlotte, North Carolina

Associate Editors

C. D. Jones, Director of Purchasing, Diamond Alkali Company, Cleveland, Ohio

E. M. Krech, Director of Purchases, J. M. Huber Corporation, Hillside, New Jersey

The purpose of this section is to present and discuss collectively some of the problems and considerations involved in nonrepetitive major purchases, namely, purchases of major capital equipment and construction certain phases of which are discussed in other parts of this handbook While it is hoped that this section may serve as a useful reference to any one in the purchasing field, it is directed particularly to the purchasing agent or department that is called upon only infrequently to undertake procurement of this nature.

HOW DIFFERENT FROM OTHER TYPES OF PURCHASING

Much plant or company purchasing is routine and repetitive, even though it may include a variety of capital equipment purchases, from typewriters to power-plant pumps. This section deals with those items of capital equipment which are not usually manufactured repetitively but are especially fabricated to a particular design and which involve special drawings, specifications, or engineering data. The procurement of such items often entails a relatively large expenditure.

This section deals also with construction, which may involve anything from a complete new plant or building, through a major or minor alteration, to relatively small maintenance jobs. If materials are involved and labor is furnished by an outside party who exercises supervision as an independent contractor and comes upon the company's property to perform the work, it is construction, for the purposes of this section.

Special Considerations in Purchasing

From the purchasing standpoint, there are certain common considerations in buying both major capital equipment and construction. First of all, there may be less familiarity or experience with the particular item r class of work due to the fact that it is special or infrequent. Second, he transaction may involve engineering features which are new or complex and which in any event will be controlling. The inquiry or invitaion to bid, the designation of bidders, the terms of the purchase (whether ontained in a purchase order form or special contract form), and the valuation of bids will all involve special engineering factors and unusual urchasing features which demand the closest kind of cooperation beween the engineering and purchasing departments. These factors are iscussed to some extent in the paragraphs immediately following, but re gone into at greater length later on in the two main subdivisions on najor capital equipment and construction.

Preparation of Terms of Inquiry. In the equipment purchase, the basis f the inquiry will be the request issued by technical or engineering peronnel. The inquiry should cover, however, such additional information s may have been developed from conferences between such personnel nd the buyer, in which the description and characteristics of the desired najor equipment were further elaborated upon. In addition, the inquiry hould request the usual quotation of price, f.o.b. point, terms of paynent, shipping date, warranties, and inspection.

Where construction on a fixed-price basis is involved, it too can be nitiated by a form of inquiry, in which the description of the work and eferences to drawings and specifications should be set forth. Whether the ommitment is to be made by means of a special form of contract or by he usual purchase order form, the most important items to be covered in the inquiry are price and completion date, since the qualifications and uitability of workmanship of the bidders should have been considered nd found acceptable before they were invited to bid. Payment and other erms are more or less standardized.

Bidders to Be Considered. In their requisitions or otherwise, technical personnel sometimes recommend a vendor or contractor. Now and then they even recommend that only a particular vendor be considered. It is then the duty of the buyer to consult with them as to the reasons for such recommendations. In the absence of special circumstances (since competitive bids are to be preferred) it is incumbent upon the buyer to determine whether the recommended course is to be followed.

Sometimes in the course of designing or selecting special equipment, technical personnel must spend considerable time in consultation and collaboration with a vendor's technical people, the result of which may be a specially worked-out arrangement. There is rarely any competition obtainable in such cases without having the whole thing done over with another vendor, which is generally impractical. To ensure that purchasing interests receive proper consideration, no formal technical or engineering work should be done until an agreement has been reached on the selection of the vendor. The sole bidder is then dealt with on a negotiated basis, and the buyer should see that the terms of the purchase are made as favorable as possible.

Evaluation of Bids. Suppliers' proposals covering major equipment should be checked against the requisition and each analyzed and compared. Omissions or deviations from the specification should be noted. The proposals should be submitted to and discussed with the technical source. After joint evaluation of the proposals has been completed and agreement reached on the selection of the vendor, the buyer is then in a position to issue the purchase order, or in those cases where the vendor insists, arrange for the execution of a formal agreemeent.

In purchasing construction on a lump-sum or fixed-price basis, the comparison of bids should be made by purchasing and then submitted to and discussed with engineering. Where contractors have been requested to bid on alternates as to part of the work or where additions and changes have been made in the original invitation to bid, these should be carefully analyzed and compared by the buyer in order for him to arrive at the proper final figure.

In cost-plus-fee construction work which is bid or negotiated on incomplete drawings and specifications, the ultimate evaluation of the proposal should be based upon the comparison of the owner's estimate of cost with the contractor's estimate. Engineering necessarily plays the big role here. The fee, however, is a matter that comes well within the province of purchasing. Whether the fee is fixed in dollars or as a percentage, it will be based in either case on some estimate of cost made by the contractor. It can be compared with fees agreed to in previous jobs of similar type or with the current offerings of other contractors whether invited to bid or not. More about this subject will be found in the part of this section on "How to Buy Construction."

Preparation of Purchase Order or Contract. The decision having been made as to the vendor or contractor to be awarded the work, the next and final step of reducing the terms of the agreement to writing, either in a purchase order or contract, falls upon the purchasing agent. He now knows what his technical personnel's complete requirements are and what they will accept, and he is familiar with the terms and conditions upon which the vendor or contractor will agree to undertake the work. It is up to the buyer, then, to prepare a document that will fully embrace the agreement and provide the necessary protection for both parties.

Many of the terms of the purchase order that should be considered in the purchase of major capital equipment are discussed in "How to Buy Major Capital Equipment," the main subdivision of this section which immediately follows. The terms of the contract for the purchase of construction are covered in some detail in the third main subdivision of this section. Therefore, reference should be made to these sections.

Some special attention should be given at this point to the terms of a purchase order that may be used to cover small construction work, such as building or plant alterations or additions, repaving of roadways, painting, reroofing, and equipment repairs and maintenance services of a somewhat substantial nature. The agreement can be set up in a regular purchase order form, with proper consideration being given, however, to special terms that apply beyond those that normally are used in the purchase of equipment or materials.

The purchase order[1] should describe the scope of the work as definitely as possible and the price limits of the work should be established. If the work is let for a lump sum or fixed price, then that is the only figure that need be shown. If the work is let on a cost basis plus a fixed fee or percentage, the price of the material can be covered in the order by a statement to that effect, or by actually showing the cost prices and the amount of the markup. The price of the labor involved should be spelled out similarly, for example, cost plus a percentage for overhead plus a percentage for profit. The total price of the order could be shown as "To be determined." The determination of final price requires verification by engineering of the amount of materials and labor supplied.

If the job involves excavation, as in the case of water or sewer lines, the contractor may quote such work at a unit price per lineal foot or, where rock excavation may be encountered, at a unit price per cubic yard. These prices should be included in the terms of the order.

The buyer should also include in the order such general terms dealing with construction work as may be applicable to the particular job. These would cover subcontracting, title to materials, indemnity, termination, etc. At the end of this section are typical or suggested terms[2] (that may be typed or printed) which could be used in the average case. The order can be written to include these terms by reference by using a statement such as "The additional terms and conditions set forth in form (identify by name, date or number) attached hereto, are hereby made a part of this order" or the terms of this form can be typed in the body of the purchase order itself with equal effect. However, the buyer should make certain the terms of this form are adequate for the case at hand.

Consideration must be given also to insurance requirements, which are no less important in small construction jobs than in large. The risks should be evaluated by the engineering department acting in conjunction

[1] Also see Sections 4 and 5.

[2] See Exhibit 16–4 at end of this section.

with the insurance department. Purchasing should see that proper consideration is given to insurance and that the insurance requirements are set forth in the order and complied with promptly by the contractor. Insurance is discussed further in the subdivision of this section dealing with construction.

HOW TO BUY MAJOR CAPITAL EQUIPMENT

This subdivision deals with the purchase of major capital equipment only. Though the discussion is pointed to direct purchases, it could apply equally to purchases under a construction contract through a contractor where the owner's approval is required for such purchases.

New Equipment versus Used

As a fundamental principle new equipment is to be preferred over used equipment. However, there are situations where delivery or cost is of such vital importance that used equipment, if available, must be bought.

Sources of Used Equipment. The sources of used equipment are many. When a manufacturing business is discontinued, assets usually are liquidated and equipment is offered for sale. Nearly all operating companies have stand-by and surplus equipment which is put on the market for sale from time to time. Upon the completion of large construction jobs, large surpluses of equipment often result. Government agencies are continually offering surplus equipment for sale. There are also many reputable dealers and brokers engaged in the sale of used equipment. (The farsighted buyer accumulates a special file on their names and addresses.) In all these cases, whether the equipment has ever been put into service or not, it is assumed that the equipment is sold as used and not new. It must be remembered, however, that at best, the availability of used equipment is unpredictable and relatively restricted.

Condition of Used Equipment. Used equipment is often sold on an "as is, where is" basis. For the most part, no warranty or guarantee of any kind is given and the purchaser buys at his peril. It is, therefore, incumbent on the buyer to make a thorough inspection of the equipment beforehand. Even if he does that, it is unlikely that he will be able to see it in operation to test all its moving parts. Moreover, the machine may have a latent defect not observable on inspection, which could cause an early breakdown and costly repairs, all of which the purchaser usually would have to bear without recourse to the seller. New equipment on the other hand is almost always warranted by the manufacturer against defects in material and workmanship.

Miscellaneous Terms of Sale. Used equipment, while sometimes sold on terms of deferred payment, most commonly is transferred on a cash basis only. The dismantling, crating, loading, transporting, unloading, uncrating, reassembling, mounting, leveling, and aligning of the equipment usually are all the responsibility of the purchaser. The services of the equipment manufacturer's engineer in supervising installation or initial operation of used equipment usually are not obtainable.

Delivery and Price. The decision to purchase used equipment usually is based upon considerations of price or delivery or both. The manufacture or fabrication of a particular new piece of equipment may take weeks or months. Where it is obtainable in the used equipment field, it is available at once for immediate use. Again, the cost of new equipment may be high, even prohibitive in some circumstances, whereas used equipment may be priced much lower. The purchase of used equipment in a given case may make possible the early start-up of a new manufacturing operation or the resumption of one that has been discontinued due to equipment failure.

Lease versus Purchase

There are occasions when the buyer has to decide if he should lease or buy an item of major equipment. It may arise because of a number of considerations, such as availability of funds, length of time the equipment is to be used, or the necessity of having to obtain equipment for immediate use where the purchase of equipment would entail an extended delivery period. Also there are those instances where the equipment may be obtainable only on lease.

Some of the more important economic considerations of leasing versus purchasing major equipment are given below:

Lease

1. It may be more economical to lease where the equipment is needed for a temporary period of relatively short duration.
2. Where the suitability of the equipment for a particular purpose is uncertain, the expense of a purchase is saved in the event the equipment is not found acceptable.
3. When a new or improved design is imminent, leasing of an older type in the interim would avoid the purchase of a less efficient piece of equipment.

Purchase

1. Since most leases are for definite terms or are terminable on some short period of notice, there is a danger that the leased equipment will be recaptured, resulting in depriving the lessee of a needed facility.
2. In a purchase either the equipment is sold at a delivered price or the transportation costs are paid but one way, from manufacturer's plant to purchaser's. In a lease the lessee pays transportation expense both ways, from lessor's location to les-

Lease	*Purchase*
4. On an occasion when the purchase price exceeds the amount of appropriated or available funds, leasing permits a production operation to start or to continue.	see's and return. In addition, dismantling and loading costs are also paid by lessee.
5. The rent is an item of expense, and usually may be treated so for tax purposes.	3. The purchase price represents a capital investment which must be depreciated over a period of years.

Terms of Lease Agreement. Most equipment-renting companies have their own forms of rental agreement. While there is considerable variation in them, the basic terms are essentially the same. There are a few special points to look out for in such agreements which are highly advantageous to lessee.

Option to Purchase. Whenever possible the lessee of rented equipment should obtain the right to purchase it outright. The sales price should be set forth in the agreement. Not infrequently the lessor will also agree to apply the rental paid under the lease toward the purchase price when the option to purchase is exercised by the lessee.

In leasing equipment with an option to purchase, it is important to remember that there is a possible tax pitfall involved which could result in the loss of the deduction for rental payments as a business expense, assuming the latter is desired. The Internal Revenue Service might determine that the transaction is not actually a true lease but is intended to transfer ownership of or an equity in the equipment to the lessee, thus making it, in effect, a conditional sale of the equipment. In that case it would disallow ordinary deductions for rental payments and would require the equipment to be treated as a capital asset and depreciated over its life.

If the lease provisions are conventional, fixing the rental payments on an hourly, daily, or weekly basis or on the basis of mileage operated or units produced, and if the price at which the equipment can be purchased is fixed in advance at a sum which will approximate the fair market value of the equipment at the time the option is exercised, the likelihood is that the rental would be allowed as a business expense.

In any event the buyer should scrutinize such transactions and in case of any doubt should consult legal or tax counsel to assure himself of the legality of this feature of the lease.

Maintenance Provisions. The rental agreement usually will provide that the equipment is to be returned to the lessor at the end of the rental period in the same condition as it was in at the time it was rented, less reasonable wear and tear. In most agreements ordinary repairs are the responsibility of the lessee. However, some agreements provide that the lessor will keep the equipment in good working order, in which case the rental price includes an amount to cover the cost of repairs. Where a latent defect arises which could not be observed at the time the rental started, the cost of repairing should be borne by the lessor and the agreement should so provide.

Check of Rates. Rental rates vary from one location to another. It is not too difficult to check rates by getting prices from competitors. The Associated Equipment Dealers can be consulted as an outside source in checking rental rates.

A word might be said here about overtime rates, especially in connection with the rental of construction equipment. A basic rental period should be stipulated, such as a 40-hr week, and a formula of some kind should be agreed upon in relation to overtime use. In the absence of such provisions, overtime charges can be burdensome.

Considerations in Purchasing

In the purchase of major capital equipment, considerations vary with the type of equipment being bought. Design drawings and specifications are almost always a prime element in the purchase. These should be referred to and identified in the purchase order and made a part of it. The usual description should be set forth along with shipping date, f.o.b. point, price and payment terms, and performance or other guarantees wherever applicable.

Common Types of Equipment. It may be helpful to deal with some of the principal types of major capital equipment separately so that features peculiar to each can be better discussed.

Structural steel, vessels, power generating units, piping, and insulation have been selected because they are typical and essential equipment in most manufacturing and industrial plants. The purchasing considerations involved are therefore of more common interest and application and the discussion of them should be of assistance in buying other major industrial equipment.

Structural Steel. The vendor usually is furnished with a plot plan, foundation plan and details, framing plan, erection sections, miscellaneous steel details, and platform details. The order should call for the vendor to furnish, fabricate, and (if erection is included) erect all structural steel shown in the drawings and specifications, which should be made part of the order by reference. The order should state that where there is a variation between the specifications and drawings, the specifications control. Specific reference should be made to column anchor bolts, setting plates, and shims which are usually furnished by the steel fabricator but installed by the foundation contractor. Where miscellaneous steel, such as stairs, is not to form part of the erection services, it should be specifically excluded in the terms of the order.

The time for the vendor to prepare and submit setting plans and detail drawings for approval should be stated, as well as the period during which the steel is to be delivered. The time for erection to commence and be completed should be shown. These schedules are usually made subject to change due to delays caused by inclement weather and last-minute changes that lead to complications involving field fabrications.

Riveting, bolting, and welding should be covered by a special reference as to what is required in any particular part of the work. Where the method to be used is optional, it should be so stated. General code references may be made in the order even though they appear in the drawings, as for example, reference to the code for welding in building construction as adopted by the American Welding Society in its "Welding Handbook," or to the specifications of the American Institute of Steel Construction as to steel fabrication and erection, or that the steel furnished shall conform with ASTM standards for structural steel buildings.

Painting requirements should be made part of the order. It is customary to require one shop coat of metal primer of rust-inhibitive paint. In this connection it is very important to specify in detail the method of preparing the metal for painting. The method of cleaning, such as wire brushing and chipping to remove all loose scale and pickling or sand blasting, should be indicated. In special circumstances where the expense is warranted, it can be provided that "all steel shall be cleaned to bright metal."

The tonnage of the steel is the big factor in establishing price, because the fabricator usually has worked out a unit tonnage price for all material and labor. When erection is included, the price of the order should state separately the figure for the fabricated steel and that for the erection cost. In many states only the cost of the steel itself is subject to sales or use tax.

Towers, Vessels, and Heat Exchangers. Equipment of this kind is usually of special design and is tailor-made. Whether the process is the purchaser's own or that of an outside engineering firm, it calls most often for equipment peculiar to that process. The fabricator therefore may be called upon to bid on design drawings and specifications furnished by the purchaser. On the other hand, he may be asked to bid on performance specifications. In the latter case the vendor is given definite processing information on materials involved, quantities, rates, temperatures, pressures, etc., and then is asked to design the equipment and to warrant that it will perform the service and produce the results required by the purchaser.

In most cases the vendor is called upon to prepare detailed drawings for submission to and approval by the purchaser before any fabrication is started. After the drawings have been approved by the purchaser, certified prints are made up by the vendor and sent to the purchaser. When finally fabricated, the equipment must be in strict accordance therewith.

The purchase order should include in the description the size and type of material for the shell, heads, nozzles, and supports. If the vessel is to be made to conform to a code such as the ASME code or API–ASME code, this should be stated. In the code provisions, such things as the qualifications of welders, type of welding, periodic inspections, hydrostatic tests, and stress relieving are set forth. Where the equipment is made of alloy metal or is going into critical service, a request should be made in the order for mill test reports covering the physical and chemical properties of the metal from which it is made. An outline sketch is often required from the vendor showing the location of each heat of the metals used. If a code vessel is purchased, it should be so stamped by the fabricator and a pencil rubbing of the name plate sent to the buyer. It might be well to point out here that despite the protection the purchaser gets from code provisions, this in itself does not ensure that the equipment will necessarily be efficient or of the proper materials for the service.

Power Generating Units. The purchase of a steam generator or turbogenerator is a complex and involved transaction. Such equipment is usually purchased on the basis of specifications and a guarantee of performance and efficiency.

It may be helpful to the purchasing agent to consider steam generating units from the standpoint of the many component parts that make them up. A large capacity unit for the most part will be made up of boiler, tubes, superheater, preheater, burners, soot blowers, steel casing, safety and vent valves, feedwater regulators, fans, structural steel, firebrick, and insulation materials.

The over-all capacity of the unit is the basic criterion; but efficiency also is critical, and it depends largely on the components. The type of burners or soot blowers designated by the vendor, for instance, may not be the most desirable kind in that they would not be equal to those made by manufacturing specialists in this field. The quotation could be questioned on this point. The amount of insulation specified in one bid may be less than the amount in another. The horsepower and overload characteristics of the motors should be compared. The make of fans might be checked. If the fuel is coal, the comparative cost of disposing of waste, such as fly ash, should not be overlooked. All points of this kind that come to the buyer's mind when analyzing and evaluating the quotations should be discussed with his technical or engineering people. Unless each item is gone into thoroughly and the specifications clearly established, it will be difficult to hold the vendor to either a firm price or definite delivery. For every change or subsequent "clarification" there may be a revision in price or deferment of delivery.

It should be pointed out here too that some manufacturers have more or less standard size units. If a 70,000-lb per hour steam generating unit is required, one manufacturer may make this size regularly whereas the nearest the next bidder may come to it may be a 90,000-lb unit. In the latter case the bid would reflect the difference in initial cost. The operating expense of the larger unit would be greater. There is room here for the buyer to do some shopping.

Steam generating units are made to ASME code specifications. This is necessary for insurance purposes and to satisfy state or municipal regulations. However, as was pointed out above, the code provisions exist chiefly for safety reasons and are not concerned with efficiency of operation. Hence, while the unit may pass the test of the code, it still could be something short of what is desired in power plant performance.

Turbogenerator units as a source of power are more a package type of purchase. If it is a condensing unit, the buyer should check thoroughly with his technical people concerning the adequacy of the size of the condenser. If it is undersized for the operation, it means more water has to be used. In a year's operation this can amount to many thousands of dollars in expense. The type of governor used is also a big factor. If it is of inadequate design or becomes defective in use, the turbine may fail or even break up. Static and dynamic balancing are of extreme importance. If these are not satisfactorily developed in preoperation tests, trouble lies ahead. The buyer might consider the size and type of construction of the casing and the effect on balancing of stresses set up in the casing by the steam lines attached to the unit. Some manufacturers normally design stronger casings that avoid this problem, without any appreciable increase in cost.

In all power generating equipment the buyer should insist that installation and initial operation of the unit be supervised by the vendor. Unless this is done, the manufacturer may fairly claim that the reason guarantees are not being met is that the equipment was not properly installed. The cost of the services of the vendor's engineer can be arranged for on a per diem basis plus reimbursement of his reasonable traveling and living expenses. It is well worth the expenditure because in no other way can the buyer be sure that the equipment manufacturer can be held to his warranties of performance. Insurance coverage for the vendor's engineer in the complete course of his performance should be provided for.

Piping. There are several types of piping from the service standpoint that are used in the operation of a plant, such as sewer, water, steam, and process piping. Where the type of service requires the use of prefabricated piping, a complicated procurement problem sometimes arises. The usual arrangement is to purchase the pipe in fully fabricated form, bent, welded, and fitted as required. The vendor, in such a case, obtains his own mill form pipe, fittings, and other materials. However, it is not uncommon to agree that part or all of the material may be procured and furnished by the purchaser, in which instances the vendor is paid for the fabrication work only. In some cases, part of the work may have to be done in the field instead of in the shop, which might call for some special terms to be arranged. Where drawings are complete enough, the purchase of prefabricated pipe can be made on a competitive lump-sum basis. It is also possible to use a combination arrangement of fixed price and unit price.

In many cases involving extensive new pipe installations where it is not practical to have all the drawing information available, the work must be let and started on a material cost plus a fabrication charge basis. Although this practice is often necessary, it should be pointed out that the measuring, counting, checking, and accounting may be quite expensive. Consequently, even where drawings are not immediately available, there may be cases where a fixed-fee arrangement can be worked out. In such instances, it would be advantageous for the buyer to do so. Where elevation drawings or bills of material may not be available and the work proceeds on a cost-plus basis, the final price of the order then must await completion of the work. The material prices per hundred lineal feet for the size and pipe schedule of the particular pipe involved are set forth in a schedule submitted by the vendor. The price is graduated downward as the quantity of the one size increases. Labor is charged for on a fabrication or welding schedule unit price, based on pipe size and service pressure rating. These schedules should be made part of the order by reference.

Drawings in this type of transaction are released to the vendor as they are completed. He in turn usually makes his own shop drawings from these. Since the fabrication cost will depend upon the number of welds, it is well to make some provision to guard against unnecessary welds being made. Short lengths of pipe might well be discarded, rather than used at the expense of additional welding costs, and an agreement on this point reached beforehand; or an inspector may be used in the shop to approve the welds in shop sketches before the work is done. The checking of invoices in this kind of purchase is complicated. The vendor should be required to show separately in his invoices the price of fittings, valves, and other pipe accessories, as well as the price, type, and quantity of welds, and he should also be required to attach a marked-up sketch of each fabrication.

Insulation. The purchase of insulation material and services for its installation also usually makes for an involved transaction. The work may include insulation of process and service piping, tanks, vessels, heat exchangers, ducting, and a host of other equipment. It is often possible to purchase insulation work on a fixed-price basis, which should be done whenever definite information is available. Otherwise the cost of necessary material may be paid for in accordance with an agreed upon price list of actual cost. The cost of services then would involve reimbursement of the wages of the vendor's employees on the job and the payment of a fee covering overhead and profit. Sometimes the work may be paid for on a unit-cost basis according to a price schedule based on square footage for various thicknesses and finishes.

Drawings and specifications are furnished the vendor and he is required to supply and install the materials as called for therein. Checking of invoices in this type of work is as difficult as in the case of prefabricated pipe. A procedure should be established for proper documents to be furnished by the vendor similar to the procedure recommended for piping.

Other Types of Equipment. The major equipment field is both broad and varied and includes anything from an electric motor to a major distributing system; from a pump to a large process installation; from a drill press to a complex manufacturing facility. In many cases a standard, commercially manufactured item will be available to satisfy requirements. In other cases, some special or peculiar purchasing considerations may be involved. It would serve little purpose to go into such special features even if space were not limited, since it is believed that the considerations discussed in the foregoing selected examples will be of assistance in the purchase of most types of major capital equipment.

Performance Guarantees. Regardless of the type of equipment, it is well to remember that the fundamental method of purchasing by performance specifications and guarantee often can be employed and should be employed whenever possible.

For the purchase of less complicated machinery and equipment where a statement of definite capacities, ratings, or speeds of operation can be made, a performance guarantee such as the following can be used:

> Vendor guarantees that the equipment supplied hereunder will be capable of the performance set forth in the specifications referred to herein, and agrees to make such changes, adjustments, or replacements as are necessary to meet the guarantee, at no cost to the purchaser.

In the unusual case where more complex machinery and equipment is to be purchased with the requirement that it perform to fit a particular purpose and assure a specified quantity or quality of product, a special performance guarantee should be used. In such cases, engineering and purchasing should collaborate on having the vendor agree beforehand to a performance guarantee providing for the definite results desired and the manner of testing and determining whether the results have been attained. The following is an example of such a performance guarantee:

> The vendor guarantees that the complete equipment sold hereunder will produce at least ________ per hour of finished product ________ from ________ components, the properties and characteristics of each component and each finished product being set forth below. To determine if the complete equipment meets this guarantee, the vendor will submit it to a continuous test of ________ hours and a minimum of ________ samples of said finished product shall be taken at approximately equal intervals and analyzed to determine whether the properties or characteristics of the finished product are as set forth below. If the equipment does not meet said performance guarantee, the vendor agrees to revise, replace, or recondition the equipment in a manner calculated by the vendor to correct the unsatisfactory performance, at the vendor's own expense. Upon completion thereof, the equipment shall again be subjected to a further continuous test of a minimum of ________ hours during which a minimum of ________ samples of said finished product shall be taken at approximately equal intervals and analyzed to determine whether the properties or characteristics of the finished product are as set forth below. Only when the equipment shall meet the full performance requirements shall it be deemed acceptable to the purchaser. If after a reasonable time the equipment has failed to meet the full performance guarantees, then, upon the request of the purchaser, the vendor agrees to dismantle and remove all the equipment at the vendor's own expense and to refund to the purchaser the purchase price paid.

Special Terms for the Purchase Order. Aside from reference to drawings, specifications, codes, texts, and test reports, which should be made as found necessary with respect to particular types of equipment, there are some other points that are worth attention in preparing the purchase order. They include references to payment for the equipment, approval of drawings, etc., wording of the proposal, inspection and expediting conditions, and installation and initial operating services.

Reference to Payment. It is customary in the purchase of major equipment to provide for a withholding of part of the purchase price (usually 10 per cent) until installation has been completed and the equipment properly tested and finally accepted. The payment terms of the purchase order should specifically provide for such retention.

Reference to Drawings, etc. The type and number of drawings that purchaser requires should be set forth in the purchase order. A statement should appear to the effect that fabrication of the equipment is not to start until the drawings have been approved by purchaser. After they have been approved, with or without changes or revisions, the vendor should be called upon to supply certified copies of the finally approved drawings, so that there can be no mistake thereafter as to the full nature and description of the equipment that the purchaser requires or that vendor agrees to furnish.

Reference to Proposal. It is customary to refer to the vendor's proposal or quotation in the order, identifying it by date or number or both. The wording of this reference clause is important because there may be general provisions of the quotation that are objectionable.

Expressions such as "all in accordance with your proposal of ______" or "all the terms and conditions of your proposal of ______ are made a part of this order" will usually incorporate all the terms of the proposal whether objectionable or not. Where the proposal is short, all the acceptable terms can be typed in the order, and an identifying clause such as "refer to your proposal of ______" can be used without too much danger of incorporating unacceptable clauses into the order. Of course, where the proposal contains no objectionable provisions, a simple statement of acceptance can be incorporated into the order.

Where the proposal contains unfavorable provisions or long and involved descriptions of equipment and performance which cannot be typed readily in the order, something along the following lines could be used:

> All material and equipment furnished to us shall comply in all respects with the physical description, specifications, performance characteristics, and warranties contained in your proposal ______, but no other terms and conditions of your proposal shall be a part of this agreement.

The foregoing is all based on the fact that the average purchase order issued in business today is an offer to buy and is subject to the vendor's acceptance.

In those instances where the vendor insists on having a formal proposal executed by both parties, the objectionable terms must be made a matter of negotiation, after which the changes agreed upon can be made in the proposal before signing.

Inspection and Expediting. Vendors usually agree without question to the right of the purchaser to inspect major equipment. This includes inspection as the fabrication work progresses as well as final inspection before acceptance. Where the right of inspection is desired, the order should so provide and the vendor should be required to agree not to ship until inspection has been made or waived.

Before an order for major equipment is placed, the supply situation on materials and component parts should be reviewed carefully with the vendor and the final shipping date agreed upon after due regard for the realities of the supply situation. Arrangements should be made for periodic progress reports to be prepared by the vendor and sent to the purchaser. An understanding should be reached ensuring that buyer will be advised promptly of any developments likely to affect delivery. The necessary provisions to this effect should be written into the order.

The extent to which the purchaser must actively participate in solving a supply problem affecting delivery of equipment he has on order depends on the circumstances of each case. The vendor's willingness and ability to handle the situation adequately are the important factors. A purchaser should be free to take any action necessary to help himself and yet avoid doing expediting work the vendor has contracted to do.

In following up and expediting the fabrication and delivery of some types of major capital equipment, it is not uncommon to request the vendor to send the purchaser copies of his orders (prices deleted) for mill materials and component parts. This is largely for the purpose of enabling a purchaser to expedite materials from the seller's subvendors where the purchaser feels such action is necessary.

Some vendors will agree to this readily, while others will refuse. Although the purchaser has no motive in the expediting of his suppliers' subvendors' materials other than to be of assistance, the purchaser must recognize the reason why some sellers refuse to furnish information regarding their specific supply problems. For example, if a manufacturer of large generators with dozens of shaft forgings on order permitted his customers to expedite deliveries of this item from his subvendors, it would upset his whole production schedule. On the other hand, an equipment manufacturer who had only one shaft on order for a customer's special order would have nothing to lose by his customer trying to improve delivery from the subvendor.

Installation and Initial Operating Services. The supplier of major equipment frequently offers to supervise installation or initial operation. The offer is usually made on the basis of the purchaser's paying the vendor's engineer assigned to the work a stipulated per diem fee plus all reasonable transportation and living expenses. Such offers are customarily accepted by the purchaser (though the practice varies depending on the type of equipment) to expedite start-up, to minimize difficulties connected therewith, and to avoid any conflict of responsibility which might affect vendor's performance guarantees. The purchase order for the equipment should provide that the services will be rendered upon the request of buyer and should set forth the terms of reimbursement. The order should also provide for the vendor to furnish the required number of copies of operating instructions. Where a vendor's practice is to issue a guarantee of the equipment after installation is completed and by a separate document, the buyer should make certain he obtains it for protection against future trouble.

Selection of Vendor. The general rule should be that vendors are to be selected on the basis of competitive bids. Bids should be requested only from suppliers who are qualified by competence and experience to furnish the required equipment. When only one source of supply exists or when for other reasons peculiar to the transaction only one vendor may be dealt with, a negotiated purchase is then in order.

Further considerations of this question appear in the first and third subdivisions of this section, to which reference should be made.

HOW TO BUY CONSTRUCTION

In purchasing construction there are several factors that must be considered before any final decision should be made. The scope and nature of the services required must be determined. Thought should be given to the current material and labor situation as well as to other aspects of the existing circumstances. The type of contract must be selected after weighing the relative advantages and disadvantages of each. A detailed consideration of these factors appears below.

Types of Services Involved

In terms of the kind of services to be rendered, there are four general classes of construction contracts.

Engineering. In the construction of a new facility, a contract covering the engineering only is frequently entered into.[3] The purchasing and actual construction are done by the owner or by others.

Engineering and Purchasing. This type of contract, which is less common than one for engineering only, provides for the one contractor to do both the engineering and purchasing. The actual construction is done by the owner or by others.

[3] See Exhibit 16–5 at the end of this section.

Construction. This contract covers the actual construction and erection of a facility. The engineering and purchasing are done by the owner or by others.

Engineering, Purchasing, and Construction. This type of contract provides that one contractor do all the engineering, purchasing, and construction of the facility. It is a package arrangement that dispenses with the need for the owner to employ any other contractors.

Some Factors to Be Considered in Selection of Type of Services

The considerations described here are those most susceptible to variation. What may be true one year or at one particular location may not be true for another year or place.

Material Situation. Contractors, because of their past purchasing volume and long experience with mills and suppliers, often can secure better delivery or price on certain materials and equipment than can the owner. For example, when steel is in short supply, the contractor may be in the advantageous position of having an adequate inventory of his own or of maintaining an open tonnage at a mill which can be converted by order to the requirements of a particular job. Blanket orders may be maintained by the contractor on motor manufacturers, etc., under which the owner's requirements can be met adequately. This factor should be considered in deciding whether the contractor is to be given the purchasing to do.

On the other hand, it may be that the owner has large surpluses of material and equipment available for use in the job so that there is no need for depending on the contractor's sources of supply.

Labor Situation. An owner who is otherwise capable of acting as his own general contractor may find that the market for skilled and unskilled labor is tight. The contractor may be far less affected by this condition because he may have a good number of men already on his staff and greater experience in recruiting may enable him to secure additional workers more readily than could the owner. Similarly, the question of adequate personnel also may affect the decision as to who will do the engineering and the purchasing. If the owner has to increase his staff to handle the increase in engineering and purchasing services required by the construction project, he may find it difficult to do so.

Engineering and Purchasing Situation. The design or process may be a matter of the specialized knowledge of the contractor, or may be under patent or license, and therefore obtainable only from that particular contractor who then must do the engineering. If the design or process is special, the contractor would have greater knowledge of and experience with the sources of supply and thus probably would be better able to do the purchasing as well.

In cases where the design or process cannot be divulged to third parties, the owner may decide to do the engineering himself, although, as an alternative, he might let the engineering out after requiring the contractor to enter into a secrecy agreement.

The size of the job often is controlling in determining who will do the engineering or purchasing best. Many operating companies are staffed to engineer and purchase for production, maintenance, and minor capital improvements only. In such cases engineering and purchasing almost without question would be given to the contractor. In other organizations which may be set up to handle some construction, the size of the job might well be beyond the ability of the staff to execute. It might be possible to increase the staff, but due to the infrequency of large capital expansions this would result in a subsequent reduction in and discharge of personnel. The preferred course of action in such cases would appear to be to contract for the engineering and purchasing.

Time Requirements. Where the contractor is capable of doing a first-class job in all three fields of engineering, purchasing, and construction, this is by far the best contract from the standpoint of time alone. The contractor who has prepared the plans, drawings, and specifications is already familiar with the material and equipment required and can proceed with the purchasing with a minimum loss of time. The field construction program and organization likewise can be set up to move more smoothly and rapidly.

For similar reasons, contracts for engineering and purchasing where actual construction is done by the owner or others are preferred next. There is a factor here too that works in favor of the job progressing faster.

As to the construction work itself, contractors, being specialists in their field, usually can do the job far faster than owners. Most operating companies do not maintain construction departments with the high-cost personnel and equipment that necessarily are involved. Even where an owner is capable of acting as his own general contractor by having almost all the construction work done by subcontractors, it is questionable whether time is on his side, regardless of how much he keeps on top of the job.

Economics of Operations. The owner's decision to launch upon a construction project is usually based upon improving or expanding his facilities. It may stem from the need to increase volume or efficiency and to lower production costs or to produce a new product. In any event the owner must weigh the financial income from the new production against the total cost of the enterprise. Where his competitive position in the market is dependent on the speed with which he gets into production or where the loss of potential sales of the new product during the construction period is of considerable proportions, the owner may be willing to expend more funds on the construction work that he would otherwise. He may contract more or all of the work and even pay the contractor a premium, to the end that the project be completed in the shortest possible time.

Supervisory Aspects. A decidedly advantageous feature of having construction work done under contract is the supervision that is provided by the contractor. It relieves the owner of this big responsibility. In fact, the owner may not be capable of performing such supervisory functions. This does not mean, however, that the owner should not keep a close watch on costs, quality of materials and workmanship, efficiency of equipment, or pace of construction.

Types of Contracts

There are various types and combinations of construction contracts. The ones more commonly used are listed below. Typical examples of such contracts with terms and conditions will be found in the five exhibits at the end of this section.

Cost-plus-fixed-fee Contract. This type of contract provides that the contractor will be reimbursed by the owner for all costs actually incurred to perform the work in accordance with the contract and in addition paid a definite fee. The fee remains the same regardless of whether the final actual cost of work is higher or lower than the parties expected when the fee was agreed to, provided of course that there has been no change in scope of work (see Exhibit 16–1 at the end of this section).

Lump-sum or Fixed-price Contract. This type of contract provides for payment of a definite amount for which the contractor agrees to perform the work. If contractor's actual cost is higher or lower than the stated definite amount he loses or gains accordingly (see Exhibit 16–2).

Cost-plus-percentage-fee Contract. This type of contract provides that the contractor will be reimbursed by the owner for all costs actually incurred to perform the work in accordance with the contract and, in addition, paid a fee specified as a definite *percentage* of cost. The amount of the fee, therefore, increases or decreases in accordance with the final, actual cost of the work.

Guaranteed Maximum Price with or without Share Savings. A cost-plus-fixed-fee contract or a cost-plus-percentage-fee contract which provides for a maximum total price of cost and fee, beyond which the owner need not pay, is called a guaranteed maximum-price contract (see Exhibit 16–3). If the cost and fee together amount to less than the maximum price, the owner saves the difference. This type of contract may also provide for sharing of savings and excess cost. If the final amount of cost and fee is less than the maximum price, the difference is divided by an agreed upon percentage between the contractor and the owner. If the final amount of cost and fee is more than the maximum price, the contractor pays owner a portion of the excess in accordance with an agreed upon percentage.

Labor. There are contracts for furnishing labor alone. In such an agreement, the contractor agrees to furnish skilled or unskilled labor, or both, at cost plus a percentage fee. The cost is the actual wages and salaries of the employees for the time they are engaged in the specified work.

Unit Price. The contractor in this type of contract agrees to do the work at a unit price specified in money for each unit of work. The final cost including fee is the product in money of the number of units of work performed multiplied by the corresponding unit price. Example: Contracting for paving work at a price per square yard or concrete work at a price per cubic yard.

Combination Fixed-price and Unit-price Contract. A contract of this type is a lump-sum arrangement for designated parts of the work and a unit-price arrangement for other designated parts. Example: Contracting for erection of a building for a fixed price excluding concrete work inside and paving work outside, which are contracted for on a unit-price basis.

Management and Supervisory Services with or without Engineering. This is a form of construction contract which provides for the contractor to furnish management and supervisory services necessary for the construction of facilities. These services include preparation of contract documents covering the various portions of the work to be let, scheduling of the work, purchasing of items of materials and equipment, taking bids and making recommendations as to awards, and directing and supervising the construction contractors. It may also include engineering services covering the preparation of plans, drawings, and specifications. The fee is based on reimbursement of cost of salaries, wages, and expenses of the contractor's employees engaged in the work, plus a percentage of the actual cost to the owner of all the construction work, as determined by purchases made and contracts awarded. The fee for engineering services includes reimbursement of salaries, wages, and expenses of the contractor's employees for time spent by them on the engineering work plus a percentage fee thereon.

Some Distinguishing Characteristics of Basic Contracts

There are really two fundamental types of construction contracts. One is based on a fixed price and the other on cost plus fee. While, as previously pointed out, there are many combinations and variations of them, the basic difference is always the same. For that reason the discussion of contracts from here on will be for the most part confined to one or the other of these two basic types.

Lump-sum or Fixed-price Contracts

Advantages

1. The cost including fee or profit is set and is known beforehand. Where owner's management has approved an appropriation of a definite amount based upon the best estimate of cost, the lump-sum agreement restricts the construction commitment at the outset to the approved limits.
2. The contractor will work to complete the job as fast as possible because the less time he spends, the less his costs and the more his profits.
3. The owner is required to spend less time in supervising the pace and progress of the job because contractor for his own good will be on top of the job at all times to complete as fast as possible.
4. Protects against mistakes of contractor and rising costs.

Disadvantages

1. Before a lump-sum job can be let, practically all engineering must be completed. During all the time this is being done no construction work is going on or even started.
2. Owner might pay more in this type of contract for the work performed, because the contractor may be put to the expense of making estimates based on subcontractors' bids. Sometimes, for unsuccessful bids he himself has made on past contracts, the contractor includes an extra factor of cost in his own general bid.
3. Since there are phases of the contractor's estimate of the job that are not certain, he will tend to include in his price contingencies for playing it safe as a cushion against a wrong guess. In the actual construction work where he finds he has not allowed enough contingency in his bid, the tendency will be to cut costs and squeeze to the point where the job may suffer.
4. Changes by owner in this type of contract cost dearly. If the contractor pinches on his original bid to get the job, he will often try to make it up on extras. Disputes often arise as to whether a change is within the original scope of work or is an extra entitling the contractor to an additional charge.
5. Contractor may figure the minimum that can be demanded by plans and specifications on which contract is based and owner may therefore have to exercise a close check on quality.

Cost-plus-fee Contract

Advantages

1. Construction can start with engineering. The job can thus be completed sooner and the owner can get into production earlier than he otherwise might.
2. As engineering and construction proceed, the advice of the contractor can be utilized as problems arise and decisions have to be made. He will be acquainted with current practices and costs and be able to give the owner the benefit of this knowledge.
3. The owner exercises a greater degree of control in this type of job and indeed must do so to control costs.
4. Competitive bids can be dispensed with except as to evaluation of fee. This saves much time in awarding the contract.
5. In a cost-plus-fixed-fee arrangement, contractor's and owner's interests are practically identical.
6. Because work can start sooner, savings of interest on money borrowed by owner and on taxes can be made.

Disadvantages

1. Contractor assumes none of the risk.
2. Where his fee is a percentage, the contractor, at least theoretically, has less incentive to push the work, since the more cost, the more fee. Thus the owner undergoes greater concern to see that the job does not drag.
3. To keep the work moving and the costs down, the owner must exercise close supervision and follow-up through properly qualified personnel who may or may not be readily available.
4. Owner does not know in advance what the work will finally cost.

Guaranteed Maximum Price with or without Share of Savings

Advantages

1. The owner knows beforehand that the cost of the job to him will not exceed a definite amount.
2. Where a division of savings is provided for, the contractor has a big incentive to complete the work rapidly and economically.
3. The owner benefits also in sharing the savings, which reduces the ultimate cost of the job.

Disadvantages

1. Contractor, in a share-savings arrangement, will usually limit absorption of excess costs to a small percentage of the total cost of the job after which the owner will be required to reimburse costs to contractor. The common provision is to limit both the contractor's sharing of savings and absorption of excess costs to a definite percentage of his fee.

Advantages

4. The owner has the benefit of an accurate and close estimate which the contractor must prepare as a basis for his guaranteed price.

Disadvantages

2. The contractor may make a fairly accurate estimate of cost of the job and then allow considerable contingencies in the various items of the estimate as a margin of safety. This will require the owner to do extensive evaluating of the estimate.
3. Carefully detailed estimates required for this type of contract are part of cost and may be quite expensive.
4. Owner cannot expect to exercise same degree of control over purchasing and subcontracting as he does in a straight cost-plus-fee contract.
5. Contractor is likely to insist on broadest possible *force majeure* provisions.

THE CONSTRUCTION CONTRACT

The terms of the construction contract will depend, in important respects, upon the type of contract to be entered into. The lump-sum contract will differ from the cost-plus-fee agreement. For example, the former will not contain provisions on reimbursable costs, but the latter will. So it is with a number of other considerations, all arising from the nature of the basic business arrangement that is made covering the construction work. At the same time there are many terms that are common to both types of contract. The *force majeure* clause dealing with acts of God and causes not within the reasonable control of the parties is an example of this. Insurance provisions would be another.

Most contractors have standard forms of contract they prefer to use and seldom are any two forms alike. There is such a wide variation in the terms of these forms that consternation to the owner often results, even though all cover the main points of a construction agreement. Where two contractors use the standard forms recommended by the Associated General Contractors organization they might be the same.

In considering what terms should be in a construction contract, a most valuable aid to the owner is a check list of terms. This helps in comparing different contract forms and in making sure that the final contract contains the provisions necessary for the protection of the owner. The following paragraphs under this subdivision contain many points that might help in great part to serve as such a check list. Since the lump-sum and cost-plus-fee contracts are the basic ones, these alone are discussed. Reference also should be made to the exhibits at the end of this section for examples of actual clauses and terms of the construction contract.

In the discussion which follows, some terms will apply to both types of contract and others will be applicable to only one. In the first sentence of each paragraph, an appropriate note will appear in this respect.

The Scope of the Work. In *both* types of contract the facilities to be furnished and constructed should be described and defined. The necessary references to drawings and specifications must be made. A statement as to what constitutes performance of the work in regard to the furnishing of labor, supervision, materials, and services should be included as well as any other special arrangements that affect the nature and extent of such performance. If part of the work of engineering, purchasing, or construction is to be done by owner or others, it must be explicitly excluded. When the contractor agrees to complete the work, he does not necessarily agree to test the work. The same applies to starting up the work in initial operation. These items should be specifically provided for.

Increases in the scope of work after the contract has been entered into mean additional expense in cost and fee. Where a change is made in the work, it may or may not constitute a change in scope. Questions of this kind frequently arise, leading to differences of opinion between owner and contractor. While changes in the work are often unavoidable, they are costly. Since in each case the determination as to whether the change is an increase in scope or not will be based upon the description and definition of the work set forth in the contract, too much emphasis cannot be placed upon the desirability of making it as comprehensive as it possibly can be.

Changes in Scope

Lump-sum Contract	*Cost-plus-fee Contract*
Changes that result in an addition to the cost of the work are increases in scope since the cost is paid for by contractor.	Changes that result in an addition to the cost of work are not necessarily increases in scope since the cost is paid for by owner.

EXAMPLE: Change of one manufacturer's pump for that of another with all other things remaining equal.

No increase in scope	No increase in scope

Lump-sum Contract	*Cost-plus-fee Contract*
EXAMPLE: Change of one manufacturer's pump for that of another at increased cost.	
Increase in scope	No increase in scope
EXAMPLE: Increase in square footage of a building.	
Increase in scope	Increase in scope

Specifications and Drawings. It is customary in *both* kinds of contracts to require the contractor to examine the specifications and drawings and to report any discrepancies between them to owner. The agreement also makes the contractor solely responsible for correct interpretation of sizes and dimensions. The contractor likewise agrees to prepare and submit to owner for approval necessary detail, arrangement, construction, and fabrication drawings which should be confined by prior agreement to only those that are necessary since they will all contribute to the cost.

Procurement of Materials. The contractor in *both* forms of contract procures the material and equipment on his own.

Lump-sum Contract	*Cost-plus-fee Contract*
1. No right of control by owner although contractor may agreee, here and there, to request a bid from a favored vendor of owner.	1. Control in some measure is retained by owner by requiring prior approval of purchase orders or bid tabulations.
2. Owner may reserve right to furnish certain materials himself.	2. Owner may reserve right to furnish certain materials himself.

Aside from the actual purchasing, the owner could well require the contractor to keep him informed of difficulties that arise in delivery of materials after the orders are placed. To be able to help out in expediting a shipment of material or equipment is a right that should be reserved.

Quality of Materials, Equipment, and Work. Contracts of *both* types commonly provide that unless otherwise arranged, all materials and equipment shall be new and that the workmanship and material shall be of the best quality. Some contractors will object to "best quality" as being an onerous requirement they should not be called upon to meet. Others accept it as reasonable. In any event the contractor should not offer less than the warranties given him by his suppliers.

Cooperation and Understanding of Contractor. The contractor in *both* classes of contract is called upon to act in good faith in carrying out the contract. He is asked to pledge that he will adhere to the spirit of the agreement in the event questions arise that are subject to different interpretations because they are not clearly or completely covered by the contract terms. He agrees to work with other contractors in such a way as to avoid any delay of the job. The burden is also upon the owner to act in the same way.

The contractor is asked to state in the contract that he has an understanding beforehand of the nature, location, and scope of the work which entails the obligation on his part to inspect visually the physical condition at the job site. The owner and the contractor agree on the utilities that are to be furnished by the owner, such as steam, electric power, and water. A thorough study of all the plans, drawings, and specifications by the contractor is required.

In the clause on the understanding of the contractor it is customary to provide for the turning over of completed portions of the work to the owner. Where the owner is to install the operating equipment in a building or is desirous of operating a unit of a plant, he is then enabled to proceed without awaiting completion of the whole construction project.

Contractor's Supervision and Labor. Contractors maintain as a permanent part of their staffs construction superintendents who are assigned the full responsibility of the work in the field in *both* types of contract. They are highly trained and experienced men in all phases of construction work. The manner in which a construction job proceeds and the time in which it is completed depend more upon the construction superintendent than upon any other person. Therefore, it is important to the owner to safeguard his right to have a competent superintendent assigned to the job, one who is satisfactory to the owner, and to require the contractor to keep him on the job site at all times and not change superintendents without the owner's consent unless he becomes unsatisfactory or leaves the contractor's employ.

The executive officers, being the ones who make up the management of a competent and reputable construction company, are likewise required by the contract terms to give the work such personal supervision as may be required for the proper execution of it.

Control by the contractor of his labor is an ordinary contract provision, making him responsible for proper workmanship and discipline.

Owner's Engineer. The counterpart of the contractor's superintendent in *both* forms of contract is the owner's engineer. The owner is required to appoint and maintain one on the job at all times. The two, acting in close cooperation, are essential to the proper progress of the work. In cost-plus contracts *only*, usually the owner's engineer is given the authority to approve costs, to reject or accept work, and to stop work when it becomes necessary to the proper execution of the job. The owner's engineer is mentioned in many places throughout the contract and his further duties and powers are set forth in such parts of the agreement.

Changes in and Completion of the Work. The right to change the work is reserved to the owner in most cases by specific provision in *both* kinds of contract. The owner is required to notify the contractor of the nature of any alteration, increase, or decrease in the work and the duty is imposed on the contractor to estimate the value thereof. When the estimate is approved by the owner, the fee in the cost-plus-fixed-fee contract is negotiated. The estimated amount in lump-sum contracts will include the contractor's profit. In a cost-plus-percentage contract the percentage will be automatically applied to the approved estimated amount. Where work is omitted, the contractor is further required to submit a net unit-price schedule, when the nature of the work is such that it can be computed in this way. This is to be used in computing the amount of an equitable deduction from the original contract price.

Completion of the work, always a matter of such vital importance to the owner, must be provided for in the contract. It can be done by stating a fixed date, with or without penalties in the nature of liquidated damages to be paid by the contractor in the event that he overruns the completion date. Such an arrangement is difficult to obtain from a contractor. An estimated time, either a fixed date or number of months, can be used. There is of course less protection for the owner when an estimated date is used. Where an agreement on an actual time of completion cannot be reached, the problem usually can be resolved by providing that time is of the essence or of importance to the owner (preferably the former because of its stronger legal significance) and that the contractor agrees to complete the work in a minimum of time consistent with good construction practices under the existing circumstances or conditions.

Cost of Work. In a cost-plus-fee contract *only,* the owner pays all costs. In a lump-sum contract all costs are paid by the contractor out of his fixed price. Although the term "all costs" as generally used in connection with cost-plus-fee agreements actually coincides with the basic theory of such contracts, nevertheless there are some expenditures made by the contractor in the course of the work which are either limited as to reimbursement by the owner or are not reimbursable at all. For these reasons it is preferable to set forth in the contract as many specific items of cost as is practicable rather than merely to provide for owner's payment of all costs except for a few standard exclusions. In the following paragraphs under this heading are listed and briefly discussed the more common elements of cost that appear in a cost-plus-fee contract.

Wages and Salaries. This item of cost generally covers the time put in on the work by the contractor's employees. The contractor is paid the amount of such employees' wages or salaries. Even though the services are rendered elsewhere than at the job site, they will be paid for, provided they were performed in connection with the work. Wage and salary classifications are usually submitted to and approved by the owner beforehand. In some cases it is agreed that they are not subject to change at all during the length of the term of the contract. In other cases they may be changed, but only upon the owner's approval. Overtime and holiday pay, as well as vacation and sick-leave pay, is made a matter of special agreement in each contract.

Materials, Equipment, etc. The costs of necessary materials, equipment, tools, supplies, fuel, freight and demurrage charges, and services including telegrams, telephone charges, postage, etc., are made reimbursable. Where temporary structures or facilities at the job site are necessary and approved by the owner, the costs of constructing, maintaining, and dismantling them are considered items of cost.

Traveling Expenses. Such expenses for travel as are directly chargeable to the work and have received the owner's prior approval are reimbursable to the contractor. Arrangements for blanket approval of certain classes of this type of expense can be made.

Moving Expenses. Expenses for moving contractor's personnel necessary for prosecuting the work are reimbursable, provided owner's approval is obtained. One point to be watched for here is the possibility that the contractor's employee may be moved from his home base to the job site and then upon completion of the work be assigned to a location far removed from the original base and so claim moving expenses for the longer trip. To guard against this, a provision restricting this cost to not more than twice the initial moving expense should be made part of the contract.

Control of Construction Equipment, etc. The reasonable rental charges for construction equipment, tools, warehouses and offices, trucks and automobiles are costs of work for which the contractor should be reimbursed, provided they are approved by the owner prior to rental. Transportation charges for such equipment, costs of loading, unloading, installing, dismantling, and removal are also expenses payable by owner to contractor. It is well to limit rental rates to the standard rates existing in the local area. An agreement on a scale of rates for the rental of the contractor's own equipment might be made before the contract is signed. Sometimes it is advantageous to agree that tools and equipment not exceeding a certain amount, such as $300, will be purchased outright by contractor for the owner and charged as cost of the job.

Where the cumulative rental charges for an item of equipment owned by the contractor may eventually, during the period of rental, equal the preagreed upon market value of the equipment, a provision can be incorporated into the contract to the effect that no further rental charge shall be made for additional, continuous use of such equipment. This would not apply to rentals of equipment from third parties.

Repairs should be excluded as an item of cost from the rental agreement except when they are minor and previously authorized by owner. The contractor should also agree to safeguard and turn over to owner upon completion of the job all tools and equipment purchased by contractor and charged as cost of work.

Payroll Taxes and Contributions. Social security, employment taxes, and contributions applicable to wages and salaries of the contractor's employees engaged in the work are considered costs to be reimbursed. The same is true of sales and other excise taxes paid by the contractor on materials, equipment, and services chargeable to the job. Where a business or occupational tax is involved, it is well to require the complete cooperation of the contractor in consulting on the preparation of returns, taking appeals from assessments, and all other steps required to protect the owner's interests. In such cases the contractor is the original party liable and will insist upon indemnification of any liability he may incur as well as reimbursement for all expenses.

Subcontracts. Construction work of any size is seldom executed without subcontracting portions of the work. The subcontractors, being specialists in their particular line, have the experience and skill to do that part of the work more efficiently and quickly than the general contractor. The owner should reserve the right to direct the contractor to subcontract work. The cost of subcontracts is a reimbursable expense. However, the contract should provide that all subcontracts must receive the owner's prior approval.

Licenses, Permits, and Bonds. Municipalities and other governmental bodies require that licenses or permits of one kind or another be obtained in connection with construction work. The fees for these are cost of the work. If a bond is required by law or by the contract, the premium for it is also considered cost. The contract accordingly should so provide.

Royalties, Infringement Damage, and Costs. The owner may require in the drawings or specifications or otherwise the use of a patented process or piece of equipment which the contractor would have to use or furnish. In such cases any royalties payable to the patent holder are cost of work. If the use of the patented process or equipment is claimed by a third party to be an infringement, the damages resulting and the expense and court costs of any suit brought on such a claim are properly considered cost of the work. The contract therefore should cover this.

Reconstruction of Work–Damaged or Destroyed. The cost involved in reconstruction of work that is damaged or destroyed, whether or not the casualty was caused by the contractor, is ordinarily made a reimbursable cost where the loss is covered by insurance.

When the loss is not covered by insurance, either because there was none at all or because the damage exceeds the amount of the insurance limits, the contractor will generally expect the owner to pay the cost of reconstruction, provided the damage was not caused by the negligence of contractor's officials or supervisory employees under the conditions specified in the particular contract. Contractors who take this position maintain that there is no provision in their business or financial setup for paying contingent liabilities of this nature and that it is impracticable for them to supervise every employee on the job to the extent of avoiding all possibility of damage.

Contractors often will request protection against loss, damage, or expense of any kind not covered by insurance and not caused by negligence of contractor's officials or supervisory employees, as mentioned above. The risks covered by such a provision might include not only reconstruction of the work but also such things as loss or damage to the contractor's employees' tools and personal effects, contractor's loss of payroll, and losses due to dishonesty of employees. The owner should consider the nature, size, and location of the particular job and the hazards that might arise, and he should see that the terms of this contract provision are such that he assumes no liability which the contractor reasonably should be expected to accept. The owner should consider what risks should be insured against and arrange for the necessary insurance coverage.

In the preceding paragraphs under this heading, costs of reconstruction were discussed but not fee. Some contractors, however, in jobs involving excessive risk, will insist upon payment of an additional fee on the cost of reconstruction, even if the loss is caused by negligence of any of contractor's employees. If the owner agrees to this, he is lessening the contractor's incentive to exercise due care, since in strict logic, the more damage that occurs, the more fee he earns. The contractor will maintain that where the damage is covered by insurance, the owner is in no way out of pocket, since claims paid by the insurance carrier are based on replacement value which will include the contractor's fee. Even though there is no insurance coverage, he may yet claim he is entitled to the fee since he is doing the work a second time.

If the reconstruction work involves a loss of a couple of thousand dollars or so and could be completed in a few days, this question of fee would be a matter of small consequence. However, where the loss is in the hundreds of thousands of dollars and the reworking would involve a number of weeks or months, the point of view of the contractor can be appreciated. It would mean the employment of a large staff of workers for a long period without any profit to the contractor, whereas without such contract obligation he could have this staff working elsewhere for a profit.

The answer to this question sometimes lies in the owner's agreeing to pay the contractor when he is not at fault a fee to the extent that it is included in the amount of the insurance claim paid. This would take care of the possibility of the claim payment being less in amount than the actual cost of reconstructing plus contractor's fee thereon. As to fee on reconstructing damaged work caused by the contractor's negligence, no fee would be paid in any event.

Pre-contract Expenses under Letter of Intent. Often, construction jobs are started before the contract negotiations are concluded or the contract signed. The owner and the contractor are in basic agreement, but some terms have not yet been gone into. In such cases a letter of intent is commonly used to authorize the contractor to proceed. In the interim, between the issuance of the letter of intent and the execution of the contract, expenses in cost and fee are incurred which constitute pre-contract expenses. Where these circumstances exist, the letter of intent and pre-contract expenses are usually referred to in the contract.

Items Not Cost of Work. In cost-plus-fee jobs *only,* certain expenses of the contractor incurred in the cost of the work are customarily excluded as elements of cost. These include overhead or general expenses of operating contractor's main or regular branch offices, including salaries of officers or members of the firm. No interest on capital employed or on money borrowed is considered cost. Special arrangements on other costs such as vacation pay or payment for illness of the contractor's employees may be made in the particular contract. It should then be stated that such items are or are not to be considered costs.

Contractor's Fee. The provisions dealing with the contractor's fee differ with the type of contract involved, as is shown in the comparison appearing below:

Lump-sum Contract

1. Fee is not specifically set forth but is included in the lump-sum price as profit. The owner does not know, nor may contractor care to reveal, what it is.
2. Changes in the work that alter the scope require the fixed price to be adjusted by adding or subtracting

Cost-plus-fee Contract

1. Fee is specifically set forth either in amount or by a definite percentage.
2. Changes in the work that alter the scope require that a previously agreed upon percentage be applied to the estimated cost of the work added or omitted, in order to adjust the fixed fee up or down. In a

Lump-sum Contract

the amount that is agreed upon for the work added or omitted.

3. Payments at agreed upon intervals are made against the full fixed price which includes cost and profit, based upon the work done but preferably upon the percentage of job completion without regard to materials delivered and uninstalled.

Cost-plus-fee Contract

percentage-fee contract the fee is automatically adjusted by applying it to the cost of the change.

3. Payments at agreed upon intervals are made for reimbursement of costs incurred and for the portion of fee earned, preferably based upon the percentage of job completion.

In *both* types of contracts it is customary to withhold a percentage, such as 10 per cent, of the fee payments on cost-plus-fee jobs and 10 per cent of the total payment on lump-sum jobs. This withheld portion is paid to the contractor on completion and acceptance of the work. Occasionally arrangements are made for the owner to establish a fund from which the contractor can make payments as the work progresses, this fund to be kept at an agreed upon level. Each week or month the owner makes an additional deposit to bring the fund up to the required amount.

Miscellaneous Provisions. There are many general terms of construction contracts that can be used to advantage, depending upon the type of agreement that is entered into. Some of the more common clauses of this kind appear below.

Discounts, Rebates, and Refunds. In the cost-plus-fee contract *only,* all discounts, rebates, and refunds should accrue to the owner, and the contractor should agree to take such steps as are necessary to secure them. In a lump-sum agreement there is no such provision, since these belong to the contractor who very well might have based his bid in part on retaining them.

Records, Accounting, and Inspection. Normally, a provision is found in cost-plus-fee contracts *only* to the effect that the contractor shall keep records in a manner approved by the owner and that all such records and documents of the contractor pertaining to the work shall be accessible to the owner at all times and open to his inspection. The contractor usually is required to preserve such records as are agreed upon for a period of about three years. No provision of this kind is found in a lump-sum contract since the owner has no need for checking or preserving records of the job. The foregoing is not to be confused with the requirement that under the lump-sum contract the contractor is to submit statements and supporting documents verifying the amounts he is to be paid over the course of the job.

Disposal of Surplus Materials. In cost-plus-fee contracts *only,* all returns on sales of surplus materials, equipment, supplies, and scrap should be credited to the cost of work. The owner's prior approval of all such sales should be required. The contractor alone is concerned with such sales in lump-sum contracts.

Continuance of Work. Because in the case of disputes the contractor, in *both* types of contracts, may feel he has no obligation to continue work until the dispute is settled to his satisfaction, a provision is usually incorporated in the contract requiring his continuing the work unless he is requested by the owner to suspend.

Protection of Work and Property. The contractor is required in *both* kinds of contracts to protect all materials, equipment, and partially completed work from loss and damage.

Inspection. The right of inspection by the owner is reserved in *both* classes of contract, not only as it applies to the facilities constructed by the contractor, but to the materials and equipment in the course of fabrication by the contractor's suppliers.

Safety Requirements. The contractor in *both* forms of contract is required to take reasonable precautions to keep the owner's premises free from hazards and to see that all applicable building codes and other pertinent provisions of law are complied with. He is called upon also to agree to observe all the safety rules of the owner's plant.

Subcontracting and Assignment. In *both* types of contract the right of the contractor to subcontract any part of the work should be made subject to the prior approval of the owner. The owner ought to be given the right to require the contractor to bind the subcontractor to the terms of the general contractor's contract to the extent that such terms are applicable.

As to assigning the main contract itself, the contractor is ordinarily denied the right unless the owner's written permission is first obtained. The owner, on the other hand, reserves the right to assign the contract to a parent, subsidiary, or affiliated company or to the transferee of its business. A change in contractor may be of much more serious concern to the owner than a change in owner is to the contractor.

Owner's Drawings. The contractor is called upon to agree in *both* forms of contract that all owner's plans, drawings, and specifications remain the property of owner, that the contractor will not use them or permit them to be used on other work, and that they will be returned to the owner on completion of the work.

Cleanup of Owner's Premises. The owner requires in *both* classes of contract that the contractor agree to clean up the premises in a thorough and workmanlike manner as required or requested by the owner.

Title to Materials and Equipment. The idea here is to make sure that when the owner's money is paid for anything, he gets title to what he has paid for.

Lump-sum Contract	*Cost-plus-fee Contract*
It should be provided that owner shall have title to all work completed or in course of construction or installation; and that title to all materials, equipment, tools, and supplies shall pass to owner simultaneously with payment therefor by owner to contractor.	It should be provided that owner shall have title to all work completed or in course of construction or installation; and that simultaneously with the passage of title in materials, equipment, tools, and supplies to contractor, the title therein shall pass to owner.

Liens. The owner in *both* kinds of contract requires the contractor to agree to keep owner's properties free from liens and charges arising from the work and give the owner prompt notice of any prospective liens. The contractor usually agrees further to indemnify the owner for all expenses, damages, and costs connected with the satisfaction of such liens.

Patents. In *both* types of contract defense of patent infringement suits brought by third parties and indemnification for damages incurred thereby are made a provision of the contract. Where the owner specifies a particular process or piece of equipment to be used by mention thereof in the plans, drawings, specifications, or otherwise, the owner will agree to bear the responsibility. Where the process or equipment relates to the contractor's design or fabrication, then the contractor will assume the liability for infringement.

Confidential Information. The contractor in *both* forms of contract is called upon to keep confidential and not disclose secret processes, apparatus, or trade secrets of owner except to the extent required in the performance of the contract. He also is required to take all reasonable precautions to prevent his subcontractors from disclosing such information. The obligation is made to survive the completion, termination, or cancellation of the contract.

Indemnity. The contractor in *both* classes of contract should be required to agree to indemnify against and save the owner harmless from all losses and liability to which owner may be subjected by reason of any acts or omissions of the contractor, his subcontractors, or employees arising from the performance of the work. This should be made to include but not be limited to personal injury and loss of or damage to property of the owner or others.

The obligations of the contractor under this provision of the contract are insurable. Previously it was pointed out, under reconstruction of the work, how the liability for the cost of it was tied up with insurance. Here is another feature of the construction contract that is connected with insurance. The three clauses, namely, reconstruction of work, indemnity, and insurance, must often be read and considered together. Thus, even though contractors can obtain insurance coverage for the indemnity risks they assume, some will insist that their liability under this clause shall be limited to the hazards insured against and not exceed the monetary limits of the insurance called for under the contract. By virtue of this, a ceiling is put on the monetary limit of the indemnity as well as on the types of risk that are covered. This clause will be further discussed later on under the subject of insurance.

Compliance with Laws. The owner in *both* forms of contract requires the contractor to comply with all laws and regulations of Federal, state, or local government in connection with the work. The contractor takes on the task of giving all notices and obtaining all permits and licenses required under such laws.

Force Majeure. A clause in *both* types of contract covering contingencies that may occur through no fault of either party to the contract is a necessary provision of the agreement. Acts of God, such as fires or floods, could play havoc with the new construction or existing facilities of an owner, causing serious delay and expense. The clause excuses either party from liability in such cases. However, it does require that the party affected do something to remove the cause in an adequate manner and with reasonable dispatch so that the construction can proceed. The party obligated to so act should keep the other party informed.

Termination. A clause usually appearing in *both* classes of contract permits the owner to terminate the agreement for his own business reasons. If the contract were silent as to termination, both parties still would have their legal remedies under the general law in cases of default in carrying out the terms of the contract. However, the right of the owner to terminate voluntarily, and the reservation of broader rights than the law usually allows to the owner in the event of default, can be given only by contract.

The contract, therefore, should provide that where conditions arise making it advisable or necessary, in the owner's opinion, to discontinue the work, the owner reserves the right to terminate. In a lump-sum contract the owner upon voluntary termination is usually willing to agree that the contractor will be paid such an amount which when added to amounts previously paid will equal the contract price less an equitable deduction for the unperformed portion of the work. In a cost-plus-fee agreement, the contractor is paid all his unpaid costs that were authorized and properly incurred by him plus the balance of his earned fee, computed preferably on percentage of job completion up to the time of termination. Some contractors will not agree to the right of the owner to terminate by will unless a greater amount of the fee is guaranteed to them. They will want to be paid the amount of their earned fee plus a percentage of their unearned fee, even sometimes with a minimum of a certain percentage of the entire fee.

The contractor in the latter instance maintains that he has planned his organization's activities to take care of the owner's particular job, even to the point of turning away other business. He contends that if owner terminates without cause, a greater payment of fee over and above the amount earned should be paid by owner as compensation to cover the contractor's expense in readjusting for the loss of the work. He may also urge that by agreeing to give the owner the right of voluntary termination, the contractor is giving up a legal right that he otherwise would have and so the owner should be willing to pay a penalty in the form of additional fee when the contract is so terminated.

In such cases, a percentage of unearned fee might be set which would result in the payment of a reasonable sum to compensate the contractor for the costs of organizational readjustment. The establishment of a percentage of the total fee as a minimum payment should be avoided, because if the termination occurs in the beginning of the job, the owner would have to pay a large penalty. If, for example, the owner agreed to pay earned fee plus 20 per cent of unearned fee, when the job was 10 per cent completed he would have to pay 28 per cent of the entire fee, representing 10 per cent earned fee and 18 per cent (20 per cent of 90 per cent) unearned fee. If, in addition, the owner agreed to pay a minimum percentage of, say, 50 per cent of the total fee, he would be obligated for an additional 22 per cent.

When a contractor defaults, the owner has several recourses, one or more of which may be provided for in a contract. He may recover damages caused by the default, or he may terminate. In the event of termination of a lump-sum contract, if the unpaid balance of the contract price exceeds the cost of finishing the work, the excess is to be paid to the contractor. On the other hand, if the cost of finishing exceeds the unpaid balance of the contract price, the contractor agrees to pay the difference to the owner. In cost-plus-fee contracts, the owner agrees to pay the contractor all unpaid, authorized costs of work done prior to the termination as well as the balance of the earned fee less any amounts subject to withholding under the contract (usually 10 per cent of the earned fee).

Notices. A provision usually appears in *both* kinds of agreements setting forth the manner in which written notices required under the contract are to be given. The addresses to which notices are to be sent are stated and also whether registered or ordinary mail is to be used.

Insurance. In *both* types of contract, each party's responsibility for insurance coverage is specified in detail. The various types of coverage, the monetary limits, and the special endorsements required are all set forth. Most contractors are prepared to furnish the necessary coverage. However, for one reason or another an owner may wish to be responsible for obtaining some part of the coverage himself. In any event, the owner must keep in mind that the premiums will be paid by him regardless of the type of contract he enters into. It is important, therefore, that the owner concern himself particularly with the limits of the insurance policies, since these have a direct bearing on the amounts of the premiums. Also, wherever possible, he should compare his own premium cost for a particular coverage with that of the contractor's; premiums vary with loss experience ratings and his may be better or worse than the contractor's.

Reference is made to the indemnity clause of construction contracts previously discussed. The owner should assure himself of proper protection, by requiring the contractor to have his insurance policy (usually his general public liability policy) cover all the risks the contractor assumes under the contract and in monetary limits that the owner considers adequate. Of course, the owner may have to assume higher premium costs to secure greater protection.

The various types of insurance coverage should be decided upon in the light of the nature of the hazards and risks involved. The monetary limits should be established to cover the size of the particular job. The following are some of the principal types of coverage required:

Workmen's compensation covering contractor's employees. Owner should also have his own policy for his employees.

Employer's liability covering employees, which applies to accidents that may not come under the workmen's compensation law of the state in which the job is located. This coverage is usually included in the workmen's compensation policy, but in most states only for a maximum of $25,000, and in some states less. The limits on an average construction job should be much higher and should have a spread covering injuries or death to one employee and to two or more employees in the same accident.

Contractor's contingent (protective) bodily injury and property damage liability where contractor employs any subcontractor. Although the contractor is obligated to see that all his subcontractors agree to act as independent contractors which legally would make them liable alone for their negligence, in cases involving inherently dangerous work such as the use of explosives this would not apply. Because the contractor would also be liable in such cases, the owner requires him to insure against this contingent liability. It is also protective to the contractor where he is sued in other cases in the mistaken belief that he is liable, in saving him expense of defending the suit, which would be assumed by the insurance carrier.

Comprehensive general public liability (including liability assumed by contract) for bodily injuries and property damage. The property damage coverage usually excludes the new construction work but should be made to apply to property of third parties and to property of the owner other than the work.

All-risk insurance which should cover the material and equipment at the job site for the new construction, both before and after it is installed and until the facility is completed and accepted by owner. It often covers also the owner's property other than the work.

Fire and extended coverage insurance which protects the new construction as well as owner's other property against fire or other hazards set forth in the policy.

Automobile insurance for bodily injuries and property damage, which should cover accidents involving the contractor's owned, hired, or nonowned vehicles.

There are other types of coverage which often need to be considered, such as boiler insurance; comprehensive, fire and theft and collision coverage on trucks and automobiles rented by the contractor, without operators, from third parties; all-risk insurance on tools and equipment rented by the contractor, without operators, from third parties; etc. Expert insurance advice should be obtained in all cases to ensure adequate coverage.

Certificates of insurance and/or copies of the policies should be obtained and interchanged between parties for purposes of checking and approving the coverage.

The question of which policies should be made payable to both parties as their interests may appear and which should provide for a waiver of subrogation of the other party by the insurance carrier should be settled in advance and set forth in the insurance requirements of the contract. By being named as assured in the contractor's insurance policy, the owner is free from suit by the carrier, even where damage to others is caused by his negligence. The other way of effecting the same thing is by having the carrier waive its right to sue the owner for any damages which it has to pay to others due to the owner's negligence. This is called a waiver of subrogation or the giving up of the insurance carrier's right to succeed to the rights of its assured.

General Provisions. A number of clauses on general matters affecting *both* forms of contract may be included as subdivisions of one article. They might consist of any or all of the following:

Contract constitutes the entire agreement between the parties relating to the work and there are no other representations or warranties not set forth in the contract.

No modification, waiver, termination, recision, discharge, or cancellation of the contract or any of its terms shall be binding on owner unless executed in writing by an officer or authorized official of owner.

No waiver of any provision of or default under the contract shall affect owner's right to enforce such provision in case of any other default.

All rights and remedies of owner specified in the contract are in addition to any other rights and remedies owner has.

The contractor shall remain an independent contractor and shall have no power to bind the owner.

This last provision in regard to independent contractor should be made part of the contract in any event, because by this statement the intention is shown that the contractor is to work on his own and be solely responsible for all his acts. The legal effect of this relationship is well established so that, except in rare instances, the owner is relieved of all responsibility for contractor's acts. The others are more or less formal provisions that owner may desire to include. If he does, there is seldom any objection raised by the contractor.

In conclusion, it is well to repeat that the terms of any two construction contracts are never the same. Special features of a construction agreement always should be specifically provided for in the contract. As to the more common features, the foregoing considerations may be used as a guide.

SELECTION OF CONTRACTOR

The greatest care is required in choosing the contractor. Regardless of the form of the contract or the consideration given to its provisions and terms, if the contractor is not the proper one for the job, trouble lies ahead for the owner. It is of the utmost importance for the owner to obtain all the information he can concerning a contractor's reputation, competence, and experience preparatory to deciding to deal with any particular contractor at all. Methods of selection and some general considerations connected therewith are gone into below.

By Competitive Bids. Where a job has been fully engineered beforehand and the plans, drawings, and specifications are complete, competitive bids for a lump-sum contract are in order. Selecting a list of prospective bidders, preparing invitations to bid, and making drawings and specifications available to general and subcontractors are steps which take considerable time. However, this time is compensated for by time saved in evaluating the final bids and deciding upon the contractor. If the owner adheres strictly to the drawings and specifications, with only a minimum of changes, he merely has to compare the few figures of final bids to make his decision. It should be emphasized most strongly that no bid should ever be requested from a contractor that the owner would not find acceptable to do the job.

In cost-plus-fee jobs also, competitive proposals can be invited. However, there is usually no formal or precise means of obtaining bids. The method is one of informal discussion of what the job involves (there being no complete drawings or specifications available) and the contractor must estimate the job roughly so that he can fix a monetary or percentage fee in his bid. In evaluating the bid, the owner also must estimate the cost in order to determine whether the fee is reasonable.

By Negotiation. Often the owner has had such successful experience with one contractor that he deals from the outset with him; competition is eliminated. There is the advantage here of mutual familiarity with each other's methods and systems. However, blind continuation of such a relationship easily can result in obtaining something less than the best services or price. The point is that the owner should never lose sight of what the competition is currently offering.

CPM and PERT. The terms CPM (Critical Path Method) and PERT (Program Evaluation and Review Technique) represent a method of planning and scheduling a project by means of a network diagram. Arrows on a network represent individual jobs that comprise the project. Events are junctions of arrows, or in some cases, milestones or important time points in the project. The diagram shows the order in which the jobs or activities should be performed and the event sequences. It also shows the relationships and dependencies of the jobs on each other.

When time estimates are applied to the jobs, the diagram can be used to predict the project duration and to indicate the longest job sequence, known as the "critical path." Simple calculations show the amount of slack or float time available on the noncritical jobs. With this information, the network diagram becomes a tool which can be used for scheduling and monitoring a project.

Perhaps the most valuable features are the forced planning that accompanies the construction of the diagram, the ability to "manage by exception," and the ease of evaluating the logic if alteration of plans is required. The diagram provides a simple, clear-cut means of communicating and fixing responsibility. An important ground rule, and one of the secrets of success of network techniques, is the separation of planning from scheduling.

One of the major functions in a PERT-managed project is purchasing, particularly when long-delivery items are critical. A diagram prepared in the early stages of the project can effectively aid the purchasing agent in improving purchasing performance, thus avoiding costly delays. Purchasing people should have more than a cursory knowledge of CPM and PERT in order to participate in the planning and aid in the management of a project. The attitude of the contractor toward the use of CPM or PERT and his opinion on their applicability to the work under consideration should be developed.

PERT, or Program Evaluation and Review Technique, is used variously. It is increasingly being used as a general term for any network technique, of which CPM would be a version. CPM, or Critical Path Method, was designed for construction projects and other projects where considerable knowledge of the details is available. The term CPM refers to the "activity oriented" version of the technique. PERT was originally conceived for use on projects with areas of high uncertainty, such as in research and development. A form of statistics was used to establish probability factors on the outcome of the project. The term PERT may also refer to the "event oriented" version of the technique, with or without the application of statistics.

Performance Bonds. If the owner is interested in a performance bond, this should be made known to the prospective contractors during the bid-taking or contract-negotiating period, in order that the terms and cost can be developed for consideration by the owner. Before calling for a performance bond, the owner should clearly understand how much it will add to the cost of the job and just what protection it will afford him. Basically, a performance bond is intended to assure that in case of default by the contractor the job will be completed without financial loss to the owner, as an obligation of the surety within the monetary limit stated in the bond.

Some people are under the impression that upon the contractor's default a sum of money in the nature of a penalty payment (similar to those made under a penalty provision in the purchase of equipment) will be paid to the owner by the surety on the bond. This is not the case, however, and where there is a default, efforts will be made by the surety to have the contractor complete performance. If the contractor cannot or will not do so, another contractor will then be employed to complete the job. There is also a rather widespread impression that a performance bond will always assure that the job will be completed on time. In practice, however, by the time the surety's efforts result in getting the work moving again it is more probable that a delay in completion of the job will be encountered.

It is questionable whether a performance bond should be used as protection against a contractor's doubtful financial standing or a lack of confidence in his ability to perform the contract. A problem such as this should preferably be resolved by eliminating such a contractor by the application of the principles set forth under the general considerations mentioned in the following paragraph.

General Considerations. This subject is concerned with the contractor's experience, accomplishments, and reputation, and his organization and method of operation. The owner should have as much information as possible on these points:

How well has the contractor performed on other jobs of similar size and scope?
Has he met schedules?
Have there been unwarranted delays in completion and start-up?
Have there been failures of structure or equipment?
Does the contractor have the necessary financial responsibility?

These and many more questions should be asked and answered.

Where design and process know-how on the part of the contractor is to be relied upon, it would be well to make inquiries regarding the performance of similar plants he has constructed in the past. Did they have the necessary throughput, quality of plant and product, and did they operate at a reasonably low maintenance cost?

Where the owner depends to a considerable extent on the contractor's estimate of cost, it is well to know how closely the contractor has met his estimates in the past.

How about the contractor's organization? Is it properly geared for the project under consideration and qualified by experience?

Some organizations use a form of questionnaire to develop and keep current the necessary information on contractors. The questions listed in the form are quite comprehensive, and the data supplied are of great assistance in judging a contractor's suitability for a particular job.

The owner's decision as to choice of a contractor involves answers to the type of questions mentioned above. Answers are usually obtainable by:

Checking with others who have dealt with the contractor
Checking with banks and credit institutions
Checking with inspection agencies
Checking with manufacturers of equipment
Checking with professional people in related fields

To repeat, there is no single element in a construction job more important than the qualifications of the contractor.

EXHIBIT 16–1. TYPICAL COST-PLUS-FIXED-FEE CONSTRUCTION CONTRACT

CONTRACT made the ______________ day of ______________,
9___, by and between ______________
______________ corporation of ______________
______________, hereinafter called the Contractor, and ______________
______________, a ______________ corporation with an office at
______________, hereinafter called the
ompany. The Contractor and the Company mutually agree as follows:

SCOPE OF WORK

The Contractor shall construct for the Company ______________
____
t ______________, as hereinafter rovided. Under the direction of the Company Engineer, the Contractor shall perform all work shown n or reasonably implied by the plans, specifications, and drawings furnished and to be furnished the ontractor by the Company entitled ______________
______________.
nsert caption descriptive of the work as used on plans and specifications.)
rawings mentioned therein are an integral part of the contract as if attached hereto. Performing he work shall include the furnishing of all labor, supervision, materials, process equipment, services, acilities, and all other things necessary or proper to complete the work in accordance with the General onditions set forth herein.

Except as otherwise provided herein, the Contractor shall perform and have full responsibility for urchasing, estimating quantities, material take-offs, scheduling, and expediting and coordinating elivery of all materials and equipment, so as to permit most rapid and economical completion f the work.

The Contractor shall provide, at intervals prescribed by the Company, schedules, charts, estimates, eports, and other data which will keep the Company fully informed of the progress of the work, urrent and total construction costs, the conditions at the site, labor status, and such other data as ay be requested by the Company or is customarily prepared for recording construction and intallation progress.

The Contractor shall unload all rail and truck deliveries and transport to and unload at the job te all materials and equipment intended for the work, whether or not furnished by the Company. he Contractor shall use designated routes and places for hauling, unloading, and storing materials, nd they shall at all times be unloaded promptly to keep tracks as clear as possible and to avoid emurrage charges.

The work shall be commenced not later than ______________ and hall be completed as provided in Article ______ of the General Conditions.

GENERAL CONDITIONS

Article 1. Specifications and Drawings. a. Any work mentioned in the specifications and not shown n the drawings, or shown on the drawings and not mentioned in the specifications, shall be of like ffect as if shown or mentioned in both. The Contractor shall examine the specifications and drawings nd check all dimensions and notify the Company of any discrepancies between the specifications nd drawings, and any deficiencies, omissions, or errors therein before any work is done in accordance erewith.

b. The Contractor shall be solely responsible for correct interpretation and use of all sizes and imensions and proper joining of all new work required to match existing work. The Contractor shall o all necessary cutting and fitting to make the Contractor's work properly come together with nd attach to existing work.

c. The Contractor before proceeding with the work shall prepare or have prepared detail, rrangement, construction, fabrication, and other drawings not supplied by the Company, and shall ubmit ______ prints of these drawings for the Company's approval. Promptly following return y the Company of any one set of the prints corrected and approved, the Contractor shall supply e Company with ______ additional sets of prints with approved corrections, for the use and ecords of the Company.

Article 2. Procurement of Materials. Unless otherwise specified by the Company in writing, all purchasing shall be accomplished by purchase order, and the Contractor shall submit all purchase orders to the Company for its prior approval, but the Company reserves the right to purchase any items directly on its own account. Each party shall forward to the other party copies of all purchase orders on the same day they are sent out.

Article 3. Quality. Unless otherwise provided in the specifications, all materials and equipment shall be new. Workmanship and materials shall be of the best quality, and all fabrications shall be done in a good and workmanlike manner and in accordance with the best shop practices. The Contractor shall, if required, furnish satisfactory evidence of the kind and quality of materials purchased by the Contractor. The Contractor shall not substitute materials for those specified without the Company Engineer's prior written approval.

Article 4. Cooperation. The Contractor shall perform the work so as to maintain plant traffic and manufacturing operations as nearly normal as possible, and shall not interfere therewith without receipt of written authority from the Company Engineer. The Contractor shall assist in keeping clear walks, roadways, railroad sidings, all passageways, working space, and storage areas adjacent to the zone of operations. The Contractor shall cooperate with and shall not in any way interfere with other contractors, their employees, and agents.

Article 5. Understanding of the Contractor. The Contractor understands the nature and location and scope of the work, the character of equipment and facilities needed preliminary to and during the prosecution of the work, the general and local conditions, and all other matters which can in any way affect the work, and is not relying on any representations or promises of the Company except those contained in this contract. The Contractor understands that from time to time the Company may require the Contractor to turn over to the Company for acceptance portions of the work when they are designated by the Company Engineer as being completed.

Article 6. Supervision and Labor. a. The Contractor shall provide a competent superintendent, satisfactory to the Company Engineer, authorized to act for the Contractor. The Contractor shall promptly remove from the work and the Company's premises any superintendent or employee of the Contractor whose work is not satisfactory to the Company Engineer. The superintendent shall not be changed except with the consent of the Company Engineer, unless the superintendent proves to be unsatisfactory to the Contractor and ceases to be in his employ.

b. The Contractor's superintendent or a competent assistant superintendent shall be on the premises at all times during working hours and in responsible charge of the work on behalf of the Contractor. The Contractor's executive officers shall give the work such personal supervision as may be necessary in the opinion of the Company.

c. All labor shall be performed in a thorough and workmanlike manner in strict accordance with this contract. The Contractor shall enforce strict discipline and good order among the Contractor's employees. The Contractor shall exercise the necessary supervision and control to prevent the Contractor's employees from violating any of the plant rules and regulations.

Article 7. Authority of Company Engineer. The Company shall provide a competent Company Engineer, who shall have authority to direct all phases of the work and to approve all authorized costs except as otherwise provided herein. The Company Engineer shall have authority to reject work and material which does not conform to the contract. He shall also have authority to stop the work whenever such stoppage may, in his opinion, be necessary to ensure the proper execution of the contract.

Article 8. Changes in the Work. Upon written order of the Company, the work may be altered, increased, or decreased. In such event, the Contractor shall furnish a written cost estimate of the work to be added or omitted.

Article 9. Completion of Work. It is understood that time is of the essence and that, subject to the directions of the Company Engineer, the Contractor shall complete all authorized work in a minimum of time consistent with good construction practices under the existing conditions or circumstances

Article 10. Cost of Work. The Company will pay the Contractor for actual costs necessarily and reasonably incurred for the proper performance of the work, such costs to include the following items

a. Wages and salaries of Contractor's employees performing authorized work at the job site, o engaged elsewhere in purchasing, expediting the procurement and delivery of materials and equip ment, and in engineering and drafting, for such part of their time as is employed on this work. A wage and salary classifications and rates and any other compensatory agreements covering em ployees, and the methods of calculation thereof, must have the Company Engineer's written approva before the Contractor makes commitments relating thereto. The Contractor shall make no changes in any labor contracts or employment agreements relating to the work without the Company Engineer's prior written approval. No overtime or holiday work shall be performed without the prior approval of the Company Engineer.

b. Cost of necessary materials, equipment, tools, supplies, fuel, freight charges, and services. Cost of construction of temporary structures and facilities at the job site and the maintenance thereof, provided the Company Engineer's prior written approval was obtained for their installation.

c. Traveling expenses directly chargeable to the work, provided the Company Engineer's prior approval was obtained.

d. Actual initial moving expenses to and final moving expenses from the job site of the Contractor's key personnel necessary for prosecuting the work, provided the Company Engineer's prior approval was obtained. Such initial moving expense of any employee is not to exceed the amount which would be incurred by his moving from the Contractor's main office to the job site, and total moving expense for any employee is not to exceed twice such initial expense.

e. Reasonable rentals on construction equipment, tools, warehouses, and offices, whether rented from the Contractor or others, in accordance with written rental agreements which must have the prior written approval of the Company Engineer; transportation of construction equipment, costs of loading, unloading, installation, dismantling, and removal, as provided in the rental agreements. Rental rates shall not be higher than the existing local standard rates. When the total rental charges for any item of rental equipment owned by the Contractor or by a party controlled by the Contractor equals the market value of such equipment at the time of rental by the Company, which value shall be mutually agreed upon before rental thereof, no further rental charge shall be made for additional continuous use of such equipment. Repair and replacement costs shall be excluded from the rental agreements and shall only be authorized as cost of work when they are minor, do not constitute a major overhauling, do not add materially to the life of the equipment, and have received the prior written approval of the Company Engineer.

f. Social Security and employment taxes and contributions applicable to the wages and salaries of the Contractor's employees performing authorized work under this contract and all sales, excise, or other taxes paid by the Contractor on materials, equipment, supplies, and services chargeable to the contract.

g. The cost of all subcontracts which have the prior written approval of the Company Engineer.

h. Cost of necessary licenses, permit fees, insurance policies, and bonds required by the contract or by law.

i. Royalties, damages for patent infringement, and costs of defending suits therefor arising out of the use of inventions required by the Company or designated in the plans or specifications, subject to Article 26.

j. The cost of reconstructing any work destroyed or damaged, not covered by insurance, and not caused by failure on the part of any officers or members of the Contractor's firm, or of its other representatives having supervision or direction of the work in whole or in part, to exercise good faith or the standard of care which is normally exercised in the conduct of the business of a contractor; but expenditures under this paragraph must have the prior written approval of the Company.

Article 11. Items Not Cost of Work. a. The Contractor will not be paid for expenses of operating the Contractor's main or regular branch offices, for interest on capital employed or on money borrowed, or for overhead or general expenses of any kind incurred at the Contractor's main or regualr branch offices, including salaries of officers, owners, or partners of the Contractor.

b. The Contractor will not be paid for any illness or vacation pay for any of the Contractor's employees.

Article 12. Contractor's Fee. a. The Contractor will be paid a fee of ______________________ ______________________________________ ($__________) as complete compensation for services in performing the contract in its entirety, including administration, home and branch office overhead and salaries, and profit.

b. If a change made by the Company as provided in Article 8 substantially alters the scope of the work, the Contractor's fee will be adjusted by an amount equal to __________ per cent of the cost of the work added or omitted, as determined by mutual agreement.

Article 13. Payment. a. Promptly after the first of each month during the progress of the work, the Contractor shall furnish the Company ______________________________________ a full detailed written statement of all authorized costs incurred during the preceding calendar month in performing the work, accompanied by receipted bills for all labor and materials furnished, payments made to subcontractors, and other authorized expenses, or other proof of the correctness of the statements satisfactory to the Company. If any bills are outstanding against the Contractor for labor, materials, or other costs, the Company may pay such bills and deduct the amount from the monthly statement. The Company ______________________ will promptly check the monthly statement, and upon his written approval the Company will pay the Contractor the approved amount by the ________ day of the month, provided ________ copies of the statement have been delivered to the Company ______________________ by the ________ day of the month.

b. The monthly statement shall also include an application for payment of ________ per cent of the Contractor's fee earned during the preceding month based upon the percentage of job completion as estimated by the Contractor and approved by the Company Engineer. The remaining ________ per cent of the Contractor's fee will be withheld until the work shall have been completed, inspected, tested, and finally accepted in writing by the Company. Within 30 days thereafter the total balance shall be paid to the Contractor.

c. No certificate or approval given or payment made to the Contractor under this contract, or partial or entire acceptance, use, or occupancy of the work by the Company shall constitute acceptance of work not in compliance with the contract. When the work is completed, the Contractor shall apply to the Company Engineer for final acceptance and payment and furnish a complete release of all liens arising out of this contract or receipts in full in lieu thereof and a certificate that such releases and receipts include all the labor and material for which a lien could be filed. Prior to final payment, and as a condition thereto, the Contractor shall furnish the Company a certificate that all bills and claims have been satisfied, except those listed therein and agreed to by the Company, and a release of all claims against the Company, its officers, and employees, arising out of this contract, except such claims as may be excepted therefrom by the Contractor and agreed to by the Company, and except claims of third persons as may be unknown to the Contractor. Final acceptance and payment shall constitute a release and waiver of all claims by the Company except those arising from unsettled liens, from defective work appearing after final payment, or from failure to comply with the specifications.

Article 14. Discounts, Rebates, Refunds. All discounts, rebates, and refunds shall accrue to the Company and the Contractor shall take the necessary steps to secure them.

Article 15. Records, Accounting, Inspection. The Contractor shall keep full and detailed records and accounts in a manner approved by the Company. The Contractor shall afford the Company's authorized personnel and independent auditors, if any, full access to the work and to all of the Contractor's books, records, correspondence, instructions, drawings, receipts, vouchers, and other documents, relating to work under this contract, and the Contractor shall preserve all such records for ________ years after final payment.

Article 16. Disposal of Surplus Materials. All sales of surplus materials, equipment, supplies, and scrap must have the prior written approval of the Company Engineer. All returns from such sales shall belong to the Company.

Article 17. Continuance of Work. In case of any dispute, the Contractor shall continue to prosecute the work pending determination thereof, unless requested by the Company to suspend work.

Article 18. Protection of Work and Property. The Contractor shall protect all materials, equipment, and completed and partially completed work from loss and damage, including theft and damage by weather, and, if necessary, shall provide suitable housing therefor, and shall correct any damage or disfigurement to contiguous work or property resulting from the work.

Article 19. Inspection. The Contractor shall at all times provide the Company Engineer complete opportunity and facilities for the inspection of the work done by the Contractor, and also of materials and equipment during the course of fabrication by the Contractor's suppliers, and the Contractor shall abide by inspection procedures and requirements established by the Company Engineer.

Article 20. Safety Requirements and Equipment. The Contractor shall take all necessary precautions to keep the premises free of safety hazards and shall comply with all applicable provisions of law and building codes relating to injury to persons and property on or about the premises where the work is being performed. The Contractor shall prevent all agents, employees, licensees, and invitees of the Contractor from smoking on the Company's premises and from operating or using any flame, spark, or explosion hazard-producing device anywhere upon such premises without the written approval of the Company Engineer. No cutting of any structural member of any part of the existing buildings which might weaken same in any way shall be done without the written approval of the Company Engineer. The Contractor shall observe the safety practices listed in the *Manual of Accident Prevention in Construction,* prepared by the Associated General Contractors of America, and shall adhere to the accident and fire-prevention regulations of the plant concerned.

Article 21. Subcontracting and Assignment. This contract may not be assigned or encumbered, nor may the Contractor subcontract the work in whole or in part, unless written permission is first obtained from the Company, but the Company may assign this contract to any of its parent, subsidiary, or affiliated corporations or to the transferee of the whole or any part of the Company's business. The Company shall have the right to direct the Contractor to subcontract such portions of the work as the Company may deem advisable. The Contractor shall be as fully responsible to the Company for the acts, omissions, materials, and workmanship of subcontractors and their employees as for the acts, omissions, materials, and workmanship of the Contractor. The Contractor will bind every subcontractor by written contract to observe all the terms of this contract to the extent that they may be applicable to such subcontractors.

Article 22. Company's Drawings. All plans, drawings, prints, and specifications, and all copies thereof supplied to the Contractor by the Company or prepared by the Contractor as part of the work, shall be the property of the Company. Contractor will not use them or permit them to be used on other work and shall return them to the Company upon completion of the work.

Article 23. Cleanup of Company's Premises. The Contractor shall clean up the Company's premises in a thorough and workmanlike manner to the satisfaction of the Company Engineer whenever necessary during the progress of the work and also whenever requested to do so by the Company Engineer.

Article 24. Title to Materials and Equipment. The Company shall have title to all work completed or in the course of construction or installation, and shall also have title to all construction materials, equipment, tools, and supplies, the cost of which is chargeable to the work, and title to the same shall pass to the Company simultaneously with the passage of title from the vendors thereof to the Contractor.

Article 25. Liens. The Contractor shall keep the Company's properties free and clear from all liens and charges arising out of the work, including materialmen's, laborers', and mechanics' liens, and shall give the Company prompt written notice of actual and prospective claims of any such liens or charges known to the Contractor.

Article 26. Patents. The Contractor shall defend all suits or claims for infringement of any alleged patent rights arising under this contract, and shall indemnify the Company from loss on account thereof and pay any judgments awarded thereunder, including attorneys' fees, except that the Company shall be responsible for all such loss and shall indemnify the Contractor therefor when a particular process or the product of a particular manufacturer is specified in writing by the Company or is specified in plans, specifications, or drawings furnished by the Company; but if the Contractor has information that any process or product specified by the Company may be an infringement of a patent, the Contractor shall be responsible for such loss unless he promptly gives such information to the Company Engineer. The Contractor hereby grants to the Company a nonexclusive, royalty-free license under patents now or hereafter owned by the Contractor covering any machines, apparatus, processes, articles, or products employed or produced in the execution of the work.

Article 27. Confidential Information. The Contractor shall not disclose any information relating to the secret processes, machinery, apparatus, or trade secrets of the Company or of any affiliated company, or any other confidential information acquired during the term of or as a result of this contract, except to the extent required by the proper performance of this contract. The Contractor shall take all reasonable precautions to prevent its subcontractors and all officers, employees, and agents of the Contractor and its subcontractors from disclosing any such information. This obligation shall survive the performance of the contract, or any termination, discharge, or cancellation thereof.

Article 28. Indemnity. The Contractor shall indemnify against and save the Company harmless from all losses and all liability, expenses, and other detriments of every nature and description (including attorneys' fees) to which the Company may be subjected by reason of any act or omission of the Contractor or of any of the Contractor's subcontractors, employees, agents, invitees, or licensees, where such loss, liability, expense, or other detriment arises out of or in connection with the performance of work under this contract, including but not limited to personal injury and loss of or damage to property of the Company or others.

Article 29. Compliance with Laws. The Contractor shall give all notices required by and compl with all Federal, state, and local laws, ordinances, rules, and regulations relating to the work, an shall secure, at the Company's request, documents evidencing compliance therewith, and the Contractor shall secure and deliver to the Company all necessary permits and licenses required thereunder If the drawings or specifications are at variance therewith, the Contractor shall promptly notify th Company Engineer in writing.

Article 30. Force Majeure. Both parties shall be absolved from liability for any act, omission, o circumstance occasioned by any cause whatsoever not within the control of the party claiming suspension and which such party could not, by reasonable diligence, have avoided. Such acts, omissions or circumstances, however, shall not relieve such party of liability in the event of its failure to us reasonable diligence to remedy the situation and remove the cause in an adequate manner an with all reasonable dispatch and to give notice and full particulars of the same in writing to the othe party as soon as possible after the occurrence of the cause relied on. The requirement that an *force majeure* be remedied with all reasonable dispatch shall not require the settlement of strike or labor controversies by acceding to the demand of the opposing party or parties.

Article 31. Termination. a. Should conditions arise which, in the Company's opinion, make it advisable or necessary to discontinue work under the contract, the Company may terminate this contrac in whole or in part without fault of the Contractor by giving seven days' written notice to the Contracto specifying the date and the extent to which the contract is terminated. Upon any such termination the Company shall take possession of the premises and of all or any part of the materials and equipment delivered or en route to the site. The Contractor will be paid all unpaid authorized costs o work properly incurred plus the balance of earned fee. Earned fee shall be computed by applyin the percentage of job completion at the date of termination to the total fee provided for in Articl 12. The percentage of job completion shall be agreed upon in writing by the Contractor and th Company Engineer. Such payments shall be made within thirty days after receipt of Contractor' statement as provided in Article 13, and such statement shall include the balance of earned fee computed as above provided.

b. If the Contractor should fail to prosecute the work with reasonable promptness and diligence or fail to make prompt payment to subcontractors or for material or labor, or should fail or refuse t supply sufficient skilled workmen or materials of the proper quality, or should become insolvent o be unable to pay its debts as they mature, or make a general assignment for the benefit of creditors or if a receiver should be appointed for the whole or any substantial part of the Contractor's property, or if the Contractor should become in any way the subject of a bankruptcy petition, or if th Contractor defaults in the performance of any material provision of the contract, the Company ma exercise any one or more of the following rights:

1. Make an equitable deduction from any sums due the Contractor to compensate the Company for the default, recover from the Contractor either the estimated or the actual cost to the Company of correcting the default, and recover from the Contractor all other damages sustained by th Company as a result of any of the Contractor's defaults not covered by the foregoing.

2. The Company shall be under no obligation to make any payment to the Contractor so lon as the Contractor is in default under this or any other contract with the Company.

3. The Company may terminate the contract by giving at least seven days' written notice to th Contractor specifying the default and the effective date of termination and, without prejudice to othe rights or remedies provided by law or by this contract, may take possession of the premises and o all or any part of the materials or equipment delivered or in transit to the site and finish the work b whatever method it may deem expedient.

4. On receipt of notice of termination the Contractor shall, unless otherwise directed by th Company Engineer, immediately discontinue the work and shall, if requested by the Compan Engineer, make every reasonable effort to procure cancellation of all existing orders or contract upon terms satisfactory to the Company and shall thereafter do only such work as may be necessar to preserve and protect work completed or in progress and to protect material, plant, and equipment at the job site or in transit.

5. If requested by the Company Engineer, the Contractor shall assign to the Company any o all contracts or options made by the Contractor in performance of the work and shall execute an deliver all such papers and take such steps as the Company may request for the purpose of vestin in the Company all rights, privileges, and benefits therein.

6. In the event of termination under this Article 31*b*, the Contractor shall be paid for unpaid authorized costs of work prior to termination and all reasonable costs incurred at the Company's request after termination, subject to Company approval in the manner specified in this contract. The Contractor shall also be paid the balance of earned fee less all amounts subject to withholding under the contract. Earned fee shall be computed by applying the percentage of job completion at the date of termination to the total fee provided for in Article 12. The percentage of job completion shall be determined by the Company Engineer.

Article 32. Rental Equipment. a. During the progress of the work, the Contractor shall not remove any items of rental equipment from the work without the approval of the Company Engineer. When items are no longer needed in the work, the Contractor shall promptly request the Company Engineer's permission to remove them, and shall do so when and as directed by the Company Engineer.

b. In the event the contract is terminated for default of the Contractor, the Contractor shall assign to the Company at its option all existing leases of rental equipment belonging to others, and the Company shall have the right to retain all equipment at that time being rented from the Contractor, upon existing terms and conditions as governed by Article 10e hereof, for a period not exceeding the time utilized by the Company in completing the work.

Article 33. Notices. All notices hereunder shall be deemed to be made properly if sent by registered mail to the Contractor at ________ (Address) and to the Company at ________ (Address). The address may be changed by either party by similar notice. Notice so mailed shall be effective upon mailing. Either party giving such notice shall also notify promptly the other party's Superintendent or Engineer, as appropriate.

Article 34. Insurance. The Contractor shall comply with the insurance obligations set forth in Schedule A, "Insurance to be Carried by Contractor," attached hereto and incorporated in the contract.

Article 35. Miscellaneous Provisions. a. This contract constitutes the entire agreement between the Contractor and the Company relating to the work. There are no previous or contemporary representations or warranties of the Company or the Contractor not set forth herein.

b. Except as specifically provided herein, no modification, waiver, termination, recision, discharge, or cancellation of this contract or of any terms thereof shall be binding on the Company unless in writing and executed by an officer or employee of the Company specifically authorized to do so.

c. No waiver of any provision of or a default under this contract shall affect the right of the Company thereafter to enforce said provision or to exercise any right or remedy in the event of any other default, whether or not similar.

d. No modification, waiver, termination, discharge, or cancellation of this contract or any term thereof shall impair the Company's rights with respect to any liabilities, whether or not liquidated, of the Contractor to the Company theretofore accrued.

e. All rights and remedies of the Company specified in this contract are in addition to the Company's other rights and remedies.

f. The Contractor shall remain an independent contractor and shall have no power, nor shall the Contractor represent that the Contractor has any power, to bind the Company or to assume or to create any obligation express or implied on behalf of the Company.

IN WITNESS WHEREOF, the Contractor and the Company have caused this contract to be executed as of the day and year first above written.

____________________	____________________
Contractor	Owner
By: ____________________	By: ____________________
(Title)	(Title)

SCHEDULE A: INSURANCE COVERAGE

By Contractor

The Contractor and Contractor's subcontractors shall obtain, pay for, and keep in force the following insurance effective in all localities where the Contractor may perform any work hereunder, with such carrier or carriers as shall be acceptable to the Company. Prior to starting work hereunder, the Contractor shall deliver to the Company one copy of policies and certificates in triplicate evidencing that such insurance is in effect and providing that the insurer will give the Company at leas 10 days' written notice of any material change in or cancellation of such insurance; the policy cop and three copies of certificates shall be delivered to the Company's Purchasing Department c ______________________.

Contractor's Insurance

a. Workmen's Compensation (including coverage for occupational diseases) or equivalent require by law and in any event covering all of the Contractor's employees who may be engaged directl or indirectly in any work hereunder. (Certificates indicating coverage for a limited time onl shall not be compliance herewith.)

b. Employer's Liability (including coverage for occupational diseases), $ for the injury or deat of any one employee in any one accident; $ for the injury or death of more than one em ployee in any one accident.

c. Comprehensive General Public Liability (including liability assumed by contract):
   1. Bodily Injury, $ for the injury or death of any one person in any one accident, $ for the injury or death of more than one person in any one accident.
   2. Property Damage, $ per accident; $ in the aggregate.

d. Comprehensive Automobile Liability covering owned, hired, and other nonowned vehicles of th Contractor:
   1. Bodily Injury, $ for the injury or death of any one person in any one accident; $ for the injury or death of more than one person in any one accident.
   2. Property Damage, $

e. If the Contractor employs any subcontractor, the Contractor shall, in addition to the insuranc referred to above, carry Contractor's Contingent (Protective) Bodily Injury and Property Damag Liability Insurance in the above specified amounts.

If any policy of insurance or any term or condition thereof shall not be satisfactory to the Company the Contractor shall make all reasonable efforts to secure insurance satisfactory to the Company Nothing herein shall be construed to authorize the Contractor to secure policies of insurance nc specified above covering risks against which the Company has insurance.

The Contractor shall give prompt notice to the Company of all personal injuries and of all losse of or damages to property arising out of work under this contract or for which a claim might be mad against the Company and shall promptly report to the Company all such claims of which the Contracto has notice, whether relating to matters insured or uninsured. No settlement or payment of any clair for loss, injury or damage or other matter as to which the Company may be charged with obligatio to make any payment or reimbursement shall be made by the Contractor without the written approva of the Company.

Each certificate of insurance delivered by the Contractor hereunder shall contain the followin endorsement: "All rights of subrogation under this contract are hereby waived by the insurer wit respect to claims against ______________________ and/or any of its subsidiary o affiliated companies or corporations."

In reduction of any liability to the Contractor, the Company shall be entitled to the benefit of an insurance of the Contractor covering the loss in question and to any payments made or to be mad by or on behalf of insurers to the Contractor, whether absolute or in the form of advances, loans o otherwise, except to the extent that the rights of the Contractor under such insurance would b thereby impaired.

By Company

The Company shall place and maintain in force with responsible insurance carriers during the lif of the work, fire and extended coverage insurance covering the Company's property and all-ris property damage insurance insuring the work and the Company's property other than the work The Company shall furnish the Contractor with certificates in triplicate evidencing that such insuranc is in effect and providing that the insurance will give the Contractor at least 10 days' written notic of any material change in or cancellaton of such insurance. The Company agrees that each certificat of insurance delivered by it hereunder shall contain the following endorsement: "All rights of subro gation under this contract are hereby waived by the insurer with respect to claims against ________ ______________________ its agents, employees, officers, and subcontractors doing work for th Contractor in connection with this contract."

EXHIBIT 16–2. TYPICAL LUMP-SUM CONTRACT

CONTRACT made the ________ day of ____________________, 19___, by and between ____, a ______________________________ corporation of ____________________ ____________________, hereinafter called the Contractor, and ____________________ ______________________________, hereinafter called the Company. The Contractor and the Company mutually agree as follows:

DESCRIPTION OF WORK

The Contractor shall construct for the Company ______________________________ ____

at ______________________________, as hereinafter provided. The Contractor shall perform all work shown on and in accordance with the plans, specifications, and drawings which are attached hereto and incorporated herein entitled __________ (Insert caption ______________________________ Drawings mentioned therein are descriptive of the work as used on plans and specifications.) an integral part of this contract as if attached hereto. The plans and specifications are listed and identified on Schedule A attached hereto.

Performing the work shall include the furnishing of and paying for all labor, supervision, materials, equipment, services, utilities, and facilities necessary or proper to complete the work, in accordance with the General Conditions set forth herein.

The work shall be commenced not later than ________ and shall be completed not later than ________. It is agreed that time of performance by the Contractor is of the essence. The Contractor shall furnish the Company copies of such progress reports as the Contractor ordinarily prepares in scheduling and performing the work.

The total sum to be paid to the Contractor for the performance of the contract in its entirety shall be $________, herein called the contract price.

Changes in the Work. Upon written order of the Company, the work may be altered, increased, or decreased. The Contractor's price for work added shall be submitted to the Company in writing, and only when the Company's written approval has been given may additional work be commenced and the contract price increased accordingly. An equitable deduction will be made from the contract price for work omitted. To facilitate the computation of such deduction, the Contractor shall, upon request of the Company, submit a net unit price schedule making clear the basis upon which the contract price was computed.

Payment. a. The Contractor shall furnish to the Company ____________________ a written monthly statement of the portion of the contract price represented by the value of the work completed by the Contractor during each calendar month, exclusive of materials and equipment not installed. The Company ____________________ will promptly check the monthly statement, and upon his written approval the Company will pay the Contractor a sum equal to ______ per cent of the amount approved. Such payment will be made by the ________ day of the month provided ________ copies of the statement have been delivered to the Company __________ __________ by the ________ day of the month. The monthly statements shall be prepared in such detail and in such manner and shall be supported by such evidence as to enable the Company Engineer readily to verify the same.

b. The remaining ________ per cent balance of each monthly statement shall be withheld until all the work shall have been completed, inspected, tested, and finally accepted in writing by the Company. Within thirty days thereafter, the total balance shall be paid to the Contractor.

c. No certificate or approval given or payment made to the Contractor under this contract, or partial or entire acceptance, use, or occupancy of the work by the Company shall constitute acceptance of work not in compliance with the contract.

d. When the work is completed, the Contractor shall apply to the Company Engineer for final acceptance and payment and furnish a complete release of all liens arising out of this contract or receipts in full in lieu thereof and a certificate that such releases and receipts include all the labor and material for which a lien could be filed. If any subcontractor refuses to furnish a release or receipt, the Contractor may furnish a bond satisfactory to the Company Engineer to indemnify the Company against any lien which may be filed by such subcontractor.

e. Final acceptance and payment shall constitute a release and waiver of all claims by the Company except those arising from unsettled liens, from defective work appearing after final payment, or from failure to comply with the specifications. Acceptance by the Contractor of final payment shall constitute a release and waiver of all claims by the Contractor against the Company, its officers and employees.

Expediting Procurement. In each instance where the Contractor is unable to furnish materials and equipment at a rate which will permit the Contractor to meet any of the completion dates, the Contractor will immediately give the Company written notice of such circumstances. If the Contractor should fail to use such reasonable diligence in expediting the purchase and delivery of any items of materials or equipment as is consistent with good construction and purchasing practices, the Company shall then have the right to expedite the purchase and delivery of such items and may deduct the reasonable cost thereof from the contract price.

Title to Materials and Equipment. The Company shall have title to all work completed or in course of construction or installation, and shall also have title to all equipment, materials, and supplies for which any payment has been made to the Contractor by the Company. The Contractor shall at the Company's request furnish proof of the Contractor's ownership, free from all liens and encumbrances, of any equipment, materials, and supplies furnished by the Contractor.

Liens. The Contractor shall keep the Company's properties free and clear from and indemnify the Company against all liens and charges arising out of the work, including materialmen's, laborers', and mechanics' liens. In case any such liens or charges are claimed or filed, the Company may deduct or withhold from any monies due or owing to the Contractor such amounts as may be reasonably necessary to pay off and discharge any such liens and charges and may pay off and discharge any such liens and charges, and the Contractor shall in any case indemnify the Company for all expenses, damages, and costs in connection therewith, including attorneys' fees. The Contractor shall deliver to the Company prompt written notice of actual or prospective claims of any such liens or charges known to the Contractor.

Patents. The Contractor shall pay all royalties and license fees and shall defend all suits or claims for infringement of any alleged patent rights and shall indemnify the Company from loss on account thereof, and pay any judgments awarded thereunder, including attorneys' fees, except that the Company shall be responsible for all such loss when a particular process or the product of a particular manufacturer is specified in writing by the Company; but if the Contractor has information that the process or product specified is an infringement of a patent, the Contractor shall be responsible for such loss unless he promptly gives such information to the Company Engineer. The Contractor hereby grants to the Company a nonexclusive, royalty-free license under patents now or hereafter owned by the Contractor covering any machines, apparatus, processes, articles, or products employed or produced in the execution of the work.

Termination. a. Should conditions arise which, in the Company's opinion, make it advisable or necessary to discontinue work under the contract, the Company may terminate this contract in whole or in part without fault of the Contractor by giving seven days' written notice to the Contractor specifying the date and the extent to which the contract is terminated. Upon any such termination, the Company shall take possession of the premises and of all or any part of the materials and equipment delivered or en route to the site. Within thirty days after such termination, the Contractor shall be paid such an amount as when added to amounts previously paid will equal the contract price less an equitable deduction for the unperformed portion of the work. To facilitate the computation of such deduction, the Contractor shall, upon request of the Company, submit to the Company a net unit price schedule showing the basis upon which the Contractor's price was computed.

b. If the Contractor should fail to prosecute the work with reasonable promptness and diligence, or fail to make prompt payment to subcontractors or for material or labor, or should fail or refuse to supply sufficient skilled workmen or materials of the proper quality, or should become insolvent or be unable to pay its debts as they mature, or make a general assignment of the benefit of creditors or if a receiver should be appointed for the whole or any substantial part of the Contractor's property, or if the Contractor should become in any way the subject of a bankruptcy petition, or if the Contractor defaults in the performance of any material provision of the contract, the Company may exercise any one or more of the following rights:

1. The Company may require the Contractor, without cost to the Company, to remove any work not in accordance with the contract and perform the work in compliance therewith; make an equitable deduction from the contract price and from any monthly payments thereon to compensate the Company for the default; recover from the Contractor, at the Company's option, either the estimated or actual cost to the Company of correcting the default; and recover from the Contractor all damages sustained by the Company as the result of any of the Contractor's defaults not otherwise covered herein.

2. The Company shall be under no obligation to make any payment to the Contractor so long as the Contractor is in default under this or any other contract with the Company.

3. The Company may terminate the contract by giving at least seven days' written notice to the Contractor specifying the default and the effective date of termination and, without prejudice to other rights or remedies provided by law or by this contract, may take possession of the premises and of all or any part of the materials or equipment delivered or in transit to the site and finish the work by whatever method it may deem expedient.

4. On receipt of notice of termination the Contractor shall, unless otherwise directed by the Company Engineer, immediately discontinue the work and shall thereafter do only such work as may be necessary to preserve and protect work completed or in progress and to protect material, plant, and equipment at the job site or in transit.

5. If requested by the Company Engineer, the Contractor shall assign to the Company any or all contracts or options made by the Contractor in performance of the work and shall execute and deliver all such papers and take such steps as the Company may request for the purpose of vesting in the Company all rights, privileges, and benefits therein.

6. In the event of termination under this article, the Contractor shall not be entitled to receive any further payment until the work is finished. If the unpaid balance of the contract price shall exceed the cost of finishing the work, such excess shall be paid to the Contractor. If such cost shall exceed the unpaid balance of the contract price, the Contractor shall pay the difference to the Company.

NOTE: For the additional terms to be used in this type of contract, reference should be made to the text of this section and also the typical cost-plus-fixed-fee contract in Exhibit 16–1.

EXHIBIT 16–3. TYPICAL GUARANTEED MAXIMUM-PRICE CONTRACT

Contractor's Fee and Guaranteed Maximum Cost. The Contractor will be paid a fee of ________ ____________________ ($________) as complete compensation for services in performing the contract in its entirety, including administration, home and branch office overhead and salaries, and profit. Contractor agrees that the total cost of the work, exclusive of the fee, will not exceed the guaranteed maximum cost of ____________________ ($________). Should the cost of the work exceed said guaranteed maximum cost, contractor will absorb the excess.

OR

Share Excess Costs. It is agreed, however, that contractor's liability for any costs in excess of the aforesaid guaranteed maximum cost shall in no event exceed the amount of ________ per cent (________%) of contractor's fee. Owner shall be responsible for the payment of costs in excess of contractor's said liability which shall be chargeable to the cost of the work in the same manner as any other costs.

OR

Share Savings. If the work is completed for an amount less than the total guaranteed maximum cost, the savings shall be divided ________ per cent (________%) to contractor and ________ per cent (________%) to owner. In computing the savings, the actual cost of the work shall be subtracted from the guaranteed maximum cost stated herein exclusive of the contractor's fee.

NOTE: For the additional terms to be used in this type of contract, reference should be made to the text of this section and also the typical cost-plus-fixed-fee contract in Exhibit 16–1.

EXHIBIT 16–4. TYPICAL ADDITIONAL TERMS AND CONDITIONS OF PURCHASE ORDERS INVOLVING CONSTRUCTION

1. *Performing the Work.* Unless otherwise provided, performing the work shall include the furnishing of and paying for all labor, supervision, materials, equipment, services, utilities, and facilities necessary or proper to complete the work in accordance with plans and specifications. Time of performance by the Contractor is of the essence.

2. *Quality.* Unless otherwise provided, all materials and equipment shall be new. Workmanship and materials shall be of the best quality.

3. *Cooperation.* Contractor shall perform the work so as to maintain plant traffic and manufacturing operations as nearly normal as possible, assist in keeping clear walks, roadways, and railroad sidings, shall cooperate with, and shall not in any way interfere with operations of, other contractors and the Company.

4. *Understanding of the Contractor.* Contractor understands the nature and location of the work and all matters which can in any way affect the work, and is not relying on any representations or promises of Company except those contained in this contract.

5. *Supervision.* Contractor's Superintendent or assistant shall be on the premises at all times during working hours and in charge of the work. Contractor shall enforce strict discipline among its employees and require them to observe all plant working rules and safety regulations.

6. *Changes in the Work.* The Company may order the work to be altered, increased, or decreased, and the contract price will be adjusted accordingly by mutual agreement.

7. *Payment.* Company may withhold payment until 30 days after it has accepted the work. Neither payment nor acceptance, use or occupancy shall relieve Contractor of responsibility for defective work not in accordance with the contract.

8. *Protection of Work.* Contractor shall protect all materials, equipment, and completed and partially completed work from loss and damage.

9. *Inspection.* The Contractor shall at all times provide the Company complete opportunity and facilities for the inspection of the work done by the Contractor, and also of materials and equipment during the course of fabrication by the Contractor's suppliers.

10. *Plant Safety Rules.* The Contractor shall comply with and require its employees to comply with all plant safety rules and shall perform the work in a safe manner; shall keep the premises free of safety hazards; and shall likewise comply with all applicable laws and building codes. The Contractor will not start any work involving the use of arc or gas welding or cutting, fires, rock drills, power chisels, electrically operated tools, or any gasoline-driven tools or equipment or other flame, spark, or explosion hazard-producing device until a fire permit has been posted by the Plant Fire Authority in a conspicuous place at the site of the work. No such work will be continued by the Contractor after the fire permit has been removed by the Plant Fire Authority.

11. *Subcontracting and Assignment.* This contract may not be assigned or encumbered, nor may the Contractor subcontract the work in whole or in part, unless written permission is first obtained from the Company; but the Company may assign this contract to any of its parent, subsidiary, or affiliated corporations or to the transferee of the whole or any part of the Company's business.

12. *Title to Materials and Equipment.* The Company shall have title to all work completed or in course of construction or installation, and shall also have title to all equipment, materials, and supplies for which any payment has been made to the Contractor by the Company.

13. *Indemnity.* The Contractor hereby releases and discharges the Company from liability for and hereby assumes the risk of loss of or damage to property of the Contractor. The Contractor shall indemnify against and save the Company harmless from all losses and all liability, expenses, and other detriments of every nature and description (including attorneys' fees), to which the Company may be subjected by reason of any act or omission of the Contractor or of any of the Contractor's subcontractors, employees, agents, invitees, or licensees, where such loss, liability, expense, or other detriment arises out of or in connection with the performance of work under this contract, including but not limited to unpaid taxes, liens, personal injury, and loss of or damage to property of the Company or others.

14. *Termination. a.* Should conditions arise which, in the Company's opinion, make it advisable or necessary to discontinue work under the contract, the Company may terminate this contract in whole or in part without fault of the Contractor by giving two days' written notice to the Contractor specifying

the date and the extent to which the contract is terminated, and payment to the Contractor for work performed shall be determined by mutual agreement.

b. If the Contractor should default in any material provision of the contract, the Company, in addition to all other rights provided by law, may require the Contractor, without cost to the Company, to remove any work not in accordance with the contract and perform the work in compliance therewith.

15. *Insurance.* Contractor shall comply with all insurance obligations specified in the attachment entitled, "Insurance to be Carried by the Contractor."

16. *Bonds.* If required by the Company, the Contractor shall furnish a performance and payment bond in form and amount and with such surety or sureties as shall be approved by the Company. If such bond is required, the Company will reimburse the Contractor for its actual cost.

17. *General.* The provisions on the face of the purchase order hereto attached shall prevail over any conflicting provisions hereof and the provisions hereof shall prevail over any conflicting provisions on the reverse side of the purchase order.

EXHIBIT 16–5. TYPICAL ENGINEERING LETTER CONTRACT

Gentlemen:

This will constitute an agreement between us covering engineering services you agree to render us in connection with ______ at our ______ ______ Plant in ______.

Under our direction and in accordance with our request, and from information and data supplied by us, you are to perform ______ engineering services as required for a detailed cost estimate and schedule. This work shall include ______ ______.

You shall make such studies as are necessary to determine the economical and technical advantages of alternatives, and you will prepare a detailed estimate of the installed cost of the plant and the overall engineering, purchasing, and construction schedule. This work shall all be directed towards establishing a firm basis for detailed design and purchasing for the complete plant.

It is understood that time is important and that the work is to start about ______ ______ and is to be completed within a minimum of time consistent with good engineering and professional practices.

For the time of your personnel engaged on the work, we shall pay you at the rates shown in Schedule A[4] attached, plus ______ per cent to cover Federal and State social security, workmen's compensation, unemployment, life, health, and other insurances, other ______ company benefits, overhead, burden and fee. Reproduction prints made in your offices, and work on your data processing machines and computers will be charged at the rates and in accordance with the provisions set forth in the attached Schedule B.[5] Reproduction prints made elsewhere or purchased by you from others will be paid at their cost. Automobiles owned by you or your employees and used on the work will be paid for at the rate of ______ cents per mile. All other costs and expenses incurred by you on the work, such as, but not limited to, travel, telegraph and telephone, postage, and the like, will be paid at their cost. You agree to work overtime if we so request, but no overtime or holiday work shall be performed without our prior authorization.

You shall furnish us monthly an invoice, in triplicate, of the wages and salaries paid by you to your personnel for work done by them hereunder and of the other reimbursable expenditures made by you in accordance with the terms of this agreement. The invoice shall also include a charge for the payment of your markup based upon the portion of the wage and salary payments shown in the invoice and approved by us. The invoice shall be prepared in such form and

[4] Schedule A is a list of salary rate ranges by job category as agreed to with the engineering contractor—for example, designers and draftsmen—$400 to $800 per month.

[5] Schedule B is a list of reimbursable costs, not subject to a percentage markup, as agreed to with the engineering contractor.

in such detail and be accompanied by such proof of the correctness thereof as shall meet with our satisfaction. Payment of the invoice will be made by us within fifteen (15) days of our approval thereof.

You agree not to disclose any information relating to our secret processes, machinery, apparatus, or trade secrets, or any other confidential information acquired during the term of or as a result of this contract, except to the extent required by the proper performance of this contract. You agree to take all reasonable precautions to prevent all of your officers, employees, and agents from disclosing any such information. This obligation shall survive the performance of the contract or any termination, discharge, or cancellation thereof.

All plans, drawings, prints and specifications, and all copies thereof supplied to you by us or prepared by you as a part of the work shall be our property. You agree not to use them or permit them to be used on other work and to return them to us upon completion of the work.

This work may not be assigned or encumbered by you nor may you subcontract any part thereof without our permission.

If at any time prior to the completion of the work, we should decide, for whatever cause or reason, that we do not desire to proceed with the work, then we shall have the right to terminate the work and your services, and you will be paid compensation and reimbursable costs on the basis aforementioned up to the date of termination.

You agree to comply with the insurance requirements set forth in Schedule C[6] attached.

The return to us of a signed copy of this letter will evidence your acceptance of this agreement.

Yours very truly,

(Owner's Signature)

ACCEPTED:

(Engineering Company's Signature)

By: ______________________________

Title: ____________________________

Date: ____________________________

SELECTED BIBLIOGRPHY

Clauser, H. R., ed.: *Encyclopedia of Engineering Materials and Processes,* Reinhold Publishing Co., New York, 1963

Leasing of Industrial Equipment, Machinery and Allied Products Institute and the Council for Technological Advancement, Washington, D.C., 1965

Leasing versus Buying, National Association of Purchasing Agents, New York, 1963

Sadler, Walter C.: *Legal Aspects of Construction,* McGraw-Hill Book Company, New York, 1959

Stires, D. M., and M. M. Murphy: *PERT and CPM,* Materials Management Institute, Boston, Mass., 1963

Taking Stock of Leasing, American Management Association, New York, 1965

Vancil, Richard F.: *Leasing of Industrial Equipment,* McGraw-Hill Book Company, New York, 1962

Others—Refer to Section 26, "Library and Catalog File."

[6] The need for insurance on an engineering contract is determined by the facts of each situation, depending upon the location where the work will be done. If insurance is required, use the applicable portions of Schedule A, Exhibit 16–1.

SECTION 17

PURCHASING INTERNATIONALLY

Editor

James M. Berry, Purchasing Agent, Vick Manufacturing Division, Richardson-Merrell Inc., Hatboro, Pennsylvania

Associate Editor

T. I. Elliott Shircore, B.A., Director (Purchasing), Chiswick Products Ltd., London W. 4, England

Purchasing internationally means simply the broadening of procurement to a world-wide basis.

Just as the family social and economic unit was merged into the community, so national concepts inevitably are evolving into world-wide relationships. Following the two major wars of the first half of the twentieth century and the quickening of social changes, there have developed throughout the world, paradoxically, strong nationalistic movements and opposing groupings of nations, seeking both political and economic advantages.

REGIONAL PACTS

Ideological conflicts and power struggles have arisen, with the issues blurred in many cases by nationalistic and political ambitions and aspirations. A brief review of some of the more important movements of the post-World War II period affords a background for better understanding of the nature and problems arising in purchasing internationally.

United Nations. All major countries, except (so far) the People's Republic of China, and most of the other smaller nations of the world including the numerous newly emerging independent African states, are banded together in the loose political and cultural organization of the United Nations. Having weathered varying stresses and cross-currents for a much longer period than the former League of Nations, the UN appears likely to continue to assume an increasing role in world affairs.

Common Market. The most notably successful economic, and to a lesser degree political, development has been the European Economic Community (EEC), or Common Market, referred to also as "The Six." Growing out of the European coal and steel community, the Common Market includes France, Western Germany, the Netherlands, Belgium, Luxembourg, and Italy, with Greece and several West African countries as associate members. The objective of the six full members is to establish progressively a single, unified market, with goods produced and marketed without regard to national boundaries, under common rules for the entire area administered in part by common governmental institutions.

A corollary of this development is the bringing into conformity of the tariff relationships between the EEC members and other countries throughout the world, and to undertake closer political cooperation, in the direction of a United States of Europe. Implementation of the perimeter protective tariff barrier involves, of course, problems in relation to the reciprocal tariff concessions negotiated bilaterally by various nations under the General Agreement on Tariffs and Trade (GATT).

European Free Trade Association. Although involved in preliminary discussions, the United Kingdom at first remained aloof from the Common Market, having preferential tariff relations with members of the British Commonwealth of Nations. The Commonwealth essentially represents an evolution from the British Empire, and with its long-standing and effective system of preferential trading predates the other economic groups. In competitive buying for Commonwealth countries this system has proved quite influential.

Immediately following formation of The Six, Great Britain instigated a customs union of other European states, the European Free Trade Association (EFTA), popularly called the "Outer Seven," consisting of, in addition to the U.K., Austria, Denmark, Norway, Portugal, Sweden, and Switzerland, with Finland as an associate member. Unlike the EEC, the EFTA objectives have been solely economic—concerned with gradual elimination of duty among member nations, but not unification of external tariffs.

North and South America. Formed before the turn of the century, the Organization of American States (OAS)—covering most of the countries of Central and South America with the United States (now excluding Cuba)—has been supplemented more recently by the Latin American Free Trade Area and the Central American Common Market as regional pacts for trade advantage formed since World War II.

Other Pacts. Other regional pacts formed variously after World War II for defensive and trade advantages include (as of February, 1964):

The North Atlantic Treaty Organization (NATO)—including members of both EEC and EFTA (except Austria, Sweden, and Switzerland) and Greece, Turkey, Iceland, Canada, and the United States.

The South East Asia Treaty Organization (SEATO)—containing Australia, France, New Zealand, Pakistan, the Philippine Republic, Thailand, the United Kingdom, and the United States.

The Warsaw Pact—consisting of the Union of Soviet Socialist Republics (Russia) and East Germany, Poland, Czechoslovakia, Hungary, Romania, Bulgaria, and Albania.

Pan African Freedom Movement for East, Central, and Southern Africa (PAFMECSA)—including Republic of the Congo, Ethiopia, Somalia, Tanganyika, Uganda, Rwanda, Burundi, and leading nationalistic "movements" in other British Commonwealth and High Commission Territories and Portuguese colonies (subsequently inactive and in a state of almost constant flux and realignment with shifting political currents and changing governments).

MONETARY PROBLEMS

Monetary problems relating to balance of payments, the expansion of foreign investments, both by United States corporations in other countries and by British and European business enterprises in the United States and other countries, and military and economic grants and loans to newly developing economies inject additional problems. However, they afford a broadened scope of source development for purchasing executives of the respective countries involved.

TYPES OF INTERNATIONAL PROCUREMENT

Purchasing internationally involves three distinct types of procurement: *import purchasing—the obtaining of goods from foreign countries; export purchasing—domestic procurement for supplying foreign manufacturing operations; and what might be termed "inter-national purchasing"—the procurement of goods in one foreign country for use in another.* Discussions of import and export purchasing will furnish generally the guidelines and cautions enabling adaptation to the problems of "inter-national purchasing," and therefore the third type will not be covered specifically hereafter. There may be, however, greater complications in overseas to overseas shipments—relating principally to problems with import licenses, currency differences, and quotas.

To participate effectively in any of the three types of purchasing, it is necessary to follow the evolution of the complex movements between and among various nations and the groups of nations briefly listed above. The difficulties inherent should not be underestimated, as leadership and economic developments change, the political struggles ebb and flow, and refinements in the control of information tend to obscure facts. As leading exponents of trade, purchasing executives are destined to, and should, provide leadership in promoting increasing and closer commercial relationships on an international scale.

Canada. Purchasing principles, policies, and procedures in Canada are not unlike those in the United States. Differences that do exist between the two countries are enumerated and explained in Section 20, "Purchasing in Canada."

IMPORT PURCHASING

There has been a consistent trend throughout postwar national administrations of both political parties in the United States to encourage imports by reducing tariffs through reciprocal trade agreements. Rapid industrialization throughout the world, particularly in formerly underdeveloped countries, the "shrinking" of the world through faster means of transportation and communication, and the increasing use of the English language in international trade encourage and facilitate the increase of imports and the need for their consideration by purchasing executives.

An increase in the volume and diversity of materials and products available from foreign countries is evident, demanding the inclusion of foreign sources of supply in the competitive field of industrial purchasing, and requiring an understanding of the many unusual aspects and problems involved in import purchasing.

Unusual Aspects. Problems peculiar to import purchasing relate, to a much greater degree than for domestic purchasing, to the nature and customs of the people abroad, currency and exchange, documentation, payment terms, quality and acceptance, insurance, government controls and restrictions, and transportation.

Consideration of the nature and customs of the people is important because there frequently is lacking, and must be created, the broad mutuality of interests and understanding which exists in domestic trade, arising from the common language, citizenship, and laws and customs. A knowledge of the exporting country, its history, political stability, climate, population, principal cities and ports, language, currency, principal products, imports, and exports, and its markets and problems tends to furnish an insight into the desire and ability of its people to trade, the honesty of their dealings, their regard for contracts, and how they fulfill their commitments. Such knowledge will help to evaluate and anticipate political decisions that may either hinder or improve opportunities for purchasing from its nationals and for export of merchandise from its shores.

It is important to recognize that the nationals of the various countries with which an importer may deal have much the same economic objectives as an American businessman. They recognize fair dealing, business ethics and loyalty, and other principles we seek to uphold in our domestic business. An importer must realize, however, that, just as among domestic sellers, there are foreigners who will take advantage of the unwary. The foreign exporter, moreover, may face problems having no parallel in the United States, perhaps arising from differing moral standards, a more competitive existence, or involving production difficulties, transportation delays, or governmental intervention. If to overcome some of these difficulties, the import buyer considers financial assistance, he must bear in mind that there is some tendency abroad to regard foreign investment as a new form of colonialism. It is necessary, therefore, to be extremely cautious, and to show patience and understanding in dealing with these problems.

There may be combined political and economic considerations involved in the importation of certain strategic or critical materials, advantages to be served in supplementing and conserving whatever supplies are available in the United States, by locating and supporting foreign sources for such materials. A healthy foreign source also may be desirable for any material which is not available domestically, either in sufficient quantity or competitively. In addition, it may be advantageous to tie imports to the export sale of the buyer's own products, because the sometime shortages of dollars abroad often may limit opportunities for exporting American products. Initial export sales of machinery, for example, also could create a continuing market for spare parts and replacements; thus by providing a potential market with the dollars paid for imports, a new outlet may be created or preserved.

Fluctuating rates of exchange for foreign currencies, including the hazard of unexpected devaluation by government fiat, interest, and exchange charges, and their influence on methods and costs of payment, have no parallel in domestic purchasing. For the American buyer, payment in United States currency is the ideal solution, but sometimes may be difficult to arrange. As the shipment or delivery of commodities or products usually follows the purchase by a considerable interval, agreements to pay in foreign currency suggest the desirability of purchasing, immediately upon execution of the purchase contract, foreign currency futures—to be available in the amount and at the time needed to make payment for the goods purchased. Most commercial banks are familiar with foreign exchange, and can arrange for your purchase of foreign currency futures.[1]

There are several reasons why determination of quality at source is important to a buyer of imported commodities. Payment under letter of credit, almost invariably before receipt of goods, places the buyer in a poor bargaining position, in seeking adjustment for failure of the goods to meet his specifications, or to conform to the U.S. Customs regulations. In the latter case, there would be delays, and perhaps even denial of entry of the goods into the United States. If payment after receipt and inspection on arrival in the United States cannot be arranged, and it seldom can, it is necessary to clearly specify the quality required, and if possible have the goods inspected at origin by an agent of the buyer, or a reliable commercial or governmental inspecting agency.[2]

Distance in itself creates many problems in import purchasing. Visits, though highly desirable in effective procurement, cannot be made as conveniently to the supplier's place of business to evaluate his facilities and personnel. Delivery time is increased and less definite than in domestic trade, necessitating larger inventories of the commodities being imported. Foreign shippers are not always as conscious of the time element of contracts as American manufacturers. In addition to manufacturing delays, there may be certain unavoidable delays due to steamer chartering, especially if delivery is desired at particular United States ports which are less frequently visited by foreign or United States vessels than others. At the time the contract is made the buyer should impress upon the seller the necessity of meeting delivery promises.

The integrity of the individual supplier is of prime importance.[3] The buyer should check carefully on the responsibility of the seller (supplier), to satisfy himself as far as possible that delivery, weights, and quality will be met, or that he is accurately informed of any circumstances arising to affect the ability of the source to meet agreed contract provisions. If the supplier will not honor claims arising under import contracts, it is a tedious, expensive process to handle lawsuits through foreign courts. It is common practice to settle disputes arising in international trade by conciliation or arbitration, avoiding costly, involved, and extended litigation before the courts. Available sources of conciliators and arbitrators and of recognized rules and procedures are:

American Arbitration Association, 140 West 51st Street, New York, N.Y. 10020 (described in Section 28, "Appendix.")

[1] See also later discussion under "Payments."

[2] See later discussion of certification under "Documents."

[3] See listing, *World Trade Directory Reports,* under "References."

Inter-American Commercial Arbitration Commission, 140 West 51st Street, New York, N.Y. 10020
United States Council of the International Chamber of Commerce, 103 Park Avenue, New York, N.Y. 10017
Court of Arbitration, 38 Cours Albert 1er, Paris 8^{e}, France

Provision for conciliation or arbitration can be included and made effective for settling disputes arising under export and import purchase contracts by simple agreement of buyer and seller, clearly stated in the contract. A typical *arbitration clause,* common in printed foreign trade contracts is:[4]

> Any controversy or claim arising out of or relating to this contract or to the breach thereof shall be settled by conciliation or arbitration, in accordance with the rules, then obtaining, of the Court of Arbitration of the International Chamber of Commerce. This agreement shall be enforceable and judgment upon any award rendered by all or a majority of the arbitrators may be entered in any court having jurisdiction. The arbitration shall be held in New York unless otherwise agreed by and where jurisdiction may be obtained over the parties.

There always is the possibility that *war* could break out in some part of the world, while fulfillment of an import contract is pending. This might have the effect of curtailing exports from a particular section of the world or from a single country, or of the placing of an embargo by the United States upon imports from certain areas. There also could be the possibility of danger to ocean shipping. *War-risk insurance* is a partial protection, but it does not cover inability of the exporter to ship or of the importer to receive, due to governmental action. It should be understood clearly that war-risk insurance[5] usually only covers actual shipments against perils while water-borne. The possibility of war, therefore, is one of the hazards involved in import purchasing.

It is clearly evident that the buyer must acquaint himself fully with a considerable field of knowledge not required for domestic purchasing, such as tariffs and import quotas, currency fluctuations, and the voluminous and exacting detail required for smooth execution and delivery under his contracts. As against direct importing by the buyer from the foreign manufacturer or seller, the purchase of goods of foreign origin from or through a commercial importer, regularly engaged in this activity, may be found to have definite advantages, and some foreign manufac-

[4] See also, in "References" later in this section, *Commercial Arbitration and the Law throughout the World, Rules of Conciliation and Arbitration,* and *Guide to ICC Arbitration.*

[5] See also later discussion on "Insurance."

turers will sell only by this method. The frequent and unexpected changes in ocean freight rates and schedules, insurance rates, governmental regulations, and other conditions surrounding importing suggest the desirability of any buyer consulting constantly with Customs and insurance brokers, bankers, government agencies, and other qualified experts in this field.

Governmental Regulations

The United States government imposes certain controls on the importation of goods of foreign origin, both to implement restrictions applying from time to time and to collect import duties exacted upon all commodities not specifically exempted under current tariff laws and executive orders (covering reciprocal trade agreements). Foreign governments, moreover, usually require their exporters to obtain export licenses—some by way of encouraging various industries or the production of certain goods—differing regulations applying, depending upon the nature and amount of goods being exported, and also sometimes due to the country of destination or currency offered by the buyer.

An example of restrictions (and actual prohibitions) on imports by the United States government is afforded by the *Foreign Assets Control regulations*[6] issued in February, 1953, prohibiting the importation of commodities or products known or presumed to have originated in Communist China, and requiring import licenses on all such or similar merchandise originating elsewhere. Under these regulations, control of imports was placed with the Federal Reserve Bank of New York, acting as agent for the Foreign Assets Control, to issue specific *import licenses* upon application, in advance of actual shipment, and requiring special certificates of origin to ensure that the goods did not originate in Communist China nor have been owned by nor of interest to any of its nationals. The same restrictions apply to North Korea and its nationals.

To make the FAC (Foreign Assets Control) regulations more effective, they covered persons subject to United States jurisdiction purchasing merchandise known or presumed to be of Communist Chinese origin in a country outside the United States for delivery to another outside country, or the purchase by such persons of any items on the "positive list" (items considered to be strategic material) in a country outside the United States for ultimate delivery to any country in "Sub-group A" (countries of the so-called Communist Bloc). The items on the positive list and Sub-group A are published in the Comprehensive Export Schedule, issued annually by the Bureau of International Commerce of the U.S. Depart-

[6] Available only from Foreign Assets Control Department, Federal Reserve Bank of New York, 33 Liberty Street, New York, N.Y. 10001.

ment of Commerce.[7] Any current FAC regulations are extremely important, and must be understood and complied with to an exactness to avoid delays and often absolute denial of entry of various stated commodities.

All imports must comply with U.S. Customs Rules and Regulations,[8] requiring exact documentation and correct procedures for clearance through Customs and payment of applicable import duties. Import duties are of several kinds: *ad valorem,* a percentage of the value of the goods; *specific,* a specified amount per unit of weight or measure; or *compound,* composed both of ad valorem and specific imposts on the same and a single item; and in application: *full duty,* at the rates specified; or *preferential,* assessed at a stated percentage of the full duty rate, depending upon the country of origin. There also are, of course, *duty-free* entries of items exempted, or originating in territories or possessions of the United States or other countries similarly favored by treaty. Reciprocal trade agreements reached by negotiation with any specified foreign country for reduction in United States import duties also are applicable equally to many other countries under the provisions of GATT (General Agreement on Tariffs and Trade) and the "most-favored nations" principle.

In addition, any imports of certain specified commodities must comply fully with the regulations of the Food, Drug, and Cosmetic Act, or other classified commodity legislation, before being offered for sale to the public in the United States, and all raw botanicals and roots are subject to quarantine inspection by the Plant Pest Control and Quarantine branches of the Department of Agriculture. Similarly, importation of livestock, other animals and poultry, hides, wool, and meats and certain other animal and poultry products must comply with current regulations of and are subject to quarantine inspection by the Animal Inspection and Quarantine Branch of the Department of Agriculture. Certain items, originating in areas of the world where specified diseases of animals are known to exist, are prohibited importation into the United States. Imports of all narcotic drugs are strictly controlled by the Bureau of Narcotics of the Treasury Department, requiring licenses, issued only to importers approved by the Bureau of Narcotics.

There exist adjacent to certain major United States and foreign ports isolated and enclosed areas known as *foreign-trade or free-trade zones* (sometimes called free ports—but not to be confused with "free cities," which because of their location and world trade and finance often are re-

[7] See listing under "References."

[8] It is essential to keep in constant contact with and consult from the outset on any import purchasing negotiations a reliable Customs broker. See listing, *Custom House Guide* and *Exporters' Encyclopedia,* in "References" later in this section.

ferred to also as free ports). Free zones permit the loading and unloading, breaking up and repacking, sorting, grading, cleaning, mixing or blending (also with indigenous materials), storing and otherwise handling, and reshipping of foreign merchandise—without payment of duties and without intervention of Customs officials. It may be of advantage, for example, to use free zones for inspection and reexportation of imports without Customs formalities, but in some cases it may be found cheaper and simpler to use "bonded" facilities under U.S. Customs supervision. For locations of free-trade zones of the world see Table 17–1 at the end of this section.

The U.S. Customs rules and regulations are so complex and subject to such frequent changes, that it is strongly recommended that qualified and licensed Customs brokers be consulted before and at each step in purchasing any commodity for importation into the United States. The Customs Brokers and Forwarders Association of America, Inc., 8–10 Bridge Street, New York, N.Y. 10004, can supply the names of licensed Customs brokers.[9] This is the major trade association and, although it includes "freight forwarders" in its title, the organization is composed primarily of Customs brokers, but many Customs brokers also perform the function of freight forwarding. The classified telephone directories of most major port cities also include extensive lists of Customs brokers and freight forwarders operating at such ports.

An example of the complexity which may be found in the export controls of foreign countries, and the absolute necessity for keeping posted on current regulations or utilizing the services of foreign trade experts (such as found in commercial banks with foreign branches or correspondents), is afforded by the bounty on exchange granted by Brazil on exports of coffee to the United States. Under regulations in effect early in 1958, the exporter was obliged to sell dollars (realized from the sale price to the United States importer of the coffee) to the Banco do Brasil, operating under the supervision of the Council of the Superintendency of Currency and Credit, at the official rate of U.S.$0.0545 per cruzeiro, but he received in addition a bonus of Cr$18.70 (cruzeiros), or 101.85 per cent per dollar of the price. This would figure, say:

10,000 lb coffee	@ U.S.$0.65 per lb.	$6,500
Official exchange	@ U.S.$0.0545.	Cr$119,627
Bonus	@ Cr$18.70 per U.S.$1.00.	121,550
Exporter receives	(equivalent to exchange @ U.S.$0.0269567).	Cr$241,177

[9] See also *Custom House Guide* and *Exporters' Encyclopedia* in "References" later in this section.

(In comparison, the free exchange rate was at that time U.S.$0.0156 per cruzeiro or Cr$64.10 per dollar.)

It is obvious that in negotiating the purchase of the coffee, the price the importer in the United States had to pay was influenced by the actual return to the Brazilian exporter in the currency of that country, and that the currency of the two countries would not have exchanged at the par value, if free exchange were permitted. Brazilian control of currency exchange for imports has been even more complicated.

Documentation

Special documents,[10] not common for domestic transactions, customarily are required on direct import purchases under letter of credit, against which the seller abroad draws and obtains payment in the country of origin, or upon presentation of his draft on the American buyer to a bank in the United States—usually sometime before the merchandise is received. Because of liability to penalty for failure to have proper documents to enter merchandise into the United States, the matter of documentation is of prime concern to the importer. At the time the order is placed, it is desirable to specify exactly the documents that are required, the number of copies of each, and the destination to which they are to be sent. Those usually required are:

Bills of Lading

There should be a "clean" on board order–notify bill of lading, issued by the steamship company, accepting the shipment and stating the quantity, description, and markings of the goods to be transported. Exact quantity should be specified, not "shipper's load and count," which often appears on domestic straight railroad bills of lading. Title to the materials covered usually is conveyed by endorsement.

Invoices

Shipments to the United States of goods exceeding $500 in value require a consular or certified invoice (Foreign Service Form 138) unless the shipment comes within one or more of the provisions of section 8.15, Customs Regulations of 1943, which exempts certain classes of goods or specified commodities from this requirement. The requirement for signature of consular invoices or certification of them by United States government representatives in the countries or ports of origin was eliminated in the fall of 1955, with certain specific exceptions, but a consular invoice did not carry, even prior to this relaxation, any assurance in itself that

[10] See listing of *Revised American Foreign Trade Definitions—1941,* in the "References" and inclusion complete near the end of this section.

the material covered would be permitted entry into the United States nor guarantee of the quantity or quality of the merchandise referred to therein. *Commercial invoices,* similar to domestic invoices, detailing the exact quantity, description, price and terms, total value, marks, weights, and method of shipment (vessel name) are customary and required as the seller's statement of fulfillment of the terms of the contract. In the absence of consular or commercial invoice at the time the goods are entered through U.S. Customs, a statement in the form of an invoice, and called a "pro-forma invoice," must be filed with the entry and a bond given for the production of the required invoice(s) not later than six months from the date of entry.

Certificate of Origin

As its name implies, this document is a statement, for purposes of Customs entry into the importing country, certifying the country from which the goods originated. A certificate of origin is required in some cases to comply with special restrictions or controls on imports and in some cases because transshipments en route can obscure the identity of the actual country of origin.

Weight Certificate

When the weight is determined by an independent certified weighmaster, government agency, or private party, a weight certificate is used as a basis for determination of the quantity shipped. In some cases a buyer may be willing to accept the seller's own weight certificate, without certification by an independent agency.

Analysis Certificate

Some goods are bought on chemical or other analysis or quality specifications, and in such instances certificate of a governmental or commercial analyst or assayer will be the basis for determination of the quality for acceptance or settlement, as provided in the purchase contract.

Certificate of Survey

A certificate of survey is somewhat similar to and may include, or be incorporated in, weight and analysis certificates, and identifies the exact material shipped against the other documents or the contract. When the importer or bank desires authoritative assurance that the goods ready for shipment are exactly as specified, an independent *cargo surveyor*[11] specializing in this function may be engaged to examine the goods and issue a certificate that they are as specified. Examination and certification

[11] Such as General Superintendence Company, Ltd. or Lloyd's, Ltd.

will be made for those particular qualities which may be authorized, such as chemical or metallurgical analysis, determining specifications, count, weight, and especially identifying markings. This service usually is paid for by the buyer unless specified otherwise in the purchase agreement.

Insurance Policy or Certificate

This document is an important part of all import shipping requirements. The type of insurance and the extent of the coverage is in accordance with agreements between buyer and seller, the risks specifically covering the particular transaction and those inherent in the general terms or trade customs.[12]

Markings of Packages

Importers should familiarize themselves with the markings required by port and Customs authorities for both inside and outside packages, such as cans, bottles, boxes, crates, rolls, bags, etc., and transmit this information in detail to the shipper for his guidance and inclusion on invoices.

Payments

To obtain the most advantageous purchase, the buyer should have a knowledge of foreign currencies and be familiar with the workings of some of the methods of payment for imported commodities. It is important that he recognize the fact that many countries impose and modify from time to time, for reasons both economic and political, restrictions and controls on the use of their currencies. Authoritative lists of *rates of exchange* for various foreign currencies are published weekly and (by averages) monthly by the Board of Governors of the Federal Reserve System.[13]

The term "free currency" usually is interpreted as meaning that the currency of a specific country is free of all restrictions, and can be converted freely into any currency of the world by its owner. Since World War II, major countries whose currencies (for the most part) have been freely convertible have been limited to Canada and the United States. Among other countries whose currencies have been essentially free are Western Germany, Lebanon, Mexico, and Switzerland. The Japanese and most European currencies by 1963 were convertible on an external basis. Commercial banks with foreign connections keep posted on currency and exchange controls of various countries.[14]

[12] See also later discussion on "Insurance."

[13] See listings under "References."

[14] See listing of *Foreign Information Service* of the First National City Bank of New York under "References."

By a controlled currency is meant that the currency of a specific country is controlled by regulations within that country, and may not be converted into the currency of another country without specific approval of the fiscal authorities of the controlled currency country. Controls can be established at a fixed rate in relation to the United States dollar, or on a system of variable rates, by which is meant that different commodities or classes of merchandise (or even varying quantities of them) are entitled to different rates of exchange in relation to the dollar. For foreign exchange rates existing on January 4, 1965, refer to Table 17–2 later in this section. The fact that a currency is controlled may be an indication that it is overvalued, or it may reflect governmental efforts to encourage or control particular industries or segments of the economy of the country involved—or of its trade relationships with various or any particular other country or countries.

Wherever currencies are freely convertible, or in free money areas, it usually is found that exchange values of controlled currencies are much lower than the controlled rates. This situation tends to give rise to illegal transactions involving currency smuggling, falsification of documents, and bribing of officials. Anyone engaged in international trade is likely to find that some illegal transactions are fairly common, and must be alert continually to detect them in any unusual circumstances encountered in his purchase negotiations.

Apart from illegal transactions, there are other devices used by some countries which are perfectly legal, and which if used by the buyer often can accomplish a more advantageous purchase. One of these is the *compensation deal,* which is a refinement of the original simple barter arrangement. The compensation deal assumes:

1. The country is short of foreign exchange, particularly dollars.
2. It has an exportable commodity which is not moving too readily.
3. It needs an imported commodity which must be purchased with a "hard" currency (dollars or freely convertible currency).

Under such conditions the government officials controlling the granting of export and import licenses often will consider a "compensation" or barter arrangement. In its simplest terms the "compensation" deal is authorization to export from the foreign country a quantity of the slow-moving commodity and to use the resultant dollars or hard currency to import a certain commodity which is needed by the foreign country. The end result is that the exported commodity usually is sold at a low price and the imported commodity, which is needed urgently by the exporting country, must be bought at a very high price. In actual practice, one individual in the foreign country usually arranges the compensation deal, obtaining the export and import licenses and exchange permits simultaneously. He serves as both the exporter of the indigenous goods and the importer of the needed items, generally in close cooperation with governmental officials or agencies of his country.

There are many different ways in which compensation deals can be arranged, always under strict surveillance and close control by the trade and currency control authorities. They are a realistic approach to the old free trade in international exchanges, representing a relaxation of strict controls in a sort of "face-saving" procedure. Similarly, and with many variations, there are so-called "switch deals," involving essentially three-cornered exchange settlements—payment in the currency of a third country rather than in that of either exporting or importing country. Finally, there also are actual three-cornered trades, in which commodities, as well as currencies, of three countries are involved.

As an example of a three-cornered trade, assume that a Spanish importer desires to purchase hops from an exporter in Sweden who is anxious to sell, but wants United States dollars or their equivalent in Swedish kronor for his hops. Being unable to obtain exchange from the Spanish control authorities, the exporter in Sweden agrees to assist the importer in Spain in the sale of a shipment of olives to the United States, provided the Spanish exporter can obtain the necessary approval from the exchange control authorities in Spain. Final arrangements for a three-cornered trade of this kind are usually made by giving the United States importer of the olives a more favorable price than he could obtain otherwise, and the premium or difference is paid by the Spanish importer in a higher price for his hops.

In some cases the discounts available are sufficiently attractive to warrant devious, although possibly "acceptable," arrangements, whereby the merchandise is shipped actually to a certain country, from which it is reshipped to its final destination. For this reason and many others, an importer in the United States entering into a three-cornered deal should discuss all angles of the transaction with the foreign department of his bank before making final commitments, to avoid jeopardizing either his cash or his reputation. Like compensation deals, switch deals and three-cornered trades are not new. They are practically the same as those which took place in the free exchange markets of the late twenties, except that control restrictions make it necessary to go through much time-consuming negotiation to obtain all required approvals.

The importer in the United States must decide whether or not he wants to conduct his business operations to make a profit in the handling of the merchandise or in speculation in the exchange markets. A combination of the two objectives seldom is compatible. Risks in currency fluctuations since World War II, however, have been limited, because most of the world currencies were handled, at least in legitimate channels, at controlled rates. Most of the "soft currency" countries, such as Brazil, Chile, Greece, and Turkey established controls which necessitated payments in dollars for all their exports to importers in the United States. Under such controls it would be unwise for an importer in the United States to speculate with the currencies of such countries, since their rates of exchange could be changed by governmental action without warning or apparent economic reason.

In free markets, such as Canada, the buyer can ensure himself against loss and, of course, forego any prospect of gain on exchange fluctuations by purchasing "futures," that is, buying Canadian dollars for future delivery to cover payments for future imports from Canada. If an importer purchases material abroad for which he agrees to pay in sterling, for example, he cannot determine the actual cost of the import until he has fixed the cost of the sterling exchange. Should the import buyer feel that there would be no appreciable change in the sterling market until payment would be due, he could wait to cover his exchange commitment until required to pay for his purchase. There also exists a market for sterling for future delivery, enabling the import purchaser to buy the sterling exchange and to fix the rate at the time he completes his import purchase arrangements.

Naturally, an importer in the United States is interested in securing the most favorable foreign exchange rate and in taking precautions against loss due to rate fluctuations. He should seek and follow the advice of a reputable domestic bank whose foreign department is engaged actively in exchange transactions. Furthermore, he should make all commitments possible in United States dollars, and by so doing he will not be subject to loss in exchange, nor will he be in a position to gain by exchange fluctuations. It also is possible to buy "futures" in many foreign currencies, usually depending upon the degree of convertibility of their currencies. Once "futures" are purchased, the importer can establish his cost in the same manner as if he had made his commitment in United States dollars.

Letters of credit constitute the most common method of financing and handling payments for imports. Letters of credit are issued by banks which deal in international trade, and may be either revocable or irrevocable. The specimen application for letter of credit (see Fig. 17–1) indicates the details which are involved in and covered by these instruments. A revocable letter of credit, after issuance by a bank, can be cancelled, changed, or amended by the buyer in any way desired, and at any time before payment has been effected. Under a revocable letter of credit there are many disadvantages to the seller or exporter abroad, and many advantages to the buyer or importer, but they are rarely used for imports into the United States.

APPLICATION FOR COMMERCIAL LETTER OF CREDIT

Morgan Guaranty Trust Company of New York,
International Banking Division,
Commercial Credits Department,
23 Wall Street,
New York 15, New York

.... (Date)

Please issue an Irrevocable Letter of Credit for our account and transmit it

Through Your Correspondent by
☐ Air Mail
☐ Cable
or
☐ Return to us for Transmission
} Check One

In favor of............................
(Name of beneficiary)

....
(Address)

Available by drafts at ☐ Sight ☐ 30 days sight ☐ 60 " " ☐ 90 " " } Check One

for............................invoice value
(full invoice value unless otherwise stated)

NOT EXCEEDING A TOTAL OF............................

Drafts to be accompanied by:

Commercial Invoice describing the merchandise as indicated below
and
Special Customs Invoice

On board ocean steamer bills of lading drawn to the order of **Morgan Guaranty Trust Company of New York,** indicating ***Notify Party*** as............................

Any other required documents to be indicated here } ....

....

Indicate merchandise here (omitting details as to grade, quality, price, etc., if possible).

....

from ☐ F.O.B. STEAMER ☐ F.A.S. STEAMER ....to ☐ C. & F. ☐ C. I. F. .... } Check One

Partial shipments ☐ prohibited. ☐ permitted. } Check One

Transshipments ☐ prohibited. ☐ permitted. } Check One

Marine and War Risk Insurance to be effected by............................
(indicate whether shipper or the undersigned)

Drawings must be either negotiated or presented at the office of the drawee on or before............................

Special Instructions............................

Unless otherwise expressly stated, the Letter of Credit is to be issued subject to the Uniform Customs and Practice for Commercial Documentary Credits fixed by the International Chamber of Commerce, as well as subject to your Letter of Credit Agreement, which agreement has been or will be duly executed by us. In case of any conflict, your rights under your Letter of Credit Agreement shall prevail.

....

....
Authorized Official(s)

Form 11-4-671B
3-63–10M

FIG. 17–1. Form of application for letter of credit.

Under an irrevocable letter of credit there are no disadvantages to the seller and the principal advantages to him are that, provided documents corresponding to the terms of the credit are presented to the issuing bank, it must make payment even though its customer, the importer, might be in difficulties or for any other reason whatsoever does not want the merchandise. Another advantage to the seller is that he may be able to use the letter of credit issued in the United States to establish credit in his own country in instances in which he otherwise might not be able to do so. The disadvantages to the buyer or importer are that he cannot cancel, change, or amend in any way the terms of the letter of credit after issuance, except upon agreement of seller, even though he might learn something which would cause him to desire to do so. It is the type of letter of credit most commonly used, however, and the one the buyer usually will find himself obliged to arrange for his payments.

Instead of making payment for imports by letter of credit, a foreign exporter may draw drafts against the importer in the United States, if he is entirely satisfied with the standing of the importer, and that the draft will be paid or accepted according to its tenor, and all conditions of the sales contract with respect to payment will be fulfilled. Unless the importing company, and the exporting company, are of excellent standing, much more difficulty would be incurred by the exporter in discounting such drafts than those drawn against letters of credit. When only drafts are used by the exporter, the importer is relieved of the obligation of arranging with his bank for the issuing of a letter of credit in favor of the exporter.

Drafts may be either sight drafts or payable 30, 60, or 90 days after sight or presentation, depending upon arrangements made between buyer and seller. Under draft only, the seller waives the protection afforded by an irrevocable letter of credit, and could encounter difficulty in discounting such drafts against shipments to obtain immediate funds. From the standpoint of the buyer, of course, letter of credit charges are avoided (although admittedly they are quite small). It is conceivable that some unscrupulous buyers might take advantage of adverse developments, such as falling markets, to refuse payment upon presentation of a draft.

In the majority of cases, payment against letter of credit is available by sight draft for 100 per cent of invoice value. Partial draft (for less than 100 per cent of agreed total payment) may be used to protect the buyer when there are doubts as to the reliability of the seller, or the nature of the commodity is such that its quality or quantity cannot be determined accurately or finally by immediate inspection or analysis. Balance due the seller is remitted subsequently by the buyer, less any agreed deductions or adjustments. Time drafts, payable in 30, 60, or 90 days, enable the buyer to use the seller as a banker, deferring actual payment for the period indicated. Time drafts usually can be discounted by the seller or exporter, but charges involved generally are for the account of the buyer, either directly or in the price of the merchandise. When partial or delayed payment drafts are required, they must be provided for definitely in the original contract of purchase.

It is very important that there be a complete understanding between the importer and the exporter as to just what fees or charges are included in the agreed price in the contract. Usually the price will include such items as export taxes, consular and documentary fees, wharfage, loading, lightering, and other similar charges involved in delivering goods into the vessel at loading port. If sampling is required, its cost assumption should be agreed upon between the two parties in advance. Charges for freight and insurance are in accordance with the terms of the contract, while the importer normally pays import duty, customs entrance fees, unloading charges at port of discharge, and various fees charged by the banks for handling documents. For most well-regarded importers there generally is no issuance charge, but in the case of very small companies it is possible that some banks may make a nominal issuance charge. The usual charge for payments under sight dollar credits is 1/8 of 1 per cent, and on time credits 1½ per cent per annum, or 1/8 of 1 per cent per month, i.e., 30 days 1/8 per cent, 60 days ¼ per cent, and 90 days 3/8 per cent. A few banks make no charge for amendments; others charge from $2.50 to $5. The charges vary for the collection of drafts drawn by foreign shippers on importers in the United States, which are not under letters of credit, from 1/8 to ½ of 1 per cent. Generally, such charges are deducted from the proceeds to its client, the exporter, or the exporter's bank in the foreign country, which sent the draft to its American correspondent.

Insurance

Marine insurance[15] is the oldest form of insurance of record, antedating the Middle Ages. *Ocean marine insurance* covers shipments of cargo by overseas vessels and domestic shipments by coastal (U.S. Atlantic or Pacific) and intercoastal (between U.S. Atlantic and/or Gulf and Pacific) vessels. This type of insurance has certain terms and conditions which are distinctly different from other types. With the increasing importance of foreign trade, a better understanding of marine insurance is essential, but its ramifications necessitate early and thorough consultation on any intended import purchases with an experienced insurance agent or broker.

An adequate insured value is of utmost importance. This value usually is computed by adding the invoice value, guaranteed freight, all charges, including the insurance premium, plus a percentage markup. The markup, commonly 10 per cent, is to allow for possible market value increase between the date of purchase of the goods and the date of un-

[15] See listings under "References."

loading at destination. If the cargo is a total loss, the full insured value, including markup, is collectible. This is the value used for general average purposes and it is important that the insured value equal or exceed the wholesale market value on the final date of discharge; otherwise the owner of the shipment would be obliged to contribute to the general average on the excess value, if any, as an uninsured interest.

The term "average" as used in marine insurance means "loss less than total." A "general average" loss is one that results from action of the master of a vessel in time of stress, which in his judgment is for the best interest of both ship and cargo. Such action may include jettison of cargo to lighten a stranded vessel, damage resulting from fighting a fire, engaging salvage assistance, or putting into a port of refuge following breakdown of machinery (including cost of repairs). From the earliest times, maritime laws have universally held that such loss should be borne by all parties of interest (for whose benefit the sacrifice was made, ship owners and owners of cargo alike).

A "particular average" loss is one that affects specific interests only (the owner of a specific shipment which is damaged or partially lost), and is caused by an insured peril which does not result in a general average loss. Insured perils are described as *of* the sea or *on* the sea; hazards from natural forces, such as unusually heavy weather, stranding, lightning, collision, and sinking are *of* the sea; whereas fire, assailing thieves, smoke, steam, or water from efforts to extinguish fires, and jettison are *on* the sea. The extent of insurance coverage of particular average (partial loss) is specified in the ocean marine policy, in clauses termed as follows:

a. FPAAC—Free of Particular Average—American Conditions. This is the most limited of the average clauses, covering losses resulting from perils *of* the sea. Under this clause no loss is paid unless caused by fire, stranding, sinking, or collision.

b. FPAEC—Free of Particular Average—English Conditions. Under this clause losses are paid not only when they are caused by stranding, sinking, burning, or collision, but also when caused by sea perils, irrespective of percentage, if the vessel at any time during the voyage is involved in a stranding, sinking, burning, or collision, even if the loss has no connection with the accident to the vessel.

c. WA or WPA—With Average or With Particular Average. This clause gives protection for partial losses by insured sea perils if the damage amounts to a certain percentage of the whole shipment or of a shipping package. A 3 per cent particular average is usual. This clause applies if there is a loss from insured sea perils and the loss amounts to more than 3 per cent. In this insurance the loss is paid in full, as the 3 per cent is not a deductible amount, but is set as a minimum figure to eliminate small claims. The minimum is waived if the vessel is involved in a fire, stranding, sinking, or collision. Theft, pilferage, nondelivery, fresh-water damage, breakage, leakage, and contamination from other cargo may be added specifically to the WA clause as needed for particular shipments.

d. Average Irrespective of Percentage. This is the broadest average clause. Under it, losses by insured perils are paid regardless of the amount of the loss.

Where a general average occurs, the owner of the cargo must sign an average agreement under which he binds himself to pay all proper general average which may be assessed against his shipment. If the shipment is insured under an ocean marine policy, the insurance company will file a guarantee as additional security. If not insured, the additional security may consist of a cash deposit, surety bond, or bank guarantee for the amount of the assessment against his shipment. As a general average can be very involved, sometimes several years elapse before final negotiations are completed. Without insurance, cash deposits can be tied up for long periods of time.

Protection under ocean marine insurance now generally covers warehouse to warehouse, the policy stating when the insuring conditions attach and terminate. Under the warehouse to warehouse clause, the insurance covers from the time the goods leave the premises of the shipper, during ordinary transit, and until arrival at the premises of the consignee at final destination, or until the expiration of 15 days (30 days if an inland destination), whichever shall occur first. Should cargo be delayed at some point through no fault of the insured, it is customary to hold the shipment covered.

Marine extension clauses, developed during World War II, continue the coverage on cargo during deviation of voyage, delays, reshipment, transshipment, or other variations beyond the control of the insured, and eliminate the 15- or 30-day time limit at destination. While coverage under marine extension clauses is only for interruption and suspension of transit beyond the control of the insured, he can secure additional protection upon payment of extra rates to cover interruption in transit within his control and extension beyond the ordinary time limit.

War-risk insurance is written by endorsement to a regular marine policy, or more commonly under a separate policy, at the time the original cargo policy is taken out. It covers only while the shipment is waterborne. It is very vital coverage, even during peaceful periods. Floating or stationary mines and stray or derelict torpedoes remain from prior wars and create a serious threat to shipping. It is wise for shippers to continue to protect their cargoes against these hazards for extended periods after the cessation of hostilities, as many ships are sunk by undetected floating mines, even after the lapse of several years.

The degree of protection given by insurance is in accordance with the wishes of the shipper. The cost, naturally, increases as the risk assumed by the underwriter increases. The property usually is insured for the benefit of the consignee, and as he pays the premium one way or the other, he quite frequently is the one who arranges for the desired protection. When letters of credit are used as a method of payment, the insurance usually is in the same currency as that in which the latter is issued. A definite understanding should exist between buyer and seller as to which party will place the insurance. The starting point for the setting of insurance rates is known as the *base rate*. Unlike most other insurance rates, those for marine insurance are not standardized, and may vary among several insurance companies. It will depend upon the relationship between the importer and the insurance company, the amount and type of cargo involved, and the claim experience, if any, which the underwriter may have with the importer or with the type of movement under consideration. Each transaction is an individual matter between the importer and the underwriter. To the initial base rate will often be added extras, depending upon various considerations, such as the flag under which carrying vessels will sail, age of the vessel, and other conditions of the voyage.

Hand in hand with the individual character of marine insurance rates, and to simplify covering repetitive risks, extensive use is made of a form of blanket, or open cargo, or reporting contract. Under an open policy an insured may obtain continuous coverage for all shipments for an extended period of time or until cancelled by either party. He has automatic protection, subject to limits and to various conditions stated in the policy, from the time the goods leave the original warehouse until delivered into the consignee's warehouse. It is not necessary that the insurance agent or broker be notified prior to the sailing of each shipment, but the declarations of shipments insured under an open policy should be made monthly, or as soon as practicable after the commencement of the transit of the goods.

The open cargo policy usually carries a limit of liability by any one conveyance, or in any one place, at any one time. It is most important for all open-policy holders to make sure that their limit of liability is sufficient to cover all the shipments that they may make (or have made for their account and risk). It is quite possible to have an accumulation of goods made up of several separate shipments go forward on the same vessel or conveyance, or arrive at the same pier or Customs warehouse at the same time. An open cargo policy covering general merchandise is usually written on an "all-risks" basis. The all-risks clause which is widely used and which is the most complete of the coverages available reads as follows:

> To cover against all risks of physical loss or damage from any external cause, irrespective of percentage (excepting risks excluded by the F.C.&.S. and Strikes, Riots and Civil Commotions warranties, unless covered elsewhere herein).

Under a blanket or open policy, both amount and character of individual coverage are determined, the details of shipment are reported to the insurance agent or broker by the insurer, and (in the case a negotiable document is required under letter of credit terms) a certificate, in lieu of policy, is issued. If full information is not known at the time a certificate is required, the insured can bind a specific shipment by submitting to the underwriter a provisional declaration, which is finalized when full particulars are available. The declarations of the insured are the basis for issuance by the underwriter of invoices covering the requisite premiums, either for individual shipments or monthly, as may have been arranged in the open policy.

There are many forms and methods of operations available, and with new systems of communications and accounting, it is possible to work out procedures for reporting and billing under open cargo policies that will help broker, underwriter, and insured to reduce operating and administrative costs. Coupled with the lower selling costs of the open policy, the simplification and reduction in administrative costs tend to result in the lowest possible rates consistent with the coverage; and since coverage is automatic, the importer runs no risk of overlooking insuring a shipment due to failure of receipt of notice of shipment by the time of sailing.

When someone who is insured suffers a loss to merchandise insured under a special marine or open policy, it is up to him to notify the nearest agent of the insurance company of the loss and to make a written notice of claim upon the carrier of the goods. Policies or certificates of insurance, which have been arranged by the shippers, contain listing of names and addresses of representatives of the insurance companies issuing them. If the insurance has been arranged by the importer, he should notify his underwriter through the agent or broker. The insurance company will arrange for a survey and report, to enable discussion of all details surrounding the loss and to make the appropriate settlement. The importer will be allowed as part of his claim any charges incurred, such as survey fees, repacking, and reconditioning expenses.

Procedure

The buyer of imported materials may avail himself of many channels of importation, the choice of which, depending upon the size and capability of his organization, the nature of his business, its financial structure and policies, and the practices of the trade, is of vital concern. Thus, a buyer may deal directly with foreign manufacturers or producers, or he may deal through a foreign export merchant or foreign broker or manufacturer's agent, or through an import commission house, an import merchant, broker, or wholesaler. In considering the problems involved, it is in order to examine the nature of various intermediate channels through which he may purchase import materials.

The import merchant contracts (in his own name) directly with the domestic buyer, and thereafter buys (in his own name) from the country of exportation, delivers to the United States port of entry, and bills the buyer, according to the contract. In the same manner, he may buy before he has a contract with the import buyer, on the strength of his knowledge of the market and anticipated requirements. In dealing with an import merchant, the buyer has the advantage, which may not be present in dealing directly with a foreign exporter or agent, of recourse to the United States courts in the event of any claim or controversy arising under the contract. He is not concerned with fluctuations in foreign exchange, chartering shipping space, or arranging for insurance; and he has the advantage of inspection of the goods in the United States, and has contact with the other party to the contract, an experienced domestic organization, often with warehouse stocks available on short notice in the United States.

The import broker acts as an intermediary between buyer and seller, and receives for his knowledge and services a stipulated fee. In so far as protection to the buyer is concerned, the broker in the United States must, of course, maintain his reputation, if he expects to continue doing business. Thus, he is inclined to see to it that the merchandise involved is as good as represented and may, in some instances, be in a position to supply technical knowledge which he has acquired in the course of doing business. All of this is of value and assistance to an import buyer.

The import wholesaler generally imports materials to serve the smaller buyer who needs a dependable source of supply and perhaps also credit. He also fixes prices, as in the case of the import merchant, and the buyer has an opportunity to inspect the merchandise and to look to the wholesaler for performance under his contract.

The disadvantages in dealing through various import agents are that whatever type of intermediary is employed, he is in business for a profit, and the buyer is one step removed from direct and immediate sources of foreign market information. The buyer, in dealing with any import agent, generally must expect to pay a little more for the goods than if he were importing directly, and he must be very much aware of the reputation of the intermediary in the foreign country, because by the mere fact of his association, the buyer might at some future time be either helped or harmed, in direct contacts with foreign exporters. The buyer of the imported commodities recognizes, of course, and bargains for the insulation from hazards of import purchasing in dealing through an intermediary.

In dealing with a foreign agent, a foreign export merchant, or a foreign broker, the buyer has, generally speaking, some advantages similar to those arising from dealing with an import house in the United States, namely, grading and sorting of goods, technical knowledge, warehousing and/or stockpiling, booking of steamer space, and arranging for insurance coverage. Just as in the case of selecting an import merchant, broker, or wholesaler, the choice of such an intermediary in the foreign country depends on the policy of the trade, the commodity involved and its characteristics, and the insulation to be furnished, and required, against possible loss.

Freight charters generally are arranged through ship or charter brokers, in part because ocean freight rates customarily are keyed to an agreed time or rate of loading and unloading, and liability for demurrage charges or dispatch premiums is incurred depending upon synchronization of the scheduling of arrival of cargo for loading and the handling of the cargo and documentation by the forwarding agent, working with the broker. The demurrage rate normally is twice or three times the rate of dispatch. The charter broker earns for his services (usually paid by ship's owners unless otherwise specified) a commission, which customarily is 1¼ per cent of the gross freight, dead freight, and any demurrage which is paid by the charterer to the ship's owners. When more than one broker is involved, duplicate brokerage normally is paid, and so most of the current coal, grain, and oil full cargo charters carry brokerage commissions totaling 2½ per cent of the charges paid by the charterer.

For companies having well-staffed traffic departments, it frequently is desirable to make foreign purchases either f.o.b. or f.a.s.[16] the foreign port, so that the buyer can arrange both the means and the cost of transportation. It is not uncommon for "deals" to be available on transportation, just as on foreign exchange, and some other portions of importing costs. In cases where the buyer finds it more convenient or

[16] See *Revised American Foreign Trade Definitions—1941,* and also listing, *Incoterms —1953,* in the "References" both later in this section.

customary to buy c.&f. or c.i.f. an American port, he should insure himself obtaining the benefit of any decreases in transportation charges which the seller may obtain, because he certainly will be liable for increases.

EXPORT PURCHASING

The evolution of foreign policy of the United States since World War II has involved to an increasing extent interest in the economic development and well-being of foreign countries. With government encouragement by special tax inducements, there has been an increase in the movement of American capital abroad, both for the manufacture of American products in branch plants and for promoting the sale of American-made goods in foreign markets. The opening of foreign branches has created problems of maintaining American quality standards for trade-marked items, of costs or the economy of mass production and procurement which is denied, initially at least, by the smaller demand of the foreign markets.

Purchasing for export involves peculiar problems which require (as for importing) specialized knowledge and handling not common with domestic industrial procurement. An understanding of the distinguishing characteristics, hazards, and sources of information is essential, therefore, to the undertaking of export purchasing. As discussed herein, export purchasing is considered to mean the purchasing of materials in the United States, by an American buyer, for the purpose of exporting such materials from the United States to a foreign country or countries.

Unusual Aspects

Purchasing for export involves considerations for the buyer, which in domestic transactions usually are the responsibility of the seller. Such responsibilities include specification of unit of packing, weight and dimensional limitations, type and adequacy of packing; scheduling and control of inland transportation; booking of ocean shipping; documentation and banking; insurance;[17] and forwarding through port of exportation. Whether such factors will be handled by the buyer, elsewhere in his own organization, or through outside agencies is a question which only can be decided on an individual basis, depending upon the circumstances involved, knowledge and experience in export procedure, and the nature, volume, and continuity of the purchasing for export.

Valuable information and assistance is available to the buyer from manufacturers or sellers familiar with or engaged regularly in exporting,

[17] See "Insurance," under "Import Purchasing," principles of which are applicable equally to coverage of export shipments.

and this factor becomes, therefore, an additional consideration in the selection of sources of supply for items being purchased for export. To the extent purchases are made from sellers experienced in export procedure, the complexities of handling can revert to the seller, as is common in domestic trade. It is necessary in every case, however, to reach a clear understanding as to the respective responsibilities of buyer and seller—to a much greater extent than in domestic transactions—because there is no such universally understood and accepted body of practice and law applicable to foreign trade.[18]

For loading and stowage aboard ship, the size and nature of packing of small articles, as well as bulk commodities, must be given special consideration. The packing must be such as to withstand dock and ship-side handling at both ends of the overseas voyage, discourage pilferage, and at the same time be of minimum bulk, since *ocean freight rates* are influenced by cubic measurement (space occupied in stowage) as well as weight. Differing trade customs and the nature of handling and inland transportation upon discharge at overseas port also influence the determination of the packing.

Helpful suggestions covering packing for export shipment can be obtained from marine insurance agents or brokers, from various foreign trade associations, and from United States government specifications.[19] For those preferring not to handle the details of packing, there are experienced commercial packing and crating services, listed extensively in the classified telephone directories of major port cities. Freight forwarders and ocean shipping agencies are readily available, also, and can be found in large numbers in the same telephone directories. It is essential that their services be utilized in this highly specialized field, and much time and expense can be saved if they are consulted at an early stage of export purchasing.

Other sources of information to buyers for export are banks with foreign branches or correspondents. The *foreign departments* of many commercial banks are experienced in handling details of documentation, shipping, financing, collection, and exchange service. They also can pro-

[18] Codes of practice, however, adopted by various foreign trade groups, are available and can be incorporated in contracts by agreement. Examples, cited in the "References" later in this section, are *Revised American Foreign Trade Definitions—1941* and *Uniform Customs and Practice for Documentary Credits.* The discussion of arbitration under "Import Purchasing" is pertinent also for exporting. See also *Arbitration* in the "References" later in this section.

[19] Typical pertinent titles include: *PPP-B-621A—Boxes; Wood, nailed and lock-cornered; MIL-P-116—Packaging and Packing for Overseas Shipment, Preservation, Methods of;* and *MIL-B-107—Boxes; Wood, wirebound (overseas type).* See also listings in the "References" later in this section of *Indexes.*

vide valuable information on exchange and import restrictions of various foreign countries, as well as the export regulations of the United States government, all of which must be carefully followed in handling export shipments.

United States Export Regulations

All exports from the United States, its territories, and its possessions are subject to export controls by the government. In practice, however, the great bulk of exports take place under *general licenses* which may be used by anyone without application to or specific authority from the government.[20] The basic document covering export regulations is *Schedule B–Statistical Classification of Foreign and Domestic Commodities Exported from the United States*.[21] Current government listings of exports by type of commodity are based on this classification. Specific export controls are covered in the *Comprehensive Export Schedule* and supplementary *Current Export Bulletins*.[21] Since all references in the Export Schedule are in terms of Schedule B, it is desirable to have the latter available when referring to the former.

The Bureau of International Commerce of the U.S. Department of Commerce is the primary export control agency, and complete information and help with export problems relating to controls, as well as procedures, is available from foreign trade specialists in any of the Department of Commerce field offices, located in 39 major cities throughout the country, or from the Exporters' Service Section of the Bureau of International Commerce in Washington. As stated in the foreword to "Selling Around the World–How Commerce Helps," one of the major responsibilities of the Department of Commerce is "to serve business directly in increasing international sales of U.S. goods," and there are located in the Bureau of International Commerce of the Department economists, statisticians, marketing, and other specialists on various areas of the world. The export of munitions, arms, and airplanes is controlled by the Department of State, and current information and regulations governing such exports require direct contact with the Munitions Office, U.S. Department of State, Washington, D.C. 20520. The Atomic Energy Commission exercises control of materials under its supervision. Inquiries covering such items as geiger counters, complete reactors, and various radioactive materials should be addressed to the Division of Licensing, Atomic Energy Commission, Washington, D.C. 20545, but radioactive isotopes are dealt with directly by the Isotopes Division, Atomic Energy

[20] *Selling Around the World–How Commerce Helps* (1965), p. 21.
[21] See listings under "References."

Commission, Oak Ridge, Tennessee 37830. The export or reexport of narcotic drugs requires special licenses, issued by the U.S. Bureau of Narcotics, Washington, D.C. 20226.

The United States government also has imposed restrictions and controls on the flow of funds and exchange of currencies in foreign trade. Under the Agricultural Trade Assistance Act (1954), also called Public Law No. 480, the Treasury Department encouraged the sale of certain farm products abroad by paying exporters in dollars, keeping the foreign currencies paid by overseas purchasers for use in various government programs abroad. The Cooley Amendment in 1957 further provided that up to 25 per cent of local funds arising from such sales might be lent to overseas subsidiaries of U.S. companies. Various other government programs, administered since 1961 by the Agency for International Development, include assistance to Latin American countries under the Alianza para Progreso (Alliance for Progress).

Special export purchasing opportunities and advantages exist from time to time because of legislation designed to assist certain domestic industries and agricultural groups. There may be available direct government subsidies on the export of certain commodities, usually agricultural products in surplus supply. Restrictions and special taxes on imports of various commodities frequently result in the maintenance of domestic prices for such commodities at levels higher than those prevailing in other countries. In such instances, it is possible either to purchase the commodity in question in the foreign country of origin for shipment to a third foreign country or to purchase from the country of origin (or an American importer) "ex-quota" at "world" prices for reexport from the United States.

By execution of a *surety bond* to the government, involving heavy penalties for default, and guaranteeing the reexportation of such imported "ex-quota" items, they may be permitted entry free of restrictions, usually acting to limit the supply, which results in the higher prices prevailing in the domestic market. Such bonds cover, generally, commodities which are further processed or enter into the manufacture of other commodities in the United States, and the reexportation may not be of the same identity or form—only products or commodities containing the equivalent amounts of the materials imported. It is necessary to have paid the scheduled import duties levied on such imports and any special processing or manufacturing taxes, but both these imposts are refunded upon application when the commodities are reexported and the surety bonds are cancelled.

The above procedure is not to be confused with transshipment through United States ports, or retention of imported materials at port of entry "in bond." In this instance, no import duty has been paid, the materials never are cleared through United States Customs, and, consequently, they have not "entered" the country officially—merely being impounded in "bonded" storage, supervised to ensure against release into the country without compliance with governmental regulations and payment of import duties.[22] As the practice of holding imported commodities at United States ports "in bond" is quite common, it often is possible to purchase such materials for export at prices below the domestic market by the equivalent of the import duty.

Under certain conditions, imported items upon which the duty has been paid, on the other hand, are subject to refund or "drawback" of the duty upon reexportation. Usually, such imports will have been refined, further processed, or incorporated into other products by manufacture. The duty drawback allowed upon reexportation is based upon the item or component of the exported material which had been imported, less any refining or manufacturing loss—not the entire quantity or amount of duty which had been paid. Prescribed certification is required with application for duty drawback, and purchase agreements covering such materials should include specifically this requirement.

The complexities and the frequency of changes in applicable regulations, only suggested herein, make it almost mandatory for the average exporter, and even many maintaining extensive export departments, to utilize the services of *foreign freight forwarders* or *commercial exporters.* In addition to the classified telephone directories previously mentioned, the names of competent freight forwarders operating in most major ports in the United States can be obtained from the New York Foreign Freight Forwarders and Brokers Association, Incorporated, 1 Broadway, New York, N.Y. 10004. Good freight forwarders are staffed and equipped to comply with all applicable export regulations and to take advantage of any subsidies or refunds available. They also should be able to furnish information in advance as to "in bond" or "ex-quota" opportunities, and can handle the requisite details covering such purchases.

Foreign Legal Requirements

Of recent years, particularly since World War II, a majority of nations have imposed restrictions on the foreign trade of their nationals. In other countries restrictions are generally more restrictive and more complicated than enumerated herein for the United States. Most foreign countries have specifically limited the importation of merchandise from other countries. These limitations have appeared in the following forms:

[22] See also discussion of "free zones," under "Import Purchasing," and Table 17–1 later in this section.

1. *Foreign exchange restrictions,*[23] usually requiring licenses for the purchase of exact amounts of foreign currencies for specified purposes
2. *Import regulations,* requiring prior permission for the importation of foreign merchandise, often by exact kind and quantity
3. *Tariffs,* restricting imports of foreign merchandise through high import duties, sometimes selectively by country of origin

These forms, either separately or in combination, for the most part have been the rule rather than the exception.

It is to be presumed, of course, that any purchase for export is the reflection of a need originating in a foreign country, and the foreign agent, principal, or ultimate buyer or consignee in the foreign country should be able to furnish detailed information and instructions relating to the governmental *controls and documentation* required for the particular transaction contemplated. Import permits usually are required, and while obtained by and in the name of the foreign agent or consignee, the American buyer for export should request a copy in order to be fully informed of its terms. *Import permits* may be expected to include statement of the exchange conversion authorized, commodity, amount, specifications, documentation,[24] payment, and the time limit within which either shipment or arrival is valid.

Careful attention must be paid to the terms of the import permit, because strict compliance is required to avoid penalties, delays, and even revocation of the permit. One of the most frequent difficulties encountered is the exact limitation on both quantity of the goods and the amount of currency available for payment, restricting within close limits in advance both price and quantity of the purchase by the exporter in the United States. Fluctuating prices or overruns on made-to-order goods often necessitate withholding small portions of the purchase from shipment to the foreign country. The time limitation usually included in import permits often presents a problem, particularly if based upon arrival date at destination port, and shipment is delayed afloat, or in leaving the port of exportation in the United States. The multitude of foreign exchange and import regulations prevailing, differing widely from country to country, and with frequent modifications, make it almost impossible for any one person to maintain complete knowledge of the legal requirements existing at any certain time, or applying to various commodities

[23] See also discussion of foreign exchange restrictions relating to payments, under "Import Purchasing."

[24] The discussion of documentation under "Import Purchasing," is equally applicable to exports. In addition to the *Revised American Foreign Trade Definitions—1941* and *Uniform Customs and Practice for Documentary Credits,* see also *Incoterms—1953,* listed later in "References."

being considered for export from the United States. In addition to (or instead of) the foreign agent or consignee of the goods, and the suggestions previously included herein, there are several sources of information and simple rules available to assist the purchaser who is faced with these problems. For example, specification of payment in terms of United States currency will avoid any risk of exchange fluctuations, and conducting all negotiations and writing the contract in the English language can prevent misunderstandings from errors in translation. Incorporating recognized codes of definitions and practice should make for complete and enforceable agreements.

Many large American *banks* make it their business to keep customers informed of the most important regulations involving trade with foreign countries. For example, the First National City Bank of New York publishes annually a summary of exchange and foreign trade regulations, which is kept up to date throughout the year by periodic *Customers' Confidential Bulletins.*[25] Among other banks offering extensive foreign trade service, the Morgan Guaranty Trust Company of New York has issued a well indexed informational pamphlet covering *Export and Import Procedures,*[25] and the Manufacturers Hanover Trust Company, also of New York, provides an *Exporters' Handbook* in loose-leaf form, which is kept current by frequent supplements.[25]

A majority of the leading trading nations also maintain *consulates* in many American cities, and *information services,* governmental *buying agencies,* and other offices at most port cities in the United States and at some inland manufacturing and trading centers. It is the function of such foreign governmental agencies to foster American trade with their respective countries. They can be located readily in telephone directories or through inquiry of the U.S. Department of State in Washington, or of any of the field offices of the U.S. Department of Commerce (or directly of the Bureau of International Commerce of the Department in Washington).

REFERENCES

The following partial list of references includes descriptions of the contents of representative publications dealing with both importing and exporting. The value of familiarity with the nature and sources of such information cannot be overemphasized, regardless of whether the buyer intends to handle import and export transactions in their entirety or through commercial agents, freight forwarders, or brokers. The periodicals listed provide the best-known current and up-to-date information

[25] See listings in "References."

on United States and foreign controls and exchange rates in usable form (other than the daily general and business newspapers). Information found in any of these references provides good general guidance, but should be checked in every vital particular with authoritative sources, because important changes are apt to occur at any time without notice.

Periodical Publications

Business Reports, Overseas (annually, and continuous), Superintendent of Documents, U.S. Government Printing Office, Washington, D.C. 20402, or any of the field offices of the U.S. Department of Commerce, located throughout the country ($18 per year, 15 cents per single copy)

Replacing (since 1961) the three-part World Trade Information Service in reporting basic and authoritative information needed by exporters, importers, investors, manufacturers, researchers, and all who are concerned with international trade and economic conditions throughout the world. The data are presented on specific countries.

Commerce of the United States, Quarterly Summary of Foreign, Superintendent of Documents, U.S. Government Printing Office, Washington, D.C. 20402, or any of the field offices of U.S. Department of Commerce, located throughout the country ($1 per year, 30 cents per single issue)

Contains information on imports and exports by commodities, countries, customs districts, and economic classes, on a cumulative basis through each quarter; compiled by the Bureau of the Census, U.S. Department of Commerce.

Commerce, International (weekly), Superintendent of Documents, U.S. Government Printing Office, Washington, D.C. 20402, or any of the field offices of U.S. Department of Commerce, located throughout the country ($16 per year, foreign $21)

Includes concise, authoritative international marketing information and news and reports on significant developments in the U.S. export trade expansion and other programs, and reports on outstanding activities of such organizations as GATT, the Common Market, Eximbank, the World Bank, ECAFE, and ECSC; and explains potential advantages to American businessmen in profitable sales of U.S. products around the world; compiled by Commercial Intelligence Division of the Bureau of International Commerce, U.S. Department of Commerce.

Commerce Handbook, Foreign (annually), Chamber of Commerce of the United States, Foreign Commerce–Foreign Policy Department, 1615 H Street, N.W., Washington, D.C. 20206 ($2)

A comprehensive reference to organization services and current published information on all important phases of international trade and investment, procedures, practices, techniques, and policy.

Comprehensive Export Schedule (see *Export Schedule, Comprehensive*)

Custom House Guide (annually, with monthly supplements), Custom House Guide, Box 7, Station P, New York, N.Y. 10004 ($35, supplements only annually $5)

Directory containing for each United States port of entry: Customs house brokers, freight forwarders, steamship lines and agents, stevedores, U.S. Customs bonded truckmen, U.S. Customs bonded warehouses, general warehouses, foreign consuls, chambers of commerce, port authorities; Canadian Customs brokers, freight forwarders, and Customs bonded warehouses; foreign forwarding agents, and Customs headquarters of foreign countries. Includes alphabetical index of 26,000 commodities showing rates of duty in accordance with the new "Tariff Schedules of the United States"; all revised by GATT, special and administrative provisions of the U.S. Customs Tariff Act, the U.S. Customs Regulations and Internal Revenue Code, affecting imports. Monthly supplements also available separately, known as *American Import and Export Bulletin* (see *Import and Export Bulletin*).

Exchange Rates, Monthly Foreign, Division of Administrative Services, Board of Governors of the Federal Reserve System, Washington, D.C. 20551

Lists average rates of exchange on various countries in current month, with comparable figures for preceding two months and corresponding month previous year. Based on daily noon buying rates in New York City for cable transfers, as certified for Customs purposes by the Federal Reserve Bank of New York; compiled at Board of Governors, and issued the first day of the following month; available without charge.

Exchange Rates, Weekly Foreign, Division of Administrative Services, Board of Governors of the Federal Reserve System, Washington, D.C. 20551

Lists daily noon buying rates in New York City for cable transfers payable in various foreign currencies, as certified for Customs purposes by the Federal Reserve Bank of New York, for five days of week ending Friday; compiled at Board of Governors, and issued following Monday; available without charge.

Exchange Restrictions, Annual Report on, The Secretary, International Monetary Fund, 1818 H Street, N.W., Washington, D.C. 20431

Contains review for preceding year covering world payments situation, progress in relaxation of restrictions, fiscal, and monetary measures (in lieu of exchange restrictions), and simplification of exchange controls; includes series of country surveys of all members of the International Monetary Fund and of certain nonmember countries, describing their exchange systems, giving basic exchange rates, nature of exchange systems, authorities administering the controls, arrangements applying to settlements with other countries, operation of accounts of nonresidents, and requirements affecting payments of import, export, invisible, and capital transactions; contains listing of the more significant changes in exchange practices taking place during the year under review; issued annually about seven months after end of each year, (*Sixteenth Annual Report,* covering 1964, announced in International Financial News Survey, October 8, 1965) and available without charge.

Export Bulletin, Current (generally twice monthly), Superintendent of Documents, U.S. Government Printing Office, Washington, D.C. 20402, or any of the field offices of U.S. Department of Commerce, located throughout the country (25 cents per issue)

Contains loose-leaf replacement pages to keep up to date the *Comprehensive Export Schedule,* together with brief summaries and explanations of changes in export regulations; compiled by offices of the Bureau of International Commerce, U.S. Department of Commerce. (Included as issued without extra charge with annual subscriptions to *Comprehensive Export Schedule.*)

Export Bulletin, American Import and (see *Import and Export Bulletin*)

Export Schedule, Comprehensive (annually), Superintendent of Documents, U.S. Government Printing Office, Washington, D.C. 20402, or any of the field offices of U.S. Department of Commerce, located throughout the country ($6 per year including periodic "Current Export Bulletins," foreign $7.50)

Contains all rules, regulations, and explanations covering the basic export controls; in loose-leaf form (kept up to date by periodic "Current Export Bulletins," containing replacement pages); compiled by the offices of the Bureau of International Commerce, U.S. Department of Commerce.

Exporters' Encyclopedia (annually), Thomas Ashwell and Company, Inc., 20 Vesey Street, New York, N.Y. 10007 ($40 per year, including Supplementary Bulletins twice monthly)

Handbook of information on shipments to all foreign countries and U.S. possessions, including the following: index of ports and trade centers; index by countries of consular regulations, shipping routes, mail, radio, cable, telephone, exchange restrictions, money, weights, and holidays; radio and cable rates; parcel post, regular and air mail, and air cargo regulations, carriers, and rates to various parts of the world; reference tables of weights, measures, time charts, political and geographical groups; foreign trade organizations in the United States; government agencies, consulates abroad, chambers of commerce, clubs, associations, and organizations; general information covering laws and regulations affecting export trade, insurance, export terms and practice, financing foreign trade, trademarks, and other items; description of export and shipping practices in principal foreign countries, including customs treatment of weights, packing hints, and shippers export declarations; United States licensing system, and the Webb-Pomerene Law; steamship companies, ports of the United States, and freight forwarders in principal cities of the United States.

Import and Export Bulletin, American (monthly), Custom House Guide, Box 7, Station P, New York, N.Y. 10004 ($5 per year)

Reports on latest changes in customs tariffs, newest regulations of various governmental departments and bureaus; port information; import and export opportunities; world trade personalities; industry news. Includes columns devoted to port activities, air transportation news, railroads in foreign trade, steamship notes. (Included as supplements with subscription to the *Custom House Guide*.)

Imports of Merchandise for Consumption in Commodity by Country of Origin, United States—Report FT 125 (monthly), Superintendent of Documents, U.S. Government Printing Office, Washington, D.C. 20402, or any of the field offices of U.S. Department of Commerce, located throughout the country ($10 per year, $1.50 per single issue)

Lists by Schedule A commodity groupings, totals imported from all countries, and for certain commodities the amount from each country from which imports total $10,000 or more; compiled by the Foreign Trade Division of the Bureau of the Census, U.S. Department of Commerce.

Information Service, Foreign (annually, with monthly supplements), First National City Bank, 399 Park Avenue, New York, N.Y. 10022

A monthly review of economic conditions in overseas countries where branches of First National City Bank are located; also periodic reports regarding exchange and foreign trade regulations; available to clients in foreign trade.

Information Service, World Trade (see *World Trade Information Service*)

News Survey, International Financial (weekly, except in Christmas and New Year weeks), The Secretary, International Monetary Fund, 1818 H Street, N.W., Washington, D.C. 20431

Digest of foreign trade and finance (developments, regulatory announcements, and statistics), based on material published in newspapers, periodicals, and official documents; written by members of the staff of the International Monetary Fund, and available without charge.

Overseas Business Reports (see *Business Reports, Overseas*)

Publications, Catalog of U.S. Census (quarterly), Superintendent of Documents, U.S. Government Printing Office, Washington, D.C. 20402 ($1.25 per year, foreign $2, single copies vary in price)

Complete listing of publications of the Bureau of the Census during the period covered, including those on agriculture, business, governments, manufacturers, population, housing, and U.S. foreign trade; compiled and issued quarterly and cumulative-to-annual; includes 12 issues of the Monthly Supplement.

Schedule, Comprehensive Export (see *Export Schedule, Comprehensive*)

Trade Lists (by commodity groups) (generally biennially), Commercial Intelligence Division, Bureau of International Commerce, U.S. Department of Commerce, Washington, D.C. 20230, or any of the field offices, U.S. Department of Commerce, located throughout the country ($1 each)

Covers names and addresses of foreign manufacturers or producers, importers and exporters, distributors, and service organizations, classified under major commodity groups, and by countries; compiled by the Commercial Intelligence Division of the Bureau of International Commerce, U.S. Department of Commerce.

World Trade Information Service (obsolescent, formerly annually, and continuous), Superintendent of Documents, U.S. Government Printing Office, Washington, D.C. 20402, or any of the field offices, U.S. Department of Commerce, located throughout the country (priced variously as still available)

A series (being superseded by *Overseas Business Reports*) compiled and issued by the offices of the Bureau of Foreign Commerce (now Bureau of International Commerce), U.S. Department of Commerce, affording detailed analytical reports on trade and investment conditions and developments in (one each) particular countries or areas, arranged in three parts by type of information covered in each, as follows:

1. *Economic Reports*—basic data on country covered with respect to economic conditions and recent developments, regulations governing establishment of new businesses, marketing areas, insurance conditions, and related subjects.
2. *Operations Reports*—information on preparing shipments, marking and labelling requirements, licensing and exchange controls, the import tariff system, pharmaceutical regulations, patent and trademark regulations, and other practical guides.
3. *Statistical Reports*—tables and charts of United States trade with particular foreign countries, and the total export and import trade monthly of the United States and of the foreign countries.

Nonperiodical Publications

Arbitration and the Law throughout the World, Commercial (1958), United States Council of the International Chamber of Commerce, 103 Park Avenue, New York, N.Y. 10017 ($12.65)

Summary of the legislation in 56 countries governing arbitration agreements, procedure, arbitral awards, enforcement of awards, and means of recourse; a loose-leaf publication, supplements covering additional countries will be published; compiled by the International Chamber of Commerce.

Arbitration of the ICC, International Commercial (1956), United States Council of the International Chamber of Commerce, 103 Park Avenue, New York, N.Y. 10017 (free)

Brief outline of ICC conciliation and arbitration as means of settling international commercial disputes; published by the International Chamber of Commerce (3d edition, 1961).

Arbitration, Rules of Conciliation and (1955), United States Council of the International Chamber of Commerce, 103 Park Avenue, New York, N.Y. 10017 (45 cents)

Rules of the Court of International Commercial Arbitration of the International Chamber of Commerce in force from June 1, 1955; published by the International Chamber of Commerce.

Arbitration, Guide to ICC (1963), United States Council of the International Chamber of Commerce, 103 Park Avenue, New York, N.Y. 10017 ($1.05)

Describes characteristics of and information on the ICC's system of international commercial arbitration and its rules of conciliation and arbitration; takes as a basis for reference the 300 most recent cases submitted to the Court of Arbitration, and contains a list of the members of the Court together with the names of some of its best-known arbitrators; published by the International Chamber of Commerce.

Classification of Foreign and Domestic Commodities Exported (see *Schedule B*)

Commodities Exported, Classification of Foreign and Domestic (see *Schedule B*)

Countries, Specified Foreign (see *Handbooks, Investment*)

Credits, Uniform Customs and Practice for Documentary (1962),[26] United States Council of the International Chamber of Commerce, 103 Park Avenue, New York, N.Y. 10017 (65 cents)

A compilation of provisions, definitions, interpretations, instructions, and documents for use in handling payments under letters of credit, and effective with United States banks subscribing July 1, 1963; revised by the International Chamber of Commerce; translations also available in German, Italian, and Spanish (regular edition contains text both in English and French); designated as Brochure No. 222.

Definitions—1941, Revised American Foreign Trade (1941),[26] National Foreign Trade Council, Inc., 10 Rockefeller Plaza, New York, N.Y. 10020

[26] Reprinted hereinafter.

A detailed definition of principal terms used in foreign trade, with general comments and cautions covering their use, and procedural outline of responsibilities of buyer and seller implied in each term or phrase; adopted July 30, 1941, by a joint committee representing the Chamber of Commerce of the United States, National Council of American Importers, Inc., and National Foreign Trade Council, Inc.

Definitions (see *Incoterms—1953,* and *Terms, Trade*)

Documents (see *Credits, Uniform Customs and Practice*)

Exporters' Handbook, Manufacturers Hanover Trust Company, 44 Wall Street, New York, N.Y. 10015

A manual consisting of three parts: (1) Collection tariff and schedule of stamp duty throughout the world, (2) Protest of drafts (cost of protest, time limit for protesting, legal benefits derived from protest, days of grace and method of extending an accepted draft), (3) Exchange regulations prevailing in foreign countries as they affect exporters in the United States; in loose-leaf form and under continual revision (latest basic edition, copyright 1962); available to clients interested in exporting.

Exporting to the United States (1962), Superintendent of Documents, U.S. Government Printing Office, Washington, D.C. 20402, or Commissioner of Customs, U.S. Treasury Department, Washington, D.C. 20226 (50 cents)

Outlines procedures, documents, restrictions, quotas, and other information necessary to the foreign exporter to the United States (or the United States importer), to promote a wider understanding of U.S. Customs requirements; includes lists of Customs collection districts and ports of entry (and airports of entry), and instructions and exhibits of required forms; includes list of senior Customs representatives in foreign countries; compiled by the Bureau of Customs, U.S. Treasury Department.

Forms for the Opening of Documentary Credits, Standard (1952), United States Council of the International Chamber of Commerce, 103 Park Avenue, New York, N.Y. 10017 (65 cents)

A pamphlet containing exhibits of forms designed to obtain greater accuracy and clearness in correspondence between banks, by establishing uniform terminology and forms of a uniform tenor for the opening of documentary credits; adopted by the Thirteenth Congress of the International Chamber of Commerce, Lisbon, Portugal, June 11–16, 1951; designated as Brochure No. 159.

Handbooks, Investment (for various countries) (variously), Superintendent of Documents, U.S. Government Printing Office, Washington, D.C. 20402, or any of the field offices of the U.S. Department of Commerce, located throughout the country (prices variable, depending on country)

Gives factual information on all sectors of the economy of (one each) particular countries, the role of government in the country's economic life, details on pertinent business and tax laws and policies, climate for foreign investment, marketing areas and potentials, and statistical data; prepared by the offices of the Bureau of International Commerce, U.S. Department of Commerce from time to time. Now available are Investment in Chile, Investment in India, Investment in Peru, and Investment in Taiwan.

Handbook of International Marketing (see *Marketing, Handbook of International*)

Holidays, Bank and Public throughout the World (1964), Morgan Guaranty Trust Company of New York, 23 Wall Street, New York, N.Y. 10015

A book listing currently available information on bank and public holidays observed in various parts of the world in 1964; includes schedule of daylight saving time in 1964 in various states of the United States; compiled by Morgan Guaranty Trust Company of New York, November, 1963.

Incoterms—1953, United States Council of the International Chamber of Commerce, 103 Park Avenue, New York, N.Y. 10017 ($1.05)

A compilation of standardized interpretations, agreed upon by representatives attending the Vienna Congress of the International Chamber of Commerce in 1953, of trade terms applying to international transactions; designated as Brochure No. 166.

Indexes to U.S. Government Specifications (see *Specifications*)

Information on American Firms for International Buyers, Sources of (1963). Superintendent of Documents, U.S. Government Printing Office, Washington, D.C. 20402 (15 cents)

A guide to the principal sources of commercial information on U.S. firms.

Insurance, Marine (see *Marine Insurance*)

Letters of Credit, The ABC of Commercial (1963), Manufacturers Hanover Trust Company, 44 Wall Street, New York, N.Y. 10015

A thesis outlining the fundamental aspects of Letter of Credit financing; discussing filing of application, procedure in handling credit from inception to liquidation; including examination in detail of documents; exhibits of forms, prepared by John L. O'Halloran of Manufacturers Hanover Trust Company (Sixth Edition, August, 1963); available to clients interested in foreign trade.

Marine Insurance: Practical Notes and Comments on Cargo Insurance (1951), Insurance Company of North America, 1600 Arch Street, Philadelphia, Pa. 19101

A pamphlet describing nature, types, provisions, and handling of marine cargo insurance, including reprint of *Revised American Foreign Trade Definitions—1941* and selected references; published by the Insurance Companies of North America.

Marine Insurance: Its Principles and Practice (1952), by William D. Winter, 3d ed., McGraw-Hill Book Company, 330 West 42d Street, New York, N.Y. 10036 ($9.50)

A 551-page book describing nature, types, provisions, and procedures (including appraisals, adjustments, and settlements), revised to reflect marked changes occurring in recent years in the practice of marine insurance.

Marketing, Handbook of International (1963), by Alexander O. Stanley, McGraw-Hill Book Company, 330 West 42d Street, New York, N.Y. 10036 ($17.50)

A 680-page book covering exporting, importing, and investing overseas; contains information on modern research methods in commercial intelligence, the international communications grid, with emphasis on cost cutting, methods and resources available to convert purchases abroad into profits at home; includes data on common markets in existence and in the planning stages, guide to U.S. Department of Commerce facilities (and those of other government agencies), and discussions of new U.S. Tax Law, U.S. Foreign Credit Insurance Program, and the New Trade Expansion Acts.

Packing Specifications (see *Specifications, Indexes to U.S. Government*)

Procedures, Export and Import (1963), Morgan Guaranty Trust Company of New York, 23 Wall Street, New York, N.Y. 10015

An informational pamphlet covering background, governmental and intergovernmental agencies, and procedures for both importing and exporting; includes reprints of *Uniform Customs and Practice for Documentary Credits* (International Chamber of Commerce) and *Revised American Foreign Trade Definitions—1941* (Chamber of Commerce of the United States, National Council of American Importers, and National Foreign Trade Council); revised edition, 1962, third printing with revisions, October, 1963; available to clients engaged in foreign trade.

Reports on Individual Foreign Firms (see *Trade Directory Reports*)

Schedule B—Statistical Classification of Foreign and Domestic Commodities Exported from the United States (1958, with new reprint pages provided when sufficient number of changes warrant), Superintendent of Documents, Government Printing Office, Washington, D.C. 20402 ($6.00, foreign $7.50)

The basic document for export regulations of the United States government, and essential to understanding of references in the Comprehensive Export Schedule, prepared and issued by the Foreign Trade Division of the Bureau of the Census, and the Bureau of International Commerce, U.S. Department of Commerce. (January 1, 1958 edition reprinted January, 1962.)

Selling Around the World—How Commerce Helps (1965), Superintendent of Documents, U.S. Government Printing Office, Washington, D.C. 20402 (15 cents)

A description of the Department of Commerce services to the international business community; simple treatment (with cartoon illustrations) of marketing information, covering trade centers, fairs, missions, National and Regional Export Expansion Councils, Free Trade Zones, export controls, and listing of 39 field offices of U.S. Department of Commerce.

Specifications, Indexes to U.S. Government (variously, separately)

Army, Navy, and Air Force specifications listed in respective indexes include several (MIL) describing packing materials and methods, reflecting experience gained in recent large-scale operations throughout the world, and may be obtained from the following sources:

Army—Army Materiel Command installations throughout the United States
Navy—Commanding Officer, BUSANDA, Washington, D.C.
Air Force—Commander, Air Logistics Command, Wright-Patterson Air Force Base, Ohio

Federal Specifications include various standard shipping containers and are available from the General Services Administration, Regional Office 3, Washington, D.C. 20407. Four separate indexes and a directory to specifications and standards are available from Superintendent of Documents, Government Printing Office, Washington, D.C. 20402, as follows:

Department of the Army, with supplemental service
Department of the Navy, with supplemental service

Department of the Air Force, with supplemental service
Federal Specifications, with supplemental service
U.S. Government Specifications Directory

Specifications Directory, U.S. Government (see *Specifications, Indexes*)

Terms, Trade (1955), United States Council of the International Chamber of Commerce, 103 Park Avenue, New York, N.Y. 10017 ($2.48)

A booklet containing tables, comparing interpretations of the ten most commonly used contractual terms in international trade in 18 important trading countries; designated as Document No. 16.

Trade Directory Reports, World (variously), Commercial Intelligence Division, Bureau of International Commerce, U.S. Department of Commerce, Washington, D.C. 20230, or any of the field offices, U.S. Department of Commerce, located throughout the country ($1 each)

Give data of specified foreign firms (one each) covering type of organization, lines handled, size of firm and extent of operating territory, names of owners and/or officers, capital, volume of business handled, general reputation in trade and financial circles, and names of any United States firms, associated with or representing; compiled by the commercial attachés of United States embassies, consulates, or representatives of the U.S. Department of Commerce or other governmental agencies in foreign countries; available for many foreign firms, but a specific request to the Commercia Intelligence Division of the Bureau of International Commerce, U.S. Department o Commerce (or in some instances to the United States Embassy abroad) will result in investigation and preparation of such report for any recognized foreign business organization.

Trade, Techniques of International (1950), by Morris S. Rosenthal, McGraw-Hill Book Company, 330 West 42d Street, New York, N.Y. 10036 ($8.95)

A 554-page book covering international trade practices, with examples from the initial transaction through completion of the shipment, problems, techniques, rule laws, and obligations assumed by buyer and seller; includes discussions of contract packing for overseas trade, financing of export and import shipments, transportation (including air), foreign exchange, customs procedures, marine insurance, and communications; contains an appendix giving definitions, regulations, agreements, suggestions, cost analysis, and procedures.

REVISED AMERICAN FOREIGN TRADE DEFINITIONS

In order to ensure clear-cut understanding of the terms of foreign trade it is essential that exact definitions be followed. The principal America reference, available for almost half a century, is the *Revised America Foreign Trade Definitions* reprinted below with the permission of th National Foreign Trade Council, Inc., 10 Rockefeller Plaza, New Yor N.Y. 10020. It is used by both exporters and importers, and no furth revision has been made since adopted July 30, 1941, by a Joint Committee representing the Chamber of Commerce of the United States America, the National Council of American Importers, Inc., and the National Foreign Trade Council, Inc.

Table 17–1. Free-trade Zones of the World

Austria:	Graz, Innsbruck, Linz, and Vienna
Bahamas:	Freeport (Grand Bahama Island)
Bermuda:	Freeport (Ireland Island)
Brazil:	Manaus
Cambodia:	Sihanoukville
Chile:	Arica and Punta Arenas
Colombia:	Barranquilla (not yet in operation)
Denmark:	Copenhagen
Dominican Republic:	Puerto Plata (not yet in operation)
Finland:	Hanko
Fed. Republic of Germany:	Bremen, Bremerhaven, Cuxhaven, Emden, Hamburg, and Kiel
Greece:	Piraeus and Salonika (Thessaloniki)
India:	Kandla
Ireland:	Shannon Free Airport
Italy:	(In Italy, Free-trade Zones are known as "Free Points.") Naples, Torre Annunziata, Trieste, and Venice. Authorized, but not yet in operation: Brindisi, Genoa, and Messina
Lebanon:	Beirut, Beirut International Airport, and Tripoli
Liberia:	Monrovia
Libya:	Tripoli (authorized, but not yet in operation)
Mexico:	Coatzacoalcos (also known as Puerto Mexico) and Salina Cruz; Topolobampo (authorized, but not yet in operation)
Morocco:	Tangier
Netherlands Antilles:	Oranjestad (Aruba) and Willemstad (Curacao)
Okinawa:	Naha
Panama:	Colon and Tocumen International Airport
Spain:	Barcelona, Cadiz, and Vigo*
Sweden:	Göteborg, Malmo, and Stockholm
Switzerland:	Aarau, Basel-Dreispitz, Basel-Rheinhafen, Basel-CFF, Chiasso-Stazione P.V., Geneva, Geneva-Aerodrome de Cointrin, Geneva-Cornavin, Lausanne, St. Gallen, St. Margrethen, Zurich-Albisrieden, Zurich-Aerodrome
Syria:	Latakia
Turkey:	Iskenderun
United Arab Republic:	Alexandria, Port Said, and Port Tewfick (City of Suez)
United States:	(In the United States, Free-trade Zones are known as Foreign-trade Zones.) Mayaguez (Puerto Rico), New Orleans, New York, San Francisco, Seattle, and Toledo
Uruguay:	Colonia and Nuevo Palmira

* Spain also has established the following depositos francos (free depots), which provide rather limited free-trade-zone facilities: Aguilas, Algeciras, Alicante, Almeria, Aviles, Bilbao, Cartegena, Castellon, El Ferrol del Caudillo, Gijon, Huelva, La Coruna, Mahon, Malaga, Palamos, Palma de Mallorca, Pasajes, Ribadeo, San Sebastian, Santander, Sevilla, Tarragona, Valencia, Villa-Garcia, and Vinaroz.

SOURCE: Transportation and Insurance Division, Bureau of International Commerce, U.S. Department of Commerce, Washington, D.C. 20230 (March, 1964).

Table 17–2. Foreign Exchange Rates

As of January 4, 1965

Country	Monetary unit	Consisting of	Free selling rate (U.S.$)[a]	Official rates[b]		
				Par value established with I.M.F.	Per U.S. dollars	
					Buying	Selling
Algeria	Algerian dinar	100 centimes	0.2041			
Argentina	Peso	100 centavos	0.0067			
Australia	Pound	20 shillings 240 pence	2.2330	2.24		
Austria	Schilling	100 groschen	0.0389	0.03846	S25.80	S26.20
Bahamas	Pound	20 shillings 240 pence	2.7982			
Belgium	Franc	100 centimes	0.02015	0.02	BF49.625	BF50.375
Bermuda	Pound	20 shillings 240 pence	2.7912			
Brazil	Cruzeiro	100 centavos	0.00056			
Burma	Kyat	100 pyas	0.2100	0.21		
Canada	Dollar	100 cents	0.93 5/32	0.9250	C$1.070377	C$1.092001
Ceylon	Rupee	100 cents	0.2110	0.21		
Chile	Escudo	100 centesimos	0.3150			
Colombia	Peso	100 centavos	0.0740			
Congo (Leopoldville)	Franc	100 centimes	0.0067			
Costa Rica	Colon	100 centimes	0.1525	0.15094	¢6.62	¢6.65
Cuba	Peso	100 centavos	no market	[c]		
Czechoslovakia	Crown	100 hellers	0.1400	[c]		
Denmark	Krone	100 ore	0.1446 3/4	0.14477	DKr6.8575	DKr6.9575
Ecuador	Sucre	100 centavos	0.0545	0.05555	S/17.82	S/18.18
Egypt (U.A.R.)	Pound	100 piasters 1,000 mils	2.32	2.87156[d]	£E0.434782	£E0.437390

Table 17–2. Foreign Exchange Rates (*Continued*)

As of January 4, 1965

Country	Monetary unit	Consisting of	Free selling rate (U.S.$)[a]	Official rates[b]		
				Par value established with I.M.F.	Per U.S. dollars	
					Buying	Selling
El Salvador	Colon	100 centavos	0.405	0.40	¢2.49	¢2.51
Ethiopia	Dollar	100 cents	0.405	0.40	Eth$2.4750	Eth$2.520
Finland	Finmark	100 pennis	0.3150	0.3125		
France	Franc	100 centimes	0.2041	0.20255	F4.90	F4.974
French Somaliland	Djibouti Franc	100 centimes	0.0047	0.00466		
Germany (West)	Mark	100 pfennig	0.2513¾	0.25	DM3.97	DM4.03
Greece	Drachma	100 lepta	0.0336	0.03333	Dr29.85	Dr30.15
Guatemala	Quetzal	100 centavos	1.00	1.00	Q1.00	Q1.01
Haiti	Gourde	100 centimes	0.2000	0.20		
Honduras (British)	Dollar	100 cents	0.7000	0.7000		
Honduras (Republic)	Lempira	100 centavos	0.5000	0.50	L1.98	L2.02
Hong Kong	Dollar	100 cents	0.1755	0.1750		
India	Rupee	100 naye paise	0.2094	0.21		
Indonesia	Rupiah	100 sen	0.0020			
Iran (Persia)	Rial	100 dinars	0.0135	0.0132	RIs75.00	RIs76.50
Iraq	Dinar	1,000 fils	2.7950	2.80		
Ireland (Eire)	Pound	20 shillings 240 pence	2.7977	2.80	£—/7/1[e]	£—/7/2⅓[e]
Israel	Pound	100 agorot	0.34	0.3333		
Italy	Lira	100 centesimi	0.001604	0.0016	Lire 620.50	Lire 629.50
Jamaica	Pound	20 shillings 240 pence	2.7972	2.80		
Japan	Yen	100 sen	0.002792	0.00277	¥357.30	¥362.70

Table 17–2. Foreign Exchange Rates (*Continued*)

As of January 4, 1965

Country	Monetary unit	Consisting of	Free selling rate (U.S.$)[a]	Official rates[b]		
				Par value established with I.M.F.	Per U.S. dollars	
					Buying	Selling
Jordan	Dinar	100 fils	2.82	2.80	Dr.35461[e]	Dr.35971[e]
Korea (South)	Won	100 chon	0.00392			Won 255
Lebanon	Pound	100 piasters	0.3255	0.45631		
Libya	Pound	100 piasters 1,000 mils	2.80	2.80		
Macao	Pataca	100 avos	0.20	[c]		
Mexico	Peso	100 centavos	0.0802	0.0800	Mex12.49	Mex12.51
Morocco	Dirham	100 francs	0.2000	0.19760		
Netherlands	Guilder (florin)	100 cents	0.2783	0.27624	f3.59¼	f3.64¾
New Zealand	Pound	20 shillings 240 pence	2.7812	2.7809		
Nicaragua	Cordoba	100 centavos	0.1425	0.14285	C7.00	C7.0525
Norway	Krone	100 ore	0.1398½	0.1400	NKr7.09	NKr7.20
Okinawa	U.S. dollar	100 cents	1.00			
Pakistan	Rupee	100 paisa	0.2096	0.2100		
Panama	Balboa	100 centismos	1.00	1.00		
Peru	Sol	100 centavos	0.0374			
Philippines	Peso	100 centavos	0.2569	0.50		
Portugal	Escudo	100 centavos	0.0350	0.03478		
Portuguese Guinea	Portuguese escudo	100 centavos	0.0352			
Saudi Arabia	Riyal	20 guirsh 100 hillal	0.2250	0.2222		
Spain	Peseta	100 centimes	0.01675	0.01666	Pts59.55	Pts60.45

Table 17–2. Foreign Exchange Rates (*Continued*)

As of January 4, 1965

Country	Monetary unit	Consisting of	Free selling rate (U.S.$)[a]	Official rates[b]		
				Par value established with I.M.F.	Per U.S. dollars	
					Buying	Selling
Sweden	Krona	100 ore	0.1946	0.19330	SKr5.135	SKr5.2125
Switzerland	Franc	100 centimes	0.2316¾	[c]	SwF4.295	SwF4.45
Syria (U.A.R.)	Pound	100 piasters	0.2640	0.45631[d]	£s3.80	£s3.82
Taiwan (Formosa)	Dollar	100 cents	0.0250			
Thailand	Baht (tiscal)	100 satang	0.0490	0.04807		
Tunisia	Dinar	1,000 mils	1.95			
Turkey	Pound	100 piasters	0.1125	0.1111	£T9.00	£T9.045
Republic of South Africa	Rand	100 cents	1.3973	1.40		
United Kingdom	Pound	20 shillings 240 pence	2.7912	2.80	£–/7/1[e]	£–/7/2⅓[e]
Uruguay	Peso	100 centesimos	0.0415	0.1351		
Venezuela	Bolivar	100 centimes	0.2228	0.2985	Various[f]	Various[f]
Vietnam (South)	Piastre	100 cents	0.01428		VN59.65	VN60.35

[a] Free to the extent governmental restrictions permit.

[b] Official fixed Central Bank buying and selling rates where applicable; otherwise official trading limits within which spot rate is permitted to fluctuate.

[c] Not a member of the Fund.

[d] No transactions done at this rate.

[e] Actually Central Bank buys and sells pounds to maintain rate within limits of $2.78 and $2.82.

[f] Venezuela has several official buying and selling rates: (1) Central Bank's buying rate for U.S. dollars for local currency payments of oil and iron companies, buying Bs4.40; (2) proceeds from export of coffee and cocoa may be sold to Central Bank at Bs4.485; (3) "Official Free" Market buying Bs4.45, selling Bs4.50.

SOURCE: Compiled by Foreign Exchange Department, First National City Bank, 399 Park Avenue, New York, N.Y. 10022.

Foreword

Since the issuance of *American Foreign Trade Definitions* in 1919, many changes in practice have occurred. The 1919 Definitions did much to clarify and simplify foreign trade practice, and received wide recognition and use by buyers and sellers throughout the world. At the Twenty-Seventh National Foreign Trade Convention, 1940, further revision and clarification of these Definitions was urged as necessary to assist the foreign trader in the handling of his transactions.

The following *Revised American Foreign Trade Definitions—1941* are recommended for general use by both exporters and importers. These revised definitions have no status at law unless there is specific legislation providing for them, or unless they are confirmed by court decisions. Hence, it is suggested that sellers and buyers agree to their acceptance as part of the contract of sale. These revised definitions will then become legally binding upon all parties.

In view of changes in practice and procedure since 1919, certain new responsibilities for sellers and buyers are included in these revised definitions. Also, in many instances, the old responsibilities are more clearly defined than in the 1919 Definitions, and the changes should be beneficial both to sellers and buyers. Widespread acceptance will lead to a greater standardization of foreign trade procedure, and to the avoidance of much misunderstanding.

Adoption by exporters and importers of these revised terms will impress on all parties concerned their respective responsibilities and rights.

General Notes of Caution

1. As foreign trade definitions have been issued by organizations in various parts of the world, and as the courts of countries have interpreted these definitions in different ways, it is important that sellers and buyers agree that their contracts are subject to the *Revised American Foreign Trade Definitions—1941* and that the various points listed are accepted by both parties.

2. In addition to the foreign trade terms listed herein, there are terms that are at times used, such as Free Harbor, C.I.F.&C. (Cost, Insurance, Freight, and Commission), C.I.F.C.&I. (Cost, Insurance, Freight, Commission, and Interest), C.I.F. Landed (Cost, Insurance, Freight, Landed), and others. None of these should be used unless there has first been a definite understanding as to the exact meaning thereof. It is unwise to attempt to interpret other terms in the light of the terms given herein. Hence, whenever possible, one of the terms defined herein should be used.

3. It is unwise to use abbreviations in quotations or in contracts which might be subject to misunderstanding.

4. When making quotations, the familiar terms "hundredweight" or "ton" should be avoided. A hundredweight can be 100 pounds of the short ton, or 112 pounds of the long ton. A ton can be a short ton of 2,000 pounds, or a metric ton of 2,204.6 pounds, or a long ton of 2,240 pounds. Hence, the type of

hundredweight or ton should be clearly stated in quotations and in sales confirmations. Also, all terms referring to quantity, weight, volume, length, or surface should be clearly defined and agreed upon.

5. If inspection, or certificate of inspection, is required, it should be agreed, in advance, whether the cost thereof is for account of seller or buyer.

6. Unless otherwise agreed upon, all expenses are for the account of seller up to the point at which the buyer must handle the subsequent movement of goods.

7. There are a number of elements in a contract that do not fall within the scope of these foreign trade definitions. Hence, no mention of these is made herein. Seller and buyer should agree to these separately when negotiating contracts. This particularly applies to so-called "customary" practices.

Definitions of Quotations

(I) Ex (Point of Origin)

"EX FACTORY," "EX MILL," "EX MINE," "EX PLANTATION," "EX WAREHOUSE," etc. (named point of origin)

Under this term, the price quoted applies only at the point of origin, and the seller agrees to place the goods at the disposal of the buyer at the agreed place on the date or within the period fixed.

Under this quotation:

Seller must

(1) bear all costs and risks of the goods until such time as the buyer is obliged to take delivery thereof;

(2) render the buyer, at the buyer's request and expense, assistance in obtaining the documents issued in the country of origin, or of shipment, or of both, which the buyer may require either for purposes of exportation, or of importation at destination.

Buyer must

(1) take delivery of the goods as soon as they have been placed at his disposal at the agreed place on the date or within the period fixed;

(2) pay export taxes, or other fees or charges, if any, levied because of exportation;

(3) bear all costs and risks of the goods from the time when he is obligated to take delivery thereof;

(4) pay all costs and charges incurred in obtaining the documents issued in the country of origin, or of shipment, or of both, which may be required either for purposes of exportation, or of importation at destination.

(II) F.O.B. (Free on Board)—Six Definitions

Seller and buyer should consider not only the definitions but also the "Comments on All F.O.B. Terms" given at end of this section (page 17–53), in order to understand fully their respective responsibilities and rights under the several classes of "F.O.B." terms.

(II-A) F.O.B. (named inland carrier at named inland point of departure)

Under this term, the price quoted applies only at inland shipping point, and the seller arranges for loading of the goods on, or in, railway cars, trucks, lighters, barges, aircraft, or other conveyance furnished for transportation.

Under this quotation:

Seller must

(1) place goods on, or in, conveyance, or deliver to inland carrier for loading;

(2) provide clean bill of lading or other transportation receipt, freight collect;

(3) be responsible for any loss or damage, or both, until goods have been placed in, or on, conveyance at loading point, and clean bill of lading or other transportation receipt has been furnished by the carrier;

(4) render the buyer, at the buyer's request and expense, assistance in obtaining the documents issued in the country of origin, or of shipment, or of both, which the buyer may require either for purposes of exportation, or of importation at destination.

Buyer must

(1) be responsible for all movement of the goods from inland point of loading, and pay all transportation costs;

(2) pay export taxes, or other fees or charges, if any, levied because of exportation;

(3) be responsible for any loss or damage, or both, incurred after loading at named inland point of departure;

(4) pay all costs and charges incurred in obtaining the documents issued in the country of origin, or of shipment, or of both, which may be required either for purposes of exportation, or of importation at destination.

(II-B) F.O.B. (named inland carrier at named inland point of departure) FREIGHT PREPAID TO (named point of exportation)

Under this term, the seller quotes a price including transportation charges to the named point of exportation and prepays freight to named point of exportation, without assuming responsibility for the goods after obtaining a clean bill of lading or other transportation receipt at named inland point of departure.

Under this quotation:

Seller must

(1) assume the seller's obligations as under II-A, except that under (2) he must provide clean bill of lading or other transportation receipt, freight prepaid to named point of exportation.

Buyer must

(1) assume the same buyer's obligations as under II-A, except that he does not pay freight from loading point to named point of exportation.

(II-C) F.O.B. (named inland carrier at named inland point of departure) FREIGHT ALLOWED TO (named point)

Under this term, the seller quotes a price including the transportation charges to the named point, shipping freight collect and deducting the cost of transportation, without assuming responsibility for the goods after obtaining a clean bill of lading or other transportation receipt at named inland point of departure.

Under this quotation:

Seller must

(1) assume the same seller's obligations as under II-A, but deducts from his invoice the transportation cost to named point.

Buyer must

(1) assume the same buyer's obligations as under II-A, including payment of freight from inland loading point to named point, for which seller has made deduction.

(II-D) F.O.B. (named inland carrier at named point of exportation)

Under this term, the seller quotes a price including the costs of transportation of the goods to named point of exportation, bearing any loss or damage, or both, incurred up to that point.

Under this quotation:

Seller must

(1) place goods on, or in, conveyance, or deliver to inland carrier for loading;

(2) provide clean bill of lading or other transportation receipt, paying all transportation costs from loading point to named point of exportation;

(3) be responsible for any loss or damage, or both, until goods have arrived in, or on, inland conveyance at the named point of exportation;

(4) render the buyer, at the buyer's request and expense, assistance in obtaining the documents issued in the country of origin, or of shipment, or of both, which the buyer may require either for purposes of exportation, or of importation at destination.

Buyer must

(1) be responsible for all movement of the goods from inland conveyance at named point of exportation;

(2) pay export taxes, or other fees or charges, if any, levied because of exportation;

(3) be responsible for any loss or damage, or both, incurred after goods have arrived in, or on, inland conveyance at the named point of exportation;

(4) pay all costs and charges incurred in obtaining the documents issued in the country of origin, or of shipment, or of both, which may be required either for purposes of exportation, or of importation at destination.

(II-E) F.O.B. Vessel (named port of shipment)

Under this term, the seller quotes a price covering all expenses up to, and including, delivery of the goods upon the overseas vessel provided by, or for, the buyer at the named port of shipment.

Under this quotation:

Seller must

(1) pay all charges incurred in placing goods actually on board the vessel designated and provided by, or for, the buyer on the date or within the period fixed;

(2) provide clean ship's receipt or on-board bill of lading;

(3) be responsible for any loss or damage, or both, until goods have been placed on board the vessel on the date or within the period fixed;

(4) render the buyer, at the buyer's request and expense, assistance in obtaining the documents issued in the country of origin, or of shipment, or of both, which the buyer may require either for purposes of exportation, or of importation at destination.

Buyer must

(1) give seller adequate notice of name, sailing date, loading berth of, and delivery time to, the vessel;

(2) bear the additional costs incurred and all risks of the goods from the time when the seller has placed them at his disposal if the vessel named by him fails to arrive or to load within the designated time;

(3) handle all subsequent movement of the goods to destination:

(a) provide and pay for insurance;

(b) provide and pay for ocean and other transportation;

(4) pay export taxes, or other fees or charges, if any, levied because of exportation;

(5) be responsible for any loss or damage, or both, after goods have been loaded on board the vessel;

(6) pay all costs and charges incurred in obtaining the documents, other than clean ship's receipt or bill of lading, issued in the country of origin, or of shipment, or of both, which may be required either for purposes of exportation, or of importation at destination.

(II-F) F.O.B. (named inland point in country of importation)

Under this term, the seller quotes a price including the cost of the merchandise and all costs of transportation to the named inland point in the country of importation.

Under this quotation:

Seller must

(1) provide and pay for all transportation to the named inland point in the country of importation;

(2) pay export taxes, or other fees or charges, if any, levied because of exportation;

(3) provide and pay for marine insurance;

(4) provide and pay for war risk insurance, unless otherwise agreed upon between the seller and buyer;
(5) be responsible for any loss or damage, or both, until arrival of goods on conveyance at the named inland point in the country of importation;
(6) pay the costs of certificates of origin, consular invoices, or any other documents issued in the country of origin, or of shipment, or of both, which the buyer may require for the importation of goods into the country of destination and, where necessary, for their passage in transit through another country;
(7) pay all costs of landing, including wharfage, landing charges, and taxes, if any;
(8) pay all costs of customs entry in the country of importation;
(9) pay customs duties and all taxes applicable to imports, if any, in the country of importation.

The seller under this quotation must realize that he is accepting important responsibilities, costs, and risks, and should therefore be certain to obtain adequate insurance. On the other hand, the importer or buyer may desire such quotations to relieve him of the risks of the voyage and to assure him of his landed costs at inland point in country of importation. When competition is keen, or the buyer is accustomed to such quotations from other sellers, seller may quote such terms, being careful to protect himself in an appropriate manner.

Buyer must
(1) take prompt delivery of goods from conveyance upon arrival at destination;
(2) bear any costs and be responsible for all loss or damage, or both, after arrival at destination.

Comments on All F.O.B. Terms

In connection with F.O.B. terms, the following points of caution are recommended:

1. The method of inland transportation, such as trucks, railroad cars, lighters, barges, or aircraft should be specified.

2. If any switching charges are involved during the inland transportation, it should be agreed, in advance, whether these charges are for account of the seller or the buyer.

3. The term "F.O.B. (named port)," without designating the exact point at which the liability of the seller terminates and the liability of the buyer begins, should be avoided. The use of this term gives rise to disputes as to the liability of the seller or the buyer in the event of loss or damage arising while the goods are in port, and before delivery to or on board the ocean carrier. Misunderstandings may be avoided by naming the specific point of delivery.

4. If lighterage or trucking is required in the transfer of goods from the inland conveyance to ship's side, and there is a cost therefor, it should be understood, in advance, whether this cost is for account of the seller or the buyer.

5. The seller should be certain to notify the buyer of the minimum quantity required to obtain a carload, a truckload, or a barge-load freight rate.

6. Under F.O.B. terms, excepting "F.O.B. (named inland point in country of importation)," the obligation to obtain ocean freight space, and marine and war risk insurance, rests with the buyer. Despite this obligation on the part of the buyer, in many trades the seller obtains the ocean freight space, and marine and war risk insurance, and provides for shipment on behalf of the buyer. Hence, seller and buyer must have an understanding as to whether the buyer will obtain the ocean freight space, and marine and war risk insurance, as is his obligation, or whether the seller agrees to do this for the buyer.

7. For the seller's protection, he should provide in his contract of sale that marine insurance obtained by the buyer include standard warehouse to warehouse coverage.

(III) F.A.S. (Free Along Side)

Seller and buyer should consider not only the definitions but also the "Comments" given later in this section (page 17–55), in order to understand fully their respective responsibilities and rights under "F.A.S." terms.

F.A.S. VESSEL (named port of shipment)

Under this term, the seller quotes a price including delivery of the goods along side overseas vessel and within reach of its loading tackle.

Under this quotation:

Seller must

(1) place goods along side vessel or on dock designated and provided by, or for, buyer on the date or within the period fixed; pay any heavy lift charges, where necessary, up to this point;

(2) provide clean dock or ship's receipt;

(3) be responsible for any loss or damage, or both, until goods have been delivered along side the vessel or on the dock;

(4) render the buyer, at the buyer's request and expense, assistance in obtaining the documents issued in the country of origin, or of shipment, or of both, which the buyer may require either for purposes of exportation, or of importation at destination.

Buyer must

(1) give seller adequate notice of name, sailing date, loading berth of, and delivery time to, the vessel;

(2) handle all subsequent movement of the goods from along side the vessel:

- (a) arrange and pay for demurrage or storage charges, or both, in warehouse or on wharf, where necessary;
- (b) provide and pay for insurance;
- (c) provide and pay for ocean and other transportation;

(3) pay export taxes, or other fees or charges, if any, levied because of exportation;

(4) be responsible for any loss or damage, or both, while the goods are

on a lighter or other conveyance along side vessel within reach of its loading tackle, or on the dock awaiting loading, or until actually loaded on board the vessel, and subsequent thereto;

(5) pay all costs and charges incurred in obtaining the documents, other than clean dock or ship's receipt, issued in the country of origin, or of shipment, or of both, which may be required either for purposes of exportation, or of importation at destination.

F.A.S. Comments

1. Under F.A.S. terms, the obligation to obtain ocean freight space, and marine and war risk insurance, rests with the buyer. Despite this obligation on the part of the buyer, in many trades the seller obtains ocean freight space, and marine and war risk insurance, and provides for shipment on behalf of the buyer. In others, the buyer notifies the seller to make delivery along side a vessel designated by the buyer and the buyer provides his own marine and war risk insurance. Hence, seller and buyer must have an understanding as to whether the buyer will obtain the ocean freight space, and marine and war risk insurance, as is his obligation, or whether the seller agrees to do this for the buyer.

2. For the seller's protection, he should provide in his contract of sale that marine insurance obtained by the buyer include standard warehouse to warehouse coverage.

(IV) C.&F. (Cost and Freight)

Seller and buyer should consider not only the definition but also the "C.&F. Comments" (page 17–56) and the "C.&F. and C.I.F. Comments" (page 17–57), in order to understand fully their respective responsibilities and rights under "C.&F." terms.

C.&F. (named point of destination)

Under this term, the seller quotes a price including the cost of transportation to the named point of destination.

Under this quotation:

Seller must

(1) provide and pay for transportation to named point of destination;

(2) pay export taxes, or other fees or charges, if any, levied because of exportation;

(3) obtain and dispatch promptly to buyer, or his agent, clean bill of lading to named point of destination;

(4) where received-for-shipment ocean bill of lading may be tendered, be responsible for any loss or damage, or both, until the goods have been delivered into the custody of the ocean carrier;

(5) where on-board ocean bill of lading is required, be responsible for any loss or damage, or both, until the goods have been delivered on board the vessel;

(6) provide, at the buyer's request and expense, certificates of origin, consular invoices, or any other documents issued in the country of

origin, or of shipment, or of both, which the buyer may require for importation of goods into country of destination and, where necessary, for their passage in transit through another country.

Buyer must

(1) accept the documents when presented;

(2) receive goods upon arrival, handle and pay for all subsequent movement of the goods, including taking delivery from vessel in accordance with bill of lading clauses and terms; pay all costs of landing, including any duties, taxes, and other expenses at named point of destination;

(3) provide and pay for insurance;

(4) be responsible for loss of or damage to goods, or both, from time and place at which seller's obligations under (4) or (5) above have ceased;

(5) pay the costs of certificates of origin, consular invoices, or any other documents issued in the country of origin, or of shipment, or of both, which may be required for the importation of goods into the country of destination and, where necessary, for their passage in transit through another country.

C.&F. Comments

1. For the seller's protection, he should provide in his contract of sale that marine insurance obtained by the buyer include standard warehouse to warehouse coverage.

2. The comments listed under the following C.I.F. terms in many cases apply to C.&F. terms as well, and should be read and understood by the C.&F. seller and buyer.

(V) *C.I.F.* (*Cost, Insurance, Freight*)

Seller and buyer should consider not only the definitions but also the "Comments" starting on the next page, in order to understand fully their respective responsibilities and rights under "C.I.F." terms.

C.I.F. (*named point of destination*)

Under this term, the seller quotes a price including the cost of the goods, the marine insurance, and all transportation charges to the named point of destination.

Under this quotation:

Seller must

(1) provide and pay for transportation to named point of destination;

(2) pay export taxes, or other fees or charges, if any, levied because of exportation;

(3) provide and pay for marine insurance;

(4) provide war risk insurance as obtainable in seller's market at time of shipment at buyer's expense, unless seller has agreed that buyer provide for war risk coverage (See Comment 10 (c), page 17–58);

(5) obtain and dispatch promptly to buyer, or his agent, clean bill of lad-

ing to named point of destination, and also insurance policy or negotiable insurance certificate;

(6) where received-for-shipment ocean bill of lading may be tendered, be responsible for any loss or damage, or both, until the goods have been delivered into the custody of the ocean carrier;

(7) where on-board ocean bill of lading is required, be responsible for any loss or damage, or both, until the goods have been delivered on board the vessel;

(8) provide, at the buyer's request and expense, certificates of origin, consular invoices, or any other documents issued in the country of origin, or of shipment, or both, which the buyer may require for importation of goods into country of destination and, where necessary, for their passage in transit through another country.

Buyer must

(1) accept the documents when presented;

(2) receive the goods upon arrival, handle and pay for all subsequent movement of the goods, including taking delivery from vessel in accordance with bill of lading clauses and terms; pay all costs of landing, including any duties, taxes, and other expenses at named point of destination;

(3) pay for war risk insurance provided by seller;

(4) be responsible for loss of or damage to goods, or both, from time and place at which seller's obligations under (6) or (7) above have ceased;

(5) pay the cost of certificates of origin, consular invoices, or any other documents issued in the country of origin, or of shipment, or both, which may be required for importation of the goods into the country of destination and, where necessary, for their passage in transit through another country.

C.&F. and C.I.F. Comments

Under C.&F. and C.I.F. contracts there are the following points on which the seller and the buyer should be in complete agreement at the time that the contract is concluded:

1. It should be agreed upon, in advance, who is to pay for miscellaneous expenses, such as weighing or inspection charges.

2. The quantity to be shipped on any one vessel should be agreed upon, in advance, with a view to the buyer's capacity to take delivery upon arrival and discharge of the vessel; within the free time allowed at the port of importation.

3. Although the terms C.&F. and C.I.F. are generally interpreted to provide that charges for consular invoices and certificates of origin are for the account of the buyer, and are charged separately, in many trades these charges are included by the seller in his price. Hence, seller and buyer should agree, in advance, whether these charges are part of the selling price, or will be invoiced separately.

4. The point of final destination should be definitely known in the event the vessel discharges at a port other than the actual destination of the goods.

5. When ocean freight space is difficult to obtain, or forward freight contracts cannot be made at firm rates, it is advisable that sales contracts, as an exception to regular C.&F. or C.I.F. terms, should provide that shipment within the contract period be subject to ocean freight space being available to the seller, and should also provide that changes in the cost of ocean transportation between the time of sale and the time of shipment be for account of the buyer.

6. Normally, the seller is obligated to prepay the ocean freight. In some instances, shipments are made freight collect and the amount of the freight is deducted from the invoice rendered by the seller. It is necessary to be in agreement on this, in advance, in order to avoid misunderstanding which arises from foreign exchange fluctuations which might affect the actual cost of transportation, and from interest charges which might accrue under letter of credit financing. Hence, the seller should always prepay the ocean freight unless he has a specific agreement with the buyer, in advance, that goods can be shipped freight collect.

7. The buyer should recognize that he does not have the right to insist on inspection of goods prior to accepting the documents. The buyer should not refuse to take delivery of goods on account of delay in the receipt of documents, provided the seller has used due diligence in their dispatch through the regular channels.

8. Sellers and buyers are advised against including in a C.I.F. contract any indefinite clause at variance with the obligations of a C.I.F. contract as specified in these Definitions. There have been numerous court decisions in the United States and other countries invalidating C.I.F. contracts because of the inclusion of indefinite clauses.

9. Interest charges should be included in cost computations and should not be charged as a separate item in C.I.F. contracts, unless otherwise agreed upon, in advance, between the seller and buyer; in which case, however, the term C.I.F. and I. (Cost, Insurance, Freight, and Interest) should be used.

10. In connection with insurance under C.I.F. sales, it is necessary that seller and buyer be definitely in accord upon the following points:

(a) The character of the marine insurance should be agreed upon in so far as being W.A. (With Average) or F.P.A. (Free of Particular Average), as well as any other special risks that are covered in specific trades, or against which the buyer may wish individual protection. Among the special risks that should be considered and agreed upon between seller and buyer are theft, pilferage, leakage, breakage, sweat, contact with other cargoes, and others peculiar to any particular trade. It is important that contingent or collect freight and customs duty should be insured to cover Particular Average losses, as well as total loss after arrival and entry but before delivery.

(b) The seller is obligated to exercise ordinary care and diligence in selecting an underwriter that is in good financial standing. However, the risk of obtaining settlement of insurance claims rests with the buyer.

(c) War risk insurance under this term is to be obtained by the seller at the expense and risk of the buyer. It is important that the seller be in definite accord with the buyer on this point, particularly as to the cost. It is desirable that the goods be insured against both marine and war risk with the same underwriter, so that there can be no difficulty arising from the determination of the cause of the loss.

(d) Seller should make certain that in his marine or war risk insurance, there be included the standard protection against strikes, riots and civil commotions.

(e) Seller and buyer should be in accord as to the insured valuation, bearing in mind that merchandise contributes in General Average on certain bases of valuation which differ in various trades. It is desirable that a competent insurance broker be consulted, in order that full value be covered and trouble avoided.

(VI) Ex Dock

EX DOCK (named port of importation)

Seller and buyer should consider not only the definitions but also the "Ex Dock Comments" at the end of this section (page 17-60), in order to understand fully their respective responsibilities and rights under "Ex Dock" terms.

Under this term, seller quotes a price including the cost of the goods and all additional costs necessary to place the goods on the dock at the named port of importation, duty paid, if any.

Under this quotation:

Seller must

(1) provide and pay for transportation to named port of importation;
(2) pay export taxes, or other fees or charges, if any, levied because of exportation;
(3) provide and pay for marine insurance;
(4) provide and pay for war risk insurance, unless otherwise agreed upon between the buyer and seller;
(5) be responsible for any loss or damage, or both, until the expiration of the free time allowed on the dock at the named port of importation;
(6) pay the costs of certificates of origin, consular invoices, legalization of bill of lading, or any other documents issued in the country of origin, or of shipment, or of both, which the buyer may require for the importation of goods into the country of destination and, where necessary, for their passage in transit through another country;
(7) pay all costs of landing, including wharfage, landing charges, and taxes, if any;
(8) pay all costs of customs entry in the country of importation;
(9) pay customs duties and all taxes applicable to imports, if any, in the country of importation, unless otherwise agreed upon.

Buyer must

(1) take delivery of the goods on the dock at the named port of importation within the free time allowed;
(2) bear the cost and risk of the goods if delivery is not taken within the free time allowed.

Ex Dock Comments

This term is used principally in United States import trade. It has various modifications, such as "Ex Quay," "Ex Pier," etc., but it is seldom, if ever, used in American export practice. Its use in quotations for export is not recommended.

UNIFORM CUSTOMS AND PRACTICE FOR DOCUMENTARY CREDITS

Purchasing internationally requires a clear understanding of customs and practices of commercial documentary credits. For provisions, definitions, interpretations, instructions, and documents used in handling payments under letters of credit, readers are referred to *Uniform Customs and Practice for Documentary Credits* (1962 Revision), reprinted below.[27]

General Provisions and Definitions

a. These provisions and definitions and the following articles apply to all documentary credits and are binding upon all parties thereto unless otherwise expressly agreed.

b. For the purposes of such provisions, definitions and articles the expressions "documentary credit (s) " and "credit (s) " used therein mean any arrangement, however named or described, whereby a bank (the issuing bank), acting at the request and in accordance with the instructions of a customer (the applicant for the credit), is to make payment to or to the order of a third party (the beneficiary) or is to pay, accept or negotiate bills of exchange (drafts) drawn by the beneficiary, or authorises such payments to be made or such drafts to be paid, accepted or negotiated by another bank, against stipulated documents and compliance with stipulated terms and conditions.

c. Credits, by their nature, are separate transactions from the sales or other contracts on which they may be based and banks are in no way concerned with or bound by such contracts.

d. Credit instructions and the credits themselves must be complete and precise and, in order to guard against confusion and misunderstanding, issuing banks should discourage any attempt by the applicant for the credit to include excessive detail.

e. When the bank first entitled to avail itself of an option it enjoys under the following articles does so, its decision shall be binding upon all the parties concerned.

[27] Copyright by International Chamber of Commerce, Br. No. 222, *Uniform Customs and Practice for Documentary Credits.* Published by the International Chamber of Commerce, 38, Cours Albert 1er, Paris 8e, France (U.S. Council of the ICC, 103 Park Avenue, New York, N.Y. 10017) in English-French and English-German editions. Obtainable from International Headquarters of the ICC and from the various National Committees. (Effective for accepting U.S. banks July 1, 1963.)

f. A beneficiary can in no case avail himself of the contractual relationships existing between banks or between the applicant for the credit and the issuing bank.

A.—Form and Notification of Credits

Article 1

Credits may be either

a) revocable, or
b) irrevocable.

All credits, therefore, should clearly indicate whether they are revocable or irrevocable.

In the absence of such indication the credit shall be deemed to be revocable, even though an expiry date is stipulated.

Article 2

A revocable credit does not constitute a legally binding undertaking between the bank or banks concerned and the beneficiary because such a credit may be modified or cancelled at any moment without notice to the beneficiary.

When, however, a revocable credit has been transmitted to and made available at a branch or other bank, its modification or cancellation shall become effective only upon receipt of notice thereof by such branch or other bank and shall not affect the right of that branch or other bank to be reimbursed for any payment, acceptance or negotiation made by it prior to receipt of such notice.

Article 3

An irrevocable credit is a definite undertaking on the part of an issuing bank and constitutes the engagement of that bank to the beneficiary or, as the case may be, to the beneficiary and bona fide holders of drafts drawn and/or documents presented thereunder, that the provisions for payment, acceptance or negotiation contained in the credit will be duly fulfilled, provided that all the terms and conditions of the credit are complied with.

An irrevocable credit may be advised to a beneficiary through another bank without engagement on the part of that other bank (the advising bank), but when an issuing bank authorises another bank to confirm its irrevocable credit and the latter does so, such confirmation constitutes a definite undertaking on the part of the confirming bank either that the provisions for payment or acceptance will be duly fulfilled or, in the case of a credit available by negotiation of drafts, that the confirming bank will negotiate drafts without recourse to drawer.

Such undertakings can neither be modified nor cancelled without the agreement of all concerned.

Article 4

When an issuing bank instructs a bank by cable, telegram or telex to notify a credit and the original letter of credit itself is to be the operative credit instrument, the issuing bank must send the original letter of credit, and any subsequent amendments thereto, to the beneficiary through the notifying bank.

The issuing bank will be responsible for any consequences arising from its failure to follow this procedure.

ARTICLE 5

When a bank is instructed by cable, telegram or telex to issue, confirm or advise a credit similar in terms to one previously established and which has been the subject of amendments, it shall be understood that the details of the credit being issued, confirmed or advised will be transmitted to the beneficiary excluding the amendments, unless the instructions specify clearly any amendments which are to apply.

ARTICLE 6

If incomplete or unclear instructions are received to issue, confirm or advise a credit, the bank requested to act on such instructions may give preliminary notification of the credit to the beneficiary for information only and without responsibility; and in that case the credit will be issued, confirmed or advised only when the necessary information has been received.

B.—Liabilities and Responsibilities

ARTICLE 7

Banks must examine all documents with reasonable care to ascertain that they appear on their face to be in accordance with the terms and conditions of the credit.

ARTICLE 8

In documentary credit operations all parties concerned deal in documents and not in goods.

Payment, acceptance or negotiation against documents which appear on their face to be in accordance with the terms and conditions of a credit by a bank authorised to do so, binds the party giving the authorisation to take up the documents and reimburse the bank which has effected the payment, acceptance or negotiation.

If, upon receipt of the documents, the issuing bank considers that they appear on their face not to be in accordance with the terms and conditions of the credit, that bank must determine, on the basis of the documents alone, whether to claim that payment, acceptance or neogtiation was not effected in accordance with the terms and conditions of the credit.

If such claim is to be made, notice to that effect, stating the reasons therefor, must be given by cable or other expeditious means to the bank from which the documents have been received and such notice must state that the documents are being held at the disposal of such bank or are being returned thereto. The issuing bank shall have a reasonable time to examine the documents.

Article 9

Banks assume no liability or responsibility for the form, sufficiency, accuracy, genuineness, falsification or legal effect of any documents, or for the general and/or particular conditions stipulated in the documents or superimposed thereon; nor do they assume any liability or responsibility for the description, quantity, weight, quality, condition, packing, delivery, value or existence of the goods represented thereby, or for the good faith or acts and/or omissions, solvency, performance or standing of the consignor, the carriers or the insurers of the goods or any other person whomsoever.

Article 10

Banks assume no liability or responsibility for the consequences arising out of delay and/or loss in transit of any messages, letters or documents, or for delay, mutilation or other errors arising in the transmission of cables, telegrams or telex, or for errors in translation or interpretation of technical terms, and banks reserve the right to transmit credit terms without translating them.

Article 11

Banks assume no liability or responsibility for consequences arising out of the interruption of their business by strikes, lock-outs, riots, civil commotions, insurrections, wars, Acts of God or any other causes beyond their control. Unless specifically authorised, banks will not effect payment, acceptance or negotiation after expiration under credits expiring during such interruption of business.

Article 12

Banks utilising the services of another bank for the purpose of giving effect to the instructions of the applicant for the credit do so for the account and at the risk of the latter.

They assume no liability or responsibility should the instructions they transmit not be carried out, even if they have themselves taken the initiative in the choice of such other bank.

The applicant for the credit shall be bound by and liable to indemnify the banks against all obligations and responsibilities imposed by foreign laws and usages.

C.—Documents

Article 13

All instructions to issue, confirm or advise a credit must state precisely the documents against which payment, acceptance or negotiation is to be made.

Terms such as "first class", "well known", "qualified" and the like shall not be used to describe the issuers of any documents called for under credits and if they are incorporated in the credit terms banks will accept documents as presented without further responsibility on their part.

DOCUMENTS EVIDENCING SHIPMENT OR DESPATCH
(Shipping Documents)

ARTICLE 14

Except as stated in Article 18, the date of the Bill of Lading, or date indicated in the reception stamp or by notation on any other document evidencing shipment or despatch, will be taken in each case to be the date of shipment or despatch of the goods.

ARTICLE 15

If the words "freight paid" or "freight prepaid" appear by stamp or otherwise on documents evidencing shipment or despatch they will be accepted as constituting evidence of the payment of freight.

If the words "freight prepayable" or "freight to be prepaid" or words of similar effect appear by stamp or otherwise on such documents they will not be accepted as constituting evidence of the payment of freight.

Unless otherwise specified in the credit or inconsistent with any of the documents presented under the credit, banks may honour documents stating that freight or transportation charges are payable on delivery.

ARTICLE 16

A clean shipping document is one which bears no superimposed clause or notation which expressly declares a defective condition of the goods and/or the packaging.

Banks will refuse shipping documents bearing such clauses or notations unless the credit expressly states clauses or notations which may be accepted.

MARINE BILLS OF LADING

ARTICLE 17

Unless specifically authorised in the credit, Bills of Lading of the following nature will be rejected:

a) Bills of Lading issued by forwarding agents.
b) Bills of Lading which are issued under and are subject to the conditions of a Charter-Party.
c) Bills of Lading covering shipment by sailing vessels.

However, unless otherwise specified in the credit, Bills of Lading of the following nature will be accepted:

a) "Port" or "Custody" Bills of Lading for shipments of cotton from the United States of America.
b) "Through" Bills of Lading issued by steamship companies or their agents even though they cover several modes of transport.

ARTICLE 18

Unless otherwise specified in the credit, Bills of Lading must show that the goods are loaded on board.

Loading on board may be evidenced by an on board Bill of Lading or by means of a notation to that effect dated and signed or initialled by the carrier or his agent, and the date of this notation shall be regarded as the date of loading on board and shipment.

ARTICLE 19

Unless transhipment is prohibited by the terms of the credit, Bills of Lading will be accepted which indicate that the goods will be transhipped en route, provided the entire voyage is covered by one and the same Bill of Lading.

Bills of Lading incorporating printed clauses stating that the carriers have the right to tranship will be accepted notwithstanding the fact that the credit prohibits transhipment.

ARTICLE 20

Banks will refuse a Bill of Lading showing the stowage of goods on deck, unless specifically authorised in the credit.

ARTICLE 21

Banks may require the name of the beneficiary to appear on the Bill of Lading as shipper or endorser, unless the terms of the credit provide otherwise.

OTHER SHIPPING DOCUMENTS, ETC.

ARTICLE 22

Banks will consider a Railway or Inland Waterway Bill of Lading or Consignment Note, Counterfoil Waybill, Postal Receipt, Certificate of Mailing, Air Mail Receipt, Air Transportation Waybill, Air Consignment Note or Air Receipt, Trucking Company Bill of Lading or any other similar document as regular when such document bears the reception stamp of the carrier or issuer, or when it bears a signature.

ARTICLE 23

When a credit calls for an attestation or certification of weight in the case of transport other than by sea, banks will accept a weight stamp or any other official indication of weight on the shipping documents unless the credit calls for a separate or independent certificate of weight.

INSURANCE DOCUMENTS

ARTICLE 24

Insurance documents must be as specifically described in the credit, and must be issued and/or signed by insurance companies or their agents or by underwriters.

Cover notes issued by brokers will not be accepted, unless specifically authorised in the credit.

ARTICLE 25

Unless otherwise specified in the credit, banks may refuse any insurance documents presented if they bear a date later than the date of shipment as evidenced by the shipping documents.

ARTICLE 26

Unless otherwise specified in the credit, the insurance document must be expressed in the same currency as the credit.

The minimum amount for which insurance must be effected is the CIF value of the goods concerned. However, when the CIF value of the goods cannot be determined from the documents on their face, banks will accept as such minimum amount the amount of the drawing under the credit or the amount of the relative commercial invoice, whichever is the greater.

ARTICLE 27

Credits must expressly state the type of insurance required and, if any, the additional risks which are to be covered. Imprecise terms such as "usual risks" or "customary risks" shall not be used.

Failing specific instructions, banks will accept insurance cover as tendered.

ARTICLE 28

When a credit stipulates "insurance against all risks", banks will accept an insurance document which contains any "all risks" notation or clause, and will assume no responsibility if any particular risk is not covered.

ARTICLE 29

Banks may accept an insurance document which indicates that the cover is subject to a franchise, unless it is specifically stated in the credit that the insurance must be issued irrespective of percentage.

COMMERCIAL INVOICES

ARTICLE 30

Unless otherwise specified in the credit, commercial invoices must be made out in the name of the applicant for the credit.

Unless otherwise specified in the credit, banks may refuse invoices issued for amounts in excess of the amount permitted by the credit.

The description of the goods in the commercial invoice must correspond with the description in the credit. In the remaining documents the goods may be described in general terms.

OTHER DOCUMENTS

ARTICLE 31

When other documents are required, such as Warehouse Receipts, Delivery Orders, Consular Invoices, Certificates of Origin, of Weight, of Quality or of Analysis, etc., without further definition, banks may accept such documents as tendered, without responsibility on their part.

D.—MISCELLANEOUS PROVISIONS

QUANTITY AND AMOUNT

ARTICLE 32

The words "about", "circa" or similar expressions are to be construed as allowing a difference not to exceed 10% more or 10% less, applicable, according to their place in the instructions, to the amount of the credit or to the quantity or unit price of the goods.

Unless a credit stipulates that the quantity of the goods specified must not be exceeded or reduced, a tolerance of 3% more or 3% less will be permissible, always provided that the total amount of the drawings does not exceed the amount of the credit. This tolerance does not apply when the credit specifies quantity in terms of packing units or containers or individual items.

PARTIAL SHIPMENTS

ARTICLE 33

Partial shipments are allowed, unless the credit specifically states otherwise.

Shipments made on the same ship and for the same voyage, even if the Bills of Lading evidencing shipment "on board" bear different dates, will not be regarded as partial shipments.

ARTICLE 34

If shipment by instalments within given periods is stipulated and any instalment is not shipped within the period allowed for that instalment, the credit ceases to be available for that or any subsequent instalment, unless otherwise specified in the credit.

VALIDITY AND EXPIRY DATE

ARTICLE 35

All irrevocable credits must stipulate an expiry date for presentation of documents for payment, acceptance or negotiation, notwithstanding the indication of a latest date for shipment.

ARTICLE 36

The words "to", "until", "till" and words of similar import applying to the expiry date for presentation of documents for payment, acceptance or negotiation, or to the stipulated latest date for shipment, will be understood to include the date mentioned.

Article 37

When the stipulated expiry date falls on a day on which banks are closed for reasons other than those mentioned in Article 11, the period of validity will be extended until the first following business day.

This does not apply to the date for shipment which, if stipulated, must be respected.

Banks paying, accepting or negotiating on such extended expiry date must add to the documents their certification in the following wording:

> "Presented for payment (or acceptance or negotiation as the case may be) within the expiry date extended in accordance with Article 37 of the Uniform Customs."

Article 38

The validity of a revocable credit, if no date is stipulated, will be considered to have expired six months from the date of the notification sent to the beneficiary by the bank with which the credit is available.

Article 39

Unless otherwise expressly stated, any extension of the stipulated latest date for shipment shall extend for an equal period the validity of the credit.

Where a credit stipulates a latest date for shipment, an extension of the period of validity shall not extend the period permitted for shipment unless otherwise expressly stated.

SHIPMENT, LOADING OR DESPATCH

Article 40

Unless the terms of the credit indicate otherwise, the words "departure", "despatch", "loading" or "sailing" used in stipulating the latest date for shipment of the goods will be understood to be synonymous with "shipment".

Expressions such as "prompt", "immediately", "as soon as possible" and the like should not be used. If they are used, banks will interpret them as a request for shipment within thirty days from the date on the advice of the credit to the beneficiary by the issuing bank or by an advising bank, as the case may be.

PRESENTATION

Article 41

Documents must be presented within a reasonable time after issuance. Paying, accepting or negotiating banks may refuse documents if, in their judgment, they are presented to them with undue delay.

ARTICLE 42

Banks are under no obligation to accept presentation of documents outside their banking hours.

DATE TERMS

ARTICLE 43

The terms "first half", "second half" of a month shall be construed respectively as from the 1st to the 15th, and the 16th to the last day of each month, inclusive.

ARTICLE 44

The terms "beginning", "middle" or "end" of a month shall be construed respectively as from the 1st to the 10th, the 11th to the 20th, and the 21st to the last day of each month, inclusive.

ARTICLE 45

When a bank issuing a credit instructs that the credit be confirmed or advised as available "for one month", "for six months" or the like, but does not specify the date from which the time is to run, the confirming or advising bank will confirm or advise the credit as expiring at the end of such indicated period from the date of its confirmation or advice.

E.—TRANSFER

ARTICLE 46

A transferable credit is a credit under which the beneficiary has the right to give instructions to the bank called upon to effect payment or acceptance or to any bank entitled to effect negotiation to make the credit available in whole or in part to one or more third parties (second beneficiaries).

A credit can be transferred only if it is expressly designated as "transferable" by the issuing bank. Terms such as "divisible", "fractionable", "assignable" and "transmissible" add nothing to the meaning of the term "transferable" and shall not be used.

A transferable credit can be transferred once only. Fractions of a transferable credit (not exceeding in the aggregate the amount of the credit) can be transferred separately, provided partial shipments are not prohibited, and the aggregate of such transfers will be considered as constituting only one transfer of the credit. The credit can be transferred only on the terms and conditions specified in the original credit, with the exception of the amount of the credit, of any unit price stated therein, and of the period of validity or period for shipment, any or all of which may be reduced or curtailed. Additionally, the name of the first beneficiary can be substituted for that of the applicant for the credit, but if the name of the applicant for the credit is specifically required by the original credit to appear in any document other than the invoice, such requirement must be fulfilled.

The first beneficiary has the right to substitute his own invoices for those of the second beneficiary, for amounts not in excess of the original amount stipulated in the credit and for the original unit prices stipulated in the credit, and upon such substitution of invoices the first beneficiary can draw under the credit for the difference, if any, between his invoices and the second beneficiary's invoices. When a credit has been transferred and the first beneficiary is to supply his own invoices in exchange for the second beneficiary's invoices but fails to do so on demand, the paying, accepting or negotiating bank has the right to deliver to the issuing bank the documents received under the credit, including the second beneficiary's invoices, without further responsibility to the first beneficiary.

The first beneficiary of a transferable credit can transfer the credit to a second beneficiary in the same country, but if he is to be permitted to transfer the credit to a second beneficiary in another country this must be expressly stated in the credit. The first beneficiary shall have the right to request that payment or negotiation be effected to the second beneficiary at the place to which the credit has been transferred, up to and including the expiry date of the original credit, and without prejudice to the first beneficiary's right subsequently to substitute his own invoices for those of the second beneficiary and to claim any difference due to him.

The bank requested to effect the transfer, whether it has confirmed the credit or not, shall be under no obligation to make such transfer except to the extent and in the manner expressly consented to by such bank, and until such bank's charges for transfer are paid.

Bank charges entailed by transfers are payable by the first beneficiary unless otherwise specified.

BIBLIOGRAPHY

Refer to list of periodical and nonperiodical publications listed under "References," starting on page 17–33.

SECTION 18

TRAFFIC AND TRANSPORTATION CONSIDERATIONS

Editor

W. H. Chaffee, Vice-president, Purchases and Traffic, American Radiator & Standard Sanitary Corporation, New York, New York

Associate Editors

J. P. Nelligan, Manager, Transportation Services, American Radiator & Standard Sanitary Corporation, New Brunswick, New Jersey

J. A. Schilpp, Director, Traffic & Purchases, H. K. Porter Company, Inc., Refractories Division, Pittsburgh, Pennsylvania

ACKNOWLEDGMENTS: In the preparation of material contained in this section, reference was made to the following publications:

Transport Topics (National newspaper of the motor freight carriers). Published by American Trucking Association, Inc., Washington, D.C. Editor, J. Paul Wilson.

Traffic World. Published by Traffic Service Corporation, Washington, D.C. Editorial Director, Joseph C. Scheleen.

Distribution Age. Published by Chilton Company, Philadelphia. Editor, Ronald G. Ray.

Freight Traffic Redbook. Published by the Traffic Publishing Company, Inc., New York. Compiled and edited by Charles J. Fagg and Walter W. Weller.

"Practical Handbook of Industrial Traffic Management," 3d ed. Published by Traffic Service Corporation, Washington, D.C. By Richard C. Colton, Vice-president, Lykes Bros. Company, Inc., and Edmund S. Ward, Department Chief, Freight Audit & Rate Development, Traffic Division, Western Electric Company, Inc.

The editors gratefully acknowledge the assistance obtained from these publications.

It is essential for any industrial organization to procure a variety of materials, supplies, and services. The responsibility for procurement is vested in the purchasing department. Effective control of the funds expended in this procurement is essential to maintaining the profit and competitive position of any business.

Purchasing agents are well aware of this in relation to materials and supplies. The importance of control of cost for services may not be so readily recognized.

This is particularly true with regard to the cost of transportation services.

The functions of shipping, receiving, paying freight charges, and filing claims are important but they can be resolved by application of suitable clerical routines. The control or "management" of expenditures for "transportation services" lies in routing shipments of raw material and other goods so as to obtain the maximum of efficient service at the lowest possible cost.

There are many types of carriers offering a variety of services so that the buying of transportation service is a very complicated purchasing activity. Even the traffic terminology varies from that normally used in purchasing departments. Some of the common terms are defined in Section 27, "Glossary of Terms." For overseas shipments, traffic terminology is fully spelled out in Section 17, "Purchasing Internationally."

In addition to the selection of routes, negotiation of rate and classification changes, design and use of the right kind of shipping containers, packaging and labeling of shipments, proper material-handling methods, strategic warehousing, and proper handling of a host of other technical matters are essential to obtain the maximum value in transportation. All these considerations require the application of specialized training, experience, and judgment, all as collectively outlined in this section with certain phases mentioned in many other sections of this handbook.

It is of prime importance that these matters are properly handled if control is to be exercised over transportation costs. Proper performance of the traffic function is an important factor in reducing operating costs and increasing profits. It can help to widen company markets, and careful analysis may open up new sources of raw materials. It can be a material factor in building up customer good will.

When the purchasing agent buys raw materials, supplies, and equipment, he should know the freight costs from the various sources of supply. The cost of transportation is a major factor on many raw materials and supplies. By considering shipping costs as well as unit prices, he is equipped to buy at the lowest delivered cost.

He should also know the proper description to use to obtain the lowest applicable freight rates. Rates usually vary in reverse proportion to the quantities shipped, and he should buy in quantities that will provide the lowest cost that is applicable to the rate of usage of the goods in his plant.

Often the use of special equipment, tank cars, bulk hopper cars, open-top trucks, and others, will reduce loading or unloading costs.

Frequently it is necessary to arrange for expedited service or for the tracing of shipments to ensure prompt delivery.

In spite of the best efforts of both shippers and carriers, loss or damage sometimes occurs to goods in transit. Loss or damage claims must be filed and collected to avoid undue costs of repair or replacement by the buyer.

Many companies purchase from foreign countries and not only must arrange for economical transport of the goods but must also provide proper documents for clearance through customs, such as preparing and filing of entries, paying duty, providing surety bonds, obtaining permits, affidavits, certificates, and other necessary papers, as described in Section 17, "Purchasing Internationally." Transportation of goods in import or export trade is more complex than domestic shipping and requires additional training and experience.

The problems of transportation are so complex and ever-changing that a vast number of traffic experts devote their entire business careers to the study and application of rates, routes, and other technical aspects of the shipping and receiving of goods.

Many companies employ personnel with this training and experience in their traffic departments. The purchasing agent can improve his efforts to obtain the maximum of value in procurement by cooperating closely with his traffic department on all matters pertaining to transportation.

Many companies do not have a sufficient volume of transportation to warrant the employment of technically trained traffic personnel. However, no company that buys or sells goods is entirely free from the costs of transportation and most companies can achieve lower operating costs by giving careful attention to these costs.

As the costs of transportation are closely related to the cost of goods purchased, it seems logical that the purchasing agent should concern himself with the degree of control that is exercised over them and in the absence of a traffic department assume the responsibility for establishing the desired degree of control over these expenditures.

This section of the handbook is intended to aid in appraising the problem and to assist in setting up a procedure for good control over transportation purchases. Many purchasing departments are well aware of these problems. In fact, a survey of 350 purchasing officers indicated responsibilities for the traffic function were about equally divided between the traffic and purchasing departments. Table 2–6 lists the departments responsible for complete traffic duties, i.e., final product as well as purchased goods. An abbreviated summary of this table follows:

Departments Responsible for Traffic

	Small depart- ments,* %	Medium depart- ments,* %	Large depart- ments,* %	Total
Purchasing department........	61.2	35.0	24.2	45.3
Traffic department............	28.1	52.6	63.6	43.1
Other departments............	10.7	12.4	12.2	11.6

* Small purchasing departments: Annual purchases under $5 million
Medium purchasing departments: Annual purchases $5 to $50 million
Large purchasing departments: Annual purchases over $50 million

SELECTION OF CARRIER AND ROUTING INSTRUCTIONS

The selection of the initial carrier to transport freight shipments has always been the prerogative of the shipper or receiver. This right is subject, of course, to agreements on routing as outlined between the seller and buyer in the contract of sale. The privilege of routing is vested in the owner of the goods. For this reason, the terms of sale relevant to each shipment must be borne in mind; f.o.b. terms are extremely important in determining (1) the point at which title to the goods passes from the vendor to the buyer and (2) the responsibility for payment of freight charges. Risk in transit and the responsibility for filing claim in the event of loss, damage, or delay accompanies the passage of title. Care should be exercised to avoid routing shipments of goods to which title is not held. An attempt to specify carrier preference on such shipments may relieve the other party to the sale of liability for damage in transit or excessive rates and charges as a result of obeying the routing instructions furnished.

In choosing the various routes over which freight may be forwarded, the person charged with the responsibility of routing is purchasing given quantities and qualities of transportation service at specified prices, namely, the rates as published in the tariffs, or price lists, of the carriers.

There are three separate and distinct steps that should be taken when preparing freight routings. The first step is to determine the type of service to be purchased, whether it may be via air, truck, rail, water, pipeline, etc. Second, the choice must be narrowed to a specific carrier within the realm of the type of service chosen. Third, the routing supervisor should check periodically the quality of the service which has been rendered by the carrier and make sure the lowest practical rate has not been adversely revised.

The selection of the type of service to purchase is influenced by numerous factors. These are outlined in the following pages. The chart shown in Fig. 18–1 represents the *approximate* relationship between various types of transportation with regard to transit time and freight costs.[1]

Available Services at Point of Origin and Destination

In some instances an origin or destination station may be serviced by a single carrier. This is especially true in the case of railroad routings. Shipping and receiving facilites of the consignor and consignee should be known and be borne in mind by the party routing the freight. For example, are the consignee and consignor both located on rail sidings and, if so, which railroads? When routing freight consigned to a destination serviced by two or more railroads, the shipper must know by which railroad delivery is desired by the consignee, so that the freight may be routed accordingly and extra expense of trucking or switching to the consignee's plant be eliminated. Thought must be given to the loading and unloading facilities existing at the shipper's and receiver's plants. Certain companies prefer that open-top or flat-bed truck trailers be utilized since loading or unloading practices necessitate the use of overhead cranes. Congestion and lack of space in the shipping and receiving areas are conditions prevalent with many companies today. Consequently, routings are usually limited to one or two carriers in an effort to alleviate a crowded situation. Another restriction to be kept in mind when routing via rail is the matter of open and prepay stations. Shipments consigned to prepay stations must always be forwarded on a prepaid basis, and any additional balance-due amounts accrue to the account of the shipper.

In routing freight, one must be acquainted with the various services offered by the different forms of transportation. The most expeditious and dependable route for carload freight may not be the best route for less-than-carload movements; and, conversely, the most advantageous service may be provided for less-than-carload traffic and only ordinary service for carload freight. Normally this holds true in the matter of long-distance hauls. Distance and congestion are the two primary factors influencing the transit time of carload shipments, while the transit time of less-than-carload traffic is dependent almost entirely upon the number of times it must be transferred en route. Therefore it is very much to the advantage of the person routing to investigate and learn to which points

[1] Rail "Piggyback" Service (trailers or containers on flatcars) transit time is similar to Motortruck-TL. Costs vary with degree of complete service desired and total weight of shipment.

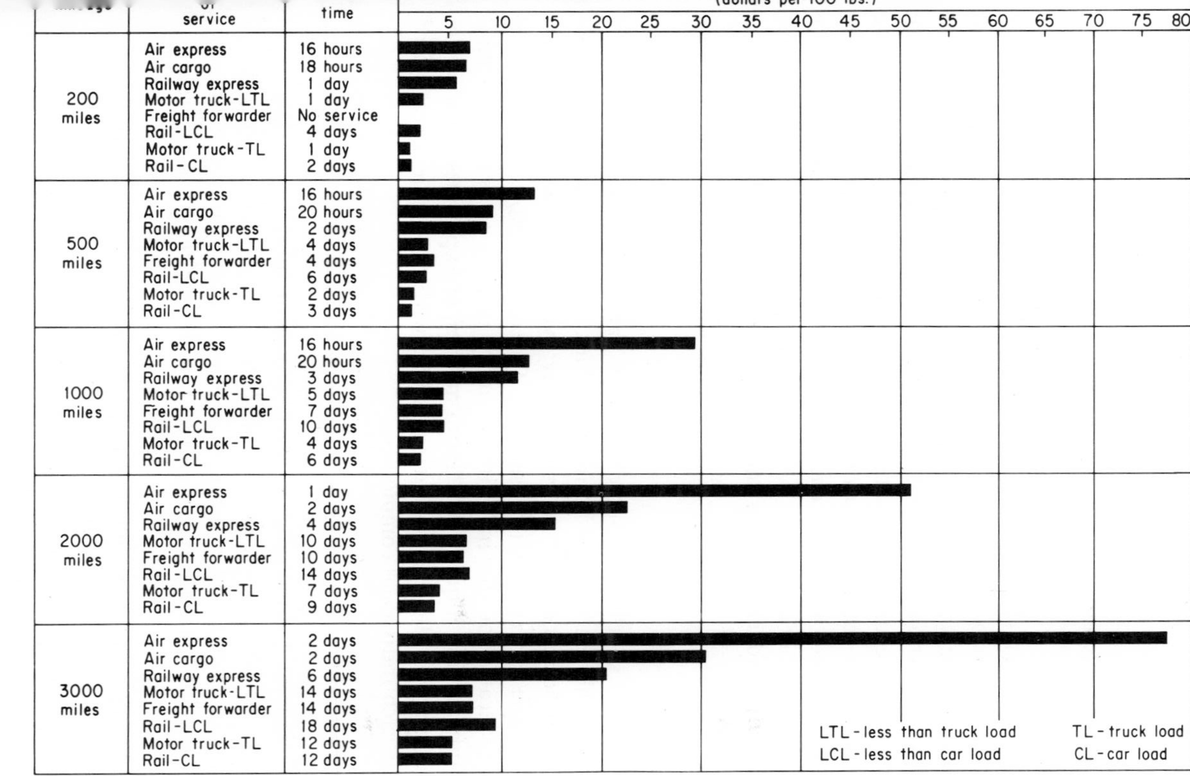

service
time
(dollars per 100 lbs.)
5 10 15 20 25 30 35 40 45 50 55 60 65 70 75 80
200 miles
Air express 16 hours
Air cargo 18 hours
Railway express 1 day
Motor truck-LTL 1 day
Freight forwarder No service
Rail-LCL 4 days
Motor truck-TL 1 day
Rail-CL 2 days
500 miles
Air express 16 hours
Air cargo 20 hours
Railway express 2 days
Motor truck-LTL 4 days
Freight forwarder 4 days
Rail-LCL 6 days
Motor truck-TL 2 days
Rail-CL 3 days
1000 miles
Air express 16 hours
Air cargo 20 hours
Railway express 3 days
Motor truck-LTL 5 days
Freight forwarder 7 days
Rail-LCL 10 days
Motor truck-TL 4 days
Rail-CL 6 days
2000 miles
Air express 1 day
Air cargo 2 days
Railway express 4 days
Motor truck-LTL 10 days
Freight forwarder 10 days
Rail-LCL 14 days
Motor truck-TL 7 days
Rail-CL 9 days
3000 miles
Air express 2 days
Air cargo 2 days
Railway express 6 days
Motor truck-LTL 14 days
Freight forwarder 14 days
Rail-LCL 18 days
Motor truck-TL 12 days
Rail-CL 12 days
LTL - less than truck load
LCL - less than car load
TL - truck load
CL - car load

FIG. 18–1. **Approximate time and cost relationships of various types of transportation.** (From Richard C. Colton and Edmund S. Ward, "Practical Handbook of Industrial Traffic Management," Traffic Service Corporation, Washington, D.C.)

the available carriers have solid carloads of less-than-carload freight. Routings should be made via the line over which such movements are operated. This knowledge can be best obtained through wide reading of traffic publications, contact with carrier representatives, and actual routing experience.

Transit-time Requirements

An elementary step in the intelligent selection of the type of service to be used for each shipment is to determine the period of time available for transportation between the expected shipping date and the promised or required delivery date. When this fact is known, the most economical method of transportation, consistent with the predetermined service needs, may be selected. Most carriers have available upon request routing guides specifying routes to various points and the service that may be normally expected. Constant checks should be made as to the service advertised and the service actually received. By following this practice, the inefficient and lax carriers may be eliminated from further routing consideration.

Nature of Shipment

Bulk liquids should be routed via tank car, tank truck, or pipeline. Volume coal shipments are limited to truck, barge, or rail movement. Perishable products should be routed only over those lines whose tariffs provide heater or refrigerator services. Often, the choice of routes is restricted because of the inability of many carriers to transport items such as inflammable liquids, dangerous articles, or explosives. The person specifying routing should familiarize himself with the carriers best suited to handle each individual commodity.

Size of Shipment

The weight and dimensions of each shipment must be considered to choose successfully the correct type of service. Very small shipments will move most economically via parcel post or railway express. Shipments of heavy machinery with extreme height, width, or length measurements will generally be limited to rail movement, but at times special permits can be obtained to permit movement by truck if it is particularly advantageous to the consignee to have truck delivery.

After the choice of the mode of transportation is completed, the next step is the selection of the carrier or carriers within that mode. As was the case in choosing the type of service to be used, there are additional factors to be considered in selecting the actual carrier. A few of the more important ones follow.

Value of Shipment

Most freight classifications governing railroad, motor-carrier, and air-freight shipments have incorporated in their text a rule stipulating that bank bills, coin, or currency, deeds, drafts, notes or valuable papers, precious metals or articles manufactured therein, precious stones, antiques, or other articles of extraordinary value are not accepted for transportation. Such items are limited, generally, to routing via Railway Express under a category called the "money classification," which requires handling under armed guard. Also, shipments exceeding $25,000 in value will necessitate making prior arrangements with certain carriers, particularly air freight, in order that additional insurance coverage may be obtained. Many rail and motor-carrier tariffs contain released value rates on certain commodities which require payment of freight charges in accordance with the shipper's declared value of the merchandise. A savings in freight costs can be realized by avoiding, when possible, those carriers who publish released value rates.

Susceptibility of the Commodity to Damage

Many items such as glassware, precision machinery, and neon signs have inherent characteristics making them more susceptible to damage than others. Articles with these qualities should be routed via carriers over whose lines numerous transfers and jostling of freight are eliminated.

Cost of the Service

This is an extremely important phase of narrowing the choice of carriers. Intelligent and economical freight routing cannot be accomplished without a wealth of information regarding the costs that will be incurred. Rates and routes are inseparable. It is most important that the route selected is one over which the rate used for cost purposes is applicable. The factor of cost must be weighed by the shipper or receiver and a compromise made as to whether faster service at a higher cost is to take precedence over slower service at a lower cost. Many different types of rates are published by the transportation companies. Among these are class, exception, specific and general commodity rates. Rates may be local, joint, or proportional. Only by familiarizing himself thoroughly with the meaning of these rates can the person routing the freight be assured of any degree of success in obtaining economical freight transport for his company.

Provision of Accessorial Services

Another factor entering into the selection of specific carriers is transit privileges. Many manufacturers utilize very efficiently such rights as milling, fabricating, storing in transit, and stop-offs for partial loading or unloading. These provisions, however, are not granted universally by all carriers, and it is wise for one to be informed of the carriers whose tariffs permit the granting of these privileges. Plenty of imagination and curiosity is needed, since it is a constant chore of checking and studying the numerous combinations possible in adapting these transit privileges to the routing program. Other examples of accessorial services are heater and refrigerator service. Commodities requiring this type of protection should be routed only via those carriers which are able to furnish this type of special equipment. Many carriers take exception in their tariffs to handling shipments that demand the use of refrigerated or heated equipment.

Availability of Adequate and Safe Equipment

The problem of acquiring sufficient and correct type of equipment is one that confronts every shipper. Special equipment is often needed for shipments of excessive height, width, length, or weight measurements. Car improvements such as DF and cushion underframe cars have reduced loading, unloading, and damage expenses. Certain motor carriers specialize in steel hauling and, consequently, have a large fleet of flat-bed trailers. Some motor carriers are general commodity haulers with their entire fleet consisting of trailers suited for dry freight. A working knowledge of the different types of equipment and the carriers possessing this equipment will simplify the routing problem.

Certain commodities (such as steel sheet and strip) are loaded and wrapped to buyers' specifications. Specification instructions for proper loading, spacing, and protection may result in lower prices and/or safe arrival.

Financial Condition of the Carrier

In routing, the company's interest must be protected at all times. For this reason it is wise to use only sound and well-financed carriers. Responsibility of the carrier could be very important in the event of a valuable shipment being damaged in transit. If the carrier were to become insolvent, considerable difficulty would be experienced in collecting any outstanding loss or damage claims. An investigation of the carrier's insurance coverage is imperative and a copy of the insurance coverage, if obtainable, should be kept on file for reference.

Quality of Service

The quality of the product is a basic criterion for measuring the efficiency of any type of procurement. In transportation the product is service and because of constant changes in rates, carrier operations, and the addition or elimination of certain types of service, the quality of transportation service never remains static. It is essential in freight routing that one be cognizant of all changes which may affect his company's operations. Quality of service is a broad term which encompasses quite a few tangible and intangible elements. In judging the relative merits of the service offered by the different carriers, one routing freight should consider the following factors.

Transit Time

This is a very important consideration. This information can be gained by scanning past delivery receipts of the various carriers being considered and striking a norm for service of different weight shipments between the points over which future freight may be routed. Carriers will have a tendency to specialize in fast service between certain cities on their line which is much better than the service given other cities served by the same carrier. Volume of freight, directional flow of movement, cost of operation, and varying carrier policy have a decided influence on the speed of service given any two points. In routing, this information will enable one to use those carriers which feature expedited service between two cities rather than select a carrier which has not developed the traffic and, therefore, provides a slower service. By using the faster carrier, the minimum transit time possible between the two points will have been purchased and the greatest value for the freight dollar spent will have been achieved.

Claims

Controversial loss and damage claims are matters for the courts to decide and not the Interstate Commerce Commission; therefore, it is wise in routing to select carriers whose record includes fair and prompt settlement of claims.

If, over a period of time, it is apparent that numerous loss or damage claims are being filed against a single carrier, it may be best to eliminate the carrier from any future freight routings. Sound advice to remember in routing freight is the fact that a claim prevented is better than a claim collected. A claim may be submitted by either party to the bill of lading to any one of the carriers which is party to the haul.

Tariffs

All carriers that participate in the transportation of commodities or passengers in intrastate or interstate commerce are compelled by law to file their various charges with either state or Federal regulatory agencies in either their own tariff issues or those published in their behalf by tariff agencies.

There are many types of tariffs—class, commodity, class and commodity, special service, etc. The regulatory agencies of state and Federal government prescribe the rules for the construction of tariffs.

Tariffs usually quote rates for certain geographical territories, governed by specific routing as well as on-line rates for certain types of carriers.

Most agency tariffs are moderately priced and easily obtained. Carrier's individual issues are furnished for the asking.

Tariff interpretation can be acquired through direct study of the rules and regulations of state and interstate commerce. Tariffs necessary to an industry vary in accordance with the procurement and distribution areas participated in by an industry as well as the type of goods procured and distributed.

Rates

There is no single formula for rate making by public carriers. Rates are generally based on carrier's cost of service and/or value of the service to customer, i.e., "what the traffic will bear." Other factors include value of the article, nature of the article—crude or finished, semifinished, liquid, dry—type of packaging, distance, volume, rates on similar articles, competition, and geographical area.

Charges are usually assessed on the basis of weight. Rates and rate structures are highly complex. For a better understanding it is recommended that a more thorough study be made.

Relations with Carriers

In striving for an efficient routing program, it is desirable to employ carriers that maintain a freight sales department composed of competent and highly respected personnel. The old adage "it is not so much knowing it all yourself as it is knowing where to go to get help" certainly holds true in transportation. The key man in shipper-carrier relations is the freight sales representative, and a friendly personal and business relationship with the carrier's representative will be of inestimable value in expediting that "hot" shipment, gaining carrier support for a rate reduction on one's commodity, or obtaining assistance in establishing proper routing instructions.

References to Traffic Publications and Services[2]

In the preceding pages an attempt has been made to focus attention on the most important factors to be considered in selecting a routing. Equally important in freight routing is the data available from com-

[2] Others listed in Section 26.

mercial sources. In addition to the complex and technical routing tariffs, purchasing personnel responsible for traffic may receive helpful routing information from (1) traffic publications, (2) carriers, (3) traffic bureaus or consultants, and (4) civic organizations. A few of the most useful traffic publications are the following:

American Trucking Association's Motor Carrier Directory. This practical routing guide is leased to subscribers by the Motor Carrier Directory Company, Atlanta, Georgia, and is kept current through the issuance of supplements. It contains a list of all trucklines, their equipment, points served, list of officers, insurance coverage, and the tariff bureaus in whose rates the various trucklines concur. It is possible to obtain from this guide truck routings between many cities throughout the United States with a minimum of difficulty on the part of the user. Routings obtained through the use of this directory without reference to freight tariffs may not always result in a route which protects the lowest possible rate.

Official List of Open and Prepay Stations. This is a railroad publication which is issued twice a year by A. P. Leland, Agent, St. Louis, Missouri, and is supplemented frequently. It contains an alphabetical and geographical list of all the railroad stations in the United States, Mexico, and Canada. Also, it shows the facilities available at each station as well as special notes applying to consignees. Many railroad stations do not have agents and in such cases all freight charges on shipments to these stations must be prepaid.

Various Commercial Routing and Rate Services. This list consists of *Leonard's Rate Guide, Reliance Traffic Service, Bullinger's Postal and Shipping Guide, Albrecht's Routing Guide, National Freight Rate Service,* and *National Highway and Airway Carrier.* These publications follow the same format in that information is furnished the subscriber relevant to rates, rules, and routes applicable to freight shipments via rail, express, motor carrier, or parcel post.

Official Railway Equipment Register. This book is issued quarterly by the Railway Equipment and Publication Company, New York. A complete listing of all the railroads' equipment and its dimensions is shown. Also included is a list of junction points between the various railroads.

Official Railway Guide. This guide contains an alphabetical list of railroad stations and the carrier or carriers serving each, railroad maps, and timetables. This guide is issued monthly by the National Railway Publication Company, New York. Passenger train schedules and accommodations are in effect as published in the month's issue.

Official Airline Guide. This guide is published monthly by American Aviation Publications, Chicago, Illinois, and contains an alphabetical list of airport cities and the airlines serving each city. A complete list of all the airlines' flights and timetables is printed.

U.S. Official Postal Guide. This is a government issue outlining the regulations and rates governing postal shipments.

Books for Useful Reference.[3] See Richard C. Colton, "Practical Handbook of Industrial Traffic Management." This book is published by Traffic Service Corporation, Washington, D.C. As the title indicates, it is a practical reference for those engaged in daily traffic problems, particularly concerning the routing of freight.

Also see Thomas G. Bugan, "When Does Title Pass?", published by W. C. Brown, Dubuque, Iowa. This book goes more deeply into the subject of when title passes from shipper to consignee and who has risk of loss or damage in transit. Rather involved legal aspects of these questions have been made comparatively easy to read and apply under most circumstances.

Magazines, Bulletins, or Periodicals. A great deal of routing data can be obtained through articles regarding carrier services, routes, and pending rate increases or reductions contained in *Traffic World, Transport Topics, American Import and Export Bulletin,* and other publications.

Another source available to purchasing for routing assistance is the carrier. Each type of carrier, whether it be rail, motor carrier, or air, provides point lists and memorandum rate charts which are helpful in routing. Carrier freight solicitors welcome the opportunity to assist industrial traffic men and through carrier cooperation the shipper or receiver has at his disposal an established traffic department composed of skilled traffic personnel who are trained in the intricacies of freight routing.

Aid from a carrier, while undoubtedly offered with the best of intentions, may at times be unintentionally biased in favor of the carrier offering assistance. It is not always possible for one type of carrier to be fully familiar with charges and services of other types of carriers with whom they compete. Therefore, it is important for an industrial traffic department, or any other department routing freight, to take a look "across the board," examining the services and charges of all carriers.

The transportation department of the local chamber of commerce or the manufacturer's trade association may be another source for routing assistance. This type of organization will assist the smaller company with routing problems and the development of a routing system.

Routing System

The final phase of routing is the establishment of a routing system. A list should be compiled of the regular sources of supply and the steady

[3] Also see *Freight Traffic Redbook* published by the Traffic Publishing Company, Inc., New York. Covers all aspects of transportation from fundamental principles to the governing laws.

outbound shipping points. From this list an individual routing card can be completed with information pertinent to the commodity trade name, freight classification, rates, tariff authority, terms of sale, and the various weight breakdowns. Routing cards should be indexed alphabetically ac-

INBOUND ROUTING

SHIPPER: ANY Machine Company **ORIGIN:** Bridgeport, Connecticut

MATERIAL			DATE	ROUTE
Milling machinery and replacement parts as				To 20 pounds - Parcel Post
Machinery, NOI, or Machine Parts, NOI, Iron or Steel				20 lbs. - 27 lbs. - Railway Express
CLASS	RATE	MIN.		27 lbs. - 11,690 lbs. - Rail LCL service
LTL-100	3.13 cwt.	to 5000 lbs.		11,690 lbs. - over - NH-NYO&W-DLW-NKP
	2.93 cwt.	over 5000 lbs.		
TL-45	1.32 cwt.	20,000 lbs.		
LCL-100	2.93 cwt.	to 5000 lbs.		Only When Authorized
	2.71 cwt.	over 5000 lbs.		
CL-45	1.32 cwt.	24,000R lbs.		0 to 34 lbs. via Air Express
TERMS:				34 lbs. & over via American Airlines Air Freight
F.O.B. Seller's Plant				
TARIFF AUTHORITY: Parcel Post Zone 4, Express Zone 16				
Item 67570-NMFC#A-2 MF-1.C.C.6				
Rate basis 600-ECMCA #31-A MF-1.C.C.A113				
Item 29662-UFC#3 - I.C.C. #A-3				
Rate basis 600-CTR E-1009 - I.C.C. 4487				

OUTBOUND ROUTING

CONSIGNEE: ABC Manufacturing Co. **DESTINATION:** Flint, Michigan

MATERIAL			DATE	ROUTE
Intake and exhaust valves as Auto, Engine,				To 20 lbs. - Parcel Post
Driving or Steering Gear Parts, NOI, Iron or Steel				20 to 39 lbs. - Railway Express
CLASS	RATE	MIN.		39 lbs. & over - Norwalk Truck Lines
LTL-2	1.93 cwt.	to 2000 lbs.		
LTL-2	1.73 cwt.	2000 to 5000 lbs.		
LTL-2	1.43 cwt.	over 5000 lbs.		
TL-CR	.55 cwt.	20,000 lbs.		Only When Authorized
				0 to 75 lbs. - Air Express
TERMS:				75 lbs. & over - Capitol Air Freight
F.O.B. Our Plant				
TARIFF AUTHORITY: Parcel Post Zone 3, Rail Express Scale 10				
Item 6480 - NMFC#13 MF-I.C.C. 7				
Item 3700 - CSMFT 565 MF-I.C.C. 699				
Rate basis 210 - CSMFT 226-B MF-I.C.C. 196				

FIG. 18–2. Inbound and outbound routing cards.

cording to consignor or consignee and filed. It is possible, as stated in an earlier paragraph, to have routing cards furnished by a commercial traffic bureau. An accepted method for recording routing data is shown in Fig. 18–2.

On inbound routings, it is the policy of many companies to apply the routing instructions shown in these records to the applicable purchase order. In addition, standard routing instructions can be sent to each supplier's traffic department. They should be requested to acknowledge these instructions. By following this procedure, the chance of misrouting by the vendor is kept to a minimum. If the vendor should disregard the furnished routing instructions, the buyer has a basis for debiting the vendor for any excess transportation costs incurred as a result of misrouting. On outbound shipments, the general practice is to furnish the shipping department a duplicate copy of the outbound routing instruction for each customer. Since the carrier's rates and services are constantly changing, the importance of keeping the inbound and outbound routing cards current cannot be overstressed.

Traffic Consultants

There are companies organized to handle the traffic management activities of smaller businesses. They are known as "traffic consultants" or "commercial traffic bureaus." In the absence of trained and qualified technicians in the purchasing organization, it is sometimes feasible to have one of them establish standard routes on consistent inbound and outbound shipments. Usually these service companies charge a flat fee for each routing and assess a retaining fee for keeping the established routing records up to date.

FREIGHT–BILL AUDIT

Freight bills are carrier invoices for transportation services rendered, the cost of having goods transported from one place to another. Freight bills may be said to have three principal functions, namely, (1) a receipt to the consignor or consignee and as prima facie evidence of payment of freight charges, (2) a receipt to the carrier and as prima facie evidence of the delivery of the goods, and (3) a notice to the consignee of the arrival of the shipment.

In an opinion expressed by the Interstate Commerce Commission, it was stated a carrier's duty exists in rendering freight bills to state thereon such information as will permit the consignor or consignee with the aid of published price lists to verify the correctness of the charges which he is expected to pay. As a result of this Commission report, a uniform freight-bill form generally exists throughout the transportation industry. This form lists the point of origin, date of shipment, weight, route of movement, initials and number of any railroad cars, adequate description of property transported, rate applicable to the service rendered, a separate listing of each accessorial charge (such as stoppage in transit, reconsignment, switching, drayage, car service, or storage), and a total charge for the services provided.

The verification of a carrier's freight bill, or invoice, is extremely important. The correct audit of freight bills is as essential to the profit and loss statement as the audit of any other commercial invoice. The audit of a transportation company's invoice necessitates a detailed knowledge and experience in the application of carriers' classifications and freight rate tariffs.

The complexity of the various carriers' price lists (tariffs) makes it desirable to have freight bills authenticated by persons who are trained and experienced in conducting intelligent freight-bill audits. Any company making substantial freight-bill payments should give careful consideration to providing a traffic technician to perform this operation. Smaller companies can negotiate with commercial traffic service bureaus to have the freight bills audited. This service may be obtained on a flat fee per bill basis or on a percentage of the overcharge claims filed and recovered.

In freight-bill auditing, the individual performing this exacting task must search for the errors that may occur in the issuance of a carrier's freight bill. One must be alert to discover undercharges or overcharges resulting from mathematical errors in extension; transposition of freight charges in improper charge columns; incorrect shipping points, when different rates apply from the different points; incorrect shipping dates, when rates change upon dates just prior to shipment; variance between shipping and billing dates, when rate changes have occurred between these dates; incorrect car numbers, which may alter freight charges by higher carload minimum weights applying to larger cars on certain commodities as stipulated in Rule 34; incorrect weights at which the freight charge is billed; application of incorrect tariffs; misdescription of commodities; transposition of figures in the weight or rate column; improper description of containers, which in turn alters the applicable freight rating; failure of carrier to protect the lowest rated route; failure of carrier to protect reciprocal switching agreements; improper addition of connecting carrier charges; application of higher combination of rail rates instead of a lower through rate; charges based on through rail rates which are higher than the lawful aggregate of intermediate rates; failure to allow for dunnage or bracing when permissible; unauthorized higher rates for shorter haul than for longer haul over same route without fourth section relief; incorrect delivery arrangements which result in extra cartage expenses.

The freight-bill audit may be accomplished before payment or after payment of the freight charges. Many companies that are staffed with competent traffic personnel find it very advantageous to audit the freight bills prior to payment. By adhering to this procedure, a company can save much accounting and filing of overcharge claim expense. If the freight bill is increased or decreased prior to payment, it is imperative the new charges be placed on the bill and complete tariff authority substantiating the correct charge be furnished the carrier. It is good practice to attach a freight-bill correction form to a carrier's check when the audit discloses any error. This form lists the name and address of the company filing the correction; the date of the correction; the freight-bill number; the description of the commodity as shown on the incorrect bill; the weight of the shipment as originally billed; the total charges as originally billed; the correct commodity description; the correct weight; the correct rate; the correct charges; tariff authority; the nature of the error; additional remarks; and the signature of the individual issuing the correction. Through the use of such a form, the carrier is able to reconcile instantly any differences in charges existing between the billed and paid amount.

If a company requires the audit of freight bills be performed after payment of the freight charges, a different procedure is necessary in correcting the carrier's error. Any overcharge in freight charges discovered after payment to the carrier must be recovered by the filing of an overcharge claim. This is done by preparing a standard form for presentation of overcharge claims, which lists the name of the carrier to whom the claim is presented; current date; claimant's number; amount of claim; description of shipment; name and address of consignor and consignee; shipping point; destination; route; date of bill of lading; paid freight-bill number; detailed statement of charges paid, statement of charges that should have been paid; tariff authority in support of overcharge claim; and signature of person presenting the claim. This document is attached to the original paid freight bill and forwarded to the negligent carrier for action. In the event a company may be reluctant to release the original paid freight bill, it is permissible to issue in lieu thereof a bond of indemnity agreement which guarantees the carrier full protection against any action taken by anyone who obtains possession of the original freight bill at a later date. As provided in the Interstate Commerce Act, an overcharge claim may be instituted during a three-year period from the time the cause of action accrues.

The fundamental purpose of any freight-bill audit is to detect the legal rates that are applicable to any given shipment. This holds true in the case of undercharges as well as overcharges. It is sheer folly for a company to accept continuously and pay freight charges lower than the legal tariff rate. Over a period of time the undercharges will accumulate and develop into a sizable amount. The same statute of limitations provision in the Act, guaranteeing the right of the shipper or receiver to collect overcharge claims within the three-year period, also protects the carrier in collecting undercharges. To avoid this unpleasant occurrence, and the accompanying additional paper work, it is a wise policy to pay the correct legal charges at all times.

Sample Check List to Lower Costs

In addition to the tangible freight savings that may be realized promptly through an efficient freight-bill audit, many other benefits can be obtained. A conscientious buyer is thinking constantly in terms of what could have been done to ship this material in a more economical manner. A few of the possibilities in lowering the cost of procurement or distribution are the following:

1. Does the weight shown on the bill of lading appear accurate, or should a scale ticket be requested to support the figure?
2. Are railroad demurrage and truck detention charges excessive, and, if so, what steps are necessary to control this expenditure?
3. Depending on comparative rates, can rail shipments move more economically via truck or piggyback, or vice versa?
4. Is there excessive transportation cost as a result of unwarranted use of premium transportation; namely, air freight, air or rail express?
5. Is it possible to incorporate into the routing program the lower rated services of freight forwarders or water carriers?
6. Are mixed carload or truckload shipments forwarded in such a manner as to protect the lowest total freight charge?
7. Is it possible to consolidate numerous small-lot shipments into fewer larger carload or truckload shipments with resulting freight savings?
8. Is trucking expense being squandered on unnecessary pickup or deliveries of freight at carrier's platform when such pickup or delivery service by the carrier is included in the tariff rate?
9. Is the freight classification of the commodity shipped specific or is an improper description being utilized which results in the assessment of higher freight charges?
10. Is it possible to order or ship materials in greater weight quantities in order to take advantage of the lower rates afforded in the higher weight brackets? Many less truckload and less carload rates decrease in direct proportion to the amount of weight offered for transportation.

FREIGHT–BILL PAYMENT

The actual payment of freight bills can be accomplished through the issuance of checks by the company's accounting department or through the deposit of funds in a local bank upon which a commercial traffic service bureau is authorized to draw in the payment of a subscriber's freight bills. In either method of payment, caution must be exercised in approving for payment only those freight bills against which delivery of the goods has been performed. This can be accomplished through the matching of the carrier's delivery receipt to the corresponding freight bill prior to payment.

A recent innovation in the method of payment of freight bills has been gaining wide acceptance from many concerns and carriers. This freight-payment plan is originated by and operated through a local bank and eligibility for membership in the plan is extended to all freight-paying concerns and carriers. Each member company deposits with the bank money which is designated as a freight-payment account. Briefly, the carrier renders to the bank all freight bills outstanding against member shippers or receivers. The bank credits the carrier's account and debits the member company's account in the amount of the freight bills deposited. The bank forwards all paid freight bills to the member company for validation. In the event an incorrect amount is charged or a bill is paid for which a concern is not responsible, the member company can return the paid freight bill with an explanatory correction form and receive prompt credit for the amount of the overcharge. For the member company, this plan is designed to eliminate costly check writing and signing, simplifies accounting, reduces check filing and record keeping, and eliminates the need of a "petty cash" fund for the payment of small collect shipments. The carrier benefits from the elimination of numerous statements, credit risk, double handling of freight bills, and the provision of immediate cash. In most bank freight-payment plans there is no charge for this service to the member company and only a minor fee per freight bill assessed against the carrier for the convenience of immediate collection.

EXPEDITING AND TRACING

In the language of the layman, the terms "expediting" and "tracing" in regard to transportation are used interchangeably. This usage is not true, however, in the vernacular of the traffic man. The term "expediting" means clearing the way and making arrangements for fast transportation service. By making contact with the carrier in advance of shipment, the way can be paved for fast, efficient handling of the shipment. Many of the pitfalls of transportation, such as misloading, delay until the following evening, or wrong connections at intermediate transfer points, can be avoided through alerting and impressing the carrier with the need for expeditious service.

Tracing, on the other hand, is the locating of a shipment after it has entered the transportation process in an effort to obtain a record of its movement. Tracing is the following or pushing of a shipment, whereas expediting is the act of clearing the path for obtaining the fastest possible delivery service.

Tracing is a voluntary service provided by the carrier and it is a wise policy for a company not to abuse the privilege. Ordinarily, before a tracer request is instituted, an opportunity should be given the carrier to make delivery. Too often this is not the case. However, if prompt delivery is imperative, it is not always possible to wait. It should be understood that tracing is nowhere near as effective a means of speeding delivery as expediting referred to above. However, there are certain things that can be done to clear the path between the point where the shipment is located and its destination. It is a mistaken belief that by constantly calling and pressuring the carrier a faster service will be obtained than if the material is permitted to receive normal handling. The end result of unnecessary tracer requests is overburdening of the carrier's facilities to the point where actual delay may be encountered. The sole purpose of tracing is to establish a record of movement and to locate the shipment. Then the decision can be made as to whether expediting from that point on is worthwhile.

Whether one is expediting or tracing, it is advantageous to become conversant with the available carrier services and the traffic terminology employed. It is important to successful tracing and expediting to understand the meaning of such terms as pro, waybill, carding point, merchandise car, diversion, reconsignment, classification yards, relay stations, and manifest. Also, one must acquire a fundamental understanding of the various methods of handling freight used by the different types of carriers. Valuable information can be obtained through frequent visits to the local carrier's terminal and studying the various methods of forwarding freight.

While tracing and expediting generally follow a similar pattern among the different kinds of carriers, there are a few differences to be explained. A brief résumé of tracing by the various carriers follows.

Rail. Rail shipments are either carload or less than carload in nature. Of the two types, the carload shipment is the easier to trace. In the carload shipment, the shipper loads a full carload of material and, when finished, applies a car seal. A bill of lading is furnished the railroad and the loaded car is removed from the company's private siding or public team track, whichever the case may be. At the railroad's classification yards, the car is assigned to an outbound train and routed, either by shipper or railroad, to its destination. The selected route may be via the originating railroad exclusively, or it may require transfers to many connecting railroads en route. The efficient tracing of carload shipments requires a knowledge of the shipping date, car initial and number, consignor, consignee, origin, destination, commodity, and the route of movement. Also, it is helpful if the junction points to be used in the route are known. With this information, one may ask the originating or delivering carrier to locate the car and advise the approximate delivery date. The carrier should be in a position to state the waybill number, engine and train number, and destination of the train to which the car in question is assigned. Routine tracing or expediting may be handled with the local tracing clerk of the carrier, but in the event of an emergency shipment requiring immediate information or assistance, it will be worthwhile to make contact directly with the yardmaster's office of the carrier and obtain the train-forwarding information.

Less-than-carload shipments are more complex in nature than carload shipments, which results in greater difficulty to trace. Small-lot shipments are received by the railroad's pickup trucks or ferry cars, sometimes called "trap cars," from the various shippers. The freight is delivered to the local freight terminal of the originating railroad and is loaded into merchandise cars. Each less-than-carload shipment is assigned a waybill number and scheduled for placement into a car destined to a point nearest the final destination of the less-than-carload shipment. The destination of the merchandise car is known as the carding point. The carding point may be the ultimate destination of the small-lot shipment or it may be just one of the numerous unloading and reloading stations the shipment will encounter en route. In tracing such a shipment, one has an advantage in knowing the consignor, consignee, origin, destination, date of shipment, number of containers and weight, route, merchandise car number, carding point (transfer station), and waybill number. The waybill number, car initial and number, route and first carding point can be obtained by contacting the originating railroad. If additional transfers of freight are necessary, the tracer must contact each transfer station and obtain the new car initial and number and carding point. At each freight transfer station, the arriving merchandise car is unloaded and the freight is reloaded into the other merchandise cars destined to nearer final destination of the small-lot shipment. Less-than-carload shipments moving between major cities do not experience the numerous transfers of freight often encountered by those shipments addressed to the smaller off-line points. Upon arrival of the merchandise car at the ultimate destination, the car is unloaded by the carrier at its local freight terminal and the shipment is usually scheduled for delivery to the consignee the following day by the railroad's delivery truck—or by ferry or trap car if sufficient weight is involved.

Truck. With the exception of terminology, the tracing and expediting of truckload or less-than-truckload shipments is similar to the procedure followed via rail. Truckload shipments are loaded into a trailer at the origin and unloaded at the destination, and unless repairs are necessary to the trailer, the material is not transferred en route. Trailers are interchanged by the trucklines just as the railroads exchange their equipment. In tracing a truckload shipment, one must possess the usual shipping data such as date of shipment, consignor, consignee, origin, destination, and weight. A telephone call to the originating truckline will enable one to get the carrier's "pro" (freight-bill number), tractor-trailer number, driver's name, and destination of the trailer. Often the originating truckline's office can estimate accurately when delivery will be made. By furnishing the above acquired forwarding information to the destination terminal of the delivering truckline, the expected arrival and delivery date can be learned.

In locating less-than-truckload shipments, the tracer is faced with a situation identical to the one found in rail less-than-carload shipments. Numerous transfers of freight may be involved in forwarding small shipments. Each time a new truckline transports the material, a new freight-bill number is issued, and it is imperative that the tracer know the correct freight bill to trace the shipment properly. This is especially true in the movement of goods via two or more trucklines, or in the movement via a single carrier in cities receiving less frequent service than the others.

Freight Forwarders. In tracing this type of shipment, one must remember that freight forwarders do not own any equipment which operates intercity. They may possess a fleet of trucks performing pickup and delivery service, but in the physical movement of the goods the freight forwarder utilizes the established facilities of the rail, truck, boat, or air carrier. It is the practice of the freight forwarder to accumulate numerous small-lot shipments from different consignors and consolidate into one volume shipment, which is tendered to the carrier on a truckload or carload basis. The consignor or consignee can obtain from the origin terminal of the freight forwarder the freight-bill number assigned to the shipper's portion of the volume shipment, the manifest number (a packing list showing the contents of the car or trailer), the car initial, number, and carding point when forwarded via rail carrier, and the trailer number and destination when forwarded via truck. With this information, the destination terminal of the freight forwarder will advise the tracer in regard to the expected arrival and delivery date.

Railway Express Agency.[4] The tracing and expediting of Railway Express is difficult and oftentimes frustrating. All records are maintained by date and waybill number. On outbound shipment, such records do not furnish any information as to which train or car a specific shipment was forwarded on. The originating station can only assume a certain shipment was placed on a particular train because that is the train which normally would handle the shipment. Once an express shipment has been placed in transportation, very little can be done by the consignor or consignee to locate the shipment. In the event of an emergency or breakdown order, this lack of information is very irritating to the anxious shipper or receiver. Upon arrival of the Railway Express car at the final destination, the car is unloaded and delivery is made to the consignee via Railway Express trucks. At destination station, the consignee is cognizant of the whereabouts of his shipment when it is delivered to his receiving department. The best method of acquiring forwarding information on Railway Express shipments is to request the shipper to alert the originating Railway Express agent in advance and ask to be informed of the train and express car number into which the shipment will be loaded. The consignor or consignee may contact the destination Railway Express agent and provide the forwarding information. Arrangements may be completed with the destination agent to hold the shipment at the depot for consignee's pickup or to have Railway Express unload the car and deliver as promptly as possible. For an additional charge, the Railway Express Agency does provide a service which is beneficial to the consignor and consignee in tracing an urgently needed shipment. This service is designed as "protective signature service" and must be requested by the shipper at the time of shipment. Also, a notation must be shown on the express bill of lading "protective signature service requested." By this arrangement Railway Express shipments are handled under a person-to-person signature from the time of receipt at origin to delivery at the destination. In many instances, the nominal fee assessed for this service is offset by the peace of mind gained by the desperate shipper or receiver in knowing the location of the shipment. If an express shipment is overdue, a written tracer request can be started with the origin or destination Railway Express office. The tracing procedure is time-consuming, however, since the tracing action by the Rail-

[4] Now commonly known as REA Express.

way Express Agency is accomplished through correspondence with the regional accounting office. While information regarding either delivery or nondelivery of the freight is received eventually, it is of little consolation to the consignor or consignee who sought immediate assistance.

Air Express. Air Express is a division of the Railway Express Agency. Because of the smaller volume of shipments forwarded, the Air Express arm is able to maintain a more efficient set of records in regard to forwardings. A telephone call to the originating Air Express office will obtain for the person tracing a shipment the waybill number, the transporting airline, and the flight number, departure time, arrival time, and destination applicable to the shipment in question. If the airline flight is through to the destination of the shipment, it is simple to arrange for company pickup at destination airport or to determine the approximate delivery time via Air Express truck. If the airline flight terminates short of the final destination of the shipment, it is necessary for the tracer to contact the intermediate Air Express station and request the connecting airline's flight number, departure time, and destination. Whenever shipments originate or terminate in cities other than airport cities, freight is forwarded via train through the facilities of the Railway Express Agency. Because of the high priority given to Air Express shipments, a fast and economical service for the small shipment can be provided. The priority system applicable to airline flight space is as follows: (1) gasoline, (2) passengers, (3) mail, (4) air express, (5) air freight of the airline, and (6) air freight of the freight forwarders. Another advantage of air express is that it can choose from a multiude of flights and airlines in transporting its freight, whereas the airlines are restricted to their own flights in the movement of their shipments. Such flexibility permits Air Express to forward the shipments immediately.

Air Freight. Most airlines operate their own air cargo service. The cartage agent of the airline receives freight at the consignor's plant and delivers to the airline at the originating airport. The airline uses only its own flights in transporting the freight to the final destination unless, of course, it is necessary to turn it over to a second airline in order to reach the destination city. The originating airline will furnish, upon request, the air-bill number and flight assigned to the shipment. If the shipment requires movement via two or more different airlines, a new air-bill number is issued by each connecting airline. In order to trace such a shipment successfully, it is necessary to contact each airline and obtain the new air-bill number. Shipments consigned to destinations outside the delivery limits of the airport city are flown to the nearest airport city and released to surface transportation for movement to ultimate destination.

Parcel Post. Once a parcel has been mailed, there is no way of expediting or immediately tracing it, except to be on friendly terms with the postmaster and ask him to watch personally for the package. To do this, one should know the approximate size, shape, and weight of the package and who the shipper was. If the addressor has insured the package and it is undelivered after a reasonable time has elapsed, it is possible to begin a tracer request form with the U.S. Post Office. Such tracers are handled by the origin and destination postmasters, however, and it is a relatively slow and tedious process in getting a reply. If the addressor failed to insure the parcel, there is no recourse against the Post Office for the addressor or addressee.

TRACING SHIPMENTS AND CARTAGE PICKUPS
TPFC-1230

ATTENTION: TRAFFIC DEPARTMENT GK DATE 4/17/

PLEASE SECURE [X] PROOF OF DELIVERY [ ] CARTAGE PICK-UP ON THE FOLLOWING DESCRIBED SHIPMENT:

SHIPPER			ORIGIN		
John Doe Company			N.Y.C.		
CONSIGNED TO			DESTINATION		
All Industries, Inc.			Cleveland, Ohio		
INVOICE NO.	CHARGED TO		DATE SHIPPED	VIA	AIR BILL OR PRO. NO.
13569			4/8/	S ates Frgt. Fwdg.	
ORDER NO.	NO. OF: BOXES / CARTONS / CRATES	WEIGHT	MATERIAL		FLT. OR TRAILER NO.
V-4732	4 BOXES X	3600#	Castings		

REMARKS:

Buyer informed Traffic material urgently needed. Shipment overdue. Trace vigorously.

Carrier advises shipment not on hand. Apparently misloaded. Will contact all parties concerned.

IN THE EVENT ADVICE IS RECEIVED THAT SHIPMENT HAS BEEN DELIVERED I WILL NOTIFY YOU SO TRACER CAN BE CANCELLED.

REQUESTED BY	DEPT.	EXT.
Buyer	124	678

PRINTED IN U.S.A.

FIG. 18–3. Tracer request form.

Most industrial traffic departments assign the tracing and expediting work to one or two key employees who are skilled in this phase of traffic management. In developing a sound and efficient tracing and expediting program, one must avoid superfluous tracing and expediting, furnish accurate and complete shipping data to the carrier, develop good public relations with the carrier's representatives, and maintain written records of all tracing and expediting requests. To assist in incorporating these points in the tracing and expediting program, many traffic departments utilize a tracer request form similar to the one shown in Fig. 18–3. On this form is recorded all pertinent information necessary to trace the shipment. Upon delivery of the shipment, the tracer form is completed and filed for later reference.

CLAIMS FOR LOSS AND DAMAGE

The loss or damage of goods in transit is a problem of major importance to any manufacturer. Because of the controversial nature of loss and damage claims, the preparation, filing, and collection can be very time-consuming and expensive. A basic step in the efficient handling of loss and damage claims is the need for one to know when to file a claim. The terms of sale applicable to each purchase order must be studied thoroughly in order to interpret the effect on transportation. Whenever material is purchased f.o.b. buyer's plant, the purchaser should take full advantage of these terms and debit the seller for invoice value of the goods damaged or lost. The buyer should forward all supporting data and documents to the claim (paid freight bill, original bill of lading, carrier inspection report, etc.) to the vendor for actual presentation against the carrier. On the other hand, a vendor whose terms of sale are f.o.b. seller's plant is quoting such terms in order to remove from his company the responsibility for safe and proper delivery of the goods to the buyer's plant. Under these terms, delivery to the carrier specified by the buyer is comparable to delivery to the buyer. It must be remembered that the risk in transit and the responsibility for filing claim in the event of loss or damage accompanies the passage of title.

The bill of lading is as fundamental to the shipper-carrier relationship as the purchase order is to the buyer-seller. The bill of lading is a legal contract between the shipper and carrier, a receipt to the shipper for the goods, documentary evidence of title to the goods, and, in the case of the order bill of lading, a negotiable instrument. Since this document defines the duties, rights, and responsibilities of the shipper and carrier, it is of special import in the just settlement of loss and damage claims. In receipting the bill of lading, the carrier is a bailee of the goods and is entrusted with the safe and reasonable dispatch. With certain exceptions, the carrier is a complete insurer of the goods while in transit. Section 1, paragraph (a) of the contract terms of bill of lading utilized by the various carriers reads as follows: "The carrier or party in possession of any of the property herein described shall be liable as at common law for any loss thereof or damage thereto, except as hereinafter provided."

Exceptions for Relief of Responsibility

The exceptions for which a carrier may be relieved of responsibility in the event of loss or damage to the goods while in transit are an act of

God, act of public enemy, authority of law, act or default of shipper, and nature of the commodity. A brief explanation of these exceptions follows:

1. *Act of God.* It has been ruled by the courts than an act of God is a justification for failure to perform a contract of carriage and relieves a carrier of liability for the loss or injury of goods entrusted to its care. An act of God is an event which could not occur by the intervention of man. It includes extraordinary floods, storms, lightning, severe frost, and earthquakes. It must be of such an unusual manifestation of the forces of nature that the carrier, under normal conditions, could not have anticipated or expected such an event. Bear in mind, however, the act of God must be the immediate and direct cause of loss or injury in order to relieve the carrier of liability. If the carrier, after being aware of an impending act of God, fails to exercise such care as a man of ordinary prudence would have exercised in protecting the goods from damage, this provision of the bill of lading will not absolve the carrier of negligence.

2. *Act of Public Enemy.* A carrier may not be held liable for destruction or conversion of goods by enemy military forces or by reason of robbery.

3. *Authority of Law.* Liability of a carrier ceases whenever goods are removed from its custody by legal process. Such a course of action may stem from Federal or state quarantines or acts of violence by rioters or strikers.

4. *Act or Default of Shipper.* The common law liability of a carrier is altered if loss or damage to the goods is the result of an act or omission of the shipper or owner of the property. An example would be improper loading or packing of the freight. The shipper is in a much better position than the carrier to know how the goods should be and are packed, and if the defect in packing or loading is not apparent through ordinary carrier observance, the carrier cannot be held responsible for damage or loss in transportation due to the improper loading or packing.

5. *Inherent Characteristics of the Commodity.* Certain commodities possess qualities which may make them more susceptible to loss or damage than other articles. For instance, many common grains are subject to deterioration, articles of iron or steel tend to rust under unfavorable atmospheric conditions, and some commodities have a tendency to heat in a confined area. Loss or damage arising strictly from the inherent nature of the article is not collectible from the carrier.

Types of Claims

Claims may be divided into known loss, concealed loss, known damage, concealed damage, and loss or damage by reason of delay.

A known loss refers to any freight which the carrier fails to deliver t the consignee. Such failure to deliver may be attributed to the destruction, disappearance, conversion of the goods, or to its being so damaged by the carrier as to render it worthless to the consignee. This is the simplest of claims. The carrier has contracted to provide carriage for a definite quantity of freight and at time of delivery there exists an apparent shortage of material. At the time of delivery, the consignee should request the carrier's agent to acknowledge the shortage by endorsement on the original freight bill. This action will expedite the settlement of any loss claim filed and, in addition, immediately places the burden for locating the shortage on the carrier.

A concealed loss means a loss that is not apparent visibly at the time of delivery by the carrier, but is discovered by the consignee upon later opening of the containers and checking the contents. The material received does not agree with the quantity invoiced by the seller. It is imperative in this type of a loss that the carrier be contacted immediately and the cartons and inner packing be set aside for later inspection. If the appearance of the package indicates the goods were packed therein, or if it bears evidence of tampering, pilfering or rifling, every opportunity should be extended to the carrier to make a thorough inspection.

Known damage is defined as damage that is apparent and acknowledged by the carrier at the time of delivery to the consignee. Such evident damage to containers or contents should be noted on carrier's receipt and copy before receiving signature is applied. A meticulous inspection of the damaged goods should be completed by the consignee and a notation specifying the extent of the damage should be applied to the carrier's original freight bill. As is the case in known loss, it is necessary for the carrier's agent to acknowledge by signature the damage notation in order for it to have any legal status. The consignee should not refuse damaged freight since it is his legal duty to accept the property and to employ every available and reasonable means to protect the shipment and minimize the loss. Acceptance of a damaged shipment does not imperil any legitimate claim the consignee may have against the carrier for damage. If the consignee fails to observe the legal duty to accept damaged freight, the carrier may consider it abandoned. After properly notifying the consignor and consignee of his intentions, the carrier may dispose of the material at public sale. This procedure is in accordance with the disposition of abandoned shipments as outlined in section 4 of the contract terms of the bill of lading.

Concealed damage means damage to the contents of a package or container which is not readily visible at the time of delivery by the carrier. The goods are received in apparent good order and a clear delivery receipt is given the carrier, but upon later opening of the packages breakage or damage is found. Carrier inspection is of extreme importance in facilitating the settlement of the concealed damage type of claim.

Rules Governing Loss or Damage Claims

In an effort to avoid charges of discrimination and to maintain fair and just practices in the settlement of highly controversial loss or damage claims, the carriers and the National Industrial Traffic League have prescribed a set of rules[5] to govern the inspection of freight and the adjustment of claims for loss or damage thereon. The full text of these rules is listed below.

Rule 1. When a package bears indication of having been pilfered while in possession of carrier, it shall be carefully weighed by the delivering agent before delivery and such weight endorsed on the freight bill and a joint inventory of contents of package by carrier and consignee shall be made before delivery or immediately upon receipt by consignee, and claim for shortage so discovered shall be promptly adjusted.

Rule 2. Loss or damage discovered after delivery of shipments to consignee shall be reported by consignee or consignor to agent of carrier immediately upon discovery, and in any event within fifteen days after receipt, and contents and container held for inspection by carrier, with a statement of facts or circumstances evidencing loss prior to delivery by carrier. Inspection shall be made by carrier when practicable, in any event within forty-eight hours, and shall include examination of package and contents for evidence of abstraction of the missing goods, checking contents with invoice and weighing for comparison with shipping weight; also, investigation of cartman's record of handling shipment. Report of inspection shall be made in duplicate on standard form and signed by carrier's agent and consignee, one copy thereof to be retained by consignee and attached to claim for loss, if made. In case no inspection is made by carrier's agent, consignee's inspection shall be accepted as carrier's inspection. If investigation develops that the loss occurred with carriers, the fifteen day clause shall not be invoked. (See Rule 7.)

Rule 3. Shortage from a package delivered to consignee without exception, when based only upon consignee's failure to find the entire invoice quantity in package, or when package remains in consignee's possession more than fifteen days before the goods are unpacked and shortage discovered, shall not be regarded as a responsibility of the carrier unless investigation develops that loss occurred with carrier. When package remains in possession of cartman overnight and not in warehouse, carrier shall require proof that loss did not occur with cartman.

Rule 4. When a package bears evidence of damage while in possession of carrier, a joint examination of contents by carrier and consignee shall be made

[5] Agreed upon by the National Industrial Traffic League and the Freight Claim Division of the Association of American Railroads. A similar set of rules exists for motor carriers.

before delivery or immediately upon receipt by consignee, and claim for damage so discovered shall be promptly adjusted upon its merits.

Rule 5. Damage to contents of package discovered after delivery of shipment to consignee shall be reported to agent of carrier immediately upon discovery, or in any event within fifteen days after receipt, with a statement of facts or circumstances evidencing damage prior to delivery by carrier, unless investigation develops that the damage occurred with carriers, then the fifteen day clause shall not be invoked. Inspection shall be made by carriers when practicable, and in any event within forty-eight hours after notice. In case no inspection is made by carrier's agent, consignee's inspection shall be accepted as carrier's inspection. Report of inspection shall be made in duplicate on standard form and signed by carrier's agent and consignee, one copy thereof to be retained by consignee and attached to claim for damage, if made. (See Rule 7.)

Rule 6. Shortage or damage discovered by consignee at time of receiving freight in any quantity from car, warehouse or other premises of carrier shall be reported to agent of carrier before removal of entire shipment in order that the cause and extent of loss or damage may, if possible, definitely be determined and proper record made thereof. Unloading of freight should not be retarded or discontinued awaiting inspection.

Rule 7. Notice of loss or damage may be given carrier's agent by telephone or in person and in either event shall be confirmed by mail. In case of loss or damage as provided for in Rules 2 and 5, and inspection is not made by carrier's agent, details of finds of inspection by consignee shall be furnished carrier's agent immediately upon completion of inspection.

Rule 8. Failure of consignee to comply with the foregoing regulations shall be regarded as indicating complete delivery of freight by carrier in good order.

Rule 9. When packages which indicate loss or damage to contents are recoopered by the carrier, proper record of this exception shall be noted on the waybill and station records and shall be available to consignee.

These regulations have no legal status and are not considered as binding on shipper, consignee, or carrier, but one can understand the reasonableness of complying with the rules. Through observance of these regulations, much can be accomplished in removing the suspicion and doubt surrounding any concealed loss or damage claim.

The final category of loss and damage is by reason of delay. The deciding factor in this type of claim is the length of time in transit. Loss or damage may be suffered by the consignor or consignee as a result of the goods declining in market value when delivered at destination or by actual physical deterioration of the commodity through reason of delay. In loss or damage by delay claims, the transit time provided is compared with the normal movement of goods over the same route, and if the transit time is excessive, the carrier must determine whether or not the delay was beyond its control. Although one of the bill of lading contract terms stipulates the carrier does not guarantee to transport a ship-

Standard Form for Presentation of Loss and Damage Claims

Freight Claim Agent (Name of person to whom claim is presented)	1341 E. 222nd St. Cleveland, Ohio (Address of claimant)	(Claimant's Number) § 394
X Truck Line, Inc. (Name of Carrier)	10/15/ (Date)	(Carrier's Number)
Broadway & Vine Streets, Lima, Ohio (Address)		

This claim for $5,313.60 (Amount of claim) is made against the carrier named above by ABC Products, Inc. (Name of claimant)

for Loss and Damage (loss or damage) in connection with the following described shipment(s):

Description of shipment Electric Motors

Name and address of consignor (shipper) Motor Electric Co., Lima, Ohio

Shipped from Lima, Ohio (City, town or station), To Cleveland, Ohio (City, town or station)

Final Destination Cleveland, Ohio (City, town or station) Routed via X Truck Line, Inc.

Bill of Lading issued by Motor Electric Co. Co.; Date of Bill of Lading 10/1/

Paid Freight Bill (Pro) Number 34870 ; Original Car Number and Initial

Truck or Trailer Number Connecting Line Reference

Name and address of consignee (Whom shipped to) ABC Products, Inc., 1341 E. 222nd St., Cleveland, Ohio

If shipment reconsigned enroute, state particulars:

DETAILED STATEMENT SHOWING HOW AMOUNT CLAIMED IS DETERMINED

(Number and description of articles, nature and extent of loss or damage, invoice price of articles, amount of claim, etc.)

Costs incurred at ABC Products, Inc. inspecting all motors repack & reship motors to be repaired	$ 361.80
Freight charges on returned motors to Lima. Mohawk Pro. C-800576.	21.30
5 motors lost - A35A 9064-2 at $76.30 ea. (Copy invoices attached)	381.50
Repair charges on motors as outlined on attached copy of invoices	4549.00
Total Amount Claimed	$5313.60

IN ADDITION TO THE INFORMATION GIVEN ABOVE, THE FOLLOWING DOCUMENTS ARE SUBMITTED IN SUPPORT OF THIS CLAIM*

( ) 1. Original bill of lading, if not previously surrendered to carrier.
( ) 2. Original paid freight ("expense") bill.
(X) 3. Original invoice or certified copy.
X 4. Other particulars obtainable in proof of loss or damage claimed.

Remarks Bond of Indemnity, issued in lieu of original paid freight bill and bill of lading.

The foregoing statement of facts is hereby certified to as correct.

ABC Products, Inc.
(Signature of claimant) Traffic Manager

§Claimant should assign to each claim a number, inserting same in the space provided at the upper right hand corner of this form. Reference should be made thereto in all correspondence pertaining to this claim.

*Claimant will please place check (x) before such of the documents mentioned as have been attached, and explain under "Remarks" the absence of any of the documents called for in connection with this claim. When for any reason it is impossible for claimant to produce original bill of lading, or paid freight bill, claimant should indemnify carrier or carriers against duplicate claim supported by original documents.

TOPS Form 3208 Litho in U.S.A.

FIG. 18–4. Standard form for presentation of loss and damage claim.

ment by any particular train or vessel, or in time for any particular market, the carrier is obligated to forward a shipment with reasonable dispatch. If a carrier can be proven negligent in this duty, claim can be filed for reimbursement of the damages suffered.

Filing Claims

In preparing a claim against a negligent carrier, the claimant is entitled to indemnification for full actual loss or damage. Because of the con-

TOPS FORM 3207

Printed in U.S.A.

Standard Form for Presentation of Overcharge Claims

Approved by the Interstate Commerce Commission; Freight Claim Division, Association of American Railroads; National Industrial Traffic League, and the National Association of Railway Commissioners.

Freight Claim Agent
(Name of person to whom claim is presented)

1341 E. 222nd St.
Cleveland, Ohio
(Address of claimant)

(Claimant's Number)‡ 56-1062

All Freight, Inc.
(Name of Carrier)

10/15/
(Date)

(Carrier's Number)

P. O. Box 7036, Akron 6, Ohio
(Address)

This claim for $63.86 is made against the carrier named above by ABC Products Inc. (Name of claimant)
for Overcharge in connection with the following described shipment(s):
Description of shipment 3 Skids Machines (Drilling) IOS, NOIBN
Name and address of consignor (shipper) Special Machine Co.
Shipped from Simsbury, Connecticut (City, town or station) To, Cleveland, Ohio (City, town or station)
Final Destination Cleveland, Ohio (City, town or station) Routed via All Freight, Inc.
Bill of Lading issued by Shipper Co.; Date of Bill of Lading 10/1/
Paid Freight Bill (Pro) Number 16-100390 ; Original Car Number and Initial
Truck or Trailer Number Connecting Line Reference
Name and address of consignee (Whom shipped to) ABC Products, Inc., 1341 E. 222nd St., Cleveland, Ohio
If shipment reconsigned enroute, state particulars:
Nature of Overcharge Rate (Weight, rate or classification, etc.)

DETAILED STATEMENT OF CLAIM

NOTE—If claim covers more than one item taking different rates and classification, attach separate statement showing how overcharge is determined and insert totals in space below.

	No. of Pkgs.	Articles	Weight	Rate	Charges	Amount of Overcharge
Charges Paid	3 Skids	Machines (Drilling) IOS, NOI	15470 as 20,000	1.40	$280.00 8.40	
		Total			$288.40	
Should have been	Same	Same	15470 as 20,000	1.09	$218.00 6.54	
		Total			$224.54	$63.86

Interest demanded on this claim at the rate of 6 % per annum from date of collection until paid.
Authority for rate or classification claimed EC-15-K, IT. 110, Simsbury takes Hartford rates; Item 6757
Give, as far as practicable, Tariff reference (I. C. C. number, effective date and page or item).

IN ADDITION TO THE INFORMATION GIVEN ABOVE, THE FOLLOWING DOCUMENTS ARE SUBMITTED IN SUPPORT OF THIS CLAIM*

( ) 1. Original paid freight ("expense") bill.
( ) 2. Original invoice, or certified copy, when claim is based on weight or valuation, or when shipment has been improperly described.
( ) 3. Original Bill of Lading, if not previously surrendered to carrier, when shipment was prepaid, or when claim is based on misrouting or valuation.
( ) 4. Weight certificate or certified statement when claim is based on weight.
( ) 5. Other particulars obtainable in proof of Overcharge claimed:†

Remarks Bond of Indemnity issued in lieu of original paid freight bill and Bill of Lading.

The foregoing statement of facts is hereby certified to as correct.

ABC Products, Inc.
(Signature of claimant) Traffic Mgr.

‡Claimant should assign to each claim a number, inserting same in the space provided at the upper right hand corner of this form. Reference should be made thereto in all correspondence pertaining to this claim.
*Claimant will please place check (X) before such of the documents mentioned as have been attached, and explain under "Remarks" the absence of any of the documents called for in connection with this claim. When for any reason it is impossible for claimant to produce original bill of lading if required, or paid freight bill, claimant should indemnify carrier or carriers against duplicate claim supported by original documents.
†Claims for overcharge on shipments of lumber should also be supported by a statement of the number of feet, dimensions, kind of lumber and length of time on sticks before being shipped.
Claims based on rates quoted in letters from traffic officials should be supported by the original or copies of such letters.

FIG. 18–5. Standard form for presentation of overcharge claims.

troversial nature of claims and the fact that final recourse in the event of carrier declination lies with the courts and not the Interstate Commerce Commission, it must be stressed that claims of a doubtful nature are not to be filed. Once a claim is filed, however, there should be no compromise and it should stand on its own merits. Ample time should be given the carrier to investigate fully the claim, since a carrier may be cited by the Commission for rebating in the event of payment of loss and damage claims not justified by the facts. Generally speaking, either a check in full

BOND OF INDEMNITY

Whereas, the undersigned cannot produce the original bill of lading
paid freight bill and in consideration of the payment of $________ in full settlement of loss & damage
overcharge
Claim No. ________ on shipment covered thereby, the undersigned hereby agree to protect and indemnify the

____

or any other carrier or carriers interested in this adjustment, against any other claim or claims which may be presented thereon, whether supported by the original bill of lading
paid freight bill or otherwise; and further protect the said ________________________________
and other interested carriers, if any, against legal proceedings, counsel fees, costs or other expenses which may be incurred by reason of claim referred to above, without surrender of the original bill of lading.
paid freight bill.

XYZ PRODUCTS, INC.

Witness: ________________ Signed: ________________

TRAFFIC DEPARTMENT

FIG. 18–6. Bond of indemnity.

payment or a letter of declination will be forwarded to the claimant within a period of one or two months. If a legitimate claim is declined, the claimant has full access to the courts for establishing the carrier's guilt.

The claim file to be presented to the negligent carrier should include a standard form for presentation of loss and damage claims, certified copies of original invoices, carrier inspection report, original paid freight bill and bill of lading or in lieu thereof a bond of indemnity agreement, and copies of correspondence applicable to the claim. Samples of the above-mentioned documents are shown in Figs. 18–4 to 18–6.

Claims for loss or damage must be filed with either the originating or delivering carrier during a period of nine months from date of delivery or, in the case of loss, after reasonable time for delivery has elapsed.

Loss, damage, and delay exist because of the innumerable unforeseeable incidents which may affect the transportation of goods. Despite the prevalance of loss, damage, and delay, there should be no relaxation on the part of the shipper, receiver, or carrier in the maintenance of an effective claim prevention program. Since goods destroyed are lost forever, the payment of loss and damage claims by the carrier is economic waste. The carrier in preparing his price lists must consider the risk element pertaining to loss or damage of property in transit. If claim payments continue to rise, the inevitable result is an upward revision in the rate structure. In the final analysis, the prevention of claims is of far greater benefit to the shipper, receiver, and carrier than the monetary reimbursement actually received.

BIBLIOGRAPHY

Reference publications and services on traffic and transportation considerations are cited on the following pages of this section: 18–1, 18–12, 18–13, and 18–14. Additional ones are listed in Section 26, "Library and Catalog File."

SECTION 19

PUBLIC PURCHASING

Editor

John F. Ward, Director of Purchases, Contracts and Supplies, City of Chicago, Chicago, Illinois

Associate Editors

STATE

G. Lloyd Nunnally, Director, Department of Purchases and Supply, Commonwealth of Virginia, Richmond, Virginia

COUNTY

Verne O. Gehringer, Purchasing Agent, County of San Diego, San Diego, California

CITY

John G. Krieg, City Purchasing Agent, City of Cincinnati, Cincinnati, Ohio

PUBLIC INSTITUTIONS

Aldan F. O'Hearn, Director of Purchases, Board of Education, Chicago, Illinois

QUASI-PUBLIC ACTIVITIES

Edward R. Jones, Director of Purchasing, New York State Thruway Authority, Albany, New York

It is the purpose of this section to describe the processes and practices involved in the purchasing programs of such public entities as state, county, and city governments; the Federal government; education, hospital, and other nonprofit public institutions; and quasi-public organizations.

It is *not* the purpose of this section to instruct the public purchasing agent on how to buy the variegated commodity classes which are required for use by public entities; or to supply detailed guidance on other technical aspects of the purchasing function. The public purchasing agent should read *all* the sections of this handbook, since the principles and practices discussed in other sections are generally applicable to both private and public buying. He will, however, find in this section a discussion of those principles and requirements which are peculiar to public purchasing. A selected bibliography on the subject of governmental purchasing will be found at the end of this section.

Although the principles of both public and private purchasing are basically the same, purchasing for a nonprofit, tax-supported organization involves special considerations which do not affect the purchaser for a private business or corporation. Both are concerned with obtaining the proper quality of merchandise at the best price and at the right time. Both take into consideration the assurance of supplier's performance as to satisfactory service, adequate production and distribution facilities, prompt delivery schedules, and other necessary contract requirements.

The important additional considerations in public purchasing result primarily from the use of public funds and certain restrictions designed to control the expenditure of the taxpayer's dollar. Such controls are in the form of specific laws and regulations, competitive bidding, fixed budgetary limitations, rigid auditing of accounts, and prescribed specifications.

GROWTH AND DEVELOPMENT OF PUBLIC BUYING

On May 8, 1792, the Second Congress passed the first law regulating government procurement. This authority, contained in section 5, 1 Stat. 280, provided that all purchases and contracts for supplies or articles for use by the Department of War be made by or under the direction of the Treasury Department.[1]

It was not until 1861 that the first Federal statute requiring advertising for competitive bids in public purchasing was enacted.[2] This law is the cornerstone of public purchasing in this country. Since that time the same basic principles have been adopted by most cities, counties, and states.

The growth of public buying since 1950 is illustrated by the following table in calendar years:

Government Purchases of Goods and Services
(In Billions of Dollars)

	1950	1954	1957	1960	1962	1963	1964
Federal	19.5	49.5	50.1	53.8	63.8	65.5	65.3
National Defense	14.3	43.2	44.4	45.7	53.6	55.2	49.9
Other	5.2	6.3	5.7	8.1	10.2	10.3	15.4
State and local	19.7	27.8	36.8	46.5	53.5	57.9	63.1
Total	39.2	77.3	86.9	100.3	117.3	123.4	128.4

SOURCE: *Federal Reserve Bulletin.*

UNIQUE FACTORS IN PUBLIC PURCHASING

Public Purchases for Use Rather than Resale or Manufacture

Because of the general policy that government should not engage in manufacturing operations in competition with private industry, public

[1] Clifton E. Mack, "Federal Procurement," Government Printing Office, Washington, D.C., 1943.

[2] Civil Sundry Appropriations Act, March 2, 1861 (12 Stat. 220; later section 3709 R.S., also section 3710).

purchases are almost exclusively for use rather than for resale or manufacture.

The public purchasing agent is, therefore, not ordinarily involved in coordinating purchases and deliveries of various raw materials for use in the manufacturing process, nor is he entangled in the complications of speculative buying and like problems so common to industrial buying.

The emphasis in public purchasing has therefore been to obtain greater value for the tax dollar by developing specifications and standards of quality and performance which apply to end products rather than to raw materials.

Purchasing Records Open for Public Inspection

Of considerable importance to the private buyer is his prerogative of secret negotiations. It has been alleged that this confidential relationship between buyer and seller is the basis for many special discounts and reduced prices which under competitive bidding would not be possible. Such pricing practices, however, fall within the limitations of the Robinson-Patman Act and care must be exercised to avoid jeopardizing the legal position of both buyer and seller. In public purchasing the bidder knows his bid prices will be available to his competition when bids are publicly opened. While public opening minimizes illegal price cutting, it encourages the submission of the bidder's "best price" in his bid tender.

Restricted Use of Public Funds

In general, the private purchasing agent is concerned with budget limitations only to the extent that he may be required to stay within the limits of an over-all operating fund, without restrictions on the purchase of any class of supplies or commodities.[3] This is particularly true because of the many uncertainties and fluctuations of supply requirements in commercial enterprise. If he has the opportunity to make a particularly advantageous purchase he may, in most cases, do so without regard to budgetary restrictions.

In contrast, the public purchasing agent usually operates under a restrictive budget which depends, either directly or indirectly (through a working capital fund) upon yearly appropriations for support. These budgets are prepared many months in advance. Unless budgeted purchase programs are based on firm requirements, the buyer may encounter shortages or overages in funds near the close of the fiscal year, both of which create problems.

Because of the necessity for strict control over public funds, purchase requests must be certified by the financial department and funds must be

[3] See Section 22, "Purchasing Department Budgets."

obligated before a purchase can be made. In most cases there are specific limitations in the budget on how much money may be expended for each class of commodity. Special provisions in Federal and in some state and local agencies require that listings of excess and surplus public property be checked to determine if present inventories can be used to fill current requirements. There are also specific controls on inventory "ceilings."

The auditing of public purchase transactions is also an exacting process intended to reveal any variations from prescribed laws and regulations.

Incentives

Procurement savings and economies are an important segment of the responsibilities of the private purchasing agent. A capable and successful buyer may be rewarded for outstanding accomplishment by salary increases, by company dividends, or by promotion. These incentives are usually sufficient to attract and retain competent, well-qualified personnel.

In the field of public purchasing the retention of competent procurement officials is a constant problem. Civil Service grades for purchasing officials are low by industry standards, particularly in the higher brackets. Public purchasing employees must be adequately trained and have to their credit years of procurement experience before they can qualify as experts in this field. There are many outstanding public purchasing officials whose initiative and foresight are saving the taxpayer millions of dollars, but whose efforts go unnoticed.

PUBLIC PURCHASING LAWS AND ADMINISTRATIVE REGULATIONS

In government as well as private industry purchasing procedures must conform to the diverse needs of the using agency. Most laws which establish public purchasing departments also prescribe the basic principles under which they must operate. The individual and varied requirements of state, local, and Federal governments, as interpreted by officials with a limited tenure of office, make *complete* standardization of purchasing laws neither practicable nor desirable.

Similarities and Variations in Public Purchasing Laws

Definite progress is being made, however, in unifying certain basic laws which apply to common purchasing practices. There is a marked similarity for instance between the various Federal, state, county, and city laws and regulations which require competitive bidding on contracts above a specified dollar value, public advertising for solicitation of bids, circulation of invitations to bid (use of bidders' list), public opening of bids, and the awarding of the contract to the lowest responsible bidder. Also public purchasing records are generally available for inspection by any interested party.

There are many variations in state, county, and city purchasing laws, with regard to the purchasing department's scope of authority. In some jurisdictions, the purchasing agency has the statutory responsibility for all procurement operations involving real and personal property, as well as contractual services. In others, procurement of real and personal property is divided, with personal property being procured by a purchasing agency, and real property by a public works or similar agency. Some laws and ordinances specifically exempt certain agencies, such as educational institutions, liquor commissions, and highway departments, from central purchasing control. In other instances, specific commodities such as textbooks, perishables, and scientific equipment are exempted. Recent trends are toward total centralization of procurement.

Public laws and adminstrative regulations have, in general, tended to reduce the exercise of individual judgment and discretion by public purchasing agents. Sound specifications under the lowest responsible bid authority do much to overcome this restrictive factor. It is possible to obtain the "best buy" regardless of the implications of the competitive bid requirements. Public advertising is the safest method to protect the public interest.

Every public purchasing agent should have a sufficient knowledge of his governing law to understand the legal relationship between himself, the agency he serves, and the general public with whom he deals. He should also be able to recognize situations where there is a need for obtaining legal guidance. In addition, public purchasing officials must also have knowledge, in varying degrees, of literally hundreds of ever-changing government policies and regulations affecting the expenditure of public funds.

Public Competitive Bidding versus Industrial Negotiation

Most governmental regulations require that purchases in excess of a specified amount, usually within the range of $500 to $5,000, shall be supported by a written contract, after public advertisement and receipt of sealed bids. Such bids must be publicly opened and the award must be made to the lowest or lowest responsible bidder.

These rules are intended to secure the lowest price for the government and also to protect the interest of the seller by providing an equal competitive opportunity to bid on government contracts. In private purchasing the buyer, in most cases, may buy without competitive bidding, may negotiate for any quantity regardless of its dollar value, may buy from any vendor, and may keep all purchase records on a confidential basis.

"Buy at Home" Policy

Some state laws require local purchase on certain commodities such as coal, and a few make all "in-state" manufactured products mandatory, with varied price differentials up to 5 per cent. More than half of the states, however, have no provisions for mandatory local purchase. Currently, 15 state laws specify that local sources of supply should be given some form of preference.

In the case of the Federal government, the basic policy, as contained in the "Buy American Act" of March, 1933, is to use domestic sources when the requirement is available in sufficient quantity. Exceptions may be granted when the application of the act would be inconsistent with the public interest, or when it would unreasonably increase the cost.

City ordinances vary on the policy of buying locally produced merchandise. Most large cities have adopted specific policies for the control of foreign-made goods. Many now permit the purchase of foreign-made goods offered by the low responsible bidder when such goods are fully comparable to those made in the United States, quality, service, and availability of repair parts being duly considered.

There appears to be a general trend in governmental purchasing not to use public funds for the support of local sources of supply unless they can compete on an equal basis. The private purchasing agent, however, can often benefit from advantages in his evalution of local sources of supply, such as prompt deliveries, better service, savings in transportation, and convenience of inspection at the source.

Extent of Purchasing Authority

One of the fundamental goals of public purchasing is to meet supply needs with the minimum expenditure of public funds. Efforts to further this objective have resulted in three major progressive developments in public purchasing: (1) centralized purchasing; (2) centralized *procurement* which emphasizes some of the supply functions traditionally excluded from *purchase* (procurement includes the obtaining of supplies through utilization of excess property, the repair or rehabilitation of used property, and consideration of all aspects of a new purchase from its receipt to payment of the invoice, including storage, inspection, and distribution); and (3) centralized supply management.

There is a definite trend toward consolidating purchasing with other "supply management" functions as a means of achieving efficiency, better customer service, and more economic operations. The "supply management" concept includes principle considerations as follows:

1. Minimizing new purchases through an adequate property management system

2. Consideration of all costs for supplies up to delivery at point of use
3. Current information on inventories, commodities, markets, and prices
4. Information relative to new developments of materials, methods of distribution, and improved methods of packing and packaging
5. Increasing competition on purchases through the use of purchase specifications and carefully selected, qualified sources of supply

State statutes are not uniform in prescribing the extent of authority vested in the purchasing division or department. To a large degree this is due to conditions such as the population and the geographical area to be served.

Some state statutes specify that the purchasing division shall prescribe the manner in which supplies, materials, and equipment shall be purchased, delivered, stored, and distributed. Some place the responsibility in the purchasing division for fixing standards of quality and quantity; developing standard specifications; control of central storerooms; transfer of surplus, obsolete, or unused property; and inspection and testing. Under this broad authority the purchase division has direct control over all supply management functions and can coordinate them in a manner best designed to achieve maximum effectiveness and economy of operations. Many states have recognized the advantages of this type of control and have provided the necessary authority in their statutes. Some states, however, have supply management functions divided between two or more departments.

A large number of *cities* with centralized purchasing have placed supply management functions under the control of their purchasing office. Milwaukee, Chicago, and Richmond, Virginia, are specific examples.

Dollar Limitation Determines Type of Purchase

Public purchasing statutes vary to a considerable degree in the maximum dollar limitation on open-market purchases. Such purchases are of relatively small value and do not usually require public advertising for bids or the furnishing of bid deposits and performance bonds. Nevertheless, in many governments, sealed bids are usually obtained and in most cases at least three competitive bids are secured. Almost invariably, purchases over the maximum dollar limitation must be made by formal *contracts.*

More than half of *state* statutes permit informal bids for open-market purchases in an amount ranging from $1,000 to as high as $3,000. Some larger *cities* have found it necessary to establish an even higher limitation, as is the case in Milwaukee where the limit is $5,000.

The limitation on *Federal* agencies is usually set at $500, although there are certain exceptions. For instance, the General Services Administration and the Department of Defense are permitted to buy up to $1,000 without formal advertising.

Quasi-public organizations report a limitation range of from $50 to $5,000, averaging $1,000.

Many purchasing officials feel that an extremely low dollar limitation on informal bids for open-market purchases impairs the efficiency of a purchasing office. Actual experience indicates that the requirement for advertising for bids on low-value purchases causes unnecessary delays and extra costs. Also a $500 limitation established fifteen years ago will buy but a fraction of that total at today's prices. A review or special study by each public purchasing entity to determine the satisfactory dividing line between formal and informal purchases would appear advisable.

Management Tools for Administrative Control

In order to keep abreast of his operations and be able to take prompt remedial action where necessary, the purchasing agent must use specific reporting and statistical devices. These may include any of the following:

Dollar volume by commodity, department, or buyer
Number of purchase orders issued and purchases completed
Number of items per purchase order and number of bids per invitation
Number of emergency orders by buyer, department, and dollar volume
Petty cash and small-order activities
Cost data per purchase order, per total operations, per department, etc.
Data on volume of cash and quantity discounts
Transfers and sales of excess and surplus property
Warehouse stock turnover, inventory, operating costs, stock ratios, etc.
Standardization statistics and activities
Rejections, sales interviews, clerical production, and miscellaneous such as commodity code revisions

Also of importance are regular monthly, annual, and special reports on operations, which are directed to the heads of government or management, or for use in press or public relations.

While the above management tools are based on *quantity* controls and statistics, it is also equally important that purchase transactions be constantly reviewed to determine the *quality* of the buying job.[4]

CENTRALIZED PUBLIC PURCHASING

Centralized procurement is now quite generally recognized as a basic element in good management. It is important, however, to point out that

[4] "Method by Which Quantity and Quality Performance of a Public Purchasing Agency May Be Measured," National Institute of Governmental Purchasing, Inc., 1963.

the term "centralized," as used herein, does not mean full or complete consolidation of all purchase requirements. As a general rule most centralized purchasing systems allow certain departments or commodities to be under separate procurement jurisdiction.

Very few state and local governments have complete centralization. In most cases such departments as state colleges and universities, public libraries, water works, alcohol control boards, highway departments, or commodities such as "perishables," are under separate control.

Nevertheless, *the basis for exemption should be commodities rather than agencies.* As illustration, a public library usually desires to be exempt because the purchasing of books is a highly specialized function. On the other hand, the fuel, furniture, and other commodities required by a library are admirably adapted to centralized procurement.

Principles and Objectives

The objectives of centralized purchasing in governments are fundamental to any efficient administration. They include lower unit costs of commodity requirements, reduction in personnel and other administrative costs, less paper work, closer control over expenditures, advancement of standardization, better utilization of property procured at public expense, and other related facets of efficient management.

Such benefits should not be expected to follow automatically the establishment of a centralized purchasing system unless it is properly organized and basic purchasing principles are intelligently applied. It is also essential that the purchasing agent have *authority* commensurate with his *responsibility.*

Legal Authority for Centralized Purchasing

The basic requirements in any authorizing public law or charter should establish the title of the purchasing agency, its place in the government structure, and the scope of its powers and duties. In general practice these provisions are usually determined by local conditions.[5]

State statutes establishing centralized purchasing vary in the detail of authority and scope of operations. In general, most state statutes vest authority in the purchasing official for the procurement of commodities and services for all state agencies, but authorize him to prescribe conditions under which an agency can be delegated direct purchasing authority. They also authorize the purchasing official to prescribe the methods for purchase, delivery, storage, and distribution; requisitioning; establishing standards; transfer or sale of surpluses; inspection and other related purchasing or supply management functions.

[5] Russell Forbes, Ph.D., "Purchasing Laws," National Association of Purchasing Agents, 1941.

State laws, in many cases, were established without adequate recognition of the rapid growth in population, and resulting problems in such fields as purchasing. Consequently, some state purchasing statutes are vague and incomplete in their coverage.

County governments in most states are regulated by state law which provides for a purchasing system either by a special or a general statute. Because of vast differences in population, county purchasing requirements vary to a considerable degree. Since a heavily populated urban county requires an elaborate purchasing system, far beyond the means of the sparsely populated rural county, it is important that the general state statute give wide latitude to the county board in adopting rules and regulations which will best meet local conditions.

Centralized *city purchasing* is also best established by charter, without restrictive detail. Detailed policies can be provided by ordinances of the city council and thus be subject to revision as required by changing conditions. These should include salaries, the maximum amount which may be purchased without formal advertising, and amounts of bid deposits and contract performance bonds. Operating methods and procedures should be established by the purchasing department.

To illustrate centralization techniques in municipal procurement, part of the model city statute developed by the National Institute of Municipal Law Officers is included at the end of this section. This is an excerpt from the booklet "NIMLO Model Purchasing Ordinance–Annotated" (which is available from their Wasington, D.C., office at 726 Jackson Place, N.W.).

In public institutions the authority of the purchasing department should be based on a resolution, or standing orders, issued by the governing board. Generally, the governing boards, whether they be school boards, boards of directors, or other groups, delegate this basic authority to a vice-president, administrator, or business manager, with the understanding that he can, in turn, redelegate the authority to someone on his staff, such as the purchasing agent.

Quasi-public organizations of the "authority type," such as the Port of New York Authority, are engaged in such varied activities that their laws must be flexible with regard to purchasing policies and practices. In many cases such policies are developed by management officials of the authority in cooperation with the director of purchases.

The magnitude and technical nature of Federal government procurement makes it almost impossible to establish a completely centralized purchasing system. Consolidation of purchasing of certain common-use items for all departments might, however, be a practical and economical development.

Congress has recognized the above limitations and has directed its laws and recommendations concerning centralized procurement to classes of commodities common to all agencies. This was the basis for establishing the Federal Supply Service in the General Services Administration.

Organization

In most states, the purchasing agency is a division of an integrated management department, such as a department of administration or finance. In approximately one-fourth of the states, the purchasing agency is a separate department, generally responsible to the governor.

In county and city governments the purchasing agency is usually established as a department or bureau.

In the Federal government most agencies have a purchasing division which controls procurement functions. In larger agencies consisting of several bureaus, purchasing is usually the responsibility of an "office of administrative operations," or similar title, which office normally delegates purchasing authority for bureau requirements to each bureau. In the case of the General Services Administration the purchasing of common-use items for use by the executive agencies is the responsibility of the Federal Supply Service headed by a Commissioner, who is directly responsible to the Administrator of General Services.

In public institutions the location of the purchasing department in the organizational structure depends upon the size of the institution and the magnitude of the purchase volume. Under a centralized system in a large institution, purchasing and related functions are usually assigned to a separately established department responsible to the board of directors, and exercising such authority as the board may delegate.

Selection of Purchasing Department Personnel

In government and other public organizations the head of the purchasing department is usually appointed, or his appointment is approved, by the executive head, such as the administrator, governor, city manager or council, county manager or board, mayor, or institutional president.

Appointment of the head of the purchasing department is often effective only for the duration of the term of the appointing officer. In some states, counties, and cities, however, appointment is made for a specific term, usually two or four years. A total of 24 states currently provide for an indefinite or "no limit" term of office for the head of the purchasing department. In many of the public agencies in which the purchasing head is appointed rather than selected through civil service procedures, the subordinate purchasing staff is selected by the purchasing head from civil service registers.

The purchasing head, in eleven states, is selected on the basis of civil service examination, and his appointment is on a permanent basis. Subordinate employees in these states are likewise under the merit system.

It should be recognized that, under central control of purchases, a purchasing agent cannot devote all of his time to "buying." A purchase is not completed until the article has been received, inspected, tested for compliance with specifications, and the invoice has been paid. In a successful centralized purchasing department, the director must be a capable administrator as well as a thoroughly qualified, experienced buyer. See Section 23, "Selection and Training of Purchasing Personnel."

The purchasing organization should provide for specialized qualifications for subordinate personnel. The functions of buying, inspection, salvage, storeskeeping, inventory control, development, revision and control of forms, etc., should be handled by those especially trained for such operations.

Ethics and Political Influence[6]

In the administration of public purchasing, the influence of politics too often plays an important role. Any administration which recognizes its obligations to the taxpayer should, however, be aware of the desirability and importance of selecting and retaining a "career staff" of professionally qualified, experienced purchasing personnel. Such policy will inspire the public's faith in the administration's desire to achieve an honest, efficient, and economical purchasing system. Sound business administration is the best politics.

The complexities of a large centralized purchasing operation cannot be solved in a brief period of time. Nor can one develop a modern, efficient purchasing system which does not depend to some degree upon the ability and ingenuity of the experienced purchasing agent to solve emergency problems caused by ever-changing requirements and market conditions. The purchasing agent whose tenure of office is "at the pleasure" of an elective official or political appointee does not ordinarily have sufficient time or incentive to determine and promote the necessary measures to achieve maximum economy and efficiency in all areas of purchasing and supply management operations. This fact is acknowledged by the Federal government, by many states, and by some counties and cities. In such instances, competent purchasing personnel have been retained through changes of administration.

Purchasing personnel are more likely to have long tenure in office if they adhere to the following principles:

[6] Also see Section 6, "Ethical Practices in Purchasing."

1. Impartial relationship with bidders, vendors, industry groups, associations, and political factions.
2. The preparation of well-written reports to management which will gain recognition and publicity.
3. Continuous and good press relations which will constantly bring to the public's attention the work of the department and demonstrate their sound purchasing policies.
4. Manuals of operation which set forth the details of policy and procedures.[7] Wide distribution of manuals to all interested parties in sales, industry, and the press. Clear and informative instructions on how to sell to the government, which instructions should explain the so-called "red tape" and other common condemnations of public purchasing practices.

Civil Service Employees

It is generally accepted that civil service registers provide an excellent source of capable, qualified job candidates. Where the civil service system may be inadequate to provide the type of experienced personnel needed by the public purchasing department, it is advisable to cooperate with civil service officials in suggesting helpful revisions or changes in procedure.

Salaries

The salary of the purchasing agent or head of the purchasing department should depend upon the scope and nature of his responsibility. An annual salary of $25,000–$30,000 may be commensurate with the function of directing the centralized purchasing functions of a large densely populated city whereas a city having less purchasing activity may pay as little as $6,000. A purchasing agent whose functions are limited to buying should not receive as much salary as one who has additional responsibility for the operation of central stores, inspection, surplus, and other supply management functions.

Salary ranges of public purchasing agents in cities with a population of 10,000 to 25,000 average $6,000,[8] with the amount increasing in relationship with the size of the city. In cities with a population over 500,000 the average is around $12,685.[9] Salaries of state purchasing agents average close to $9,000 with the top reported salary being $20,000.[10] Civil service classifications, which cover Federal and some state and local

[7] See Section 3, "Policy and Procedure Manuals."

[8] *Municipal Year Book,* Cushing-Malloy, Inc., Ann Arbor, Michigan, 1960.

[9] *Municipal Year Book,* International City Manager's Association, Chicago, Ill., 1960.

[10] Survey conducted by Council of State Governments, 1737 K Street, N.W., Washington, D.C. See "Purchasing by the States."

purchasing officials range in the Federal government from Grade GS-4 procurement clerk, whose base salary is $4,110, up to a supervisory procurement officer, grade GS-15, whose salary range is from $15,665 to $19,270. Although it is possible to advance as high as grade GS-18, salary $20,000, purchasing in such positions is only one of many administrative responsibilities.

Considerations in Establishing a Centralized Public Purchasing Department

In determining the advisability of converting to a centralized public purchasing system the initial step is, of course, the decision by competent authority that such a policy is justified by reason of expected savings, a more satisfactory purchasing system, and more efficient management. Once this decision is made, it becomes necessary to draft adequate laws and regulations which will establish basic authority and organization.

In comparing the advantages and disadvantages of centralized purchasing, it is elementary that the efficiency and effectiveness of the existing decentralized system will play an important part. Thus in a large organization with volume purchases it may be found that consolidation of requirements may not substantially decrease acquisition costs, but will reduce personnel, paper work, and overhead costs. Perhaps the major advantage will be in better-quality goods at the same price, greater utilization, or better service. In most cases, however, the savings achieved through bulk purchasing are most widely quoted.

Advantages of Centralized Purchasing

1. *Lower unit costs* should be obtained by bulk purchases resulting from consolidation of the requirements of many using departments. In analyzing such savings, one must discount those reductions in cost through bulk purchases which are caused by policy changes rather than by a consolidation of requirements. Procurement of a three years' supply of an item, for instance, in place of a normal one year's supply, falls in this category.

2. *Small orders and emergency purchases* will be reduced to a minimum under an efficiently operated centralized purchasing system by consolidating and scheduling requirements.

3. *Reduction in overhead costs through reduction of personnel* should be achieved through the elimination or consolidation of the purchasing personnel in many separate buying organizations.

4. *The volume of paper work will be reduced* by reason of fewer purchase orders, bids, invoices, vouchers, and related accounting documents.

5. *Procedures and processes will be standardized* because of centralized control, resulting in savings of time and labor and increased efficiency.

6. *Standards and specifications should be reduced or unified* to a large degree since a centralized purchasing system will usually require a special group or "board of standardization." Under decentralized purchasing various buying departments are usually not large enough to bear the additional cost of assigning the responsibility to full-time employees.

7. *Delayed deliveries and rush orders will be minimized* because of centralized control. Systematic schedules can be developed because bids and orders will be processed in a normal, orderly fashion. Central maintenance of purchasing records on repetitive items will anticipate departmental requirements in sufficient time for "assurance of supply when needed."

8. *Increased efficiency should result from centralized supervision over inspection* by sampling and testing of deliveries; storage, issuance, and distribution of stocks; interdepartmental transfers; and trade-in or sale of surplus or obsolete commodities.

9. *Closer accounting control over expenditures* should bring savings through the consolidation of purchasing budgets and cooperation between the purchasing and budget offices. Unexpended appropriation balances at the close of the fiscal year will be under better control and expenditures will be subject to specific approval. Cash discounts can be more closely supervised and important savings effected. Exemptions from Federal excise taxes are granted to states and their political subdivisions *if the proper exemption certificates are filed.* Under centralized control the filing of such certificates would be systematic routine.

10. *Buying techniques should be improved and favoritism discouraged* through a consolidated grouping of full-time, trained buyers with a combined knowledge of supply sources, requirements, market trends, prices, manufacturing processes, past purchasing records, and other pertinent purchasing information. Uniform quality and price are difficult to control when the same item is purchased by a multiplicity of buying offices.

11. *Problems of the supplier should be simplified* by a reduction in the number of orders and deliveries, by less paper work and account keeping, and by the convenience of having the purchasing activities in one location so that salesmen can conduct their business on a "one-stop" basis with experienced purchasing personnel.

12. *Unified prices for the same commodity.* One of the more important advantages of centralized purchasing is the opportunity it automatically creates to check the prices paid by various departments for identical items. In numerous instances it has been found that one department is paying several cents a pound or a gallon more than another for such common items as bread, gasoline, fuel oil, liquid soap, and paint, even though the quantity purchased is comparable.

Comments on Savings

Although it is generally estimated that centralized buying should result in average savings of around 15 per cent there are no exact statistics to prove or disprove any given percentage. As previously indicated, the percentage of savings depends to a large degree upon the efficiency of the prior decentralized purchasing organization.

Substantial discounts may be obtained by states and local governments by consolidating contracts for incandescent lamps and similar articles purchased in large quantities. Such an area-wide contract may not be desirable if only a few individual contracts are involved, each with a sufficiently large volume to warrant maximum discounts.

It may well be, however, that, as is the case in many public utility contracts, an area-wide contract may result in the elimination of several hundred individual contracts and worthwhile savings in administrative costs and contract simplification. Such was the case in New York City where the separate contracts of 400 government agencies were consolidated under one area-wide contract, with each agency billed separately. Throughout the United States there is a general trend for area-wide contracts at filed rates, approved by the commission with jurisdiction.

Beverly Hills, California, for example, showed savings on annual costs of office supplies of 42 per cent, less an estimated 2 per cent to cover overhead expenses of the purchasing system. A large eastern city reduced the number of full- and part-time employees engaged in purchasing activities from approximately 250 to 37 through centralized purchasing. When a central buying office was established in one western state a staff of 8 people took over the work of approximately 50 former employees. These cases are more extreme than the average, for which any number of examples could be cited.

The above comments are not intended to prove the infallibility of centralized purchasing. They indicate that, under normal conditions, centralized buying should reduce the over-all cost of supplies, personnel costs, and administrative expenses. It should also be noted that certain of these advantages must be carefully analyzed with a clear and complete understanding of ultimate objectives and policies involved. For example, lower unit costs may not always be the most desirable factor, since greater value may sometimes be obtained by the purchase of higher-quality and higher-priced merchandise.

The Cost of Centralized Purchasing

In 1948 the average cost of operating centralized purchasing departments was slightly over 1 per cent. Present surveys (1964) indicate very little change and range up to 1.2 per cent. Professional purchasing agents and consultants seldom rely on these criteria as measuring devices of purchase performance because the elements of costs and purchase functions vary widely in even centralized systems. Poor buying and higher prices appear to enhance the percentage factor.

The *state* survey previously mentioned[11] showed a $939,783,000 volume of centralized purchases for the 37 states reporting, at a cost of $6,000,535 or 0.64 per cent of the value of purchases made. These figures are for the fiscal year 1954.

Federal government costs are difficult to determine since administrative expenses in most cases cover portions of centralized, partially centralized, and decentralized operations. Headquarters purchasing and related personnel are often used to control all three types of systems. In some cases agency accounting procedures do not permit a segregation of centralized purchasing costs.

Experience shows that the cost of large Federal procurement programs may figure but a fraction of 1 per cent of the dollar value of the product involved, whereas low dollar volume purchases usually result in an extremely high cost percentage. Thus an agency or system with a preponderance of large purchases would reflect a much lower cost percentage by volume than the low dollar volume agency, even though the latter's operations are more efficient.

Extent of Centralized Public Buying

Governmental agencies buy supplies, materials, and equipment of practically every known type and description. More recently, the trend in public buying goes beyond the purchase or lease of personal property. Public Works Construction Contracts are being let by the Centralized Buying Agency.

The *Federal government* has made steady progress toward centralized control over purchasing. The General Services Administration was created July 1, 1949, by Public Law 152 (81st Cong.). It is charged, among other functions, with responsibility for central procurement of Federal personal property, and for the development of procurement policies applicable to other Federal buying agencies. The discharge of these responsibilities requires a certain degree of decentralization to each of the ten General Services Administration regional offices.

General Services Administration procurement programs for personal property are in two major categories: (1) regular procurement programs for supplies and services, mostly of the types in common use in Federal

[11] See footnote 10 on page 19–15.

executive agencies; and (2) emergency procurement programs for the national stockpile, foreign aid, and defense production.

Important advancements have also been made in centralized *military procurement* of certain product classes whereby one department buys all military requirements, or where one service, bureau, or command buys for all the other units of its department.

Centralized purchasing is indicated to have had its initial trial in *state government* as early as 1899 when Texas created the office of purchasing agent for certain state institutions.[12] Several partially centralized systems were established soon after the turn of the century and by 1915 the movement was rapidly gaining momentum.

A survey of all forty-eight states was conducted by the Council of State Governments in Washington, D.C., in June, 1955.[13] Replies indicated that all except three states had centralized their purchasing to at least a partial degree.

Vigorous activities on the part of the National Association of County Officials during the past few years has had its effect on centralizing purchases in county governments. While many of the 3,074 counties are small, with relatively minor purchasing volume, more and more of the counties faced with an urban growth now have successfully centralized their purchasing operations. Today, 37 of the 58 counties in California have centralized purchasing. *The Municipal Year Book* for the year 1963 indicates 10 additional counties across the nation have instituted a centralized purchasing system.

Of eighteen *quasi-public organizations* of the "authority" type, all have centralized their purchasing operations.

An "authority" is a governmental business corporation set up outside the normal structure of traditional government to give continuity, business efficiency, and elastic management to the construction or operation of a self-supporting or revenue-producing public enterprise.[14]

These authorities are generally organized for the construction or operation of seaports, turnpikes, toll bridges, water systems and terminals, tunnels, public housing developments, and, in some instances, such unusual activities as gymnasiums, theaters, and even factory buildings. In general, they follow the same purchasing policies and practices in use by other governmental entities.

Centralized purchasing practices predominate in these organizations despite the variety of requirements and the area in terms of miles of high-

[12] Russell Forbes, Ph.D., "Governmental Purchasing," Harper & Brothers, New York, 1929.

[13] In "Purchasing by the States," published July, 1956.

[14] "Authorities and How to Use Them," *The Tax Review,* Tax Foundation, New York.

way that some cover. The top purchasing official is selected through civil service in only 5 of 19 agencies. In seven cases, appointment is by the Board, and the balance are appointed by members of management.

Authorities usually are independent of the state purchasing department but most cooperate with the state office and take advantage of its contracts. The annual volume of authority purchases ranges from $40,000 to $15,000,000. Most authorities have a dollar limit above which sealed bids are required. This limit ranges from $100 to $2,500 and appears to depend on the annual dollar purchase volume.

In the larger authorities purchasing is a separate department or bureau. In the smaller ones it is generally a unit within a department or combined with the finance department.

The following table shows the status of centralized purchasing in *cities* of over 10,000 population in 1957:[15]

	No. of cities	Per cent of cities reporting	Cities with central purchasing departments
Cities over 500,000	17	100.0	17
Cities 250,000 to 500,000	21	100.0	21
Cities 100,000 to 250,000	57	82.4	47
Cities 50,000 to 100,000	106	79.2	84
Cities 25,000 to 50,000	226	68.5	155
Cities 10,000 to 25,000	584	65.7	384
All cities over 10,000	1,011	70.0	708

The above table is the latest information compiled by *The Municipal Year Book*. However, many additional municipalities have established centralized systems since these data were developed.

The larger hospitals, universities, and other *public institutions* have found centralized purchasing very adaptable to their type of operations, which are generally limited to a relatively homogeneous personnel.

THE PURCHASING PROCESS

Under the competitive system it is necessary to ensure a clear undertanding between buyer and seller as to the exact nature of the product o be purchased, to avoid difficulty in evaluating bids, to obtain the maxinum number of bids, to receive the best price, and to ensure delivery of he exact product desired.

[15] *The Municipal Year Book,* International City Manager's Association, Chicago, Ill.

The public purchasing agent must avoid any semblance of favoritism, patronage, and personal preference in his selection of suppliers. Formal advertising for competitive bids is the basic rule and negotiated purchases are authorized only as "exceptions." His selection of a source of supply must conform to regulations or be subject to public criticism. Under these circumstances, the government's source of supply is usually limited to the lowest or lowest responsible bidder.

To achieve maximum effectiveness a centralized purchasing organization should, as one of its first steps, standardize requirements by reducing to the minimum the varieties of commodities used by the different agencies or departments. When this is done, it becomes possible to consolidate requirements for common-use items into bulk purchases.

Most large public purchasing organizations have established a special unit which is responsible for standardization of the commodities purchased.

Standards and Specifications

In public purchasing, standardization is essential to efficient and effective supply management because it adopts as standard those items which are most economical and best suited to serve the needs of using departments. The process eliminates duplicate items, and those which are unnecessary or wasteful, and establishes a clear basis to consolidate the items being used by several departments. Otherwise, each may purchase unnecessary or undesirable variations of similar types of equipment and supplies. Uniform standard purchase specifications are necessary to obtain free and open competition in bids on a fair and equitable basis. They ensure that the public buying agency obtains the item it specifies and pays for—at lowest cost.[16]

In centralized public purchasing, standardization is a normal requirement because of the consolidation of many buying departments, many of which may be purchasing the same type of equipment or supplies. The grouping of like items under a single purchase order or contract necessitates a common specification.

It is important that all specifications be reviewed periodically to keep pace with technological advances. This will prevent the purchase of obsolete designs and types of merchandise and will give the community the benefit of the latest and most modern and adaptable materials, supplies, and equipment.

Purchase specifications should concisely define that quality level or levels of a product that are required to meet user needs and at the same time provide as wide competition in sources of supply as is possible. The

[16] See Section 9, "Pricing Considerations."

provisions should be so stated as to avoid misinterpretation and to ensure that bids can be equitably compared and evaluated.

Commodity standardization has for its goal the establishment of standard items agreed upon by using departments. Savings are effected by reducing to the minimum the number of qualities, sizes, colors, varieties, and types of commodities. To be practicable, standardization must meet user needs, take into account commercially available products, and reflect supply-demand requirements and established inventory levels.

The preparation of standards can be done on a decentralized basis. Standardization or specification projects may be assigned to a specific department having engineering competence and major interest in the supply item to be standardized. Such assignments should always be supervised by the responsible authority, that is, the chief purchasing official or standardization board. On such assignments they must be coordinated with other departments having an interest through the central authority.

Many local governments have standing committees on standards and specifications. Such committees meet at the request of the purchasing agent to examine tentative or proposed specifications, to assist in formulating new specifications, to interview prospective bidders with reference to specifications proposed for use, and to decide whether specifications will provide maximum competition.

Federal Specifications. General Services Administration issues Federal specifications which cover common-use items regularly used by all Federal agencies. They establish the minimum standards of quality or performance which are required to meet the Federal government's needs consistent with regularly available commercial production.

More than 5,500 Federal specifications covering over 850,000 items have been developed and issued to date. An index to Federal specifications may be obtained from the Superintendent of Documents, Government Printing Office, Washington, D.C. 20025. Individual specifications are available for inspection at regional offices of the General Services Administration. Federal specifications may be purchased from the General Services Administration, Regional Business Service Center, Washington, D.C. 20025.

The Department of Defense has made notable progress in standardizing military equipment. For example, by standardizing specifications 47 various types of combat tanks have been reduced to 13, with only 4 different engines needed to service *all 13 types of tanks.* Previously a selection of 5 engines for *each tank* was required. Tank parts were reduced from 5,364 to 2,066.

Federal Standards. The General Services Administration has standardized a number of categories of administrative type, commonly used items such as furniture, paper, janitorial and office supplies, and electrical appliances. Approximately 150 such standards have been promulgated to date and much more remains to be done.

Development of Public Purchase Specifications. To be of maximum value, purchase specifications should describe the article clearly and in sufficient detail to ensure delivery of the product desired. They should provide for free and open competition and for inspection by the purchaser. They should, as far as possible, provide for the purchase of standard products rather than special manufacture. Consideration should be given to provisions that will ensure availability of local repair services and availability of parts in connection with mechanical and technical equipment.

In recent years there has been a definite trend toward the use of "performance" type specifications. This type sets forth the end use performance needs rather than detailed formulations or construction details. This gives manufacturers a chance to use their best technical "know-how" resources to provide an item which will serve the customers declared needs. It is one medium of avoiding "closed specifications." Customers' detailed specifications, many times, result in unintentionally excluding some desirable bidder from competition.

In all cases justified by the purchase volume, or where safety of human life or property is a consideration, there should be full-time assignments to individuals or groups for developing top-quality, standardized specifications. If possible this group should include engineers, chemists, and other qualified technicians as well as representatives from the using agencies or departments. Participation through consultation with, and comments of, representative suppliers is important to ensure that the requirements of the specification are practical in terms of regularly manufactured competitive items.

More and more state, county, and municipal purchasing agencies are establishing standards units within their organizations. These units are usually headed by a qualified engineer, whose full-time duties are devoted to the development of commodity standards. In addition, some public agencies employ the use of advisory committees which include representatives of the various using agencies. The use of such advisory committees makes available a large force of individuals who are expert in various commodity fields and who are technically qualified to render valuable assistance in furthering a sound standards program. Such advisory committees also help to speed up the program of standardization, and attain the desirable end of having the active participation of the using agency in establishing and developing sound specifications describing such standards. Standards and specifications, to be really effective and worthwhile must produce results in the form of commodities which will most effectively serve the needs of the users, at the lowest unit of service cost.

In practically all *states* where purchasing is centralized, the purchasing agency has authority to write or adopt standard specifications.

Standards and Specifications Developed at National Level. Increasingly wider use is being made of standards and specifications developed at the national level, including specifications developed by the Federal government, American Standards Association, American Society for Testing and Materials, and the numerous national trade organizations.

Such organizations as the National Association of Purchasing Agents[17] and the National Institute of Governmental Purchasing[18] are vitally concerned with the importance of standards and specifications and in many instances can provide valuable information and technical assistance.

The National Association of State Purchasing Officials, for which the Council of State Governments[19] serves as secretariat, has conducted industry surveys through its member states on all Federal specifications to determine their suitability for use in state purchasing. The program was supervised by a Committee on Standards, which issues specification reports to all states recommending the use of those Federal specifications which the surveys indicate as being suitable for state use. Current plans call for the program to encompass specifications prepared by other Federal agencies as well as specifications developed on a national scale by technical standards organizations and trade associations. It is expected that substantial progress toward standardization of state purchasing specifications on a nationwide basis will result from this program.

Buying by Qualified Products or Acceptable Brands Lists. The Federal Qualified Products List is a list of products which have been tested and found to conform to the requirements of the applicable Federal specifications. These lists are developed only where it is not possible to write specification requirements adequate to the quality and performance required of the item, or where the tests necessary to determine compliance with the specification are lengthy, costly, and require complicated technical equipment. The Federal QPLs are confidential and are not available except to authorized Federal government purchasing personnel. Manufacturers are not permitted to use the qualification certification in their promotional and sales activities or advertising.

State and local governments can benefit from the development and use of a comparable list known as the Acceptable Brands List. This list indicates products by brand name which have been accepted as meeting the

[17] 11 Park Place, New York, 10007.

[18] 1001 Connecticut Avenue, N.W., Washington, D.C. 20006.

[19] The Council of State Governments, 1737 K Street, N.W., Washington, D.C.

desired quality standards. The Acceptable Brands List is used in lieu of the preparation of detailed specifications in instances where the latter process is neither possible nor practicable. Among the practical considerations which appear to favor the development of "acceptable brands list" are the following: (1) the difficulty of developing detailed specifications for products manufactured by secret processes; (2) the difficulty of developing detailed specifications in such a manner as to eliminate inferior products; (3) the variability of designs, features, or compositions of a product acceptable for a common end use purpose; (4) intended use of the product—so that different qualities of merchandise can be provided in accordance with the importance of end use; (5) minor quantities or dollar volume involved; and (6) the absence of, or extreme cost, or time involved in testing against a detailed specification for compliance.

Types of Specifications Used in Public Buying. Most public purchasing, under the competitive bidding system, is accomplished through the use of five basic types of specifications, as follows:

1. *Uniform standard* purchase specifications approved and promulgated for use by all departments and agencies of the government. Examples: Federal specifications, state specifications, county specifications, and city specifications.
2. *Nationally accepted* specifications and standards adopted for use by all departments and agencies of the government, i.e., Federal, state, county, and city.
3. Departmental or agency specifications applicable to the needs *of a single departmental activity*. Examples: military department specifications, Veterans Administration specifications, sanitation department of a city, a state roads commission, or a state, county, or city department of welfare.
4. Standard purchase descriptions *for a given supply item* applicable to all agencies or to a particular department where a specification or standard is not justified and where the description can adequately define the requirements to be met for the item.
5. Prototype standard, i.e., typical *brand or equal,* with determination of equality by best means of comparison, examination or test.

Use of the fifth, brand name "or equal," method is not a satisfactory procedure for formal bids or contracts. This method should be limited, in so far as possible, to open-market purchases, where quantities are limited or where time does not permit the development of one of the first four types of specifications listed above.

A variation of the fourth and fifth types, applicable to certain transactions, is the use of "descriptive performance" and "prototype sample" specifications. The former is used where an item is a special manufacture and is usually described by general dimensions and by its intended purpose or use. In the latter case bidders are required to furnish a sample or a drawing which meets general performance requirements. The use of these two types of specifications is an acceptable and sound practice. It should be noted, however, that where such purchases become repetitive, are bought in quantity, and are of sufficient value, it may be practicable to draft a *standard* purchase specification. If this is done, the advice of using departments and representative suppliers should be obtained.

Examples of the "descriptive performance" or "prototype sample" forms of specifications are fireworks displays, certain items of office equipment, office machines, and specialized instruments having limited application. Specification by sample should be avoided whenever possible because of the difficulty in making comparisons of equality and in evaluating competitive bids.

In both contract and open-market purchases, the public buyer should follow the same general practice as the private purchasing agent in using the type of specification which best suits his needs.

Standard Purchase Requisitions, Contracts, Bids, and Other Forms. The standardization of purchase requisitions, contracts, bids, invoices, and related forms would result in tremendous savings, not only to the public purchasing agencies but to the vendor as well. Such savings would be in the form of time, paper work, lower acquisition costs because of increased competition, and better service.

Many counties, cities, and public institutions buy from the same source as their state purchasing office. The use of the same format, wording, legal clauses, and specifications could be accomplished in most cases with the cooperation of the proper authorities.

Determining Purchase Requirements

The public buyer must be particularly careful in the control he exercises over the *quantity* to be purchased. Buying too little may mean the sacrifice of volume discounts; the extra costs of emergency orders; and strained relationships with the using departments. Too much may create problems of excess inventories; the need for additional storage space; increased loss of merchandise due to shelf age and obsolescence; and a general waste of public funds.

It is an often-heard criticism of public purchasing that the buyer has little to do with the actual determination of requirements—that he merely buys what is requested by the using department. In such cases it is especially important that the requisitioning department work closely with the buyer in coordinating the problems of both departments.

Economic or Correct Ordering Quantity. There has been a tendency in recent years to adapt statistical and mathematical principles to supply management and inventory control. One element of such usage is the development of a mathematical formula which can be used in establishing the most economic quantity of material to be ordered for inventory replenishment.

The right amount to buy at any given time is ordinarily that quantity which results in the lowest total cost, including the cost of carrying the merchandise in stock as well as its procurement costs. Where no quantity discounts are involved, the right amount is the quantity at which the order costs equal the carrying costs. If such costs are known, or can be computed, management can apply the mathematical formula and prepare tables or calculator charts for use by assistant buyers or stock clerks.

In public purchasing, procurement costs should include the costs of inventory management, the preparation and servicing of the purchase order, receiving, inspection, and payment of the invoice. Carrying costs would include inventory losses, obsolescence and deterioration, interest, warehouse space, and possibly insurance. The formula is based on variable costs rather than fixed costs.[20]

The computation of this formula may be obtained from any one of several sources, including "The Theory of Inventory Management" by Thomson M. Whitin (Princeton University Press, Princeton, N.J.) or "Industrial Purchasing" by J. H. Westing and I. V. Fine (John Wiley & Sons, Inc., New York).

The economic ordering quantity formula, as well as other statistical principles, is being used to some degree in many large industrial and public purchasing activities in connection with inventory and supply management.

The General Services Administration has recently published a comprehensive handbook entitled "The Economic Order Quantity" for use by Federal government agencies, or other interested public agencies or private concerns. It is available to Federal agencies as a stores stock item under Federal stock number 7610–543–6765. Others may order it from the Superintendent of Documents, Government Printing Office, Washington, D.C. 20025.

Market Research. The use of market research as an aid to more efficient purchasing is receiving increased attention by many public purchasing departments, particularly those which have centralized their purchasing activities. Market research includes the preparation of statistical charts

[20] See Section 13, "Quantity Determination through Inventory Management"; also Section 29, EOV Tables.

and data for use in analyzing purchase performance and budgetary controls; reports covering current market conditions in connection with products bought on major contracts; analysis of current and long-range problems created by increased purchasing activity, or changes in programs created by improved designs and technical progress; and the review of requirements which are seasonal or subject to fluctuating markets, for determining the best time and quantity to buy.

Also included in market research is the review of trade magazines, newspapers, and other publications and the analysis of those articles which report new purchasing techniques or recent developments in related subjects.

Other ancillary functions include investigation and research on many subjects related to purchasing. Where the volume of purchases does not justify a separate division for traffic management, market research could study tariff changes and rulings affecting transportation rates and other pertinent problems.

Recent annual reports of the Department of Purchases, Contracts and Supplies, city of Chicago, commend the efficient operation of their Market Research Division and point out substantial savings effected as the result of its efforts.

Advance Estimates of Requirements. The use of established purchase schedules is common in state purchasing and in the larger local governments. Such schedules provide for purchases of common-use items to be made in accordance with a predetermined timing schedule, ranging from weekly to annual periods depending upon the nature of the commodity and the controlling market.

Many purchasing agents in state and local governments have clearly defined authority to anticipate the needs of using departments and to make contracts for deliveries, either direct or through the central stores warehouse, to supply common-use articles which are estimated to be required within reasonable future periods.

Increasing use is being made of so-called *preitemized purchase requisitions.* Such requisitions list commodities to be purchased at a specified time to cover future requirements. Prepared in the central purchasing agency, preitemized purchase requisitions are forwarded to all using agencies in advance of the time the purchase is scheduled. The using agency merely indicates quantity required against those items listed for which they have need.

Preitemized requisitions have many advantages. They establish uniform and standard item description and packaging, thus eliminating the necessity for editing by the purchasing office and sometimes eliminating the need for contacting a distant agency for clarification of their needs, which is a contributing factor to purchasing cost and program delays. They also provide a check list to guide the requisitioning agency, thus eliminating many out-of-schedule requisitions. The requisitioning agency's job of preparing requisitions is made easier and speeded up by eliminating the necessity for the preparation of item description. Preitemized requisitions received in the purchasing office are easily and quickly tabulated to determine total over-all requirements, as the lists are uniform as to item description and sequence.

Nonschedule purchase requirements are made known to the purchasing agency by means of a standard purchase requisition which originates within the using agency, and usually represents a single purchase and delivery of the item or items requisitioned. Such current requirements are filled either by individual purchase orders or by a delivery order against an existing contract.

Minimizing New Purchases through Use of Current Inventory or Transfer of Excess Stocks. There has been a gradual breakdown of the "ownership concept," traditionally held by most government agencies and departments, that property they have acquired belongs to them and should not be made available for use by other departments, even when it is in excess of foreseeable needs.

Federal agencies, and most large state and local governments, have provided authority for the transfer of excess or surplus property between using departments. Such regulations, in most cases, make it mandatory to check the listings of excess property available for transfer before new procurement is effected. This desirable and economic procedure is saving millions of dollars of public funds each year. Utilization of excess or surplus property should not be limited to that property which meets exact specifications but should include property which is satisfactory as a substitute because of the potential savings.

Certification of Funds and Justification of Need. In government procurement the requisitioning or contracting officer must ascertain that adequate funds are available, and are obligated or set aside to cover any proposed purchase. An appropriate copy of the purchase order is ordinarily used for this purpose. It should have the approval signature of the proper finance authority and should be returned to the purchasing office prior to the signing and release of the purchase order, with a certification that funds are available. Also, the requisitioning department should certify on the requisition that the requested material or service is needed.

If payment is to be made from a revolving fund, the receipt of a properly authenticated requisition citing such funds is sufficient.

Follow-up and Expediting. Follow-up procedures are essential in ensuring the delivery of orders at the right time and right place, even though the vendor's reliability has been verified. Such follow-up should be the function of the purchasing department, in keeping with its procurement responsibilities.

The procedure of checking on delivery time consists mainly of liaison with the supplier and attempting to secure a firm commitment. In most cases the value of the order and urgency of need should determine the amount of time and related costs expended in follow-up procedures.

Expediting the delivery involves not only follow-up but also taking certain actions which will help clear the way so that delivery can be accomplished on or ahead of schedule. These actions include the coordination of related activities in other departments or divisions, such as transportation and inspection. The expediter, in urgent cases, arranges to have certain orders delivered ahead of others on the supplier's schedule. In some cases it may be necessary to assist the supplier to obtain materials in short supply which he needs to complete the order.

Representative Forms and Documents Used in the Purchasing Process. The number of forms necessary in the public purchasing process vary in accordance with the systems in use. In general they include the requisition; the purchase order; the invitation to bid, which should provide for acceptance and award; applicable specifications; the summary or tabulation of bids; the standard bid and contract form; special contract forms; the inspection and receiving report; and compliance and complaint reports. Related forms would include the application for inclusion on the bidders' list; statement of supplier's financial status, or such form as may be used to verify the responsible character of the supplier or his company; direct delivery invoice; request for price quotation; request for invoice; and many others.

A sample copy of the purchase requisition used by the city of Chicago is illustrated by Fig. 19–1.

Methods of Procurement

Government purchasing involves one of the following methods:

1. Informal bids for open-market purchases
2. Formal bids for contract purchases
3. Purchase by negotiation
4. Emergency purchases
5. Small-order purchases
6. Transfer or disposal of excess or surplus property
7. Trade-in or exchange

Securing Competitive Bids—Informal or Formal

If the estimated amount of the transaction exceeds the amount established by law for informal bids and open-market purchases, it is necessary, in most cases, to advertise formally, send out invitations to bid,

CITY OF CHICAGO **PURCHASE REQUISITION** DEPT. OF PURCHASES CONTRACTS & SUPPLIES

NAME OF DEPARTMENT

BUREAU

DIVISION

DATE | DEPT. REG. NO.

FOR PURCHASING DEPT. ONLY

OPEN DATE | P.O. NO.

Q | T | E

BIDDERS

DELIVER TO:

(LOCATION)

ATTENTION ____ TEL NO. ____

THIS REQUISITION COVERS OUR NEED FOR ☐ ONE YEAR ☐ 6 MONTHS ☐ 3 MONTHS ☐ ____ ☐ ONE TIME PURCHASE

ACCOUNT CODE NUMBERS

FUND	DEPARTMENT	ACCOUNT

DATE TO BE DELIVERED

COMMODITY CODE NO.	FULL DESCRIPTION OF NEED	QUANTITY	EST. COST	★ END USE

EMER. NO. ____ STOREROOM NO. ____

CERTIFICATION
I HEREBY APPROVE THE PURCHASE OF THE ITEM (S) AND/OR SERVICES LISTED ABOVE AND CERTIFY THAT THERE ARE SUFFICIENT UNENCUMBERED FUNDS TO GRANT SAME. AND WHERE SUCH FUNDS ARE TO BE EXPENDED UPON COUNCIL AUTHORITY THAT SUCH AUTHORITY HAS BEEN OBTAINED.

BUREAU OR DIVISION HEAD

DEPARTMENT HEAD

★ WHERE A COMMODITY IS FOR A PARTICULAR OR PECULIAR USE REQUIRING OTHER THAN STANDARD QUALITY, GRADES, COLOR, SIZE OR OTHER CHARACTERISTICS, GIVE DETAILS OF HOW IT WILL BE USED AND FOR WHAT PURPOSE.

(USE REVERSE SIDE IF NECESSARY)

1 DEPARTMENT OF PURCHASES, CONTRACTS AND SUPPLIES COPY

FIG. 19–1. Purchase requisition. Varied color snap-out form of four copies; one copy kept by originator of requisition.

receive sealed bids, and award a contract to the lowest responsible bidder. If the amount is under the maximum limitation for open-market purchases, an informal contract or a purchase order may be issued to the lowest of three or more competitive bidders, without advertising. In many cases competitive bids are not required, as for instance on emergency and small-order purchases. Under some circumstances only one bid is required.

While the detailed process of securing competitive bids varies, the principal factors include the establishment and maintenance of a current bidders' list, the solicitation of bids, the terms and conditions of the bid, the opening and evaluation of bids, the handling of late bids, and the award of the purchase order or contract to the successful bidder.

In compiling and maintaining a *bidders' list,* it is necessary, in the interest of economy, to limit the list to prospective bidders who are interested in the specific items contained in various commodity classes. In order to obtain maximum competition, the list should include all responsible interested and prospective bidders. Provision must also be made for the addition and removal of names from the list and for the reinstatement of bidders.

It is important that regulations specify the measures which should be taken to accomplish these purposes. In large-volume public purchasing, the use of automatic selecting and addressing equipment is advisable, to facilitate the selection of names and preparation of the list. In smaller purchasing activities such an elaborate system is usually not feasible.

Much time can be saved in the final evaluation of bids if the bidders' mailing list is restricted to responsible and eligible bidders. However, it is not always practicable to do so.

Figure 19–2 shows a sample of a bidders' mailing list application, as

STANDARD FORM 129—AUGUST 1952
PRESCRIBED BY GENERAL SERVICES ADMINISTRATION
REG. 1-II-206

BIDDER'S MAILING LIST APPLICATION

☐ INITIAL APPLICATION
☐ REVISION

All answers should be typed or printed. See reverse for information and instructions.

TO:
GENERAL SERVICES ADMINISTRATION
REGION 3, FEDERAL SUPPLY SERVICE
7TH AND D STREETS SW., WASHINGTON, D. C. 20025

DATE OF THIS APPLICATION

1. NAME OF APPLICANT

2. ADDRESS TO WHICH BIDDING FORMS ARE TO BE MAILED

3. ADDRESS OF MAIN BUSINESS OFFICE

4. HOW LONG IN PRESENT BUSINESS

5. TYPE OF ORGANIZATION (*Check one*)
☐ INDIVIDUAL ☐ PARTNERSHIP ☐ CORPORATION

6. IF INCORPORATED, INDICATE IN WHICH STATE

7. NAMES OF OFFICERS, MEMBERS OR OWNERS OF CONCERN, PARTNERSHIP, ETC.
(A) PRESIDENT
(B) VICE PRESIDENT
(C) SECRETARY
(D) TREASURER
(E) OWNERS OR PARTNERS

8. AFFILIATED CONCERNS (*Name, location, and in detail, controlling interest in each*)

9. PERSONS OR CONCERNS AUTHORIZED TO SIGN BIDS AND CONTRACTS IN YOUR NAME (*If agent, so specify*)

NAME	OFFICIAL CAPACITY

10. PERSONS TO CONTACT ON MATTERS CONCERNING BIDS AND CONTRACTS (*If agent, so specify*)

NAME	OFFICIAL CAPACITY	TELEPHONE NO.

11. INDICATE CLASSES OF EQUIPMENT, SUPPLIES, MATERIAL, AND/OR SERVICES ON WHICH YOU DESIRE TO BID (*Use attached list, if any*)

12. CATEGORY (*See definitions on the reverse of this form and check below the category which applies to the applicant*)
☐ (A) MANUFACTURER OR PRODUCER ☐ (C) REGULAR DEALER (*Type 2*)
☐ (B) REGULAR DEALER (*Type 1*) ☐ (D) SERVICE ESTABLISHMENT

13. NUMBER OF PERSONS NOW EMPLOYED	14. FLOOR SPACE (*Square feet*)		15. NET WORTH	
	MANUFACTURING	WAREHOUSE	DATE	AMOUNT

16. THIS SPACE FOR USE BY THE GOVERNMENT

17. I certify that the information supplied herein (*including all pages attached*) is correct and that neither the applicant nor any person (*or concern*) in any connection with the applicant as a principal or officer, so far as is known, is now debarred or otherwise declared ineligible by any agency of the Federal Government from bidding for furnishing materials, supplies or services to the Government or any agency thereof.

SIGNATURE OF PERSON AUTHORIZED TO SIGN THIS APPLICATION

18. NAME AND TITLE OF PERSON SIGNING (*Please type or print*)

FIG. 19–2. Bidders' mailing list application. Reverse side defines categories of manufacturer, producer, regular dealer, and service establishment.

prescribed by the General Services Administration for use by Federal government agencies.

In state governments, the manner of maintaining the bidders' list varies widely. Some states employ the use of a more or less formal application in which a prospective bidder submits data concerning the nature of his business, references, etc., as well as a check list of commodities on which bid invitations are desired. States employing the more formal approach to establishing bidders' mailing lists usually send out inquiries to the applicant's references and, on the basis of the evidence developed, the decision is made on whether or not the applicant is to be placed on the bidders' list. In other states, bidders' mailing lists are established merely by letter request from a prospective bidder. Various methods are employed for applying the bidders' lists. Some states and local governments maintain such lists in a central location on mechanized addressing equipment, while in others mailing lists are maintained by the buyer responsible for the procurement of the item to be obtained.

A prequalification questionnaire, plus a Dun and Bradstreet report,[21] are used by many state and local purchasing agencies to determine the responsibility of prospective bidders.

Bidders should be debarred from bidding when performance is unsatisfactory. Such debarring may be made for either a specified or indefinite period of time depending on the circumstances which led to the debarment.

It is an accepted practice in some governments to remove a prospective bidder from the mailing list followng his failure to respond to three successive invitations. Where many products and supplies are involved, this procedure is impracticable. The trend is to permit qualified supply personnel to use individual judgment in determining when a bidder's name should be removed, after he has failed to respond to one or more bids.

Solicitation of bids not only is based on the bidders' list but also includes names obtained from national lists, classified telephone directories, personal knowledge, trade magazines, and many other sources. Examples of such sources include *Thomas' Register of American Manufacturers, McRae's Blue Book, Machine and Tool Bluebook,* the *Institutions Cataloging Directory, Lockwood's Directory of Paper and Allied Trades, The Paper Yearbook, Machinery,* and others listed in Section 26.

Written and, in some cases, telegraphic invitations should be sent to all names on the bidders' list, provided such action is warranted by the size of the order.

In the interest of securing maximum competition consistent with the

[21] See sample report in Section 28, "Appendix."

nature and size of the requirement involved, and having a better selection of quality and price, every available means, within the limits of economy, should be utilized in publicizing the bid. Copies should be posted on public bulletin boards, newspapers and trade papers should be used to the extent feasible, and other media, such as the *Synopsis of Proposed Purchases* published by the Department of Commerce, should be consulted. Copies should also be distributed to the requisitioning office concerned. A bulletin board in the outer office of the purchasing department serves a very useful purpose for posting invitations to bid, tabulations of bids received, and contract awards.

The invitation to bid should be a standard form which provides for the identification and description of the desired commodities, the quantity, unit, unit price, and total price. It should clearly specify the date and time for opening of the bids, for delivery of the commodities involved, and information on cash discounts. It may provide an appropriate section for notification of acceptance of the bid, signed by the purchasing or contracting officer. The invitation should be sent to prospective bidders together with an official bidding envelope for their use in returning the completed sealed bid. A colored envelope may be used for easy identification.

Both informal and formal bid forms as used by the city of Cincinnati are reproduced in Figs. 19–3 and 19–4. The former is used for purchases under $2,500.

Securing competitive bids is a basic requirement in public purchasing. There are certain exceptions such as small-order purchases, emergency purchases, and, under certain limited conditions, some negotiated contracts. Requirements for competitive bidding are usually set forth in state and local laws as amended, but certain Federal agencies have special laws or regulations. Notable among these are the Armed Services Procurement Regulations and the Federal Property and Administrative Services Act of 1949 as amended.

Newspaper advertising is required by law in most public purchasing activities, although in some state and local governments such advertising is left to the discretion of the purchasing agent, or limited to certain classes of contracts, i.e., construction, coal, and fuel. The dollar value of the contract involved in the requirement for newspaper advertising varies from zero to $7,000, averaging $2,500.

If such advertising is required by law, care should be taken to minimize costs by consolidating ads and using as little space as possible. Specification data need not be included in the advertisement.

The terms and conditions of the invitation to bid should be specific and should be stated in simple and clear terminology. If desirable, the

FORM 3–100M–6-62

C. A. HARRELL
City Manager

JOHN G. KRIEG
City Purchasing Agent

CITY OF CINCINNATI
DEPARTMENT OF PURCHASING
Room 162 City Hall, Cincinnati 2, Ohio
INVITATION

Quotations, subject to the conditions on the reverse hereof, are requested on the following list of materials, supplies, equipment or services, for the department as mentioned, with delivery to destination as shown below. Quotations shall include all charges for delivery, packing, etc. Address your quotation to the City Purchasing Agent, Room 162, City Hall, Cincinnati 2, Ohio.

Ref. No. ____________
Date ____________
Buyer ____________
Fund ____________

REQUIRED FOR DELIVERY TO:

Department or Division ____________

Address ____________

Mail Invoices to ____________

Closing Time of Bids ____________

TAXES: THE CITY IS EXEMPT FROM FEDERAL EXCISE AND OHIO STATE SALES TAX. THE CITY'S TAX EXEMPTION REGISTRY NUMBER IS NO. A-135976. PRICES SHOULD NOT INCLUDE THESE TAXES. See "Instructions to Bidders" No. 9 on reverse hereof for details.

TAX EXEMPT (Unless otherwise indicated)

Quantity	Unit	Materials, Supplies, Equipment or Services	Unit Price	Total Amount
		THIS IS AN INQUIRY FOR PRICE—NOT AN ORDER		

Terms________% cash discount if paid within________days from delivery and acceptance of goods or completion of services.

PROPOSAL OR BID

In compliance with the above invitation for bids and subject to all conditions thereof, the undersigned offers and agrees, if this bid be accepted within a reasonable time from date of closing, to furnish any or all of the items or render such services upon which prices are quoted, in accordance with the specifications applying and at the price set opposite each item.

Delivery of any or all of the items or completion of services indicated shall be made within________days from receipt of order

IMPORTANT As delivery may be a deciding factor in the award of an order, it is important that bidders furnish the information requested above.

Sign Here:

.... Name of Company

Per............Title............

Address............

City............Date............

FIG. 19–3. Informal bid form.

formal bid invitation can be accompanied by standard bid and contract terms which spell out detailed instructions on bidding, awarding, contracting, delivery, and methods of payment. In most cases the bid and the purchase order accepting the bid represent an acceptable and binding contract.

In determining the lowest competitive bidder, the purchasing department must know the exact price each bidder asks for the material to be delivered to the same location. Since there is no traffic or freight bureau in most state and local government agencies, properly qualified clerks are usually not available to figure the exact delivery cost on goods which originate in different and widely separated locations, and goods may be handled by several carriers. State and local government purchase invitations and contracts, therefore, usually provide for prepaid delivery to the using department at the address shown in the invitation and in the contract or purchase order. If this cannot be accomplished, the bidder should be required to include information in his bid regarding delivery charges.

FORM 1A-10-63-25M

BID DOCUMENT

W. C. WICHMAN, City Manager

CITY OF CINCINNATI
DEPARTMENT OF PURCHASING
Room 162, City Hall, Cincinnati, Ohio 45202

JOHN G. KRIEG, City Purchasing Agent

Proposal from

Name of Bidder (Print or Type)

Reference No. ....

Date ....

Buyer ....

This space for City Use Only

Type of Bid Surety

EXCERPT FROM LEGAL ADVERTISEMENT OF BIDS WANTED

LEGAL NOTICE – BIDS WANTED

Sealed proposals will be received at the Office of the City Purchasing Agent, Room 162, City Hall, Cincinnati, Ohio, 45202, until *12 o'clock noon E.S.T.*, on the dates hereinafter stated at which time they will be opened and publicly read, for furnishing the materials, supplies, equipment, or services, or for supplying the materials and/or doing the work necessary for the repair, construction, or improvement, as the case may be, as indicated by the items hereunder listed and in accordance with the applicable specifications.

Unless otherwise specifically indicated under the individual listing in the legal advertisement, all bids shall be subject to the following:

a) A Bid Bond, deposit of cash, or Certified Check, Bank Cashier's or Bank Official's Check drawn on a solvent bank payable to the Treasurer of the City of Cincinnati, in the amount of not less than ten percent (10%) of the total amount of the bid must accompany each proposal as a guarantee that if the proposal is accepted a contract will be entered into.

b) The successful bidder will be required to furnish a bond or a *Certified Check* on a solvent bank, payable to the Treasurer of the City of Cincinnati, in an amount of not less than fifty percent (50%) of the total amount of the contract as a guarantee for the faithful performance thereof.

c) The City reserves the right to waive informalities not inconsistent with law or to reject any or all bids.

d) *Bidder must use the bid document proposal forms furnished by the City as none other will be accepted. Proposal forms must be returned intact. Removal of any part thereof may invalidate the bid.*

Proposal forms, specifications, etc. may be obtained upon application at the Office of the City Purchasing Agent, Room 162, City Hall, Cincinnati, Ohio 45202.

NOTICE OF BIDS WANTED BY THE CITY MANAGER

ITEM DESCRIPTION	REFERENCE NO.	BIDS DUE 12 NOON

W. C. WICHMAN,
City Manager

INVITATION TO BID

Sealed proposals are requested on the list of materials, supplies, equipment, or services set forth herein, subject to all conditions outlined in the bid document, including the General Conditions, Instructions to Bidders, and Information for Bidders on the Reverse hereof.

FIG. 19–4. Formal bid form. For purchases exceeding $2,500. Four-page form, with other three pages as bid sheet, information on the supplier, and general information for bidding.

Bid bonds or *bid deposits* are required where security is necessary to protect the interest of the public agency in the event the low bidder attempts to withdraw his bid. Bid bonds or deposits are not usually required unless the invitation requires the furnishing of a performance bond by the successful bidder.

The amount of the bid bond or deposit should be determined by the purchasing agent in relationship to the cost of the supplies or services. Theoretically, the amount of the bond should be equal to the probable difference between the two lowest bids. The degree of responsibility of the prospective bidder is a major consideration. Most state statutes provide for bid and performance bonds but sometimes limit the requirement to certain classes of products, such as building or construction. In many cases the purchasing agent can use his own discretion as to whether bonds are necessary or desirable. This is considered the most satisfactory procedure since it reduces the cost of bidding and, therefore, tends to increase competition.

There appears to be some question as to the advisability of requiring performance bonds, since they do not always guarantee the faithful performance of a contract.

Bond requirements also discourage some suppliers from submitting bids and tend to reduce competition. This is particularly true of small business. One large city found it more satisfactory to substitute a sworn statement showing the bidder's financial position and other pertinent data, which statement had to be signed by a certified public accountant. Such other data could include equipment and production facilities, personnel and management, pending litigations, mercantile ratings, credit ratings at banks, union and labor relations, and many others, depending upon the nature of the investigation.

Bid deposits are becoming more common than bid bonds since they represent cash (or equivalent) *in hand* which the bidder agrees shall be retained to cover liquidated damages in the event of failure to sign the contract, or failure to provide a satisfactory performance bond, if such is required. Such personal control of deposits has many advantages.

The Federal government and some state and local governments permit regular bidders to file annual bid bonds and annual performance bonds, in lieu of surety, with each bid and contract. This practice reduces the cost of bidding and tends to increase competition. It is worthy of consideration by governments where surety is a legal requirement. Figures 19–5 and 19–6 illustrate the front and back of the performance bond, as prescribed for use by Federal agencies.

As a *safeguard against tampering* with the bids, the sealed envelopes containing the bids should, upon receipt, be stamped to indicate the date, time, and place of receipt. Special colored and marked envelopes are recommended. They should then be placed in a locked receptacle until the time specified for opening. Under no circumstances should any bids be allowed to pass out of the hands of a responsible government employee. Telegraphic bids may be opened for purposes of identification. Prior to the fixed time for opening, bids may be modified or withdrawn.

Telephone quotations on small orders are generally authorized in all

STANDARD FORM 25
REVISED NOVEMBER 1950
PRESCRIBED BY GENERAL SERVICES ADMINISTRATION
GENERAL REGULATION NO. 5

PERFORMANCE BOND
(See Instructions on Reverse)

DATE BOND EXECUTED

PRINCIPAL

SURETY

PENAL SUM OF BOND (*express in words and figures*)	CONTRACT NO.	DATE OF CONTRACT

KNOW ALL MEN BY THESE PRESENTS, That we, the PRINCIPAL and SURETY above named, are held and firmly bound unto the United States of America, hereinafter called the Government, in the penal sum of the amount stated above, for the payment of which sum well and truly to be made, we bind ourselves, our heirs, executors, administrators, and successors, jointly and severally, firmly by these presents.

THE CONDITION OF THIS OBLIGATION IS SUCH, that whereas the principal entered into a certain contract with the Government, numbered and dated as shown above and hereto attached;

NOW THEREFORE, if the principal shall well and truly perform and fulfill all the undertakings, covenants, terms, conditions, and agreements of said contract during the original term of said contract and any extensions thereof that may be granted by the Government, with or without notice to the surety, and during the life of any guaranty required under the contract, and shall also well and truly perform and fulfill all the undertakings, covenants, terms, conditions, and agreements of any and all duly authorized modifications of said contract that may hereafter be made, notice of which modifications to the surety being hereby waived, then, this obligation to be void; otherwise to remain in full force and virtue.

IN WITNESS WHEREOF, the above-bounden parties have executed this instrument under their several seals on the date indicated above, the name and corporate seal of each corporate party being hereto affixed and these presents duly signed by its undersigned representative, pursuant to authority of its governing body.

In Presence of:

WITNESS — INDIVIDUAL PRINCIPAL

1. .... as to .... [SEAL]
2. .... as to .... [SEAL]
3. .... as to .... [SEAL]
4. .... as to .... [SEAL]

WITNESS — INDIVIDUAL SURETY

1. .... as to .... [SEAL]
2. .... as to .... [SEAL]

Attest: — CORPORATE PRINCIPAL
BUSINESS ADDRESS
BY
TITLE
AFFIX CORPORATE SEAL

Attest: — CORPORATE SURETY
BUSINESS ADDRESS
BY
TITLE
AFFIX CORPORATE SEAL

STANDARD FORM 25
NOVEMBER 1950 EDITION
16—30441-2

FIG. 19–5. Performance bond (front).

The rate of premium on this bond is .... per thousand.

Total amount of premium charged, $..............................

(The above must be filled in by corporate surety)

CERTIFICATE AS TO CORPORATE PRINCIPAL

I, ..., certify that I am the .... secretary of the corporation named as principal in the within bond; that ...., who signed the said bond on behalf of the principal, was then .... of said corporation; that I know his signature, and his signature thereto is genuine; and that said bond was duly signed, sealed, and attested for and in behalf of said corporation by authority of its governing body.

.... [CORPORATE SEAL]

INSTRUCTIONS

1. This form shall be used for construction work or the furnishing of supplies or services, whenever a performance bond is required. There shall be no deviation from this form except as authorized by the General Services Administration.

2. The surety on the bond may be any corporation authorized by the Secretary of the Treasury to act as surety, or two responsible individual sureties. Where individual sureties are used, this bond must be accompanied by a completed Affidavit of Individual Surety for each individual surety (Standard Form 28).

3. The name, including full Christian name, and business or residence address of each individual party to the bond shall be inserted in the space provided therefor, and each such party shall sign the bond with his usual signature on the line opposite the scroll seal, and if signed in Maine or New Hampshire, an adhesive seal shall be affixed opposite the signature.

4. If the principals are partners, their individual names shall appear in the space provided therefor, with the recital that they are partners composing a firm, naming it, and all the members of the firm shall execute the bond as individuals.

5. If the principal or surety is a corporation, the name of the State in which incorporated shall be inserted in the space provided therefor, and said instrument shall be executed and attested under the corporate seal as indicated in the form. If the corporation has no corporate seal the fact shall be stated, in which case a scroll or adhesive seal shall appear following the corporate name.

6. The official character and authority of the person or persons executing the bond for the principal, if a corporation, shall be certified by the secretary or assistant secretary, according to the form herein provided. In lieu of such certificate there may be attached to the bond copies of so much of the records of the corporation as will show the official character and authority of the officer signing, duly certified by the secretary or assistant secretary, under the corporate seal, to be true copies.

7. The date of this bond must not be prior to the date of the instrument in connection with which it is given.

U. S. GOVERNMENT PRINTING OFFICE 16—30441-9

FIG. 19–6. Performance bond (back).

public purchasing activities within specified dollar limits. Such limit varies in each instance, but is usually in line with limitations established for informal purchases. In many cases the limit is left to the discretion of the purchasing agent. The higher the dollar value, the more important it becomes to secure written confirmation. In the Federal government there has been a trend to liberalize the requirements for written confirmation.

Most regulations provide that telephone quotations be received from at least two suppliers, except for small orders such as would be paid from an imprest fund. Administrative costs should not be out of proportion with the amount of the purchase.

Where telephone quotations are practicable, a buyer has the advantage of a personal contact and can obtain detailed information on new or improved items, current market conditions, and other pertinent data.

The opening and tabulation of bids should be under the control of a responsible purchasing department official and the quotations and contents of bids should be open to the public. Bids should, in most cases, be read aloud when opened, for the benefit of those present. The tabulation of bids should include the names of the bidders, the price bid, and other pertinent information. The original copy of the tabulation or abstract should be kept on file, along with the originals of all bids. In those cases where strict security measures are necessary, tape recordings or microfilming of bids is advisable.

In the handling of late bids, it is common practice in state and local governments that bids received in the purchasing office after the time and date specified for bid opening must be rejected, except in those rare circumstances where the bid is misplaced or mishandled after receipt in the purchasing office. Late bids may either be returned unopened to the bidder, or retained, opened, and filed. The latter procedure permits a comparison of such bids with those received and officially opened, and aids in the decision of whether or not the purchasing department would be justified in rejecting all bids and soliciting new bids. If retained, the bidder should be notified that his bid was not considered because it was late. This is a debatable procedure since it may place the late bidder in an embarrassing or unfair position if bids are readvertised.

Evaluation of bids and the award to the successful bidders involves checking all wording, figures, and content against the invitation, and against standard rules and regulations, or any special rules applying to the specific invitation to bid. If the conditions of the invitation are satisfactorily met, and price and other factors make the lowest responsible bid the most advantageous to the government, and all policies and procedures which apply to evaluating the bid are complied with, the award is then officially made and the successful bidder is notified.

Procedures should spell out the details for determining or identifying a "responsible" bidder, the various causes for rejecting bids, the reinstatement of ineligible bidders, and other pertinent factors considered in evaluating bids. For instance, in deciding whether the prospective supplier is capable of fulfilling all obligations of the contract, it should be determined that he has the necessary organization, adequate financial resources, technical qualifications, facilities, and experience. If he does not have a well-established reputation, or a satisfactory performance record with the procuring activity, the purchasing officer should, where possible, obtain the technical assistance of inspectors in verifying the supplier's ability to produce a quality product in the quantities required.

Practically all public purchasing laws now specify that the award be made to the *lowest responsible bidder.* There are apparently a few isolated cases where the "low bid" is still required to be accepted, in some smaller cities and authorities. As an accepted practice, however, the latitude permitted purchasing personnel in selecting the lowest responsible bidder results in a contract which is based, not on net price alone, but on quality and on assurance that the vendor will satisfy the terms and conditions of the contract. By this practice the government achieves a more "advantageous buy" for the taxpayers' dollar.

In the case of *equal low bids* procedures should establish a certain priority for awarding the contract. Such factors as small business concerns versus big business, firms located in areas which have a substantial surplus of labor, and the use of locally manufactured products and materials could be considered. Other factors would include the advantageous location of a bidder, lower transportation costs, and the assurance of better service. All such factors being equal, the practice of public "drawing of lots" is acceptable.

Successful bidders must be notified of the award within the time specified for acceptance. Provision should be made for *advance* notice of awards under certain specified circumstances. As an example, prompt action is sometimes required by a bidder to obtain critical materials necessary for use in the performance of the contract. Under some contracts there are important preliminaries which the bidder can be working on while awaiting release of formal contract documents. Because of the time required to prepare and issue a formal contract a "notice of award and authorization to proceed with contract" is used by some awarding authorities. A sample copy of such form as used by the city of Milwaukee is shown in Fig. 19–7. The contract or purchase order form used by the County of San Diego, California, is illustrated by Figs. 19–8 and 19–9 (front and back). The "blank check" type of purchase order, as used by the County of Los Angeles, is reproduced in Fig. 19–16.

Purchase by Negotiation

Although government procurement by formal advertising is the preferred method, it should be noted that most public purchasing regulations permit some latitude in negotiation, even though the dollar quantity is above the maximum for informal bids. It is the *basic governmental policy* to obtain maximum competition, consistent with the nature and size of the requirement, to the end that purchases will be made to the

City of **MILWAUKEE**

CENTRAL BOARD AND DEPT. OF PURCHASES
SUITE 607 • CITY HALL • BR. 6-3711 • MILWAUKEE 2, WISCONSIN

ANDREW L. LEHRBAUMMER
City Purchasing Agent

HOWARD A. McMILLAN
Deputy City Purchasing Agent

Date____________________

____

____

____

Gentlemen:

NOTICE OF AWARD AND AUTHORIZATION TO
PROCEED WITH CONTRACT

On__________________________ the Central Board of Purchases awarded your firm a contract for furnishing____________

____

____

in accordance with Formal Advertisement No. CP- __________, and Specification No.__________________________________.

This is your authority to proceed with this contract.

Delivery shall be made________________________________.

Kindly acknowledge receipt of this authorization.

Contract forms will follow as soon as possible. Contract No._________has been assigned. Please refer to this in all communications.

Very truly yours,

Andrew L. Lehrbaummer
City Purchasing Agent

Member National Institute of Governmental Purchasing and National Association of Purchasing Agents

FIG. 19–7. Notice of award and authorization to proceed with contract. City of Milwaukee departmental form.

best advantage of the government, price and other factors considered. In keeping with such policy, government regulations usually provide that bids may be rejected for such causes as unreasonable prices, failure to receive bids from responsible bidders, and failure to meet quality, delivery, or other specification requirements.

Where competitive bidding has failed to provide an acceptable source

PURCH. FORM 103 REV. 3-64

THE PURCHASE ORDER NUMBER AND DEPARTMENT NAME SHOWN BELOW MUST APPEAR ON ALL INVOICES AND SHIPMENTS.

COUNTY OF SAN DIEGO
PURCHASING DEPARTMENT
PURCHASE ORDER
BLDG. 11, 5555 OVERLAND AVE.
SAN DIEGO, CALIFORNIA 92123

PURCHASE ORDER NO.

DATE	REQ. NO.
DEPT.	DIV.
FUND	CLASS.
OBJ'T	

TO:

CHARGE TO:

SHIP TO:

DELIVER ON OR BEFORE

VIA

F.O.B.

QUANTITY	UNIT	CHANGE ORDER MUST BE OBTAINED FROM PURCHASING DEPARTMENT PRIOR TO SHIPMENT IF UNABLE TO FILL ORDER OR RENDER INVOICES EXACTLY AS DESCRIBED HEREON.	CLASS & ITEM NO.	PRICE	UNIT	DISCOUNTS
		IF DELIVERY IS NOT COMPLETED WITHIN SIX MONTHS FROM DATE OF THIS ORDER, UNFILLED PORTIONS WILL BE AUTOMATICALLY CANCELLED.				

IMPORTANT NOTICE

1. INVOICES MUST BE PREPARED IN TRIPLICATE TO "THE COUNTY OF SAN DIEGO."
2. AFTER DELIVERY MAIL INVOICES TO "COUNTY AUDITOR & CONTROLLER" ROOM 166, CIVIC CENTER, SAN DIEGO.
3. PURCHASE ORDER NUMBER MUST APPEAR ON FACE OF INVOICE.
4. FREIGHT CHARGES MUST BE PREPAID ON MATERIAL SHIPPED F.O.B. DESTINATION.
5. FILE SEPARATE INVOICES FOR EACH PURCHASE ORDER.
6. NO MERCHANDISE SHOULD BE ACCEPTED FOR RETURN OR EXCHANGE WITHOUT APPROVAL OF THE PURCHASING AGENT.
7. INVOICES WILL NOT BE APPROVED FOR PAYMENT UNTIL THE ABOVE REQUIREMENTS ARE MET.

THIS ORDER IS SUBJECT TO CONDITIONS ON THE REVERSE SIDE HEREOF.

VERNE O. GEHRINGER
COUNTY PURCHASING AGENT

BY ______________________

PRINTED BY THE STANDARD REGISTER COMPANY, U.S.A. ZIPSET ®

FIG. 19–8. Purchase order (front).

because of the above reasons, it is possible, under certain conditions, to negotiate. Negotiation is also permitted in cases of emergency or public exigency if time does not permit advertising. In most public purchasing regulations negotiations are also permitted in the following cases: (1) where there is only one acceptable source, such as sometimes occurs in the case of professional services; (2) the services of educational institutions; (3) certain supplies such as drugs and medicines; (4) technical equipment; (5) experimental and research requirements; (6) classified supplies or services which should not be publicly disclosed.

The authority to negotiate does not excuse the public buyer from his responsibility to obtain maximum competition and to obtain goods and services at the best advantage to the government. It is therefore a usual requirement that competitive bids must be secured if the dollar value of the purchase is sufficiently high to justify the extra cost and effort.

SPECIAL INSTRUCTIONS

1. This county reserves the right to cancel this order if goods are not shipped as directed.
2. Each shipment must be plainly marked and show the order number and the department in whose care shipped.
3. No charge will be allowed for packing, boxing or cartage, unless agreed upon at the time of purchase.
4. Freight charges must be prepaid on all material sold F.O.B. destination.
5. Merchandise must not be shipped C.O.D.
6. On shipments sold F.O.B. point of origin—prepay charges and add to invoice. Original copy of paid express or freight bill must be attached to invoice.
7. In case any article sold hereunder shall be covered, or purport to be covered by any patent or copyright, you will indemnify this county and save it harmless from and against any and all suits, claims, judgments and costs instituted or recovered against it by any person or persons whomsoever, on account of the purchase, use or resale of such article by this county in violation or claimed violation of any rights under patent or copyright.

PURCHASE OF MATERIALS AND SUPPLIES

(An act to require the use of materials and supplies substantially produced in the United States, in public works and for public purposes.) Government Code Sections 4301-4305.

4300 G.C. When used in this act "United States" means the United States of America, and includes any Territory or insular possession of the United States.

4303. CONTRACTS TO BE LET ONLY ON AGREEMENT TO USE OR SUPPLY MATERIALS PRODUCED OR MANUFACTURED IN UNITED STATES. The governing body of any political subdivision, municipal corporation, or district, and any public officer or person charged with the letting of contracts for (1) the construction, alteration, or repair of public works or (2) for the purchasing of materials for public use, shall let such contracts only to persons who agree to use or supply only such unmanufactured materials as have been produced in the United States, and only such manufactured materials as have been manufactured in the United States, substantially all from materials produced in the United States.

4303.5. PURCHASE OF OFFICE MACHINES OR SUPPLIES THEREFOR. Any provision of this article to the contrary notwithstanding, any such body or person may let a contract for the purchase of office machines or supplies therefor without regard to the place of their manufacture or the source of the materials from which such machines or supplies are manufactured, except that such contracts or purchases shall be subject to the provisions of Section 4334. (Added by Stats 1955 ch 1335 s 1.)

4304. PROVISION THAT ONLY MATERIALS PRODUCED AND MANUFACTURED IN UNITED STATES SHALL BE USED.

(Contract to contain provision.) Every contract for the construction, alteration or repair of public works or for the purchase of materials for public use shall contain a provision that only unmanufactured materials produced in the United States, and only manufactured materials manufactured in the United States, substantially all from materials produced in the United States, shall be used in the performance of the contract.

(Noncomplying person not to be awarded contract.) Any person who fails to comply with such provision shall not be awarded any contract to which this article applies for a period of three years from the date of the violation.

4305. POSTING NAME OF NONCOMPLYING PERSON WITH REPORT OF FACTS. The name of the person failing to comply, together with a report of the facts constituting the violation, shall be posted by the governing board or person who let the contract in at least three public places in the county in which the contract was made.

FEDERAL FOOD & DRUG ACT

By acceptance hereof, Seller guarantees that no article furnished herein is adulterated or misbranded within the meaning of the federal food, drug, and cosmetic act, or is an article which may not, under the provisions of section 404 or 505 of the act, be introduced into interstate commerce.

FIG. 19–9. Purchase order (back).

The number of bids requested depends to a large degree upon the value or characteristics of the requirement and the judgment of the buyer. He selects the qualified sources he considers necessary to ensure adequate competition. Price quotations, and other pertinent data, are then solicited. The same type of form used for invitation to bid under formally advertised purchasing can be utilized for negotiated bids by omitting reference to the public opening of bids.

Upon receiving the quotations the buyer or contracting officer negotiates the contract. In making the award, he should take into account the same factors which govern his decision in the case of contracts awarded on open competitive bids.

Emergency Purchases

Emergency purchases are occasioned primarily by fire, flood, explosion, drought or other disasters, or by breakdown of machinery and services. Under such conditions special provisions in agency regulations permit purchases without formal advertising. Usually such emergencies in the Federal government are proclaimed by the President, and in the public interest purchases may be negotiated for immediate delivery of needed supplies or services. Telephone quotations are sometimes necessary where savings of time are essential.

Some state and local governments permit using agencies to make emergency purchases up to a specified dollar limit, which in some instances is as high as $300. Emergency purchases above the specified amount generally require the prior approval of the purchasing agency. It is the usual practice to require confirming requisitions or purchase orders to be accompanied by a statement explaining the nature of the emergency, the purpose of which, obviously, is to serve as a deterrent against unjustifiable purchase transactions being made under the guise of emergencies.

In some cases provision is made for emergency purchases to enable repair of equipment in service departments which breaks down during a period when the purchasing department is not open for business.

Small-order Purchases

The cost of preparing and servicing a government purchase order varies in accordance with the system in use, the technical nature of the item being purchased, and the efficiency of the particular agency's purchasing process. The administrative expense of making a small purchase is proportionately much greater than that of a large purchase, and may sometimes be greater than the cost of the goods or services purchased.

While the need for buying small requirements cannot be eliminated entirely, there are certain methods which can be used to minimize the number of small purchase orders. The best known and most widely used of these methods is the "imprest" or petty cash fund. Depending on the volume of small purchases, the imprest fund may be replenished on a monthly basis, and the dollar amount of the fund can be established in accordance with the requirements for such periods of time. All expenditures from the fund must be authorized, but the authority to make small purchases should be at the lowest practicable working level. All purchases, except those of very minor nature, must be supported by a receipt. Purchases of several dollars should be itemized and require a receipt signed by the vendor or his agent.

Small repeat requirements purchased from the same local source may be economically serviced by local term contracts. Under such a contract, price discounts from the contractor's price list should be obtained and arrangements made for consolidated billing. Items and services such as plumbing, hardware, and electrical supplies are typical examples.

COMMONWEALTH OF VIRGINIA
COMP. FORM 5-(11-63) 300M SETS
ORIGINAL

INVOICE

Purchase Order No. ______
Requisition No. ______
Date of invoice ______
How Shipped ______
Terms and discount ______

SOLD TO (Name and address of State Agency receiving goods or service)

BY (Name and address of Vendor)

NOTICE TO VENDOR

All invoices against agencies of the Commonwealth of Virginia must be prepared on this form and four copies sent directly to the agency to which merchandise was shipped or for which service was rendered. Invoices must be complete in detail. Render a separate invoice for each purchase order promptly upon completion of shipment, or performance of service. Retain last copy for your records. If charges for freight or express are added to invoice, original bill of lading or receipt must be attached.

DATE OF SHIPMENT OR SERVICE	DESCRIPTION OF ARTICLES OR SERVICES	QUANTITY	UNIT	UNIT PRICE	AMOUNT	LEAVE BLANK

VENDORS SHOULD NOT WRITE BELOW THIS LINE — VENDOR'S TOTAL

Purchase Order:—Complete ☐ **Incomplete** ☐
Voucher No. ______ Month ______
Approp.-Activity-Object (Allotment) (E.O.) Amount

DEDUCTIONS
Discounts..........% ....
Other (Specify):
....
....
Amount certified for payment

Audited:
Charged:
Tabulated:
Receiving stamp. — Dept. of Accts.
Entered on Comptroller's register of warrants

TO THE COMPTROLLER:
It is hereby certified that the goods or services specified above have been received, or performed, payment therefor has not been previously authorized and that this expenditure is a proper charge to the appropriation indicated. This account is approved for payment.
Signature of approving officer ______
(*Use ink or indelible*)
Title ______

FIG. 19–10. Invoice voucher form.

Other methods include the planned scheduling of small-order requisitions, the use of standard purchase order-invoice-voucher forms. Figure 19–10 illustrates a copy of such a form, which is widely used by Federal government agencies.

Transfer or Disposal of Excess and Surplus Property

One of the functions of a good purchasing organization is the development of buyers who become specialists in their field, and who are cognizant of market trends and technological advances. The application of such skills tends to decrease materially the chances of generating large volumes of excess or surplus property, most of which are caused by overbuying or obsolescence.

All Federal and a large number of state and local government agencies have specific regulations which require that published listings of excess property available for transfer be checked prior to new procurement. This procedure is saving the taxpayer millions of dollars each year. Payment, if required, is made by the receiving agency on a sliding scale percentage of the original purchase price, depending upon the condition of the property. Federal government excess personal property is reported on a form such as that reproduced in Figs. 19–11 and 19–12 (front and back).

STANDARD FORM 120
AUGUST 1950
PRESCRIBED BY GENERAL SERVICES ADMINISTRATION
PERSONAL PROPERTY MANAGEMENT
REGULATION NO. 3

REPORT OF EXCESS PERSONAL PROPERTY

See Instructions on Reverse

1. REPORT NUMBER
2. DATE MAILED
PAGE 1 OF NO. OF PAGES
3. TOTAL COST
4. TYPE OF REPORT ☐ ORIGINAL REPORT ☐ PARTIAL WITHDRAWAL ☐ AMENDED REPORT ☐ TOTAL WITHDRAWAL
4A. NUMBER AND DATE OF PRIOR REPORT, IF ANY
5. TO (*Name and address of reportee agency*)
6. FROM (*Name and address of reporting agency*)
7. LOCATION OF PROPERTY
8. CUSTODIAN (*Name, address, and telephone number*)
9. DOES RAIL CARRIER SERVE LOCATION? ☐ YES ☐ NO IF ANSWER IS "YES," GIVE NAME OF CARRIER
10. FOR FURTHER INFORMATION CONTACT (*Name, title, address, and telephone number*)
11. SEND PURCHASE ORDERS TO (*Name, address, and telephone number*)
12. IF LOCATION TO BE ABANDONED GIVE DATE ☐ CHECK IF LOCATED ON EXCESS REALTY
DO NOT WRITE IN THIS SPACE — DATE RELEASED AS SURPLUS | NUMBER — SPECIAL ACTION
13. IS PROPERTY REIMBURSABLE? ☐ YES ☐ NO IF ANSWER IS "YES," SEE INSTRUCTIONS ON REVERSE
14. IS PROPERTY CONTRACTOR INVENTORY? ☐ YES ☐ NO
15. REPORT APPROVED BY (*Name and title*)
16. COMMODITY GROUP NUMBER
17. EXCESS PROPERTY LIST

ITEM NO. (a)	DESCRIPTION (b)	CODE		UNIT (e)	NUMBER OF UNITS (f)	ACQUISITION COST		FAIR VALUE	
		S.C.C. (c)	COND. (d)			PER UNIT (g)	TOTAL (h)	CODE (i)	PER UNIT (j)

STANDARD FORM 120 AUGUST 1950 EDITION (*Use Standard Form 120a for continuation sheets*) 10—02382-1

FIG. 19–11. Report of excess personal property (front).

State and local governments are paying increased attention to the utilization of excess and surplus property as an economic measure for reducing new purchases. They are particularly interested in the "donation program" under which state educational and health institutions, and certain other nonprofit organizations, can obtain Federal surplus personal property free of charge, except for certain handling and shipping costs. Only fourteen of the fifty states have placed control over Federal donation program surplus in the purchasing department.

The sale of *scrap and salvage* is usually a function of the centralized purchasing department. In decentralized purchasing it should be cen-

GENERAL INSTRUCTIONS

This form and, when continuation sheets are necessary, Standard Form 120a shall be used to report excess personal property in accordance with Personal Property Management Regulation No. 3 and to make amendment or withdrawal of prior reports.

Reports shall be confined to property at one location constituting a single commodity group, as defined in detailed instructions below. Contractor inventory, reimbursable property, and nonreimbursable property shall not be included on the same report but shall be the subject of separate reports.

Legal restrictions (including patent) on the power of the holding agency to dispose of property being reported excess shall be fully explained in the listing of such items.

Reports shall be submitted in the number of copies required by Personal Property Management Regulation No. 3.

DETAILED INSTRUCTIONS

No. of Pages. Enter here total number of pages in the report.

1. *Report Number.* Insert the serial number of the report and any other identifying number or symbol the reporting agency may desire. If the report is an amendment or withdrawal of a prior report, the prior report number shall be entered followed by the letter (*a*), (*b*), or (*c*), etc. to identify the respective successive amending and withdrawing reports.

2. *Date Mailed.* Insert the date the report is mailed (not date on which prepared).

3. *Total Cost.* Insert the sum of all amounts shown in column (*h*) of the property listing except that, when reporting an adjustment or withdrawal of a prior report, the net amount by which the "Total Cost" of the prior report is increased or decreased shall be entered followed, respectively, by the letters "Inc." or "Dec."

4. *Type of Report.* Indicate the type of report by inserting an (X) in the appropriate box. If the report is an amendment or withdrawal of a prior report enter the number and date of mailing such prior report in 4A. In preparing such reports observe the following:

   a. If the report amends a prior report, each line item amended shall be restated under its original consecutive line item number in column (*a*) and as it should be in columns (*b*) through (*j*).
   b. If the report withdraws in part a prior report the line items withdrawn shall be restated in columns (*a*) through (*c*) as they appeared in the original report. The word "withdrawn" should be written across the remaining columns (*d*) through (*j*).
   c. If the report withdraws in total a prior report the word "withdrawn" should be written across columns (*a*) through (*j*) of the Excess Property List.
   d. The amount by which the "Total Cost" of the prior report is increased or decreased by the amending or withdrawing report shall be entered in box 3 as an "Inc." or "Dec." amount, respectively.

5. *To.* Enter name and address of the executive agency and office to which the report, in accordance with Personal Property Management Regulation No. 3, is to be made.

6. *From.* Enter the name and address of the Federal agency or department, and bureau, office, or other subdivision making the report.

7. *Location of Property.* Give the warehouse, building, or other specific location and the address at which the property is located.

8. *Custodian.* Enter name, address, and telephone number of the custodian of the property. If the property is in the custody of another agency enter also the name of such agency.

9. *Rail Carrier.* Indicate by (X) in appropriate box whether location is served by rail carrier. If so, enter name of carrier. Any clear, commonly understood abbreviation may be used.

10. *Further Information Contact.* Enter name, title, address, and telephone number of the person who may be contacted for further information about the property.

11. *Send Purchase Orders To.* Give name, address, and telephone number of the person, or office, to whom purchase orders are to be sent.

12. If the property is at a location to be abandoned give date for such abandonment. If located on excess realty indicate such fact by an (X) in the appropriate square.

13. *Reimbursable.* Indicate by (X) in appropriate box whether the property is or is not reimbursable and if reimbursable enter the appropriation symbol and title or the name and address of the Government corporation to receive the net proceeds from disposition.

14. *Contractor Inventory.* Indicate whether the property is or is not contractor inventory.

15. *Report Approved By.* Type the name and title of the person authorized to approve the report by signature on the original copy.

16. *Commodity Group Number.* Enter the number of the following commodity group to which the property being reported belongs. (In cases of uncertainty as to the correct category in which to report certain items, the reporting office shall make the determination, using its best judgment and such information as is available, including a visual inspection when feasible):

No.	*Commodity Group Description*
01.	Automotive equipment, including trucks, trailers, passenger cars, busses, and motorcycles.
02.1	Office furniture, machines, and equipment.
02.2	Stationery and office supplies.
02.3	Household furniture, appliances, and equipment.
03.	Construction equipment, including building materials and supplies, earth moving equipment (except trucks), tractors, agriculture machinery, and implements.
04.	Electrical equipment, including electrical equipment and supplies (other than office and household), communication, and electronic equipment.
05.	Machine tools, including general industrial and production equipment, industrial air conditioning and refrigeration equipment.
06.	Miscellaneous hardware and hand tools.
07.	Textiles, including textile products, apparel, and footwear.
08.	Hospital equipment, including medical and laboratory equipment, and supplies, drugs, and medicines.
09.	Agricultural products, including animals, foodstuffs, and related products and manufactures.
10.	Crude and basic materials, including ores, coal, petroleum, oils, chemicals, and metals.
11.1	Miscellaneous materials and supplies.
11.2	Miscellaneous equipment.

17. *Excess Property List.* For the purpose of this list a line item of property shall consist of a single unit of property or a number of identical units each of which meets the descriptions in columns (*b*) through (*e*), (*g*), (*i*), and (*j*).

(*a*) *Item.* Enter the consecutive number of the line items in the report, beginning with number one for the first line item on the first page.

For example, if 10 line items are being reported excess and there is room for only 6 on the first page of the report they will be given consecutive numbers "(1)" through "(6)" on the first page of the report and the remaining 4 line items will be given consecutive numbers "(7)" through "(10)" on the continuation sheet. Leave a blank line space across all columns between line items.

(*b*) *Description.* In this column describe each line item in commercial terms and in sufficient detail to permit transfer or sale without further reference to the holding agency. Stock numbers and prefixes, manufacturer's part number, and standard catalog reference numbers should be stated. The condition of the most important components of an item should be noted. Specify the type of container or package and the quantities in each.

(*c*) *S. C. C. Code.* The Standard Commodity Classification code may be entered in this column as additional descriptive identification of a line item.

(*d*) *Cond. Code.* Enter the appropriate letter and number code combination taken from the following code system:

Code	*Means*	*Code*	*Means*
N	New	1	Excellent
E	Used—reconditioned	2	Good
O	Used—usable without repairs	3	Fair
R	Used—repairs required	4	Poor
X	Items of no further value for use as originally intended but of possible value other than as scrap.		

If condition of a line item cannot be adequately described by code, describe condition in column (*b*).

(*e*) *Unit.* Enter the unit of measure, such as: Each, pounds, tons, dozen, gross, etc. Distinguish between long, short, and metric tons. Standard abbreviations may be used.

(*f*) *Number of Units.* Enter the quantity of each line item in terms of the unit of measure given in column (*e*).

(*g*) *Acquisition Cost—Per Unit.* Enter the recorded acquisition cost per unit (column (*e*)). If acquisition cost is not known, enter the estimated original cost per unit excluding transportation and handling charges incurred after purchase. Identify an estimated cost by the prefix (E).

(*h*) *Acquisition Cost—Total.* Enter the computed total cost of each line item (number of units in column (*f*) times the cost per unit in column (*g*)).

(*i*) *Fair Value—Code.* Insert the following fair value letter code which describes the fair value condition of the property.

Code	*Fair Value Condition*
A	"New—excellent" means unused personal property, ready for use in a condition identical with new items delivered by a supplier.
B	"Usable—without repairs" means personal property which has been used and requires no reconditioning or repair; and property which, although unused and requiring no reconditioning or repair, does not qualify for Code A.
C	"Usable—minor repairs required" means personal property requiring minor repairs, to put into usable condition, whether used or unused.
D	"All other" means property requiring major repairs, conversion, or rehabilitation, and all other items which through deterioration, obsolescence, or other factors do not fit Codes A, B, or C and includes scrap and salvage.

(*j*) *Fair Value—Per Unit.* Enter the fair value per unit determined by applying the following percentages to the base price (current delivered market price, new; or acquisition cost) arrived at in accordance with Personal Property Management Regulation No. 3.

Fair Value Code	*Percentage of Base Price*
A	50%
B	35%
C	20%
D	0% (None)

U. S. GOVERNMENT PRINTING OFFICE 16—62382-1

FIG. 19–12. Report of excess personal property (back).

trally controlled as to policy. If possible, it should be coordinated by purchasing personnel who know the market and have had specific experience in dealing with competitive salvage and scrap sales and with the lotting and grading of materials for auction. Such knowledge will usually result in a far greater return to the government.

Special care should be exercised in determining whether an item is economical to repair, or otherwise may be further utilized, before being disposed of as salvage or scrap. In many cases its value to some other department, as a useful item, far exceeds the salvage return.

Experience has proved the need for qualified evaluation of the physical qualities of metal which is being sold as scrap or salvage, and the advantages, in some cases, of "cannibalizing," or selling component parts of machinery and equipment, in order to realize the greatest return. There are some instances in government sales where mixed lots of metals are sold at the market price of the metal having the lowest value. Much greater income will result from proper segregation. Segregation and baling will also be an advantage in the sale of waste, such as paper and rags.

It is of great importance that the proper method of sale be used in disposing of salvage and scrap items and material. In many cases, particularly those where high value and high potential use are involved, a greater return may result from the use of sealed competitive bids rather than auction.

The disposal of surplus property is commonly accepted as a responsibility of the purchasing department. The purchasing personnel have many existing records of the original purchase, are familiar with its use, possible markets, merchandising or sales techniques, and used-equipment prices. Most sales of scrap, salvage, and surplus in the larger government organizations are made by surplus disposal officers. It is important that such officers be well qualified, capable, and experienced in their field, with a thorough knowledge of markets and prices. Responsibility for surplus disposal, and experience gained (in those cases where surplus results from overbuying) can be used to advantage by the purchasing department in developing more efficient procurement policies and procedures, and in determining or verifying requirements.

The disposal of surplus materials is, of course, directly related to the transfer and utilization of property which is excess to the requirements of any given department, since failure to find a use for such excess results in its becoming surplus to the over-all needs of the agency.

Records show that the average return to the Federal government on the sale of surplus is between 7 and 8 per cent of its original cost. State and local government proceeds should be considerably higher since most of their surplus is commercially usable and not affected by the low returns from special-purpose military-type items.

At the state and local government level, the relatively low volume of surplus generated would not require the variety of techniques involved in the sale of Federal surplus property. They should, however, be concerned with the basic principles of using the most effective media for reaching prospective markets; of fully describing surplus for sale, in terms of commercial use and condition; and of applying the basic rules of good merchandising in their disposition of surplus.

If the volume of surplus at any one location is sufficiently large, it should be sold "at site" since the cost of any movement of surplus amounts to a reduction from the net proceeds of its sale. If consolidation with quantities at another location is necessary, transportation costs should be kept as low as possible. If handling equipment and manpower are available, surplus goods may be segregated from regular stocks and physically moved to another point in the same warehouse or general area.

Sales methods for surplus include sealed bids, auction, site sales, and negotiated sales. Each method has its advantages under certain conditions. It is the responsibility of the individual or group in the controlling office to determine the best and most advantageous method to be used in each case rather than to adopt a single method for use in all disposals of surplus. Experience shows that, as a general rule, the sealed-bid method results in more satisfactory returns. Further information on sale of surplus will be found in Section 21, "Disposal of Reclamation and Salvage Materials."

Trade-in or Exchange

Under certain conditions used government personal property which has outlived its economic usefulness, but which is not excess to requirements, may be traded in or exchanged for similar property. General Services Administration regulations control such "trade-in and exchange" procedures for all Federal agencies and provide a listing of those items or classes of property which are so controlled. Included are such items as trucks, passenger cars, refrigerators, air-conditioning units, fans, typewriters, and numerous other categories of machinery and equipment.

In cases where bids for the items to be purchased are not required by applicable laws and regulations, the items to be traded in may be sold and the proceeds applied to the purchase of new "similar" equipment, provided such purchase is approved and funds obligated. If bids are required, and it is determined that the property should be traded in, the bid must contain a full description of the items involved. Such bids are called "cash and trade-in" bids.

In some instances the used property is still in excellent condition, or only slightly used, and is being disposed of in the interest of economy, such as where a large truck or tractor is desired to replace two smaller ones. In such cases it is to the best advantage of the government to offer the used equipment to other departments at a cost commensurate with its trade-in or sale value. Such utilization of property proposed for exchange or sale is also specifically covered in General Services Administration regulations and applies to all Federal agencies. Copies of these regulations have been furnished, upon request, to various states through their national associations.

Some state statutes specify that the purchasing agency shall arrange for the transfer to or between agencies of personal property which is surplus with one but which may be needed by others. Some states are carrying on an effective program for the utilization of state-generated surplus property, with the result that many purchases of new and additional property are avoided, with resultant savings in tax funds.

Types of Contracts

In public purchasing the fixed-price, definite-quantity contract is usually preferred over other types. There are, however, circumstances where other-type contracts are more advantageous to both parties. Cost-type contracts, fixed-price incentive contracts, cost-plus-incentive-fee, and like varieties of contracts with special features are not discussed since they are used primarily in connection with military-type production programs. The use of "cost plus a percentage of cost" contracts is specifically forbidden in General Services Administration regulations of the Federal government. The following categories and specific types of contracts represent those in general use in public purchasing departments.

Indefinite-quantity or *open-end contracts* are widely used in government purchasing because of two major advantages. First, they permit contracting for total requirements of all departments or agencies on a long-term basis and provide minimum prices in those situations where exact-quantity requirements cannot be determined. Second, they have a tendency to minimize the number of items being ordered since the process of consolidating requirements results in a definite standardization of the best types or qualities of products. The relative simplicity of purchase actions under this type of contract, and the elimination of duplicative supply contracts by the various departments or agencies, results in substantial economies and many administrative advantages.

The General Services Administration uses *indefinite-quantity* or *term contracts* in the procurement of common-use items under its Federal Supply Schedules. Under such schedules all Federal agencies have the benefit of prices based on total quantity requirements even though the orders issued by each for direct delivery are relatively small. Federal Supply Schedules cover approximately 50,000 items or categories of items, including office supplies, office furnishings and equipment, and tires and tubes.

Some states using the indefinite-quantity contract refer to it as a "supply" or a "requirements" contract. Whatever the name used, it represents an agreement whereby the supplier contracts to furnish the total requirements of the government for a specified item over a stated period of time, for delivery as ordered. The price may be a "fixed price," or it may be subject to fluctuation of an established pricing medium such as posted prices for gasoline.

Counties, cities, and public institutions also use the supply contract or agreement to cover such items as chemicals, lamps, fuels, paper products, sand and gravel, laundry supplies, and photographic and duplicating supplies.

Long-term contracts are used in practically all public purchasing activities as a means of securing quantity discounts, and because of the savings effected by only advertising for bids once during the period covered by the contract. Such contracts may require performance bonds and do not ordinarily extend beyond one year.

Definite-quantity contracts, which may also be *term* contracts, are used where requirements are known or can be estimated with reasonable accuracy. They may provide for "one-time" delivery or "scheduled" delivery, and the price may be a *fixed price* with or without provisions for an escalation clause. Definite-quantity contracts make it possible to take advantage of quantity prices prevailing at the time of the contract while spreading delivery over future periods. Other advantages are (1) the vendor can use such contracts as a backlog to keep his plant busy and as a result will usually give the buyer a better price; (2) the number of purchase orders and related forms are reduced; (3) the cost of advertising on formal contracts is limited to the initial contract for the period covered; (4) many small orders are eliminated; and (5) price advantage is obtained while inventory carrying costs are maintained at a low level.

Price-agreement contracts are those where certain discounts from list prices are incorporated in the agreement. Such discounts may be part of any contract that covers the procurement of either cataloged items or standard production items, where the price is reflected by published price lists.

Service contracts are normally used to cover requirements for services such as window washing, utilities, laundry, insect extermination, guard service, truck rental, and repair services. They may be formally advertised or negotiated contracts depending upon considerations such as the number of sources of supply and the dollar value of the contract.

Samples of general provisions prescribed for use in the Federal government and also by the state of Connecticut will be found at the end of this section.

Escalation Clauses

In long-term contracts, where the possibility of increased labor or material costs may affect the supplier's willingness to set an acceptable price, escalator or price revision clauses may be used. Such "flexible" contracts apply to both definite- and indefinite-quantity agreements.

Escalation or price-revision clauses in bids are not usually desirable. They were in general use, however, during World War II and the Korean conflict. Under certain circumstances they serve a useful purpose in protecting both the government and the supplier *from either a rising or falling market.* In some cases suppliers must quote an obviously excessive price to provide for the contingencies of rising costs of labor and materials. Under these conditions it may prove advantageous for the bid or contract to provide for escalation clauses, if such clauses contain a maximum price, percentage ceiling, or are related to a public price information service such as the *Wall Street Journal* or *Chicago Journal of Commerce.* In some instances where no bids are received because of unstable market conditions it may be necessary to readvertise and include an escalation clause.

Where escalation clauses are used, they should be included in the invitation to bid and contain a maximum price or percentage ceiling. Such maximum should be based on the best estimate which can be made of expected increases in labor or raw materials, plus any other pertinent factors. Current Armed Services' and certain civilian agency regulations use a 10 per cent figure. However, the circumstances of each individual case should determine the maximum percentage of increase.

Regulations should include *specific* instructions concerning the use of escalation clauses, and should provide for approval by the head of the purchasing department, prior to use.

Inspection of Deliveries

The inspection of materials and equipment prior to their acceptance is one of the most important responsibilities in the entire procurement operation. This is especially true in public purchasing as the act of acceptance by inspection may be irrevocable. Once the goods are accepted, litigation is sometimes required to effect adjustment on items found to be of inferior quality.

Inspection is defined, for use herein, as the method or process of determining that materials, equipment, and services supplied by a contractor or vendor meet the quality requirements stipulated in the contract or other purchase documents.

Most of the larger public agencies have a sufficient volume of purchases to warrant a full-time inspection force. Some Federal agencies, such as the General Services Administration and the military departments, require a separate headquarters division and large field staffs to control their inspection operations, because of the large volume and diverse nature of supplies under contract.

A few of the larger states, counties, and cities operate with a limited number of full-time, qualified inspectors and depend to a large degree, like most of the smaller-volume purchasing activities, upon receiving or using agency personnel to inspect deliveries. Such using agency personnel receive various degrees of training, but in some instances depend almost entirely on inspection handbooks.

Responsibility for Inspection

Inspection, as a supply management function, is a responsibility of the centralized purchasing office. Even though the inspection function is delegated to the receiving department, the over-all responsibility should remain in the purchasing organization. In some cases it is feasible to have a full-time inspector from one department inspect for one or more other departments.

Because of the distance between activities within state and Federal agencies, and within some counties, it is generally desirable to have using agencies perform inspection duties. It may be advisable, in some instances, to utilize commercial inspection firms or other government agencies when special equipment or technical competence is required. Department of Agriculture inspectors, for example, are available in most areas for the inspection of food and subsistence items at a reasonable cost. Such cost may be borne by the purchaser or supplier, depending on contractual arrangements.

Inspection Methods

Inspection techniques are too numerous to discuss in detail. They include preaward inspections of the prospective supplier's product or facilities; origin and destination inspections; sampling; visual and dimensional checks; chemical and laboratory analyses; and physical, functional, and endurance tests.

The proper inspection method to be used depends upon the individual order, the responsible character of the supplier, the specification requirements, the volume and destination, and many other considerations. Experience has proved that a complete inspection of each product, or unit of a product, is neither practical nor desirable—100 per cent inspection would be costly and wasteful. Economy and accepted practice dictate the premise that on most products a reasonable allowance for nonconformance is necessary.

Inspection of a representative sample of a lot for the purpose of acceptance or rejection of the entire lot may be made on *attributes* or *variables*. Space does not permit a detailed discussion of these two sampling techniques; however, a full description of such procedures is contained in Military Standard 105A (available from the Government Printing Office, Washington, D.C. 20025) and in A. H. Bowker and H. P. Goode, "Sampling Inspection by Variables" (McGraw-Hill Book Company, Inc., New York).

Special emphasis should be placed on the inspection of any particular supplier's merchandise which has been the subject of past complaints, or classes of property which are known to have a marked variation in quality or performance.

Purchase Documents Necessary for Inspection

The personnel responsible for inspection must be provided with all the purchase documents used in the procurement in order to perform a complete and intelligent job. This includes the contract, purchase order, applicable technical specifications and drawings, any amendments to these documents, and any other pertinent information or correspondence. All agreements made with the supplier which have a bearing on the contract should be documented, and a copy provided for inspection. Verbal agreements should be avoided.

A copy of Standard Form 32 (General Provisions–Supply Contract) which has been satisfactorily used by Federal agencies for a wide variety of procurement will be found at the end of this section. Section 5 of such form covering "Inspection" completely protects the rights of the buyer and at the same time provides flexibility to purchasing and inspection personnel in determining the acceptability of materials offered by a supplier.

Place of Inspection

In public purchasing, other than Federal, inspection is generally made at destination. This is traceable to several factors, such as small-volume purchases, commercial items of simple specification, brand-name purchases, and buying from distributors rather than manufacturers.

It should be noted, however, that under certain circumstances origin inspection (at the manufacturer's plant) is either essential or highly desirable. Such is the case where quality, defects, or analyses of the product or its ingredients can be determined only during the manufacturing process; where testing apparatus or facilities are available only at the manufacturer's plant; where costly packaging or preservation would be destroyed by destination or in-transit inspection; and where a large volume of merchandise is being shipped to several widely separated destinations.

Experience has shown that origin inspection and sampling at overseas sources of supply cannot always be relied upon. Receipts from foreign sources should preferably be inspected when unloaded in United States ports, before acceptance of the shipment.

Laboratory Analysis or Testing

In Federal government procurement, ample facilities are available for laboratory testing and analysis at centralized locations. State and local governments, and public institutions, with very minor exceptions, do not have their own laboratories for testing purchased products and as a result must utilize the laboratory facilities of other departments, government agencies, colleges, or those of commercial laboratories. Only six state purchasing agencies indicate that they maintain, or are in the process of establishing, laboratories for checking quality requirements on purchased commodities. (A *Directory of Commercial and College Testing Laboratories,* published by the American Society for Testing and Materials, may be obtained from their headquarters at 1916 Race Street, Philadelphia, Pa. 19103. This publication lists 278 commercial and 86 college laboratories and outlines their specialties and testing facilities.)

It is noted that the National Bureau of Standards, U.S. Department of Commerce, has a substantial program for testing certain supplies bought by the Federal government. Many large cities have recently organized their own testing and inspection laboratories under the authority of the Purchasing Department, Philadelphia, Pennsylvania, being the most recent to do so.

Inspection and Receiving Reports

Commodity or service inspection reports should be prepared upon completion of inspection and copies should be distributed to all parties and departments concerned. Separate reports may be required for origin inspections as compared to destination or warehouse inspections. In the interest of standardization, and to save labor and materials, effort should be made to minimize the number and variety of inspection reports.

Goods which have been inspected should be stamped or labeled in a permanent manner to indicate and identify such action.

In cases where inspection is a specified condition of the contract, suppliers should be promptly notified by the use of prescribed letters, forms, or telegrams if the goods contracted for were rejected; and the reasons for rejection should be cited in the communication. See Fig. 19–13 to illustrate one type of complaint report sent to vendors.

STATE OF CONNECTICUT
DEPARTMENT OF FINANCE AND CONTROL
PURCHASING DIVISION
70 ARCH STREET HARTFORD, CONNECTICUT 06115

COMPLAINT REPORT

Complete this form to report complaints against vendors, commodities, or to report any unsatisfactory service by the Purchasing Division.

Be sure to furnish all necessary detail so that a satisfactory settlement of the complaint can be made.

Please verify all information to insure accuracy. Complaint reports become a permanent record of the commodity or vendor concerned and must be accurate to guarantee intelligent and equitable settlement and to serve as a guide for future action.

AGENCY

DATE OF COMPLAINT | PURCHASE REQUISITION NUMBER

CONTRACT AWARD NUMBER | PURCHASE ORDER NUMBER

NAME OF VENDOR

ADDRESS OF VENDOR

COMMODITY OR COMMODITIES COVERED BY COMPLAINT

NATURE OF COMPLAINT

DELIVERY	QUALITY	OTHER
Delivery not made on date ordered or promised	Quality of commodity is inferior	Purchase authorization or contract award not received
Delivery made at an unsatisfactory hour	Unsatisfactory and unauthorized substitute delivered by vendor	Invoice price higher than authorized
Delivery made at wrong destination	Unsatisfactory workmanship in installation of commodity	Weight received at variance with invoice or shipping ticket
Improper method of delivery	Commodity lacks required inspection stamps	Quantity delivered in excess of order.
Unauthorized delivery made before issuance of order		Quantity delivered less than ordered.
Delivery in damaged condition		

REMARKS Note:
Give detailed explanation of complaint in this space, using reverse side, if additional space is necessary. Indicate manner in which you suggest complaint be settled. Be specific.

COMPLAINT INITIATED BY: .... Name .... Title

COMPLAINT FORM EXECUTED BY: .... Name .... Title

ORIGINAL—TO PURCHASING DIVISION
DUPLICATE—RETAINED BY AGENCY

FIG. 19–13. Complaint report.

The accounting copy of the receiving report, or related forms, should provide for certification that goods or services were received and were in conformance with inspection and specification requirements. Payment of the invoice should not be approved unless so certified by a responsible designee. Figure 19–14 typifies the type of inspection report used by the state of Connecticut.

FORM—INSP 5

STATE OF CONNECTICUT
DEPARTMENT OF FINANCE AND CONTROL
PURCHASING DIVISION

REQUEST FOR INSPECTION AND/OR SAMPLING

DATE ________________

FROM: ________________________________
TO: INSPECTION SECTION
REF: ________________________________
Contract Award No. Or Authorization No.

AGENCY ________________________________
POINT OF DELIVERY ________________________________
PROMISED DATE OF DELIVERY ________________________________
MATERIAL ________________________________
SPECIFICATION ________________________________
VENDOR ________________________________
SPECIAL INSTRUCTIONS ________________________________

REPORT OF INSPECTION AND/OR LABORATORY ANALYSIS

DATE ________________

FINDING ________________________________

RECOMMENDATION ________________________________

____
INSPECTOR

FIG. 19–14. Request for inspection and/or sampling.

OTHER SUPPLY MANAGEMENT FUNCTIONS UNDER CENTRALIZED PURCHASING

Centralized purchasing often changes a purchasing department from a relatively small operation to one of considerable magnitude. In consolidating the purchasing function of several departments there are a number of methods for effecting economies and efficiency which are not practicable under the decentralized purchasing system. Among these are the establishment of a central stores and warehouse system for common-use items; the use of prescribed inventory-level standards for departmental stockrooms; transportation and traffic management; and the processing of invoices.

Establishment of a Central Stores System for Common-use Items

To store or not to store is a big question. This problem must be evaluated from all angles, including such factors as storage space and distribution costs, depreciation and obsolescence, availability of local commodity, private warehousing, and classes of products involved. Some large municipalities have found it desirable to reduce or eliminate some of their warehouse and stores facilities through the use of term requirement contracts or blanket purchase orders, described in Section 5. They are able to secure direct delivery from contractor warehouses to the operating departments at the same prices as for warehouse delivery and consequently save the total warehousing cost. The decision to store or not to store should be placed under the purchasing authority.

Because of geographical areas serviced by state purchasing agencies, few states have central warehouses in operation for the storage and distribution of common-use commodities. Twenty states, however, maintain within the purchasing agency central stockrooms from which using agencies requisition common-use office supplies. In several instances such warehouse systems handle food, textiles, and other selected categories of stocks not ordinarily found in central warehouse stocks.

Many large cities and counties maintain central warehouses. However, the trend is toward "stockless buying." This requires the contractor to warehouse and deliver common-use items when and if needed, similar to "term supply" contract buying.

Quasi-public organizations of the "authority" type have, in most cases, established stockrooms for common-use items. The majority of these are under the supervision of the purchasing department.

In analyzing the total cost of supplying common-use items from a central stores warehouse it is important that all direct and indirect costs be included. Several different sources have made studies on the cost of carrying average warehouse stocks and most of them are in approximate agreement that total annual costs are close to 18 to 25 per cent of the value of such stocks. Public purchasing departments usually ignore some costs which must be considered in the operation of a private warehouse, such as insurance, taxes, and interest, which account for approximately 7 per cent of the above 25 per cent. There are some instances where minor costs are incurred by public agencies for these items. In computing total costs, they should be included. The breakdown is as follows:[22]

[22] Thomson M. Whitin, "The Theory of Inventory Management," p. 231, Princeton University Press, Princeton, N.J. See Section 13 for additional cost data.

	Per cent
Storage facilities	0.25
Transportation	0.50
Handling and distribution	2.50
Depreciation	5.00
Obsolescence	10.00
Insurance, taxes, and interest (if any)	6.75
Total	25.00

The savings available from quantity purchases of warehouse stocks, from reduced paper work, and from lower transportation costs should be estimated as accurately as possible. Consideration should be given to the savings resulting from reducing or eliminating departmental stockrooms and all other tangible and intangible savings and advantages.

When total costs of establishing and operating a central stores warehouse are determined, a comparison with estimated savings and advantages should provide reliable guidance on whether or not to stock an item or class of items.

Establishing Inventory Levels for Departmental Stockrooms

In both centralized and decentralized public purchasing systems, there is inclined to be a lack of uniform standards with regard to the inventory level of stocks carried in departmental storerooms. Based on the preceding discussion of the costs of carrying warehouse stocks, it is apparent that uniform inventory standards are an important part of good administration. It follows, therefore, that in decentralized purchasing operations a central authority, such as the director of the department of administration, should take the initiative in establishing standards for mandatory use by all departments in the maintenance of economic inventory levels. Under centralized procurement this responsibility should be vested in the purchasing department.

It has been found in Federal agency storerooms that shortages and overages are usually not the fault of the system. It is important, therefore, under any system, periodically to review and evaluate its effectiveness.

Realistic methods must be used in establishing standards for replenishment of stocks on hand and economic inventory levels. Such methods should consider all pertinent factors, including stock on hand, average issue experience and records, stock due in, delivery dates of supplies en route or on order, and cost data. The "economic ordering quantity," previously discussed under that heading, is only one of many systems which uses the realistic approach to the problem of economic inventory levels. Production and delivery lead times on each item should be on record and allowances should be made, where applicable, for contingency reserves. Cost data should include information on quantity discounts. Physical inventories should be taken at least annually.

The individual requirements of each department must be analyzed to determine if special circumstances exist and, if so, whether separate standards are required.

Inventory standards, if properly developed, will ordinarily divide various classes of products into stock retention levels of three, six, nine, or twelve months. In general, items with the fastest turnover should have the lowest inventory level. All other considerations being equal, a quantity discount may justify increasing the inventory level of an item from three to six months or more, because of savings in excess of carrying costs.

Traffic and Transportation Management

If the volume of purchases makes it feasible for a state or local government to maintain a traffic or transportation organization, it is essential that there should be close cooperation between the purchasing department and those divisions, groups, or individuals who are responsible for developing and coordinating the transportation program. The policy in public purchasing is to secure the lowest possible cost, commensurate with the type of service required, in the handling and movement of supplies and equipment.

In the distribution of centrally warehoused government-owned stocks advantage should be taken of any method of shipment which will result in the lowest rate plus satisfactory service. Combinations of motor and rail, rail and water, barge and rail or motor should be considered, as well as air, Railway Express, and parcel post for package or crate deliveries.

If carriers provide for free pickup and delivery, service, government-owned vehicles should not be used. If government trucks are not being fully utilized they should be used, where extra charges are made for delivery service, in preference to paying for local drayage.

Traffic personnel should also advise the purchasing personnel with regard to packaging and marking so that advantage may be taken of lower rates based on carriers' requirements. For further information on traffic, refer to Section 18, "Traffic and Transportation Considerations."

Processing of Invoices

The large-scale operations of public procurement agencies result in complicated procedures for the control of appropriated and rotating funds. Because of the many departments involved in public purchasing activities, the many supply systems, the different types of contracts, and the numerous warehouses and distribution points for supplies, a variety of different forms are required to report the receipt of material to the finance or accounting office so that payment may be effected.

The receiving report copy of the purchase order, the purchase order–invoice-voucher used for small orders, and the requisition for equipment, supplies, or services are used, where applicable, for payment of government purchases.

In state and local governments the payment of invoices is generally not as complex as in the Federal government because of more localized deliveries and lesser volume. In most cases delivery is certified on a copy

CP 45 40M 2:57 445 NGS

CITY OF CHICAGO
INVOICE FORM

VOUCHER NUMBER — MAIL IN TRIPLICATE TO DEPARTMENT OF PURCHASE, ROOM 400, CITY HALL, CHICAGO, ILL. 60602

TO BE FILLED IN BY CREDITOR — DATE:

CITY OF CHICAGO, DR.: — GOODS AND/OR SERVICE FURNISHED TO: — CITY PURCHASE ORDER NO.

NAME OF CREDITOR — DEPARTMENT

ADDRESS — BUREAU — REQ. NO.

ADDRESS — CONTRACT NO.

SELLER'S ORDER NO. — INVOICE NO. — TERMS: — SUB-ORDER NO.

QUANTITY	DESCRIPTION	UNIT PRICE	AMOUNT

We hereby certify that this invoice is rendered in full conformity with the Purchase Order or Contract and meets the Specifications contained therein. Federal Regulations are also complied with:

Signed ______ (vendor)

ACCOUNT CODE NUMBERS			AMOUNT
FUND	DEPARTMENT	ACCOUNT	
		TOTAL	

FOR OFFICE USE ONLY

PURCHASING AGENT'S APPROVAL

I HEREBY CERTIFY THAT I HAVE EXAMINED THE RECEIVING REPORT FROM THE USING DEPARTMENT AND IT AGREES WITH THIS INVOICE AND THAT SATISFACTORY EVIDENCE IS ON FILE IN MY OFFICE OF RECEIPT OF GOODS AND/OR SERVICES.

PRICES CORRECT. INVOICE APPROVED AND PASSED TO COMPTROLLER FOR PAYMENT

PURCHASING AGENT

BY ______

AUDITOR'S APPROVAL

EXAMINED AND APPROVED

DATE:

DATE:

AUDITORS

WARRANT ISSUED:

POSTED:

INDEXED:

FIG. 19–15. Invoice form.

of the purchase order. In a few instances a uniform invoice form supplied by the buyer is required. This practice, although helping governmental agency accounting and filing systems, does not impose an inconvenience on the vendor. Some use is made of a separate receiving report document for partial deliveries. Use is also made of a notarized expenditure certificate as to the correctness and propriety of invoices submitted for payment. A copy of the invoice and voucher form used by the city of Chicago is shown in Fig. 19–15.

Receiving reports, in whatever form, should be channeled through the purchasing office, combined with the approved invoice, and transmitted to the finance office for payment. This should be done as quickly as possible in order to secure cash discounts.

In some cases, the Federal government permits *advance payments* in order to assist the supplier to finance performance of his government contract. Provisions for advance payments and the terms and conditions thereof must be approved by proper legal authority prior to use in a contract.

NIMLO MODEL PURCHASING ORDINANCE*

SECTION 2–103. *Establishment of Department of Purchase.*[1] There is hereby established in the Administrative Service of the City the Department of Purchase, and in said Department the office of City Purchasing Agent.

ALTERNATE SECTION 2–103. *Establishment of Bureau of Purchases.* There is hereby established in the Department of .... a Bureau of Purchases.

SECTION 2–104. *City Purchasing Agent.* The City Purchasing Agent shall be the head, and have general supervision of the Department (Bureau) of Purchases. The Agent shall perform all duties required of a department head by law, and shall have the powers and duties prescribed by this Ordinance.

(1) *Position Specifications.* The Agent shall:

(a) *Appointment.* Be appointed by the..................[2] according to Personnel System regulations.[3]

(b) *Experience Requirement.* Have had, prior to his appointment, at least ....years experience in a purchasing office of a public or private corporation in an executive capacity.

(c) *Bond.* Give an official bond, to be approved by the City Attorney, in the sum of $..................[4]

[1] In a case where a city official also serves as city purchasing agent the sentence should read: "The city manager (city clerk or other official in whom the purchasing authority rests) shall also serve as city purchasing agent, and shall be the head of the Department (or Bureau) of Purchase."

[2] See Section 1–303 of the NIMLO Model Administrative Code for duty of Chief Administrator to appoint officials in the administrative service under his control. Generally, the power of appointment depends upon the form of government, with the appointing power vesting at times in the Mayor, Council, city manager or department head.

[3] It is generally agreed that for best results centralized purchasing should not labor under the impediment of insecure tenure in the city purchasing agent. Thus, if the municipality has no Personnel System, subsection (a) should be limited to the appointing statement and followed by this subsection: "Tenure. The City Purchasing Agent shall hold office until his successor shall have been appointed and qualified, or until his resignation or removal on written charges preferred against him by the appointing officer and sustained at a hearing."

[4] See Section 1–306 of the NIMLO Model Administrative Code for suggested language requiring bonds of certain officers and Section 1–305 for "Oaths of Office."

* SOURCE: Reproduced from NIMLO Model Administrative Code, by permission of the National Institute of Municipal Law Officers, Washington, D.C.

(2) *Scope of Purchasing Authority.* The Agent shall have the power and it shall be his duty:

(a) *Purchase or Contract.* To purchase or contract for all supplies and contractual services needed by any using agency which derives its support wholly or in part from the City, in accordance with purchasing procedures as prescribed by this Ordinance and such rules and regulations as the Agent shall adopt for the internal management and operation of the Department of Purchasing and such other rules and regulations as shall be prescribed by the Chief Administrator and the City Council.

(a–1) *Exceptions prohibited.* The authority of the Agent to negotiate all purchases for all using agencies shall not be abridged by excepting any particular using agency.[5]

(a–2) *Unauthorized purchases.* Except as herein provided, it shall be unlawful for any City officer or officers to order the purchase of any supplies or make any contract within the purview of this Ordinance other than through the Department of Purchasing, and any purchase ordered or contract made contrary to the provisions hereof shall not be approved by the City officials, and the City shall not be bound thereby.

(3) *Other Powers and Duties.*[6] In addition to the purchasing authority conferred in subsection (2) above and in addition to any other powers and duties conferred by this Ordinance the Agent shall:

(a) *Minimum Expenditure.* Act to procure for the City the highest quality in supplies and contractual services at least expense to the City.

(b) *Encourage Competition.* Discourage uniform bidding and endeavor to obtain as full and open competition as possible on all purchases and sales.

(c) *Rules and Regulations.* Establish, and amend when necessary, all rules and regulations authorized by this Ordinance and any others necessary to its operation.

(d) *Purchasing Analysis.* Keep informed of current developments in the field of purchasing, prices, market conditions and new products, and secure for the City the benefits of research done in the field of purchasing by other governmental jurisdictions, national technical societies, trade associations having national recognition, and by private businesses and organizations.

(e) *Forms.* Prescribe and maintain such forms as he shall find reasonably necessary to the operation of this Ordinance.

(f) *Standard Nomenclature.* Prepare and adopt a standard purchasing nomenclature for using agencies and suppliers.

[5] If there are to be exceptions to the purchasing authority of the Agent they should be made on the basis of specified types of supplies rather than in terms of using agencies. Where a more strict policy of exception is desired, the Agent can be given the power to delegate authority to make specific purchases.

[6] See Section 1–307 of the NIMLO Model Administrative Code, "Administrative Policy and Procedures," for subsectional duties of department heads entitled (1) "Responsibility to Administrator"; (2) "Inaugurate Sound Practices"; (3) "Report to Administrator"; (4) "Maintain Records"; (5) "Authority Over Employees"; (6) "Maintain Equipment."

(g) *Vendors' Catalog File.* Prepare, adopt and maintain a vendors' catalog file. Said catalog shall be filed according to materials and shall contain descriptions of vendors' commodities, prices, and discounts.

(h) *Bulk Purchases.* Exploit the possibilities of buying "in bulk" so as to take full advantage of discounts.

(i) *Federal Tax Exemptions.* Act so as to procure for the City all Federal Tax Exemptions to which it is entitled.

(j) *Cooperation with Department of Finance.* Cooperate with the Department of Finance so as to secure for the City the maximum efficiency in budgeting and accounting.

(k) *Disqualification of Bidders.* Have the authority to declare vendors who default on their quotations irresponsible bidders and to disqualify them from receiving any business from the municipality for a stated period of time.

SECTION 2–105. *Committee on Standardization and Specification.* There is hereby established in the Administrative Service of the City the Committee on Standardization and Specification.[7]

(1) *Composition.* The Committee shall consist of the following five officials or their duly designated representatives who shall serve without additional compensation:[8]

Specifications Engineer from the Department of Purchases
Chief Administrator
Director of Finance
Executives from private industry
Chief of Police
Fire Chief
Director of Public Works
Director of Welfare
Superintendent of Schools
Supervisor of Cafeterias
City Engineer
Technician or chemist from the city testing laboratory
Supervisor of Hospitals

(2) *Capacity of Agent.* The Agent shall enforce the written specifications adopted by the Committee. He shall attend all meetings of the Committee in an advisory capacity and shall have the authority to present his recommendations on any proposed standardization or specification.

[7] A municipality which feels that its purchasing volume does not warrant the creation of a committee as herein provided for should substitute the following provision: "The City Purchasing Agent shall prepare and secure with the cooperation of the City departments standard and written specifications for supplies used by the various branches of the City government."

[8] This list of committeemen is suggestive only of five possible appointees and does not purport to be exhaustive of those officials or persons whose service on such a committee would be to the city's advantage. The membership figure of five appointees was adopted on recommendation of competent authority who felt that a greater number would prove unwieldy.

(3) *Committee Duties.* It shall be the duty of the Committee:

(a) *Classification.* To classify all the supplies used by the various branches of the City government.

(b) *Standardization.* To adopt as standards the minimum number of qualities, sizes, and varieties of supplies consistent with the successful operation of the City government.

(c) *Specifications.* To prepare and adopt written specifications of all such standard supplies.

(d) *Meetings.* To hold official meetings at least once every two months.

(4) *Effect of Adoption.* After its adoption, each standard specification shall until revised or rescinded, apply alike in terms and effect to every future purchase and contract for the supply described in such specification.

(a) *Exception.* The Agent, with the approval of the Committee, shall have the authority to exempt any using agency of the City for use of the supply described in such standard specification.

(5) *Laboratory Facilities.* The Committee shall have the authority to make use of the laboratory and engineering facilities of the City and the technical staffs thereof in connection with its work of preparing and adopting standards and written specifications.

(6) *Consultation with Using Agencies.* The Committee shall consult with the heads and other officials of the using agencies to determine their precise requirements and shall endeavor to prescribe those standards which meet the needs of the majority of such agencies.

(7) *Nature of Specifications.* All specifications shall be definite and certain and shall permit of competition.

(a) *Exception.* Provided, however, that the provisions of this subsection shall not apply to non-competitive types and kinds of supplies.

SECTION 2–106. *Requisition and Estimates.* All using agencies, either by or with the authorization of the Head of the Department under which the using agency operates, shall file with the Agent detailed requisitions or estimates of their requirements in supplies and contractual services in such manner, at such times, and for such future periods as the Agent shall prescribe.

(1) *Unforeseen Requirements.* A using agency shall not be prevented from filing, in the same manner, with the Agent at any time a requisition or estimate for any supplies and contractual services, the need for which was not foreseen when the detailed estimates were filed.

(2) *Revisory Power in Agent.* The Agent shall examine each requisition or estimate and shall have the authority to revise it as to quantity, quality, or estimated cost; but revision as to quality shall be in accordance with the standards and specifications established pursuant to this Ordinance.

SECTION 2–107. *Encumbrance of Funds.* Except in cases of emergency, the Agent shall not issue any order for delivery on a contract or open market purchase until the .... (City Treasurer, Auditor, Comptroller or other designated official) shall have certified, after pre-audit, that there is to the credit of the using agencies concerned a sufficient unencumbered appropriation balance, in excess of all unpaid obligations, to defray the amount of such order.

SECTION 2–108. *Prohibition of Interest.* Any purchase order or contract within the purview of this Ordinance in which the Agent, or any officer or employee of the City is financially interested, directly or indirectly, shall be void, except that before the execution of a purchase order or contract the Council shall have the authority to waive compliance with this Section when it finds such action to be in the best interests of the City.[9]

(a) *Gifts and Rebates.* The Agent and every officer and employee of the City are expressly prohibited from accepting, directly or indirectly, from any person, company, firm or corporation to which any purchase order or contract is, or might be awarded, any rebate, gift, money, or anything of value whatsoever, except where given for the use and benefit of the City.

SECTION 2–109. *Competitive Bidding Required.* All purchases of, and contracts for supplies and contractual services, and all sales of personal property which has become obsolete and unusable shall, except as specifically provided herein, be based wherever possible on competitive bids.

SECTION 2–110. *Formal Contract Procedure.* All supplies and contractual services, except as otherwise provided herein, when the estimated cost thereof shall exceed five thousand dollars ($5,000), shall be purchased by formal, written contract from the lowest responsible bidder, after due notice inviting proposals. All sales of personal property which has become obsolete and unusable, when the estimated value shall exceed five thousand dollars ($5,000), shall be sold by formal written contract to the highest responsible bidder, after due notice inviting proposals.

(1) *Notice Inviting Bids.*

(a) *Newspaper.* Notice inviting bids shall be published once in at least one official newspaper in the City and at least five days preceding the last day set for the receipt of proposals.

(a–1) *Scope of Notice.* The newspaper notice required herein shall include a general description of the articles to be purchased or sold, shall state where bid blanks and specifications may be secured, and the time and place for opening bids.

(b) *Bidders' List.* The Agent shall also solicit sealed bids from all responsible prospective suppliers who have requested their names to be added to a "Bidders' List" which the Agent shall maintain, by sending them a copy of such newspaper notice or such other notice as will acquaint them with the proposed purchase or sale. In any case, invitations sent to the vendors on the bidders' list shall be limited to commodities that are similar in character and ordinarily handled by the trade group to which the invitations are sent.

(c) *Bulletin Board.* The Agent shall also advertise all pending purchases or sales by a notice posted on the public bulletin board in the City Hall.

[9] This sentence must be drafted with care and in light of governing charter or statutory considerations. It aims to by-pass a situation of this general nature: Candidate for City Council is president of only company in town selling X autos, trucks and parts. Under existing law the City could not purchase any equipment from the candidate during his term of office and the City would be hard pressed to find a source of parts for the X trucks and autos it now operates.

(2) *Bid Deposits.* When deemed necessary by the Agent, bid deposits shall be prescribed in the public notices inviting bids. Unsuccessful bidders shall be entitled to return of surety where the Agent has required such. A successful bidder shall forfeit any surety required by the Agent upon failure on his part to enter a contract within ten (10) days after the award.

(3) *Bid Opening Procedure.*

(a) *Sealed.* Bids shall be submitted sealed to the Agent and shall be identified as bids on the envelope.

(b) *Opening.* Bids shall be opened in public at the time and place stated in the public notices.

(c) *Tabulation.* A tabulation of all bids received shall be posted for public inspection.

(4) *Rejection of Bids.* The Agent shall have the authority to reject all bids, parts of all bids, or all bids for any one or more supplies or contractual services included in the proposed contract, when the public interest will be served thereby.

(a) *Bidders in Default to City.* The Agent shall not accept the bid of a contractor who is in default on the payment of taxes, licenses or other monies due the City.

(5) *Award of Contract.*

(a) *Authority in Agent.* The Agent shall have the authority to award contracts within the purview of this Ordinance.

(b) *Lowest Responsible Bidder.* Contracts shall be awarded to the lowest responsible bidder. In determining "lowest responsible bidder," in addition to price, the Agent shall consider:

(b–1) The ability, capacity and skill of the bidder to perform the contract or provide the service required;

(b–2) Whether the bidder can perform the contract or provide the service promptly, or within the time specified, without delay or interference;

(b–3) The character, integrity, reputation, judgment, experience and efficiency of the bidder;

(b–4) The quality of performance of previous contracts or services;

(b–5) The previous and existing compliance by the bidder with laws and ordinances relating to the contract or service;

(b–6) The sufficiency of the financial resources and ability of the bidder to perform the contract or provide the service;

(b–7) The quality, availability and adaptability of the supplies, or contractual services to the particular use required;

(b–8) The ability of the bidder to provide future maintenance and service for the use of the subject of the contract;

(b–9) The number and scope of conditions attached to the bid.

(c) *Award to Other Than Low Bidder.* When the award is not given to the lowest bidder, a full and complete statement of the reasons for placing the order elsewhere shall be prepared by the Agent and filed with the other papers relating to the transaction.

(d) *Tie Bids.*

(d–1) *Local vendors.* If all bids received are for the same total amount or unit price, quality and service being equal, the contract shall be awarded to a local bidder.

(d–2) *Outside vendors.* Where subsection (d–1) is not in effect, the Agent shall award the contract to one of the tie bidders by drawing lots in public.

(e) *Performance Bonds.* The Agent shall have the authority to require a performance bond, before entering a contract, in such amount as he shall find reasonably necessary to protect the best interests of the City.

(6) *Prohibition Against Subdivision.* No contract or purchase shall be subdivided to avoid the requirements of this Section.

SECTION 2–111. *Open Market Procedure.* All purchases of supplies, and contractual services, and all sales of personal property which has become obsolete and unusable, of less than the estimated value of five thousand dollars ($5,000) may be made in the open market, without newspaper advertisement and without observing the procedure prescribed by Section 2–110 for the award of formal contracts.

(1) *Minimum Number of Bids.* All open market purchases shall, wherever possible, be based on at least three competitive bids, and shall be awarded to the lowest responsible bidder in accordance with the standards set forth in subsection (5) (b) of Section 2–110 above.

(2) *Notice Inviting Bids.* The Agent shall solicit bids by (a) direct mail request to prospective vendors, (b) by telephone and (c) by public notice posted on the bulletin board of the City Hall.

(3) *Recording.* The Agent shall keep a record of all open market orders and the bids submitted in competition thereon, and such records shall also be open to public inspection.

SECTION 2–112. *Petty Expenditures Revolving Fund.* There is hereby appropriated out of any money in the City Treasury, not otherwise appropriated, ... hundred dollars ($..........), which shall be known as the Petty Expenditures Revolving Fund. From this Fund shall be paid all purchases not in excess of .... dollars ($..........) each, made by the heads of using agencies for incidentals, with the approval of the Agent.

(1) *Accounting.* At the end of each month, the Agent shall render to the .... (City Treasurer, Auditor, Comptroller or other designated official) a statement showing the actual expenditures for each using agency so made out of such Petty Expenditures Revolving Fund, and the City Treasurer shall reimburse said revolving fund for such expenditures in the same manner as other expenditures of such using agencies are paid.

(2) *Rules and Regulations.* The Agent shall promulgate rules and regulations for use of the Petty Expenditures Revolving Fund.

SECTION 2–113. *Central Warehousing.* The Agent shall control and supervise storerooms and warehouses and shall administer the Storerooms Revolving Fund

(1) *Storerooms Revolving Fund.* There is hereby appropriated out of any money in the City treasury, not other wise appropriated, ...

thousand dollars ($..................), which shall be known as the Storerooms Revolving Fund.

(a) *Accounting Procedure.* Requisitions from supplies, in a storeroom or warehouse shall be credited by the Agent to the Storerooms Revolving Fund by a charge against the appropriation of the using Agency.

(b) *Inventory.* The Agent shall maintain a perpetual inventory record of all materials, supplies or equipment stored in storerooms and warehouses.

SECTION 2–114. *Price Agreement Contract Procedure.* The Head of the using Agency shall have the authority to submit requisitions to the Agent for supplies available under the terms of a "price agreement" contract made by the Agent.

SECTION 2–115. *Emergency Purchases.*

(1) *By Agent.* In case of an apparent emergency which requires immediate purchase of supplies or contractual services, the Chief Administrator shall be empowered to authorize the Agent to secure by open market procedure as herein set forth, at the lowest obtainable price, any supplies or contractual services regardless of the amount of the expenditure.

(a) *Recorded Explanation.* A full report of the circumstances of an emergency purchase shall be filed by the Agent with the City Council and shall be entered in the minutes of the Council and shall be open to public inspection.

(2) *By Head of Departments.* In case of actual emergency, and with the consent of the Agent, and the approval of the Chief Administrator, the head of any using agency may purchase directly any supplies whose immediate procurement is essential to prevent delays in the work of the using agency which may vitally affect the life, health or convenience of citizens.

(a) *Recorded Explanation.* The head of such using agency shall send to the Agent a requisition and a copy of the delivery record together with a full written report of the circumstances of the emergency. The report shall be filed with the Council as provided in subsection (a) above.

(b) *Emergency Procedure.* The Agent shall prescribe by rules and regulations the procedure under which emergency purchases by heads of using agencies may be made.

SECTION 2–116. *Inspection and Testing.* The Agent shall inspect, or supervise the inspection of, all deliveries of supplies or contractual services to determine their conformance with the specifications set forth in the order or contract.

(1) *Inspection by Using Agency.* The Agent shall have the authority to authorize using agencies having the staff and facilities for adequate inspection to inspect all deliveries made to such using agencies under rules and regulations which the Agent shall prescribe.

(2) *Tests.* The Agent shall have the authority to require chemical and physical tests of samples submitted with bids and samples of deliveries which are necessary to determine their quality and conformance with the specifications. In the performance of such tests, the Agent shall have the authority to make use of laboratory facilities of any agency of the City government or of any outside laboratory.

SECTION 2–117. *Surplus Stock.* All using agencies shall submit to the Agent, at such times and in such form as he shall prescribe, reports showing stocks of all supplies which are no longer used or which have become obsolete, worn out or scrapped.

(1) *Transfer.* The Agent shall have the authority to transfer surplus stock to other using agencies.

(2) *Sale.* The Agent shall have the authority to sell all supplies which have become unsuitable for public use, or to exchange the same for, or trade in the same on, new supplies.

(a) *Competitive Bidding.* Sales under this Section shall be made to the highest responsible bidder and in conformance with Section 2–110 or Section 2–111 hereof, whichever is applicable.

SECTION 2–118. *Cooperative Purchasing.* The Agent shall have the authority to join with other units of government in cooperative purchasing plans when the best interests of the City would be served thereby.

STANDARD BID AND CONTRACT—TERMS AND CONDITIONS

STATE OF CONNECTICUT
DEPARTMENT OF FINANCE AND CONTROL
PURCHASING DIVISION
HARTFORD, CONNECTICUT

Scope

These Standard Bid and Contract Terms and Conditions are definitely a part of each bid, proposal and contract, and apply in like force to contracts for the purchase of personal property and contractual services.

All bids issued by the Supervisor will bind Bidders to the terms and conditions herein set forth, except as specifically qualified in Special Bid and Contract Terms and Conditions issued in connection with any individual bid.

Definitions

As used herein, as well as in all specifications, bids, awards, contracts, etc. issued by the Supervisor, the following definitions shall apply, unless otherwise indicated:

STATE: The State of Connecticut.

SUPERVISOR: Supervisor of Purchases for the State of Connecticut.

DIVISION: Purchasing Division, Department of Finance and Control, State of Connecticut.

AGENCY: All State Departments, Institutions and Agencies, or any one of them.

BIDDER: Any Individual, Firm or Corporation submitting proposals on bids issued by the Supervisor.

CONTRACTOR: Any Individual, Firm or Corporation to whom contract is awarded against a proposal submitted.

BID: The documents comprising an invitation to bid for furnishing commodities or services.

PROPOSAL: The offer of a Bidder to furnish commodities or services in response to a bid.

CONTRACT: The acceptance by the State of a proposal by a Bidder to furnish commodities or services.

All qualified prospective Bidders on the mailing lists of the Division will be eligible to receive copies of bids issued by the Supervisor on all commodity groups on which a desire to receive bids has been indicated. Failure to submit proposals on or reply to three consecutive bids mailed to a prospective Bidder will cause the name of such Bidder to be removed from the mailing list for such group.

ANY ALLEGED ORAL AGREEMENT OR ARRANGEMENT MADE BY A BIDDER OR CONTRACTOR WITH ANY AGENCY, OR THE SUPERVISOR, OR AN EMPLOYEE OF THE DIVISION, WILL BE DISREGARDED.

Submission of Proposal

1. Proposals must be submitted on and in accordance with forms supplied by the Supervisor. Telegraphic proposals will not be accepted unless so stated in the bid. In the event telegraphic proposals are acceptable under the terms of a bid, the proposal forms supplied by the Supervisor must be properly and completely executed with the exception of prices and returned in time to be received by the Supervisor not later than the time and date specified for opening of proposals. Telephone proposals will not be accepted under any circumstances.

2. The time and date proposals are to be opened is given in each bid issued. All proposals must be sealed in envelopes furnished by the Division or those supplied by the Bidder. All proposals must be addressed to the Supervisor of Purchases, State of Connecticut, Hartford 15, Connecticut. Proposal envelopes must clearly indicate the bid number as well as the date and time of the opening of the proposal. The name and address of the Bidder should appear in the upper left hand corner of the envelope.

3. Bidders are cautioned to verify their proposals before submission, as amendments to, or withdrawal of proposals submitted, if received by the Supervisor after time specified for opening of proposals, will not be considered. This applies to proposals sent by mail, those delivered in person, as well as telegraphic proposals.

4. All information required in bid forms in connection with each item against which a proposal is submitted must be given to constitute a regular proposal.

5. Qualified proposals are subject to rejection in whole or in part.

6. Proposals may be submitted for all or any part of total quantities, or for any or all agency requirements listed in the bid, unless otherwise specifically indicated.

7. Alternate proposals will not be considered unless specifically called for in the bid.

8. Unless qualified by the provision "NO SUBSTITUTE," the use of the name of a manufacturer, brand, make or catalog designation in specifying an item does not restrict bidders to that manufacturer, brand, make or catalog designation identification. This is used simply to indicate the character, quality and/or performance equivalence of the commodity desired, but the commodity on which proposals are submitted must be of such character, quality and/or performance equivalence that it will serve the purpose for which it is to be used equally as well as that specified. In submitting a proposal on a commodity other than as specified, Bidder shall furnish complete data and identification with respect to the alternate commodity he proposes to furnish. Consideration will be given to proposals submitted on alternate commodities to the extent that such action is deemed to serve best the interests of the State. If a Bidder does not indicate that the commodity he proposes to furnish is other than as specified, it will be construed to mean that the Bidder proposes to furnish the exact commodity as described.

9. If the Bidder proposes to furnish any item of a foreign make or product, he should write the word "Foreign" together with the name of the originating country opposite such item on the proposal. All items not so designated will be considered to be of domestic origin.

10. Prices should be extended in decimals, not fractions; to be net, and shall include transportation and delivery charges fully prepaid by the Contractor to the destination specified in the bid, and subject only to cash discount.

11. The State of Connecticut is exempt from the payment of excise, transportation and sales taxes imposed by the Federal Government and/or the State. Such taxes must not be included in proposal prices. Federal excise exemption certificates will be furnished, on request, by either the ordering Agency or the Division.

12. In the event of a discrepancy between the unit price and the extension, the unit price shall govern.

13. Bidder declares that the proposal is not made in connection with any other Bidder submitting a proposal for the same commodity or commodities, and is in all respects fair and without collusion or fraud.

14. All proposals will be opened and read publicly and are subject to public inspection. Bidders may be present or be represented at all openings. Abstracts of proposals received are not prepared for distribution by the Division.

15. A guaranty that bidder will execute contract and furnish performance surety, when requested and within ten (10) days after execution date of contract, shall, if required, be submitted with proposal. Guaranty may be submitted in any one of the following forms:

a. Annual Proposal Bond in the amount of $2,500.00 to cover all pro posals up to $50,000.00 submitted within one year.
b. Individual proposal bond for five (5) per cent of the total amount o each separate proposal.
c. Certified check made payable to Treasurer, State of Connecticut fo five (5) per cent of the total amount of each separate proposal.

16. Performance surety binding the Contractor faithfully to fulfill the obligations of his proposal as accepted, may be required. Such surety, in an amount up to 25 per cent of each separate award, may be submitted in the form of a performance bond or certified check.

17. Standard bond forms will be furnished by the Division on request.

18. Bonds must meet the following requirements:

a. Corporation. The bond must be signed by an official of the corporation above his official title and the corporate seal must be affixed over his signature.

b. Firm or Partnership. The bond must be signed by all of the partners, and indicate they are "Doing Business As (name of firm)."

c. Individual. The bond must be signed by the individual owning the business, and indicated "Owner."

d. The surety company executing the bond must be licensed to do business in the State of Connecticut, or bond must be countersigned by a company so licensed.

e. The bond must be signed by an official of the surety company and the corporate seal must be affixed over his signature.

f. Signatures of two witnesses for both the principal and the surety must appear on the bond.

g. A Power of Attorney for the official signing the bond for the surety company must be submitted with the bond, unless such Power of Attorney has previously been filed with the Division.

Samples

19. All specifications are minimum standards and accepted proposal samples do not supersede specification for quality unless proposal sample is superior, in which case deliveries must have the same identity and quality as the accepted proposal sample.

20. Samples, when required, must be submitted strictly in accordance with instructions; otherwise proposal may not be considered. If samples are requested subsequent to opening of proposals, they shall be delivered within ten (10) days following request, unless additional time is granted. Samples must be furnished free of charge and must be accompanied by descriptive memorandum invoices indicating if the Bidder desires their return, provided they have not been used or made useless by tests. Award samples may be held for comparison with deliveries. Samples will be returned at the Bidder's risk and subject to his expense.

21. When the bid indicates that an item to be purchased is to be equivalent to a sample, such samples will be on display in the Division, unless another location is specified. Failure on the part of a Bidder to examine sample shall not entitle him to any relief from the conditions imposed by the bid.

Award

22. Award will be made to the lowest responsible qualified Bidder. The quality of the articles to be supplied, their conformity with the specifications, their suit-

ability to the requirements of the State, and the delivery terms will be taken into consideration in making the award.

23. The Supervisor reserves the right to award by item, or part thereof, groups of items, or parts thereof, or all items of the bid, and to award contracts to one or more bidders submitting identical proposals as to price; to reject any and all bids in whole or in part; to waive technical defects, irregularities and omissions if, in his judgment, the best interest of the State will be served.

24. The Supervisor reserves the right to make awards within thirty (30) calendar days from the date proposals are opened, unless otherwise specified in the bid, during which period proposals shall not be withdrawn unless the Bidder distinctly states in his proposal that acceptance thereof must be made within a shorter specified time. Should award, in whole or in part, be delayed beyond the period of thirty (30) days or an earlier date specified by a Bidder in his proposal, such award shall be conditioned upon Bidder's acceptance.

25. A Bidder, if requested, must be prepared to present evidence of experience, ability, service facilities and financial standing necessary to meet satisfactorily the requirements set forth or implied in the bid.

26. The quantities listed in the proposal schedule may be increased or decreased by the Supervisor to meet new or amended requirements of state agencies between the time the bid is issued and the time award is made, subject to the Bidder's acceptance.

27. Other things being equal, preference will be given to resident bidders of the State and to commodities produced or manufactured in the State.

28. Cash discount may be offered by Bidder for prompt payment of bills, but such cash discount will not be taken into consideration in determining low bidder[23] except in the case of tie bids and then only provided such discount is based on payment of invoice not less than thirty (30) days after satisfactory delivery and/or receipt of invoice, whichever is later.

29. The Supervisor reserves the right to reject the bid of any bidder in default of any prior contract or guilty of misrepresentation, or of any company having as its sales agent or representative, or member of the firm, any individual in default or guilty of misrepresentation.

Contract

30. Each proposal will be received, with the understanding that the acceptance[24] in writing by the Supervisor of the offer to furnish any or all of the commodities described therein, shall constitute a contract between the Bidder and the State, which shall bind the Bidder on his part to furnish and deliver

[23] Some cities which have mechanized the processing of invoices do consider discounts in determining the lowest responsible bidder. Chicago and Baltimore are in this category.

[24] Some municipalities have the bidders sign three copies of their bid at time bidder submits his sealed bid. The same bid form contains a section for the government's "acceptance." When signed by the government officials, it constitutes "offer and acceptance, for a consideration," therefore a binding contract by law.

the commodities at the prices given and in accordance with conditions of said accepted proposal and specification and Standard Bid and Contract Terms and Conditions Form SP–7A (Rev. 6–54) and the State on its part to order from such contractor, except for causes beyond reasonable control, and subject to the availability of appropriated funds, and to pay for at the contract prices, all commodities or services ordered and delivered. The State reserves the right to order up to ten (10) per cent more or less than the quantity listed in the bid or as amended in the award. This acceptance is not an order to ship—See No. 40.

31. Quantities are subject to order against contracts by State agencies not specifically mentioned, or to transfer between agencies under an adjustment in transportation costs, providing such transportation costs are based on separately determined delivery costs to individual agencies.

32. No alterations or variations of the terms of contract shall be valid or binding upon the State unless made in writing and signed by the Supervisor.

33. Contracts will remain in force for full period specified and until all articles ordered before date of termination shall have been satisfactorily delivered and accepted (and thereafter until all terms and conditions have been met), unless:

a. Terminated prior to expiration by satisfactory delivery against orders of entire quantities contracted for.

b. Extended upon written authorization of the Supervisor and accepted by Contractor, to permit ordering of unordered balances or additional quantities at contract price and in accordance with contract terms.

34. Contract quantities will be assumed to have been ordered out at expiration period according to contract terms. Contractor must furnish Supervisor with a statement of unordered balances at least ten (10) days prior to termination of contract.

35. It is mutually understood and agreed that the Contractor shall not assign, transfer, convey, sublet, or otherwise dispose of his contract or his right, title or interest therein, or his power to execute such contract, to any other person, firm or corporation, without the previous written consent of the Supervisor.

36. The placing in the mail to the address given in his bid or delivery of a notice of award to a bidder will constitute notice of acceptance of contract. When so requested by the Supervisor, the Contractor shall execute a formal contract with the State for the complete performance specified therein.

37. The contract may be cancelled or annulled by the Supervisor upon nonperformance of contract terms or failure of the Contractor to furnish performance surety within ten (10) days from date of request. Any unfulfilled deliveries against such contract may be purchased from other sources at the Contractor's expense.

38. Failure of a Contractor to deliver within the time specified or within reasonable time as interpreted by the Supervisor or failure to make replacements of rejected commodities when so requested, immediately or as directed by the Supervisor, will constitute authority for the Supervisor to purchase in the open market to replace the commodities rejected or not delivered. The Supervisor reserves the right to authorize immediate purchases in the open market against

rejections on any contract when necessary. On all such purchases, the Contractor agrees promptly to reimburse the State for excess costs occasioned by such purchases. Such purchases will be deducted from contract quantities. However, should public necessity demand it, the State reserves the right to use or consume commodities delivered which are substandard in quality, subject to an adjustment in price to be determined by the Supervisor.

39. When commodities are rejected, same must be removed by the Contractor from the premises of the Agency within forty-eight (48) hours after notification, unless public health and safety require immediate destruction or other disposal of such rejected delivery. Rejected items left longer than forty-eight (48) hours will be considered as abandoned and the State shall have the right to dispose of them as its own property.

40. Orders against Contracts will be placed by Agencies directly with the Contractor. All orders must be in writing and must bear the contract number and approval of the State Comptroller. Contractor making delivery without formal written order does so at his own risk.

41. The Supervisor reserves the right to remove from mailing lists for future bids for an indeterminate period, the name of any Bidder for failure to accept contract, or the name of any Contractor for unsatisfactory performance of contract.

Contract Guaranty

42. Contractor hereby guarantees to:

a. Perform contract in accordance with the specifications and proposal under which the contract was awarded.

b. Save the State, its agents, or employees harmless from liability of any kind for the use of any copyrighted or uncopyrighted composition, secret process, patented or unpatented invention, article or appliance furnished or used in the performance of the contract of which the contractor is not the patentee, assignee, or licensee.

c. Guarantee his products against defective material or workmanship and to repair or replace any damage or marring occasioned in transit.

d. Furnish adequate protection from damage for all work and to repair damages of any kind, for which he or his workmen are responsible, to the premises or equipment, to his own work or to the work of other contractors.

e. Pay for all permits, licenses, and fees, and to give all notices and comply with all laws, ordinances, rules and regulations of the city or town in which the installation is to be made, and of the State of Connecticut

f. Carry proper insurance to protect the State from loss.

Delivery

43. It shall be understood and agreed that any and all commodities furnished shall comply fully with all applicable Federal and State laws and regulations.

44. Any equipment delivered must be standard new equipment, latest model, except as otherwise specifically stated in bid. Where any part or nominal appurtenances of equipment is not described, it shall be understood that all the equipment and appurtenances which are usually provided in the manufacturer's stock model shall be furnished.

45. Materials and supplies delivered must be new items except as otherwise specifically stated in bid.

46. Delivery must be made as ordered and in accordance with proposal. If no delivery instructions appear on order, it will be interpreted to mean prompt delivery. The decision of the Supervisor as to reasonable compliance with delivery terms shall be final. Burden of proof of delay in receipt of order shall rest with the Contractor.

47. Any request for extension of time of delivery from that specified must be approved by the State, such extension applying only to the particular item or shipment.

48. Commodities shall be securely and properly packed for shipment, according to accepted standard commercial practice, without extra charge for packing cases, baling or sacks, the containers to remain the property of the State unless otherwise stated in the bid or proposal.

49. Deliveries are subject to reweighing over official sealed scales designated by the State and payment will be made on the basis of net weight of materials received.

Inspections and Tests

50. The Inspection of all commodities and the making of chemical and physical tests of samples submitted with bids and samples of deliveries to determine whether or not the specifications are being complied with shall be made in the manner prescribed by the Supervisor.

51. Any item which fails in any way to meet the terms of the contract is subject to rejection or to be paid for at an adjusted price basis. The decision of the Supervisor shall be final.

Payment

52. Payment for all accepted commodities and services shall be due within thirty (30) days after receipt thereof, or the date invoice is received, whichever is later. Where there is a question of non-performance involved, payment in whole or in part against which to charge back any adjustment required, will be withheld. In the event cash discount is involved, the withholding of payment as provided herein shall not deprive the State from taking such discount.

53. Payment will be made only after presentation of state invoice forms. Additional forms may be obtained from the ordering Agency and/or the Division. All invoices shall be sent directly to the ordering Agency. Inquiries regarding the status of unpaid invoices shall likewise be directed to the ordering Agency.

54. All charges against a Contractor shall be deducted from current obligations

that are due or may become due. In the event that collection is not made in this manner, the Contractor shall pay the State, on demand, the amount of such charges. All remittances shall be made payable to Treasurer, State of Connecticut.

55. Payment for the used portion of an inferior delivery will be made by the State on an adjusted price basis determined by the Supervisor.

Saving Clause

56. It is understood and agreed that the Contractor shall not be held liable for any losses resulting if the fulfillment of the terms of the contract shall be delayed or prevented by wars, acts of public enemies, strikes, fires, floods, acts of God, or for any other acts not within the control of the Contractor and which by the exercise of reasonable diligency, the Contractor is unable to prevent.

57. Should the performance of any contract be delayed or prevented as set forth in Paragraph 56, the Contractor agrees to give immediate written notice and explanation of the cause and probable duration of any such delay.

Effective July 1, 1954 SUPERVISOR OF PURCHASES

GENERAL PROVISIONS—SUPPLY CONTRACT—FEDERAL GOVERNMENT*

(as prescribed by General Services Administration)

1. DEFINITIONS

As used throughout this contract, the following terms shall have the meanings set forth below:

(*a*) The term "Secretary" means the Secretary, the Under Secretary, or any Assistant Secretary of the Department, and the head or any assistant head of the Federal agency; and the term "his duly authorized representative" means any person or persons or board (other than the Contracting Officer) authorized to act for the Secretary.

(*b*) The term "Contracting Officer" means the person executing this contract on behalf of the Government, and any other officer or civilian employee who is a properly designated Contracting Officer; and the term includes, except as otherwise provided in this contract, the authorized representative of a Contracting Officer acting within the limits of his authority.

(*c*) Except as otherwise provided in this contract, the term "subcontracts" includes purchase orders under this contract.

2. CHANGES

The Contracting Officer may at any time, by a written order, and without notice to the sureties, make changes, within the general scope of this contract, in any one or more of the following: (i) Drawings, designs, or specifications, where

* Standard form 32, October, 1957, edition.

the supplies to be furnished are to be specially manufactured for the Government in accordance therewith; (ii) method of shipment or packing; and (iii) place of delivery. If any such change causes an increase or decrease in the cost of, or the time required for, the performance of any part of the work under this contract, whether changed or not changed by any such order, an equitable adjustment shall be made in the contract price or delivery schedule, or both, and the contract shall be modified in writing accordingly. Any claim by the Contractor for adjustment under this clause must be asserted within 30 days from the date of receipt by the Contractor of the notification of change: *Provided, however,* That the Contracting Officer, if he decides that the facts justify such action, may receive and act upon any such claim asserted at any time prior to final payment under this contract. Where the cost of property made obsolete or excess as a result of a change is included in the Contractor's claim for adjustment, the Contracting Officer shall have the right to prescribe the manner of disposition of such property. Failure to agree to any adjustment shall be a dispute concerning a question of fact within the meaning of the clause of this contract entitled "Disputes." However, nothing in this clause shall excuse the Contractor from proceeding with the contract as changed.

3. EXTRAS

Except as otherwise provided in this contract, no payment for extras shall be made unless such extras and the price therefor have been authorized in writing by the Contracting Officer.

4. VARIATION IN QUANTITY

No variation in the quantity of any item called for by this contract will be accepted unless such variation has been caused by conditions of loading, shipping, or packing, or allowances in manufacturing processes, and then only to the extent, if any, specified elsewhere in this contract.

5. INSPECTION

(*a*) All supplies (which term throughout this clause includes without limitation raw materials, components, intermediate assemblies, and end products) shall be subject to inspection and test by the Government, to the extent practicable at all times and places including the period of manufacture, and in any event prior to acceptance.

(*b*) In case any supplies or lots of supplies are defective in material or workmanship or otherwise not in conformity with the requirements of this contract, the Government shall have the right either to reject them (with or without instructions as to their disposition) or to require their correction. Supplies or lots of supplies which have been rejected or required to be corrected shall be removed or, if permitted or required by the Contracting Officer, corrected in place by and at the expense of the Contractor promptly after notice, and shall not thereafter be tendered for acceptance unless the former rejection or requirement of correction is disclosed. If the Contractor fails promptly to remove such supplies or lots of supplies which are required to be removed, or promptly to replace or correct such supplies or lots of supplies, the Government either (i) may by contract or otherwise replace or correct such supplies and charge to the Contractor the cost occasioned the Government thereby, or (ii) may terminate this contract for default as provided in the clause of this contract entitled "Default." Unless the Contractor corrects or replaces such supplies within the delivery schedule, the Contracting Officer may require the delivery of such supplies at a reduction in price which is equitable under the circumstances. Failure to agree to such reduction of price shall be a dispute concerning a question of fact within the meaning of the clause of this contract entitled "Disputes."

(*c*) If any inspection or test is made by the Government on the premises of the Contractor or a subcontractor, the Contractor without additional charge shall provide all reasonable facilities and assistance for the safety and convenience of the Government inspectors in the performance of their duties. If Government inspection or test is made at a point other than the premises of the Contractor or a subcontractor, it shall be at the expense of the Government except as otherwise provided in this contract: *Provided,* That in case of rejection the Government shall not be liable for any reduction in value of samples used in connection with such inspection or test. All inspections and tests by the Government shall be performed in such a manner as not to unduly delay the work. The Government reserves the right to charge to the Contractor any additional cost of Government inspection and test when supplies are not ready at the time such inspection and test is requested by the Contractor or when reinspection or retest is necessitated by prior rejection. Acceptance or rejection of the supplies shall be made as promptly as practicable after delivery, except as otherwise provided in this contract; but failure to inspect and accept or reject supplies shall neither relieve the Contractor from responsibility for such supplies as are not in accordance with the contract requirements nor impose liability on the Government therefor.

(*d*) The inspection and test by the Government of any supplies or lots thereof does not relieve the Contractor from any responsibility regarding defects or other failures to meet the contract requirements which may be discovered prior to acceptance. Except as otherwise provided in this contract, acceptance shall be conclusive except as regards latent defects, fraud, or such gross mistakes as amount to fraud.

(*e*) The Contractor shall provide and maintain an inspection system acceptable to the Government covering the supplies hereunder. Records of all inspection work by the Contractor shall be kept complete and available to the Government during the performance of this contract and for such longer period as may be specified elsewhere in this contract.

6. RESPONSIBILITY FOR SUPPLIES

Except as otherwise provided in this contract, (i) the Contractor shall be responsible for the supplies covered by this contract until they are delivered a the designated delivery point, regardless of the point of inspection; (ii) after delivery to the Government at the designated point and prior to acceptance by the Government or rejection and giving notice thereof by the Government, the Government shall be responsible for the loss or destruction of or damage to the supplies only if such loss, destruction, or damage results from the negligence of officers, agents, or employees of the Government acting within the scope of their employment; and (iii) the Contractor shall bear all risks as to rejected supplies after notice of rejection, except that the Government shall be responsible for the loss, or destruction of, or damage to the supplies only if such loss, destruction or damage results from the gross negligence of officers, agents, or employees of the Government acting within the scope of their employment.

7. PAYMENTS

The Contractor shall be paid, upon the submission of proper invoices or vouchers, the prices stipulated herein for supplies delivered and accepted or services rendered and accepted, less deductions, if any, as herein provided. Unless otherwise specified, payment will be made on partial deliveries accepted by the Government when the amount due on such deliveries so warrants; or, when requested by the Contractor, payment for accepted partial deliveries shall be made whenever such payment would equal or exceed either $1,000 or 50 per cent of the total amount of this contract.

8. ASSIGNMENT OF CLAIMS

(*a*) Pursuant to the provisions of the Assignment of Claims Act of 1940, as amended (31 U.S. Code 203, 41 U.S. Code 15), if this contract provides for payments aggregating $1,000 or more, claims for monies due or to become due the Contractor from the Government under this contract may be assigned to a bank, trust company, or other financing institution, including any Federal lending agency, and may thereafter be further assigned and reassigned to any such institution. Any such assignment or reassignment shall cover all amounts payable under this contract and not already paid, and shall not be made to more than one party, except that any such assignment or reassignment may be made to one party as agent or trustee for two or more parties participating in such financing. Notwithstanding any provisions of this contract, payments to an assignee of any monies due or to become due under this contract shall not, to the extent provided in said Act, as amended, be subject to reduction or set-off. (*The preceding sentence applies only if this contract is with the Department of Defense, the General Services Administration, the Atomic Energy Commission, or any other department or agency of the United States designated by the President pursuant to clause 4 of the proviso of section 1 of the Assignment of Claims Act of 1940, as amended by the Act of May 15, 1951, 65 Stat. 41.*)

(*b*) In no event shall copies of this contract or of any plans, specifications, or other similar documents relating to work under this contract, if marked "Top Secret," "Secret," or "Confidential," be furnished to any assignee of any claim arising under this contract or to any other person not entitled to receive the same: *Provided,* That a copy of any part or all of this contract so marked may be furnished, or any information contained therein may be disclosed, to such assignee upon the prior written authorization of the Contracting Officer.

9. ADDITIONAL BOND SECURITY

If any surety upon any bond furnished in connection with this contract becomes unacceptable to the Government, or if any such surety fails to furnish reports as to his financial condition from time to time as requested by the Government, the Contractor shall promptly furnish such additional security as may be required from time to time to protect the interests of the Government and of persons supplying labor or materials in the prosecution of the work contemplated by this contract.

10. EXAMINATION OF RECORDS

(The following clause is applicable if the amount of this contract exceeds $1,000 and was entered into by means of negotiation, but is not applicable if this contract was entered into by means of formal advertising.)

(*a*) The Contractor agrees that the Comptroller General of the United States or any of his duly authorized representatives shall, until the expiration of three years after final payment under this contract, have access to and the right to examine any directly pertinent books, documents, papers, and records of the Contractor involving transactions related to this contract.

(*b*) The Contractor further agrees to include in all his subcontracts hereunder a provision to the effect that the subcontractor agrees that the Comptroller General of the United States or any of his duly authorized representatives shall, until the expiration of three years after final payment under the subcontract, have access to and the right to examine any directly pertinent books, documents, papers, and records of such subcontractor, involving transactions related to the subcontract. The term "subcontract" as used in this clause excludes (i) purchase orders not exceeding $1,000 and (ii) subcontracts or purchase orders for public utility services at rates established for uniform applicability to the general public.

11. DEFAULT

(*a*) The Government may, subject to the provisions of paragraph (*c*) below, by written notice of default to the Contractor, terminate the whole or any part of this contract in any one of the following circumstances:
(i) if the Contractor fails to make delivery of the supplies or to perform the services within the time specified herein or any extension thereof; or
(ii) if the Contractor fails to perform any of the other provisions of thi contract, or so fails to make progress as to endanger performance of thi

contract in accordance with its terms, and in either of these two circumstances does not cure such failure within a period of 10 days (or such longer period as the Contracting Officer may authorize in writing) after receipt of notice from the Contracting Officer specifying such failure.

(*b*) In the event the Government terminates this contract in whole or in part as provided in paragraph (*a*) of this clause, the Government may procure, upon such terms and in such manner as the Contracting Officer may deem appropriate, supplies or services similar to those so terminated, and the Contractor shall be liable to the Government for any excess costs for such similar supplies or services: *Provided,* That the Contractor shall continue the performance of this contract to the extent not terminated under the provisions of this clause.

(*c*) Except with respect to defaults of subcontractors, the Contractor shall not be liable for any excess costs if the failure to perform the contract arises out of causes beyond the control and without the fault or negligence of the Contractor. Such causes may include, but are not restricted to, acts of God or of the public enemy, acts of the Government in either its sovereign or contractual capacity, fires, floods, epidemics, quarantine restrictions, strikes, freight embargoes, and unusually severe weather; but in every case the failure to perform must be beyond the control and without the fault or negligence of the Contractor. If the failure to perform is caused by the default of a subcontractor, and if such default arises out of causes beyond the control of both the Contractor and subcontractor, and without the fault or negligence of either of them, the Contractor shall not be liable for any excess costs for failure to perform, unless the supplies or services to be furnished by the subcontractor were obtainable from other sources in sufficient time to permit the Contractor to meet the required delivery schedule.

(*d*) If this contract is terminated as provided in paragraph (*a*) of this clause, the Government, in addition to any other rights provided in this clause, may require the Contractor to transfer title and deliver to the Government, in the manner and to the extent directed by the Contracting Officer, (i) any completed supplies, and (ii) such partially completed supplies and materials, parts, tools, dies, jigs, fixtures, plans, drawings, information, and contract rights (hereinafter called "manufacturing materials") as the Contractor has specifically produced or specifically acquired for the performance of such part of this contract as has been terminated; and the Contractor shall, upon direction of the Contracting Officer, protect and preserve property in possession of the Contractor in which the Government has an interest. Payment for completed supplies delivered to and accepted by the Government shall be at the contract price. Payment for manufacturing materials delivered to and accepted by the Government and for the protection and preservation of property shall be in an amount agreed upon by the Contractor and Contracting Officer; failure to agree to such amount shall be a dispute concerning a question of fact within the meaning of the clause of this contract entitled "Disputes."

(*e*) If, after notice of termination of this contract under the provisions of paragraph (*a*) of this clause, it is determined that the failure to perform this contract is due to causes beyond the control and without the fault or negligence of the Contractor or subcontractor pursuant to the provisions of paragraph (*c*) of this clause, such notice of default shall be deemed to have been issued pursuant to the clause of this contract entitled "Termination for Convenience of the Government," and the rights and obligations of the parties hereto shall in such event be governed by such clause. (*Except as otherwise provided in this contract, this paragraph* (*e*) *applies only if this contract contains such clause.*)

(*f*) The rights and remedies of the Government provided in this clause shall not be exclusive and are in addition to any other rights and remedies provided by law or under this contract.

12. DISPUTES

(*a*) Except as otherwise provided in this contract, any dispute concerning a question of fact arising under this contract which is not disposed of by agreement shall be decided by the Contracting Officer, who shall reduce his decision to writing and mail or otherwise furnish a copy thereof to the Contractor. The decision of the Contracting Officer shall be final and conclusive unless, within 30 days from the date of receipt of such copy, the Contractor mails or otherwise furnishes to the Contracting Officer a written appeal addressed to the Secretary. The decision of the Secretary or his duly authorized representative for the determination of such appeals shall be final and conclusive unless determined by a court of competent jurisdiction to have been fraudulent, or capricious, or arbitrary, or so grossly erroneous as necessarily to imply bad faith, or not supported by substantial evidence. In connection with any appeal proceeding under this clause, the Contractor shall be afforded an opportunity to be heard and to offer evidence in support of its appeal. Pending final decision of a dispute hereunder, the Contractor shall proceed diligently with the performance of the contract and in accordance with the Contracting Officer's decision.

(*b*) This "Disputes" clause does not preclude consideration of law questions in connection with decisions provided for in paragraph (*a*) above: *Provided,* That nothing in this contract shall be construed as making final the decision of any administrative official, representative, or board on a question of law.

13. NOTICE AND ASSISTANCE REGARDING PATENT INFRINGEMENT

The provisions of this clause shall be applicable only if the amount of this contract exceeds $5,000.

(*a*) The Contractor shall report to the Contracting Officer, promptly and in reasonable written detail, each notice or claim of patent infringement based on the performance of this contract of which the Contractor has knowledge.

(*b*) In the event of litigation against the Government on account of any claim of patent infringement arising out of the performance of this contract or out of the use of any supplies furnished or work or service performed hereunder, the Contractor shall furnish to the Government, upon request, all evidence and information in possession of the Contractor pertaining to such litigation. Such evidence and information shall be furnished at the expense of the Government except in those cases in which the Contractor has agreed to indemnify the Government against the claim being asserted.

14. BUY AMERICAN ACT

(*a*) In acquiring end products, the Buy American Act (41 U.S. Code 10 a–d) provides that the Government give preference to domestic source end products. For the purpose of this clause:
(i) "components" means those articles, materials, and supplies, which are directly incorporated in the end products;
(ii) "end products" means those articles, materials, and supplies, which are to be acquired under this contract for public use; and
(iii) a "domestic source end product" means (A) an unmanufactured end product which has been mined or produced in the United States and (B) an end product manufactured in the United States if the cost of the components thereof which are mined, produced, or manufactured in the United States exceeds 50 per cent of the cost of all its components. For the purposes of this (*a*) (iii) (B), components of foreign origin of the same type or kind as the products referred to in (*b*) (ii) or (iii) of this clause shall be treated as components mined, produced, or manufactured in the United States.

(*b*) The Contractor agrees that there will be delivered under this contract only domestic source end products, except end products:
(i) which are for use outside the United States;
(ii) which the Government determines are not mined, produced, or manufactured in the United States in sufficient and reasonably available commercial quantities and of a satisfactory quality;
(iii) as to which the Secretary determines the domestic preference to be inconsistent with the public interest; or
(iv) as to which the Secretary determines the cost to the Government to be unreasonable.
(The foregoing requirements are administered in accordance with Executive Order No. 10582, dated December 17, 1954.)

5. CONVICT LABOR

In connection with the performance of work under this contract, the Contractor grees not to employ any person undergoing sentence of imprisonment at hard abor.

16. EIGHT-HOUR LAW OF 1912—OVERTIME COMPENSATION

This contract, to the extent that it is of a character specified in the Eight-Hour Law of 1912, as amended (40 U.S. Code 324–326) and is not covered by the Walsh-Healey Public Contracts Act (41 U.S. Code 35–45), is subject to the following provisions and exceptions of said Eight-Hour Law of 1912, as amended, and to all other provisions and exceptions of said Law:

No laborer or mechanic doing any part of the work contemplated by this contract, in the employ of the Contractor or any subcontractor contracting for any part of said work contemplated, shall be required or permitted to work more than eight hours in any one calendar day upon such work, except upon the condition that compensation is paid to such laborer or mechanic in accordance with the provisions of this clause. The wages of every laborer and mechanic employed by the Contractor or any subcontractor engaged in the performance of this contract shall be computed on a basic day rate of eight hours per day; and work in excess of eight hours per day is permitted only upon the condition that every such laborer and mechanic shall be compensated for all hours worked in excess of eight hours per day at not less than one and one-half times the basic rate of pay. For each violation of the requirements of this clause a penalty of five dollars shall be imposed for each laborer or mechanic for every calendar day in which such employee is required or permitted to labor more than eight hours upon said work without receiving compensation computed in accordance with this clause, and all penalties thus imposed shall be withheld for the use and benefit of the Government.

17. WALSH-HEALEY PUBLIC CONTRACTS ACT

If this contract is for the manufacture or furnishing of materials, supplies, articles, or equipment in an amount which exceeds or may exceed $10,000 and is otherwise subject to the Walsh-Healey Public Contracts Act, as amended (41 U.S. Code 35–45), there are hereby incorporated by reference all representations and stipulations required by said Act and regulations issued thereunder by the Secretary of Labor, such representations and stipulations being subject to all applicable rulings and interpretations of the Secretary of Labor which are now or may hereafter be in effect.

18. NONDISCRIMINATION IN EMPLOYMENT

(*a*) In connection with the performance of work under this contract, the Contractor agrees not to discriminate against any employee or applicant for employment because of race, religion, color, or national origin. The aforesaid provision shall include, but not be limited to, the following: employment, upgrading, demotion or transfer; recruitment or recruitment advertising; layoff or termination; rates of pay or other forms of compensation; and selection for training, including apprenticeship. The Contractor agrees to post hereafter in conspicuous places, available for employees and applicants for employment, notices to be provided by the

Contracting Officer setting forth the provisions of the nondiscrimination clause.

(*b*) The Contractor further agrees to insert the foregoing provision in all subcontracts hereunder, except subcontracts for standard commercial supplies or raw materials.

19. OFFICIALS NOT TO BENEFIT

No member of or delegate to Congress, or resident commissioner, shall be admitted to any share or part of this contract, or to any benefit that may arise therefrom; but this provision shall not be construed to extend to this contract if made with a corporation for its general benefit.

20. COVENANT AGAINST CONTINGENT FEES

The Contractor warrants that no person or selling agency has been employed or retained to solicit or secure this contract upon an agreement or understanding for a commission, percentage, brokerage, or contingent fee, excepting bona fide employees or bona fide established commercial or selling agencies maintained by the Contractor for the purpose of securing business. For breach or violation of this warranty the Government shall have the right to annul this contract without liability or in its discretion to deduct from the contract price or consideration, or otherwise recover, the full amount of such commission, percentage, brokerage, or contingent fee.

21. UTILIZATION OF SMALL BUSINESS CONCERNS

(*a*) It is the policy of the Government as declared by the Congress that a fair proportion of the purchases and contracts for supplies and services for the Government be placed with small business concerns.

(*b*) The Contractor agrees to accomplish the maximum amount of subcontracting to small business concerns that the Contractor finds to be consistent with the efficient performance of this contract.

PURCHASE ORDER DRAFT SYSTEM

This system, described in Section 5, "Purchase Order Essentials," has been adopted by public agencies for the same reason, i.e., to reduce paper work on relatively inexpensive items. The County of Los Angeles inaugurated such a plan in 1964 as its "Purchase Order–Check System," also referred to as "instant money" or "blank check." It retains some of the features used by industry while incorporating others essential to operation and control of public agencies.

In the year before the adoption of this system, the Purchasing and Stores Department of the County of Los Angeles issued 15,235 orders having individual values of less than $25 and a total value of $169,527. Thus 13 per cent of all orders were issued for only ⅓ of 1 per cent of

INVOICE YOUR REF NO

ITEM #	QUANTITY	UNIT PRICE	EXTENSION	CASH DISC.
				–
				SALES USE TAX * +
				P'PAID FRT +
				NET AMOUNT
SALES USE TAX PERMIT # *			TOTAL	

* IF INVOICING FOR TAX, SHOW CALIFORNIA SALES USE TAX PERMIT NUMBER.

COUNTY OF LOS ANGELES 16-61 / 1220

PURCHASING AND STORES DEPARTMENT
2011 N. SOTO ST., LOS ANGELES, CALIFORNIA, 90032

PURCHASE ORDER ACCOUNT | VOID 90 DAYS AFTER | CHECK NO. 999998

PAY TO THE ORDER OF — NOT VALID FOR MORE THAN $25

SAMPLE — $ ______

BANK OF AMERICA
INDUSTRIAL OFFICE
112 S. MAIN STREET
LOS ANGELES, CALIF. 90012

FRED CALIN, PURCHASING AGENT

BY ______
DEPUTY PURCHASING AGENT

⑆1220⑈0061⑈ 216⑈8010 1⑈

⑆1220⑈0061⑈ 216⑈8010 1⑈

PURCHASE ORDER AND MEMORANDUM OF PAYMENT

SHIP TO

GENERAL	FUNCTION
FINANCE P& SD STORES	ACTIVITY
STORES	BUDGET UNIT APP'N
GENERAL	FUND

DELIVER ______ DAYS FROM RECEIPT OF ORDER

F.O.B. DELIVERED

THIS ORDER SUBJECT TO CONDITIONS ON REVERSE

	QUANTITY ORDERED	FILL EXACTLY IN ACCORDANCE WITH INSTRUCTIONS NO BACK ORDERS PERMITTED	UNIT PRICE	UNIT	% CASH DISC'T

SUBJECT TO SALES/USE TAX — DEPOSIT ON CONTAINERS NOT SUBJECT TO SALES OR USE TAX

DEPT'L REQN. NO.	SOURCE OF QUOTATION		SHOW ORDER NUMBER ON SHIPMENT

ENTER THIS ORDER SUBJECT TO TERMS AND CONDITIONS ON REVERSE.
NO BACK ORDERS. ORDER WILL BE CONSIDERED COMPLETE ON FIRST SHIPMENT.

TO SECURE PAYMENT:

1. Complete invoice portion of check for items and quantities shipped.
2. Allow applicable cash discount.
3. Enter net amount on check.
4. Do not send separate invoice.
5. If order is priced, your check entries must conform thereto.
6. If you collect California Sales or Use Tax, show your permit number on check.
7. Detach check, endorse and deposit in your bank.
8. All shipments must be fully prepaid to destination.

IF UNABLE TO SHIP, RETURN ORDER AND CHECK TO PURCHASING & STORES DEPARTMENT.

FIG. 19–16. Purchase order–check form, prenumbered–snap-out; check detached from purchase order. Both are mailed simultaneously to vendor, who inserts the correct amount on the check before depositing it to his account in the bank. (*Reproduced by permission.*)

the dollar volume. Reducing paper work on this 13 per cent of the orders was the main object of the system, which provides that:

1. A "purchase order account" in the amount of $50,000 be established in a commercial bank for the use of the Purchasing Agent and his deputies.

2. Its use be restricted to purchases of $25 or less for books, periodicals, pamphlets, and other services and supply items wherein combination orders are not feasible. This system is not used in any way to restrict competitive bidding.
3. The deputy purchasing agent will determine the source of supply and indicate the issuance of purchase order check.
4. The vendor will be provided with a purchase order and a signed blank check limited to $25, payable to his account. All checks are void after 90 days. Illustrated by Fig. 19–16.

FRED CALIN
PURCHASING AGENT

COUNTY OF LOS ANGELES
PURCHASING AND STORES DEPARTMENT
2011 NORTH SOTO STREET
LOS ANGELES, CALIFORNIA 90032
TELEPHONE 221-4121

VICTOR W. QUAM
CHIEF DEPUTY

FRANK W. RADDATZ
CHIEF, PURCHASING DIVISION

Gentlemen:

Our purchase order, which accompanies this letter, utilizes a recent development in purchasing procedures. You will be pleased to note that a "blank check" is attached to the order so that you can receive immediate payment.

As soon as you have shipped the order and calculated the amount due you, you need only do the following:

(1) Complete the detail of the invoice section of the check and fill in the amount due you on the face of the check. Be sure you allow applicable cash discount. If order is priced, your check entries must conform thereto.

(2) Detach the check and endorse it.

(3) Deposit it in your bank.

We ask you to observe the following rules to help us in handling this type of purchase:

(1) No back orders are allowed. The order will be considered complete as shipped. If you are unable to ship, please advise us at once, returning both check and order.

(2) Please ship on a prepaid basis. Add any freight charge assessable to us to your invoice and include this charge in the check amount.

We feel certain that you will be pleased to receive immediate payment upon shipment. We both will gain through your careful attention to the details of processing this order.

Very truly yours,

Fred Calin

Purchasing Agent

FIG. 19–17. Form letter to vendors which accompanies initial mailing of purchase order–check. (*Reproduced by permission.*)

5. The requisitioning department will be provided with two copies of a "report of goods received," one copy of which, after completion, will be forwarded to the auditor-controller.
6. The auditor-controller will be provided with two copies of an "invoice for merchandise delivered," one copy of which, after summarization, will be forwarded to the requisitioning department.
7. The purchasing agent will retain one copy of the order check for statistical and record purposes.
8. The purchasing agent will reconcile monthly his file of issued orders with the cancelled checks and bank statement.
9. The auditor-controller will audit monthly the above reconciliation, will file a claim for reimbursement of the purchase order account with the value of audited cancelled checks, and will prepare an exception listing of those checks which exceed an established variance.
10. The purchasing agent will examine the exception listing to determine whether or not the variations are warranted.
11. A form letter, Fig. 19–17, will accompany initial mailings of the new order form to the vendor.

CERTIFICATION IN PUBLIC PURCHASING

United States—Two plans are now in effect:

California Association of Public Purchasing Officers, adopted 1961
National Institute of Governmental Purchasing, Inc., adopted 1964

Both plans require college-level training and substantial purchasing experience. Written and oral examinations are required.

Canada—There is no separate program for public purchasing people. The program adopted in 1963 by the Canadian Association of Purchasing Agents is open to all purchasers. This program establishes 11 routes for achieving a "Professional Purchaser Diploma." It provides for association-sponsored college purchasing seminars and courses.

Details in "Appendix," Section 28—Details regarding the above certification programs are given in Section 28 of this handbook. Brief reference also is made to the programs in the United Kingdom.

BUYING EQUIPMENT ON A LIFE BASIS

Early in 1966, *The American City Magazine,* a national publication, presented to the Department of Purchases of the City of Chicago a Certificate of Award for its leadership in introducing a new buying concept in the field of public purchasing.

Vehicular equipment is purchased on the basis of original cost plus guaranteed maintenance for the life of the vehicle. The sum total deter mines the lowest responsible bidder. The idea has proven successful with substantial savings, better equipment, and less downtime.

SELECTED BIBLIOGRAPHY FOR GOVERNMENTAL AND INSTITUTIONAL PURCHASING

Bean, Clarence D.: *Procurement Handbook,* General Services Administration, Government Printing Office, 1959

Bradley, L. A.: *Hotel Textile Purchasing Guide,* American Hotel Association, New York, 1956

Cohen, Henry: *Public Construction Contracts and the Law,* McGraw-Hill Publications, New York, 1961

Forbes, Russell, Ph.D.: *Centralized Purchasing,* National Association of Purchasing Agents, New York, 1941

Forbes, Russell, and members of the PAS Staff: *Purchasing for Small Cities,* Public Administration Service, Chicago, Ill., 1939

Gerzin, Joseph F., city purchasing agent: *Purchasing Manual,* Springfield, Ill., 1956

Gray, Albert: *Purchase Law Manual,* Conover-Mast Publications, Inc., New York, 1954

Hall, Albert H.: *NIGP Letter,* National Institute of Governmental Purchasing, Washington, D.C. (Issued monthly and variously paged. Distribution restricted to Institute members.)

Kitchen, James D.: *Cooperative Governmental Purchasing,* Bureau of Governmental Research, University of California, Los Angeles, Calif., 1953

Lowry, Robert K., city purchasing agent: *Purchasing Manual,* Fort Lauderdale, Fla., 1956

McGee, John F.: *Production Planning and Inventory Control,* McGraw-Hill Publications, New York, 1958

Morrison, Alex, Purchasing Agent for the City of London, England: *Storage and Control of Stock for Industry and Public Undertakings,* Sir Isaac Pitman & Sons, Ltd., London, 1962

Nicholson, Joseph W.: *County Purchasing,* National Association of Purchasing Agents, New York, 1940

Nicholson, Joseph W., city purchasing agent: *Stores Manual and Catalog,* Central Board of Purchases and Department of Purchases, Milwaukee, Wis., 1956

Nicholson, Joseph W., Thomas J. Nammacher, and Keith L. Smith: *Guide to Governmental Purchasing,* Lakewood Publications, Minneapolis, Minn., 1965

Prerequisites for Certification of Public Purchasing Agents, National Institute of Governmental Purchasing, Washington, D.C., 1964 (See Section 28, "Appendix," for the essentials of this publication.)

Purchases and Stores, School Business Management Handbook No. 5, The University of the State of New York, The State Education Department, Albany, N.Y., 1964

"Purchasing Methods Manual," *Purchasing,* Conover-Mast Publications, Inc., New York, 1952

Restrictions upon the Interest of Municipal and Other Public Officials in Governmental Contracts, American Municipal Association, Washington, D.C., Report 135, January, 1940

Ritterskamp, James J., Jr., et al., *Purchasing for Educational Institutions,* Bureau of Publications, Teachers College, Columbia University, New York, 1961

Rosenbaum, Nelson: *Criteria for Awarding Public Contracts to Lowest Responsible Bidder,* Cornell Law Quarterly, vol. 28, Cornell University, Ithaca, N.Y., 1942

Rydland, Leiv N.: *A "Buy-Michigan" Purchasing Policy?* Bureau of Government, Institute of Public Administration, University of Michigan, Ann Arbor, Mich., 1956

Ward, John F.: *Commodity Code Catalog,* 2nd edition, 2 vols., Department of Purchases, City of Chicago, Chicago, Ill., 1965

Ward, John F.: *Manual of Purchasing Organization and Procedure,* Civic Federation, Chicago, Ill., 1943

U.S. Government Purchasing Directory, Small Business Administration, Superintendent of Documents, Government Printing Office, Washington, D.C., 1956

SECTION 20

PURCHASING IN CANADA

Editor

Allan S. Harrison, formerly Director of Purchasing, Ford Motor Company of Canada Limited, Oakville, Ontario, Canada

Associate Editors

H. A. Cole, Purchasing Agent, Bendix Eclipse of Canada, Limited, Windsor, Ontario, Canada

George A. Harrap, Purchasing Agent, Disston Division, H. K. Porter Company (Canada) Limited, Acton, Ontario, Canada

J. T. Rapson, Manager, Traffic Services, Ford Motor Company of Canada Limited, Oakville, Ontario, Canada

Ian M. Young, Purchasing Agent, Toronto General Hospital, Toronto, Ontario, Canada

EDITOR-IN-CHIEF'S NOTE: Principles, policies, and procedures in Canada are in general similar to those used in the United States, as enumerated in the other 28 sections of this handbook. Major differences that do exist, as mentioned on page 20–3, are defined in this section, "Purchasing in Canada." Although in Canada there are many parallels to the United States in the application of the legal aspects of purchasing, there are, at points, marked differences which would require study in detail and could hardly be handled in a handbook of this type.

Canada, our friendly neighbor to the north, resembles the United States in many ways. Its economy, people, and customs are linked closely with our own and, therefore, it is not surprising that purchasing in Canada differs but slightly from that in the United States. To avoid repetition, the next few pages will be used not to outline purchasing in Canada but rather to describe those differences that exist between the two countries.

First, a brief description of the country whose southern boundary adjoins the United States for approximately 3,000 miles. It is some 20 per cent larger than the United States; however, its population is but one-tenth that of the United States. The country is divided into ten self-governing provinces which respond to a central federal control in Ottawa, Ontario, similar to the fifty states which respond to Washington, D.C.

The large majority of its people reside within a belt some 100 miles wide paralleling the United States border. Apart from minerals, crops, and other natural resources, industrial Canada lies within this belt, mostly in the area north of the states of New York and Ohio.

There is extensive trade between the two countries, each being the other's largest customer. In 1963 Canada made purchases of approximately \$4½ billion from the United States, compared to a little over \$3¾ billion in the reverse direction.

Canada is linked together, east to west, by two large transcontinental railways with minor branch lines running north and with southern connections to United States railroads. Highways more or less parallel these systems and the huge inland waterway extending from the Great Lakes to the ocean is common to both countries for a great part of its length.

The following subsections will deal with the Government and Constitution of Canada; Federal and provincial laws; trade laws and regulations; government controls, the Combines Investigation Act; Federal, provincial, and municipal taxes; customs, traffic regulations; banking and foreign exchange—only to the extent whereby they affect purchasing.

The purchasing fraternity in Canada is organized as it is in the United

States, and the several local associations form the Canadian Association of Purchasing Agents (CAPA) with offices in Toronto at 357 Bay Street. These offices are well staffed and their services are available to members of the purchasing profession, all as described in the booklet "A Membership That Pays Dividends."

CANADA'S GOVERNMENT

The Dominion of Canada came into being July 1, 1867, as the result of a federation of the British Colonies of Canada, New Brunswick, and Nova Scotia.

The Colony of Canada represented an earlier federation of Upper Canada and Lower Canada, the Act of Union passing the British Parliament in 1840 and becoming operative February 1, 1841. After 1867, other provinces were created, Manitoba joining the Dominion in 1870, British Columbia in 1871, and Prince Edward Island in 1873. In 1905, the territories of Assiniboia, Saskatchewan, Athabasca, and Alberta were made into two provinces—Saskatchewan and Alberta—and joined the Dominion. In 1949, Newfoundland, which had occupied the unique position of being a separate Dominion in the Commonwealth, but with its Dominion status suspended, voted to join as Canada's tenth province.

There are still existent two territories—the Yukon and the North West Territories—which do not have provincial legislatures but do send members to the House of Commons in Ottawa. These two territories await further development before they can be set up as fully legislative provinces. In recent years, the title Dominion has been dropped, and the country is now known as Canada, and its government as the Government of Canada.

Canada came into being at the request of the legislatures of the three Colonies, who petitioned the British Government to act upon their request. The act by which the provinces joined to form one country is officially known as the British North America Act. This Act can only be amended by the British Government at the request of the Canadian Government, after the consent of each province has been obtained. Unanimity is essential to safeguard the rights of each province, particularly the Province of Quebec, which as we will see, occupies an unusual position.

The Constitution—the British North America Act

The British North America Act is often spoken of as the Constitution of Canada, but the term is erroneous as it does not embody all the laws by which Canada is governed. The Statute of Westminster, proclaimed by the British Government in 1931, is also a part of Canada's Constitution as to its application. Except for the Province of Quebec, in which particular conditions prevail, much of Canada's laws follow the "unwritten" laws of England, and are built up by precedent, tested in the courts. Sufficient has been written that no one in purchasing need ever be embarrassed by being confronted by an "unwritten" law.

Throughout Canada, English criminal law prevails, and in all the provinces except Quebec, English civil law is in effect. This strange anomaly came about from the conditions granted by General Murray when the province passed into the hands of the British. Confirmed by the Quebec Act of 1774, the Magna Charta of French Canada, the French-speaking Canadian in what is now Quebec was guaranteed three of the four essentials of French Canadian survival—free exercise of the Catholic religion, almost complete restoration of the ancient boundaries of New France, and the right to practice French civil law. The fourth essential, that of language, was left unsettled by legislation. But circumstances soon decided the whole matter of language.

It was inexpedient to call together a French-speaking Assembly; there were no French-speaking English barristers in the whole province to conduct cases in the courts; the Catholic clergy were entirely French speaking. The pragmatic British accepted the only course. The use of the French language has long been accepted as a right and this has established itself so firmly that nothing short of a national eruption could disturb it.

In the interval since 1760, unassisted by outside immigration, the French-speaking population has grown from a scant 60,000 to 5½ million people. Cut off from contact with France by the peace treaty of 1763, and lacking sympathy with the French revolution of 1789, the French-speaking Canadians have continued to retain and to exercise all the privileges granted under the earlier treaties. As we shall see later, this has had a marked effect upon all Canadian legislation since 1760. Canada then is a dual language country with many of its laws designed to safeguard constitutional rights of a French-speaking minority.

Legislative Make-up of Canada's Government

The Canadian legislative branch consists of four divisions.

The Governor General. The Governor General is appointed by the British Government for a five-year term, after consultation with the Prime Minister of Canada. The Governor General represents the Sovereign, and carries on all the duties of state performed in England by Her Majesty, Queen Elizabeth II. The Governor General may not act except on the advice of his Canadian ministers, who are in effect the Prime Minister of Canada and the members of his Cabinet. The present Governor General is the first Canadian appointed to that office.

The Cabinet. No mention is made of the Cabinet in the enabling acts. It is a body of counselors to the Prime Minister, selected from the governing party, usually with an eye to balance among the provinces. Each Cabinet member must have been elected to the House of Commons by popular vote, and he must regularly take his seat in the House. Most members of the Cabinet are assigned to portfolios although there are sometimes members of the Cabinet described as ministers without portfolio. When the House of Commons is sitting, most members of the Cabinet will be present to answer questions arising in the House pertaining to the functioning of his department. He is thus responsible to the House for the conduct of his department, as well as to the Prime Minister in Cabinet sessions.

The Senate. The Senate is composed of men, with a sprinkling of women, appointed by the Prime Minister, and usually from his own party. Members of the Senate need not have had previous legislative experience, and hold office for life unless disqualified by misconduct or by absence from the sittings for two consecutive sessions. Legislation, except on finance, may be inaugurated in the Senate but seldom is so introduced. In the main, the Senate passes on the legislation brought to it by the House of Commons for confirmation, before it is passed to the Governor General for signature.

The House of Commons. The House of Commons is elected by the voters of Canada for a period of five years, unless dissolved earlier by the Governor General at the request of the Prime Minister. With minor exceptions as in the case of Prince Edward Island brought about by the small population of that province, representation in the House is based on population.

The total House membership in 1964 was 265, based on proportionment to the total population; the Province of Quebec elects 75 members and the Province of Ontario 85 members. It is not strictly true that representation by population prevails entirely throughout, as some rural constituencies require a much smaller population to elect a member than do some urban constituencies, but considerable effort is made to equalize representation. Constituency boundaries are redrawn following each ten year census.

For all practical purposes, the House of Commons through the Cabinet govern the country, the Prime Minister being the leader of the party with the greatest number of seats in the House.

Legal Status of the Government of Canada as It Affects Industry

Once a bill has been read three times in the House of Commons, and has been passed by that body, it is sent to the Senate for similar reading and endorsement, and then to the Governor General for signature. Copies of the legislation are circulated to all interested bodies, and by paying a small sum, any private citizen may secure a stenographic record of the discussions and legislation enacted in the House of Commons. This record is known as Hansard, and the cost of securing copies of Hansard does not exceed $5 annually.

It is the privilege of any citizen to appeal to the courts against the operation of any piece of legislation that is felt to be detrimental to that citizen or group of citizens, and not beneficial to the country as a whole. The courts strive to be fair and equitable. Judges are appointed for life to protect the rights of the citizens. Should a lower court rule the legislation effective, the appeal can be carried through successive courts to the Supreme Court of Canada. Such procedure is expensive and is seldom resorted to, unless the case be an extreme one.

Legislation thrown out by the courts as being incapable of enforcement is declared *ultra vires.* Frequently in such a case, the House of Commons takes appropriate action to revise the Statute to bring it within the compass of enforcement by legal means.

The desire for a strong central government loomed so largely in the thinking of those who framed the British North America Act that the responsibilities allocated to the provinces are relatively limited. These include education; financing of matters within the province; sale of public lands and timber; municipal institutions; licensing for sale of alcoholic beverages, for auctioneering, etc., and other matters of lesser character.

In the course of time, the provinces introduced taxation on motor vehicles and on gasoline, provincial sales tax acts, and other forms of taxation. During the years of World War II, to allow the Government of Canada to prosecute the war successfully, forms of taxation in the provinces were temporarily suspended to allow the Government of Canada to enter these taxing fields in return for grants to each of the provinces. These grants have been modified from time to time and the whole matter has yet to be finalized.

Provincial sales taxes are still levied in some of the provinces, as well as other taxes mentioned earlier. But in an effort to build a strong central government, the bulk of the powers was transferred to the central government. It was granted also powers of disallowance of provincial legislation for just cause, and it was granted all residual powers, that is, powers of legislation not specifically defined in the act as it then stood.

Tariffs, excise taxes, and sales taxes come within the sphere of the Federal Government, and any sales tax levied by the provinces is, therefore, a supplementary tax. Generally speaking, purchasing is little affected by provincial legislation, except for such taxes as the gasoline tax and provincial sales taxes where they are in effect.

Municipal governments derive their powers from provincial legislation.

In general, the legislation of municipal governments relates strictly to municipal affairs, to the levying of taxes on property, and to laws affecting the life of the citizens of the municipality. Purchasing is not greatly affected by municipal governments.

Canada's Bilingual Situation. Reference has already been made to the surprising fact that Canada is a bilingual country. Either French or English is an official language. House of Commons debates are in both languages, official documents are printed in French and in English, even the postage stamps and paper currency are printed in the two languages. The use of the French language in general conversation is practiced by

Date

No 6195

A
TO

F. O. B.

Veuillez fournir à:
Please ship to:

Date d'expédition:
When wanted:

Mode d'expédition:
Via:

Les articles suivant:
The following goods:

Conditions:
Terms:

Quantité Quantity	DESCRIPTION	Prix Price

Veuillez accuser réception de cette commande et inscrire son numéro d'ordre sur le colis et sur les factures.

Please acknowledge receipt and mention the number of the order on each parcel and invoice.

FIG. 20–1. Sample of purchase order form in French and English as used in the Province of Quebec, Canada.

the majority in Quebec, a large segment of the population in New Brunswick, and by comparatively small segments of the population in Ontario, Manitoba, and Nova Scotia. However, even in Quebec, English is the language of business and business correspondence except for the domestic trade of the smaller French businesses and their French clientele, as is illustrated by Fig. 20–1 for a purchase order used in Quebec. The use of English is widespread among the French except in the large rural areas.

Government Emergency Controls. The emergencies of World War II introduced a larger measure of controls not previously experienced. Control of foreign exchange became effective on September 16, 1939, largely to control the use of United States dollars in the most salutary way.

While the government made available foreign exchange for the import of essential goods, luxuries were generally barred. Sale of foreign exchange realized from exports was compulsory. For a brief period in 1947–1948, there was a limited list of articles banned as imports, another limited list of quota goods, and on iron and steel capital goods there were limitations. During World War II, controls were exercised on some food products such as meats, sugar, and articles made from sugar, butter, tea and coffee, and similar products. Shipping also was controlled.

But what affected industry more generally was the government control exercised on the use of steel, copper, and aluminum. By legislation, the government was authorized, under a priorities system, to allocate these vital necessities on the basis of need. After much experimentation and a great deal of paper work, the Controlled Materials Plan was introduced and operated successfully for imports from the United States.

In effect, the government granted to individual industries allocations of scarce materials which were used like a bank account, although imported steels could only be obtained on direct application. On domestic steels the control was more elastic and those handling such steels were allowed to issue them on the basis of need. When the Korean War came, with its attendant shortages, previous experience allowed the introduction of controls with the minimum of annoyance. Even today, the government has stand-by powers for a similar emergency.

Distress Merchandise. During the early days of the depression of 1929–1936, distress merchandise came into the market. To prevent dumping into Canada at lower than cost-plus-reasonable-profit prices, the government took steps that allowed a revaluation of any imports where it seemed apparent that the full resale value had not been shown. Very generally, as operative at the present time, the practice is to show on the importing invoice the value of the merchandise to the purchaser, and in a second column there is shown, under oath, the fair market value as sold for home consumption in like quantities at the time and date of shipment into Canada. In actual practice the procedure is somewhat more involved, as each item is considered on conditions and individual circumstances.

If the goods being imported are ruled to be of a class or kind made in Canada, any difference between the two columns is assessed as a dump duty, which added to the duty paid on imported articles makes the import an expensive one. It becomes difficult, therefore, to import any merchandise that is being sold for less than its fair market value.

Combines Investigation Act. The Government of Canada has been active in recent years in prosecuting under existing laws members of an industry where it has appeared that these members, far from acting competitively, have joined for the maintenance of a price schedule or otherwise in restraint of trade.

Where convictions have been registered, fines have been levied. Some of the legislation is of long standing, but a recent investigation produced the Combines Investigation Act, known as the McQuarrie Act, which is designed to prevent a fixed retail selling price on an article. Thus, a manufacturer may sell an article to a wholesaler and he in turn to a retailer, but the manufacturer cannot control the selling price of the article in the retail store. Nor may he do so, if a department store instead of the usual retail store is the outlet.

There can be, then, no "manufacturer's selling price" but the retailer is free to set his own selling price. Manufacturers can, and frequently do, suggest a retail selling price, but this is a suggestion that need not be acted upon and is often ignored.

There are severe penalties for conviction for violating these regulations, under sections 498 and 498A of the Criminal Code, to which one is referred.

TAXATION IN CANADA

Taxation should be of serious concern to all Canadians because about one of every five dollars in circulation ends up in the Canadian Treasury as taxes. Purchasing agents handle up to fifty cents of every sales dollar in their company's operation and should, therefore, be vitally concerned with taxes. They should understand the evolution and scope—and particularly the details—of all taxes which directly affect their daily work.

Many types of Federal, provincial, and municipal taxes are of little or no direct concern to purchasing people. They need only be mentioned to round out the tax story and to permit a broader treatment of the taxes more applicable to the function of the purchasing agent.

Other taxes are of daily importance. For example, imports into Canada represent a substantial portion of the gross national product. Customs duties, or taxes, levied on imports produce about 10 per cent of the Federal tax revenue. This tax impost is an important and complex one which all buyers must include in their competitive considerations.

A key point in considering the development of Canadian taxation is the basic tax powers granted the various levels of government by the Constitution of 1867. The Federal Government was empowered to levy any type of taxation, either direct or indirect. The provinces and the municipalities were restricted to direct taxation only.

The early revenue of the Federal Government was obtained largely from duty on imports, even though taxing powers conferred by confederation permitted the use of much broader fields for raising funds to meet government expenses.

Subsequent growth of course could not be foreseen with accuracy. Therefore, developments have presented many problems which only loyalty and statesmanship have solved and can continue to solve for the good of all. It is readily apparent that taxation must be from a source of money and only where there is money can taxes be collected. The wealthy parts of the country, therefore, produce most of the tax dollars.

The rapid expansion of Canada and the increasing demand for facilities and services in all of the spheres of government made apparent the necessity of broadening the tax base. The Federal Government during World War I moved into the field of direct taxation which up to this time had been exercised by the provinces and the municipalities only.

During and after World War I all taxation expanded on direct applications so extensively that during the 1930s practically chaotic conditions developed between Federal, provincial, and to some extent municipal interests. Only through heavy and extended negotiation has some clarification been achieved. From all of this the Federal Government now has tax rental agreements with most of the provinces which eliminate many major duplications particularly in the area of personal income taxes.

In the latter half of World War I and through the following twenty years, many new forms of taxation appeared. The business profits tax, personal income tax, sales tax, and many luxury taxes appeared in the Federal field. In the provinces the entertainment tax, gasoline tax, and liquor taxes appeared and most have been retained. In 1936 the first provincial sales tax appeared in Alberta (repealed the following year) and is now in use in five of the provinces and in some cities. Rate adjustments have occurred, mostly upward, as revenue need expanded.

Summary of the Tax Structure as of 1964

Personal Income Tax. Federal tax by rental agreements. Currently Ontario has a personal income tax. This tax is imposed upon income allocable to Ontario. The rate of tax is a percentage of the Federal tax payable on this income allocated to Ontario. Since the Federal Government is collecting the tax imposed by Ontario, joint payments including withholding at source are required under a combination of the Federal and Ontario Acts.

Corporation Income Tax. Federal tax of 21 per cent on the first $35,000 of corporate income with 50 per cent on any excess. In addition there is 9 per cent in Quebec Province; effective 1957 11 per cent in Ontario. The Federal Government allows an abatement of tax of 9 per cent of profits earned in Quebec and Ontario.

Corporation and Business Taxes. Provincial tax of 2 per cent on insurance premiums; taxes in Quebec on paid-up capital, places of business, insurance premiums, railway mileage, etc., in most cases in lieu of (but in some in addition to) the tax on profits; municipal business taxes, mainly levied on business premises (capital value, rental value, floor space) or on gross receipts.

Commodity Taxes. Federal manufacturers' sales tax of 10 per cent; additional Federal taxes and duties on liquor, tobacco, automobiles, radios, cosmetics, jewelry, etc., and, of course, the customs tariff; provincial retail sales tax in Newfoundland, New Brunswick, Quebec, Saskatchewan, and British Columbia at rates from 2 to 5 per cent; provincial gasoline taxes of from 10 to 17 cents per gallon in all provinces; special taxes on tobacco in Prince Edward Island, New Brunswick, and Quebec, and special tax on meals in Quebec; retail sales taxes in Montreal, Quebec City, and several other Quebec municipalities.

Other Sources of Revenue. In the provinces, motor vehicle licenses, monopoly sale of liquor, and natural resources including mining profits taxes; in the municipalities, principally the tax on property, supplemented by business, sales, and poll taxes, and miscellaneous charges. The tax rental agreements between the Federal Government and the provinces are being reviewed for the years 1957 to 1962. All but Ontario and Quebec will rent to the Federal Government all three direct tax fields, i.e., succession duties, personal, and corporate income taxes. Quebec will continue to levy all three taxes and Ontario has rented only the personal income tax.

Municipal Taxes

There is a very broad field here for impost. Ninety per cent of the population of Canada live in the area of municipal taxation and these taxes raise a revenue about one-seventh as large as the Federal revenue.

Property Tax. If purchasing work takes you into municipal areas where you rent or must purchase warehouse space, it is of value to know that municipal property taxes are based on real property, that is, land and improvements on land. Interpretations of the application of taxes on real property vary from one municipality to the other and will, no doubt, continue to do so. Only by direct reference to the particular municipal assessment act can the details be secured.

Much development has taken place in assessing real property, and through court decisions and education of assessors, reasonably simple rules have been established and are applied to local conditions through the intimate knowledge of the individuals involved.

Depending upon the requirements of the municipality, taxes are collected by an assessor, collector, treasurer, or one acting for one or all.

Other municipal revenue comes from the poll tax, an ancient tax still used by many of the cities and towns, amusement taxes in Saskatchewan and Newfoundland, such licenses as store, restaurant, tavern, theater, dance hall, pawnshop, bicycle, taxi, hawker and peddler, and some others.

Sales Tax. In municipal taxation, the purchasing agent will meet, more often than any other, problems involving the municipal retail sales tax which has spread from one municipality to another until at present it is used by many municipalities (all in Quebec province). With Montreal and Quebec City included this represents a large portion of the population and can be very burdensome to some. Not only does population indicate its particular importance, but the rates which apply that run from 2 to 3 per cent mean a very heavy impost.

In Quebec, collection of the municipal sales tax is all handled by the Province and all exemptions are the same as those allowed by the Province in its provincial sales tax. These exemptions will be referred to later when dealing with provincial taxes.

It will be easily seen that with the mass movement of people and goods through uncontrolled gateways, there is a great opportunity for evasion of this form of taxation and much of the success of its operation rests with the residents of the areas.

One other form of sales tax exists in Canadian municipalities. This is a tax of 5 per cent and 2½ per cent on gas and electricity, respectively, in the city of Winnipeg.

"Taxation in Canada" furnishes much statutory reference for those who need complete and current details. It quotes assessment acts, statutes, and reference to charters all too lengthy for complete inclusion here.

Provincial Taxes

It has been stated earlier in this work that the provinces are restricted by the Constitution to direct taxation. However, there has been much litigation centering around interpretation of direct taxation and much clarification has been obtained. Much more simplification will come from closer Federal-provincial cooperation and understanding in the field of taxation in the future. This is a must, regardless of petty politics, but it can be well understood that every step will not be a forward one.

Here, as in the municipal field, much of the taxation may have little effect on the day-to-day operations of the buyer, but summary comment could be of value in an understanding of the whole structure.

Corporation Tax. Provincial corporation income taxes have been in effect in most provinces since the early 1930s. All were suspended during 1941 to 1946 under the wartime tax rental agreements between the provinces and the Federal Government but were reintroduced in 1947 alongside the Federal profits tax. Since 1952, Quebec has used this form of taxation; their rate is 9 per cent and that of Ontario is now at 11 per cent.

Personal Income Tax. Personal income taxes have been eliminated in all the provinces except Quebec and Ontario through the rental agreements. How long this will continue it is difficult to predict but the present Federal Government is doing its utmost to encourage complete elimination. Quebec appears to seek autonomy all along the line.

Succession Duties. Succession duties are still a large factor in provincial taxation in Ontario and Quebec. All the other provinces surrendered this field through the Federal-provincial tax agreements. Ontario and Quebec regulations are somewhat close to those of the Dominion, but this field is still a complicated one and of little interest to the buyer.

Property Tax. Property taxes in the provinces have practically disappeared except in British Columbia, leaving this field to the municipalities. The provinces, however, raise considerable revenue from property rentals and royalties or taxes, if you will, on natural resources known as revenue from the public domain. Provincial wealth of natural resources varies greatly, and therefore these imposts vary from province to province but taxes on mining, lumbering, and on water power are common.

Sales Tax. Retail sales taxes are much more popular in the provinces than are the municipal sales taxes (which are restricted at present to the Province of Quebec municipalities only) and are in effect in about 50 per cent of the provinces. It appears quite likely that this percentage will increase rather than diminish.

This type of tax at first might not be considered as direct taxation and therefore unconstitutional, but this has been skillfully handled by the provinces that collect tax on all goods purchased by every person in the province. Such items as machinery and equipment for manufacturing are fully exempt in some provinces.

The intent of the provinces is to collect the tax at the consumers' level only and they, therefore, license manufacturers to purchase raw materials tax free and wholesalers and retailers to purchase goods for resale tax free. Licensed vendors then collect the tax from consumers.

There are, of course, many loopholes, as goods pass freely from one province to another. The provinces hold consumers, retailers, and manufacturers liable to pay taxes on goods sold or brought into the province and attempt to police this vigorously.

Real property, food, and service are exempt from this provincial tax and, of course, goods shipped out of the province are specially exempted.

The rates vary from province to province, for instance, Quebec collects 2 per cent, while New Brunswick collects 3 per cent and the other provinces are in the area from 3 to 5 per cent where this type of taxation is in effect. These taxes, of course, are in addition to the Federal sales tax on all goods.

Other Taxes. Other provincial taxes include those on gasoline, meals, tobacco, amusements, bets on pari-mutuels, and liquor. The provinces also license motor vehicles, fishermen, hunters, and some other miscellaneous functions. These produce a substantial portion of provincial revenues varying up to 17 per cent.

Gasoline is taxed in all the provinces and was taxed during World War II by the Federal Government as well; this tax was withdrawn in 1947 but was immediately absorbed into the provincial levies by increases. This tax applies to all products which can be used to operate a motor vehicle including benzol, natural gas, or even coal in liquid form. Provision for rebate, however, is available on application where the product is used for other than highway propulsion. The rebates vary from province to province as do the rates of tax. The range of taxes is from 10 to 17 cents per Imperial gallon.

Motor vehicles are licensed by all provinces and the charges are based on horsepower in some and on wheel base in others. Commercial vehicles are based on gross weight or seating capacity. These annual license fees vary widely from $7 to $10 on light cars in some provinces to $20 and $25 in others. Operators' licenses are all nominal, from $1 to $2 each.

Federal Taxation

In the field of Federal taxation there is, of course, a broad scope because of the powers conferred on the Dominion Parliament in the Constitution to tax either directly or indirectly. Many of the imposts have no consequence to the buyer, but he or she will most certainly be involved in sales and excise taxes and customs duties.

Corporation Tax. A Federal tax on corporation income dates back to 1917 and has been in effect continuously since that time. As well as the normal tax a form of excess profits tax was in effect in both World War I and World War II.

The corporation income tax is based on income derived from business and property with certain allowable deductions for depreciation, depletion, bad debts, etc., in manufacturing, mining, and other activities.

There are exemptions from this tax for organizations operated for social welfare, some credit unions, and a few others, but this group is small. It does not include cooperatives.

The rates of tax have varied from a flat 4 per cent in 1917 to the present 18 and 47 per cent wherein a portion of profit is taxed at the low rate and another portion at the high one. In addition there is a 3 per cent old age security tax. (Statutory reference: Income Tax Act, 12 Geo. 6 (Can.) as amended.)

Personal Income Tax. Federal personal income tax is levied on residents—not necessarily citizens—and is levied even on those who under certain circumstances only reside in Canada for more than 183 days per year. This tax has been in effect for the same length of time as the corporation levy and raises approximately the same revenue.

The tax is based on income from all sources including foreign income, salaries, dividends, wages, annuities, pensions, death benefits, alimony, directors' fees, and many others.

There are many allowances or deductions and exemptions. These include payments to pension funds, depletion allowances on dividends from Canadian mining companies, allowances for dependents, charitable donations, alimony payments, salesmen's expenses and other expenses of employment only to mention a few of the more common.

Rates of tax have been established on a basis of income bracket, that is, lower rates in the lower brackets and higher rates for larger incomes (statutory reference: Income Tax Act, 12 Geo. 6, (Can.) as amended; also for ready reference *Income Tax Preparation* by Lancelot Smith).

Succession Duties. Succession duties in the Federal field, as has been mentioned earlier, are not duplicated in the provinces except in Quebec where there is no tax rental agreement and in Ontario where this tax is an exception in the agreement. The rates are graduated according to the size of the estate, the amount of the succession, and the relationship of the beneficiary to the deceased.

Excise Taxes and Duties. Excise taxes and duties are most important to the buyer, as these are levied along with sales taxes and customs duties on commodities and services which are the daily needs of all in the buying profession.

Excise taxes first came into being during World War I and one form or another of these has been in effect ever since.

Excise duties have been an impost ever since 1867 and differ from excise taxes in that they are collected when the goods are taken out of bonded warehouses, whereas the taxes are collected on a monthly basis under licenses similar to the method of collection for the Federal sales tax.

Administration of both is by the Department of National Revenue, Excise Division, Ottawa, and this is the headquarters of administration for Canada for both sales and excise taxes. Payment of sales and excise tax, however, is made at port offices of the Customs and Excise Department located at various points across Canada.

Excise tax is applied on a specific list of goods as contained in Schedule I of the Excise Tax Act and applies on goods which are either manufactured or imported into Canada. It is applied on the sale price of the manufacturer of the goods to the wholesaler or retailer if manufactured in Canada and on the duty-paid value if imported into Canada.

The list of goods contains articles which are usually regarded as luxuries and the present rate of tax is 10 per cent in most cases, with the rate being 15 per cent in the case of phonograph, radio, television, and combination sets.

In addition to the goods contained in Schedule I, there are goods listed under Schedule II as follows for excise taxes:

Cigarettes, manufactured tobacco

a. For each five cigarettes or fraction of five cigarettes contained in any package . . . 2½ cents

b. Manufactured tobacco, including snuff, but not including cigars and cigarettes . . . 80 cents per pound

Regulations quoted under sales tax regarding licenses, returns, penalties, and appeals are also applicable to the excise tax.

Excise duties under the provisions of the Excise Act are imposed and are quoted on the goods, whether manufactured in Canada or imported into Canada.

I. Spirits
   1. On every Imperial gallon of the strength of proof distilled in Canada, except as hereinafter otherwise provided, Twelve Dollars, and so in proportion for any greater or less strength than the strength of proof and for any less quantity than a gallon.
   2. Spirits used in any bonded manufactory in the production of goods, manufactured in bond are subject to the following duties of excise and no other, that is to say:
      a. On every gallon of the strength of proof used in the manufacture of patent and proprietary medicines, extracts, essences and pharmaceutical preparations, One Dollar and Fifty cents, and so in proportion for any greater or less strength than the strength of proof and for any less quantity than a gallon.
      b. On every gallon of the strength of proof used in the production of such chemical compositions as are from time to time approved by the Governor in Council, Fifteen cents, and so in proportion for any greater or less strength than the strength of proof and for any less quantity than a gallon.
   3. Upon spirits sold to any druggist licensed under this Act, and used exclusively in the preparation of prescriptions for medicines and pharmaceutical preparations, the duty of excise shall be, on

every gallon of the strength of proof, One Dollar and Fifty cents, and so in proportion for any greater or less strength than the strength of proof and for any less quantity than a gallon.

4. Spirits used solely in the manufacture of vinegar by a manufacturer of vinegar licensed under this Act are subject to no duty of excise.
5. Spirits distilled from wine produced from native fruits and used in any bonded manufactory for the treatment of domestic wine are subject to no duty of excise.
6. Spirits used directly in the manufacture of toilet preparations or cosmetics on which excise tax is applicable under Schedule I of the Excise Tax Act, are subject to no duty of excise.
7. Upon imported spirits when taken into a bonded manufactory, in addition to any of the duties otherwise imposed, upon every gallon of the strength of proof, Thirty cents, and so in proportion for any greater or less strength than the strength of proof and for any less quantity than a gallon.

II. Canadian brandy

On every gallon of the strength of proof, Eleven Dollars, and so in proportion for any greater or less strength than the strength of proof and for any less quantity than a gallon.

III. Beer

Upon all beer or malt liquor, per gallon Thirty-eight cents, subject to an allowance for loss in production based on the duty assessed on beer or malt liquor produced, of (*a*) five per cent when yeast sediment is included, or (*b*) three per cent when yeast sediment is not included.

IV. Tobacco, cigars, and cigarettes

1. Manufactured tobacco of all descriptions except cigarettes, per pound actual weight, Thirty-five cents.
2. Cigarettes weighing not more than two and one-half pounds per thousand, Four Dollars per thousand.
3. Cigarettes weighing more than two and one-half pounds per thousand, Five Dollars per thousand.
4. Cigars, Two Dollars per thousand.
5. Canadian raw leaf tobacco when sold for consumption, per pound, actual weight, Ten cents.

References. Sales and excise taxes are imposed under the provisions of the Excise Tax Act, chapter 100, Revised Statutes of Canada, 1952, and amendments thereto. An office consolidation of the Excise Tax Act is available from the Queens Printer, Ottawa, and in addition a booklet of regulations under the Excise Tax Act is available from the same source. There is also available from the Canadian Manufacturers Association an excellent handbook on sales tax under the title of "Sales Tax Canada." This book is highly recommended for the complete detail which it contains. Also *Sales and Excise Tax Guide* by CCH Canadian Limited.

Federal Sales Tax. Federal sales tax is applied on goods which are either manufactured or imported into Canada. It is applied on the sale price of the manufacturer of the goods to the wholesaler or retailer if manufactured in Canada, and on the duty-paid value if imported. There is a list of articles which are subject to various rates of tax, and these are shown as Schedule III of the Excise Tax Act. It should also be noted that sales tax is applied only at time of sale from the manufacturer and is not applied at other points of sale.

In order to prevent the pyramiding of sales tax on articles processed and/or manufactured in Canada, a sales tax license system has been developed together with certificates which permit tax-free purchase. These are available both to manufacturers and wholesalers, depending upon the category in which they function.

The following is a summary of the various exemption certificates which are presently in effect and which relieve the vendor from adding sales tax to his sale price.

1. I/we certify that the goods ordered/imported hereby are to be used in, wrought into, or attached to taxable goods for sale.
   License Number ....
   Name of Purchaser

This certificate is given by a licensed manufacturer when purchasing or importing goods or materials to be further manufactured in Canada.

2. I/we certify that the machinery, apparatus or complete parts thereof ordered/imported hereby are to be use directly in the process of manufacture or production of goods.

This certificate can be used by a manufacturer or producer when purchasing or importing machinery or apparatus or complete parts thereof for use in the manufacture or production of his product.

3. I/we certify that the materials ordered/imported hereby are for use exclusively in the manufacture or production of foodstuffs exempted by Schedule III of the Excise Tax Act, under the heading "Foodstuffs."

This certificate can be used by a manufacturer or producer of foodstuffs exempted by the Excise Tax Act when purchasing materials to be used in the manufacture or production of such foodstuffs.

4. I/we certify that the materials ordered/imported hereby are to be consumed or expended directly in the process of manufacture or production of goods.

....
Name of Purchaser

This certificate can be used by a manufacturer or producer when purchasing materials (not including lubricating oils) to be consumed or expended directly in the process of manufacture or production of goods.

5. I/we certify that the goods ordered/imported hereby are for resale.
License Number ....
Name of Purchaser

This certificate can be used by a licensed wholesaler or jobber, when purchasing or importing goods for resale.

NOTE: Application for wholesale licenses will not be considered unless and until the applicants have been in business for a period of at least three months.

No such license shall be issued unless fifty per cent of the wholesaler's sales of goods, ordinarily subject to sales tax, were made under sales tax exempt conditions for the three months immediately preceding his application.

6. I certify that the articles or materials being purchased/imported hereby are for the sole use of ....
(Name of Hospital)
and are not in any case for resale.

....
(Signature)

....
(Office Held by Signatory)

....
(Place and Date)

This certificate can be used when bona fide public hospitals which have been certified as such by the Department of National Health and Welfare purchase or import articles or materials for their own use and not for resale under the conditions of the exemption.

7. I certify that the goods being purchased/imported by ....
....
(Name of Provincial Government or Department)
are being purchased with Crown funds, and are for a purpose other than for resale.

....
(Name of Authorized Official)

....
(Rank or Official Designation)

This certificate can be used by purchasing agents for provincial government departments entitled to purchase or import goods free from excise taxes.

8. I/we hereby certify that the goods which we will purchase from you during the period from .... to ....
   Date Date
   are to be used in the manufacture of taxable goods for sale.
   License No. ....
   Name of Purchaser

This blanket certificate can be given by licensed manufacturers and licensed wholesalers who in the regular course of their business repeatedly order specific goods by telephone or telegraph or where written orders are not given. (Maximum period allowed for such a certificate is three months.)

NOTE: Licensed wholesalers will certify that the goods are for resale.

Regulations regarding use of certificates:

1. All certificates entitling the purchaser to exemption from sales tax are to be signed, or the name of the company may be stamped or typewritten if initialed by a responsible officer.

   Where a purchaser quotes a license number only on his order for goods, the vendor is responsible for sales tax on the sale.

   Where a purchaser erroneously quotes both license number and certificate on his order, the purchaser is liable for the tax, except in such cases where it is obvious to the vendor that the quotation was made in error.
2. A licensed manufacturer or producer, or a licensed wholesaler or jobber, who also conducts a retail branch or branches shall not use his license when purchasing or importing merchandise for such retail branch or branches.
3. Licensed manufacturers and licensed wholesalers must not have their license numbers printed on their stationery or order forms, but should place their license numbers and certificates on orders given only in cases where exemption is applicable.

General regulations:

1. Specific exemptions—all goods
   a. Sold by a licensed manufacturer to another licensed manufacturer if the goods are partly manufactured goods.
   b. Imported by a licensed manufacturer if the goods are partly manufactured goods.
   c. Imported by a licensed wholesaler, or importation.
   d. Sold by a licensed manufacturer to a licensed wholesaler.
   e. Sold by a licensed wholesaler to a licensed manufacturer if the goods are partly manufactured goods.
   f. Sold by a licensed wholesaler to another licensed wholesaler.

g. Goods which have been exported from Canada by the manufacturer, producer or licensed wholesaler.

h. There shall be imposed, levied, and collected only fifty per cent of the tax on the sale and delivery of the articles enumerated in Schedule IV.

Schedule IV covers articles manufactured or processed by the labor of the blind and the deaf in institutions in Canada established for their care or under the control or direction of such institutions.

2. Licenses

a. Every manufacturer or producer shall take out an annual license and the Minister may prescribe a fee therefor, not exceeding Two Dollars.

b. A bona fide wholesaler or jobber may be granted an annual license and the Minister may prescribe a fee therefor not exceeding Two Dollars, but no such license shall be issued to him unless fifty per cent of his sales for the three months immediately preceding his application were exempt from the sales tax under the provisions of this act.

c. Every person who is required to pay or collect sales tax shall apply for a sales tax license and failure to do so is an offence.

3. Sales tax returns

a. Every person who is required to pay or to collect taxes shall make each month a true return of his taxable sales for the last preceding month, containing such information and in such form as may be required by regulations.

b. Every person holding a license shall, if no taxable sales have been made during the last preceding month, make a return stating that no taxable sales have been made.

4. Penalties

Upon default in payment of the tax or any portion thereof within the time prescribed there shall be paid in addition to the amount of the default a penalty of two-thirds of one per cent of the amount in default in respect of each month or fraction of a month during which the default continues.

5. Appeals

Where any difference arises or where any doubt exists as to whether any, or what rate of tax is payable on any article under this Act and there is no previous decision upon the question by any competent tribunal binding throughout Canada, the Tariff Board constituted by the Tariff Board Act may declare what amount of tax is payable thereon or that the article is exempt from tax under this Act. A further appeal from the decision of the Tariff Board may be made to the Exchequer Court under certain conditions.

Customs Duties. Customs administration for Canada is by the Department of National Revenue, Customs Division, Ottawa. Port offices are maintained at many points across the country and these port offices are the points at which customs entries are made.

Every shipment of goods imported into Canada must be formally cleared through customs. Parcel-post, express, and rail freight shipments are usually bonded on the nearest customs port to the destination of the shipment, where the shipments are held until customs clearance and examination of the goods have been completed. Truck shipments are held for clearance either at the border point of entry to Canada or are bonded to inland sufferance warehouses, at which point customs clearance is made before delivery of the shipment.

Clearances are made on behalf of a company either by an employee or a licensed customs broker. In either case powers of attorney must be properly executed and filed with the actual port of entry.

Canadian customs tariff provides three levels of classification, namely, British preferential, most-favored nation, and general, and shipments are rated for duty according to the category to which the country of exportation belongs. To qualify for British preferential or most-favored-nation tariff treatment, certain requirements are necessary such as customs invoices being produced on the proper forms and shipments being made direct from qualifying country without transshipment.

Protection to Industry. While the primary function of the customs tariff is to provide revenue for the government, the direct result of customs tariffs is protection to Canadian industry. This protection has assisted Canadian companies to become established and to survive against competition from imported goods of a similar nature where such goods are manufactured in greater volume and at lower cost. In meeting such competition from foreign imports, Canadian manufacturers need only be competitive with the duty-paid value of similar imported goods.

Tariff classification is as listed in Schedule A of the Customs Tariff.

Tariff Changes. The Customs Tariff is reviewed from time to time and changes are made as the Government sees fit by the following methods.

1. The annual budget is the usual process for making tariff changes and after presentation by the Minister of Finance, the changes are debated by the Government, and if passed become law, effective from the date of the budget.
2. Special tariff items are provided from time to time by order in council on the recommendation of the Minister of Finance for a temporary period, as stated in the order in council.
3. Tariff changes are also affected by direct negotiations with individual countries under trade agreements and also with groups of countries under such special negotiations as the General Agreement on Tariffs and Trade.

Each shipment imported into Canada is required to be classified according to the provisions of the Customs Tariff under the specific tariff item which the customs appraisers consider applicable. Some shipments are classified by being specifically covered by name in the tariff; others by being included in a group classification, e.g., machinery. Other articles are classified by material content and/or finish and still others are classified by reason of their end use.

Appeals may be made if an importer disagrees with the classification made by the examining appraiser. He has recourse to appeal his case to the Department of National Revenue, Customs and Excise Branch, Ottawa for further consideration. If still dissatisfied, he can appeal the decision of the Deputy Minister to the Tariff Board with further appeal to the Exchequer Court being permitted under certain conditions. It is recommended that a customs specialist be engaged to assist in the preparation and presentation of the case.

Value for duty is subject to government control. Basically, this is the fair market value at which similar articles are sold in the exporting country in like quantity to similar customers. The Customs Act also provides other methods of determining value for duty when this formula is not ascertainable.

Special or "dumping duty" to protect Canadian manufacturers is provided for in Section 6 of the Customs Tariff Act where goods "of a class or kind made in Canada" are offered for entry at a selling price to purchasers in Canada lower than the actual fair market value of the shipment in the country of exportation. The duty assessed is equal to the difference and must be paid by the importer. Freight allowances to customers in Canada are only allowed if similar freight allowances are part of the price in the country of export; otherwise they also are subject to this special duty.

Conversion of Foreign Currency. Invoices on prescribed forms are required for all shipments imported into Canada and are required to show the fair market value in the currency of the country of export and the true price at which the goods were sold to the purchaser in the currency of the actual transaction.

In computing the value for duty of the goods in Canadian currency, the rate of exchange shall be the rate as declared from time to time by the Bank of Canada. For this purpose, the Department of National Revenue, Ottawa, issues currency bulletins every few days which show the acceptable conversion rates to be used for converting invoices from most foreign countries with a separate currency bulletin being issued from time to time, indicating the acceptable conversion rate for United States dollars.

These conversion factors are applied to the fair market value to arrive at the fair market value in Canadian dollars and then either this value or the selling price if higher, also converted to Canadian dollars, determines the value for duty.

Refund of duty paid is subject to regulations of the Customs Act, and is allowable under the following circumstances: Goods found to be "not according to order" or proved to be "ordered in error" if exported under customs supervision within six months from date of importation. Goods which are inferior in quality or deficient in quantity or incorrectly invoiced, if same reported to the customs within thirty days of entry and the appraiser given an opportunity for reexamination of the goods to verify the report. Goods which are incorrectly classified are subject to refund under reclassification. In no case is a refund allowed after a period of two years from date of payment, unless authorized for special reasons by order in council. Applications for refund must be submitted on prescribed forms to the office of the collector of customs at which duty was paid.

Domestic drawbacks, listed as Schedule B of the Customs Tariff, provide for drawback of duty for articles and materials which are used according to the provisions of the various items in this Schedule. The portion of duty payable as drawback under the home consumption items varies from 40 per cent in some cases to 100 per cent in other items.

In addition to the items listed in Schedule B of the Customs Tariff, provision is made for drawback for certain specified articles when used according to the regulations contained in the Customs Act:

1. Drawback on philosophical and scientific apparatus, utensils, and instruments when used in accordance with the provisions of Tariff Item 696. Subject to drawback of 99 per cent.
2. Drawbacks in respect of missals, benitiers, scapulars, chapelets and rosaries, and religious medals and crosses of any material—materials and articles used in the manufacture of the above are subject to drawback of 99 per cent.
3. Goods used for ships or vessels built in Canada, as per special regulations. Subject to drawback of 99 per cent.
4. Ships' stores, furnishings, or equipment, as per special regulations. Subject to drawback of 99 per cent.
5. Goods manufactured or produced in Canada and exported as per special regulations. Subject to drawback of 99 per cent.
6. Goods imported into Canada and exported therefrom, as per special regulations. Subject to drawback of 99 per cent.
7. Material used in the manufacture of wireless telegraph apparatus, as per special regulations. Subject to drawback of 99 per cent.
8. Drawback of customs and excise duty and taxes and remission or re-

fund of sales and excise taxes pertaining to Canadian Commercial Corp. purchases, as per special regulations. Subject to drawback of 99 per cent.

9. Drawback of customs duty in respect of joint Canadian–United States projects, as per special regulations. Subject to drawback of 100 per cent.

Prohibited Goods. Listed as Schedule C of the Customs Tariff (see section 12). Under this section a variety of articles and goods which are prohibited entry into Canada are listed and reference should be made to it if articles of a doubtful nature are being considered for importation. Some of these items are quite important and include used aircraft, used automobiles, and motor vehicles other than those of the current calendar year.

TRANSPORTATION IN CANADA

Canada, one of the largest countries in the world, has a total area of 3,700,000 square miles. It is over 4,000 miles in length from coast to coast. The main topographical barriers are in a north-south direction at the coasts, while the relatively small population of approximately 19 million is consolidated comparatively close to the United States border. Almost two-thirds of the population of Canada is concentrated in a narrow strip stretching from Quebec City to Windsor, Ontario. The east-west transcontinental railway system must traverse large stretches of unproductive country in order to bind together various economic regions of Canada.

Railways

With more than 43,000 miles of railway line, Canada has 1 mile of line to 442 people, possibly the lowest population density per mile of railway line in the world. Transcontinental railway mileage is under the control of two lines, the Canadian Pacific Railway and the Canadian National Railway. The Canadian Pacific is privately owned; the Canadian National is controlled by the Federal Government. As well as offering transcontinental services, these two Railways operate very substantial mileage in feeder lines across the country. Both Railways control large truck fleets, used in highway transport operations. There are in addition a number of lines in operation by other interests, but their total mileage is relatively small. These latter serve special interests, as in the case of the Ontario Northland owned by the Province of Ontario and serving the area of that province in the direction of James Bay. The Pacific Great Eastern, another example, owned by the Province of British Columbia, serves special areas in that province.

United States railway lines cross into Canada, particularly into the southern Ontario area from Buffalo and Detroit and from New York and Portland into Montreal. These lines have local rights for passenger, freight, and express equal to those on the Canadian lines.

The railways in Canada operate freight services, passenger services, and express services. Each railway controls its own freight and passenger movement, but the Canadian Pacific Express and the Canadian National Express Companies operate all the express services for the other roads with only one or two small exceptions. The Railway Express Agency, usually in conjunction with Canadian National Railway facilities, operates the express services in Canada for the United States lines.

Waterways

Canada is blessed with an extensive natural inland waterway for transportation, which extends through the St. Lawrence River and the Great Lakes to about the center of the continent. This waterway, through its location on and around the international border, is shared with the United States. Its development is also a joint function and responsibility.

This waterway has been used for many years for the movement of a very extensive tonnage of bulk and package freight. Millions of dollars have been spent by the United States and Canadian governments in the dredging of channels and construction of locks to improve this waterway. The St. Lawrence Seaway, the latest major accomplishment, was opened on April 25, 1959. It makes it possible for large ocean freighters to bring freight through the Great Lakes and pick up export material from as far inland as Chicago, Ill., permitting freight handling from and to all parts of the world without transshipment. As a result of the St. Lawrence Seaway being opened, the volume of ocean vessel movements has increased. For this reason a bill was passed in the House of Commons on November 25, 1963, to have the Welland Canal equipped with double locks.

The Federal Government assumes responsibility for clearance, dredging, and navigation aids on the waterway and in the canals and main harbor. The harbor facilities, however, are the responsibility of the municipalities.

Highways

The highway system in Canada is under the jurisdiction of the provnces. There are approximately 430,000 miles of road with a population of 44 people per mile. Only about two-thirds of this road mileage is surfaced, indicating approximately 66 people per mile of surfaced road.

Controlled access highways are limited. The greater mileage of these at present is in Ontario. Canada now has a transcontinental highway extending from coast to coast, and special emphasis is being placed on road construction.

Truck transportation on the highways is subject to provincial regulation, the extent of which varies in each province. Some provinces exercise control over motor carrier freight rates in varying degrees. Control in the Province of Ontario requires that all rates be filed with the Ontario Highway Transport Board.

Motor carriers are divided into three general classes: common carriers, contract carriers, and private carriers. A common carrier is one providing service to the public as a whole and may be a transporter of commodities generally or of certain classes of goods only. A contract carrier is one that transports for a limited number of shippers, under special and individual contracts and agreements, and is usually restricted to the handling of certain classes of material. Operations of either type of carrier may be (1) over fixed routes between certain points or (2) over irregular routes throughout a given territory. The lawful scope of the operations of most motor carriers is determined by terms and conditions of certificates and permits issued by provincial regulatory agencies. A private carrier is one that transports its own goods. There are no fixed regulations for the private carrier other than licenses and safety regulations.

The basic requirement of regulation may be summarized as follows: A motor carrier may not lawfully operate unless it holds a suitable certificate or license and must confine operations to the scope of the authority held.

Airways

Air transport in Canada handles passenger, freight, and express service. Domestic lines in Canada consist of two scheduled transcontinental carriers, Air Canada, and Canadian Pacific Airlines. Canadian Pacific Airlines operate a transcontinental service on a scheduled basis to and from certain points parallel to Air Canada, but fewer points are served. In addition there are several local or feeder lines. Unscheduled lines and aircraft operate into the mining sections of the country and many other remote areas. International lines from the United States and overseas operate into the more important cities of the country. In many instances, over parallel routes, the airlines and railways carry an equal number of passengers. Montreal is the world headquarters of the International Civil Aeronautical Organization (ICAO) which makes regulations and procedures for world civil aeronautics. It is located in its own twenty-story building.

Regulatory Control

The Board of Transport Commissioners, under the jurisdiction of the Federal Government, handles the regulation of the greater part of the transport and shipping in the country. It does not regulate air transport or truck transportation. Jurisdiction over trucking is given to the provinces. Air transport is controlled by the Air Transport Board under the jurisdiction of the Federal Government. The ocean and coastal transport of the country is controlled by a third Federal Government commission, the Maritime Commission.

The Railway Act of 1919 with its amendments and the Transport Act of 1938, both currently effective, designate the responsibility and the authority of the Board of Transport Commissioners. This legislation, of course, is the most important in the field of transportation. A completely detailed description of the responsibility and the authority of the Board of Transport Commissioners is given in the *Canada Year Book* of 1940, pages 632 to 645. The Air Transport Board is described in the 1952–1953 *Canada Year Book,* pages 740 to 741, and again in the 1954 edition, pages 783 and 784.

Tariffs

Rates charged for transportation in their current form are the result of much evolution and mass negotiation, particularly in their early stages of development. They can by no means be said to be based on any scientific or other formula. To a very great extent they have been brought into reasonably stable operation and development under the regulations of the Railway Act, sections 322 to 359. These sections prescribe the rules for the filing with, and approval by, the Board of all classifications and tariffs.

Class rates are determined by reference to the classification of the article to be transported and are outlined in the Canadian Freight Classification No. 21. After reference to the CFC No. 21 and the determination of the rating number, CFC No. 21 should also be consulted for rules governing packing, marking, and other such phases of shipping. The CFC No. 21 is issued for uniform application on railway traffic throughout Canada, with the exception of the Yukon Territory, which uses a publication known as "A Northern Freight Classification."

It is important to understand the distinction between the terms "rate" and "rating." The rate is the charge per hundred pounds (or other unit of weight), and the rating is a numbered class given to the article by

CFC No. 21. The present classification has been patterned after the United States Uniform Classification. The progression of classes is as follows: class 100, class 85, class 70, class 55, class 45, class 33, class 30, and class 27.

The lower classes are percentage ratings of class 100 which is 100 per cent. In addition, there are several multiples of class 100. The classification divides all the various articles of commerce into classes according to their transportation characteristics. It also contains the basic rules and regulations as indicated above. These rules in the Canadian Freight Classification follow the same order as those in the United States Uniform Classification. That is to say rule 3 in the Canadian Freight Classification deals with the same subject matter as rule 3 in the Uniform Classification, although the details may vary slightly.

There is no uniform classification in use by the highway transport operators and many of them use the Canadian Freight Classification as their basis.

On international rail movements, classification and rates are a joint development under the approval of the Interstate Commerce Commission and the Board of Transport Commissioners, both of whom have jurisdiction in their own territories to the international border.

Four types of freight tariffs are prescribed by the Railway Act (chapters 2, 3, and 4 of the Revised Statutes of Canada, 1952). Section 341 of this Act describes them as Class Rate Tariffs, Commodity Rate Tariffs, Competitive Rate Tariffs, and Special Arrangement Tariffs. A class rate is the rate applicable to a class rating to which articles are assigned in the freight classification. Class rates apply to all articles offered for transportation, unless a lower commodity rate or competitive rate can be used. Effective March 1, 1955, a uniform scale of class rates was prescribed by the Board of Transport Commissioners for Canada, to be applicable throughout the Dominion except on the White Pass and Yukon Route and within the Maritime Freight Rate Territory (that is, the territory east and south of Diamond and Levis, Quebec).

Commodity rates, as the name implies, are established for movements of named or described commodities. In the case of raw materials, commodity rates are necessary because most raw materials could not or would not move on the very high basis of class rates provided for them. The system of commodity rates for manufactured goods is the result of negotiations between shippers and carriers, to assist the former in reaching new markets and to enable the latter to obtain traffic which might not move freely at the higher class rates.

Competitive rates are class or commodity rates that are issued to meet the competition of other railway carriers, as well as the competition of alternative forms of transportation.

The agreed charge system of rate making was introduced first in Great Britain and did not become law in Canada until 1938, the legislation for which can be found in Part IV of the Transport Act of 1938. It applies only in Canada and not between Canada and the United States, nor has it ever been made law within the United States.

A brief definition of an agreed charge is that it is contract between one shipper and/or a group of shippers of similar commodities and the railways, by which the shipper agrees to give the railways a certain percentage of his shipping tonnage in exchange for a lower basis of rates and/or conditions of carriage.

At times the contract calls for 100 per cent of the traffic to be delivered to the railways. However, the percentage is frequently lower but, at the time of writing, no agreed charge has ever been published guaranteeing the railways less than 50 per cent.

After an agreed charge has been contracted, the shipper or railway must honor it for at least one year from date of publication and it can then only be terminated by either participant after a three-month notice in writing.

Special arrangements are charges, allowances, rules, and regulations respecting demurrage, protection, storage, switching, elevation, cartage, loading, unloading, weighing, diversion, and all other accessory or special arrangements that in any way increase or decrease the charges to be paid on any shipment, or that increase or decrease the value of the service provided by the railway.

Maximum charges are merely stated in many of the rules of both classification and tariffs. For example, the maximum charge for less-than-carload shipment is the carload rate multiplied by the carload minimum weight; in pickup and delivery tariffs this becomes the carload rate multiplied by the minimum weight, plus cartage charges on the carload minimum weight. The total charge produced by the class rate on the actual weight of the shipment, subject to the classification minimum weight, will apply if it produces a lower total charge than the commodity rate and the commodity tariff minimum weight. When the classification provides specified individual minimum weights for articles in less-than-carload quantities, a maximum charge for a shipment is set by the total charges accruing on a similar number of pieces of greater weight. In relating rates to distance, the principle of maximum charges is stated in the "long-" and "short-haul" clause of the Railway Act. This clause states that no toll shall be approved which is greater for a shorter than a longer distance, in which such shorter distance is included, unless the toll is issued to meet competition.

Demurrage

Demurrage rules are issued by the Canadian Car Demurrage Bureau. After the expiration of the 48-hr free time allowed (for international shipments this free time is increased by one full day for customs clearance), a charge of $4 per day is made for the first four days or fraction thereof of delay. For the fifth and each succeeding day or fraction thereof, a charge of $8 per day is made. There is no average demurrage arrangement in effect in Canada.

Express

For express, as in the case of freight, all rates or tolls are governed by a classification known as the Express Classification for Canada. Unlike the Railway Classification it is not so much a classification as it is a list of exceptions to two general classes, first and second.

The Express Classification contains the condition of carriage for express shipments and applies only on traffic moving within the Dominion. For traffic moving internationally, between Canada and the United States, the Official Express Classification governs. This is the classification for use within the United States. There is also a sheet of exceptions to the Official Classification which is issued for use on international traffic between Canada and the United States.

Air Express and Freight

Air freight and air express rates are subject to the approval of the Air Transport Board and, as in the case of many other early developments, are still very high in relation to other forms of competition. Air freight charges are in the area of two to one for rail freight and air express four to one for air freight.

Comparative Summarization

The outline below attempts to list briefly the inherent advantages of each mode of transportation.

Railroad. Provides the best means of shipping bulky, heavy, or low-valued commodities, but each shipment should be judged on its individual merits as well as customers' expressed desires, in deciding whether to ship by rail or truck.

Truck. Physically, truck transportation is superior to rail in the field of shorter hauls. It is faster and more flexible and offers door-to-door service. The cost of truck transportation, however, tends to be higher than rail, particularly for long hauls and the movement of low-valued commodities. While there are exceptions to the rule, in general the natural field of the truck does not exceed one thousand miles.

Water. Accessibility is limited and is much slower than rail, but is compensated for by lower rates.

Freight Forwarder. By rail—To the west coast and far western provinces these rates are usually lower than standard l.c.l. rates. This is a good mode of transportation on less-than-carload shipments moved over great distances and is faster when moving to points where forwarders ship through cars. Service is limited to movements between large cities.

By truck—Same as by rail with the exception that all western destinations are served.

Rail Express. A fast but more expensive service adaptable particularly to small shipments of 25 to 100 lb upon which premium in transportation charges is acceptable to obtain fast delivery.

Parcel Post. Rates are usually cheaper than Express on parcels up to 25 lb. This is the weight limit for parcel post. There are also limits on size.

Air Freight. Expensive and unreliable during adverse weather. However, it offers the fastest available time in transit, with the exception of air express.

Air Express. Very expensive and used only for extremely rush and small shipments.

Carrier Liability

Bills of lading are the most important documents in transportation. The terms of these bills are not often read carefully by shippers and receivers of freight. These should be understood clearly. Highway truck bills of lading vary extensively and in each instance the carrier's liability should be clearly determined by the shipper.

In general the following applies to rail and inland water bills of lading. After the expiration of free time, the carrier is no longer an insurer of the goods and his liability becomes that of a warehouseman. If a fire occurs, and there is no negligence on the part of the carrier, there is no claim. If the shipment is stolen, there is no claim except in the case of negligence.

The carrier's liability extends for 48 hr exclusive of legal holidays, or in the case of bonded goods 72 hr exclusive of legal holidays, after written notice of arrival has been sent or given. After that the carrier can continue his liability as a warehouseman only, or he can escape further responsibility after giving written notice of intent, by removal of the goods to a public or licensed warehouse. They will be held at the risk of the owner and subject to a lien for all freight and lawful charges including a reasonable charge for storage.

Owner's risk articles are subject to some misunderstanding. If you ship at owner's risk, it does not mean that the carrier escapes responsibility for loss or damage. The risks intended to be covered by owner's risk conditions are those necessarily incidental to transportation. This condition does not release the carrier from liability for negligence and the burden of proving freedom rests with him. The carrier in this case is not an insurer of the goods, but he is bound to take all reasonable care of them and he is liable for all loss or damage occasioned by his negligence.

The carrier is liable for any loss, damage, or delay, subject to certain exceptions such as acts of God, the Queen's or public enemies, riots, strikes, defect or inherent vice, and others.

All these terms have been defined at law and your local claims agent's interpretation may be his own special one. Act of God, for example, will not hold if there is warning of it and the carrier has opportunity to get the goods to safety. The act of God must be the proximate cause of the loss.

Notice of loss, damage, or delay must be made to the carrier at the point of delivery or to the carrier at the point of origin within four months after delivery of the goods, or in the case of failure to make delivery then, within four months after a reasonable time for delivery has elapsed. Unless notice is so given, the carrier will not be liable.

The amount of any loss or damage for which any carrier is liable shall be computed on the basis of the value of the goods at the time and place of shipment under the bill of lading. This value also includes the freight and other charges if paid, and the duty if paid or payable and not refunded.

BANKING[1]

The Canadian banking system consists of the Bank of Canada, a government-owned central bank; the Industrial Development Bank, a subsidiary of the Bank of Canada; and eight privately owned commercial banks which have more than 5,000 branches and subagencies located across the country.

The Bank of Canada was established in 1934, as a central or banker's bank. All its stock is owned by the Canadian Government. The bank holds on deposit the statutory cash reserves of the chartered banks and,

[1] Excerpts by permission of Ryerson Press, Toronto, publishers of "Chartered Banking in Canada."

in effect, sets the over-all volume of bank credit, the chief ingredient of the nation's money supply. In addition, it is the fiscal agent of the government, manages the public debt, issues all paper money or notes, and is the instrument through which the nation's monetary policy is given effect.

The Bank of Canada may buy and sell securities on the open market, discount securities and commercial bills, fix minimum rates at which it will discount, and buy and sell bullion and foreign exchange.

Industrial Development Bank. The Industrial Development Bank was established under legislation passed in August, 1944. This bank extends loans to economically sound enterprises which cannot arrange necessary financing with chartered banks or on the investment market. It can extend loans over a longer period than the chartered banks.

The bank has a capital of 50 million dollars subscribed by the Bank of Canada, with 10 million dollars paid up at the time the act came into force and 23 million dollars subsequently. It can borrow through the sales of bonds and debentures up to five times its paid-up capital.

Bank Act Revision. Charters of the commercial banks in Canada are renewable every 10 years, when the Bank Act is revised by Parliament after public hearings before the Banking and Commerce Committee of the House of Commons. The latest revision was in 1954, when the following principal changes were made:

The principle of variable cash reserves was introduced and the chartered banks were required to keep a minimum of 8 per cent of their Canadian deposit liabilities in the form of deposits with, and notes of, the Bank of Canada. The central bank was empowered to raise this to a maximum of 12 per cent, gradually and after notice.

A revised National Housing Act, with parallel changes in the Bank Act, empowered the banks to make mortgage loans on new housing.

An entirely new section in the act enabled the chartered banks to make loans on the security of oil in the ground.

Banks were given the opportunity of making their shares transferable other than on the books of the bank. Other changes facilitated the offering of new shares.

By amendment banks accepted chattel mortgages as loan security.

The Chartered Banks. The nine commercial banks are called chartered because they operate under charter or license granted by Parliament. The charters are for a 10-year period, renewable at the decennial revision of the Bank Act. The public review of the basic banking law before a parliamentary committee is unique with Canada, and has resulted in banks and banking keeping pace with the changing and expanding financial and economic needs of the Canadian people.

The branch bank is perhaps the most distinctive feature of the Canadian banking system, and Canada has extended it further than any other country. In 1963 there was a branch bank for every 3,500 Canadians. Each branch has a full range of banking facilities, whether it is located in a big city or a rural hamlet. In 1868 there were only 123 branch banks in Canada. By 1902 the number, including subagencies, had risen to 747 and since then there has been a steady increase, with 1,200 new branches established in the last 7 years.

In addition to branches in Canada, most of the banks have offices in the world money centers of New York and London and some have branches in other countries. All Canadian banks maintain banking correspondents or agents throughout the world, an important factor in Canada's world trade.

The eight chartered banks are Bank of Montreal, The Bank of Nova Scotia, The Toronto-Dominion Bank, The Provincial Bank of Canada, The Canadian Imperial Bank of Commerce, The Royal Bank of Canada, Banque Canadienne Nationale, and The Mercantile Bank of Canada.

Growth of Commercial Banking. The strength of the Canadian banking system can be seen clearly in combined figures for the chartered banks. For instance, total deposits increased from $6,883 millions in December, 1945, to $14,562 millions in September, 1963. At the same time, total assets increased from $7,353 millions to $21,182 millions.

Loans and discounts in Canada stood at $1,139 millions in December, 1945, and 18 years later had jumped to $7,912 millions, not including $904 millions in housing loans.

Dividends paid in 1962 totaled $60,278,000 to 109,210 shareholders. A further indication of the growth of the system is that 5,132,000 deposit accounts have been opened in the past 10 years, with a total now of more than 14,700,000. Bank staffs total more than 55,000 men and women.

FOREIGN EXCHANGE[2]

Since foreign exchange control was abolished in Canada on December 15, 1951, residents of this country have again been able to acquire and use such exchange at their pleasure. As Canada is not on the gold standard and no parity for the Canadian dollar has been established with the International Monetary Fund since the discontinuance of controlled rates on October 2, 1950, the price at which foreign exchange may be bought or sold in terms of Canadian funds is governed by supply and demand.

[2] Excerpts by permission of Quick Canadian Facts Limited, Toronto, publishers of "Quick Canadian Facts."

The Canadian foreign exchange market is centered largely in Montreal and Toronto. Acting through foreign exchange brokers there, the banks place bids and offers in accordance with the requirements of their customers.

The banks also keep in close touch with markets in centers such as New York, London, Paris, Brussels, Amsterdam, and Zurich, by telephone, teletype, telegraph, and cable, and buy and sell there when they can do so to advantage. In this way rate changes abroad are reflected immediately in the local market.

It is not only in Montreal and Toronto that it is important to have up-to-the-minute information about changes in rates. Branches across Canada must be kept closely informed because it is through them that business houses and others transact their foreign exchange business. To do this, it is customary for some of the banks, at least, to divide the country into districts, roughly according to provinces, to designate the main branch in each district a trading branch and, through direct telephone or teletype connection with head office, keep such branches constantly advised of all changes in quotations for the principal foreign currencies.

All branches are furnished daily, usually from district headquarters, with rate bulletins containing firm quotations for all such currencies. Up to specified amounts branches are allowed to handle transactions on the basis of rates quoted in the latest bulletin. In the case of a transaction in excess of the limit, an up-to-the-minute rate must be obtained from the district trading branch.

When any unusual fluctuation occurs in a particular currency during the course of the day, trading branches telephone or telegraph branches dealing regularly in that currency.

The form in which foreign exchange is offered to a bank includes cable, telegraph, and mail transfers, checks, drafts, and money orders, demand, sight, and time bills, both clean and with documents attached, coupons, and foreign bank notes. Foreign exchange is sold by the banks in the form of cable, telegraph, and mail transfers, drafts, money orders, foreign bank notes, and so on.

According to the wishes of the customer, transactions are handled for immediate delivery, on a delayed spot basis—that is, for delivery in a day or two—on a forward basis for delivery within, say, 180 days, or on the basis of what is known as a swap.

Forward transactions are handled largely for importers and exporters buying and selling goods for future shipment, who wish to establish their costs or prices. A swap is a transaction in which a customer buys or sells foreign exchange for immediate delivery against a sale or purchase of the same amount for forward delivery. An example of one who buys is a customer who knows he will receive a certain amount of foreign currency at a future date but has immediate use for it. He buys exchange for immediate delivery on a swap basis, agreeing to deliver the same amount at a specified later date.

An example of one who sells is a customer who has exchange available which he does not require immediately, but will need at a later date. He sells the exchange for immediate delivery, against a purchase of the same amount forward on a swap basis. This gives him immediate use of an equivalent amount of local funds and assurance that the foreign funds will be available when required, at an established rate of exchange.

Usually swap transactions are handled at a very low cost, although rates vary with the rates for forward transactions. These, in turn, fluctuate with supply and demand, international interest rates, and foreign exchange regulations where in effect. Under ordinary conditions, however, the premium or discount on forwards is moderate. On the other hand, during a period of financial crisis costs of both forwards and swaps may become prohibitive.

The banks will buy from or sell to a customer any foreign exchange for which there is a market, but the major portion of Canada's trade is handled on a United States dollar or sterling basis, as these currencies have a ready market both for immediate and forward delivery.

The importance which is attached to keeping branches closely informed regarding changes in rates has been shown in the foregoing. It is equally important that the foreign exchange department at head office receives prompt advice of purchases and sales at branches, as it is the responsibility of that department to keep the bank's foreign exchange risks at a minimum. Large purchases and sales are reported immediately through the trading branch. Sundry transactions handled at bulletin rates are reported by mail to district headquarters, where they are tabulated and the totals telegraphed daily to the head office. When these totals are received, and during the day as it learns of other transactions, the foreign exchange department takes immediate steps to cover the bank's position by buying or selling the required exchange in whatever market it can be obtained.

Although it is often impossible to avoid being long or short in a certain exchange temporarily, the bank does not intentionally take a speculative position in any exchange.

Mention has been made of the necessity for dependable foreign service, either through branches or correspondent banks. Such services include the making and receiving of all types of payments, collecting clean and documentary bills, coupons, etc., clearing items payable locally, dealing with commercial and traveler's letters of credit, furnishing credit reports, and so on.

Where the agency is a correspondent bank, therefore, commensurate balances must be maintained or its services otherwise compensated. Balances in foreign currencies with correspondent banks do not necessarily represent exchange risks. Often they result from deposits of customers in foreign currencies on the books of branches in Canada or elsewhere, from swap transactions covering the purchase of spot exchange against forward sales, or float arising from the purchase of cable exchange against the sale of drafts.

Many different types of instruments have to be dealt with in connection with foreign exchange transactions, and procedures, charges, stamp tax, and so on vary in different countries. For this reason branches have to be furnished with explicit standing instructions indicating the channels through which business is to be handled, the method of accounting and settling, and covering any other features for which guidance is required.

SELECTED BIBLIOGRAPHY

Canada—Royal Commission on Banking and Finance. Report. Queen's Printer, Ottawa, Ontario, Canada, 1964

The Canada Year Book (annual), The Dominion Bureau of Statistics, Ottawa, Ontario, Canada

Canadian Official Railway Guide (monthly), International Railway Publishing Company, Montreal, Quebec, Canada

Canadian Traffic Management, vol. 1–3, Department of University Extension, The University of Toronto Press, Toronto, Ontario, Canada, 1953–1955

Cook, Ramsay: *Canada—A Modern Study,* Clarke, Irwin & Co., Ltd., Toronto, Ontario, Canada, 1963

Coyne, H. E. B.: *The Railway Law of Canada,* Canada Law Book Co., Ltd., Toronto, Ontario, Canada, 1947

Currie, W. A.: *Economics of Canadian Transportation,* The University of Toronto Press, Toronto, Ontario, Canada, 1954

Galbraith, J. A.: *The Economics of Banking Operations,* McGill University Press, Montreal, Quebec, Canada, 1963

Jamieson, A. B.: *Chartered Banking in Canada,* Ryerson Press, Toronto, Ontario, Canada, 1962

New, Chester: *Lord Durham Mission to Canada,* McClelland & Stewart, Ltd., Toronto, Ontario, Canada, 1964

O'Brien, J. W.: *Canadian Money and Banking,* McGraw-Hill Co. of Canada, Toronto, Ontario, Canada, 1964

Official Guide of the Railways (monthly), National Railway Publishing Company, New York

Assistance may be obtained in transportation matters from the Transportation Department of the Canadian Manufacturers Association, The Canadian Industrial Traffic League, Toronto, and the numerous municipal boards of trade or chambers of commerce, most of which have traffic departments.

SECTION 21

DISPOSAL OF RECLAMATION AND SALVAGE MATERIALS

Editor

R. W. Stewart, Purchasing Agent–Raw Materials and Metals, Aluminum Company of America, Pittsburgh, Pennsylvania

Associate Editors

Lyle E. Schaffer, Coordinator, Purchasing, Standard Oil Company (Indiana), Chicago, Illinois

Raymond I. Wells, Purchasing Agent, I. H. Schlezinger & Sons, Columbus, Ohio

The salvage, or saving for advantageous disposal, of a company's property which is no longer economically useful to its owner in its present condition or form, provides a means for:

1. Increasing cash income
2. Reducing the cost of the company's product or service
3. Conserving raw materials

A well-managed salvage operation provides cash income from the refuse from manufacturing processes, calls attention of the production department to apparent excesses in waste materials, and reclaims materials and parts for use in another form or for restoration to workable condition at a lower cost than buying new. These all contribute to lower costs of operation.

The conservation of raw materials is important to us as individuals, as companies, and as a nation. Salvage contributes to conservation by restoring useful material to the channel of production, thereby replacing a quantity of raw material that would otherwise have been required. Waste paper can replace a certain amount of pulpwood, rags, and chemicals; ferrous scrap reduces the need for iron ore; aluminum scrap the need for bauxite; etc.

GENERAL CONSIDERATIONS

The purchase and sale of scrap and waste material is a big business. It is estimated that in recent years the gross sales value of salvage materials of all kinds in the United States has run well over 3 billion dollars annually. The table on page 21–4 is illustrative of the volume of sales of ferrous scrap and certain of the metals for which statistics are available. In addition to copper, lead, nickel, and aluminum, substantial tonnages of antimony, tin, zinc, and the precious metals are also salvaged.

Types of Reclamation and Salvage Material

The materials with which the salvage and reclamation operation of a company is concerned are:

1. *Surplus and obsolete stocks.* These may consist of raw materials, parts, or supplies no longer needed because of changes in design, different method of manufacture, or unforeseen reduction in volume of production or change of product.

2. *Scrap.* As generally used, the word "scrap" applies to any ferrous materials or object which is suitable for remelting to produce iron, steel, or its alloys. It may be sold as prepared scrap, ready for use as it is, or it may require preparation before it is acceptable to the ultimate user. Some scrap, called rerolling grades, is not remelted, but is heated and re-formed.

3. *Metals (nonferrous scrap).* All salvaged materials which are chiefly composed of any of the nonferrous metals, or of any alloy of those metals, are usually referred to as "metals" rather than as "scrap," although the term "nonferrous scrap" is often used to distinguish metals from "ferrous scrap."

Consumption of Purchased Metal Scrap in the United States*

Nonferrous: net tons; ferrous: gross tons of 2,240 lb

Year	Nonferrous				Ferrous
	Copper	Lead	Nickel	Aluminum	
1958	1,109,479	520,682	7,797	375,564	27,755,840
1959	1,267,916	581,151	13,900	475,964	32,239,200
1960	1,208,434	610,029	15,251	441,479	29,562,400
1961	1,170,097	587,274	13,590	498,116	28,430,080
1962	1,265,301	578,930	13,210	594,873	28,407,680
1963	1,360,262	640,915	12,714	647,489	33,255,040
1964	1,512,600	705,163	24,864	712,251	35,700,000

* Nonferrous figures reported by the U.S. Department of the Interior; ferrous figures are estimated, and reported by the Institute of Scrap Iron & Steel, Inc.

The metals may be melted, refined, and poured into ingots without change in their basic metal content, or alloys may be resmelted, in which process certain metals or impurities are removed or separated.

4. *Waste.* This term is applied to all nonmetallic refuse from an operation. It includes paper, rags, rubber, and wood, or any other material not useful to the company, but which has a market value.

5. *Surplus and obsolete equipment.* Changes in method of production, or the company's product, or permanent reduction in demand for the product, can result in machinery and other facilities being no longer required. Similarly, improved design of machinery may make it uneconomical to continue an old machine in operation although its service life has not been expended. Equipment of this kind may have a sales value as it is. If not, it can usually be sold as scrap.

Types of Purchasers

The purchasers of salvage materials fall into four categories:

The *consumer* who actually puts the material to use in making his product is, of course, the ultimate purchaser, and a considerable quantity of scrap, metals, waste, etc., is bought directly from the producer of the material by the ultimate consumer.

There is, however, a large industry in its own right, devoted to the purchase, preparation, and resale of salvage materials to the consumers. Most of the waste materials resulting from the operation of industry, which have reusable value, are handled in one way or another by this industry. It is composed of the following types of firms.

Dealers who purchase, often collect local purchases in their own trucks, and prepare the material into a form suitable for sale. Small dealers may do little more than collect material for resale to other yards. Large, well-equipped dealers, however, may have a substantial investment in machinery, such as presses, shears, and cranes, which facilitate the sorting, cutting up, and preparation into the forms best suited to the customers who buy the material from them. A fully integrated operator will have the personnel and facilities for demolition of structures at the site and removal of the material to his yard.

Nonferrous metal resmelters perform much the same functions as the large yard operator, except that resmelters have the special facilities required for the proper preparation of salvaged metals into usable form.

Brokers of scrap, metals, and machinery buy and sell the material, usually without taking physical possession at any time. They have an important part to play in the often involved transfer of salvaged materials from the producer to the consumer.

Purchasing Department Responsibility

The purchasing officer, with his knowledge of materials and how his company uses them, is the logical person to be held responsible for reclamation and salvage disposal. He is familiar with the companies which make various materials and where they are located. He knows how the items his company buys are made and what they cost.

This is the proper background for deciding which items should be reclaimed or disposed of as scrap, and then finding the most favorable outlets for the scrap. Since the purchasing officer is familiar with various purchasing techniques, he is in a position to weigh the merits of having certain scrap or metals converted into a usable product for his company or of selling the material outright.

That the purchasing officer should handle the reclamation and salvage function was verified in a survey taken by the NAPA as far back as 1939. That analysis indicated that 88 per cent of the firms questioned have this phase of their operation handled by the purchasing agent.

If another department is held responsible for the disposal of waste material, the purchasing officer should be constantly consulted, in order that maximum benefits may be derived from his knowledge of the market, material sources, and the other factors which are the basis for his daily buying operations.

The policies and procedures outlined in this section have been taken from the manuals of large companies. Exactly the same policies, however, can be modified in whole or in part for any company producing reclamation and salvage material *regardless of size*. For example, the single-plant company can disregard the problems arising in multiple-plant operations. Furthermore, the smaller company can assign the reclamation and salvage duties to a part-time function of a buyer. The main point is that all companies, regardless of size, have complete, clearly defined policies and procedures in writing, if possible, for profitable disposal of reclamation and salvage material.

Besides deriving the maximum for efficient disposal, some companies do not overlook checking ways and means of reducing production in their plants. Causes of salvage vary from misuse of machine tools and other equipment, inexperience and carelessness on the part of the operators, to hundreds of other possibilities that require close scrutiny of the plant management. The purchasing official in the smaller companies is usually very helpful in furnishing information and data on how to reduce the salvage right at the source, all as described later in this section.

ORGANIZING AND OPERATING A RECLAMATION AND SALVAGE DEPARTMENT

Every year plants lose thousands of dollars because of lack of an organized reclamation and salvage program. One large utility company which recently instituted and organized such a program found that its sales of reclamation and salvage materials jumped from $40,000 per year to well over $300,000. Reclamation of materials for further use in their company's operations went from zero to approximately $50,000 per year. Many other such examples could be cited.

Objectives and Activities. In setting up any reclamation and salvage program the first step is to determine the objectives and specific activities of the reclamation and salvage department. Its basic objectives, whether in a large or a small reclamation and salvage department, are:

1. To ensure that all scrap, metals, waste, surplus stocks, and equipment produced are properly located, collected, and handled. Waste may include gases or liquids as well as solids
2. To obtain maximum reuse and economic value of such reclamation and salvage materials
3. To assist in minimizing the generation of reclamation and salvage material by observing sources and by close cooperation with other departments

The specific activities of the reclamation and salvage department will include the following:

1. Collecting or supervising the collecting of reclamation and salvage materials from various areas in the plant and taking them to a central location
2. Storing reclamation and salvage materials until they are disposed of or reused
3. Sorting and preparing scrap, metal, and waste to obtain maximum sale value
4. Reviewing all purchase requisitions before they are forwarded to purchasing department to determine if material can be furnished from reclamation and salvage material
5. Restoring reclaimable materials to usable condition or transferring such materials to other departments if they are not to be reconditioned by the reclamation and salvage department
6. Seeking out possible plant uses for reclamation and salvage materials
7. Assisting in the sale of reclamation and salvage materials

Selection and Duties of Reclamation and Salvage Manager. When the objectives and activities of the reclamation and salvage department have been determined, the next step is to decide who is going to run the department. This will depend upon the size of the plant, quantity of reclamation and salvage materials produced, and the personnel available. If supervision of the job requires only the part-time attention of one man, it may be assigned to the purchasing agent or some member of the production or stores department. If supervising the job requires at least one man full time, it should be set up as a separate department. In this case the reclamation and salvage supervisor will usually report to some member of management other than the purchasing agent. In most cases a separate reclamation and salvage department will report to the head of the production department.

The selection of a man to head the reclamation and salvage activities should be done with great care. This is true whether the reclamation and salvage department is to be a separate function or a part of some department. As the head of a new department the reclamation and salvage manager will find that many of his activities have in the past been performed by other departments. This is certain to create jealousies and resentments. He must have the tact and diplomacy to handle these situations at the outset or be in for continual trouble. He must be able to sell his department to all levels from the lowest shopworker to the boss. He will be required to use considerable initiative. He must be able to work and cooperate with all people in the plant and outsiders. He must know materials and material handling.

After the reclamation and salvage manager has been appointed, his first step will be to determine the dormant and potential reclamation and salvage materials. This will include unused idle or surplus supplies and equipment, production scrap, metals, and waste, and salvageable materials. This knowledge will be required in presenting his program to management. In addition he should be able to recommend to management the type and size of organization required, the equipment and facilities needed, the cost of operating his department, and what profit or loss can be expected.

This information should be supplied to management in a written report. The purpose obviously is to get the backing of management. This point cannot be stressed too much. *No reclamation and salvage program has succeeded fully without the backing of management.* A letter should be issued by top management clearly outlining the function of the reclamation and salvage department and the authority of the reclamation and salvage manager. The reclamation and salvage manager must have the authority to do his job properly. He should be on the same level as other department heads and report directly to top management.

Reclamation and Salvage Manual. The reclamation and salvage manager should prepare a manual describing the functions and operations of his department. One portion of the manual should be prepared for other department heads and should give a general picture of the reclamation and salvage department. The other portion of the manual should be written giving specific details for the men in the department who are actually going to do the work. The two portions may be issued as two separate manuals or incorporated into one. The manual or manuals should include:

1. Foreword written and signed by the top management man
2. Organization of reclamation and salvage department
3. Functions of reclamation and salvage department
4. Methods of collecting, handling, sorting, preparing, storing, and disposing of scrap, metals, and waste
5. Procedure for reporting, transferring, and disposing of surplus and obsolete equipment and stocks
6. Reclamation procedures
7. Economic limitations, i.e., cost to reclaim versus value received
8. Procedure for sales to employees of reclamation and salvage materials
9. Procedure for donations of reclamation and salvage materials to educational and charitable institutions
10. Handling of returnable containers
11. Disposal of surplus or obsolete land and buildings
12. Examples of all forms and an explanation of their use

A properly prepared manual has the advantage of making the position of the reclamation and salvage department clear to all plant personnel. The preparation of such a task may seem like an endless job, but the rewards are worth the work. Manuals of other companies can usually be borrowed to serve as a guide. The manual should be prepared one section at a time. Each section should be reviewed with all interested parties upon completion. Provisions should be made for revisions. A loose-leaf manual is excellent in this respect.

Operation of Reclamation and Salvage Department. The number of people required to operate the reclamation and salvage department will depend upon the quantity of material produced and how much sorting and preparation is performed. Whether it is one worker or a hundred, the personnel should be selected with care. Their judgment and care or lack of it in sorting and preparing reclamation and salvage material will have considerable effect upon the return to the company. They should also be able to get along well with people since they will normally come in contact with many workers in other departments.

The reclamation and salvage manager should schedule regular surveys of the plant. He should be accompanied by a member—preferably the head—of the purchasing, production, and engineering departments. The purpose of these surveys is to turn up any dormant reclamation and salvage materials, detect practices which result in excessive waste, develop new possibilities for reclamation and salvage, and check performance of reclaimed materials being used in the plant. They are also helpful in bringing to light any cases of individuals or departments who have set up their own individual little storerooms.

The reclamation and salvage manager can aid his cause by the proper use of publicity within the plant. One method is to hold regular informative meetings with plant personnel to outline the over-all purpose of the program and spell out the "who, what, where, when, and why" objectives of the reclamation and salvage department. Other methods of publicity include bulletin boards, pamphlets, and posters. Many plants have contests to decrease the output of scrap, metal, and waste between two or more groups of workers doing the same job.

The reclamation and salvage manager will have to keep the necessary records to provide the following information:

1. Quantities of reclamation and salvage materials collected and their source
2. Equipment declared surplus and location
3. Record of sales including purchaser, date, quantity, description of material, unit price, and total price
4. Inventory of materials on hand
5. Materials reclaimed for further use and cost of reclaiming
6. Departmental operating costs

It will be necessary to work out with the accounting department how the revenue received from the sale of reclamation and salvage materials will be distributed. Some companies credit each department with a proportionate share of the revenues based on the amount of reclamation and salvage materials produced by the department. Other companies prefer to credit the revenue to the over-all plant rather than to individual departments.

The reclamation and salvage manager should report the activities of his department to top management on a weekly or monthly basis. This report should include changes in inventory, summary of material disposed of, and a brief profit and loss statement. Following is an example of the profit and loss statement used by one company:

Sales and Expense
Reclamation and Salvage Department
June, 19—

Sales		
Ferrous metals—outside	$ 6.69	
Ferrous metals—plant	54.64	
Nonferrous metals—plant	220.96	
Nonferrous metals—outside	.00	
Miscellaneous sales—plant	.00	
Miscellaneous sales—employees	67.98	
Miscellaneous sales—outside	.00	
Materials returned to stores	.00	
Total sales		$ 350.27

Expenses		
Fixed expense	$ .75	
Miscellaneous expense	28.10	
Operating supplies	.00	
Labor	46.74	
Total reclamation expense		$ 75.59
Total sales		$ 350.27
Total expense		$ 75.59
Total profit or loss		$ 274.68
Total sales for year to date (sales)		$12,654.77
Total expense for year to date		$ 1,071.74
Total profit or loss for year to date (net profit)		$11,583.03

NOTE: This report does not include labor or sales of returned containers.

In addition to review of over-all profit or loss, cost studies should be made from time to time on reclamation or preparation of specific items to be sure that the value added by this work exceeds the cost of doing it.

In most cases every department connected with the reclamation and salvage function, including the purchasing, reclamation and salvage (if separate from purchasing), and accounting departments, will be faced with inspections by either or both internal and external auditors. The records of sales, procedures, policies, and accounting should be established so that there is every opportunity for the auditors to make an intelligent audit. Auditors will be interested in the following matters:

1. Is there an effective control over weight?
2. Are weights properly determined?
3. Is accountability soundly established?
4. Are materials classified for the most profitable returns?
5. Is there any possibility of collusion?

The collection and storage of scrap, metals, and waste from production areas is generally a function of the reclamation and salvage department. The great variety of plants and problems encountered make it impossible to discuss this function completely. There is one principle, however, which will apply to the majority of plants. Separate marked containers should be provided at each source where scrap, metal, and waste are generated. These containers should be removed and replaced as soon as they are full or when a new class of material is to be produced.

Investigation should be made in cases of large quantities as to the possibility of moving scrap materials directly from the operating department to buyer. This will eliminate excessive handling, such as to a central area, and then to the buyer's equipment. Removal may be daily or weekly dependent upon volume.

The central reclamation and salvage area should have separate bins for each different class of materials. Concrete bins will usually prove more economical in the long run, particularly for heavier materials. They should be laid out so that each bin is readily accessible by truck or whatever means is used to transport materials to the central area. Covers should be provided for bins containing materials which can be damaged by the weather.

Reclamation and salvage materials can be conveyed from the producing area to the central area by any one of several means. The determining factors are the weight and volume to be moved and the distance the material has to be transported. For small quantities and short distances hand trucks may be satisfactory. Larger quantities and longer distances will require lift trucks, flat-bed trucks, load-lugger-type trucks, cranes, or conveyors.

Handling at the central area will depend upon similar factors. A magnet mounted upon an electric- or gasoline-powered crane is useful for handling scrap and separating magnetic from nonmagnetic materials. The central area should have a scale or access to one nearby for determining weights produced and sold.

SURPLUS AND OBSOLETE STOCKS

Surplus and obsolete stocks are usually created by change in design, different method of manufacture, unforeseen reduction in volume of production, change of product, change in personnel, or a wrong decision by some part of management. These dormant stocks must be put to some other use or disposed of promptly if a company is to realize its maximum profit.

Surplus and obsolete stocks consist of raw materials, replacement parts, and maintenance and operating supplies. While the purchasing department may be consulted before stocks are declared surplus or obsolete, it is almost never the sole judge. The operating department is usually responsible for declaring surplus or obsolete raw materials and operating supplies, while the engineering and maintenance departments are responsible for replacement parts and maintenance supplies. The stores department will figure in these decisions if the materials are carried in stores.

Surplus and obsolete stocks should be reported to the reclamation and salvage manager or such other person who is responsible for this function. The reclamation and salvage manager should first determine if the material can be used elsewhere in the plant. This is the most profitable method of disposal since it represents the cost of new material. In a multiple-plant operation the material should also be offered to the other plants. The material is normally transferred to the other plant prepaid at its book value or at the price the other plant can buy similar material, whichever is lower.

If the material cannot be used within the company, it should be reported to the purchasing agent for disposal. The first method for the purchasing agent to investigate is return to the supplier. Most vendors will accept the return of good salable material at its original cost less a restocking charge.

Failing this, the next step will be to offer material to a jobber, second-hand dealer, or employees. Sales of this type are usually made on a bid basis and bring substantially lower returns. If the surplus material will have an eventual use within the company, the decision on whether to sell at these lower returns, or to hold it until used at full value, will depend on the length of time involved, the company's cost of capital, and the income tax rate. For example, assume material costing $5,000 has a salable present market value of $4,000 and will be used at full value in five years. At a 48 per cent tax rate, it has a total present cash-flow value, which can be realized by selling, equal to the market value plus tax credits, or $4,480. Assuming it will still be worth $5,000 in five years, the $4,480 present value in becoming $5,000 will earn the equivalent compound interest of 2.2 per cent after taxes. If, however, the company's cost of capital is 10 per cent, this is an insufficient rate of return and the material should be sold. Figure 21–1 shows the minimum sale values as

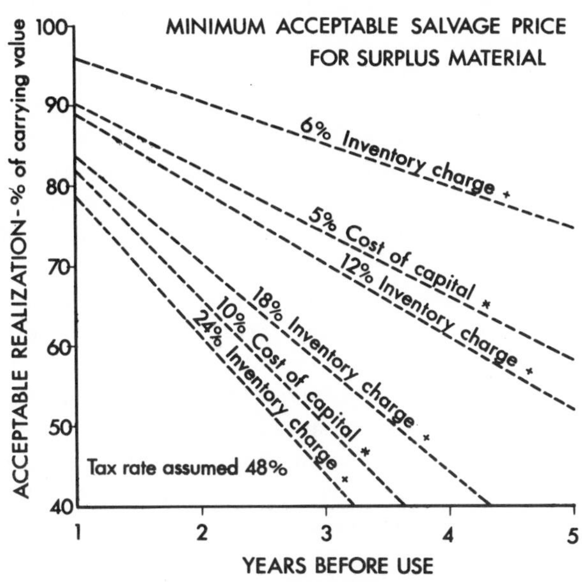

FIG. 21–1. Minimum acceptable salvage price for surplus material.

a percentage of carrying value (original cost) based on cost of capital (or inventory carrying cost, if preferred) and the holding period prior to ultimate use. No inflation factor, or obsolescence or deterioration of material, is provided for in the chart reference values. If involved, these factors must be treated separately.

Surplus and obsolete stocks may be sold as scrap for one of the following reasons:

1. Failure to sell by one of the above methods
2. The material in present form would be helpful to a competitor. In such a case the material should be destroyed before sale as scrap
3. Where the cost of attempting to transfer, return, or sell is less than the value of the material

SCRAP, METALS, AND WASTE

Throughout the United States in most every town, large or small, may be found persons gainfully employed in collecting and processing scrap, metals, and waste of every kind. The scrap industry alone is a big business.

All scrap and metals that are used in the manufacture of ferrous and nonferrous metals originate from one of two sources: first, that scrap which is known as "home or intraplant scrap" has its origin as a result of the waste or by-product of operations within the mills or foundries and is generally recycled for reuse on the premises from which it originates; second, "purchased or open-market" or dealer's scrap is the end result of obsolescence on everything ferrous and nonferrous.

The source of scrap that is most interesting to the purchasing agent is his own plant. It is his duty to dispose of these materials to advantage. In order to do so, he must know and understand the various phases of the scrap industries.

The specification and value of scrap is governed by the type of furnace that will be used in the remelting operation. Different furnaces have doors of varying size, different methods of charging, and a variety of other characteristics that must be considered. Naturally, scrap that has been segregated according to exacting specifications will have a much higher sales value than unsegregated scrap. For these reasons, scrap must be sorted according to the use for which it is intended. A practical knowledge of scrap uses will prove to be a definite advantage to those who handle scrap segregation.

Description of Scrap. The following description of scrap uses in the foundry and steel industries is from *Materials Survey, Iron and Steel*

Scrap, compiled by the National Security Resources Board, February, 1953:[1]

USE OF SCRAP IN FOUNDRY GRAY-IRON CUPOLA

The use of scrap in the gray-iron foundry, where the melting unit is predominantly the cupola, has been a widely discussed topic in the foundry industry. For many years there was a prejudice against the use of large percentages of scrap in mixtures intended for gray-iron. With the many advances in the art of melting in a cupola, as well as in the metallurgical control of the metal produced from the cupola, this prejudice has been very largely dissipated.

For example, standard practice in the automotive industry calls for roughly 20 to 30 per cent pig iron. The remainder of this mixture consists of return scrap, steel scrap, purchased automotive cast, and briquets of steel turnings and cast-iron borings. This type of mixture is being run out regularly with 70 to 80 per cent scrap and is principally a quality iron, requires very close control, and is successfully produced regularly in the best foundries in this country. Many foundries operate regularly on 70 to 100 per cent scrap in their mixtures.

The important consideration in using large percentages of scrap in the gray-iron mixture is to have it, first of all, properly classified, both in purchasing it and in having it classified on the foundry yard, so that the foundry may know at all times just what it is putting into the cupola. There is no such thing as "bad scrap," with the possible exception of such items as cast-iron retorts from the carbon disulfide industry or badly-burned grate bars.

USE OF SCRAP IN BLAST FURNACE

The blast furnace can digest nearly any iron scrap that can be charged. It can salvage iron materials that are impractical in any other furnace. It can seldom be operated on 100 per cent scrap because only peculiar conditions ever justify all scrap in a blast furnace. It can and does consume the poorer kinds of scrap such as cast-iron borings, corroded turnings, iron oxides such as mill scale, or cinders such as mill cinder with high iron content.

Usually the amount of scrap that can be used depends upon the cost of scrap and the desire for production by the operator. There is a certain excess of heat in the operation of a blast furnace. This tends to overheat the top of the stack. All this excess heat can be used to melt scrap, and in amount it is enough to melt about 10 per cent of the production. Thus any time scrap is available at a price, about 10 per cent of the production is possible at a real saving. This is the usual reason for using scrap.

The blast furnace can and does handle scrap that the cupola avoids, owing to the purification that takes place in the blast furnace. Sulfur is decreased in the blast furnace if desired, whereas the cupola usually increases the sulfur considerably.

[1] *Materials Survey, Iron and Steel Scrap,* United States Department of the Interior, Bureau of Mines, with cooperation of the Geological Survey, for the National Security Resources Board, February, 1953.

USE OF SCRAP IN OPEN-HEARTH FURNACE

The grades of scrap suitable for use in the open-hearth furnaces include most kinds of heavy steel. Weight is favored, since light scrap oxidizes much more readily. Excessively light scrap would virtually burn up, leaving only a small metallic yield. Excessive alloy content is also avoided, particularly tin and copper. Scrap with zinc coating gives a smaller percentage yield of steel, since the zinc is lost in the gases. Scrap with lead coating is damaging to the lining of the furnace, as the lead sinks to the bottom where it eats holes.

The open-hearth furnace uses the following grades of scrap: No. 1 Heavy-Melting Steel, No. 2 Heavy-Melting Steel, No. 1 Busheling, No. 1 Bundles (compressed new black-steel clippings and shearings), No. 2 Bundles (compressed automobile body and fender stock, galvanized sheets and wire), No. 3 Bundles (compressed galvanized sheets or wire), Machine-Shop Turnings, various types of railroad scrap, and all types of cast iron.

USE OF SCRAP IN ELECTRIC FURNACE

The steel produced by an electric furnace is almost entirely from scrap.

The tolerance of impurities is less for the electric furnace than for other furnaces. The size requirement is a maximum of 3 feet in length and 18 inches in width. Light scrap oxidizes in an electric furnace just as readily as in an open-hearth furnace. Because the scrap requirements of electric furnaces are more exacting than for open-hearth furnaces, in wartime electric furnaces were given priority over open-hearth furnaces for the premium grades of scrap. To be suitable for use in an electric furnace, the scrap may not have significant chemical impurities of phosphorus or sulfur.

The grades of scrap used by electric furnaces are No. 2 Heavy-Melting Steel, punchings and plate, structural, automobile steel, alloy-free turnings, heavy turnings, and small bundles. Electric-furnace users have a particular preference for obtaining scrap from specific industrial sources, in order that they may know the alloy content and be able to obtain large quantities of scrap of uniform alloy composition.

Scrap Markets. Headquarters for the principal markets in the scrap trade are found in Boston, New York, Philadelphia, Buffalo, Pittsburgh, Cincinnati, Detroit, Chicago, St. Louis, Birmingham, Los Angeles, San Francisco, Seattle, Portland, Dallas, and Houston. Market conditions and prices are reported regularly from these centers by correspondents from the trade press. Through their contacts with consumers, producers, dealers, and brokers, these correspondents are able to keep industry informed on the trends of the market.

Price of Scrap. The market price of scrap is determined by the price the consumer is willing to pay. It reacts almost directly to the law of supply and demand and does not respond to special sales inducements. In effect, scrap is bought by consumers at their price, not sold by processors.

Historically, there has been a relationship between the price of scrap and that of pig iron, a competing raw material. This held true when the great bulk of steel tonnage was produced by open-hearth furnaces which used scrap and pig iron in almost equal amounts. With the advent of the basic oxygen steelmaking furnace and its lessened reliance on scrap as a raw material, this relationship has been partially destroyed.

To review the historic pattern of prices, these excerpts from the *Materials Survey, Iron and Steel Scrap,* compiled by the National Security Resources Board, February, 1953, are useful:

> Pig iron prices normally are higher than scrap prices. When the gap between the two prices narrows, pig iron consumption increases. (This occurs because it is more economical for integrated mills to use pig iron which they themselves produce than to purchase scrap from outside sources, part of the fixed charges of the mill being attributable to pig iron facilities.) When the pig iron price increases, due to this increased consumption, there is some shift to the use of scrap as substitute for pig iron. This increased consumption of scrap causes the price of scrap to advance. The increased price of scrap may accelerate the flow of scrap to the dealer, and the narrowed gap between the price of scrap and the price of pig iron then tends to cause shift to pig iron.
>
> To a substantial extent, scrap prices are consumer-administered. Scrap consumers establish basing-point (mill) prices. From a basing-point price, a dealer may deduct freight to mill and cost of scrap preparation, and decide what is the highest price he will pay. The consumer's price-administering is, however, not complete, due to the elasticity of scrap price. Too low a mill price fails to elicit the required tonnages.

The basic oxygen method is expected to produce about one-third of the nation's ingot steel tonnage within the next five years. The most widely used basic oxygen unit uses as little as 25 per cent scrap in its formula with the remainder pig iron. This reduction in the need for scrap has given consumers much greater flexibility in purchasing it.

Except in rare instances, there are not great and sudden increases in demand for scrap now with an accompanying increase in price. With the use of oxygen-lanced open hearths and basic oxygen furnaces, most scrap needs can be satisfied from stocks on hand, or the necessary tonnages can be elicited with only mild increases in the offering price by consumers.

Major scrap processors have adjusted to this basic alteration in the scrap market by endeavoring to sell at prevailing market levels each month as much scrap as they accept in their yards for processing. This, of course, approaches the customary selling practice of manufacturers with the major difference outlined earlier: scrap is bought only when needed by consumers at a price they set. This same theory of supply and demand plus competitive or substitute material applies also to metals and waste. The difference in these industries is that technological changes in production methods have not had as serious consequences as they have in ferrous scrap.

Organization of Scrap Industry. The scrap industry is made up primarily of dealers and brokers. Their functions are described by Edwin C. Barringer in *The Story of Scrap*[2] as follows:

In a strict sense, the dealer is the man who performs the service of segregation and preparation. He is the mechanized part of the scrap industry; he hauls unprepared material from industrial plants; he buys material over his scales from collectors, auto wreckers, and farmers; he acquires bridges and buildings to demolish, and sometimes also job lots of "junkers" on auto wrecking yards which he wrecks on these yards and hauls in a semi-prepared condition to his own yard where he prepares it for use by the steel mills and foundries.

But the dealer usually has no sales department and has no direct contact with a steel mill although, because there are thousands of small iron foundries in almost as many cities, he may truck or ship by freight car cast iron scrap to his local foundry. The broker accordingly is the salesman of the scrap industry.

One type of broker is strictly what the name indicates; this broker does not operate a yard but fills orders from consumers by buying from yard dealers. By far the great majority of brokers also operate yards, to some extent as a hedge against their brokerage operation. Brokers seek to locate scrap, both unprepared and prepared; they finance dealers either on their general operations or for specific demolition projects; they book orders from consumers and fill them either from dealers or from their own yard operations; they function as the representatives of dealers who, as previously noted, have no sales departments and whose primary function is the collection, preparation, and storing of scrap.

Stated as a generality, the larger steel mills prefer to purchase their scrap through a comparatively small number of brokers. Thereby they narrow the area of responsibility for adequate supplies, minimize bookkeeping and checking on freight rates, and centralize other details. In a very direct sense, brokers are the industry's wholesalers, a sort of reverse wholesale distributor. Over the years the combination of brokers and dealers has been found to be a complementary one, and as a team they have kept steel mills and foundries supplied with a very vital raw material.

Trade Practices. Most scrap is sold on the basis of gross ton of 2,240 lb. There is sufficient sold on a net-ton basis to make it worthwhile checking bids and offers to verify which system is being used. Metals and waste are sold on the basis of pounds, 100 lb or net ton of 2,000 lb. Certified railroad weights are accepted in all cases. Although the large scrap yards are equipped with railroad scales where the cars are weighed, both light and loaded, an unwritten rule of the scrap industry permits the con

[2] By permission—Edwin C. Barringer, *The Story of Scrap,* Institute of Scrap Iron & Steel, Inc., Washington, D.C., revised edition, 1954.

sumers' weights to govern. The National Association of Waste Material Dealers list suggested terms of contract in their various specifications.

Specifications for Scrap, Metals, and Waste. Listed below are some of the more commonly used specifications for scrap metals and waste as issued by the Institute of Scrap Iron & Steel, Inc., and the National Association of Waste Material Dealers. The specifications listed are not all-inclusive but are the more general ones likely to be encountered by the average purchasing agent. More detailed information can be obtained from the Institute of Scrap Iron & Steel, Inc., 1729 H Street, N.W., Washington, D.C., and National Association of Secondary Material Industries, 271 Madison Avenue, New York 10016, New York.

Scrap

Basic Open-hearth and Blast-furnace Grades

No. 1 Heavy Melting Steel. Clean wrought-iron or carbon-steel scrap ¼ in. and over in thickness, not over 18 in. in width, and not over 5 ft in length. Individual pieces must be free from attachments, and so cut as to lie flat in the charging box. May include new mashed pipe ends, 4 in. and over.

No. 2 Heavy Melting Steel. Wrought-iron or carbon-steel scrap, black or galvanized, ⅛ in. and over in thickness, not over 18 in. in width, and not over 3 ft in length. Individual pieces must be free from attachments and so cut as to lie flat in the charging box. May include pipe cut 3 ft and under. May not include automobile body and fender stock.

No. 1 Busheling. Clean new wrought-iron or steel scrap 1/16 in. and over in thickness, not exceeding 12 in. in any dimension, including new factory busheling 20 gauge or heavier (for example, sheet clippings, stampings, etc.) and steel cartridge cases 40 mm or less. May not contain burnt material or auto body and fender stock. Must be free of metal-coated, limed, porcelain-enameled stock.

Machine-shop Turnings. Clean steel or wrought-iron turnings, free of cast or malleable iron borings, nonferrous metals in a free state, scale, or excessive oil. May not contain badly rusted or corroded stock.

No. 1 Bundles. New black steel sheet scrap, clippings, or skeleton scrap, compressed or hand bundled, to charging box size, and weighing not less than 75 lb per cu ft. (Hand bundles are tightly secured for handling with a magnet.) May include Stanley balls or mandrel wound bundles or skeleton reels, tightly secured. May include chemically detinned material. May not include old auto body or fender stock. Free of metal-coated, limed, vitreous-enameled, and electrical sheet containing over 0.5 per cent silicon.

No. 2 Bundles. Old black and galvanized steel sheet scrap, hydraulically compressed to charging box size and weighing not less than 75 lb per cu ft. May not include tin or lead-coated material or vitreous-enameled material.

Electric-furnace and Foundry Grades

Billet, Bloom, and Forge Crops. Billet, bloom, axle, slab, heavy plate, and heavy forge crops, not over 0.05 per cent phosphorus or sulfur and not over 0.5 per cent silicon, free from alloys. Must not be less than 2 in. in thickness, not over 18 in. in width, and not over 36 in. in length.

Bar Crops and Plate Scrap. Bar crops, plate scrap, forgings, bits, jars, and tool joints, containing not over 0.05 per cent phosphorus or sulfur, not over 0.5 per cent silicon, free from alloys. Must not be less than ½ in. in thickness, not over 18 in. in width, and not over 36 in. in length, except that plate scrap may not be less than ½ in. thick.

Cast Steel. Steel castings not over 48 in. long or 18 in. wide, and ¼ in. and over in thickness, containing not over 0.05 per cent phosphorus or sulfur, free from alloys and attachments. May include heads, gates, and risers.

Punchings and Plate Scrap. Punchings or stampings, plate scrap, and bar crops containing not over 0.05 per cent phosphorus or sulfur and not over 0.5 per cent silicon, free from alloys. All material must be cut 12 in. and under and with the exception of punchings or stampings must be at least ⅛ in. in thickness. Punchings or stampings may be of any gauge, but must not be more than 6 in. in diameter.

Cut Structural and Plate Scrap, Three Feet and Under. Clean open-hearth steel plates, structural shapes, crop ends, shearings, or broken steel tires. Must be not less than ¼ in. in thickness, not over 3 ft in length, and 18 in. in width. Must not contain over 0.05 per cent phosphorus or sulfur.

Cut Structural and Plate Scrap, Two Feet and Under. Clean open-hearth steel plates, structural shapes, crop ends, shearings, or broken steel tires. Must be not less than ¼ in. in thickness, not over 2 ft in length, and 18 in. in width. Must not contain over 0.05 per cent phosphorus or sulfur.

Cut Structural and Plate Scrap, One Foot and Under. Clean open-hearth steel plates, structural shapes, crop ends, shearings, or broken steel tires. Must be not less than ¼ in. in thickness or over 1 ft in length or width. Must not contain over 0.05 per cent phosphorus or sulfur.

Foundry Steel, Two Feet and Under. Steel scrap ⅛ in. and over in thickness, not over 2 ft in length, or 18 in. in width. Individual pieces must be free from attachments. May not include nonferrous metals, metal-coated material, cast or malleable iron, body and fender stock, cable, enameled or galvanized material.

Foundry Steel, One Foot and Under. Steel scrap ⅛ in. and over in thickness, not over 1 ft in length or width. Individual pieces must be free from attachments. May not include nonferrous metals, metal-coated material, cast or malleable iron, body and fender stock, cable, enameled or galvanized material.

Special Grades

No. 1 Chemical Borings. New clean cast or malleable iron borings and drillings containing not more than 1 per cent oil, free from steel turnings, or chips, lumps, scale, corroded, or rusty material.

Wrought Iron. Clean wrought-iron scrap, free of steel and with rivets and attachments removed. May include structural shapes, plates, bars, pipes, staybolts, or any other material known to have been manufactured from wrought iron.

Cast-iron Grades

Cast Iron No. 1 (Cupola Cast). Clean cast-iron scrap such as columns, pipes, plates, and castings of a miscellaneous nature, including the cast-iron parts of agricultural machinery. Must be free from stove plate, burnt iron, brake shoes, or foreign material. Must be cupola size, not over 24 by 30 in., and no piece to weigh over 150 lb.

Cast Iron No. 2 (Charging Box Cast). Clean cast-iron scrap in sizes not over 5 ft in length or 18 in. in width, suitable for charging into an open-hearth furnace without further preparation. Must be free from burnt iron, brake shoes, or stove plate.

Cast Iron No. 3 (Heavy Breakable Cast). Cast-iron scrap over charging box size or weighing more than 500 lb and which can be broken by an ordinary drop into cupola size. May include cylinders, driving-wheel centers, but may not include hammer blocks or bases. May include steel which is an integral part of the casting, which does not protrude more than 6 in. and which does not exceed 10 per cent of the weight of the casting.

Cast Iron No. 4 (Burnt Cast). Burnt cast-iron scrap such as stove parts, grate bars, and miscellaneous burnt iron. Includes sash weights or window weights.

Stove Plate. Clean cast-iron stove plate. Must be free from malleable and steel parts, window weights, plow points, or burnt cast.

Drop-broken Machinery Cast. Clean, heavy cast-iron machinery scrap that has been broken under a drop. All pieces must be in cupola size, not over 24 by 30 in. and no piece is to weigh over 150 lb or less than 5 lb.

Metals (Nonferrous Scrap)

Copper

No. 1 Copper Wire. To consist of clean untinned unalloyed copper wire not smaller than No. 16 B.&S. Wire gauge to be free from burnt copper wire which is brittle and all foreign substances.

No. 2 Copper Wire. To consist of miscellaneous clean copper wire which may contain a percentage of tinned wire and soldered ends but to be free of hair wire and burnt wire which is brittle; the tinned wire not to be over 15 per cent of the total weight.

No. 1 Heavy Copper. This shall consist of untinned copper not less than $\frac{1}{16}$ in. thick, and may include trolley wire, heavy field wire, heavy armature wire that is not tangled, and also new untinned and clean copper clippings and punchings, and copper segments that are clean. To be free of all foreign substances.

Mixed Heavy Copper. May consist of tinned and untinned copper, consisting of copper clippings, clean copper pipe and tubing, copper wire free of hair wire and burnt and brittle wire, free from nickel-plated material.

Light Copper. May consist of the bottoms of kettles and boilers, bathtub linings, hair wire, burnt copper wire which is brittle, roofing copper and similar copper, free from radiators, brass, and bronze screening, excessive lead and solder, readily removable iron, old electrotype shells, unclean gaskets, and free of excessive paint, tar, and scale.

Brass

Composition or Red Brass. May consist of red scrap brass, valves, machinery bearings, and other parts of machinery, including miscellaneous castings made of copper, tin, zinc, and/or lead, no piece to measure more than 12 in. over any one part or to weigh over 60 lb, to be free of railroad boxes, and other similarly excessively leaded material, cocks and faucets, gates, pot pieces, ingots and burned brass, aluminum composition, manganese, and iron.

Yellow Brass. May consist of heavy brass castings, rolled brass, rod brass, tubing and miscellaneous yellow brasses, to contain not over 15 per cent of nickel-plated material; no piece to measure more than 12 in. over any one part and must be in pieces not too large for crucibles. Must be free of manganese, aluminum brasses, nickel silver, iron, dirt, and excessively corroded materials.

Light Brass. May consist of miscellaneous brass, tinned or nickel-plated, that is too light for heavy brass, to be free of gun shells containing paper, ashes, or iron, loaded lamp bases, clockworks, and automobile gaskets. Free of iron unless otherwise specified.

Manganese-bronze Solids. Shall have a copper content of not less than 55 per cent, a lead content of not more than 1 per cent, and shall be free of aluminum bronze and silicon bronze.

Lead

Scrap Lead—Heavy Soft. To consist of clean, soft scrap lead, free of all foreign material such as battery plates or parts, lead-covered copper cable, foil, short lead, hard lead, dross, spatters, collapsible tubes, electro or stereotype plates, pot pieces, solder joints, zinc, and dirty chemical lead. Iron or brass fittings must be removed.

Drained Whole Batteries. Batteries to be free of liquid and extraneous material content. Aircraft (aluminum-cased) and other special batteries subject to special agreement.

Mixed Common Babbitt. Shall consist of lead-base-bearing metal containing not less than 8 per cent tin, free from Allens metal, ornamental, antimonial, and type metal. Must be free from all zinc and excessive copper in the alloy.

Zinc

Old Die-cast Scrap. Miscellaneous old zinc-base die castings, with or without iron attachments. Must be free of borings or turnings and also of dross pieces or chunks. All attachments that do not melt with the die cast will be deducted from the weight. Material containing iron in excess of 25 per cent will not constitute good delivery.

New Die-cast Scrap. Shall consist of zinc-base die castings, new, clean, and free of any iron or any foreign attachments. No plating or paint.

Old Scrap Zinc. Shall consist of old clean, dry scrap zinc such as sheets, jar lids, and clean unalloyed castings, etc. Battery zinc and die castings not acceptable. Material must not be excessively oxidized. All extraneous materials will be deducted.

New Zinc Clips. Shall consist of any new pure zinc sheets or stampings, no attachments, clean and free of any contamination. Print zinc such as engravers zinc, lithograph sheets, and addressograph plates subject to special arrangement.

Aluminum

New Pure Aluminum Clippings. Shall consist of new, clean, unalloyed sheet clippings and/or aluminum sheet cuttings. Must be free from oil, grease, and any other foreign substance. Also to be free from punchings less than ½ in. in size.

Segregated New Aluminum-alloy Clippings. Shall consist of new unpainted aluminum clippings of one aluminum alloy only and be free of stainless steel, iron, dirt, oil, grease, and any other foreign substance. Also to be free from punchings less than ½ in. in size.

Segregated Old Aluminum-alloy Sheet. Shall consist of clean old aluminum sheet of one alloy only free of wrecked airplane sheet and free from stainless steel, iron, dirt, oil, grease, and any other foreign substance.

Mixed Old Alloy Sheet Aluminum. Shall consist of clean old alloy sheet aluminum of two or more alloys not to contain wrecked airplane sheet and be free of iron, dirt, oil, grease, and all other foreign substances.

Segregated New Aluminum Forgings and Extrusions. Shall consist of new unpainted aluminum forgings and extrusions of one alloy only and be free of iron, dirt, oil, grease, and any other foreign substance.

Segregated Aluminum Borings and Turnings. Shall consist of clean, uncorroded aluminum borings and turnings of one alloy only and subject to deductions for fines in excess of 3 per cent through a 20-mesh screen of dirt, free iron, oil, moisture, and all other foreign materials. Material containing iron in excess of 10 per cent and/or free magnesium will not constitute good delivery.

Mixed Aluminum Borings and Turnings. Shall consist of clean, uncorroded aluminum borings and turnings of two or more alloys and subject to deductions for fines in excess of 3 per cent through a 20-mesh screen of dirt, free iron, oil, moisture, and all other foreign materials. Material containing iron in excess of 10 per cent and/or free magnesium will not constitute good delivery.

Nickel

New Nickel. Shall consist of clean forgings, flashings, punchings, new pipe, tubes, new bright wire, or screen, bar, rod, angles, or other structural rolled stock. Each grade to be packed and sold separately. Minimum nickel contents 98½ per cent, maximum copper contents 0.50 per cent.

Old Nickel Scrap. Shall be of 98 to 99 per cent purity, maximum 0.50 per cent copper. All rolled stock should come under this classification, such as sheet, pipe, tubes, bars, rods, same to be free of soldered, brazed, or welded alloyed material. It shall also be free of trimmed seams that have been sweated. Soldered, brazed, welded, and sweated material shall be packed and sold separately. All painted material shall be packed and sold separately.

Ferro-nickel-chrome Iron. Ferro-nickel-chrome-iron materials, whether castings, forgings, pipe, rod, tubes, wire screen, ribbon, or in any other form, should be sold on analysis basis. Physical description should accompany each inquiry. Approximate weight of pieces should accompany the inquiry. Copper content up to ½ per cent to be acceptable. The material must be free from other metals, sediments, and nonmetallic attachments.

Ferro-nickel-iron Alloy. Shall consist of alloys containing nickel and iron only. Physical description should accompany each inquiry and, in the case of the larger pieces, approximate weight should be mentioned. Copper content in the alloy up to ½ per cent to be acceptable.

Stainless Steel

New Stainless Steel. 18–8 type graded as new clippings 0.10 and under in carbon. All others are to be sold as to type numbers for which there are standard classifications.

Stainless Steel. 18–8 type. Shall consist of new and old sheet, pipe, rod, tubes, forgings, and flashings. Sold with no carbon guarantee, but to be free of all other metals and alloys.

Waste

Number 1 Mixed Paper. Consists of a mixture of various qualities of paper, packed in bales weighing not less than 500 lb and containing less than 25 per cent of soft stocks such as news. Outthrows, including a maximum of 1 per cent of prohibitive materials, may not exceed 5 per cent.

Number 2 Mixed Paper. Consists of a mixture of various qualities of paper not limited as to type of packing or soft stock content. Outthrows, including a maximum of 2 per cent of prohibitive materials, may not exceed 10 per cent.

Corrugated Containers. Consists of corrugated containers having liners of either jute or kraft, packed in bales of not less than 54 in. in length. Outthrows, including a maximum of 1 per cent of prohibitive materials, may not exceed 5 per cent.

Colored Tabulating Cards. Consists of printed colored or manila cards, predominantly sulfite or sulfate, which have been manufactured for use in tabulating machines. This grade may be shipped in securely wrapped bales or in bags or cardboard boxes. Outthrows may not exceed 1 per cent. Prohibitive materials, none permitted.

Manila Tabulating Cards. Consists of printed manila colored cards, predominantly sulfite or sulfate, which have been manufactured for use in tabulating machines. This grade may contain manila colored tabulating cards with tinted margins but may not contain beater or calender-dyed cards in excess of ½ of 1 per cent. This grade may be shipped in securely wrapped bales, or in bags, or in cardboard boxes. Outthrows may not exceed 1 per cent. Prohibitive materials, none permitted.

The American Association of Railroads publishes specifications for scrap of the various grades produced by the railroad industry. The Canadian Secondary Materials Association publishes specifications for the Canadian scrap industry. Its address is Excelsior Life Building, 36 Toronto Street, Toronto 1, Ontario.

Sorting and Preparation

While collecting, sorting, and preparation of scrap metals and waste may be the responsibility of other departments, the purchasing agent should be familiar with all phases of these operations. He should stand ready to advise current prices of various classes so that optimum return can be obtained and expenditures for unprofitable sorting or preparation avoided.

Sorting is the operation of segregating by type, alloy, grade, size, and weight, i.e., segregating No. 1 and No. 2 heavy melting grades. Preparation is the further processing of material to place it in a higher-priced classification, i.e., scrap which would meet No. 1 heavy melting classification, except that it is over 5 ft in length, can be sheared to meet this classification.

The reasons for sorting are obvious. If scrap metals or waste are mixed, somebody must sort it if it is to be of any use to the consumer. If a dealer is required to do the sorting, the price he can offer must reflect his cost of sorting. In times when there is excess scrap on the market, mixed scrap may be unsalable. Few dealers or brokers are willing to do business with plants which consistently mix or misclassify their metals. There is no excuse in any plant for not properly sorting at all steps from the time the metal is produced until it leaves the plant scrap area.

Whether scrap metals and waste are to be prepared is normally a function of the quantity produced. A dealer may easily invest a quarter of a million dollars in land, buildings, and equipment for a moderate-sized yard. Only a plant producing large quantities of all types of scrap metals and waste can justify such an expense. Plants with a small output of scrap metals and waste will undoubtedly find it better to leave the preparing to a dealer who has the equipment and experience to do the job economically. In between these two extremes lies an area where a plant producing substantial quantities of one or more grades of scrap metals and waste will find it profitable to install limited quantities of processing equipment.

Even in the most efficiently handled places, some mix-up is inevitable. This is particularly true in the case of scrap and metals. While there is almost an unlimited number of alloys and grades of ferrous and nonferrous metals, probably less than 100 different alloys and grades make up more than 95 per cent of the tonnage produced. There are three qualitative methods of testing—magnetic, spark, and chemical spot—which will provide sufficient information in most cases for a reliable sorting. The following description of these tests from the *Salvage Manual for Industry,* U.S. War Production Board, Salvage Division,[3] may be useful:

Magnetic Testing. Magnetic testing consists merely in determining whether or not the material is "ferromagnetic"—iron, nickel, and cobalt. Among the alloys, the iron-base alloys (such as cast iron, plain carbon, and low-alloy steels, etc.), are most likely to be ferromagnetic, although a few nickel alloys are also magnetic.

The magnetic test is best and simply carried out with a small permanent hand magnet. It can serve only for an initial approximate classification of alloys, and never as a final test (except to separate two alloys of known composition, one being magnetic and the other nonmagnetic).

Spark Testing. Spark testing is based upon the fact that some metals, in the finely divided state, will oxidize rapidly when heated in air to a high enough temperature. When such materials are ground by a high-speed grinding wheel, the fine particles torn loose are oxidized and raised to an incandescent temperature through the heat of friction on the wheel.

Of the commercially important alloys, only those with iron- and nickel-base compositions give characteristic sparks. Certain elements used as alloying agents in steels impart characteristic and recognizable variations to the basic plain carbon-steel sparks.

Proficiency in spark testing requires practice and reproducibility of sparking results. The lighting conditions should be approximately the same each time; sparks should be examined against a dark background. Care should be taken to exert the same amount of pressure over the same sparking area in each test. Only with such reproducibility, or unless a set of checking standards of known compositions be used, can spark testing be used for absolute identification (except, as with magnetic testing, to distinguish between two materials whose compositions are known).

The spark test is best conducted on a high-speed power grinder, with the specimen held so that the sparks fly off horizontally. The preferable setup is to hold the metal part or tool stationary and touch it with the wheel of a portable grinder. The surface speed may be about 8,000 feet per minute. A stationary grinder is satisfactory if care is taken to exert the same relative pressure in applying all specimens.

Contamination of the spark from particles retained in the wheel during previous spark tests on materials of different composition should be avoided. Frequent dressing of the wheel will serve to prevent such contamination.

Chemical Spot Testing. The chemical tests that may be used for sorting or final identification of materials range from simple drop tests to show attack or lack of

[3] *Salvage Manual for Industry,* Technical Service Section, Industrial Salvage Branch, Salvage Division, U.S. War Production Board, Superintendent of Documents, Government Printing Office, Washington, D.C., September, 1943.

attack by specific acids, to scientifically worked-out spot tests to determine the presence or absence of a specific alloying element in a metal.

Spot tests are based on the formation of characteristic colors or precipitates of the unknown elements when those elements react with various test reagents. The tests may be carried out "electrographically" on filter paper or on spot plates.

The electrographic method consists in forming a metal "sandwich" of the unknown material and a piece of aluminum or platinum or other inert alloy on the outside, with two pieces of filter paper moistened with an appropriate solution between the two. The current from two dry cells is then passed through the filter paper for a specified length of time, with the unknown metal serving as the anode and the inert metal as the cathode. The filter paper will thus be impregnated with dissolved matter from the unknown metal. The papers are removed from the sandwich and treated with suitable reagents to bring out the desired color reactions. Filter papers one-half to one inch square are large enough for this work.

More common is the solution method comprising placing one or two drops of an acid or alkali on the metal surface. The subsequent spot tests to identify the unknown may be conducted (1) on the metal surface itself, (2) by transferring the solution drop to a reagent-impregnated filter paper, or (3) by transferring it to a spot plate. Capillary tubes are best for transferring, since minimum quantities of reagents and solutions give the best results. In certain simple cases, the solution and testing reactions may be carried out in test tubes.

It is important to remember that except under *rigid laboratory control,* spot tests are no more than qualitative tests.

Disposal of Scrap, Metals, and Waste

As discussed earlier, in the great majority of cases the purchasing department is charged with the disposal of scrap, metals, and waste. Proper disposal procedures can result in one of the most profitable activities of the purchasing agent. Improper disposal procedure not only nullifies any good work done in collecting, sorting, and preparing but results in actual loss of profits. Proper disposal does not mean just selling by proper classifications to a dealer or broker. When a purchasing agent is considering disposal of material, he will normally consider the following procedures in the order listed:

1. Use within his own company
2. Return to supplier
3. Sale to outside company
4. Sale to dealer or broker

The greatest return will be realized if the material can be used within the purchasing agent's own plant. The savings are the difference between the prices of new material and scrap. Some processing may be necessary, but the savings are usually still substantial. A commonly used example is the material remaining when a part has been stamped or punched from sheet or strip material. Often a smaller part can be made from the remaining material.

In the case of a company having two or more plants, often one plant can use the scrap of another plant. Handling and transportation are the additional factors that must be considered in such instances.

Often scrap metals and waste are in such condition that they can be returned to the supplier either as an outright sale or as a deposit on future purchases. Highly alloyed scrap and some nonferrous metals—particularly semiprecious and precious—fall in this category. During periods of shortage a supplier may require that he be furnished scrap prior to furnishing any new material. Strict segregation of alloys must be practiced if they are to be returned to a supplier.

Nonferrous metals such as copper and aluminum can in some instances be returned to a supplier on a toll basis. In this case the supplier accepts the return of a certain quantity of metal to be reprocessed into new metal. The quantity of new metal returned by the supplier will be slightly less because of melting and fabricating losses.

Often the refuse of one company is the raw material of another. For example, paper scrap may be sold to a paper mill. Since this type of consumer will pay more than a dealer or broker, the purchasing agent will do well to be constantly alert for sales of this kind. One of the best sources of information regarding such possible sales is the purchasing agent of the other company.

Methods of Sale to Dealers and Brokers

If scrap, metals, and waste cannot be disposed of by the methods listed above, the best outlet is a dealer or broker. Negotiations with dealers or brokers are usually carried on by one of the following methods:

1. *Fixed-price Contract.* Contract to remove scrap metals and waste at periodic intervals. Prices for various classifications are fixed. Prices are established by bid or negotiation.

2. *Varying-price Contract.* Contract to remove materials at periodic intervals. Price to be market price at time of removal less stipulated sum or percentage of dealer's or broker's cost and profit. This sum or percentage may be established by bid or negotiation.

3. *Bid.* Each lot of one or more classes of scrap metals and waste is offered to dealers or brokers with high bidder to receive the material.

4. *Negotiation.* Prices for each lot are negotiated with a dealer or broker.

5. *Commission.* A dealer or some other party removes scrap metals and waste at periodic intervals and sells it for the highest price he can find.

The method of sale is a function of the type and volume of scrap produced and the personal preference of the purchasing agent. The varying-price contract or bid, however, is to be strongly recommended for materials that fall in standard classifications.

The term of the variable-price contract may vary from a few weeks to a year or more. This type of contract has the advantage to the purchasing agent of taking less time to administer than the bid method. The only duty of the purchasing agent if the contract has been established is to check the price against an agreed source of market prices. The price of the material may be established from one of the following:

1. Market price at the time of removal
2. Market price on specific day to govern for a period of time, i.e., market price on Monday to prevail for entire week
3. Average market price for period of time, i.e., average market price for a month to be priced for all material removed during month

This method has the disadvantage that the purchasing agent is usually confined to one dealer or broker. When a dealer or broker is overloaded with one particular grade, he may be reluctant to collect any more of this grade. Counteracting this disadvantage, when a dealer knows that he is the only outlet for a specific period of time, he is more willing to help and advise regarding sorting and preparation. He will often loan equipment to remove materials and also for other plant operations. In many cases, he will also provide containers for the various grades which relieves the producer of this expense. He may also remove the material which has no value merely as an accommodation to his customer.

The bid method has the advantage of obtaining maximum return to the producer at the time of sale. Sometimes the broker may require large quantities of a particular grade to meet commitments to the consumer. In such cases, he may be willing to pay higher than the market price. This method is also useful for nonstandard classification materials which have substantial value.

The bid has the disadvantage that it usually requires more of the purchasing agent's time than the variable-price contract. It is also necessary for the producer to provide all storage containers or bins. Rigid rules should be set up for a periodic issuance of invitations for bid. This may be done on the basis of sending out invitations for bid when certain quantities of material have been accumulated or at periodic intervals such as the first day of every month. Unless such rules are set up, there is a tendency to postpone sending out invitations for bid in favor of other work. Overaccumulation of scrap, metals, and waste creates a safety hazard and promotes mixing of grades. A typical bid form is shown in

Fig. 21–2. The normal procedure is to send two copies to the bidder. He will fill out and return one copy and retain the other for his files.

The fixed-price contract is useful in plants producing substantial quantities of scrap, metal, and waste which do not fall in standard classifications and have little value. The main purpose in this case is to have the material removed from the plant site in both good and bad times. While securing bids on each lot may result in a slight increase in revenue, the

REQUEST FOR BID

RECLAMATION AND SALVAGE DIVISION

SCRAP INQUIRY Nº 7283

LOCATION OF WORKS ____________

DATE ____________

PLEASE QUOTE BY DATE SHOWN BELOW
YOUR BEST PRICE FOR THE FOLLOWING ITEMS

____

FOR ADDITIONAL INFORMATION CONTACT

OUR MR. ____________

DISTRICT PURCHASING AGENT

ITEM NO.	DESCRIPTION OF MATERIAL	APPROXIMATE WEIGHT	UNIT AND/OR LOT PRICE

BIDS WILL BE ACCEPTED OR REJECTED AT OUR DISCRETION. WE WILL SELL MATERIALS WITHOUT INSPECTION BUT WE ACCEPT NO REJECTIONS.
TERMS ARE CASH UPON AWARD OF BID.
TRUCK SHIPMENTS:- WEIGHTS OBTAINED ON SCALES AT OUR PLANT OR AUTHORIZED SCALES IN THE VICINITY OF OUR PLANT ARE TO GOVERN SETTLEMENT.
RAIL SHIPMENTS:- WEIGHTS OBTAINED AT OUR PLANT TO GOVERN SETTLEMENT.
IF PLANT IS WITHOUT RAIL SCALES WE ACCEPT RAILROAD WEIGHTS, PROVIDING YOU FURNISH US A WEIGHT CERTIFICATE SHOWING GROSS, TARE AND NET WEIGHT.

____
COMPANY NAME

DATE ____________ BY ____________

FIG. 21–2. Request for bid form. Two copies sent to bidder.

additional time and expense required may more than offset any gain. The normal period of this type of contract is one year. Since the price of standard classification materials may vary over a wide range, the fixed-price contract is not generally used for this type of material.

Negotiation of price with a dealer or broker can be useful in disposing of small quantities of nonrecurring lots of nonstandard classification materials. It can also be used for small quantities of standard classification materials. In either case the value involved should be relatively small. Dealers and brokers are experts on market conditions prevailing for scrap, metals, and waste. Few plants are lucky enough or can afford an expert who is equally well informed. Negotiations on price should be carried on only with established dealers or brokers in whom the purchasing agent has confidence.

Some plants which generally have small quantities of scrap, metals, and waste may find it to their advantage to dispose of these materials on a commission basis. A small dealer or trucker collects the material at periodic intervals and disposes of it to the best advantage. For this service he will receive a portion of the selling price, which is usually 10 to 20 per cent, depending upon the volume and value of the material. This method still requires the producer to collect and sort the material properly in order to receive the maximum rate.

The number of dealers and brokers with which to deal will depend upon the volume and value of the scrap, metals, and waste involved, the method of disposal, and the number of reliable dealers and brokers available in the area. Generally the purchasing agent will find it advisable and more convenient to conduct his negotiations with local dealers and brokers. It is usually wise, however, to check dealers and brokers periodically in other areas particularly when there is any indication of collusion.

The purchasing agent should follow the same rules when dealing with dealers and brokers as he would with any important vendor. The dealers and brokers are part of a large industry and are usually substantial citizens in their community. A friendly dealer or broker can be of valuable help in any reclamation or salvage program.

The purchasing agent at times may be tempted to outguess the market by holding scrap, metals, or waste beyond the normal disposal time hoping for a rise in a market price. This is risky business. The purchasing agent may be a hero if the market goes up or he may lose his job if the market goes down. He must remember that he is gambling with money that does not belong to him and must be able to justify his actions at all times. In the long run the disposal of scrap, metals, and waste at regular intervals will bring as great or greater return along with peace of mind for the purchasing agent.

Contracts for Sale to Dealers and Brokers

While a given plant may use one or more methods of disposal, the following items should be included in each contract:

1. Price
2. Quantity
3. Delivery time
4. F.o.b. point
5. Cancellation privileges
6. Determining weights shipped

7. Handling shortages and overshipments
8. Terms of payment

While the purchasing agent may usually specify the conditions of the contract that best fit his convenience, it is advisable to adhere to industry practices as closely as possible. The National Association of Secondary Material Industries has published suggested contract conditions for some of its standard classifications. The following suggested conditions, taken from *Standard Classification for Non-ferrous Scrap Metals, Circular* NF-50,[4] are typical and can be used as a guide for disposing of other classes of materials.

a. Delivery of more or less on the specified quantity up to 1¼ per cent is permissible.
b. If the term "about" is used, it is understood that 5 per cent more or less of the quantity may be delivered.
c. Should the seller fail to make deliveries as specified in the contract, the purchaser has the option of canceling all of the uncompleted deliveries or holding the seller for whatever damages the purchaser may sustain through failure to deliver and if unable to agree on the amount of damages, an Arbitration Committee of the National Association of Secondary Material Industries may be appointed for this purpose, to determine the amount of such damages.
d. In the event that buyer should claim the goods delivered on a contract are not up to the proper standard, and the seller claims that they are a proper delivery, the dispute may be referred to an Arbitration Committee of the National Association of Secondary Material Industries to be appointed for that purpose.
e. A carload, unless otherwise designated, shall consist of the weight governing the minimum carload weight at the lowest carload rate of freight in the territory in which the seller is located. If destination of material requires a greater carload minimum weight, buyer must so specify.
f. A ton shall be understood to be 2,000 pounds unless otherwise specified. On material purchased for direct foreign shipment a ton shall be understood to be a gross ton of 2,240 pounds unless otherwise specified.
g. If, through embargo, a delivery cannot be made at the time specified, the contract shall remain valid, and shall be completed immediately on the lifting of the embargo, and terms of said contract shall not be changed.
h. When shipments for export for which space has been engaged have been delivered or tendered to a steamship for forwarding, and through inadequacy of cargo space the steamship cannot accept the shipment, or where steamer is delayed in sailing beyond its scheduled time, shipment on the next steamer from the port of shipment shall be deemed a compliance with the contract as to time of shipment.

[4] By permission of the National Association of Secondary Material Industries, 271 Madison Avenue, New York 10016, N.Y.

Are You Scrapping Money?

Only 80 per cent of the metal that goes into your plant will come out as finished products. That means that the other 20 per cent will be completely wasted—unless you can take advantage of the many opportunities available for cutting losses due to scrap.

Here are nine tips for saving on scrap:

1. *Keep scrap segregated.*

Scrap dealers will pay more for metal if it is kept free from extraneous materials. The place to segregate scrap is at the point of generation. Simple tote boxes or elaborate conveyor systems—depending on the kinds and quantity of scrap you handle—will help. So will proper markings: color, code, or names. Make sure the in-plant collector of scrap knows what type of material is coming off each machine.

2. *Minimize your scrap output.*

Redesign your product and its manufacture to eliminate as much scrap as possible. Buy metals that are nearest in shape, form, and size to your end product.

3. *Re-use scrap.*

Some scrap can be used as raw material for smaller parts. As scrap, this material may be worth $40 a ton; as raw material, it may be worth as much as $150 a ton.

4. *Sell scrap as salvage.*

If scrap is good enough for production but doesn't fit your needs, check with your scrap dealer. He may sell it as salvageable material; he will pay more for it than for scrap.

5. *Ask your scrap dealer for advice.*

Many experienced scrap dealers will help you with your segregation and handling problems. An increasing number of dealers can provide special equipment, such as engineered containers.

6. *Develop a rulebook.*

Some companies find it helpful to spell out the rules of scrap control in a manual.

7. *Watch your weights.*

Sell only on certified truck or rail weights, not on a lot basis using estimated weights. Be careful in loading scrap. If you load into a railroad car, see that it is clean and that no extraneous material gets into it.

8. *Check scrap as inventory.*

Scrap has value, and it should be properly accounted for.

9. *Use in-plant promotion programs.*

Posters, bulletin boards, slogans, and meetings will help minimize unnecessary scrap generation and maximize its value once it is generated.

FIG. 21–3. Tips for saving on scrap. Reproduced with permission from the Feb. 10, 1960 issue of *Steel* magazine, Cleveland, Ohio.

i. In case of a difference in weight and the seller is not willing to accept buyer's weights, a sworn public weigher shall be employed and the party most in error must pay the cost of handling and reweighing.

j. When material is such that it can be sorted by hand, consignees cannot reject the entire shipment if the percentage of rejection does not exceed 10 per cent. The disposition of the rejected material should then be arranged by negotiations; no replacement of the rejected material to be made.

Upon request of the shipper, rejections shall be returnable to the seller on domestic shipments within ten days and on foreign shipments within thirty days from the time notice of rejection is received by them, and upon payment by them of 1¢ a pound on material rejected to cover cost of sorting and packing, the seller to be responsible for freight both ways.

In order to administer a successful disposal program, the purchasing agent must keep abreast of market prices and conditions. It is suggested he subscribe to and read one or more trade publications such as these:

American Metal Market, 525 West 42d Street, New York, N.Y. 10036
The Iron Age, Chestnut and 56th Streets, Philadelphia, Pa. 19100
Steel, Penton Building, Cleveland, Ohio 44113
Waste Trade Journal, 130 West 42d Street, New York, N.Y. 10016

Interest in saving of scrap by these publications is excellently illustrated by Fig. 21–3.

SURPLUS AND OBSOLETE EQUIPMENT

Every company with few exceptions has a capital investment ranging from a typewriter and desk to plants worth many millions of dollars. While every effort is expended both in time and money to prolong the life of these investments, production changes, new and more efficient equipment, and normal obsolescence make occasional replacements a necessity. When these replacements have been made, the old equipment is available for other uses. It may be transferred to other units of the company, and when not adaptable for use within the company, disposition of the equipment is made by outright sale or scrapping.

Proper disposal of surplus and obsolete equipment will bring sufficiently higher returns which justify any extra time and effort when compared to slipshod and haphazard methods of disposal. In order to secure proper disposal, all surplus and obsolete equipment should be cleared through one outlet. Who performs this duty will vary with the size of the operation. In a small plant this function may be performed by the purchasing agent. In a large plant or multiple-plant company having a large volume of surplus and obsolete equipment this function may be the responsibility of the reclamation and salvage department. The procedures outlined in this section are based on a multiple-plant company with a reclamation and salvage department. The same procedures may be used for a smaller company by substituting the purchasing agent or other person responsible for the reclamation and salvage department and disregarding any references to other plants.

Declaration of Surplus

When equipment becomes surplus in any department, the department head in charge of the equipment should inform the chief plant engineer immediately on a departmental notice of surplus equipment (shown in Fig. 21–4). Upon receiving the departmental notice of surplus equipment, the chief plant engineer should determine at once whether the equipment can be used by other departments in his plant. If no use can be developed, the form should be returned with the recommendation that a surplus equipment report be prepared. An appropriate space is provided on the form for this purpose.

DEPARTMENTAL NOTICE OF SURPLUS EQUIPMENT

Dept. Name ______ Bldg. No. ______ Plant Name ______

QUANTITY	GIVE BRIEF DESCRIPTION BELOW	DATE AVAILABLE

DISPOSE OF AS INDICATED BELOW:

RETAIN IN PRESENT LOCATION . . . . ☐
STORE IN BLDG. No. ______ . . . ☐
HOLD FOR INTERPLANT TRANSFER . . . . . ☐
LIST AS SURPLUS ON FORM No. 4466 Rev. . . . ☐

INDICATE YOUR DECISION WITH A CHECK MARK.

FORWARDED TO CHIEF WORKS ENGINEER ______ NAME ______ DATE ______ DATE

RETURNED TO DEPARTMENT HEAD ______ NAME ______ DATE ______ DATE

FIG. 21–4. Departmental notice of surplus equipment.

Before preparing a surplus equipment report, the department head should proceed as follows:

1. Attach to the surplus item a surplus equipment tag (shown in Fig. 21–5).
2. Inspect the equipment personally to develop the following information:
   a. Name-plate data, including model number, serial number, and type of machine

b. Motor data, including horsepower, enclosure, frame number, voltage, cycle, phase, rpm, and other pertinent information
c. A list of standard and special auxiliary equipment and accessories
d. Design changes, if any, that make this machine different from a standard model
e. A list of missing parts
f. The operating condition, i.e., poor, fair, good, or excellent
g. An estimate of the cost to repair equipment (if it is worth repairing)
h. An estimate of total weight
i. Estimated cost to remove and load on cars (include cost to skid or crate)
j. An estimate of current scrap value, as scrap
k. Asset numbers

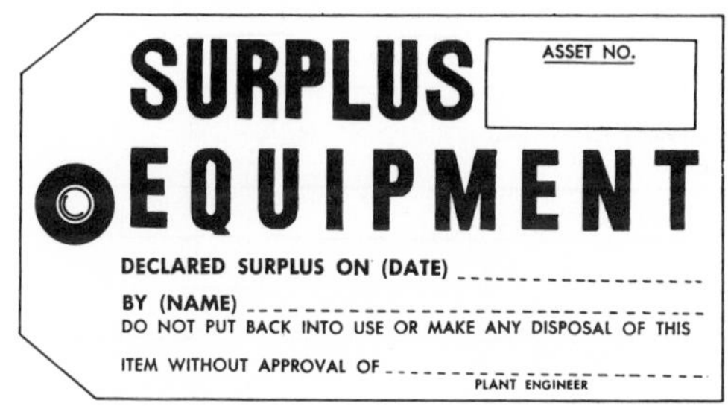

FIG. 21–5. Tag to be attached to surplus equipment.

The next step is the preparation of the surplus equipment report form, as shown in Figs. 21–6 (front) and 21–7 (back). In the case of this company this form is furnished in quadruplicate sets with the original for the main office and the others for plant engineering, plant purchasing, and plant rough draft copy.

The plant rough draft copy is used as the pencil copy on which original notes are made. Each local plant determines which department will transfer information on the rough draft copy to the final copy of the form. Both active and permanent numerical files of each surplus equipment report are kept in a binder for ready reference.

The portion of the form that calls for a list of surplus spare parts for the equipment must be completed by the stores department. Consequently, after all other information has been entered, the forms are to be forwarded to the stores department for completion. The entry on the form should include the original cost and stores card value of the surplus parts that are listed.

When surplus spare parts have been listed, all copies of the surplus re-

PAGE 1

SURPLUS EQUIPMENT REPORT No. 2316 A

COMPANY NAME AND LOCATION: ____

DESCRIPTION OF MACHINE OR EQUIPMENT: THIS MUST BE COMPLETE—GIVE MANUFACTURER'S NAME, SIZE, MODEL AND SERIAL NOS. AND CAPACITY. LIST MOTORS, STARTERS WITH FULL DESCRIPTION OF EACH. INCLUDE SPARE PARTS AND ACCESSORIES.

—NOTE: IF ADDITIONAL SPACE REQUIRED ADD PAGE NO 3.

	ORIGINAL PURCHASE ORDER NO.	ORIGINAL ORDER DATE	ORIGINAL NEW COST	CURRENT DEPRECIATED VALUE	DATE	ASSET NO.
ITEM 1						
ITEM 2						
ITEM 3						
ITEM 4						
ITEM 5						

PURCHASED FROM:
(NAME AND ADDRESS OF MANUFACTURER OR JOBBER.)

1. ____
2. ____
3. ____
4. ____
5. ____

NOTE: IF MOTORS, SPARE PARTS, ETC. FOR THIS ITEM WERE PURCHASED SEPARATELY, LIST IN SPACE PROVIDED ABOVE AS ANOTHER ITEM. IF MORE SPACE REQUIRED, CONTINUE ON PAGE 3 AS ITEMS 6, 7, 8, ETC.

FIG. 21–6. Surplus equipment report (front).

port should be sent to the asset department for checking. Personnel of the asset department should compare the items listed on the report with current asset records. The procedure provides a double check on the availability of the equipment. Date of acquisition, original cost (less freight and installation charges), whether new or used when acquired, date and degree of last rebuilding, and current depreciated value should be included for each capitalized item.

The completed, fully checked surplus equipment form is then returned to the chief plant engineer for his approval. After signing the form in the space provided, the chief plant engineer will forward all copies to the plant manager.

Before returning these reports to the plant purchasing agent for distribution, the plant manager should note "remarks of others" and add any comments that he may have before he affixes his signature. When the reports are returned to the district purchasing agent, the original copy should be mailed at once to the division manager at the main office.

PAGE 2

DESCRIBE PRESENT OPERATING CONDITION. GIVE COMPLETE INFORMATION AS TO BROKEN OR MISSING PARTS, DESIGN CHANGES, CAPACITY LOSSES CAUSED BY DETERIORATED CONDITION, ETC. IF IN YOUR OPINION THIS ITEM IS WORTHY OF REPAIR, ATTACH LETTER DESCRIBING NEEDED REPAIRS AND YOUR ESTIMATE OF COSTS INVOLVED TO PLACE THIS ITEM IN GOOD OPERATING CONDITION.

____

ESTIMATED PLANT COST TO REMOVE AND LOAD ON CARS $______

APPROXIMATE SHIPPING WEIGHT LBS.______

ESTIMATED CURRENT SCRAP VALUE $______

DO YOU CONSIDER THIS CONDITION TO BE (CHECK ONE) POOR - FAIR - GOOD - EXCELLENT?

WHY IS YOUR PLANT RELEASING THIS EQUIPMENT?______

DATE EQUIPMENT WILL BE AVAILABLE FOR RELEASE______?

IN YOUR OPINION WHICH OF THE FOLLOWING METHODS OF DISPOSAL WOULD BE TO THE BEST INTEREST OF THE COMPANY? (CHECK ONE)

INTER-COMPANY TRANSFER ( ) OUTRIGHT SALE ( ) SELL AS SCRAP ( )

THIS REPORT MADE BY (NAME)______ REPORT DATE______

EQUIPMENT INSPECTED BY (NAME)______ INSPECTION DATE______

HAVE SURPLUS SPARE PARTS BEEN INCLUDED? (______) STOREKEEPERS (NAME)______

ALL ASSET VALUES NOTED APPROVED BY (NAME)______ ASSET CUSTODIAN.

RELEASE OF EQUIPMENT FOR TRANSFER OR SALE APPROVED BY:

DEPT. HEAD OR PLANT SUPT.______ SIGNATURE ______ DATE______

PLANT ENGINEER______ SIGNATURE ______ DATE______

WORKS MANAGER______ SIGNATURE ______ DATE______

DIVISION MANAGER______ SIGNATURE ______ DATE______

REMARKS:______

SOLD OR TRANSFERRED TO______

M. S. O. NO.______ DATE______ SALES PRICE______ F. I. NO.______

FIG. 21–7. Surplus equipment report (back).

Review of Surplus Equipment Reports

The review of surplus equipment reports of division managers is an important step in properly disposing of equipment items. Their recommendations, based on the complete, comprehensive set of answers on the surplus equipment report, provide a broad view of company policy. Frequently, future developments within the company may prompt division managers to discuss the equipment and its use with other executives before approving release or transfer. In any case, their decision must be noted on the original of the form before the report is forwarded to the reclamation and salvage department.

Decisions to "retain for future company use," "transfer for a special use," or "scrap" are based on the information in the surplus equipment report. Those who review the report after it leaves the plant have no other basis for their opinions. Thus, it must be stressed again that each answer should be recorded in accurate detail. The division managers are particularly interested in the following information:

1. Description of the equipment
2. Reason for declaring it surplus
3. Original cost and present depreciated value
4. Present operating condition
5. Estimated cost to place in good operating condition
6. Plant recommendations as to disposal
7. "Remarks"—pertinent facts concerning the equipment indicated by plant manager and/or other plant personnel

Disposal of Surplus Equipment

The reclamation and salvage department is responsible for disposing of all surplus equipment within a reasonable time, and in a manner that will be of greatest benefit to the company. As stated in an earlier paragraph, proper disposition may involve transfer to another plant, sale outside the company, or authorization to scrap the equipment.

The following questions are used as a guide by the reclamation and salvage department in determining the most economical method of disposal:

1. Is the machine description complete?
2. What is the age and condition of the equipment?
3. What will it cost to remove, load, and crate the equipment?
4. How soon must the machine be removed?
5. What are the recommendations of others as to its disposal?
6. Can the equipment be used at present in other company plants?
7. Is the equipment an adequate substitute for an item that is now being purchased?
8. Would there be any economic advantage in transferring the equipment to another plant?
9. What is the potential resale value?
10. What is the estimated scrap value by weight?
11. Should it be scrapped or sold?
12. Does the decision of the reclamation and salvage department concur with recommendations of others?

Transfer of Surplus Equipment

Surplus equipment that is available for transfer within the company is announced periodically by the reclamation and salvage department, and these lists of equipment are mailed to all district purchasing agents, each of whom should receive enough copies to permit proper distribution in his plant. Lists of this equipment are also sent to the main office engineering departments and division managers. The lists itemize each piece of surplus equipment and indicate its present location. Furthermore, a description of the item is given, including its specifications, condition, date of purchase, original cost, and present depreciated value. Every effort is made to present a true picture of items that are available. Worthless equipment is never intentionally listed.

A stamped notation on the transmittal letter that accompanies the surplus equipment list indicates how long the equipment will be available. This statement, "your reply requested by *date,*" usually provides a fifteen-day period from the date the lists are mailed. At the end of this period, the equipment will be offered for sale.

Surplus equipment that is available for transfer is ordered by following the usual procedure employed in purchasing from an outside vendor. Appropriate spaces on the standard purchasing department requisition are to be used to describe the equipment to be transferred, indicate item number, and state the name and location of the owning plant. The completed requisition is then mailed to the main office, attention–reclamation and salvage department, where a transfer purchase order is prepared on the standard purchasing department order form.

Sale of Surplus Equipment

After a reasonable period, surplus equipment that is not requisitioned for transfer is offered for sale. All sales of equipment, however, must be made by, or at the direction of, the reclamation and salvage department. Consequently, no plant may make any commitments for use or disposal of equipment that has been reported as surplus to the main office without specific approval from this department.

Sale of surplus equipment is usually handled by one of the following methods:

1. Offer to selected dealers on a bid basis
2. Offer to selected dealers for a set price
3. Advertising in trade journals and papers
4. Auction

Most sales are made on a bid basis since they are easily administered and will normally result in a fair return to the seller. Offering for sale at a set price is a satisfactory method only when the person setting the price is extremely well versed in equipment and market conditions. He is of course guided by the information contained in the surplus equipment report. Advertising has the advantage that it reaches a wide market and is a good way to build up a list of dealers. When using this method, it is necessary for the purchasing agent to check closely the financial condition of the bidder. Sale by auction is a fast and convenient method when it is desired to dispose of large quantities of material. This method will usually not bring as great a return as selling on a bid or set-price basis.

When a prospective purchaser asks to inspect equipment, the reclamation and salvage department will notify the plant manager, plant purchasing agent, and chief plant engineer in advance of the visit. Upon arriving at the plant, the inspector will be instructed to ask for the plant purchasing agent, who is responsible for arrangements during the visit.

All plans for the inspection must be coordinated with the chief plant engineer's office. During the visit, the chief plant engineer should permit the inspection of only the surplus equipment in question. The inspector should be treated with utmost courtesy, because indifference to his interests may result in losing both a sale and the good will of one who may be a valuable customer.

After inspecting the equipment, the visitor should leave via the plant purchasing agent's office where an effort should be made to determine whether he is inclined to make a purchase. Any information that is obtained should be forwarded immediately to the reclamation and salvage department.

The sale of surplus equipment is, in most cases, covered by a written purchase order furnished the reclamation and salvage department by the purchaser. This order, accompanied by a transmittal letter that explains the transaction, is mailed to the plant purchasing agent for processing. Payment for most surplus equipment sold is 50 per cent in advance, balance before loading of the equipment. It is the responsibility of the reclamation and salvage department to determine the sales price and terms and to secure the first payment of 50 per cent. Those at the plant are responsible for securing the balance due before making shipment. If necessary, two notices requesting payment should be mailed to the customer within a ten-day period. When there is no response to the second notice, the reclamation and salvage department will assume responsibility for collecting the balance, if properly notified.

One point, mentioned in an earlier paragraph, should be reemphasized. *After equipment is reported as surplus, use or alteration in any way cannot be permitted without the express approval of the reclamation and salvage department.* Both the equipment as a unit, and its individual parts, have been fully relinquished to the control of the reclamation and salvage department.

Sale of surplus is based on the reported condition of the equipment. Any variation between condition represented and condition upon delivery would place the company liable to lawsuit. Neither the equipment nor its parts, therefore, may be used in any way after it is reported as surplus.

Scrapping of Surplus Equipment

The decision to scrap surplus equipment is the prerogative of the reclamation and salvage department. When it is apparent that equipment can neither be transferred nor sold, the plant will be notified to dispose of it by sale to a scrap dealer. It may also be decided to scrap a piece of equipment because of its special construction or design which would be detrimental to the company's best interest if this piece of equipment were to come into the hands of a competitor. Such a piece of equipment should be completely demolished before it leaves the plant site. This notification to scrap, originating in the reclamation and salvage department, is sent to the plant purchasing agent. Whenever possible, the equipment should be scrapped within thirty days after the date of notification. Serviceable auxiliary equipment such as motors, blowers, etc., should be removed for use at the owning plant, or be declared as surplus on a new surplus equipment report. All sales of scrap are to be handled by the plant purchasing agent only. In accepting and rejecting bids, the plant purchasing agent may use his own discretion. His decision, however, should be based on policies established by the reclamation and salvage department.

Many dealers in used equipment specialize along various lines. A dealer may handle only locomotive equipment or materials-handling equipment. The reclamation and salvage department should keep a list of dealers and the type of equipment which they handle. A tentative list can be made up from advertisements in trade journals and papers. These names can be added to a permanent list only after the purchasing agent has had time to check the financial condition and reliability of each dealer.

The reclamation and salvage department should keep management informed of its activities by providing a semiannual or annual report of all capital equipment that has been transferred, sold, or scrapped. The information included in the report should contain the following:

1. Description of equipment
2. Original cost less installation
3. Age of equipment
4. Depreciated value of equipment transferred
5. Depreciated value of equipment scrapped
6. Depreciated value of equipment sold
7. Value received for equipment sold
8. Profit or loss (difference between items 6 and 7)

RECLAMATION

Functions of a Reclamation Department

The duties of a reclamation department require a knowledge of material and plant equipment and of how it is made and used. The supervisor must be familiar with various methods and equipment available to bring worn-out parts back to serviceable condition, and on his own initiative develop improvements in techniques. Finally, there must be intelligent cost accounting or the department will not produce favorable results from the financial standpoint.

The reclamation department has the following responsibilities:

1. Know what materials are discarded in its company's operation.

   There must be a detailed knowledge as to individual items and quantities, and it is for this reason that reclamation should be a part of the over-all salvage effort of the company.
2. Determine what can be reclaimed.

   This is not limited to making material again suitable for its original purpose. An alert reclamation department will find ways to convert many discarded items to some entirely different product which its company requires.
3. Decide the method by which each part or material will be reclaimed.
4. Calculate the cost to return each item to usefulness.

   All costs, including expense of collecting, sorting, inspecting, packaging, and stocking, should be considered as well as direct labor and materials and supervisory expense required in the operation.

   There will be frequent cases where the cost to reclaim by one method will be prohibitive, whereas another procedure will be inexpensive. Constant study is necessary to reduce costs, by changes in method.

5. Determine, with the purchasing department, whether it is economical to reclaim.

   The reclamation department must follow up the performance of reclaimed articles, to know whether they are rendering service comparable to new products. In deciding whether it is more advantageous to reclaim than to buy, allowance should be made for any difference in service life.

   There can be circumstances when, because of a national emergency or some other factor, it may be desirable to reclaim items because of the necessity for preserving critical material, even though the cost is higher than the price of new material.

6. Operate as a manufacturer, regulating its production of reclaimed material to meet actual requirements of the company.

   The quantities of items reclaimed should be determined from orders placed with the reclamation department by the purchasing agent or general storeskeeper.

Organization of a Reclamation Department

In general, reclamation and salvage are so closely interwoven that they should be considered as one operation.

The reclamation department in most of the larger concerns is a separate and distinct organization guided, but not supervised, by the purchasing or procurement department. In some smaller firms, operating in one location, this function is controlled by the purchasing or procurement department. In larger companies, however, reclamation and salvage are a part of the production or operating department. The reason is that scrap materials are generated and handled by the production department, and reclamation requires much the same technical knowledge and shop equipment as is used in producing the company's product and maintaining its plant.

A reclamation and salvage department should be headed by a superintendent, or his equivalent, whose duties would include the complete supervision of reclamation and scrap handling. The superintendent should report to the chief operating officer and work closely with the purchasing agent and general storeskeeper.

Under the superintendent, in a large organization or one having plants in scattered locations, one or more assistant superintendents or general foremen may be necessary to assist in the direction of the many phases involved.

The work of the department can be divided into sections, according to functions or material handled, with a supervisor in charge of one or more. The number of sections involved in the organization of a reclamation department depends upon the variety of materials and the volume handled.

A typical arrangement in a large organization might include the following:

1. Blacksmith section
2. Welding section
3. Machine shop
4. Scrap section
5. Annealing and heating section
6. Nonferrous metal section
7. Lubricant section
8. Paper and fabric section
9. Container section
10. Stock control section
11. Clerical and accounting section

Examples of reclaimable items:

1. Oils and greases

   The most common type of oil reclaimed is lubricating oil or crank case oil which is put through a re-refining process to remove impuri ties. The impurities having been removed, it is often necessary to ad lighter-bodied oils to restore the original viscosity. Properly reclaime oils of this type may be used many times. The use of diesel engine on highways and railroads, in recent years, has greatly increased th use of re-refined lubricating oils, and the reason is economy as well a easy recovery. A well-operated re-refining plant can reclaim lubricatin oil for less than 20 cents per gallon, which is about one-half the cos of new oil.

   Cutting oils may be recovered from chips by several processes, th most simple being drainage into vats. Another widely used process r quires the use of a centrifugal extractor when both water and im purities are to be removed.

   Grease may be melted down, cleaned, pressed into cakes, and reuse

2. Tools

   a. Many hand tools may be reclaimed through various processes. Fo lowing is a list of some of the reclaimable types:

   (1) Hammers
   (2) Wrenches
   (3) Files over 6 in.
   (4) Picks
   (5) Screwdrivers
   (6) Pinch bars
   (7) Crowbars
   (8) Pneumatic tools
   (9) Jacks
   (10) Hand hoists

(11) Cutting and welding torches
(12) Handles (cut for smaller tools)
(13) Punches
(14) Shovels

b. A wide variety of cutting tools are reclaimable. The following are some:

(1) Saws
(2) Taps
(3) Dies
(4) Broaches
(5) Chisels
(6) Reamers
(7) Milling cutters
(8) Drill bits
(9) Lathe tools

3. Bearings

Economy in operation and maintenance is often realized through the repair of faulty bearings rather than the purchase of new. Practically all types of bearings may be reclaimed if existing conditions warrant, but certain types are more economically reclaimed than others. Following are a few types which may be reclaimed:

a. Worn babbitt or lead-lined solid
b. Cut or grooved bronze solid
c. Cut or grooved ball or roller races

4. Metallic items that can be reclaimed by various methods

The most widely used shop reclamation methods are welding, brazing, hard facing, metallizing, and hard chromium plating. The choice of process depends on the material of which the part is made, the character of its failure or defect, the nature of the service, the probable replacement cost and availability, etc.

Welding was originally introduced as a means of repairing machinery and other metal objects. It is not necessarily the most desirable method and each probable application should be studied as to the economy of the procedure and possible alternates.

Some examples of items which may be repaired by various methods are:

a. Brazing welding:
Shafts
Cutting tools
Machine parts
Castings
Cylinder heads

b. Hard facing or metallizing:
Shafts
Axles
Journals
Pistons
Cylinders
Rail ends
Bores

c. Reforging:
Various types of rods
Insert tips for lathes
Some hand tools
Most forgings

d. Rerolling:
Axles
Shafts
Rods

Control of Containers

Returnable Containers

1. A returnable container is one which the supplier, for various reasons, may wish returned for use in future shipments. With the emphasis on mechanical materials handling, the items classed in this category have increased to include the following:

   a. Drums
   b. Reels
   c. Carboys
   d. Gas cylinders
   e. Pallets
   f. Tote boxes
   g. Special packing cases
   h. Burlap bags

2. Containers, especially of these types, represent a large investment on the part of the suppliers. To protect their original investment, and at the same time keep the selling price of the material in line with its value rather than reflect the cost of the container as well as the material, many firms charge an amount for each container, which is refunded if the container is returned. In periods of short supply or when certain materials are pronounced critical, a larger number of firms use the returnable method to improve availability and conserve scarce materials.

3. Firms using containers of a returnable type normally stencil the firm name and deposit value on the container. This acts as an incentive to return containers promptly. Some firms, especially those using reels, designate a specified time in which the container must be returned in order to realize the return of the deposit charge. Some of these companies include the deposit on the invoices for the material, while others invoice the reel charge separately and render credit when reel is returned. It may be more economical for the buyer, in such cases, to transfer the contents of the container to a company-owned container to ensure the deposit return.

   Responsibility for transportation charges for the return of empty containers varies, and this responsibility is normally established on an industry basis, being a part of the original purchase agreement covering the basic material involved.

   Some suppliers require drums returned through a cleaning firm, returning the deposit upon advice of the receipt of the drums by the cleaner.

   Where returnable pallets are used, receiving firms sometimes find it more economical to pay the deposit fee and to keep the pallets for their own use, including the cost of the pallets as part of the cost of the commodity on which they were shipped. Where return shipments are made to the original supplier, returnable pallets may be used, realizing materials-handling economy as well as ensuring the return of the deposit fee.

Industrial gas manufacturers, in order to ensure return of cylinders, charge demurrage for cylinders not returned within a specified period. They also allow a credit for those returned before the expiration date, but this is a "paper" credit which is used only to reduce any amount due them for demurrage.

4. To ensure the proper control of returnable containers, accurate records must be established, indicating the following:
   a. Number of purchase order on which shipped
   b. Number of invoice on which billed
   c. Shipper
   d. Commodity
   e. Type of container
   f. Number of containers
   g. Deposit value
   h. Receiving date
   i. Record of transfer from original consignee to local using department or to another storehouse
   j. Deposit expiration date, if any
   k. Date returned
   l. Deposit credited
5. All records for returnable containers should be kept by the original receiver, who must also keep after users to ensure prompt return of the containers to the supplier. It is essential that one person be responsible for the container records and follow up at a given location. Sufficient copies must be made of all records to provide for local accounting, checking original receipts and returns against the invoices of the supplier.

Nonreturnable Containers

1. Practically all types of nonreturnable containers may be used in some phase of inter- or intraplant operation, whether in the condition received or altered to suit company use. Following are some, with suggested uses:
   a. Drums
      (1) Top removed and used for storage or shipments of parts between storehouses. May be equipped with skids to facilitate fork-lift operation.
      (2) Top saved and used for storage of liquids

b. Reels
   (1) Storage of cable or wire to release returnable reels
   (2) Storage of pieces of wire or cable, either new or fit for reuse
c. Cartons and boxes
   (1) Storage of materials
   (2) Shipments between or within plants
d. Pallets
   (1) Storage of materials
   (2) Transportation of materials, including company's products

2. Suppliers are at times not able to obtain sufficient containers to meet their needs and are willing to buy back from the customers all containers in good condition. Contacts between the two firms are handled by the respective purchasing departments.

   Containers, in good condition and on which a deposit has been paid, upon expiration of the return date, are also classed as nonreturnable. Frequently it is possible to realize a substantial part of the deposit by contacting the firm involved and obtaining permission to return the containers.

3. Sale to dealer

   Many companies accumulate containers of various kinds beyond the requirements of their plants. These containers, if in good condition, may be offered for sale to firms dealing in the cleaning and resale of such commodities, usually drums.

   Damaged steel drums which cannot be used in the local plants may be sold as sheet scrap. Other types of nonreturnable containers such as boxes, cartons, etc., may also be sold as scrap paper, or if they are made of wood, may be salable to secondhand lumber dealers.

SALES TO EMPLOYEES

Practically every business, large or small, has at least one part-time mechanic, home builder, or do-it-yourself fan among its employees. It has often been said that all scrap has some value. This is particularly true to an individual, since he sets little or no value on his own time and is willing to work many hours putting an object into usable shape. In most businesses surplus equipment, scrap metals, and waste are accumulated where employees can see them at some time during their working hours.

Companies usually sell certain of the materials for which they have no further use to employees as a matter of employee relations. If all factors of cost of selling to employees such as preparing forms and collecting payment are taken into account, sales to employees are usually at a financial loss to the company. A minimum amount is often set on sales to employees to keep such losses to a minimum. In some cases it may be easier and less expensive to give materials of little or no value to employees at no charge.

Nowhere in the sale of reclamation and salvage materials is uniformity of policy more important than in the sales to employees. It is not hard to imagine the effect upon employees' morale in the case where foreman A would let an employee have a discarded piece of rubber hose for free while foreman B would charge another employee a nominal sum for identical material. The easiest and only practical solution for the problem is to require that all sales of reclamation and salvage materials to employees be made through one person. This person could be the purchasing agent, reclamation and salvage clerk, or stores clerk so long as he is the sole one responsible for sales to employees. Since the price for items of reclamation and salvage being sold to employees is usually set by the company's purchasing agent, it may be well to have a person other than the purchasing agent do the actual selling as a matter of internal control.

All employees should be given an equal opportunity to purchase reclamation and salvage materials. Normally it will not be necessary to publicize materials which are constantly available such as used dunnage lumber, nonreturnable drums, scrap, and old electrical wire. Materials of this type are generally sold to employees by means of a price list prepared by the purchasing agent. The purchasing agent should remember to revise such a price list as outside markets fluctuate. One-of-a-kind items or items that infrequently come up for sales to employees should in fairness be brought to the attention of all employees. The simple way to do this is to post a notice on bulletin boards, allowing ample time before the date of sale for all employees to see it. This type of material is usually sold to employees in one of two ways. One method is to let all employees interested in purchasing the material at a price set by the purchasing agent leave their names with the person responsible for sales to employees. The lucky name is then picked at random by such means as drawing it from a hat. The other is to let all employees bid upon the material with the highest bidder getting it.

Proceeds from the sale of reclamation and salvage material to employees may be collected by payment of cash, issuing an invoice, or deducting it from the employee's paycheck. The method used is usually dictated by the accounting set up at any particular plant. If a payment is made by cash, collection should be made by some person such as the cashier who has no connection with the reclamation and salvage activities.

GOVERNMENT REGULATION AFFECTING DISPOSAL OF RECLAMATION AND SALVAGE MATERIALS

Scrap and metals are basic commodities used in the production of finished materials which have a direct bearing on national production in time of emergency. It is, therefore, to be expected that if an emergency situation necessitates establishment of government regulations applying to materials, scrap and metals would be included.

Based on experience in World War II and the Korean conflict, it is probable that government regulations over these commodities would take the form of controlled distribution to consumers under ceiling price regulations, with consumers reporting their inventory position and requirements to a government agency.

Controlled distribution of scrap and metals is accomplished by requiring producers of these materials to report at regular intervals their accumulations of each type of scrap and metals which they are in position to offer for disposal. The materials included in the different grades or classes are usually the same as those in normal periods, and are therefore known to both the consumer and the producer. Hence the records of quantities available for sale, required by regulations, can be kept without serious change from procedures followed in normal business operations, and with little or no additional clerical effort.

However, additional time and paper work are required to complete a sale of scrap under government regulations, because of the necessity of obtaining written authorization for sale to the consumers designated by the government office responsible for allocation to consumers. This is especially true with producers of large quantities of scrap or metals, because it is frequently necessary, under government allocations, to sell each class to a number of consumers, whereas under normal conditions the material in each class is awarded to a few buyers.

For the buyer of scrap under government regulations, there is additional record keeping involved, because of the necessity of registering with the responsible government office his current need for scrap. This information is required by the government office in order to determine the share of the available scrap, which may be of use to certain consumers, that should be allocated to a buyer of scrap.

Ceiling price regulations, generally speaking, will stipulate quite clearly the maximum price at which a particular grade or classification of scrap may be sold. The historic differentials in price of scrap in different market areas have been, and should continue to be, recognized in government regulations. The effect of operating under a maximum-price regulation is to eliminate the necessity for obtaining quotations as current accumulations are available for sale. This partly offsets the additional paper work involved in reporting scrap available and obtaining the proper authority for its sale.

DONATIONS TO EDUCATIONAL AND CHARITABLE ORGANIZATIONS

Every company is subject to a never-ending succession of requests for donations. While money is a commodity more often requested, machinery, equipment, instruments, and other miscellaneous items are often sought. Company officials may feel that it is advisable to donate a discarded lathe to an educational institution or a surplus typewriter to a charitable organization for purposes of good will. An employee may request scrap or waste for a local youth project. Whatever the source of the request, a uniform policy must be followed since one request for a donation will usually be followed by another. All requests should be given impartial consideration. The following paragraphs outline the policy of one company.

Donations of company-owned items is the responsibility of a group known as the donations committee. Members of this committee are appointed by top management and in the case of multiple-plant operation are located at the main office. When a request for donation has been received, before making the presentation the committee must have (*a*) assurance from the plant that the donation of the item has their approval; (*b*) assurance that the item is not usable in other company operations; (*c*) a complete detailed description of specifications and parts available and a qualified opinion as to present operating condition; (*d*) approximate time as to when the item will be available for delivery.

To correlate these needs with the demands of other company departments, the following steps are followed:

1. The owning plant or company division must prepare and complete a surplus equipment report form as shown in Figs. 21–6 and 21–7.
2. Upon receipt of a surplus equipment report, the division head should indicate his release of the equipment by placing his signature in the space provided on page 2 of the form. If he does or does not favor donating the item in question, he must state so specifically under "remarks." The form is then forwarded to the reclamation and salvage division or such person as may be in charge of this function.
3. Upon receipt of the surplus equipment report, the reclamation and salvage division will offer the items for transfer to other company operations. If not wanted for company use, a letter in which are in-

cluded detailed specifications will be written to the donations committee informing them the equipment is available for donation.

4. The donations committee may then notify the donee that the company is willing to make such a donation, all crating and freight to be at the expense of the company. They must secure a written declaration from the donee to the effect that the donation is acceptable. The letter of declaration should be acknowledged by the donation committee and the donee should be informed that the reclamation and salvage division will contact them in the near future relative to a definite time of delivery.
5. The letter of declaration must be sent to the reclamation and salvage division, and that division will contact the donee, requesting them to furnish a "no charge" purchase order containing shipping instructions.
6. When the purchase order is received, the reclamation and salvage division will notify the owning plant to crate and ship, charges prepaid, the item to be donated. The notification to the plant will also include the estimated current fair market value of the items in question. This fair market value is required in order to comply with tax accounting procedures for donation of facilities.

SALE OF SURPLUS OR OBSOLETE LAND AND BUILDINGS

Basically, surplus property, be it vacant or improved, should be sold: (1) to obtain cash, (2) to reduce real estate taxes, and (3) perhaps to obtain a loss to offset capital gains.

Sale of Land and Buildings Outright

1. Selecting the real estate agent:

   In the outright sale of land and buildings, the selection of a real estate broker is important in order to obtain the best results. Naturally such a broker should be one well-versed in the value and use possibility of industrial property. He should be in good standing in his community, have a well-organized firm, and be capable of reaching all who may be interested in acquiring properties to be sold.
2. Types of contracts with real estate agent:

   An exclusive agency contract with a well-selected broker should bring the best results. The broker is thus protected in his commission and need not hesitate in advertising and letting all that could be interested know that the property is for sale. If not protected by an "exclusive" contract, he may not feel justified in spending the money and time necessary to bring the best results. Further, a good reliable broker with an exclusive contract will normally "split" his commission with a cooperating broker who produces a purchaser. It is also not uncommon for an owner, in order to secure the best results, to agree to pay a commission and a half where an exclusive contract is given and a cooperating broker is involved.

Sale of Buildings Only—for Dismantling

Where improvements are to be sold for removal from the land, care should be exercised in offering same for sale and in the terms and conditions under which the buildings are to be sold and removed.

1. Making offer for sale:
   a. Description of building and estimate of scrap content:
   If construction plans of the building still exist, they should be made available to all bidders along with an estimated scrap content. If such information is not available, then a floor plan and perhaps recent photographs should be set up in brochure form for submission to interested parties.
   b. Provision for insurance by contractor:
   One of the conditions under which an offer is made is the insurance requirements to be furnished by the successful bidder. This insurance coverage should be such as to protect and save harmless the seller and the said lot of land, from any and all lawsuits, judgments, liens, claims, or payments of money which may arise or be made for or by reason of any accident resulting in injury to or death of any person or persons, or in damage to property of any one, happening in the conduct or through the prosecution of the work of removing, tearing down, filling or leveling as aforesaid; or for or by reason of the nonpayment of any wages, bills, or charges for anything in connection therewith, or for or by reason of anything happening during the progress of the said work, and until it is accepted as satisfactory by the seller.
   c. Arrangements for inspection:
   In offering the buildings, care should be taken that all interested parties are advised of a specific time when the buildings will be opened for inspection. A definite time should be set forth as to when bids are to have been received and a specific time when such bids will be opened. The owner, for his own protection, should reserve the right to refuse any or all bids.
   d. Description of how property is to be left (i.e., condition):
   The successful bidder shall remove within a set period, the whole of each of said buildings from the said lot of land, or tear down the said buildings and remove all the materials composing the

same from said land, including the cellar walls or foundations; and to pay all the costs and expenses for or connected with such removal.

To obtain, before commencing the work, all permits or licenses required by law in the prosecution of the work; or, if it becomes necessary for the seller to intervene and obtain such licenses or permits, to first pay the fees therefor and all other expenses connected therewith.

To comply with all laws and regulations of the board of health or of any city, county, or state authority that may have jurisdiction of or supervision over the said work, and to assume the risk of loss by reason of the said buildings or any part thereof being destroyed or damaged either by fire or otherwise.

Not to disturb the fences, pavements, or sidewalks, manholes, or other fixtures in said pavements or sidewalks; or, if disturbed to replace the same and to repair any damage which may be done thereto or thereby.

Within the above-mentioned period, to fill in to the grade of adjacent and surrounding land all cellars, basements, wells, cisterns, vaults, etc., and all other holes or depressions on said lot of land caused by the removal of the building or buildings or material composing the same, by tearing down and utilizing all foundations, chimneys, etc., as a base, the same to be finished and leveled off with ______ feet of clean earth or ashes, first removing all timber, lumber, or other combustible or inflammable matter from such excavations, sloping the surface so that it will not drain onto any adjoining pavement or sidewalk or abutting owner's property; and to leave the said lot of land and pavements or sidewalks in a safe condition both during the progress of the said work and when finished; and to pay all costs and expenses in connection with such filling and leveling.

To plug and seal all sewer and drain openings permanently, and to disconnect gas and water pipes in such manner that same shall remain permanently sealed so that no leakage shall occur, to the satisfaction of the local municipal authorities, utility companies concerned, and the seller.

e. Lump-sum price versus price per ton of scrap:

Where a large amount of scrap is involved and the tonnage indefinite, bids should be obtained based on a price per ton of scrap. Otherwise bids should be requested on a lump-sum basis.

2. Sales contract:

In asking for bids, it is well to furnish prospective bidders with the sales agreement form which the successful bidder will be required to execute.

a. Deciding award:

In requested bids, the time and method of deciding the awarding should be set forth with the further understanding the seller reserves the right to refuse any or all bids.

b. Terms of payment:

The terms of payment set forth in the sales contract should be such that a substantial certified down payment (not less than 10 per cent) is submitted with each bid, with the understanding such payment will be returned promptly to the unsuccessful bidders. The balance of the bid price should be paid upon execution of the contract, or where large sums are involved, on a percentage of the work completed as determined by the seller.

c. Time limit for execution:

When requesting bid, one of the conditions is that successful bidder will execute sales contract within 10 days of receiving such notice or forfeit his down payment submitted with his bid.

Dismantling Buildings to Reclaim Scrap or Usable Materials for Own Use

Where the seller is reclaiming scrap or usable materials for his own use, bids should be secured whereby such scrap and materials are to be turned over to owner at a specific location and in condition to meet predetermined specifications, the successful bidder to then remove all other materials. It may well be that the materials which the bidder obtains will not be of sufficient value to offset the cost of his obtaining the materials and, therefore, the bids received will in all probability require a payment by the seller to the successful bidder.

REDUCTION OF RECLAMATION AND SALVAGE MATERIALS

The purchasing agent through his knowledge of materials and methods of manufacturing is in an excellent position to offer suggestions which will decrease the output of reclamation and salvage materials. Some examples of the items the purchasing agent should look for are:

1. Replacement of items which must be machined with castings, extruded nonferrous shapes, cold-headed parts, and forgings
2. Examining width, length, and thickness requirements of raw materials to decrease process losses
3. Use of coils or longer lengths to reduce butt scrap
4. Use of standard parts instead of specially made parts

The reclamation and salvage manager (or other person responsible for this function) can assist in reducing reclamation and salvage materials resulting during production by bringing excessive and unwarranted loss to the attention of the proper people. Following are excerpts from one company's manual on this phase of reclamation and salvage department's activities:

1. Purpose:

   In order to maintain adequate control of scrap generated throughout the plant, a salvage coordination group has been established for the prime function of eliminating, to the closest possible extent, the loss of direct and indirect materials.

   This group is established as a staff activity responsible to the plant manager and will cooperate with line supervision to minimize such losses.

   The responsibility for scrap losses still remains with line supervision and it should be emphasized that such losses require expenditures on the part of the plant for materials over and above specified or budgeted quantities.

2. Organization:

   The salvage coordination group is headed by an analyst-scrap and one salvage coordinator for each shift. This group will operate full time in the plant in accordance with a definite program outlined later in this procedure.

3. Program of operation:

   There will be two phases in the operation of the salvage coordination group, namely:

   Preventive phase, to eliminate conditions contributing to or causing losses of materials before any appreciable loss occurs.

   Corrective phase, to isolate materials on which losses are being experienced and to determine causes and institute corrective measures to eliminate similar losses in the future.

4. Preventive phase of operation:

   A daily inspection of all plant areas will be made by the salvage coordinator operating on each shift, with a three-stage follow-up. It might not be possible for the coordinator to cover the entire plant each day and still leave time for his follow-up work. But coordinators will work out a program whereby they will cover the entire plant progressively which might take two or more days to complete the tour of all areas.

   During this inspection tour, the salvage coordinator will look primarily for the following conditions:

   a. Untagged scrap
   b. Material on the floor
   c. Material mislocated
   d. Material damaged in cartons
   e. Mixed stock
   f. Unrotated stock
   g. Disarranged stock
   h. Faulty equipment

A written report will be prepared by the coordinator for each daily tour. This report is so arranged as to require a minimum of written information since the form provides for checking off and rating each department visited during the tour.

These daily tours can be so arranged that only part of the total shift time will be consumed, leaving the balance for items requiring special attention.

The first stage of follow-up is to review the daily report with the superintendent involved and while no copies of the report will be made, the coordinator's work copy will be filed for future reference.

Second-stage follow-up will be made on chronic or critical conditions which have not been corrected after the first-stage follow-up has been completed. If determined necessary by the salvage coordinator, a photograph will be taken of the condition and will be attached to a report which will be given to the superintendent involved. This particular report provides space for the superintendent's disposition of the condition noted and subsequently the report, together with the superintendent's disposition, will be forwarded to the plant superintendent until corrective action is taken.

A third-stage follow-up will consist of a weekly report from the salvage coordination group to the plant manager and plant superintendent in which the five most critical conditions contributing to scrap loss will be listed. This will be restricted, however, to those items which have gone through the first two follow-up stages and still remain uncorrected.

5. Corrective phase:

While it is believed that most unnecessary loss or damage to materials should be caught in the preventive stage, it is probable that all such damage or loss cannot be so eliminated because of the high-volume production and large plant areas to be covered. For this reason, the following corrective phase will be instituted.

Through the corrective phase, damaged patterns which result in loss or misuse of materials should be detected. When such a pattern is detected, and the cause of the loss determined, appropriate corrective measures will be instituted and followed up.

It is important to determine the pattern of damage as early as possible in order to minimize the extent of resulting loss.

The first stage of the corrective phase will occur during the daily inspection tour described in the preventive phase, at which time the coordinator will check all locations where tagged scrap is accumulated prior to the movement of such scrap to the salvage area. This check should assist the coordinator in developing an early pattern of damage.

A second stage of this corrective phase will be a review of the scrap tickets accumulated in the salvage area. These tickets will be grouped by part number so that any pattern of damage not revealed in the daily plant tour can be reviewed, although in some cases this review may confirm previous observations of the coordinator.

The third stage of this corrective phase involves a review by the analyst of scrap of the weekly scrap report as issued by the salvage group and any pattern noted from this review will be referred to the coordinator for investigation.

6. Corrective action:

As damaged patterns are uncovered, the coordinator will review the matter with the foreman involved. Should this review fail to disclose cause of the damage, the matter will be referred to the appropriate staff departments for future investigation. The coordinator, however, will still follow the investigation by the staff department and expedite the investigation in any manner practical.

After the cause of the pattern is determined, the coordinator will request from supervisors and staff departments involved their opinion as to the most effective corrective action to be taken. Any disagreement at this level will be referred to superintendents or higher management, if necessary. When corrective action has been agreed upon and instigated, the coordinator will see that the indicated course of action is followed through to a conclusion.

7. Corrective phase follow-up:

A systematic follow-up will be established by the salvage coordination group to provide a record for future reference of each pattern noted and a project record will be prepared in four parts, as follows:

a. Problem: To describe completely the pattern noted together with its size and scope and the names of individuals to which the problem of determining the pattern cause has been assigned.

b. Cause: Describe the cause of the pattern as uncovered by the investigation and the names of individuals assigned to determine the course of corrective action.

c. Corrective action: Describe the corrective action decided upon and names of individuals assigned to carry out such corrective action.

d. Disposition: Describe the results and effect of the corrective action taken.

This report will start as any pattern is first noted and the other steps listed above will be completed as the project develops. All projects will remain open until final disposition is completed as outlined in item 4. Only one pencil copy of this report will be made and it will not be distributed, although each report will be indexed by area and number and will be retained in binders by the salvage coordination group.

The weekly report of the salvage coordination group to the plant manager and plant superintendent will contain a list of the five most chronic or critical patterns of loss that still remain open in this follow-up project record.

8. Cost report:

In order to emphasize to supervision the dollar value of scrap and other losses in their particular areas, as well as to indicate such costs to management, a weekly summary of the cost of tagged scrap will be issued showing each foreman's area together with the cost of scrap or loss for which each foreman is responsible.

9. Indirect materials and equipment:

Equally important losses are incurred on indirect materials which are those used in manufacturing operations, but which are not an integral part of assemblies being produced. These items can be grouped into three types, as follows:

a. Processing supplies: Such as tape used in packing, cartons, stationery supplies, and oil

b. Perishable tools: Such as needles, cutters, and sewing-machine parts

c. Safety promotion equipment: Such as grinding hoods, safety glasses, and gloves

10. Establishment of budget quotas:

Each year, based upon past experience, budgeted quantities of all indirect materials are established and any usage above these budgeted quantities becomes a plant loss, since its cost is over and above that provided for in selling prices.

11. Control of indirect materials:

Budgets will be established on indirect materials by each foreman with the approval of the general foreman and superintendent. If more than the budgeted daily quantities are required, these quantities must be requisitioned from the crib on the signature of a general foreman or higher level, and these requisitions will be marked "over budget."

12. Follow-up of indirect material usage:

The first stage of follow-up for usage of indirect materials takes place during the daily inspection tour of the salvage coordinator at which time he will observe materials being used and whether or not excessive use is apparent. The coordinator will also check any used materials being scrapped to determine whether or not full usage has been made of such materials.

The second follow-up stage involves a review of requisitions issued for "over budget" amounts, after which these requisitions will be turned over to the purchase requisition and accounting sections. The analyst of scrap will review requisitions with the purchase requisition supervisor each day and any exceptional cases will be investigated and followed up by the salvage coordination group.

The third stage of follow-up will be a review of the weekly summary of indirect material requisitions prepared by the purchase requisition section. In the event that excess or misuse of indirect materials is detected in any of the above three follow-up stages, a project will be prepared similar to the one referred to under item 7 above.

ETHICS

Considerations in selling or otherwise disposing of reclamation and salvage materials parallel policies and practices for sound departmental procedures outlined in other sections of this handbook. Accepted principles will be found in, among others, Section 2, "Purchasing Department Organization," Section 3, "Policy and Procedure Manuals," Section 4, "Legal Influences in Purchasing," Section 24, "Evaluating Purchasing

Perfomance," and of major importance, Section 6, "Ethical Practices in Purchasing."

The concept of ethics plays a major role in the disposal of salvage material, and ethics in practice poses numerous problems in the day-to-day transactions. All must be handled, as outlined in Section 6, in a sound and acceptable manner, bearing in mind the obligations to the company and to the purchasers. Questionable influences are kept at an absolute minimum. Common sense and sound judgment must govern each situation, as there are no specific rules or standards that are applicable. To be compatible with one's employment, the activity must serve the employer's interest at all times and under all circumstances.

SELECTED BIBLIOGRAPHY

Greenberg, Simon: *The Metals Handbook,* American Society of Metals, Cleveland, Ohio, published annually

Internal Audit and Control of Scrap, Salvage, and Surplus Materials, Research Committee Report No. 8, Institute of Internal Auditors, New York, N.Y., 1960

Lipsett, Charles H.: *Industrial Wastes and Salvage,* Atlas Publishing Co., Inc., New York, N.Y., 1963

Salvage Manual for Industry, U.S. War Production Board, Salvage Division, Washington, D.C., 1943

Scrap Material Guide, Institute of Scrap Iron & Steel, Inc., Washington, D.C., 1965

Surplus Record, Thos. P. Scanlon, Kemper Building, Chicago, Ill.

Used Equipment Directory, H. Cole, 30 Vesey, New York, N.Y.

Additional references on subject matter of this section are included in many of the books listed in Section 26, "Library and Catalog File."

SECTION 22

PURCHASING DEPARTMENT BUDGETS

Editor

C. F. Ogden, Administrative Vice-president, The Detroit Edison Company, Detroit, Michigan

Associate Editors

E. B. Adams, Purchasing Supervisor, Mobil Oil Company, Inc., Detroit Division, Detroit, Michigan

C. C. Chauvin, Manager–Purchasing Research, Corporate Purchasing Staff, Chrysler Corporation, Detroit, Michigan

W. J. Pierce, Supervisor–Purchase Research Division, Purchasing Department, The Detroit Edison Company, Detroit, Michigan

A budget is a formalized financial plan for balancing expenditures against income. Budget periods vary but the most common period of time is usually one year. Within this year there may be monthly or quarterly budget reviews made. The term budget is popularly applied to that portion of money allocated for a specific purpose, i.e., the "manufacturing budget," the "labor budget," or the "procurement budget." There can be as many of these individual budgets as the complexity of the organization requires. Usually, these individual budgets are parts of an over-all budget which is commonly referred to as the "master budget."

The preparation of the master budget and the presentation of it to the officers of the company is usually the responsibility of the budget director who reports to the comptroller or the controller. In a small company the budget director may be one of the officers of the company who acts only as a budget director in addition to other managerial responsibilities. It is the budget director's responsibility to coordinate the efforts of the individual departments or management groups who will be asked to submit their cash requests in the form of a budget for their projected operations.

Budget administration has been defined as the directing of a financial plan controlling future operations. The very thought of budgeting, however, has deterred many companies both large and small from adopting a budgetary system. The moment one talks about control, department heads immediately interpret that phrase as meaning "restricted expenditures." Cost reduction is certainly an ever-present responsibility as outlined throughout this handbook, particularly in Section 11, "Value Analysis Techniques." But if it is the only or even primary concept of the purpose of budget administration, then the thinking is negative. The positive approach should be taken. This is the philosophy of administration that places the responsibility for the money spent upon each member of the management team. With this concept, emphasis is placed on wise spending rather than on first reducing costs.

The purpose of budgeting, in a positive sense, is to provide these two things:

1. A forecast of the amount of money a company will have to set aside for its operations during a stated period of time.
2. A basis for measurement of the efficiency of the functional and operating components.[1]

It is much easier to budget for a month ahead than it is to budget for a year ahead. For many companies, particularly small companies with

[1] Also described in Section 24, "Evaluating Purchasing Performance."

limited capital assets and fluctuating sales revenue, the monthly budget has been found to be the most helpful.

Many small companies shy away from a budget plan because they are overwhelmed by the amount of paper work and detail which they observe large companies have in their budget systems. A budget, to be effective, does not have to involve all this detail. It should be tailor-made to fit the needs of the company installing it and kept as simple as practicable.

PROCUREMENT BUDGETING

Of the many supplementary budgets which must be prepared, one will deal with the matter of production materials, components, supplies, and services which have to be bought for production purposes and for machine tools, plant investment, nondurable tools, and shop supplies necessary for the maintenance and operation of plant facilities. The responsibility for the preparation of this budget usually rests with the production manager on production materials, components, and supplies and with the plant facilities manager on plant and office maintenance and operation.

Obviously, each working independently and then together must rely on sales forecasts for one, two, five, or more years. The purchasing agent has no direct concern or responsibility with respect to the preparation of the procurement budget unless operation or maintenance is also his direct management responsibility. He does have, however, an important secondary responsibility in that he will have to supply much of the cost and market information to the production and plant facilities managers so that they can present an accurate picture of the costs of materials needed.

The purchasing officer and his staff, if he has one, are important to any budget planning system because of the information which they can supply to those responsible for making up any of the supplemental budgets which are a part of the master budget. If a company is large enough to have a budget committee, the purchasing officer may be a member of this committee. But, as already stated, beyond this important function of furnishing information best available to him, the purchasing officer usually has no direct responsibility for the preparation of the procurement budget.

SOME CONSIDERATIONS OF PRICE FORECASTING

In furnishing information to the production head, the purchasing officer is faced with certain basic problems in arriving at realistic future price information. Some of the more important things that he should take into account in furnishing price information for the procurement budget are:

1. Material contracts containing price escalator clauses
2. Accuracy of statistical sources of information on prices
3. World political or economic factors that may influence prices
4. The world and domestic general labor situation
5. The past history of price movements in the industry
6. The position of the company in industry and the resulting influence that it can exert in controlling production, consumption, prices, and deliveries
7. Weather conditions such as droughts and floods or other acts of God (more significant in the case of agricultural commodities)
8. Possible effect on supply caused by governmental regulation
9. Recent decisions of Federal and state courts and decisions pending
10. Availability (scarcity) of any one or more commodities and components

Since purchased materials and services average 56 cents out of each sales dollar, accurate figures on market conditions and material prices are one of the more important aspects of budget planning. The sales price of a product is governed by what customers are willing to pay and the general competitive situation. It is apparent, therefore, that the cost of a product is to a proportionate degree established by the cost of the materials, machines, and tools required to produce it. By supplying accurate information concerning markets, commodity prices, and material shortages and availability in the near future as well as the more distant future, the purchasing officer can to an important degree influence the amount that will be budgeted for specific product material purchases and when. And it follows that this will influence the amount to be budgeted for all other operating expenses. Also see Sections 9 and 12 on pricing considerations and forecasting.

INVENTORY TURNOVER AS A BUDGET FACTOR

Since the purchasing officer may have a direct or indirect responsibility for inventory control in a company, he may be asked for certain information concerning inventory turnover in the preparation of the budget. Because of the interest and carrying charges assessed on inventories, it is desirable to keep inventory investment to the minimum compatible with production needs. This, however, should not be carried to the extreme that added procurement, delivery, and handling costs offset any gains in reduced carrying charges. No set formula can be prescribed for establishing a ratio of inventory on hand to turnover, since individual factors in each industry and company will have an influence on this determination. Where the purchasing officer is responsible for inventories, estimates of the dollar value of inventory to be carried from month to month or by quarters is an important factor in budget planning. Whether responsible for inventories or not, he must be concerned since inventory policy will have a direct effect on prices, deliveries, and follow-up of purchased materials, as described in detail in Section 13, "Quantity Determination through Inventory Management."

Procurement time schedules for materials, components, supplies, and services are important tools in the hands of the production, manufacturing, and engineering departments to assist in determining those items which must be engineered, ordered, and are required in the manufactur-

Item	*Weeks*
Abrasive wheels (if vendors stock)	2
Abrasive wheels (if special)	8
Adhesives, miscellaneous	3
Adhesives, rubber type	3
Asbestos cloth and tape	5
Automobile batteries	2
Belts and sheaves	3
Brushes, paint, and varnish	4
Cast-iron pipe	7
Cement	4
Common nuts	3
Composition shingles and roofing	2
Continuous forms, printed	16
Copper pipe	10
Envelopes (plain)	4
Fiberboard boxes	6
Fire extinguishers	5
Galvanized nuts, electrozinc	3
Galvanized nuts, hot dip	8
Glass, standard	4
Lacquers and synthetics	3
Lead, standard	4
Lumber, carload deliveries	8
Malleable iron castings	12
Paper towels	5
Plumbing fixtures	10–12
Rubber hose and hose fittings	3
Steel strand C coating	24
Taps, standard	3
Taps, special	8
Wire rope, regular construction	4
Wire rope, special construction	12

FIG. 22–1. Example of procurement lead time—number of weeks.

ing cycle ahead of others. These are simple to prepare: list alphabetically the major commodities, components, tools, supplies, etc., and show the number of weeks required to procure from the time the purchase order is placed. This may be issued quarterly, semiannually, or annually as circumstances warrant. An example of lead-time considerations is shown in Fig. 22–1.

INFORMATION FOR SALES ESTIMATES

Another area where the purchasing officer is called upon for information is in the preparation of sales estimates. Sales estimates are the primary source of revenue information against which expenditures are budgeted. Therefore, the first consideration in budgeting is, "How much money do we have to spend?" This determination, usually made by the sales or marketing group, forms the basis for the determination of how much money can be spent in normal operations. The need for accurate sales estimates cannot be overemphasized. It is not uncommon for the sales head to consult with purchasing before submitting his sales estimates. Many of the market statistical services used by the purchasing department can assist the sales group in analyzing markets. The purchasing department's close contact with suppliers' representatives offers another source for "ear to the ground" information that can help the sales estimate. Just as every member of management is concerned with the accuracy of the sales estimate, the purchasing officer realizes that any contribution he can make will better allow him to budget for his own operations.

Briefly, a simple summary of points to consider in the use of sales estimates is:

1. Sales estimates should be defined as to whether or not they are sales forecasts of *orders received* to be taken in a year or whether they are *sales billed* based on shipments during the same year. This is particularly important, depending upon whether the product is one of long or short manufacturing cycle.
2. If the manufacturing cycle is short, sales and manufacturing output bear almost the same relationship.
3. If the manufacturing cycle is long, sales this year may be sales billed sometime in the next twelve, eighteen, and twenty-four months.
4. If the manufacturing cycle is short, can purchasing support manufacturing output and sales billed now and in immediate months, particularly during periods of great demand? Also, can purchasing hold a price line on material input?
5. If the manufacturing cycle is long, can purchasing support manufac-

turing output and sales billed in the next twelve, eighteen, or twenty-four months and hold a price line which will prevent escalation on sales contracts?

6. The purchasing agent can, from manufacturing output and sales estimates, determine his budget much better on personnel additions, expenses, office investment, etc.

PURCHASING DEPARTMENT BUDGETS

The purchasing officer does have a direct concern and is charged with the specific responsibility of preparing the budgets necessary for the operations of those management activities specifically assigned to him. In the most restricted sense this may be only the buying function. But in many companies he may also have added management responsibilities such as traffic, salvage, invoice clearance and payment, inspection, standards, and real estate and in some companies such unrelated operations as building maintenance and other functions requiring purchased labor and services. Obviously, the purchasing officer who has many functions is going to have to present a more detailed budget than is one who is responsible for the procurement function only. The basic budget considerations, however, are the same regardless of the complexity of the operations reporting to the purchasing officer. Certainly an effective tool for the purchasing agent to have is a copy of the approved budgets for production materials, components, supplies, and services and machine tools, plant equipment, nondurable tools, and shop supplies.

To illustrate the steps that would be taken in preparing a purchasing department operating budget for a small company, the following example is used. Figure 22–2 shows an example of a completed budget request for the smaller company. The application is factual, the company fictitious.

PURCHASING DEPARTMENT OPERATING BUDGET—SMALL COMPANY

The XYZ Company is a small one-plant operation employing about 400 people. Its purchasing department is comprised of the purchasing agent, one buyer, and two girls. One of the girls, the stenographer-clerk, is used for routine expediting and follow-up in addition to her stenographic duties. The other girl is an order typist and file clerk.

The basic budget factors that will have to be taken into consideration are:

1. Payroll
2. Expendable materials and supplies
3. Miscellaneous expenses

XYZ MANUFACTURING COMPANY

Purchasing Department 19___ Budget Request

Date October 31, 19 Prepared by Purchasing Agent

ITEM	Jan.	Feb.	Mar.	Apr.	May	Jun.	Jul.	Aug.	Sept.	Oct.	Nov.	Dec.	TOTAL
SALARIES													
Purchasing Agent	1,000.00	1,000.00	1,000.00	1,000.00	1,000.00	1,000.00	1,050.00	1,050.00	1,050.00	1,050.00	1,050.00	1,050.00	12,300.00
Buyer	750.00	750.00	750.00	750.00	750.00	785.00	785.00	785.00	785.00	785.00	785.00	785.00	9,245.00
Steno-clerk	340.00	340.00	450.00	360.00	360.00	450.00	366.40	382.40	478.00	382.40	382.40	478.00	4,769.60
Typist	280.00	280.00	360.00	288.00	288.00	360.00	294.40	302.40	378.00	302.40	302.40	378.00	3,813.60
													30,128.20
SUPPLIES													
Purchase forms	20.00	20.00	20.00	20.00	20.00	20.00	20.00	20.00	20.00	20.00	20.00	20.00	240.00
Stationery	20.00	20.00	20.00	20.00	20.00	20.00	20.00	20.00	20.00	20.00	20.00	20.00	240.00
Miscellaneous	15.00	15.00	15.00	15.00	15.00	15.00	15.00	15.00	15.00	15.00	15.00	15.00	180.00
													660.00
EXPENSES													
Travel													1,100.00
Tel. and Tel.													600.00
Postage													600.00
Periodicals													120.00
Market Services													500.00
Entertainment and Meals													500.00
													3,420.00
												GRAND TOTAL	$34,208.20

FIG. 22–2. Budget request for a smaller company purchasing department.

Under payroll we will have such considerations as the salary of each of the four persons concerned as of January 1 of the budget year (for our purposes we are assuming a calendar year as a budget year), and any contemplated increases in the salaries of any of these persons during the coming year. These salary increases will include such things as normal merit increases, cost of living increases, annual improvement factors, etc. The entries for payroll costs are shown in the example in Fig. 22–2. Entries for the purchasing agent and the buyer are made on a monthly basis since they are paid monthly. However, the stenographer-clerk and the typist are paid weekly; therefore certain months with five weeks in them will have a greater amount budgeted than the other months. Also since wage increases and other factors affecting pay may take place on a date other than the first of the month, they will have to be computed in part and will appear in the month in which they took effect. In the example, the purchasing agent got a pay increase in July amounting to $50 a month and the buyer got a pay increase in June amounting to $35 a month. The stenographer-clerk got a pay increase in March and another one in August, as well as the annual improvement factor increase that was granted to all hourly workers on July 1 and amounted to four cents an hour. The typist also received two small increases during the year, one on March 1 and one on August 1, as well as the July 1 four cents an hour improvement factor.

The important thing to note is that the purchasing agent is able to budget fairly accurately what his payroll costs are going to be. In a small company, it is very desirable to make pay increases for such a compact department effective on the same date. This will simplify the preparation of the budget and also the administration of it. The example in Fig. 22–2 is used, however, to show that even if all pay increases for the people in the department do not coincide or do not fall on the same date, it is still not any great chore to prepare the budget estimate.

The next item the purchasing agent is going to consider is the budget for expendable materials and supplies required in the operation of the department, as listed in Fig. 22–3. These include such things as stationery, the various requisitions and purchase forms charged against the purchasing department, typewriter ribbons, pencils, and any other expendable items required for the operation of the department. Usually this information is best obtained by looking at past records. Certainly from old invoice records the cost of the various forms used in the purchasing department can be made available. If petty cash funds are used to obtain such things as typewriter ribbons, pencils, ink, blotters, etc., the purchasing agent should be able to find out from the girls in the office approximately how much petty cash is allocated for this purpose each year. If these miscellaneous stationery items are drawn on a memo receipt from some central stores facilities such as a stationery storeroom, perhaps these old records will be available to the purchasing agent. He will then have some idea of the past history of these expenditures. In any event, when preparing a budget for the first time, a well-thought-out estimate may be accurate enough since these items are seldom of very great significance in the total budget.

After the installation of a budget system, the purchasing officer will find that he is forced into being more concerned with the amount of money he spends for each of the various phases of his operations and will initiate a system, if one does not already exist, that will enable him to give more accurate estimates in succeeding years. Since the amount spent for expendable materials and supplies is not great in any event, it is common practice to take a year's total figure and divide it by 12, putting an equal amount in each month, as shown in Fig. 22–2. (See also discussion later in this section concerning "The Thirteen-period Budget.") If, however, more precise budgeting is required, the total amount spent for a year can be divided by 52 and again proportioned according to the months with five weeks as against those that have only four. An even further refinement enters into the consideration when it is known that certain months of the year require heavier cash demands than other months and these months are so specifically budgeted with larger requirements. A good example of this is shown where many small companies close down their whole plant for a period during the summer when all employees take their vacations at the same time. Obviously, in budgeting for this kind of an operation, that month would probably have few expenditures for expendable materials or for miscellaneous expenses. Also, in some companies the month of December may be particularly heavy while the purchasing department is placing annual contracts or blanket orders for the following year. This may draw more heavily upon the supply of expendable materials.

The next consideration for the purchasing agent in preparation of his budget is the matter of miscellaneous expenses. This is shown as the heading Expenses in Fig. 22–2. Here the purchasing agent lists all the additional operating expenses he will have or anticipates during the coming year. (Figure 22–3 lists examples of some of those he might want to consider.) These expenses have not been distributed in this illustration by months, only an annual total being shown. This is often the practice with the items of expendable materials and supplies, as well as expenses, since it is very difficult to project accurately exactly when these costs will be incurred. However, the purchasing agent will have to give some estimate of the amount of money that is going to be spent for these expenses. And, again, the best source for the information required is from past experience. If the purchasing agent is preparing his first budget, he may have to seek sources for this information outside his own department. The accounting department is always a good place to start. However, if he cannot get detailed information on the various items shown under expenses, he will have to use his best judgment and make as accurate an estimate as is possible. Here again, the purchasing agent will probably keep a closer record on such expenditures during the first and succeeding budget years, since he will recognize the need to have this information for following budgets. This awareness of the need to know is one of the important arguments for budgeting.

EXPENDABLE MATERIALS AND SUPPLIES	MISCELLANEOUS EXPENSES
Rubber stamps	Meals for business purposes
Personal cards	Travel
Stamps and postage	Reimbursement for use of personal automobile
Pens and pencils	Telephone, telegraph, and teletype
Paper and stationery	Professional association dues and incidental expenses
Market reports and surveys	Conventions and conferences
Purchase handbooks	Flowers or bereavement gifts
Desk calendars	Maintenance of office equipment
Ink and pencil leads	Consultant services
Purchasing department forms	Taxi fares (business)
Dictating machine supplies	Entertainment
Carbon paper	Utilities, heat, light, etc.
Magazines and periodicals	Photographs
Book ends	Parking fees
Filing trays	Air travel insurance
	Pool car expenses (company)
	Plant visits

Note: These are suggested items only. Many others may be added where applicable.

FIG. 22–3. Items for consideration in preparing a purchasing department operating budget.

After all the required entries have been made on this budget request sheet, it is then possible to see at a glance what the total expenditures of the department are going to be for any one month (by totaling the columns vertically) or for any one activity or item (by totaling horizontally). The purchasing agent now needs only to total his expenses for a month and compare it with his budget to see where he stands. In large companies the accounting department may furnish this information by supplying the budgeted departments with monthly expense statements. This relieves the individual departments of the necessity for keeping separate record systems.

If the purchasing agent exceeds his budget for any given month, he may be asked to explain this situation to the chief financial officer of the company. By the same token, if he does not spend as much as he budgeted, he will be expected to explain. This is the only budget control necessary.

REVIEW AND MODIFICATION TO THE SMALL COMPANY PURCHASING DEPARTMENT BUDGET

As already stated, it is very difficult to budget with any great degree of accuracy as far as a year ahead. Changes in the general economic situation, changes in the company's product line, and employment changes are but a few of the factors which can influence the budget. It is probably a good idea for the purchasing head to check sales and manufacturing regularly to determine changes in business that might affect his operations.

If the XYZ Manufacturing Company had expanded its operations to the point where four people could no longer handle the purchasing operation, it might be necessary for the purchasing agent to add another employee or two, say, sometime around the middle of the year. In this event he would also have to increase his budget request for the balance of the year. This can be done in either of two ways:

1. The purchasing agent can prepare a revised budget request for the six months from July 1 through December 31, increasing each of the various items shown on his budget.
2. He can submit a separate budget for the individual or two he adds to his staff, indicating the increased costs of payroll and expenses that will result from their addition to his staff.

This is called a budget supplement and can be stapled or clipped to his regular budget request. In succeeding years, of course, these additions would be integrated into his regular budget.

PURCHASING DEPARTMENT BUDGET FOR LARGER COMPANIES

The factors to take into consideration when preparing a budget for the purchasing department of a large company are exactly the same as those for a small company. However, in a large company the procurement officer may have responsibilities for many functions, as already mentioned, such as traffic, salvage, invoice clearance, inspection, standards, etc., involving as many as 100, 200, or more people. This means that the time and effort required to prepare this more complex budget will be increasingly greater. His basic concerns, however, are still with the amount of money he will have to request for payroll, operating supplies for the department, and other miscellaneous expenses.

Budget preparation in a large purchasing department can be made a joint effort, enhancing the value of the budget and making supervisors on the purchasing staff aware of its importance. This is done by having the supervisors in charge of the important subdivisions of the department prepare their own budget requests for their work group. This is then consolidated into one composite purchasing department budget. A sample form for requesting this budget information from division heads is included as Fig. 22–4.

PURCHASING DEPARTMENT
1966 Operating and Payroll Budget Estimate

Construction Buying Division
(62F8)

1965 Budget and Expenses	
Estimate for 1965	
Payroll	$38,000
Other Expenses	$ 1,500
Actual for 1965 (3 months estimated)	
Payroll	$37,654
Other Expenses	$ 1,350
1966 Budget Estimate	
Payroll	$40,700
Other Expenses	$ 2,000
Total for 1966	$42,700
Please add for overtime	40 Male hr
	— Female hr

FIG. 22–4. Work sheet for submitting budget data by subordinate division heads.

These are work sheets which will be used by the purchasing agent or his staff assistant in compiling the total purchasing department budget request. It will be noted that the work sheets furnished the group heads show the amount of money that was spent by each division during the past year. This serves as a guide to the group head in preparing his next year's estimate and is taken from the detailed expense sheets which are furnished to the purchasing agent by the accounting department. An example of a detailed expense sheet for one month for one division is included as Fig. 22–5. In most large companies these detailed expense sheets are furnished by the accounting department to show the department heads how they are spending money budgeted the previous year.

EXPENSE ACCOUNT STATEMENT

MONTH OF SEPTEMBER 19__

ACCOUNT NO. 62 F 7 JOB **1**

FORM AG 33 4-55

ADDRESS INQUIRIES TO GENERAL ACCOUNTING DEPT., BOOKKEEPING SECTION

DESCRIPTION	REFERENCE		AMOUNT		
BALANCE FORWARD			42	117	69
LABOR	L	21	4	637	52
LABOR	L	43		166	60
			4	804	12 *
SHAW STAMP DISBURSED	I	48152		31	25
ERS MIDWEST PIPE CO	I	48152		39	00
ASSOCIATED EQUIPMENT	I	51502		5	15
19__ RENTAL RATES FOR CONSTRUCTION EQUIPMENT	I	51502			
MCT - MEALS	I	52046		7	00
JFC - MEALS	I	52046		16	10
ERS TO ST. LOUIS	I	55138		80	00
KWH - MEALS	I	55138		12	25
				190	75 *
COPYING SERVICE WORK	J	40		3	00
MEALS SERVED	J	77		132	37
				135	37 *
COMPANY POOL CAR EXPENSE	A	47		19	30
				19	30 *
EXPENDITURES CURRENT MONTH			5	149	54
EXPENDITURES TOTAL TO DATE			47	267	23 *
BUDGET PRORATED TO DATE			47	482	40
BUDGET CURRENT MONTH			5	276	00

FIG. 22–5. Monthly expense account statement for one work order account assigned to purchasing department.

Before individual division heads in the purchasing department can be asked to prepare their own budget requests for consolidation into the purchasing department budget, there must be some system in effect in the company which permits the accumulation of expense data month by month or quarter by quarter. These figures from past experience are important in helping to arrive at a realistic budget request. If no such system of expense reporting is available, the need for budgeting may well be challenged. Obviously, the purpose of a budget is to allocate funds for specific purposes and to operate within reasonable tolerances of these estimates. An accurate system of accounting for expenses must be in effect before the establishment of realistic estimates can have any meaning. The most commonly used system of accounting for budgetary purposes is the work order system.

WORK ORDER SYSTEM

The purchasing department head can establish his own work order system in the absence of a company-wide system if he desires to keep an accurate check on his expenditures within his department. Where work order systems are in effect in a company they make budgeting much easier.

Briefly, the work order system operates like this:

1. A series of numbers or a combination of numbers and letters or any other means of identifying individual groupings is used to establish an account against which charges can be made.
2. One of these numbers or combination of numbers and letters is assigned to each of the separate functional groups within the department.
3. Any expense incurred by that group is charged directly to that work order number. This must be done before reimbursement can be made.
4. Individual sheets are kept in a journal or ledger for each of the functional groupings and its assigned work order number. As expenses are incurred against the work order number, they are entered under the appropriate page in the journal.
5. Payroll, which is more or less a fixed amount from month to month, is also entered in the journal on a monthly basis, showing the amount paid in straight time to the individuals concerned and the amount paid in premium time, and extras, if any.

In other words, any money spent, or committed, by any one of the divisions within the purchasing department for any operating purpose, is entered as a separate journal entry to the appropriate assigned work order. Some companies have a "catch-all" or separate work order assigned for expenses which should not rightfully be charged against any one division, since the costs are incurred in behalf of several of the divisions. Examples of these are certain forms that are used by all divisions or telephone charges where the cost of trying to keep a record of individual telephone calls would offset any savings that might be realized.

The work order system does permit flexibility of operation and involves more of the responsible supervisors within the department in this important cost-concern activity.

PREPARING THE PURCHASING DEPARTMENT BUDGET IN A LARGE COMPANY

In a large company, probably the most involved part of the purchasing department operating budget to prepare is that which deals with payroll. Figure 22–6 shows a payroll budget form used to prepare the payroll portion of the purchasing department budget. It is used for hourly or weekly paid employees. The department head, supervisors, and key staff are carried on a separate, "monthly" roll.

The first item on this payroll budget is for the number of full-time employees as of January 1 and as of the first of each of the months for the balance of the budget year. In this case it is 88. The second line is for the number of straight time hours per employee. This figure is going to vary from month to month, depending upon the number of weeks in the payroll month. In the example shown, January had five weeks with 200 hr, whereas February had only four weeks with 160 hr. The third item asked for is the total number of straight time man-hours, which is the number of employees multiplied by the straight time hours per employee. This, too, is going to vary with the number of pay weeks in each payroll month.

Items 4 and 5 deal with the same factors covered under 1, 2, and 3 only with respect to part-time employees. In the example no part-time employees were scheduled for this budget year. Item 6 then asks for the total straight time man-hours including both full- and part-time employees. In this case, it is the same as item 3 since there were no part-time employees. Item 7 is the estimate by months of the paid overtime hours. This estimate is arrived at by totaling the overtime hours reported on the work sheets (Fig. 22–4) submitted by the individual divisions within the purchasing department. Item 8 shows employee additions or exits and is taken from item 26 on the sheet. This is a summary of the employee additions or exits by month. In the illustration shown, students from high school and college are employed during the summer months. They assist

PAYROLL BUDGET

PAYROLL NUMBER 21

DEPARTMENT Purchasing DIVISION ______ YEAR 19__

	JANUARY	FEBRUARY	MARCH	APRIL	MAY	JUNE	JULY	AUGUST	SEPTEMBER	OCTOBER	NOVEMBER	DECEMBER	TOTAL
FULL TIME EMPLOYES													
1 NUMBER OF EMPLOYES AT JAN. 1	88	88	88	88	88	88	88	88	88	88	88	88	88
2 STRAIGHT TIME HOURS PER EMPLOYE	200	160	160	200	160	160	200	160	200	160	160	200	2,120
3 STRAIGHT TIME MAN HOURS (LINE 1 X 2)	17,600	14,080	14,080	17,600	14,080	14,080	17,600	14,080	17,600	14,080	14,080	17,600	186,560
PART TIME EMPLOYES													
4 NUMBER OF EMPLOYES AT JAN. 1													
5 STRAIGHT TIME MAN HOURS													
6 TOTAL STRAIGHT TIME MAN HOURS (LINE 3 + 5)	17,600	14,080	14,080	17,600	14,080	14,080	17,600	14,080	17,600	14,080	14,080	17,600	186,560
7 PAID OVERTIME HOURS	239	239	239	239	239	238	238	238	239	239	239	239	2,865
8 EMPLOYE ADDITIONS OR EXITS (LINE 26)						360	1,400	1,120	400				3,280
9 TOTAL MAN HOURS (LINE 6 + 7 + 8)	17,839	14,319	14,319	17,839	14,319	14,678	19,238	15,438	18,239	14,319	14,319	17,839	192,705
10 AVERAGE HOURLY RATE $	2.74	2.74	2.74	2.74	2.74	2.80	2.80	2.80	2.80	2.80	2.80	2.80	
11 COST BASED ON AVERAGE RATE (9 X 10) $	48,878.86	39,234.06	39,234.06	48,878.86	39,234.06	41,098.40	53,866.40	43,226.40	51,069.20	40,093.20	40,093.20	49,949.20	534,855.90
12 MERIT OR PROMOTIONAL INCREASES (LINE 39) $	256.00	287.00	351.00	555.50	530.50	567.00	776.00	704.00	1,092.50	1,026.00	1,109.50	1,476.00	8,731.00
13 TOTAL COST (LINE 11 + 12) $	49,134.86	39,521.06	39,585.06	49,434.36	39,764.56	41,665.40	54,642.40	43,930.40	52,161.70	41,119.20	41,202.70	51,425.20	543,586.90

EMPLOYE ADDITIONS OR EXITS (HOURS)

	NO.	JAN.	FEB.	MAR.	APR.	MAY	JUNE	JULY	AUG.	SEPT.	OCT.	NOV.	DEC.	TOTAL
14 JANUARY														
15 FEBRUARY														
16 MARCH														
17 APRIL														
18 MAY														
19 JUNE	7						360	1,400	1,120	400				3,280
20 JULY														
21 AUGUST														
22 SEPTEMBER														
23 OCTOBER														
24 NOVEMBER														
25 DECEMBER														
26 TOTAL	7						360	1,400	1,120	400				3,280

MERIT OR PROMOTIONAL INCREASES (DOLLARS)

	NO.	JAN.	FEB.	MAR.	APR.	MAY	JUNE	JULY	AUG.	SEPT.	OCT.	NOV.	DEC.	TOTAL
27 JANUARY	15	256.00	258.00	258.00	322.50	258.00	258.00	322.50	258.00	322.50	258.00	258.00	322.50	3,352.00
28 FEBRUARY	3		29.00	34.00	42.50	34.00	34.00	42.50	34.00	42.50	34.00	34.00	42.50	403.00
29 MARCH	10			59.00	120.00	96.00	96.00	120.00	96.00	120.00	96.00	96.00	120.00	1,019.00
30 APRIL	11				70.50	114.00	114.00	142.50	114.00	142.50	114.00	114.00	142.50	1,068.00
31 MAY	5					28.50	48.00	60.00	48.00	60.00	48.00	48.00	60.00	400.50
32 JUNE	4						17.00	62.50	50.00	62.50	50.00	50.00	62.50	354.50
33 JULY	6							26.00	50.00	62.50	50.00	50.00	62.50	301.00
34 AUGUST	3								54.00	70.00	56.00	56.00	70.00	306.00
35 SEPTEMBER	13									210.00	230.00	230.00	287.50	957.50
36 OCTOBER	10										90.00	130.00	162.50	382.50
37 NOVEMBER	6											43.50	120.00	163.50
38 DECEMBER	2												23.50	23.50
39 TOTAL	88	256.00	287.00	351.00	555.50	530.50	567.00	776.00	704.00	1,092.50	1,026.00	1,109.50	1,476.00	8,731.00

REQUESTED BY ______ DEPARTMENT HEAD RECOMMENDED BY ______ OFFICER OR MANAGER

FIG. 22–6. Payroll budget for purchasing department in a large company.

during the heavy vacation period of the regular employees. Item 9 shows the total man-hours and is the sum of lines 6, 7, and 8. Item 10 is an average hourly rate figure. This figure is derived by taking the total actual, straight time wages for 1 hr of the 88 people in the department as of January 1 and dividing it by 88. Experience has shown that using an average figure is accurate enough and greatly simplifies succeeding computations. Item 11 is arrived at by multiplying the hourly rate times the number of man-hours for each month. Item 12 is the total of contemplated promotional pay increases that will be given to some portion of the 88 employees each month of the year. It is taken from line 39 on the sheet which is a total or summation of all the increases being given for each of the months of the budget year, extended for the balance of the budget year.

Totaling items 11 and 12, regular pay plus the promotional increases, gives us the total payroll cost by month for each of the months in the budget year. This in turn is totaled by months, giving a grand total in the last column. This grand total is the total cost of payroll for operating the department of 88 employees for the budget year. Throughout the budget year minor fluctuations in employees' pay may take place. In some instances it may be holding up on promotional or merit increases; in other cases accelerating promotional or merit increase. These minor adjustments will have a very slight effect on the grand total at the end of the year. However, the experiences of companies who budget in this manner is that the total is never more than ½ to 1 per cent off from the estimate.

After the payroll budget has been computed, the next consideration is the amount of money that will be used for department operating supplies and materials and for other department expenses such as travel, hotels, meals, and the other incidentals which are incurred in the operation of the department. Here is where it is a big help to have the division heads of the functional groupings within the purchasing department supply the information. Although it is very difficult to arrive at a precise or absolutely accurate estimate of additional expenses, experience has again proved that division heads can estimate within 5 to 7 per cent the actual amount of money they will require for these additional expenses. To help them, the purchasing head or someone on his staff can prepare a list of the kinds of items each should consider in submitting his work-sheet budget estimate. These items can be taken from previous year's experience.

If the company employs a work order system, the kinds of expenses can be taken from the detailed expenditure sheets submitted to each department each month. It has been found in purchasing department operations that travel expenses are usually one of the largest additional expense considerations in budgeting. Meals and entertainment, in reciprocity for

OPERATING AND MAINTENANCE BUDGET ESTIMATE FOR 19___
MANAGER OF PURCHASES AND REAL ESTATE

Account No.	*Description of Account* Purchasing department:	*Estimate* *for 19___*	*Spent in* *19___* *(3 mos. est.)*	*Increase* *or decrease*	*Explanation of large differences or unusual items of expense*
62 F 1	Inspection division	$175,600.00	$161,450.00	$14,150.00	Includes addition of one inspector and increased travel costs
62 F 2	Standards division	76,900.00	65,260.00	11,640.00	Includes addition of one employee and increased printing costs
62 F 3	Traffic and services division	72,900.00	64,730.00	8,170.00	
62 F 4	Invoice clearance division	37,300.00	34,890.00	2,410.00	
62 F 5	Salvage sales division	38,600.00	35,290.00	3,310.00	
62 F 6	Electrical buying division	52,800.00	43,330.00	9,470.00	Vacancy for one employee will be filled
62 F 7	Mechanical buying division	72,100.00	63,020.00	9,080.00	Includes addition of one employee
62 F 8	Construction buying division	43,800.00	39,000.00	4,800.00	
62 F 9	Office equipment and supplies buying division	15,400.00	20,440.00	−5,040.00	One employee transferred to monthly payroll as of 7–1–___
62 F 10	Appliance buying division	19,900.00	17,590.00	2,310.00	
62 F 11	Food buying division	13,700.00	12,880.00	820.00	
62 F 12	Staff and general expense	56,200.00	50,500.00	5,700.00	
	Total—purchasing department	$675,200.00	$608,380.00	$66,820.00	

FIG. 22–7. Budget summary for purchasing department in a large company.

like treatment from salesmen and suppliers' representatives, are also large expense items. However, each purchasing department operating a budget system will have to make its own list of items to be considered for these additional expenses. The items in Fig. 22–3 can again serve as a guide in arriving at an acceptable list.

After the additional expenses have been determined from each of the separate functional divisions within the purchasing department, it remains now only to add these additional expenses to the payroll budget for each of these divisions and total them. In Fig. 22–7, which is a summary of a large department's budget, column 1 shows the work order number assigned to each of the divisions.

Column 2, "Description of Account," gives the divisions within the purchasing department to which the account numbers are assigned. Column 4, "Spent in 19–" (three months estimated), is included as a guide to show a comparison between past year's expenses and the estimate for the following year (column 3). Since the budget has to be submitted substantially ahead of the first of the year, so that the master budget may be prepared, it is necessary to estimate the amount of money that will be spent by each of the divisions for the last three months of the current year. This is done by taking the actual amount that was spent for the first nine months, dividing it by 9, and multiplying it by 12.

The fifth column on this sheet is the amount of increase or decrease in the budget estimate for the next year as compared with the amount that was actually spent during the current budget year. The last part of this sheet is devoted to an explanation of large differences or unusual items of expense. Note on the example, several of the items require explanation because they seemed disproportionately greater than normal or less than normal.

This summary sheet (Fig. 22–7) offers a quick bird's-eye view of the cost of operating a purchasing department for a year. The purchasing agent can quickly size up his estimated cost of operation for the coming year.

MAINTAINING THE BUDGET WITHIN THE PURCHASING DEPARTMENT

A budget is of little value as a measure of performance if the only attention given to it is at the beginning of the year when it is prepared. Between its preparation and the conclusion of the year for which it was prepared, the budget should be a living tool. If individual division heads within the purchasing department are asked to assist in preparation of the budget by supplying estimates of the cost of operating their groups,

DEPARTMENTAL BUDGET AND EXPENSE COMPARISON

DEPARTMENT PURCHASING DEPARTMENT MONTH OF SEP

ACCOUNT NUMBER		CURRENT MONTH BUDGET	CURRENT MONTH EXPENDITURES	TO DATE PRORATED BUDGET	TO DATE TOTAL EXPENDITURES
62F 1	INSPECTION DIVISION				
	LABOR		7 407		64 845
	EXPENSE		4 254		56 185
	TOTAL	10 115	11 661	98 622	121 030
62F 2	STANDARDS DIVISION				
	LABOR		4 285		41 741
	EXPENSE		688		7 203
	TOTAL	5 261	4 973	51 294	48 944
62F 3	TRAFFIC AND SERVICE DIVISION				
	LABOR		4 652		40 739
	EXPENSE		1 134		7 807
	TOTAL	6 192	5 786	60 372	48 546
62F 4	INVOICE CLEARANCE DIVISION				
	LABOR		2 827		25 456
	EXPENSE		36		710
	TOTAL	2 684	2 863	26 169	26 166
62F 5	SALVAGE SALES DIVISION				
	LABOR		2 761		24 403
	EXPENSE		200		2 061
	TOTAL	2 738	2 961	26 697	26 464
62F 6	ELECTRICAL BUYING DIVISION				
	LABOR		3 212		29 136
	EXPENSE		119		2 745
	TOTAL	3 923	3 331	38 247	31 881
62F 7	MECHANICAL BUYING DIVISION				
	LABOR		4 637		41 305
	EXPENSE		512		5 962
	TOTAL	4 469	5 149	43 572	47 267
62F 8	CONSTRUCTION BUYING DIVISION				
	LABOR		3 117		28 240
	EXPENSE		55		1 012
	TOTAL	3 038	3 172	29 622	29 252
62F 9	OFFICE EQUIP BUYING DIVISION				
	LABOR		1 036		15 116
	EXPENSE		11		212
	TOTAL	1 853	1 047	18 069	15 328
62F 10	APPLIANCE BUYING DIVISION				
	LABOR		1 361		12 737
	EXPENSE		496		749
	TOTAL	1 361	1 857	13 269	13 486
62F 11	FOOD BUYING DIVISION				
	LABOR		973		9 358
	EXPENSE				300
	TOTAL	976	973	9 519	9 658
62F 12	STAFF AND GENERAL				
	LABOR		2 283		22 531
	EXPENSE		988		15 052
	TOTAL	4 015	3 271	39 147	37 583
	TOTAL	46 625	47 044	454 599	455 605
	% OF BUDGET ESTIMATE USED			100%	

ISSUED BY BUDGET DIVISION

FIG. 22–8. Expense comparison summary for a purchasing department in a large company.

they should be periodically informed of the performance which is expected of them in adhering to their budget estimate. This is done, as has already been discussed, by giving them a monthly detailed statement of the charges made against their budget (Fig. 22–5). In this way the supervisor of the division is able to check the expenditures made against his account number. He is also able to correct expenditures charged against his account in error.

The purchasing head may not want to be concerned with such a detailed report. He probably would rather see a summary of the budget and expenses of all his divisions. Figure 22–8, "Expense Comparison Summary for a Purchasing Department in a Large Company," illustrates such a summary. On this sheet is shown a listing of the divisions, their work order numbers, and the labor and other expenses charged to each. To the right of the page is a summary of expenditures showing these four entries:

1. Budget for the current month
2. Expenditures for the current month
3. Prorated budget to date
4. Total expenditures to date

Obviously, items 1 and 2 and items 3 and 4 should be fairly close together.

The final entry is the per cent of budget estimate used. This may vary slightly from month to month. However, at the end of the year it should be very close to 100 per cent if a good job of budget preparation has been done.

BUDGET APPROVAL

In most large companies, the budget will require formal approval after submission by the purchasing officer. This same approval will be required of all other departments submitting their budget requests for the year. It is usually done by the officer responsible for preparation of the master budget. After the purchasing department budget has been approved, it will require additional approval from the budget director before changes can be made.

SPECIAL BUDGET REQUESTS

Often during the budget year it may be necessary to ask for authorization to spend money for some purpose unforeseen at the beginning of the budget year. To do this, a form such as that shown in Fig. 22–9 is used. This properly completed form follows the same channels as the original budget request.

REQUEST FOR WORK ORDER

WORK ORDER NO. (Filled in by Gen'l Acctg)

LOCATION
Purchasing Department and General Offices

DATE August 10, 19

DESCRIPTION
Study by University of Michigan

REASON
To study specific problems in connection with disposal of scrap and economies of alternate methods

STARTING DATE: August 29, 19 COMPLETION DATE: December 30, 19

DETAIL OF ESTIMATE		TOTAL
Request an amount as shown to hire University of Michigan consultants to make a comprehensive study of alternate methods of disposing of scrap materials. Purchasing Department will supervise this study since salvage operations are assigned to the Manager of Purchases.		$5,000.00
BUDGET ITEM NO. WORK REQUESTED BY		$5,000.00

Requests for work orders should be submitted in triplicate to the Property Department, Work Order Costs Group, 846 General Offices.

AUTHORIZED SIGNATURE

FIG. 22–9. Budget request for item not anticipated or included in regular budget at beginning of year.

If the request is for some out-of-the-ordinary purpose not usually considered as part of regular operating expenses, a separate work order may be established. In other instances it may be carried as a capital expense, particularly in connection with a construction program, even though in itself it is not real property. These determinations are usually made by the accounting department.

PURCHASING DEPARTMENT PROPERTY BUDGET

Each budget year there will be certain items of property, such as desks, chairs, typewriters, etc., that will have to be budgeted for in the purchasing department. These are items that are carried on the books as part of the physical assets of the company. Where the operating expenses are written off during the budget year, the property items will be carried on the books until amortized. The maintenance of capitalized items is considered part of operating expense. However, the purchase of new items, either as replacement for obsolescence or as new acquisition, must be budgeted and accounted for.

A company using a work order system of budget and financial control has a separate set of work orders against which capital expenditures are made. For this reason a separate budget request is used in asking for money for this purpose. Figure 22–10 shows a property budget request. In this case it is called a "Proposed Construction Project." No attempt is made to spell out in detail certain small items of miscellaneous furniture

PROPOSED CONSTRUCTION PROJECT

PROJECT NO.

GROUP NO. A & B CLASS OF WORK 4 & 5 DATE ISSUED October 13, 19

LOCATION AND GENERAL DESCRIPTION OF PROJECT

Miscellaneous office equipment and furniture for the Purchasing Department.

REASON FOR WORK

REQUIRED 19____$

REQUIRED 19____$ 4,345.00

TOTAL COST $

WORK TO BE STARTED WORK TO BE COMPLETED

BUDGET ITEM NO.	BY H. D. Williamson DESCRIPTION OF WORK INVOLVED	Group	Class	ESTIMATED COST
4	IBM Electric typewriters	A	4	$1,725.00
2	Desks, typist	B	5	260.00
2	Desks, standard	B	5	280.00
4	Chairs, side	B	5	180.00
2	Typewriters, standard	B	5	300.00
4	Typewriters, standard	A	4	600.00
	Miscellaneous office furniture and equipment	B	4 & 5	1,000.00
	Total			$4,345.00

RECOMMENDED BY DATE

APPROVED CONTROLLER

NOTED ASST. CONTROLLER AND BUDGET SUPERVISOR

REQUESTED BY

FIG. 22–10. Budget request for purchasing department capital additions.

and equipment that may be required during the year. The major items required, the estimated cost, and the group and class are shown. *Group* refers to the need for the items, such as:

Group A. *Essential* (projects necessary to supply demands which will exist at their completion, and other projects absolutely necessary for the current year; also includes projects required on account of government-required improvements)

Group B. *Advisable* (projects which will improve quality of service)

Group C. *Desirable* (projects which might reduce operating and maintenance costs, but may be considered deferrable beyond the budget period; these should be accompanied by a full explanation of the estimated annual savings in labor, material, etc.)

Class refers to the purpose for which the items will be used, such as:

Class 1. Extensions to provide additional capacity definitely required by growth or for new business

Class 2. Work necessitated by public improvements or requested by customers

Class 3. Elimination of hazards to life, property, or continuity of service, including jobs involving employee relations

Class 4. Replacement of worn-out, obsolete, or inadequate equipment

Class 5. Equipment to effect operating economies sufficient to justify the investment

Class 6. Refinement of equipment or conditions in ways that do not directly produce economies

Of course the request must be properly signed by the purchasing officer and approved by the responsible higher levels of management before purchases can be made against the work order. For budget purposes, it is assumed that these items are required on the first day of the budget year and hence no attempt is made to schedule their purchase during specific months of the year. Many companies do, however, seek to effect some control over these capital expenditures by requiring a separate budget release on all items costing over $500 (or some other specified amount) even though properly budgeted. This also serves to ensure that sufficient funds are on hand to meet current expenses.

THE THIRTEEN-PERIOD BUDGET

Up to now most of this discussion has dealt with conventional budget periods of calendar months. In some instances another classification is used. It is known as the thirteen-period budget. Instead of 12 calendar months, 13 equal periods of 4 weeks each are used. Newspapers in particular prefer this timing since each period includes an equal number of Saturdays and Sundays. This is understandably of particular significance to them.

The budget considerations here are no different. However, it is a more common practice to budget for each period as it comes up rather than on a yearly basis. This, of course, makes a correspondingly more sensitive budget estimate. Each month's budget request includes a comparison of the actual costs for the corresponding period of the previous year and for the immediately preceding period of the same year. Figure 22–11 shows a completed typical budget estimate form for one of these periods.

The budget estimate for the period under consideration is shown in the fourth column. When the period has been completed, the actual expenditures are entered in column 5 and the comparison of actual expenses and estimated expenses noted in the sixth column.

EXPENSE BUDGET SHEET

2nd Period 19___ Department Purchasing and Building Operation Account No. 428 -

From: Through:	13 Last Mo. Actual		Last Yr. Actual		New Budget		Actual		Over or Under	
Mis. Unclassified										
Telegrams	60	81	12	60	32	19	44	74	+ 12	55
Telephone Tolls	Cr. 48	74	32	95	20	00	Cr. 72	67	- 92	67
Telephone Exchange	1574	52	1743	22	1743	22	1743	22		00
Books and Periodicals	19	16	7	65	7	50	17	65	+ 10	15
Suppers and Lunches					5	00	1	10	- 3	90
Carfare and Taxi	3	00								
Traveling Expense			68	01	100	00				
Water	4	12			4	12	Cr. 867	79	+ 871	91
Organization Memberships							10	00	+ 10	00
Stamps	49	58	42	18	46	89	35	76	- 11	13
Stationery and Supplies	73	58	88	33	75	32	69	19	- 6	13
Sundry Supplies	256	82	7	47	75	00	83	47	+ 8	47
Freight, Express & Drayage	9	58			8	42	6	41	- 2	01
Rags, Oil and Grease										
Light and Power	8	58	8	58	8	58	8	58		00
Building Expense	2223	42	1469	63	1575	34	1582	94	+ 7	60
Electrical Maintenance										
Insurance										
Vacations	966	00	966	00	1038	00	1038	00		00
Interdepartment	Cr. 412	53	Cr. 149	41	Cr. 208	19	Cr. 89	41	+ 118	78
Total Expense Other Than Payroll	4787	90	4297	21	4531	39	3611	19	- 920	20
Total Payroll	25323	37	17275	79	18933	64	19024	19	+ 90	55
Grand Total	30111	27	21573	00	23465	03	22635	38	- 829	65

FIG. 22–11. Expense budget sheet for the thirteen-period budget.

Accompanying the expense budget sheet when it is submitted at the beginning of each budget period is an explanation of the differences between last year's actual expenses and this year's estimate. This explanation is shown in Fig. 22–12. For ease in making a quick evaluation of expenses, detail is omitted. Only *payroll* and *other expense* differences are noted.

Again, after the budget period has been completed, and all expenses tabulated, the purchasing head is required to explain actual expenses that exceeded or were less than his estimate. This is done by a form similar to that used in explaining his original estimate.

The examples used here to illustrate the application of budgeting to 13 periods resulted from a very simple, workable procedure established by one company. It has been in operation for many years and further emphasizes that budgeting need not be a cumbersome process. The account number, in this case No. 428, is used for identifying all charges made against the budget for the purchasing department. The explanation

BUDGET EXPLANATIONS

2nd Period 19__

To: L.B.
W.R.H.

Date 1/25/

From: T.A.C. Dept. Head

Dept. Purchasing & Building
No. 428-

Explanation of variances in budget compared with prior year.

Explanation	Over Last Year	Under Last Year
Payroll-straight time	1657.85	
Payroll-overtime	.00	.00
Other differences:	234.18	
Payroll straight time exceeds last year due to wage advances and one addition to executive payroll.		
Other than payroll accounts are up in nine categories, down in four, and same in two. Principal differences are in Vacation Reserve, up $72.00, and Bldg. Exp., up $105.71.		

FIG. 22–12. Explanation of differences in current period estimated budget over corresponding period a year ago—thirteen-period budget system.

given for a sizable credit, as noted in Fig. 22–13, indicates that an improper account number was used in allocating charges against the purchasing department in the previous budget period. Having been detected by the purchasing head and called to the attention of the accounting people, a credit is issued. Without the formality of a budget system such errors might go undetected for many months and might only be caught by a very careful annual audit. Indeed, they might never be uncovered at all.

ACTUAL EXPLANATIONS

2nd Period 19___

Date 3/6/

To: L.B.
W.R.H.

From: T.A.C. Dept. Head Dept. Purchasing
No. 428

Explanation of variance between actual this year and budget

Explanation	Over Budget	Under Budget
Payroll-straight time	89.09	
Payroll-overtime	1.46	
Other differences:		920.20
Both payroll straight time and overtime closely approximate budget, exceeding it by less than ½%. Other than payroll accounts are up in six categories, down in seven, and same in three. Amount under budget is due principally to credit of $872.40 for water to correct charge posted to this account in error in Period 1.		

FIG. 22-13. Explanation of actual budget expenditures for one period—thirteen-period budget system.

MATERIALS BUDGETING

A relatively new concept being employed by a growing number of enterprises whose end products remain relatively stable in design is the use of a materials budget. This approach employs the same principles used in personnel or expense budgeting, with the exception that anticipated material costs are used instead of salary, office expense, telephone, and telegraph costs, etc., as already discussed.

The major benefits of materials budgeting are:

1. To assist financial management in forecasting profits and cash flow
2. To establish a "bogey," or objective, for purchasing management against which purchasing performance can be measured

Side benefits include emphasizing the importance of the purchasing function and its ability to contribute directly to company profits.

This approach to budgeting utilizes current and historical information as a base to forecast or anticipate material cost levels. The factors that should be considered in adjusting current material cost levels are:

1. Anticipated commodity prices and supplier's labor economics.

2. Material usage:
   a. Specification
   b. Volume

Before attempting to prepare the budget, the purchasing executive must identify those areas affecting cost over which he feels he has no control, some control, or most control. For example, under commodity prices and supplier's labor economics he might list in the "no control" category:

1. Economic spirals of commodity price levels resulting from national or international developments (steel or lead price fluctuations)
2. Design changes specified by the engineering department for quality improvement or styling consideration
3. General freight rate increase
4. Significant changes in labor economics on a national scale

"Some or most control" could include:

1. Negotiations
2. Introduction of competitive conditions not previously possible
3. Reevaluation of inbound costs, including packaging and supplier's delivery methods

Under material usage the purchasing manager might detail in the "little or no control" category:

1. Operational scrap
2. Obsolescence
3. Improper interplant handling
4. Faulty specifications
5. Improper design
6. Inadequate facilities and equipment for processing

"Some or most control" might be:

1. Volume and releasing or ordering patterns (within the limits established by the sales department and imposed by prudent warehousing)
2. The establishment of some type of receiving inspection norms where the lack of such may have resulted in premium prices
3. The establishment of material specifications and quality standards (with the help of engineering) when the lack of such information has prevented clarity in purchasing
4. Timely delivery

Using the foregoing outline, a hypothetical television company making a single product might develop a simplified materials budget in the following manner:

Step 1

Complete a current, priced bill of material of purchased parts.

Television-Receiver Bill of Material

Part no.	Item	No. used	Current prices	
			Per unit	Per set
101	Chassis	1	$ 3.00	$ 3.00
102	Cabinet	1	16.00	16.00
103	Tube—picture	1	18.00	18.00
104	Tube	2	1.00	2.00
105	Tube	3	1.50	4.50
106	Tube	2	1.25	2.50
107	Tube	2	1.00	2.00
108	Tube	1	1.00	1.00
109	Wiring (per set)	1	0.75	0.75
110	Miscellaneous parts (per set)	1	0.25	0.25
Total purchased cost per set				$50.00

Step 2

Identify factors to be used in projecting possible cost changes for the duration of the forecast.

Design ($0.08 increase)

CHASSIS: $0.15 decrease anticipated in March due to reduction in gauge of steel used in chassis from .08 (inch thickness) steel to .06 steel.

CABINET: $0.25 increase expected in January due to the addition of a decal for identification.

MISCELLANEOUS: $0.02 decrease expected in April through the elimination of bolt, nut, and washer assembly.

Economics ($1.41 increase)

CABINET: $0.75 increase anticipated in April due to posted wood prices and new labor contract.

PICTURE TUBE: $0.36 increase expected in June due to new labor contract and material cost increase.

OTHER TUBES: $0.30 increase anticipated in March due to new labor contract and material cost increase.

Source ($0.81 decrease)	CHASSIS:	$0.70 decrease expected in March due to new source.
	TUBE:	$0.11 decrease anticipated in September due to expected new source.
Negotiation ($0.27 decrease)	PICTURE TUBE:	$0.20 decrease expected in May due to vendor process realignment.
	OTHER TUBES:	$0.07 decrease anticipated in March due to competitive conditions.
Other ($0.08 decrease)	CHASSIS:	$0.05 decrease expected in February due to new packaging specifications.
	PICTURE TUBE:	$0.05 decrease anticipated in March because of change in f.o.b. point.
	TUBES:	$0.02 increase expected in September due to location of new vendor plant.

Details used in the development of anticipated economic increases:

	Wood fabrication industry	Glass fabrication industry
Contract-renewal date	4-1-66	3-1-66* 6-1-66*
Present hourly labor rate	$2.35	$2.60
Anticipated settlement with union representing industry, including direct and indirect labor, would establish the following increase:		
Cost	$0.20	$0.20
Per cent	8.5	7.7
An analysis of components supplied by our vendors indicates a labor content of	30%	20%

* Two unions involved—picture tubes and vacuum tubes.

	Part number						
	102	103	104	105	106	107	108
Based on our analysis, labor-contract settlements will increase our cost as follows:							
30% labor content	$0.41						
20% labor content	...	$0.28	$0.03	$0.04	$0.04	$0.04	$0.02
Expected increase in material prices	0.34	0.08	0.03	0.04	0.03	0.02	0.01
Total anticipated economic increase	$0.75	$0.36	$0.06	$0.08	$0.07	$0.06	$0.03

Step 3 Adjust the current bill of material to reflect forecast and calendarize anticipated changes.

Television-Receiver Production Material Budget

Part no.	Item	No. used	Current prices		Anticipated changes—increase/(decrease)					Year-end prices	
			Per unit	Per set	Design	Economics	Source	Negotiation	Other	Per unit	Per set
101	Chassis	1	$ 3.00	$ 3.00	$(0.15)	$. . . .	$(0.70)	$. . . .	$(0.05)	$ 2.10	$ 2.10
102	Cabinet	1	16.00	16.00	0.25	0.75	. . . .	. . . .	. . .	17.00	17.00
103	Tube—picture	1	18.00	18.00	. . . .	0.36	. . . .	(0.20)	(0.05)	18.11	18.11
104	Tube	2	1.00	2.00	. . . .	0.06	. . . .	(0.02)	. . . .	1.02	2.04
105	Tube	3	1.50	4.50	. . . .	0.08	. . . .	(0.04)	. . . .	1.51	4.54
106	Tube	2	1.25	2.50	. . . .	0.07	(0.06)	. . . .	0.01	1.26	2.52
107	Tube	2	1.00	2.00	. . . .	0.06	(0.05)	. . . .	0.01	1.01	2.02
108	Tube	1	1.00	1.00	. . . .	0.03	. . . .	(0.01)	. . . .	1.02	1.02
109	Wiring (per set)	1	0.75	0.75	. . . .	. . . .	. . . .	. . . .	. . . .	0.75	0.75
110	Miscellaneous Parts (per set)	1	0.25	0.25	(0.02)	. . . .	. . . .	. . . .	. . . .	0.23	0.23
Total cost per set.				$50.00	$0.08	$1.41	$(0.81)	$(0.27)	$(0.08)	. . . .	$50.33

Calendarization of Anticipated Unit-price Change—increase/(decrease)

	Jan.	Feb.	Mar.	Apr.	May	June	July	Aug.	Sept.	Oct.	Nov.	Dec.
Design.	$0.25	$ 0.25	$ 0.10	$ 0.08	$ 0.08	$ 0.08	$ 0.08	$ 0.08	$ 0.08	$ 0.08	$ 0.08	$ 0.08
Economics.	. . . .	. . . .	0.30	1.05	1.05	1.41	1.41	1.41	1.41	1.41	1.41	1.41
Source.	. . . .	. . . .	(0.70)	(0.70)	(0.70)	(0.70)	(0.70)	(0.70)	(0.81)	(0.81)	(0.81)	(0.81)
Negotiation.	. . . .	. . . .	(0.07)	(0.07)	(0.27)	(0.27)	(0.27)	(0.27)	(0.27)	(0.27)	(0.27)	(0.27)
Other.	. . . .	(0.05)	(0.10)	(0.10)	(0.10)	(0.10)	(0.10)	(0.10)	(0.08)	(0.08)	(0.08)	(0.08)
Total adjustments	$ 0.25	$ 0.20	$(0.47)	$ 0.26	$ 0.06	$ 0.42	$ 0.42	$ 0.42	$ 0.33	$ 0.33	$ 0.33	$ 0.33
Sales units.	80	80	100	100	110	90	80	80	90	100	110	110
Total effect of adjustments (see step 4).	$20	$16	$(47)	$26	$7	$38	$34	$34	$30	$33	$36	$36

Step 4

Summarize the effect of anticipated changes and prepare calendarized materials budget.

Television-Receiver Production Material Budget

	Jan.	Feb.	Mar.	Apr.	May	June	July	Aug.	Sept.	Oct.	Nov.	Dec.
Sales*												
Units	80	80	100	100	110	90	80	80	90	100	110	110
Amount ($100 per unit)	$8,000	$8,000	$10,000	$10,000	$11,000	$9,000	$8,000	$8,000	$9,000	$10,000	$11,000	$11,000
Production material at current prices ($50 per unit)†	4,000	4,000	5,000	5,000	5,500	4,500	4,000	4,000	4,500	5,000	5,500	5,500
Adjustments to current prices:												
Design	20	20	10	8	9	7	5	5	7	8	9	9
Economics	...	...	30	105	116	127	115	115	127	141	155	155
Source	...	...	(70)	(70)	(77)	(63)	(56)	(56)	(73)	(81)	(89)	(89)
Negotiations	...	...	(7)	(7)	(30)	(24)	(22)	(21)	(24)	(27)	(30)	(30)
Other	...	(4)	(10)	(10)	(11)	(9)	(8)	(8)	(7)	(8)	(9)	(9)
Total adjustment	20	16	(47)	26	7	38	34	34	30	33	36	36
Total material budget	$4,020	$4,016	$ 4,953	$ 5,026	$ 5,507	$4,538	$4,034	$4,034	$4,530	$ 5,033	$ 5,536	$ 5,536

*Sales projections furnished by sales department.

†Assuming current bill of material, current prices and two month inventory build-up.

Step 5

Measure progress of actual experience against budget.

Television-Receiver Performance Measurement per Unit

	January		December	
	Authorized	Actual	Authorized	Actual
Design	$0.25	$0.25	$0.08	$0.08
Economics	...	...	1.41	1.32
Source	...	...	(0.81)	(0.81)
Negotiations	...	...	(0.27)	(0.33)
Other:				
F.o.b. point	...	...	(0.03)	(0.01)
Packaging	...	...	(0.05)	(0.05)
Total	$0.25	$0.25	$0.30	$0.20
Variance from authorized—over/(under)	0		$(0.10)	

Utilizing the materials budget approach, with a relatively simple internal reporting structure, purchasing can tabulate the effect on costs (and profits) of purchase order changes granted to suppliers. Such tabulations also permit relatively accurate estimates of the cost-change impact to be readily available at all times.

More important, this information allows before-the-fact evaluation and appraisal of cost factors which can often be avoided through timely remedial action. An added feature is that purchasing is provided with a tool that permits the reappraisal of corporate policies covering changes in cost levels in initial stages, rather than "too late" or after-the-fact.

CONCLUSION

Regardless of whether it is a large company or a small company, the very mechanics of preparing a budget make the purchasing officer more aware of costs. To the degree that establishing goals is helpful in measuring the performance of the department, there is no more realistic goal that the purchasing agent can provide for his guidance than the establishment of an operating budget. The budget should be a challenge to efficient operations rather than a millstone around his neck. Again, the consensus of companies who have used budgets is that once experience has been gained in their use, adherences to the budget within 2 or 3 per cent are commonplace. In a large company, major changes to a budget are seldom made unless it is known that expenses are going to exceed 10 per cent of the budgeted amount. Seldom are budgets changed where expenditures are going to be 10 per cent less than the budget estimate. Most large companies do require, however, that whenever a department adds to its personnel, or requires a sum of money in excess of an amount such as $500 or $1,000 that was not included in the original budget estimate, a supplemental budget request be issued. The purpose of the supplemental budget request is to serve as a check against the requesting department for unusual or extraordinary expenses which had not been included in the original budget estimate.

Summarizing, formal budgeting has come to be accepted as a necessary management tool. The involvement of all levels of management in the preparation and performance of the budget is recognized as an important part of their development. As already mentioned, budgeting must be keyed to some financial criteria established by management. It has to bear a relationship to some yardstick such as direct labor costs, manufacturing costs, sales billed, or dollars of material input. Just to set a budget figure, record expenses, and periodically review the budget is not enough. When properly administered, a budget system ensures management of a more orderly operated business.

SELECTED BIBLIOGRAPHY

Bierman, Harold, Jr., and Seymour Smidt: *Capital Budgeting Decision,* The Macmillan Company, New York, 1960

Branch, Melville C.: *Corporate Planning Process,* American Management Association, New York, 1962

Budgeting (bi-monthly, $10/yr.), Budget Executives Institute, Oxford, Ohio

Devine, Carl Thomas: *Cost Accounting and Analysis,* The Macmillan Company, New York, 1950

Eiteman, Wilford J.: *Graphic Budgets,* Masterco Press, 1949

Henrici, Stanley B.: *Standard Costs for Manufacturing,* McGraw-Hill Book Company, New York, 1947

Klingman, H. F.: *Business Budgeting,* prepared for Controllership Foundation, Inc., 1958

Knight, W. D., and E. H. Weinwurm: *Managerial Budgeting,* The Macmillan Company, New York, 1964

Lang, Theodore: *Cost Accountants' Handbook,* The Ronald Press Company, New York, 1952

Newman, Wm. H.: "Administrative Action," chap. 24, *Budgetary Control,* 7th ed., Prentice-Hall, Inc., Englewood Cliffs, N.J., 1956

Williams, R. I., and Lillian Doris: *Encyclopedia of Accounting Systems,* vols. 1–5, Prentice-Hall, Inc., Englewood Cliffs, N.J., 1957

For other references, see list of purchasing books in Section 26, "Library and Catalog File."

SECTION 23

SELECTION AND TRAINING OF PURCHASING PERSONNEL

Editor

Glenn H. Reinier, Director of Purchases, Abbott Laboratories, North Chicago, Illinois

Associate Editors

Dr. Kenneth Cox, Professor, School of Business Administration, North Texas State University, Denton, Texas

Douglas V. Smith, Consultant—Purchasing Education, General Electric Company, New York, New York

The industrial purchasing man of tomorrow will be asked to carry more and more of management's responsibilities. On the shoulders of today's purchasing manager and his management rests the sober responsibility for the selection of the right men to take over these heavier duties.

Indicative of the stature granted to the purchasing function are the increasing references to it as a management function. Heads of purchasing departments are being asked to join the "management team" in many more companies than was the case a few years ago. Solicitations by management consultant firms for men[1] of executive timber and purchasing

[1] Reference to "men" in this section, as well as throughout this handbook, includes both women and men, and the use of the word "man" rather than the word "person" is more of an effort to be conventional than to be literal. Many highly qualified women have distinguished themselves in the field of purchasing, and the future opportunities for women in the purchasing function appear unlimited. Women are especially qualified to further the profession's efforts to maintain high standards of fairness and ethics. The requirements of education, experience, background, etc., will be the same whether the person being considered is a woman or a man. Hence, it has seemed less fussy to use the single masculine reference throughout this section on the selection and training of buyers.

background emphasize the importance top management places on purchasing experience. It points up, too, the absence, all too often, of properly trained "insiders." This handbook is dedicated to the task of smoothing the path toward proper execution of one of the purchasing man's very important tasks today. By its use, not only will he be better informed, but he will assist in training others in a more effective way.

ESSENTIAL CONSIDERATIONS

Proper selection and training of new personnel is vital to the purchasing function. It is a management job. *The selection of future buyers must have top management attention.*

This section is devoted to methods of selection and training of purchasing people, with the emphasis placed on buyers, including their assistants. No less important are the requirements for qualified clerks and stenographers. Every person engaged in purchasing should be above reproach in character, integrity, thoroughness, and neatness. The buyer must be surrounded by competent and interested people.

Tried and proved techniques are described in the pages that follow. They can be adapted to the particular needs of the individual reader.

The industrial society will expect the industrial buyer in the future to hold aloft high ideals of performance. To him will come credit or discredit for changing standards of ethics in industry. Selection of men and women who believe in high standards will ensure that the purchasing profession will make its proper contribution as the years pass.

Proper attention to the selection of new employees is necessary to avoid costly failures later. Many years and many dollars of training costs are often required to train even the best selected men or women for the responsibilities of purchasing. If it is recognized that whenever a buyer negotiates a contract he commits his company to important expenditures, it will be evident to the reader that the buyer is in a strategic position to help ensure the company's success. In many companies, the purchasing department spends 50 per cent or more of the sales dollar in the procurement of the required materials, supplies, and services. Competent performance by the buyer is "profit making"; anything less is "profit taking."

Proper selection may require but a few hours and relatively little cost if the following few simple rules are followed:

1. Prepare a tentative long-range plan for the new employee now and in *the future.*
2. List responsibilities the new employee may *someday* assume.

3. Write a description of the duties the new employee will *ultimately* be expected to perform.
4. Use the company facilities; i.e., personnel department, executive training department, executives, and department heads and their records in the search for candidates.
5. Use *recognized* testing techniques to determine aptitudes, knowledge, and mental ability.
6. *Personally* investigate all references.
7. Prepare a *check list* of questions and topics for the interview.
8. Allow *adequate* time for the interviews.
9. Carefully evaluate *all* data, keeping in mind the ultimate *duties* and *responsibilities* of the man.
10. Establish *realistic* salary scales.

SALARY CONSIDERATIONS

The importance of a realistic salary scale cannot be overemphasized when hiring new employees or in the case of regular staff members during their career with the company. Of course, other important considerations are advancement potential and the reputation of the company.

According to the National Association of Purchasing Agents in its booklet, *Guide to the Selection of Competent Buyers,* the best recruiting, testing, and selecting program may be wasted if the job applicant can better himself financially elsewhere, other things being equal. Salary scales must accurately reflect the degree of responsibility. At the same time, they must also be comparable with like levels of responsibility in other phases of the company's business and with other buying positions in the industry or area in which the applicant is interested. Salary scales must also be flexible, so that they take into account varying degrees of education, experience, and pertinent abilities of the applicant. A fixed salary scale, while the easiest to administer and perhaps defend, may rule out many job applicants who feel that they have something to offer beyond the average. It is this "beyond the average" grouping from which purchasing executives are drawn.

The foregoing booklet also states: "The human element precludes any possibility of categorically listing starting salaries for buyers. Added to this are the considerations of what a company can pay, the position of purchasing in the company organization, area pay differentials, and many other variables that make it inadvisable to list specific rates of pay. The constantly changing picture in the supply and demand of qualified personnel is also a big factor in the variability of pay rates."

Affiliated associations, as well as other local agencies, are often in a position to advise on the going rates for the classification of people whom they represent, according to the NAPA. College placement services at universities can advise on the rates offered recent graduates. In large companies, wage comparison data are often kept by personnel or employment departments. These sources should be tapped by the purchasing executive as often as necessary to keep him informed. In the final analysis, salary determination must be mutually satisfactory to applicant and employer.

MAKING A PLAN

A plan is as necessary to the efficient utilization of people in industry as the proper flow of cash is essential to the efficient manufacture and marketing of its products. The "plan" may be *short range* or *long range.* It is best to have *both.* An analysis should be made to determine how the new employee will fit the plans. Both plans should provide:

1. A training schedule
2. The initial assignment
3. Probable schedule of job promotions
4. Subordinate requirements
5. New facilities contemplated

The "long-range" plan should further provide:

1. Additional personnel expansion related to probable volume increases
2. New operations necessary as business grows
3. Elimination of operations unnecessary as department grows
4. Anticipated salary adjustments
5. Supplemental education or off-the-job training
6. Purchasing association activities

DESCRIBING THE JOB

The job description will consist of a definition of the duties and responsibilities and a description of the operations required to perform them. The job description may be a detailed account or a mere outline or list, but, in any case, its existence as a ready reference is necessary for orderly training. The job description will include:

1. Title
2. Primary functions
3. Supervision received
4. Supervision or direction exercised
5. General duties and responsibilities
   a. Areas and nature of direction exercised as line responsibility

   b. Persons, firms, associations, and agencies with whom liaison shall be maintained
   c. Market and management activities of direct interest and required study
   d. Job's relationship to other jobs
6. Activities and operations
   a. Interviews—with whom and for what reasons
   b. Order placement—what materials are bought
   c. Correspondence activities demanded
   d. Relationships and activities with suppliers to be maintained
   e. Reports expected, including subject matter and periods to be covered
7. Requirements
   a. Education
   b. Experience
   c. Personal

According to a recent survey by the National Industrial Conference Board, job descriptions are less popular with procurement managers than with top management, 90 per cent of whom want written descriptions used. Their value during the recruiting and training of new people appears to justify this attitude.

Two typical purchasing job descriptions (sometimes called job specifications) follow. These are for an assistant purchasing agent and the manager of chemical purchases, respectively. They have been taken from two different industrial fields. Also following is Example 3, a buyer's model job or position description prepared by the NAPA Development Committee on Intracompany Activities, and published in the NAPA educational booklet, *Guide to the Selection of Competent Buyers.* All three provide the essential data which will be helpful to the candidate in his sizing up the job and to his supervisor in the training that must follow. Others are listed in Section 2.

Job Descriptions

EXAMPLE 1. **Assistant Purchasing Agent in Gas/Oil Pipeline Transmission Industry**

JOB SPECIFICATION

Title: Assistant Purchasing Agent
Department: Purchasing

DESCRIPTION

Primary Functions: Procure and expedite material and equipment, transfer and/or sell surplus or scrap material. Supervise and train Purchasing Department office and field personnel.

Supervision Received: Purchasing Agent/Director of Purchases.

Supervision or Direction Exercised: Expediting Section–Purchase Order Control Section–Buying Section–Field Receiving Clerks and Warehousemen.

GENERAL DUTIES AND RESPONSIBILITIES

(1) Enforce throughout the company and subsidiary companies established company purchasing policies governing negotiations, emergency purchases, disposition or sale of surplus and scrap on the level as high as comparable job classifications (Assistant Superintendent Compressor Stations, Assistant Superintendent Pipeline Department, etc.; see Job Specification Purchasing Agent/Director of Purchases).

(2) Devote sufficient time to keep abreast of current government affairs, industrial development, production and price trends–spend approximately one quarter of each year's time visiting suppliers and manufacturing plants, government agencies, the company's various field locations and construction sites.

(3) Interview sales and technical representatives relative to production and price trends in their respective industries–cultivate friendly relations with all suppliers.

(4) Review Dun & Bradstreet and financial reports (suppliers'); keep informed of Workmen's Compensation Laws, law of contracts, patents, warranty, title, etc.; refer and consult with Purchasing Agent on extraordinary problems.

(5) Correspond with and telephone frequently to vendors relative to delivery, substitutions, inquiries and quotations, damage claims, discrepancies in billing and misinterpretations of purchase orders, contracts, etc., and on the request of other departments.

(6) Process requisitions–place verbal and formal orders on suitable vendors for construction, operating and maintenance materials–office equipment, furniture, supplies, printing, etc. Issue emergency orders; tabulate bids; supervise buyers and assistant buyers in the above procedure.

(7) Make available to management material delivery and dollar commitment reports–quarterly reports on dollar value of orders placed on all vendors, dollar value of emergency purchase orders, other reports as required.

(8) Meet and discuss departmental procedures and programs with Purchasing Agent, Buyers, Expediters (weekly).

(9) Supervise Expediting Section.

(10) Supervise Purchase Order Control Section.

(11) Supervise Construction Material Field Clerks and Warehousemen.

(12) Route minor shipments via transportation arteries to the best possible advantage. Authorize the dispatch of company owned equipment.

(13) Use blueprints, drawings, and specifications in inter-company discussions–during contract negotiations, etc.

(14) Design department printed forms; issue instructions for their use; contribute to company's purchasing manual. Establish department procedures, filing systems, methods, etc.

(15) Supervise departmental personnel and review copies of their correspondence with vendors (in the numerous problems related to the completion of purchase orders) to assure no infractions of company or departmental policy.

(16) Assist in company and departmental training programs; consult with Purchasing Agent on hiring or transferring personnel; interview suggested applicants for positions directly in job classification supervised (Expediting Section, Purchase Order Control Section, etc.).

(17) Cultivate the friendship of purchasing agents in other companies; subscribe to and attend NAPA meetings and other activities applicable to company and department promotion and interest.

(18) Contribute information, suggestions, etc., to business associations and government research studies.

(19) Be capable of assuming and directing the supervision of programs necessitated by emergency government orders. If so delegated, act as Manager Priority Section, liaison man between company and government. Advise Purchasing Agent and Director of Purchases, operating and executive committees on government rules and regulations pertaining to priorities, restrictions, construction (other than F.P.C.), inventories, etc.

(20) Promote company's welfare. Visit, consult, and correspond with government officials. Explain to government the necessity for government approval or intercession in obtaining material and/or assistance in stepping up deliveries or approving the release of material.

(21) Submit reports, drawings, etc., to the government when so required.

(22) Approve overtime, time records, and expense reports.

Requirements

Education: Four years college or equivalent, plus one or more years of special courses within management curriculum.

Experience: Five years' experience in pipeline (oil or gas) transmission industry, preferably within own company.

* * *

EXAMPLE 2: **Manager of Chemical Purchases in Pharmaceutical Industry**

Job Description

Title: Manager, Chemical Purchases

Department: Purchasing

Principal Duties: Supervise all purchases of chemicals. Procure and expedite inorganic and synthetic chemicals including petrochemical solvents. Recommend policies pertinent to chemical buying. Train personnel in this division.

Supervision Received: Director of Purchases/Purchasing Agent

Supervision Exercised: Chemical Buyer, Chemicals Order Clerk, Chemicals Expediter and Assistant Chemical Buyer

General Duties and Responsibilities

(1) Approve prices, contracts, allocations of business and plant visitations by chemical buying personnel in connection with all chemical purchases.
(2) Expedite delivery of all chemicals.
(3) Recommend buying policies for the Director of Purchases' approval.
(4) Recommend promotions, transfers, and other personnel changes in this division for the Director of Purchases' approval.
(5) Maintain regular liaison with all chemical suppliers, research, product development, and using departments, and report important developments to the Director of Purchases. Attend chemical and technical group meetings.
(6) Support and participate in the NAPA and join its Chemical Group as well as the local Association of Purchasing Agents, and the local Drug and Chemical Association.
(7) Study periodicals listed in the Purchasing Library Reference Section for circulation to the Chemical Section, and recommend additions or deletions from this list.

Activities and Operations

(1) Examine all requisitions of this assigned group and select suppliers to receive the orders. Instruct the Chemical Order Clerk to prepare for typing and mailing in accordance with the Purchasing Procedure Manual.
(2) Interview sales and technical representatives of all chemical suppliers of this assigned chemical group and maintain friendly relations with all chemical suppliers' personnel.
(3) Use the telephone as much as possible for expediting, quotations, complaints and other inquiries, confirming by letter or other document operations demanded in the Procedure Manual. Machine dictation should be used whenever practicable.
(4) Visit the facilities of at least ten important suppliers annually and spend some time each week with the men who handle and use the chemicals purchased.
(5) Provide the following for the Director of Purchases:

Daily:

(a) Refer copies of new orders placed having a value in excess of $1000.
(b) Prepare a list of chemical price changes.
(c) Refer copies of correspondence on complaints and new materials.

Weekly:

(a) Prepare summaries of new suppliers under consideration.
(b) Report market trends which may affect chemicals.

Monthly:

(a) Tabulate total value of new orders placed.
(b) Estimate projected values of new orders to be placed in future months.
(c) Tabulate savings in costs of goods (profit) resulting from purchases at better than market or due to change in source or material.

Annually:

(a) Tabulate distribution of business by dollars to suppliers.
(b) List important chemicals having only one qualified source of supply.
(c) List important chemicals purchased only on spot basis.

Background and Requirements

Education:

Required: Four year college degree in Pharmacy or Chemistry
Desirable: Graduate work in Business Administration

Experience:

Required: Eight years in pharmaceutical industry, three years of which shall be in purchasing
Desirable: Pharmacy, manufacturing, and accounting

* * *

EXAMPLE 3: **Buyer**[2]

Position Description. XYZ Company

Title: Buyer

Job Summary

Purchases a wide variety of technical and nontechnical items and materials required in production, maintenance and research activities. Selects vendors, places purchase contracts and approves invoices for the classes of materials or services under his jurisdiction. Works under direct supervision of Purchasing Agent. Annual value of purchases averages $2,500,000.

Job Requirements

JOB DUTIES

May perform one or more of the following duties as buyer of a widely diversified group of raw materials, components or finished parts, such as chemicals, paper and board, office equipment and supplies, printing, electrical and electronics equipment and supplies, building supplies, metals, pipe and fittings, and various services, etc.

1. Edits requisitions and confers with departments regarding requirements, specifications, quantity and quality of merchandise, and delivery requirements. Recommends substitutes to save cost or improve delivery.
2. Carries out necessary follow-up and expediting activities to insure delivery as required by production schedules.
3. Solicits and analyzes quotations for new or nonstandard items. Recommends or approves awarding of contracts or purchase orders, insuring that all purchases comply with Government regulations and accepted trade practices.
4. Interviews vendors and their representatives personally and maintains close contact by correspondence, telephone, and plant visits.

[2] By permission of NAPA.

5. Arranges with appropriate subcontractors to fabricate special equipment to our blueprints. Checks blueprints to insure freedom from accidental errors and completeness of information so that vendor can comply with our special requirements.
6. Serves in an advisory capacity to assist other departments to obtain proper specifications, quotations, delivery terms, and costs.
7. Examines and approves all invoices covering purchase orders placed by him.
8. Handles adjustments with vendors involving replacement of materials not conforming to purchase specifications, return of material declared surplus as a result of engineering changes, cancellations of orders, etc., prepares shipping orders and insures that appropriate credit is received.
9. Maintains an appropriate file of catalogs, price lists, etc., to be available for use of departments to assist them in obtaining the latest information with reference to new products.

EDUCATION AND TRAINING

Bachelor's degree, preferably in engineering, or equivalent in technical experience.
Two to four years' experience in manufacturing, engineering or purchasing.

MENTAL REQUIREMENTS

Requires ability to analyze a variety of technical problems resulting from the diversified nature of items purchased. Requires mature judgment and initiative to locate proper sources of supply and insure deliveries to meet production schedules, to find and recommend new and substitute items, and to maintain the optimum business relations with vendors. Skill in writing business letters is essential. Must have thorough knowledge of shop practices, ability to interpret blueprints and familiarity with shop costs to determine correct price levels.

PERSONAL REQUIREMENTS

Constant personal contacts with vendors, technical and production personnel and contractors, as representative of the company. Serves as liaison between using departments of the company and vendors in placing and filling orders. Must be neat in appearance, tactful, co-operative and have a pleasing personality. Must like working with people. Must have good social adaptability. Must be very accurate and dependable and able to hold matters in the strictest confidence.

APPLICATION

No unusual physical effort required. Work requires considerable mental application and ability to work under pressure. Must be able to co-ordinate many simultaneous activities.

General Responsibilities

CUSTOMER AND PUBLIC CONTACTS

Responsible for maintaining the highest degree of amicable relations between the company and all levels of supplier personnel or other members of the public with whom contacts are essential. These contacts are for the purpose of discussing technical, financial and legal aspects of the purchases for which he is responsible and include such things as negotiations, scheduling and follow-up on such purchases.

Public contacts result from attendance at society, association and outside committee meetings at which this position represents the company.

INTERNAL CONTACTS

Responsible for consulting with and advising company personnel, usually at first and second line supervisory levels, on all matters pertaining to the planning for, purchase and follow-up of the equipment, supplies and services for which this position is responsible. Contacts first and second line supervisors and engineers on the design, schedules, acceptable substitutes, specifications and other information needed for the purchase of equipment, supplies and services for which this position is responsible. Discusses and agrees on changes where necessary or desirable.

Arranges and participates in meetings between suppliers' representatives at any level and/or company personnel, usually at intermediate levels, at which decisions are made concerning engineering and design characteristics; schedules delivery, etc., of the equipment, supplies and services for which he is responsible.

INVESTIGATION AND RESEARCH

Responsible for making technical analyses of suppliers' equipment, materials and services within his assigned area, to determine suitability for company purchase and use. On the more important items, recommends his choice of vendor to Purchasing Agent and discusses reasons for selection.

Studies and analyzes markets and makes recommendations to his supervisor on the more important items and directly to departments on items of lesser significance. These analyses take into account anticipated company use, price, delivery or other market advantages.

Studies, analyzes and co-ordinates the purchasing action necessary on purchases within assigned areas. On more important items, will discuss and get approval of Purchasing Agent.

Participates in or assists in making tests or studies with other departments on engineering or technical data concerning present or prospective purchases. Keeps Purchasing Agent informed on results of such tests or studies.

PLANNING, FORECASTING AND SCHEDULING

Furnishes departments with information relative to suppliers' capabilities and work loads, to enable them to make decisions concerning purchases of the items within his assigned area.

Assists departments in the planning and scheduling for the purchase of assigned items for construction or maintenance projects in order to meet completion dates.

Studies markets and keeps departments informed concerning advantageous purchases, shortages, or other market conditions.

Responsible for follow-up on his purchases to assure that suppliers adhere to previously agreed upon schedules and delivery promises.

Arranges for and participates in supplier-company discussions concerning the establishment or change of schedules of assigned purchases. Changes may be requested by either party.

DESCRIBING THE MAN

To save time in the selection of the man best suited to carry out the program in mind, one must first get a mental picture of him. What are his *personal habits?* What *mental capacity* is needed? What is his attitude toward the job? What *experience* is desirable? What *education* and *training* are necessary? What will be the physical and health requirements?

Preparing a Man Description. The purchasing agent should prepare a chart which will provide a check of the characteristics it is believed the candidate should possess. This will list the qualities wanted in the man and those not wanted. One must *rely on experts* when it comes to judging mental and physical health. Opinions gained only from interviews can hardly be as dependable as those gained from the interpretation of data obtained by advanced scientific methods of observing mental and physical behavior.

The purpose of the chart is to bring about an objective attitude on the employer's part toward the person to be hired. Whether it is a replacement or a new job, the same careful planning is required. A good chart will assist the interviewer to more thoroughly:

1. Analyze the job to be done.
2. Determine whether a full-time job exists.
3. Create an approximate impression of the man needed to fit the responsibility.
4. Plan a procedure for the orderly search for and examination of the man to be selected.

The more factors considered at this point, the greater likelihood there is of successful selection. Additional factors which may be of importance are requirements for his family, necessary adjustments in other departments, office space, etc. If so, they deserve consideration on the chart.

A typical chart is shown in Fig. 23–1 (Candidate's Interview Chart), which has been filled in as a guide. Generally speaking, a candidate for the responsible duties of purchasing should rate as well as or better than the levels indicated. The employment manager should fill in a similar chart to compare with that of the purchasing department. This comparison will aid in spotting questionable evaluations.

If the chart is filled in before an interview to show what is wanted, it can become the target against which to compare charts filled in later during interviews. Its use as such will be helpful to the personnel man. When so used, it is a *man description.* Used with the job description during screening, much time can be saved by quickly eliminating some who will not qualify on personal trait requirements.

√-Test	G-Good	F-Fair	P-Poor	U-Unimportant
Personal Habits—From Personal Observation				
Neatness:	.. G .. Clothes		.. G .. Person	.. F .. Writing
Bearing:	.. G .. Entrance		.. F .. Walking	.. G .. Sitting
Speech:	.. G .. Modulated		.. G .. Forthright	.. F .. Expressive
Mental Ability—From Professional Testing				
Thought:	.. G .. Perceptive		.. G .. Inductive	.. G .. Deductive
Memory:	.. G .. Verbal		.. F .. Rote	.. G .. Numerical
I.Q.*	.. .. High School		.. .. College	.. √ .. Industrial
Attitude—From Personal Observation				
Enthusiasm:	.. F .. Eager		.. G .. Thoughtful	.. G .. Cautious
Reference:	.. G .. Responsibility		.. G .. Honesty	.. G .. Loyalty
Training—From References—Application				
Education:	.. G .. High School		.. F .. College	.. U .. Other
Work:	.. U .. Other Companies		.. U .. Own Companies	.. U .. Purchasing
Health—From Observation—Professional References				
Appearance:	.. F .. Energetic		.. G .. Alert	.. √ .. Examinations
Medical:	.. √ .. Chronic		.. √ .. Handicaps	.. √ .. Lost Time
History:				

* Authorities do not agree on minimum requirements but a review of tests given to men in purchasing and similar fields indicates I.Q.'s at the level of 100 to 115 are most frequently encountered.

FIG. 23–1. Candidate's interview chart.

Educational Requirements. Experience and familiarity with the company's products and policies is, by far, the most important background for prospective purchasing personnel. However, schooling in basic mathematics, grammar, science, accounting, law, economics, composition, and speech provides sturdy blocks on which to build this experience. All interplay in the deliberations and negotiations that make up the purchasing man's workday. See Fig. 23–2*a* (Recommended Minimum Educational Requirements for Purchasing Personnel) for a brief list of recommended educational requirements that fit the modern trend toward developing purchasing people who can assume their assigned responsibility on the management team. These recommendations are taken from the author's study of the requirements of several industries engaged in the manufacture of products requiring substantial technical and research facilities.

Figure 23–10, later in this section, outlines a college course specifically pointed to purchasing as a career. Graduates with such education are not included in the above data, since the course at the Illinois Institute of Technology at Chicago was relatively new when this handbook went to print.

Position	College degrees	High School Majors
Manager of purchases Purchasing agent	Technical* and/or Business administration†	Science and mathematics
Supervising buyers Senior buyers	Technical* or Business administration†	Science and mathematics
Buyers Assistant buyers	Technical*	Science and mathematics
Order clerks Expediters		Commercial and mathematics
Secretaries Stenographers Typists		Commercial, mathematics, and language skills

* Technical in this sense refers to engineering, chemical, metallurgical, biological, or other scientific fields, as major studies with an A.B. or B.S. degree resulting.

† Business administration refers to graduate work or an A.B. degree with business administration or practices as the major study.

FIG. 23–2*a*. Recommended minimum educational requirements for purchasing personnel.

The person available may not meet the educational standards set up. If he is a good prospect otherwise, these standards may be met by outside study while on the job. Night school and correspondence courses may answer the need.

In its booklet, *Guide to the Selection of Competent Buyers,* the NAPA groups the qualifications and requirements of buyers in the six following classifications:

1. All-purpose buyers
2. Construction buyers
3. Equipment buyers
4. MRO buyers (maintenance, repair, and operating)
5. Production materials and components buyers
6. Raw materials and commodities buyers

Part 1: for technical buyers

	Number of companies reporting			
	Small	Medium	Large	Total
Minimum educational requirements				
High school	10	13	17	40
College degree	11	15	15	41
Specialized study	..	6	3	9
High school and specialized study	4	1	2	7
College and specialized study	..	3	6	9
Graduate study				
Companies not reporting on technical buyers	8	6	8	22
Total	33	44	51	128
Preferred educational requirements				
High school	1	4	4	9
College degree	14	19	20	53
Specialized study	4	8	5	17
High school and specialized study	4	1	..	5
College and specialized study	2	4	9	15
Graduate study	..	2	5	7
Companies not reporting on technical buyers	8	6	8	22
Total	33	44	51	128

Part 2: for nontechnical buyers

	Number of companies reporting			
	Small	Medium	Large	Total
Minimum educational requirements				
Grade school	5	1	1	7
High school	22	27	33	82
College degree	3	8	5	16
Specialized study	..	1	2	3
High school and specialized study	1	5	5	11
College and specialized study	..	1	1	2
Companies not reporting on nontechnical buyers	2	1	4	7
Total	33	44	51	128
Preferred educational requirements				
Grade school	2	..	..	2
High school	14	11	10	35
College degree	10	21	28	59
Specialized study	1	5	4	10
High school and specialized study	2	..	3	5
College and specialized study	2	6	2	10
Companies not reporting on nontechnical buyers	2	1	4	7
Total	33	44	51	128

Reproduced by permission of the NAPA.

FIG. 23–2*b*. Educational requirements for buyers.

However, another grouping mentioned for general discussion purposes was the technical buyers and nontechnical buyers. Some of the more interesting figures available from the Survey of Purchasing Agents made by the NAPA pertain to the minimum and preferred educational requirements for technical and nontechnical buyers. For purposes of comparison, the simple definitions of technical and nontechnical, as used in the NAPA Survey, follow:

Technical are those kinds of buying jobs where a large number of contracts or orders placed require formal technical training, such as a degree in engineering, in order to buy in accordance with a company's standards of purchasing performance.

Nontechnical are buying jobs on which formal technical training is not required in order to buy in accordance with a company's standards of purchasing performance.

Part 1 in Fig. 23–2*b* illustrates the minimum and preferred educational requirements for technical buyers, as shown by the NAPA Survey referred to above. Part 2 of Fig. 23–2*b* presents similar data for nontechnical buyers.

The references to "small," "medium," and "large" on the above charts pertain to the size of the 128 companies that were participants in the NAPA Survey.

Desirable Characteristics for Purchasing Personnel

The list of personal characteristics shown on the following page is by no means complete, but it contains the minimum requirements that might be considered in looking for the person to do the purchasing job. No amount of emphasis would be too much for the "essential" characteristics listed here. These qualities would be necessary in any man or woman who wished to compete successfully in the profession of purchasing. The characteristics listed as "desirable" would be those which must be trained into the candidate if he does not have them already developed when he is assigned the purchasing job!

By far, the most desirable candidate for today's purchasing assignment is the man who has received a degree in either a technical subject or in business administration. George A. Renard, former Executive Secretary-Treasurer of the National Association of Purchasing Agents, reports that 40 per cent of the key purchasing men in industry today have college degrees in engineering or other technical fields. Some of these men have continued their studies to obtain a master's degree in business administration. Combine this type of educational background with the personal attributes on the following list, and success in purchasing is almost ensured.

Personal Characteristics

Essential (*Needed to begin the job*)	*Desirable* (*May be acquired on the job*)
PERSONAL	
Alertness	Adaptability
Curiosity	Analytical ability
Good health	Forthrightness
Strict honesty	Human relations
Intelligence–better than average	Imagination
Loyalty to employer	Initiative
	Mechanical aptitude
	Neatness
	Orderly manner
	Punctuality
	Self-control
	Self-expression
	Tactfulness
EDUCATION	
High school diploma	College degree
Knowledge of mathematics	Knowledge of science
Knowledge of business principles	Knowledge of economics
EXPERIENCE	
Production	Warehousing
Factory costs	Inventory control
Material handling	Sales

The following lists of job and family considerations will also serve as a check list during the interview later.

Job Considerations

1. Has adequate work space been provided?
2. Is a married man more desirable than a single man?
3. Will the new person properly balance the department?
4. Is age important? If so, what age is wanted?
5. Should the new person be male? or female?
6. Should the new employee have a specialized knowledge?
7. What are the educational backgrounds of the people who will call on him.
8. Will the salary offered induce the man to stay?
9. Has the cost of training been included in department costs?
10. Is this man likely to be advanced to another department of the company at some future time?

11. What are the educational levels of people within the company who will work with this man?

Family Considerations

1. Does the community provide adequate facilities for this man's recreation?
2. What kind of church facilities will be needed?
3. What kind of schools are expected, and what will be found?
4. Will a place to live be available?
5. Is the applicant familiar with the neighborhood where he is about to make his home?
6. Will the salary offered enable him to provide adequately for his family?

SEARCHING FOR THE MAN

Now that the purchasing agent has described the job to be done (Job Description, Examples 1, 2, and 3), and has in mind approximately the person to do the job (Candidate's Interview Chart—Fig. 23–1), the search for the right man may begin. Regardless of how the purchasing agent approaches this step, he should talk with his employment manager before proceeding. The interviewer should be on equal terms with the applicant. Direct inquiries for employment should be referred to the employment manager. Interviews should be conducted by appointment if at all possible, and always with the knowledge of the employment manager.

The employment manager should be furnished with a copy of the job description and a completed personnel requisition. Most firms today have requisition forms which may be filled out very much as a requisition for purchased material would be filled out. (See Fig. 23–3.)

A good purchasing man will recognize the importance of supplying the personnel department with the complete performance specifications (Job Description). The specifications should be attached to the requisition, and the searching should be left to the personnel man. If the correct specifications have been given, a good employment manager will come up with the right person just as surely as a good purchasing man will obtain the right material at the right price.

If the purchasing agent knows of individuals whom he would like to interview, he should suggest their names to the employment department for an interview.

In the smaller company it is often necessary for the purchasing manager or another executive to do the interviewing and hiring without the benefit of an organized personnel department. Under these circumstances it would be essential to read the following procedure which differs from the foregoing only in that it is necessary to advertise, screen, interview, and evaluate the data.

Job Name	Dept. No.	Number of Persons Needed	Date Needed	Req'n. No.
Working Hours				
Replacement New Job Permanent Temporary for how Long				
Detailed description of job (see Job Spec. No.)				
Qualifications (education, previous experience, skills, etc.)				
(see Job Spec. No.)				
Approved by				

(Reverse side)

Name of Employer	Date Employed	Approved By	Started

If no job specification or description has been established, consultation between the personnel manager and purchasing agent is in order. Then prepare a job description. See Examples 1 and 2.

FIG. 23–3 A personnel requisition.

If the task of searching, as well as the selection, is the responsibility of the purchasing agent, then it is best to begin by considering the advantages and disadvantages of the five methods at his disposal. He should ask himself these questions:

1. Is there someone available in the *organization?*

2. What *outside contacts* should be interviewed?
3. What form of *advertising* should be used?
4. Should an *employment agency* be engaged?
5. Are there technical *schools* or *colleges* from which applicants might be recruited?

The National Committee on Education of the National Association of Purchasing Agents has completed a study of the purchasing personnel selection policies of its members. The Committee has compiled this information in the previously mentioned booklet, *Guide to the Selection of Competent Buyers.* Much valuable information is given therein, and its study by those responsible for recruiting purchasing personnel should prove worthwhile. The paragraphs and data on education requirements, the specialty buyers, and the interview techniques are especially valuable guides.

Selection from Within. Selection from the company's personnel may prove the most desirable. Medium- and large-sized companies should encourage this means since it provides opportunity for:

1. Careful study of the prospect's work record
2. More reliable evaluation of character and disposition
3. Time savings through experience with the company's products and policies
4. Promotion from within, thus creating better *esprit de corps*
5. Less uncertainty about the objectives during orientation

Possible disadvantages which may result from the selection of present personnel may be:

1. A tendency to perpetuate current below-grade practices
2. A possible reluctance for the employee to become as aggressive with new ideas
3. A higher pay level even though beginning a new job
4. A dissatisfaction among employees not selected

The capabilities of personnel working with them should be discussed with other executives or supervisors.

If likely prospects are mentioned, the comments and recommendations which the supervisor may make should be relied upon heavily but not altogether. The written records of the man should be checked personally. If there is former work experience, it should be discussed with his former employer. Outside help should be engaged for mental and health testing.

The interview chart should be kept in mind, and it should be made certain that all essential facts are obtained before a decision is made.

Selection from among Personal Acquaintances. Although this approach has some advantages, they are likely to be offset by the limitation of prospects. If, however, one is inclined to call in people already known, it might be best to consider them in addition to other prospects who become available through advertising in the press. Some advantages from personal recruiting are:

1. Personal knowledge of the prospect's background
2. More rapid orientation of the new employee
3. Establishment in the community

Some disadvantages are:

1. The limitation of prospects
2. The tendency to settle for less than a completely satisfactory employee

Selection by Recruiting. Most colleges have established a practice of holding "interview days." The schools invite the industries and businesses to interview men and women who will soon seek employment. Since most of those participating have stabilized programs of recruiting, their offers of starting salaries and opportunities for advancement are realistic.

If it is the intention to recruit in this manner, a recent study made by Opinion Research Corporation, Princeton, New Jersey, may be of interest. Their study was conducted in the technical schools, but it is safe to assume that their findings would differ little from those of other colleges in the country. Other surveys have been made, and help in setting up a program may be obtained through the National Association of Purchasing Agents, which has carried on extensive work with many of the leading colleges and universities currently emphasizing purchasing in their curricula. Address inquiries to the National Association of Purchasing Agents, 11 Park Place, New York, N.Y., 10007, or The Canadian Association of Purchasing Agents, 357 Bay Street, Toronto, Canada, for a list of colleges who offer purchasing or related subjects as a part of their studies. This information may also be available at local chapters of the NAPA.

Direct contact with colleges in your area will furnish information on interview arrangements. The contact should be made through your personnel department.

Selection by Advertising. Purchasing is already recognized as a specialized business profession. Advertising for men with purchasing experience occurs regularly in the daily press as well as many of the trade papers and magazines.

Positions Available—Male Positions Available—Male Positions Available—Male Positions Available—Male

DIRECTOR OF PURCHASES

This firm, a leading manufacturer of capital equipment, seeks a Director of Purchases to manage procurement for a multi-division operation involving annual purchases in excess of $20 million.

The opportunities, for the qualified individual, with this growing manufacturer are excellent. He will have an unusual opportunity to apply his professional ability in all aspects of procurement management.

Foremost qualification will be substantial experience in directing similar purchasing operations, including development of new programs in the areas of cost & quality control & performance reporting. Advanced business education (MBA) or training in methods of material management desirable. Salary open. Send resume to:

Box MEC 194, Tribune

DIRECTOR OF PURCHASES

Midwest diversified electronics manufacturer with multi-million dollar sales has growth opportunity for an aggressive executive with proven ability to assume administration of large, established military procurement department with full responsibility for buying, scheduling and expediting under ASPR Regulations. Must be capable of participation in management at a staff level. Must be familiar with all aspects of modern purchasing, management techniques, viz; incentive contracting and capable of ultimate promotion to higher levels of management. Send resume in confidence to:

ASSISTANT PURCHASING AGENT

Midwest industrial firm is seeking an Assistant Purchasing Agent. Duties will be approving supply sources, quotations, negotiating prices, and purchasing. Requirements—Degree and 5 years experience in Industrial Purchasing. Submit complete resume including salary requirements to:

PURCHASING – HEAVY CHEMICALS

Major corporation with wide diversification in chemical industries seeks man with two to five years experience in purchasing heavy chemicals and similar items for corporate purchasing office, Chicago.

Prefer college graduate, possibly a chemical engineer whose interests shifted to purchasing. Age to 35. Please send resume including salary requirements to:

DIRECTOR OF PURCHASING

Major Midwest consumer packaged goods company seeks an experienced purchasing executive to assume full responsibility for multi-plant purchasing function. Reporting to top management, position offers challenge, major responsibility and attractive salary.

REQUIREMENTS INCLUDE:

- A minimum of five years experience as a successful purchasing agent or director of purchasing in a multi-plant company with both general office and plant purchasing operations.
- Experience in purchasing packaging materials and familiarity with new developments in the packaging industry.
- Strong profit orientation, with a knowledge of modern purchasing techniques. Familiarity with traffic operations desirable.
- Intelligence and maturity to establish and maintain sound working relationships with plant, division and general office personnel.

All replies treated in strictest confidence and should include present company, position, compensation and prior experience.

DIRECTOR OF MATERIEL

A progressive metal working plant located in the Midwest, nationally-known in the aircraft and aero-space industry, is currently seeking a high caliber man to fill the position of Director of Materiel.

The man we are seeking should be a college graduate, or its equivalent with extensive knowledge of production control, purchasing and related functions.

Replies will be kept in strict confidence.

PURCHASING
Chemical Industry

Corporate expansion has created immediate openings for graduate chemists or chemical engineers with or without previous purchasing experience. Age 25 to 35. If inexperienced in purchasing, background should include either chemical sales or familiarity with the process industries. These positions offer ample opportunity for personal growth and development. Please send your confidential resume, including salary requirements, to:

PERSONNEL DIRECTOR :, CINCINNATI, OHIO 45202

Procurement Director

Major company in Southern California seeking top level experienced man to head procurement group. Will be responsible for directing all procurement activities including general commodity buying, scheduling, expediting and subcontractor liaison on large mechanical equipment. Should have engineering background and at least 10 years' procurement experience. This is an outstanding opportunity which we hope to fill at the earliest possible date.

PURCHASING ADMINISTRATOR

Nation-wide, multi-plant manufacturer of heavy machinery requires a highly qualified coordinator of purchasing. The successful candidate will be knowledgeable in the latest purchasing methods, capable of teaching same and through his efforts help improve purchasing procedures. Although the position is staffed in nature, the incumbent will be responsible for negotiating on a corporate basis in reference to selective items. Engineering degree preferred. Travel will be heavy.

Minimum 15 years experience in purchasing with a manufacturer of heavy machinery preferably produced on a job-shop basis, is desired. Future opportunities are excellent; salary commensurate with abilities and experience.

Send confidential resume and salary to:

PURCHASING AGENT/STEEL BUYER

Automotive components manufacturer requires an experienced individual to direct the purchasing function and take personal responsibility for steel buying. Knowledge of wire, sheet and coil specifications, vendors, sources and markets, both foreign and domestic is required. Training and experience in Value Engineering and Analysis is very desirable. Administrative capability, promotability, personality and executive qualities are of major importance. Degree in engineering desired. Age 35-50. Salary to $15,000 depending on background and experience, plus excellent fringe benefits. Submit resume in confidence.

MANAGER OF PURCHASING

A major division of a large metals company has a challenging opportunity for a young, aggressive man with purchasing experience. Position supervises all purchasing for $25,000,000 a year operation. Degree required.

DIRECTOR of PURCHASING

Major Michigan paper manufacturer requires aggressive person to head Purchasing Department in a highly competitive industry. Applicants must have successfully completed extensive experience as a large volume buyer and have the administrative ability to direct the activities of a purchasing department. Annual purchasing volume now exceeds $20 million. Excellent future for progressive and ambitious man. Prefer college graduate under forty. All replies confidential. Send complete resume and salary requirement to:

The Wall Street Journal

FIG. 23–4. Examples of advertisements for purchasing talent. Note the strong emphasis on experience and college degrees (the underlining is ours). These advertisements, published during the winter of 1963–64, reflect the dearth of well-trained purchasing talent in companies which have experienced rapid growth.

A study of purchasing magazines listed in Section 26 may uncover the person best adapted to the requirements. Such daily newspapers as the *Wall Street Journal, New York Journal of Commerce, Chicago Daily Tribune, Chicago Daily News,* and *The New York Times* frequently carry display advertising by experienced men who desire to change and request purchasing jobs. Figure 23–4 illustrates such advertising as well as examples of companies searching for candidates. These have appeared in the daily press.

CAUTION: If the firm has a well-established personnel department, there is no need for you to place the advertising. However, your personnel people may want assistance in phrasing the job description or any other data which the advertisement may need to include.

The Interview. The trained interviewer has many aids on which to draw at the time of the interview. If at all possible, someone in this capacity should handle the screening of the initial candidates.

The use of "pattern interviews," when done by the trained interviewer, is important in the selection of the right man.

Work references are more important than most personal references. Thus work references should be obtained from the candidate *before* the interview. This will give an opportunity to size up the man on the basis of his record.

The interview chart should be used, and the man rated by filling in the chart. His rating should be checked with the target in mind.

A man's work habits are likely to remain constant. If his record shows acceptable habits, they are likely to remain so. A new man with bad work habits should not be engaged in the hope that he can be changed. It is the exception and not the rule for work habits to change. The required personality traits must be kept constantly in mind. *Few people acquire new ones.*

TRAINING THE MAN

Careful training of the candidate is important in preparing him for his future assignments. If he has been intelligently selected, his training may be more rapid than if a "convenient" candidate has been "pressed" into the job. However, the same orderly approach to the training program is necessary. Thus his training will be thorough and consume the least amount of his time.

A new employee's training experiences, generally, fall into five classifications:

1. Orientation (learning about the company)
2. In-plant (experience in other departments)
3. On-the-job (actual experience on assigned job)

4. Off-the-job (study and Purchasing Agents Association activities)
5. Evaluation and adjustment (a continuing experience)

Care should be taken that each phase has adequate attention and that the employee's experience is orderly and logical.

On-the-job training is the oldest known method of training purchasing men. Until a few years ago, no other training effort was made. If the new purchasing man were selected from another department, he had the good fortune of company and product knowledge as a background. His further training was principally by "trial and error." He would learn "by his mistakes." Some very successful purchasing agents were developed in this way.

Today, students of the purchasing function are inclined to think that the cost of training by "total immersion" is more costly than a well-ordered program with the objective clearly stated at the outset.

In large companies "rotation" programs under the supervision of permanent training personnel frequently supply talent ready for "on-the-job" training. A "sponsor" or "big brother" is usually appointed to "guide" the trainee in the department during his early training.

On-the-job training may have several definite stages or aspects. These may be:

1. Orientation—the work is explained and demonstrated.
2. Instruction—the work is explained and demonstrated.
3. Execution—the work is done by the new man.
4. Discussion—conferences on problems and work.
5. Reports—evaluation of training progress.

Each of these will occur and recur as the new employee progresses from one station or task to another. A program wisely developed will provide the opportunity for sound groundwork to be done in each stage on each task assigned.

Orientation in the Department. Orientation is the *first important experience* the new employee will have in the purchasing department.

This period should be divided into two phases:

1. People and facilities. Introduction to his fellow purchasing department employees and the tools used in the department—machines, records, etc.
2. Reading and study. Reading manuals, textbooks, literature from the National Association of Purchasing Agents, and magazines or special guides devised as training tools.

Orientation in purchasing should take place before any in-plant work is done by the new employee. His other work experience will mean more to him in terms of purchasing. He can apply his orientation experience to the questions to be raised about his plant work.

Orientation must logically precede work experience. If proper orientation is not provided, the new employee will make his own adjustment, and he may orientate in a haphazard way. To correct *wrong impressions* so gained by him will take far more effort later than it would take to tell or show him the facts in the first place.

Company manuals, historical data, and the counsel of older employees should be used profusely during this period of becoming acquainted. If the company has no manual stating general policies, it is best to prepare a statement covering those in general practice. Otherwise, discuss the company's principal policies of:

1. Sales
2. Manufacture
3. Product development
4. Research
5. Engineering
6. Advertising
7. Relationships with:
   a. Employees
   b. Stockholders
   c. Customers
   d. Suppliers
   e. Community

Training Manuals. If the department has a purchasing manual,[3] the trainee can study it at once. He should keep it with him during the entire period of his training.

Many companies today have developed a training manual. This may be for general use as well as more specific use in purchasing. A training manual will embody many of the items discussed in this handbook. However, the manual should not contain so much detailed instruction that frequent revision will be necessary.

The importance of the purchasing manuals cannot be emphasized enough. Not only should they contain company policy on all matters pertaining to purchasing but they should:

1. Define the purchasing agent's duties, prerogatives, responsibilities, and limitations of authority.
2. Serve as a textbook for training the new employee in policy and procedure.

[3] See Section 3, "Policy and Procedure Manuals."

3. Be a reference for defining daily action within the framework of the organizational structure of the purchasing department.

A good training manual will set forth:

1. Policies of the company
2. Policies of the purchasing department
3. Objectives of the purchasing function
4. General procedures of the purchasing department
5. Organizational charts of the company and department

The new employee should be given a copy of such a manual to be kept for reference and revision while he remains in the department. See the details discussed in Section 3 of this handbook for examples to follow in the development of a procedure manual if you do not have one.

The contents of this handbook may liberally assist in planning the reading program during this "get-acquainted" period, particularly the paragraphs in this section devoted to "preparing a trainee for plant visitations" to get ideas on files and other data the new employee should learn to study.

Make frequent reference to, and assign as important reading, the following sections of this handbook:

Section 1—The Purchasing Function
Section 3—Policy and Procedure Manuals
Section 6—Ethical Practices in Purchasing
Section 7—How to Select Sources of Supply
Section 9—Pricing Considerations

See list at the end of this section for additional reading matter. Note especially the listings under the heading of "Literature of General Interest." These references contain necessary information for the new man who is looking broadly at the purchasing operation. Literature dealing more specifically with the aspects of the corporation related to purchasing will be found in the list under the heading of "Literature of Special Interest." These will prove invaluable as references when the new man prepares for his in-plant experiences.

Copies of magazines published for buyers should be obtained. They are issued by some local associations of the NAPA, by CAPA, and by magazine publishers.[4] Back copies will supply new employees with a wealth of reading material. Local associations will also have other useful literature available for the asking.

A good training program will "anticipate" the new employee by methodically referencing, indexing, and clipping articles and other ma-

[4] See complete list in Section 26, "Library and Catalog File."

terial that will help him to learn about the meaning of his new assignment.

The first week may be taken up solely with this activity. By the second week some of the reading can give way to observation. He can, for example, sit in on interviews by the buyers. He may be allowed to meet salesmen making calls. This will inspire him to someday be in a position to do likewise.

By the third week he probably can begin the department "work" schedule. He can start with the most elementary tasks. Here he can learn the "detail" of the department. His schedule should provide experience in many phases. A week on each task may be sufficient. This should include:

1. Filing purchase orders
2. Posting purchase record cards
3. Checking invoice copies against purchase order terms and prices
4. Reading outgoing and incoming correspondence
5. Posting source information
6. Filing catalogs
7. Delivering samples

Whatever time is required for the employee to grasp the mechanics of these operations should be taken. He will associate them, and, with the use of a procedure manual, put each operation in its proper place and relationship with the others. His appreciation for this detail will be a sound basis for future suggestions on procedure and office economies.

He, thus, will become acquainted with forms and simple procedures. These will give more meaning to his next experiences—his in-plant training. If he is a veteran employee with plant experience, then this handling of detail will add significance to what he has done in other departments.

During his first days, if he is given the task of delivering samples or special messages to other departments, he will become aware of the areas and departments that "do business" with and "depend on" the work of the purchasing department. Also, people outside the department are given an excellent opportunity to know about and become acquainted with the new employee. This is an opportunity, too, for the purchasing department manager to introduce the new man in other departments.

In-plant Training. By the sixth week the new employee should be ready to move into the rotation pattern of "outside-the-department" experience. It is at this time that real planning will have to be done.

In setting up the following in-plant training schedule (see Fig. 23–5, In-plant Training Schedule), selling has been omitted. Today's trend toward better public relations through ethical and understanding purchasing practices has brought many successful purchasing men from sales. Selling experience can be important. If it is possible to get a man with selling experience who sincerely wants to purchase, so much to the good. Purchasing, by its very nature, requires a more conservative and somewhat more retiring personality than selling usually demands. The purchasing man must be a *good listener.* If other work experience outlined here is fully performed, the lack of selling experience will be of little moment.

Name: P. A. Buyer	Start: July 1, —					Complete: April 1, —					
Dates to Complete Training	7/31	8/14	9/11			11/6	12/4	2/26	3/12	4/9	4/30
No. Working Days on Job	22	10	19			40	19	58	10	20	15
Jobs in Training Schedule	Conference Dates With Trainee (Notes on progress)										
Purchasing Dept. Orientation	7/31	8/7									
Receiving Dept. Dock		8/14	8/28								
Warehousing Inventory			9/11			9/25					
Production Chemical						10/8					
Production Tabletting						10/22		12/24			
Production Packaging						11/6	11/20	1/15			
Inventory Control Posting							12/4	2/5			
Factory Costs								2/26			
Purchasing-Product Identification									3/12		
Supplier Evaluation										4/9	4/16
Report on Training	Oral — written —										4/30

FIG. 23–5. In-plant training schedule; a working model.

A *training schedule* should be developed. The outline for such a schedule is shown in Fig. 23–5. It covers only in-plant training. A similar schedule will be helpful for on-the-job training.

This schedule serves the following purposes:

1. Defines the needs and area of training.
2. Sets time and efficiency goals to be met.

3. Encourages the candidate to read and investigate future study areas.
4. Provides a guide to others as to what is expected.

The training table will follow a general pattern of on-the-job training but will be modified to fit the occasion. The training schedule for a senior buyer will differ from that for an assistant buyer.

Time taken in training is seldom wasted. It is easier to err on the side of haste. Haste in training means waste in time later. Train by instruction and guided experience in accordance with a *plan*. Industry has learned that "learning by the mistakes we make" is a tortuous and costly method of training.

Experience vital to the execution of good purchasing will be found in many departments of the company. Some of the most important are:[5]

Cost accounting (6)
Engineering, design, and development (3)
Inventory control (1)
Production (12)
Production planning and scheduling (6)
Receiving (1)
Warehousing and material handling (1)

Other department managers should be consulted on how the time of the trainee will be spent. Actual contact with the material used is important. A training guide may be helpful for the prospective member of the purchasing department. One large company in the Middle West furnished the following list to each purchasing trainee progressing through the mill or factory:

1. What is the specific end product or products of the department?
   a. What measurements of output are used?
   b. What quantities are being produced at present?
   c. Approximately what quantities of various materials are required per unit of production?
2. What is the principal process or service rendered in the department?
   a. Is it an operating department: manufacturing, converting, finishing, etc.?
   b. Is the department rendering general service: engineering, planning, materials handling, etc?
   c. What is the nature of the process? If in manufacturing, what is the flow of materials and what particular function does the equip-

[5] Figures in parentheses represent average length of *experience in months* that may be necessary to make these operations meaningful.

ment play in the manufacturing of the finished product? If in a service department, how does the department contribute to the manufacturing process?

d. Process or department flow sheet?

3. What are the raw materials used or handled by the department?
   a. What are their specifications and why are specifications required?
   b. What is the function of each of the raw materials in relation to the finished product?
   c. What operating problems, if any, are created by the quality or quantity of raw materials purchased or the method of purchasing them?
   d. What characteristics of the finished product dictate the type and kind of raw materials?
   e. What raw materials involve storage and handling problems?
   f. Where do they come from geographically?
   g. Which materials are manufactured by another unit of the same firm?
4. Where does the department fit into the general flow diagram of the mill?
5. What are the major pieces of operating equipment?
   a. What function does each perform?
   b. How does the material or product get from one to another?
   c. What is the capacity of each in units of product?
6. How are costs of manufacture determined?
   a. What is general cost distribution, i.e., labor, raw materials, clothing, maintenance, etc.?
   b. How do purchased raw materials and supplies costs affect finished product costs?
7. How do staff services (engineering, research and development, purchasing, traffic, industrial relations department, etc.) assist in operation of mills?
8. Learn organizational structure of mill and its tie-in with staff organization.
9. Become familiar with physical layout of mills and storages.
10. Machine clothing, plant lubrication, painting, power and steam generation, laboratory supplies and equipment are major items other than raw materials to be observed during progression.

After completing his experience in any department, the trainee is expected to write a brief report summarizing his observations, using questions listed above as a guide, but with particular emphasis on raw materials and related items, functions, and problems. In this report he should feel free to evaluate any of the existing conditions and make as many recommendations as he can.

It may be desirable to include in the report the definition of the departmental function, the list of organization relationships, and the outline and description of the process flow. Such items as departmental layout, process procedures, equipment capacities, departmental operating problems, services received, etc., would have been observed and would be discussed in a meeting with the head of the department.

It is to be understood, however, that such reports are to be used more as a criterion of the trainee's ability to observe and to express himself than as a basis for some specific action to be taken in the department referred to.

Another firm prepares a check list pointed to specific operations that directly or indirectly affect purchasing operations. This guide is divided into operations which the trainee may experience. They are the same operations as those included on the training schedule. For each operation there are two sets of questions. One set deals with the physical aspects; the other with procedure. All questions are pertinent to purchasing matters. They direct specific attention to packaging, markings, handling, use, costs, quality, service, and internal procedure. The list follows:

Physical aspects

1. Name various materials received and handled.
2. What methods of transportation were observed?
3. What types (describe) of packaging were used?
4. Indicate volume received; trucks, railroad cars, tons, etc.
5. What are most bulky? Most compact?
6. Is palletizing used? Where? Advantage?
7. Are packages frequently damaged on arrival?
8. Are materials easy to identify? Whose gave trouble?
9. Were deliveries well scheduled to avoid dock congestion?
10. What safety measures were observed?
11. What special problems were encountered? Describe how handled.
12. What improvements can be suggested?

Procedure

1. What special precautions were taken in handling?
2. Were costly items handled differently than less costly? How?
3. What markings are necessary on the packages to identify the contents?
4. How is a dock ticket made out? Prepare an example.
5. Where do the copies of the receiving record go from the receiving department?

6. What notations are necessary on the receiving records?
7. Where is the material delivered by receiving? Chemicals? Etc.?
8. What notice is prepared when supplier fails to fully mark package?
9. Whose signature is required to complete the receiving record?
10. What procedure is followed when a shipment is damaged?
11. What procedural problems seem to exist?
12. What improvements in procedure can be suggested?

Similar lists of questions should be prepared for each in-plant function which is included in the trainee's schedule. Care should be given in the preparation of the list so that the trainee's attention is *directed* to the operations which are significant to the purchasing man.

On-the-job Training. The new employee has now had an opportunity through his orientation in the purchasing department and his in-plant experience to relate several of the company operations. His experience in purchasing should now begin. He may be given the rank of assistant buyer and assigned to one of the buying groups. A more experienced man may be ready for immediate assignment of more responsibilities as a buyer. In this case his training up to now would have been much more rapid and would have consumed only a matter of weeks rather than the months required for the inexperienced man.

In any case, the first buying duties should begin by careful introduction to the materials to be handled. The new buyer will gain invaluable experience by first handling a miscellaneous group of materials. Maintenance materials, laboratory supplies, office supplies, and shipping supplies each offer opportunities for flexing the buyer's muscles. He should be given time to pick up some of the items in one of these groups and to do a buying job. An item might be picked which has had little evaluation but might lead to an improved buying position. If possible, he should spend time discussing the subject with the using department personnel. This provides instruction in the following steps:

1. Learning the nature and use of the material
2. Searching for new sources
3. Dictating written inquiries
4. Tabulating the quotations
5. Evaluating the reliability of new sources
6. Submitting samples for approval
7. Negotiating price and terms
8. Preparing and placing the order
9. Checking and approving invoices
10. Recording necessary information

In most cases each of the foregoing steps can be taken by the new buyer under the direct supervision of the department manager or an experienced member of the purchasing department. Regular reference can be made by the supervisor to department manuals and to similar buying situations for instruction in the methods to use.

An abundance of information in the other sections of this handbook will be invaluable as reference material. Time should be taken by the new man to read these references. Time should be taken by his supervisor to answer the questions he raises and to relate his questions to the investigation of the material he is studying.

Where no centralized purchasing function has existed before and the new man is attempting to set up the operation, greater problems of procedure will exist. In this case the following outline may be helpful.

What to Do in Ten Steps of Purchasing

1. *Learning the nature and use of the material.* This investigation should be as complete as time will permit.
   a. Read and inquire about commercial uses of the material.
   b. Learn what use the company makes of it.
   c. Check on the quantity used and how frequently it is bought.
   d. Learn why this material was selected instead of another.
   e. Search files for data received from suppliers.
   f. Determine whether specifications have been established.
   g. If poisonous or dangerous, find out if the safety engineer has been informed.
   h. Examine the form of the material.
   i. Inspect the type of packing ordinarily used.
2. *Searching for new sources.* See Fig. 23–6 for a few of the references available. Lists of others will be found in Sections 26 and 28.
   a. Examine the references which list suppliers of this material.
   b. Decide the maximum distance a supplier should be located.
   c. Investigate the usual methods of distribution.
   d. Determine who are the basic manufacturers.
3. *Dictating written inquiries.* Unless time prevents, the beginner should always write for information.
   a. Learn to use a dictating machine if one is available.
   b. Double check to see that material is described completely.
   c. If the description is brief, use postal cards instead of letters if many are involved.
   d. Make one file copy of the inquiry and tabulate all sources contacted.
   e. Request samples, literature, data, price schedules, and terms of sale.

These references usually list suppliers by items or class of material:

Allen's Hand Book of the Oil & Chemical Industries, WorCo Industries Inc., Western Saving Fund Building, Philadelphia, Pa., 19107

Chemical Engineering Catalog and *Chemical Materials Catalog,* Reinhold Publishing Corporation, 430 Park Avenue, New York, 10040

Chemical Sources, Sources Directories Publishing Company, 510 Madison Avenue, New York, N.Y., 10010

Chemical Week Buyer's Guide (two parts), McGraw-Hill Publications, 330 West 42d Street, New York, N.Y., 10036

Drug and Cosmetic Catalog, Drug and Cosmetic Industry, 101 West 31st Street, New York, N.Y., 10001

Drug Topics Red Book, Topics Publishing Co., 10 East 15th Street, New York, N.Y., 10003

The Green Book, Schnell Publishing Company, Inc., 100 Church Street, New York, N.Y.

MacRae's Blue Book, MacRae's Blue Book Company, 18 East Huron Street, Chicago, Ill., 60611

Poor's Register of Corporations, Directors and Executives, Standard & Poor's Corporation, 345 Hudson Street, New York, N.Y., 10014

Purchasing Directory, Conover-Mast Publications, Inc., 205 East 42d Street, New York, N.Y., 10017

Sweet's File, Sweet's Catalog Services, F. W. Dodge Company, A Division of McGraw-Hill, Inc., 330 West 42d Street, New York, N.Y., 10036

Thomas' Register of American Manufacturers, Thomas Publishing Company, Inc., 461 Eighth Avenue, New York, N.Y., 10001

Cities and states: telephone directories, chambers of commerce, or secretaries of state

Commodities: trade associations

Countries abroad: ministers of commerce of respective countries having diplomatic relations with U.S.A.

FIG. 23–6. List of references and addresses.

4. *Tabulating the quotations.* This operation offers the beginner the opportunity to study thoroughly the suppliers' offers.
   a. Devise a uniform record for permanent filing.
   b. Record prices, terms, and availability.
   c. Note deviations from the description in the inquiry.
   d. Determine whether clarification is needed in order to understand the quotation.
   e. Indicate whether samples will be submitted.
   f. Provide space for notations of later action.
5. *Evaluating the reliability of new sources.* The important factors of evaluation are quality, financial responsibility, price, and service.
   a. Eliminate firms unable to supply material required to do the job.
   b. Obtain and study financial statements of firms likely to be considered further.
   c. Determine delivered costs from a study of prices, terms, and cartage on offers received.
   d. List suppliers who appear satisfactory as to finances, price, and service.

6. *Submitting samples for quality approval.* Samples should be approved by the quality-control department or by the user in all cases where a new source or a substitute material is considered for purchase.
   a. Use a numbered form for this purpose (see Fig. 23–7).
   b. Keep a permanent register of all samples cleared.
   c. Describe the material fully, noting dangerous features.
   d. Note date of receipt and date of approval or rejection.
   e. Indicate whether material is suggested as a substitute and reasons.
   f. Avoid expending time investigating samples from obviously undesirable sources.

Copies To:

COMMODITY INVESTIGATION REQUEST

Request No.	Date	By	Date Wanted	Project No.	Sample No. 11029
Commodity Type		Compound No.	Vendor		

Product Used With	List No.	F.E. No.	Abbott No.

Technical Specifications of Material and Nature of Problem

Refer Reply To

FIG. 23–7. Commodity investigation request. The use of this form will provide a uniform method for sample handling and a permanent record for the investigators as well as the purchasing department.

7. *Negotiating price and terms.* Usually this will take place in a personal interview and the new man will be able to apply the techniques which he has already observed.
   a. Make certain that the quantity involved is realistic.
   b. Inquire prices and terms of contracts versus single shipments.
   c. Check prices and cartage costs on various types of packing available.
   d. Determine what warranties will be given.

   e. Compare terms, etc., of the transaction with other offers before closing.
8. *Preparing and placing the order.* All orders by the new employee should be countersigned by a superior to ensure completeness and accuracy.
   a. Complete the order as to specifications, quantity, price, terms, routing, and delivery instructions.
   b. Include references to applicable trade standards of purity, construction, or performance.
   c. Clearly state warranties and guarantees expected from the supplier.
   d. Describe packing and state precautions necessary in handling the material.
   e. Provide information on time required to inspect after delivery before payment will be made.
   f. State clearly all conditions relating to rejection, damage, etc.
9. *Checking and approving invoices.* If invoices are not actually handled in the purchasing department, provision should be made that no invoice may be paid without an approval by the buyer who placed the order.
   a. Check each invoice with the price and terms on the order.
   b. Ascertain as quickly as possible whether the goods received are approved.
   c. Notify shippers promptly if quality of material is questionable.
   d. Avoid delays in payment beyond the terms of the purchase order.
10. *Recording necessary information.* Requirements will vary, but complete records of repetitive purchases on the same item are necessary for planning a good purchasing program.
   a. Record dates, quantities, vendors, and prices on established materials.
   b. Record cartage costs only if they are an important part of the cost of the material.
   c. Use visible type records on all important items.
   d. Omit order numbers, invoice numbers, and total charges on less important materials.
   e. Use only a file of copies of purchase orders for tabulation if quantity is the only important data needed.

In the foregoing outline many important references have been omitted. For the beginner the outline will suffice to start him on his purchasing career. Such activities as filing claims, requesting formal bids, holding conferences, and the like will come later as a part of his work. Reference to other sections in this handbook will provide help in these activities.

Other considerations which the new purchasing man will do well to keep in mind are:

1. The purchasing department records are often the critical evidence necessary to establish the inception of interest in a material or project for patent purposes.
2. The use of a dictating machine is easy to learn at the beginning and provides greater economy of the buyer's time.
3. The buyer accomplishes most during the interview when both the buyer and salesman are able to discuss their subjects in a relaxed atmosphere.
4. All records are costly to create and house; therefore, only those records which earn their cost by providing useful tools in purchasing should be kept.
5. A review of the circumstances and conditions of a transaction with the department manager should be made at every opportunity since these conferences will afford the best opportunity for establishing policies and methods in the mind of the new man.

Supplier Plant Visits. Company managements differ greatly in their policies toward buyers traveling to see suppliers' personnel and facilities. Some recommend that trainees travel extensively until they are familiar with all major suppliers' facilities. Others permit traveling only when a crisis in quality or service occurs. In the latter case, the situation frequently indicates that the purchasing man is replaced on such trips by expediting, development, production, or financial people. They make these evaluations by visiting the facilities of the suppliers.

Today's trend is for management to depend on purchasing people to make the decisions on supplier selection. These decisions cannot be made without adequate knowledge. A thorough knowledge of the suppliers' *facilities and problems* is a valuable background for the decision-making buyer. If not overdone, supplier visits will be useful.

Why and What to See. In modern industrial organizations, the buyer's chief responsibility is in the selection of the right supplier. All else will fall into line if the right supplier is selected. The right supplier will have the right quality, the right quantities, the right price, and the right service. A knowledge of needs is necessary to select the right supplier. Just as important is the knowledge of the supplier's facilities to furnish those needs.

The trainee must be given an opportunity to observe the supplier's:

1. Organization and management
2. Plant and manufacturing facilities
3. Research, engineering, and development facilities

4. History, specifications, and quality-control procedures
5. Packaging, warehousing, and handling methods

These observations must be meaningful to be of value. To make them meaningful, the buyer must be properly prepared for such observations. Thought must be given to this program.

Visits to suppliers' plants are recognized by many companies as necessary training in day-to-day buying. These visits keep the veteran buyer up to date on the supplier's progress in modernization, new products, etc. Even more important is this program to the new man in buying. When he sees the item made or processed, he understands its nature and characteristics better.

Trainee's Behavior Important. The first call at a supplier's plant by a trainee should be in company with a veteran purchasing man. This affords, *by example,* an opportunity for the new man to observe the older man's behavior and attitude.

The purchasing man represents his management. He must think like management. His training should take this fact into consideration. It is especially important that he learn this early.

Good manners away from home are important. A veteran purchasing man will instinctively react to the supplier's overtures, while the new man must find his way. It is easier to learn the proper reaction *by example.* The trainee is there to learn about products, methods, and facilities. He can learn and retain this information if he is at ease. His older associate will make him feel more "at home" on this initial call.

Other advantages gained by this method of introduction are:

1. Greater prestige for the new man
2. Greater chance to meet management men
3. More positive direction of trainee's interest
4. Less likelihood of distracting activities

Ethics.[6] A good buyer never violates his supplier's confidence. Any buyer who discusses with a supplier's competitor what he has seen in the supplier's plant will be unwelcome in either plant. *Even though it might be to the buyer's immediate benefit, he is morally obligated never to divulge methods, new developments, procedures, or confidential information gained by his visit, without that supplier's permission.* He must be careful that requests for such permission will result in an advantage for the supplier granting the permission as well as for his company.

Visits to suppliers' plants are for the purpose of informing the buyer. How he uses this information will be the test of its value to him. Properly

[6] See Section 6, "Ethical Practices in Purchasing."

used, this information will usually result in better relations between the buyer and the supplier he visited.

Using the Information Gained by Plant Visits. The buyer who knows about the supplier's plant and methods by firsthand observation can make good use of his knowledge. He will be better able to:

1. Judge the supplier's capabilities to handle new items.
2. Decide what technical assistance the supplier can furnish on new products.
3. Suggest revisions in material specifications to gain:
   a. Better quality at same or less cost
   b. Lower costs by improvement in supplier's methods, etc.[7]
   c. Lower costs through substituted materials
4. Contribute more effectively in "make or buy" deliberations.
5. Advise more accurately about deliveries, etc.
6. Determine plant personnel who are most effective in accelerating production.

Planning the Visits. Inadequate planning of the buyer's trips to suppliers' plants is a woeful waste of money and time. Advance plans must be made to gain the desired advantages. Failure to plan may result in:

1. Too much time away from the desk
2. Inadequate time allowed for essential observations
3. Lack of direction of interest by the trainee
4. Haphazard and diverting entertainment by the supplier
5. Extra expense in traveling

The plan should:

1. Allow for selection of the supplier having high standards of quality.
2. Allow for trainee to see research and development facilities.
3. Allow for adequate time to observe production methods, etc.
4. Allow planning with the supplier in advance:
   a. To permit him to arrange for the right people to be on hand
   b. To permit him to organize a program of observation and study
   c. To permit the purchasing agent an opportunity to check the supplier's plans and schedule
5. Allow the purchasing agent or one of the older buyers to accompany him on his first trip during this training

[7] A multitude of examples testify to the importance of the buyer's contribution in this area. The section editor's personal experience has included several such instances where costs were reduced from 20 to 50 per cent, saving sizable sums. See Section 11, "Value Analyses Techniques," for further details.

Selecting Plant of Industry Leader. Selection of the right plant to visit by the new man must be carefully made. Nearness is not enough. Often the nearest supplier of a commodity is a poor representative of the industry. The first call should be on the leader of the industry, if at all possible. Usually this will permit the new man the opportunity to:

1. Meet an aggressive and confident management.
2. See the best research and development facilities.
3. Observe the most mechanized production methods.
4. Study the strictest quality control.
5. Know the reasons for tolerances set for their products.
6. Learn the newest packaging and handling techniques for the material.
7. Properly evaluate competitors' facilities when he visits them later.

Evaluation of competitors' facilities is easier when the best facilities are already familiar to the buyer.

Timing of Visit Is Important. Training costs money. Visiting vendors and their plants costs in time and money. To make the expenditure worthwhile, the trainee must be ready for the experience. He must be sent at the right time. If he goes too early, he will not know how to interpret what he sees. If he goes too late, he will not have the experience to apply to his buying chores.

The right time is when the new man knows all that can be learned about the manufacturer's material and organization without going to see his plant.

He can learn about the purchased material by:

1. Seeing and handling it
2. Reviewing purchasing department files on its development and adoption
3. Discussing specifications with control and production people
4. Reviewing complaints on quality and service
5. Reviewing purchase records of quantity, price, and delivery

He can learn about the company by referring to:

1. Trade information services such as Dun and Bradstreet, Inc., Standard & Poor, etc.
2. Trade registers such as *Sweet's Catalog Service, Thomas' Register of American Manufacturers, MacRae's Blue Book,* etc.
3. Most recent financial statement available from the company
4. Daily and trade newspapers such as:
   a. Wall Street Journal
   b. Journal of Commerce
   c. Specialized papers published for the trade or industry

Vendor

Telephone

S CODE	SALESMEN	DATE

PRINCIPLE PRODUCTS

P CODE		P CODE	
	1.		11.
	2.		12.
	3.		13.
	4.		14.
	5.		15.
	6.		16.
	7.		17.
	8.		18.
	9.		19.
	10.		20.

DATE	SPECIAL ADVANTAGES

SOURCE STATUS	1	2	3	4	5	6	7	8	9	10	11	12	13	14	15	16	17	18	19	20
Major																				
Secondary																				
Alternate																				
Emergency																				

S CODE	DATE	P CODE	SALESMEN'S PRESENTATION AND REMARKS

FIG. 23–8*a*. Consolidated record on the supplier (front).

Things the trainee should know before he visits supplier's plant:

1. What and how much his company buys from that supplier
2. What contracts and orders are currently open
3. What methods of shipment are used by the supplier
4. How this supplier's material is handled, etc., when it is received
5. What use his company makes of the material
6. What specifications are established and why
7. The financial structure and who the supplier's owners are
8. Supplier's type of management and principal officers
9. How the supplier rates in size, etc., in the industry
10. Method of distribution commonly used by the supplier
11. Local sales representative
12. How competitors' quality and prices compare on the same material

If the department does not regularly keep a consolidated record on each supplier, i.e., data sheet or rating chart, the trainee should be encouraged to develop such a record on each supplier with whom he will

Vendor

D145-1M

COMPANY DATA

OFFICERS	PLANT LOCATION	PRODUCTS
1. President	1.	1.
2. Exec. Vice-President	2.	2.
3. Sales Manager	3.	3.
4.	4.	4.
5.	5.	5.
	Home Office	

FINANCIAL STABILITY AND ANALYSIS

PD	SALES	DIV.	$ VALUE	NET ASSETS	DATE

RECENT FINANCIAL TRENDS AND CHANGES

SOURCE: NEWSPAPER CLIPPINGS AND SALES REMARKS

DATE	

BUYER'S RATING

DATE					
Price					
Service					
Quality					
Fin Resp					

1. Excellent 2. Very Good 3. Good 4. Fair 5. Poor

DATE	GENERAL REMARKS

FIG. 23–8*b*. Consolidated record on the supplier (back).

deal. An example of such a chart in the form of a file folder is reproduced in Figs. 23–8*a* and 23–8*b*. It provides spaces on both sides for recording information on:

1. Supplier's management and sales personnel
2. Products purchased and on which business is solicited
3. Rating of the supplier
4. Financial data and clippings
5. Interview summaries

The use of a folder provides for the accumulation of financial statements, trade reports, and other data related to the company's activities.

Reporting on the Visit. The report should be simple, brief, and thoughtful in its preparation. It should be related to the questions or directions given before the visit, and should include brief comments on:

1. People met and positions they hold
2. Materials discussed
3. Processes and procedures observed

4. New ideas resulting from the experience
5. Recommendations for future visits
6. The expenses incurred during the trip

Such a report should be required of older as well as newer men *after each plant visit.* A simple form used by one company is reproduced in Fig. 23–9 (Purchasing Department Buyer's Trip Report).

I Went	I Was Away	I Traveled	I Stayed At:	Transportation	Acc't No.
				Cashier———	
				Traffic———	
				Other———	43———
				Cash Spent———	
	Hours	Miles		Total———	67———

Where I went: ___________

Why I went: ___________

People I saw were: ___________

My activities were: ___________

I learned that: ___________

I suggest that: ___________

If you go there: ___________

Date___________ ___________ Reported by

FIG. 23–9. Purchasing department buyer's trip report.

The report should be discussed with the new man. An interest in his experience will be stimulating to him. His comments will be more of an aid than his written report in judging the value of his experience.

The real worth of the written report is to require him to *think about* his experience and to try to evaluate it.

Continuing the Employee's Education. Education is never-ending. Each new experience adds to knowledge and leaves its memory record. Each job changes, and purchasing's responsibilities multiply with the increase in the complexity of the firm's organization and size. Added knowledge is necessary to meet this challange. "As a company management exerts more pressure on purchasing to reduce cost of purchased parts, the need for capable people becomes more apparent," states Dr. Douglas Basil,

Associate Professor of Management of the School of Business Administration at the University of Minnesota. When asked who should head up a training program, he replied, "The top man in purchasing. Unless he is directly involved in both the planning and the implementation of a purchasing training program, it won't be successful. If the 'big boss' is behind the program and also directly involved in some phase of teaching, the rest of the staff will accept the program." He is supported in this view by management surveys that show that the top purchasing man selects his people in more than 75 per cent of companies.

Although Dr. Basil feels strongly that much of the training is the responsibility of the purchasing head, he believes that supplemental off-the-job training and study can be furnished by local colleges and universities. In this opinion, he is joined by many other university people. Former Professor of the Commerce School of Business Administration at the University of Pittsburgh, Keith E. MacEachron, has said, "Although the training of purchasing personnel can, to a significant degree, be conducted within the purchasing organization, there are cases where it is advisable to supplement the program with the coordinated use of outside resources. Among the tools available to train purchasing personnel are special courses offered by colleges, universities and other institutions. These courses may be either related directly to the purchasing profession or they may be of a general management nature. Most institutions of higher education offer courses in purchasing principles, which are a most valuable supplement to on-the-job training offered within the purchasing organization."

Although Stuart F. Heinritz has raised the question, "Is professionalism purchasing's goal?" he points out: "Management respects professional training, but in an objective fashion. It may elect to pick a man with potential promise, rather than immediate qualifications, and to undertake training and seasoning on its own account. If we look for precedence here, we shall find many instances where men have been chosen from the professions of engineering, accounting, or the law, or men who have a practical rather than a professional background in some other phase of the business, to direct purchasing activities. Sometimes this is done with the specific purpose of using those attributes in a particular buying situation; more often, probably, it is done on a basis of personality, for management too has an image to project, the company man."

John Van de Water of *Purchasing* magazine in an article entitled "The Problem of Purchasing Training" writes: "The young man expects to achieve in a few years, the economic status his parent now enjoys. Often not too far from that of the boss himself. He is challenged, not frightened by automation, materials management, and value analysis. He wants to move quickly and is not easily content with secure anonymity.

"While this does not imply that the established purchasing manager should look upon the newcomers as immediate competition, it does suggest that he must not be content to rest upon past achievements.

"Again, the seminars and refresher courses may not have all the answers. Perhaps the P.A. or his buyers need to go back to college. Perhaps they should work through their Purchasing association to provide sensible courses that meet specific needs."

This is precisely what has been done by the joint effort of the Graduate School of Business Administration at Harvard University and The National Association of Purchasing Agents. In 1962, Harold A. Berry, former President of the NAPA, conceived the notion that a joint effort by Harvard and the Association would attract top purchasing executives. The effort was successful, and the program is expected to continue as a fortnight of intensive workshop activity. Howard T. Lewis has quoted Mr. Berry as saying, "We still feel that a good, sound basic bachelor degree in business administration, engineering, or even in the liberal arts school should precede in the Purchasing education. Included in the undergraduate schools, regardless of the major, we should like to see one or two semesters of Purchasing for all who enter business. We are not eager to develop Purchasing majors at this point, but feel that Purchasing education in depth should follow undergraduate training."

Nevertheless, it is obvious that both Mr. Lewis of Harvard and Mr. Berry of NAPA believe in continuing education for the buyer. Every employee should be encouraged to continue his study. His work should inspire him to learn all there is to know about it and its related activities.

Make generous use of Section 26 of this handbook. Much of the literature listed is new and useful for reading.

The reading list at the end of this section as well as supplier catalogs, trade magazines, business periodicals, and newspapers will provide an abundance of information for voluntary reading. Other organized study programs may be arranged by consulting the local librarian or nearby college faculty.

Classroom instruction is available to many employees as a part of their employee activities. These are usually conducted as a part of a vocational or educational program in large companies. Other programs are available in night classes in the local high school or college. Purchasing personnel near metropolitan centers have many opportunities for study. College credit is frequently given for this study.

Figure 23–10 gives in detail the course of study available for four years at the Illinois Institute of Technology in Chicago. This course was encouraged and counseled by the Purchasing Agents Association of Chicago. Students may enroll and upon completion of the requirements receive the degree of Bachelor of Science in Business and Economics. Courses are available in *both day* and *evening* classes. Similar programs are available

FIRST SEMESTER

BE	101	Prin. of Econ. I	3	0	3
BE	122	Introd. to Acct.	3	0	3
Engl	101	Reading, Writing, and Thinking I	3	0	3
Math	121	Elem. Anal.	3	0	3
PE	101	Physical Education	2	0	0
Soc	281	Introd. Soc.	3	0	3
		Totals	17	0	15

SECOND SEMESTER

BE	102	Prin. of Econ. II	3	0	3
BE	342	Cost Accounting	3	0	3
Engl	102	Reading, Writing, and Thinking II	3	0	3
Math	122	Elem. Anal.	3	0	3
PE	102	Physical Education	2	0	0
Psy	201	Introd. Psy.	3	0	3
		Totals	17	0	15

THIRD SEMESTER

*Math	220	Elem. Calculus or	3	0	3
Approved Elective			3	0	3
BE	321	Bus. Law: Cont.	3	0	3
BE	371	Marketing	3	0	3
BE	421	Acct. Theory Underlying Finan. Statements	3	0	3
Approved Elective			3	0	3
		Totals	15	0	15

FOURTH SEMESTER

BE	315	Economics Statistics I	3	0	3
BE	322	Business Law and the Market	3	0	3
†Departmental Elective			3	0	3
Approved Elective			6	0	6
		Totals	15	0	15

FIFTH SEMESTER

BE	351	Theory of Organ. and Management	3	0	3
BE	373	Purchasing	3	0	3
BE	375	Indust. Relations	3	0	3
ME	448	Manufacturing Processes	4	3	5
Natural Science			—	—	3 to 5
		Totals	—	—	17 or 19

SIXTH SEMESTER

BE	307	Devel. of Economic Thought	3	0	3
BE	360	Money, Bkg. & Pr.	3	0	3
BE	374	Purch. Problems	3	0	3
BE	312	Prin. Indust. Mgt.	3	0	3
Sp	409	Public Speaking	2	0	1
Natural Science			—	—	3 to 5
		Totals	—	—	16 or 18

SEVENTH SEMESTER

BE	305	Am. Ind. Hist.	3	0	3
BE	376	Buying from Specific Industries	3	0	3
BE	450	Prosperity and Depression	3	0	3
BE	427	Engineering Econ.	3	0	3
TD	204	Blueprint Reading	1	5	2
Humanities Elective			3	0	3
		Totals	15	0	15

EIGHTH SEMESTER

BE	470	Indust. Marketing	3	0	3
BE	472	Sales Management	3	0	3
BE	496	Analysis and Research or	3	0	3
Approved Elective			3	0	3
BE	377	Purchasing Admin. for Institutions	3	0	3
PS	420	Amer. Con. Sys.	3	0	3
		Totals	15	0	15

Minimum standard for graduation—123 credits

† The *Departmental Elective* requirement is satisfied by BE 350, 427, 475, 455, or another course in the department approved by the adviser.

The *Approved Elective* requirement may be fulfilled by any elective approved by the student's adviser from among the offerings of this and other departments. These electives in part are designed to provide an opportunity for a student to elect a minor. In addition, these electives are designed to provide an opportunity to acquire a broad social, cultural, philosophical and historical background.

FIG. 23–10. Course of study in purchasing available at Illinois Institute of Technology, Chicago.

at such schools as: Los Angeles State College, Michigan State University, University of Pittsburgh, and the University of Wisconsin.

Recognizing that purchasing and selling are complementary activities, the course at the University of Pittsburgh is a combined program. Thus it differs somewhat from the other major purchasing courses designed to lead to "professional competence in the field of industrial purchasing." It is also offered at Pittsburgh to both day and evening classes. Junior and senior students will be required to take 68 credits of specially selected topics, 19 of which are in science and engineering. All of these courses recognize that training for purchasing cannot be narrow and must develop the individual in a broad sense. Based upon a background of liberal arts work, they include chemistry, physics, engineering, and business administration.

Dr. I. V. Fine of the University of Wisconsin lists the following nine areas of knowledge that the "beginning buyer should bring with him to the job":

1. English—both written and spoken
2. Mathematics and statistics
3. Economics
4. Accounting
5. Commercial law
6. Industrial management
7. Marketing
8. Corporate finance
9. Public relations

Lamar Lee, Jr., head of Purchasing at the Stanford Graduate School of Business, lists the following "basic subjects of business with which a Purchasing man must be familiar":

1. The principles of management
2. Business economics
3. Accounting
4. Statistics and forecasting
5. Marketing
6. Manufacturing
7. Finance
8. Human elements of management
9. Management and management science
10. English
11. Employee relations
12. Legal aspects of business

Mr. Lee goes on to say, "Unless Purchasing executives participate in educational programs, particularly those that teach them to consider problems from a viewpoint of a company as a whole, the goals of the Purchasing profession can never be met."

The National Association of Purchasing Agents, 11 Park Place, New York, compiles information about classes offered in purchasing. Many such classes are conducted by purchasing men under the auspices of a local purchasing association. Purchasing courses currently being offered are listed in Section 28, "Appendix." The costs are usually nominal.

A letter to Mark R. Greene, Executive Secretary of the American Association of Collegiate Schools of Business, 101 North Skinker Road, St. Louis 63105, Missouri, will bring information on schools of business throughout the United States.

Materials Management. In recent years, the concept of materials management as a new management function has come in for considerable attention. In general, this concept embraces all activities affecting the costs of materials prior to introduction into the product and after delivery of the finished product to the warehouse for marketing. Only a handful of managements have adopted the concept without some modification. In theory, the activities involved would be: production scheduling, inventory control, purchasing, receiving, warehousing, and traffic. The manager of this division of materials management is likely to have an important voice in management policy. He becomes responsible for material costs except those added during processing and for overheads. Purchasing people have frequently been tapped to develop and later head this function.

The American Management Association has developed studies in this field and may be contacted for further information. It is interesting that this organization, long recognized for its impact on management thinking, has, at the same time it is advancing the concept of materials management, taken a new look at purchasing. Traditionally, the AMA has treated the purchasing function as one of the other management activities. In 1961, the Association organized and conducted its first "Purchasing Division Seminar." Since then, many workshops, seminars, and conferences have been conducted under the purchasing division's auspices. Purchasing and materials management people have greeted this effort by attending in great numbers. The experience of purchasing agents associations has been similar. Workshops conducted by the Purchasing Agents Association of Chicago have been heartily co-sponsored by the Illinois Institute of Technology who have provided talent and space for the workshop. Other universities in the Chicago area have assisted the Chicago Association similarly in providing leadership. Their story is being repeated throughout the educational centers that service industrial areas.

Association Activities. The opportunity to exchange ideas with others engaged in the purchasing occupation is one of the most rewarding educational experiences. The new purchasing man should attend all local Purchasing Agents Association meetings. He will learn much through these contacts.

When the local association holds commodity group meetings in which he is interested, he should attend. The purchasing agent should encourage his subordinates to accompany him to local meetings.

Conferences and conventions of several trade associations afford excellent chances for learning. Appearances on the program at such meetings will *accelerate the study of the job.* The new man should be encouraged to offer to help in association work. This is more valuable in his early training than in later years when heavy responsibilities intervene.

Some of the larger and better known associations conduct seminars and conferences of interest to purchasing personnel. Literature is frequently available. Special studies are made and reports circulated on aspects of industry related to purchasing.

Some of the active associations which have made timely studies, conducted seminars, or compiled reports in the purchasing field are:

1. National Association of Purchasing Agents, 11 Park Place, New York[8]
2. The Canadian Association of Purchasing Agents, 357 Bay Street, Toronto, Canada
3. Local associations of the National Association of Purchasing Agents and the Canadian Association of Purchasing Agents listed in Section 28
4. The National Institute of Governmental Purchasing, 1001 Connecticut Avenue, N.W., Washington, D.C.
5. National Association of Manufacturers, 277 Park Avenue, New York
6. American Management Association, 135 West 50th Street, New York
7. Chamber of Commerce of the United States, 1615 H Street, N.W., Washington, D.C.
8. Manufacturing Chemists Association, 1625 I Street, N.W., Washington, D.C.
9. Southern Gas Association, 1932 Life of America Building, Dallas, Texas

EVALUATING THE MAN

Training without its counterpart, evaluation, is likely to become disorganized and haphazard. A sound program for measuring the progress of the new employee will permit a shift of emphasis where needed.

The objectives in the training have been set forth. The task of evaluation is simply trying to determine as we go along how effective is the

[8] In addition to its many other services, the NAPA provides many training tools to its members. Some of these include many booklets on special aspects of purchasing, reference lists, movies, and other visual aids that can be important in training programs.

instruction given. For this reason, the evaluation of the training is a necessary part of the training program.

Evaluation of the Trainee

Conferences with the trainee are perhaps the most important means of judging his progress. Regular reports from his "big brother" and supervisors are necessary. These reports should be made in his presence, if possible. He will feel that such open frankness indicates his acceptance into the family of employees. He will have no fear that vital information on his progress is being withheld from him. His confidence will remain unimpaired.

Each new employee *expects to be told* if he is in error. Any failure to do so will shake his confidence in the department's management. If the trainee is informed as to the relative importance his management attaches to each aspect of his assignment, he can direct his attentions more effectively. The standards by which he will be judged should be spelled out (see Sections 3 and 24).

Best of all, methods of evaluation should be devised that will suit the man and the job to be done. Reviewing the literature at the end of this section is suggested. There are many good articles and texts which cover this subject.

The new man, if properly chosen, will be a man who wants to learn the right way to do the job. He should be told what is the right way. Anything less than that is unfair to him, to the purchasing agent, and to the company.

Evaluation of the Buyer

Evaluating performance of the purchasing department and that of the individual buyer is the subject of Section 24. All areas are explained in detail. A study of the contents is required in order to grasp the significance of the detailed audit. In the interest of completeness in this section, a brief general summary slanted to the training objective seems warranted at this time, even though it overlaps to some extent the contents of Section 24.

The evaluation of a buyer's performance cannot be reduced to an exact science. The standards to be used must be related to the targets that were set. Spell out these targets, make use of the "Training Schedule" (Fig. 23–5), and take adequate time for the trainee to tell what he has experienced. Since it is meaningless, in the long run, to use such quantity factors as numbers of orders, dollars spent, and salesmen interviewed, it is necessary to talk with those who will receive satisfaction from the way in which the trainee does his job. These opinions will be invaluable in the final analysis of the trainee's progress. Arthur R. Pell, in an article entitled "What Makes a Good P. A. Tick," observed that "both Salesmen and Purchasing executives agreed in a general survey that product knowledge is secondary to personal characteristics." Some believed that curiosity and imagination were most important. Others believed that open-mindedness was extremely important. Some added that skepticism tempered by some humility is a valuable personal characteristic. George W. Baker, commenting in the survey, said, "Purchasing agents have to be able to work under pressure. There is a sense of urgency in their job that is always with them." Robert H. A. Davis, Executive Secretary for the New York Purchasing Agents Association said, "Attention to detail can make the difference between success and failure on the job." Paul V. Farrell of *Purchasing* magazine editorialized the need for higher standards of performance and education. He said, "The demands on Purchasing today make it imperative that buyers be better equipped and better educated than ever before. Standards of Purchasing performance and Purchasing education are inevitably going to get higher and higher. Ideally the modern Purchasing executive should try to exceed the standard in both areas."

In short term only the time factor is changed. If a buyer purchases a substitute material regularly available *because the buyer and no one else discovered it was available and thought to try it out,* then that buyer has performed a short-term creative act. The actual submission of the sample, proposal, and subsequent approval of the material is the creative act. Subsequent purchases that result in the saving of money are the productive acts.

Therefore, we can say that an act of *thought* applied to the purchasing operation is *creative.* An act of *buying* is *productive.* We might generalize by saying that the intangibles of the function are apt to be creative; the tangibles are apt to be productive.

It seems to follow, then, that *creative* acts depend on the *opportunities for them and the application of the buyer's ability* to take advantage of them. Furthermore, productive acts depend on the knowledge of the subject matter and the efficient use of the time available.

Factors That Can Be Measured

Quantitative standards and qualitative units of measure and standards applied to some of these factors may give us a measure of performance. Since the "creative" or "intangible" aspects of the performance are related to the "productive," the measurement of the productive acts can give us some idea of the buyer's over-all proficiency.

If we devise a report that tells management regularly what cost savings

Date	Product	How Accomplished						Brief Description	Actual amount saved	Est. annual saving	Actual annual saving
		A	B	C	D	E	O				
Jan.	Trousers, men's	X						Blanket order price advantage at price existing prior to increases	$ 355.00		$ 355.00
Jan.	Sisal twine		X					Research on weight used vs. adequate weight for using department; price negotiation; quick delivery	332.25		332.25
Jan.	Pallets, wood	X		X				Negotiated price advantage of 7% on carload of pallets prior to price increase	168.21		168.21
Jan.	Gloves, 12 oz.	X						Located best price vendor with acceptable glove. Constant price changes on this item	135.00		135.00
Jan.	Rags, wiping (curtain stock)		X		X			New vendor; lesser quality, but found to be adequate for applied usage	80.55		97.50
Jan.	Receptacles, metal		X					New vendor; fireproof item; best price; quick delivery	78.40		78.40
Jan.	Toweling for cafeteria		X					New vendor with better size consistency and better quality; quick delivery	15.00		30.00
Jan.	Staples, auto clench	X						New vendor having identical staples	25.20		25.20
								Total	$1,189.61		$1,221.56

A, result of favorable price negotiating with supplier.
B, due to use of new sources, research and evaluation.
C, as a result of advance buying.
D, resulting through use of substitutions.
E, as a result of recommended economical purchase quantity.
O, other.

Buyer John Doe

Period

FIG. 23–11. Report of savings resulting from effort and ingenuity of buyer.

result from the various purchasing operations, we supply a valuable means of measuring the job and function.

Figure 23–11 shows how one company requires each buyer to report cost savings each month. This form is concise and easily interpreted. A conference with the buyer on one or more of the items picked at random will give the whole story. It is not difficult to learn how much the buyer contributed to the reduction. Also, it is no task to learn how he handled the supplier during the negotiation. The buyer's remarks during the course of the conference will be a good indication of how well he is doing on his job.

SELECTED BIBLIOGRAPHY: PERSONNEL TRAINING

Literature of General Interest

Anyon, G. Jay: *Managing an Integrated Purchasing Process,* Holt, Rinehart and Winston, Inc., New York, 1963

Berry, Harold A.: *Purchasing Management,* Prentice-Hall, Inc., Englewood Cliffs, N.J., 1964

England, W. B.: *Procurement: Principles and Cases,* 4th ed., Richard D. Irwin, Inc., Homewood, Ill., 1962

Farmer, Samuel C.: *A Look at Purchasing through the President's Eye, Management Bulletin 33,* American Management Association, New York, 1963

Fearon, Harold E., and John H. Hoagland: *Purchasing Research in American Industry,* American Management Association, New York, 1963

Heinritz, S. F., and P. V. Farrell: *Purchasing: Principles and Applications,* 4th ed., Prentice-Hall, Inc., Englewood Cliffs, N.J., 1965

Lee, Lamar, Jr., and Donald W. Dobler: *Purchasing and Materials Management,* McGraw-Hill Book Company, New York, 1965

McMillan, A. L.: *The Art of Purchasing,* Exposition Press, Inc., New York, 1959

Pooler, Victor H., Jr.: *The Purchasing Man and His Job,* American Management Association, New York, 1964

Westing, Fine, et al.: *Industrial Purchasing,* 2d ed., John Wiley & Sons, Inc., New York, 1961

Many other references are listed in Section 26, "Library and Catalog File," and Section 28, "Appendix."

Literature of Special Interest

Many of these should be made available to the new employee in purchasing during orientation. They will be useful before assigning him to in-plant training.

Bethel, S. S., et al.: *Industrial Organization and Management,* 3d ed., McGraw-Hill Book Company, New York, 1956

Crissy, William, and Robert Kaplan: *Vendor Interviewing,* Michigan State University, Illinois Institute of Technology Press, Chicago, 1964

Gray, Albert Woodruff: *Purchase Law Manual,* Conover-Mast Publications, Inc., New York–Chicago, 1954

Hayes, F. Albert, and George A. Renard: *Evaluating Purchasing Performance,* American Management Association, New York, 1964

Henrici, S. B.: *Standard Costs for Manufacturing,* McGraw-Hill Book Company, New York, 1953

Imner, J. R.: *Materials Handling,* McGraw-Hill Book Company, New York, 1953

Nickerson, C. B.: *Cost Accounting,* McGraw-Hill Book Company, New York, 1954

Thau, Theodore L.: *Business Ethics* (pamphlet), Business Ethics Advisory Council, U.S. Department of Commerce, Washington, D.C.

Literature for Training Purposes

Interview Proceeding and Employee Testing Methods, The Dartnell Corporation, Ripert, 537, Chicago, Ill., 1947

Lawshe, C. H.: *Principles of Personnel Testing,* McGraw-Hill Book Company, New York, 1948

Lusardi, F. R.: *Purchasing for Industry, Studies in Business Policy No. 33,* National Industrial Conference Board, New York, September, 1948

McNair, M. P., and A. O. Hersum: *Case Method at the Harvard Business School,* McGraw-Hill Book Company, New York, 1954

National Association of Purchasing Agents, New York:
- *Guide to the Selection of Competent Buyers*
- *Outline of a Course in Industrial Procurement: Principles, Practices, and Cases*
- *Outline of an Intracompany Training Program for Purchasing Personnel*
- *Suggestions for Development–Recording-use of Purchasing Policies and Procedures for a Purchasing Department Manual*
- *The Plant Visitation*
- *Where to Find It,* Howard T. Lewis

The Public Opinion Index for Industry, Opinion Research Corporation, Princeton, N.J.

Recruiting and Selecting Employees, Studies in Personnel Policy No. 144, National Industrial Conference Board, Inc., New York, 1954

Scott, W. D., et al.: *Personnel Management,* 5th ed., chap. 10, McGraw-Hill Book Company, New York, 1949

Thorndike, R. L.: *Personnel Selection: Test and Measurement Techniques,* John Wiley & Sons, Inc., New York, 1949

Many other references are listed in Section 26, "Library and Catalog File," and Section 28, "Appendix."

SECTION 24

EVALUATING PURCHASING PERFORMANCE

Co-Editors

A. G. Pearson, Executive Assistant, North American Aviation, Inc., Downey, California

W. G. Watt, Manager—Purchasing and Packaging, California and Hawaiian Sugar Refining Corporation, Ltd., San Francisco, California

Associate Editors

Ralph W. Dixon, Purchasing Agent, Datex Corp., a Subsidiary of Gianinni Controls Corporation, Monrovia, California

Alice C. Hodnett, Purchasing Officer, U.S. Atomic Energy Commission, New York, New York

Evaluation in business is an everyday occurrence. Managers "evaluate" for the purpose of determining whether their organizations are moving toward their objectives according to agreed-upon plans. It is a function of *control.* Without evaluation, drifts could inadvertently occur which might well carry a company into unplanned and unintended areas foreign to its objectives and ultimately to financial ruin.

Evaluation should not be undertaken without understanding why it must be done, what must be done, and how to do it. Authors Newman and Summer, in *The Process of Management,*[1] sum up the control process (evaluation) as follows:

> The aim of control is to assure that the results of operations conform as closely as possible to established goals. Three elements, or phases, are always present in the control process. These are:

[1] Reproduced by permission. William H. Newman and Charles E. Summer, Jr., *The Process of Management: Concepts, Behavior, Practice,* Prentice-Hall, Inc., Englewood Cliffs, N.J., 1961.

1. Standards that represent desired performance. These standards may be tangible or intangible, vague or specific, but until everyone concerned understands what results are desired, control will create confusion.
2. A comparison of actual results against the standards. This evaluation must be reported to people who can do something about it.
3. Corrective action. Control measurements and reports serve little purpose unless corrective action is taken when it is discovered that current activities are not leading to desired results.

Evaluation thus may also be termed "measuring." In some degree, it can be considered as auditing, although, in general, an audit is considered in narrower limits than we tend to think of for evaluation or measuring. Evaluation, in terms of measuring purchasing performance, for too long has been thought to be an intercompany measurement rather than an intracompany one. Since the aims and objectives of various companies differ even within an industry, to say nothing of what happens in unrelated industries, and since management concepts of what constitutes proper purchasing also differ, it is difficult to make meaningful purchasing comparisons between companies. Large companies have long understood the need to evaluate. Too often, however, in small or even among medium-sized organizations, this either has not been done on the proper basis or simply has not been done at all. Also, for many years the idea persisted in the minds of many purchasing executives that in evaluating, they would only be compiling endless and meaningless charts and statistics. The fact that evaluation more frequently than not is of the appraisal type did not occur to them. These fallacious notions no longer exist to the same degree, and more and more purchasing executives are applying a form of evaluation in their departments.

WHY EVALUATE?

From the foregoing, it becomes clear that evaluation is needed in order to control and thus to assure being on target with respect to meeting purchasing objectives. Top management evaluates the purchasing function not only in relation to other departments. The basic responsibility of purchasing is the effective commitment of company funds, to buy at the right price, at the right time, at the right quality, and in the right quantity, and ultimately, of course, to deliver to the right place. The increasing recognition of purchasing as a profit center makes it all the more desirable that these basic functions be kept in mind. The widely advertised profit center of today is a profit center only as it performs these basic functions well.

AMERICAN MANAGEMENT ASSOCIATION SURVEY

The 1964 survey of more than 200 executives and other top-level corporate officers (American Management Association Research Study 66) found 72 per cent of the responding companies were evaluating the performance of their procurement organizations by some means. This trend has developed for three reasons. The first is the realization, though slow in coming, that the spending of over half a company's income is the responsibility of a small group, usually less than 5 per cent of the total people in the organization. This small unit can make or break an organization by the way it commits the company's funds. Next, there is the expanding scope of the function of procurement management as over-all management finds in this group the key to better coordination of company activities to achieve low over-all cost results. And there is the realization that more profit can result from improved procurement performance than will result from the same effort expended in improving any other unit in the organization.

Those responding to the AMA Survey felt very strongly about improved results from procurement performance. In summary:

1. Forty-eight per cent believed purchasing performance would be improved if some of their present employees were replaced.
2. Fifty-five per cent believed performance would improve if buying commitments made outside the purchasing department were eliminated.
3. Eighty-nine per cent believed performance would improve if purchasing responsibilities were more clearly pinpointed and capabilities of present employees were developed to a higher level.
4. Forty-four per cent believed performance would improve if there were stronger management backing for purchasing policies, programs, and budgets.
5. Forty-three per cent believed the pathway to improvement lies in more fluid communication and integration with management.

METHODS OR TECHNIQUES OF MEASUREMENT (WHO MEASURES?)

The purchasing department can be evaluated either by external organizations or internal ones. External evaluation would principally involve management consultants and would generally be resorted to for the study of individual departments only by large organizations. Smaller companies, when they employ such consultants, generally do so for the purpose of checking known troublesome areas in an over-all study of the company. Because of its cost, this method is rarely used in study of the purchasing department alone in small or even medium-sized companies. Such a study has the advantage of being performed by people whose experience is broad and who may be presumed to be entirely objective. But it has the disadvantage that such people, by the same token, have much to learn about the particular organization and that this learning is usually carried out during the process of evaluation.

Internal evaluation can be done by the company's internal auditors, by so-called "systems experts" within the company, or by the purchasing department itself. Despite the comment earlier in this chapter, internal auditors are playing an ever-larger part in evaluation of areas other than accounting and can be of inestimable value to purchasing. Their aid should be welcomed—not opposed.

A 1955 survey of the Institute of Internal Auditors indicated that about 25 per cent of the firms reporting were conducting audits of the purchasing department. A similar survey in 1961 showed that 70 per cent of a much larger reporting group were doing so. This growth in use of auditing reflects the worthwhileness of the internal audit when properly conducted.

The areas and methods of exploration set forth in this section are designed primarily with the thought in mind that evaluation will be *internal,* and carried out by the head of the purchasing department. By the same token, however, these ideas can be of value to others performing an evaluation.

The selected areas of study cover the majority of the purchasing functions which can be evaluated. They are, however, by no means all-inclusive, and as each organization evaluates its purchasing function, it should keep in mind the objectives of the department and how it goes about attaining those objectives. Purchasing as a profit center was mentioned earlier. The attainment of profits for an organization can come about insofar as purchasing is concerned by decreased costs of operating the purchasing department as well as through excellence in buying performance. Thus, purchasing evaluation should be a continuous operation of examining structure, personnel, and buying technique, rather than an occasional flurry of activity. It must be thought-out, well planned, and not haphazard. It should be performed by people who have a knowledge of such matters and not by people who either are untrained or lack interest. In performing these studies, it is well to remember that:

1. Performance measurements do not usually speak for themselves. The facts must be interpreted orally or in writing.

2. Many of the evaluation measures are not complete or exact. Performance measurement may require the combined use of several of them.
3. Quantitative measures for purchasing should never be emphasized at the expense of qualitative ones.

QUALITATIVE FUNCTIONS: MEASUREMENT OF ATTITUDES AND PEOPLE

Purchasing Climate

To properly evaluate the purchasing function, one needs to consider carefully the "climate" in which it is operating. Even the best organization with the most highly qualified personnel will not function effectively in an atmosphere of hostility or indifference or even passive tolerance. Most enlightened top management today fully recognizes and supports the procurement function. But this is by no means universal. Where active support does not exist, it must be sought. Opportunities for savings (profits) through purchasing must be called to top management's attention. Failure to perform at peak quality levels because of inadequate or unqualified personnel or facilities should also be explained.

Even when stated corporate policy may be favorable to the function, in actual practice there may be situations which cause difficulties. The reporting procedure can often be the seat of problems: reporting to the wrong member of top management; reporting to a member of management who is too far down the line to be effective in the broad picture; or even reporting to someone who, no matter how high his position, may lack understanding of and interest in the procurement function. These situations can be changed only by producing *proof* of the department's ability to aid in enhancing corporate profitability. It requires constant persuasion. But the persuasion *must* be factual, and not just "me too."

A good purchasing climate is something more than just having the purchasing department place orders. This something more is a manner of thinking, a management way of looking at the purchasing problem. When thinking is right, the resultant actions and devices take their proper places without problems. Major factors determining company climate include:

1. Does top management set clear company objectives? Are these meaningful to people down the line?
2. Has top management carefully thought through the major policies of the business? Have these been communicated skillfully so that executives down the line can act with confidence in conformity with the intent of management?

	Relative responsibility												
	Purchasing				Inventory control			Traffic and warehouse			Other departments		
	P	S	A	O	P	S	A	P	S	A	Engr.	Fin.	Mfg.
1. Recognition of need													
What ?													
How much ?													
When ?													
Where ?													
2. Inventory control													
Raw													
In-process													
Finished													
3. Specifications													
4. Authorization													
5. Appropriation													
6. Make or buy													
7. Search for vendor													
8. Screening vendors													
9. Quotations & bids													
10. Analysis of bids													
11. Selection of source													
12. Commitment													
13. Follow-up or expedite													
14. Receiving													
15. Inspection													
16. Payment													
17. Adjustments													
18. Storage													
19. Issue													
20. Purchase records													
21. Traffic													
a. inward													
b. outward													
22. Shipping													
a. finished goods													
b. other than fin.													
23. Insurance													
24. Legal													
25. Disposal or sale of													
a. Scrap													
b. Excess or obsolete													
c. Equipment													
26. Observance of results of material bought													

"P" - Prime responsibility
"A" - Advisory only
"S" - Shares in discussions and decisions
"O" - Administered by others, but purchasing is dependent on timely and efficient performance and reports

FIG. 24–1. Potential responsibilities of a purchasing department. The materials-management concept usually embraces all of these responsibilities.

3. Do executives at all levels feel a sense of proprietorship in the business? If not, what factors prevent this?
4. Does the company plan of organization provide the best harness for constructive individual action and effective executive teamwork?
5. What are company practices in delegation of responsibility?
6. What is the real effect of company practices in granting financial and nonfinancial rewards? In making promotions?
7. Does the president's approach to his job create an atmosphere that stimulates initiative and risk-taking or does it create attitudes of "play it safe" or "do not stick your neck out"?
8. Does the company atmosphere reflect the principles of free enterprise in a democracy or of corporate dictatorship, benevolent or otherwise?
9. Does the business consistently adhere to standards of conduct that men of good character can accept and live by without reservation?

Responsibility and Authority of the Department

No evaluation should be undertaken without first knowing the responsibility and authority of the department. Figure 24–1 lists potentials in this classification. The function varies greatly in organizations of different character and size. It is most desirable that the areas of responsibility and authority be set forth, whether as part of a complete organization manual or merely as a written statement from the president of the company. In smaller organizations, authority and responsibility are designated by tacit understanding, which, in most cases, is entirely satisfactory. For a proper study of this, see the examples in Section 2, "Purchasing Department Organization." In organizations of any size at all, it is most desirable that there be a purchasing manual, that the responsibility and authority of the department be set forth in the manual, and that top management approval be obtained for this statement. Figures 24–2*a* and 24–2*b* show

AUTHORITY AND RESPONSIBILITY OF THE PURCHASING DEPARTMENT

The Purchasing Department has the authority and sole responsibility of purchasing all supplies and materials required by the company. The performance of this special task is the department's primary concern.

All purchases are to be made only by the Purchasing Department, which shall conduct and conclude all negotiations affecting purchases, such as prices, terms, delivery and quality.

The responsibility for the discharge of these duties rests with the Manager of Purchasing and his staff.

FIG. 24–2*a*. Over-all policy.

PURCHASING FUNCTIONS - BASIC

The basic functions which follow are to be used as a guide by the Purchasing Department to achieve its primary objective:

1. Procure to the best advantage all materials,equipment and supplies required for the company's operations.
2. Establish general policies and procedures in connection with all purchasing operations.
3. Give effective assistance to other departments in reducing expenses by investigating and recommending alternate material.
4. To explore the market for new sources, products,materials, processes and ideas.Anticipated requirements when market trends point to an advantage.

Other Functions Performed Are:

Select vendors
Interview salesmen
Analyze quotations and prices
Negotiate with vendors
Issue purchase orders and initiate term contracts
Expedite deliveries
Process invoices,adjust claims
Dispose of scrap and surplus materials
Maintain records necessary to the functions
Maintain a reference library

Procurement Functions Not Performed by the Purchasing Department Are:

Procurement of advertising (other than printing)insurance,real estate and all traffic functions.

Functions in Which the Purchasing Department Shares Responsibilities With Other Departments:

Develop and maintain highway transportation facilities
Auditing
Inventory control of containers and stores materials
Systems development
Packaging research and quality control
Value Analysis
Make or buy studies
Reciprocal agreements with customers

The nature of our activities is such that the Purchasing Department may be called upon to assist in many functions not directly related to purchasing, per se.

\- - -

FIG. 24-2*b*. Basic policy for purchasing department.

such statements taken from a purchasing manual. A complete manual is shown in Section 3, "Policy and Procedure Manuals."

Purchasing Centralized in the Department

While in many organizations it is taken for granted that purchasing is done by purchasing personnel or through specifically authorized representatives of other departments, this is not necessarily the case. This is determined first by company policy and secondly by the effectiveness of the purchasing department itself. If a policy is not clearly set forth, one should be. If a large segment of procurement, including raw materials, is not being performed by purchasing personnel, there should be a reason for this division of functions and the reason should be understood. Division of purchasing functions is the case in a number of industries, including, for example, the sugar industry, where raw sugar is traditionally procured by a totally separate department.

There is no more validity for having buying functions performed by nonpurchasing personnel than for having engineering work done by chemists or legal work by accountants. Each function is specialized, and the efforts of the corporation as a whole are best advanced when this is recognized. For purchasing, the best argument for centralization (of the *function*—not necessarily of the location) is well-trained personnel whose performance results in *profits*. See Fig. 24–3*a* as an illustration of how one company places *buying* responsibility in purchasing without

CALIFORNIA AND HAWAIIAN SUGAR REFINING CORPORATION, LIMITED

RULE OF

PLANT PRACTICE

Date 5-26-64 Classification 5-2

Supersedes G-720-6 (4-4-39) Source Plant Manager

CROCKETT CONTACTS WITH SUPPLIERS OF

EQUIPMENT AND MATERIALS

PURPOSE

To specify the procedure at Crockett for contacting suppliers of equipment and materials.

ASSIGNMENT OF RESPONSIBILITIES

Department heads are responsible for the compliance of these provisions by members of their departments.

GENERAL POLICY

Purchasing of all supplies, materials and equipment for the refinery is the sole responsibility of the Purchasing Department. The Purchasing Department will conduct and conclude all final negotiations affecting purchases, such as prices, terms, delivery, and quality. However, certain refinery personnel, needing technical and engineering information to assist in their assigned projects, may contact supplying organizations directly for such information. In making these contacts, they are to keep the Purchasing Department fully informed. Except in the most general sense, there is to be no discussion of prices or terms except when a member of the Purchasing Department is present, and there are to be no agreements regarding orders.

Occasional small purchases and supplies for the Company House are excepted from this rule, being covered in Sections B and C of Rule of Plant Practice 11-4.

PROVISIONS

1. Certain refinery personnel, as specified by the department heads and approved by the Plant Manager, who have occasion to contact suppliers may phone, write or interview representatives of these suppliers to:

a. Obtain or exchange technical information.

b. Discuss problems concerning installation or use of equipment and supplies.

FIG. 24–3*a*. How one company spells out the relationship between plant personnel and the purchasing department.

Date 5-26-64 Classification 5-2

Supersedes G-720-6 (4-4-39)

-2-

Before such contacts are made other departments should be consulted, where they may be involved, to avoid duplication. In general, the department primarily responsible for the project should make the necessary contacts with the suppliers.

Wherever possible the Purchasing Department is to be informed in advance of any refinery contacts and is to receive copies of all correspondence.

2. Final negotiations and orders for purchases are to be referred to the Purchasing Department for their handling. Refinery personnel may make appropriate suggestions to the Purchasing Department regarding the handling of such purchases. If source of supply is specified on any requisition, Purchasing Department may develop alternate sources of supply which are acceptable to the person placing the requisition, as well as to the Purchasing Department.

In cases of emergency, purchases may be authorized by Crockett department heads. As soon as possible thereafter, however, proper requisitions are to be forwarded to the Purchasing Department with a memorandum explaining details. A copy of the memorandum is to be forwarded to the Plant Manager.

3. Except for those individuals covered in paragraph 4, salesmen desiring to contact individuals or departments at the refinery are to do so normally by appointment made through the Purchasing Department. When salesmen call at Crockett without having made previous arrangements, the Industrial Relations Department will refer them to the Purchasing Department.

When such visits are initiated by refinery personnel, both the Industrial Relations Department and the Purchasing Department are to be notified in advance.

4. Certain representatives of outside organizations who call frequently at Crockett may be admitted to the refinery without making previous arrangements. A list of such individuals is to be maintained by the Industrial Relations Department in consultation with the departments concerned at Crockett and the Purchasing Department.

5. In interviews with salesmen, no one who is not a member of the Purchasing Department is to commit himself on preference for any product, source of supply for any product, or give any information regarding competititve performance, final approval or price.

Date 5-26-64 Classification 5-2

Supersedes G-720-6 (4-4-39)

-3-

6. If necessary for anyone from the refinery to call personally at stores, office or factory of any supplier on company business, arrangements for such visit are to be made through the Purchasing Department.

CALIFORNIA AND HAWAIIAN SUGAR REFINING CORPORATION, LIMITED

FIG. 24–3*a*. (Continued.)

being overly restrictive. Figure 24–3*b* is more applicable to a small company.

Is the Department Adequately Staffed?

Proper organization of the department requires that there be the right number of buyers and clerks to do the job which is expected of the department. One needs to ask the question: Are there too many or too few buyers for the assigned responsibilities? What about the clerical func-

PLATE MANUFACTURING COMPANY
Standard Purchasing Procedural Instruction

Number 4110
Effective:July 20,1966
Supersedes:Aug.10,1961
Page 1 of 2

Subject: PURCHASE ORDER and REQUISITION CONTROL

I Purpose
  1.To define what purchases may be made at each level of management.
  2.To define who has authority to originate purchase orders.
  3.To provide a routine authorization for payment of invoices.
  4.To provide a format for Receiving Control.

II Procedure
  1.Forms used:
    A.Traveling Requisition (Form #101)
    B.Purchase Requisition (Form #411)
    C.Purchase Order (Form #412)
  2.All company purchases must be made using authorized purchase order.
    A.Exceptions are travel and entertainment expense.
    B.Petty cash purchases authorized by approved expense statements.
  3.No one in the company outside of its officers has the authority to obligate the company to purchase,lease or rent,other than the Purchasing Department.
  4.Purchase orders shall be originated by the Purchasing Department based on properly approved Purchase Requisition or Traveling Requisitions.
  5.Traveling Requisitions shall be used for all standard manufacturing raw materials, components,and purchases for resale. In every case these will originate from Production Control and must have a six digit stock number assigned before being submitted to Purchasing.
  6.Anyone in the company may requisition goods or services they feel are required to accomplish their job assignment,but before they may be accepted by Purchasing they must be approved.
  7.Requistion approvals are required based upon the following approving levels:
    A.All requisitions require the approval of a supervisor on at least the third level of management.Levels of management are defined as:
      1)The President
      2)Those reporting directly to the President
      3)Supervisors reporting to the second level
    B.Requisitions totaling over $100 but not including Traveling Requisitions,require the approval of the department manager (level 2). For Capital Expenditure see procedure #2329 "Capital Expenditures Authorization".
    C.Requisitions totalling over $500 but not including Traveling Requisitions,require the approval of the President.
    D.Traveling Requisitions under $1,000 require the Production Control Manager's approval.Traveling Requisitions over $1,000 require the additional approval of the Manager of Manufacturing.
    E.Requisitions charging a Project require the additional approval of the project head.
  8.Purchasing will honor all properly approved requisitions.The requisitioner may indicate sources to Purchasing, but Purchasing has the prerogative of buying from other sources if they can obtain equal merchandise and satisfactory delivery service at lower prices.In addition new sources for Product Components must have source approved by engineering.

FIG. 24–3*b*. Procedure policy for small company.

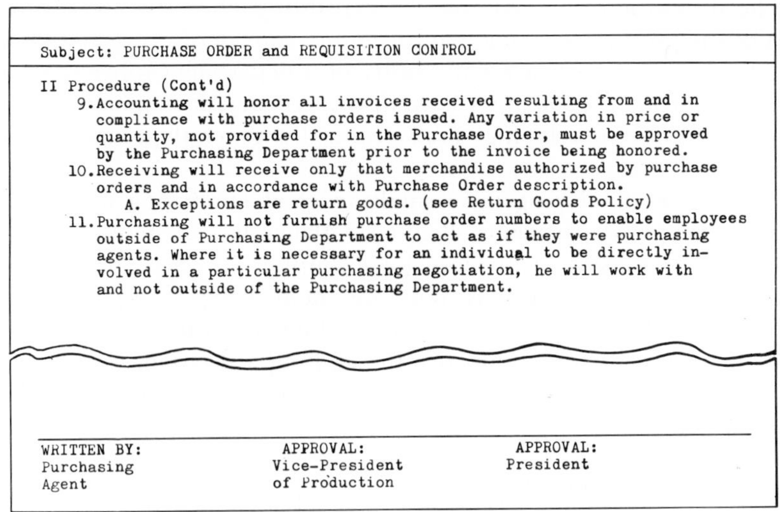

Subject: PURCHASE ORDER and REQUISITION CONTROL

II Procedure (Cont'd)

9. Accounting will honor all invoices received resulting from and in compliance with purchase orders issued. Any variation in price or quantity, not provided for in the Purchase Order, must be approved by the Purchasing Department prior to the invoice being honored.

10. Receiving will receive only that merchandise authorized by purchase orders and in accordance with Purchase Order description.
    A. Exceptions are return goods. (see Return Goods Policy)

11. Purchasing will not furnish purchase order numbers to enable employees outside of Purchasing Department to act as if they were purchasing agents. Where it is necessary for an individual to be directly involved in a particular purchasing negotiation, he will work with and not outside of the Purchasing Department.

WRITTEN BY:	APPROVAL:	APPROVAL:
Purchasing Agent	Vice-President of Production	President

FIG. 24–3*b*. Procedure policy for small company (Continued).

tions? Are there enough clerks or is the staffing such that there is an overlapping of duties? Too few buyers for the work that is expected can result in hasty decisions on buying problems, with the result that money is lost. An adequate number of personnel will make it possible for buyers to become specialists in the purchasing of important materials, to give the requisite amount of thought to each transaction, and to perform the investigative work which is necessary if profits are to be made through purchasing.

Efforts to reduce procurement costs through reduction in personnel can result in costly losses. Buyers can become mere order-placers, and opportunities for intelligent buying can evaporate. In smaller departments, illnesses and vacations can be highly disruptive if there are too few members on the purchasing staff. Where such situations exist, top management must be advised. Purchasing should not have to assume these responsibilities. A complete description of what is required is furnished in Section 2, "Purchasing Department Organization."

Are Functions Properly Distributed?

While in most companies there is agreement that the buying functions belong in purchasing, one needs to consider whether or not the responsibilities of a purchasing department include such matters as disposition of scrap, inventory control, traffic control, expediting, and invoice processing. If these are included, should they be? If they are not, why not?

The disposition of scrap and the expediting of orders are definitely part of the procurement function. Inventory control of raw materials and supplies is occasionally a responsibility of a department other than purchasing, but many companies have discovered that it is more effectively controlled under purchasing. Traffic control is generally a separate function.

The idea is developing increasingly in good purchasing management that purchasing departments should rid themselves of nonbuying functions. The processing of invoices, for example, was once predominantly a purchasing duty. Now it is more and more being transferred to the accounts payable section. Should you do this? If you do, is it in the best over-all interest of your company? In reaching a decision, consider only the net effect of all factors—cost, supplier relations, interdepartmental relations, etc.

What of the People in the Department?

The Department Head

The department head is obviously the key figure in the department. His qualifications for the job need to be carefully scrutinized. If the evaluation is being conducted by the department head himself, an objective appraisal is difficult but nevertheless necessary. He should ask himself whether he is keeping up with modern trends in purchasing, whether he is alert to changes which need to be made, if he is progressive in his views, if he listens to the advice and counsel of others, whether he delegates work properly, whether he participates in professional and trade associations, and if he is alert to changes within his company. In short, does he continue to have the attributes which presumably resulted in his being given the job to begin with?

The Buyers

Profitable purchasing on a day-in, day-out basis depends on the proper selection and training of the buyers. Working within established corporate and departmental policies, these are the people who, through proper selection, training, interest, and motivation, can do a *buying* job rather than merely *placing orders*. Section 23 of this handbook covers selection and training of purchasing personnel in detail, but no purchasing department can be expected to do a top job if it doesn't have properly qualified buyers. The qualifications of each buyer *for the job expected of him* need to be continually examined. This is doubly important if we consider that one of today's buyers can be tomorrow's department head.

Clerks, Secretaries, and Typists

Too frequently not enough attention is paid to these members of a purchasing department. While not as critical as buyers and more easily replaceable, they are nonetheless of substantial importance. Alert, intelligent, and well-trained employees can considerably lighten the work load of the buyers.

What Is the Department's Personnel Policy?

Policy of personnel recruitment, selection, training, promotion, salary administration—and even severance—needs to be clearly thought out and understood. Again, since Section 23 deals with this, let it suffice to be said here that failure to comprehend the importance of good personnel policy can result in haphazard selection, lack of training, promotion from "outside," and poor morale. A department known to have poor morale is generally avoided by good people, and thus the problem is compounded. There must be regular appraisal of employees, and good work should be rewarded just as quickly as poor work is criticized. Salary increases are an important recognition of jobs well done, but salary alone is not enough. There must be praise of exceptional accomplishments—preferably in the presence of others. Evaluation of the individual is possible with reviews of performance; a general employee review form is illustrated in Fig. 24–4*a*, and a form specifically for the review of buyers is shown in Fig. 24–4*b*.

Department Participation

Company Activities

The caliber of purchasing personnel can often be evaluated by the frequency with which they are invited to participate in company affairs, both in a direct business capacity and in corollary areas such as credit unions. Are they active participants, or are they left out? If they are not sought out, find out why.

Outside Activities

What of participation of department members in community and government affairs? Are they active in business and professional societies, or do they tend to remain aloof? Some people are natural "joiners," others are not. At least some participation in outside activities should be encouraged for the beneficial effects obtained.

Department Relations

With Other Departments

Are relations with other departments easy and friendly, or are they "at arms length"? Do other departments consult with purchasing *before* decisions are made to purchase materials? Does top management look to purchasing for information on commodities, prices, trends, etc.?

FOR THE PERIOD

EMPLOYEE PERIODIC REVIEW
MATSON NAVIGATION COMPANY

CONFIDENTIAL

FROM ________ TO ________

NAME ________ DEPARTMENT ________ LOCATION ________

POSITION ________ POSITION DATE ________ SERVICE DATE ________

Place a check mark in the box of the descriptive phrase of each factor or in the box separating two adjoining descriptive phrases that best describes the employee's performance during the period for which this record is reporting. (See instructions on reverse side)

Factor			
1. KNOWLEDGE OF WORK Understanding of all specific phases and duties of the position.	Complete and thorough understanding	Adequate understanding	Requires assistance in routine duties
	Comments, special aptitudes, recommendation for improvement, etc.		
2. KNOWLEDGE OF RELATED WORK Understanding of related jobs helpful or required for successful performance of current position.	Complete and thorough understanding	Adequate understanding	Limited understanding
	Comments, special aptitudes, recommendation for improvement, etc.		
3. PLANNING/ORGANIZATION Ability to plan ahead and schedule work with most effective use of personnel, materials and equipment.	Very effective under all conditions	Plans and organizes well	Needs assistance
	Comments, special aptitudes, recommendation for improvement, etc.		
4. VOLUME OF WORK Quantity of acceptable work.	Unusually high output	Regularly meets recognized standards	Should be increased
	Comments, special aptitudes, recommendation for improvement, etc.		
5. QUALITY OF WORK Thoroughness, neatness and accuracy of work.	Consistently maintains highest quality	Regularly meets recognized standards	Needs improvement
	Comments, special aptitudes, recommendation for improvement, etc.		
6. INITIATIVE Ability to originate or develop constructive ideas and to get things done.	Unusually active and resourceful	Has necessary drive	Inclines to follow precedent; lacks necessary drive
	Comments, special aptitudes, recommendation for improvement, etc.		
7. RELIABILITY Dependability in performing duties and following instructions.	Unfailingly dependable	Usually dependable	Needs prodding; often undependable
	Comments, special aptitudes, recommendation for improvement, etc.		
8. JUDGMENT Degree to which decisions and actions are sound.	Unusually accurate in judgment	Usually good judgment	Lacks judgment in other than routine work
	Comments, special aptitudes, recommendation for improvement, etc.		
9. COOPERATION Ability and willingness to be part of the team and work for the common interest of the job, section, department and Company.	Willingly cooperates	Generally cooperative	Inadequate teamwork and inconsiderate of others
	Comments, special aptitudes, recommendation for improvement, etc.		
10. ATTITUDE Indicated state of mind toward job and associates	Friendly and inspired	Generally contented	Somewhat disgruntled
	Comments, special aptitudes, recommendation for improvement, etc.		

FIG. 24–4*a*. Employee-review form (front).

CONFIDENTIAL

Factor			
11. ALERTNESS Intellectual awareness and response to instructions and existing and new conditions.	Shows keen perception	Shows good comprehension without undue delay	Is slow to comprehend
	Comments, special aptitudes, recommendation for improvement, etc.		
12. CONDUCT Courtesy and ethical behavior - self discipline.	Exemplary	Good	Should improve
	Comments, special aptitudes, recommendation for improvement, etc.		
13. LEADERSHIP Ability to inspires others to perform.	Highly developed leadership qualities	Usually successful	Requires some assistance
	Comments, special aptitudes, recommendation for improvement, etc.		
14. DEVELOPMENT OF SUBORDINATES Ability to train and develop subordinates for current and potential future positions.	Unusually successful in developing others	Encourages subordinates to develop their abilities	Contributes little to development of subordinates
	Comments, special aptitudes, recommendation for improvement, etc.		

POSSIBLE FUTURE ASSIGNMENTS: APPROXIMATE DATE

1. ______________________ ; ____________

2. ______________________ ; ____________

3. ______________________ ; ____________

WHAT ADDITIONAL EXPERIENCE OR TRAINING DO YOU RECOMMEND TO DEVELOP EMPLOYEE'S POTENTIAL FOR FUTURE ADVANCEMENT OR GROWTH IN PRESENT POSITION?

WHAT ARE THE EMPLOYEE'S AMBITIONS FOR HIS FUTURE?

Signature of Rating Supervisor ____________ Reviewed and Approved ____________ Department Head

Date: ____________ Date: ____________

INSTRUCTIONS

The purpose of this report is to provide an objective measurement of performance on the job for the period of time being reported. The rater should limit his evaluation to actual job performance during the period being reported and should make his judgments based upon the position level of the employee and not in comparison to employees in higher or lower positions. Care should be exercised to judge each trait or characteristic separately and independently; the evaluation of one trait should not influence another. The report may be used to determine training requirements and may be used as a basis for discussion with the employee to help him in his efforts to become better suited for his present and future position with the Company. It also will provide a permanent record for the employee's personnel file.

This form will be prepared during the third and twelfth months of employment, at times of promotion or transfer, and annually thereafter. Each review will cover the period of time since the last report. The form will be prepared by the employee's immediate supervisor and will be reviewed and approved by the department head. A Personnel Relations Department representative may be called upon by the department head to assist in the completion of the report.

There are fourteen factors on which supervisory and managerial employees are to be rated (twelve factors for non-supervisory employees); each factor has three descriptive phrases. The rater will use a check mark (✓) to indicate his rating of the employee. The check mark should be placed in the box on one of the descriptive phrases of each factor. The mark may be placed in the box separating two adjoining descriptive phrases to indicate that the appraisal falls between the two. The "Comments" section may be used by the rater to provide any additional comment he feels is needed to supplement or clarify any part of the rating or the over-all report.

Completed forms are confidential. No file copy will be retained by the raters. Completed forms will be sealed and forwarded to the Personnel Relations Department, 215 Market Street, San Francisco, where they will be maintained as a supplement to the master personnel files.

FIG. 24–4*a*. Employee-review form (back).

With Vendors

Vendors are often a buyer's most valuable allies. Are relations with vendors on a frank, friendly basis? Do vendors merely tolerate your buyers, or can their active cooperation be relied upon in times of material shortages? Is the relationship one of mutual respect, or are your buyers too straitlaced or too quick to accept favors? This is an area in which policy should be clearly stated—policy with respect to meals, entertainment, gifts. Entertainment and gifts should not be tolerated, but an occasional friendly lunch can do more good than harm. Do buyers have expense accounts so that luncheons can be reciprocated? For a further discussion of such policy, see Section 6, "Ethical Practices in Purchasing."

Vendor Selection

Of all the responsibilities of purchasing, this is one of the most important. The selection of suppliers is solely a matter for purchasing to decide. One way of evaluating how well sources have been selected is by how few complaints are received from departments using the purchased

PACIFIC GAS &
ELECTRIC COMPANY

PURCHASING AND STORES DEPARTMENT

BUYER PERFORMANCE REVIEW

Buyer's Name________________ Review Date________

Supervisor________________ Counseling Date________

The following are the principal areas in which a Buyer is to be evaluated for his past performance to determine his qualifications for a merit increase. In areas I-IV you are to rate the Buyer numerically from 0 to 100, 0 representing complete failure and 100 absolute perfection; 50 will represent an average performance. Ratings on either side of this figure should represent the degree in which performance falls below or exceeds average. In addition, in the sub-areas listed explain the Buyer's strength or weakness on the subject in question. Give specific examples, where possible, of outstanding or unusual accomplishments. In area V, please provide written comments.

	Item Rating	Category Rating
I. Product Knowledge		
A. Knowledge of function, and product life	____	
B. Knowledge of Manufacturing methods	____	
C. Knowledge of competing or alternate products	____	____
II. Source Knowledge		
A. Knowledge of supplier personnel	____	
B. Knowledge of supplier corporate structure, fiscal strength	____	
C. Knowledge of supplier stocking policies and service available	____	
D. Activity in developing new sources	____	
E. Knowledge of Supplier's Plant Location	____	____
III. Price Knowledge		
A. Knowledge of his product prices	____	
B. What action does he take when advised of price changes?	____	
C. What does he do to achieve better prices or value on his material?	____	____

FIG. 24–4*b*. Buyer-review form.

Buyer Performance Review Page 2

IV. Efficiency — Item Rating — Category Rating

A. How does he handle sales calls? ________

B. What steps has he taken or suggestions has he made to improve his own or the Department' efficiency? ________

C. How well does he communicate? Orally? In writing? ________

____

V. Inter-Personal Relationships

A. How does he react to criticism?
Comment________________

____

B. To what degree does he require supervision?
Comment________________

____

C. What is his attitude toward his job? His supervisors? The Company?
Comment________________

____

D. How well does he get along with other people? In the Company? With suppliers' representatives?
Comments________________

____

FIG. 24–4*b*. Buyer-review form (continued).

material. However, this can also be highly misleading. To check on whether selection is effective, determine if the vendor:

1. Furnishes quality specified
2. Sells at reasonable prices
3. Meets delivery promises
4. Provides technical or other useful assistance if required
5. Keeps up to date on technological improvements
6. Settles complaints promptly
7. Is financially sound, and can be expected to continue as supplier
8. Operates on his money, not yours
9. Has good labor relations
10. Has intelligent and helpful sales personnel
11. Has competent management which carries out commitments

Frequent complaints about quality, service, or any of the above items should be adequate reason to consider changing suppliers.

Negotiation

Price *negotiation* is too often confused with mere *bidding* or is considered a form of price haggling. If purchasing is doing its proper job, there are times when negotiation, in the full sense of the word, must be practiced.

It is not the purpose here to instruct the uninformed *how* to negotiate. Techniques are described in Section 10. To negotiate properly, the buyer must know exactly what he wants, and must have at least a reasonably good idea of what the vendor is capable of producing, and at *what cost.* Haggling has no part in negotiating. An efficient supplier must be permitted a fair profit if he is to remain a good supplier.

Generally speaking, negotiation is most useful when items of special manufacture are involved. However, there are occasions when the prices of even standard items of commerce are open to negotiation. Nor is price the only item of negotiation. Delivery date, quality, etc., are all factors. Do buyers really know how and when to negotiate? Or do they always accept a supplier's offer without determining whether something better may be available which would save money for their own company and still leave the supplier with a fair profit?

PORTER MANUFACTURING CO.

COMMODITY PURCHASE ANALYSIS

History

Item ______ Contract No. ______

Stock Car No. (or Using Craft) ______ Reorder Point ______ Maximum Inventory ______

Annual Purchase (Qty) ______

Specifications ______

______

______

______ Authority for Spec. ______

Use and Location ______

How consumption is determined ______

Storage space available: Location ______

Quantity ______

How bought: Open Market ______ Sealed Bids ______
Annual Contract ______ Indefinite Contract ______
Other ______

Present Supplier (s) ______

______

Reason for choice of Supplier ______

Price ______ F.O.B. ______

TERMS ______ Transit Time ______ Lead Time ______

Manufacturer ______

FIG. 24–5*a*. Example of value analysis or profit improvement form (front).

QUANTITATIVE FUNCTIONS: MEASUREMENT OF AREAS OF ACTION AND OF RESULTS

Value Analysis

A good buyer is always on the alert to purchase exactly the right material for a given application. He knows the use to which his purchases are put and is ready with suggestions which will result in *cost* reductions.

Section 11 covers value analysis in detail, but the following questions should serve as a check list.

1. Is the buyer familiar with the end use of his purchases?
2. Does the buyer have the confidence of his engineers?
3. Does he call attention to possible changes to achieve *cost* (not necessarily *price*) reductions?
4. Do suppliers actively cooperate in presenting ideas?
5. Does the department head insist on ideas for cost reduction?
6. Do personnel have enough time to perform value analysis studies?

POSSIBLE IMPROVEMENT IN PURCHASE PROCEDURE

I. A. POSSIBLE NEW SOURCE:
(Lower Prices, Service, Equal Quality)

Price
Potential
Annual Saving

B. ALTERNATE QUALITIES OR CHANGE IN SPECIFICATIONS:
(Obsolescence, Specials vs Standard Items)

Price
Potential
Annual Saving

C. CHANGE IN METHOD OF BUYING:
(Quantity Differentials, Packing, Routing, Factory vs Warehouse Origin)

Price
Potential
Annual Saving

D. OTHER POSSIBILITIES:
(Reduce Consumption, Waste, Combine Similar Items or Uses)

Price
Potential
Annual Saving

II. RECOMMENDATIONS:

III. REMARKS:

DATE

BY

FIG. 24–5*a*. Example of value analysis or profit improvement form (back).

7. Is there a form available for this use? (Figures 24–5*a*, 24–5*b*, and 24–5*c* are good examples of value analysis or profit improvement forms.)

Standardization

One excellent way to reduce costs through better prices and lower obsolescence is by standardization. This makes consolidation of orders

Date ______________

PROFIT IMPROVEMENT REPORT
Union Oil Company

SUBJECT:

Where and How Used:

Previous Method:

New Method:

What brought this situation to your attention?

Estimated Annual Cost of Subject, Previous Method: $ ______________

Annual Savings: ______________

Other Savings: ______________

Are the Savings Repetitive? ______________

Signed ______________________________

Original - C. S. Perkins
Duplicate - Supervisor
*Triplicate - Operating Personnel Assisting in Saving
*Quadruplicate - Operating Personnel's Supervisor

*Where applicable

FIG. 24–5*b*. Example of value analysis or profit improvement form.

possible and hence lowers unit cost through larger purchases. With fewer items, inventory control also is simplified, and danger of loss through obsolescence is reduced. Standardization also reduces "brand" buying and increases purchasing by specification.

Standardization can be achieved only through the active cooperation of engineering, technical, and using personnel. How effective is purchasing in getting this cooperation? Do the buyers take the initiative, or do they wait for others?

Search for New and/or Better Products

While this search is closely allied to value analysis, there is a distinct difference between the two procedures. A new product could, for example, be a new container in which to package the company's product. The new container might result in increased costs, but greater sales could offset the increase in cost. The point to keep in mind is the contention that purchasing is the company's eyes and ears. Is this so? Are widespread supplier contacts being used to advantage? Are new ideas called to the attention of others? Are they followed up and followed through?

PURCHASING COST REDUCTION SUMMARY

1. Value Analysis
2. Standardization
3. Quantity
4. Negotiation
5. Substitution
6. New Vendor
7. Market Conditions
8. Terms (Cash Disc., etc.)
9. Estimated Savings (Subject to Cost Dept. Confirmation)
10. Savings--all others

Item No.	Date of Change	ITEM	Old Unit Price	New Unit Price	SAVINGS Known & Proved	SAVINGS Est.*	Code	Explanation & Comments
1								
2								
3								
4								
5								
6								
TOTALS								

* Savings which involve clerical, handling, etc., and cannot readily be measured. Buyer ______________ For Month of __________

FIG. 24–5*c*. Example of value analysis or profit improvement form.

Price Paid

Sections 9 and 10 of this handbook cover pricing in detail, with Section 10 devoted entirely to price evaluation. Price paid for materials, services, and supplies is still the major responsibility on which the effectiveness of the department is judged by others. Purchasing can make highly significant contributions to a company's financial well-being through purchases which reflect *value* in their end use and through prices paid that are more favorable than the general prevailing prices (see "Value Analysis Techniques," Section 11).

Value analysis and *negotiation* are separately covered in this section. Favorable pricing, however, also results from buying at the right time, in the right quantity, and from the right supplier. This means that buyers must have a thorough knowledge of market conditions, domestically and, if applicable, internationally (NOTE: this is why certain industries, such as cane sugar refining, have separate departments for the purchase of their principal raw material). A buyer should keep charts or tabulations which not only show past price performance, but may reasonably be used to predict future pricing. Applicable trade journals and such daily publications as the *Wall Street Journal* and the *Journal of Commerce* provide excellent information.

Is such informative material available? Is it being used? Are competitive prices obtained? If competition is not available, are prices negotiated? Are the quantities purchased the most favorable from a pricing standpoint? Are cash discounts taken? Are purchases made from primary sources or as close thereto as possible (e.g., from the manufacturer or wholesaler rather than from a retail outlet)? Who pays the freight, insurance, taxes, etc.? And finally, as a check, should the item be purchased at all, or should it be made? See Section 10 for a discussion on "Make or Buy."

Price Analysis

For the price analysis function, one or all of the following methods can be utilized:

1. Comparison of proposed price with that of similar or identical items previously or currently purchased on a competitively priced basis.
2. Comparison of proposed price using estimate of cost independently developed by personnel within the organization.
3. Comparisons using pricing (learning) curves, trend data, or pricing factors appropriate for the industry involved.
4. Published price lists to be used as the basis for pricing when it can be demonstrated that published prices are issued on a price competitive basis. Consideration should be given to discounts, most favored customer clauses, and other appropriate arrangements.

At times, price competition is not present. A competitive bid may have been received, but competition may appear to be lacking. Technical considerations may have reduced or eliminated price competition. In such cases, the supplier should be requested to support proposals with cost data. Analysis and evaluation of cost data for each procurement will vary with the complexity and value of the item, the degree of competition, and other matters of relevance. The appraisal should find the following things being considered in an analysis and evaluation of cost proposals.

1. Knowledge of suppliers' costing, accounting, and estimating methods
2. Knowledge of areas where judgment factors have been used and evaluation of the reasonableness of these factors
3. Need for verification of cost data
4. Need for data to supplement those included in the proposal
5. Need for assistance from technical specialists within or without the purchasing organization

Price analysis is covered in detail in Section 10. In evaluating this activity, however, the guideline must be the fact that fair and reasonable prices result from sound business principles and approaches, competent practices, fairness and equity, readiness to compromise, and considerations of public policy. In any organization, the extent to which these factors are applied depends upon management support and action.

Inventory Control[2]

While inventory control is sometimes a responsibility of purchasing, a more normal practice is to locate this control elsewhere. But purchasing can always make a major contribution to inventory control and here are some of the measures which can be applied to such purchasing performance.

Scheduling

Careful scheduling of shipments to avoid overstocks and shortages is obtained by close cooperation with departments where plans are made, schedules set and changed, materials controls exercised, and requisitions written.

It should be possible to measure purchasing's contribution by:

1. The frequency of material shortages controllable by purchasing (see Figs. 24–6 and 24–7).
2. The extent to which inventories can be reduced by purchasing's dealings with those suppliers whose delivery promises are most dependable (see Figs. 24–6 and 24–7). In some cases measures might be kept for single commodities or suppliers.

Records may be kept of vendor's performance on overdue shipments. These can be used as an indication of such supplier's share of future business. Purchasing can often arrange with vendors to supply periodic

[2] Also see Section 13, "Quantity Determination through Inventory Management."

open-order shipping schedules. These give purchasing an early indicator of the need for expediting and, if delayed shipments are unavoidable, a chance to prepare the using departments for the delay.

Vendor Stocking

In an increasing number of cases purchasing people have been able to persuade some of their suppliers to carry in stock for their use quantities of items which enable the purchaser to reduce substantially his own in-

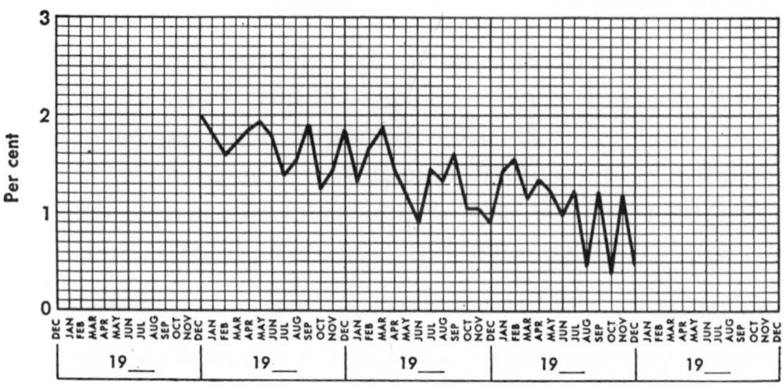

FIG. 24–6. Ratio of rejections to total number of completed purchase orders. Measure of vendor performance.

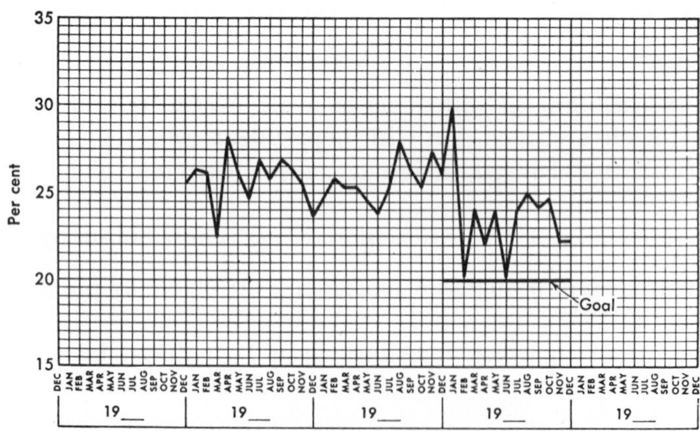

FIG. 24–7. Number of purchase orders that were overdue when received as a percentage of total orders completed. Another measure of vendor performance.

ventory. This practice is usually termed "stockless purchasing." Savings from this practice can be measured by actual inventory reduction or by the number of units or the dollar value of stocks kept by the vendor for this purpose.

Consigned Stocks

These are materials physically in possession of the purchaser but actually the property of the supplier until they are used. The consigned stock method has some advantages, particularly on repetitive use items, in that it ensures the purchasing company a supply to the extent of the quantity consigned, but avoids a corresponding investment of capital in inventory. The measure of the value of consigned stocks can be determined in units or dollars which effect a direct reduction of the user's own inventory.

Economical Ordering Quantities

Many persons in purchasing, in collaboration with others responsible for materials control, have developed formulas for determining more economical ordering quantities for repetitive purchase items. The graph

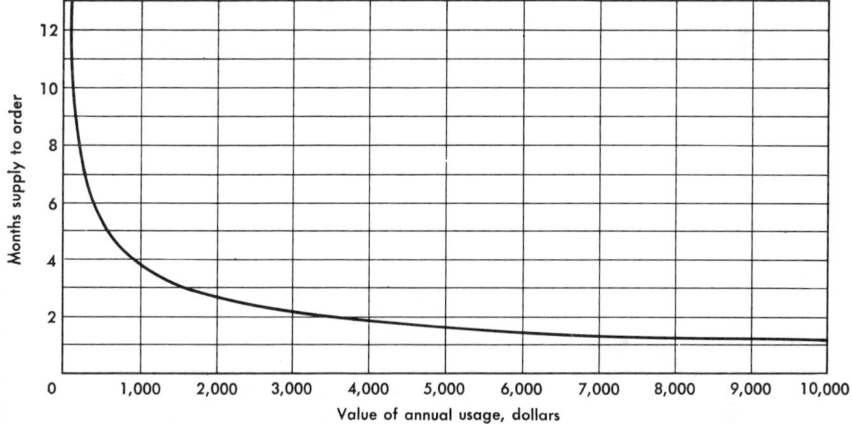

FIG. 24–8. Economic ordering quantities. This curve was arrived at by balancing the cost of stock replenishment in stores, purchasing, and accounting operations against the cost of maintaining inventory in stores and internal auditing operations. The appropriate overheads were added to each cost. The curve gives a graphic example of the need for concentrating time and attention on the more expensive items of stock, ordering them in smaller quantities for more frequent delivery. At the same time, it points up the fact that items whose consumption amounts to only a small number of dollars per year should be ordered in large quantities that will last a considerable period of time.

and text in Fig. 24–8 show a typical yardstick of this kind. The search for and use of similar programs in any company will contribute to better inventory controls and a reduction in operating and handling costs in purchasing and stores operations.

Turnover Rate

One of the best measures of effective inventory control is its turnover rate. All the contributions purchasing makes to inventory controls should reflect a better turnover rate and hence are measurable (see Fig. 24–9).

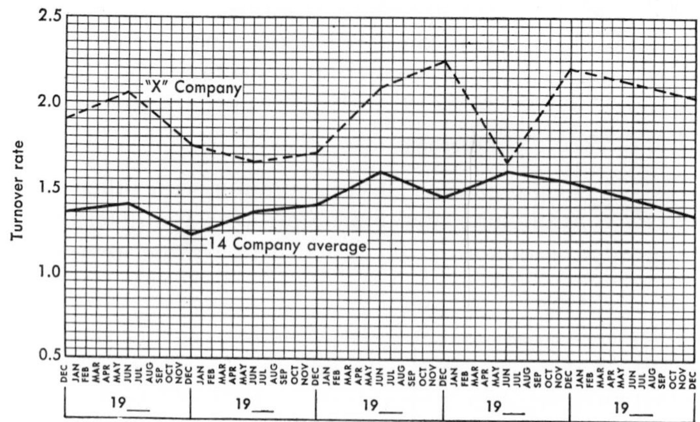

FIG. 24–9. Inventory turnover. This chart is based on an industry with a relatively low rate of inventory turnover. Fourteen companies, of comparable size, exchange inventory statistics semiannually which enables each company to measure and interpret its own performance and trends in comparison with industry averages.

The relationship of inventory levels or inventory turnover to a company's sales volume can also be a measure of progress made.

Traffic and Transportation

The traffic function is in some organizations a responsibility of the purchasing department, but more often it is handled by a separate department. Section 18 covers this operation in detail, but in evaluating the purchasing function, one needs to consider the importance of the traffic function. The price of a purchase includes the cost of delivery, and the buyer must be sure that materials purchased, regardless of f.o.b. point, reach destination by the most economical means. Involved in this is not only rate charged by the carrier, but also his record of delivery. Is he generally prompt? Have repeated delays been encountered?

Where purchasing and traffic are separate responsibilities, is there close cooperation? Do the buyers give ample notice of requirements? And does traffic provide purchasing with up-to-date information on routings, cost, etc.?

Reciprocity

Among buyers, reciprocity is too often considered emotionally rather than subjectively. Actually, there are times when reciprocal dealings are plain common sense. However, one needs to be sure of the legal and ethical considerations, as well as the financial. Sections 1 and 7 deal with reciprocity in greater length. In evaluating the department, ask the questions: "Are any of our customers also our suppliers, or potential suppliers? Should they be? What would be the *full* effect on my company if they were?" Purchasing should take the initiative with respect to reciprocity, but must consult with the sales and law departments before making commitments. Is this being done?

Foreign Purchases

Section 17, "Purchasing Internationally," discusses this subject in detail. It is listed here as an area for evaluation only so that evaluators will ask the questions: "Can our needs be better fulfilled—quality, price, and service factors considered—through foreign rather than domestic purchases? Should they be?" Questions of corporate policy, in addition to quality, price, and service, need to be understood.

Sale of Surplus, Scrap, and Obsolete Materials

This is a responsibility generally assigned to the purchasing department. Section 21, "Disposal of Reclamation and Salvage Materials," details the subject. Purchasing performance is clearly measurable here. The following are suggested checks:

1. Are the materials for disposal sold by the buyers responsible for new materials of the same category?
2. Are the available markets and channels of distribution known and *constantly* reviewed?
3. Are usable or reclaimed materials disposed of as such, rather than as scrap?
4. Are *second-hand* dealers (as opposed to scrap dealers) known and used?
5. Are materials properly sorted or segregated?
6. Are fluctuations in scrap markets watched and taken advantage of?
7. Are disposal procedures such as to avoid loss of value through deterioration in storage?
8. Are trade practices among scrap dealers known?
9. Should material be disposed of, or reclaimed and reused?

10. Is scrap used in place of new materials (i.e., scrap paper bags used as dunnage, or as containers for other scraps)?

Substantial income can be generated from this area. Practices and procedures should be carefully understood and evaluated.

Expediting

This is an important function of purchasing. But it can also be overemphasized. In times of material shortages, its proper conduct can be absolutely essential. On the other hand, expediting materials from suppliers of known good performance can often be wasteful of time—both the buyer's and the seller's.

Expediting and follow-up are often thought of as the same thing. *Follow-up* is usually "tracing" to ensure that a promised delivery date will be met. *Expediting,* in the true sense of the word, is an effort to *improve* a delivery date and could call for technical assistance. Is there a definite department policy on *both* follow-up and expediting? Is the time spent on each proportioned to the need? Is the work systematic, or haphazard? Does the using department have to prod purchasing, or is information on the status of an order readily available? Is the method of follow-up and expediting one which conserves time? (In many cases, post cards, such as those illustrated in Figs. 24–10*a* and 24–10*b,* can be substituted for phone calls.) Are records kept of suppliers requiring constant expediting? What action is being taken to reduce this need?

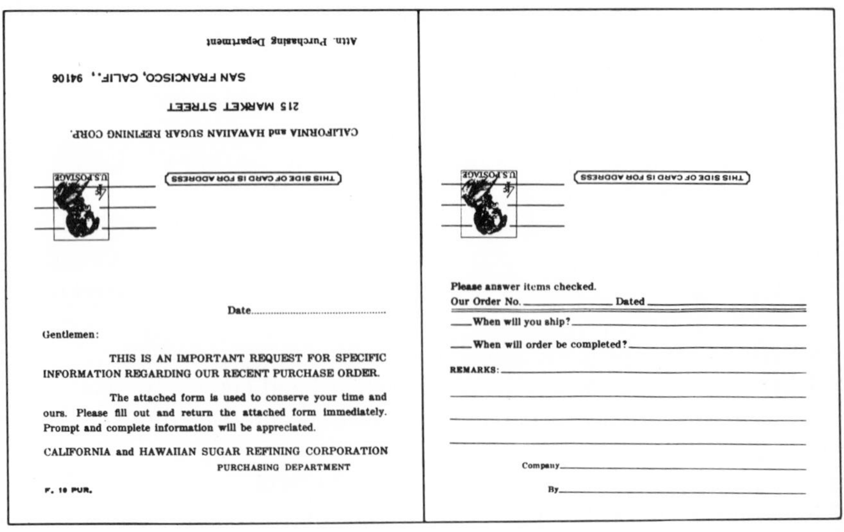

Attn. Purchasing Department

CALIFORNIA and HAWAIIAN SUGAR REFINING CORP.
215 MARKET STREET
SAN FRANCISCO, CALIF., 94106

THIS SIDE OF CARD IS FOR ADDRESS

U.S. POSTAGE 4¢

Date..

Gentlemen:

THIS IS AN IMPORTANT REQUEST FOR SPECIFIC INFORMATION REGARDING OUR RECENT PURCHASE ORDER.

The attached form is used to conserve your time and ours. Please fill out and return the attached form immediately. Prompt and complete information will be appreciated.

CALIFORNIA and HAWAIIAN SUGAR REFINING CORPORATION
PURCHASING DEPARTMENT

F. 10 PUR.

THIS SIDE OF CARD IS FOR ADDRESS

U.S. POSTAGE 4¢

Please answer items checked.
Our Order No. ____________ Dated ____________
___When will you ship? ____________
___When will order be completed? ____________
REMARKS: ____________

Company ____________
By ____________

FIG. 24–10*a*. Self-addressed expediting post card—deliveries.

Date:_________

URGENT REQUEST FOR:

INVOICE ☐
CREDIT MEMO ☐
(In Triplicate)

Refers to our order

No.__________________

CALIFORNIA MANUFACTURING CO.
215 MARKET STREET
SAN FRANCISCO, CALIF., 94106
Purchasing Dept.

F.6 PUR.

FIG. 24–10*b*. Expediting post card—missing documents.

Invoice Checking and Approval

This is often a function of accounting, but it is also in whole or in part the function of purchasing in some companies. In an evaluation, ask these questions:

1. Should this function be included in purchasing?
2. Where can it most economically be performed?
3. Should there be a dollar limit on invoices checked?
4. Is cash discount always taken?
5. How frequently is improper pricing detected?

Departmental Efficiency

The most effective and profitable departments are generally those that are the most efficient. But it does not always follow that a low cost department is necessarily either effective or a proper contributer to profits. In judging departmental efficiency, one needs to know clearly what is expected of the department and what support can be counted on. For example, mere holding down of manpower does not, of itself, contribute to profitability. Output of orders per buyer may be very high, but profits can be lost in hurried selection of suppliers, failure to get competitive quotations, etc. Additional buyers, above the essential minimum, might easily justify their positions through *proper* buying. In judging department efficiency, one needs to appraise the effectiveness of each individual, how he is performing his work, how he uses his time, how good his judgment is. In short, the qualifications of each man must be appraised.

Closely tied in are department procedures. Can they be simplified? Can they be mechanized? (See Section 14, "Electronic Data Processing Applications in Purchasing.") Are blanket orders[3] utilized to the fullest extent possible? Potentials are indicated in Fig. 24–11. Are requisitions being combined for fewer purchasing orders (and better price)? Are the best

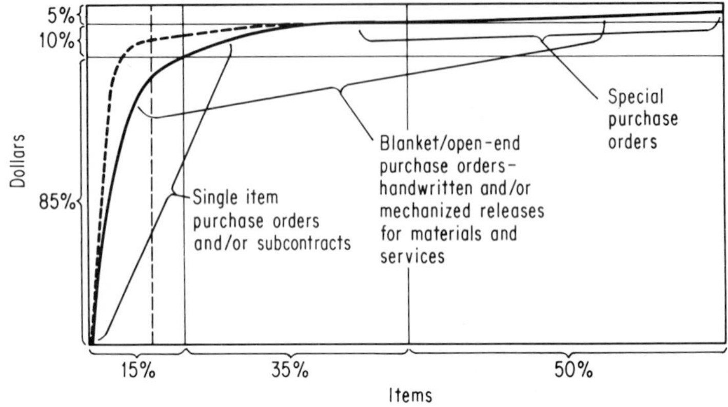

FIG. 24–11. Distribution by item of dollars committed.

order quantities utilized for few purchases of repetitive items? Are telephone conversations limited to business matters, with pleasantries kept to the minimum needed for good manners and pleasant relations? Is correspondence kept to the minimum needed? Are personal interviews with salesmen kept to essentials, consistent with getting the whole story? Analysis of a time utilization chart, such as that shown in Fig. 24–12, will help in this evaluation.

Other items can be added to this list, depending on the scope of activities, size of department, and nature of materials purchased.

SCORE SHEET: PERFORMANCE EVALUATION

Earlier in this section, it was cautioned that quantitative measures should not be emphasized at the expense of qualitative considerations. Nevertheless, the person who heads up the purchasing department, or others evaluating the procurement function, must be prepared to demonstrate to management the contributions of the department to cost reduction in the areas in which the department can logically be expected to

[3] Described fully in Section 5, "Purchase Order Essentials."

15 minute segements of day

1 2 3 4 5 6 7 8 9 10 11 12 13 14 15 16 17 18 19 20 21 22 23 24 25 26 27 28 29 30 31 32

Wednesday September 19th

Telephone	62.4%
Misc.	18.8%
Write-up	9.4%
Vendors	9.4%

Thursday September 20th

Telephone	59.3%
Misc.	20.0%
Write-up	9.4%
Vendors	6.2%
*Special	3.1%

Friday September 21st

Telephone	43.6%
Misc.	15.7%
Write-up	9.4%
Vendors	3.1%
*Special	28.2%

Average day

Telephone	55.1%
Misc.	18.8%
Write-up	9.4%
Vendors	6.2%
*Special	10.5%

Telephone: time spent placing orders, phone quotations, follow-up (both in plant and with vendors).

Miscellaneous: time spent obtaining information for requesters, checking on lost material, etc.

Write-up: time spent writing up orders, vendors codes, etc.

Vendors: time spent seeing salesmen in person.

* Special: time spent trying to straighten out three purchase orders from one East Coast vendor, including complete examination of the material on the dock and comparison of goods against catalog material that was ordered. (This is not normally included in time.)

FIG. 24–12. Time utilization chart in 15 min segments.

Quantitative

	Total dollars per period
Price	
Lowered prices through negotiation, competition, quantity or cash discounts, etc.	
Fewer rejects through better suppliers, more feasible routing, packaging, etc. ..	
Value analysis—suggested by purchasing	
Substitutes that have reduced costs of raw materials, supplies, MRO, etc.	
Standardization, resulting in reduced cost of goods, freight, paper work, etc. ..	
Inventory	
Decreased dollar volume by stockless purchasing, better scheduling, better deliveries, improved transportation, etc.—based on accounting department actual carrying costs (usually 1 to 2 per cent per month)	
Scrap and salvage	
Increased return through better classification, improved price, faster disposal, etc.	
Departmental	
Reduced work load through blanket purchase ordering, automation, reducing paper work, expediting by mail, or other techniques that eventually will reduce cost of purchasing department, particularly through reductions in personnel ..	
Other Savings	
Gross savings per period	
Cost of effecting savings	
Net savings per period	

Qualitative

To the above must be added other suggestions and improvements that eventually will be translated into profits for the company. These could include such matters as:

1. Purchasing climate which encourages top effort
2. Written purchasing department policy and procedure manual
3. Centralization of function
4. Top quality staffing and training
5. Optimum distribution of functions within department
6. Participation in company and professional and community affairs
7. Good working relationships with other departments
8. Better suppliers, and better supplier and public relations
9. Awareness of how to deal effectively with reciprocity
10. Better quality of purchased products, with no increase in costs
11. Improved deliveries
12. Awareness of make-or-buy possibilities
13. Reduced frequency of rush orders
14. Recommendations for improvement of company products, procedures, etc.
15. Contributions to company's short- and long-range planning

FIG. 24–13. Score sheet: performance evaluation.

be effective. These are *quantitative* factors, factors which can be measured. But whether or not a department is effective in this area is usually determined by the *qualitative* considerations.

Figure 24–13 is a score sheet used in a relatively small company. This is but one example of what purchasing executives, auditors, and management consultants can compile for a receptive and understanding management. The performance score given top management must not be prepared without a full knowledge of what is back of it. Is performance good, bad, or indifferent? Improvement generally depends on how we evaluate the *qualitative* factors.

CONCLUSION

While the areas and functions of purchasing which have been set forth here for evaluation are intended primarily for small and medium-sized companies, they can also be effectively followed for large organizations. Obviously, in large departments, evaluation will be of greater scope than in smaller ones. Because larger departments are also probably more complex and of greater scope in variety of purchases, dollar volume, and, of course, personnel, their evaluation and measurement is also likely to be more formalized.

It is important to keep in mind that in measuring purchasing performance, the compilation of endless charts and statistics is not needed. Evaluation is a form of control. It is getting the answers to the question, "How are we doing?" It should not be engaged in haphazardly, but neither should it be regarded as such a formidable task that it is not done at all. Equally important, evaluation is *not* an end in itself. Where indicated by the findings, action must be taken to keep on the course toward the department's objectives.

SELECTED BIBLIOGRAPHY

Foster, Roy R.: "How to Measure Performance," *Purchasing,* October 22, 1962

Hayes, F. Albert, and George A. Renard: *Evaluating Purchasing Performance,* AMA Research Study No. 66, American Management Association, Inc., 1964

Heinritz, Stuart F.: "Can't Measure Purchasing?", *Purchasing,* April and May, 1951

"Internal Audit and Control of a Purchasing Department," *Research Committee Report No. 2,* Institute of Internal Auditors, 1955

Kellogg, Marion S.: "What to Do about Performance Appraisal," American Management Association, Inc., 1965

Kennedy, George Thomas: *Evaluating Purchasing Performance,* Ohio State University, 1964. (An excerpt is published by the National Association of Purchasing Agents.)

A Look at Purchasing through the President's Eye, AMA Special Study No. 5, American Management Association, Inc., May, 1962

Pooler, Victor H., Jr.: "Developing the Negotiation Skills of the Buyer," *AMA Management Bulletin No. 50,* American Management Association, Inc., 1964

Seybold, Geneva: "Personnel Audits & Reports to Top Management," *Studies in Personnel Policy No. 191,* National Industrial Conference Board, Inc., 1964

Many other references are included in purchasing books listed in Section 26, "Library and Catalog File."

SECTION 25

FORMS AND RECORDS

Editor

Frank W. Wodrich, Director of Material, Science Services Division, Texas Instruments Incorporated, Dallas, Texas

Associate Editors

Irene Gordon, Purchasing Agent, Wallace & Tiernan Inc., Belleville, New Jersey

Charles W. Hayes, Director of Purchases, Emory University, Atlanta, Georgia

Purchasing forms are devices for pinpointing the relevant and important factors involved in the (1) what, (2) when, (3) how much, (4) from what source, and (5) at what cost—in the expression of the need for purchasing.

Purchasing records are the body of forms and correspondence which give the day-to-day as well as the historical operating picture and essential documentation.

Purchasing files are devices to make readily available the forms in their various stages of implementation, vendor and product information, price information, and potential source information, to all purchasing personnel, and, as necessary, to other personnel within the company.

Forms and procedures are designed to perform necessary functions and not to be ends in themselves. Simplicity of use and usefulness, as demonstrated by the pragmatic test of workability, are basic considerations.

Each company will require somewhat different forms and records because of inherent differences in organization, size, and complexity caused by differences in policies and operating procedures. It is the function of this section to describe and briefly discuss those forms and records that are generally accepted as standard because of their wide adoption and general usefulness.

This section essentially deals with these four phases of purchasing: forms, records, filing, and forms design and procurement. It takes up, in sequence, each of these phases.

No attempt will be made to describe all the forms that may be used. Three of the forms covered, purchase requisition, purchase order, and material receipt, are basic to all purchasing departments. The other forms discussed and illustrated also may be found valuable in smaller departments. The principal types of forms are covered in the following order.

Purchase requisition
Invitation to bid
Acknowledgment of quotation
Purchase order
Follow-up
Material receipt
Returned materials
Purchase order change notice
Invoice adjustments or corrections

Of equal importance is the matter of records, and these will be treated in the following sequence:

Order index
Vendor index
Price records
Contract index
Tests on new products and materials

On the filing phase, this section will cover correspondence, commodities, suppliers' catalogs, purchase orders, purchase requisitions, general, the intelligent usage of files, and retention of records.

It should be recognized that there is no such thing as a standard form which will apply to all purchasing departments, regardless of the company size.[1] While the forms covered in this section are basic, the printed matter may vary according to the type of business involved, company policy, or laws in certain states. The forms used as illustrations are flexible to the extent that additions or deletions may be made to meet the user's requirements.

The forms, records, filing, and forms design and procurement procedures covered in this section should be sufficient for the smaller departments, and are basic in the larger departments. For the very large companies, forms might involve mechanization, such as described in Section 14, "Electronic Data Processing Applications in Purchasing."

Also, it is assumed, in this section, that the purchasing function is handled to conclusion in the purchasing department. No attempt is made to cover those larger organizations where the checking of invoices and material receipts may be handled by the accounting department.

[1] Best illustrated by the variety of similar forms shown in this and other sections of this handbook. Refer to Index for location of additional illustrations.

Similarly, there are excluded procedures in governmental purchases, city, county, state, or Federal, where those procedures may be covered by special legislation, as discussed in Section 19, "Public Purchasing." The basic forms and records treated herein should, however, apply to all lines of endeavor.

FORMS

Purchase Requisition. The purchase requisition (Fig. 25–1*a,* Purchase Requisition Form) is the form requesting the purchasing department to purchase materials, parts, supplies, equipment, or services as described thereon. (Also see Figs. 5–1, 9–2 and 19–3.)

The standard requisition ordinarily originates in engineering, plant, research, operating, or other consuming or using departments, except on regularly stocked items. Requisitions for stock items usually originate in stores.

Certain essential information is required when a standard requisition is received by a purchasing department. These data are filled in on the requisition by its originator or by the person authorized to approve it:

1. Requisition number
2. The quantity of material required
3. The complete description of the material, goods, or services with specification number, blueprint reference, or catalog number as may be applicable so that there will be no misunderstanding of the requirement
4. The date on which the material is required by the using department
5. Delivery information to show which plant, department, or individual is to receive the material
6. The account number and the authorization number to be charged, when required by company procedure
7. Special packaging or other data if there are any deviations from normal or standard procedures

As a further guide to the purchasing department, some companies require that additional information be furnished on purchase requisitions, such as quantity on hand, quantity on order, and estimated usage for a given period.

In order for the purchase requisition to be completed for issuance of the purchase order, these forms provide for the buyer to add:

1. Vendor's name and address
2. Purchase order number
3. Shipping point

4. F.o.b. point
5. Terms of payment
6. Routing instructions
7. Whether taxable or tax exempt
8. Date delivery is required
9. Complete price information
10. Any special terms or conditions

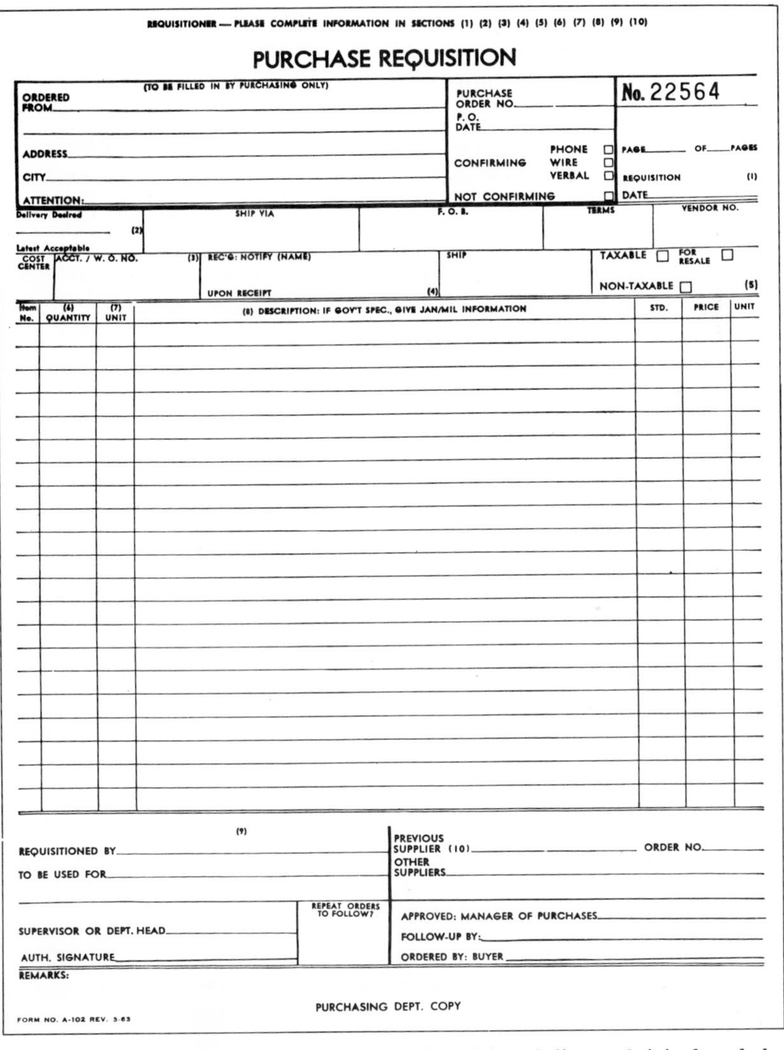

REQUISITIONER — PLEASE COMPLETE INFORMATION IN SECTIONS (1) (2) (3) (4) (5) (6) (7) (8) (9) (10)

PURCHASE REQUISITION

(TO BE FILLED IN BY PURCHASING ONLY)

ORDERED FROM ______
ADDRESS ______
CITY ______
ATTENTION: ______

PURCHASE ORDER NO. ______
P. O. DATE ______
CONFIRMING PHONE ☐ WIRE ☐ VERBAL ☐
NOT CONFIRMING ☐

No. 22564

PAGE ______ OF ______ PAGES
REQUISITION (1)
DATE ______

Delivery Desired ______ (2) Latest Acceptable	SHIP VIA	F. O. B.	TERMS	VENDOR NO.

COST CENTER	ACCT. / W. O. NO. (3)	REC'G: NOTIFY (NAME) UPON RECEIPT (4)	SHIP	TAXABLE ☐ FOR RESALE ☐ NON-TAXABLE ☐ (5)

Item No.	(6) QUANTITY	(7) UNIT	(8) DESCRIPTION: IF GOV'T SPEC., GIVE JAN/MIL INFORMATION	STD.	PRICE	UNIT

(9)

REQUISITIONED BY ______
TO BE USED FOR ______

PREVIOUS SUPPLIER (10) ______ ORDER NO. ______
OTHER SUPPLIERS ______

SUPERVISOR OR DEPT. HEAD ______
AUTH. SIGNATURE ______

REPEAT ORDERS TO FOLLOW?

APPROVED: MANAGER OF PURCHASES ______
FOLLOW-UP BY: ______
ORDERED BY: BUYER ______

REMARKS:

PURCHASING DEPT. COPY

FORM NO. A-102 REV. 3-63

FIG. 25–1*a*. Purchase requisition form. Prenumbered in triplicate. Original and duplicate to purchasing department; triplicate, originator's copy. (*Reproduced by permission.*)

It is best to print the information referred to in the preceding paragraph on the requisition, so arranged that it will be in logical sequence for the order typist to transpose to the purchase order.

Standard purchase requisitions are of various sizes and shapes and the specifications are designed to fit the needs of individual companies. Most, however, are 8½ in. wide and 7 to 11 in. long. The minimum number of copies provides for the originator to retain one copy and send the original to the purchasing department.

Purchase requisitions should be provided with space at the bottom for signature at the originating office, along with the approvals necessary in keeping with policy of the company.

CALIFORNIA AND HAWAIIAN SUGAR REFINING CORPORATION

STOCK NUMBER 50-72396 | ACCOUNT NUMBER

SPECIFICATIONS
½-13 x 2" Finished Hexagon Head
Type 316 Stainless Steel Machine
Bolts

MANUFACTURER
Everlasting Machine Works
XYZ Corporation

SUBSTITUTE
Type 18-8 Stainless Steel
Everdur (Silicon Bronze)

SUPPLIER
1 A.Z. INDUSTRIAL SUPPLY
2 SPECIALTY METALS CORP.
3 B-C HARDWARE & TOOL CO.
4 STAINLESS NUTS & BOLTS INC.

EQUIPMENT | NO. OF PARTS INSTALLED
Maintenance throughout plant | -

PRICE BREAKS AT 1-49, 50-499, 500 or over
WHEN DOWN TO 50 ORDER 100 UNIT Each

STOCK HISTORY CARD FORM S-59A

SENT TO P.D.	QUANTITY REQUIRED	DEL'Y DSRD	PURCHASE ORDER NUMBER	DATE	PRICE	F.O.B.	SUP
2/6/	100	2/20	53012	2/7	33.90 c	S.F.	2
6/11/	100	6/25	54150	6/13	33.90 c	S.F.	1
10/2/	100	10/16	55260	10/3	34.90 c	S.F.	3
2/18/	100	3/4	56403	2/19	34.90 c	S.F.	4

FIG. 25–1*b*. Traveling purchase requisition form. Used between stores and purchasing department for repetitive materials, mostly MRO.

Traveling Purchase Requisition. A traveling purchase requisition (Fig. 25–1*b,* Traveling Purchase Requisition Form) is used for reordering materials, *repetitive in nature,* whether for production, processing, maintenance, repair, or operating supplies. Most involve MRO (maintenance, repair, and operating supplies) purchases in the average company. They are kept in the stores department, which stocks the materials, and are forwarded to the purchasing department whenever additional quantities are needed. This requisition may or may not contain the purchase price, before returning it to the stores department once the material has been ordered and suitable notation made thereon by the buyer or the purchase order typist.

"Traveling purchase requisitions" are printed on card stock for ease in filing and handling. This is necessary, as they are intended to be reused and transferred many times for a number of years between the stores and purchasing departments.

Invitation to Bid. Invitation to bid, or request for quotation, is the means of conveying to various vendors equipment specifications, a list of materials and/or supplies that the purchaser intends to order, and invites bid, or bids, from vendors.

It originates in the purchasing department, under the supervision or direction of the individual who has been designated to make such purchases.

In general usage, there are three forms of invitation to bid: verbal, letter, and bid forms. Verbal invitations are used by many organizations where minor purchases are being made. Usually the bid is obtained in an interview, or over the telephone, and pertinent information is inserted on the purchase requisition by the responsible buyer. More important purchase requirements should be handled by written invitation in letter form, or on a specially designed bid form.

The specially designed bid form (Fig. 25-2, Request for Quotation) is usually sent out in duplicate, with one copy to be returned to the buyer as the bid. The form should provide space for the following pertinent information which is filled in by the purchasing department:

1. Bid number
2. Date of bid request
3. Date by which proposal is to be submitted
4. Name of buyer or purchasing agent (may be printed)
5. Quantity and description of material
6. Any other special information that may affect vendor's quotation, such as requirement for prepaying transportation, required delivery date, etc.

Space should also be provided for vendor to fill in the following information:

1. Unit price
2. Total price (optional)
3. Shipping point
4. F.o.b. point
5. Time required before shipment can be made
6. Payment terms and cash discount terms

The form has advantage over the letter invitation in that it is more likely to obtain all desired information; and since the invitation form is largely printed, less time is required in preparation in the purchasing department.

FORM 2233 REV 8-59-5M

WALLACE & TIERNAN INCORPORATED

25 MAIN STREET, BELLEVILLE 9, NEW JERSEY

REQUEST FOR QUOTATION

I. GORDON
Purchasing Agent DATE:

1

2

3

IMPORTANT

THIS IS NOT AN ORDER

RETURN YELLOW COPY

Bidder retains this copy

PLEASE FURNISH ALL INFORMATION REQUESTED AND MAIL THIS BID BY (DATE)

QUANTITY	DESCRIPTION	UNIT PRICE	DISCOUNT	NET PRICE

IN REPLY REFER TO ______ PURCHASING DEPARTMENT

1. If interested, your quotation is desired upon this form. Retain your copy.
2. We reserve the right to accept all or any part of your bid.
3. Packing charges will not be allowed unless provided in Bidder's quotation.
4. F.O.B. ______
5. Terms and Cash Discount ______
6. Shipment can be made within ______ days

from ______

VENDOR ______

By ______ Date ______

FIG. 25–2. Invitation to bid or request for quotation form. Two copies sent to each vendor invited to quote; one copy returned with vendor's quotation. (*Reproduced by permission.*)

Care should be taken to see that the form is complete in its coverage of desired information, as to quantity and description, so that when properly completed by the vendor all information necessary will be immediately available for making the purchase order. The form should show clearly that it is a request for bid, and not a purchase order. The size of this form is usually 8½ in. wide and 7 to 11 in. long.

Acknowledgment of Quotation. It is desirable that an acknowledgment be made of all quotations, where bidder did not receive order. This can be a simple postal card form (Fig. 25–3, Acknowledgment of Quotation Form), and will show bidder what disposition was made of material on which bid was requested.

Thank You for Your Quotation of________________19 __

Concerning Our Request No.____________

( ) Your proposal is being considered and we will order or notify you later.

( ) Our plans have been changed.

( ) Order placed with another company.

( ) ________________________

Yours very truly,

J. M. HUBER CORPORATION

By________________
Purchasing Department

FIG. 25–3. Acknowledgment of quotation form. Postal card form sent to each vendor who submitted quotation. (*Reproduced by permission.*)

To facilitate analyzing quotations, particularly when several items or vendors are involved, a *quotation summary sheet* can be prepared. This may be done by listing on a single sheet of plain paper the essential information from the quotations of all vendors for ready comparison. Or, if the volume is large, use of a "summary of quotations or tabulation of bids" form may be desirable. An example is illustrated by Fig. 7–6.

Purchase Order.[2] The purchase order is a written commitment to vendor requesting shipment of various items of material, supplies, equipment, and/or services.

At least three types of purchase order forms may be in use by a company: regular purchase order, local supply order, and cash purchase order. The latter two types of orders are intended for small or emergency purchases when it is not convenient to use the regular purchase order. System Purchase Order Draft, explained in Section 5, is also used for small orders.

The purchase order is the most important purchasing form. It is the essential contract form and as such is the basic document which would

[2] See Section 5, "Purchase Order Essentials," for more complete facts and explanations of purchase orders. Purchase order forms are illustrated in other sections. Refer to Index.

PURCHASE ORDER

TEXAS INSTRUMENTS
INCORPORATED
13500 NORTH CENTRAL EXPRESSWAY
P.O. BOX 5474 • DALLAS 22, TEXAS • ADAMS 5-3111

PURCHASE ORDER NO.
H 47298
PAGE OF

TEXAS SALES AND USE TAX EXEMPTION
☐ EXEMPT ☐ TAXABLE

DATE | SHIP VIA | F.O.B. | TERMS

SHIPPING SCHEDULE | REQUESTED ON OR BEFORE | PROMISED | ☐ IMMEDIATE SHIPMENT REQUESTED | REFER ALL QUESTIONS TO → | BUYER | EXTN.

ADDRESS CORRESPONDENCE TO: P.O. BOX 5474

OTHER:

SHIP TO: ☐ P. O. BOX 5474
☐ RESEARCH BUILDING 13500 N. CENTRAL EXPRESSWAY
☐

PLEASE ACKNOWLEDGE PROMPTLY CONFIRMING SHIPPING SCHEDULE DALLAS 22, TEXAS

ITEM	QUANTITY	DESCRIPTION	PRICE	UNIT

SUBMIT INVOICES IN DUPLICATE SHOWING OUR ORDER NUMBER AND ACCOMPANY WITH ORIGINAL BILL OF LADING OR EXPRESS RECEIPT.

BY ACCEPTANCE OF THIS PURCHASE ORDER AND PERFORMANCE HEREUNDER YOU AGREE TO COMPLY FULLY WITH THE CONDITIONS OF PURCHASE STATED ON THE REVERSE SIDE HEREOF AND HEREBY MADE A PART OF THIS ORDER.

TEXAS INSTRUMENTS
INCORPORATED

CORPORATE PURCHASING OFFICE

PURCHASE ORDER NO.
H 47298

THIS NUMBER MUST APPEAR ON ALL PACKAGES, ACKNOWLEDGMENTS, INVOICES, AND PACKING LISTS.

TI–1293-A

FIG. 25–4*a*. A regular purchase order form (front). Prenumbered-snap-out.
Original to vendor.
Copy 1: Acknowledgment copy.
Copy 2: Accounting department copy.
Copies 3 and 4: Purchasing department copies.
Copy 5: Receiving department copy.
(*Reproduced by permission.*)

be used by courts for interpreting the contract. Extreme care should be exercised in preparation of the purchase order so that it will be clear, unambiguous, and will accurately represent your requirements and also make reference to prior verbal and/or written negotiations.

The Regular Form. The purchase order design (Fig. 25–4*a*, Purchase Order Form) must suitably represent the company by attractive printing of company name, address, and trademark.

Purchase orders should include provision for:

1. Vendor's name and address
2. Date of order
3. Purchase order number
4. Requisition number
5. Where to ship
6. F.o.b. point (and shipping point if not the same as f.o.b. point)
7. Terms of payment—when cash discount period begins
8. Routing instructions

CONDITIONS

1. This form, properly signed, constitutes the entire agreement. Terms stated by Seller in accepting or acknowledging this order shall not be binding unless accepted in writing by Kaiser. Seller may not assign this order without Kaiser's prior written consent.

2. Seller shall suitably pack, mark, and ship in accordance with any instructions from Kaiser and the requirements of common carriers to secure the lowest transportation costs. Seller shall be liable for any difference in freight charges or damage to the materials by its failure to comply therewith. Seller will send Kaiser a "Notice of Shipment" giving the number of the order, kind and amount of materials, and route at or prior to time of shipment.

3. Invoices must show the name of the plant to which materials were delivered or shipped. If any sales, use, duty, excise or other similar tax or charge, for which Kaiser has not furnished or agreed to furnish an exemption certificate, is applicable to this order, it must be stated separately on the invoices.

4. Kaiser may return any materials which are defective, unsatisfactory, or of inferior quality or workmanship, or fail to meet the specifications or other requirements of this order. Such materials shall, unless used by Kaiser, remain the property of Seller and may be returned at Seller's risk and expense; and Seller shall reimburse Kaiser for all prior payments therefor and/or costs incurred in connection with delivery or return of such materials.

5. Seller warrants the materials will conform to the description and applicable specifications, shall be of good merchantable quality and fit for the known purpose for which sold, that the materials are free and clear of all liens and encumbrances, and that Seller has good and merchantable title. This is in addition to any warranty or service guarantee given by Seller to Kaiser as provided by law.

6. Seller shall comply, and has complied with all State, Federal and local laws, regulations or orders applicable to the purchase, manufacture, processing and delivery of materials, including but not limited to the Fair Labor Standards Act of 1938, as amended. The provisions of Executive Orders 10925 and 11114, as amended, and any subsequent executive orders relating to equal opportunity for employment on government contracts and all Rules and Regulations of the President's Committee on Equal Employment Opportunity are incorporated by reference.

7. If Seller shall default in any respect, or become insolvent, or if a petition in bankruptcy or insolvency is filed by or against Seller under any State or Federal law, Kaiser, in addition to other rights or remedies, may terminate and cancel this order. A waiver of a breach of any provision shall not be a waiver of any other breach of such provision or of any other provisions. Kaiser shall not, in any event, be liable to Seller for special, contingent or consequential damages.

8. Seller shall defend any suit or proceeding brought against Kaiser, its officers, agents and/or employees based on a claim that the manufacture or sale or Kaiser's intended use or resale of any of the materials covered by this order constitutes infringement of any United States Letters Patent, now or hereafter issued, or violates any other proprietary interest (including copyrights, trademarks and trade secrets), if notified promptly in writing and given authority, information, and assistance (at Seller's expense) for the defense of same; and Seller shall pay all damages and costs, including attorneys' fees, awarded against Kaiser in such suit or proceeding. In the event Kaiser is enjoined from use and/or resale of any of the materials covered by this order as a result of said suit or proceeding, Seller shall (at its expense) expend all reasonable efforts to procure for Kaiser the right to use and/or resell said materials. If Seller cannot so procure the aforementioned right within a reasonable time, Seller shall then promptly (at Seller's expense): (1) modify said materials so as to avoid infringement of any patent or other proprietary interest, or (2) replace said materials with materials which do not infringe or violate said proprietary interest and reimburse Kaiser for any additional transportation and reinstallation costs in connection therewith, or (3) remove said materials and refund the purchase price and reimburse Kaiser for the transportation and installation costs thereof. Seller shall have the same obligations with respect to any claim for infringement of foreign patents or violation of other foreign proprietary interests if Kaiser purchases hereunder for shipment to and for use or resale in a foreign country and Seller is so advised. This paragraph 8 shall constitute the sole agreement relating to liability for infringement or violation of proprietary rights unless expressly revised or revoked in writing.

9. Buyer's remedies, in the event of default by Seller, shall be as provided by law, except as otherwise provided herein.

FIG. 25–4*b*. A regular purchase order form (back). (*Reproduced by permission.*)

9. Whether taxable or tax exempt
10. Shipping schedule
11. Quantity and unit
12. Description of material ordered
13. Unit price and discount
14. Invoicing instructions
15. Any general or special terms or conditions
16. Signature

Purchase order terms and conditions vary from one company to another due to the various important clauses that the purchaser wishes to emphasize as being a part of each purchase order.

In some companies such terms are brief enough to be printed on the face of the purchase order (see Fig. 5–9 for one example of this type). In most companies, however, it is desirable to print only a few conditions on the face of the purchase order, and then print the more lengthy and extended terms and conditions on the reverse side of the purchase order and purchase order acknowledgment copy. See Fig. 25–4*b* for one example of conditions applicable to purchase order. It is not necessary to print them on the reverse side of the other copies of the purchase order as they are for internal company use.

These conditions may include:

1. Acceptance
2. Inspection
3. Packing requirements
4. Billing, marking, and routing
5. Release authorizations
6. Suspension of work and shipment
7. Changes
8. Termination at option of buyer
9. Excusable delays
10. Patents
11. Liability for injury
12. Remedies
13. Modification of purchase order and nonassignment
14. Warranties
15. Fair Labor Standards Act

It is important to note that only the terms and conditions appearing on the purchase order are a part of the contract. Acceptance of the order is conditional on acceptance of all terms and conditions. See Sections 4 and 5 of this handbook for detailed explanation of purchase order essentials and their legal obligations.

Purchase Order Copies. In addition to the original purchase order sent to vendor, copies are necessary for purchasing, receiving, and accounting. Purchasing must have a record of every purchase order. The receiving department is furnished a copy of the purchase order to be used when material is received. The accounting department may also be furnished a copy when that department is responsible for checking the invoice to see that it is in accordance with the purchase order. Following is a list of copies that may be needed:

1. Purchasing department copy
2. Acknowledgment copy
3. Follow-up copy
4. Accounting department copy
5. Inspection copy
6. Requisitioner's copy
7. Inventory control copy
8. Receiving department copy. (May need several to be distributed, when material is received, to departments such as inspection, production,

cost, accounting, or purchasing; the second receiving department copy often accompanies the material to identify it during handling and inspection by the requisitioner.)

Purchase Order Acknowledgment. The extra copy of the order provided to serve as an acknowledgment by the vendor is of special design, with space provided for the vendor's acceptance and the date of anticipated shipment. This copy must carry all printed matter that is on the original. When the vendor signs the acknowledgment copy and takes no exceptions, a legal contract exists. A vendor's failure to sign, and submission of his acknowledgment copy as an alternate also consummates the contract, but on the vendor's terms instead of the buyer's. It behooves the buyer to determine the differences immediately and take necessary action to correct the situation. For small dollar purchases or purchases for immediate delivery, an acknowledgment copy usually is not required. Instead of a copy of the order, an acknowledgment in the form of a self-addressed post card is very satisfactory (Fig. 25–5, Acknowledgment of Order Form) with acceptance clause and space for vendor's signature.

Date____________________

Gentlemen:

The acknowledgment of receipt of order No.________________, constitutes a representation and an agreement to abide by the conditions and provisions contained therein.

Shipment was made from____________________
will be
on (Date)____________________Via____________________

Remarks:____________________

Yours very truly,

____

NOTICE: Please fill in this card and mail to addressee at once. By____________________

FIG. 25–5. Acknowledgment of order form. Postal card form sent to vendor with original order; vendor fills and returns.

Minimizing paper work on small dollar purchases is possible by the Purchase Order Draft system, at times referred to as the "instant money" or "blank check" plan. Details and sample forms are included in Sections 5 and 19.

The Local Supply Order (Fig. 25–6, Local Supply Order Form). This is an order form used by authorized persons to cover emergency purchases, and small purchases, restricted in value as determined by management on recommendations made by the purchasing department. The orders are issued only to cover materials, supplies, and services which are readily available and on which delivery is taken at the time order is issued. It is imperative that the individual issuing the order fill in all spaces on the form. It covers a company transaction, the terms of which are familiar only to him and the vendor. The copy of order furnishes the necessary information for the purchasing department to identify the items covered before invoice can be approved for payment.

LOCAL SUPPLY ORDER
ORIGINAL

No.

To ____________________

At ____________________ ____________________ 19____
Town State Date

Please Deliver the Following Material and Supplies to:

____________________, Care ____________________

Send Invoice, in Duplicate, TO SAME COMPANY, Care PURCHASING DEPT., 1915 WOOD STREET, DALLAS, TEXAS. Fully itemize Invoice, showing quantity description and unit price of each item, discounts and order number. Keep this order for future reference.

QUANTITY	SIZE	DESCRIPTION	PRICE	TO BE USED FOR

The Above Material Received

Approved ____________________ Signed ____________________
Foreman

FIG. 25–6. Local supply order form.

Local supply order forms should provide space for the following to be filled in by originator:

1. Vendor's name and address
2. Order number and date
3. Where to ship or deliver
4. Quantity and unit
5. Description of material ordered
6. Unit price and discount
7. Invoicing instructions
8. Any special conditions or comments
9. Signature of originator

Usually a minimum of three copies of the local supply order are required:

1. To vendor
2. To purchasing department
3. Originator's copy

Copy sent to purchasing department may also be used as the receiving copy, in which event space should also be provided for acknowledgment of receipt by the receiving department which is done prior to sending to purchasing. Size 8½ by 4¼ in. is a convenient pocket size for this form.

The Cash Purchase Order. It is the policy in many companies to supply their operating departments with a petty cash fund, with which to pay authorized local service bills as well as invoices for authorized small-value purchases of materials and supplies (Fig. 25–7, Cash Purchase Order Form). This is particularly popular with small vendors, who do not make regular volume sales to the purchasing company. It gives them payment at the time sales are made, and they do not have a waiting period for their money, as is the case if the sale had been made on a charge basis.

CASH PURCHASE ORDER THIS NUMBER MUST BE SHOWN ON INVOICE CPO No.______
ORIGINAL.

To______ Req. No.______

At______ ______ 19____
Town State Date

Please Deliver the Following to:

______Co., Care______

PAYMENT OF INVOICE COVERING THIS ORDER TO BE MADE BY OUR LOCAL OFFICE AT THE ABOVE ADDRESS.

QUANTITY	UNIT	SIZE	DESCRIPTION OF MATERIAL	PRICE	AMOUNT
			TOTAL		

USED FOR

Approved______ Signed______
Supt. - Mgr. - Foreman

FIG. 25–7. Cash purchase order form.

One copy of the order serves as a notice of receipt and accompanies the invoice in the petty cash voucher. Another copy is mailed to purchasing department for checking of prices, and for seeing that the operating departments are not exceeding their authority on such purchases. The cash purchase order may be further justified in the savings effected over handling on requisition, involving approval, details of buying, and securing receiving information. Cash purchase orders should be used only to purchase materials, etc., readily available at the point where order is issued.

Follow-up. This form can be a two-section single-page form or two-section postal card form, with perforations between sections (Fig. 25–8, Follow-up Form). The top section is addressed to vendor and signed by purchaser. It requests vendor to use the bottom section to advise purchaser definite shipping information on items covered by purchaser's specific order. The bottom section is addressed to purchaser and furnishes information as to how and when shipment has been, or will be, made. Signature space is provided for vendor. This form is a timesaver, as it is quickly completed in the purchasing department for mailing.

J. M. HUBER CORPORATION
PURCHASING DEPARTMENT
BOX 831
BORGER, TEXAS

Date .... Our Order No. .... Dated .... Your Order No. ....

ATTENTION: EXPEDITING SECTION

Gentlemen:

We are particularly interested as to the deliveries of the following items on the above order. We must know immediately when, and how the contents of this order will be shipped.

Please fill out, detach, and return the lower half of this form giving complete details. We will appreciate your immediate reply to this request.

Yours very truly,

Purchasing Department

PLEASE DETACH AND MAIL

J. M. Huber Corporation
Box 831
Borger, Texas — Attn: Purchasing Department — Date ....

Gentlemen:

We (have not) (have) made (partial shipment) (shipment) of your order No. ....

ITEMS NO.	BRIEF DESCRIPTION	SHIPPING INFORMATION

ENTIRE ORDER

Shipment (will go) (went) forward by (Express) (Parcel Post) (Carload) (L.C.L.) (Pkg. Frt) (Motor Frt.) on (date)..

and routed via ....

REMARKS: ....

Yours truly,

By: ....

FIG. 25–8. Follow-up form. Sent to vendor to trace for delivery of material on order. Purchasing department fills out upper portion and sends to vendor. After detaching and filling out, vendor returns lower portion to purchasing department. (*Reproduced by permission.*)

Material Receipt. This form, when completed, is evidence that material has been received (Fig. 25–9, Material Receipt Form).

It originates with the receiving location, and if the material received checks with that ordered and invoiced, the original is attached to invoice and passed for payment.

The size of form may conform to the purchase order form, but should fit in the voucher when folded.

PURCHASING DEPT. **J. M. HUBER CORPORATION** RECEIVING REPORT No. 72501

CHARGE TO | DATE RECEIVED

THE FOLLOWING MATERIAL RECEIVED AT

PURCHASE ORDER NO. | DATE SHIPPED

REC'D FROM

TRANSPORTATION CHARGES | PREPAID COLLECT

CARRIER | VEND. TRK | P. P. | EXP. | TRUCK | RAIL FRT. | OUR P. U. | WAYBILL NO. | CAR NO.

NO. OF PCKGS.	TYPE	GROSS WEIGHT	QUANTITY	DESCRIPTION	CONDITION

REMARKS

RECEIVED BY

FIG. 25–9. Material receipt form. Prenumbered. (*Reproduced by permission.*)

The material receipt form should include provision for:

1. Date
2. Order number
3. Vendor s name and address
4. Origin point of shipment
5. How received
6. Weight of shipment
7. Condition of shipment
8. Transportation charges
9. Prepaid or collect
10. Waybill reference
11. Complete listing of material received
12. Where to be used
13. Space for special notation as to receipt in full or part or of any discrepancy existing between material ordered and received
14. Signature of receiving agent

An extra copy of the purchase order is used by many companies. This avoids copying much of the information that is needed and which is already on the purchase order copy. This receiving report copy can be printed at the same time as the purchase order (Fig. 25–4*a*) by omitting *instructions* and *conditions* at the bottom, and by having, in that space, printed instructions for the receiving office to fill in all blank spaces and return to purchasing department when material on order has been received. Spaces are provided for such information listed above as does not already appear on the receiving report copy of the purchase order.

To use this system, an arrangement must be made to handle partial receipts. This may be done with a partial-receipt form or by use of a copying machine in the receiving department. Accumulative receipts may be recorded by retaining the first copy as a master. Procedures must be established to check merchandise and to process receiving reports promptly so that material may be quickly available to the requisitioner and to those requiring the report for invoice payment.

Returned Materials. The returned materials form (Fig. 25–10) is an 8½ by 11 in. form addressed to original vendor, and is used to cover ma-

WALLACE & TIERNAN INC.
25 MAIN STREET, BELLEVILLE 9, NEW JERSEY
CODE 201: TEL. 759-8000 - TWX 759-3985 -- CABLE WALTIERNAN NEWARK -- TELEX 081-813

PLEASE REPLY TO:
BOX 178, NEWARK 1, N. J.

Re: P.O.#
Your#

Gentlemen:

We have had to reject the following material on the above order for the reason noted below:

Material ordered:

Amount rejected:

Reason for rejection:

☐ Please pick up above in our Receiving Department on our Purchasing Shipping Order #

☐ Above will be returned to ____________________ on our Purchasing Shipping Order #

☐ Please issue credit.

☐ Please send us replacement on order # ____________ enclosed.

Very truly yours,
WALLACE & TIERNAN INC.

Purchasing Department

FIG. 25–10. Returned material form. (*Reproduced by permission.*)

terial that is being returned. It may be defective material, damaged material returned for repairs, overshipment on order, or material returned for other reasons. Space should be provided for:

1. Vendor's name and address
2. Purchaser's order number reference
3. Complete listing and description of material
4. Authority for returning
5. Reference to shipping document attached
6. Amount of credit due for material returned

Purchase Order Change Notice. Purchase order adjustments are change notices or revisions issued to a vendor to cancel, alter, change the price, or otherwise modify the purchase order as originally issued. This can be accomplished by correspondence or by use of an order change notice form (Fig. 25–11, Change Notice Form). Small departments usually handle changes by correspondence.

The simplest method of accomplishing such a change is to have a supply of unnumbered purchase orders bearing in heavy type across the face, "Purchase Order Change Notice," "Purchase Order Revision," or some other designation to distinguish them from a company's standard purchase order.

Space should be provided on the order change notice form for the following:

1. Vendor's name and address
2. Date
3. Reference to order number and date
4. Details of change desired
5. Signature

For larger organizations where semiautomatic typing or other types of control require the use of a continuous perforated form, frequently the original purchase order form is used for a change order. In this case, it is necessary to type the words "Change Notice" either directly above the words "Purchase Order" or to otherwise call the vendor's attention to the fact that it is a change instead of an original order. If the volume is nominal, a rubber stamp may be used for this purpose.

One of the most frequent uses for change orders in industries where purchases are made by controlled drawings is to use the change order as a notice of correction of drawings. Use of change letters on the change notice becomes vital in such instances so that there may be no disagreement with the vendor at a later date as to which change drawing is the one actually to be used for manufacture by the vendor.

WALLACE & TIERNAN INC.

25 MAIN STREET, BELLEVILLE, NEW JERSEY 07109

PURCHASE ORDER CHANGE NOTICE

TO:

P. O. NO.

REQ. NO.

DATED

PLEASE CHANGE OUR ORIGINAL PURCHASE ORDER AS FOLLOWS:

☐ SHIP TO:

☐ SHIP VIA:

☐ SHIPPING DATE:

☐ RELEASE FOR SHIPMENT AT THE EARLIEST POSSIBLE DATE:

☐ CHANGE QUANTITY TO:

☐ CHANGE DESCRIPTION TO READ:

☐ OTHER CHANGES:

ALL TERMS AND CONDITIONS SHOWN ON ORIGINAL ORDER SHALL REMAIN UNCHANGED.

WALLACE & TIERNAN INC

BY..

FORM 2122A 9-63 -5M

ORIGINAL

FIG. 25–11. Purchase order change notice form. (*Reproduced by permission.*)

Usually all departments receiving copies of the original order are given copies of the change notice so that they will have complete details of changes. An acknowledgment copy is also sent to the vendor, to sign and return to indicate that vendor has received and accepted the change notice.

The change notice form is usually the same size as the original order.

Invoice Adjustments or Corrections (Fig. 25–12, Invoice Return Notice). It is advisable for the purchasing department to handle the correction of errors on invoices direct with the vendors, whether or not the accounting department or the purchasing department handles the invoice audit function. When the accounting department handles the function, many of the minor invoice errors may be corrected directly by accounting without the necessity of involving the purchasing department. The use of an invoice return notice is helpful in handling the majority of details involved, whether issued by accounting or purchasing. Since the form is normally attached to the invoice and both are returned to the vendor together, it is not necessary to repeat invoice information on the form.

INVOICE RETURN NOTICE TI-5875

THE ATTACHED INVOICE RETURNED FOR REASON CHECKED BELOW:

☐ INCORRECT PRICE ☐ TERMS NOT IN AGREEMENT WITH PURCHASE ORDER ☐ INCORRECT DATING

☐ INCORRECT EXTENSION ☐ INCORRECT PURCHASE ORDER NO. ☐ SUPPORTING FREIGHT BILL REQUIRED

☐ INCORRECT TOTAL ☐ PURCHASE ORDER NO. MISSING — IF NO PURCHASE ORDER ISSUED, PLEASE ADVISE NAME OF PURCHASER ☐ WE REQUIRE______COPIES

REMARKS

DISCOUNT PERIOD WILL BE FIGURED FROM DATE CORRECT INVOICE IS RECEIVED.

TEXAS INSTRUMENTS INCORPORATED

DIVISION ______ BY ______ ACCOUNTS PAYABLE

ADDRESS ______ DATE ______

FIG. 25–12. Invoice return notice. (*Reproduced by permission.*)

The reasons for issuing the invoice return notice are printed on the form with a box provided for each to permit marking the applicable situation. Use of a form of this type simplifies the handling of this process with resultant time and cost saving. For the same reason, the vendor's name and other purchase order data have been omitted from the form.

Space should be provided on the Invoice Return Notice for the following:

1. Incorrect price
2. Incorrect extension
3. Incorrect total
4. Terms not in agreement with purchase order
5. Incorrect purchase order number
6. Purchase order number missing
7. Incorrect dating
8. Supporting freight bill required
9. We require _____ copies

The "remarks" portion of the form is used whenever any special explanation of unusual circumstances is required concerning one or more of the items marked in the boxes or when an invoice variance occurs which the listed errors do not cover.

The form illustrated does not have a box for quantity differences because when quantity variance occurs, the buyer must negotiate with the vendor. In this case, a special letter is usually required and the form may or may not be used. Variance in quantity, whether above or below that specified on the purchase order, should be checked with the requisitioner to determine whether he is in a position to close the purchase order quantity short or accept the overage.

RECORDS

Records are valuable to a department only if they serve a particular purpose and can be made readily available for future use. Before adopting the use of a particular record, careful consideration should be given to whether the effort involved in maintaining it will be less than would be necessary without the record. If effort is saved or an essential purpose is served, a record can be very useful.

Order Index. There is advantage in having a record on purchase orders issued: the numerical listing or the vendor index.

If purchasing department copies of orders are filed by vendors, the numerical listing provides the cross index to vendor's name; if filed by number, the vendor index provides the numbers of the orders placed with a particular vendor.

The numerical listing can be on either a loose-leaf form or preferably in a book. The pages should have columns to provide for order number and vendor's name. If desired, provision can be made for supplemental information such as material ordered and shipping destination. All entries in these columns are made with pen or pencil at the time order number is assigned.

The index by vendors can be on either a card or loose-leaf form with one card or leaf assigned for each vendor, and filed in order by vendor name. On this form will be shown vendor's name with order numbers being entered as orders are issued. (NOTE: Where this form is used, it can also serve as the vendor index record described below.)

Vendor Index. A complete vendor record is not only convenient but also saves much time in securing information that would otherwise have to be developed on each occasion where information will be needed. This is a valuable record for buyers. It should include each vendor, its mailing address and telephone number, from which a company makes purchases.

It should show name of representative calling, important personnel of the vendor, and products handled. It can also provide space to list orders placed, date promised, and date shipped as an instant record of vendor's dependability in performance on his promises. Card forms or loose-leaf forms are usually used, filed in order by vendor name. One such card is illustrated by Fig. 7–1.

A separate record, similar to the vendor record, for all potential vendors may also be desirable. When a purchase is made from a listed potential vendor, its listing should be transferred to the regular, or active, vendor record.

Price Record. The price record form (Fig. 25–13) is a form for tabulating purchases of a particular item or material. It is useful to the buyer

CLASS ITEM

ORDER	DATE	VEN	QUANTITY	NET OR LIST	DISCOUNT	UNIT	F. O. B.	DESCRIPTION

VENDOR	ADDRESS	VENDOR	ADDRESS
1		5	
2		6	
3		7	
4		8	

LONE STAR GAS CO

FIG. 25–13. Price record form. (*Reproduced by permission.*)

in marking the purchase requisition for preparation of the purchase order. It is also useful for checking on future bids on like materials, and will furnish information for developing trends in prices.

The successful bidder's quotation is recorded on the form, and as orders are placed, the order number and date are entered.

Price record forms are usually filed by item or commodity in visible record filing equipment, of the cabinet type, or loose-leaf binders. The commodity or item designation is listed at the top or bottom of the form, or both, so that it may be readily visible when the usual lapping method of filing is used. Both sides can be printed, leaving vendor details off the reverse side.

Price record forms should provide space for purchasing department to insert the following essential information:

1. Item or commodity designation
2. Price and discount, and price unit
3. F.o.b. point
4. Vendors' names and addresses
5. Order number and date
6. Comments which may be pertinent to a particular item, commodity, or transaction

Contract Index. A varying number of periodic contracts with vendors are in force at all times. These contracts may cover equipment, material, supplies, and services, and a permanent record should be made of each contract when it becomes effective.

The index of contracts is suitable for card form application, and the form should have space for contractor's name and address, material or service contracted for, effective dates of contract, price information, and delivery points covered. The index may be filed by contractor's name or by material or service contracted for.

Tests on New Products and Materials. With many new materials coming on the market, along with older materials with which the purchasing company has no experience record, it is often necessary that these materials be put through a test period to determine their adaptability to company's use. In other cases, a specific investigation may be required. The system followed in one large company will be found in Section 28, "Appendix," under "Procedure for Initiating and Concluding Trials or Tests of Materials or Equipment."

In order to save repetition in testing, a record should be maintained on each item tested. The final summary of the test file should contain the essential information obtained through the test, the results, and recommendations regarding use of the product or material. The complete test record and report are retained together in a letter folder, and the completed test files are filed together. A consecutive numbering system may be used, or the files may be maintained in an alphabetical filing system. If a numerical system is used, a cross-index alphabetical card record is needed to locate any given file, and it can also provide a ready reference to the tests run and to the results obtained.

FILING

The filing system employed in the purchasing department will be of maximum value only if it provides ready access to information needed, is not too complicated, and is all-inclusive of the many phases of the department's activities. These phases cover such subjects as correspondence; publications of suppliers, such as catalogs and pamphlets, along with correspondence with suppliers from whom catalogs or pamphlets are not obtainable; purchase requisitions; bids; purchase orders; contracts; commodity specifications and correspondence; records; etc.

Many purchasing departments do not file material that is useless and unnecessary. Purchasing agents and buyers thus save the time of their secretaries and filing clerks by throwing out a large part of the material received in the mail or left with them by salesmen.

They agree that unsolicited advertising material, letters, brochures, catalogs, form letters, and postal cards do not justify the use of clerical labor and the expense of maintaining departmental files unless they are of immediate use to the recipient. The reason for this is that in the majority of purchases it is necessary to secure current price information along with catalogs or brochures which are up to date.

Correspondence. Much general correspondence is had by a purchasing department, which has no direct bearing on a purchase order, contract, or purchase requisition. Such correspondence will involve numerous subjects. Among these will be personnel, bulletins on purchasing policy, procedural bulletins that may be of either a temporary or permanent nature, and vendor correspondence of a general coverage.

This correspondence will generally fall under two classes, namely, open and closed. Open correspondence is that on which answers are desired, and is the most active of the files. When correspondence is completed, it is transferred to the closed file. Closed correspondence falls in two classes, temporary and permanent.

The temporary, or short-life, correspondence may cover subjects that have no general bearing on the company's operations, and should be destroyed after its purpose has been served.

The permanent files are the archives of the purchasing department. While seldom referred to, if they have probable future value, they should not be destroyed. After twelve months, as a rule, reference is seldom made to closed correspondence and it (particularly originals of contracts on major construction) should be transferred to the permanent "dead" files. To minimize use of filing space, care should be exercised so that only essential material is placed in permanent files.

Commodities. It is a good practice to maintain a card file under the heading of "specific commodities," with pertinent data relating to purchase of such commodities listed on the cards. This file can include data on tests of new products and materials if desired. Such records are usually filed in visible form, either in cabinets or in loose-leaf binders.

An alphabetical letter folder file may be used to file correspondence on commodities important to a company's operation. All pertinent data relating to the particular commodity, should be filed in that folder.

Where studies are made of the advisabiilty and feasibility of certain commodity or material purchases, a permanent file should be kept of such studies. A file number may be assigned for each such study, with a cross reference showing parties interested and all pertinent information developed, filed in such folders.

Suppliers' Catalogs, etc. Probably the most difficult filing in a purchasing department is that of suppliers' catalogs, pamphlets, and correspondence with noncataloged suppliers. There being no standard format for catalogs and pamphlets, they come in varying sizes and thicknesses. To be of value, these must be filed and cross-indexed so as to be readily available when needed. Also refer to Section 26, "Library and Catalog File."

Many catalogs contain items of a number of classifications that are not suitable for filing by any specific class of commodity. The best and neatest system for catalog filing is by catalog size. Each catalog should have a number applied on the back, which number should be visible when catalog is on the shelf. An alphabetical cross index should be maintained for all catalogs in the library. The index should show commodity and the vendor's name. Each listing should have the same number as that on the back of the catalog to which it refers. This index may be preserved in a loose-leaf ring binder, with alphabetical guides inserted.

The proper time for discarding catalogs and pamphlets is a comprehensive problem in the purchasing department. Obsolete catalogs and pamphlets should be eliminated at the time they have no future value. Filing space is expensive, and should not be maintained for useless catalogs and pamphlets. They take space, and, when mixed with current ones, only make it more difficult to locate the proper catalog and pamphlet when needed.

Pamphlets can be filed in letter folders, on a commodity or item basis, since they are issued on that basis, as a rule. Folders should be tabbed with commodity, or item name, and all pamphlets on a given commodity, or item, should be filed in a folder set up for that particular commodity or item.

Various communications are received from suppliers that do not publish a catalog. These may pertain to specific items regularly used by purchaser; may cover new items to be considered as substitutes for items currently in use; and may cover items not currently used, but for which there is a possible future use. It is desirable to keep much of this correspondence, and it should be filed satisfactorily for ready future reference. The letter-size file folder makes a good filing medium for all such correspondence. The folder should be tabbed by the commodity name, and all correspondence pertaining to that commodity should be placed in that folder. It is not necessary to index this file, but folders should be filed in alphabetical sequence.

Any communications from vendors referring to specific purchase orders or requisitions should be filed with the purchase order. If correspondence is with purchaser's company personnel and has reference to a requisition, such correspondence should be filed with that requisition.

Purchase Orders. A satisfactory method for filing purchase orders is by vendors, arranged alphabetically, in the open working file. When order is completed, the file copy and its attachments are transferred to the closed file, under vendor name, and arranged alphabetically. This method of filing lends itself to quick reference, particularly if a numerical order index record is maintained.

If, for any reason, it is desirable to file purchase orders in numerical sequence, instead of by vendors, a vendor index record should be maintained as a cross index to the order file so that an order file can be readily located when vendor name only is available.

All correspondence pertaining to questions that relate to material ordered, along with copy of invoice and material receipt, should be attached to file copy of the order.

It is well to have an extra copy of the order, known as the tracing copy, in order to prevent disturbing the file copy of order until completion. The tracing copy will often be out of its file location while being expedited. The tracing copy should be filed so as to come up for attention on a specified tracing date, regardless of vendor name, classification, or commodity. A letter-size file folder should be made for each tracing date and should contain all orders due for tracing on that date. So that there will be no duplication in clerical effort, the tracing desk must work very closely with the order desk. When shipment is made and received, the tracing copy may be destroyed. Before destroying, all correspondence should be transferred to the file containing file copy of the order.

In many lines of business it is not necessary to keep all files. It may be found advisable, to conserve filing space, to destroy certain orders, particularly those of small money value. Most companies, however, will want all orders kept in a permanent file when they cover investment items, including machinery and special equipment.

Purchase Requisitions. An effective and accessible method for filing requisitions is by requisitioning departments, and in letter-sized folders tabbed for each authorized requisitioner. These folders should be arranged alphabetically in the files. Since each requisitioner is assigned a series of numbers, or begins each year with number one, requisitions should be placed in designated folders in numerical order. This enables easy notice of any missing numbers, and gives a cross reference to order numbers.

There is some preference for filing requisitions with the file copy of orders. This is not practical, unless single-item requisitions are in use. Even then a cross index will be needed in order to locate a particular requisition, when necessary. This increases the departmental work load.

General. The letter-size file folder makes for good filing of purchase contracts. These folders should be tabbed with vendor's name and filed alphabetically. For easy reference, a cross index is needed of materials or services contracted for.

Competitive bids on invitation to bid forms should be filed together, with the successful bidder form on top. These would be filed alphabetically, by classification, and not under vendor name.

The Intelligent Usage of Files. Two fundamental objectives for files are to support and identify the purchase decision, and to guide the purchasing personnel in their decisions and actions. Irrespective of the filing system selected, simplification should be an important factor. Filing should be kept current. The need for a document will occur immediately after it is received by the vendor, the requisitioner, or accounting. Papers should be placed in their proper places daily. A large number of files are referred to regularly in a purchasing department, and the efficiency of that department can almost be judged by its filing system.

Considerable assistance may be obtained from filing equipment vendors in helping to establish or revise purchasing department files to obtain best efficiency.

Retention of Records. There is no quick-and-easy solution to the problem of what records to retain. The basic factors to consider in the light of each company's operations and experience involve: (1) legal requirements, (2) administrative requirements, (3) historical requirements, and (4) administrative discretion. A booklet entitled "Retention and Preservation of Records with Destruction Schedules" is available from Record Controls, Inc., 209 South LaSalle Street, Chicago, Illinois. This publication contains information on organizing a records retention program and a summary of state laws as well as Federal laws and regulations.[3]

FORMS DESIGN AND PROCUREMENT

Factors in Forms Design. When consideration is to be given to the adoption of a form, the following three factors should be kept in mind:

1. Will the purpose for which intended be better or more economically served by utilizing a form than it will by other means? Perhaps a

[3] For detailed Federal regulations on what records must be kept, who must keep them, and for how long, refer to "Guide to Records Retention Requirements," available from Superintendent of Documents, Washington, D.C. Single-copy price is 40 cents. Ask for catalog number GS 4.107/a:R245.

letter, memorandum, or telephone call will do the job more quickly and at less cost. Forms cost money to buy and use.

2. If a form is to be used, is there a standard one available? Most printing vendors or stationery supply houses carry in stock some standard forms which are adaptable to use in any company, and since these are printed in large quantities, they may be much more economical to use than a custom-printed form.
3. If a custom-printed form is to be used, what is the best size, style, and type and the essential printed matter needed?

Forms Design. In general, forms which will be sent outside the company should be of good quality and appearance. Those for internal use should emphasize utility and economy. All should be simple and easy to use.

Repetitive information should be printed on the form, but care must be taken to avoid including any that must be frequently crossed out or changed. To avoid this use of the box-check method, such as that employed on the Invoice Return Notice Form illustrated by Fig. 25–12.

Spaces to be filled in should be large enough to accommodate the maximum volume of information that may be entered, so as to avoid crowding. Vertical spacing of headings should correspond to standard typewriter spacing. Headings should be placed in the same order in which information will logically be entered, whether by machine or hand. If handwritten entries are to be made, supply lines on which to write.

If copies are to be made, consideration should be given to whether plain or printed copies are necessary. The plain copy is obviously the most economical and may serve the purpose as well as the printed one. When several copies are necessary, such as on the purchase order form, utilization of specialized forms may be more economical or more expeditious. Among these are the carbon-interleaved type of form which incorporates single-use snap-out carbon paper, and the continuous folded type used with a carbon-paper-holder attachment on the typewriter. One of the various copy-producing duplicating processes may also be used.

The economical printing of complicated forms requires specialized machinery, and some printers thus specialize in their production. Furthermore, there are companies which make a specialty of designing and producing business forms to fit the need. Such specialists are regularly consulted when designing and procuring forms for the purchasing department.

Elements of Cost of Forms. Cost of forms is materially affected by paper quality and size. Design should incorporate the minimum weight and quality of paper suitable for the purpose.

Standard sizes should be used to avoid extra costs resulting from necessity of cutting paper to special size with attendant trimming wastage.

Booklets on standard qualities, weights, types, and sizes of paper are available from paper vendors.

Usually, the lowest unit price obtainable for printed material is for the largest quantity. To obtain low unit cost, yet keep quantity to a realistic figure based on actual or anticipated usage, it is well to ascertain prices on quantities representing six, nine, or twelve months' requirements. On large quantities some vendors will offer to print as much as a year's needs and permit withdrawal from their stock as needed, with payment being made for quantity drawn. On a newly adopted form it is well to have only a small quantity printed initially, as it may be found after it is placed in use that revisions are necessary.

There are several printing processes, two or more of which can do the same printing job well, but one may be more economical. Discussion with printing vendors can be very fruitful.

Check List of Forms Design. The following check list may be helpful in verifying that factors outlined above have been considered before adopting a form:

1. Is a form actually needed?
2. Is a standard form available?
3. Best selection made for:

Size and style	Spacing and location of headings
Appearance	Preparation of copies that may be needed
Utilization	Paper stock
Printed matter	Printing process
Allocation of space	Over-all economy of production and use

Procurement of Forms. Control of inventory of forms and initiation of purchase requisitions is usually best handled in the stores or purchasing office. It is preferable to treat forms as a regular stock item to ensure that requests to replenish will be initiated far enough in advance of stock depletion to have replacement stock ordered, produced, and received.

The same purchasing procedures as those utilized for other materials are employed in purchase of forms and printing service. However, combining into one purchase (and printing) two or more forms of the same style, size, paper, etc., frequently results in lower printing costs because the printer can double up on a single press run. This is value analysis purchasing in its simplest application.

BIBLIOGRAPHY

For reference books, refer to Section 26, "Library and Catalog File." This lists current books containing further illustrations of forms and records used in purchasing departments.

SECTION 26

LIBRARY AND CATALOG FILE

Editor

D. R. Coultrip, Manager of Administrative Services, Dow Corning Corporation, Midland, Michigan

Associate Editors

Wilbur B. England, Professor of Business Administration, Harvard University, Boston, Massachusetts

Roland E. Neal, Purchasing Agent, Dow Corning Corporation, Midland, Michigan

Purchasing in modern business requires a wide range of knowledge in most fields of endeavor. Every department, whether small, medium, or large, calls for not only a rudimentary knowledge of all branches of business, but a familiarity with human relations, economics, geography, law, etc.

Purchasing personnel cannot hope to gain more than a mere smattering of all this knowledge through courses in schools and colleges. Even a lifetime of actual contacts would not give the required information because methods and procedures are constantly changing. Facts as now known are outmoded and superseded by others tomorrow. Thus purchasing keeps in tune with these changes if the heads of departments and the buyers are to satisfactorily perform their duties and responsibilities.

Reading is to be looked upon as the principal source of ideas, information, and inspiration. Through reading, purchasing augments its experience a thousandfold by sharing the knowledge of others. That makes the purchasing department library with its books and magazines on business in general, and purchasing in particular, an essential tool of any department. In fact, one of the most beneficial features of the magazines is the advertising they carry. Frequently they provide information of great value to buyers.

Purchasing is particularly fortunate in the wealth of information contained in easily available books, bulletins, and magazines. Many of them have been prepared and published specifically for purchasing by the professional associations in the United States and Canada, such as the NAPA, CAPA, and the NIGP.[1]

Many other sections (particularly in the "Selected Bibliography" at the end of most sections and in Section 28, "Appendix") in this handbook contain reference to individual books, magazines, and other publications where applicable to their subject matter. This section, however, itemizes a list of more general classifications for men and women in purchasing.

BOOKS IN THE PURCHASING LIBRARY

The purchasing library, to be most effectively used by members of the purchasing department, must be located where it is easily accessible. It should either be situated in the department itself or certainly nearby. The library should be in a room devoted entirely to this purpose if the

[1] National Association of Purchasing Agents.
Canadian Association of Purchasing Agents.
National Institute of Governmental Purchasing.

size of the library and the number of people who will use it warrant the use of sufficient space for this purpose. Many small purchasing departments will find that a bookcase or set of shelves will be adequate to house their books and magazines. In practically all cases it is desirable to have the purchasing library separate from any other library or central file room maintained by the company.

Ease in finding and using the desired book or magazine is the key to the success of a purchasing department library. The library, whatever its size and scope, must be the responsibility of a librarian, either a full- or a part-time member of the purchasing department. Records must be kept of books loaned out. Obsolete issues must be discarded and current editions obtained and recorded.

Checking latest editions is possible by referring to *Books in Print,* published each fall by R. R. Bowker Co., 1180 Avenue of the Americas, New York, 10036. The purchasing department library should include books and magazines typical of those indicated on the following lists. The type of industry, the size and responsibilities of the department, and the performance of its personnel will determine the selection of books and magazines to be retained. Physical separation by categories, as well as indexing, is very desirable.

Investment in the proper facilities, with subscriptions to pertinent magazines and the purchase of books relating to the industry to be served, will pay dividends in time and dollars saved. The manner in which subsequent reading and its profitable application is absorbed into regular procedures largely determines the measure of success which many purchasing departments eventually achieve.

Books on Purchasing

With the increased importance of purchasing in industry, government, and institutions, and the resulting educational influences on hundreds of schools, colleges, and associations, more books are becoming available to students of purchasing. Following is a list of books published since 1954 on this particular subject. It represents the types usually found in libraries of purchasing departments.

American Management Association, "Report No. 68, Guides to More Effective Purchasing," New York, 1962

Ammer, Dean S.: "Materials Management," Richard D. Irwin, Inc., Homewood, Ill., 1962

Anyon, G. Jay: "Managing an Integrated Purchasing Process," Holt, Rinehart and Winston, Inc., New York, 1963

Berry, H. A., "Purchasing Management," National Foremen's Institute, Division of Prentice-Hall, Inc., New York, 1964

Colton, R. R.: "Industrial Purchasing: Principles and Practices," Charles E. Merrill Books, Inc., Columbus, Ohio, 1962

DeRose, L. J.: "Negotiated Purchasing," Materials Management Institute, Boston, Mass., 1962

England, Wilbur B.: "Procurement: Principles and Cases," Richard D. Irwin, Inc., Homewood, Ill., 1962

Farrell, P. V.: "The First Fifty Years of the N.A.P.A.," National Association of Purchasing Agents, New York, 1965

Fearon, H. E., and J. H. Hoagland, "Research Study No. 58, Purchasing Research in American Industry," American Management Association, New York, 1963

Hayes, F. Albert, and George A. Renard: "Research Study No. 66, Evaluating Purchasing Performance," American Management Association, New York, 1964

Heinritz, S. F., and P. V. Farrell: "Purchasing: Principles and Applications," 4th ed., Prentice-Hall, Inc., Englewood Cliffs, N.J., 1965

Hodges, Henry G.: "Procurement: The Modern Science of Purchasing," Harper & Row, Publishers, Incorporated, New York, 1961

Kinnard, Dr. William N., Jr.: "How Small Manufacturers Buy," The University of Connecticut Press, Storrs, Conn., 1964

Lee, Lamar, Jr., and Donald Dobler: "Purchasing and Materials Management," McGraw-Hill Book Company, New York, 1965

McDonald, Paul R.: "Government Prime Contracts and Subcontracts," Procurement Associates, Glendora, Calif., 1964

McMillan, A. L.: "The Art of Purchasing," Exposition Press, New York, 1959

Miles, Lawrence D.: "Techniques of Value Analysis and Engineering," McGraw-Hill Book Company, New York, 1962

National Association of Purchasing Agents, "Guide to Purchasing," New York, 1965

Pooler, Victor H., Jr.: "The Purchasing Man and His Job," American Management Association, New York, 1964

Ritterskamp, James J., Jr., et al.: "Purchasing for Educational Institutions," Bureau of Publications, Teachers College, Columbia University, New York, 1961

Westing, J. H., et al.: "Industrial Purchasing," 2d ed., John Wiley and Sons, Inc., New York, 1961

Weston, J. F.: "Procurement and Profit Renegotiation," Wadsworth Publishing Co., San Francisco, Calif., 1960

Books on Purchasing, International

AUSTRALIA

Tyler, M., "Save Money through Better Purchasing," *The Australian Businessman's Handbook,* Rydges Business Journal, Sydney, 1960

FRANCE

Ammer, Dean S., *Materials Management,* Richard D. Irwin, Inc., Homewood, Ill., 1962 (French edition in course of publication by Dunod, Paris)

Bernatené, Henri, *L'Achat,* Les Editions d'Organisation, Paris, 1964

Heinritz, Stuart F., *L'Approvisionnement,* Editions de l'Entreprise Moderne, Paris, 1963

Kaufman, A., and G. Desbazeilles, *La Methode du Chemin Critique* (*Pert*), Dunod, Paris, 1965

Rambaux, A., *Gestion Economique des Stocks,* Dunod, Paris, 1959

GERMANY

Degelmann, Dr. Alfred (ed.), *Einkaufsleiter-Handbuch,* Verlag Moderne Industrie, München, 1965

Trautmann, Dr. W. P., *Moderne Einkaufs-Praxis,* Forkel-Verlag, Stuttgart, 1962

Lahde, Fein, and Müller, *Handbuch Moderner Lagerorganisation und Lagertechnik,* Verlag Moderne Industrie, München, 1962

GREAT BRITAIN

Bailey, J. H., *Purchasing and Supply Management,* Chapman & Hall, Ltd., London, 1963

Kay, F., *Purchasing for Industry and Public Undertakings,* Sir Isaac Pitman & Sons, Ltd., London, 1961

JAPAN

Handbook on Purchasing and Material Management, Japan Materials Management Association, Marusen Publishing Co., Tokyo, 1964

NETHERLANDS

Groot, Dr. A. M., *Voorraadbeheersing en inkoopbeleid,* Nederlands Instituut Voor Efficiency, Den Haag, 1959

Verdoorn, P. J., *Conjunctuur en inkoopbeleid,* Nederland Instituut Voor Efficiency, Den Haag, 1962

Verdoorn, P. J., *Het commercieel beleid bij verkoop en inkoop,* Stenfert Kroese, Leiden, 1964

NORWAY

Purchasing in the Industry (*Innkjøp I Industrien*), Norsk Innkjøpslederforbund, Oslo, 1964

SWEDEN

Lindquist, Hans, *En Praktisk Handbok om Inköp,* Bokförlaget Forum AB, Stockholm, 1961

Books on Subjects Directly Related to Phases of Purchasing

Many purchasing departments are not responsible for inventory or quality control. However, a basic knowledge of their techniques is essential to purchasing. That also applies to other operations directly related to the procurement function. Typical examples of books in this and corollary categories are listed below:

Bartells, R.: "Ethics in Business," Ohio State University College of Business Administration, Columbus, Ohio, 1963

Bratt, E. C.: "Business Cycles and Forecasting," 5th ed., Richard D. Irwin, Inc., Homewood, Ill., 1961

Brown, R. G.: "Statistical Forecasting for Inventory Control," McGraw-Hill Book Company, New York, 1959

Clement, E. J., and C. C. Harrington: "Plant Maintenance Manual," 2d ed., Chilton Company—Book Division, Philadelphia, Pa., 1952

Duncan, Delbert J.: "Some Basic Determinants of Behavior in Industrial Purchasing," University of California, Berkeley, Calif., 1965

General Services Administration, "Economic Order Quantity," Federal Stock Number 7610–543–6765, Supt. of Documents, Washington, D.C., 1961

Gray, A. W.: "Purchase Law Manual," Chilton Company—Book Division, Philadelphia, Pa., 1954

Hadley, G., and T. M. Whitin: "Analysis of Inventory Systems," Prentice-Hall, Inc., Englewood Cliffs, N.J., 1963

Hansen, B. L.: "Quality Control," Prentice-Hall, Inc., Englewood Cliffs, N.J., 1963

Henrici, S.: "Standard Costs for Manufacturing," 3d ed., McGraw-Hill Book Company, New York, 1960

Jiler, H.: "Commodity: 1963 Year Book," Commodity Research Bureau, Inc., New York, 1963

Leenders, Michiel R.: "Improving Purchasing Effectiveness through Supplier Development," Division of Research, Harvard University, School of Business Administration, Boston, Mass., 1965

Lusk, H. F.: "Business Law: Principles and Cases," 7th ed., Richard D. Irwin, Inc., Homewood, Ill., 1963

Magee, J. F.: "Planning and Inventory Control," McGraw-Hill Book Company, New York, 1958

Mee, John F.: "Management Thought in a Dynamic Economy," New York University Press, New York, 1963

Melnitsky, B.: "Profiting from Industrial Standardization," Chilton Company—Book Division, Philadelphia, 1953

National Association of Purchasing Agents, 11 Park Place, New York, 10007, pamphlets on the following subjects:[2]

Basic Steps in Value Analysis
The Cost of Operating a Purchasing Department
Cutting Costs by Analyzing Values

[2] Additional educational articles are distributed to members for inserting in a looseleaf binder entitled "NAPA Guide to Purchasing." This guide and supplementary articles are available to nonmembers at a cost.

Effective Meeting Leadership
Evaluation of Supplier Performance
Guide to the Selection of Competent Buyers
Interdepartmental Relations
Inventory Management of Purchased Materials
Leasing versus Buying
Materials-You-Buy Articles
Aluminum, Chemicals, Copper, Glass, Plastics, Plating, Refractory Metals, Scales, Sponge Rubber, Tires
NAPA Standards of Conduct
Purchasing as a Career
The Small Order Problem
Standardization Manual
Steel Product Manual—Hot Rolled Carbon and Alloy Bars
Steel Product Manual—Hot Rolled Steel Sheets
Training Purchasing Department Personnel and "Quick Scan" and Other Useful Tools for Public Speakers
Your Career in Purchasing

Neet, R., and S. A. Hetzler: "An Introduction to Electronic Data Processing," The Free Press of Glencoe, New York, 1963

Pritchard, James W., and Robert H. Eagle: "Modern Inventory Management," John Wiley & Sons, Inc., New York, 1965

Schmidt, Richard, and William E. Meyers: "Electronic Business Data Processing," Holt, Rinehart and Winston, Inc., New York, 1963

Welch, W. E.: "Scientific Inventory Control," Management Publishing Corporation, Greenwich, Conn., 1956

Whitin, T. M.: "Theory of Inventory Management," Princeton University Press, Princeton, N.J., 1953

Wyatt, J. W., and M. B. Wyatt: "Business Law," McGraw-Hill Book Company, New York, 1958

Books on General Business Matters

Men and women charged with the responsibility of purchasing have found that a knowledge of many phases of business is essential to do the purchasing job expected of them. It is essential that they have an understanding of other management functions and problems, particularly those dealing with other people. Listed below are the types of books used for this purpose.

Jones, M. H.: "Executive Decision Making," Richard D. Irwin, Inc., Homewood, Ill., 1962

Juran, J. M.: "Managerial Breakthrough," McGraw-Hill Book Company, New York, 1964

McGuire, J. W.: "Theories of Business Behavior," Prentice-Hall, Inc., Englewood Cliffs, N.J., 1964

Raymond, T. C.: "Problems in Business Behavior," 2d ed., McGraw-Hill Book Company, New York, 1964

Sampson, R. C.: "Managing the Managers," McGraw-Hill Book Company, New York, 1965

Scott, W. G.: "Human Relations in Management," Richard D. Irwin, Inc., Homewood, Ill., 1962

Spriegel, W. R., and R. H. Lansburgh: "Industrial Management," 5th ed., John Wiley & Sons, Inc., New York, 1955

Summer, C. E., and J. J. O'Connell (eds.): "The Managerial Mind," Richard D. Irwin, Inc., Homewood, Ill., 1964

Terry, G. R.: "Principles of Management," Richard D. Irwin, Inc., Homewood, Ill., 1964

Handbooks

Frequently the versatility of the purchasing man is demonstrated when called in conference to discuss new products, construction contracts for new plants, new production facilities or expansion, and revision of existing facilities. He may, for example, be valuable in determining the type and quality of fuel to be used in new boilers or revision of present steam or power generation equipment. The purchasing man may be the only person, in a smaller company, who deals in chemical and physical properties of commodities, printing, quality control, and a host of other areas, which makes his working knowledge of handbooks in his library of great value. Some of the reference handbooks that are helpful are shown below.

American Foundrymen's Association: "Cast Metals Handbook," 3d ed., The Association, Chicago, Ill., 1944

American Society of Metals: "The Metals Handbook," The Society, Cleveland, Ohio (published annually)

American Society of Tool and Manufacturing Engineers: "Manufacturing Planning and Estimating Handbook," McGraw-Hill Book Company, New York, 1963

American Welding Society: "Welding Handbook," 3d ed., The Society, New York, 1950

Brady, G. S.: "Materials Handbook," 9th ed., McGraw-Hill Book Company, New York, 1963

Brantly, J. E.: "Rotary Drilling Handbook," 5th ed., Palmer Publications, New York, 1952

California Association of Public School Business Officials: "Handbook of Public School Purchasing," The Association, Inglewood, Calif., 1957

Crocker, S.: "Piping Handbook," 4th ed., McGraw-Hill Book Company, New York, 1954

Croft, T.: "American Electricians' Handbook" (revised by C. C. Carr), 8th ed., McGraw-Hill Book Company, New York, 1961

Davis, C. V.: "Handbook of Applied Hydraulics," 2d ed., McGraw-Hill Book Company, New York, 1952

Eshbach, O. W.: "Handbook of Engineering Fundamentals," 2d ed., John Wiley & Sons, Inc., New York, 1952

Fiske, W. P., and S. A. Beckett: "Industrial Accountants' Handbook," Prentice-Hall, Inc., Englewood Cliffs, N.J., 1954

"Handbook of Chemistry and Physics," 36th ed. (revised annually), Chemical Rubber Co., Cleveland, Ohio

Henney, K.: "Radio Engineering Handbook," 5th ed., McGraw-Hill Book Company, New York, 1959

Ingham, H. F., and A. P. Shepard: "Metco Metallizing Handbook," Metallizing Engineering Company, Westbury, Long Island, N.Y., 1959

Juran, J. M.: "Quality Control Handbook," 2d ed., McGraw-Hill Book Company, New York, 1962

Kidder, F. E., and H. Parker: "Architects' and Builders' Handbook," 18th ed., John Wiley & Sons, Inc., New York, 1953

Knowlton, A. E.: "Standard Handbook for Electrical Engineers," 9th ed., McGraw-Hill Book Company, New York, 1957

Lange, N. A.: "Handbook of Chemistry," 10th ed., McGraw-Hill Book Company, New York, 1961

Lasser, J. K.: "Business Management Handbook," 2d ed., McGraw-Hill Book Company, New York, 1960

LeGrand, R.: "The New American Machinists' Handbook," McGraw-Hill Book Company, New York, 1955

Marks, L. S.: "Mechanical Engineers' Handbook," 6th ed., McGraw-Hill Book Company, New York, 1958

Markus, J., and V. Zeluff: "Handbook of Industrial Electronic Control Circuits," McGraw-Hill Book Company, New York, 1956

Marsden, C.: "Solvents Guide," 2d ed., Interscience Publishers Division, John Wiley & Sons, Inc., New York, 1963

Maynard, H. B.: "Industrial Engineering Handbook," 2d ed., McGraw-Hill Book Company, New York, 1963

Melcher, D., and N. Larrick: "Printing and Promotion Handbook," 2d ed., McGraw-Hill Book Company, New York, 1956

Miner, D. F., and J. B. Seastone: "Handbook of Engineering Materials," John Wiley & Sons, Inc., New York, 1955

Mulligan, J. A.: "Handbook of Brick Masonry Construction," McGraw-Hill Book Company, New York, 1942

Oberg, E., and F. D. Jones: "Machinery's Handbook," 17th ed., The Industrial Press, New York, 1964

O'Rourke, C. E.: "General Engineering Handbook," 2d ed., McGraw-Hill Book Company, New York, 1940

Peele, R.: "Mining Engineers' Handbook," 3d ed., John Wiley & Sons, Inc., New York, 1941

Perry, J. H.: "Chemical Business Handbook," McGraw-Hill Book Company, New York, 1954

Perry, R. H.: "Chemical Engineers' Handbook," 4th ed., McGraw-Hill Book Company, New York, 1963

Smithells, C. J.: "Metals Reference Book," 2d ed., Interscience Publishers, Inc., New York, 1955

Society of the Plastics Industry, "Plastics Engineering Handbook," 3d ed., Reinhold Publishing Corporation, New York, 1960

Uhlig, H. H.: "Corrosion Handbook," John Wiley & Sons, Inc., New York, 1948

Urquhart, L. C.: "Civil Engineering Handbook," 4th ed., McGraw-Hill Book Co., New York, 1959

Miscellaneous Books

Bound volumes of association material
Dictionary—Webster's Third New International
Encyclopedia
Industrial directories
Rand McNally Trading Area Manual No. 4555
So-called "society membership lists"
Special types of dictionaries—foreign language, special subjects, trade names
"Who's Who" directories—in America, in Industry, in Science, in Engineering, etc.
World Almanac (annual)

MAGAZINES IN THE PURCHASING LIBRARY

Magazines are a very good source of information on new developments, new products, substitute and new materials, and new methods of handling both old and new problems. Purchasing men agree that business and trade papers are an essential tool of purchasing, and of management generally. Thus they receive the same attention as other important "tools of the trade."

Since it is almost impossible to read all the magazines that are available to the purchasing man, it has been found worthwhile to establish a magazine section in the library. It is essential to remove periodically obsolete and unused magazines from this section so that the space can be utilized for current and usable issues. A suggested control is shown by Fig. 26–1.

Numerous publications are available to purchasing departments and the main problem comes in picking and selecting those of maximum advantage to the department. This again depends to a great extent on the location and type of industry involved. Magazines useful to purchasing generally fall into three classifications: purchasing, business and professional, and trade magazines.

Purchasing Magazines

A large number and variety of monthly magazines devoted exclusively to purchasing are published in Canada, Great Britain, and the United

States. Not only the editorial content, but the advertising sections as well, are carefully planned with a view to providing helpful information

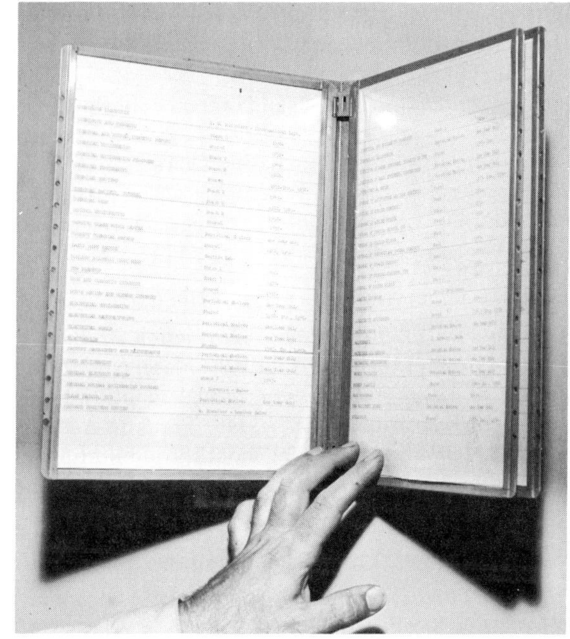

FIG. 26–1. Typical visible-file post index showing location and length of time magazines are retained.

for the buyer. Most are published for and/or by purchasing associations as indicated below:

SUBSCRIPTION MAGAZINES

Air Purchasing and Traffic, APT Publishing, Inc., Chicago, Ill.
Buyers Purchasing Digest, Buyers Purchasing Digest Company, Cleveland, Ohio
Electronic Procurement, Ojibway Press, Inc., Duluth, Minn.
Purchasing, Conover-Mast Publications, Inc., New York
Purchasing Week, McGraw-Hill Publications, New York
Railway Purchases & Stores, Simmons-Boardman Publishing Corporation, New York
Utility Purchasing & Stores, Charleson-Myers Publishing Company, Darien, Conn.

ASSOCIATION MAGAZINES—INTERNATIONAL

Acheteurs, Compagnie des Chefs D'Approvisionnement et Acheteurs, France
Canadian Purchasor, Fullerton-Weston Publishing Ltd., Don Mills, Ontario, Canada (official publication, Canadian Association of Purchasing Agents)

The Eastern Purchasing Journal, National Association of Purchasing Executives, India

Inkoop, Netherlands Purchasing Agents' Association, The Hague, Holland

Inköp, Swedish Purchasing Agents' Associations, Stockholm, Sweden

Innkjøp, Purchasing Agents' Association of Norway, Oslo, Norway

Materials and Purchasing Management, Japan Materials Management Association, Tokyo, Japan

Modern Purchasing, Maclean-Hunter Publishing Company, Toronto, Ontario, Canada

Purchasing, Australian Purchasing Officers' Association, Sydney, Australia

The Purchasing Journal, Purchasing Officers Association, London, England

Purchasing in Western Canada, Purchasing Agents' Association of British Columbia, Vancouver, B.C., Canada

NATIONAL ASSOCIATION BULLETINS IN THE UNITED STATES[3]

The Bulletin of the National Association of Purchasing Agents, official weekly publication of the NAPA, 11 Park Place, New York, 10007

Buying for Higher Education, official monthly bulletin of the National Association of Educational Buyers, 1461 Franklin Avenue, Garden City, N.Y. 11530

NIGP Letter Service, official monthly publication of the National Institute of Governmental Purchasing, 1001 Connecticut Avenue, N.W., Washington, D.C. 20036

ASSOCIATION MAGAZINES IN THE UNITED STATES[4]

Alabama Purchasor, Purchasing Agents' Association of Alabama, Inc., Birmingham, Ala. 35203

Baltimore Purchaser, The Purchasing Agents' Association of Baltimore, Inc., Baltimore, Md. 21212

Buy Lines, Milwaukee Association of Purchasing Agents, Inc., Milwaukee, Wis.

Central Michigan Association Bulletin, Purchasing Association of Central Michigan, Lansing, Mich. 48933

The Chicago Purchasor, Purchasing Agents' Association of Chicago, Chicago, Ill. 60602

The Cincinnati Purchasor, Cincinnati Association of Purchasing Agents, Inc., Cincinnati, Ohio 45203

Connecticut Purchasor, Purchasing Agents' Association of Connecticut, Inc., Ansonia, Conn. 06401

Detroit Purchasor, Ricker Publishing, Inc., Detroit, Mich. 48202

Dixie Purchasor, P. Buford Harris, Publisher, Atlanta, Ga. 30305

Florida Purchaser, Purchasing Agents' Association of Florida, Jacksonville, Fla.

The Genesee Valley Buyer, Purchasing Agents' Association of Rochester, Inc., Rochester, N.Y. 14608

[3] Do not contain advertisements, and are available only to members of the respective national association.

[4] Affiliated associations: NAPA. A few do not contain advertisements, and thus are available only to members of the respective affiliated association.

Heart of America Purchaser, Financial Publications, Inc., Kansas City, Mo. 64105

The Hoosier Purchasor, Purchasing Agents' Association of Indianapolis, Indianapolis, Ind. 46207

The Kentuckiana Purchasor, Purchasing Agents' Association of Louisville, Louisville, Ky. 40201

Journal of Purchasing (quarterly), National Association of Purchasing Agents, New York, 10007

Mid-Continent Purchaser, Purchasing Agents' Association of Tulsa and Oklahoma City, Tulsa, Okla. 74103

The Midwest Purchasing Agent, Purchasing Agents' Association of Cleveland, Inc., Cleveland, Ohio 44115

Mid-South Purchaser, Mississippi Association of Purchasing Agents, State College, Miss. 39762

New England Purchaser, New England Purchasing Agents' Association, Inc., Boston, Mass. 02110

New Jersey Purchaser, Purchasing Agents' Association of North Jersey, New Brunswick, N.J. 08903

New York Purchasing Review, The Purchasing Agents' Association of New York, Inc., New York, 10005

Niagara Frontier Purchaser, Purchasing Agents' Association of Buffalo, Buffalo, N.Y. 14214

North Central Purchasor, Twin City Association of Purchasing Agents, St. Paul, Minn. 55114

Oregon Purchasor, Purchasing Agents' Association of Oregon, Portland, Ore. 97204

Pacific Purchasor, Purchasing Agents' Association of Northern California, Inc., San Francisco, Calif. 94105

The Philadelphia Purchasor, Purchasing Agents' Association of Philadelphia, Inc., Philadelphia, Pa. 19102

Purchasing Pictorial, Purchasing Agents' Association of Western Massachusetts, Inc., Springfield, Mass. 01101

Purchasor, Purchasing Agents' Association of Syracuse and Central New York, Inc., Syracuse, N.Y. 13203

Rock River News, Purchasing Agents' Association of Rock River Valley, Rockford, Ill. 61101

St. Louis Purchaser, Purchasing Agents' Association of St. Louis, St. Louis, Mo. 63102

The Southwestern Purchaser, Purchasing Agents' Associations of Texas, Western Louisiana, and Wichita, Kansas, Dallas, Tex. 75201

Southwestern Purchasing Agent, Purchasing Agents' Association of Los Angeles, Los Angeles, Calif. 90014

The Tennessee Journal of Purchasing, Purchasing Agents' Association of Tennessee, Knoxville, Tenn. 37901

Washington Purchaser, Purchasing Agents' Association of Washington, Inc., Seattle, Wash. 98109

Business and Professional Magazines

Some of the business and professional magazines to be considered may include the following:

ASTM Bulletin, American Society for Testing and Materials, Philadelphia, Pa. 19103
Business Week, McGraw-Hill Publications, New York, 10036
Dun's Review & Modern Industry, Dun & Bradstreet Publications Corp., New York, 10008
Factory, McGraw-Hill Publications, New York, 10036
Fortune, Time, Inc., New York, 10020
Harvard Business Review, Graduate School of Business Administration, Harvard University, Boston, Mass. 02163
Mill & Factory, Conover-Mast Publications, Inc., New York, 10017
Nation's Business, Chamber of Commerce of the U.S., Washington, D.C. 20006
New Equipment Digest, Penton Publishing Company, Cleveland, Ohio 44113
Time, Time, Inc., New York, 10020
U.S. News & World Report, U.S. News Publishing Corp., Washington, D.C. 20006

Trade Magazines

The publication of trade magazines covers so many subjects that it is impossible to specify trade magazines used by any particular purchasing department library. The listing that follows plus those in Sections 15 and 28 are typical of the more prominent magazines, but selection remains with the individual purchasing executive and with the variety of products purchased by his department.

Automotive Industries, Chilton Company, Philadelphia, Pa. 19139
Chemical & Engineering News, American Chemical Society, Washington, D.C. 20006
Chemical Week, McGraw-Hill Publications, New York, 10036
Drug & Cosmetic Industry, Drug Markets, Inc., New York, 10001
Electro Technology, C-M Technical Publications Corp., New York, 10017
Electronics, McGraw-Hill Publications, New York, 10036
Food Engineering, Chilton Company, Philadelphia, Pa. 19139
Food Processing, Putnam Publishing Co., Chicago, Ill. 60611
Glass Packaging, The Reuben H. Donnelly Corp., Chicago, Ill. 60605
Good Packaging, Pacific Trade Journals, Inc., San Francisco, Calif. 94105
Hydraulics & Pneumatics, Industrial Publishing Corp., Cleveland, Ohio 44115
Hydrocarbon Processing & Petroleum Refiner, Gulf Publishing Company, Houston, Tex. 77001
IEEE Spectrum, The Institute of Electrical and Electronics Engineers, New York, 10036
Industrial & Engineering Chemistry, American Chemical Society, New York, 10022

Iron Age, Chilton Company, Philadelphia, Pa. 19139
Lubrication Engineering, American Society of Lubrication Engineers, Chicago, Ill. 60602
Machine Design, Penton Publishing Company, Cleveland, Ohio 44113
Materials in Design Engineering, Reinhold Publishing Corporation, New York, 10022
Mechanical Engineering, The American Society of Mechanical Engineers, New York, 10017
Modern Packaging, Modern Packaging Corp., New York, 10022
Plastics Technology, Bill Brothers Publishing Corp., New York, 10017
Plastics World, Cleworth Publishing Co., Inc., Cos Cob, Conn. 06807
Printers' Ink, Printers' Ink Publishing Co., Inc., New York, 10022
Product Design & Development, Chilton Company, Philadelphia, Pa. 19139
Review of Scientific Instruments, American Institute of Physics, Inc., New York, 10017
Rubber Age, Palmerton Publishing Co., Inc., New York, 10001
Safety Maintenance, Alfred M. Best Co., Inc., New York, 10038
Scientific American, Scientific American, Inc., New York, 10017
Space/Aeronautics, Conover-Mast Publications, Inc., New York, 10017
Steel, Penton Publishing Company, Cleveland, Ohio 44113
Sugar y Azucar, Palmer Publications, New York, 10036
Magazines published by large manufacturers on their products

Many articles of potential value are printed in trade magazines. The problem of keeping these articles and finding them when needed, without the problem of storage of the complete magazine, can be solved quite simply and inexpensively. The articles can be removed from the magazine, placed in properly indexed file folders, and stored in a regular steel file. This preserves the article which may be of interest to purchasing, engineering, or operating departments, and enables it to be easily found when needed but requires little space or expenditure. This also applies to clippings from newspapers, particularly from issues like the *New York Journal of Commerce* and the *Wall Street Journal.* Even the smaller purchasing departments purchase these and other newspapers for short-time use in their libraries.

Advertisements in magazines occupy prominence in the minds of purchasing people. Editorial matter especially attracts the heads of departments and their principal assistants. Buyers, however, are chiefly concerned with advertising matter, because from this source comes suggestions of new sources of supplies, and equally, if not more important, suggestions for changing specifications that help in better procurement, particularly in the value analysis field.

Some purchasing executives even claim that industrial advertising helps overcome inertia and fixed buying habits. Just how important one large company considers industrial advertising reading is indicated by the fact that its purchasing staff receives and reads through some 200 publications carrying advertising. Usually, different magazines are assigned to various buyers for reading. Most agree that time prevents doing much reading in the office; thus it has become customary in many firms to do a great deal of reading at home or while commuting. Despite this handicap, nearly 70 per cent of purchasing personnel, according to a recent survey of leading firms, make an effort to read advertisements in business magazines.

BUYERS' GUIDES[5]

The use and value of buyers' guides of various types varies in all purchasing departments. Their use is controlled by several factors, the age and experience of the buyer and whether the buyer handles only a limited number of specific items, as in the case of a large department with highly specialized buyers. In the smaller department they are of considerable value at many times. They offer possible sources of supply for many infrequently purchased supplies, equipment, and materials. They are usually quite well indexed and cross-referenced and are usually either free or quite inexpensive. Some of the more prominent types of buyers' guides are enumerated below.

Thomas' Register of American Manufacturers is a very complete guide issued annually by Thomas Publishing Company, 461 Eighth Avenue, New York, 10001. This guide consists of five volumes each year, includes a trade-name section, is completely cross-referenced by products, and has an alphabetical section of leading manufacturers, their offices and officials, their capital rating, and presently consists of 10,000 pages.

Visual Search Microfilm File is a library of 16mm microfilm cartridges issued by VSMF, 800 Acoma St., Denver, Colo. 80204. This guide contains over 100,000 pages of product data from more than 3,100 vendors serving the aerospace and electronic industries.

Conover-Mast Purchasing Directory. A single volume published semiannually by Industrial Directories, Inc., 205 East 42d Street, New York, 10017.

Sweet's Catalogs. This group consists of several complete sets of catalogs, published annually. The catalogs are free to qualified users but distribution is restricted. Sweet's Catalog Service, F. W. Dodge Company, Division of McGraw-Hill, Inc., 330 W. 42d St., New York, 10036.

MacRae's Blue Book, MacRae's Blue Book Co., 18 East Huron Street, Chicago, Ill. 60611. A two-volume guide with a classified material section with index to advertisers and an address trade-name section.

Guides for specific industries and their purchasing such as *Chemical Engineering Catalog,* published annually by Reinhold Publishing Corporation, 430 Park

[5] Others are listed in Section 28, "Appendix."

Avenue, New York, 10022. Another example is the *Chemical Week Buyers Guide Section* published annually by McGraw-Hill Publications, 330 West 42d Street, New York, 10036, as a part of a subscription to *Chemical Week.* This lists manufacturers and distributors of practically all chemicals used in industry and laboratories.

Guides published by cities, states, or geographic sectors covering the products produced or sold in their specific area.

Many companies find that the classified telephone directories, from the major cities where their purchasing is done, provide a quick and easy reference for infrequently purchased materials, supplies, or services. These are available from local telephone offices upon request.

CATALOG FILES

The catalog file can and should be an excellent source of information, a timesaving and moneysaving device for any purchasing department. Whether for one part-time buyer or a great number of purchasing executives, their assistants and buyers, the success in using the catalog file depends chiefly on its location, indexing, and cross reference and its status as a current and complete section. The size of a catalog file adequate for purchasing use may well vary from a small bookcase in a one-man department to a central file with a catalog librarian in the large plant.

Types of catalog files usually fall into three categories:

1. Central file
2. Individual files kept by buyers
3. Combination central and individual file
   a. General catalogs, those less frequently used and those used by other departments kept in the central file
   b. Specific and most frequently used retained in buyer's office

Central File

This file should consist of all the catalogs to be used by the purchasing department, or if used in conjunction with another department such as engineering, by them also. Each catalog should be carefully reviewed by a responsible person before decision is rendered to retain it in the central file. If such care is not exercised, the room for the central file will soon be filled with unused and unneeded catalogs. A person should be designated as responsible for the central catalog file to ensure proper indexing, proper filing, and the return of the catalogs by those who use them. See Figs. 26–2 and 26–3 for suggestions on filing catalogs in large and medium-size purchasing departments.

FIG. 26–2. Catalog file in larger department showing Flexoline index as two separate units. One unit by product, the second unit by manufacturer or supplier.

FIG. 26–3. Typical catalog file for medium-size department using Flexoline index. One index unit accommodates two types of indexes, one by product, the other by manufacturer or vendor.

Indexing of the catalog file is probably its greatest problem. Catalogs come in all sizes, shapes, colors, types of bindings, and thicknesses. It is often advisable to combine a group of related catalogs in one labeled binder instead of trying to file such a number of thin catalogs of various sizes on a shelf. Small departments may find that the best system is a pair of simple card files. One file should contain a list of the catalogs by manufacturer or vendor. The second file should contain a listing by product. Each catalog should be assigned a permanent identification

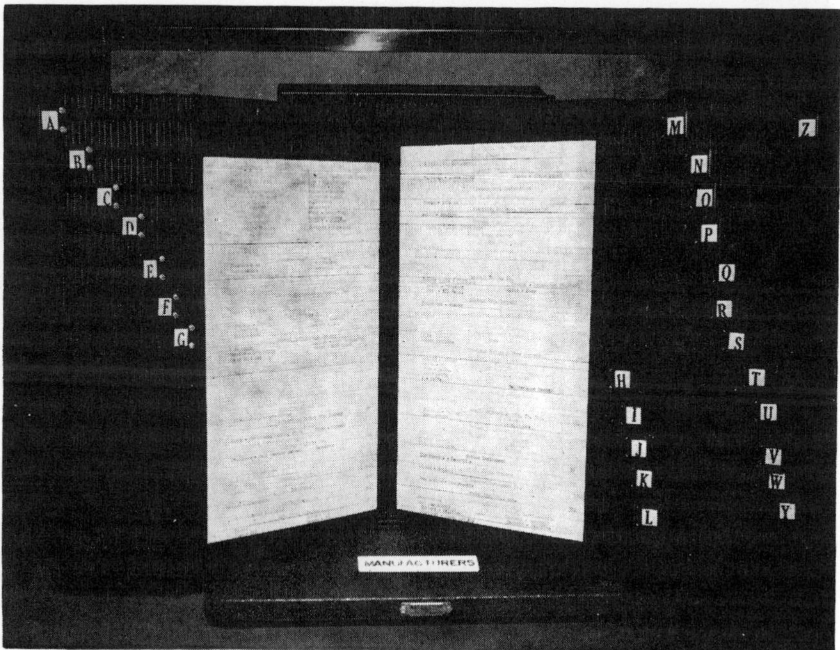

FIG. 26–4. Flexoline catalog filing index by manufacturer or vendor. Close-up view of Flexoline index. Strips are easily added or deleted, allowing expansion of the index to match addition of catalogs to the file. This index is by manufacturer or vendor.

number. Identification on the card file should be by use of the number assigned to the catalog. Larger departments find that card files are usually not satisfactory unless an elaborate system of indexing and numbering is used.

A much more flexible system involves the use of strips inserted in books, rotary units, or stands similar to those shown in Figs. 26–4 to 26–6. This type of index allows plenty of freedom for addition of new catalogs and deletion of obsolete and unused issues. It also provides excellent facilities for cross referencing which is so important in good catalog filing.

The central file has the advantage of having all the catalogs in one closely defined area. This usually means that the catalogs are also used by members of other departments, which may or may not be desirable. Care must be taken to file and keep only those catalogs that will actually be used. Establishing, indexing, and maintaining a good central catalog file is a time-consuming and fairly costly undertaking and should only be done when the need is apparent.

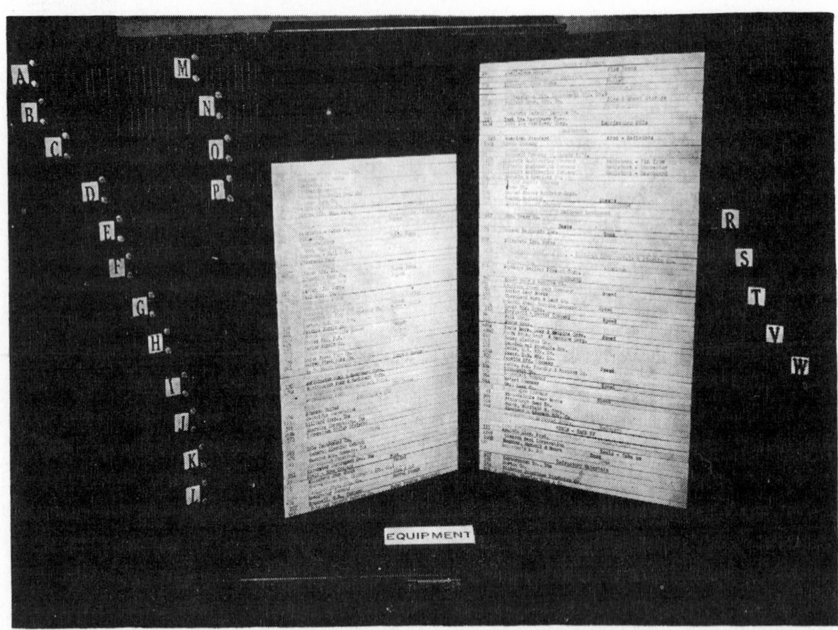

FIG. 26–5. Flexoline catalog filing index by product. Flexoline index identical to Fig. 26–6 except indexing is by product. Cross referencing, which is so essential, is easily accomplished with this type of unit.

Individual Files Kept by Buyers

The individual file, kept by the buyer or otherwise defined purchasing man, is usually desirable. In the small department, and this comprises nearly 90 per cent of all purchasing departments, it enables the buyer to have close at hand the catalogs that he uses most frequently. It enables him to use the catalog while he confers with salesmen or plant people when they are in his office or via telephone, as illustrated by Fig. 26–7. Again the space is usually limited, and care must be used in selecting only the catalogs that will be used. Periodic review of catalogs in the file usually reveals some that should be discarded.

FIG. 26–6. Rotary-type visible file for listing catalogs either by vendor or product.

FIG. 26–7. Typical catalog file in the individual buyer's office. In small departments, this, in itself, may be adequate. In larger departments, the buyer can use a file of this type for his most frequently used catalogs, in conjunction with the file shown in Figs. 26–2 and 26–3.

Combination Central and Individual File

In the medium- and larger-size departments this combination proves quite satisfactory. It has the advantages of the central file, usually ensures a complete catalog file for use by the purchasing department, and may be used by other people. It offers the advantages and flexibility of the individual file since the buyer has the most frequently used catalogs and bulletins within easy reach.

SECTION 27

GLOSSARY OF TERMS[1]

Editor

Frank E. Whyte, Director of Purchasing, SKF Industries, Inc., Philadelphia, Pennsylvania

Associate Editor

Jack S. Rutherford, Buyer–Industrial, Aluminum Company of America, Pittsburgh, Pennsylvania

This glossary contains selected terms and symbols on purchasing and transportation that in many cases have acquired a special meaning and thus cannot be found in a general-purpose desk dictionary of current edition. It aims to make definitions understandable to those engaged in day-to-day purchasing activity, not to make them legally unassailable.

The *words or phrases* marked with an *asterisk* are primarily associated with *transportation. Numerical symbols* in text indicate source of reference listed below:

[1] By permission from *A Dictionary for Accountants,* by Eric L. Kohler, Prentice-Hall, Inc., Englewood Cliffs, N.J.

[2] By permission from "Glossary of Supply Terms for General Usage in Government Agencies"

[3] Reprint from the *Freight Traffic Red Book,* with permission, by Traffic Publishing Company, Inc., New York

Definitions of highly technical terms and symbols have been excluded, with the possible exception of certain ones on transportation. In such cases, only the broadest definitions are shown in this glossary, since more concise meanings in most terms will be found in Section 17, "Purchasing Internationally," and in Section 18, "Traffic and Transportation Con-

[1] Not all of the words, terms, and symbols in this section are included in the "Index" to this handbook. The glossary is in alphabetical order and thus is an index in itself.

siderations." Other sections will include explanations and illustrations of many terms in this glossary.

abandonment* Refusal to receive freight so damaged in transit as to be worthless and render carrier liable for its value. [2]

absorption* The assumption by a carrier of switching or other special charges without increasing the charge to the shipper. [2]

abstract of title A condensed history of the title to property, based on the records.

acceptance (1) A promise to pay, by the drawee of a bill of exchange, usually evidenced by inscribing across the face of the bill "accepted," followed by the date, the place payable, and the acceptor's signature. Any words showing the intention of the drawee to accept or honor the bill are sufficient, however. The effect of the acceptance is to make the bill equivalent to a promissory note, with the acceptor as maker and the drawer as endorser. [1]. cf. "bank acceptance."

(2)* Receipt by the consignee for a shipment, thus terminating the common carrier liability subject to claim for shortages or damages if such exist.

accessorial service* A service rendered by a carrier in addition to a transportation service, such as assorting, packing, precooling, heating, storage, substitution of tonnage, etc. [3]

acknowledgment A form used by a vendor to advise a purchaser that his order has been received. It usually implies acceptance of the order.

acquittance A written receipt in full, or discharge from all claims.

act of God A term used to denote a danger beyond control of avoidance by human power; any accident produced by a physical cause which is irresistible, such as hurricane, flood, lightning, etc., which is in no way connected with negligence. See Sections 4 and 18.

ad valorem (according to value) Ad valorem is usually applied to a customs duty charged upon the value only of goods that are dutiable, irrespective of quality, weight, or other considerations. The ad valorem rates of duty are expressed in percentages of the value of the goods, usually ascertained from the invoice. See Section 9.

advanced charges* The amount of freight or other charge on a shipment advanced by one transportation line to another, or to the shipper, to be collected from the consignee. [3]

advice of shipment A notice sent a purchaser advising that shipment has gone forward and usually containing details of packing, routing, etc.

affidavit A written statement sworn to before a notary.

after sight An expression used on bills of exchange and meaning "after presentation to the drawee for acceptance."

agency The term "agency" signifies relations existing between two parties by which one is authorized to perform or transact certain business for the other; also applies to the office of the agent.

agent One acting for another, called principal, in dealing with third parties.

aggregated shipments* Numerous shipments, from different shippers to one consignee, consolidated and treated as a single consignment. [3]

agreed valuations* The value of a shipment agreed upon in order to secure a specific rating and/or liability. [3]

agreed weight* The weight prescribed by agreement between carrier and shipper for goods shipped in certain packages or in a certain manner. [3]

allonge A paper attached to a bill of exchange, on which additional endorsements may be placed when the back of the bill has already been filled with names.

anticipation An allowance, usually expressed as a percentage, granted for payment of an invoice in advance of the discount or net due date. It is calculated at the stated percentage rate for the number of days between that of actual payment and the due date, and is allowed in addition to any discounts.

any-quantity rate* A rate applied irrespective of quantity shipped.

arbitrage A term applied to transactions in which the trader buys in the cheaper market and sells in the dearer at the same time. The margin between the two prices, though necessarily small, must be sufficient to do more than cover the costs of exchange in order to yield a profit. The objects of such arbitrage transactions may be bills of exchange. bonds, stocks, coin, or bullion.

arbitrary* A stipulated and unvarying amount over a rate between two points, and used to make a through rate. Besides being a rate itself, an arbitrary generally represents the amount of division allowed the delivering carrier.

arbitration The investigation and decision of a cause or matter between parties in controversies, by chosen persons. See Section 28.

arrival notice* A notice sent by the carrier to the consignee advising of the arrival of a shipment.

artisan's lien The lien of a mechanic or other skilled worker in connection with something on which he has bestowed labor or materials, giving him a right to retain possession of it until paid.

as is A term indicating that goods offered for sale are without warranty or guarantee. The purchaser has no recourse on the vendor for the quality or condition of the goods.

assigned siding* A side or team track owned by a carrier and assigned to one or several industrial concerns for loading or unloading.

assignment Transference of some property right or title to another party.

This term is frequently used in connection with bills of lading which are endorsed (assigned) over to another party (the assignee) by the owner of the bill (assignor). Such endorsement gives to the party named the title to the property covered by the bill of lading. [2]

astray freight* Freight bearing marks indicating owner and destination, but separated from the waybill. [3]

attachment A legal proceeding accompanying an action in court by which a plaintiff may acquire a lien on a defendant's property as a security for the payment of any judgment which the plaintiff may obtain.

authorized deviation A permission to a supplier authorizing the production or delivery on a restricted basis of items not in conformance with the applicable drawings or specifications. [2]

average demurrage agreement* An agreement made between a shipper and a transportation line whereby the shipper is debited for the time cars are held for loading or unloading beyond a certain period and credited for the time cars are released by him within a certain period, demurrage charges being assessed by the transportation line, usually at the end of the month, for any outstanding debits. [3]

back order That portion of an order which the vendor cannot deliver at the scheduled time and which he has reentered for a shipment at a later date.

bailee A person into whose possession personal property is delivered.

bailment The delivery of personal property to another for a special purpose, on condition that the property will be returned pursuant to agreement.

bailor One who entrusts goods to another.

bank(er's) acceptance An instrument utilized in the financing of foreign trade, making possible the payment of cash to an exporter covering all or a part of the amount of a shipment made by him. Such an arrangement originates with the foreign importer who instructs his local bank to provide for a "commercial acceptance credit" with, for example, a New York bank in favor of a named American exporter; the New York bank then issues an acceptance credit, in effect guaranteed by the foreign bank, to the exporter, under the terms of which he may draw a time bill of exchange maturing in 60 or 90 days. Supported by the required evidence of shipment, the bill of exchange is accepted by the bank, by endorsement on the face of the bill, thus signifying that it will pay the bill at maturity. The exporter may retain the bill until maturity or sell it on the so-called "discount market." [1]

barge A generic term for a class of vessels having shallow draft or flat bottoms, used chiefly on rivers and canals. [2]

barratry In maritime law, any willful breach of duty or trust by master or crew, without consent of owners or insurers. Barratry refers to such acts as desertion or willful damage to a vessel.

barrel A round bulging vessel or cask, usually of greater length than breadth, having flat ends or heads. The quantity constituting a full barrel, for liquids, in the United States is usually 31½ U.S. gal; in England, 36 Imperial gal. However, a barrel as a unit of measurement in the petroleum industry is 42 U.S. gal; in flour milling and trade 196 lb, in the cement industry 376 lb. Wherever "barrel" is used as a unit of measurement, a purchaser should determine the volume or weight described as a "barrel." Abbreviation: bbl.

barter The act of exchanging one kind of goods for another, as distinct from trading by the use of money.

basing point* A particular geographic point to which fixed transportation rates are established to be used for the purpose of constructing rates to adjacent points by adding to, or deducting from, the basing point rate.

basing rate* A transportation rate on which other rates are constructed or based. For example, the rates from New York to Chicago constitute the basis on which rates are constructed between western points on the one hand and points in central territory on the other.

bedding charge* At most of the large stockyards, bedding for livestock cars is furnished by the stockyard companies, and a charge, usually assessed per car, is made for the service in addition to the rate.

bid An offer, as a price, whether for payment or acceptance. A quotation specifically given to a prospective purchaser upon his request, usually in competition with other vendors. An offer, by a buyer, to a vendor, as at an auction.

bill* A form used by a carrier as an invoice showing consignee, consignor, description of shipment, weight, freight rate, freight charges, and other pertinent information about goods being transported.

billed weight* The weight on the basis of which charges are assessed by the carrier and shown in freight bill and waybill.

bill of entry The detailed statement by the importer of the nature and value of goods entered at the customhouse and used for statistical purposes.

bill of exchange An unconditional order in writing addressed by one person to another, signed by the person giving it, requiring the person to whom it is addressed to pay on demand or at a fixed or determinable future time a certain sum in money to order or to bearer (Uniform Negotiable Instruments Law) ; in commercial usage, often synonymous with draft or acceptance. The term is by custom generally confined to an order to pay money arising out of a foreign transaction, "draft" being the term relating to a domestic transaction. [1]

bill of lading (uniform)* Abbreviation: B/L or b/l. A carrier's contract and receipt for goods which it agrees to transport from one place to another and to deliver to a designated person or assigns for compensation and upon such conditions as are stated therein.

The *straight bill of lading* is a nonnegotiable document and provides that a shipment is to be delivered direct to the party whose name is shown as consignee. The carriers do not require its surrender upon delivery except when necessary that the consignee be identified.

The *order bill of lading* is negotiable. Its surrender, endorsed by the shipper, is required by the carriers upon delivery, in accordance with the terms thereon. The object of an order bill of lading is to enable a shipper to collect for his shipment before it reaches destination. This is done by sending the original bill of lading, with draft drawn on the consignee, through a bank. The drawee, or the one to whom delivery is made, receives the lading upon payment of the draft and surrenders it to the carrier's agent for the shipment of goods. It is customary for shipper, when forwarding goods on this form of lading, to consign the shipment to himself to be delivered only upon his order, designating the person or firm to be notified of its arrival at destination.

A *clean bill of lading* is one receipted by carrier for merchandise in good condition (no damage, loss, etc., apparent), and which does not bear such notations as "shipper's load and count," etc.

An *export bill of lading* (through) is one issued by an inland carrier covering contract of carriage from interior point of origin to foreign destination.

A *foul bill of lading* is one indicating that a damage or shortage existed at the time of shipment.

A *government bill of lading* is one supplied by the United States government for shipment of government-owned property or of goods being delivered to the government.

An *ocean bill of lading* is one issued by an ocean carrier for marine transport of goods.

bill of materials A list specifying the quantity and character of materials and parts required to produce or assemble a stated quantity of a particular product.

bill of sale A written agreement under the terms of which the title or interest in a property is transferred by the seller (s) to the buyer or other designated person (s).

bill of sight A customhouse document, allowing consignee to see goods before paying duties. Such inspection is made in the presence of a customs officer and is requested by an importer for the purpose of obtaining details which will enable him to prepare a correct bill of entry. This latter document must be completed within three days of the bill of sight; otherwise goods are removed to government warehouse.

bill of sufferance A document giving a coasting vessel authority to carry goods in bond.

binder A tentative but binding commitment, as by the owner of real property, or by a fire insurance company. cf. "earnest money."

blind check* The tallying or checking of freight without access to records disclosing kind and amount of freight contained in the shipment.

block (express)* Groups of points considered together for the purpose of rate making in connection with express transportation.

block rate* A rate applying between a point in one express block and a point in another.

board An abbreviation for "paperboard." Paperboard is essentially paper, but the term is generally applied to the heavier and thicker grades. The terms "board" and "paperboard" cover substantially the entire range of forms of paper used to manufacture paper containers and cartons.

bond (performance) A bond executed in connection with a contract and which secures the performance and fulfillment of all the undertakings, covenants, terms, conditions, and agreements contained in the contract. [2]

bonded warehouse Place owned by persons approved of by the Secretary of the Treasury, and who have given guarantees or bonds for the strict observance of revenue laws. Such warehouses are used for the storage and custody of import merchandise, subject to duty, until the duties are paid or the goods reshipped without entry.

booking space* The act of contracting space aboard a vessel for cargo which is to be transported.

boycott A concerted effort to persuade people not to deal with a particular person or organization or to buy a certain product.

bulky A term applied to goods which take up considerable space in comparison to their weight.

bunching (cars)* Cars placed for loading or unloading in excess of orders or track and unloading facilities.

bursting strength The bursting pressure per square inch required to rupture a board sample, as determined by a Mullen or Cady test. Under Rule 41 (freight) and Rule 18 (express), bursting strength must be shown in the boxmaker's certificate.

buyer's market A "buyer's market" is considered to exist when goods can easily be secured and when the economic forces of business tend to cause goods to be priced at the purchaser's estimate of value.

buyer's option The privilege of buying a commodity, security, merchandise, or other property within a given period of time, usually at a price and under conditions agreed upon in advance of the actual sale. A seller usually requires a prospective buyer to pay for an option.

buyer's right of routing When the seller does not pay freight charges, buyer has option of routing. When seller is to prepay freight, the buyer's right to name the carrier must be made a part of the contract of sale; such right to be exercised before actual shipment of goods. If seller disobeys buyer's orders as to carrier or route, he incurs all risks of transportation.

caliper The thickness of a sheet of board, expressed in thousandths of an inch. In the paper box industry, thousandths of an inch are referred to as "points."

c.&f.[2] ***(cost and freight)****** A term used when goods are to be conveyed by ocean marine transportation and meaning that the price stated includes both the cost of the goods and the transportation charges to the named point of destination. The seller is liable for the ocean freight charges and for all risks and other charges, until he has received a clean ocean bill of lading from the carrier (either a "received for shipment" or an "on-board," as agreed between seller and buyer) at which point title passes to the buyer. The buyer is liable for all risks and charges, except ocean freight, after title has passed. The buyer is responsible for arranging for insurance on the goods from the point of ocean shipment.

car float* A large flat-bottomed boat equipped with tracks, which is used to transport railway cars over water in harbors or sheltered waters. [2]

cargo* The freight transported in a vehicle. The load for transportation as differentiated from things carried as operating equipment and supplies for the conveyance.

Flatted: Cargo all of one type placed in the bottom of a ship's hold and covered with dunnage. There is usually room left above it for loading other cargo which may be moved without interference with the flatted cargo.

Frustrated: Cargo which, while in transit, has been stopped pending issuance of new, or amended, shipping instructions.

Labeled: Cargo of a dangerous nature, such as explosives, inflam-

[2] Also see Sections 17 and 18.

mable or corrosive liquids, and the like, identified by different-colored labels to indicate requirements for special handling and stowage.

Heavy-lift: A cargo unit of excessive weight which requires special handling.

Cubic measurement: Cargo on which transportation and stevedoring charges are assessed on the basis of cubic measurement. [2]

cargo (manifest)* A document listing all cargo consignments on board a truck, vessel, or aircraft, and giving the quantity, identifying marks, consignor, and consignee of each item. [2]

car initials Initials used to indicate carrier owning a car. cf. "car number."

carload* Abbreviation: C/L or c/l. (1) A quantity of freight to which carload rates apply, or a shipment tendered as a carload; (2) a car loaded to its carrying capacity. [2]

carload minimum weight* Abbreviation: C/L min. The least weight at which a shipment is handled at a carload rate. [3]

carload rate* The rate applying to a carload quantity of freight.

car number* A number given a car in conjunction with owner's initials as a means of identification.

carrier's lien A carrier's claim on goods for the collection of freight charges.

car seal* A device to secure against unauthorized opening of the doors of a railroad car. The seal is usually registered and individually identifiable and can be used to identify the place where it was affixed. [2]

cartage* Drayage; a charge for local hauling.

carton This term is usually applied to the interior package commonly used to enclose cereals, dried fruit, sugar, soap, etc. A carton is not normally a shipping container and is not intended by itself to meet shipping requirements and regulations.

cash in advance Same as "cash with order."

cash on delivery Abbreviation: C.O.D. Payment due and payable upon delivery of goods.

cash with order Payment accompanies order when given to seller.

caveat emptor "Let the buyer beware"—the purchase is at the buyer's risk.

caveat venditor "Let the seller beware"—the seller, in some situations, is liable to the buyer if the goods delivered are different in kind, quality, use, and purpose from those described in the contract of sale.

certificate of compliance A supplier's certification to the effect that the supplies or services in question meet certain specified requirements. [2]

certificate of damage A document issued by dock companies in regard to merchandise received or unloaded in a damaged condition.

certificate of origin A certified document as to the origin of goods. [3]

certificate of weight An authoritative statement of the weight of a shipment. [3]

certified bill of lading An ocean bill of lading certified by a consular officer to meet certain requirements of his country as to goods imported.

certified check A check drawn on a bank and accepted by it.

cetane number An index of the relative ignition quality of diesel engine fuels. cf. "octane number."

change order The purchaser's document used to amend a purchase transaction previously formalized by a purchase order.

charter* The mercantile lease or hire of a vessel, aircraft, etc. Also the written evidence of such an agreement or contract. The following phrases apply to marine charters:

Bare boat: A charter obligating the charterer to provide the personnel and equipment, including all voyage and cargo expenses, marine and war risks, necessary to operate a privately owned ship.

Space: A charter which specifies that a certain cubic volume of shipping space is allocated to the charterer for use on specified voyages between designated ports. Such agreements are made by means of voyage commitment orders.

Time: A charter of a vessel which provides that the vessel shall be operated, maintained, manned, and equipped by the owner.

Voyage: A charter of a given vessel for a single voyage.

charterer One leasing a ship or part of its cargo space.

charter party A document which forms the contract between the ship owner and the one leasing the ship.

chattel The word "chattel" is derived from the word "cattle." It is a very broad term and includes every kind of property that is not real property.

check A check is a bill of exchange or draft drawn on a bank and payable on demand.

c.i.f.[3] ***(cost, insurance, and freight)**** Similar to c.&f. except that the cost of ocean marine insurance is also for the account of the seller. "War risk" insurance is not for the seller's account unless otherwise agreed upon between the parties.

classification* A publication containing a list of articles and the classes to which they are assigned for the purpose of applying class rates, together with governing rules and regulations. [3]

classification of purchaser Purchasers are classified by vendors into categories and often are given prices or discounts established by the vendor for such classification. Typical classifications are: ultimate consumer,

[3] Also see Sections 17 and 18.

retailer, wholesaler, distributor, and original equipment manufacturer.

class rate* An article not given a special or commodity rate, and not covered by an exception, comes under the class basis. Such rates are absolute in their nature, and apply to the numbered or lettered groups or classes of articles that are contained in the territorial rating column in the classification schedule.

cleaning in transit* The stopping of articles, such as peanuts, etc., at a point located between the points of origin and destination to be cleaned. [3]

clearance A customhouse certificate that a ship is free to leave, all legal requirements having been met. A term also applied to space or measurements above and beside tracks and highways, where they pass through tunnels, under and over bridges, and when published are known as "clearance tables."

collateral Security placed with a creditor to assure performance of an obligation.

collector of customs The chief officer of a customhouse. The representative of the Treasury Department of the Federal government with respect to foreign traffic.

combination rate* A rate made by combining two or more rates published in different tariffs. [3]

commercial attaçhé A representative of a government located in a foreign country for the purpose of assisting and fostering the foreign trade of that government.

commercial law That branch of the law used to designate the rules that determine the rights and duties of persons engaged in trade and commerce.

commission merchant An agent, broker, or factor employed to sell "goods. wares, and merchandise" consigned or delivered to him by his principal, for a compensation called a commission.

commodity rate* A rate applicable to an article described or named in the tariff containing the rate, and which applies to, from, or between specific points.

common carrier A person or corporation, licensed by an authorized state, Federal, or other governmental agency, engaged in the business of transporting personal property from one place to another for compensation. A common carrier is bound to carry for all who tender their goods and the price for transportation.

common law Law based on precedent expressed in judicial decisions, from the early English days down to the present in this country.

compelled rate* This is a term used to describe a rate which is established lower than the general adjustment of its related rates; usually due to water competition, and in some cases because of direct rail competition. Rates between points adjacent to rivers, lakes, etc., are often compelled rates.

competitive bidding The offer of estimates by individuals or firms competing for a contract, privilege, or right to supply specified services or merchandise.

competitive rate* A rate established by a carrier to meet the competition of another carrier.

composition of creditors An agreement among creditors and with their debtor by which they agree to take a lesser amount in complete satisfaction of the total debt due.

compromise An agreement between two or more persons, to settle the matters of a controversy without resort to litigation.

concealed damage Damage to the contents of a package which is in good order externally. [2]

concealed loss A loss from a package bearing no indication of having been opened. [3]

condemnation proceedings An action or proceeding in court for the purpose of taking private property for public use.

conditional sale A sale in which title is retained by the vendor as security for the purchase price, although possession is surrendered to the buyer.

confirming order A purchase order issued to a vendor, listing the goods or services and terms of an order placed verbally, or otherwise, in advance of the issuance of the usual purchase document.

confusion of goods The intermingling of the goods of two or more persons by either of the owners to such extent that the several portions cannot be distinguished. The person so commingling has the duty of distinguishing his own property or losing it.

consideration Something of value given for a promise to make the promise binding. cf. "binder," "earnest money."

consignee* The person or organization to whom a shipper directs the carrier to deliver goods. Such person or organization is generally the buyer of goods and is called a consignee on a bill of lading.

consignee marks* A symbol placed on packages for export generally consisting of a square, triangle, diamond, circle, cross, etc., with designated letters and/or numbers for the purpose of identification.

consignment* Goods shipped for future sale or other purpose, title remaining with the shipper (consignor), for which the receiver (consignee), upon his acceptance, is accountable. Consigned goods are a part of the consignor's inventory until sold. The consignee may be the eventual purchaser, may act as the agent through whom the sale is effected, or may otherwise dispose of the goods in accordance with his agreement with the consignor. [1]

consignor* The person or organization who delivers freight to a carrier for shipment is called a consignor or shipper and is the one who directs the bill of lading to be executed by the carrier. Such a person or organization may be the consignor-consignee, if the bill of lading is made to his own order.

consist* An itemized descriptive listing of freight carried by a particular train; usually there is a list for each car in the train. Also, the listing of the cars included in the train. "Consist" is comparable to "manifest" in maritime shipping usage. [2]. cf. "cargo (manifest)."

consolidated classification* The schedule which has superseded the individual classifications formerly issued by committees in the Official, Southern, and Western territories. The consolidated classification unifies minimum carload weights, number of classes, assignment of articles to classes, as well as descriptions of articles and rules and regulations governing their preparation and handling.

consolidation* As applied to shipments, consolidation is the act of combining a number of small (less-than-carload) shipments into a carload, generally confined to articles taking the same rating and usually carried on at point of origin.

constructive delivery Although physical delivery of personal property has not occurred, yet by the conduct of the parties, it may be inferred that as between them possession and title has passed.

constructive placement* When, due to some disability on the part of consignor or consignee, a railroad car cannot be placed for loading or unloading at a point previously designated by the consignor or consignee, and it is placed elsewhere, it is considered as being under constructive placement and subject to demurrage rules and charges, the same as if it were actually placed at the designated point. [2]

consul A government official residing in a foreign country to care for the interest of his country.

consular invoice A document in prescribed form required by a foreign government showing exact information as to consignor, consignee, value, description, etc., of a shipment being imported.

container An item in which or around which another item or items are kept and maintained as an entity, mainly for shipping or issue purposes. Examples: barrel, bottle, can, drum, reel, spool. [2]

continuing guaranty An undertaking by one person to another person to answer from time to time for money to be loaned or goods to be sold to a third person. The term refers to the future liability of the principal for a series of future transactions. It is usually revocable upon actual notice as to all future transactions.

continuous seals* A term denoting that the seals on a car or truck remained intact during the movement of the car or truck from point of origin to destination; or, if broken in transit, that it was done by proper authority and without opportunity for loss to occur before new seals were applied. [2]

contract A deliberate agreement between two or more competent persons to perform or not to perform a specific act or acts. A contract may be verbal or written. A purchase order, when accepted by a vendor, becomes a contract. Acceptance may be either in writing or by performance, unless the purchase order requires acceptance thereof to be in writing, in which case it must be thus accepted. A unilateral contract is one where only one party promises performance, the performance being in exchange for an act by the other. A bilateral contract is one where both parties promise performance, each promise being given in exchange for the other. See Sections 4 and 5.

contract carrier* By motor vehicle, any person or corporation, not a common carrier, who under special and individual contracts or agreements, transports passengers or property by motor vehicle for compensation. [3]

contract date The date when a contract is accepted by all parties thereto. [2]

contractor (1) Any one of the parties to a contract. (2) One who contracts to perform work or furnish materials in accordance with a contract.

conveyance (1) A formal written instrument usually called a deed by which the title or other interests in land (real property) is transferred from one person to another. (2) The equipment in which goods are transported by a carrier, such as a railroad, car, truck, vessel, barge, airplane, etc.

conveyor A generic term for a class of materials-handling devices used to move things over a fixed line of travel. [2]

cooperage The charge for putting hoops on casks or barrels, or the reconditioning of any packages to make them suitable for safe transportation. One engaged in this work is called a cooper.

cordage A general term covering the products of the twine, cord, and rope industry.

corporation A collection of individuals created by statute as a legal person, vested with powers and capacity to contract, own, control, convey property, and transact business within the limits of the powers granted.

cost-plus A pricing method whereby the purchaser agrees to pay the vendor an amount determined by the costs incurred by the vendor to produce the goods and/or services purchased and to which costs are added a stated percentage or fixed sum. See Section 16.

counteroffer An offer to enter into a transaction on terms differing from those first proposed. It should be noted that vendors' "acknowledgment forms" given to a purchaser in response to a purchase order may be, in fact, a counteroffer.

covenant A promise in writing under seal. It is often used as a substitute for the word contract.

currency Lawful money in current circulation. The terms "currency" and "current funds" now seem to include not only coin, silver, United States notes, and treasury notes, but also silver certificates, Federal Reserve notes, and national-bank notes.

customs (duties) Customary taxes, tolls, or duties levied upon goods which pass a frontier, generally upon goods imported.

customs tariff A schedule of charges assessed by the government on imported or exported goods.

cwt See "hundredweight."

cylinder One of two principal types of board machines or board produced on a cylinder machine. The other principal type is "fourdrinier."

damages Compensation, usually in money, for injury to goods, person, or property.

dating A method of granting extended credit terms used by sellers to induce buyers to receive goods in advance of their required delivery date, thus permitting the seller to ship goods earlier than the buyer would ordinarily wish to receive them. An example of dating would be for a purchase of spring-season goods shipped in the winter, by a manufacturer whose normal selling terms were 2 per cent discount for payment in 10 days from date of invoice or net payment in 30 days. Assuming an invoice of December 30, the terms would be stated: "2 per cent 10 days, net 30 days as of March 15." "Dating" may be extended on open account or on a secured account by use of a time draft or other instrument.

d.b.a. An abbreviation meaning "doing business as."

dead storage Storage of goods for a relatively long period of time. Frequently, goods so stored are preserved and protected in such a way that they are not readily available for immediate issue in usable condition.

deadweight tonnage The total carrying capacity of a ship in tons of 2,240 lb. [2]

debt Any obligation to pay money. Ordinarily the term debt means a sum of money due by reason of a contract expressed or implied. Broadly, the word may include obligations other than to pay money, such as the duty to render services or deliver goods.

_declared valuation_* The valuation placed on a shipment when it is delivered to the carrier.

deed A written instrument in a special form that is used to pass the legal title of real property from one person to another. See "conveyance." In order that the public may know about the title to real property, deeds are recorded in the deed record office of the county or town where the land is situated.

_defective car_* When a car has defects which are liable to injure contents, it is known as defective or in "bad order"; but if the car is loaded by the shipper the carrier is still liable for loss or damage to the contents, unless the shipper has authorized the carrier to supply a defective car and relieved the carrier of liability for loss or damage.

delivery The transfer of possession; as applied to shipping, it occurs when lading is surrendered and title to goods passes to the receiver or consignee.

delivery schedule The required or agreed time or rate of delivery of goods or services purchased for a future period.

demand charge That part of charges for a utility service which is based on the demand factor of a customer's load. [2]

demand (public utility) The utility load at a particular junction point of a utility distributing system averaged over a specified period of time, and expressed in suitable units such as kilowatts, hundreds of cubic feet, etc. [2]

_demurrage_* A charge, allowed in tariffs, or by contract, assessed against a consignor, consignee, or other responsible person for delays to transportation equipment in excess of "free time" for loading, unloading, reconsigning, or stopping in transit.

_demurrage agreement_* _average_ An agreement between a carrier and a consignor (or consignee) whereby delays in excess of the allowed free time, provided in tariffs, are debited against the consignor (or consignee), and delays less than those allowed are credited to the consignor (or consignee). In rail-carrier demurrage agreements charges are assessed by the carrier on the net debits on a periodic basis, usually at the end of a month.

deposition The written testimony of a witness taken in proper form.

depreciation Decline in value of a capital asset through wear and tear, age, inadequacy, and obsolescence without loss of substance. [2]

desiccant A material which will absorb relatively large amounts of water vapor and which is used to protect against deterioration items which are harmed by prolonged exposure to humid conditions, often by placing the item and the desiccant in one protective container or wrapper. [2]

despatch money An agreement that charterer is to receive a fixed sum per day for each day saved in loading out of a number of lay days specified in the charter party.

destination The place to which a shipment is consigned. [3]

direct delivery The consignment of goods directly from the vendor to the buyer. Frequently used where a third party acts as intermediary agent between vendor and buyer. [2]

discount An allowance or deduction granted by the seller to the buyer, usually when certain stipulated conditions are met by the buyer, which reduces the cost of the goods purchased. However, discounts may be granted by the seller without reference to stipulated conditions. An example of such use of discount is the application of discount to a nominal or "list" price to establish the "net" or actual price.

An *arbitrary discount* is one agreed upon between vendor and purchaser which has no relation to the vendor's usual basis for discount.

A *broken package discount* is one applying on a quantity of goods less than the quantity contained in a vendor's regular package.

A *cash discount* is an allowance extended to encourage payment of invoice on or before a stated date which is earlier than the NET date. The per cent of discount allowed is as agreed between buyer and seller and is often established by industry or trade custom. Usual discounts are ½, 1, 2 per cent with occasional discount allowances to 10 per cent. Typical cash discount terms are shown below and in Table 29–13.

½ per cent 10 days—½ per cent discount allowed if paid on or before the 10th day

1 per cent e.o.m.—1 per cent discount allowed if paid on or before the end of the month

2 per cent e.o.m.—10—2 per cent discount allowed if paid on or before the 10th of the following month.

2 per cent 10—60X or 2 per cent 10—60 extra—2 per cent discount allowed if paid on or before the 70th day.

2 per cent 10th prox. Same as 2 per cent e.o.m. 10.

2 per cent 10th & 25th or 2 per cent 25th & 10th—2 per cent discount allowed for payment on or before the 25th of the month for billings of the first half of the month; 2 per cent discount allowed for payment on or before the 10th of the succeeding month for billings of the last half of the month.

NOTE: Discount payment dates, other than with e.o.m. or prox. terms, are interpreted in various ways. The usual interpretation is that the discount date is calculated from the invoice date. Other interpretations should be specifically agreed upon between the buyer and seller. Other interpretations are based on (*a*) the date goods are shipped, (*b*) the date goods are received by the buyer, and (*c*) the date the goods are inspected and found acceptable by the buyer.

Discount payment terms usually are stated in conjunction with a net term. Typical are:

1 per cent 10 days, net 30 . . . or 1–10–30.
2 per cent 10 days, net 60 . . . or 2–10–60.
2 per cent 10 days 60 extra, net 90 . . . or 2–10–60X, net 90.
2 per cent 30 net 31.

Where the net date is not stated in conjunction with a discount date, the presumption is that the invoice is due net the day following the discount date.

Net terms require that vendors' invoices be paid without discount on or before due date. Typical statements of net terms are:

Net—payment due immediately.
Net 10 days—due on or before the tenth day.
Net e.o.m. Due on or before the end of the month.
Net e.o.m. 10, net 10 e.o.m., or net 10th prox.—due on or before the 10th of the month following.
Net 10–60X or net 10–60 extra—due on or before the 70th day.
Net 10th & 25th or net 25th & 10th—payment due on the 25th of the month for billings of the first half month; due on the 10th of the following month for billings of the last half of the month.

A *chain discount* is a series of discounts, the per cent of each discount in the chain applying to the amount resulting from application of the immediately preceding per cent of discount. A chain discount can be reduced to a single discount by multiplying the complement of each of the discounts and determining the complement of the result. For example:

The single discount figure equal to the chain discount 30% + 20% + 10% = 49.6% and is calculated as follows: $70 \times 80 \times 90 = 50.4$ whose complement is 49.6%. Detailed computations will be found in Tables 29–12A and 29–12B.

A *quantity discount* is an allowance determined by the quantity or value of a purchase.

A *standard package discount* is one applying to goods supplied in the vendor's regular package.

A *trade discount* is a deduction from an established price for items or services, often varying in percentage with volume of transactions, made by the seller to those engaged in certain businesses and allowed irrespective of the time when payment is made.

discount schedule The list of discounts applying to varying quantities of goods or applicable to differing classifications of purchasers.

dishonor Failure or refusal to discharge an obligation on an instrument.

dispatch cf. despatch money.

disposal The act of getting rid of excess or surplus property. Disposal may be by, but not limited to, sale, donation, abandonment, destruction, or transfer to others.

distributor A purchaser who acquires goods for resale to a wholesaler, retailer, or ultimate consumer. A distributor may sell goods from his own inventory, from a consignment inventory in his possession, or may sell for shipment to be made directly from the manufacturer's stocks.

diversion* A change made in the designation of consignee, destination, or route of a shipment while in transit; reconsignment. [2]

dockage* Charges made for the use of a dock. [2]

dock receipt* A receipt given for a shipment received or delivered at a pier or dock.

domicile That place that a person intends as his fixed and permanent home and establishment and to which, if he is absent, he intends to return. A person can have but one domicile. The old one continues until the acquisition of a new one; thus, while in transit the old domicile exists. One can have more than one residence at a time, but only one domicile. The word is not synonymous with residence.

draft A written order drawn by one party (drawer) ordering a second party (drawee) to pay a specified sum of money to a third party (payee). An *arrival draft* is prepared by the seller and, with invoice and shipping receipt for the goods sold, is deposited at his bank for collection. The bank forwards the documents to its correspondent bank at the buyer's city. The buyer secures the invoice and shipping receipt from the bank upon payment or acceptance of the draft, usually at the time the goods have arrived at destination. A *sight draft* is payable upon presentation to the drawee (as distinguished from an *arrival* or *time draft*). A *time draft* is one which is payable a stated time after acceptance by the drawee. cf. "check."

drawback A refund of customs duties paid on material imported and later exported.

drayage* Cartage. A charge for transfer and cartage between stations or to and from vessels on carts, drays, or trucks.

due bill* A bill rendered by carrier for undercharges. [3]

due care The words express that standard of conduct which is exercised by an ordinary, reasonable, prudent person.

dunnage* Materials such as boards, planks, blocks, cushions, paulins, straps, etc., used to support, secure, protect, or to facilitate handling of goods loaded in a carrier's transportation equipment.

duty A tax levied by a government on the importation, exportation, or use and consumption of goods.

e. and o.e. (***errors and omissions excepted***) An abbreviation sometimes placed on a quotation or invoice by a vendor to reserve the right to correct the amount charged if this amount is later found to be incorrect.

earnest "Earnest money" is a term used to describe money that one contracting party gives to another at the time of entering into the contract in order to "bind the bargain" and which will be forfeited by the donor if he fails to carry out the contract. Generally, in real estate contracts, such money is used as part payment of the purchase price. cf. "binder."

easement An easement is an interest in land—a right that one person has to some profit, benefit, or use in or over the land of another. Such right is created by a deed, or it may be acquired by prescription (the continued use of another's land for a statutory period).

elevator A specially constructed building for the storing, sorting, mixing, cleaning, and similar operations involved in the handling and treatment of grain.

embargo* An order issued by a carrier, carriers or their agent, or by a government, prohibiting the acceptance of freight, in any kind or of a specific nature, for shipment; generally applying to certain areas, or to and from particular points, and resulting from congestion, labor troubles, etc.; in marine usage, a detention of vessels in port; a prohibition from sailing.

endorsement cf. indorsement.

en route On the way; in transit.

entire contract A contract which by its terms requires full and complete performance on one side in return for the full and complete performance on the other. The term "entire contract" is used in contradistinction to the term "divisible contract," wherein a part of the performance required may be set over against a part of the performance on the other side.

entry (***customs***) A statement of the kinds, quantities, and values of goods imported together with duties due, if any, and declared before a customs officer or other designated officer.

equipment-trust certificate An interest-bearing document evidencing a part ownership of a trust created for the purpose of purchasing equipment and selling or leasing it to a user. An equipment trust serves as a device for avoiding direct ownership by the user, particularly in the case of railroads where such ownership would bring the newly acquired asset under existing mortgages and thus make it impossible to have it serve at the same time as security under a conditional-sales or installment-purchase contract. [1]

escalation An amount or per cent by which a contract price may be adjusted if specified contingencies occur, such as changes in the vendor's raw material or labor costs.

escrow An agreement under which a grantor, promisor, or obligor places a sum of money or the instrument upon which he is bound with a third person, called escrow holder, until the performance of a condition or the happening of an event stated in the agreement permits the escrow holder to make delivery of the money or instrument to the grantee, promisee, or obligee.

ex A prefix meaning "out of" or "from." Used in conjunction with a noun of location, such as, ex-mill, ex-mine, ex-warehouse. "Ex (named point of origin)" means that all charges for transportation and all risks of loss and damage are for the account of the buyer when the goods are delivered to a carrier at the "ex-" location. Where local cartage costs are incurred between the "ex-" location and a common carrier receiving point, such costs are for the buyer's account. On ocean marine shipments, the term "ex-dock (named port of importation)," means all transportation costs, all insurances, risks of loss and damage, export and import duties, taxes, and levies, consular and entry fees are for the account of the seller. Title passes to the buyer either when he takes possession of the goods at point of import or when the free time allowed on the dock at the point of importation expires, whichever occurs first.

examiner (customhouse) A customhouse officer who compares goods with invoice.

excess freight* Freight in excess of amount billed; also called "over" freight.

excise tax A tax imposed on the manufacture, sale, or consumption of a product.

ex parte (Latin) "From only one side or party."

expedite To hasten or to assure delivery of goods purchased in accordance with a time schedule, usually by contact by the purchaser with the vendor.

export To send goods to a foreign country.

export declaration A form required by the U.S. Treasury Department and filled out by a shipper showing the value, weight, consignee destination, etc., of shipments to be exported.

export license A certificate granting the holder permission to export goods.

express classification* A schedule containing the classes to which articles accepted for transportation are assigned. Compared with freight classification of the rail carriers, the "express classification" is a list of exceptions to three standard classes, first, second, and third, and includes a "money" section, which provides rules, regulations, and rates for the transportation or transfer of coin, currency, bullion, and securities.

express warranty When a seller makes some positive representation concerning the nature, quality, character, use, and purpose of goods, which induces the buyer to buy, and the seller intends the buyer to rely thereon, the seller has made an express warranty. See page 4–21.

factor A factor is an agent for the sale of merchandise. He may hold possession of the goods in his own name or in the name of his principal. He is authorized to sell and to receive payment for the goods.

fair market value The value of an item as determined by negotiation between buyers and sellers and which value would be acceptable as a basis of a purchase and sale.

f.a.s.* (***free alongside ship***) The term f.a.s. must be qualified by a named port. The seller is liable for all charges and risks until the goods sold are delivered alongside a vessel at such port or are delivered to the port on a dock which will be used by the vessel. Title passes to the buyer when the seller has secured a clean dock or ship's receipt for the goods. See Section 17.

ferry car* See "trap car," "station order car."

fifo First in, first out; as lifo except the first put in is taken out first instead of the last in.

finder A person who acts to bring together a purchaser and a vendor and who is not in the employ of either. A finder usually is paid a fee by the party engaging his service.

firm offer A definite proposal to sell something on stated terms, such offer binding the proposer up to stipulated time of expiration. A "firm bid" is a similar proposal to buy something. Although both are referred to colloquially as "firm offers," the distinction between bids and offers is usually preserved in cable codes.

floatage* A charge for the floating or transfer of rail freight cars across water.

floating-in rates* A low basis of rates that applies on shipments of flat cotton from ginning points to compress or concentration points, at the same time assures the inbound carrier of the outbound haul. The floating-in rate is only of a temporary measure. When cotton is reshipped, the through rate is that applicable from the original point of shipment to the final destination, based on the weight reshipped from the concentration point, plus a small transit charge.

floating policy An insurance policy that covers a class of goods located in a particular place which the insured has on hand at the time the policy was issued, but which goods at the time of a loss may not be the identical items that were on hand at the time the policy was issued. A fire policy covering the inventory of a grocery store is an example.

floor-load capacity A general term giving for a particular location in a building the maximum weight that the floor can safely support, expressed in pounds per square foot. [2]

f.o.b. (free on board)* The term means the seller is required to place the goods aboard the equipment of the transporting carrier without cost to the buyer. The term "f.o.b." must be qualified by a name of location, such as shipping point, destination; name of a city, mill, warehouse, etc. The stated f.o.b. point is usually the location where title to the goods passes from the seller to the buyer. The seller is liable for transportation charges and the risks of loss or damage to the goods up to the point where title passes to the buyer. The buyer is liable for such charges and risks after passing of title. Also see Sections 17 and 28.

follow-up To review a transaction to determine its status. In connection with purchase transactions often synonymous with "expedite."

f.o.r. (free on rails)* A term meaning that seller will make delivery as far as the railroad terminal named, or in case of overseas shipment, in harbor at port of departure, name of port stated. To avoid misunderstanding, since term is often considered to be the equivalent of "f.o.b. vessel (   )," or "f.a.s. vessel (   )," the phrase is amplified further thus, "f.o.r., cartage to vessel extra."

forwarder (freight) A commercial organization engaged in the business of consolidating less-than-carload, less-than-truckload, or less-than-planeload shipments and making arrangements for their transportation in carload, truckload, or planeload lots under applicable tariffs. [2]

fourdrinier One of the two principal types of paper machines or board machines, the other type being "cylinder."

fourth-section order* An order issued by the Interstate Commerce Commission permitting transportation lines to charge higher rates for a shorter haul than for a longer haul over the same route to avoid violation of Section 4 of the Interstate Commerce Act. [2]

free astray* A shipment miscarried or unloaded at the wrong station is billed for and forwarded to the correct station, free of charges, account of being astray, and hence the term "free astray." [3]

free goods Goods not subject to duty.

free lighterage* A privilege accorded export freight shipped in carlots.

free lighterage (New York City)* Export shipments in carlots are granted free lighterage at New York if inland bill of lading is marked "lighterage free." The inland carrier is entitled to hold the goods without charge for a longer period than it can hold domestic shipment without imposing demurrage, if the words "for export" are added.

free list A list of articles exempt from customs duties.

free port A restricted area at a seaport for the handling of duty exempted import goods, a "foreign trade zone."

free time* The period allowed to load or unload transportation equipment before demurrage or storage charges begin to accrue. See "lay time."

freight Goods being moved from one place to another by transportation lines.

freight at destination An expression meaning that freight charges will be paid by the consignee of goods upon their arrival at a specified destination.

freight (customs) bonded* Cargo imported and subject to customs inspections on entry to the United States, which is transported to destination in government-sealed conveyances under surety bond, and inspected and released by customs authorities at destination in lieu of initial port of entry. [2]

fungible goods Fungible goods are goods of which any unit is from its nature of mercantile usage treated as equivalent of any other unit. Grain, wine, and similar items are examples.

futures Contracts for the sale and delivery of commodities at a future time, made with the intention that no commodity be delivered or received immediately.

general average* In marine usage, the equitable and proportionate distribution of a loss through sacrifice or expense incurred intentionally for the safety of all interests involved in a common risk and which loss is less than the total to the ship or cargo. The loss or expense is assessed against the ship and cargo and levied against the owners thereof, or the underwriters, if there are any. [2]

good title A title free from encumbrances such as mortgages and liens.

government bill of lading A special form of bill of lading employed for shipments made by the government or by others to the government when its use is authorized.

grain Paper or paperboard, as made on modern high-speed machines, has grain, which is roughly comparable to the grain of wood. In the formation of the sheet on the machine, the individual fibers tend to be aligned in machine direction more than in cross-machine direction, thus producing grain in machine direction. This is neither always good nor always bad.

gross negligence The want of even slight care. cf. "due care."

gross register (***tonnage of a ship***) A measure of the total enclosed space, or internal capacity, of a ship expressed in measurement tons of 100 cubic feet each. In the United States it is the basis for calculating dry-dock charges. [2]

group (***or blanket***) ***rate**** Rates covering a large number of related points or a definite section of territory. The blanket system of rate application is very pronounced in cases of long-distance traffic, such as from defined groups to transcontinental and southwestern territories.

heated-car service* Warming a car to keep perishable freight from freezing and usually performed by caretakers.

heavy-lift charge* A charge by a transportation service for lifting articles of excessive weight. Heavy-lift charges are usually specified in carrier's tariffs.

hedge Any purchase or sale transaction having as its purpose the elimination of profit or loss arising from price fluctuations; specifically, a purchase or sale entered into for the purpose of balancing, a sale or purchase already made, or under contract, in order to offset the effect of price fluctuation. [1]. See Section 12.

hold A below-decks cargo stowage space aboard ship. [2]

holder in due course A person who takes a negotiable instrument under the following conditions: (1) that it is complete and regular on its face; (2) that he becomes the holder of it before it was overdue and without notice that it had been previously dishonored, if such was the fact; (3) that he took it in good faith and for value; (4) that at the time it was negotiated to him he had no notice of any infirmity in the instrument or defect in the title of the person negotiating it.

hundredweight In United States measurement and in domestic rail freight, 100 lb; in English measurement and in ocean freight parlance a hundredweight, or "cwt," is 112 lb, or one-twentieth of a long ton of 2,240 lb. Care should be taken in the use of this phrase to avoid confusion as to the exact meaning.

import To receive goods from a foreign country.

importer A buyer or merchant who imports goods.

in bond The storage or transport of goods in the custody of a warehouse or carrier from whom the goods can be taken only upon payment of taxes or duties to a governmental agency.

independent contractor The following elements are essential to establish the relation of independent contractor in contradistinction to principal and agent. An independent contractor must: (1) exercise his independent judgment as to the means used to accomplish the result; (2) be free from control or orders from any other person; (3) be responsible only under his contract for the result obtained.

indorsement Writing one's name upon paper for the purpose of transferring the title. When a payee of a negotiable instrument writes his name on the back of the instrument, such writing is an indorsement.

installment payments A schedule of payment arranged in connection with a purchase transaction requiring periodic payment of a specific sum for each of a stated number of payments. The first payment is usually at the time of delivery of the purchase or soon thereafter. Installment payment terms may be either on an open-account basis or on a secured-account basis. Secured installment accounts are usually evidenced by a mortgage or a series of promissory notes or time drafts.

insurance By an insurance contract, one party, for an agreed premium, binds himself to another, called the insured, to pay to the insured a sum of money conditioned upon the loss or damage to the property of the insured.

in-transit privileges* Changes in degree of manufacture, treatment, and other accessorial services provided for in tariffs on commodities between points of origin and destination.

inventory (1) The amount of property on hand at any given time; (2) an itemized listing of amounts of property indicated as on hand at a particular time. A "physical inventory" is one determined by actual physical count of the items. A "book inventory" is one determined from records maintained in connection with day-to-day business activities. [2]. See Section 13.

invitation for bids A request, verbal or written, which is made to prospective suppliers for their quotation on goods or services desired by the prospective purchaser.

invoice A document showing the character, quantity, price, terms, nature of delivery, and other particulars of goods sold or of services rendered; a bill.

jacket A covering of wood or fiber, placed around containers, such as bottles and cans, for protection.

jobber A middleman or dealer who purchases goods or commodities from manufacturers or importers and sells them to retailers. Also called dealer or wholesale merchant.

joint adventure Sometimes "joint venture." When two persons enter into a single enterprise for their mutual benefit without the intention of continuous pursuit, they have entered a joint adventure. They are essentially partners.

joint rate* A joint rate is one agreed upon by two or more carriers and applies between a point on the line of one and a point on the line of another. Such a rate may include one or more intermediate carriers in its route.

junction point* A point at which two or more carriers interchange freight. This term is also applied to a point where a branch-line railroad track connects with the mainline track.

k.d. (knocked down) An abbreviation meaning that the article described is supplied unassembled. When an article is shipped "k.d.," it must be reduced in size by one-third or as specified in the carrier's tariff, to secure the applicable freight rate.

kraft The term "kraft" is synonymous with sulfate and refers to the paper-pulping process. It is made from virgin pulp, coming directly from wood.

labels* Under Interstate Commerce Commission regulations, certain classes of items require specified warning labels affixed to the goods being shipped. The requirements for labeling are stated in ICC regulations, Sec. 73.400 to Sec. 73.414. Generally, a "red label" is for flammable liquids and gases; a "yellow label" for flammable solids and oxidizing materials; a "white label" for acids, caustics, and corrosive liquids; a "green label" for compressed gasses (other than flammable or tear gas). Labeling is also required for poisons, fireworks, tear gas, explosives, and radioactive materials.

lading* That which constitutes a load, as the freight in a vessel or car.

landed price A price which includes the cost of the goods, transportation, and other costs incident to ultimate delivery to the location specified by the purchaser.

landing certificate A document requiring the oath of the foreign consignee, taken before an American consul or merchant or "two respectable foreign merchants," that goods described have actually been delivered to him.

lay time* The period of time in which a ship is to be loaded or unloaded and for which time no demurrage is charged.

lead time The period of time from date of ordering to the date of delivery which the buyer must reasonably allow the vendor to prepare goods for shipment.

lease A contract conveying from one person (lessee) to another (lessor) real estate or personal property for a term in return for a specified rent or other compensation.

leased car* A car rented by a shipper or a carrier for a through movement.

legal tender Currency or coin which a government has declared shall be received in payment of duties or debts.

legal weight A foreign term denoting the weight of a shipment not including the container.

less-than-carloads* Abbreviation: l.c.l. A quantity of freight which is less than the amount necessary to constitute a carload.

less-than-carload rate* A rate applicable to less than a carload shipment.

less-than-truckload* Abbreviation: l.t.l. A quantity of freight which is less than the amount necessary to constitute a truckload.

less-than-truckload rate* A rate applicable to less than a truckload shipment.

letter of credit A letter containing a request that the party to whom it is addressed pay the bearer or person named therein money, sell him commodities on credit, or give him something of value, with the intention that the addressee later seek payment from the writer of the letter. It is used by a buyer to secure goods without the necessity of having cash in hand.

letter of intent A preliminary contractual arrangement customarily used in situations where the items, quantities, price, and delivery dates are known, but where the principal contract provisions require additional time-consuming negotiations. It is used to enter into interim agreement, pending a definitive contract, so as to permit the start of construction, production, or delivery of the supplies or materials.

license A certificate granting permission to do a specific act or acts. An *export license* is granted by a government to ship goods out of the country; an *import license* is granted to permit goods to be received into the country.

lien A right one person, usually a creditor, has to keep possession of or control the property of another for the purpose of satisfying a debt.

lifo Last in, first out; referring to accounting, handling, and pricing of materials held in inventories.

lighter A flat-bottomed boat, usually moved by tugs, and employed for transferring freight between cars, piers, and vessels.

lighterage* The charge for loading, unloading, or transferring freight by means of lighters or barges.

line haul* The movement or act of carriage over the tracks of a carrier from one city to another, not including the switching service.

liquidated damages A sum agreed upon between the parties to a contract, to be paid as ascertained damages by that party who breaches the contract.

loading and unloading* In domestic shipping, a service usually performed by the consignor and consignee in carload lots and by the carrier in less-than-carload quantities.

l.s. The letters are an abbreviation for the Latin phrase *locus sigilli,* meaning "place of the seal." cf. "seal."

lump sum The price agreed upon between vendor and purchaser for a group of items without breakdown of individual values; a lot price.

machine tools An important class of production tools basic to many manufacturing industries; nonportable, power-driven, precision metal-working machines which remove metal in the form of chips by cutting or grinding, such as lathes, drill presses, boring mills, planers, milling machines, shapers, and grinders. [2]

manifest See "cargo (manifest)."

manufacturer One who (1) controls the design and production of an item, or (2) produces an item from crude or fabricated materials, or (3) assembles materials or components, with or without modification, into more complex items. [2]

marked capacity* The stenciled or marked weight on a car denoting its carrying capacity.

marketable title A title of such character that no apprehension as to its validity would occur to the mind of a reasonable and intelligent person.

measurement goods (cargo)* Merchandise on which freight is assessed on the basis of measurement.

measurement ton* In marine usage, a term meaning 40 cu ft.

mechanic's lien A mechanic's lien is created by statute to secure laborers for their wages. Such lien has for its purpose to subject the land of an owner to a lien for material and labor expended in the construction of buildings, which buildings having been placed on the land become a part thereof by the law of accession.

minimum carload weight* The least weight at which a shipment is handled at a carload rate. [3]

minimum truckload weight* The least weight at which a shipment is handled at a truckload rate. [3]

mock-up A model, usually full size and constructed of inexpensive material, made for the purpose of studying the construction and use of an article or mechanical device. [2]

mortgage A lien on land, buildings, machinery, equipment, or other fixed or movable property given by a buyer to the seller as security for payment of the purchase price or given to the lender by the borrower as security for a loan. A *real estate mortgage* applies to lands and buildings. A *chattel mortgage* applies to all other types of property.

Mullen test A test of the pressure required to puncture a paper sample under specific conditions, as indicated on a piece of testing equipment known as a Mullen tester. The Mullen test is a requirement in connection with various shipping regulations.

mutual assent In every contract each party must agree to the same thing. Each must know what the other intends; they must mutually assent to be in agreement.

national security clause Particular stipulations made in instruments which accomplish the sale or lease of certain government property; they specify conditions and restrictions and other rights which the government reserves to itself in the transaction in order to guarantee that the property will be available for national defense purposes when the Secretary of Defense deems necessary. [2]

negligence The failure to do that which an ordinary, reasonable, prudent man would do, or the doing of some act which an ordinary, prudent man would not do. Reference must always be made to the situation, the circumstances, and the knowledge of the parties.

nested The packing of items for storage or shipment one within another to reduce bulk and facilitate handling.

net register (***tonnage of a ship***) A measure of earning power of a ship in terms of pay-load capacity. Its gross register tonnage less space needed for engines and other operating equipment, fuel, crew accommodation, operating supplies, and the like. Net register tonnage is used as a basis for charges for harbor dues, canal tolls, and similar tariffs. [2]. cf. "gross register."

net terms See "discount."

net weight The weight of an article exclusive of the weights of all packing materials and containers. [3]

n.o.i.b.n. (***not otherwise indexed by name***)* An abbreviation indicating an article not specifically included in the list of items named under a general class in the consolidated freight classification.

n.o.s. (***not otherwise specified***)* An abbreviation indicating an article within a general class in the consolidated freight classification but not completely identified.

notary A public officer authorized to administer oaths by way of affidavits and depositions; also to attest deeds and other formal papers in order that such papers may be used as evidence and be qualified for recording.

octane number An index of the relative ignition quality of liquid motor fuel. cf. "cetane number."

open-account purchase A purchase made by a buyer who has established credit with the seller. Payment terms are usually stated to require payment of invoice on or before a specific date or dates; also, to require payment of invoice in full, or less a certain percentage for prompt payment. Such terms are agreed upon between buyer and seller at time of placing order, or before.

open and prepay stations* An official list of freight stations in the United States with information as to whether goods may be consigned collect or whether charges must be prepaid.

open insurance policy A form of insurance covering shipments for a specified time or a stated value and not limited to a single shipment.

open-to-buy A term used in retailing to designate the value or quantity of goods beyond which a buyer may not purchase; the value or quantity remaining to be purchased against a specific appropriation or requisition.

original equipment manufacturer A classification assigned by a seller to a purchaser who acquires goods for incorporation into a product which he manufactures for sale, usually without changing the item which he acquires.

over, short, and damage report* A report submitted by a freight agent showing discrepancies in billing received and freight on hand. For example, if he has freight not covered by billing, he is "over," if less freight than the amount billed, he is "short," and if freight is received in bad condition, he reports "damage." Abbreviation: O.S.&D. report.

package car* A car containing less-than-carload shipments destined for one or more distant points.

packaging The use of wrappings, cushioning materials, containers, markings, and related techniques to protect items from deterioration, to prevent loss or damage, to facilitate handling, and to identify the item packaged. Packaging does not include that additional processing which may be required to prepare the packaged item for shipment. [2]

packing The preparation of an item for shipment or storage; includes required bracing, cushioning, wrapping, strapping, placement in shipping container, and marking. [2]

packing list A document which itemizes in detail the contents of a particular package or shipment.

pallet A portable platform upon which goods are placed in unit loads to facilitate stacking and handling by mechanical equipment such as fork-lift trucks. cf. "skid."

palletainer A collapsible container designed for transporting and stacking, with its contents, by means of a fork-lift truck. The container's sides and ends fold down to the deck for space savings of empty units.

palletizing The loading of supplies and equipment on a pallet. [2]

particular average In marine insurance, particular average refers to partial loss on an individual shipment from one of the perils insured against, irrespective of the balance of the cargo, and thus differs from "general average." Such insurance can usually be obtained, but the loss must be in excess of a certain percentage of the insured value of the shipment, usually 3 to 5 per cent, before a claim will be allowed by the company. See Section 17.

partnership An agreement under which two or more persons agree to carry on a business for profit.

par value (at par) The face or nominal value of a commercial paper.

patent A grant made by the Register of Patents of the United States under the authority of Federal legislation to an inventor, which gives the patentee the exclusive right to make, use, and sell the patented article. The word "patent" is also used to name the original grant of title to public lands. Such patent is a government deed of public lands to the first grantee. See Section 4.

peddler car* A car handled by carriers for less-than-carload shipments from only one consignor over a specified route, the shipments being delivered at points along the route direct from the car to the various consignees. [3]

per diem (Latin) "By the day."

permit (customs) A written authority to remove dutiable goods from a bonded warehouse or from a bonded carrier's possession.

pilot model A model, usually handmade, used in production planning for production engineering studies. [2]. cf. "mock-up."

pledge The deposit or placing of personal property as security for a debt or other obligation with a person called the pledgee. The pledgee has the implied power to sell the property if the debt is not paid. If the debt is paid, the right to possession returns to the pledgor.

point of origin* The station at which a shipment is received by a transportation line from the shipper. [3]

policy of insurance In insurance law, the word policy means the formal document delivered by the insurance company to the insured, which evidences the rights and duties between the parties.

port mark* In marine shipping, a mark affixed to packages indicating the final destination—not the port of entry, except when such port is the final destination.

port of entry A port at which foreign goods and persons are admitted legally into the receiving country. Ports of entry are officially designated by the government.

prepaid* A term denoting that transportation charges have been or are to be paid at the point of shipment. [3]

prepay station* A station (generally nonagency) to which freight charges must be prepaid.

price maintenance The price of an item established by a manufacturer or wholesaler below which he will not sell or permit his product to be sold by others.

price prevailing at date of shipment An agreement between the purchaser and the vendor that the price of the goods ordered is subject to change at the vendor's discretion between the date the order is placed and the date the vendor makes shipment and that the then-established price is the contract price.

price protection An agreement by a vendor with a purchaser to grant the purchaser any reduction in price which the vendor may establish on his goods prior to shipment of the purchaser's order. Price protection is sometimes extended for an additional period beyond the date of shipment.

price schedule The list of prices applying to varying quantities or kinds of goods.

private car* A car having other than railroad ownership.

private car line* A private concern owning its own rolling equipment, or leasing cars to, or from, railroads and operating them as private cars.

private carrier* A transportation line not engaged in business as a general public employment. [3]

production center A unit of production, usually a processing machine or production line-up, against which certain overhead charges are prorated.

proforma invoice An invoice prepared by a vendor in advance of a sale to show the form and amount of the invoice which will be rendered to the purchaser if the sale is consummated. Proforma invoices are often used in export transactions to support the purchaser's request to governmental authorities for import permits and foreign exchange.

progress payments Payments arranged in connection with purchase transactions requiring periodic payments in advance of delivery for certain stated amounts or for certain percentages of the purchase price. The whole of the purchase price may be due in advance of delivery or partially in advance and partially after delivery. Progress payments are usually required in contracts for building construction and often for specially designed plant machinery and equipment. Purchases calling for progress payments may be either on open account or be secured, usually by a contract between the buyer and seller.

prohibited articles* Articles which will not be handled, as listed in carrier's tariffs.

promissory note An unconditional written promise, signed by the maker, to pay a certain sum in money, on demand or at a fixed or determinable future date, either to the bearer or to the order of a designated person. [1]

pro-number* In freight offices, records of shipments are kept and agents' numbers are placed on freight bills, with the prefix pro- (derived from the word "progressive"), so that a specific consignment may be referred to instantly.

proprietary article An item made and marketed by a person or persons having the exclusive right to manufacture and sell it. [2]

purchase To procure property or services for a price; includes obtaining by barter. [2]

purchase change order See "change order."

purchase order The purchaser's document used to formalize a purchase transaction with a vendor. A purchase order, when given to a vendor, should contain statements as to the quantity, description, and price of the goods or services ordered; agreed terms as to payment, discounts, date of performance, transportation terms, and all other agreements pertinent to the purchase and its execution by the vendor. See Section 5.

purchase requisition A form used to request the purchasing department to procure goods or services from vendors. cf. "traveling purchase requisition."

quotation A statement of price, terms of sale, and description of goods or services offered by a vendor to a prospective purchaser; a bid. When given in response to an inquiry is usually considered an offer to sell. Also, the stating of the current price of a commodity; the price so stated.

rate* As applied to transportation or the movement and handling of goods and persons, the cost of, or charge for, service to be or which has been rendered.

rebate A sum of money returned by the vendor to a purchaser in consideration of the purchase of a stipulated quantity or value of goods, usually within a stated period.

rebilling* Issuing a new waybill at junction point to which shipment has been billed by connecting line.

receiver (in bankruptcy) A person appointed by the courts in an action in bankruptcy who takes charge of the bankrupt's assets for the benefit of the creditors of the bankrupt.

receiver (of freight)* One to whom a shipment is consigned; the consignee.

receiving report A form used by the receiving function of a company to inform others of the receipt of goods purchased. Usually, copies are distributed to the purchasing and accounting departments and the stores room.

reconsignment* A privilege extended to shippers whereby goods may be forwarded to a point other than the original destination without removal from car and at the through rate from the initial point to that of final delivery. This privilege exists only under the permission granted in a carrier's tariffs and must only be exercised in accordance with the rules and conditions contained therein.

reefer* A colloquialism meaning refrigerator. A motor vehicle, railroad freight car, ship, airplane, or other conveyance, especially constructed and insulated to protect its cargo from heat and cold. [2]

refused shipment* Freight which the consignee refuses to accept.

reinsurance A contract of reinsurance is one where one insurance company agrees to indemnify another insurance company in whole or in part against risks which the first company has assumed. The original contract of insurance and the reinsurance contract are distinct contracts. There is no privity between the original insured and the reinsurer.

released rate* A released rate is one based upon the value of an article (or articles) to which it applies, and directly conditioned upon the assumption of part or all of the risk of transportation by the consignor.

released (valuation)* A condition whereby the carrier's liability is limited.

restricted articles* Goods which are handled only under certain conditions, as listed in the carrier's tariff.

retailer A purchaser who acquires goods for resale to an ultimate consumer.

retention The practice of withholding a portion of the sum due a vendor until the purchase has been finally accepted as fully meeting specifications. The amount or percentage withheld is agreed between the parties at the time of purchase as is the period of retention.

Retention is commonly agreed upon in the purchase of building construction, and occasionally in purchase of equipment which has to be "proved-out" after delivery.

royalty Compensation for the use of land, equipment, or process payable to the owner, vendor, or lessor. Royalty payments are usually calculated as a per cent of income derived by the user from the property or process, as a stated sum per unit produced therefrom, or, a stated sum per period, such as a month or a year.

sales tax A tax imposed specifically on a sale made by a vendor. See Section 9.

salvage (1) Property that has some value in addition to its value as scrap, but which is no longer useful as a unit in its present condition and whose restoration to usefulness as a unit is economically not practicable. (2) The act of saving or recovering condemned, discarded, or abandoned property in order to obtain useful parts and scrap therefrom. [2]. See Section 21.

same as* A term meaning that the classified ratings for such articles are identical.

sample A small portion of merchandise taken as a specimen of quality.

scrap Material that has no value except for its basic material content. [2]

seal A seal is to show that an instrument was executed in a formal manner. At early common law sealing legal documents was of great legal significance. A promise under seal was binding by virtue of the seal. Today under most statutes any stamp, wafer, mark, scroll, or impression made, adopted, and affixed is adequate. The printed word "seal," or "l.s.," is sufficient. See also "car seal."

seal record* A record of the number, condition, and marks of identification of car seals made at various times and places in connection with movement of car between points of origin and destination.

seasonal rate* A rate instituted for specified articles or commodities and effective only certain periods of the year.

secured account An account on which liability is evidenced by a negotiable instrument signed by the purchaser at the time the purchase transaction is arranged or at the time of delivery. The usual types of instruments are draft, letter of credit, mortgage, promissory note, bill of exchange, or trade acceptance.

seller's lien The right of a seller to retain possession of goods until the price is paid. Such right does not exist where goods are sold on credit.

seller's market A seller's market is considered to exist when goods cannot easily be secured and when the economic forces of business tend to cause goods to be priced at the vendor's estimate of value.

seller's option The right of a seller to require the buyer to purchase merchandise, or other property at an agreed price and within a given period of time.

shipper's load and count* A term denoting that the contents of a conveyance were loaded and counted by the shipper and not checked or verified by the transportation agency. [2]

shipping release A form used by the purchaser to specify shipping instructions of goods purchased for delivery at an unstated future date or to an undisclosed destination. Also used to specify quantities to be shipped when the purchase was for an unspecified quantity or when delivery is to be made in partial lots at the purchaser's discretion.

ship's tackle The rigging, blocks, and other paraphernalia used on a ship for hoisting freight. [2]

short sale The sale of a commodity for future delivery which the seller does not possess but intends to purchase prior to the required delivery date, expecting that the market price will be no higher or will decline during the intervening period.

sight entry A procedure that must be put through to release goods from customs, occasioned by the use of incorrect invoice form, and particularly applicable to traffic into Canada.

skid A wood or metal platform fitted with two sled-type runners, or with legs, upon which material is placed and transported. It differs from a pallet in that its construction does not permit stacking of loaded skids one atop another. [2]. cf. "pallet."

sling* A net of rope, chain, or other device into which goods are placed to be hoisted into and out of a ship or other conveyance.

specification A clear, complete, and accurate statement of the technical requirements descriptive of a material, an item, or a service, and of the procedure to be followed to determine if the requirements are met.

Federal: A specification established in accordance with procedures prescribed by the Federal Specifications Board and approved for use by all government activities. [2]. See Section 19.

spotting* The act of placing a car, truck, or trailer to be loaded or unloaded.

statement of account A detailed listing, usually prepared by the vendor, of transactions between vendor and purchaser for a stated period of time, usually a month, concluding with the open or unpaid balance.

station order car* A car loaded by a shipper with several less-than-carload shipments in destination order for different points along the same route. Unlike the trap car or ferry car, this car is placed into a train without its contents being rehandled at the carrier's terminal at point of shipment. cf. "trap car," "peddler car."

stevedore One who has charge of the work of loading or unloading a vessel. The stevedore is not one of the vessel's officers or crew.

stock A supply of goods maintained on hand at the storage points in a supply system to meet demands that it is anticipated will be made.

stopover* Many carriers allow a "stopover" privilege on carload freight shipments at stations between points of origin and final destination, for the purpose of finishing loading or partly unloading or of taking advantage of transit or other privileges permitted in accordance with tariff rules and regulations.

stopping in transit* The holding of a shipment by the carrier on order of the owner after the transportation movement has started and before it is completed. [3]

storage (1) The act of storing, or state of being stored, in a designated storage place for safekeeping. (2) Space, or a place, for the safekeeping of goods. [2]

storage in transit* The stopping of freight traffic at a point located between the point of origin and destination to be stored and reforwarded at a later date. [3]

store-door delivery* The movement of goods to the consignee's place of business.

stow To arrange in a compact mass; as to stow cargo in hold of a ship. Stowing is the detailed technique of placing goods in storage.

strapping A technique of reinforcing containers by which metal straps, bands, or wires are placed around them at intervals, drawn taut, and fastened in place. [2]

s.u. Setup. An abbreviation meaning that the article described is supplied fully assembled.

subcontractor A party who contracts with a prime contractor to perform all or any part of the prime contractor's obligations in a particular prime contract. [2]

subrogation The substitution of one person in another's place, whether as a creditor or as the possessor of any lawful right, so that the substituted person may succeed to the rights, remedies, or proceeds of the claim.

surrender The abandonment of leased premises by a tenant. If a landlord accepts the abandonment as a termination of the lease, a surrender has occurred.

switching charge* The charge made for moving freight cars within the switching limits of a station. [3]

tally To count; the process of counting the pieces of an incoming or outgoing consignment and recording the particular data obtained by visual inspection, such as number of pieces, weight, commodity, and the like. Also, the number of pieces determined by counting.

tariff (freight)* A schedule containing matter relative to transportation movements, rates, rules, and regulations. An *alternative tariff* is one containing two or more rates from and to the same points, on the same goods, with authority to use the one which produces the lowest charge. A *commodity tariff* is one containing only commodity rates. A *class tariff* is one containing rates applicable to classifications of goods as established by the carriers. See also "customs tariff."

team track A track on which cars are placed for the use of the public in loading or unloading freight. [3]

terms of payment All purchase transactions require a payment for the goods or services received and, excepting an unusual exchange or barter deal, payment is made in negotiable funds in accordance with the terms agreed between buyer and seller. There are three basic payment terms: cash, open account, and secured account.

through package car* A through package or "merchandise car" is one loaded with less-than-carload shipments to break bulk at a given point; in some cases containing package freight for one station only and in other cases shipments for stations beyond.

through rate* A rate applicable through from point of origin to destination. A through rate may be either a joint rate or a combination of two or more rates. [3]

total loss Nothing salvageable; completely destroyed.

tracer (1) A request for an answer to a communication, or for advice concerning the status of a subject; (2) a request upon a transportation line to trace a shipment for the purpose of expediting its movement or establishing delivery.

track storage* A charge made on cars held on carrier's tracks for loading or unloading after the expiration of free time allowed. The charge is generally made in addition to demurrage charges. [3]

trade acceptance A non-interest-bearing bill of exchange or draft covering the sale of goods, drawn by the seller on, and accepted by, the buyer. Its purpose is to put into negotiable form an open account having a short maturity. To be eligible for discount it must contain the statement that the acceptor's obligation arises out of the purchase of goods from the drawer and it may be accompanied by a record of the purchase. [1]

trade terms The broad classification applicable to purchase transactions with reference to understandings between buyer and seller, either as to the meanings of certain abbreviations, words, or phrases or to customs applicable to transactions as established by agreement between the parties or as established by general usage. "Trade terms" includes agreed or arbitrary classifications of buyers and sellers, or their agents; types and methods of discounts, delivery terms, allowances; practices peculiar to an industry, etc.

trademark No complete definition can be given for a trademark. Generally it is any sign, symbol, mark, work, or arrangement of words in the form of a label adopted and used by a manufacturer or distributor to designate his particular goods, and which no other person has the legal right to use. Originally, the design or trademark indicated origin, but today it is used more as an advertising mechanism. See Section 4.

transit charges* Charges made for services rendered while a shipment is in transit.

transit privilege* A tariff provision authorizing a shipper to stop specified commodities at some point between origin and destination for processing or storage and later complete their movement to destination at the through rate. [2]

transship* A term commonly used to denote the transfer of goods from one steamer or conveyance to another; the rehandling or transshipment of goods en route.

trap car* A freight car, also known as a "ferry car," which is placed on a shipper's siding and in which is loaded several less-than-carload shipments destined for different points. Shipments are distributed at carrier's terminal at point of origin into other cars for forwarding to their respective destinations.

traveling purchase requisition A purchase requisition designed for repetitive use. After a purchase order has been prepared for the goods requisitioned, the form is returned to the originator who holds it until a repurchase of the goods is required. The name is derived from the repetitive travel between the originating and purchasing departments.

truckload* Abbreviation t.l. (1) A quantity of freight to which truckload rates apply or a shipment tendered as a truckload; (2) a highway truck or trailer loaded to its carrying capacity.

truckload minimum weight* The least weight at which a shipment is handled at a truckload rate.

truckload rate* The rate applying to a truckload quantity of freight.

trust receipt A document given banks by exporters and importers in exchange for bill of lading.

trustee in bankruptcy An agent of the court authorized to liquidate the assets of the bankrupt, protect them, and to bring them to the court for final distribution for the benefit of the bankrupt and all the creditors.

ultimate consumer A purchaser who acquires and consumes the goods in their entirety or who converts them into another product entirely unlike the goods received, or who secures the goods with no intention of resale.

uniform express receipt* A receipt furnished the shipper for goods entrusted to the express company for transportation.

use tax A tax imposed on the user of goods. Specifically, a use tax is levied on the purchaser of goods acquired outside the jurisdiction of the taxing authority if a sales tax would have been applicable had the goods been purchased within such jurisdiction. See Section 9.

valued policy As used in fire insurance, a valued policy is one in which the sum to be paid in case of loss is fixed by the terms of the policy. No reference can be made to the real value of the property that is lost.

vendee A purchaser of property. The term is generally applied to the purchaser of real property. The word "buyer" is usually applied to the purchaser of personal property.

vendor One who sells something; a "seller."

vendor's lien An unpaid seller's right to hold possession of property until he has recovered the purchase price.

visual inspection A term generally used to indicate inspection performed without the aid of test instruments. [2]

voucher A written instrument that bears witness or "vouches" for something. Generally a voucher is an instrument showing services have been performed, or goods purchased, and authorizes payment to be made to the vendor.

warehouse (bonded) A warehouse in which goods are held under bond to the government subject to payment of customs duties or taxes on the goods. [2]

warehouse (public) A place of storage for the use of the general public; usually embracing merchandise and/or household goods, or sometimes limited to certain commodities. In addition to the service of storage many public warehouses are performing the functions of distributing agent and forwarder.

warehouse receipt An instrument showing that the signer has in his possession certain described goods for storage, and which obligates the signer, the warehouseman, to deliver the goods to a specified person or to his order or bearer upon the return of the instrument. Consult Uniform Warehouse Receipts Act.

warranty An undertaking, either expressed or implied, that a certain fact regarding the subject matter of a contract is presently true or will be true. The word should be distinguished from "guaranty" which means a contract or promise by one person to answer for the performance of another. See Section 4.

waybill* A document prepared by a transportation line at the point of origin of a shipment, showing the point of origin, destination, route, consignor, consignee, description of shipment and amount charged for the transportation service, and forwarded to the carrier's agent at transfer point or destination. An *astray waybill* is used for freight miscarried or separated from its proper waybill. A *blanket waybill* is one covering two or more consignments of freight. An *interline waybill* is one covering the movement of freight over two or more transportation lines.

weight, gross The weight of an article together with the weight of its container and the material used for packing. [3]

weight, net The actual weight of the contents of a container or of the cargo of a vehicle. It is the total weight less the tare weight. [2]

weight, tare The weight of an empty container and the other material used for packing its contents. *Actual tare* is determined when each cask, bag, etc., is weighed; *average tare,* when one is weighed as a sample; and *estimated tare,* when a fixed percentage is allowed.

wharfage* A charge against a vessel for lying at a wharf. It is often used synonymously with "dockage" and "moorage."

wholesaler A purchaser who acquires goods for resale to a retailer or a jobber.

without engagement A phrase incorporated in a quotation and used to avoid having to accept an order at the price quoted. A safeguard against prices fluctuating in the interval between the giving of the quotation and the order being placed.

w/o An abbreviation meaning (1) without or (2) with order, as cash w/o.

zip code Numbering of U.S. post offices to facilitate delivery of mail. The Zip Code number is part of the address to be used on all mail immediately after the name of the state. Example: York, Pa. 17405.

zones (express) Portions of the country employed in rate making in connection with express traffic and rates.

zones (parcel post) The United States and its possessions are divided into eight zones for the application of parcel-post charges, the rate from a point to any of the points located in one of the zones being the same.

SECTION 28

APPENDIX

Editor

H. A. Hamilton, Jr., Purchasing Agent, Afro-American Purchasing Center, Inc., New York, N.Y. (Section written while Purchasing Agent, Sperry Rand Research Center, Sperry Rand Corporation, Sudbury, Massachusetts)

Associate Editors

H. Bloom, Materiel Manager, Avco-Everett Research Laboratory, Division of Avco Corporation, Everett, Massachusetts

George A. Cumming, Deputy State Purchasing Agent, State of California, San Francisco, California

R. S. Mullen, Purchasing Agent, Harvard University, Boston, Massachusetts

The Purchasing function is efficient only as long as it keeps up-to-date in the various areas in which it requires information. Current market trends (local, national, and international) sources of supply, standards for materials and processes, commodity prices, and operating techniques are only a few. Sources of information for these data are vital to the progressive purchasing official if his operation is to keep his company in step with or ahead of his competition.

Purchasing association meetings provide an excellent opportunity to discuss mutual problems with fellow purchasers. They also furnish a chance to learn new techniques of operation and to hear progressive leaders in the purchasing and management fields. As one example, the professional development activities of the National Association of Purchasing Agents (NAPA) and its affiliated associations are designed to satisfy the need of purchasing people to become more enlightened regarding their profession and to create new bodies of knowledge on which to draw in the future. Similar educational activities are sponsored by the other national and foreign purchasing associations listed in this section.

It is the purpose of this section to provide a ready reference for data to satisfy the above-mentioned needs—a reference both for statistics, which are shown under the first division, "Basic Sources of Information," and for purchasing associations, which are shown under the second division, "Information on Purchasing Associations." Obviously, this material is of value to anyone involved in purchasing, irrespective of membership in such a group.

The third and last division, "Reference Material," has been set up to provide information to supplement other sections of this handbook. This information is strictly of a reference nature and is thus more appropriately located in this section. The Uniform Sales Act, which was the first major step in providing interstate uniformity in marketing and purchasing terms and conditions of sale, is still in effect in many states. This is printed here in full because of its importance to the purchasing function. The Uniform Commercial Code, which is being adopted by many states, is a further refinement of methods being used to obtain uniform laws governing buying and selling. Articles covering the use of this code and its adoption have been included in this section.

Included under "Supreme Court Decisions Affecting Purchasing" are the decisions handed down on two major cases involving purchasing, the "Automatic Canteen" case and the "Cement" case. The first deals with buyer responsibilities under the Robinson-Patman Act, and the second with the basing point system of pricing.

Source selection has many facets, not the least of which are the financial responsibility of the supplier and the quality of his product. The most common source of information for financial analysis is the Dun & Bradstreet report, and an explanation of this report is included here. A supplement to Section 8 on quality control is the "Procedure for Initiating and Concluding Trials or Tests of Materials or Equipment," also found in this section.

Education is the key to progress in any field, and thus United States colleges and universities offering courses on purchasing are listed. Also included in this last division are a curriculum of a typical comprehensive course in purchasing management, how to resolve disputes by arbitration, and certification programs in purchasing.

BASIC SOURCES OF INFORMATION

On Purchasing and General Directories

Bibliography of Purchasing Literature, Guide to Purchasing, compiled by Howard T. Lewis, National Association of Purchasing Agents, 11 Park Place, New York, N.Y. 10007, 1965

Provides a basic working list of selected references on all phases of industrial procurement. References consist of books and articles in magazines of national circulation.

Guide to American Directories, 6th ed., McGraw-Hill Book Co., 330 West 42nd St., New York, N.Y. 10036, 1965

A guide to the major business directories of the United States, covering all industrial, professional, and mercantile categories and including a section as well on selected foreign directories. This publication can be valuable in locating new sources of supply of products and services through the various directories listed.

Sources of Business Information, Edwin T. Coman, Jr., University of California Press, Berkeley, Calif. 94720, 1964

The most complete guide to business information, with descriptive annotations for the publications listed.

Business Information: How to Find and Use It, Marin C. Manley, Harper & Row, Publishers, Incorporated, 49 East 33rd Street, New York 10016, 1955

Information for Administrators, Paul Wasserman, Cornell University Press, Ithaca, N.Y. 14850, 1956

A guide to publications and services for management in business and government.

Encyclopedia of Associations, 2 vols., Gale Research Co., Detroit, Mich., 1964

Vol. I, "National Organizations of the United States"–Trade, business, and other organizations, and 17 other classifications, with a subject and an alphabetical and keyword index; Vol. II, "Geographic and Executive Index."

Industrial Marketing, "Market Data and Directory Number" (annual, mid-June), Advertising Publications, Inc., 200 E. Illinois Street, Chicago, Ill. 60611

A guide to industrial markets giving trends in the major fields of industry, basic statistics, names of trade associations and trade journals which serve them.

Foreign Commerce Handbook; Information and a Guide to Sources, Chamber of Commerce of the United States, 1615 H Street, N.W., Washington, D.C., 1960

Includes an annotated bibliography of selected books, pamphlets, reference works, and periodicals useful in gathering data on foreign commerce.

Monthly Catalog of U.S. Government Publications, Government Printing Office, Washington, D.C. 20025 (December issue complete)

On Current Business Statistics

NAPA Bulletin (weekly), National Association of Purchasing Agents, 11 Park Place, New York, N.Y. 10007

Contains monthly business survey summarizing nationwide purchasing agents' reports on general business, purchased materials, inventories, buying policies, employment, commodity price trends, and specific commodity price changes. Also contains monthly graphic presentations of trends in new orders, production, employment, inventories, and prices both on national and regional basis.

Survey of Current Business (monthly), Office of Business Economics, U.S. Department of Commerce, Superintendent of Documents, U.S. Government Printing Office, Washington, D.C. 20025

Indexes of the major fields of business activity are carried on for the current month and the preceding twelve. Each monthly issue analyzes the current business situation and forecasts trends. Usually there are other articles on some new developments affecting business. The biennial supplements consolidate all this information into one volume.

Survey of Current Business (weekly supplement), Office of Business Economics, U.S. Department of Commerce, Superintendent of Documents, U.S. Government Printing Office, Washington, D.C. 20025

On a weekly basis, some of the business indicators which appear in the monthly *Survey of Current Business* are kept current by this leaflet.

Federal Reserve Bulletin (monthly), U.S. Board of Governors of the Federal Reserve System, Constitution Avenue, N.W., Washington, D.C. 20551

The majority of statistics presented are related to finance, but indices of industrial production, employment and earnings, department store sales, and wholesale and consumer prices are of general interest. The industrial production index is one of the most widely used.

Conference Board Business Management Record (monthly), National Industrial Conference Board, 845 Third Avenue, New York, N.Y. 10022

The discussion and analysis of current statistics help interpret the tabulated data. "Selected Business Indicators" brings the information in *The Economic Almanac* (listed below) up to date each month.

Current Statistics (monthly), Standard & Poor's Corporation, 345 Hudson Street, New York, N.Y. 10014

Indices of activity in basic industries and production as a whole are furnished each month. Figures on stocks and prices of commodities are also included. This keeps the Basic Statistics section of *Trade and Securities Statistics* up to date. Latter is mentioned under the next heading.

On General Business Statistics

Statistical Abstract of the United States (annual), U.S. Bureau of the Census, Superintendent of Documents, U.S. Government Printing Office, Washington, D.C. 20025

All the important government statistical agencies are represented, and many of the commonly used private agencies' statistics are included. All sources are given and any changes in method of calculation are indicated at the foot of each table. The "Bibliography of Sources of Statistical Data" is an almost complete list of statistics-collecting agencies.

Economic Indicators (monthly), Council of Economic Advisers for the Joint Economic Committee, U.S. Congress, Superintendent of Documents, U.S. Government Printing Office, Washington, D.C. 20025

Printed by the Joint Committee on the Economic Report, this publication supplies the reader with a quick look at the current economic situation without his having to look through a large number of specialized publications. The material is presented in chart form and also in tables. Mostly figures are given for the preceding two years and frequently monthly averages are given back to 1939.

The Economic Almanac (annual), National Industrial Conference Board, 845 Third Avenue, New York, N.Y. 10022

This brings together a large body of statistics of interest to business and the general public. The "Glossary of Selected Terms" defines in a strictly business sense many of the terms ordinarily found in business reports.

Trade and Securities Statistics (annual, with monthly supplements), Standard & Poor's Corporation, 345 Hudson Street, New York, N.Y. 10014

This service brings together a tremendous mass of statistical information. Although the heaviest emphasis is on financial data, there is a large amount of statistical material on general business conditions, cost of living, and prices. The more important Canadian statistics are also included.

On Trade Periodicals

One source for finding the names of trade magazines is *Industrial Marketing, Media-Market Planning Guide Issue,* issued by Advertising Publications, Inc., 200 E. Illinois Street, Chicago, Ill. 60611. Another source is *Business Publication Rates and Data,* issued by Standard Rate and Data Service, Inc., 5201 Old Orchard Road, Skokie, Ill. 60076

For listing of other trade magazines and periodicals, see Section 26, "Library and Catalog File"; also other sections, particularly Section 9, "Pricing Considerations," and Section 15, "Buying Considerations: Representative Commodities."

On Financial Matters

Keeping up to date on financial conditions of major suppliers and especially prospective suppliers is a major responsibility of purchasing. The following includes reliable references to three types in that category.

NEWSPAPERS

The Journal of Commerce of New York (daily), 99 Wall Street, New York, N.Y. 10013

The New York Times (daily), The New York Times Company, 229 West 43d Street, New York, N.Y. 10036

The Wall Street Journal (daily), New York, Chicago, and West Coast editions, Dow Jones & Co., Inc. New York address: 30 Broad Street, New York, N.Y. 10004. Chicago address: 711 West Monroe Street, Chicago, Ill. 60666. Los Angeles address: 2999 West 6th Street, Los Angeles, Calif., 90014. San Francisco address: 1540 Market Street, San Francisco, Calif. 94119

PERIODICALS

The Financial Analysts' Journal (published five times a year), The National Federation of Financial Analysis Societies, 509 Madison Avenue, New York, N.Y. 10022

Bank and Quotation Record (monthly), William B. Dana Company, 25 Park Place, New York, N.Y. 10007

Barron's National Business and Financial Weekly, Barron's Publishing Company, 50 Broadway, New York, N.Y. 10004

The Bond Buyer (daily and weekly), The Bond Buyer, Inc., 67 Pearl Street, New York, N.Y. 10004

Commercial and Financial Chronicle (semiweekly), William B. Dana Company, 25 Park Place, New York, N.Y. 10007

Financial World (weekly), Guenther Publishing Corporation, 17 Battery Place, New York, N.Y. 10004

Funk and Scott Index of Corporations and Industries, 10550 Park Lane, University Circle, Cleveland, Ohio 44106

SERVICES

The following security services attempt to give as complete a picture on all phases of investment as possible. Some of the publications of these companies are shown below.

Dun & Bradstreet, Inc., 99 Church Street, New York, N.Y. 10007

Million Dollar Directory (annual, with supplements). Lists 23,000 U.S. companies with an indicated worth of $1 million or over, giving officers, products (if manufacturer), standard industrial classification, approximate sales, and number of employees.

Fitch Investors Service, 129 Front St., New York, N.Y.

Fitch Bond Book. An annual publication containing statistical descriptions and ratings of government, railroad, public utility, industrial, and real estate mortgage bonds.

Fitch Statistical Service. A daily service on stocks, bonds, and trade, consisting of *Fitch Corporation Manuals, Fitch Bond Record,* and *Fitch Stock Record.*

International Statistical Bureau, Inc., 350 Fifth Avenue, New York, N.Y. 10001

Business and Investment Service. A weekly publication containing data on and analysis of current and indicated general business tendencies as reflected by production, distribution, cost of money, prices, and individual industries. Also included is *Washington Interpreter,* which analyzes the effects on general business of important economic, political, and social tendencies.

Selected Securities Guide. A weekly outlook for security markets including special recommendations and *Common Stock Selector,* basic data for individual companies and earnings projections, the *Market Timer,* giving specific buying and selling signals, as well as recording the sentiment of the market. Buying and selling signals are specific and definite. Quarterly supervised list of bonds and preferred stocks indicating prices, yields, and price ranges of the most desirable bonds and preferred stocks broken down by major classifications.

Trend of Distribution. A monthly service containing basic information on the consumer's position, as well as retailing. Analyses and forecasts of consumer buying are provided.

Moody's Investors Service, 99 Church Street, New York, N.Y. 10007

Moody's Dividend Record. A semiweekly cumulative record of dividends and dates of payments and corporate meetings.

Moody's Bond Record. A pocket guide to bond information.

Moody's Manual of Investments, American and Foreign. Annual volumes containing full information about the issuers of the following kinds of securities: governments and municipals, banks, insurance, real estate, investment trusts, industrials, public utilities and railroads.

Standard & Poor's Corporation, 345 Hudson Street, New York, N.Y. 10014

Standard Corporation Records. Complete factual information on 6,000 major American and Canadian corporations and important developments affecting 5,000 smaller concerns. Six loose-leaf volumes, revised monthly, supply the bulk of the data on balance sheets, earnings, and market prices.

Standard & Poor's Trade and Securities Service. Three sections include: Weekly Outlook for Securities Markets, Monthly Earnings and Ratings Stock Guide, and a Statistical Section.

Standard & Poor's Bond Guide. Pocket-size booklet with information all on one line for each security.

On Regulation of Business

Business is subject to numerous Federal and state laws and regulations. Below is a list of services in the fields indicated by the titles. In each of these fields there are similar loose-leaf services published by Commerce Clearing House, Inc., 4025 West Peterson Street, Chicago, Ill. 60646. In the labor field there are also loose-leaf services published by the Bureau of National Affairs, Inc., 1231 24th Street, N.W., Washington, D.C. 20037

Martindale-Hubbell Law Directory (annual, 3 volumes), Martindale-Hubbell, Inc., 1 Prospect Street, Summit, N.J. 07901

Law digest directory for excellent quick-reference source for information on state laws covering a large range of business subjects. Volume 1 contains a list of lawyers and their addresses in the United States, Canada, and Newfoundland. Volumes 2 and 3 contain digests of laws in the various states and other legal information.

Prentice-Hall Trade Regulation Edition of the Labor Guide (1 volume, with biweekly supplements), Prentice-Hall, Inc., Englewood Cliffs, N.J. 07631

For concise information on the regulation of unfair competition, price discrimination, and other practices prohibited by law, this service is particularly helpful. It explains the Federal Trade Commission Act, the Robinson-Patman Act, and the various state fair trade laws.

Prentice-Hall Installment and Conditional Sales Service (1 volume, with biweekly supplements), Prentice-Hall, Inc., Englewood Cliffs, N.J. 07631

In clear, simple business English, this service describes the nature of installment sales, the procedure in financing them, the laws, regulations, and rules that govern them in each of the states of the United States as well as Canada.

Prentice-Hall Labor Service (3 volumes, with weekly supplements), Prentice-Hall, Inc., Englewood Cliffs, N.J. 07631

All Federal and state labor laws are treated fully in this comprehensive loose-leaf service. The full text of each Federal labor law and digests of the state labor laws are provided. The latest decisions, rulings, and opinions by government agencies and officials are reported with editorial explanations and examples. Volume 1 deals with the Federal Wage and Hour Act and related laws, Volume 2 covers the National Labor Relations Act and laws related to it, and Volume 3 covers the state labor laws. Another volume, American Labor Cases, gives the full text of labor court decisions.

Trade Regulation Reporter, vol. I–V, Commerce Clearing House, Inc., 420 Lexington Avenue, New York, N.Y. 10017

Contains current information with respect to governmental trade regulations, rulings, court decisions, and State and Federal laws regulating trade.

Armed Services Procurement Regulation, U.S. Government Printing Office, Washington, D.C. 20025

Contains specific instructions for the conduct of business with the Armed Services of the United States, outlining methods of procurement, accounting principles, contract clauses, government property, etc. A very comprehensive publication stemming from the Armed Services Procurement Act of 1947.

On Other Reference Books

FOR LOCATING NAMES AND ADDRESSES OF MANUFACTURERS

Composite Catalog of Oil Field and Pipeline Equipment, Gulf Publishing Company, 3301 Buffalo Drive, P.O. Box 2608, Houston, Tex. 77001

This catalog service is designed specifically for those who select, specify, requisition, and purchase equipment, service, and supplies for the oil and gas exploration, drilling, producing, and pipeline industry. It is an up-to-date file of catalog data of most leading equipment and service concerns serving this world-wide industry.

Conover-Mast Purchasing Directory (semiannual), Industrial Directories, Inc., 205 East 42d Street, New York, N.Y. 10017. Divided equally into two semiannual editions. This contains a product classification section, a chemical section, a mechanical data section, a trade name section, and an address section.

Dun & Bradstreet Reference Book (semiannual), Dun & Bradstreet, Inc., 99 Church Street, New York, N.Y. 10007

Available only to subscribers. Supplies credit and capital ratings of large and small businesses, their addresses, and types of business.

Kelley's Directory of Merchants, Manufacturers and Shippers of the World—A Guide to the Export, Import, Shipping and Manufacturing Industries (annual, 2 volumes), Kelley's Directory, Ltd., 186 Strand, London W.C. 2, England

Volume 1 covers all countries except the British Empire. Volume 2 is devoted to the British Empire. The two volumes give the names and addresses of merchants and manufacturers in each city within a country.

MacRae's Blue Book (annual), MacRae's Blue Book Company, 18 East Huron Street, Chicago, Ill. 60611

The information in this directory is less detailed and complete than that in the *Thomas Register,* although the *Address and Local Distributors* is somewhat more complete for branch offices. It includes a classified materials section and lists trade names.

The Radio Electronic Master (annual), United Catalog Publishers, Inc., 645 Stewart Avenue, Garden City, N.Y. 11533

Electronic Engineers Master (annual), Tech Publishers, Inc., 645 Stewart Ave., Garden City, N.Y. 11533

Two separate publications containing extensive reference material on electronic components, materials, and manufacturers. The latter is organized into a numerically indexed catalog system which may also be used to set up a purchasing catalog file.

The Refinery Catalog, Gulf Publishing Company, 3301 Buffalo Drive, P.O. Box 2608, Houston, Tex. 77001

The function of *The Refinery Catalog* is to provide companies with quick and constant access to manufacturers' materials. There is condensed data on the products of more than 300 leading concerns. It is a composite catalog for the refining, natural gasoline, and petrochemical industry.

Sweet's File (annual), Sweet's Catalog Service Division, F. W. Dodge Company, a Division of McGraw-Hill, Inc., 330 West 42d Street, New York, N.Y. 10036

A compilation of manufacturers' catalogs for specific industries, which lists firms, products, and trade names.

Thomas Register of American Manufacturers (annual), Thomas Publishing Company, Inc., 461 Eighth Avenue, New York, N.Y. 10001

This shows who manufactures what. More than 70,000 products are listed, with names of the manufacturers under each product, arranged by state and city. The compilation of trade names and trademarks is excellent for locating the manufacturers of widely advertised products.

Thomas Micro Catalogs, Thomas Publishing Company, Inc., 461 Eighth Avenue, New York, N.Y. 10001

A microfilm file of catalog pages from subscribing advertisers. Limited at present.

Vendor Specs Microfilm File (VSMF), Rogers Publishing Co., Denver, Colo. 80204

A microfilm file of catalog pages and specifications from subscribing advertisers.

On Trade and Professional Associations

Below is a representative but certainly not complete list of trade associations and professional groups that publish their own standards on commodities. The "Encyclopedia of Associations," issued by Gale Research Company, Book Tower, Detroit, Mich. 48226, contains a comprehensive list of trade associations. The names of officers, size of membership, objectives, scope of activities, and publications issued are indicated. Purchasing agents subscribe to one or more of these publications in order to keep abreast of developments that will aid in the pursuit of value and in the maintenance of a competitive position in their own field.

Abrasive Grain Assn., Keith Building, Cleveland, Ohio 44115

Acoustical Materials Assn., 335 East 45th Street, New York, N.Y. 10017

Aeronautical Materials Division (see Society of Automotive Engineers), 485 Lexington Avenue, New York, N.Y. 10017

Aerospace Industries Assn., Value Engineering Committee, Shoreham Building, N.W., Washington, D.C. 20005

Air Conditioning and Refrigeration Institute, 1346 Connecticut Avenue, N.W., Washington, D.C. 20006

Air Moving and Conditioning Assn., 2159 Guardian Building, Detroit, Mich. 48226

American Assn. of Hospital Purchasing Agents, 420 East 34th Street, New York, N.Y. 10016

American Assn. of State Highway Officials, National Press Building, Washington, D.C. 20004

American Assn. of Textile Chemists and Colorists, Box 28, Lowell, Mass. 01850

American Bankers Assn., 90 Park Avenue, New York, N.Y. 10016

American Boiler Manufacturers Assn., 1180 Raymond Boulevard, Newark, N.J. 07102

American Bureau of Shipping, 45 Broad Street, New York, N.Y. 10004

American Concrete Institute, P.O. Box 4754, Redford Station, Detroit, Mich. 48219

American Electroplaters Society, 445 Broad Street, Newark, N.J. 07102

American Foundrymen's Society, Golf and Wolf Roads, Des Plaines, Ill. 60016

American Gas Assn., 605 Third Avenue, New York, N.Y. 10017

American Gear Manufacturers Assn., 1 Thomas Circle, N.W., Washington, D.C. 20005

American Institute of Architects, 1735 New York Avenue, N.W., Washington, D.C. 20006

American Institute of Chemical Engineers, 345 East 47th Street, New York, N.Y. 10017

American Institute of Steel Construction, 101 Park Avenue, New York, N.Y. 10017

American Iron & Steel Institute, 150 East 42d Street, New York, N.Y. 10017

American Ladder Institute, 666 Lake Shore Drive, Chicago, Ill. 60611

American Oil Chemists Society, 35 East Wacker Drive, Chicago, Ill. 60606

American Ordinance Assn., Value Engineering Committee, Mills Building, Washington, D.C. 20006

American Petroleum Institute, 1271 Avenue of the Americas, New York, N.Y. 10020

American Railway Car Institute, 11 East 44th Street, New York, N.Y. 10017

American Railway Engineering Assn., 59 East Van Buren Street, Chicago, Ill. 60605

American Society of Agricultural Engineers, 420 Main Street, St. Joseph, Mich. 49085

American Society of Civil Engineers, 345 East 47th Street, New York, N.Y. 10017

American Society of Heating, Refrigerating and Air-Conditioning Engineers, Inc., 345 East 47th Street, New York, N.Y. 10017

American Society of Lubrication Engineers, 5 North Wabash Avenue, Chicago, Ill. 60602

American Society of Mechanical Engineers, 345 East 47th Street, New York, N.Y. 10017

American Society for Testing and Materials, 1916 Race Street, Philadelphia, Pa. 19103

American Society of Tool and Manufacturing Engineers, 10700 Puritan Avenue, Detroit, Mich. 48238

American Standards Assn., 10 East 40th Street, New York, N.Y. 10016

American Transit Assn., 355 Lexington Avenue, New York, N.Y. 10017

American Trucking Assn., 1616 P Street, N.W., Washington, D.C. 20006

American Veneer Package Assn., 1225½ North Orange Avenue, Orlando, Fla. 32804

American Water Works Assn., 2 Park Avenue, New York, N.Y. 10016

American Welding Society, 345 East 47th Street, New York, N.Y. 10018

Anthracite Institute, 237 Old River Road, Wilkes-Barre, Pa. 18702

Anti-Friction Bearing Manufacturers Assn., 60 East 42d Street, New York, N.Y. 10017

Asphalt Institute, Asphalt Institute Building, University of Maryland, College Park, Md. 20740

Associated Factory Mutual Fire Insurance Companies, 355 Lexington Avenue, New York, N.Y. 10017

Association of American Railroads, Transportation Building, N.W., Washington, D.C. 20006

Association of Casualty and Surety Companies, Accident Prevention Bureau, 110 William St., New York, N.Y. 10038

Association of Edison Illuminating Companies, 51 East 42d Street, New York, N.Y. 10017

Association of Iron and Steel Engineers, Empire Building, Pittsburgh, Pa. 15222

Association of Roller and Silent Chain Manufacturers, 3343 Central Avenue, Indianapolis, Ind. 46205

Automobile Manufacturers Assn., New Center Building, Detroit, Mich. 48202

Cast Iron Pipe Research Assn., Prudential Plaza, Chicago, Ill. 60601

Clay Sewer Pipe Assn., 5 East Long Street, Columbus, Ohio 43215

Compressed Gass Assn., 500 Fifth Avenue, New York, N.Y. 10036

Concrete Reinforcing Steel Institute, 38 South Dearborn Street, Chicago, Ill. 60603

Copper and Brass Research Assn., 420 Lexington Avenue, New York, N.Y. 10017

Diesel Engine Manufacturers Assn., 2000 K Street, Washington, D.C. 20006

Edison Electric Institute, 750 Third Avenue, New York, N.Y. 10017

Electronics Industries Assn., Value Engineering Committee, 1721 DeSales Street, N.W., Washington, D.C. 20006

Fine Hardwoods Assn., 666 North Lake Shore Drive, Chicago, Ill. 60611

Fine and Specialty Wire Manufacturers Assn., 839 17th Street, N.W., Washington, D.C. 20006

Gas Appliance Manufacturers Assn., Inc., 60 East 42d Street, New York, N.Y. 10017

Government Contract Management Assn. of America, 425 Park Avenue, New York, N.Y. 10022

Gray Iron Founders Society, National City East 6th Building, Cleveland, Ohio 44114

Grinding Wheel Institute, Keith Building, Cleveland, Ohio 44115

Gypsum Assn., 201 North Wells Street, Chicago, Ill. 60606

Hack and Band Saw Assn. of America, 1718 Sherman Avenue, Evanston, Ill. 60201

Heat Exchange Institute, 122 East 42d Street, New York, N.Y. 10017

Helical Washer Institute, 2583 Union Lake Road, Union Lake, Mich. 48085

Home Manufacturers Assn., Barr Building, Washington, D.C. 20006

Hydraulic Institute, 122 East 42d Street, New York, N.Y. 10017

Illuminating Engineering Society, 345 East 47th Street, New York, N.Y. 10017

Industrial Fasteners Institute, Terminal Tower, Cleveland, Ohio 44113

Industrial Mineral Fiber Institute, 441 Lexington Avenue, New York, N.Y. 10017

Industrial Safety Equipment Assn., Inc., 630 Third Avenue, New York, N.Y. 10017

Institute of Boiler and Radiator Manufacturers, 393 Seventh Avenue, New York, N.Y. 10020

Institute of Appliance Manufacturers, Shoreham Hotel, Washington, D.C. 20008

Institute of Makers of Explosives, 420 Lexington Avenue, New York, N.Y. 10017

Institute of Electrical and Electronic Engineers, 345 East 47th Street, New York, N.Y. 10017

Instrument Society of America, 313 Sixth Avenue, Pittsburgh, Pa. 15222

Insulated Power Cable Engineers Assn., 283 Valley Road, Montclair, N.J. 07042

Insulation Board Institute, 111 West Washington Street, Chicago, Ill. 60602

Internal Combustion Engine Institute, 201 North Wells Street, Chicago, Ill. 60606

International Acetylene Assn., 270 Park Avenue, New York, N.Y. 10017

Lead Industries Assn., 292 Madison Avenue, New York, N.Y. 10017

Malleable Founders' Society, Union Commerce Building, Cleveland, Ohio 44114

Manufacturers Standardization Society of the Valve and Fittings Industry, 420 Lexington Avenue, New York, N.Y. 10017

Manufacturing Chemists Assn., 1825 Connecticut Avenue, N.W., Washington, D.C. 20009

Mechanical Contractors Association of America, 666 Third Avenue, New York, N.Y. 10020

Mechanical Power Transmission Assn., 3525 West Peterson Street, Chicago, Ill. 60603

Metal Lath Manufacturers Assn., Engineers Building, Cleveland, Ohio 44114

Metal Powder Industries Federation, 60 East 42d Street, New York, N.Y. 10017

National Assn. of Chain Manufacturers, 111 West Washington Street, Chicago, Ill. 60602

National Assn. of Educational Buyers, 1461 Franklin Avenue, Garden City, Long Island, N.Y. 11530

National Assn. of Mutual Casualty Companies, 20 North Wacker Drive, Chicago, Ill. 60606

National Assn. of Pipe Nipple Manufacturers, 501 Fifth Avenue, New York, N.Y. 10017

National Assn. of Purchasing Agents, 11 Park Place, New York, N.Y. 10007

National Assn. of Wiping Cloth Manufacturers, 173 West Madison Street, Chicago, Ill. 60602

National Board of Boiler and Pressure Vessel Inspectors, 1155 North High Street, Columbus, Ohio 43201

National Board of Fire Underwriters, 85 John Street, New York, N.Y. 10038

National Coal Assn., 1130 17th Street, N.W., Washington, D.C. 20006

National Electrical Manufacturers Assn., 155 East 44th Street, New York, N.Y. 10017

National Elevator Manufacturing Industry, 101 Park Avenue, New York, N.Y. 10017

National Foundry Assn., 4321 St. Charles Road, Bellwood, Ill. 60104

National Institute of Governmental Purchasing, 1001 Connecticut Avenue, N.W., Washington, D.C. 20006

National Lime Assn., 925 15th Street, N.W., Washington, D.C. 20005

National Lubricating Grease Institute, 4638 J. C. Nichols Parkway, Kansas City, Mo. 64112

National Lumber Manufacturers Assn., 1319 18th Street, N.W., Washington, D.C. 20006

National Machine Tool Builders Assn., 2139 Wisconsin Avenue, N.W., Washington, D.C. 20007

National Office Management Assn., 1927 Old York Road, Willow Grove, Pa. 19090

National Oil Fuel Institute, 60 East 42d Street, New York, N.Y. 10017

National Paint, Varnish and Lacquer Assn., 1500 Rhode Island Avenue, N.W., Washington, D.C. 20005

National Petroleum Assn., Munsey Building, N.W., Washington, D.C. 20004

National Safety Council, 425 North Michigan Avenue, Chicago, Ill. 60611

National Screw Machine Products Assn., 2860 East 130th Street, Cleveland, Ohio 44120

National Security Industrial Assn., Value Engineering Committee, 1107 19th Street, N.W., Washington, D.C. 20006

National Slag Assn., Perpetual Building, N.W., Washington, D.C. 20004

National Tool and Die Manufacturers Assn., Public Square Building, Cleveland, Ohio 44113

National Warm Air Heating and Air Conditioning Assn., Engineers Building, Cleveland, Ohio 44114

National Wooden Box Assn., Barr Building, Washington, D.C. 20006

Natural Gasoline Assn. of America, Kennedy Building, Tulsa, Okla. 74103

Non-Ferrous Founders Society, 1604 Chicago Avenue, Evanston, Ill. 60201

Optical Society of America, 1155 16th Street, N.W., Washington, D.C. 20006

Packaging Machinery Manufacturers Institute, Inc., 60 East 42d Street, New York, N.Y. 10017

Paper Bag Institute, 41 East 42d Street, New York, N.Y. 10017

Pipe Fabrication Institute, 1 Gateway Center, Pittsburgh, Pa. 15222

Porcelain Enamel Institute, 1145 19th Street, N.W., Washington, D.C. 20006

Portland Cement Assn., 33 West Grand Avenue, Chicago, Ill. 60610

Producers Council, 2029 K Street, N.W., Washington, D.C. 20006

Rail Steel Bar Assn., 38 South Dearborn Street, Chicago, Ill. 60603

Railway and Industrial Spring Research Institute, 1581 East 48th Street, Brooklyn, N.Y. 11234

Railway Tie Assn., 1373 Grandview Avenue, Columbus, Ohio 43212

Railway Wheel Association, 445 North Sacramento Boulevard, Chicago, Ill. 60612

Resistance Welder Manufacturers Assn., 1900 Arch Street, Philadelphia, Pa. 19103

Rubber Manufacturers Assn., 444 Madison Avenue, New York, N.Y. 10022

Rubber Reclaimers Assn., 101 West 31st Street, New York, N.Y. 10001

Safe Manufacturers National Assn., 366 Madison Avenue, New York, N.Y. 10017

Scientific Apparatus Makers Assn., 20 North Wacker Drive, Chicago, Ill. 60606

Society of American Value Engineers, 40 Sylvan Road, Waltham, Mass. 02154

Society of Automotive Engineers, 485 Lexington Avenue, New York, N.Y. 10017

Society of the Plastics Industry, 250 Park Avenue, New York, N.Y. 10017

Society of Protection Engineers, National Fire Protection Assn. (Parent), 60 Batterymarch Street, Boston, Mass. 02110

Southern Pine Assn., National Bank of Commerce Building, New Orleans, La. 70112

Steel Boiler Institute, Land Title Building, Broad and Chestnut Streets, Philadelphia, Pa. 19110

Steel Founders Society of America, Terminal Tower, Cleveland, Ohio 44113

Steel Joist Institute, 1346 Connecticut Avenue, N.W., Washington, D.C. 20006

Steel Kitchen Cabinet Manufacturers Assn., Park Building, Cleveland, Ohio 44114

Stoker Manufacturers Assn., P.O. Box 669, Evanston, Ill. 60201

Structural Clay Products Institute, 1520 18th Street, N.W., Washington, D.C. 20006

Synthetic Organic Chemical Manufacturers Assn. of the United States, 261 Madison Avenue, New York, N.Y. 10017

Tag and Label Manufacturers Institute, 211 East 43rd Street, New York, N.Y. 10017

Tanners' Council of America, 411 Fifth Avenue, New York, N.Y. 10016

Technical Assn. of the Pulp and Paper Industry, 360 Lexington Avenue, New York, N.Y. 10017

Tile Manufacturers Assn., 50 East 42d Street, New York, N.Y. 10017

Tire and Rim Assn., 34 North Hawkins Ave., Akron, Ohio 10013

The Tool and Die Institute, 2435 North Laramie Avenue, Chicago, Ill. 60639

Tubular Exchanger Manufacturers Assn., 53 Park Place, New York, N.Y. 10007

Underwriters' Laboratories, Inc., 207 East Ohio Street, Chicago, Ill. 60611

United States Cap Screw Service Bureau, 53 Park Place, New York, N.Y. 10007

United States Machine Screw Service Bureau, 53 Park Place, New York, N.Y. 10007

United States Wood Screw Service Bureau, 53 Park Place, New York, N.Y. 10007

Value Engineering Committee, Aerospace Industries Assn., Shoreham Building, N.W., Washington, D.C. 20005

Value Engineering Committee, American Ordinance Assn., Mills Building, Washington, D.C. 20006

Value Engineering Committee, Electronics Industries Assn., 1721 DeSales Street, N.W., Washington, D.C. 20006

Value Engineering Committee, National Security Industrial Assn., 1107 19th Street, N.W., Washington, D.C. 20006

Wirebound Box Manufacturers Assn., 222 West Adams Street, Chicago, Ill. 60606

On Commodities

Listed below are names of organizations and publications (name printed in italics) that specialize in study and distribution of information and data on commodities in general. For more detailed commodity information, consult references listed in Section 15 as well as *Sources of Commodity Prices* compiled by Paul Wasserman, Special Libraries Association, New York, 1959.

Agricultural Marketing Service, U.S. Department of Agriculture, Independence Avenue, between 12th and 14th, S.W., Washington, D.C. 20250

The Aluminum Association, 420 Lexington Avenue, New York, N.Y. 10017

American Institute of Food Distribution, 420 Lexington Avenue, New York, N.Y. 10017

American Metal Market, published by American Metal Market Co., 525 West 42d Street, New York, N.Y. 10036

American Paper and Pulp Association, 122 East 42d Street, New York, N.Y. 10017

American Supply and Machinery Manufacturers Association, Keith Building, Cleveland, Ohio 44115

Automotive Service Digest (A Division of National Market Reports, Inc.), 900 South Wabash Avenue, Chicago, Ill. 60605

Babson's Washington Forecast, Babson's Reports, Inc., 370 Washington Street, Wellesley, Mass. 02181

Chemical and Engineering News, American Chemical Society, 1155 16th Street, N.W., Washington, D.C. 20006

Chemical Week, McGraw-Hill Publications, 330 West 42d Street, New York, N.Y. 10036

The Commercial Analysts Co., 579 Fifth Avenue, New York, N.Y. 10017

The Commercial Bulletin, Commercial Bulletin Publishing Co., 177 Milk Street, Boston, Mass. 02109

Dominion Bureau of Statistics, Department of Trade and Commerce, Ottawa, Canada

Economic Notes, Labor Research Association, 80 East 11th Street, New York, N.Y. 10003

The Economist, 22 Ryder Street, St. James, London, S.W. 1, England

Electric Light and Power, Illinois Haywood Publishing Co., 6 North Michigan Avenue, Chicago, Ill. 60602

Iron Age, Chilton Company, Chestnut and 56th Streets, Philadelphia, Pa. 19139

Journal of Commerce, Eric Ridder, Publisher, 99 Wall Street, New York, N.Y. 10013

LaSalle Extension University, *Business Bulletins,* 417 South Dearborn Street, Chicago, Ill. 60603

Materials in Design Engineering, Reinhold Publishing Corporation, 430 Park Avenue, New York, N.Y. 10022

Nation's Business (Washington Letter), Chamber of Commerce of the United States, 1615 H. Street, N.W., Washington, D.C. 20006

National Association of Manufacturers News, 277 Park Avenue, New York, N.Y. 10017

National Association of Purchasing Agents, 11 Park Place, New York, N.Y. 10007

National Better Business Bureau, Inc., 230 Park Avenue, New York, N.Y. 10017

National Coal Association, 1130 17th Avenue, N.W., Washington, D.C. 20005

National Industrial Conference Board, 845 Third Avenue, New York, N.Y. 10022

National Industrial Relations Reporter, Industrial Relations Institute, 82 Beaver Street, New York, N.Y. 10005

Oil, Paint and Drug Reporter, Schnell Publishing Co., Inc., 100 Church Street, New York, N.Y. 10007

Petroleum Facts and Figures, American Petroleum Institute, 1271 Avenue of the Americas, New York, N.Y. 10020

Steel, Penton Publishing Company, Penton Building, Cleveland, Ohio 44113

United Business Service Co., 210 Newbury Street, Boston, Mass. 02116

U.S. Agriculture Marketing Service, published by U.S. Government Printing Office, Washington, D.C. 20025

U.S. Department of Labor, Bureau of Labor Statistics, Constitution Avenue and 14th Street, N.W., Washington, D.C. 20250

"Commodity Statistics," *The 1942 Commodity Year Book,* Commodity Research Bureau, 82 Beaver Street, New York, N.Y. 10005

Production, stock, price, and consumption figures are supplied on some 60 commodities. Data include prices, production, and consumption of these commodities in both the raw and semifinished state. Figures are carried back for varying periods of years, some as far back as 80 years. This work is helpful for locating trends and markets of previous years.

Commodity Year Book (annual), Commodity Research Bureau, 82 Beaver Street, New York, N.Y. 10005

This work describes the commodities of commerce. Points covered are physical characteristics, methods of production and areas of origin, principal uses, marketing and transportation methods, comparative recent prices, and principal types and grades. Any person desirous of obtaining brief information on commodities will find it a useful reference book.

On Government Technical Reports

Clearinghouse, U.S. Commerce Department, Springfield, Va. 22151

The Clearinghouse has been established to provide a central source from which Federal Scientific and Technical Information can be obtained and disseminated. Copies of all *unclassified* and *unlimited* Government Technical Reports will be furnished by the Clearinghouse for a small fee. Information on State-of-the-Art in Government research as well as the names of people working in the various fields of research will be supplied upon request. A literature search of the Clearinghouse on a given subject will be made for a few dollars providing bibliographies, report titles, abstracts, etc.

INFORMATION ON PURCHASING ASSOCIATIONS

Purchasing Associations of the World

United States

GENERAL

National Association of Purchasing Agents, 11 Park Place, New York, N.Y. 10007

Affiliates of NAPA

The Purchasing Agents' Association of:

Akron, Cuyahoga Falls, Ohio 44221
Alabama, Birmingham, Ala. 35202
Arizona, Phoenix, Ariz. 85001
Arkansas, Little Rock, Ark. 72206
Baltimore, Baltimore, Md. 21203
Buffalo, Buffalo, N.Y. 14216
Canada, Toronto 1, Ontario, Canada
Canton, Canton, Ohio 44701
Carolinas-Virginia, Asheville, N.C. 28800
Central Illinois, Decatur, Ill. 62521
Central Iowa, Des Moines, Iowa 50302
Central Michigan, Jackson, Mich. 49202
Central Pennsylvania, Lancaster, Pa. 17600
Chattanooga, Chattanooga, Tenn. 37402
Chicago, Chicago, Ill. 60602
Cincinnati, Cincinnati, Ohio 45216
Cleveland, Cleveland, Ohio 44113
Columbus Area, Columbus, Ohio 43221
Connecticut, Ansonia, Conn. 06401
Dallas, Dallas, Tex. 75204
Dayton, Dayton, Ohio 45407
Denver, Denver, Colo. 80216
Detroit, Detroit, Mich. 48202
East Tennessee, Knoxville, Tenn. 37918
East Texas, Longview, Tex. 75603
Eastern Indiana, Muncie, Ind. 47302
Eastern New York, Castleton-on-Hudson, N.Y. 12033
Elmira, Elmira, N.Y. 14901
El Paso, El Paso, Tex. 79902
Erie, Erie, Pa. 16500
Evansville, Evansville, Ind. 47711
Florida, Winter Park, Fla. 32789
Fort Wayne, Fort Wayne, Ind. 46803
Fort Worth, Fort Worth, Tex. 76101
Georgia, Hapeville, Ga. 30054
Grand Rapids, Grand Rapids, Mich. 49502
Greater Lafayette, Crawfordsville, Ind. 47933
Greater Omaha, Omaha, Neb. 68102
Hawaii, Honolulu, Hawaii 96813
Houston, Houston, Tex. 77004
Illiamo, Keokuk, Iowa 52632
Indianapolis, Indianapolis, Ind. 46207
Kalamazoo Valley, Kalamazoo, Mich. 49003
Kansas City, Kansas City, Mo. 64141
Lehigh Valley, Columbia, N.J. 07832
Lima Area, Bluffton, Ohio 45817
Los Angeles, Los Angeles, Calif. 90014
Louisville, Louisville, Ky. 40202
Memphis, Memphis, Tenn. 38105
Milwaukee, Milwaukee, Wis. 53201
Mississippi, Jackson, Miss. 39200
Mobile, Mobile, Ala. 36600
Nashville, Nashville, Tenn. 37201
New Castle, Sharon, Pa. 16146
New England, Boston, Mass. 02110
New Mexico, Albuquerque, N. Mex. 87103
New Orleans, New Orleans, La. 70112
New York, New York, N.Y. 10005
North Alabama, Decatur, Ala. 35602
North Central Ohio, Shelby, Ohio 44875
North Jersey, New Brunswick, N.J. 08903
Northern Pennsylvania, Wilkes-Barre, Pa. 18701
Northern California, San Francisco, Calif. 94105
Northwestern Pennsylvania, Port Allegany, Pa. 16743
Oklahoma City, Oklahoma City, Okla. 73101
Old Dominion, Roanoke, Va. 23200
Orange County, Fullerton, Calif. 92631
Oregon, Portland, Ore. 97204
Ozarks, Springfield, Mo. 65802
Philadelphia, Philadelphia, Pa. 19102
Pittsburgh, Pittsburgh, Pa. 15203
Reading, Reading, Pa. 19603
Rhode Island, Providence, R.I. 02903

Rochester, Rochester, N.Y. 14603
Rock River Valley, Rockford, Ill. 61103
Sabine-Neches, Beaumont, Tex. 77704
Saginaw Valley, Saginaw, Mich. 48601
St. Louis, St. Louis, Mo. 63136
San Antonio, San Antonio, Tex. 78202
San Diego, San Diego, Calif. 92112
Shreveport, Shreveport, La. 71100
South Bend, Elkhart, Ind. 46514
Spokane, Spokane, Wash. 99207
Springfield, Springfield, Ohio 45500
Syracuse, Syracuse, N.Y. 13203
Tenneva, Kingsport, Tenn. 37662
Texas Panhandle, Amarillo, Tex. 79105
Toledo, Toledo, Ohio 43609
Tri-City, Davenport, Iowa, 52801
Tri-State, Charleston, W.Va. 25326
Tulsa, Tulsa, Okla. 74103
Twin City, St. Paul, Minn. 55101
Twin Ports, Duluth, Minn. 55802
Utah, Provo, Utah 84601
Washington, Seattle, Wash. 98134
Washington, D.C., Simpsonville, Md. 21150
Western Michigan, Muskegon Heights, Mich. 49440
Western New England, Springfield, Mass. 01101
Wichita, Wichita, Kans. 67215
Wilmington, Wilmington, Del. 19899
Youngstown District, Youngstown, Ohio 44512

Above addresses subject to annual change with election of officers. For current and complete address, contact NAPA at address given on the previous page.

GOVERNMENTAL

National Institute of Governmental Purchasing, 1001 Connecticut Avenue, N.W., Washington, D.C. 20006
National Association of State Purchasing Officials
California Association of Public Purchasing Officers
Federal Procurement Officers Association of Chicago
Federal Procurement Officers Association of Los Angeles
Federal Procurement Officers Association of Greater New York
Federal Procurement Officers Association of Northern California
Pacific Northwest Public Buyers Association

EDUCATIONAL AND INSTITUTIONAL

National Association of Educational Buyers
National Association of Hospital Purchasing Agents

Canada

GENERAL

Canadian Association of Purchasing Agents, 357 Bay Street, Toronto 1, Ontario, Canada

Member-Associations of CAPA

Brant-Norfolk District, Brantford, Ont.
British Columbia District, Vancouver, B.C.
Calgary District, Calgary, Alta.
Central Ontario District, Kitchener, Ont.
Eastern Ontario District, Kingston, Ont.
Eastern Townships District, Sherbrooke, Que.
Edmonton District, Edmonton, Alta.
Essex-Kent District, Windsor, Ont.

Georgian Bay District, Barrie, Ont.
Hamilton District, Hamilton, Ont.
Montreal District, Montreal, Que.
Niagara District, Niagara Falls, Ont.
Northwestern Ontario District, Fort William, Ont.
Nova Scotia District, Halifax, N.S.
Oakville District, Oakville, Ont.
Ottawa District, Ottawa, Ont.
Quebec District, Quebec, Que.
Sarnia District, Sarnia, Ont.
Toronto District, Toronto, Ont.
Western Ontario District, London, Ont.
Winnipeg District, Winnipeg, Man.

As the majority of the member-associations of the Canadian Association of Purchasing Agents do not have fixed postal addresses, they can best be contacted through the Canadian Association of Purchasing Agents, 357 Bay Street, Toronto 1, Ontario, Canada.

Foreign

AMERICA, SOUTH

Argentina

Association Argentina de Compradores, Defensa 320, Buenos Aires, Agentina

ASIA

India

National Association of Purchasing Executives, Cecil Court, Lansdowne Road, Bombay 1, India

Japan

Japan Materials Management Association, Terashima Building 2–1, Hon-cho, Nihonbashi Chuo-ku, Tokyo, Japan

AUSTRALIA

The Australian Purchasing Officers Association, Broughton House, 181 Clarence Street, Sydney, Australia

EUROPE

Belgium

L'Association Belge des Chefs d'Approvisionnement, 27 Rue de la Science, Brussels 4, Belgium

Denmark

Danske Indkobschefers Landsforening, Postbox 8, Gentofte, Denmark

Finland

Suomen Ostopäälliköiden Yhdistys r.y., Oy Rastor Ab, Satamakatu, 4, Helsinki, Finland

France

Compagnie des Chefs d'Approvisionnement et Acheteurs de France, 27, Rue Bleue, Paris 9e, France

Germany

Bundesverband, industrieller Einkauf e.V. (BIE), 25 Waidmannstrasse, Frankfurt/Main–Sud 6000, Germany

Netherlands

Nederlendse Vereniging voor Inkoop-Efficiency, Parkstraat 18, The Hague, Holland

Norway

Norsk Innkjøpslederforbund, Trondheimsvn 80, Oslo, Norway

Sweden

Swedish Purchasing Officers Association, Teatergatan, 3, 1 tr. Stockholm C, Sweden

Switzerland

Schweizerische Einkaufer-vereinigung, Postfach 545, Schaffhausen, Switzerland

United Kingdom

Purchasing Officers Association, York House, Westminster Bridge Road, London, S.E. 1, England

The Institute of Public Supplies, 24 Park Crescent, London, W. 1, England

International Federation of Purchasing

The International Federation of Purchasing was formed by delegates representing nine purchasing associations from eight nations who met in New York City on May 14 and 15, 1965. This organization succeeds the former International Committee of Purchasing, which was formed in London in April, 1964. The first officers of the Federation are: Chairman–P. Boney, U.S.A. (NAPA); President–H. Themoin, France (CCAAF); Vice-president and Treasurer–A. Colston, Great Britain (POA); Secretary-general–John Blinch, Great Britain.

Charter members of the Federation (subject to ratification by each association) are the national purchasing associations of Australia, Belgium, Canada, Finland, France, West Germany, Great Britain, The Netherlands, India, Japan, Norway, Sweden, and Switzerland. The United States is represented by the National Association of Purchasing Agents and the National Institute of Governmental Purchasing.

The objectives of the Federation are:

1. To further the principles and practices of purchasing and the other functions of supply management, considered as a basic and distinct function of the management structure of trade, industry, and public undertakings.
2. To ensure the highest standard of the business ethics of those engaged throughout the world in the professions of purchasing and the other functions of supply management.
3. To provide an international body to represent purchasing and its allied functions in supply management in world affairs.
4. To promote throughout the world the international consideration of and to further possible solutions to problems affecting purchasing and the other functions of supply management.
5. To encourage and assist those engaged in purchasing and the other functions of supply management to develop their national associations and their national education schemes, bearing on the principles and practices of the profession. To assist in founding national associations in countries where such bodies do not as yet exist.
6. To provide the forum for furthering of the concept of the International Federation and to undertake by means of conferences, meetings, international committees, the publication and interchange of information, or by any other method considered suitable, any task or enterprise in order to achieve these objects.

The Federation has undertaken a series of studies on world-wide purchasing practices which will be coordinated by various individual delegates. The areas to be covered in these initial studies include: conditions and customs of sale and purchase; quality, reliability and standardization; transportation; customs regulations; codification of purchase and stores terminology, leading eventually to a multilingual dictionary; and purchasing education. It is planned that as these studies are completed, they will be released through the various individual associations' publications to the memberships. The Federation also plans to publish periodically international news of interest to the various memberships in the official publication of each association.

The creation of an international body through which purchasing associations throughout the world could exchange information and act cooperatively on matters of mutual interest has been a long-sought objective of many purchasing leaders in the United States and other countries. It is expected that the newly formed Federation will provide the medium through which purchasing executives can benefit from sharing ideas and experiences and can strengthen the influence of the purchasing function as a major contributor to the effective and efficient management of public and private enterprise in all nations.

PRINCIPLES OF PURCHASING PRACTICE ADVOCATED BY ASSOCIATIONS

Purchasing the world over has benefited materially by the activities of associations of purchasing men and women in industry, government, institutions, etc. Their keen interest in education, ethics, and other areas of development that enhance the stature of purchasing has created certain sound basic aims, objectives, principles, standards, and codes of ethics of purchasing practice. The growth, position, and prestige of purchasing is attributed by many to these goals set forth at the start of the professional associations. Goals are listed below for some of the better known associations.

The areas of interest and the activities of the National Association of Purchasing Agents are extremely broad. In addition to its "Standards of Conduct," information has been included here covering its "Policy of Operation," "Board of Basic Policy," and its "Professional Development Program."

NAPA Standards of Conduct[1]

Officially adopted by the NAPA Executive Committee, June 11, 1959

Principles and Standards of Purchasing Practice

Loyalty To His Company
Justice To Those With Whom He Deals
Faith In His Profession

From these principles are derived the N.A.P.A. standards of purchasing practice.

1. To consider, first, the interests of his company in all transactions and to carry out and believe in its established policies.
2. To be receptive to competent counsel from his colleagues and to be guided by such counsel without impairing the dignity and responsibility of his office.
3. To buy without prejudice, seeking to obtain the maximum ultimate value for each dollar of expenditure.
4. To strive consistently for knowledge of the materials and processes of manufacture, and to establish practical methods for the conduct of his office.
5. To subscribe to and work for honesty and truth in buying and selling, and to denounce all forms and manifestations of commercial bribery.

[1] Reproduced by permission of NAPA.

6. To accord a prompt and courteous reception, so far as conditions will permit, to all who call on a legitimate business mission.
7. To respect his obligations and to require that obligations to him and to his concern be respected, consistent with good business practice.
8. To avoid sharp practice.
9. To counsel and assist fellow purchasing agents in the performance of their duties, whenever occasion permits.
10. To co-operate with all organizations and individuals engaged in activities designed to enhance the development and standing of purchasing.

Standards and Ethics of Buying and Selling

Unnecessary sales and purchasing expense is an economic waste—a tax on legitimate industry. Its elimination will assure satisfactory profits to the producer, economy to the consumer, and greater efficiency in commercial relations.

We recognize that the concern which buys must also sell, that buying and selling are companionate functions, that sound commercial transactions must be mutually profitable, and that cooperation between buyer and seller will reduce the cost to purchasing, sales, and distribution with consequent benefits to industry as a whole.

In furtherance of these principles, we subscribe to the following standards in our buying and selling:

1. To buy and sell on the basis of value, recognizing that value represents that combination of quality, service, and price which assures greatest ultimate economy to the user.
2. To respect our obligations and neither expressly nor impliedly to promise a performance which we cannot reasonably expect to fulfill.
3. To avoid misrepresentation and sharp practice in our purchases and sales, recognizing that permanent business relations can be maintained only on a structure of honesty and fair dealing.
4. To be courteous and considerate of those with whom we deal, to be prompt and businesslike in our appointments, and to carry on negotiations with all reasonable expedition so as to avoid trespassing on the rights of others to the time of buyers and salesmen.
5. To avoid statements tending to injure or discredit a legitimate competitor, and to divulge no information acquired in confidence with the intent of giving or receiving an unfair advantage in a competitive business transaction.
6. To strive for simplification and standardization within the bounds of utility and industrial economy, and to further the development of products and methods which will improve industrial efficiency.
7. To recognize that character is the greatest asset in commerce, and to give it major consideration in the selection of customers and source of supply.
8. To adjust claims and settle disputes on the basis of facts and fairness, to submit the facts to arbitration if a mutual agreement cannot be reached, to abide by the decisions of the arbiters and to resort to legal measures in commercial disputes only when the preceding courses prove ineffective.

9. To provide or accept no gifts or entertainment in the guise of sales expense, where the intent or effect is to unduly prejudice the recipients in favor of the donor as against legitimate competitors.
10. To give or receive no bribes, in the form of money or otherwise, in any commercial transaction and to expose commercial bribery wherever encountered for the purpose of maintaining the highest standard of ethics in industry.

In this manual we are going to elaborate on a few principles which are mentioned rather briefly and which have come in for considerable discussion in Association meetings. We believe we should maintain our standards on an even higher plane than that generally accepted by society. This is the true test of greatness.

Gifts and Gratuities

This is a subject of increasing concern to all clear-thinking purchasing people. There is a lot of precedent involved and it is difficult to reconcile the philosophy of a Purchasing Department which does not desire to receive gifts with that of a Sales Department in the same company which makes it a regular practice to present gifts. However, a firm and understandable attitude on our part will go a long way to attain the position of dignity and repute for which we are striving. Time and concerted action will eventually bring about the desired results.

There is nothing that can undermine respect for the purchasing profession more than improper action on the part of its members with regard to gifts, gratuities, favors, etc. People engaged in purchasing should not accept from any supplier or prospective supplier any money, gift or favor which might influence, or be suspected of influencing their buying decisions. We must decline to accept or must return any such gift or favor offered us or *members of our immediate family*. The declination of these gifts or favors must be done discreetly and courteously. Possible embarrassment resulting from refusals does not constitute a basis for an exception.

The term "Gifts, Gratuities and Favors" includes, but is not limited to, monies, credits, discounts, seasonal or special occasion presents (Christmas, birthday, weddings, etc.), edibles, drinks, household appliances and furnishings, clothing, loans of goods or money, tickets to sporting events, theaters, etc., dinners, parties, transportation, vacations, travel or hotel expenses and various forms of entertainment. In any case, where the return of a gift is impracticable because of its perishability, disposition may be made to a charitable institution, and the donor informed of the disposition.

Personal business transactions with suppliers or prospective suppliers should be scrupulously avoided. Personal loans must not be accepted from such companies on any basis. Offers of hospitality, business courtesies, or favors, no matter how innocent in appearance, can be a source of embarrassment to all parties concerned.

We should not allow ourselves to become involved in situations where unnecessary embarrassment may result from an offer or refusal of a hospitality or a business courtesy from our suppliers or potential suppliers. It is generally the best policy to decline *any* sort of favor, hospitality or entertainment, to insure that all relationships are above reproach at all times. Situations requiring common sense and good judgment will develop, such as a company-provided luncheon during the course of a visit to a supplier's plant located in some remote area. Another example is the case of a buyer or a purchasing expeditor-inspector accepting free company-provided automobile transportation on a temporary or emergency basis where other means are not available.

A purchasing man may ethically attend periodic meetings or dinners of trade associations, professional and technical societies or other industrial organizations as the guest of a supplier where the meetings are of an educational and informative nature and where it is considered to be in the best interest of buyer-seller relationships. The repeated appearance of an individual at such regularly scheduled meetings, as the guest of the same company, is the type of situation which should be tactfully avoided.

The simple casual luncheon or cocktail with a supplier's representative are merely normal expressions of a friendly business relationship or a time-saving expediency. It would be prudish to raise any serious question on this score. The purchasing man himself is in the best position to judge when this point has been exceeded. It is the time-saving expediency which makes up the great majority of such instances and, since the buyer's company prestige is also involved, there is every reason why an adequate expense account should be available to the buyer. It is a small price for maintaining a position free from any taint of obligation. Mature purchasing people know that they are quickly classified among the sales' fraternity by the amount of entertainment they expect or will accept. Salesmen usually speak with real respect of the buyer who pays his share of entertainment expenses. The purchasing expense account is the most effective answer to this ethical problem.

Outside Business Affiliations

Since we are engaged in the administration and expenditure of funds of the company we represent, our conduct must necessarily be subject to more restrictions and to higher standards not only on the job, but in our outside activities as well. We should not be involved in purchasing transactions with any companies in which we, our family or relatives, are owners or have a substantial financial interest. We should not engage in business and professional activities from which we might derive financial profit or other benefits resulting from our employment as a buyer.

Ethical Responsibility of Groups

If we will concede that it is important for purchasing people to conform to high ethical standards as individuals, then it will inexorably follow that it is more important that purchasing people in groups do so. The impact of group deviation from the highest of ethical standards will be infinitely greater than deviations of a single individual. And this is true if only for the fact that more people are involved. A single person can be guilty of unethical conduct and this does not necessarily reflect discredit upon the organization nor upon purchasing generally. But, when a group commits an error of this kind the charge can justifiably be made that someone in the group should have known better. And, the next step by someone who is so inclined would very likely be to generalize and say they're all alike.

It is quite possible for an individual who personally observes the highest degree of ethical conduct to accede to the majority opinion or remain silent when a questionable act is being considered by a group. The individual may hide behind the cloak of anonymity provided by the fact that action is being taken as a group. He may also feel that criticism which might be justly directed toward an individual act would be withheld in the case of a group. Lack of respect and vocal criticism do not necessarily go hand in hand. We can well have the former without the latter. And, if we are to engender that respect for our profession which we so earnestly desire then we must be extremely careful that group action is such that the highest order of respect is commanded—that our actions are above criticism.

In most organizations, there are developed over the years habits and patterns of action which tend to be taken for granted as being perfectly natural and in conformance with the aims and ideals of the group. Newcomers into the group and, particularly, newly appointed or elected officials of the group, tend to automatically continue these action patterns. Periodic scrutiny to determine conformance with current aims and ideals is minimized. Minor changes from year to year, although insignificant in themselves, can cumulatively distort the action pattern so that it no longer represents the ideals of the group.

It is necessary, therefore, to take stock periodically to see that programs are consistent with the high ideals for which we strive. Each element of the program should be subjected to a searching examination to determine whether it does or does not conform to the highest of standards. And, if it does not, it should be discontinued. It will probably be well to consider here some group actions which may be considered to be at least questionable. This is not to say that those practices discussed below are all-inclusive. Rather, it is the intent that they should be considered as examples.

There has grown up among groups of purchasing people and particularly local associations of the National Association of Purchasing Agents, the custom of holding periodic joint meetings with sales organizations, such as local affiliates of the National Sales Executives' organization. This can be an estimable practice and can be beneficial to both groups. Quite frequently, a "hospitality hour" becomes part of the program. And, more than likely, the entire meeting can be enhanced by a custom of this kind. However, consideration should be given to each organization acting as host on an alternate basis. In this way, there is no obligation incurred by anyone and no one is penalized.

The temptations are many and sometimes the pressure is great to let a salesman's organization or a supplier company provide the cocktail party, the prizes for the Christmas party or the golf outing or the annual picnic. There is frequently the implied if not the direct offer to provide more than the proper degree of hospitality during a plant visit. But those in authority on the purchasing side of the coin will think twice before departing from the strictest interpretation of the highest standards of conduct.

Purchasing organizations which publish magazines or other periodicals containing advertising must be especially conscious of the proprieti the temptation (admittedly with only the good of the organiza great to subject the advertiser or prospective advertiser to press

In this area of association activities it is well to conform to Practice" established by the Editors' Group of the National Asso chasing Agents, which are:

We, the publishers of magazines, published by, and/or for Associations affiliated with the National Association of Purchasing Agents, pledge ourselves to the following Standards of Practice:

1. To disseminate information relative to and to promote the welfare of industry in general and the purchasing profession in particular.
2. To promote a better understanding of the ethics and functions of purchasing.
3. To decline any advertisement that has a tendency to mislead or that does not conform to business integrity.
4. To establish and maintain suitable contacts with Association members.
5. To establish contacts with, and arouse interest of prospective members in our local Associations and the National Association of Purchasing Agents.
6. To maintain our editorial pages in accordance with the highest journalistic practice . . . to maintain balanced publications . . . to publish nothing that will reflect upon the good name of an individual, an association, a firm, or the purchasing profession.
7. To accept advertising solely upon the basis of value of the medium to the advertiser . . . to accept no advertising given as a favor to any purchaser or group of purchasers . . . to recognize a definite responsibility to the advertiser . . . to keep our reading columns independent of advertising consideration.

Actions of all purchasing people on ethical questions must not only be meticulous at all times and under all circumstances, but must also be constant and consistent. Relations of a compromising nature, or even the appearance of such relations must be scrupulously avoided.

NAPA Statement of Policies[2]

As a professional association, as distinguished from a trade group, or a commercial or management membership with widely diversified interests, NAPA policies limit the scope of its activities and services to those having a common and beneficial value to progressive purchasing personnel.

Those NAPA policies have their foundation in the objectives of the association which are specified in its Constitution. The association's activities and services that have a common interest and value must implement those objectives, and meet the needs of a membership which is also restricted by the NAPA Constitution, in its clear eligibility specifications.

In a professional organization, the leadership and contributions of members are the keystones of such developments. NAPA is, and has been, fortunate in that respect; and the continued development, use and recognition of activity leadership, and member cooperation, are major responsibilities of the Executive

[2] Reproduced by permission of NAPA.

Committee. Staff assistance is not a suitable substitute for the practical contributions the members should make to the program of a professional association.

The outstanding keynote of the association's activities is *purchasing education*—for both current and prospective members, and for other professional and business groups and segments of our business and industrial world.

NAPA's operations are highly decentralized into the local associations which enjoy wide ranges of latitude in their activities, within the limitations specified in the NAPA Constitution and By-Laws.

Democratic control and government of NAPA is largely "from the bottom up"—i.e., each individual member can make recommendations through his local association officers to his National Director, who in turn acts through his District Council and thence to the National Executive Committee. No dictatorial or autocratic control is permitted "from the top down."

The headquarters staff remains neutral on all questions of elections and "internal politics," of both local associations and the National Association.

Freedom of Speech for Consultants of NAPA

The association freely and impartially presents information from nationally recognized sources and consultants through its Bulletin and otherwise upon which members may base their determinations, but recognizes their individual rights which place a corresponding limitation on representations by a professional organization. Information on business and commodity trends and on purchasing policies and procedure is supplied, as well as forecasts from authoritative and representative sources. However, the association does not edit or censor statements prepared by its consultants, or others whose comments and opinions may be published from time to time in the Bulletin or other association material. The association considers them to be personal opinions, for which it takes no responsibility.

NAPA Board of Basic Policy[3]

Over the years the policy of the National Association of Purchasing Agents has been to take a neutral stand on political and controversial matters. In May 1960, however, it amended its by-laws by restating its policy of neutrality on these matters in so far as the officers and employees of NAPA were concerned, but it created a Board of Basic Policy for the sole purpose of reviewing ". . . any matters having to do with philosophies, theories, or legislation which are, or may be, in the opinion of the Said District Council, the Executive Committee, the said President, or the Executive Secretary-Treasurer, a threat to our free enterprise and capitalistic system and are of sufficient importance as to merit the attention and consideration of the said Board of Basic Policy. Said Board shall have the power to consider such matters on its own recognizance . . ."

This board is composed of nine of the "ablest and most experienced members of NAPA" and provides the association a means of dealing effectively with important controversial and political matters. The board recommends to the Executive Committee the actions and procedures, if any, which it feels should be followed. The Executive Committee then takes necessary action, at its discretion,

[3] Reproduced by permission of NAPA.

to present NAPA's position on the situation under consideration to the public or to the interested body.

NAPA Professional Development

Recognizing the increasingly competitive requirements of people in purchasing positions in the modern business world, the National Association of Purchasing Agents has developed a broad program of professional development activities.

All Association members are encouraged to recognize their personal needs for self-improvement in order that they can accept steadily increasing responsibilities. NAPA tries to identify these needs and to provide the tools for filling them.

The over-all program in NAPA is under the direction of a national Professional Development and Review Committee which reviews and coordinates all of the Association activities which are of a professional nature.

Five national committees carry on these activities.

1. *Professional Development Activities.* This committee is organized on a local, district, and national basis to promote the professional concept among all members and to make all association activities constructive and educational. Toward this end the local association committees conduct workshops, seminars, discussion groups, classes and regular meeting programs on current purchasing philosophy techniques and ethical considerations providing direct value for purchasing people.

2. *Development Projects.* This is the research area. At least ten study groups are at work at all times on purchasing problem areas (1) to determine whether there is need for literature or other training material and then (2) to develop training material to fill this need. Among the currently active study groups are those on the subjects of data processing, evaluating purchasing performance, internal controls, make or buy, negotiations, and reports to management.

Resulting from the work of these research committees through NAPA's history have come more than one hundred publications on specific purchasing problems. Examples of these publications are: *Purchasing as a Career, Evaluation of Supplier Performance, Leasing versus Buying, Inventory Management of Purchased Materials* and *Competent Buyers.*

3. *Literature Review.* To review all literature relating to purchasing is the job of the committee. Literature produced by the Association must have this committee's approval before publication. Outside publications are reviewed and reported to the membership. (With the encouragement of the Association an average of five books per year has been published in recent years.)

4. *Value Techniques.* To encourage the effective use of job-related purchasing techniques, a full national committee has been engaged in intensive promotion and training within the Association organization. Beginning with standardization and then value analysis, this committee has successively emphasized the use of current purchasing techniques such as those used in evaluating supplier performance and solving small order problems.

NAPA was one of the pioneers in promoting value analysis with its first publication on this subject "Cutting Costs by Analyzing Values," released in 1952. This committee has used publications, filmstrips, a motion picture, and cooperative university seminars in its work.

5. *Universities and Colleges.* In order to develop a long-range understanding of the purchasing function in business, NAPA has intensified its cooperative efforts with the universities. A group of prominent educators who are academic members of the Association have been organized as a national committee. In this capacity they advise the Association on constructive relations with the universities and administer specific programs toward this objective.

Three key programs are:

1. A doctoral research grant program which awards grants up to $5,000 to doctoral candidates doing their dissertation research in areas relating to purchasing. Since the beginning of this program in 1961, it has resulted in important contributions to basic purchasing research and has caused considerable interest in academic circles.
2. A faculty internship program makes it possible for educators to spend a summer in a purchasing department gaining first-hand experience in modern purchasing operations. This provides better informed purchasing instructors and advisors in the universities.
3. A management seminar for purchasing executives is being held annually. Purchasing executives who have achieved management responsibilities in their companies meet for a two-week intensive course in management techniques at the Harvard Graduate School of Business Administration.

Teaming with the Public Relations Committee of NAPA, the Professional Development Committee brings career information to high-school and college students all over the United States. A relationship with the Junior Achievement Program has also been established for this purpose. Lectures, brochures, leaflets, and motion pictures are used in this promotional program.

The objective of the career program is to establish throughout the educational system a better understanding of the purchasing function and its place in business operations.

All of these programs and many others sponsored by NAPA strive to provide adequate training and incentives at all levels for purchasing people of the present and the future.

NIGP Aims and Objectives

THE NATIONAL INSTITUTE OF GOVERNMENTAL PURCHASING, INC.[4]
1001 Connecticut Avenue, N.W.
Washington, D.C. 20036

Founded in 1944

A Non-Profit Educational and Technical Organization of Governmental Buying Agencies of the United States, Canada and Puerto Rico, Chartered as an Educational Corporation Under the Laws of the State of Wisconsin

Its Aims and Objectives

Organized

To study, discuss, and recommend improvements in governmental purchasing.

[4] Reproduced by permission of NIGP.

To interchange ideas and experiences and obtain expert advice on local, state and national governmental purchasing problems.

To collect and distribute to governmental purchasing officials information on the organization and administration of governmental buying.

To develop and promote simplified standards and specifications for governmental buying.

To promote effective purchasing structures and uniform purchasing laws and procedures.

To promote and foster the professional competence and stature of all persons engaged in governmental buying.

To set an academic and professional standard for all such persons and to award diplomas, certificates and distinctions to any such persons after examination or otherwise.

To achieve recognition of the place of public purchasing in the governmental structure with emphasis on cabinet or top-management status for the public purchasing official.

To work for or against proposals affecting the welfare of governmental buying agencies.

To give to taxpayers information on governmental buying problems in order to foster interest in public affairs and cooperation between governmental buyers and those they serve.

NAEB Code of Ethics

THE NATIONAL ASSOCIATION OF EDUCATIONAL BUYERS

Code of Ethics[5]

1. To give first consideration to the objectives and policies of my institution.
2. To strive to obtain the maximum ultimate value of each dollar of expenditure.
3. To co-operate with trade and industrial associations, governmental and private agencies engaged in the promotion and development of sound business methods.
4. To demand honesty in sales representation whether offered through the medium of a verbal or written statement, an advertisement, or a sample of the product.
5. To decline personal gifts or gratuities which might in any way influence the purchase of materials.
6. To grant all competitive bidders equal consideration, to regard each transaction on its own merits; to foster and promote fair, ethical and legal trade practices.
7. To use only by consent original ideas and designs devised by one vendor for competitive purchasing purposes.
8. To be willing to submit to arbitration on any major controversies.
9. To accord a prompt and courteous reception insofar as conditions permit to all who call on legitimate business missions.

[5] Reproduced by permission of NAEB.

10. To counsel and co-operate with NAEB members and to promote a spirit of unity among them.

PAANC Objectives[6]

Associations affiliated with the NAPA include similar objectives in their official Articles of Incorporation to accomplish the purposes for which they were formed. Below is a representative statement from the constitution and by-laws of the Purchasing Agents' Association of Northern California, Inc., which is one of about 100 associations affiliated with the NAPA.

The primary purposes of this Association are:

a. To foster and promote interchange of ideas and cooperation among its members.
b. To promote the study, development and application of improved purchasing methods and practices.
c. To collect and disseminate information of interest and benefit to its members, including current production and market data, information on business trends, manufacturing methods and practices, products and their uses, sources of supply, and channels of distribution.
d. To correct trade abuses and encourage maintenance of ethical standards in buying and selling.
e. To encourage and cooperate in the institution and development of courses in the subject of purchasing in colleges and universities.
f. To strive by all legitimate means to advance the purchasing profession.

JMMA Object and Activities

Object—The object of the Japan Materials Management Association is mutual study, education and friendship as well as contribution to accelerating modernization of materials and purchasing management. Members of the Association are business managers, materials, purchasing, storehouse and conveyance managers and the personnel in charge of above function.

Activities—In order to attain the object we perform the following:

1. Research conference, lecture meeting course, field study tour, annual study convention and social gathering for materials and purchasing and storehouse management.
2. Specific guidance for implementing materials, purchasing and storehouse management.
3. Education and upbringing of materials, purchasing and storehouse managers.
4. Dissemination of managerial concept of materials, purchasing and storehouse management.
5. Collection and distribution of organ, pamphlets and other books and leaflets.
6. Compilation and distribution of organ, pamphlets and other leaflets.
7. Acceptance of requests for researches and investigations.
8. Proper liaison and tie-up with relevant domestic and foreign organizations.
9. Other activities necessary to attain our object.

[6] Reproduced by permission of PAANC.

EXAMPLE—APPLICATION OF PRINCIPLES AND STANDARDS

Reflection of such principles, practices, aims, and objectives will be found in the many hundreds, if not thousands, of organization procedures issued by purchasing departments throughout the United States, Canada, and other countries. Figure 6–1 gives the statement for the Xerox Corporation of Rochester, N.Y.

Following is the one in the informational booklet prepared by the purchasing department of The Detroit Edison Company of Detroit, Michigan, to assist in the orientation of its employees and such other employees of the company as would benefit by such information.

THE DETROIT EDISON COMPANY

PURCHASING POLICIES[7]

The following policies should govern our business relationships with the Company's suppliers. They are necessarily broad enough to allow for the reasonable exercise of judgment and discretion.

C. F. OGDEN

1. *Develop and maintain the maximum of competition* compatible with the quality and service required by the Company and the degree of reliability we desire in our suppliers.
2. *Develop and maintain dependable sources of supply*—ask for quotations only from those vendors from whom we are willing to buy. However, if a vendor requests to quote, permit him to bid as he might have something worth while.
3. *Deal fairly*—avoid favoritism and make each transaction both a good buy for the Company and a satisfactory sale for the supplier.
4. *Do not bargain with suppliers*—obtain each bidder's best price on his first quotation; don't ask for a second quotation on a particular purchase or to meet a competitive bid.
5. *Pay no premium for reciprocal business*—award orders to the lowest bidder, provided the elements of quality, service, delivery, and reliability are equal.
6. *Keep prices confidential*—do not divulge prices to competitors.
7. *Receive supplier representatives promptly and courteously.*
8. *Establish good personal relationships with supplier representatives*—this can be better accomplished when incidental social expenses are shared equally by buyer and seller.
9. *Do not accept gratuities*—it is not in accordance with Company policies and has no place in our purchasing transactions.
10. *Know each product we buy*—increase our knowledge of materials and manufacturing processes.
11. *Always cooperate with other Company Departments* and be receptive to suggestions from them.
12. *Promote good will*—make purchasing a real service function in all our dealings.

[7] Reproduced by permission of The Detroit Edison Company.

REFERENCE MATERIAL

Legal (Section 4)

UNIFORM SALES ACT [8]

The rules governing the sale of goods come from the old "law merchant," the decisions of the courts, and the statutes enacted by Congress and state legislative bodies. These rules have been "hammered-out" of experience and for workability. The basic contractual concepts are applicable for the most part.

But there are some problems in connection with the sale of goods which have caused the development of rules peculiar to this branch of contract law. For instance, there is the matter of the Statute of Frauds. This statute sets forth the requirements as to the amount involved, the receipt of part or all the goods, and the presence of a signed note or memorandum by the party to pay, if the sale or contract is to be enforced.

Rules developed concerning bulk sales, conditional sales, passing of title, chattel mortgages, etc. The amounts and terms varied from state to state. It was felt desirable to have a uniform set of rules governing sales. The Uniform Sales Act was developed to smooth out differences between states and to aid and encourage business.

This statute has now been adopted in more than half of the states of the Union. The courts in most of the other states follow the rules of the Uniform Sales Act or have a similar sales act statute of their own.

It would be wise also to keep an eye on the Uniform Commercial Code, adopted by Pennsylvania in 1954. As other states adopt the Code, it will be of increasing importance to purchasing executives. Comments on the Code will be found in the section following the Sales Act.

The following is a copy of the Uniform Sales Act and should be of interest to all purchasing people and used as a ready reference for the items covered.

PART I

The Contract

Formation of the Contract

SEC. 1. *Contracts to Sell and Sales.* (1) A contract to sell goods is a contract whereby the seller agrees to transfer the property in goods to the buyer for a consideration called the price.

(2) A sale of goods is an agreement whereby the seller transfers the property in goods to the buyer for a consideration called the price.

(3) A contract to sell or a sale may be absolute or conditional.

[8] Application to purchasing explained in Section 4, "Legal Influences in Purchasing."

(4) There may be a contract to sell or a sale between one part owner and another.

SEC. 2. *Capacity—Liabilities for Necessaries.* Capacity to buy and sell is regulated by the general law concerning capacity to contract, and to transfer and acquire property.

Where necessaries are sold and delivered to an infant, or to a person who by reason of mental incapacity or drunkenness is incompetent to contract, he must pay a reasonable price therefor.

Necessaries in this section means goods suitable to the condition in life of such infant or other person, and to his actual requirements at the time of delivery.

FORMALITIES OF THE CONTRACT

SEC. 3. *Form of Contract or Sale.* Subject to the provisions of this act and of any statute in that behalf, a contract to sell or a sale may be made in writing (either with or without seal), or by word of mouth, or partly in writing and partly by word of mouth or may be inferred from the conduct of the parties.

SEC. 4. *Statute of Frauds.* (1) A contract to sell or a sale of any goods or choses in action of the value of five hundred dollars or upwards shall not be enforceable by action unless the buyer shall accept part of the goods or choses in action so contracted to be sold or sold, and actually receive the same, or give something in earnest to bind the contract, or in part payment, or unless some note or memorandum in writing of the contract or sale be signed by the party to be charged or his agent in that behalf.

(2) The provisions of this section apply to every such contract or sale, notwithstanding that the goods may be intended to be delivered at some future time or may not at the time of such contract or sale be actually made, procured, or provided, or fit or ready for delivery, or some act may be requisite for the making or completing thereof, or rendering the same fit for delivery; but if the goods are to be manufactured by the seller especially for the buyer and are not suitable for sale to others in the ordinary course of the seller's business, the provisions of this section shall not apply.

(3) There is an acceptance of goods within the meaning of this section when the buyer, either before or after delivery of the goods, expresses by words or conduct his assent to becoming the owner of those specific goods.

SUBJECT MATTER OF CONTRACT

SEC. 5. *Existing and Future Goods.* (1) The goods which form the subject of a contract to sell may be either existing goods, owned or possessed by the seller, or goods to be manufactured or acquired by the seller after the making of the contract to sell, in this act called "future goods."

(2) There may be a contract to sell goods, the acquisition of which by the seller depends upon a contingency which may or may not happen.

(3) Where the parties purport to effect a present sale of future goods, the agreement operates as a contract to sell the goods.

SEC. 6. *Undivided Shares.* (1) There may be a contract to sell or a sale of an undivided share of goods. If the parties intend to effect a present sale, the buyer, by force of the agreement, becomes an owner in common with the owner or owners of the remaining shares.

(2) In the case of fungible goods, there may be a sale of an undivided share of a specific mass, though the seller purports to sell and the buyer to buy a definite number, weight or measure of the goods in the mass, and though the number, weight or measure of the goods in the mass is undetermined. By such a sale the buyer becomes owner in common of such a share of the mass as the number, weight or measure bought bears to the number, weight or measure of the mass. If the mass contains less than the number, weight or measure bought, the buyer becomes the owner of the whole mass and the seller is bound to make good the deficiency from similar goods unless a contrary intent appears.

SEC. 7. *Destruction of Goods Sold.* (1) Where the parties purport to sell specific goods, and the goods without the knowledge of the seller have wholly perished at the time when the agreement is made, the agreement is void.

(2) Where the parties purport to sell specific goods, and the goods without the knowledge of the seller have perished in part or have wholly or in a material part so deteriorated in quality as to be substantially changed in character, the buyer may at his option treat the contract:

(a) As avoided, or

(b) As transferring the property in all of the existing goods or in so much thereof as have not deteriorated, and as binding the buyer to pay the full agreed price if the sale was indivisible, or to pay the agreed price for the goods in which the property passes if the sale was divisible.

SEC. 8. *Destruction of Goods Contracted to Be Sold.* (1) Where there is a contract to sell specific goods, and subsequently, but before the risk passes to the buyer, without any fault on the part of the seller or the buyer, the goods wholly perish, the contract is thereby avoided.

(2) Where there is a contract to sell specific goods, and subsequently, but before the risk passes to the buyer, without any fault of the seller or the buyer, part of the goods perish or the whole or a material part of the goods so deteriorates in quality as to be substantially changed in character, the buyer may at his option treat the contract:

(a) As avoided, or

(b) As binding the seller to transfer the property in all of the existing goods or in so much thereof as have not deteriorated, and as binding the buyer to pay the full agreed price if the contract was indivisible, or to pay the agreed price for so much of the goods as the seller, by the buyer's option, is bound to transfer if the contract was divisible.

THE PRICE

SEC. 9. *Definition and Ascertainment of Price.* (1) The price may be fixed by the contract, or may be left to be fixed in such manner as may be agreed, or it may be determined by the course of dealing between the parties.

(2) The price may be made payable in any personal property.

(3) Where transferring or promising to transfer any interest in real estate constitutes the whole or part of the consideration for transferring or for promising to transfer the property in goods, this act shall not apply.

(4) Where the price is not determined in accordance with the foregoing provisions the buyer must pay a reasonable price. What is a reasonable price is a question of fact dependent on the circumstances of each particular case.

SEC. 10. *Sale at a Valuation.* (1) Where there is a contract to sell or a sale of goods at a price or on terms to be fixed by a third person, and such third person without fault of the seller or the buyer, cannot or does not fix the price or terms, the contract or the sale is thereby avoided; but if the goods or any part thereof have been delivered to and appropriated by the buyer he must pay a reasonable price therefor.

(2) Where such third person is prevented from fixing the price or terms by fault of the seller or the buyer, the party not in fault may have such remedies against the party in fault as are allowed by Parts IV and V of this act.

Conditions and Warranties

SEC. 11. *Effect of Conditions.* (1) Where the obligation of either party to a contract to sell or a sale is subject to any condition which is not performed, such party may refuse to proceed with the contract or sale or he may waive performance of the condition. If the other party has promised that the condition should happen or be performed, such first-mentioned party may also treat the non-performance of the condition as a breach of warranty.

(2) Where the property in the goods has not passed, the buyer may treat the fulfillment by the seller of his obligation to furnish goods as described and as warranted expressly or by implication in the contract to sell as a condition of the obligation of the buyer to perform his promise to accept and pay for the goods.

SEC. 12. *Definition of Express Warranty.* Any affirmation of fact or any promise by the seller relating to the goods is an express warranty if the natural tendency of such affirmation or promise is to induce the buyer to purchase the goods, and if the buyer purchases the goods relying thereon. No affirmation of the value of the goods, nor any statement purporting to be a statement of the seller's opinion only shall be construed as a warranty.

SEC. 13. *Implied Warranties of Title.* In a contract to sell or a sale, unless a contrary intention appears, there is:

(1) An implied warranty on the part of the seller that in case of a sale he has a right to sell the goods, and that in case of a contract to sell he will have a right to sell the goods at the time when the property is to pass.

(2) An implied warranty that the buyer shall have and enjoy quiet possession of the goods as against any lawful claims existing at the time of the sale.

(3) An implied warranty that the goods shall be free at the time of the sale from any charge or encumbrance in favor of any third person, not declared or known to the buyer before or at the time when the contract or sale is made.

(4) This section shall not, however, be held to render liable a sheriff, auctioneer, mortgagee, or other person professing to sell by virtue of authority in fact or law, goods in which a third person has a legal or equitable interest.

SEC. 14. *Implied Warranty in Sale by Description.* Where there is a contract to sell or a sale of goods by description, there is an implied warranty that the goods shall correspond with the description and if the contract or sale be by sample, as well as by description, it is not sufficient that the bulk of the goods corresponds with the sample if the goods do not also correspond with the description.

SEC. 15. *Implied Warranties of Quality.* Subject to the provisions of this act and of any statute in that behalf, there is no implied warranty or condition as to the quality or fitness for any particular purpose of goods supplied under a contract to sell or a sale, except as follows:

(1) Where the buyer, expressly or by implication, makes known to the seller the particular purpose for which the goods are required, and it appears that the buyer relies on the seller's skill or judgment (whether he be the grower or manufacturer or not), there is an implied warranty that the goods shall be reasonably fit for such purpose.

(2) Where the goods are bought by description from a seller who deals in goods of that description (whether he be the grower or manufacturer or not), there is an implied warranty that the goods shall be of merchantable quality.

(3) If the buyer has examined the goods, there is no implied warranty as regards defects which such examination ought to have revealed.

(4) In the case of a contract to sell or a sale of a specified article under its patent or other trade name, there is no implied warranty as to its fitness for any particular purpose.

(5) An implied warranty or condition as to the quality or fitness for a particular purpose may be annexed by the usage of trade.

(6) An express warranty or condition does not negative a warranty or condition implied under this act unless inconsistent therewith.

Sale by Sample

SEC. 16. *Implied Warranties in Sale by Sample.* In the case of a contract to sell or a sale by sample:

(a) There is an implied warranty that the bulk shall correspond with the sample in quality.

(b) There is an implied warranty that the buyer shall have a reasonable opportunity of comparing the bulk with the sample, except so far as otherwise provided in section 47 (3).

(c) If the seller is a dealer in goods of that kind, there is an implied warranty that the goods shall be free from any defect rendering them unmerchantable which would not be apparent on reasonable examination of the sample.

PART II

Transfer of Property and Title

TRANSFER OF PROPERTY AS BETWEEN SELLER AND BUYER

SEC. 17. *No Property Passes Until Goods Are Ascertained.* Where there is a contract to sell unascertained goods, no property in the goods is transferred to the buyer unless and until the goods are ascertained, but property in an undivided share of ascertained goods may be transferred as provided in section 6.

SEC. 18. *Property in Specific Goods Passes When Parties So Intend.*

(1) Where there is a contract to sell specific or ascertained goods, the property in them is transferred to the buyer at such time as the parties to the contract intend it to be transferred.

(2) For the purpose of ascertaining the intention of the parties, regard shall be had to the terms of the contract, the conduct of the parties, usages of trade and the circumstances of the case.

SEC. 19. *Rules for Ascertaining Intention.* Unless a different intention appears, the following are rules for ascertaining the intention of the parties as to the time at which the property in the goods is to pass to the buyer.

Rule 1. Where there is an unconditional contract to sell specific goods, in a deliverable state, the property in the goods passes to the buyer when the contract is made and it is immaterial whether the time of payment, or the time of delivery, or both, be postponed.

Rule 2. Where there is a contract to sell specific goods and the seller is bound to do something to the goods, for the purpose of putting them into a deliverable state, the property does not pass until such thing be done.

Rule 3. (1) When goods are delivered to the buyer "on sale or return," or on other terms indicating an intention to make a present sale, but to give the buyer an option to return the goods instead of paying the price, the property passes to the buyer on delivery, but he may revest the property in the seller by returning or tendering the goods within the time fixed in the contract, or, if no time has been fixed, within a reasonable time.

(2) When goods are delivered to the buyer on approval or on trial or on satisfaction, or other similar terms, the property therein passes to the buyer—

(a) When he signifies his approval or acceptance to the seller or does any other act adopting the transaction,

(b) If he does not signify his approval or acceptance to the seller, but retains the goods without giving notice of rejection, then if a time has been fixed for the return of the goods, on the expiration of such time, and, if no time has been fixed, on the expiration of a reasonable time. What is a reasonable time is a question of fact.

Rule 4. (1) Where there is a contract to sell unascertained or future goods by description, and goods of that description and in a deliverable state are unconditionally appropriated to the contract, either by the seller with the assent of the buyer, or by the buyer with the assent of the seller, the property in the goods thereupon passes to the buyer. Such assent may be expressed or implied, and may be given either before or after the appropriation is made.

(2) Where, in pursuance of a contract to sell, the seller delivers the goods to the buyer, or to a carrier or other bailee (whether named by the buyer or not) for the purpose of transmission to or holding for the buyer, he is presumed to have unconditionally appropriated the goods to the contract, except in the cases provided for in the next rule and in section 20. This presumption is applicable, although by the terms of the contract, the buyer is to pay the price before receiving delivery of the goods, and the goods are marked with the words "collect on delivery" or their equivalents.

Rule 5. If the contract to sell requires the seller to deliver the goods to the buyer, or at a particular place, or to pay the freight or cost of transportation to the buyer, or to a particular place, the property does not pass until the goods have been delivered to the buyer or reached the place agreed upon.

SEC. 20. *Reservation of Right of Possession or Property When Goods Are Shipped.* (1) Where there is a contract to sell specific goods, or where goods are subsequently appropriated to the contract, the seller may, by the terms of the contract or appropriation, reserve the right of possession or property in the goods until certain conditions have been fulfilled. The right of possession or property may be thus reserved notwithstanding the delivery of the goods to the buyer or to a carrier or other bailee for the purpose of transmission to the buyer.

(2) Where goods are shipped, and by the bill of lading the goods are deliverable to the seller or his agent, or to the order of the seller or of his agent, the seller thereby reserves the property in the goods. But, if except for the form of the bill of lading, the property would have passed to the buyer on shipment of the goods, the seller's property in the goods shall be deemed to be only for the purpose of securing performance by the buyer of his obligations under the contract.

(3) Where goods are shipped, and by the bill of lading the goods are deliverable to the order of the buyer or of his agent, but possession of the bill of lading is retained by the seller or his agent, the seller thereby reserves a right to the possession of the goods as against the buyer.

(4) Where the seller of goods draws on the buyer for the price and transmits the bill of exchange and bill of lading together to the buyer to secure acceptance or payment of the bill of exchange, the buyer is bound to return the bill of lading if he does not honor the bill of exchange, and if he wrongfully retains the bill of lading he acquires no added right thereby. If, however, the bill of lading provides that the goods are deliverable to the buyer or to the order of the buyer, or is indorsed in blank, or to the buyer by the consignee named therein, one who purchases in good faith, for value, the bill of lading, or goods from the buyer will obtain the property in the goods, although the bill of exchange has not been honored, provided that such purchaser has received delivery of the bill of lading indorsed by the consignee named therein, or of the goods, without notice of the facts, making the transfer wrongful.

SEC. 21. *Sale by Auction.* In the case of a sale by auction—

(1) Where goods are put up for sale by auction in lots, each lot is the subject of a separate contract of sale.

(2) A sale by auction is complete when the auctioneer announces its completion by the fall of the hammer, or in other customary manner. Until such announcement is made, any bidder may retract his bid; and the auctioneer may withdraw the goods from sale unless the auction has been announced to be without reserve.

(3) A right to bid may be reserved expressly by or on behalf of the seller.

(4) Where notice has not been given that a sale by auction is subject to a right to bid on behalf of the seller, it shall not be lawful for the seller to bid himself or to employ or induce any person to bid at such sale on his behalf, or for the

auctioneer to employ or induce any person to bid at such sale on behalf of the seller or knowingly to take any bid from the seller or any person employed by him. Any sale contravening this rule may be treated as fraudulent by the buyer.

SEC. 22. *Risk of Loss.* Unless otherwise agreed, the goods remain at the seller's risk until the property therein is transferred to the buyer, but when the property therein is transferred to the buyer the goods are at the buyer's risk whether delivery has been made or not, except that—

(a) Where delivery of the goods has been made to the buyer or to a bailee for the buyer, in pursuance of the contract and the property in the goods has been retained by the seller merely to secure performance by the buyer of his obligations under the contract, the goods are at the buyer's risk from the time of such delivery.

(b) Where delivery has been delayed through the fault of either the buyer or seller the goods are at the risk of the party in fault as regards any loss which might not have occurred but for such fault.

Transfer of Title

SEC. 23. *Sale by a Person Not the Owner.* (1) Subject to the provision of this act, where goods are sold by a person who is not the owner thereof, and who does not sell them under the authority or with the consent of the owner, the buyer acquires no better title to the goods than the seller had, unless the owner of the goods is by his conduct precluded from denying the seller's authority to sell.

(2) Nothing in this act, however, shall affect:

(a) The provisions of any factors' acts, recording acts, or any enactment enabling the apparent owner of goods to dispose of them as if he were the true owner thereof.

(b) The validity of any contract to sell or sale under any special common law or statutory power of sale or under the order of a court of competent jurisdiction.

SEC. 24. *Sale by One Having a Voidable Title.* Where the seller of goods has a voidable title thereto, but his title has not been avoided at the time of the sale, the buyer acquires a good title to the goods, provided he buys them in good faith, for value, and without notice of the seller's defect of title.

SEC. 25. *Sale by Seller in Possession of Goods Already Sold.* Where a person having sold goods continues in possession of the goods, or of negotiable documents of title to the goods, the delivery or transfer by that person, or by an agent acting for him, of the goods or documents of title under any sale, pledge, or other disposition thereof, to any person receiving and paying value for the same in good faith and without notice of the previous sale, shall have the same effect as if the person making the delivery or transfer were expressly authorized by the owner of the goods to make the same.

SEC. 26. *Creditors' Rights Against Sold Goods in Seller's Possession.* Where a person having sold goods continues in possession of the goods, or of negotiable documents of title to the goods and such retention of possession is fraudulent in fact or is deemed fraudulent under any rule of law, a creditor or creditors of the seller may treat the sale as void.

SEC. 27. *Definition of Negotiable Documents of Title.* A document of title in which it is stated that the goods referred to therein will be delivered to the bearer, or to the order of any person named in such document is a negotiable document of title.

SEC. 28. *Negotiation of Negotiable Documents by Delivery.* A negotiable document of title may be negotiated by delivery—

(a) Where by the terms of the document the carrier, warehouseman or other bailee issuing the same undertakes to deliver the goods to the bearer, or

(b) Where by the terms of the document the carrier, warehouseman or other bailee issuing the same undertakes to deliver the goods to the order of a specified person, and such person or a subsequent indorsee of the document has indorsed it in blank or to bearer.

Where by the terms of a negotiable document of title the goods are deliverable to bearer or where a negotiable document of title has been indorsed in blank or to bearer, any holder may indorse the same to himself or to any specified person, and in such case the document shall thereafter be negotiated only by the indorsement of such indorsee.

SEC. 29. *Negotiation of Negotiable Documents by Indorsement.* A negotiable document of title may be negotiated by the indorsement of the person to whose order the goods are by the terms of the document deliverable. Such indorsement may be in blank, to bearer or to a specified person. If indorsed to a specified person, it may be again negotiated by the indorsement of such person in blank, to bearer or to another specified person. Subsequent negotiations may be made in like manner.

SEC. 30. *Negotiable Documents of Title Marked "Not Negotiable."* If a document of title which contains an undertaking by a carrier, warehouseman or other bailee to deliver the goods to the bearer, to a specified person or order, or to the order of a specified person, or which contains words of like import, has placed upon it the words "not negotiable," "non-negotiable" or the like, such a document may nevertheless be negotiated by the holder and is a negotiable document of title within the meaning of this act. But nothing in this act contained shall be construed as limiting or defining the effect upon the obligations of the carrier, warehouseman, or other bailee issuing a document of title or placing thereon the words "not negotiable," "non-negotiable," or the like.

SEC. 31. *Transfer of Non-negotiable Documents.* A document of title which is not in such form that it can be negotiated by delivery may be transferred by the holder by delivery to a purchaser or donee. A non-negotiable document cannot be negotiated and the indorsement of such a document gives the transferee no additional right.

SEC. 32. *Who May Negotiate a Document.* A negotiable document of title may be negotiated—

(a) By the owner thereof, or

(b) By any person to whom the possession or custody of the document has been entrusted by the owner, if, by the terms of the document the bailee issuing the document undertakes to deliver the goods to the order of the person to whom the possession or custody of the document has been entrusted, or if at the time of such entrusting the document is in such form that it may be negotiated by delivery.[9]

SEC. 33. *Rights of Person to Whom Document Has Been Negotiated.* A person to whom a negotiable document of title has been duly negotiated acquires thereby:

(a) Such title to the goods as the person negotiating the document to him had or had ability to convey to a purchaser in good faith for value and also such title to the goods as the person to whose order the goods were to be delivered by the terms of the document had or had ability to convey to a purchaser in good faith for value, and

(b) The direct obligation of the bailee issuing the document to hold possession of the goods for him according to the terms of the document as fully as if such bailee had contracted directly with him.

SEC. 34. *Rights of Person to Whom Document Has Been Transferred.* A person to whom a document of title has been transferred, but not negotiated, acquires thereby, as against the transferor, the title to the goods, subject to the terms of any agreement with the transferor.

If the document is non-negotiable, such person also acquires the right to notify the bailee who issued the document of the transfer thereof, and thereby to acquire the direct obligation of such bailee to hold possession of the goods for him according to the terms of the document.

Prior to the notification of such bailee by the transferor or transferee of a non-negotiable document of title, the title of the transferee to the goods and the right to acquire the obligation of such bailee may be defeated by the levy of an attachment or execution upon the goods by a creditor of the transferor, or by a notification to such bailee by the transferor or a subsequent purchaser from the transferor of a subsequent sale of the goods by the transferor.

SEC. 35. *Transfer of Negotiable Document without Indorsement.* Where a negotiable document of title is transferred for value by delivery, and the indorsement of the transferor is essential for negotiation, the transferee acquires a right against the transferor to compel him to indorse the document unless a contrary intention appears. The negotiation shall take effect as of the time when the indorsement is actually made.

SEC. 36. *Warranties on Sale of Document.* A person who for value negotiates or transfers a document of title by indorsement or delivery, including one who assigns for value a claim secured by a document of title unless a contrary intention appears, warrants:

[9] In a jurisdiction where it is desired that the Sales Act and the Bills of Lading Act should both be passed and should be in harmony, the Commissioners on Uniform State Laws have suggested the following substitute for section 32 of the Sales Act as printed above:

> "A negotiable document may be negotiated by any person in possession of the same; however such possession may have been acquired if, by the terms of the document, the bailee issuing it undertakes to deliver the goods to the order of such person, or if at the time of negotiation the document is in such form that it may be negotiated by delivery."

The substitute section 32 has been adopted by eighteen jurisdictions.

(a) That the document is genuine;

(b) That he has a legal right to negotiate or transfer it;

(c) That he has knowledge of no fact which would impair the validity or worth of the document; and

(d) That he has a right to transfer the title to the goods and that the goods are merchantable or fit for a particular purpose, whenever such warranties would have been implied if the contract of the parties had been to transfer without a document of title the goods represented thereby.

SEC. 37. *Indorser Not a Guarantor.* The indorsement of a document of title shall not make the indorser liable for any failure on the part of the bailee who issues the document or previous indorsers thereof to fulfill their respective obligations.

SEC. 38. *When Negotiation Not Impaired by Fraud, Mistake or Duress.* The validity of the negotiation of a negotiable document of title is not impaired by the fact that the negotiation was a breach of duty on the part of the person making the negotiation, or by the fact that the owner of the document was deprived of the possession of the same by loss, theft, fraud, accident, mistake, duress or conversion, if the person to whom the document was negotiated or a person to whom the document was subsequently negotiated paid value therefor in good faith without notice of the breach of duty, or loss, theft, fraud, accident, mistake, duress or conversion.[10]

SEC. 39. *Attachment or Levy upon Goods for Which a Negotiable Document Has Been Issued.* If goods are delivered to a bailee by the owner or by a person whose act in conveying the title to them to a purchaser in good faith for value would bind the owner and a negotiable document of title is issued for them they cannot thereafter, while in the possession of such bailee, be attached by garnishment or otherwise or be levied under an execution unless the document be first surrendered to the bailee or its negotiation enjoined. The bailee shall in no case be compelled to deliver up the actual possession of the goods until the document is surrendered to him or impounded by the court.

SEC. 40. *Creditors' Remedies to Reach Negotiable Documents.* A creditor whose debtor is the owner of a negotiable document of title shall be entitled to such aid from courts of appropriate jurisdiction by injunction and otherwise in attaching such document or in satisfying the claim by means thereof as is allowed at law or in equity in regard to property which cannot readily be attached or levied upon by ordinary legal process.

[10] As amended 1922. Prior to the 1922 amendment this section read as follows:

SEC. 38. *When Negotiation Not Impaired by Fraud, Mistake or Duress.* The validity of the negotiation of the negotiable document of title is not impaired by the fact that the negotiation was a breach of duty on the part of the person making the negotiation, or by the fact that the owner of the document was induced by fraud, mistake or duress to entrust the possession or custody thereof to such person, if the person to whom the document was negotiated or a person to whom the document was subsequently negotiated paid value therefor, without notice of the breach of duty, or fraud, mistake or duress.

The section in its original form continues in force in twenty-two jurisdictions.

PART III

PERFORMANCE OF THE CONTRACT

SEC. 41. *Seller Must Deliver and Buyer Accept Goods.* It is the duty of the seller to deliver the goods, and of the buyer to accept and pay for them, in accordance with the terms of the contract to sell or sale.

SEC. 42. *Delivery and Payment Are Concurrent Conditions.* Unless otherwise agreed, delivery of the goods and payment of the price are concurrent conditions; that is to say, the seller must be ready and willing to give possession of the goods to the buyer in exchange for the price and the buyer must be ready and willing to pay the price in exchange for possession of the goods.

SEC. 43. *Place, Time and Manner of Delivery.* (1) Whether it is for the buyer to take possession of the goods or for the seller to send them to the buyer is a question depending in each case on the contract, express or implied, between the parties. Apart from any such contract, express or implied, or usage of trade to the contrary, the place of delivery is the seller's place of business if he has one, and if not his residence; but in case of a contract to sell or a sale of specific goods, which to the knowledge of the parties when the contract or the sale was made were in some other place, then that place is the place of delivery.

(2) Where by a contract to sell or a sale the seller is bound to send the goods to the buyer, but no time for sending them is fixed, the seller is bound to send them within a reasonable time.

(3) Where the goods at the time of sale are in the possession of a third person, the seller has not fulfilled his obligation to deliver to the buyer unless and until such third person acknowledges to the buyer that he holds the goods on the buyer's behalf; but as against all others than the seller the buyer shall be regarded as having received delivery from the time when such third person first has notice of the sale. Nothing in this section, however, shall affect the operation of the issue or transfer of any document of title to goods.

(4) Demand or tender of delivery may be treated as ineffectual unless made at a reasonable hour. What is a reasonable hour is a question of fact.

(5) Unless otherwise agreed, the expenses of and incidental to putting the goods into a deliverable state must be borne by the seller.

SEC. 44. *Delivery of Wrong Quantity.* (1) Where the seller delivers to the buyer a quantity of goods less than he contracted to sell, the buyer may reject them, but if the buyer accepts or retains the goods so delivered, knowing that the seller is not going to perform the contract in full, he must pay for them at the contract rate. If, however, the buyer has used or disposed of the goods delivered before he knows that the seller is not going to perform his contract in full, the buyer shall not be liable for more than the fair value to him of the goods so received.

(2) Where the seller delivers to the buyer a quantity of goods larger than he contracted to sell, the buyer may accept the goods included in the contract and reject the rest, or he may reject the whole. If the buyer accepts the whole of the goods so delivered he must pay for them at the contract rate.

(3) Where the seller delivers to the buyer the goods he contracted to sell mixed with goods of a different description not included in the contract, the buyer may accept the goods which are in accordance with the contract and reject the rest, or he may reject the whole.

(4) The provisions of this section are subject to any usage of trade, special agreement, or course of dealing between the parties.

SEC. 45. *Delivery in Installments.* (1) Unless otherwise agreed, the buyer of goods is not bound to accept delivery thereof by installments.

(2) Where there is a contract to sell goods to be delivered by stated installments, which are to be separately paid for, and the seller makes defective deliveries in respect of one or more installments, or the buyer neglects or refuses to take delivery of or pay for one or more installments, it depends in each case on the terms of the contract and the circumstances of the case, whether the breach of contract is so material as to justify the injured party in refusing to proceed further and suing for damages for breach of the entire contract, or whether the breach is severable, giving rise to a claim for compensation but not to a right to treat the whole contract as broken.

SEC. 46. *Delivery to a Carrier on Behalf of the Buyer.* (1) Where, in pursuance of a contract to sell or a sale, the seller is authorized or required to send the goods to the buyer, delivery of the goods to a carrier, whether named by the buyer or not, for the purpose of transmission to the buyer is deemed to be a delivery of the goods to the buyer, except in the cases provided for in section 19, rule 5, or unless a contrary intent appears.

(2) Unless otherwise authorized by the buyer, the seller must make such contract with the carrier on behalf of the buyer as may be reasonable, having regard to the nature of the goods and the other circumstances of the case. If the seller omit so to do, and the goods are lost or damaged in course of transit, the buyer may decline to treat the delivery to the carrier as a delivery to himself, or may hold the seller responsible in damages.

(3) Unless otherwise agreed, where goods are sent by the seller to the buyer under circumstances in which the seller knows or ought to know that it is usual to insure, the seller must give such notice to the buyer as may enable him to insure them during their transit, and, if the seller fails to do so, the goods shall be deemed to be at his risk during such transit.

SEC. 47. *Right to Examine the Goods.* (1) Where goods are delivered to the buyer, which he has not previously examined, he is not deemed to have accepted them unless and until he has had a reasonable opportunity of examining them for the purpose of ascertaining whether they are in conformity with the contract.

(2) Unless otherwise agreed, when the seller tenders delivery of goods to the buyer, he is bound, on request, to afford the buyer a reasonable opportunity of examining the goods for the purpose of ascertaining whether they are in conformity with the contract.

(3) Where goods are delivered to a carrier by the seller, in accordance with an order from or agreement with the buyer, upon the terms that the goods shall not be delivered by the carrier to the buyer until he has paid the price,

whether such terms are indicated by marking the goods with words "collect on delivery," or otherwise, the buyer is not entitled to examine the goods before payment of the price in the absence of agreement permitting such examination.

SEC. 48. *What Constitutes Acceptance.* The buyer is deemed to have accepted the goods when he intimates to the seller that he has accepted them, or when the goods have been delivered to him, and he does any act in relation to them which is inconsistent with the ownership of the seller, or when, after the lapse of a reasonable time, he retains the goods without intimating to the seller that he has rejected them.

SEC. 49. *Acceptance Does Not Bar Action for Damages.* In the absence of express or implied agreement of the parties, acceptance of the goods by the buyer shall not discharge the seller from liability in damages or other legal remedy for breach of any promise or warranty in the contract to sell or the sale. But, if, after acceptance of the goods, the buyer fails to give notice to the seller of the breach of any promise or warranty within a reasonable time after the buyer knows, or ought to know of such breach, the seller shall not be liable therefor.

SEC. 50. *Buyer Is Not Bound to Return Goods Wrongly Delivered.* Unless otherwise agreed, where goods are delivered to the buyer, and he refuses to accept them, having the right so to do, he is not bound to return them to the seller, but it is sufficient if he notifies the seller that he refuses to accept them.

SEC. 51. *Buyer's Liability for Failing to Accept Delivery.* When the seller is ready and willing to deliver the goods, and requests the buyer to take delivery, and the buyer does not within a reasonable time after such request take delivery of the goods, he is liable to the seller for any loss occasioned by his neglect or refusal to take delivery, and also for a reasonable charge for the care and custody of the goods. If the neglect or refusal of the buyer to take delivery amounts to a repudiation or breach of the entire contract, the seller shall have the right against the goods and on the contract hereinafter provided in favor of the seller when the buyer is in default.

PART IV

UNPAID SELLER

RIGHTS OF UNPAID SELLER AGAINST THE GOODS

SEC. 52. *Definition of Unpaid Seller.* (1) The seller of goods is deemed to be an unpaid seller within the meaning of this act—

(a) When the whole of the price has not been paid or tendered.

(b) When a bill of exchange or other negotiable instrument has been received as conditional payment, and the condition on which it was received has been broken by reason of the dishonor of the instrument, the insolvency of the buyer, or otherwise.

(2) In this part of this act the term "seller" includes an agent of the seller to whom the bill of lading has been indorsed, or a consignor or agent who has himself paid, or is directly responsible for, the price, or any other person who is in the position of a seller.

SEC. 53. *Remedies of Unpaid Seller.* (1) Subject to the provisions of this act, notwithstanding that the property in the goods may have passed to the buyer, the unpaid seller of goods, as such, has—

(a) A lien on the goods or right to retain them for the price while he is in possession of them;

(b) In case of the insolvency of the buyer, a right of stopping the goods in transitu after he has parted with the possession of them;

(c) A right of resale as limited by this act;

(d) A right to rescind the sale as limited by this act.

(2) Where the property in goods has not passed to the buyer, the unpaid seller has, in addition to his other remedies, a right of withholding delivery similar to and coextensive with his rights of lien and stoppage in transitu where the property has passed to the buyer.

UNPAID SELLER'S LIEN

SEC. 54. *When Right of Lien May Be Exercised.* (1) Subject to the provisions of this act, the unpaid seller of goods who is in possession of them is entitled to retain possession of them until payment or tender of the price in the following cases, namely:

(a) Where the goods have been sold without any stipulation as to credit;

(b) Where the goods have been sold on credit, but the term of credit has expired;

(c) Where the buyer becomes insolvent.

(2) The seller may exercise his right of lien notwithstanding that he is in possession of the goods as agent or bailee for the buyer.

SEC. 55. *Lien After Part Delivery.* Where an unpaid seller has made part delivery of the goods, he may exercise his right of lien on the remainder, unless such part delivery has been made under such circumstances as to show an intent to waive the lien or right of retention.

SEC. 56. *When Lien Is Lost.* (1) The unpaid seller of goods loses his lien thereon—

(a) When he delivers the goods to a carrier or other bailee for the purpose of transmission to the buyer without reserving the property in the goods or the right to the possession thereof;

(b) When the buyer or his agent lawfully obtains possession of the goods;

(c) By waiver thereof.

(2) The unpaid seller of goods, having a lien thereon, does not lose his lien by reason only that he has obtained judgment or decree for the price of the goods.

STOPPAGE IN TRANSIT

SEC. 57. *Seller May Stop Goods on Buyer's Insolvency.* Subject to the provisions of this act, when the buyer of goods is or becomes insolvent, the unpaid seller who has parted with the possession of the goods has the right of stopping them *in transitu,* that is to say, he may resume possession of the goods at any time while they are *in transitu,* and he will then become entitled to the same rights in regard to the goods as he would have had if he had never parted with the possession.

SEC. 58. *When Goods Are in Transit.* (1) Goods are in transit within the meaning of section 57—

(a) From the time when they are delivered to a carrier by land or water, or other bailee for the purpose of transmission to the buyer, until the buyer, or his agent in that behalf, takes delivery of them from such carrier or other bailee;

(b) If the goods are rejected by the buyer, and the carrier or other bailee continues in possession of them, even if the seller has refused to receive them back.

(2) Goods are no longer in transit within the meaning of section 57—

(a) If the buyer, or his agent in that behalf, obtains delivery of the goods before their arrival at the appointed destination;

(b) If, after the arrival of the goods at the appointed destination, the carrier or other bailee acknowledges to the buyer or his agent that he holds the goods on his behalf and continues in possession of them as bailee for the buyer or his agent; and it is immaterial that a further destination for the goods may have been indicated by the buyer;

(c) If the carrier or other bailee wrongfully refuses to deliver the goods to the buyer or his agent in that behalf.

(3) If goods are delivered to a ship chartered by the buyer, it is a question depending on the circumstances of the particular case, whether they are in the possession of the master as a carrier or as agent of the buyer.

(4) If part delivery of the goods has been made to the buyer, or his agent in that behalf, the remainder of the goods may be stopped *in transitu,* unless such part delivery has been under such circumstances as to show as agreement with the buyer to give up possession of the whole of the goods.

SEC. 59. *Ways of Exercising the Right to Stop.* (1) The unpaid seller may exercise his right of stoppage *in transitu* either by obtaining actual possession of the goods or by giving notice of his claim to the carrier or other bailee in whose possession the goods are. Such notice may be given either to the person in actual possession of the goods or to his principal. In the latter case the notice, to be effectual, must be given at such time and under such circumstances that the principal, by the exercise of reasonable diligence, may prevent a delivery to the buyer.

(2) When notice of stoppage *in transitu* is given by the seller to the carrier, or other bailee in possession of the goods, he must redeliver the goods to, or according to the directions of, the seller. The expenses of such delivery must be borne by the seller. If, however, a negotiable document of title representing the goods has been issued by the carrier or other bailee, he shall not be obliged to deliver or justified in delivering the goods to the seller unless such document is first surrendered for cancellation.

Resale by the Seller

SEC. 60. *When and How Resale May Be Made.* (1) Where the goods are of perishable nature, or where the seller expressly reserves the right of resale in case the buyer should make default, or where the buyer has been in default in the payment of the price an unreasonable time, an unpaid seller having a right of lien or having stopped the goods *in transitu* may resell the goods. He shall not thereafter be liable to the original buyer upon the contract to sell or the sale or for any profit made by such resale, but may recover from the buyer damages for any loss occasioned by the breach of the contract or the sale.

(2) Where a resale is made, as authorized in this section, the buyer acquires a good title as against the original buyer.

(3) It is not essential to the validity of a resale that notice of an intention to resell the goods be given by the seller to the original buyer. But where the right to resell is not based on the perishable nature of the goods or upon an express provision of the contract or the sale, the giving or failure to give such notice shall be relevant in any issue involving the question whether the buyer had been in default an unreasonable time before the resale was made.

(4) It is not essential to the validity of a resale that notice of the time and place of such resale should be given by the seller to the original buyer.

(5) The seller is bound to exercise reasonable care and judgment in making a resale, and subject to this requirement may make a resale either by public or private sale.

Rescission by the Seller

SEC. 61. *When and How the Seller May Rescind the Sale.* (1) An unpaid seller having the right of lien or having stopped the goods *in transitu,* may rescind the transfer of title and resume the property in the goods, where he expressly reserved the right to do so in case the buyer should make default, or where the buyer has been in default in the payment of the price an unreasonable time. The seller shall not thereafter be liable to the buyer upon the contract to sell or the sale, but may recover from the buyer damages for any loss occasioned by the breach of the contract or the sale.

(2) The transfer of title shall not be held to have been rescinded by an unpaid seller until he has manifested by notice to the buyer or by some other overt act an intention to rescind. It is not necessary that such overt act should be communicated to the buyer, but the giving or failure to give notice to the buyer of the intention to rescind shall be relevant in any issue involving the question whether the buyer had been in default an unreasonable time before the right of rescission was asserted.

SEC. 62. *Effect of Sale of Goods Subject to Lien or Stoppage in Transitu.* Subject to the provisions of this act, the unpaid seller's right of lien or stoppage *in transitu* is not affected by any sale, or other disposition of the goods which the buyer may have made, unless the seller has assented thereto.

If, however, a negotiable document of title has been issued for goods, no seller's lien or right of stoppage *in transitu* shall defeat the right of any purchaser for value in good faith to whom such document has been negotiated, whether such negotiations be prior or subsequent to the notification to the carrier, or other bailee who issued such document, of the seller's claim to a lien or right of stoppage *in transitu*.

PART V

Action for Breach of the Contract

REMEDIES OF THE SELLER

SEC. 63. *Action for the Price.* (1) Where, under a contract to sell or a sale, the property in the goods has passed to the buyer, and the buyer wrongfully neglects or refuses to pay for the goods according to the terms of the contract or the sale, the seller may maintain an action against him for the price of the goods.

(2) Where, under a contract to sell or a sale, the price is payable on a day certain, irrespective of delivery or of transfer of title, and the buyer wrongfully neglects or refuses to pay such price, the seller may maintain an action for the price, although the property in the goods has not passed, and the goods have not been appropriated to the contract. But it shall be a defense to such an action that the seller at any time before judgment in such action has manifested an inability to perform the contract or the sale on his part or an intention not to perform it.

(3) Although the property in the goods has not passed, if they cannot readily be resold for a reasonable price, and if the provisions of section 64 (4) are not applicable, the seller may offer to deliver the goods to the buyer, and, if the buyer refuses to receive them, may notify the buyer that the goods are thereafter held by the seller as bailee for the buyer. Thereafter the seller may treat the goods as the buyer's and may maintain an action for the price.

SEC. 64. *Action for Damages for Non-acceptance of Goods.* (1) Where the buyer wrongfully neglects or refuses to accept and pay for the goods, the seller may maintain an action against him for damages for non-acceptance.

(2) The measure of damages is the estimated loss directly and naturally resulting, in the ordinary course of events, from the buyer's breach of contract.

(3) Where there is an available market for the goods in question, the measure of damages is, in the absence of special circumstances showing proximate damage of a greater amount, the difference between the contract price and the market or current price at the time or times when the goods ought to have been accepted, or, if no time was fixed for acceptance, then at the time of the refusal to accept.

(4) If, while labor or expense of material amount are necessary on the part of the seller to enable him to fulfill his obligations under the contract to sell or the sale, the buyer repudiates the contract or the sale, or notifies the seller to proceed no further therewith, the buyer shall be liable to the seller for no greater damages than the seller would have suffered if he did nothing towards carrying out the contract or the sale after receiving notice of the buyer's repudiation or countermand. The profit the seller would have made if the

contract or the sale had been fully performed shall be considered in estimating such damages.

SEC. 65. *When Seller May Rescind Contract or Sale.* Where the goods have not been delivered to the buyer, and the buyer has repudiated the contract to sell or sale, or has manifested his inability to perform his obligations thereunder, or has committed a material breach thereof, the seller may totally rescind the contract or the sale by giving notice of his election so to do to the buyer.

Remedies of the Buyer

SEC. 66. *Action for Converting or Detaining Goods.* Where the property in the goods has passed to the buyer and the seller wrongfully neglects or refuses to deliver the goods, the buyer may maintain any action allowed by law to the owner of goods of similar kind when wrongfully converted or withheld.

SEC. 67. *Action for Failing to Deliver Goods.* (1) Where the property in the goods has not passed to the buyer, and the seller wrongfully neglects or refuses to deliver the goods, the buyer may maintain an action against the seller for damages for non-delivery.

(2) The measure of damages is the loss directly and naturally resulting in the ordinary course of events, from the seller's breach of contract.

(3) Where there is an available market for the goods in question, the measure of damages, in the absence of special circumstances showing proximate damages of a greater amount, is the difference between the contract price and the market or current price of the goods at the time or times when they ought to have been delivered, or, if no time was fixed, then at the time of the refusal to deliver.

SEC. 68. *Specific Performance.* Where the seller has broken a contract to deliver specific or ascertained goods, a court having the powers of a court of equity may, if it thinks fit, on the application of the buyer, by its judgment or decree, direct that the contract shall be performed specifically, without giving the seller the option of retaining the goods on payment of damages. The judgment or decree may be unconditional, or upon such terms and conditions as to damages, payment of the price and otherwise, as to the court may seem just.

SEC. 69. *Remedies for Breach of Warranty.* (1) Where there is a breach of warranty by the seller, the buyer may, at his election—

(a) Accept or keep the goods and set up against the seller, the breach of warranty by way of recoupment in diminution or extinction of the price;

(b) Accept or keep the goods and maintain an action against the seller for damages for the breach of warranty;

(c) Refuse to accept the goods, if the property therein has not passed, and maintain an action against the seller for damages for the breach of warranty;

(d) Rescind the contract to sell or the sale and refuse to receive the goods or if the goods have already been received, return them or offer to return them to the seller and recover the price or any part thereof which has been paid.

(2) When the buyer has claimed and been granted a remedy in any one of these ways, no other remedy can thereafter be granted.

(3) Where the goods have been delivered to the buyer, he cannot rescind the sale if he knew of the breach of warranty when he accepted the goods, or if he fails to notify the seller within a reasonable time of the election to rescind, or if he fails to return or to offer to return the goods to the seller in substantially as good condition as they were in at the time the property was transferred to the buyer. But if deterioration or injury of the goods is due to the breach of warranty, such deterioration or injury shall not prevent the buyer from returning or offering to return the goods to the seller and rescinding the sale.

(4) Where the buyer is entitled to rescind the sale and elects to do so, the buyer shall cease to be liable for the price upon returning or offering to return the goods. If the price or any part thereof has already been paid, the seller shall be liable to repay so much thereof as has been paid, concurrently with the return of the goods, or immediately after an offer to return the goods in exchange for repayment of the price.

(5) Where the buyer is entitled to rescind the sale and elects to do so, if the seller refuses to accept an offer of the buyer to return the goods, the buyer shall thereafter be deemed to hold the goods as bailee for the seller, but subject to a lien to secure the repayment of any portion of the price which has been paid, and with the remedies for the enforcement of such lien allowed to an unpaid seller by section 53.

(6) The measure of damages for breach of warranty is the loss directly and naturally resulting, in the ordinary course of events, from the breach of warranty.

(7) In the case of breach of warranty of quality, such loss, in the absence of special circumstances showing proximate damage of a greater amount, is the difference between the value of the goods at the time of delivery to the buyer and the value they would have had if they had answered to the warranty.

SEC. 70. *Interest and Special Damages.* Nothing in this act shall affect the right of the buyer or the seller to recover interest or special damages in any case where by law interest or special damages may be recoverable, or to recover money paid where the consideration for the payment of it has failed.

PART VI

INTERPRETATION

SEC. 71. *Variation of Implied Obligations.* Where any right, duty or liability would arise under a contract to sell or a sale by implication of law, it may be negatived or varied by express agreement or by the course of dealing between the parties, or by custom, if the custom be such as to bind both parties to the contract or the sale.

SEC. 72. *Rights May Be Enforced by Action.* Where any right, duty or liability is declared by this act, it may, unless otherwise by this act provided, be enforced by action.

SEC. 73. *Rule for Cases Not Provided for by This Act.* In any case not provided for in this act, the rules of law and equity, including the law merchant, and in particular the rules relating to the law of principal and agent and to the effect of fraud, misrepresentation, duress or coercion, mistake, bankruptcy, or other invalidating cause, shall continue to apply to contracts to sell and to sales of goods.

SEC. 74. *Interpretation Shall Give Effect to Purpose of Uniformity.* This act shall be so interpreted and construed, as to effectuate its general purpose to make uniform the laws of those states which enact it.

SEC. 75. *Provisions Not Applicable to Mortgages.* The provisions of this act relating to contracts to sell and to sales do not apply, unless so stated, to any transaction in the form of a contract to sell or a sale which is intended to operate by way of mortgage, pledge, charge, or other security.

SEC. 76. *Definitions.* (1) In this act, unless the context or subject matter otherwise requires—

"Action" includes counterclaim, set-off and suit in equity.

"Buyer" means a person who buys or agrees to buy goods or any legal successor in interest of such person.

"Defendant" includes a plaintiff against whom a right of set-off or counterclaim is asserted.

"Delivery" means voluntary transfer of possession from one person to another.

"Divisible contract to sell or sale" means a contract to sell or a sale in which by its terms the price for a portion or portions of the goods less than the whole is fixed or ascertainable by computation.

"Document of title to goods" includes any bill of lading, dock warrant, warehouse receipt or order for the delivery of goods, or any other document used in the ordinary course of business in the sale or transfer of goods, as proof of the possession or control of the goods, or authorizing or purporting to authorize the possessor of the document to transfer or receive, either by indorsement or by delivery, goods represented by such document.

"Fault" means wrongful act or default.

"Fungible goods" means goods of which any unit is from its nature or by mercantile usage treated as the equivalent of any other unit.

"Future goods" means goods to be manufactured or acquired by the seller after the making of the contract of sale.

"Goods" include all chattels personal other than things in action and money. The term includes emblements, industrial growing crops, and things attached to or forming part of the land which are agreed to be severed before sale or under the contract of sale.

"Order" in sections of this act relating to documents of title means an order by indorsement on the documents.

"Person" includes a corporation or partnership or two or more persons having a joint or common interest.

"Plaintiff" includes defendant asserting a right of set-off or counterclaim.

"Property" means the general property in goods, and not merely a special property.

"Purchaser" includes mortgagee and pledgee.

"Purchases" includes taking as a mortgagee or as a pledgee.

"Quality of goods" includes their state or condition.

"Sale" includes a bargain and sale as well as a sale and delivery.

"Seller" means a person who sells or agrees to sell goods, or any legal successor in interest of such person.

"Specific goods" means goods identified and agreed upon at the time a contract to sell or a sale is made.

"Value" is any consideration sufficient to support a simple contract. An antecedent or pre-existing claim, whether for money or not, constitutes value where goods or documents of title are taken either in satisfaction thereof or as security therefor.

(2) A thing is done "in good faith" within the meaning of this act when it is in fact done honestly, whether it be done negligently or not.

(3) A person is insolvent within the meaning of this act who either has ceased to pay his debts in the ordinary course of business or cannot pay his debts as they become due, whether he has committed an act of bankruptcy or not, and whether he is insolvent within the meaning of the Federal bankruptcy law or not.

(4) Goods are in a "deliverable state" within the meaning of this act when they are in such a state that the buyer would, under the contract, be bound to take delivery of them.

SEC. 76a. *Act Does Not Apply to Existing Sales or Contracts to Sell.* None of the provisions of this act shall apply to any sale, or to any contract to sell, made prior to the taking effect of this act.

SEC. 76b. *No Repeal of Uniform Warehouse Receipts Act or Uniform Bills of Lading Act.* Nothing in this act or in any repealing clause thereof shall be construed to repeal or limit any of the provisions of the Act to Make Uniform the Law of Warehouse Receipts, or of the Act to Make Uniform the Law of Bills of Lading.

SEC. 77. *Inconsistent Legislation Repealed.* All acts or parts of acts inconsistent with this act are hereby repealed except as provided in section 76b.

SEC. 78. *Time When Act Takes Effect.* This act shall take effect on the ________ day of ________ one thousand nine hundred and ________.

SEC. 79. *Name of Act.* This act may be cited as the Uniform Sales Act.

UNIFORM COMMERCIAL CODE[11]

The Uniform Commercial Code is of increasing importance to purchasing officials, as it sets the ground rules for every purchase and sale made in the United States.

Reproduction of this lengthy code is not possible in this handbook. Interested parties may wish to obtain a copy from the American Law Institute, 133 South 36th Street, Philadelphia, Pa. The following three references, however, all reproduced by permission, are included in this chapter to familiarize the purchasing profession with its implications.

[11] Applicability mentioned in Section 4, "Legal Influences in Purchasing."

1. "Purchasing Under the Uniform Commercial Code." Extracts from an article under this title specially prepared for the October 17, 1956, issue of the *NAPA Bulletin* by L. E. Treadway, member of the NAPA and the Ohio Bar, and Purchasing Agent of The Federal Glass Co., Columbus, Ohio. The text of this extract was revised slightly by L. E. Treadway in June, 1958, to update the material in anticipation of the enactment of a Uniform Commercial Code on October 1, 1958, by the State of Massachusetts.
2. "Purchasing Under Conflicting State Laws." Sequel article also by L. E. Treadway, prepared for the February 20, 1957, issue of the *NAPA Bulletin* to clarify certain questions raised by readers of the foregoing article. For the same reason mentioned in the preceding paragraph, this article was also slightly revised by L. E. Treadway in June, 1958.
3. "Pennsylvania Pioneers in Adopting Uniform Commercial Code." "From One P.A. to Another," editorial under this title in the July 17, 1956, issue of the *Journal of Commerce* by George A. Renard, then associate editor for purchasing economics.

Purchasing Under the Uniform Commercial Code

Pennsylvania adopted the Uniform Commercial Code to become effective July 1, 1954, and in so doing became the first state to accept a basic revision of commercial law which has been recommended for adoption in every state. More than four years later, Massachusetts became the second state to adopt this important legislation, but action by other states is expected to come at an accelerated rate.

The first uniform code dealing with the law of sales was promulgated by the Conference of Commissioners in 1906 and is known as the Uniform Sales Act. A total of 34 states subsequently passed the Act, some with minor variations. The Uniform Commercial Code covers a much wider area and the law of sales is only a part of this statute which is, undoubtedly, the most comprehensive codification of commercial law ever attempted.

In formulating the new Uniform Code, the central viewpoint and emphasis are on the contract and its incidents, as intended by the parties, and not questions of title. Fair play, commercial reasonableness, and the customs and usages of trade are accentuated. While it will pose many problems of interpretation and application for the courts and the legal profession, the purchasing agent can welcome this new legislation as a progressive step conforming the law closer to the practices and ethics of modern industry with which he is familiar.

The Commercial Code clearly broadens and liberalizes the rules of contract formation to fit the informal, high-speed methods of modern business. The requirements of offer and acceptance are much relaxed by provisions stating that "a contract for sale of goods may be made in any manner sufficient to show agreement." It also provides that "conduct by both parties which recognizes the existence of a contract is sufficient to establish a contract even though the moment of making the agreement cannot be determined."

Where it is clear that the parties intended to make a contract, the Uniform

Code empowers the courts to do justice by enforcing the agreement through a provision that "even though one or more terms are left open, a contract does not fail for indefiniteness if the parties intended a contract and there is a reasonably certain basis for giving an appropriate remedy."

It has been a time-honored axiom of the common law that, in order to form an enforceable contract, there must be an offer coupled with an acceptance identical in terms. Any variation in the acceptance was construed, not as an acceptance, but as a counteroffer. The Uniform Code, however, contains important modifications of this rule.

Taking a realistic view of modern business practices, section 2–207 provides "(1) A definite and seasonable expression of acceptance . . . operates as an acceptance even though it states terms additional to or different from those offered or agreed upon; (2) The additional terms are to be construed as proposals for addition to the contract and between merchants become part of the contract unless they materially alter it, or notification of objection to them has already been given or is given within a reasonable time."

The problem involved in this section is quite familiar to the professional buyer. Many times the supplier's acknowledgment comes back with much legalistic "fine print" which certainly does not agree with the order. In most jurisdictions, there is then a serious question as to whether any contract of purchase has been created. If, as often occurs, the seller proceeds with performance even though the offer and acceptance do not agree, the buyer may then be deemed to accept performance on the seller's terms.

Under the Uniform Commercial Code, however, the buyer can protect himself against modifications of his purchase order. This is achieved by use of an order form which, by its terms, has the effect of giving advance notice of objection to any modification. This feature of the code will certainly be welcomed by purchasing agents.

Purchasing Under Conflicting State Laws

Do you place orders with out-of-state suppliers? If so, which law governs when a dispute arises—those of your state or the law of the state in which your supplier is located?

Discussion in a recent article of significant changes in the law of buying and selling contained in the Uniform Commercial Code has raised questions as to whether the new rules apply when out-of-state buyers place orders with suppliers located in states which have adopted the code. Likewise, purchasing agents in these states (such as Pennsylvania and Massachusetts) need to know whether their new Commercial Code applies to purchases they make from out-of-state sources.

The answers to these questions involve a wider field of legal investigation than first impressions might indicate. The general principles of law affecting interstate purchases must be considered.

For the benefit of the purchasing agent, a single, clear rule covering out-of-state purchases would be highly desirable. Unfortunately, such a rule cannot be supplied under the present state of the law. However, a few basic principles can be outlined which may be sufficient to provide the professional buyer with "rules of thumb" for use in daily decisions affecting his out-of-state purchases. These principles must be given, however, with the caution that they are good "rules of thumb" only, and may be subject to important exceptions in specific situations.

By way of introduction, it should be made very clear that this discussion does *not* suggest that the new Uniform Commercial Code involves special hazards for the purchasing agent, or that doing business in states having the code should be avoided because of legal pitfalls. References herein to the statutes of Pennsylvania are for the sole purpose of indicating the conditions under which the courts of other states may give effect to those statutes.

The Principle of "Comity"

The rules that determine which laws govern the contract of purchase are included within a body of legal doctrines and principles which, perhaps for want of a better term, is known to the legal profession as the "conflict of laws." One of the fundamental principles of this branch of the law is that the laws of a state never apply outside its own boundaries. However, each state, through the decisions of its courts, develops a set of rules under which, in certain situations, it will voluntarily *give effect* to the laws of other states. Essentially, these situations are ones in which the transaction or event which determines the rights of the parties took place in another state.

The principle under which one state will give effect to laws of another is known as "comity." This is, in reality, a theory or method whereby justice can be done between parties by enforcing in one state a claim arising in another state.

Courts have generally held that a claim enforceable in the state in which it was created should be given effect in any jurisdiction in which the claim is asserted. This is true even though the claim would not be enforceable if created in the state where suit is brought. However, this rule is subject to the definite exception that claims will not be enforced if they are contrary to the criminal law or public policy of the state in which they are asserted. For example, gambling debts are generally not collectible even if valid at the place created.

The weight of opinion is that foreign claims should be upheld unless they are clearly and strongly contrary to public policy. A mere conflict in the rules of commercial law does not justify refusal to recognize a foreign claim. *Loucks v. Standard Oil Company of New York,* 224 N.Y. 99.

Creation of the Contract to Buy

Every purchase is, of course, a "contract" in contemplation of law, and the rules which apply to contracts under the general subject of "conflict of laws" will govern the rights and obligations of the buyer. Fortunately for the purchasing agent, the decisions of state and Federal courts on this subject have been reasonably consistent (with a few notable exceptions). As a result, there have emerged a number of well defined principles determining the laws which govern the relationship of buyers and sellers doing business across state lines.

For the purpose of determining which law governs, the entire purchasing transaction must be broken down into its various elements or stages. Beginning with issuance of the purchase order, following through to inspection or testing of materials after delivery, and ending with payment of the supplier's invoice, the laws which govern will generally depend on the place or places where various parts of the transaction are performed.

One of the leading cases on this subject is *Scudder v. Union National Bank,* 92 U.S. 406, in which the United States Supreme Court said "Matters bearing upon the execution, the interpretation, and the validity of a contract are determined by the law of the place where the contract is made. Matters connected with its performance are regulated by the law prevailing at the place of performance."

In line with the rule expressed in this decision, state courts have generally held that formation of the contract of purchase, including questions of offer and acceptance, legality of subject matter, etc., is governed by the law of the place of contracting. In law, this is often referred to as the *lex loci contractus.* For the professional buyer, therefore, it becomes important to know the rules which determine, from a legal standpoint, the place where the contract is made.

As a general rule, the place of contracting is defined as the place where the last act occurs which is necessary to make the contract binding and enforceable. In the usual situation, this means that the law of the place where the buyer's order is accepted will govern much of the transaction. From a legal point of view, most purchase orders are regarded only as offers until accepted by the principal office of the vendor. Unless he is vested with special authority, the salesman normally serves only to convey the buyer's offer (order) to his employer.

This rule, when strictly applied, sometimes results in unusual legal situations. Suppose that a Maryland buyer and a New York seller meet in Philadelphia and agree on the purchase of goods. The weight of authority would hold that the formation of the agreement is governed by the new Uniform Commercial Code of Pennsylvania, even though neither party does business in that state.

There have been cases in which a purchase was held governed by the law of Florida because the official of the supplier who accepted the order was vacationing in that state when he gave acceptance by mail, telegram, or by telephone. This, again, is an application of the rule that the contract is governed by the law of the place where the act is done which makes the contract binding.

In some instances, of course, the purchasing agent's order is an acceptance of a prior offer or proposal made by the seller. In that event, formation of the contract will be governed by the law of the state in which the buyer issues his order.

In many purchasing departments, it is routine procedure to mail a purchase order to an out-of-state supplier who immediately ships without giving the buyer a prior formal acknowledgment. This is especially true in dealing with well-established suppliers. In this situation, the supplier has, in contemplation of law, given "acceptance by performance." The place of contracting then becomes the location from which the seller makes shipment.

Referring again to possible application of the Uniform Commercial Code to purchasers outside Pennsylvania, the laws of that state may apply if shipment is made from a plant or warehouse in Pennsylvania, even though the supplier's home office may be elsewhere. The same principle should apply, of course, to shipments made from Massachusetts or any other state which has adopted the code.

The foregoing rules are the ones generally applied in determining the place of contracting. When this place has been established, the professional buyer should bear in mind that the law of that state will govern the contract of purchase with respect to:

(1) The capacity of the parties to make the purchase and sale.

(2) The formalities required in making certain kinds of sales and purchases; e.g., those which must be in writing under the so-called "statute of frauds."

(3) The rules of offer and acceptance, including the vital question of conflicting provisions between the buyer's order and the seller's acknowledgment.

(4) Legality of the subject matter of the contract, including questions of fraud.

Contrary Opinions

While the law of the place where the contract is made is usually applied to the problems just described, it should be mentioned that there are decisions in some jurisdictions to the effect that the intention of the parties will govern regardless of where the contract is made. This view is supported by logic in some situations. In the example previously given of the Maryland buyer and New York seller meeting in Philadelphia, we can readily understand the view of some courts that the intention of the parties to be governed, let us say, by the laws of New York should prevail (even though this intention was not expressed in writing).

The rule that the intent of the parties shall govern is, however, a minority view. It is open to the criticism that the parties can choose the law of any jurisdiction, however remote and unrelated, in order to justify their agreement. As one jurist put it, "The parties could elect to be governed by the law of China."

Performance of the Purchase Contract

We have seen that the law of the place where the contract is made generally governs formation of the purchase contract. With respect to performance of the contract, however, it is generally held that the law of the place of performance shall govern. In legal terminology this is referred to as the *lex loci solutionis.*

For example, in an early South Carolina decision, it was held that the measure of liability for care of cotton shipped from that state to Georgia was, after arrival in Georgia, governed by the law of the latter state. (Even though the contract was made and suit brought in South Carolina.) *Spring v. South Bound Railroad Company,* 46 S.C. 104.

The place of performance is usually defined as (1) the place specifically provided in the written contract or, failing this, (2) the place intended by the parties as inferred from the language of the contract or the circumstances of the transaction. The intent of the parties is sometimes difficult to determine and the courts must hear evidence on the facts of the entire transaction in order to fix the place of performance.

The law of the place of performance generally determines, among other questions, the following rights and obligations of buyer and seller:

(1) The manner and method of performance by the supplier.

(2) The time and place of delivery of goods or performance of services ordered by the buyer.

(3) The sufficiency of performance; e.g., whether goods meet the specifications of the buyer and comply with seller's warranties.

(4) The obligation of the buyer to pay for goods and services received and the application of the buyer's payments.

(5) Whether a breach of contract or warranty has occurred and, if so, the measure of damages for the breach.

The purchasing agent should note that the place of performance is often not the location where goods are received by the buyer. Many sales are made f.o.b. seller's plant or place of business. In that event, the seller performs in his own state when goods are delivered to a carrier for shipment to the buyer. On the other hand, the buyer's state will generally be the place of performance when goods are shipped f.o.b. buyer's plant.

Under the rules just indicated, the place of performance may be in a state in which neither the buyer nor the seller maintains his principal office. The place of performance may be where delivery is made to a branch plant, sales office, or warehouse.

Practical Solutions

As a solution to the problem of which law shall govern the contract of purchase, some purchasing agents follow the practice of inserting a specific provision in the purchase order form, stipulating that the laws of a particular state shall apply. If the order is accepted without objection by the supplier, the stipulation will generally be upheld, especially if the contract is made in the state indicated or the goods are to be shipped to that state.

If the buyer inserts a provision concerning which law is to govern his order, he should be alert to contrary provisions which may appear in the supplier's acknowledgment. Any discrepancy should be reconciled with the supplier. Otherwise, if the buyer accepts shipment without objection, he may be legally deemed to accept, as a counterproposal, the stipulation as to jurisdiction contained in the supplier's acknowledgment.

From a practical point of view, most professional buyers probably do not have frequent concern with technical rules of the conflict of laws. Recently, these questions have been highlighted by the innovations in purchasing law contained in the Uniform Commercial Code. However, the purchasing agent can derive benefit from a general knowledge of the problems involved and, thereby, recognize the need for study in particular situations before commitments are made which might involve misunderstandings with out-of-state sources of supply.

Pennsylvania Pioneers in Adopting Uniform Commercial Code

It is no secret that Philadelphia and Pittsburgh are in the top flight of candidates for leadership in the municipal modernization league. But the State of Pennsylvania, in which those cities are located, is probably better known for a transport-speeding turnpike than for its three-year-old trail blazer into the field of commercial law.

Its new model legal highway for purchases and sales is known as the Uniform Commercial Code.

Other States . . . more than 30 of them . . . operate under the Uniform Sales Act. That lower-case u.s.a. was drawn up, 50 years ago, by the Conference of Commissioners on Uniform State Laws. It was based, naturally, on the commercial, economic and legal traffic conditions of the days before automobiles.

Caveat Emptor Was Early Rule

As we get the story, the early effort to attain uniformity in the commercial laws of the several States came before purchasing rated a tuxedo; so that the early edition was infiltrated by more than a smidgen of the rural relic called *caveat emptor*—"let the buyer beware."

A free-wheeling decoding of that latin lingo leaves us with: "You should know that many peddlers slip in wooden nutmegs, and ignorance is no excuse; so when you buy and take title, you are stuck."

The nutmeg treatment went out with buggy whips, and court decisions have done quite a remodeling job on the law. With purchasing achieving management stature, the arbitration of commercial disputes became a quite common practice. In fact, the courts now generally recognize and encourage the fair and friendly arbitration procedure.

New Ground Rules Are Established

As a result, the old u.s.a. (lower case) ain't what she used to be, but some of the frayed fringes of *caveat emptor* show up now and then to slow the parade of progress. Consequently, its authors decided the old law should be debarnacled and streamlined.

From that decision came action. The Conference of Commissioners on Uniform State Laws this time, with an assist by the Philadelphia-based American Law Institute, drew up the Uniform Commercial Code, with the recommendation it be adopted by all the States.

Although the State of Pennsylvania was several laps ahead of the field in making the new Code effective July 1, 1954, that State's embrace of the Code's provisions merits a pause to look and listen.

The Code establishes new ground rules for eight common commercial transactions, with the Law of Sales only one of the major classifications.

Important? Where do you buy? He must be a rare industrial purchasing executive who does not shop now and then in Pittsburgh, Philadelphia, or other well-known spots in Pennsylvania where many prominent producers nest.

A contract to purchase generally is governed by the law of the State where the contract is made. Most purchase orders do not become binding contracts until accepted at the home office of the supplier . . . and that could well be in Pennsylvania.

On the other hand, our information indicates that the buyer may find there are advantages in doing business in Pennsylvania under the the Uniform Commercial Code; that he has nothing to fear and much in his favor. That is the conclusion of Lyle Treadway, an Ohio lawyer—purchasing executive and prominent officer of the National Association of Purchasing Agents.

Lyle likes the emancipation from an exchange of fine print, which the Code concedes by: "A contract for the sale of goods may be made in any manner sufficient to show agreement. Conduct of both parties which recognizes the existence of a contract is sufficient to establish a contract."

Industry Practices Show Many Changes

Then, get this interpretation by the American Law Institute, which puts a damper on the running rhubarbs over whose terms take the trick: "Where clauses on confirming forms sent by both parties conflict, each party must be assumed to object to a clause of the other conflicting with one on the confirmation sent by himself.

"The enforceable contract resulting is only that agreed upon plus non-conflicting terms in the confirmation."

Bet you know some Keystone State executives whose correspondence on sales terms would lead you to believe that they believe that they are still operating under the old Uniform Sales Act!

Lawyer-buyer Treadway wrote for the NAPA: "There have been great changes in the methods and practices of industry since the turn of the century when the Uniform Sales Act was formulated. I believe the purchasing executive can welcome this new legislation as a progressive step conforming the law closer to the practices and ethics of modern industry with which he is familiar.

"Fair play, commercial reasonableness and the customs and usages of trade are accentuated in the Uniform Code, with emphasis on the intentions of the parties to the contract rather than questions of title."

If that whets the information appetite of management and of teachers of management, copy of the Uniform Commercial Code costs $6, and the hefty volume is obtainable from American Law Institute, 133 South 36th Street, Philadelphia, Pa., or from West Publishing Company, St. Paul, Minn. 55102.

Since Pennsylvanians are proud of their modernization programs, buyers may find that samples of the Code's section on the Law of Sales are as easy to come by as some widely-distributed and well-known brands of cigars.

States That Have Adopted Code

Since Pennsylvania adopted the Uniform Commercial Code on July 1, 1954, twenty-eight additional states and the District of Columbia have enacted this modern code of commercial law which has been recommended for passage to every state legislature in the U.S.A. The states which have adopted the Code and the dates on which it became effective are as follows:

Alaska	January 1, 1963	Nebraska	September 1, 1965
Arkansas	December 31, 1961	New Hampshire	July 1, 1961
California	January 1, 1965	New Jersey	January 1, 1963
Connecticut	October 1, 1961	New Mexico	December 31, 1961
District of Columbia	January 1, 1965	New York	September 27, 1964
Georgia	January 1, 1964	Ohio	July 1, 1962
Illinois	July 1, 1962	Oklahoma	December 31, 1962
Indiana	July 1, 1964	Oregon	September 1, 1963
Kentucky	July 1, 1960	Pennsylvania	July 1, 1954
Maine	December 31, 1964	Rhode Island	January 2, 1962
Maryland	February 1, 1964	Tennessee	June 30, 1964
Massachusetts	October 1, 1958	Virginia	January 1, 1966
Michigan	January 1, 1964	West Virginia	July 1, 1964
Missouri	July 1, 1965	Wisconsin	July 1, 1965
Montana	January 1, 1965	Wyoming	January 1, 1962

A number of additional states, including Florida, Iowa, Kansas, Nevada, South Carolina and South Dakota, have adopted bills to study and consider the Uniform Commercial Code. It is therefore anticipated that further enactments of the Code will follow in the near future.

SUPREME COURT DECISIONS AFFECTING PURCHASING[12]

Antitrust, unfair competition, price discrimination, and similar regulatory law problems have come not only from the enactments of the laws but also from the rules enunciated by the commissions and bureaus set up for the administration and enforcement of the acts.

The antimonopoly rules are calculated to keep business from being "controlled" or manipulated by a few or by a representative organization of an industry or group, with the net result of a fixed and unfair price. The line of reasoning in these cases would seem to call for unlimited opportunities for bargaining and a search and "pushing" for lower competitive prices.

Businessmen are also concerned about the rules against price discrim-

[12] In the United States, when credits are transferred to a beneficiary in another place whether in the same country or not, the credits may be changed from one requiring payment on or before a certain date to one requiring negotiation on or before that date, and during the validity of the credit as transferred, payment or negotiation may be made at the place to which the credit has been transferred.

ination and unfair wage and hour practices. From a casual reading of the rules, one might unwisely assume that prices are set to a point where there is no need for bargaining or for a purchasing agent.

The two Supreme Court decisions that are given in full below should clearly show the need of competent legal advice in such matters.

In the "Canteen" case the purchaser was charged with the violation of knowingly receiving price discriminations in connection with its purchases of confectionery products. In 1953 the Supreme Court remanded the case after holding that the "FTC Must Prove Price Received by Buyer Was Not Justified and That Buyer Knew of Such Lack" (see *NAPA Bulletin,* vol. 24, no. 27, July 22, 1953). And from the same article: "Contrary to certain wild-eyed misinformation that this decision gave the green light to high pressure bargaining and unjustified special prices, the opinion does no more than settle the principle that (1) guilty knowledge must be shown (and not presumed), and (2) that the FTC *must* show that the price received by the buyer was an unjustified price."

Automatic Canteen Co. of America, Petitioner v. Federal Trade Commission[13]

(On Writ of Certiorari to the United States Court
of Appeals for the Seventh Court)
June 8, 1953

Mr. Justice Frankfurter delivered the opinion of the Court.

The Robinson-Patman Act, directed primarily against sellers who discriminate in favor of large buyers, includes a provision under which proceedings may be had against buyers who knowingly induce or receive discriminatory prices. That provision, Section 2 (f) of the Act, is here for construction for the first time as a result of a complaint issued by the Federal Trade Commission against petitioner, a large buyer of candy and other confectionary products for resale through 230,000-odd automatic vending machines operated in 33 States and the District of Columbia. Petitioner, incorporated in 1931, has enjoyed rapid growth and has attained, so we are told, a dominant position in the sale of confectionary products through vending machines.

The Commission introduced evidence that petitioner received, and in some instances solicited, prices it knew were as much as 33% lower than prices quoted other purchasers, but the Commission has not attempted to show that the price differentials exceeded any cost savings that sellers may have enjoyed in sales to petitioner. Petitioner moved to dismiss the complaint on the ground that the

[13] Because of the profound effect of this decision on the buyer, it is reprinted in full text. However, footnotes contained in the decision and the dissenting opinion have been omitted. Full text of the decision is reported in 346 U.S. 61, 73. S. Ct. 1017.

Commission had not made a prima facie case. This motion was denied; the Commission stated that a prima facie case of violation had been established by proof that the buyer received lower prices on like goods than other buyers, "well knowing that it was being favored over competing purchasers," under circumstances where the requisite effect on competition had been shown. The question whether the price differentials made more than due allowance for cost differentials did not need to be decided "at this stage of the proceeding." On petitioner's failure to introduce evidence, the Commission made findings that petitioner knew the prices it induced were below list prices and that it induced them without inquiry of the seller, or assurance from the seller, as to cost indifferentials which might justify the price differentials. The Commission thereupon entered a cease and desist order. 46 F.T.C. 861. On review, the Court of Appeals affirmed, holding that the Commission's prima facie case under Section 2 (f) does not require showing absence of a cost justification. 194 F.2d 433.

Section 2 (f) of the Robinson-Patman Act, roughly the counterpart, as to buyers, of sections of the Act dealing with discrimination by sellers, is a vital prohibition in the enforcement scheme of the Act. In situations where buyers may have difficulty in proving their sellers' costs, Section 2 (f) could, if the Commission's view in this case prevails, become a major reliance for simplified enforcement of the Act not only by the Commission but by plaintiffs suing for treble damages. Such enforcement, however, might readily extend beyond the prohibitions of the Act and, in doing so, help give rise to a price uniformity and rigidity in open conflict with the purposes of other antitrust legislation. We therefore thought it necessary to grant certiorari. 344 U.S. 809.

Enforcement of the Clayton Act's original declaration against price discrimination was so frustrated by inadequacies in the statutory language that Congress in 1936 enacted the sweeping amendments to that Act contained in what is known as the Robinson-Patman Act. 49 Stat. 1526, 15 U.S.C. Section 13. Chief among the inadequacies had been express exemption of price discrimination in the sales of different quantities of like goods, an exemption that was interpreted as leaving quantity-discount sellers free to grant discounts to quantity buyers that exceeded any cost savings in selling to such buyers. *Goodyear Tire and Rubber Co. v. F.T.C.*, 6 Cir., 101 F.2d 620. In an effort to tighten the restriction against price discrimination inimical to the public interest, Congress enacted two provisions bearing on the issues in this case. It made price discrimination in the sale of like goods unlawful without regard to quantity, although quantity discounts, like other price differentials, could still be justified if they made "no more than due allowance" for cost differences in sales to different buyers. Congress in addition sought to reach the large buyer, capable of exerting pressure on smaller sellers, by making it unlawful "knowingly to induce or receive a discrimination in price which is prohibited by this section."

Since precision of expression is not an outstanding characteristic of the Robinson-Patman Act, exact formulation of the issue before us is necessary to avoid inadvertent pronouncement on statutory language in one context when the same language may require separate consideration in other settings. Familiar but loose language affords too ready a temptation for comprehensive but loose construction. We therefore think it imperative in this case to confine ourselves as much as possible to what is in dispute here.

We are here asked to settle a controversy involving simply the burden of coming forward with evidence under Section 2 (f) of the Act. The record, so abundant in its instances of individual transactions that the Commission itself felt bound to animadvert on undue proliferation of the evidence by Government lawyers, may be taken as presenting varying degrees of bargaining pressure exerted by a buyer on a seller to obtain prices below those quoted other purchasers. In some instances, so the Commission found, petitioner's method was to "inform prospective suppliers of the prices and terms of sale which would be acceptable to (petitioner) without consideration or inquiry as to whether such supplier could justify such a price on a cost basis or whether it was being offered to other customers of the supplier." 46 F.T.C., at 888. A typical instance of the maximum pressure found by the Commission was a series of negotiations in which representatives of petitioner sought to explain to a prospective supplier the kind of savings he might enjoy in sales to petitioner and might make the basis of a price differential. In such instances, petitioner sometimes gave the supplier estimates of what it considered "representative" percentage savings on various costs such as freight, sales costs, packaging, and returns and allowances.

The Commission made no finding negativing the existence of cost savings or stating that whatever cost savings there were did not at least equal price differentials petitioner may have received. It did not make any findings as to petitioner's knowledge of actual cost savings of particular sellers and found only, as to knowledge, that petitioner knew what the list prices to other buyers were. Petitioner, for its part, filed offers of proof that many sellers would testify that they had never told petitioner that the price differential exceeded cost savings. An offer of proof was in turn made by the Commission as to the testimony of these sellers on cross-examination; such proof would have brought out that petitioner never inquired of its suppliers whether the price differential was in excess of cost savings, never asked for a written statement or affidavit that the price differentials did not exceed such savings, and never inquired whether the seller had made up "any exact cost figures" showing cost savings in serving petitioner.

Petitioner claims that the Commission has not, on this record, made a prima facie case of "knowing inducement of prices that made more than due allowance for cost differences," while the Commission contends that it has established a prima facie case, justifying entry of a cease and desist order where the buyer fails to introduce evidence. Before proceeding to an examination of the statutory provisions, it is desirable to consider the kind of evidence about which this dispute centers. Petitioner is saying in effect that under the Commission's view, the burden of introducing evidence as to the seller's cost savings and the buyer's knowledge thereof is put on the buyer; this burden, petitioner insists, is so difficult to meet that it would be unreasonable to construe the language Congress has used as imposing it. If so construed, the statute, petitioner contends, would create a presumption so lacking rational connection with the fact established as to violate due process.

We have been invited to consider in this connection some of the intricacies inherent in the attempt to show costs in a Robinson-Patman Act proceeding. The elusiveness of cost data, which apparently cannot be obtained from ordinary business records, is reflected in proceedings against sellers. Such proceedings make us aware of how difficult these problems are, but this record happily does not require us to examine cost problems in detail. It is sufficient to note that, whenever costs have been in issue, the Commission has not been content with accounting estimates; a study seems to be required, involving perhaps stop-watch studies of time spent by some personnel such as salesmen and truck drivers, numerical counts of invoices or bills and in some instances of the number of items or entries on such records, or other such quantitative measurement of the operation of a business. What kind of proof would be required of a buyer we do not know. The Commission argues that knowledge generally available to the buyer from published data or experience in the trade could be used by petitioner to make a reasonable showing of his sellers' costs. There was no suggestion in the Commission's opinion, however, that it would take a different attitude toward cost showings by a buyer than it has taken with respect to sellers, and "general knowledge of the trade," to use the Commission's phrase, unsupported by factual analysis has as yet been far from acceptable, and indeed has been strongly reproved by Commission accountants, as the basis for cost showings in other proceedings before the Commission.

No doubt the burden placed on petitioner to show his sellers' costs, under present Commission standards, is heavy. Added to the considerable burden that a seller himself may have in demonstrating costs is the fact that the data not only are not in the buyer's hands but are ordinarily obtainable even by the seller only after detailed investigation of the business. A subpoena of the seller's records is not likely to be adequate. It is not a question of obtaining information in the seller's hands. It is a matter of studying the seller's business afresh. Insistence on proof of costs by the buyer might thus have other implications; it would almost inevitably require a degree of cooperation between buyer and seller, as against other buyers, that may offend other antitrust policies, and it might also expose the seller's cost secrets to the prejudice of arm's-length bargaining in the future. Finally, not one but, as here, approximately 80 different sellers' costs may be in issue.

It is against this background that the present dispute arises. The legislative setting indicates congressional recognition of the need to charge buyers with a responsibility for price discrimination comparable, so far as possible, to that placed on sellers. Thus, at the least, we can be confident in reading the words in Section 2 (f), "a discrimination in price which is prohibited by this section," as a reference to the substantive prohibitions against discrimination by sellers defined elsewhere in the Act. It is therefore apparent that the discriminatory price that buyers are forbidden by Section 2 (f) to induce cannot include price differentials that are not forbidden to sellers in other sections of the Act, and, what is pertinent in this case, a buyer is not precluded from inducing a lower price based on cost differences that would provide the seller with a defense. This reading is, indeed, not seriously disputed by the parties. For we are not dealing simply with a "discrimination in price"; the "discrimination in price" in Section 2 (f) must be one "which is prohibited by this section." Even if any price differential were to be comprehended within the term "discrimination in price," Section 2 (f), which speaks of prohibited discriminations, cannot be read as declaring out of bounds price differentials within one or more of the "defenses" available to sellers, such as that the price differentials reflect cost differences, fluctuating market conditions, or bona fide attempts to meet competition, as those defenses are set out in the provisos of Sections 2 (a) and 2 (b).

This is not to say, however, that the converse follows, for Section 2 (f) does not reach all cases of buyer receipt of a prohibited discrimination in prices. It limits itself to cases of knowing receipt of such prices. The Commission seems to argue, in part, that the substantive violation occurs if the buyer knows only that the prices are lower than those offered other buyers. Such a reading not only distorts the language but would leave the word "knowingly" almost entirely without significance in Section 2 (f). A buyer with no knowledge whatsoever of facts indicating the possibility that price differences were not based on cost differences would be liable if in fact they were not. We have seen above that Section 2 (f) does not refer to all price differentials. But we do not think that price differentials, even as a matter of uncritical impression, come so often within the prohibited range of price discriminations that the language can in any way be read one way for some purposes and another in relation to the word "knowingly."

The Commission's attempts in this case to limit the word "knowingly" to a more reasonable area of prohibition are not, we think, justified by the language Congress has used. The Commission argues that Congress was attempting to reach buyers who through their own activities obtain a special price and that "knowingly to induce or receive" can be read as charging such buyers with responsibility for whatever unlawful prices result. But that argument would comprehend any buyer who engages in bargaining over price. If the Commission means buyers who exert undue pressure, the argument might find greater support in the legislative background but less in the language Congress has employed. Such a reading not only ignores the word "receive" but opens up even more entangling difficulties with interpretation of what is undue pressure.

The Commission also urges, from legislative explanation of similar language in Section 2 (a), that the word "receive" can in some way be limited to a continued and systematic receipt of lower prices that could fairly charge the recipient with knowledge of illegality. While we need not decide whether systematic receipt of prices in itself could ever be sufficient to give the buyer the requisite knowledge, we think, as the argument itself recognizes, that the inquiry must be into the buyer's knowledge of the illegality.

Not only are the arguments of the Commission unsatisfying, but we think a fairer reading of the language and of what limited legislative elucidation we have points toward a reading of Section 2 (f) making it unlawful only to induce or receive prices known to be prohibited discriminations. For Section 2(f) was explained in Congress as a provision under which a seller, by informing the buyer that a proposed discount was unlawful under the Act could discourage undue pressure from the buyer. Of course, such devices for private enforcement of the Act through fear of prosecution could equally well have been achieved by providing that the buyer would be liable if, through the seller or otherwise, he learned that the price he sought or received was lower than that accorded competitors, but we are unable, in the light of congressional policy as expressed in other antitrust legislation, to read this ambiguous language as putting the buyer at his peril whenever he engages in price bargaining. Such a reading must be rejected in view of the effect it might have on that sturdy bargaining between buyer and seller for which scope was presumably left in the areas of our economy not otherwise regulated. Although due consideration is to be accorded to administrative construction where alternative interpretation is fairly open, it is our duty to reconcile such interpretation, except where Congress has told us not to, with the broader antitrust policies that have been laid down by Congress. Even if the Commission has, by virtue of the Robinson-Patman Act, been given some authority to develop policies in conflict with those of the Sherman Act in order to meet the special problems created by price discrimination, we cannot say that the Commission here has adequately made manifest reasons for engendering such a conflict so as to enable us to accept its conclusion. Cf. *Eastern-Central Motor Carriers Ass'n v. United States,* 321 U.S. 194, 211–212.

We therefore conclude that a buyer is not liable under Section 2(f) if the lower prices he induces are either within one of the seller's defenses such as the cost justification or not known by him not to be within one of those defenses. This conclusion is of course only a necessary preliminary in this case. As we have noted earlier, the precise issue in the case before us is the burden of introducing evidence—a separate issue, though of course related to the substantive prohibition. This issue, involving as it does some of the same considerations, requires us further to consider a balance of convenience in the light of whatever evidentiary rules Congress has laid down for proceedings under the Act. Assuming, as we have found, that there is no substantive violation if the buyer did not know that the prices it induced or received were not cost-justified, we must in this case determine whether proof that the buyer knew that the price was lower is sufficient to shift the burden of introducing evidence to the buyer.

The Commission, in support of its position that it need only show the buyer's knowledge that the prices were lower, employs familiar interpretative tools without adequate regard to their immediate serviceability. It labels a seller's defense, such as the cost-justification, as an "exception to the general prohibition" and from this argues that under conventional rules of evidence the Commission need come forward with evidence of violation only of the "general prohibition." This interpretation has foundation in the many commonsensical readings of comparable prohibitions so as to put the burden of showing a justification on the one who claims its benefits. We have said as much even in connection with that part of Section 2 (b) of the Robinson-Patman Act which attempts to lay down the rules of evidence under the Act. That section provides, "Upon proof being made . . . that there has been discrimination in price . . . the burden of rebutting the prima-facie case thus made by showing justification shall be upon the person charged with a violation of this section." The Commission points out that it was under this section that we held in the Morton Salt case that the burden of showing a cost-justification is on the seller in a Section 2 (a) proceeding, and argues that the same burden is on the buyer. It argues that the "prima facie case thus made" clearly refers back to "proof (of) discrimination in price" and thus, from our decision in Morton Salt, that the prima facie case of a prohibited discrimination to which Section 2 (b) refers consists only of proof of a difference in prices in the sale of like goods having the requisite effect on competition. Saying that Section 2 (f) differs from Section 2 (a) "only in containing the express requirement that the buyer shall have 'knowingly' induced or received such price discriminations," the Commission asks us to hold that a prima facie case under Section 2 (f), is made out with a showing of the prima facie case of Section 2 (a) violation "plus the additional element of having induced or received such discrimination with knowledge of the facts which made it violative of Section 2 (a)."

We need not concern ourselves with the Commission's interpretation of the words "prima facie case thus made" in Section 2 (b) and the resulting conclusion that if Section 2 (a) and Section 2 (f) are to be read as counterparts, the elements necessary for a prima facie case under Section 2 (a) are sufficient for a prima facie showing of the "discrimination in price which is prohibited by this section" in Section 2 (f). However that may be, the Commission recognizes that there is an "additional element" resulting from the word "knowingly" in Section 2 (f), and, of course, it is that element about which the controversy here centers and to which we must address ourselves. We may, however, note in passing that consistency between Section 2 (a) and Section 2 (f) both as to what constitutes the prohibited "discrimination in price" and as to the elements of a prima facie showing of the prohibited "discrimination in price" would not be disturbed by a holding against the Commission in this case, for we are concerned here with the prima facie showing of knowledge, admittedly an independent and separate requirement of Section 2 (f) above and beyond that of Section 2 (a).

The Commission argues that a prima facie case of knowledge is made out when it is shown that the buyer knew the facts making the price differential violative of Section 2 (a). At another point it urges that it must now show only "that the buyer affirmatively contributed to obtaining the discriminatory prices by special solicitation, negotiation or other action taken by him." However the argument is phrased, the Commission is, on this record, insisting that once knowledge of a price differential is shown, the burden of introducing evidence shifts to the buyer. The Commission's main reliance in this argument is Section 2 (b), which, as we have stated above, we interpreted in the Morton Salt case as putting the burden of coming forward with evidence of a cost justification on the seller, on the one, that is, who claimed the benefits of the justification.

To this it is answered that although Section 2 (b) does speak not of the seller but of the "person charged with a violation of this section," other language in Section 2 (b) and its proviso seems directed mainly to sellers, that the legislative chronology of the various provisions ultimately resulting in the Robinson-Patman Act indicates that Section 2 (b) was drafted with sellers in mind, and that the few cases so far decided have dealt only with sellers.

A confident answer cannot be given; some answer must be given. We think we must read the infelicitous language of Section 2 (b) as enacting what we take to be its purpose, that of making it clear that ordinary rules of evidence were to apply in Robinson-Patman Act proceedings. If Section 2 (b) is to apply to Section 2 (f), although we do not decide that it does because we reach the same result without it we think it must so be read. Considerations of fairness and convenience operative in other proceedings must, we think, have been controlling in the drafting of Section 2 (b), for it would require far clearer language than we have here to reach a contrary result. Cf. *Addison v. Holly Hill Co., Fruit Products,* 322 U.S. 607, 617–618. If that is so, however, decisions striking the balance of convenience for Commission proceedings against sellers are beside the point. And we think the fact that the buyer does not have the required information, and for good reason should not be required to obtain it, has controlling importance in striking the balance in this case. This result most nearly accommodates this case to the reasons that have been given by judges and legislators for the rule of Section 2 (b), that is, that the burden of justifying a price differential ought to be on the one who "has at his peculiar command the cost and other record data by which to justify such discriminations." Where, as here, such considerations are inapplicable, we think we must disregard whatever contrary indications may be drawn from a merely literal reading of the language Congress has used. It would not give fair effect to Section 2 (b) to say that the burden of coming forward with evidence as to costs and the buyer's knowledge thereof shifts to the buyer as soon as it is shown that the buyer knew the prices differed. Certainly the Commission with its broad power of investigation and subpoena, prior to the filing of a complaint, is on a better footing to obtain this information than the buyer. Indeed, though it is of course not for us to enter the domain of the Commission's discretion in such matters, the Commission may in many instances find it not inconvenient to join the offending seller in the proceedings.

If the requirement of knowledge in Section 2 (f) has any significant function, it is to indicate that the buyer whom Congress in the main sought to reach was the one who, knowing full well that there was little likelihood of a defense for the seller, nevertheless proceeded to exert pressure for lower prices. Enforcement of the provisions of Section 2 (f) against such a buyer should not be difficult. Proof of a cost justification being what it is, too often no one can ascertain whether a price is cost-justified. But trade experience in a particular situation can afford a sufficient degree of knowledge to provide a basis for prosecution. By way of example a buyer who knows that he buys in the same quantities as his competitor and is served by the seller in the same manner or with the same amount of exertion as the other buyer can fairly be charged with notice that a substantial price differential cannot be justified. The Commission need only to show, to establish its prima facie case, that the buyer knew that the methods by which he was served and quantities in which he purchased were the same as in the case of his competitor. If the methods or quantities differ, the Commission must only show that such differences could not give rise to sufficient savings in the cost of manufacture, sale or delivery to justify the price differential, and that the buyer, knowing these were the only differences, should have known that they could not give rise to sufficient cost savings. The showing of knowledge, of course, will depend to some extent on the size of the discrepancy between cost differential and price differential, so that the two questions are not isolated. A showing that the cost differences are very small compared with the price differential and could not reasonably have been thought to justify the price difference should be sufficient.

What other circumstances can be shown to indicate knowledge on the buyer's part that the prices cannot be justified we need not now attempt to illustrate; but surely it will not be an undue administrative burden to explain why other proof may be sufficient to justify shifting the burden of introducing evidence that the buyer is or is not an unsuspecting recipient of prohibited discriminations. We think, in any event, it is for the Commission to spell out the need for imposition of such a harsh burden of introducing evidence as it appears to have sought in this case. Certainly we should have a more solid basis than an unexplained conclusion before we sanction a rule of evidence that contradicts antitrust policy and the ordinary requirements of fairness. While this Court ought scrupulously to abstain from requiring of the Commission particularization in its findings so exacting as to make this Court in effect a court of review on the facts, it is no less important, since we are charged with the duty of reviewing the correctness of the standards which the Commission applies and the essential fairness of the mode by which it reaches its conclusions, that the Commission do not shelter behind uncritical generalities or such looseness of expression as to make it essentially impossible for us to determine what really lay behind the conclusions which we are to review. Cf. *United States v. Chicago, M., St.P. & P.R.Co.,* 294 U.S. 499, 510–511.

Because of our view of the balance of convenience in these circumstances, we do not reach petitioner's claim that the Commission is in effect saying that knowledge of a difference in prices creates a presumption of knowledge that the price was unlawful, a presumption it claims would fall for lack of rational connection under *Tot v. United States,* 319 U.S. 463. Cf. *Note,* E (dmund) M. M (organ), *56 Harv. L. Rev.* 1324. It has seemed to us unnecessary in this case to speak of presumptions, and we need only call attention to the fact that in this case, as in the Tot case, we have dealt only with the burden of introducing evidence and not with the burden of persuasion, as to which different considerations may apply.

The judgment of the Court of Appeals, accordingly, is reversed as to the charges in Count II of the complaint (Count I is not before us), and the case is remanded to that court with instructions to remand it to the Federal Trade Commission for such further action as is open under this opinion.

It is so ordered.

[EDITOR'S NOTE: On January 12, 1955, the Federal Trade Commission issued an order dismissing Count II of the original complaint.]

Federal Trade Commission v. Cement Institute et al.

Excerpts from the Supreme Court Decision

In the Supreme Court of the United States, Nos. 23–34 October Term, 1947. Decided April 26, 1948, 333 U.S. 683.

Mr. Justice Black delivered the opinion of the court.

We granted certiorari to review the decree of the Circuit Court of Appeals which, with one judge dissenting, vacated and set aside a cease and desist order issued by the Federal Trade Commission against the respondents. 157 F.2d 533. Those respondents are: The Cement Institute, an unincorporated trade association composed of 74 corporations which manufacture, sell and distribute cement; the 74 corporate members of the Institute, and 21 individuals who are associated with the Institute. It took three years for a trial examiner to hear the evidence which consists of about 49,000 pages of oral testimony and 50,000 pages of exhibits. Even the findings and conclusions of the Commission cover 176 pages. The briefs with accompanying appendixes submitted by the parties contain more than 4,000 pages. The legal questions raised by the Commission and by the different respondents are many and varied. Some contentions are urged by all respondents and can be jointly considered. Others require separate treatment. In order to keep our opinion within reasonable limits, we must restrict our record references to the minimum consistent with an adequate consideration of the legal questions we discuss.

The proceedings were begun by a Commission complaint of two counts. The first charged that certain alleged conduct set out at length constituted an unfair method of competition in violation of Sec. 5 of the Federal Trade Commission Act. 38 Stat. 719, 15 U.S.C. Sec. 45. The core of the charge was that the respondents had restrained and hindered competition in the sale and distribution of cement by means of a combination among themselves made effective through mutual understanding or agreement to employ a multiple basing point system of pricing. It was alleged that this system resulted in the quotation of identical terms of sale and identical prices for cement by the respondents at any given point in the United States. This system had worked so successfully, it was further charged, that for many years prior to the filing of the complaint, all cement buyers throughout the nation, with rare exceptions, had been unable to purchase cement for delivery in any given locality from any one of the respondents at a lower price or on more favorable terms than from any of the other respondents.

The second count of the complaint, resting chiefly on the same allegations of fact set out in Count I, charged that the multiple basing point system of sales resulted in systematic price discriminations between the customers of each respondent. These discriminations were made, it was alleged, with the purpose of destroying competition in price between the various respondents in violation of Section 2 of the Clayton Act, 38 Stat. 730, as amended by the Robinson-Patman Act, 49 Stat. 1526. That section, with certain conditions which need not here be set out, makes it "unlawful for any person engaged in commerce, . . . either directly or indirectly, to discriminate in price between different purchases of commodities of like grade and quality. . . ." 15 U.S.C. Sec. 13.

Resting upon its findings, the Commission ordered that respondents cease and desist from "carrying out any planned common course of action, understanding, agreement, combination, or conspiracy" to do a number of things, 37 F.T.C. 97, 258–262, all of which things, the Commission argues, had to be restrained in order effectively to restore individual freedom of action among the separate units in the cement industry. Certain contentions with reference to the order will later require a more detailed discussion of its terms. For the present it is sufficient to say that, if the order stands, its terms are broad enough to bar respondents from acting in concert to sell cement on a basing point delivered price plan which so eliminates competition that respondents' prices are always identical at any given point in the United States.

UNFAIR METHODS OF COMPETITION

We sustain the Commission's holding that concerted maintenance of the basing point delivered price system is an unfair method of competition prohibited by the Federal Trade Commission Act. In so doing we give great weight to the Commission's conclusions, as this Court has done in other cases. *Federal Trade Commission v. R. F. Keppel and Bro.*, 291 U.S. 304, 314; *Federal Trade Commission v. Pacific States Paper Trade Ass'n,* 273 U.S. 52, 63. In the Keppel case the Court called attention to the express intention of Congress to create an agency whose membership would at all times be experienced, so that its conclusions would be the result of an expertness coming from experience. We are persuaded that the Commission's long and close examination of the questions it here decided has provided it with precisely the experience that fits it for performance of its statutory duty. The kind of specialized knowledge Congress wanted its agency to have was an expertness that would fit it to stop at the threshold every unfair trade practice—that kind of practice, which if left alone, "destroys competition and establishes monopoly." *Federal Trade Commission v. Raladam Co.,* 283 U.S. 643, 647, 650. And see *Federal Trade Commission v. Raladam Co.,* 316 U.S. 149, 152.

We cannot say that the Commission is wrong in concluding that the delivered price system as here used provides an effective instrument which, if left free for use of the respondents, would result in complete destruction of competition and the establishment of monopoly in the cement industry. That the basing point price system may lend itself to industry-wide anti-competitive practices is illustrated in the following among other cases: *United States v. United States Gypsum Co., et al.,* 333 U.S. 364; *Sugar Institute v. United States,* 297 U.S. 553. We uphold the Commission's conclusion that the basing point delivered price system employed by respondents is an unfair trade practice which the Trade Commission may suppress. ([footnote] While we hold that the Commission's findings of combination were supported by evidence, that does not mean that existence of a "combination" is an indispensable ingredient of an "unfair method of competition" under the Trade Commission Act. See *Federal Trade Commission v. Beech-Nut Packing Co.,* 257 U.S. 441,455.)

THE PRICE DISCRIMINATION CHARGE IN COUNT TWO

The Commission found that respondents' combination to use the multiple basing point delivered price system had effected systematic price discrimination in violation of Section 2 of the Clayton Act as amended by the Robinson-Patman Act, 49 Stat. 1526, 15 U.S.C. Sec. 13. Section 2 (a) of that Act declares it to "be unlawful for any person engaged in commerce . . . either directly or indirectly, to discriminate in price between different purchasers of commodities of like grade and quality . . . where the effect of such discrimination may be substantially to lessen competition or tend to create a monopoly in any line of commerce, or to injure, destroy, or prevent competition with any person who either grants or knowingly receives the benefit of such discrimination, or with customers of either of them. . . ." Section 2 (b) provides that proof of discrimination in price (selling the same kind of goods cheaper to one purchaser than to another), makes out a prima facie case of violation, but permits the seller to rebut "the prima facie case thus made by showing that his lower price . . . was made in good faith to meet an equally low price of a competitor. . . ."

The Commission held that the varying mill nets received by respondents on sales between customers in different localities constituted a "discrimination in price between different purchasers" within the prohibition of Sec. 2 (a), and that the effect of this discrimination was the substantial lessening of competition between respondents. The Circuit Court of Appeals reversed the Commission on this count. It agreed that respondent's prices were unlawful insofar as they involved the collection of phantom freight, but it held that prices involving only freight absorption came within the "good faith" proviso of Section 2 (b).

The respondents contend that the differences in their net returns from sales in different localities which result from use of the multiple basing point delivered price system are not price discriminations within the meaning of Sec. 2 (a). If held that these net return differences are price discriminations prohibited by Section 2 (a), they contend that the discriminations were justified under Section 2 (b) because "made in good faith to meet an equally low price of a competitor." Practically all the arguments presented by respondents in support of their contentions were considered by this Court and rejected in 1945 in *Corn Products Co. v. Federal Trade Commission,* 324 U.S. 726, and in the related case of *Federal Trade Commission v. A. E. Staley Mfg. Co.,* 324 U.S. 746. As stated in the Corn Products opinion at page 730, certiorari was granted in those two cases because the "questions involved" were "of importance in the administration of the Clayton Act in view of the widespread use of basing point price systems." For this reason the questions there raised were given thorough consideration. Consequently, we see no reason for again reviewing the questions that were there decided.

In the Corn Products case the Court, in holding illegal a single basing point system, specifically reserved decision upon the legality under the Clayton Act of a multiple basing point price system, but only in view of the "good faith" proviso of Section 2 (b), and referred at that point to the companion Staley opinion, 324 U.S. at page 735. The latter case held that a seller could not justify the adoption of a competitor's basing point price system under Sec. 2 (b) as a good faith attempt to meet the latter's equally low price. Thus the combined effect of the two cases was to forbid the adoption for sales purposes of any basing point pricing system. It is true that the Commission's complaint in the Corn Products and Staley cases simply charged the individual respondents with discrimination in price through use of a basing point price system, and did not, as here, allege a conspiracy or combination to use that system. But the holdings in those two cases that Section 2 forbids a basing point price system are equally controlling here, where the use of such a system is found to have been the result of a combination. Respondents deny, however, that the Corn Products and Staley cases passed on the questions they here urge.

Corn Products Co. was engaged in the manufacture and sale of glucose. It had two plants, one in Chicago, one in Kansas City. Both plants sold "only at delivered prices, computed by adding to a base price at Chicago the published freight tariff from Chicago to the several points of delivery, even though deliveries are in fact made from their factory at Kansas City as well as from their Chicago factory," 324 U.S. at page 729. This price system we held resulted in Corn Products Co. receiving from different purchasers different net amounts corresponding to differences in the amounts of phantom freight collected or of actual freight charges absorbed. We further held that "price discriminations are necessarily involved where the price basing point is distant from the point of production," because in such situations prices "usually include an item of unearned or phantom freight or require the absorption of freight with the consequent variations in the seller's net factory prices. Since such freight differentials bear no relation to the actual cost of delivery, they are systematic discriminations prohibited by Section 2 (a) whenever they have the defined effect upon competition." *Federal Trade Commission v. A. E. Staley Mfg. Co.,* 324 U.S. 746, at pages 750–751. This was a direct holding that a pricing system involving both phantom freight and freight absorption violates Sec. 2 (a) if under that system prices are computed for products actually shipped from one locality on the fiction that they were shipped from another. This Court made the holding despite arguments, which are now repeated here, that in passing the Robinson-Patman Act, Congress manifested its purpose to sanction such pricing systems; that this Court had approved the system in *Maple Flooring Mfgrs'. Ass'n v. United States,* 268 U.S. 563 and in *Cement Mfgr's. Ass'n v. United States,* 268 U.S. 588; and that there was no discrimination under this system between buyers at the same point of delivery.

Respondents attempt to distinguish their multiple basing point pricing system from those previously held unlawful by pointing out that in some situations their system involves neither phantom freight nor freight absorption, and that is correct; for example, sales by a base mill at its base price plus actual freight from the mill to the point of delivery involve neither phantom freight nor freight absorption. But the Corn Products pricing system which was condemned by this Court related to a base mill, that at Chicago, as well as to a non-base mill, at Kansas City. The Court did not permit this fact to relieve the pricing system from application of Section 2, or to require any modification of the Commission's order. So here, we could not require the Commission to attempt to distinguish between sales made by a base mill involving actual freight costs and all other sales made by both base and non-base mills, when all mills adhere to a common pricing system.

Section 2 (b) permits a single company to sell to one customer at a lower price than it sells to another if the price is "made in good faith to meet an equally low price of a competitor." But this does not mean that Section 2 (b) permits a seller to use a sales system which constantly results in his getting more money for like goods from some customers than he does from others. We held to the contrary in the Staley case. There we said that the Act "speaks only of the seller's 'lower' price and of that only to the extent that it is made 'in good faith to meet an equally low price of a competitor.' The Act thus places emphasis on individual competitive situations, rather than upon a general system of competition." *Federal Trade Commission v. A. E. Staley Mfg. Co.,* 324 U.S. 746, at page 753. Each of the respondents, whether all its mills were basing points or not, sold some cement at prices determined by the basing point formula and governed by other base mills. Thus, all respondents to this extent adopted a discriminatory pricing system condemned by Section 2. As this in itself was evidence of the employment of the multiple basing point system by the respondents as a practice rather than as a good faith effort to meet "individual competitive situations," we think the Federal Trade Commission correctly concluded that the use of this cement basing point system violated the Act. Nor can we discern under these circumstances any distinction between the "good faith" proviso as applied to a situation involving only phantom freight and one involving only freight absorption. Neither comes within its terms.

We hold that the Commission properly concluded that respondents' pricing system results in price discriminations. Its finding that the discriminations substantially lessen competition between respondents and that they were not made in good faith to meet a competitor's price are supported by evidence. Accordingly, the Commission was justified in issuing a cease and desist order against a continuation of the unlawful discriminatory pricing system.

Many other arguments have been presented by respondents. All have been examined, but we find them without merit.

The Commission's order should not have been set aside by the Circuit Court of Appeals. Its judgment is reversed and the cause is remanded to that Court with directions to enforce the order.

It is so ordered.

Mr. Justice Jackson and Mr. Justice Douglas took no part in the consideration or decision of these cases.
Mr. Justice Burton wrote the dissenting opinion.

Many years have passed since these decisions were given. Those interested should ask an attorney for any changes, cases, or new opinions in relation thereto.

Arbitration (Sections 5 and 17)

Resolving Disputes by Arbitration[14]

Businessmen want to *do* business, not argue about it.

But in the world of trade and commerce, disputes are inevitable. One person may understand his rights and obligations differently from another no matter how carefully a contract is written. This may lead to delayed shipments, complaints about quality of merchandise, claims of non-performance of contracts, and similar misunderstandings. And even with the best of intentions parties often perform less than they promise.

These controversies seldom involve great legal issues. On the contrary, they concern the same evaluation of facts and interpretation of contract terms that businessmen and their attorneys are accustomed to deal with every day. Consequently, when differences arise out of day-to-day commercial affairs parties often prefer to settle them privately and informally, in the kind of businesslike way that encourages continued business relationships. That is what commercial arbitration is for.

Arbitration is the reference of a dispute to one or more impartial persons for final and binding determination. It is private and informal, designed for quick, practical and inexpensive settlements. But at the same time arbitration is an *orderly* proceeding, governed by rules of procedure and standards of conduct prescribed by law. This is so especially where proceedings are administered by an impartial agency dedicated exclusively to arbitration. Such an agency is the American Arbitration Association.

The above four paragraphs were taken from a booklet entitled *A Businessman's Guide to Commercial Arbitration.* Published by the American Arbitration Association, it describes very briefly the basis for existence of the AAA.

Solution of business disputes by litigation can be costly both in time and in dollars. The advantages of arbitration as an alternative can best be illustrated by the fact that the number of cases solved by this method climbed from 3,988 cases in 1960 to approximately 9,000 cases in 1963.

[14] Reproduced by permission of AAA.

Process for Arbitration

The AAA maintains a National Panel of Arbitrators numbering some 13,000 men and women in 1,600 communities of the United States. These panel members are screened for knowledge of their field and reputation, and they serve without compensation, as a service to the business community. The process has four steps.

THE FIRST STEP—THE AGREEMENT TO ARBITRATE

In some contracts the agreement to arbitrate is written in when the contract is first prepared. In this case, arbitration is automatic in case of a dispute arising out of performance of the contract.

Where there is no previous agreement, a demand for arbitration may be made by an offended party and the process is started if the second party is agreeable to this method of settlement.

Contact with the AAA is made at this point and a tribunal clerk is appointed to coordinate the case.

THE SECOND STEP—SELECTION OF AN ARBITRATOR

Names of arbitrators are provided by the AAA and an agreement is reached by the parties involved on a mutually satisfactory arbitrator. If agreement cannot be reached, the AAA appoints an arbitrator.

THE THIRD STEP—PREPARATION FOR THE HEARING

Each side prepares its evidence and witnesses.

THE FOURTH STEP—PRESENTATION OF THE CASE

Each side presents its case to the arbitrator with or without counsel, similar to a court presentation except that emphasis is on informality.

An award is made within 30 days and is binding upon both parties unless the case is reopened by mutual consent of both parties.

Administrative Fee Schedule[15]

The administrative fee of the AAA is based upon the amount of each claim as disclosed when the claim is filed, and is due and payable at the time of filing.

Amount of Claim	***Fee***
Up to \$10,000	3% (minimum \$50)
\$ 10,000 to \$ 25,000	\$ 300, plus 2% of excess over \$ 10,000
\$ 25,000 to \$100,000	\$ 600, plus 1% of excess over \$ 25,000
\$100,000 to \$200,000	\$1350, plus ½% of excess over \$100,000

[15] Reproduced by permission of AAA.

The fee for claims in excess of $200,000 should be discussed with the AAA in advance of filing.

When no amount can be stated at the time of filing, the administrative fee is $200, subject to adjustment in accordance with the above schedule if an amount is subsequently disclosed.

Fees are charged to cover secretarial and administrative costs only.

AAA has tribunals in the fields of commerce, labor, international, inter-American, and accident-claims arbitration.

A number of variations in the above process are available, and further information may be obtained by writing the American Arbitration Association, 140 West 51st Street, New York, N.Y. 10019.

Available sources of conciliators and arbitrators and of recognized rules and procedures for *international* trade are listed in Section 17, "Purchasing Internationally."

Credit Reports (Section 7)

Credit reports serve purchasing in creatively and constructively telling an impartial and sometimes eloquent story on current and potential vendors. They provide a check on the basic financial structure of suppliers and thus constitute a most valuable tool for purchasing men and women in their choice of new vendors or their retention of old ones. Such reports are available from various agencies, one of which is Dun & Bradstreet, Inc., with headquarter offices at 99 Church Street, New York, N.Y. 10008.

Figures 28–1 to 28–4 illustrate such an analytical report on the Bristol Candy Corporation, a fictitious firm. This report covers four basic areas of information, each of which has its own and special use to a buyer. The key elements of the credit reports, and uses buyers make of them, follow:

1. *Trade.* This section of the credit report shows how the supplier pays his bills. If a supplier is soundly financed and pays his bills according to terms, it is reasonable to assume he can get the materials he needs when he needs them. On the other hand, often the first sign of approaching difficulty is the inability to meet bills as they fall due. If the trend is toward tardiness, the possibility arises that the supplier will be unable to get prompt shipment of materials he needs to meet delivery schedules.
2. *Financial Information.* This section of the report usually shows a recent financial statement, the sales volume, and a summary of recent trends. From this section of the report the buyer can tell which suppliers have capital enough to handle his requirements, information which can be just as important as knowing whether the equipment at their disposal

Dun & Bradstreet ANALYTICAL Report

20 71 — 123-4567 — A- AD 4 AUG 18 19 - N

BRISTOL CANDY CORP — MFG

100 EDGELY RD
BRISTOL 3 PA — TEL215-000-0000

1930 — B+ 1
See History — Formerly B 1

TRADE DISC-PPT
SALES $1,106,165
WORTH $719,008
EMPLS 135

SUMMARY

LAST MARCH THE PLANT WAS EXPANDED GREATLY TO INCREASE PRODUCTION AND LOWER COSTS. CURRENT FIGURES SHOW THE INITIAL RESULTS. SALES ARE UP ABOUT 40% AND EARNINGS ARE UP EVEN MORE. THE FINANCIAL POSITION CONTINUES STRONG.

TRADE

Sugar, the basic raw material used, is purchased on a sight draft basis under annual contract with one broker. Such drafts have been honored on presentation. Other raw materials, such as cocoa, flavorings, nut meats, and packaging materials are purchased from seven suppliers. Recent experiences of the principal suppliers follow:

HC	OWE	P DUE	TERMS	Aug 12 19 -	SOLD
30000	3450		2-10-30	Disc	Over 3 yrs
25000			2-10-30	Disc	Over 3 yrs
5555			2-10	Disc	Over 3 yrs
5399			2-10-31	Disc	
5000			2-10	Disc	2 yrs
4939	264		2-10-30	Disc	Over 3 yrs
3000			2-10-30	Disc	Over 3 yrs
658			2-10	Disc	
Req			Sight Draft	Ppt	Over 3 yrs

BANKING

An account is maintained at a local bank. Balances average in medium to high five figures. In 19 -, a five year, unsecured term loan of $150,000 was granted and is payable $12,500 semi-annually for six years. A low six figure line of short term, unsecured bank credit which is available has not been used in recent years.

CURRENT

On August 14, 196-, Henry T. Conroy, Secretary and Treasurer, stated that the uptrend in sales and earnings is continuing with unit volume well ahead of last year. He furnished a copy of the June 30, 196- auditor's report from which the balance sheet and income statement are quoted in the CD section of this report.
8-18-- (803 49)

PLEASE NOTE WHETHER NAME, BUSINESS AND STREET ADDRESS CORRESPOND WITH YOUR INQUIRY.
This report is furnished by DUN & BRADSTREET, Inc. in STRICT CONFIDENCE at your request under your subscription agreement for your exclusive use as an aid in determining the advisability of granting credit or insurance, and for no other purpose. DUN & BRADSTREET, Inc. does not guarantee the correctness of this report and shall not be liable for any loss or injury caused by the neglect or other act or failure to act on the part of said company and/or its agents in procuring, collecting or communicating any information. 9R4-3 (1-63)

FIG. 28–1. Example of credit report. (*Reproduced by permission of Dun and Bradstreet, Inc., New York.*)

can effectively handle the necessary volume. This section is an important factor in assigning the credit rating.

3. *History*. The history section of the report describes the background of the business. When it was started, by whom, starting capital, authorized and paid-in capital, when present management assumed control, and any other pertinent facts are all outlined. This section also describes the previous experience of the owner, partners, officers, and directors. When a buyer plans to enter into what he hopes will be a long-term, continuing arrangement, or if he plans to buy equipment that will be around a long time, a record of stability in management puts added meaning into his supplier's guarantee to ship. The history section also lists outside business interests of partners or officers, and subsidiary and

BRISTOL CANDY CORP
BRISTOL 3 PA

A CD Page I

Figures were prepared from annual financial reports of the auditors, James Wheaton & Co., CPA, Philadelphia, Pa.

FINANCIAL STATEMENTS

	Jun 30 19 -	Jun 30 19 -	Jun 30 19 -
CASH	$ 78,171	$ 72,913	$ 87,486
MARKETABLE SECURITIES	36,710	70,126	-
NOTES RECEIVABLE			
ACCOUNTS RECEIVABLE	38,040	29,584	68,640
INVENTORY	58,053	71,874	138,442
.....			
OTHER CURRENT ASSETS			
TOTAL CURRENT ASSETS	210,975	244,499	294,570
FIXED ASSETS	31,232	28,549	253,755
INVESTMENTS			
PREPAID – DEFERRED	2,036	1,947	6,496
.....			
OTHER ASSETS	4,154	5,047	6,416
TOTAL ASSETS	248,398	280,043	561,237
DUE BANKS	-	-	25,000
NOTES PAYABLE			
ACCOUNTS PAYABLE	20,179	9,802	10,654
ACCRUALS	18,049	12,816	8,635
TAXES (Except Federal Income)			
FEDERAL INCOME TAXES	30,395	38,712	79,131
LONG TERM LIABILITIES (Current)			
.....			
OTHER CURRENT LIABILITIES			
TOTAL CURRENT LIABILITIES	68,624	61,331	123,420
LONG TERM LIABILITIES	-	-	125,000
.....			
RESERVES			
PREFERRED STOCK			
COMMON STOCK	150,000	150,000	150,000
CAPITAL SURPLUS			
EARNED SURPLUS	29,774	68,712	162,817
NET WORTH (Prop or Part)			
TOTAL LIABILITIES	248,398	280,043	561,237
NET WORKING CAPITAL	142,350	183,168	171,150
CURRENT RATIO	3.07	3.98	2.38
TANGIBLE NET WORTH	179,774	218,712	312.817
IF USED: D=DEFICIT, L=LOSS			

Inventory valued at lower of cost or market. Accounts receivable are less reserves of $3,106. Fixed assets are less reserves of $31,612. Full fire insurance carried on inventory and fixed assets under reporting policy. No contingent liabilities reported.
8-18- -

(CONTINUED)

FIG. 28–2. Example of credit report. (*Reproduced by permission of Dun and Bradstreet, Inc., New York.*)

affiliated companies of a corporation. Knowledge of such relationships can forestall collusion on competitive bidding.

4. *Operation-Location.* This section of a Dun & Bradstreet report is the one the buyer probably scrutinizes most closely. It lists the physical facilities of the business, including size and location of plants and warehouses; proximity to transportation facilities such as rail sidings and docks; machinery and equipment, in instances when considerable volume is under contract or made to individual specifications; number of employees; active seasons; and usual selling terms. In addition, other aspects of the business needed for a complete understanding of the company's operations are included.

BRISTOL CANDY CORP
BRISTOL 3 PA

A CD Page 2

INCOME STATEMENTS AND SURPLUS OR NET WORTH RECONCILIATIONS

FOR THE YEARS ENDED	Jun 30 19 -	Jun 30 19 -	Jun 30 19 -
NET SALES	$ 720,198	$ 771,035	$ 1,106,165
COST OF GOODS SOLD	510,639	521,015	719,008
GROSS PROFIT	209,559	250,020	387,157
EXPENSES	114,526	116,872	143,432
DEPRECIATION	1,242	1,019	5,122
NET INCOME ON SALES	93,791	142,129	238,633
OTHER INCOME			
OTHER EXPENSES			
FEDERAL INCOME TAXES	49,017	73,191	114,528
OTHER TAXES			
FINAL NET INCOME	44,774	68,938	124,105
SURPLUS—NET WORTH—START	-	29,774	68,712
ADD: NET INCOME	44,774	68,938	124,105
ADJUSTMENTS			
DEDUCT: NET LOSS			
ADJUSTMENTS			
DIVIDENDS-WITHDRAWALS	15,000	30,000	30,000
SURPLUS—NET WORTH – END	29,774	68,712	162,817
IF USED: D=DEFICIT, L=LOSS			

ANALYSIS Annual sales volume has been at a high level since formation of this corporation. Net profits were correspondingly high and, except for moderate dividends, were retained and invested in Government Bonds to finance a plan of plant modernization and expansion. Construction under this plan of fixed asset expansion was started early in the last fiscal year and completed in March. The cost of approximately $250,000 was financed with an unsecured term bank loan of $150,000 and liquidation of Government Bonds. The term bank loan is payable $12,500 semi-annually for six years.

Net sales were 43% larger in the last fiscal year. This increase in the dollar volume resulted from both a 25% price increase in August, following a rise in raw material and labor costs, and increased unit sales subsequent to March. Net profit also was higher as a result of the sales expansion and lower unit production costs subsequent to March, when the plant and manufacturing improvements were completed.

In prior years, seasonal use was made of unsecured bank loans up to $100,000. There has been no recourse to this type of financing during the last three years as inventories were turned rapidly and the collection experience was excellent. Financial position at the last fiscal closing was sound. Compared to net sales of that period inventory comprised primarily of raw materials was equivalent to 45 days sales while accounts receivable were equivalent to 22 days sales.
8-18- -

(CONTINUED)

FIG. 28–3. Example of credit report. (*Reproduced by permission of Dun and Bradstreet, Inc., New York.*)

Purchasing uses credit reports on suppliers to establish:

1. Experience and capability of new suppliers
2. Background of "ups" and "downs" of established suppliers; changes in their performance and the reasons
3. Continuity at times of management or ownership change
4. Fiscal integrity, financial soundness, promptness in meeting obligations
5. Character of management people and their individual experience

In summary, credit reports provide the facts which the buyer, as well as the credit manager or sales manager, needs in making decisions. No man likes to step into the dark. When a buyer sees where his goods are coming from and knows something about the vendor, he can make prompt buying decisions with confidence.

```
            BRISTOL CANDY CORP                                        A CD Page 3
            100 EDGELY RD
            BRISTOL 3 PA

MANAGEMENT  Chester G. Hoover, Pres                        F. Charles Young, V Pres
            Henry T. Conroy, Sec-Treas
            DIRECTORS: The Officers with Mrs. Mary S. Lawrence.

HISTORY     Started: October 1930 by F. Bradford Lawrence, who died in March 1960.
            Under the provisions of his will, the three key employees were bequeathed
a 50% interest in the business and the subject corporation was formed to carry out
this provision.

Incorporated: Pennsylvania June 29, 1960.
Authorized Capital Stock: 250,000 shares Common $1.00 par value.
Outstanding Capital Stock: 150,000 shares. Mary S. Lawrence, the widow of F. Bradford
Lawrence, the founder, owns 50% of the outstanding capital stock. The remainder is
owned by Chester G. Hoover (25%), Henry T. Conroy (15%), and F. Charles Young (10%).
Life insurance of $25,000 is carried on each officer with the corporation as benefici-
ary.

Chester G. Hoover, born 1900, married. Employed sales department, Federal Biscuit
Company, Philadelphia, 1927-1937. Since associated with this business as General Sales
Manager to June 1960 when he was elected President and General Manager. He is the
chief executive officer.

Henry T. Conroy, born 1917, married. Cashier of Fidelity Trust Company, Baltimore,
1938-1951. Then employed as Office Manager of this business to 1960 when he was
elected Secretary and Treasurer.

F. Charles Young, born 1912, married, was employed in the plant from 1937 to 1942 when
he became Plant Superintendent. Elected Vice President in June 1960.

Mrs. Mary S. Lawrence takes no active part in the management.

OPERATION    Products: Manufactures packaged confections, including chocolates, hard
             candies and novelty sweets. Seventy-five percent of the volume is in choc-
olates which retail from $1.25 to $2.50 a pound. Brand Name: "Honey Crunch".

Distribution: To retail candy (35%), chain (25%), drug (20%), grocery (10%) and depart-
ment stores (10%).
Accounts: 2,000 active.
Terms of Sale: 2%-15-Net 30.
Territory: The Eastern Seaboard from Maine to Florida.
Seasons: Sales are highest in November and December (40%).
Salesmen: 10 on salary and commission.
Employees: 125

Facilities: Owns and fully occupies a three-story brick building, sprinkler equipped,
comprising 50,000 square feet of floor space. Also an adjacent two-story brick build-
ing which formerly housed the plant but is now used for warehousing. The buildings,
machinery and equipment are in excellent condition.
8-18-- -  (803 49)
```

FIG. 28–4. Example of credit report. (*Reproduced by permission of Dun and Bradstreet, Inc., New York.*)

Quality Control (Section 8)

PROCEDURE FOR INITIATING AND CONCLUDING TRIALS OR TESTS OF MATERIALS OR EQUIPMENT

(Example of One Company's Written Procedure)

This procedure outlines the handling for trials or tests of material or equipment and the dissemination of the results of these tests to interested parties. Its main objective is to help select vendors as outlined on page 8–3 of Section 8, "Quality: The Major Assignment."

Since even the simplest trial or test is expensive, extreme care must be taken to screen all material and equipment before submitting a request. Bear in mind that trials and tests must be limited to materials and equipment which show definite promise of future savings, operating advantages, or improved efficiency.

It is not the desire of this company to be a general proving ground for various manufacturers or vendors.

Further, when tests are initiated, a definite effort should be made to include other acceptable competitive makes. This will eliminate the need of soon repeating the test of those competitive materials.

METHOD OF INITIATION

A trial or test may be initiated or recommended by any operating or staff supervisor of this company in accordance with departmental policy. The originator shall prepare the form shown by Fig. 28–5, "Proposed Material Test," in quadruplicate. The original and two copies are to be sent to the manager of purchases. The quadruplicate copy is to be retained by the originator.

FORM HANDLING

The purchasing department will review the request, assign a test number, attach pertinent information from its files, and will return, with suggestions and comments, one copy to the local purchasing office and the original copy to the originator's department head or his designated representative. The third copy will be retained in the purchasing department test files. The department head will forward the file to the originator with his further instructions.

PROCUREMENT OF MATERIAL OR EQUIPMENT

A requisition and a purchase order must be issued whether or not there is to be a charge for the material or equipment. The items to be tested are to be ordered by standard requisitioning procedures with the following additions:

1. The requisition must be clearly marked "For Trial" or "For Test."
2. The requisition must refer to the test number assigned on Fig. 28–5, "Proposed Material Test."

Upon receiving the requisition, the purchasing department will issue the proper purchase order, showing reference to the assigned test number. Copies of the purchase order will be made for the manager of purchases and the originator.

All details of the transaction must be clearly shown on the order, and the material must be delivered through normal channels so that proper receiving records can be maintained.

The purchase order will be issued in the usual manner. One of the following clauses must appear on the purchase order:

1. On Trial/Test for a ________ period. If not proved satisfactory in our estimation, the material can be returned for full credit.
2. On Trial/Test for a ________ period. Not to be paid for unless proved satisfactory in our estimation. Invoice to be approved by ______________________ before payment.
3. On Trial/Test for an estimated ________ period. The company is not obligated to purchase regardless of outcome of said Trial/Test.

1. ORIGINATOR (Complete section 1 in quadruplicate; and forward original and 2 copies to manager of purchases)

NAME________ DATE________

DEPARTMENT________ LOCATION________

COMPLETE DESCRIPTION OF MATERIAL OR EQUIPMENT TO BE TESTED________

MANUFACTURERS________

SUGGESTED VENDORS________

TEST CONDITIONS (explain in detail)________

SPECIFIC LOCATION OF TEST________

SPECIFIC SERVICE________

REASON FOR TEST (Including estimate of savings to be gained if article is designed to achieve savings. When savings are intangible, the non-monetary advantages shall be explained.)

ESTIMATED PERIOD OF TEST________ SIGNED________

2. PURCHASING DEPARTMENT

ASSIGNED TEST NO.________ DATE________

REFERENCES________

COMMENTS________

SIGNED________

3. ORIGINATOR'S DEPARTMENT HEAD

APPROVED FOR TEST YES ☐ NO ☐ DATE________

COMMENTS________

SIGNED________

FIG. 28–5. Proposed material test form.

The foregoing is a general outline and may be changed as required to meet a condition. Clause 1 should not be used unless absolutely necessary, and then only with a reliable supplier.

CONDUCTING TESTS

All testing shall be done in an impartial, workmanlike manner. Care must be taken to comply with manufacturer's recommendations. Progress reports are to be made at least once every three months to purchasing on the form shown in Fig. 28–6, "Material and Equipment Test, Progress and Final Report." These forms will be prepared by purchasing and forwarded to the originator upon receipt of the purchase order by the manager of purchases. The number of copies supplied will be determined by the estimated period of test. Additional copies of Fig. 28–6 may be secured on request to the manager of purchases.

REPORTS OF TEST

Copies of each completed form will be sent to selected purchasing department offices for their information and determination of distribution of in-progress and final reports. After the final report is received by the local purchasing office, it will prepare a follow sheet to the original purchase order, authorizing payment, return of material, or other disposition in accordance with test results.

TEST REFERENCE FILE

Copies will be sent annually to the operating departments. If information is desired on any test, it may be obtained by writing to the manager of purchases specifying the test number, the individual's name, and company mailing address.

RESPONSIBILITIES OF ORIGINATOR

It shall be the responsibility of the originator to:

1. Properly initiate the trial or test by the preparation of form, Fig. 28–5, "Proposed Material Test."
2. Design the test to consider competitive makes whenever possible.
3. Conduct the test in an impartial, workmanlike manner.
4. Conscientiously prepare the provided report forms and return copies to the manager of purchases.

RESPONSIBILITIES OF PURCHASING DEPARTMENT

It shall be the responsibility of the purchasing department to:

1. Provide the manager of purchases with a copy of the purchase order for the test file.
2. Maintain a complete reference file on all tests conducted throughout the company.
3. Review all forms, Fig. 28–5, "Proposed Material Test," and provide pertinent data and information to the originator.
4. Assign test numbers.
5. Aid the originator in obtaining desirable competition.
6. Act as adviser or observer, if required.

7. Duplicate and distribute to select purchasing department offices copies of form, Fig. 28–5.
8. Accumulate, summarize, and distribute to interested parties copies of form, Fig. 28–6.
9. Trace overdue progress reports.
10. Distribute annually to the operating departments copies of the test reference file.

TEST NO.________________

REQUESTED BY________________

TO BE COMPLETED BY PURCHASING DEPARTMENT

MATERIAL OR EQUIPMENT UNDER TEST________________

PURCHASE ORDER NO.________ DATE________

VENDOR________________

MANUFACTURER________________

UNIT COST________________

SPECIFIC LOCATION OF TEST________________

SPECIFIC SERVICE________________

REASON FOR TEST________________

ORIGINATOR (Please supply complete history of test for future reference)

PROGRESS REPORT NO.____ FINAL REPORT ☐ DATE OF REPORT________

DATE OF INSTALLATION____ MONTHS ON TEST____ EST. CONCLUSION DATE________

REPORT: (Use reverse side of this form if additional space required)

SIGNED________________

ANALYSIS SLIPS, REVIEWS OR ANY MEMORANDA THAT HAS BEARING ON RESULTS OF TEST, SHOULD BE ATTACHED TO PURCHASING DEPARTMENT COPY.

KEEP DUPLICATE FOR YOUR FILE, SEND ORIGINAL TO PURCHASING DEPARTMENT

FIG. 28–6. Material and equipment test, progress and final report form.

Educational (*Section 23*)

COLLEGES AND UNIVERSITIES IN THE UNITED STATES OFFERING COURSES IN PURCHASING[16]

Since its origin, the National Association of Purchasing Agents has encouraged the teaching of purchasing courses in colleges and universities. A recent study shows that 168 schools teach one or more separate purchasing courses, offering a total of 267 courses. The 267 separate courses reported were divided as follows: undergraduate, 172 (basic, 130; advanced, 42); graduate, 18 (basic, 12; advanced, 6); extension, 67.

Following are the schools reporting that purchasing is included in their curriculum as a separate course (note: U = Undergraduate; G = Graduate; E = Extension):

ALABAMA (*3 colleges*)

Florence State College, Florence (U)
Auburn University, Auburn (U)
University of Alabama, University (U)

ARIZONA (*2 colleges*)

Arizona State College, Flagstaff (U)
Arizona State University, Tempe (U)

ARKANSAS (*1 college*)

Southern State College, Magnolia (U-E)

CALIFORNIA (*28 colleges*)

Armstrong College, Berkeley (U)
California State College, Long Beach (U-E)
California State College at Los Angeles, Los Angeles (U)
California State Polytechnic College, San Luis Obispo (U)
East Los Angeles College, Los Angeles (U)
Fullerton Junior College, Fullerton (U)
Humboldt State College, Arcata (U)
Long Beach State College, Long Beach (U)
Los Angeles State College, Los Angeles (E)
Menlo College, Menlo Park (U)
Mount San Antonio College, Walnut (U)
Orange Coast College, Costa Mesa (U)
Pasadena College, Pasadena, (E)
Pierce College, Woodland Hills (U-E)
Sacramento State College, Sacramento (U)
San Diego State College, San Diego (U)
San Fernando Valley State College, Northridge (U)
San Francisco State College, San Francisco (U)
San Jose State College, San Jose (U-E)
Stanford University, Stanford (G)
University of California, Berkeley (U-G); Los Angeles (E); Riverside (E); Santa Barbara (E)
University of San Francisco, San Francisco (E)
University of Santa Clara, Santa Clara (U)
University of Southern California, Los Angeles (U-G-E)
Woodbury College, Los Angeles (U)

COLORADO (*2 colleges*)

University of Colorado, Boulder (U-E)
University of Denver, Denver (U)

CONNECTICUT (*5 colleges*)

Fairfield University, Fairfield (U)
New Haven College, West Haven (E)
Quinnipiac College, Hamden (U)
University of Connecticut, Storrs (U-E)
University of Hartford, Hartford (U)

DISTRICT OF COLUMBIA (*3 colleges*)

The American University, Washington (U-E)

[16] Result of 1965 Survey conducted by NAPA; reproduced by permission of NAPA.

The George Washington University, Washington (G)
Southeastern University, Washington (U)

FLORIDA (*2 colleges*)

Florida State University, Tallahassee (U)
University of Miami, Coral Gables (U)

GEORGIA (*1 college*)

Georgia State College, Atlanta (U)

ILLINOIS (*6 colleges*)

Bradley University, Peoria (G)
Illinois Institute of Technology, Chicago (U)
Loyola University, Chicago (U)
Northern Illinois University, De Kalb (U)
Northwestern University, Evanston (E)
Roosevelt University, Chicago (U-E)

INDIANA (*4 colleges*)

Butler University, Indianapolis (U)
Evansville College, Evansville (U-E)
Tri-State College, Angola (U)
University of Notre Dame, Notre Dame (U)

IOWA (*1 college*)

University of Iowa, Iowa City (U-G-E)

KANSAS (*3 colleges*)

Friends University, Wichita (U)
Wichita State University, Wichita (U)
University of Kansas, Lawrence (E)

KENTUCKY (*2 colleges*)

University of Kentucky, Lexington (U)
University of Louisville, Louisville (E)

LOUISIANA (*4 colleges*)

Louisiana Polytechnic Institute, Ruston (U)
Louisiana State University, Baton Rouge (U)
Northeast Louisiana State College, Monroe (U-G)
Tulane University, New Orleans (E)

MAINE (*1 college*)

Husson College, Bangor (U)

MARYLAND (*2 colleges*)

University of Baltimore, Baltimore (U)
University of Maryland, College Park (U)

MASSACHUSETTS (*6 colleges*)

American International College, Springfield (U-G)
Babson Institute, Babson Park (G)
Boston University, Boston (U-G-E)
Harvard University, Graduate School of Business Administration, Boston (G)
Northeastern University, Boston (G-E)
University of Massachusetts, Amherst (U)

MICHIGAN (*10 schools*)

Central Michigan University, Mt. Pleasant (U)
Detroit Institute of Technology, Detroit (U)
Eastern Michigan University, Ypsilanti (U)
Ferris State College, Big Rapids (U)
Michigan State University, E. Lansing (U-G)
Oakland University, Rochester (E)
University of Detroit, Detroit (E)
University of Michigan, Ann Arbor (G)
Wayne State University, Detroit (U-G-E)
Western Michigan U., Kalamazoo (U-G-E)

MINNESOTA (*2 schools*)

St. Cloud State College, St. Cloud (U)
University of Minnesota, Minneapolis (U-G)

MISSOURI (*4 schools*)

Rockhurst College, Kansas City (U)
St. Louis University, St. Louis (E)
University of Missouri, Columbia (U-G)
Washington University, St. Louis (E)

MISSISSIPPI (*2 schools*)

Mississippi State University, State College (U)
University of Mississippi, University (U)

NEBRASKA (*1 school*)

University of Omaha, Omaha (U)

NEW JERSEY *(6 schools)*

College of Saint Elizabeth, Convent Station (U)
Fairleigh Dickinson University, Rutherford (U-E)
Monmouth College, West Long Branch (U)
Rider College, Lawrenceville (U)
Saint Peter's College, Jersey City (U)
Seton Hall University, South Orange (U)

NEW YORK *(11 schools)*

Canisius College, Buffalo (E)
City University of New York, New York (U-E)
Clarkson College of Technology, Potsdam (U)
Corning Community College, Corning (U-E)
Fordham University, New York (U)
Hofstra University, Hempstead (U-E)
Pace College, New York (U)
Rochester Institute of Technology, Rochester (E)
Russell Sage College, Troy (E)
St. Bonaventure University, St. Bonaventure (U)
St. John's University, Brooklyn (U)

NORTH DAKOTA *(1 school)*

University of North Dakota, Grand Forks (U)

OHIO *(16 schools)*

Bowling Green State University, Bowling Green (U)
Dyke College, Cleveland (U)
Fenn College, Cleveland (U)
John Carroll University, Cleveland (U)
Kent State University, Kent (U)
Miami University, Oxford (U)
Ohio State University, Columbus (U)
Also School of Systems and Logistics
Ohio University, Athens (U)
Sinclair College, Dayton (E)
University of Akron, Akron (U-E)
University of Cincinnati, Cincinnati (U)
University of Dayton, Dayton (U)
University of Toledo, Toledo (U)
Wittenberg University, Springfield (U)
Xavier University, Cincinnati (U-G)
Youngstown University, Youngstown (U)

OKLAHOMA *(2 schools)*

University of Oklahoma, Norman (U-E)
University of Tulsa, Tulsa (U-E)

OREGON *(2 schools)*

Portland State College, Portland (U-E)
University of Portland, Portland (U)

PENNSYLVANIA *(10 schools)*

Beaver College, Glenside (U)
Duquesne University, Pittsburgh (E)
LaSalle College, Philadelphia (U)
Pennsylvania State University, University Park (E)
Philadelphia College of Textiles & Science, Philadelphia (U)
St. Joseph's College, Philadelphia (U)
Temple University, Philadelphia (U)
University of Pennsylvania, Philadelphia (G)
University of Pittsburgh, Pittsburgh (U)
University of Scranton, Scranton (U-E)

RHODE ISLAND *(1 school)*

Bryant College, Providence (E)

SOUTH CAROLINA *(1 school)*

Presbyterian College, Clinton (U)

TENNESSEE *(5 schools)*

East Tennessee State University, Johnson City (U)
Memphis State University, Memphis (U)
Tennessee Polytechnic Institute, Cookeville (U)
University of Chattanooga, Chattanooga (U)
University of Tennessee, Knoxville (U-E)

TEXAS *(6 schools)*

Lamar State College of Technology, Beaumont (E)
North Texas State University, Denton (U)
Texas Christian University, Fort Worth (U)
Texas Western College, El Paso (U)
University of Houston, Houston (U)
West Texas State University, Canyon (U)

UTAH *(2 schools)*

University of Utah, Salt Lake City (U)
Utah State University, Logan (U)

WEST VIRGINIA *(2 schools)*

Morris Harvey, Charleston (U)
West Virginia University, Morgantown (U)

VIRGINIA *(4 schools)*

Richmond Professional Institute, Richmond (U)
Roanoke College, Salem (U-E)
University of Richmond, Richmond (U)
Virginia Polytechnic Institute, Blacksburg (U)

WASHINGTON *(1 school)*

Pacific Lutheran University, Tacoma (U-E)

WISCONSIN *(3 schools)*

Marquette University, Milwaukee (U)
University of Wisconsin, Madison (U-G-E)
University of Wisconsin, Milwaukee (U-E)

CORRESPONDENCE COURSES

Sometimes although a basic purchasing course is needed, location makes it impossible to attend an organized class. In such cases correspondence courses fill important needs. The following schools offer such courses:

(1) International Correspondence Schools, Scranton, Pa., Course No. 6103 Purchasing. For the Purchasing Agent they also recommend a series of courses including: Accounting, Inventory Control, Commercial Law, Letter-Writing Improvement, Sales Analysis and other special related subjects.

(2) University Extension Division, University of Wisconsin, 606 West Wisconsin Avenue, Milwaukee, Wisconsin. Course No. 180CS Industrial Purchasing. This is a broad basic course divided into sixteen assignments and using one of the well-known basic purchasing textbooks. Thirty-nine courses are listed in the commerce section of this school's catalogue. Many of these would be useful to the Purchasing Agent, such as: Accounting, Business Law, Business Management, Personnel Management, Business Ethics, and Business Letter Writing.

Two other schools offer related correspondence courses:

(1) Division of University Extension, Indiana University, Bloomington, Indiana. Course No. P423 Operations Planning and Control. The course syllabus indicates that this course deals heavily in Purchasing and Materials Management. Principles of Management, Course No. P300 is listed as a prerequisite for this course. Listed in the business section of this school's catalogue are 33 courses many of which are related and would be of interest to purchasing people.

(2) Lincoln Extension Institute, 1401 West 75th Street, Cleveland, Ohio. This school lists Materials Control as one of twenty-two units in its Management Development program.

In Canada, the Canadian Association of Purchasing Agents has recently revised its correspondence course in purchasing. The Procurement Course, by correspondence, will be administered by C.A.P.A., 357 Bay Street, Toronto 1, Ontario. This course which aims at an advanced level of training uses two standard textbooks and has eight broad assignments. One of these areas relates directly to Canadian purchasing problems. The Procurement Course is a part of the broad Professional Development Programme of C.A.P.A.

COURSES IN PURCHASING MANAGEMENT

Some colleges and universities offer comprehensive courses in purchasing management. Typical of these is the one at the University of California at Los Angeles, which is outlined below. This program of 66 semester-hour units is equal to 2 years of full-time college work. Persons holding a bachelor's degree are exempt from Section 2, "Certificate in Business Program," which totals 33 units.

SENIOR AWARD IN PURCHASING MANAGEMENT[17]

Developed by University of California Extension in cooperation with the National Association of Purchasing Agents, this Program leading to the Senior Award provides an educational foundation for the professional practice of purchasing management.

The Senior Award Program is a carefully selected sequence of courses designed to meet the specialized needs of those in the broad field of purchasing management, as well as to provide a familiarity with the major facets of business administration. The courses are arranged to provide a balance between background information and specialized training. They are taught at a down-to-earth level by faculty members of the University of California, industrial leaders, and experienced practitioners in the various professions related to the subject areas of the program.

The Senior Award in Purchasing Management is awarded by University of California Extension in cooperation with the National Association of Purchasing Agents upon the satisfactory completion of the three phases (22 courses) outlined below:

1. The Professional Designation in Purchasing Management Program
2. The Certificate in Business Program
3. Six Advanced Courses in Purchasing Management

All appropriate University of California courses taken on any one of the several campuses or through the Department of Correspondence Instruction are accepted.

THE PROGRAM REQUIREMENTS (number of units in parentheses)

1. Professional Designation in Purchasing Management
   Industrial Purchasing (3)
   Advanced Purchasing (3)
   Mathematics of Purchasing (3)
   Legal Aspects of Purchasing
   Organization and Management Theory (3)

[17] Reproduced by permission of the University of California

2. Certificate in Business Program (recommended courses)
   Economics (3)
   Accounting 1A (3) and 1B (3)
   Business Finance (3)
   Elements of Industrial Relations (3)
   Elements of Production Management (3)
   Elements of Marketing (3)
   Managerial Accounting (3)
   Business Statistics (3)
   Legal Analysis for Business Managers (4)
   Business Economics (3)
3. Advanced Courses in Purchasing Management (required)
   Subcontract Management (3)
   Price and Cost Analysis (3)

Electives (select four):
   Organization Planning and Control (3)
   Defense Contract Types and Incentive Procurement Procedures (3)
   Marketing Research Techniques (3)
   Office Organization and Management (3)
   Work Improvement Principles and Practices (3)
   Production Planning and Control (3)
   Government Contract Administration (3)
   Principles and Applications of Value Analysis (2)

CERTIFICATION IN PURCHASING

Certification programs have been developed by purchasing associations in the United Kingdom, Australia, Canada, and the United States.

The Purchasing Officers Association in the United Kingdom was founded in 1931. It presently has a certified membership in excess of 7,000 plus over 1,400 registered students. At first, admission was based on age, experience, and the nature of the job held by candidates. About 1937, an educational program was established to produce a formal technical or professional qualification for membership. Briefly, it calls for college study leading to intermediate and final examinations. This procedure was developed in conjunction with the British Institute of Management. The candidate also must satisfy an examining board regarding the nature of his experience and his general qualifications for membership. Two levels of membership exist—full member and associate member. Both must pass the intermediate and final examinations. A full member must have more experience and be at least 28 years of age. An associate member is eligible at 25. Four to five years of college-level education are necessary to qualify. There is a close bond between the Purchasing Officers Association and many technical colleges.

Institute of Public Supplies in the United Kingdom, an association of purchasers employed by public bodies, has an educational certification program for membership qualification closely paralleling that of the Purchasing Officers Association. In fact, for the first eight years of their existence they were virtually the same, with the added requirement of the Institute of one paper in the final syllabus on public purchasing.

The Australian Purchasing Officers Association membership, unlike the two British systems, is not confined exclusively to certified members. The organization has two grades of membership, corporate and non-corporate. The latter kind of member may be either a student studying purchasing in an approved course or someone actively engaged in purchasing, 21 years of age or older, but not otherwise qualified to meet the requirements of corporate membership. Corporate membership consists of two grades—associate and full member. An associate member must be 25 years of age with three years' experience in a responsible capacity in purchasing. A full member must be 28 years of age with five years of responsible purchasing experience. The Association, in conjunction with the technical-education authorities in each of the Australian States, has sponsored a two-year purchasing and supply-management certificate course consisting of 255 college hours of classwork plus outside assignments. Present plans call for extension to 463 hours of college work over a period of three years. In January, 1966, holding of the above certificate will be a condition of corporate membership for all new applicants. An applicant 38 years of age at that date, who is otherwise qualified, may file an application requesting exception.

The California Association of Public Purchasing Officers adopted in 1961 the first formal North American system. There are two levels of certification—"Certified Public Purchasing Officer" (CPPO) and "Associate Public Purchasing Officer" (APPO). Both levels require college graduation with majors in public administration, business administration, engineering, or closely related fields. A four-hour written examination in purchasing, inventory control, traffic management, commercial law, business organization, market conditions, and other aspects of purchasing specialization is required for both levels. This written test is followed by an oral examination (for those candidates achieving a passing written score) by an advisory panel of recognized authorities on purchasing. The basic difference between the two certifications is in experience. The upper level requires ten years of active purchasing, of which five must be public purchasing, and three must be in a position of administrative responsibility. An applicant for APPO must have five years' purchasing experience. While there are no residence restrictions nor is eligibility restricted to its members, over 50 per cent of applicants have been members of the Association.

The Canadian Association of Purchasing Agents reached agreement in 1963 on a desirable professional development program leading to a Professional Purchaser Diploma. The Canadian plan, while unique, compares more to the British than to the California system. Its basic contribution is in the establishment of purchasing seminars and more extensive courses, including correspondence courses, in close cooperation with many colleges and universities. Eleven routes for the achievement of a Purchasing Diploma have been adopted. The highest diploma, the "Route to Eminence," is awarded at the discretion of the National Board of Examiners to persons who have achieved outstanding eminence in the field of purchasing. Route 11 requires four years' purchasing experience, a university degree, 12 semester seminar credits, plus the Association's Procurement Course. The other nine routes reflect varying combinations of age, experience, and academic training.

The National Association of Purchasing Agents started in 1965 a study as to the feasibility of establishing a program of professional standards and/or professional certification, with the ultimate object of instituting a common ground for professionalism based on education, knowledge, and experience.

The National Institute of Governmental Purchasing (NIGP) approved in 1964 the most recent and most comprehensive North American system. Its program is based on an academic syllabus, a purchasing syllabus, a written examination, and an oral examination. Again, two levels of certification are established—"Certified Public Purchasing Officer" (CPPO) and "Associate Certified Public Purchasing Officer" (ACPPO).

The upper level requires a minimum age of 30 and five years of administrative experience in a public purchasing agency. Candidates who meet all requirements, except experience and age, are certified as associates, subject to later review by the examination board.

While the program is far too new to be evaluated, it is being covered here in more detail because its total requirements are broader.

Academic Syllabus

The basic academic requirements are the same as those normally found in a business administration course consisting of, but not restricted to, economics, accounting, business and contract law, principles of management, marketing, statistics, and work measurements, totaling approximately 20 units or semester hours. There is no requirement for college graduation, but a graduate in these fields will be assumed to have met these requirements.

Purchasing Syllabus

At this point, a new element is added. NIGP has outlined the contents of three courses—Purchasing I, II, and III. These courses, yet to be offered, would give the student a very diversified coverage of purchasing theory and practices. No academic semester-hour appraisal is given, but the three courses approximate 15 college units. Courses would be given in colleges approved by the NIGP Board of Examiners. The final steps of written and oral examination vary from those already described only in methods of administration.

ESSENTIALS OF THE NIGP PROFESSIONAL CERTIFICATION PROGRAM[18]

1. NIGP provides a program for professional development leading a candidate to obtain, by examination, a qualification of "Certified Public Purchasing Officer" (CPPO).
2. To qualify, candidates must pass an examination of two parts conducted separately:
   (a) a written part, prepared by NIGP and graded by university faculty, on the basis of specific type questions;
   (b) an oral part, to be conducted by the NIGP Examining Board within 90 days after results of the written exams are determined. All oral examinations to be tape recorded and held for one (1) year by NIGP.
3. To take the examination a candidate must
   (a) meet subject requirements of the academic syllabus and the purchasing syllabus;
   (b) attain the age of 30 and have acquired 5 years' administrative experience in a public purchasing agency.
4. All candidates must take and pass the *oral* part of the examination.
5. Some requirements may be waived:
   (a) a candidate will be exempted from the "academic syllabus" requirement if he has graduated from a recognized institution with a major in a specified field;
   (b) a candidate may be exempted from the "purchasing syllabus" requirements and the written part of the exam if he has attended a graduate school in which he covered the necessary subjects;
   (c) a candidate may be exempted from the "academic syllabus" and the written part of the exam if he has received a high school diploma, if he is 40 years old or more, and has acquired 15 years' experience including 5 years in a responsible administrative capacity, and is currently employed in public purchasing;

[18] Reproduced by permission of NIGP, 1001 Connecticut Avenue, N.W., Washington, D.C. 20036.

(d) a candidate who has satisfied all requirements except age or the 5 years' public purchasing experience factor may take the oral exam if he proves he has maturity and comparable experience and is an outstanding candidate *and* currently holds an executive position in a recognized purchasing agency.

6. All candidates who do not qualify for exemptions may take the entire examination upon completion of the "academic syllabus" and "purchasing syllabus."
7. Part of the written exam will be a thesis on public purchasing principles and problems.
8. Candidates who pass the examination and fulfill all requirements will receive a certificate of "Certified Public Purchasing Officer" (CPPO).
9. Candidates who pass the exam but have not met age requirements will receive a certificate of "Associate Certified Public Purchasing Officer" (ACPPO).
10. Administrative details of the program will be handled by NIGP.
11. A quick summary of required courses is set forth as follows:
    1. Economics I
    2. Economics II
    3. Business Law I
    4. Business Law II
    5. Accounting I
    6. Accounting II
    7. Statistics
    8. Office Management
    9. Business Ethics
    10. Inventory Control
    11. Personnel Management
    12. Principles of Management
    13. Electronic Data Processing
    14. Business Report Writing
    15. Quality Control
    16. Government Finance
    17. Principles of Purchasing
    18. Public Purchasing I
    19. Public Purchasing II
    20. Public Purchasing III

Summary

The two British systems require certification as a condition of membership. While at first this was based largely on experience, "blanketing-in" has passed and is now replaced by examination. The Australian system parallels the British systems but is in the process of evolution toward certification. Effective in 1966, membership and certification will be synonymous.

The California association's program assumes a body of knowledge and academic background. It makes no attempt to establish training programs, but relies on the existence of such courses in colleges and universities. It permits variance from the college-graduation requirement only in exceptional cases. There is no blanketing-in or requirement for membership in a purchasing association.

The Canadian program sets up through its 11 routes various recommended minimum requirements which are a combination of age, experience, formal university training, and association-sponsored courses. A unique contribution is the recognition that many of the courses can be taken by persons already in the purchasing field on a part-time and/or correspondence basis.

No summary of the NIGP program is necessary since full details are shown above.

Sources of Information on Certification

Purchasing Officers Association
York House, Westminster Bridge Road
London, S.E. 1, England

The Institute of Public Supplies
24 Park Crescent
London, W. 1, England

The Australian Purchasing Officers' Association
Broughton House
181 Clarence Street
Sydney, Australia

California Association of Public Purchasing Officers
P.O. Box 3381
San Francisco, Calif. 94119

Canadian Association of Purchasing Agents
357 Bay Street
Toronto 1, Ontario, Canada

National Association of Purchasing Agents
11 Park Place
New York, N.Y. 10007

National Institute of Governmental Purchasing, Inc.
1001 Connecticut Avenue, N.W.
Washington, D.C. 20036

SECTION 29

REFERENCE TABLES

Editor

Chas. F. Smith, Director of Purchases, American Oil Company, Chicago, Illinois

Associate Editors

G. E. Priester, Manager–Purchasing Planning, American Oil Company, Chicago, Illinois

Scott W. Tyree, Assistant Purchasing Agent, Container Corporation of America, Chicago, Illinois

TABLES OF WEIGHTS AND MEASURES

Table 29–1. U.S. Weights and Measures

	WEIGHTS
Apothecaries' 20 grains (gr)	= 1 scruple (s ap. or ℈)
3 scruples	= 1 dram (dr ap. or ʒ)
8 drams	= 1 ounce (oz ap. or ℥)
12 ounces	= 1 pound (lb ap. or ℔)
Avoirdupois 27–11/32 grains (gr)	= 1 dram (dr)
16 drams	= 1 ounce (oz)
16 ounces	= 1 pound (lb)
25 pounds	= 1 quarter
4 quarters	= 1 hundredweight (cwt)
20 hundredweights or 2,000 pounds	= 1 ton (tn or t) or short ton (s.t.)
2,240 pounds	= 1 long ton (l.t.)
Troy 24 grains (gr)	= 1 pennyweight (dwt)
20 pennyweights	= 1 ounce (oz t.)
12 ounces	= 1 pound (lb t.)
	MEASURES
Circular 60 seconds (″)	= 1 minute (′)
60 minutes	= 1 degree (°)
30 degrees	= 1 sign
3 signs	= 1 quadrant or 90 degrees
4 quadrants	= 1 circle or 1 circumference or 360 degrees
Cubic 1,728 cubic inches (cu in.)	= 1 cubic foot (cu ft)
27 cubic feet	= 1 cubic yard (cu yd)
128 cubic feet	= 1 cord (cd)
Dry 2 pints (pt)	= 1 quart (qt)
8 quarts	= 1 peck (pk)
4 pecks	= 1 bushel (bu) or 2,150.42 cubic inches (cu in.)
Linear or Long 12 inches (in.)	= 1 foot (ft)
3 feet	= 1 yard (yd)
5½ yards	= 1 rod (rd) or pole (p) or perch (p)
40 rods	= 1 furlong (fur.)
8 furlongs or 1,760 yards or 5,280 feet	= 1 mile (mi)
3 miles	= 1 league
Liquid 8 fluid drams (f ʒ)	= 1 fluid ounce (f ℥)
4 fluid ounces	= 1 gill (gi)
4 gills	= 1 pint (pt)
2 pints	= 1 quart (qt)
4 quarts	= 1 gallon (gal) or 231 cubic inches (cu in.)
31½ gallons	= 1 barrel (bbl)
Mariners' or Nautical 6 feet (ft)	= 1 fathom (f or fm)
100 fathoms	= 1 cable's length (ordinary)
10 cables' lengths	= 1 nautical mile or 6,080.20 feet
1 nautical mile	= 1.1516 statute miles
1 knot	= a speed of 1 nautical mile, or 1.1516 statute miles per hour
Paper 24 sheets (sh)	= 1 quire (qr)
20 quires	= 1 ream (rm)
2 reams	= 1 bundle (bdl)
5 bundles	= 1 bale (B/-)

Table 29–1. U.S. Weights and Measures (*Continued*)

Square 144 square inches (sq in.)	= 1 square foot (sq ft)
9 square feet	= 1 square yard (sq yd)
30¼ square yards	= 1 square rod (sq rd) or square pole (sq p) or square perch (sq p)
160 square rods or 4,840 square yards	= 1 acre (A)
640 acres	= 1 square mile (sq mi)
36 square miles	= 1 township (tp)

Table 29–2. Metric Weights and Measures

AREA	
100 square millimeters (sq mm or mm^2)	= 1 square centimeter (sq cm or cm^2)
100 square centimeters	= 1 square decimeter (sq dm or dm^2)
100 square decimeters	= 1 square meter (sq m or m^2) or 1 centiare (ca)
100 square meters	= 1 are (a)
100 ares	= 1 hectare (ha)
100 hectares	= 1 square kilometer (sq km or km^2)
CAPACITY	
10 milliliters (ml)	= 1 centiliter (cl)
10 centiliters	= 1 deciliter (dl)
10 deciliters	= 1 liter (l)
10 liters	= 1 decaliter (dkl)
10 decaliters	= 1 hectoliter (hl)
10 hectoliters or 1,000 liters	= 1 kiloliter (kl)
LENGTH	
10 millimeters (mm)	= 1 centimeter (cm)
10 centimeters	= 1 decimeter (dm)
10 decimeters	= 1 meter (m)
10 meters	= 1 decameter (dkm)
10 decameters	= 1 hectometer (hm)
10 hectometers or 1,000 meters	= 1 kilometer (km)
VOLUME	
1,000 cubic millimeters (cu mm or mm^3)	= 1 cubic centimeter (cu cm or cm^3)
1,000 cubic centimeters	= 1 cubic decimeter (cu dm or dm^3)
1,000 cubic decimeters	= 1 cubic meter (cu m or m^3)
WEIGHT	
10 milligrams (mg)	= 1 centigram (cg)
10 centigrams	= 1 decigram (dg)
10 decigrams	= 1 gram (g)
1,000 grams	= 1 kilogram or kilo (kg)
100 kilograms	= 1 quintal (q)
10 quintals or 1,000 kilograms	= 1 metric ton (MT)

CONVERSION TABLES AND EQUIVALENTS

Table 29–3. Metric Equivalents of U.S. Weights and Measures

APOTHECARIES' WEIGHT

1 scruple	= 1.296 grams
1 dram	= 3.888 grams

AVOIRDUPOIS WEIGHT

1 dram	= 1.772 grams
1 ounce	= 28.3495 grams
1 pound	= 453.59 grams or 0.4536 kilogram
1 hundredweight	= 45.36 kilograms
1 short ton	= 907.18 kilograms or 0.9072 metric ton
1 long ton	= 1,016.05 kilograms or 1.0160 metric tons

TROY WEIGHT

1 pennyweight	= 1.555 grams
1 ounce	= 31.1035 grams
1 pound	= 373.24 grams or 0.3732 kilogram

CUBIC MEASURE

1 cubic inch	= 16.387 cubic centimeters
1 cubic foot	= 0.0283 cubic meter
1 cubic yard	= 0.7646 cubic meter
1 cord	= 3.625 cubic meters

LIQUID MEASURE

1 fluid ounce	= 0.0297 liter
1 gill	= 0.118 liter
1 pint	= 0.4732 liter
1 quart	= 0.9463 liter
1 gallon	= 3.7853 liters

DRY MEASURE

1 quart	= 1.1012 liters
1 peck	= 8.8096 liters
1 bushel	= 35.2383 liters

LINEAR OR LONG MEASURE

1 inch	= 2.54 centimeters
1 foot	= 0.3048 meter
1 yard	= 0.9144 meter
1 rod	= 5.029 meters
1 furlong	= 201.17 meters
1 mile	= 1.6093 kilometers
1 league	= 4.83 kilometers

MARINERS' OR NAUTICAL MEASURE

1 fathom	= 1.829 meters
1 nautical mile	= 1,853.248 meters

SQUARE MEASURE

1 square inch	= 6.452 square centimeters
1 square foot	= 929 square centimeters
1 square yard	= 0.8361 square meter
1 square rod	= 25.29 square meters
1 acre	= 40.4687 ares or 0.4047 hectare
1 square mile	= 259 hectares or 2.59 square kilometers
1 township	= 9,324 hectares or 93.24 square kilometers

Table 29–4. U.S. Equivalents of Metric Weights and Measures

AREA

1 square centimeter	= 0.155 square inch
1 centiare	= 1,550 square inches
1 are	= 119.6 square yards
1 hectare	= 2.471 acres
1 square kilometer	= 0.3861 square mile

CAPACITY

1 centiliter	= 0.338 fluid ounce
1 deciliter	= 6.1025 cubic inches
1 liter	= 0.9081 dry quart or 1.0567 liquid quarts
1 decaliter	= 0.284 bushel or 2.64 gallons
1 hectoliter	= 2.838 bushels or 26.418 gallons
1 kiloliter	= 35.315 cubic feet or 264.18 gallons

LENGTH

1 centimeter	= 0.3937 inch
1 decimeter	= 3.937 inches
1 meter	= 39.37 inches
1 decameter	= 393.7 inches
1 hectometer	= 328 feet 1 inch
1 kilometer	= 0.62137 mile

VOLUME

1 cubic centimeter	= 0.061 cubic inch
1 cubic meter	= 1.308 cubic yards

WEIGHT

1 centigram	= 0.1543 grain
1 decigram	= 1.5432 grains
1 gram	= 15.432 grains
1 kilogram	= 2.2046 pounds
1 quintal	= 220.46 pounds
1 metric ton	= 2,204.6 pounds

Table 29–5. Engineering Units

1 British thermal unit (Btu or B)	= 1,055 watt-seconds
	= 778 foot-pounds (ft-lb)
	= 0.000293 kilowatthour
	= 0.000393 horsepower-hour
1 horsepower-hour (hp-hr)	= 0.746 kilowatthour
	= 1,980,000 foot-pounds
	= 2545 heat units (Btu or B)
1 horsepower (hp)	= 33,000 foot-pounds per minute
	= 550 foot-pounds per second
	= 746 watts
	= 0.746 kilowatt
1 kilowatt (kw)	= 1,000 watts
	= 1.34 horsepower
	= 737.3 foot-pounds per second

Table 29–5. Engineering Units (*Continued*)

	= 44,240 foot-pounds per minute
	= 56.9 heat units (Btu or B) per minute
1 kilowatthour (kwhr)	= 1,000 watthours (whr)
	= 1.34 horsepower-hours
	= 2,654,200 foot-pounds
	= 3412 heat units (Btu or B)
1 watt (w)	= 1 joule per second
	= 0.00134 horsepower
	= 3412 heat units (Btu or B) per hour
	= 0.7373 foot-pound per second
	= 44.24 foot-pounds per minute

Table 29–6. Fractions and Their Decimal Equivalents

Fraction	*Decimal Equivalent*	*Fraction*	*Decimal Equivalent*
1/64	.0156	33/64	.5156
1/32	.0312	17/32	.5312
3/64	.0468	35/64	.5468
1/16	.0625	9/16	.5625
5/64	.07812	37/64	.5781
3/32	.09375	19/32	.5937
7/64	.10937	39/64	.6093
1/8	.125	5/8	.6250
9/64	.14062	41/64	.6406
5/32	.15625	21/32	.6562
11/64	.17187	43/64	.6718
3/16	.1875	11/16	.6875
13/64	.20312	45/64	.7031
7/32	.21875	23/32	.7187
15/64	.23437	47/64	.7343
1/4	.25	3/4	.7500
17/64	.26562	49/64	.7656
9/32	.28125	25/32	.7812
19/64	.29687	51/64	.7968
5/16	.3125	13/16	.8125
21/64	.32812	53/64	.8281
11/32	.34375	27/32	.8437
23/64	.35937	55/64	.8593
3/8	.375	7/8	.8750
25/64	.39062	57/64	.8906
13/32	.40625	29/32	.9062
27/64	.42187	59/64	.9218
7/16	.4375	15/16	.9375
29/64	.45312	61/64	.9531
15/32	.46875	31/32	.9687
31/64	.48437	63/64	.9843
1/2	.50	1	1.0000

Table 29–7. Temperature Conversion*

General formula: °F = (°C × 9/5) + 32; °C = (°F − 32) × 5/9

C		F	C		F	C		F	C		F	C		F	C		F	C		F	C		F
−273.1	**−459.4**		−17.8	**0**	32	10.0	**50**	122.0	38	**100**	212	260	**500**	932	538	**1000**	1832	816	**1500**	2732	1093	**2000**	3632
−268	**−450**		−17.2	**1**	33.8	10.6	**51**	123.8	43	**109**	230	266	**510**	950	543	**1010**	1850	821	**1510**	2750	1099	**2010**	3650
−262	**−440**		−16.7	**2**	35.6	11.1	**52**	125.6	49	**120**	248	271	**520**	968	549	**1020**	1868	827	**1520**	2768	1104	**2020**	3668
−257	**−430**		−16.1	**3**	37.4	11.7	**53**	127.4	54	**130**	266	277	**530**	986	554	**1030**	1886	832	**1530**	2786	1110	**2030**	3686
−251	**−420**		−15.6	**4**	39.2	12.2	**54**	129.2	60	**140**	284	282	**540**	1004	560	**1040**	1904	838	**1540**	2804	1116	**2040**	3704
−246	**−410**		−15.0	**5**	41.0	12.8	**55**	131.0	66	**150**	302	288	**550**	1022	566	**1050**	1922	843	**1550**	2822	1121	**2050**	3722
−240	**−400**		−14.4	**6**	42.8	13.3	**56**	132.8	71	**160**	320	293	**560**	1040	571	**1060**	1940	849	**1560**	2840	1127	**2060**	3740
−234	**−390**		−13.9	**7**	44.6	13.9	**57**	134.6	77	**170**	338	299	**570**	1058	577	**1070**	1958	854	**1570**	2858	1132	**2070**	3758
−229	**−380**		−13.3	**8**	46.4	14.4	**58**	136.4	82	**180**	356	304	**580**	1076	582	**1080**	1976	860	**1580**	2876	1138	**2080**	3776
−223	**−370**		−12.8	**9**	48.2	15.0	**59**	138.2	88	**190**	374	310	**590**	1094	588	**1090**	1994	866	**1590**	2894	1143	**2090**	3794
−218	**−360**		−12.2	**10**	50.0	15.6	**60**	140.0	93	**200**	392	316	**600**	1112	593	**1100**	2012	871	**1600**	2912	1149	**2100**	3812
−212	**−350**		−11.7	**11**	51.8	16.1	**61**	141.8	99	**210**	410	321	**610**	1130	599	**1110**	2030	877	**1610**	2930	1154	**2110**	3830
−207	**−340**		−11.1	**12**	53.6	16.7	**62**	143.6	100	**212**	413	327	**620**	1148	604	**1120**	2048	882	**1620**	2948	1160	**2120**	3848
−201	**−330**		−10.6	**13**	55.4	17.2	**63**	145.4	104	**220**	428	332	**630**	1166	610	**1130**	2066	888	**1630**	2966	1166	**2130**	3866
−196	**−320**		−10.0	**14**	57.2	17.8	**64**	147.2	110	**230**	446	338	**640**	1184	616	**1140**	2084	893	**1640**	2984	1171	**2140**	3884
−190	**−310**		− 9.44	**15**	59.0	18.3	**65**	149.0	116	**240**	464	343	**650**	1202	621	**1150**	2102	899	**1650**	3002	1177	**2150**	3902
−184	**−300**		− 8.89	**16**	60.8	18.9	**66**	150.8	121	**250**	482	349	**660**	1220	627	**1160**	2120	904	**1660**	3020	1182	**2160**	3920
−179	**−290**		− 8.33	**17**	62.6	19.4	**67**	152.6	127	**260**	500	354	**670**	1238	632	**1170**	2138	910	**1670**	3038	1188	**2170**	3938
−173	**−280**		− 7.78	**18**	64.4	20.0	**68**	154.4	132	**270**	518	360	**680**	1256	638	**1180**	2156	916	**1680**	3056	1193	**2180**	3956
−169	**−273**	−459.4	− 7.22	**19**	66.2	20.6	**69**	156.2	138	**280**	536	366	**690**	1274	643	**1190**	2174	921	**1690**	3074	1199	**2190**	3974
−168	**−270**	−454	− 6.67	**20**	68.0	21.1	**70**	158.0	143	**290**	554	371	**700**	1292	649	**1200**	2192	927	**1700**	3092	1204	**2200**	3992
−162	**−260**	−436	− 6.11	**21**	69.8	21.7	**71**	159.8	149	**300**	572	377	**710**	1310	654	**1210**	2210	932	**1710**	3110	1210	**2210**	4010
−157	**−250**	−418	− 5.56	**22**	71.6	22.2	**72**	161.6	154	**310**	590	382	**720**	1328	660	**1220**	2228	938	**1720**	3128	1216	**2220**	4028
−151	**−240**	−400	− 5.00	**23**	73.4	22.8	**73**	163.4	160	**320**	608	388	**730**	1346	666	**1230**	2246	943	**1730**	3146	1221	**2230**	4046
−146	**−230**	−382	− 4.44	**24**	75.2	23.3	**74**	165.2	166	**330**	626	393	**740**	1364	671	**1240**	2264	949	**1740**	3164	1227	**2240**	4064
−140	**−220**	−364	− 3.89	**25**	77.0	23.9	**75**	167.0	171	**340**	644	399	**750**	1382	677	**1250**	2282	954	**1750**	3182	1232	**2250**	4082
−134	**−210**	−346	− 3.33	**26**	78.8	24.4	**76**	168.8	177	**350**	662	404	**760**	1400	682	**1260**	2300	960	**1760**	3200	1238	**2260**	4100
−129	**−200**	−328	− 2.78	**27**	80.6	25.0	**77**	170.6	182	**360**	680	410	**770**	1418	688	**1270**	2318	966	**1770**	3218	1243	**2270**	4118
−123	**−190**	−310	− 2.22	**28**	82.4	25.6	**78**	172.4	188	**370**	698	416	**780**	1436	693	**1280**	2336	971	**1780**	3236	1249	**2280**	4136
−118	**−180**	−292	− 1.67	**29**	84.2	26.1	**79**	174.2	193	**380**	716	421	**790**	1454	699	**1290**	2354	977	**1790**	3254	1254	**2290**	4154
−112	**−170**	−274	− 1.11	**30**	86.0	26.7	**80**	176.0	199	**390**	734	427	**800**	1472	704	**1300**	2372	982	**1800**	3272	1260	**2300**	4172
−107	**−160**	−256	− 0.56	**31**	87.8	27.2	**81**	177.8	204	**400**	752	432	**810**	1490	710	**1310**	2390	988	**1810**	3290	1266	**2310**	4190
−101	**−150**	−238	0	**32**	89.6	27.8	**82**	179.6	210	**410**	770	438	**820**	1508	716	**1320**	2408	993	**1820**	3308	1271	**2320**	4208
− 95.6	**−140**	−220	0.56	**33**	91.4	28.3	**83**	181.4	216	**420**	788	443	**830**	1526	721	**1330**	2426	999	**1830**	3326	1277	**2330**	4226
− 90.0	**−130**	−202	1.11	**34**	93.2	28.9	**84**	183.2	221	**430**	806	449	**840**	1544	727	**1340**	2444	1004	**1840**	3344	1282	**2340**	4244

C		F
1371	**2500**	4532
1377	**2510**	4550
1382	**2520**	4568
1388	**2530**	4586
1393	**2540**	4604
1399	**2550**	4622
1404	**2560**	4640
1410	**2570**	4658
1416	**2580**	4676
1421	**2590**	4694
1427	**2600**	4712
1432	**2610**	4730
1438	**2620**	4748
1443	**2630**	4766
1449	**2640**	4784
1454	**2650**	4802
1460	**2660**	4820
1466	**2670**	4838
1471	**2680**	4856
1477	**2690**	4874
1482	**2700**	4892
1488	**2710**	4910
1493	**2720**	4928
1499	**2730**	4946
1504	**2740**	4964
1510	**2750**	4982
1516	**2760**	5000
1521	**2770**	5018
1527	**2780**	5036
1532	**2790**	5054
1538	**2800**	5072
1543	**2810**	5090
1549	**2820**	5108
1554	**2830**	5126
1560	**2840**	5144

C		F	C		F	C		F	C		F	C		F	C		F	C		F	C		F	C		F
– 84.4	**–120**	–184	1.67	**35**	95.0	29.4	**85**	185.0	227	**440**	824	454	**850**	1562	732	**1350**	2462	1010	**1850**	3362	1288	**2350**	4262	1566	**2850**	5162
– 78.9	**–110**	–166	2.22	**36**	96.8	30.0	**86**	186.8	232	**450**	842	460	**860**	1580	738	**1360**	2480	1016	**1860**	3380	1293	**2360**	4280	1571	**2860**	5180
– 73.3	**–100**	–148	2.78	**37**	98.6	30.6	**87**	188.6	238	**460**	860	466	**870**	1598	743	**1370**	2498	1021	**1870**	3398	1299	**2370**	4298	1577	**2870**	5198
– 67.8	**– 90**	–130	3.33	**38**	100.4	31.1	**88**	190.4	243	**470**	878	471	**880**	1616	749	**1380**	2516	1027	**1880**	3416	1304	**2380**	4316	1582	**2880**	5216
– 62.2	**– 80**	–112	3.89	**39**	102.2	31.7	**89**	192.2	249	**480**	896	477	**890**	1634	754	**1390**	2534	1032	**1890**	3434	1310	**2390**	4334	1588	**2890**	5234
– 56.7	**– 70**	– 94	4.44	**40**	104.0	32.2	**90**	194.0	254	**490**	914	482	**900**	1652	760	**1400**	2552	1038	**1900**	3452	1316	**2400**	4352	1593	**2900**	5252
– 51.1	**– 60**	– 76	5.00	**41**	105.8	32.8	**91**	195.8				488	**910**	1670	766	**1410**	2570	1043	**1910**	3470	1321	**2410**	4370	1599	**2910**	5270
– 45.6	**– 50**	– 58	5.56	**42**	107.6	33.3	**92**	197.6				493	**920**	1688	771	**1420**	2588	1049	**1920**	3488	1327	**2420**	4388	1604	**2920**	5288
– 40.0	**– 40**	– 40	6.11	**43**	109.4	33.9	**93**	199.4				499	**930**	1706	777	**1430**	2606	1054	**1930**	3506	1332	**2430**	4406	1610	**2930**	5306
– 34.4	**– 30**	– 22	6.67	**44**	111.2	34.4	**94**	201.2				504	**940**	1724	782	**1440**	2624	1060	**1940**	3524	1338	**2440**	4424	1616	**2940**	5324
– 28.9	**– 20**	– 4	7.22	**45**	113.0	35.0	**95**	203.0				510	**950**	1742	788	**1450**	2642	1066	**1950**	3542	1343	**2450**	4442	1621	**2950**	5342
– 23.3	**– 10**	14	7.78	**46**	114.8	35.6	**96**	204.8				516	**960**	1760	793	**1460**	2660	1071	**1960**	3560	1349	**2460**	4460	1627	**2960**	5360
– 17.8	**0**	32	8.33	**47**	116.6	36.1	**97**	206.6				521	**970**	1778	799	**1470**	2678	1077	**1970**	3578	1354	**2470**	4478	1632	**2970**	5378
			8.89	**48**	118.4	36.7	**98**	208.4				527	**980**	1796	804	**1480**	2696	1082	**1980**	3596	1360	**2480**	4496	1638	**2980**	5396
			9.44	**49**	120.2	37.2	**99**	210.2				532	**990**	1814	810	**1490**	2714	1088	**1990**	3614	1366	**2490**	4514	1643	**2990**	5414
						37.8	**100**	212.0										1093	**2000**	3632				1649	**3000**	5432

* *Note.* The numbers in boldface type refer to the temperature (in either centigrade or Fahrenheit degrees) which it is desired to convert into the other scale. If converting from Fahrenheit degrees to centigrade degrees the equivalent temperature is in the left column, while if converting from degrees centigrade to degrees Fahrenheit, the equivalent temperature is in the column on the right. This table, made by Professor Albert Sauveur, is published by permission of the heirs and next of kin of Mrs. Albert Sauveur.

Reprinted from Robert H. Perry et al., "Chemical Engineers' Handbook," 4th ed., McGraw-Hill Book Company, Inc., New York, 1963.

Interpolation Factors

C		F	C		F
0.56	**1**	1.8	3.33	**6**	10.8
1.11	**2**	3.6	3.89	**7**	12.6
1.67	**3**	5.4	4.44	**8**	14.4
2.22	**4**	7.2	5.00	**9**	16.2
2.78	**5**	9.0	5.56	**10**	18.0

Table 29–8. Viscosity Conversion

(Approximate)

Gardner Holt	*Seconds Saybolt Universal*	*Seconds Saybolt Furol*	*Engler degrees*	*Engler time*	*Barbey*	*Redwood Standard*	*Approximate seconds No. 4 Ford cup*	*Centistokes or kinematic viscosity, centipoises with specific gravity of 1*
	35		1.2	60	2,800	32		2.6
	50		1.6	82	880	44		7.4
	75		2.3	102	460	65		14.1
	100	15	3.0	153	320	88	10	20.2
	150	19	4.4	230	205	128	12	31.8
A	200	23	5.9	305	148	170	21	43.1
B	250	28	7.6	375	118	212	24	54.3
B	300	33	8.9	450	98	254	27	65.1
C	400	42	11.8	550	72	338	32	87.6
D	500	52	14.5	750	59	423	37	110
E	600	61	17.5	900	48	518	44	132
F	700	71	20.6	1,050	41	592	51	154
G	800	81	23	1,200	36.5	677	54	176
H	900	91	27	1,300	32	762	57	198
J	1,000	100	29	1,500	29.5	846	63	220
M	1,500	150	42	2,300	19.5	1,270	79	330
P	2,000	200	59	3,000	14.5	1,695	95	440
S	2,500	250	73	3,750	11.5	2,120		550
U	3,000	300	87	4,500	9.6	2,540		660
V	4,000	400	117	6,000	7.4	3,380		880
W	5,000	500	145	7,500	6.0	4,230		1,100
X	6,000	600	175	9,000	5.2	5,080		1,320
Y	7,000	700	205	10,500	4.1	5,925		1,540
	8,000	800	230	12,000	3.7	6,770		1,760
	9,000	900	260	13,500	3.2	7,620		1,980
Z-1	10,000	1,000	290	15,000	2.9	8,460		2,200
Z-3	20,000	2,000	590	30,000	1.4	16,920		4,400
Z-5	40,000	4,000	1,170	60,000		33,850		8,800
Z-6	60,000	6,000	1,750	90,000		50,800		13,200
Z-6	80,000	8,000	2,300	120,000		67,700		17,600

Table 29–9. Volume, Weight, and Energy Units

To convert from	Multiply by														
	To cu in.	To cu ft	To cu yd	To fl oz	To pt	To qt	To gal	To grain	To oz troy	To oz av	To lb troy	To lb av	To ml or g	To l or kg	To cu m
Cu in.	1.00000	$.0_3 5787$	$.0_4 2143$	.554112	.034632	.017316	.004329	252.891	.526857	.578037	.043905	.036127	16.3871	.016387	$.0_4 1639$
Cu ft.	1728.00	1.00000	.037037	957.505	59.8442	29.9221	7.48052	436996	910.408	998.848	75.8674	62.4280	28316.9	28.3169	.028317
Cu yd.	46656.0	27.0000	1.00000	25852.6	1615.79	807.896	201.974	117990_3	24581.0	26968.9	2048.42	1685.56	764556	764.556	.764556
Fl oz.	1.80469	.001044	$.0_4 3868$	1.00000	.062500	.031250	.007813	456.390	.950813	1.04318	.079234	.065199	29.5736	.029573	$.0_4 2957$
Pt.	28.8750	.016710	$.0_3 6189$	16.0000	1.00000	.500000	.125000	7302.23	15.2130	16.6908	1.26775	1.04318	473.177	.473177	$.0_4 4732$
Qt.	57.7500	.033420	.001238	32.0000	2.00000	1.00000	.250000	1460.45	30.4260	33.3816	2.53550	2.08635	946.354	.946354	$.0_3 9463$
Gal.	231.000	.133681	.004951	128.000	8.00000	4.00000	1.00000	58417.9	121.704	133.527	10.1420	8.34541	3785.42	3.78542	.003785
Grain.	.003954	$.0_5 2288$	$.0_7 8475$	.002191	$.0_3 1369$	$.0_4 6850$	$.0_4 1712$	1.00000	.002083	.002286	$.0_3 1736$	$.0_3 1428$	.064799	$.0_4 6479$	$.0_7 6479$
Oz troy.	1.89805	.001098	$.0_4 4068$	1.05173	.065733	.032867	.008217	480.000	1.00000	1.09714	.083333	.068571	31.1035	.031104	$.0_4 3110$
Oz av.	1.72999	.001001	$.0_4 3708$	.958608	.059913	.029957	.007489	437.500	.911457	1.00000	.075955	.062500	28.3495	.028350	$.0_4 2835$
Lb troy.	22.7766	.013181	$.0_3 4882$	12.6208	.788800	.394400	.098600	5760.00	12.0000	13.1657	1.00000	.822857	373.242	.373242	$.0_3 3732$
Lb av.	27.6799	.016018	$.0_3 5933$	15.3378	.958611	.479306	.119826	7000.00	14.5833	16.0000	1.21528	1.00000	453.593	.453593	$.0_3 4536$
Ml or gram.	.061024	$.0_4 3531$	$.0_5 1308$	.033814	.002113	.001057	$.0_3 2642$	15.4323	.032151	.035274	.002679	.002205	1.00000	.001000	.000001
Liter or kg.	61.0237	.035315	.001308	33.8140	2.11337	1.05669	.264172	15432.3	32.1507	35.2739	2.67923	2.20462	1000.00	1.00000	.001000
Cu m.	61023.7	35.3146	1.30795	33814.0	2113.37	1056.69	264.172	154320_3	32150.7	35273.9	2679.23	2204.62	1000000	1000.00	1.00000

NOTE: The small subnumeral following a zero indicates that the zero is to be taken that number of times; thus, $0.0_3 1428$ is equivalent to 0.0001428.

Values used in constructing table:

1 in. = 2.540001 cm.

∴ 1 cu in. = 16.387083 ml = 16.387083 g H_2O at 4°C (39°F)

1 lb av = 453.5926 g

∴ 1 gal = 8.34541 lb

∴ 1 lb av = 27.679886 cu in. H_2O at 4°C

1 lb av = 7000 grains

∴ 1 gal = 58417.87 grains

231 cu in. = 1 gal = 3785.4162 g

When volume and weight interconversions are given, water is the medium the calculations are based upon. By the introduction of specific gravity factors the medium can be changed, giving the weight of any volume of any material, etc.

Table continued on next page.

Table 29–9. Volume, Weight, and Energy Units (*Continued*)

To convert from	Multiply by										
	To Btu	To pcu	To cal	To ft-lb	To ft-tons	To kg-m	To hp-hr	To kw-hr	To joules	To lb C	To lb H_2O
Btu	1.00000	.555556	.251996	778.000	.389001	107.563	$.0_3 3929$	$.0_3 2931$	1055.20	$.0_4 6876$	.001031
Pcu	1.80000	1.00000	45.3593	1400.40	.700202	193.613	$.0_3 7072$	$.0_3 5276$	1899.36	$.0_3 1238$	.001855
Calories	3.96832	2.20462	1.00000	3091.36	1.54368	426.844	.001559	.001163	4187.37	$.0_3 2729$	.004089
Ft-lb	.001285	$.0_3 7141$	$.0_3 3239$	1.00000	.000500	.138255	$.0_6 5050$	$.0_6 3767$	1.35625	$.0_7 8840$	$.0_5 1325$
Ft-tons	2.57069	1.42816	.647804	2000.00	1.00000	276.511	.001010	$.0_3 7535$	2712.59	$.0_3 1768$	002649
Kg-m	.009297	.005165	.002343	7.23301	.003617	1.00000	$.0_5 3653$	$.0_5 2725$	9.81009	$.0_6 6394$	$.0_5 9580$
Hp-hr	2544.99	141388	641.327	1980000	990.004	273747	1.00000	.746000	2685473	.175044	2.62261
Kwhr	3411.57	1895.32	859.702	2654200	1327.10	366959	1.34041	1.00000	3599889	.234648	3.51562
Joules	$.0_3 9477$	$.0_3 5265$	$.0_3 2388$	.737311	$.0_3 3687$	.101937	$.0_6 3724$	$.0_6 2778$	1.00000	$.0_7 6518$	$.0_6 9766$
Lb C	14544.0	8080.00	3665.03	113150_3	5657.63	1564396	5.71434	4.26285	153470_3	1.00000	14.9876
Lb H_2O	970.400	539.111	244.537	754971	377.487	104379	.381270	.284424	1023966	.066744	1.00000

"Pcu" refers to the pound-centigrade unit. "Lb C" refers to pounds of carbon oxidized, 100% efficiency, equivalent to the corresponding number of heat units.

"Lb H_2O" refers to the pounds of water evaporated at 100°C, at 100% efficiency.

Extract from *Chemical & Metallurgical Engineering* magazine.

Table 29–10. Wire and Sheet-metal Gauges

Values in approximate decimals of an inch

As a number of gauges are in use for various shapes and metals, it is **advisable to state the thickness in thousandths when specifying gauge number.**

Gauge number	**American** (A.W.G.) or **Brown & Sharpe** (B. & S.) (for nonferrous wire and sheet) *	**U.S. Steel Wire** (Stl. W.G.) or **Washburn & Moen** or **Roebling** or **Am. Steel & Wire Co.** [A. (steel) W.G.] (for steel wire)	**Birmingham** (B.W.G.) (for steel wire) or **Stubs Iron Wire** (for iron or brass wire) †	**U.S. Standard** (for sheet and plate metal, wrought iron)	**Standard Birmingham** (B.G.) (for sheet and hoop metal)	**Imperial Standard Wire Gauge** (S.W.G.) (British legal standard)	**Gauge** number
0000000	. . .	.4900	. . .	.500	.6666	.500	**0000000**
000000	. . .	.4615	. . .	.469	.6250	.464	**000000** *
00000	. . .	.4305	. . .	.438	.5883	.432	**00000**
0000	.460	.3938	.454	.406	.5416	.400	**0000**
000	.410	.3625	.425	.375	.5000	.372	**000**
00	.365	.3310	.380	.344	.4452	.348	**00**
0	.325	.3065	.340	.312	.3964	.324	**0**
1	.289	.2830	.300	.281	.3532	.300	**1**
2	.258	.2625	.284	.266	.3147	.276	**2**
3	.229	.2437	.259	.250	.2804	.252	**3**
4	.204	.2253	.238	.234	.2500	.232	**4**
5	.182	.2070	.220	.219	.2225	.212	**5**
6	.162	.1920	.203	.203	.1981	.192	**6**
7	.144	.1770	.180	.188	.1764	.176	**7**
8	.128	.1620	.165	.172	.1570	.160	**8**
9	.114	.1483	.148	.156	.1398	.144	**9**
10	.102	.1350	.134	.141	.1250	.128	**10**
11	.091	.1205	.120	.125	.1113	.116	**11**
12	.081	.1055	.109	.109	.0991	.104	**12**
13	.072	.0915	.095	.094	.0882	.092	**13**
14	.064	.0800	.083	.078	.0785	.080	**14**
15	.057	.0720	.072	.070	.0699	.072	**15**
16	.051	.0625	.065	.062	.0625	.064	**16**
17	.045	.0540	.058	.056	.0556	.056	**17**
18	.040	.0475	.049	.050	.0495	.048	**18**
19	.036	.0410	.042	.0438	.0440	.040	**19**
20	.032	.0348	.035	.0375	.0392	.036	**20**
21	.0285	.0317	.032	.0344	.0349	.032	**21**
22	.0253	.0286	.028	.0312	.0313	.028	**22**
23	.0226	.0258	.025	.0281	.0278	.024	**23**
24	.0201	.0230	.022	.0250	.0248	.022	**24**
25	.0179	.0204	.020	.0219	.0220	.020	**25**

Table 29–10. Wire and Sheet-metal Gauges (*Continued*)

Values in approximate decimals of an inch

As a number of gauges are in use for various shapes and metals, it is **advisable to state the thickness in thousandths when specifying gauge number.**

Gauge number	**American** (A.W.G.) or **Brown & Sharpe** (B. & S.) (for nonferrous wire and sheet) *	**U.S. Steel Wire** (Stl. W.G.) or **Washburn & Moen** or **Roebling** or **Am. Steel & Wire Co.** [A. (steel) W.G.] (for steel wire)	**Birmingham** (B.W.G.) (for steel wire) or **Stubs Iron Wire** (for iron or brass wire)†	**U.S. Standard** (for sheet and plate metal, wrought iron)	**Standard Birmingham** (B.G.) (for sheet and hoop metal)	**Imperial Standard Wire Gauge** (S.W.G.) (British legal standard)	**Gauge** number
26	.0159	.0181	.018	.0188	.0196	.018	**26**
27	.0142	.0173	.016	.0172	.0175	.0164	**27**
28	.0126	.0162	.014	.0156	.0156	.0148	**28**
29	.0113	.0150	.013	.0141	.0139	.0136	**29**
30	.0100	.0140	.012	.0125	.0123	.0124	**30**
31	.0089	.0132	.010	.0109	.0110	.0116	**31**
32	.0080	.0128	.009	.0102	.0098	.0108	**32**
33	.0071	.0118	.008	.0094	.0087	.0100	**33**
34	.0063	.0104	.007	.0086	.0077	.0092	**34**
35	.0056	.0095	.005	.0078	.0069	.0084	**35**
36	.0050	.0090	.004	.0070	.0061	.0076	**36**
37	.0045	.0085	....	.0066	.0054	.0068	**37**
38	.0040	.0080	....	.0062	.0048	.0060	**38**
39	.0035	.0075	....	.....	.0043	.0052	**39**
40	.0031	.0070	....	.....	.0039	.0048	**40**
41	.....	.0066	....	.....	.0034	.0044	**41**
42	.....	.0062	....	.....	.0031	.0040	**42**
43	.....	.0060	....	.....	.0027	.0036	**43**
44	.....	.0058	....	.....	.0024	.0032	**44**
45	.....	.0055	....	.....	.0022	.0028	**45**
46	.....	.0052	....	.....	.0019	.0024	**46**
47	.....	.0050	....	.....	.0017	.0020	**47**
48	.....	.0048	....	.....	.0015	.0016	**48**
49	.....	.0046	....	.....	.0014	.0012	**49**
50	.....	.0044	....	.....	.0012	.0010	**50**

Metric wire gauge is ten times the diameter in millimeters.

* Sometimes used for iron wire.

† Sometimes used for copper plate and for steel plate 12 gauge and heavier and for steel tubes.

From Dr. Lewis V. Judson with I. H. Fullmer, National Bureau of Standards.

Reprinted from Robert H. Perry et al., "Chemical Engineers' Handbook," 4th ed., McGraw-Hill Book Company, Inc., New York, 1963.

MISCELLANEOUS TABLES

Table 29-11A. Relative Atomic Weights—1961

Based on the Atomic Mass of ^{12}C = 12

The values for atomic weights given in the table apply to elements as they exist in nature, without artificial alteration of their isotopic composition, and, further, to natural mixtures that do not include isotopes of radiogenic origin.

Alphabetical Order

Name	Symbol	Atomic number	Atomic weight	Name	Symbol	Atomic number	Atomic weight
Actinium	Ac	89		Iron	Fe	26	55.847[b]
Aluminum	Al	13	26.9815	Krypton	Kr	36	83.80
Americium	Am	95		Lanthanum	La	57	138.91
Antimony	Sb	51	121.75	Lead	Pb	82	207.19
Argon	Ar	18	39.948	Lithium	Li	3	6.939
Arsenic	As	33	74.9216	Lutetium	Lu	71	174.97
Astatine	At	85		Magnesium	Mg	12	24.312
Barium	Ba	56	137.34	Manganese	Mn	25	54.9380
Berkelium	Bk	97		Mendelevium	Md	101	
Beryllium	Be	4	9.0122	Mercury	Hg	80	200.59
Bismuth	Bi	83	208.980	Molybdenum	Mo	42	95.94
Boron	B	5	10.811[a]	Neodymium	Nd	60	144.24
Bromine	Br	35	79.909[b]	Neon	Ne	10	20.183
Cadmium	Cd	48	112.40	Neptunium	Np	93	
Calcium	Ca	20	40.08	Nickel	Ni	28	58.71
Californium	Cf	98		Niobium	Nb	41	92.906
Carbon	C	6	12.01115[a]	Nitrogen	N	7	14.0067
Cerium	Ce	58	140.12	Nobelium	No	102	
Cesium	Cs	55	132.905	Osmium	Os	76	190.2
Chlorine	Cl	17	35.453[b]	Oxygen	O	8	15.9994[a]
Chromium	Cr	24	51.996[b]	Palladium	Pd	46	106.4
Cobalt	Co	27	58.9332	Phosphorus	P	15	30.9738
Copper	Cd	29	63.54	Platinum	Pt	78	195.09
Curium	Cm	96		Plutonium	Pu	94	
Dysprosium	Dy	66	162.50	Polonium	Po	84	
Einsteinium	Es	99		Potassium	K	19	39.102
Erbium	Er	68	167.26	Praseodymium	Pr	59	140.907
Europium	Eu	63	151.96	Promethium	Pm	61	
Fermium	Fm	100		Protactinium	Pa	91	
Fluorine	F	9	18.9984	Radium	Ra	88	
Francium	Fr	87		Radon	Rn	86	
Gadolinium	Gd	64	157.25	Rhenium	Re	75	186.2
Gallium	Ga	31	69.72	Rhodium	Rh	45	102.905
Germanium	Ge	32	72.59	Rubidium	Rb	37	85.47
Gold	Au	79	196.967	Ruthenium	Ru	44	101.07
Hafnium	Hf	72	178.49	Samarium	Sm	62	150.35
Helium	He	2	4.0026	Scandium	Sc	21	44.956
Holmium	Ho	67	164.930	Selenium	Se	34	78.96
Hydrogen	H	1	1.00797[a]	Silicon	Si	14	28.086[a]
Indium	In	49	114.82	Silver	Ag	47	107.870[b]
Iodine	I	53	126.9044	Sodium	Na	11	22.9898
Iridium	Ir	77	192.2	Strontium	Sr	38	87.62

Table 29-11A. Relative Atomic Weights—1961 (*Continued*)

Name	Symbol	Atomic number	Atomic weight	Name	Symbol	Atomic number	Atomic weight
Sulfur	S	16	32.064[a]	Titanium	Ti	22	47.90
Tantalum	Ta	73	180.948	Tungsten	W	74	183.85
Technetium	Tc	43		Uranium	U	92	238.03
Tellurium	Te	52	127.60	Vanadium	V	23	50.942
Terbium	Tb	65	158.924	Xenon	Xe	54	131.30
Thallium	Tl	81	204.37	Ytterbium	Yb	70	173.04
Thorium	Th	90	232.038	Yttrium	Y	39	88.905
Thulium	Tm	69	168.934	Zinc	Zn	30	65.37
Tin	Sn	50	118.69	Zirconium	Zr	40	91.22

[a] Atomic weights so designated are known to be variable because of natural variations in isotopic composition. The observed ranges are:

Hydrogen	±0.00001
Boron	±0.003
Carbon	±0.00005
Oxygen	±0.0001
Silicon	±0.001
Sulfur	±0.003

[b] Atomic weights so designated are believed to have the following experimental uncertainties:

Chlorine	±0.001
Chromium	±0.001
Iron	±0.003
Bromine	±0.002
Silver	±0.003

Table 29-11B. The Radioactive Elements—1961

Alphabetical Order

Name	Symbol	Atomic number	Isotope	Half life	Mode of disintegration
Actinium	Ac	89	227	21 year	β^-, α
Americium	Am	95	243	7.8×10^3 years	α
Astatine	At	85	210	8.3 hours	α
Berkelium	Bk	97	247	*ca.* 10^4 years	α
Californium	Cf	98	249	360 years	α
Curium	Cm	96	247	$>4 \times 10^7$ years	α
Einsteinium	Es	99	254	*ca.* 320 days	α
Fermium	Fm	100	253	3 days	α
Francium	Fr	87	223	22 minutes	β^-
Mendelevium	Md	101	256	*ca.* 1.5 hours	electron capture
Neptunium	Np	93	237	2.1×10^6 years	α
Nobelium	No	102		*ca.* 10 minutes	α
Plutonium	Pu	94	242	3.8×10^5 years	α
Polonium	Po	84	210*	138 days	α
Promethium	Pm	61	147*	2.6 years	β^-
Protactinium	Pa	91	231	3.4×10^4 years	α
Radium	Ra	88	226	1622 years	α
Radon	Rn	86	222	3.8 days	α
Technetium	Tc	43	99*	2.1×10^5 years	β^-
Thorium	Th	90	232	1.4×10^{10} years	α
Uranium	U	92	238	4.5×10^9 years	α

This table lists selected isotopes of the chemical elements, whether occurring in nature or known only through synthesis, that are commonly classed as radioactive. The listed isotope may be either the one of longest known half-life, or, for those marked with an asterisk, a better known one.

Reprinted by permission of copyright owner, the American Chemical Society, from "The Report of the International Commission on Atomic Weights" by A. E. Cameron and Edward Wichers appearing in the *Journal of the American Chemical Society*, vol. 84, no. 22, Dec. 6, 1962.

Table 29–12A. Discount Computer 1

Discount, per cent	Equiv-alent	Net	Discount, per cent	Equiv-alent	Net	Discount, per cent	Equiv-alent	Net
2½	.025	.975	25	.25	.75	30, 7½, & 7½	.4011	.5989
2½ & 2½	.0494	.9506	25 & 2½	.2688	.7312	30, 7½, & 10	.4173	.5827
2½ & 5	.0737	.9263	25, 2½, & 2½	.2870	.713	30 & 10	.37	.63
2½, 5, & 2½	.0969	.9031	25, 2½, & 5	.3053	.6947	30, 10, & 2½	.3858	.6142
2½, 5, & 5	.1201	.8799	24, 2½, & 7½	.3236	.6764	30, 10, & 5	.4015	.5985
2½, 5, 5, & 2½	.1421	.8579	25, 2½, & 10	.3419	.6581	30, 10, & 7½	.4173	.5827
2½ & 10	.1225	.8775	25 & 5	.2875	.7125	30, 10, & 10	.433	.567
2½, 10, & 2½	.1444	.8556	25, 5, & 2½	.3053	.6947	32½	.325	.675
2½, 10, & 5	.166	.834	25, 5, & 5	.3231	.6769	32½ & 2½	.3419	.6581
2½, 10, 5, & 2½	.1872	.8128	25, 5, & 7½	.3409	.6591	32½, 2½, & 2½	.3583	.6417
2½, 10, & 10	.2102	.7898	25, 5, & 10	.3588	.6412	32½, 2½, & 5	.3748	.6252
5	.05	.95	25 & 7½	.3063	.6937	32½, 2½, & 7½	.3912	.6088
5 & 2½	.0738	.9262	25, 7½, & 2½	.3236	.6764	32½, 2½, & 10	.4077	.5923
5 & 5	.0975	.9025	25, 7½, & 5	.3409	.6591	32½ & 5	.3588	.6412
5, 5, & 2½	.1201	.8799	25, 7½, & 7½	.3583	.6417	32½, 5, & 2½	.3748	.6252
5, 5, & 5	.1426	.8574	25, 7½, & 10	.3756	.6244	32½, 5, & 5	.3908	.6092
5, 5, 5, & 2½	.164	.836	25 & 10	.325	.675	32½, 5, & 7½	.4068	.5932
5 & 10	.145	.855	25, 10, & 2½	.3419	.6581	32½, 5, & 10	.4229	.5771
5, 10, & 2½	.1664	.8336	25, 10, & 5	.3588	.6412	32½ & 7½	.3756	.6244
5, 10, & 5	.1877	.8123	25, 10, & 7½	.3756	.6244	32½, 7½, & 2½	.3912	.6088
5, 10, 5, & 2½	.2081	.7919	25, 10, & 10	.392	.6075	32½, 7½, & 5	.4068	.5932
5, 10, & 10	.2305	.7695	27½	.275	.725	32½, 7½, & 7½	.4225	.5775
10	.10	.90	27½ & 2½	.2931	.7069	32½, 7½, & 10	.4381	.5619
10 & 2½	.1225	.8775	27½, 2½, & 2½	.3108	.6892	32½ & 10	.3925	.6075
10 & 5	.145	.855	27½, 2½, & 5	.3285	.6715	32½, 10, & 2½	.4077	.5923
10, 5, & 2½	.1664	.8336	27½, 2½, & 7½	.3461	.6539	32½, 10, & 5	.4229	.5771
10, 5, & 5	.1878	.8122	27½, 2½, & 10	.3638	.6362	32½, 10, & 7½	.4381	.5619
10, 5, 5, & 2½	.2081	.7919	27½ & 5	.3113	.6887	32½, 10, & 10	.4533	.5467
10 & 10	.190	.81	27½, 5, & 2½	.3285	.6715	32½ & 20	.460	.54
10, 10, & 2½	.2103	.7897	27½, 5, & 5	.3457	.6543	32½, 20, & 2½	.4735	.5625
10, 10, & 5	.2305	.7695	27½, 5, & 7½	.3629	.6371	32½, 20, & 5	.4870	.5130
10, 10, 5, & 2½	.2497	.7503	27½, 5, & 10	.3801	.6199	32½, 20, & 7½	.5005	.4995
10, 10, & 10	.271	.729	27½ & 7½	.3294	.6706	32½, 20, & 10	.514	.486
15	.150	.85	27½, 7½, & 2½	.3461	.6539	32½, 20, & 20	.5680	.4320
15 & 2½	.1713	.8287	27½, 7½, & 5	.3629	.6471	35	.35	.65
15 & 5	.1925	.8075	27½, 7½, & 7½	.3797	.6203	35 & 2½	.3663	.6337
15, 5, & 2½	.2127	.7873	27½, 7½, & 10	.3964	.6036	35, 2½, & 2½	.3821	.6179
15, 5, & 5	.2329	.7671	27½ & 10	.3475	.6525	35, 2½, & 5	.3979	.6021
15, 5, 5, & 2½	.2521	.7479	27½, 10, & 2½	.3638	.6362	35, 2½, & 7½	.4138	.5862
15 & 10	.235	.765	27½, 10, & 5	.3801	.6199	35, 2½, & 10	.4296	.5704
15, 10, & 2½	.2541	.7459	27½, 10, & 7½	.3964	.6036	35 & 5	.3825	.6175
15, 10, & 5	.2733	.7267	27½, 10, & 10	.4128	.5872	35, 5, & 2½	.3979	.6021
15, 10, 5, & 2½	.2914	.7086	30	.30	.70	35, 5, & 5	.4134	.5866
15, 10, & 10	.3115	.6885	30 & 2½	.3175	.6825	35, 5, & 7½	.4288	.5712
20	.20	.80	30, 2½, & 2½	.3346	.6654	35, 5, & 10	.4443	.5557
20 & 2½	.220	.78	30, 2½, & 5	.3516	.6484	35 & 7½	.3988	.6012
20 & 5	.240	.76	30, 2½, & 7½	.3687	.6313	35, 7½, & 2½	.4138	.5862
20, 5, & 2½	.259	.741	30, 2½, & 10	.3858	.6142	35, 7½, & 5	.4288	.5712
20, 5, & 5	.278	.722	30 & 5	.335	.665	35, 7½, & 7½	.4438	.5562
20, 5, 5, & 2½	.2961	.7039	30, 5, & 2½	.3516	.6484	35, 7½, & 10	.4589	.5511
20 & 10	.280	.72	30, 5, & 5	.3683	.6317	35 & 10	.415	.585
20, 10, & 2½	.298	.702	30, 5, & 7½	.3849	.6151	35, 10, & 2½	.4296	.5704
20, 10, & 5	.316	.684	30, 5, & 10	.4015	.5985	35, 10, & 5	.4443	.5557
20, 10, 5, & 2½	.3331	.6669	30 & 7½	.3525	.6475	35, 10, & 7½	.4589	.5411
20, 10, & 10	.352	.648	30, 7½, & 2½	.3687	.6313	35, 10, & 10	.4735	.5265
			30, 7½, & 5	.3849	.6151	35 & 20	.48	.52

Table 29-12A. Discount Computer 1 (*Continued*)

Discount, per cent	Equivalent	Net	Discount, per cent	Equivalent	Net	Discount, per cent	Equivalent	Net
35, 20, & 2½	.493	.507	40, 20, & 7½	.556	.444	45, 20, & 20	.648	.352
35, 20, & 5	.5060	.4940	40, 20, & 10	.568	.432	47½	.475	.525
35, 20, & 7½	.4190	.5810	40, 20, & 20	.616	.384	47½ & 2½	.4881	.5119
35, 20, & 10	.3520	.6480	42½	.425	.575	47½, 2½, & 2½	.5009	.4991
35, 20, & 20	.5840	.4160	42½ & 2½	.4394	.5606	47½, 2½, & 5	.5237	.4863
37½	.375	.625	42½, 2½, & 2½	.4534	.5466	47½, 2½, & 7½	.5265	.4735
37½ & 2½	.3906	.6094	42½, 2½, & 5	.4674	.5326	47½, 2½, & 10	.5393	.4607
37½, 2½, & 2½	.4059	.5941	42½, 2½, & 7½	.4814	.5186	47½ & 5	.5013	.4987
37½, 2½, & 5	.4211	.5789	42½, 2½, & 10	.4954	.5046	47½, 5, & 2½	.5137	.4863
37½, 2½, & 7½	.4363	.5637	42½ & 5	.4538	.5462	47½, 5, & 5	.5262	.4738
37½, 2½, & 10	.4516	.5484	42½, 5, & 2½	.4674	.5326	47½, 5, & 7½	.5386	.4614
37½ & 5	.4063	.5937	42½, 5, & 5	.4811	.5189	47½, 5, & 10	.5511	.4489
37½, 5, & 2½	.4211	.5789	42½, 5, & 7½	.4947	.5053	47½ & 7½	.5144	.4856
37½, 5, & 5	.4359	.5641	42½, 5, & 10	.5084	.4916	47½, 7½, & 2½	.5265	.4735
37½, 5, & 7½	.4508	.5492	42½ & 7½	.4681	.5319	47½, 7½, & 5	.5387	.4613
37½, 5, & 10	.4656	.5344	42½, 7½, & 2½	.4814	.5186	47½, 7½, & 7½	.5508	.4492
37½ & 7½	.4219	.5781	42½, 7½, & 5	.4947	.5053	47½, 7½, & 10	.5629	.4371
37½, 7½, & 2½	.4363	.5637	42½, 7½, & 7½	.508	.492	47½ & 10	.5275	.4725
37½, 7½, & 5	.4508	.5492	42½, 7½, & 10	.5213	.4787	47½, 10, & 2½	.5393	.4607
37½, 7½, & 7½	.4652	.5348	42½ & 10	.4825	.5175	47½, 10, & 5	.5511	.4489
37½, 7½, & 10	.4797	.5203	42½, 10, & 2½	.4954	.5046	47½, 10, & 7½	.5629	.4371
37½ & 10	.4375	.5625	42½, 10, & 5	.5084	.4916	47½, 10, & 10	.5748	.4252
37½, 10, & 2½	.4516	.5484	42½, 10, & 7½	.5213	.4787	47½ & 20	.58	.42
37½, 10, & 5	.4656	.5344	42½, 10, & 10	.5343	.4657	47½, 20, & 2½	.5905	.4095
37½, 10, & 7½	.4797	.5203	42½ & 20	.54	.46	47½, 20, & 5	.601	.399
37½, 10, & 10	.4938	.5062	42½, 20, & 2½	.5515	.4485	47½, 20, & 7½	.6115	.3885
37½ & 20	.50	.50	42½, 20, & 5	.563	.437	47½, 20, & 10	.622	.378
37½, 20, & 2½	.5125	.4875	42½, 20, & 7½	.5745	.4255	47½, 20, & 20	.664	.336
37½, 20, & 5	.5250	.4750	42½, 20, & 10	.586	.414	50	.50	.50
37½, 20, & 7½	.5375	.4625	42½, 20, & 20	.632	.368	50 & 2½	.5125	.4875
37½, 20, & 10	.55	.45	45	.45	.55	50, 2½, & 2½	.5247	.4753
37½, 20, & 20	.60	.40	45 & 2½	.4638	.5362	50, 2½, & 5	.5369	.4631
40	.40	.60	45, 2½, & 2½	.4772	.5228	50, 2½, & 7½	.5491	.4509
40 & 2½	.415	.585	45, 2½, & 5	.4906	.5094	50, 2½, & 10	.5613	.4387
40, 2½, & 2½	.4296	.5704	45, 2½, & 7½	.504	.496	50 & 5	.515	.475
40, 2½, & 5	.4443	.5557	45, 2½, & 10	.5174	.4826	50, 5, & 2½	.5369	.4631
40, 2½, & 7½	.4589	.5411	45 & 5	.4775	.5225	50, 5, & 5	.5488	.4512
40, 2½, & 10	.4735	.5265	45, 5, & 2½	.4906	.5094	50, 5, & 7½	.5606	.4394
40 & 5	.43	.57	45, 5, & 5	.5036	.4964	50, 5, & 10	.5725	.4275
40, 5, & 2½	.4443	.5557	45, 5, & 7½	.5167	.4833	50 & 7½	.5375	.4625
40, 5, & 5	.4585	.5415	45, 5, & 10	.5298	.4702	50, 7½, & 2½	.5491	.4509
40, 5, & 7½	.4728	.5272	45 & 7½	.4913	.5087	50, 7½, & 5	.5606	.4394
40, 5, & 10	.487	.513	45, 7½, & 2½	.504	.496	50, 7½, & 7½	.5722	.4278
40 & 7½	.445	.555	45, 7½, & 5	5167	.4833	50, 7½, & 10	.5838	.4162
40, 7½, & 2½	.4589	.5411	45, 7½, & 7½	.5294	.4706	50 & 10	.55	.45
40, 7½, & 5	.4728	.5272	45, 7½, & 10	.5421	.4579	50, 10, & 2½	.5613	.4387
40, 7½, & 7½	.4866	.5134	45 & 10	.505	.495	50, 10, & 5	.5725	.4275
40, 7½, & 10	.5005	.4995	45, 10, & 2½	.5174	.4826	50, 10, & 7½	.5838	.4162
40 & 10	.46	.54	45, 10, & 5	.5298	.4702	50, 10, & 10	.595	.405
40, 10, & 2½	.4735	.5265	45, 10, & 7½	.5421	.4579	50 & 20	.60	.40
40, 10, & 5	.487	.513	45, 10, & 10	.5545	.4455	50, 20, & 2½	.61	.39
40, 10, & 7½	.5005	.4995	45 & 20	.56	.44	50, 20, & 5	.62	.38
40, 10, & 10	.514	.486	45, 20, & 2½	.571	.429	50, 20, & 7½	.63	.37
40 & 20	.52	.48	45, 20, & 5	.582	.418	50, 20, & 10	.64	.36
40, 20, & 2½	.532	.468	45, 20, & 7½	.593	.407	50, 20, & 20	.68	.32
40, 20, & 5	.544	.456	45, 20, & 10	.604	.396	52½	.525	.475

Reprinted with permission from the "Personal Record Book for Executives," published by the Dartnell Corporation, Chicago.

Table 29–12B. Discount Computer 2

To find a net price, multiply list price by the decimal net equivalent of the given discount.

Example. What will be the net price if a discount of 40–10–10–5 is allowed on a list price of $65?

Solution. In the column for Leading Discount 40, and in the horizontal line for Supplementary Discount 10–10–5 at the left, find the decimal net equivalent .4617. Then $65 by .4617 equals $30.01, the net price.

Discount	Leading discount										
	10	20	25	30	33⅓	40	50	60	66⅔	75	80
	Decimal net equivalent										
2½	.8775	.7800	.7313	.6825	.6500	.5850	.4875	.3900	.325	.2438	.1950
5	.8550	.7600	.7125	.6650	.6333	.5700	.4750	.3800	.3167	.2375	.1900
5–2½	.8336	.7410	.6947	.6484	.6175	.5558	.4631	.3705	.3087	.2316	.1853
5–5	.8123	.7220	.6769	.6318	.6017	.5415	.4513	.3610	.3008	.2256	.1805
10	.8100	.7200	.6750	.6300	.6000	.5400	.4500	.3600	.3000	.2250	.1800
10–2½	.7898	.7020	.6581	.6143	.5850	.5265	.4388	.3510	.2925	.2194	.1755
10–5	.7695	.6840	.6413	.5985	.5700	.5130	.4275	.3420	.2850	.2138	.1710
10–5–2½	.7503	.6669	.6252	.5835	.5558	.5002	.4168	.3334	.2779	.2084	.1667
10–10	.7290	.6480	.6075	.5670	.5400	.4860	.4050	.3240	.2700	.2025	.1620
10–10–5	.6925	.6156	.5771	.5387	.5130	.4617	.3848	.3078	.2565	.1924	.1539
10–10–5–2½	.6752	.6002	.5627	.5252	.5002	.4502	.3752	.3001	.2501	.1876	.1501
10–10–10	.6561	.5832	.5468	.5103	.4860	.4374	.3645	.2916	.2430	.1823	.1458
10–10–10–10	.5905	.5249	.4921	.4593	.4374	.3937	.3281	.2624	.2187	.1640	.1312
10–10–10–10–5	.5610	.4987	.4675	.4363	.4155	.3740	.3116	.2493	.2078	.1558	.1246
15	.7650	.6800	.6375	.5950	.5667	.5100	.4250	.3400	.2833	.2125	.1700
15–2½	.7459	.6630	.6216	.5801	.5525	.4973	.4144	.3315	.2762	.2072	.1658
15–5	.7268	.6460	.6056	.5653	.5383	.4845	.4038	.3230	.2692	.2019	.1615
15–10	.6885	.6120	.5738	.5355	.5100	.4590	.3825	.3060	.2550	.1913	.1530
20	.7200	.6400	.6000	.5600	.5333	.4800	.4000	.3200	.2667	.2000	.1600
20–5	.6840	.6080	.5700	.5320	.5067	.4560	.3800	.3040	.2533	.1900	.1520
20–10	.6480	.5760	.5400	.5040	.4800	.4320	.3600	.2880	.2400	.1800	.1440
20–10–5	.6156	.5472	.5130	.4788	.4560	.4104	.3420	.2736	.2280	.1710	.1368
25	.6750	.6000	.5625	.5250	.5000	.4500	.3750	.3000	.2500	.1875	.1500
25–5	.6413	.5700	.5344	.4987	.4750	.4275	.3563	.2850	.2375	.1781	.1425
25–10	.6075	.5400	.5063	.4725	.4500	.4050	.3375	.2700	.2250	.1688	.1350
25–10–5	.5771	.5130	.4809	.4489	.4275	.3848	.3206	.2565	.2137	.1603	.1283

Reprinted by permission of the *New England Purchaser* magazine, Boston, Mass.

Table 29–13. Cash Discounts

The cash discount is what a seller is willing to give his customers for paying his bill *20 days* before the expiration of the full 30-day period. A 2 per cent cash discount thus gives the buyer an inducement of 36 per cent a year, since there are eighteen periods of 20 days each, which might be anticipated by the buyer if he were having shipments made to him constantly through the year.

½% 10 days—net 30 days = 9% per annum
1 % 10 days—net 30 days = 18% per annum
1½% 10 days—net 30 days = 27% per annum
2 % 30 days—net 4 mos. = 8% per annum
2 % 10 days—net 60 days = 14% per annum
2 % 30 days—net 60 days = 24% per annum
2 % 10 days—net 30 days = 36% per annum
3 % 10 days—net 4 mos. = 10% per annum
3 % 30 days—net 60 days = 36% per annum
3 % 10 days—net 30 days = 54% per annum

Reprinted with permission from the "Personal Record Book for Executives," published by the Dartnell Corporation, Chicago.

Table 29–14. Greek Alphabet

Name	Greek	English
Alpha	Α, α	A, a
Beta	Β, β	B, b
Gamma	Γ, γ	G, g
Delta	Δ, δ	D, d
Epsilon	Ε, ϵ	E, e
Zeta	Ζ, ζ	Z, z
Eta	Η, η	E, e
Theta	Θ, θ	Th, th
Iota	Ι, ι	I, i
Kappa	Κ, κ	K, k
Lambda	Λ, λ	L, l
Mu	Μ, μ	M, m
Nu	Ν, ν	N, n
Xi	Ξ, ξ	X, x
Omicron	Ο, ο	O, o
Pi	Π, π	P, p
Rho	Ρ, ρ	R, r
Sigma	Σ, σ	S, s
Tau	Τ, τ	T, t
Upsilon	ϒ, υ	U, u
Phi	Φ, ϕ	Ph, ph
Chi	Χ, χ	Ch, ch
Psi	Ψ, ψ	Ps, ps
Omega	Ω, ω	O, o

Table 29–15. Profits and Markups

Cost per dozen	Each	Profit per cent on selling price							
		20%	23.10%	25%	28.57%	33⅓%	37½%	42.86%	50%
$ 0.12	$0.01	0.013	0.013	.013	0.014	.015	0.016	0.018	0.02
0.15	0.013	0.015	0.016	.016	0.017	.019	0.02	0.022	0.025
0.20	0.017	0.021	0.022	.022	0.023	.025	0.027	0.029	0.033
0.24	0.02	0.025	0.026	.027	0.028	.03	0.032	0.035	0.04
0.25	0.021	0.026	0.027	.028	0.029	.031	0.033	0.037	0.042
0.30	0.025	0.031	0.033	.033	0.035	.038	0.04	0.044	0.05
0.35	0.030	0.037	0.038	.039	0.041	.044	0.047	0.051	0.058
0.36	0.03	0.038	0.039	.04	0.042	.045	0.048	0.053	0.06
0.40	0.033	0.042	0.043	.044	0.047	.05	0.053	0.058	0.067
0.45	0.038	0.047	0.049	.05	0.053	.056	0.06	0.066	0.075
0.48	0.04	0.05	0.052	.053	0.056	.06	0.064	0.07	0.08
0.50	0.042	0.053	0.055	.056	0.059	.063	0.067	0.074	0.084
0.60	0.05	0.063	0.065	.067	0.07	.075	0.08	0.088	0.10
0.72	0.06	0.075	0.078	.08	0.084	.09	0.096	0.105	0.12
0.75	0.063	0.078	0.081	.083	0.088	.094	0.10	0.11	0.125
0.84	0.07	0.088	0.091	.093	0.098	.105	0.112	0.123	0.14
0.96	0.08	0.10	0.101	.107	0.112	.12	0.128	0.14	0.16
1.00	0.083	0.104	0.108	.111	0.116	.125	0.133	0.145	0.166
1.20	0.10	0.125	0.13	.133	0.14	.15	0.16	0.175	0.20
1.25	0.104	0.13	0.135	.139	0.146	.156	0.166	0.182	0.208
1.50	0.125	0.156	0.163	.167	0.175	.188	0.20	0.219	0.25
1.75	0.146	0.183	0.19	.195	0.204	.219	0.234	0.256	0.292
2.00	0.167	0.209	0.217	.223	0.234	.251	0.267	0.292	0.334
2.25	0.188	0.235	0.244	.251	0.263	.282	0.30	0.329	0.376
2.50	0.208	0.26	0.27	.277	0.291	.312	0.333	0.364	0.416
2.75	0.229	0.286	0.298	.305	0.321	.344	0.366	0.40	0.458

Table 29–15. Profits and Markups (*Continued*)

Cost per dozen	Each	Profit per cent on selling price							
		20%	23.10%	25%	28.57%	33⅓%	37½%	42.86%	50%
$ 3.00	$0.25	0.312	0.325	.333	0.35	.375	0.40	0.437	0.50
3.25	0.27	0.337	0.351	.36	0.378	.405	0.432	0.473	0.54
3.75	0.312	0.39	0.406	.416	0.437	.468	0.499	0.546	0.624
4.00	0.333	0.416	0.433	.444	0.466	.50	0.533	0.583	0.666
4.25	0.354	0.443	0.460	.472	0.496	.531	0.566	0.62	0.708
4.50	0.375	0.469	0.488	.50	0.525	.563	0.60	0.656	0.75
5.00	0.417	0.524	0.542	.556	0.584	.626	0.667	0.73	0.834
6.00	0.50	0.625	0.65	.667	0.70	.75	0.80	0.875	1.00
6.50	0.541	0.676	0.703	.721	0.757	.812	0.866	0.947	1.08
6.75	0.562	0.703	0.731	.749	0.787	.843	0.899	0.984	1.12
7.00	0.583	0.729	0.758	.777	0.816	.875	0.933	1.02	1.17
7.25	0.604	0.755	0.785	.805	0.846	.906	0.956	1.06	1.21
7.50	0.625	0.781	0.813	.833	0.875	.938	1.00	1.09	1.25
8.00	0.666	0.833	0.866	.888	0.932	.999	1.07	1.17	1.33
8.50	0.708	0.885	0.92	.944	0.991	1.06	1.13	1.24	1.41
9.00	0.75	0.938	0.975	1.00	1.05	1.13	1.20	1.31	1.50
10.50	0.88	1.09	1.14	1.17	1.23	1.31	1.40	1.53	1.75
12.00	1.00	1.25	1.30	1.33	1.40	1.50	1.60	1.75	2.00
13.50	1.13	1.41	1.46	1.50	1.58	1.69	1.80	1.97	2.25
15.00	1.25	1.56	1.63	1.66	1.75	1.88	2.00	2.19	2.50
16.50	1.38	1.72	1.79	1.83	1.93	2.06	2.20	2.41	2.75
18.00	1.50	1.87	1.95	2.00	2.18	2.25	2.40	2.63	3.00
19.50	1.63	2.04	2.12	2.17	2.28	2.45	2.61	2.85	3.26
21.00	1.75	2.19	2.28	2.33	2.45	2.63	2.80	3.06	3.50
22.50	1.88	2.34	2.44	2.50	2.63	2.81	3.00	3.28	3.75
24.00	2.00	2.50	2.60	2.67	2.80	3.00	3.20	3.50	4.00
27.00	2.25	2.81	2.93	3.00	3.15	3.38	3.60	3.96	4.50
30.00	2.50	3.12	3.25	3.33	3.50	3.75	4.00	4.38	5.00
33.00	2.75	3.44	3.58	3.67	3.85	4.13	4.40	4.81	5.50
36.00	3.00	3.75	3.90	4.00	4.20	4.50	4.80	5.25	6.00
39.00	3.25	4.06	4.23	4.33	4.55	4.88	5.20	5.69	6.50
42.00	3.50	4.37	4.55	4.67	4.90	5.25	5.60	6.12	7.00
45.00	3.75	4.69	4.88	5.00	5.25	5.63	6.00	6.56	7.50
48.00	4.00	5.00	5.20	5.33	5.60	6.00	6.40	7.00	8.00
54.00	4.50	5.62	5.85	6.00	6.30	6.75	7.20	7.87	9.00
60.00	5.00	6.25	6.50	6.67	7.00	7.50	8.00	8.75	10.00
66.00	5.50	6.87	7.15	7.33	7.70	8.25	8.80	9.62	11.00
69.00	5.75	7.19	7.48	7.67	8.05	8.63	9.20	10.06	11.50
72.00	6.00	7.50	7.80	8.00	8.40	9.00	9.60	10.50	12.00
Per dozen	Each	25%	30%	33⅓%	40%	50%	60%	75%	100%
		Profit per cent on cost							

Reprinted by permission from the "Personal Record Book for Executives," published by the Dartnell Corporation, Chicago.

Table 29–16. Economic Order Value (EOV)

(Refer to Section 13 for explanation of Economic Order Quantity, EOQ. EOV and EOQ are solutions to the same problem, but may not be identical.)

What is EOV?

Economic Order Value is a scientific way of finding the right size-lot of orders. Behind it is this common-sense thinking:

• If you cut down on the number of orders you place, you'll save labor and paperwork, but

• If you increase their individual size to the point where you tie up too much money and storage, you'll erase—or exceed—your gains.

EOV tells you exactly where the balance lies.

What has made this subject so difficult heretofore is computation of the balance. The mathematics involved is time-consuming, painstaking, dreaded by everybody.

How We Can Help You

This special study eliminates computation drudgery. If you can read a railroad timetable, you can handle the figures that follow in a wink. Moreover, they not only tell you how to buy precisely, they also tell you 1) how big a penalty you will incur if you over-buy or under-buy, 2) how to judge quantity discounts, and 3) how to evaluate transportation rate savings.

True, you must know something about expenses and carrying charges in advance. So we have included instructions to show you how to get—or estimate—this information. *Read this section carefully first.*

Step I

What to Include in Your EOV Program

Your Economic Order Value Program will work best if you concentrate on items that:

- Consume the bulk of your expenditures, and
- Have a high turnover.

FORGET about such purchases as custom-made products, capital equipment, or items bought on tricky world markets.

CHOOSE products whose:

1) Annual use can be predicted fairly well.
2) Price is reasonably stable.
3) Shelf life is longer than the inventory cycle.
4) Chance of obsolescence is small.

Such a list should include:

- Many raw materials
- Standardized components

- Sub-assemblies
- Industrial supplies
- Stationery-office supplies
- Spare parts

Step II

How to Figure Your Order Cost

For EOV purposes, "order cost" is NOT based on the expense of running your entire department (which obviously would stay in existence whether you use EOV or not).

"Order cost" here applies only to extra cost—specifically, that extra expense (mainly labor and paperwork) which you incur when you place one more order. Economists call this concept "marginal cost." *You must have marginal cost data to use the tables.*

To get it, first have your accounting department supply—or estimate—the information required below (small errors won't matter):

	Per year
1. Salaries and fringe benefits for:	
Purchasing Administrator	$......*
Buyers	......*
Expediters	......*
Secretaries	......*
Clerical	......*
2. Telephone, telegraph	......*
3. Travel, expense accounts	......
4. Printing, stationery, postage	......*
5. Other charges (rent, etc.)	......
TOTAL FOR PURCHASING DEPARTMENT	$......
6. Get same costs for Receiving & Stores, Inspection, Accounts Payable, and Requisitioning	......
GRAND TOTAL	$......

* Components of marginal cost.

Armed with this information, you now can determine your "marginal" order cost in one of three ways:

1. *Simple Method:* Suppose your total purchasing department cost was $10,000 and that 1,000 orders were placed. You estimate that if you bought the same volume but used only 800 orders, the total cost would be $9,000—a difference of $1,000, or $5 per order. Similarly you estimate that reductions in other departments would come to $3 per order. Your "marginal" order cost in this case is $8 per order.

2. *Sophisticated Method:* If your accounting department keeps extremely detailed records, it can estimate the "extra" factor in the items starred above and give you a per-order total.

3. *Comparison Method:* If you are in a small or medium sized manufacturing firm, pick a low order cost—say $2 or $3. Also pick a low figure if you are in a relatively low profit industry—metalworking, textiles, food processing.

Take a high figure (say $6) if you are a larger firm, or in a comparatively high profit industry—electronics, chemicals.

Now try the tables on some regular purchases. Follow this up by using the next higher order cost—say $3 if you started with $2—and see the effect of it on the order quantity. If there's not much difference, take the lower figure. If there is a big dollar difference, split the difference between the two tables.

Step III

How to Figure Carrying Charges

Here again, you want only extra (or "marginal") charges.

Typically, such marginal charges range from 12% to 24% of inventory cost per year (or 1% to 2% per month).

The table below is a composite of estimates made by a number of experts to show you 1) the factors involved in carrying charges, and 2) their possible magnitude:

Cost Component	*Range Pct. per year*
1. Interest on investment	5% to 6%
2. Space charge	¼%
3. Handling charges	1% to 3%
4. Supplies	¼%
5. Insurance	¼%
6. Taxes	¼% to ½%
7. Obsolescence	5% to 10%
8. Depreciation	5%
9. Deterioration	3%
10. Use of money elsewhere	4½% to 8%
TOTAL IN PCT. PER YEAR	12% to 24¼%

Now try to figure your own carrying charges in one of the four following ways:

1. *Accurate Method:* Have your accounting department supply data to fit the categories above.

2. *Profit Method:* If your firm is in a high-profit, fast-moving industry like electronics, chemicals, services, etc., pick 24% (or 2% per month). This figure is O.K., too, if your inventory has high handling charges, obsolescence, or deterioration.

3. *Industry Method:* If you are in metalworking, textiles, or general manufacturing, where profits are more modest and inventories relatively spoil-proof, pick 12% (or 1% per month).

4. *Trial Method:* If in doubt, pick 18% (or 1½% per month)—then refine this figure as you gain experience under EOV.

Step IV

How to Use the Tables

Now that you have your marginal order and carrying costs, you're set to use the tables we have compiled for you.

Note their versatility:

1) They cover order costs of \$2, \$3, and \$6; carrying charges of 1%, 1½%, and 2% per month; and will fit any item whose monthly usage ranges from \$25 to \$10,000. (If your own figures don't match exactly, pick the closest ones in the tables.)

2) The tables not only show you how much to buy per order, but how big a monthly penalty you will incur if you order uneconomically.

Let's try some examples:

MONTHLY USAGE ➧		$25	50 ★	75	100
ORDER	CORRECT PURCHASE 25	2	4	6	9
COST	50	0	1	2	3
$3	75	0	0	1	1
	100	0	0	0	1
	200	1	0	0	0
	300	2	1	1	0
	400	2	2	2	1
	500	3	3	2	2
	600	4	4	3	3
	700	5	5	4	4
	800	6	6	5	5
	900	7	7	6	6
CARRYING	1,000	8	8	7	7
CHARGE	1,500	13	13	12	12
2%	2,000	18	18	17	17
Per Mo.	2,500	23	23	22	22
	3,000	28	28	27	27
	4,000	38	38	37	37
	5,000	48	48	47	47
	6,000	58	58	57	57
	8,000	78	78	77	77
	10,000	98	98	97	97

Example No. 1

You want to buy an item whose carrying cost is 24% per year (2% per month), and whose order cost is \$3. You consume \$50 worth of this item per month, and get no discounts. Here's what you do:

1. Pick the table which is geared to 2% carrying charges and \$3 order charges. (For convenience a part of it is reproduced herewith.)

2. Locate the \$50 usage figure on the horizontal line at the top. (We've put a star over it.)

3. Follow the arrow down the \$50 column until you hit the first zero.*

4. Now turn left and follow the horizontal arrow to the left scale. Here you will find \$75. That's your answer. In other words, for this \$50 monthly-usage item, your order size should be \$75.

* Whenever several zeros are stacked, choose the top one. It will give you the lowest economic order value.

MONTHLY USAGE ➧	CORRECT PURCHASE	$25	50	75	100	200	300	400	500 ★	600
ORDER	25	2	4	6	9	19	30	41	53	64
COST	50	0	1	2	3	8	13	18	23	28
$3	75	0	0	1	1	4	7	10	13	16
	100	0	0	0	1	2	4	6	8	11
	200	1	0	0	0	1	1	1	2	
	300	2	1	1	0	0	0	0	0	
	400	2	2	2	1	1	0	0	0	0
	500	3	3	2	2	1	1	1	0	0
	600	4	4	3	3	2	2	1	1	
	700	5	5	4	4	3	2	2	1	
	800	6	6	5	5	4	3	3	2	
	900	7	7	6	6	5	4	3	3	
CARRYING	1,000	8	8	7	7	6	5	4	4	
CHARGE	1,500	13	.13	12	12	11	10	9	8	[illegible]
2%	2,000	18	18	17	17	16	15	14	13	13
Per Mo.	2,500	23	23	22	22	21	20	19	18	17
	3,000	28	28	27	27	26	25	24	23	23
	4,000	38	38	37	37	36	35	34	33	32
	5,000	48	48	47	47	46	45	44	43	42
	6,000	58	58	57	57	56	55	54	53	52
	8,000	78	78	77	77	75	74	73	73	72
	10,000	98	98	97	97	95	94	93	92	92

Example No. 2

Suppose you used $500 of a similar item per month. Again:

1. Start with $500 on the top scale.
2. Go down the column to the first zero.
3. Turn left and proceed to the vertical scale which says $300.

That's your answer—order $300 at a time.

* * *

Now for the wages of sin—*How to Figure Penalties.*

Let's take the $50 monthly-usage item. All the figures above zero in the same column show the monthly penalty for buying too little; all the figures below zero show the monthly penalty for buying too much.

Had you ordered $25 worth of this item (instead of $75), you would have wasted $4 per month. Had you ordered $10,000, you would have wasted $98 per month. (Just think what that would be in one year!)

Similarly, on the $500 monthly-usage item, your penalty would range from $53 to $92 a month.

Step V

How to Evaluate Quantity Discounts and Transportation Savings

Suppose a supplier says, "I'll give you a discount if you order more than your EOV tables tell you to."

Should you listen?

Yes—if the discount is bigger than the penalty for overbuying.

No—if the discount is less than the penalty.

This example will show you how to form your judgment:

Once more, let's take our familiar $500-monthly-usage item with a $3 order cost and 2% per-month carrying charges. The EOV table says you should order $300 at a time.

However, your supplier promises, "If you buy $6,000, I'll give you a 5% discount."

Here's what you do:

1. Figure out how many months' supply the vendor is trying to sell you. (In this case it's 12.)
2. Now locate $6,000 on the vertical (left) scale and follow this row until it intersects with the $500 monthly-usage column.
3. The box at the intersection says $53. That's your monthly penalty for overbuying.
4. Since you would incur this penalty 12 times. your aggregate penalty would be $636.
5. Match this against the supplier's discount (in this case $300) and see how you make out. In our example, his offer is a dud because the discount covers less than half the penalty.

* * *

Use the same method to figure whether it's worthwhile to buy in large lots to gain volume freight rates.

If the saving in freight is greater than the penalty for buying more, you are ahead. If not, stick to your original EOV order-size.

ORDER COST $2 — CARRYING CHARGE 1% Per Mo.

CORRECT PURCHASE \ MONTHLY USAGE	$25	50	75	100	200	300	400	500	600	700	800	900	1,000	1,500	2,000	2,500	3,000	4,000	5,000	6,000	8,000	10,000
25	1	3	4	6	13	21	28	36	43	51	58	66	74	112	151	180	229	337	386	465	622	780
50	0	1	1	2	5	9	12	16	19	23	26	30	34	52	71	90	109	147	186	225	302	380
75	0	0	1	1	3	5	7	9	11	14	16	18	21	33	45	57	69	95	119	145	186	247
100	0	0	0	1	2	3	5	6	8	9	11	13	14	23	32	41	50	68	86	105	143	181
200	0	0	0	0	0	1	1	2	2	3	3	4	5	8	12	16	20	28	37	46	63	81
300	1	0	0	0	0	0	0	0	1	1	1	2	2	4	6	8	11	16	21	27	39	48
400	1	1	1	1	0	0	0	0	0	0	0	1	1	2	3	5	6	9	13	17	24	32
500	2	1	1	1	1	0	0	0	0	0	0	0	0	1	2	3	4	6	8	11	17	23
600	2	2	2	1	1	1	0	0	0	0	0	0	0	0	1	1	2	4	6	8	12	16
700	3	2	2	2	1	1	1	0	0	0	0	0	0	0	0	1	1	2	4	5	8	12
800	3	3	2	2	2	1	1	1	1	0	0	0	0	0	0	0	1	1	3	4	6	9
900	4	3	3	3	2	2	1	1	1	1	1	1	0	0	0	0	0	1	2	2	4	8
1,000	4	4	3	3	3	2	2	2	1	1	1	1	1	0	0	0	0	0	1	2	3	5
1,500	7	6	6	6	5	4	4	4	3	3	3	3	3	2	1	1	1	0	0	0	0	1
2,000	9	9	8	8	7	7	6	6	6	5	5	5	5	4	3	2	1	1	1	1	0	0
2,500	12	11	11	11	10	9	9	8	8	8	7	7	7	6	5	4	3	3	2	2	1	1
3,000	14	14	13	13	13	12	11	11	11	10	10	10	9	8	7	7	6	5	4	4	3	2
4,000	19	19	18	18	17	17	16	16	15	15	15	14	14	13	12	11	11	9	8	8	6	5
5,000	24	24	23	23	22	22	21	20	20	20	19	19	19	18	17	16	15	14	13	12	10	9
6,000	29	29	28	28	27	27	26	26	25	25	25	24	24	23	22	21	20	19	18	17	15	13
8,000	39	39	38	38	37	37	37	37	36	36	35	35	34	33	32	31	30	28	27	26	24	22
10,000	49	49	48	48	47	47	46	46	45	45	44	44	44	43	42	41	40	38	37	36	34	32

ORDER COST $2 — CARRYING CHARGE 1 1/2% Per Mo.

CORRECT PURCHASE \ MONTHLY USAGE	$25	50	75	100	200	300	400	500	600	700	800	900	1,000	1,500	2,000	2,500	3,000	4,000	5,000	6,000	8,000	10,000
25	1	2	4	6	13	20	27	35	42	49	57	65	73	112	149	188	227	305	383	461	618	776
50	0	1	1	2	5	8	12	15	18	22	26	29	33	52	69	89	107	145	183	221	299	376
75	0	0	1	1	3	4	6	8	11	13	15	17	20	32	43	55	67	91	117	142	192	243
100	0	0	0	0	1	3	4	5	7	8	10	12	13	22	30	39	47	65	84	102	139	176
200	1	0	0	0	0	0	1	2	2	2	3	3	4	8	11	14	18	26	34	43	60	77
300	1	1	1	1	0	0	0	0	0	0	1	1	1	4	5	7	10	13	18	23	33	44
400	2	2	1	1	1	0	0	0	0	0	0	0	0	2	2	3	5	8	11	14	21	29
500	3	2	2	2	1	1	1	0	0	0	0	0	0	1	1	2	2	4	7	9	14	19
600	3	3	3	2	2	1	1	1	1	0	0	0	0	0	0	1	1	2	4	6	9	13
700	4	4	3	3	2	2	2	1	1	1	1	1	0	0	0	0	1	1	2	4	6	9
800	5	4	4	4	3	3	2	2	2	1	1	1	1	1	0	0	0	1	1	2	4	7
900	6	5	5	5	4	3	3	2	2	2	2	2	1	1	0	0	0	0	1	1	5	5
1,000	6	6	6	5	4	4	3	3	3	2	2	2	2	2	1	0	0	0	0	1	2	3
1,500	10	10	9	9	8	8	7	6	6	6	5	5	5	5	3	3	2	1	1	0	0	0
2,000	14	13	13	13	12	11	11	10	10	9	9	9	8	8	6	5	5	4	3	2	1	1
2,500	18	17	17	16	15	15	14	14	13	13	13	12	12	11	9	9	9	7	6	5	3	2
3,000	21	21	20	20	19	19	18	17	17	16	16	16	15	15	13	12	11	10	9	8	6	5
4,000	29	28	28	28	27	26	25	25	24	24	24	23	23	22	20	19	18	17	15	14	12	11
5,000	36	36	35	35	34	33	33	32	32	31	31	31	30	29	27	26	25	24	22	21	19	17
6,000	44	43	43	43	42	41	40	40	39	39	38	38	38	37	35	34	33	31	29	28	26	24
8,000	59	58	58	58	57	56	55	55	54	54	53	53	53	52	50	48	47	46	44	43	40	38
10,000	74	73	73	73	72	71	70	70	69	69	68	68	68	67	64	63	62	60	59	57	55	53

ECONOMIC ORDER VALUE TABLES

ORDER COST $2 — CARRYING CHARGE 2% Per Mo. — CORRECT PURCHASE

MONTHLY USAGE ▶	$25	50	75	100	200	300	400	500	600	700	800	900	1,000	1,500	2,000	2,500	3,000	4,000	5,000	6,000	8,000	10,000
25	1	2	4	6	12	19	27	34	41	49	56	64	71	109	148	186	225	302	380	458	615	772
50	0	1	1	2	5	8	11	14	18	21	25	28	32	50	68	86	105	143	181	219	295	372
75	0	0	0	1	2	4	6	8	10	12	13	16	18	30	42	53	65	89	114	139	188	239
100	0	0	0	0	1	2	3	5	6	8	9	11	12	20	28	37	46	63	81	100	136	172
200	1	1	0	0	0	0	0	1	1	2	2	3	3	6	9	13	17	24	32	40	57	74
300	2	1	1	1	0	0	0	0	0	0	0	1	1	2	4	6	8	12	16	21	31	41
400	3	2	2	2	1	1	0	0	0	0	0	0	0	1	1	3	4	6	9	12	19	26
500	4	3	3	3	2	1	1	1	1	0	0	0	0	0	0	1	2	3	5	7	12	17
600	5	4	4	4	3	2	2	1	1	1	1	1	0	0	0	0	1	2	3	4	7	11
700	6	5	5	4	4	3	2	2	2	2	1	1	1	0	0	0	0	1	1	2	5	7
800	7	6	6	5	4	4	3	3	3	2	2	2	2	1	0	0	0	0	0	1	3	5
900	8	7	7	6	5	5	4	4	3	3	3	3	2	1	1	1	0	0	0	1	2	3
1,000	9	8	8	7	6	6	5	5	4	4	4	3	3	2	1	1	1	0	0	0	1	2
1,500	14	13	13	12	11	11	10	9	9	8	8	8	7	5	5	4	4	3	2	1	0	0
2,000	19	18	18	17	16	16	15	14	14	13	13	12	12	10	9	8	8	6	5	4	3	2
2,500	25	24	24	23	22	22	20	19	19	18	18	17	17	15	14	13	12	10	9	8	6	5
3,000	29	28	28	27	26	25	25	24	24	23	23	22	22	20	19	18	17	15	13	12	10	8
4,000	39	38	38	37	36	35	35	34	33	33	32	32	32	30	28	27	26	24	22	21	19	17
5,000	49	48	48	47	46	45	44	44	43	43	42	42	42	40	38	37	36	34	32	31	28	26
6,000	59	58	57	57	56	55	54	54	53	53	52	52	51	50	48	47	46	43	42	40	37	35
8,000	79	78	78	77	76	75	74	74	73	73	72	72	71	69	68	67	65	63	61	60	57	54
10,000	99	98	98	97	96	95	94	94	93	93	92	92	91	89	88	87	85	83	81	79	76	74

ORDER COST $3 — CARRYING CHARGE 1% Per Mo. — CORRECT PURCHASE

MONTHLY USAGE ▶	$25	50	75	100	200	300	400	500	600	700	800	900	1,000	1,500	2,000	2,500	3,000	4,000	5,000	6,000	8,000	10,000
25	2	4	7	10	21	32	43	55	66	78	89	101	112	171	229	288	348	465	583	701	938	1176
50	0	2	3	4	9	14	19	25	30	36	41	47	53	82	109	138	167	225	283	341	458	576
75	0	1	1	2	5	8	11	15	18	22	26	29	32	52	69	88	107	135	183	221	299	376
100	0	0	1	1	3	5	8	10	13	15	18	20	23	37	50	63	77	105	133	162	218	276
200	0	0	0	0	1	1	2	3	4	5	6	7	8	15	20	26	33	46	59	72	99	127
300	1	0	1	1	1	1	1	1	2	2	3	3	4	8	11	14	18	26	34	43	59	77
400	1	1	0	0	0	0	0	0	1	1	1	2	2	5	6	9	11	17	22	28	40	53
500	1	1	1	1	0	0	0	0	0	0	0	1	1	3	4	5	7	11	15	20	29	38
600	2	2	1	1	0	0	0	0	0	0	0	0	0	2	2	3	5	8	11	14	21	26
700	2	2	2	2	1	1	0	0	0	0	0	0	0	1	1	2	3	5	8	10	16	22
800	3	2	2	2	1	1	1	0	0	0	0	0	0	1	1	1	2	4	6	8	12	17
900	3	3	3	2	2	1	1	1	0	0	0	0	0	0	0	1	1	2	4	6	9	13
1,000	4	3	3	3	2	2	1	1	1	1	1	0	0	0	0	0	1	2	3	4	7	11
1,500	6	6	6	5	4	4	3	3	3	2	2	2	2	2	0	0	0	0	0	1	2	3
2,000	9	8	8	8	7	6	6	5	5	5	4	4	4	4	2	1	1	1	0	0	0	1
2,500	11	11	10	10	9	9	8	8	7	7	7	6	6	6	4	3	3	2	1	1	0	0
3,000	14	13	13	13	12	11	10	10	10	9	9	9	9	8	6	5	5	3	3	2	1	0
4,000	19	18	18	18	17	16	15	15	14	14	14	13	13	12	11	10	9	8	6	6	4	3
5,000	24	23	23	23	22	21	20	20	19	19	19	18	18	17	15	14	13	12	11	10	8	7
6,000	29	28	28	28	27	26	25	25	24	24	23	23	23	22	20	19	18	17	15	14	12	11
8,000	39	38	38	38	37	36	35	35	34	34	33	33	33	32	30	29	28	26	25	23	21	19

ORDER COST $3 — CARRYING CHARGE 1½% Per Mo. — CORRECT PURCHASE

MONTHLY USAGE ➧	$25	50	75	100	200	300	400	500	600	700	800	900	1,000	1,500	2,000	2,500	3,000	4,000	5,000	6,000	8,000	10,000
25	2	4	7	9	20	31	42	54	65	76	88	99	111	169	227	285	344	461	579	679	933	1170
50	0	1	2	3	8	13	18	24	29	35	40	45	51	79	107	135	164	221	279	337	454	570
75	0	1	1	2	5	7	11	14	17	21	24	28	31	49	67	86	104	142	179	217	293	371
100	0	0	0	1	3	5	7	9	12	14	16	19	21	34	47	61	74	102	130	158	214	271
200	0	0	0	0	0	1	2	2	3	4	5	6	7	12	18	24	30	43	55	68	95	122
300	1	1	0	0	0	0	0	0	1	1	2	2	3	6	9	12	16	23	31	39	55	72
400	2	1	1	1	0	0	0	0	0	0	1	1	1	3	5	7	9	14	19	25	36	48
500	2	2	2	1	1	0	0	0	0	0	0	0	0	1	2	4	5	9	13	17	25	34
600	3	3	2	2	1	1	0	0	0	0	0	0	0	0	1	2	3	6	8	11	18	25
700	4	3	3	3	2	1	1	1	1	0	0	0	0	0	1	1	2	3	5	8	13	18
800	5	4	4	3	3	2	2	1	1	1	1	0	0	0	0	0	1	2	4	5	9	14
900	5	5	4	4	3	3	2	2	1	1	1	1	1	0	0	0	0	1	2	4	7	10
1,000	6	5	5	5	4	3	3	2	2	2	1	1	1	0	0	0	0	1	1	2	5	8
1,500	10	9	9	9	7	7	6	6	5	5	4	4	4	3	2	1	1	0	0	0	0	1
2,000	14	13	12	12	11	10	10	9	9	8	8	7	7	6	5	4	3	2	1	1	0	0
2,500	17	17	16	16	15	14	13	13	12	12	11	11	11	9	8	7	6	5	4	3	2	1
3,000	21	20	20	20	19	18	17	16	16	15	15	14	14	12	11	10	9	7	6	5	4	2
4,000	29	28	27	27	26	25	24	24	23	23	22	22	21	20	18	17	16	14	12	11	9	8
5,000	36	35	35	35	33	32	32	31	31	30	29	29	29	27	25	24	23	21	19	18	16	14
6,000	44	43	42	42	41	40	39	39	38	37	37	36	36	34	33	31	29	28	26	25	22	20
8,000	59	58	57	57	56	55	54	54	53	52	52	51	51	49	47	46	45	43	41	39	36	34
10,000	74	73	72	72	71	70	69	68	68	67	67	66	66	64	62	61	60	57	55	54	51	48

ORDER COST $3 — CARRYING CHARGE 2% Per Mo. — CORRECT PURCHASE

MONTHLY USAGE ➧	$25	50	75	100	200	300	400	500	600	700	800	900	1,000	1,500	2,000	2,500	3,000	4,000	5,000	6,000	8,000	10,000
25	2	4	6	9	19	30	41	53	64	75	87	98	109	167	225	283	341	458	576	694	929	1166
50	0	1	2	3	8	13	18	23	28	33	39	44	50	77	105	133	162	219	276	334	450	566
75	0	0	1	1	4	7	10	13	16	19	23	26	30	47	65	83	102	139	176	214	289	366
100	0	0	0	1	2	4	6	8	11	13	15	18	20	33	46	59	72	99	127	154	210	266
200	1	0	0	0	1	1	1	2	3	3	4	5	6	11	17	20	28	40	53	65	91	117
300	2	1	1	0	0	0	0	0	1	1	1	2	2	5	8	11	14	21	29	36	52	68
400	2	2	2	1	1	0	0	0	0	0	0	1	1	2	4	6	7	12	17	22	33	44
500	3	3	2	2	1	1	1	0	0	0	0	0	0	1	2	3	4	7	11	14	22	30
600	4	4	3	3	2	2	1	1	1	0	0	0	0	0	0	1	2	4	6	12	15	22
700	5	5	4	4	3	2	2	1	1	1	1	0	0	0	0	0	1	2	4	6	10	15
800	6	6	5	5	4	3	3	2	2	1	1	1	1	0	0	0	0	1	2	4	7	11
900	7	7	6	6	5	4	3	3	2	2	2	2	1	1	0	0	0	0	1	2	5	8
1,000	8	8	7	7	6	5	4	4	3	3	3	2	2	1	1	0	0	0	0	1	3	5
1,500	13	13	12	12	11	10	9	8	8	7	7	6	6	5	5	4	2	1	0	0	0	0
2,000	18	18	17	17	16	15	14	13	13	11	11	11	11	9	8	6	6	4	3	2	1	0
2,500	23	23	22	22	21	20	19	18	17	17	16	16	15	13	12	11	10	8	7	5	4	2
3,000	28	28	27	27	26	25	24	23	23	22	21	21	20	18	17	15	14	12	11	9	7	5
4,000	38	38	37	37	36	35	34	33	32	31	31	30	30	28	26	25	23	20	19	18	15	13
5,000	48	48	47	47	46	45	44	43	42	41	41	40	40	38	36	34	33	31	29	27	24	21
6,000	58	58	57	57	56	55	54	53	52	51	51	50	50	47	45	44	43	40	38	36	33	31
8,000	78	78	77	77	75	74	73	73	72	71	71	70	69	67	65	63	62	60	57	55	52	49
10,000	98	98	97	97	95	94	93	92	92	91	90	90	89	87	85	83	82	79	77	75	71	68

ECONOMIC ORDER VALUE TABLES

ORDER COST $4 — CARRYING CHARGE 1% Per Mo.

CORRECT PURCHASE / MONTHLY USAGE ➡	$25	50	75	100	200	300	400	500	600	700	800	900	1,000	1,500	2,000	2,500	3,000	4,000	5,000	6,000	8,000	10,000
25	3	6	10	13	28	43	58	74	89	105	120	136	151	239	308	386	465	622	780	938	1255	1572
50	1	2	4	5	12	19	27	34	41	49	56	64	71	109	148	185	222	302	380	458	615	772
75	1	1	2	3	7	11	16	21	25	30	35	40	45	69	95	119	145	196	247	298	402	505
100	0	1	1	2	5	8	11	14	18	21	25	28	32	50	68	86	105	143	179	219	295	372
200	0	0	0	0	1	2	3	5	6	8	9	11	12	20	28	37	46	63	81	99	136	173
300	0	0	0	0	0	1	1	2	3	3	4	5	6	11	16	21	26	37	48	60	82	106
400	1	1	0	0	0	0	0	1	1	2	2	3	3	6	9	13	17	24	32	40	57	74
500	1	1	1	0	0	0	0	0	0	1	1	1	2	4	6	8	11	17	23	29	41	54
600	2	1	1	1	0	0	0	0	0	0	0	1	1	2	4	5	8	12	16	21	31	42
700	2	2	1	1	1	0	0	0	0	0	0	0	0	1	3	4	5	8	12	16	24	32
800	3	2	2	2	1	1	0	0	0	0	0	0	0	1	1	2	4	6	9	12	19	26
900	3	3	2	2	1	1	1	0	0	0	0	0	0	0	1	2	2	5	7	9	15	21
1,000	4	3	3	3	2	1	1	1	1	0	0	0	0	0	0	1	2	3	5	7	12	17
1,500	6	6	5	5	4	3	3	3	2	2	2	1	1	1	0	0	0	0	1	2	3	6
2,000	9	8	8	7	6	6	5	5	4	4	4	3	3	2	1	1	1	0	0	0	1	2
2,500	11	11	10	9	8	7	7	7	7	6	6	5	5	4	3	2	2	1	1	0	0	0
3,000	14	13	13	13	12	11	10	9	9	8	8	8	7	6	5	4	4	2	2	1	1	0
4,000	19	18	18	17	16	15	15	14	14	13	13	12	12	10	9	9	8	6	5	4	3	2
5,000	24	23	23	22	21	20	20	19	19	18	18	18	15	14	13	12	10	10	8	7	5	4
6,000	29	28	28	27	26	25	24	24	24	23	23	22	22	20	19	18	17	15	13	12	10	9
8,000	39	38	38	37	36	35	35	34	34	33	33	32	32	30	29	27	26	24	23	21	19	18
10,000	49	48	48	47	46	45	44	44	43	43	42	41	39	38	38	37	35	34	32	32	28	26

ORDER COST $4 — CARRYING CHARGE 1½% Per Mo.

CORRECT PURCHASE / MONTHLY USAGE ➡	$25	50	75	100	200	300	400	500	600	700	800	900	1,000	1,500	2,000	2,500	3,000	4,000	5,000	6,000	8,000	10,000
25	3	6	9	13	28	42	57	73	88	103	118	134	149	227	305	383	461	618	776	933	1249	1566
50	1	2	3	5	12	18	26	33	40	47	55	62	69	107	145	183	221	299	376	454	609	766
75	0	1	2	2	7	11	15	20	24	29	34	38	43	67	92	117	139	192	243	294	396	499
100	0	0	1	1	4	7	10	13	16	20	23	26	30	47	65	83	102	139	176	214	290	366
200	0	0	0	0	1	2	3	4	5	6	8	9	11	18	26	34	43	60	77	95	131	167
300	1	1	0	0	0	0	1	1	2	2	3	4	5	9	14	18	23	34	45	56	77	101
400	2	1	1	1	0	0	0	1	1	1	1	2	2	5	8	11	14	21	29	36	53	68
500	2	2	1	1	1	0	0	0	0	0	0	1	1	2	4	7	9	14	19	25	37	49
600	3	2	2	2	1	1	0	0	0	0	0	0	0	1	2	4	6	9	13	18	27	37
700	4	3	3	2	2	1	1	0	0	0	0	0	0	0	1	2	4	6	9	13	20	28
800	4	4	3	3	2	2	1	1	1	0	0	0	0	0	0	1	2	4	7	9	15	21
900	5	5	4	4	3	2	2	1	1	1	1	0	0	0	0	0	1	3	5	7	11	17
1,000	6	5	5	4	3	3	2	2	1	1	1	1	1	0	0	0	1	2	3	5	9	13
1,500	10	9	9	8	7	6	5	5	4	4	4	3	3	2	1	1	0	0	0	1	2	4
2,000	13	13	12	12	11	10	9	8	8	7	7	6	6	5	4	3	2	1	1	0	0	0
2,500	17	16	16	15	14	13	13	12	11	11	10	10	9	8	7	6	5	3	2	2	1	0
3,000	21	20	20	19	18	17	16	15	15	14	14	13	13	11	10	9	8	6	5	4	2	1
4,000	28	28	27	27	25	24	24	23	22	21	21	20	20	18	17	15	14	12	10	9	7	5
5,000	36	35	35	34	33	32	31	30	29	29	28	28	27	25	24	22	21	19	17	16	13	11
6,000	43	42	42	42	40	39	38	38	37	36	36	35	35	33	31	29	28	26	24	22	19	17
8,000	58	57	57	57	55	54	53	53	52	51	51	50	50	48	46	44	42	40	38	36	33	30

ORDER COST $4 — CARRYING CHARGE 2% Per Mo.

CORRECT PURCHASE / MONTHLY USAGE ➡	$25	50	75	100	200	300	400	500	600	700	800	900	1,000	1,500	2,000	2,500	3,000	4,000	5,000	6,000	8,000	10,000
25	2	5	9	12	27	41	56	71	86	102	117	132	148	225	302	380	458	615	772	929	1245	1560
50	1	2	3	5	11	18	25	32	39	46	53	61	68	105	143	181	219	295	372	450	606	761
75	0	1	1	2	6	10	14	19	23	27	32	36	41	65	89	113	139	188	239	290	393	494
100	0	0	1	1	3	6	9	12	15	18	22	25	28	46	63	81	99	136	173	210	285	361
200	1	0	0	0	0	1	2	3	4	5	7	8	9	17	24	32	40	57	74	91	127	162
300	1	1	1	0	0	0	0	1	1	2	3	3	4	8	12	16	21	31	42	52	71	96
400	2	2	1	1	0	0	0	0	0	1	1	1	1	4	6	9	12	19	26	33	49	64
500	3	3	2	2	1	1	0	0	0	0	0	0	0	2	3	5	7	12	17	22	34	45
600	4	4	3	3	2	1	1	0	0	0	0	0	0	1	1	2	4	8	11	15	24	33
700	5	4	4	4	2	2	1	1	1	0	0	0	0	0	1	1	2	5	7	10	18	24
800	6	5	5	5	3	3	2	2	1	1	1	0	0	0	0	0	1	3	5	7	13	18
900	7	6	6	5	4	3	3	2	2	1	1	1	1	0	0	0	0	1	3	5	10	13
1,000	8	7	7	6	5	4	4	3	3	2	2	2	1	1	0	0	0	1	2	3	7	10
1,500	13	12	12	11	10	9	8	7	7	6	6	5	5	4	2	2	1	1	0	0	1	2
2,000	18	17	17	16	15	14	13	12	11	11	10	10	9	8	6	5	4	3	2	1	1	0
2,500	23	22	22	21	20	18	18	17	16	16	15	14	14	12	10	9	8	6	5	4	3	1
3,000	28	27	27	26	25	24	23	22	21	20	20	19	19	17	15	13	12	10	9	7	6	3
4,000	38	37	37	36	35	33	32	32	31	30	30	29	28	26	24	23	21	19	17	15	13	10
5,000	48	47	47	46	45	43	42	42	41	40	39	39	38	36	34	32	31	28	26	24	21	18
6,000	58	57	57	56	55	53	52	52	51	50	49	49	48	46	43	42	40	37	36	33	30	27
8,000	78	77	77	76	75	73	72	71	71	70	69	68	68	65	63	61	60	57	54	52	49	45
10,000	98	97	97	96	95	93	92	91	91	90	89	88	88	85	83	81	79	76	74	71	68	64

ORDER COST $6 — CARRYING CHARGE 1% Per Mo.

CORRECT PURCHASE / MONTHLY USAGE ➡	$25	50	75	100	200	300	400	500	600	700	800	900	1,000	1,500	2,000	2,500	3,000	4,000	5,000	6,000	8,000	10,000
25	4	10	15	21	27	66	89	112	136	159	182	206	229	347	465	583	701	938	1176	1414	1889	2366
50	2	4	6	9	19	30	41	53	64	75	86	98	109	167	225	283	341	558	576	693	929	1166
75	1	2	3	5	12	18	25	33	40	57	54	62	69	107	145	183	221	299	375	454	610	766
100	1	1	2	3	8	13	18	23	28	33	39	44	50	67	105	133	162	219	276	334	450	566
200	0	0	0	1	2	4	6	8	11	13	15	18	20	33	46	59	72	99	127	154	210	266
300	0	0	0	0	1	2	2	3	5	6	8	9	10	18	26	34	43	59	77	95	130	167
400	0	0	0	0	1	1	2	3	4	4	4	5	6	11	17	22	28	40	53	65	91	117
500	1	1	0	0	0	0	0	1	2	2	2	3	4	7	11	15	20	29	38	48	68	88
600	2	1	1	1	0	0	0	0	1	1	1	2	2	5	7	10	14	21	28	36	52	69
700	2	2	1	1	0	0	0	0	0	0	0	1	1	3	5	8	10	16	22	28	41	55
800	2	2	2	1	1	0	0	0	0	0	0	0	1	2	4	5	8	12	17	22	33	44
900	3	2	2	2	1	0	0	0	0	0	0	0	0	1	2	4	5	9	14	18	27	37
1,000	3	3	2	2	1	1	1	0	0	0	0	0	0	1	2	3	4	7	11	14	22	30
1,500	6	5	5	4	3	3	2	2	1	1	1	1	1	0	0	0	1	2	3	5	8	13
2,000	8	8	7	7	6	5	4	4	3	3	3	2	2	1	1	0	0	0	1	1	3	5
2,500	11	10	10	9	8	7	7	6	5	5	5	4	4	3	2	1	1	0	0	0	1	2
3,000	14	13	12	12	11	10	9	8	8	7	7	6	6	5	4	3	2	1	1	0	0	0
4,000	18	18	17	17	15	14	14	13	12	12	11	11	11	9	8	7	6	4	3	2	1	0
5,000	23	23	22	22	20	19	19	18	17	17	16	16	15	13	12	11	10	8	7	5	4	2
6,000	28	28	27	27	25	24	24	23	22	21	21	21	20	18	16	15	14	12	10	9	7	6
8,000	38	38	37	37	35	34	33	33	32	31	31	30	30	28	26	25	23	21	19	18	15	13
10,000	48	48	47	47	45	44	43	43	42	41	41	40	40	38	36	34	33	31	29	27	24	21

ECONOMIC ORDER VALUE TABLES

ORDER COST $6 — CARRYING CHARGE $1\frac{1}{2}$% Per Mo.

CORRECT PURCHASE ↓ / MONTHLY USAGE ➡	$25	50	75	100	200	300	400	500	600	700	800	900	1,000	1,500	2,000	2,500	3,000	4,000	5,000	6,000	8,000	10,000
25	4	9	15	20	42	65	88	111	134	157	180	204	227	344	461	579	697	933	1170	1407	1883	2358
50	1	3	6	8	18	29	40	51	62	73	84	96	107	164	221	279	337	454	570	688	923	1158
75	0	2	3	4	11	17	24	31	38	45	53	60	67	104	142	179	217	321	370	448	603	758
100	0	1	2	3	7	11	16	21	26	32	37	42	47	74	102	130	158	214	271	328	443	558
200	0	0	0	0	2	3	5	7	9	11	13	16	18	30	43	55	68	95	122	149	204	259
300	1	0	0	0	0	1	2	2	4	5	7	8	9	16	24	31	39	55	73	89	124	160
400	1	1	0	0	0	0	1	1	2	3	3	4	5	9	14	20	25	36	48	60	86	111
500	2	1	1	0	0	0	0	0	1	1	1	2	2	5	9	13	17	25	34	43	62	81
600	3	2	2	1	0	0	0	0	0	1	1	1	1	3	5	8	11	18	24	32	47	62
700	3	3	2	2	1	1	0	0	0	0	0	0	0	2	4	6	7	13	18	24	36	49
800	4	3	3	3	2	1	1	0	0	0	0	0	0	1	2	3	5	9	14	18	29	39
900	5	4	4	3	2	1	1	1	0	0	0	0	0	0	1	2	3	6	10	14	23	31
1,000	6	5	4	4	3	2	1	1	1	1	0	0	0	0	1	1	2	5	8	11	18	25
1,500	9	8	8	8	6	5	4	4	3	3	2	2	2	1	0	0	0	1	1	2	6	9
2,000	13	12	11	11	10	9	8	7	6	6	5	5	5	3	2	2	1	0	0	0	2	3
2,500	17	16	15	15	13	12	11	11	10	9	9	8	8	6	5	4	3	2	1	0	0	0
3,000	20	20	19	18	17	16	15	14	13	13	12	12	11	9	8	6	5	4	3	2	1	0
4,000	28	27	27	26	24	23	22	21	21	20	19	19	18	16	14	13	11	9	7	6	5	3
5,000	35	35	34	33	31	31	29	29	28	27	26	26	25	23	21	19	18	16	14	12	10	7
6,000	43	42	41	41	39	38	37	36	35	34	34	33	33	30	28	26	25	22	20	18	15	13
8,000	58	57	56	56	54	53	52	51	50	49	49	48	47	45	42	41	39	36	34	32	29	26
10,000	73	72	71	71	69	68	67	66	65	64	63	63	62	60	57	55	54	51	48	46	42	39

ORDER COST $6 — CARRYING CHARGE 2% Per Mo.

CORRECT PURCHASE ↓ / MONTHLY USAGE ➡	$25	50	75	100	200	300	400	500	600	700	800	900	1,000	1,500	2,000	2,500	3,000	4,000	5,000	6,000	8,000	10,000
25	4	9	14	19	41	64	86	109	132	155	178	202	225	341	458	576	693	929	1166	1402	1876	2351
50	1	3	5	8	18	28	39	50	61	72	83	94	105	162	219	276	334	450	566	683	917	1152
75	0	1	3	5	9	16	23	30	37	43	50	58	65	102	139	176	214	290	366	447	597	752
100	0	1	1	2	6	11	15	20	25	30	35	40	46	72	99	127	154	210	266	323	437	552
200	0	0	0	0	1	3	4	6	8	10	12	13	17	28	40	53	65	91	117	144	198	253
300	1	1	0	0	0	1	1	2	3	4	5	6	7	14	21	28	36	52	69	85	118	154
400	2	1	1	1	0	0	0	1	1	2	2	3	4	8	12	17	22	33	44	56	80	105
500	3	2	2	1	1	0	0	0	0	0	1	1	2	4	7	11	14	22	30	39	57	76
600	4	3	3	3	2	2	1	0	0	0	0	0	1	2	4	6	9	15	21	28	42	57
700	5	4	3	3	2	1	1	0	0	0	0	0	0	1	3	4	6	10	15	21	32	44
800	6	5	4	4	3	2	1	1	1	0	0	0	0	0	2	2	4	7	11	15	24	34
900	7	6	5	5	3	2	2	1	1	1	0	0	0	0	0	1	2	4	8	11	19	27
1,000	8	7	6	6	4	3	3	2	2	1	1	1	1	0	0	1	1	3	5	8	14	21
1,500	13	12	11	11	9	8	7	6	5	5	4	4	4	2	1	1	0	0	0	1	3	6
2,000	18	17	16	15	14	12	11	11	10	9	9	8	8	6	4	3	2	1	0	0	0	1
2,500	23	22	21	20	19	17	16	15	14	14	13	12	12	10	8	7	5	4	2	1	0	0
3,000	28	27	26	25	24	22	21	20	19	18	18	17	16	14	12	10	9	7	6	4	2	1
4,000	38	37	36	35	34	32	31	30	29	28	27	27	26	23	21	20	18	15	13	11	8	6
5,000	48	47	46	45	44	42	41	40	39	38	37	36	36	33	31	29	27	24	21	19	16	13
6,000	58	57	56	55	54	52	51	50	49	48	47	46	46	43	40	38	36	33	30	28	24	21
8,000	78	77	76	75	73	72	71	69	68	68	67	66	65	62	60	57	55	52	49	47	42	38

GENERAL INFORMATION

Table 29–17. Geometric Formulas

Area of a circle = half diameter × half circumference
Area of a circle = square of diameter × 0.7854
Area of a circle = square of circumference × 0.07958
Area of a sector of circle = length of arc × one-half radius
Area of a segment of circle = area of sector of equal radius minus area of triangle, when the segment is less, and plus area of triangle, when segment is greater than the semicircle
Area of ellipse = product of the two diameters × 0.7854
Area of a parabola = base × two-thirds of the altitude
Area of parallelogram = base × altitude
Area of a regular polygon = sum of its sides × perpendicular from its center to one of its sides divided by 2
Area of a rectangle = length × breadth or height
Area of circular ring = sum of the diameter of the two circles × difference of the diameter of the two circles and that product × 0.7854
Area of a square = length × breadth or height
Area of trapezium = divide into two triangles, total their areas
Area of trapezoid = altitude × one-half of the sum of parallel sides
Area of a triangle = base × one-half of the altitude
Circumference of circle = diameter × 3.1416
Circumference of circle = radius × 6.283185
Circumference of sphere = square root of surface × 1.772454
Circumference of sphere = cube root of solidity × 3.8978
Contents of pyramid or cone = area of base × one-third of the altitude
Contents of frustum of pyramid or cone = sum of circumference at both ends × one-half of the slant height plus area of both ends
Contents of frustum of pyramid or cone = multiply areas of two ends together and extract square root; add to this root the two areas and × one-third of the altitude
Contents of a sphere = diameter × 0.5236
Contents of segment of sphere = (height squared plus three times the square of radius of base) × (height × 0.5236)
Contents of a wedge = area of base × one-half of the altitude
Diameter of circle = circumference × 0.3183
Diameter of circle = square root of area × 1.12838
Diameter of circle that shall contain area of a given square = side of square × 1.1284
Diameter of sphere = cube root of solidity × 1.2407
Diameter of sphere = square root of surface × 0.56419
Radius of a circle = circumference × 0.0159155
Side of inscribed cube of sphere = radius × 1.1547
Side of inscribed cube of sphere = square root of diameter
Side of inscribed square = diameter × 0.7071
Side of inscribed square = circumference × 0.225
Side of square that shall equal area of circle = diameter × 0.8862
Side of square that shall equal area of circle = circumference × 0.2821
Side of inscribed equilateral triangle = diameter × 0.86
Surface of cylinder or prism = area of both ends plus length and × circumference
Surface of pyramid or cone = circumference of base × one-half of the slant height plus area of base
Surface of sphere = diameter × circumference
Volume of sphere = surface × one-sixth of the diameter
Volume of sphere = cube of diameter × 0.5236
Volume of sphere = cube of radius × 4.1888
Volume of sphere = cube of circumference × 0.016887

Table 29–18. How to Analyze Operating Statements and Inventory Figures

Use Ratio Analysis to Gauge Over-All Strength

A sample balance sheet and income statement (sometimes referred to as a profit and loss statement) are given below. They are over-simplified—with many key items omitted—to emphasize some of the more commonly used financial yardsticks for evaluating vendors.

XYZ CORPORATION BALANCE SHEET
on December 31, 1965 (Millions of $)

ITEM	ASSETS		ITEM	LIABILITIES	
	Current Assets			*Current Liabilities*	
A	Cash	$ 6	J	Accounts Payable	$ 5
B	Government Securities	5	K	Accrued Taxes	3
C	Accounts Receivable	4	L	Accrued Wages & Int.	2
D	Inventories	6	M	Total Current	$10
E	Total Current	$21			
	Fixed Assets		N	*Long-term Bonds*	15
F	Building & Eqpt.	$79		*Stockholders Equity*	
G	Less Accumulated Depreciation	20	O	Preferred Stock	12
			P	Common Stock	28
H	Net Fixed Assets	$59	Q	Surplus	15
I	*Total Assets*	$80	R	*Total Liab. & Equity*	$80

XYZ CORPORATION INCOME STATEMENT
Year Ended December 31, 1965

ITEM		(MIL. OF $)
S	Sales	$21
T	Less Cost of Goods Sold	$15
U	Gross Profit	$ 6
V	Less Administrative & Selling Expenses	$ 1
W	Less Depreciation	$ 1
X	Less Interest Charges	$ 1
Y	Net Profit (Before Taxes)	$ 3
Z	Less Income Taxes	$ 1.5
AA	Net Profit (After Taxes)	$ 1.5

The balance sheet presented above gives the condition of the XYZ Corp. as it existed on December 31, 1965. It's not a history of a year's operations, but rather a "snapshot" of the firm on that day. The accompanying income statement gives a summary of how the company operated over the entire year ending December 31, 1965.

All the yardsticks given immediately below can be derived from the figures appearing in these two simple financial statements:

• *Current ratio* (E/M)—This is a commonly used measure which indicates a firm's liquidity (ability to meet current obligations). Defined as the ratio of current assets to current liabilities, it can be obtained by comparing item E to item M in the balance sheet. That would be $21-million compared to $10-million for a ratio of 2.1:1.

Since a figure of 2:1 is generally considered satisfactory, there seems to be nothing to worry about on this score. A firm with a less than 1:1 ratio has a real problem, according to the experts.

• *Quick ratio* $\left(\frac{A + B + C}{M}\right)$—This is another liquidity measure. It's defined as the total of cash, current investments, and accounts receivable to total current liabilities. Inventories are eliminated in the asset section because they can't usually be converted into cash as quickly as accounts receivable or government securities. For the XYZ Corp., the ratio is determined by adding items A, B, and C and comparing them to item M. That's $15-million compared to $10-million—or a ratio of 1.5:1. A 1:1 ratio is generally considered normal so the XYZ Corp. also passes this test.

• *Sales-receivable ratio* (S/C)—A comparison of these items aims to show whether customers are paying their bills on time. In the above example, sales are $21-million (item S from the income statement). Assuming terms of net 90 days for the industry, then you wouldn't want much more than $5¼-million (the equivalent of 90 days sales) in receivables. If receivables were more, it might indicate slow payment, difficulties in collection, and a general "aging" of debt. Since the XYZ Corp. only has $4-million in accounts receivable, the firm is again in pretty good shape.

• *Cash flow* (W + AA)—This represents the sum of net income (after taxes) plus depreciation, or how much money is coming in. In many cases, this is as important as the simple profit figures. Reason: With new accelerated depreciation, a reduction in profit figures is often offset by additional cash inflows resulting from lower income taxes. For the mythical XYZ Corp., cash flow consists of item W and AA, or $1-million plus $1.5-million or $2.5-million.

• *Margins* (U/S & Y/S)—A study of gross and net profits (before taxes) relative to sales also provides a lot of interesting information about the vendor. Profits are the lifeblood of the firm and if they're down, it may spell trouble. A look at profits also gives some guidelines for price negotiations. If a vendor's profits are above the industry average then some questioning on his listed prices might be in order.

Also of particular interest as far as prices are concerned is the gap between gross profit and net profit. This gives information on operating expenses—a factor which often weighs heavy in vendor pricing decisions. In the case of the XYZ Corp., gross profit margins (item U divided by item S or 6/21) comes out to 28.6%. The net profit margin before taxes (item Y divided by item S or 3/21) comes out 14.5%. That's a gap of more than 14%—though, of course, whether it is too large or too small again depends upon the industry. If, for example, the gap is much larger than the industry average it could mean vendor is padding his payroll or else he might have a relatively inefficient administrative and sales setup.

• *Inventory turnover* (T/D)—This figure (cost of goods sold divided by inventories) is designed to show how successful the vendor has been in controlling total inventories. It also can give some hints on the quality of inventories. Thus, if the ratio is relatively low it could mean that the firm has a lot of obsolete materials or unsaleable finished goods on hand—and hence may be in some sort of trouble. It follows then that a high turnover rate is always preferable to a lower one.

But since these figures vary sharply by industry (see chart below), no rule of thumb can be given on what constitutes a high or low rate. Generally speaking, a firm's turnover rate must be compared to that of its industry. In the case of our own XYZ Co., the ratio T over D comes out $15/$6, which boils down to a turnover rate of 2½ times a year.

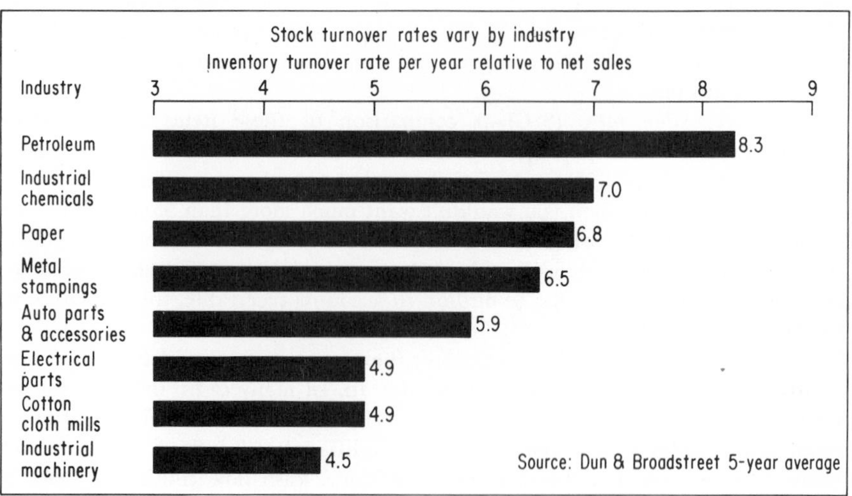

Review Inventory Methods for Price Strategy

Inventories constitute one of the most important items in financial statements. Considerable emphasis is put on this area by top analysts and accountants because:

• Material costs almost always add up to a large—sometimes the largest—expense item on the income statement.

• Inventories are usually a substantial part of the net assets of a company—and hence figure importantly in any liquidity evaluation.

• Inventories can, and usually are, evaluated in many different ways. For example, whether a firm uses LIFO, FIFO, average costs, etc., can make a big difference in the inventory figures and a firm's overall profit position.

The whole question of inventory valuation can be illustrated by a simple example. Here's how a merchandising firm (no labor or fabricating expense needed to convert from purchases to sales) might show up using the three major types of inventory accounting:

Assume the following: The firm has no stocks at the beginning of the year but makes purchases of 50 units at $1 each in January, and another purchase of

50 units at $1.50 each later on in the year. In other words, the actual cost of the year's purchases comes to $125. Further assume that 50 units are sold during the year at $3 each—for a sales volume of $150.

Note from the table below that under FIFO you would charge out as cost the price of the first 50 items purchased (line 3). In this case, it would be 50 units at $1 or a total cost of $50 for the 50 items sold.

Under the LIFO technique you would charge off as cost the price of the last 50 inventory items purchased. In this case, it would be $1.50 per unit or a total cost of $75 for the 50 items sold.

Under the average cost method, divide the 100 units purchased during the year into the total purchase cost ($125) and you come up with $1.25 per unit cost or a total cost of $62.50 for the 50 units sold.

*Comparison of Inventory Methods**

	FIFO	LIFO	AVG. COST
(1) Purchases During year	125	125	125
(2) Sales	150	150	150
(3) Cost of Sales	50	75	62.50
(4) Gross Profit [(2)—(3)]	100	75	87.50
(5) Inv. End of Year [(1)—(3)]	75	50	62.50

* Under any of the above methods it's still possible for the current market value to be below the resulting inventory value. If such is the case, inventories are written down to market value to conform to "the lower of cost or market" rule. This is used to prevent over-valuation of inventories on financial statements.

Note that LIFO shows the smallest end-of-year inventory (line 5) and the smallest profit (line 4). This is always the case in times of rising prices, as assumed in the above example. Under such conditions, LIFO generally has inventories which are valued at less than their current market-value.

Many companies prefer this method during periods of rising prices because the resulting lower profits mean lower taxes. Therefore over the past decade when prices were generally rising, it's no surprise that many firms switched to this method of valuing inventories. But the government won't allow you to switch back.

There are many other yardsticks used in financial analysis, but they are mostly concerned with evaluation for investment purposes and not for review of a supplier. For a good summary of these measures, get "How to Understand Financial Statements," available free from the New York Stock Exchange, New York City. Another valuable aid is Dun & Bradstreet's pamphlet, "How Does Your Business Compare With Others In Your Line," which gives typical industry averages for 14 key performance ratios. Single copies are available from D & B, 99 Church Street, New York.

1. How to Get Important Price, Inventory Clues

A close look at financial statements can give some pretty knowledgeable hints on:

• Prices—A low rate of profit in a firm relative to the industry, for example, reveals that costs are too high, or selling prices too low, plant outdated or inefficiently run. In either case, it's possible that prices may be subject to some upward pressures. On the other hand, if the firm's low profit is caused by inadequate volume, it may be willing to negotiate a lower price to build sales.

Conversely, a too-high rate of profit has also some important price implications. It may give the buyer leverage in negotiations. It possibly can be used to put the supplier on the defensive—in that he might be asked to justify the price he is quoting. This may be possible if your requirements are a substantial part of the firm's capacity. You can get an idea of this from the statements, too.

• Inventories—The size of vendor's inventories relative to sales also can give some pretty important clues. For example, a slow inventory turnover rate relative to others in the same industry might indicate that a vendor is overstocked and hence vulnerable to P.A. bargaining pressure.

The inventory figures for companies with few product lines also can give some clues as to how fast the P.A. can get delivery in a pinch. If figures are broken down into raw materials, goods in process, and finished goods, the P.A. may get some idea of any inventory imbalance and distress merchandise on supplier shelves.

How inventories are valued is also an important consideration. Whether last in, first out (LIFO), first in, first out (FIFO), or average cost methods are used can make a big difference in inventories, cost of goods sold, and profits (see below).

• Reliability—The financial condition of a vendor affects quality, delivery, and (as noted above) prices. The solvent firm is more likely to meet its contractual obligations than the firm that is bordering on the brink of bankruptcy. A vendor that is one step ahead of the bill collector is more likely to cut corners on quality, figuring that only by squeezing nickels and dimes can he stay in business. Put another way, it's the creditors rather than the buyers who must get top priority.

2. *Where to Go for Information and Comparisons*

There are certain standard ways of going about obtaining information on a vendor's financial status: Generally speaking, data for a listed company (a company whose stock appears on the New York or American Stock Exchange) is easiest to obtain. All that is required is a note to the treasurer of the vendor asking for the latest copies of company's financial statements.

For unlisted companies, proprietorships, or family-owned businesses, the situation is more difficult. In some cases, writing to the treasurer of the company might get results. Often however these "unlisted" vendors are under no obligation to send this information out and might refuse to do so.

If you don't meet with success, a check with Dun and Bradstreet credit reporting service might be in order. But this is generally less satisfactory than receiving audited financial statements. That's because the information given to credit rating services comes directly from the corporation—without any audit.

Another information source is the local bank used by the vendor. Since almost all firms need and use credit, the bank that the vendor does business with usually knows a good deal about the firm's financial status. And, generally speaking, they are willing to cooperate. Check directly or through your company's bank.

Finally there's the time-tested technique of comparing notes with other P.A.'s. While this is the weakest method of all, it's better than none, because chances are if the vendor has performed well before, he will do so again.

For more general information—about an over-all industry—there are several other sources available. Trade associations, for example, very often collect data on sales, costs, and profits of all reporting members. A useful list of associations is "The Directory of National Associations of Businessmen," published by the Dept. of Commerce (50¢). Other government sources include Securities & Exchange Commission and Federal Trade Commission which put out quarterly financial reports for major manufacturing industries. They are composite financial statements giving assets, liabilities, sales and profit margins for some 25 industries.

3. *But Watch Out for Misleading Conclusions*

In any evaluation of financial statements, there are several pitfalls to be avoided. Generally, it's important to check for:

• Reliability—One major question all analysts ask: Are the reports audited by an accredited accounting firm? Generally speaking, an audited report puts the reputation of the accountant behind the statement. It's not likely that these auditors would jeopardize their whole practice to cover up for just one firm. It's a pretty good rule to accept an audited report rather than one that has not been audited.

• Comparability—Don't automatically put one firm's inventory or profit figures up against another's. For individual companies often have different methods of valuing inventories, taking depreciation, etc. And differences here lead to differences in profits and profit margins. The thing to remember: Check the specific accounting methods which underlie each figure in the balance sheet and income statement and read the footnote to statements.

• Industry differences—Don't compare profit margins blindly. Each industry has its own norm, and it's usually much more important to check against the industry average than any national average.

• Short-run problems—Often a strike or other unusual event can distort operating results because what happened in that year is not a typical occurrence.

Most analysts, however, prefer to look over a firm's history for several years. For in addition to washing out "one-shot" affairs, it helps give a clearer picture of the trend over time—and therefore the basic health of a particular firm.

Table 29–19. Discounted Cash-flow Factors

Time Value of Money. Purchasing decisions often require that the time value of money be considered. By time value we mean, for example, that a dollar received today is more valuable than a dollar due one year hence because interest can be earned during the one-year interval. How much interest can be earned? For purchasing decisions in a specific company, the company's rate of return on invested capital is a good guideline. Solving problems involving the time value of money can be facilitated by using Tables 29–19A and 29–19B. These tables list discount factors to apply against cash flows which commute their value to a common reference time—the present. Table A provides factors which can be applied to cash flows which occur instantaneously at some point in time. Table B provides factors which can be applied to cash flows which occur uniformly over a period of time.

Specific Problems. The use of the tables may be illustrated by the following two specific problems:

1. Is it better to pay $250 installed for a higher-quality item with 20 years life (alternative A) or to replace the item every 5 years with lower-quality merchandise costing $100 installed (alternative B)? All costs are expensed, and the company's cost of capital R is 10 per cent. In the computations that follow, note that R is taken as a whole integer and time T is expressed in years. Solution:

Alternative A

Cash flow	Time, in years	$R \times T$	Factor (Table A)	Present value
–$250	0	$ 0	1.0000	–$250

Alternative B

Cash flow	Time, in years	$R \times T$	Factor (Table A)	Present value
–$100	0	$ 0	1.0000	–$100.00
– 100	5	50	0.6065	– 60.65
– 100	10	100	0.3679	– 36.79
– 100	15	150	0.2231	– 22.31
				–$219.75

A comparison of present values indicates alternative B is $250.00 – $219.75 = $30.25 lower in cost than alternative A.

2. Is it better to make lease payments of $50 per month for 5 years or to pay a $2,000 lump-sum for an item of capital equipment? The lease provides that title cannot be taken, so the monthly payments are expensed. In the other alternative, title is taken and lump-sum payment must be capitalized. The cost of capital R is 10 per cent. Corporate tax rate is 50 per cent, and depreciation is sum-of-year digits for 5 years. The equipment is of no value at the end of 5 years. As in Example 1 above, R is a whole integer and time T is expressed in years. Solution:

Alternative A

	Cash flow	Time, in years	$R \times T$	Factor (Table B)	Present value
Expense	$-\$50 \times 12 \times 5$	0–5	\$50	0.7869	−\$2,360
Tax savings ..	$50\% \times \$50 \times 12 \times 5$	0–5	50	0.7869	+ 1,180
			Net present value of five-year lease costs		−\$1,180

Alternative B

	Cash flow	Time, in years	$R \times T$	Factor (Table A)	Present value
Investment ...	−\$2,000	0	0	1.0000	−\$2,000
Tax savings from depreciation	$\frac{5}{15} \times \$2,000 \times 50\%$	1	10	0.9048	+\$ 302
	$\frac{4}{15} \times \$2,000 \times 50\%$	2	20	0.8187	+ 218
	$\frac{3}{15} \times \$2,000 \times 50\%$	3	30	0.7408	+ 148
	$\frac{2}{15} \times \$2,000 \times 50\%$	4	40	0.6703	+ 89
	$\frac{1}{15} \times \$2,000 \times 50\%$	5	50	0.6065	+ 40
			Net present value of purchase costs		−\$1,203

The present value of alternative A is \$1,203 − \$1,180 = \$23 less over a five-year period.

Decisions Based on Economic Evaluations. The general method employed in the above two specific examples and other similar problems is as follows:

1. Quantify as many factors involved in the problem as possible, with regard to both their monetary amount and the time of their occurrence.
2. Commute their monetary value to a common reference time—the present.
3. Compare the commuted present values of the alternatives, evaluate other factors which were not quantified, and decide which alternative is best.

Factors which were not quantified in Example 1 include the probability of price rises on the future purchases of the lower-cost item and, conversely, the possibility of technological improvement obsoleting the higher-priced item before the end of the 20-year period. In Example 2, factors not quantified include corporate policy with regard to leasing. Before a final decision is made, consideration must be given to the factors which cannot be calculated.

Those wishing to pursue the subject of economic evaluation in greater depth should refer to *Principles of Engineering Economy,* 4th ed., Ronald Press Company, New York, 1960.

Text prepared by D. J. Murphy, Purchasing Planning, American Oil Company, Chicago, Ill.

Table 29-19A. Factors for Cash Effects Which Occur at a Point in Time after the Reference Point

R x T	0	1	2	3	4	5	6	7	8	9
0	1.0000	.9910	.9802	.9704	.9608	.9512	.9418	.9324	.9231	.9139
10	.9048	.8958	.8869	.8781	.8696	.8607	.8521	.8437	.8353	.8270
20	.8187	.8106	.8025	.7945	.7866	.7788	.7711	.7634	.7558	.7483
30	.7408	.7334	.7261	.7189	.7188	.7047	.6977	.6907	.6839	.6771
40	.6703	.6637	.6570	.6505	.6440	.6376	.6313	.6250	.6188	.6126
50	.6065	.6005	.5945	.5886	.5827	.5770	.5712	.5655	.5599	.5543
60	.5488	.5434	.5379	.5326	.5273	.5220	.5169	.5117	.5066	.5016
70	.4966	.4916	.4868	.4819	.4771	.4724	.4677	.4630	.4584	.4538
80	.4493	.4449	.4404	.4360	.4317	.4274	.4232	.4190	.4148	.4107
90	.4066	.4025	.3985	.3946	.3906	.3867	.3829	.3791	.3753	.3716
100	.3679	.3642	.3606	.3570	.3535	.3499	.3465	.3430	.3396	.3362
110	.3329	.3296	.3263	.3230	.3198	.3166	.3135	.3104	.3073	.3042
120	.3012	.2982	.2952	.2923	.2894	.2865	.2837	.2808	.2780	.2753
130	.2725	.2698	.2671	.2645	.2618	.2592	.2567	.2541	.2516	.2491
140	.2466	.2441	.2417	.2393	.2369	.2346	.2322	.2299	.2276	.2254
150	.2231	.2209	.2187	.2165	.2144	.2122	.2101	.2080	.2060	.2039
160	.2019	.1999	.1979	.1959	.1940	.1921	.1901	.1882	.1864	.1845
170	.1827	.1809	.1791	.1773	.1755	.1738	.1720	.1703	.1686	.1670
180	.1653	.1637	.1620	.1604	.1588	.1572	.1557	.1541	.1526	.1511
190	.1496	.1481	.1466	.1451	.1437	.1423	.1409	.1395	.1381	.1367
200	.1353	.1340	.1327	.1313	.1300	.1287	.1275	.1262	.1249	.1237
210	.1225	.1212	.1200	.1188	.1177	.1165	.1153	.1142	.1130	.1119
220	.1108	.1097	.1086	.1075	.1065	.1056	.1044	.1033	.1023	.1013
230	.1003	.0993	.0983	.0973	.0963	.0954	.0944	.0935	.0926	.0916
240	.0907	.0898	.0889	.0880	.0872	.0863	.0854	.0846	.0837	.0829
250	.0821	.0813	.0805	.0797	.0789	.0781	.0773	.0765	.0758	.0750
260	.0743	.0735	.0728	.0721	.0714	.0707	.0699	.0693	.0686	.0679
270	.0672	.0665	.0659	.0652	.0646	.0639	.0633	.0627	.0620	.0614
280	.0608	.0602	.0596	.0590	.0584	.0578	.0573	.0567	.0561	.0556
290	.0550	.0545	.0539	.0536	.0529	.0523	.0518	.0513	.0508	.0503
300	.0498	.0493	.0488	.0483	.0478	.0476	.0469	.0464	.0460	.0455
310	.0450	.0446	.0442	.0437	.0433	.0429	.0424	.0420	.0416	.0412
320	.0408	.0404	.0400	.0396	.0392	.0388	.0384	.0380	.0376	.0373
330	.0369	.0365	.0362	.0358	.0354	.0351	.0347	.0344	.0340	.0337
340	.0334	.0330	.0327	.0324	.0321	.0317	.0314	.0311	.0308	.0305
350	.0302	.0299	.0296	.0293	.0290	.0287	.0284	.0282	.0279	.0276
360	.0273	.0271	.0268	.0265	.0263	.0260	.0257	.0255	.0252	.0250
370	.0247	.0245	.0242	.0240	.0238	.0235	.0233	.0231	.0228	.0226
380	.0224	.0221	.0219	.0217	.0215	.0213	.0211	.0209	.0207	.0204
390	.0202	.0200	.0198	.0196	.0194	.0193	.0191	.0189	.0187	.0185
400	.0183	.0181	.0180	.0178	.0176	.0174	.0172	.0171	.0169	.0167
410	.0166	.0164	.0162	.0161	.0159	.0158	.0156	.0155	.0153	.0151
420	.0150	.0148	.0147	.0146	.0144	.0143	.0141	.0140	.0138	.0137
430	.0136	.0134	.0133	.1032	.0130	.0129	.0128	.0127	.0125	.0124
440	.0123	.0122	.1020	.0119	.0118	.0117	.0116	.0114	.0113	.0112

Table 29-19B. Factors for Cash Effects Which Occur Uniformly over a Period of Years Starting with the Reference Point

R x T	0	1	2	3	4	5	6	7	8	9
0	1.0000	.9950	.9901	.9851	.9803	.9754	.9706	.9658	.9610	.9563
10	.9516	.9470	.9423	.9377	.9332	.9286	.9241	.9196	.9152	.9107
20	.9063	.9020	.8976	.8933	.8891	.8848	.8806	.8764	.8722	.8681
30	.8639	.8598	.8558	.8517	.8477	.8438	.8398	.8359	.8319	.8281
40	.8242	.8204	.8166	.8128	.8090	.8053	.8016	.7979	.7942	.7906
50	.7869	.7833	.7798	.7762	.7727	.7692	.7657	.7622	.7588	.7554
60	.7520	.7486	.7452	.7419	.7386	.7353	.7320	.7288	.7256	.7224
70	.7192	.7160	.7128	.7097	.7066	.7035	.7004	.6974	.6944	.6913
80	.6883	.6854	.6824	.6795	.6765	.6736	.6707	.6679	.6650	.6622
90	.6594	.6566	.6537	.6510	.6483	.6455	.6428	.6401	.6374	.6348
100	.6321	.6295	.6269	.6243	.6217	.6191	.6166	.6140	.6115	.6090
110	.6065	.6040	.6016	.5991	.5967	.5942	.5918	.5894	.5871	.5847
120	.5823	.5800	.5777	.5754	.5731	.5708	.5685	.5663	.5641	.5618
130	.5596	.5574	.5552	.5530	.5509	.5487	.5466	.5444	.5424	.5402
140	.5381	.5361	.5340	.5320	.5299	.5279	.5259	.5239	.5219	.5199
150	.5179	.5160	.5140	.5121	.5102	.5082	.5064	.5044	.5026	.5007
160	.4988	.4970	.4952	.4933	.4915	.4897	.4879	.4861	.4843	.4825
170	.4808	.4790	.4773	.4756	.4739	.4721	.4704	.4687	.4671	.4654
180	.4637	.4621	.4605	.4588	.4571	.4555	.4540	.4523	.4508	.4491
190	.4476	.4460	.4445	.4429	.4414	.4399	.4383	.4368	.4354	.4338
200	.4323	.4308	.4294	.4279	.4265	.4250	.4236	.4221	.4207	.4193
210	.4179	.4165	.4151	.4137	.4123	.4109	.4096	.4082	.4069	.4055
220	.4042	.4029	.4015	.4002	.3989	.3976	.3963	.3950	.3937	.3925
230	.3912	.3899	.3887	.3874	.3862	.3849	.3837	.3825	.3813	.3801
240	.3789	.3777	.3765	.3753	.3741	.3729	.3718	.3706	.3695	.3683
250	.3672	.3660	.3649	.3638	.3627	.3615	.3604	.3593	.3582	.3571
260	.3560	.3550	.3539	.3528	.3517	.3507	.3496	.3486	.3476	.3465
270	.3455	.3445	.3434	.3424	.3414	.3404	.3393	.3384	.3374	.3364
280	.3354	.3344	.3335	.3325	.3315	.3306	.3296	.3287	.3277	.3268
290	.3259	.3249	.3240	.3231	.3221	.3212	.3203	.3194	.3185	.3176
300	.3167	.3158	.3150	.3141	.3132	.3123	.3115	.3106	.3098	.3089
310	.3080	.3072	.3064	.3055	.3047	.3039	.3030	.3022	.3014	.3006
320	.2998	.2990	.2982	.2974	.2966	.2958	.2950	.2942	.2934	.2926
330	.2919	.2911	.2903	.2896	.2888	.2880	.2873	.2865	.2858	.2850
340	.2843	.2936	.2828	.2821	.2814	.2807	.2799	.2792	.2785	.2778
350	.2771	.2764	.2757	.2750	.2743	.2736	.2729	.2722	.2715	.2709
360	.2702	.2695	.2688	.2682	.2675	.2669	.2662	.2655	.2649	.2642
370	.2636	.2629	.2623	.2617	.2610	.2604	.2598	.2591	.2585	.2579
380	.2573	.2567	.2560	.2554	.2548	.2542	.2536	.2530	.2524	.2518
390	.2512	.2506	.2500	.2495	.2489	.2483	.2477	.2471	.2466	.2460
400	.2454	.2449	.2443	.2437	.2432	.2426	.2421	.2415	.2410	.2404
410	.2399	.2393	.2388	.2382	.2377	.2372	.2366	.2361	.2356	.2350
420	.2345	.2340	.2335	.2330	.2325	.2319	.2314	.2309	.2304	.2299
430	.2294	.2289	.2284	.2279	.2274	.2269	.2264	.2259	.2255	.2250
440	.2245	.2240	.2235	.2230	.2226	.2221	.2216	.2212	.2207	.2202

SELECTED BIBLIOGRAPHY

International Critical Tables, McGraw-Hill Book Company, New York

Perry, Robert H., et al.: *Chemical Engineers' Handbook,* McGraw-Hill Book Company, New York, 1963

Smithsonian Physical Tables, Publication 4169, Smithsonian Institution, Washington, D.C.

Units of Weights and Measures; Definitions and Tables of Equivalents, Miscellaneous Publication 214, National Bureau of Standards, U.S. Department of Commerce, Washington, D.C.

Units and Systems of Weights and Measures; Their Origin, Development, and Present Status, Circular 570, National Bureau of Standards, U.S. Department of Commerce, Washington, D.C.

Zimmerman, O. T., and Irvin Lavine: *Conversion Factors and Tables,* Industrial Research Service, Inc., Dover, N.H., 1961

INDEX

Also refer to Section 27, "Glossary of Terms," which defines many words, terms, and symbols not included in this index. The glossary is in alphabetical order and thus is an index in itself on purchasing and allied subjects. Reference to the table of contents at the beginning of each section may also prove helpful.